THE SECRET HISTORY
OF
SOE:
THE SPECIAL OPERATIONS EXECUTIVE
1940–1945

THE SECRET HISTORY
OF
SOE:
THE SPECIAL
OPERATIONS EXECUTIVE
1940–1945

W. J. M. Mackenzie

with a Foreword and notes by
M. R. D. Foot

ST ERMIN'S
PRESS

A *St Ermin's Press* Book

First published in this form in Great Britain in 2000
by St Ermin's Press
in association with Little, Brown & Company

Copyright © 2000 by St Ermin's Press

Foreword and additional footnotes copyright © 2000
by M. R. D. Foot

The Public Record Office is the custodian of W. J. M. Mackenzie's
original manuscript.

A CIP catalogue record for this book
is available from the British Library.

ISBN 0 9536151 8 9

Typeset by Palimpsest Book Production Limited
Polmont, Stirlingshire.
Printed and bound in Great Britain
by Clays Ltd, St Ives plc

St Ermin's Press
in association with
Little, Brown and Company (UK)
Brettenham House
Lancaster Place
London WC2E 7EN

Contents

Foreword

This is in effect the in-house history of SOE, the Special Operations Executive, Great Britain's wartime secret service that handled subversion and sabotage overseas. It was compiled, just after the service had been shut down, by a distinguished don in his thirties, who had not served in it himself, but met almost all of its directing figures and several of its agents, and had unrestricted access to its surviving archive. He told the story so fully and so frankly that for over fifty years it was graded secret, and so was unavailable to the public. It now fills an important missing page in twentieth-century history.

It was written by William James Millar Mackenzie (known as Bill to his many friends), a pure Scot, born on 8 April 1909 to a writer to the signet in Edinburgh; on both sides of his family, a grandson of the manse. From Edinburgh Academy he went up to Balliol College, Oxford, where he distinguished himself as a classics scholar. He took firsts both in honour moderations and in Greats, and in 1929 won the Ireland Scholarship, the university's principal award for those of his standing. His father persuaded him to return to Edinburgh, where he graduated LL.B. from that university; Magdalen College, Oxford, in need of a classics don, persuaded him south again.

He settled to a life of teaching; but soon persuaded his colleagues to release him from teaching the ancient languages. Instead he taught politics, to undergraduates reading modern greats (now more commonly called philosophy, politics, and economics, PPE for short). With John Austin, Thomas Weldon, David Worswick and (later) A. J. P. Taylor, he helped to provide Magdalen with a formidable body of PPE tutors.

When the Second World War began, he was called up into the Civil Service and worked in the Air Ministry, where his abilities raised him to the post of secretary to the Air Council. He was privy to all the Ministry's difficulties about manpower, organisation and armament, and knew a good deal about strategy. Though not privy to ultra secret intelligence (hardly anybody in the Air Ministry was), he was aware of the existence of several secret services – in particular of SOE, which took up a slice of his Ministry's attention. He must have had frequent dealings with Portal, the brightest of the Chiefs of Staff, an acquaintance likely to cure anyone of strategic cant.

Unlike some clever dons, he had plenty of common sense, as well as a sharp mind. He was a tall, burly, well-spoken, well-mannered, good-looking man, with fair wavy hair that turned white early; not too preoccupied with work to have no private life at all. He married Pamela Muriel Malyon in 1943; she survives him, with their son and four daughters. A secure personal base was his for the rest of his life.

At the end of the war he was released back to Oxford, and at once became a leading figure in the faculty of social sciences. He did much to foster the growth of political studies in the United Kingdom. He was a founder member of the Political Studies Association, which promptly grew into a major professional body with its own learned journal. When Nuffield College was founded, he moved to it for a year, in 1948, as its politics fellow; the following year, he moved on to Manchester, where he was the founder professor of government from 1949 to 1966, working in the house in Dover Street where Engels used to entertain Marx in the 1860s. His was a name to reckon with in government as well as in academic circles. He was created CBE in 1963 and elected a fellow of the British Academy in 1968. From Manchester he moved on to Glasgow, where he had a named chair (as Edward Caird professor of politics) till he reached retirement age in 1977. He lived nearly twenty years more, dying in west Glasgow on 22 August 1996 at the age of eighty-seven.

He wrote several textbooks of political practice, two of them Pelicans, and sat on a large number of committees, public as well as academic, including several that tried to help newly liberated African countries to find their political feet. He had all the normal preoccupations of a professor in a large department – arranging for promising candidates to take further degrees, sorting out messes in the syllabus, cutting out dead wood, selecting promising new dons, and so on; his mind remained inquiring and lively to the end. He put a brief intellectual autobiography at the start of his *Explorations in Government*, a collection of essays published by Macmillan in 1975, and was given a handsome obituary by Richard Rose – one of the many former pupils who themselves became professors of politics – in the *Proceedings of the British Academy*, volume 101 (1999).

From the late 1960s, in spite of official annoyance, he mentioned in his *Who's Who* article that he had written this book; but he never discussed it in front of a television camera, or engaged in any of the many media controversies that wrestled – usually in ignorance – with SOE.

He came to write this book, just after the end of the war, by personal accident. As the world war in Europe drew to a close, (Sir) Colin Gubbins, who was then the executive head of SOE, started to look round for a suitable man to write its history. He had met Mackenzie when summoned before the Air Council to account for SOE's calls on the RAF's facilities; liked him; discovered he was a trained historian; and invited him to undertake the task. It was clear from the start that there was no immediate prospect of publication. Mackenzie's role was to explain how SOE had come into being, what it had been for, and how it had worked, so that future users of any successor body could appreciate the pros and cons of running any such service.

He wrote it mainly in three long vacations, in 1945, 1946 and 1947, in the intervals of full-time teaching at Magdalen. He often (so he once told me) carried the files he was using between London and Oxford by train in his own briefcase; later historians were forbidden to remove them from the guarded building in which they were kept. He had some initial guidance among the maze of files from Margaret Jackson, formerly Gubbins's personal assistant, but did much of the donkey-work himself, though government provided a typist for his finished text and cyclostyled it.

The Foreign Office, each Service Ministry, the Cabinet Office and the principal secret services each had their own copy, but there was long no question of making it public. This was partly because of the ancient, still valid, principle that unless a secret service remains secret it cannot do its work properly, however ill this fits with democratic or media government. Partly it was because the secret services were anxious to maintain the anonymity of a few members of SOE who were later absorbed into them. Mainly, it was due to bureaucratic inertia which thrives on Whitehall's deep-rooted cult of secrecy.

It was available to every official historian, preparing the Service histories of the Second World War; to every one of them, that is, who knew of its existence and cared to ask for it. A few of them referred to it, guardedly, in footnotes. To the later official historians of SOE it has of course been indispensable – both as the first work to consult, and as a sterling guide to the outlines of their subjects. As the first of these historians, starting work over ten years after Mackenzie had finished, and in such conditions of secrecy that I was forbidden to consult him (though I had already sat at his feet as a junior politics don at Oxford in the late 1940s), I must take this belated opportunity to testify how inordinately much I am indebted to this work for guidance. To anyone who compares its French chapters with my *SOE in France* (London, like other books for which no other place is given, 1966, 1968), the size of my debt will at once be clear. At least I could inscribe a copy for him with the motto, cribbed from Eliot, '*il miglior fabbro*'.

The late Charles Cruickshank, author of two other published official histories of SOE, *SOE in the Far East* and *SOE in Scandinavia* (1983, 1986), must have been almost equally indebted; and the complications of SOE's command structure in the Eastern Mediterranean that will emerge below help to explain why no official history of SOE in any Balkan country has yet emerged. These tangles were so dense that even an historian of Mackenzie's capacity could hardly hack his way through them.

As soon as I read his book, I started to press for its publication. Letters to successive secretaries to the Cabinet uniformly produced, from an underling, the reply that the time was not yet ripe. At last Sir Robin Butler, almost as his last act before he resigned in 1998 to become a peer and Master of University College, Oxford, let it go. It now reposes, in a laundered version, in the Public Record Office at Kew. The laundry deserves a moment's notice. (The word is used on purpose, in spite of its modern derogatory tone.) Mackenzie began his book by stating that 'The work as it now stands has not been subject to any official censorship on grounds of security or policy.' Alas, this is no longer true: one slice has been cut out of it, on grounds presumably of policy, inexplicable to the common man but supposedly defensible behind the scenes. There have also been a number of minor cuts, some readily defensible, some by now a shade old-maidish. For instance, authority still insists on drawing a veil over the precise circumstances of a Balkan escape, although they are spelt out in detail both in the autobiography of the British minister concerned and in a recent biography by the son of the SOE agent who engineered it (see page 107 below).

In parallel with the appearance of Mackenzie's history at Kew, SOE's own papers – or rather, what is left of them – are now turning up there too, under the call phrase HW. Most of the surviving operational and equipment files are now available for research; headquarters and communications files will shortly join them; and several thousand personal files, often containing items of historic importance, are to follow.

Mackenzie himself saw what he had time to see in the whole set of SOE's surviving papers, all of which were available to him; except for a few that had already been whisked down the gulf of time and are recorded as 'destroyed' in his meticulous footnotes. A steady run of archival weedings has reduced their quantity by seven-eighths, done by clerks who had not met Mackenzie's remark that they were 'certainly the best single source of material in the world for the history of European resistance' (page xxviii). Weeding has been random; many important papers have gone. Duncan Stuart read a valuable paper on this subject to the SOE conference at the Imperial War Museum in autumn 1998, due to appear in the conference papers Mark Seaman is editing.

An extra difficulty awaits those who try to take up Mackenzie's references to SOE papers. He complained himself of the troubles of trying to cope with 'two superimposed systems of filing, both radically imperfect' (page xxviii); a third system has been imposed even on them. In the early 1970s, the surviving operational and headquarter files were all gone through by Mr Townsend of the PRO and reduced to what that office regarded as a sensible arrangement. Townsend's index to them did include cross-references to the original file numbers, where they survived, but it will be a nightmare task to try to fix which of the AD/S.1 files to which Mackenzie so often refers have survived.

Mackenzie's sources consisted not only of papers, but of interviews. He talked to all but one of the principal directing characters in SOE, some of them repeatedly; he also saw a few agents and enough of the minor staff to give him the flavour of the office. The one that he missed was Dr Hugh (later Lord) Dalton, the original minister in charge; for Dalton, as Chancellor of the Exchequer in the first Attlee Government, declared himself too busy to recall SOE; and by the time he retired, under a passing cloud late in 1947, Mackenzie had got past the Dalton period in his history.

Historians will notice, in the pages that follow, how deftly Mackenzie managed to blend together what he had discovered on paper with what he had found out in interview, and with his own general knowledge of the course and conduct of the war; it was fortunate that he had had a ringside seat himself. Modern advocates of oral history need to recall that Thucydides, the greatest of historians, from studying whom Mackenzie had learned his trade at Balliol, relied even more on oral history and on his own memory than he did on archive. Mackenzie himself remarked, in his introduction to his *Explorations in Government*, that he had found nothing in the whole range of SOE's activities for which Thucydides had not prepared him.

It also deserves recall that, in a secret service, there are bound to be a few points so secret that nothing gets put on paper about them at all. A few of these may have come Mackenzie's way in the course of interviews; history will have to do without the rest. Leo Marks, SOE's agent cipher officer, whom Mackenzie did not see, has remarked recently that the signals branch of SOE knew everything (*Between Silk and Cyanide*, 1998), overlooking these few points.

There was only one respect in which Mackenzie was not perfectly fitted to his task: he had not himself been in a secret service. He had, naturally enough, been used in the Air Ministry to handling secret documents, making sure they were not left about in an unattended office, locking them up at night and not talking about them to casual friends; but he had not taken on board the extra strict rules of secrecy that bound everyone in SOE, as in its companion services. This may have helped him to take a view that Whitehall would have regarded as cavalier, if not downright insecure, about the custody of his own book, of which he took a couple of copies away with him.

Every copy bore this box on its cover:

SECRET

THIS DOCUMENT IS THE PROPERTY OF H.B.M.
GOVERNMENT, and is issued only for the information of those
officials who are concerned with its content.
    The official in possession of this document will be
responsible for its safe custody and when not in use it is to be
kept under lock and key.

Every page of the text was marked SECRET, top and bottom, as a
standing reminder to the reader.

As time passed, Mackenzie took a more relaxed view. By the middle
1960s, he kept a copy in his office in Dover Street; in a locked
cupboard, it is true, but the cupboard was glass-fronted, and anyone
who had been through Beaulieu's lock-picking course and had a hair-
pin handy could have opened it in seconds. He invited the more senior
members of his staff to read it, on the understanding that they would
not divulge its contents carelessly; and when he discovered that his
successor Brian Chapman had spent part of his war delivering agents
in secrecy to the Italian coast by small boat, he left him one copy of
the book behind when he departed for Glasgow. (Chapman let me see
the outside of it, but would not lend it to me.)

Mackenzie also lent a copy to Elisabeth Barker when she was
preparing her formidable book on *British Policy in South-East Europe
in the Second World War* (1976), further strengthening it – as she
acknowledged in it; and he helped Joan Bright Astley when she was
preparing with Sir Peter Wilkinson their equally formidable *Gubbins
and SOE* (1993). His book's help towards a fuller understanding of
the political as well as the military course of the war against Hitler
will become clear to its readers as they read on, whether they have
read the books just cited or not.

It is time to discuss what SOE was. It was one of the nine British
wartime secret services. The others were the comparatively long-stand-
ing security and intelligence services, with roots in the distant past
but dating formally back to a Cabinet decision in 1909 (they are known
for convenience as MI5 and MI6); the decipher service, miscalled in
1939 the Government Code and Cipher School (it did no teaching);
the radio security service; the escape service, MI9, set up at Christmas
1939; the deception service, covered by the name of the London
Controlling Section – which meant, and was meant to mean, nothing;

the Political Warfare Executive, which began as a part of SOE but was split from it in tangled circumstances, fully described below; and the auxiliary units, formed (like SOE) in a tearing hurry in the summer of 1940, which were to have disrupted the rear areas of the German invasion of England that, mercifully, never took place.

For over a year before Hitler attacked Poland, some efforts had been made in Whitehall to investigate, though hardly yet to practise, the arts of propaganda, subversion and sabotage. The three small bodies that dealt with them, one an obscure branch of the War Office, one an unacknowledged corner of the Foreign Office, and one an inadmissible branch of MI6, were all thrown together in the summer crisis of 1940 to form SOE: a new, full-scale secret service, the mere existence of which could not be admitted either to Parliament or to the press. All this is gone into by Mackenzie in considerable detail; no wonder, considering his post as a tutor of political institutions.

He understood how institutions can help to shape the way things happen. Hence his fascination with the siting of SOE in the wartime machine for articulating combat. SOE was never itself in Whitehall. It began, tentatively, 'across the Park' (as the Foreign Office called it), in the upper floors of the St Ermin's Hotel in Caxton Street near Broadway (where MI6 then had its headquarters), but soon moved to Baker Street, which was not even in Westminster, but in Marylebone; and was nominally subordinate to the new Ministry of Economic Warfare, which lay in Berkeley Square, Mayfair.

These were confusions enough; many more, and more complex ones, were to follow. SOE's successive heads each maintained that they ought to have sat with the Chiefs of Staff, permanently, instead of being summoned to the Chiefs' meetings only when SOE's affairs were on the agenda. (Even then, minutes were seldom taken of the decisions arrived at: an admirable measure from the point of view of security, maddening though it is for historians.) It was often necessary for SOE to make trouble in one or another enemy-occupied, or even neutral, country, to the standing annoyance of the Foreign Office, and often to the exasperation of MI6 as well.

No one should be surprised at bad blood between any two secret services; the rivalries are no odder than those between rival ships in the same squadron, or football teams in the same city. The head of MI6 had some good reasons for feeling affronted at the cutting away from his service of Section D (for destruction?), which had been a part of it; particularly because in the hurly-burly of the Battle of Britain nobody remembered for three weeks to notify him that the change had formally taken place. Individual personal dislikes, some of them on the acrid side, did not make relations any more smooth. On the other hand, it needs to be remembered that MI6 had one perfectly sound professional reason for wishing to keep SOE out of its path: its task was to collect intelligence, for which it needed as much quiet as it could get, while SOE's task was to raise mayhem, bound to attract hostile police in droves. If SOE insisted on operating in areas from which MI6 was tasked to collect news, how could MI6 do its job as it should?

Mackenzie treats this thorny subject with tact. Conspiracy theorists will probably enjoy themselves trying to whip up storms in teacups from some data below; they should remember that by the summer of 1944 SOE and MI6 had got onto such friendly terms that it is reasonable to talk of a single intelligence community, of which both formed part – as had been envisaged several years before (see Christopher Andrew, *Secret Service* [1985]). With MI5 SOE's relations were a good deal warmer; and the head of SOE's security section (Sir) Frank Soskice (who died Lord Stow Hill) moved on to be Solicitor-General in Attlee's post-war Government.

With GC&CS SOE had hardly anything to do. Gradually, during the war (so General Gubbins told me thirty years later), a drill developed by which Churchill's military secretary Ismay kept by him in a file any ultra secret decipher message which he thought would interest SOE, and showed the file once a week either to CD, the executive head, or to one of his immediate deputies; no notes were taken; that was all. Whether SOE got any help from the Radio Security Service in identifying the points from which its agents were supposed to be transmitting I do not know; presumably, if needed, it did.

With the Auxiliary Units SOE had an important link – it was from them that Dalton secured their commander, then Brigadier Gubbins, in November 1940 when the threat of invasion had somewhat receded (the threat was in fact over; this was long unclear to Whitehall). Gubbins brought with him into SOE from these units several of his most colourful supporters, such as Peter Fleming and Andrew Croft; and himself became the leading figure in SOE, well before he turned into its executive head.

Colonel Bevan, who came to head the deception service, did not think SOE secure enough to take part in his exceedingly secret work, and hardly ever used it to achieve his devious ends; Operation 'Starkey', ill fated as it was, in the summer of 1943 provided the only exception, apart from a single sharp stroke in Belgium in the summer crisis of 1944.

With MI9, the escape service, SOE got on well; indeed, there was probably more interchange, 'in the field' (as the office called the occupied countries where SOE's agents worked), between SOE's discreet escape lines and some of the lines run for the RAF than London ever knew.

PWE's birth from an early SOE that turned out unmanageably cumbrous is described in detail by Mackenzie; SOE usually thereafter looked, more or less kindly, on PWE as a sort of younger brother, and frequently acted for it as travel agent. Relations at least were warmer than they had been with MI6, with which, in a memorable phrase of David Stafford's, they had too often seemed like those between a couple who had just had a bad divorce.

Why was SOE created at all? Because, in the summer crisis of 1940, it looked as if one of the principal weapons Nazi Germany had used to secure its Blitzkrieg victories, that had carried the swastika in eleven weeks from the North Cape to the Pyrenees, had been subversion by fifth columnists, which had rotted away Germany's intended victims from within. We now know, thanks to a sound piece of historical revision – Louis de Jong (trs. C. M. Geyl), *The German Fifth Column in the Second World War* (1956) – that this is a myth; but it was a powerful myth in its day.

It was powerful enough to capture the attention of Churchill, the new Prime Minister, as well as Lord Hankey, the Civil Service's principal strategic expert, who was currently trying to reconcile various secret service quarrels. On Churchill's instructions, the document that created SOE was drawn up by his predecessor, Chamberlain, reviled today as the man who had appeased Hitler too far at Munich in September 1938. By a nice irony, Chamberlain's last political act was to devise a tool for felling Hitler. He fell ill very shortly after he had drafted what SOE always regarded as its founding charter, in mid-July 1940, and died late that year. (The charter, of which several copies survive, was published in Nigel West, *Secret War* [1992], pp. 20–21.)

Its strategic origins can be traced back directly to a meeting of the Chiefs of Staff, now famous, on 25 May 1940, to consider British policy in the light of what gave Philip Bell the title for a book – *A Certain Eventuality* (Farnborough, 1974). The eventuality, the collapse of France, followed at once. The Chiefs had already decided that, if it happened, the only hope for the British would lie in armed rescue by the still unmobilised United States of America; till the US could intervene, the best hope would lie in subversion, to rot the enemy-held countries from within.

By the late autumn of 1940 the strategic kaleidoscope had shifted again, but by then SOE was established. David Stafford's significant article, 'The Detonator Concept' (*Journal of Modern History*, x. 185, April 1975) is here in point. Normally, to set up a department of that size and importance would have taken months, years more probably, of inter-departmental wranglings in committee; but 1940 was a year of crisis. The nation was fighting for its life against the most formidable enemy it had ever faced; and even committee men were prepared to hurry, when they had to. The two head men in SOE, after Dalton – (Sir) Gladwyn Jebb, later Lord Gladwyn, the chief executive officer, and Sir Frank Nelson, a former MP, the first CD or head of the sabotage branch of the new body – spent the autumn touring Whitehall and explaining, behind closed doors, to a very few very senior people what SOE was, and how swiftly and how precisely any requests from it for help were to be handled.

It was not then – it was never – a popular department elsewhere in the public services; and it has left a degree of distaste behind it in many places, some of them unexpected. Mackenzie's account of what it was trying to do may help to set the record straight.

In competition with the rest of the armed services, it sought of course to secure armaments; indeed it helped to invent several. A host of its devices are now on show in the secret war gallery of the Imperial War Museum, assembled by Mark Seaman's staff and exhibited thanks to the generosity of John Paul Getty, Jr. For those who cannot reach Lambeth, Colonel Pierre Lorain has provided a most lucid account in print: *Secret Warfare*, translated by David Kahn (1983), includes a mass of detailed drawings, as well as descriptions, of all the weapons SOE sent into France, covering virtually the whole field.

The one of these that achieved the widest circulation was the Sten sub-machine gun, invented at the invitation of Gubbins who thought it the ideal weapon for a short-range guerilla ambush. Several million were made. At ranges of more than a few feet the short-barrelled Sten was notoriously inaccurate, but it had one advantage that commended it to the Treasury – it was cheap. It only cost thirty shillings (£1.50 in today's money), then worth $7.20. It had a countervailing disadvantage – it was liable, if jolted, to go off, a vice that made it much less useful for the ambush-layer than Gubbins had intended.

Many of SOE's other devices are described in Stuart Macrae's book, *Winston Churchill's Toyshop* (Kineton, 1971), a life of M. R. Jefferis, who had been with Holland in MIR and ran a tiny branch of Churchill's Ministry of Defence.

Supply was vital in establishing SOE's importance 'in the field'; for arms are to active resisters what rain is to farmers – nothing can be done without them – and SOE was often the only serious source of supply. When the Germans bothered to conclude an armistice with a country they had conquered, it always included a clause about the surrender of existing stocks of arms; and serious German bureaucrats arrived, to make sure the stocks were handed over. This threw would-be resisters back on theft, on bribery, or on contact with SOE; which, if it could be attained, was a great deal more productive of results than either bribery or theft.

Except in Yugoslavia and, to a lesser degree, in Denmark, arms could hardly come by sea; they had to be sent in by parachute drop. This involved much danger on the ground for the reception committees. It also involved several thousand airmen, flying and servicing the special duty squadrons, a drain SOE made on RAF manpower that has not had much attention from air historians, apart from Hugh Verity's matchless *We Landed by Moonlight* (1978, often revised), which deals with the Lysander corner. It formed Mackenzie's first point of contact with the new service. Altogether, some 10,000 tons of weapons were put into France, and nearly twice as much – some 18,000 tons – into Yugoslavia. Into Poland, by contrast, only some 600 tons could be dropped, because most of the load of an aircraft flying that far had to be fuel: Stalin would not let RAF aircraft on clandestine tasks land to refuel in the Soviet Union.

Though Mackenzie was writing in the early years of the Cold War, he did not let that struggle affect his text at all. He gave credit and discredit to Communist resisters when and where he thought it was due. Long controversies have raged on the continent about the extent to which resistance was, or was not, Communist-inspired. There would have been plenty of ammunition here for cold warriors, had they been able to get hold of it; most of it telling in an anti-Communist sense. Mackenzie's account – for instance, pages 154–5 – of the origins of the left-wing Greek resistance movement, EAM, contradicts much that has been claimed since.

Both the big international conferences that were organised by the late Henri Michel, the doyen of resistance historians, to discuss European resistance – at Liège in 1959 and at Milan in 1961 – were bedevilled by the failure of minds to meet, between the delegations of the Eastern and of the Western Blocs. (Their proceedings were published by Pergamon, entitled *European Resistance Movements 1939–1945*, in 1960 and 1964.) This was less of a difficulty at the five congresses held under French auspices in the late 1990s, in Rennes, Brussels, Toulouse, Besançon and Paris, also published in macaronic volumes, using several languages (e.g. *La Résistance et les Européens du Nord*, Brussels, n.d.), which gave the current *état des questions*, and left several questions unresolved.

In the 1970s, three scholars produced a general history of armed resistance in Europe – Michel (translated by Barry, who had been Gubbins's Chief of Staff), *The Shadow War* (1972); Jorgen Haestrup, *Europe Ablaze* (Odense 1978); and my own *Resistance* (1976). Michel and Haestrup, both now dead, would have been fascinated by Mackenzie had they been able to read him.

He emphasised the importance of SOE's Council in directing the body's affairs; but no member of Council has left a published account of his role in it, and only Jebb has gone into print at any length, leaving out much mention of SOE. Dalton devoted less than twenty pages to SOE in his memoir, *The Fateful Years* (1957). Lord Selborne published nothing on his secret work, and indeed (as a granddaughter of his once told me) kept it from his own family's knowledge. Gubbins gave one telling talk to the Royal United Services Institute, published in its journal in May 1948 (xciii. 210–23), and was persuaded to give one lecture at Manchester long afterwards (in M. R. Elliott-Bateman [ed.], *The Fourth Dimension of Warfare* [Manchester, 1970], pp. 83–110).

There are two splendid books on SOE's headquarters, viewed from a middle staff officer's level: Bickham Sweet-Escott, *Baker Street Irregular* (1965), and J. G. Beevor, *SOE: Recollections and Reflections 1940-1945* (1981). Marks's *Between Silk and Cyanide*, already mentioned, gives a much less comfortable but equally personal description.

There is also one important study of SOE's relations with the Chiefs of Staff: David Stafford, *Britain and European Resistance 1940–1945* (1980, 1983), based on a careful trawl through the then fairly recently released papers in the record office.

Mackenzie had been so much soaked in Aristotle at Oxford that he remained aware, ever thereafter, of the links between political and moral action. He began his discussion of how the British organised propaganda in war with some remarks on whether it was wise to conduct it at all; into which he threw, *obiter*, the observation that subversion was in itself unjust.

Yet, writing from England and viewing the war from its London aspects, he did not take as full account as he might have done of the moral hedge every resister had to cross, before going into resistance: to do so was illegal. That is, to resist broke the *de facto* laws, imposed by the Nazis under whom resisters had to live; even if, *de jure* – as was the case with the Dutch – Nazi laws had no validity on the spot, because the Queen of Holland had taken away with her in May 1940 both her great seal and the official without whose assent no Dutch law could pass (Herman Friedhoff, *Requiem for the Resistance* [1990], pp. 27–8).

Mackenzie did not much concern himself with SOE's supply difficulties, beyond a mention of the silk-for-parachutes crisis that almost brought its operations to a halt (page 727). He wrote a long introductory section, to explain the executive's origins; and then plunged straight into a narrative of its adventures in Yugoslavia. He was the first to notice that the field was going to be much too complex to handle in detail everywhere, and decided to concentrate on France, Norway, Yugoslavia and Greece.

To discuss Greece and Yugoslavia at all, he had of course to insert a chapter on the command arrangements in the Eastern Mediterranean, which remained a difficulty for SOE's high command all through the war; a difficulty made still more complicated by the interest taken by the Foreign Office in the area (the FO had never brought itself to hand the Egyptian protectorate over to the Colonial Office), and brought to the point of exasperation by SOE's and MI6's insistence on absolute secrecy for their ciphers. SOE's tiny cipher staff in Cairo eventually fell weeks behind in deciphering even messages of the highest priority; no wonder ministers got impatient. Artemis Cooper's *Cairo in Wartime* (1996) and Lady Ranfurly's *To War with Whitaker* (1994) add local detail to what Sweet-Escott memorably described as the uninhabitability of the Egyptian capital for exiles from England.

As for what it was actually like on the ground – a point on which Mackenzie is necessarily weak – there are a few books by former British agents in the Balkans which here deserve mention: John Mulgan's *Report on Experience* (Oxford, 1947), C. M. Woodhouse's *Apple of Discord* (1948), E. C. W. Myers's *Greek Entanglement* (1955) and Nicholas Hammond's *Venture into Greece* (1983) cover Greece, while (Sir) F. W. D. Deakin's *The Embattled Mountain* (Oxford, 1971) and Jasper Rootham's *Miss Fire* (1946) describe Yugoslavia from opposite sides in its civil war.

Mackenzie did not say much about SOE in Africa. Here, again, there is one vivid book about what it was like – J. F. A[ppleyard]'s *Geoffrey* (1946, pp. 79–110), a personal memoir of his son, describes *Maid Honor*'s cutting-out operation in Fernando Po. W. E. D. Allen's *Guerilla War in Abyssinia* was a Penguin from as early as 1943, and Mackenzie must have seen it, but he wrote little of SOE in Abyssinia (as Ethiopia was then called), not taking in its significance for further work into Europe. As Sir Douglas Dodds-Parker explained in his *Setting Europe Ablaze* (Windlesham, 1983, pp. 72–3), the expedition proved the value of small parties of knowledgeable men sent into occupied territory, with wireless sets to keep in touch with their headquarters, as foci of future armed resistance, and the scheme was re-used repeatedly in Europe. Some private lectures he started to give on this subject were discontinued at the request of the then South African Government, which was worried at the comparatively easy defeats black men in SOE had inflicted on white Italians.

For SOE's work in America we have now got the official report, compiled after the end of the war on the instructions of Sir William Stephenson, who commanded the British secret services west of the Atlantic, and was the subject of one of the many world best-sellers about SOE with which these pages do not need to be troubled (his entry in the *Dictionary of National Biography* remarks that there is no evidence that he ever met Churchill). *British Security Coordination* (1999) covers the ground soberly.

There is one other official history of SOE, not this time confined to a single country, that goes into far more detail than Mackenzie had time or information to do: *Secret Flotillas* by Sir Brooks Richards (1996), which describes how SOE's private navy was formed, and operated across the Channel between Cornwall and Brittany before it went out to North Africa to work behind the German right flank in

Tunisia. He was himself involved from an early stage, so that the book has authenticity. A useful pendant to it is Margaret Pawling, *In Obedience to Instructions* (1999), on the work done by FANYs in SOE in the Mediterranean; she too participated.

Worldwide though SOE was in principle, it had no impact in the sixth of the world that then came under Stalin. Its office in Moscow achieved no useful interchanges with the Russian staffs who were running operations comparable to SOE's through the partisans on the eastern front.

Nor did it have much impact inside Hitler's Germany. A press sensation in 1998, when the PRO published *Operation Foxley* (edited by Mark Seaman), the X section file on whether the Führer could be assassinated, overlooked its conclusion: that by that stage in the war – August 1944 – Hitler was of more use to the Allies alive than dead, because his strategy had become so erratic. And SOE is not even mentioned in either of the two best books in English on resistance in Germany, Peter Hoffmann's *The History of German Resistance 1933–1945* (1977) and Michael Balfour's *Withstanding Hitler* (1988). SOE did supply the plastic for the bomb that failed to kill Hitler on 20 July 1944, but unintentionally: it was captured by the Abwehr from an early SOE agent in France and passed on to the conspirators by an Abwehr helper.

Mackenzie found material enough for a twenty-five-page chapter, late in the book, on Germany and Austria (pages 673–713); though saying little of 'Foxley', probably because his minders were then nervous about the degree of close co-operation between SOE and SIS that the 'Foxley' files revealed.

He touches lightly (pages 322–3) on SOE's efforts into Spain, always a tricky subject, made trickier by the presence as British Ambassador in Madrid of Sir Samuel Hoare (later Lord Templewood), who had a clandestine past of his own, and was determined that SOE should not interfere with the détente he was seeking to establish with General Franco.

All through, his book illustrates both the bravery of the agents, and the ingenuity of the staffs who were doing what they could to direct them; from a base of ignorance about what conditions on the continent were actually like that was only slowly, and with intense difficulty, coped with by men and women who had to teach themselves on the job.

Inside Mussolini's Italy, again, SOE was able to do little; but after Mussolini's fall, the all-party partisan movement in occupied Northern Italy did manage to do extensive damage to the common enemy; and the Italian change of sides was organised by secret help provided by a captured SOE wireless operator, without whom it could hardly have been managed. (See Christopher Woods, 'A Tale of Two Armistices', in K. G. Robertson [ed.], *War, Resistance and Intelligence* [1999], pp. 1–18; and Woods's forthcoming official history of SOE in Italy.) SOE, again, was able to play a critical part in bringing the German forces in the Netherlands to surrender to Eisenhower, right at the end of the European war, as will be clear in my official history of SOE in the Low Countries, should it be cleared for publication.

The Low Countries, the Netherlands in particular, have long been the butt of SOE's enemies, and indeed SOE did very badly there – for eighteen months; while the Abwehr did to it what MI5 did to the Abwehr all through the war – ran almost all its agents back, undetected. Mackenzie made no attempt to cover up.

As for Poland, where resistance began, and where Gubbins's heart was always fixed, a remarkable book by Jozef Garlinski, *Poland, SOE and the Allies* (1969), covers the ground so thoroughly that no official history seems to be contemplated. Similarly, Callum Macdonald on *The Killing of SS Obergruppenfuehrer Reinhard Heydrich* (1989) deals conclusively with SOE in Czechoslovakia; Frantisek Moravec's *Master of Spies* (1975) makes a useful appendix.

In both these countries, any agents of SOE's who fell into enemy hands were likely to suffer appalling fates; indeed, almost a quarter of F Section's agents in France never returned to this country either. Many of them were done away with in concentration camps – two days were devoted, for instance, to the slaughter of two-score Dutch agents at Mauthausen; the camps' ghastly total of victims did not by any means consist only of Jews. No one in his senses would want to under-emphasise the fate of Jews at the hands of the Nazis, but it should not be forgotten that they were not Nazism's only victims.

Where France is concerned, to which Mackenzie devotes several chapters, there has been for over thirty years a published official history (my *SOE in France*, 1966, revised 1968), not yet translated. On a few minor points, he and I contradict each other; in each case, I only ventured to go against him when I was convinced, by fuller evidence than he could have seen, that he might have made a slip. Of the enormous literature on this subject I will only mention one book, which still seems to me (as it seemed to General de Gaulle) the best: George Millar, *Maquis* (1945), which Mackenzie no doubt read.

In dealing with France, as elsewhere, he showed a remarkable grasp of recent and current politics and history; in retrospect, it seems a pity that his knowledge of Europe was retained on comparatively formal duties in the Air Ministry, instead of being available to the Foreign Office or one of the secret services. This could not be helped.

He sub-titled his book 'Britain and the Resistance Movements in Europe'; and though he touched on extra-European affairs, his heart was not in them. Indeed, in 1971 a fifth volume was added to his four, which dealt with SOE's affairs in Eastern Asia. It was written by a civil servant who had himself served in SOE, reaching the rank of major, Adrian G. McLaughlin (1909–79), and can be found in the PRO at CAB 102/653. It is not included here, because it varies both in style and in subject-matter from Mackenzie's own work; however, one fragment in it deserves mention. One of SOE's most successful operators in Asia was (Sir) Walter Fletcher, *né* Fleischl, who came into it from the international rubber trade; assured Colin Mackenzie (only a clansman of Bill's, a big name in the textile world) who ran SOE in Asia that he could coax rubber out of the lost Dutch East Indies; failed to do so; and moved to China, whence he returned with £77,000,000 worth of hard cash – most of it in United States dollars. He had obtained it partly by using his wits on the Chungking foreign exchange market, partly by selling to Chinese tycoons jewelled watches smuggled for him out of Switzerland by F Section's agents in SOE, who thought they were smuggling gun sights for the RAF. SOE was thus able to bring off the unexampled feat, for a secret service, of ending its life – Attlee wound it up early in 1946 – with its accounts showing a profit.

It showed a strategic profit as well, for which it has so far had little credit from official historians inhibited from discussing secret service matters, most of them writing before the Ultra secret went public. Before ever PWE split away from it, SOE helped largely to secure the shift in United States public opinion from isolationism to the belief that Nazi predominance in the world would sit badly with the US constitution – a change of world-shaking import. Nine of its saboteurs, in Norway, scuppered the heavy-water supply from Rjukan on which Heisenberg had been relying while preparing an atom bomb for Hitler; thereafter, he was directed to drop his atomic project – another world-shaker. All over Nazi-occupied Northern, Western, and Southern Europe, SOE could provide arms for resistance to Nazism, and thus enable the citizenry to recapture the self-respect they had lost when Blitzkrieg had swept their nations' forces aside in 1939–41. Moreover the personal gallantry of many of its agents in the field has caught the imagination of two generations at least of poets, novelists and dramatists, and stimulated much interesting literature – even if not all of it is historically sound.

A closing word may be useful on the notes that have been added below to the original. All are in square brackets, [thus], a device not used by Mackenzie's typist.

He knew, off hand, as the political public then did, who had been Chancellor of the Exchequer in the spring of 1939, or Chief of the Imperial General Staff in the spring of 1940; today's readers may be glad of a reminder. Who the British minister was in a Balkan capital – in the days before the diplomatic world had turned from legations to embassies – is a point readily recoverable from the *Foreign Office*

List, but that annual is not to be found on everybody's library shelf. Moreover, as a wartime civil servant he was used to acronyms, and knew what DDSD stood for without having to pause to think; a brief spell as a Whitehall warrior has given me help in recovering stumbling-blocks like this.

Where feasible, I have done what I can to identify the characters he names, and at least to give them birth dates. Most of them came from the old ruling class, and had been brought up on Kipling's dictum of 'Respect the aged'; seniority of birth still counted for something in that society, and when men of whom he writes were knighted I have tried to date the knighthoods, which also marked advance to a position of social eminence. A great many of them appeared in the ten-yearly supplements to the *Dictionary of National Biography*. These are all marked 'In *DNB*', and are traceable by their death dates; unless they fell into the *Missing Persons* volume (Oxford, 1993), in which case I say so.

The agents, a much more various lot than the staff, will (about half of them) in due course be traceable in the PRO, when some eight thousand surviving personal files about them are released. For a few it has been possible to insert notes already.

There is no adequate bibliography of books on resistance (one is badly needed). Numerous notes below indicate (a) autobiographical notes, (b) standard biographies and (c) other notable works, not all of which Mackenzie could refer to, some of which modify to some extent his conclusions: which remain, after more than fifty years, fresh and incisive.

Those who read on will find a wise man's comments on an aspect of the war that has so far been under-studied in this country. When Mackenzie has been digested, a much greater role in securing the Allied victory will be accorded to SOE than it has yet been given credit for. His book, late in time though it appears, will help to restore the balance of truth.

M. R. D. Foot
Nuthampstead, 3 March 2000

Preface

This work is one of the series of official histories of the war of 1939–45 sponsored by the Cabinet Office: but the responsibility for any facts or opinions which it contains is entirely the author's. The work as it now stands has not been subject to any official censorship on grounds of security or of policy.

A word on sources may be useful. The narrative is based primarily on the departmental papers of SOE. After the dissolution of the department many of these were destroyed as unimportant, but there still remains an immense mass of material which contains much of historical value. Some of it helps to elucidate particular events or threads of policy, but on the whole its importance is in the fullness with which it paints the picture of the life of Europe under German occupation. There is a great deal which it does not contain, but in spite of that it is certainly the best single source of material in the world for the history of European resistance.

This material is in great confusion. Partly through inexperience, partly for reasons of security, SOE began life without a central registry or departmental filing system. Each branch kept its own papers on its own system, from the Minister down to the sub-sections of the Country Sections: if a paper existed only in a single copy, it might come to rest finally anywhere in this hierarchy of separate archives. The original confusion was made worse because in 1945, when the end was in sight, SOE made a resolute attempt to impose on the existing chaos a proper system of departmental filing by subject. This was an immense task which was scarcely begun when the department officially came to an end: the registry staff was kept in being for some time, but the work was eventually stopped on grounds of economy when it was about a quarter done. One has therefore to cope with two superimposed systems of filing, both radically imperfect.

It should be made perfectly clear that the present is not based on a survey of *all* this SOE material. It has been an overriding consideration to produce some useful narrative quickly, while events were still fresh in mind: it can be claimed that whatever appears in the narrative has been verified by some good source, but there is still an immense amount of material untouched, which may affect details and local colour though it will probably not affect general conclusions.

In selecting material and pursuing references the author's mainstay has been the patience and experience of his research assistant, Miss Winifred Close: but the following clues are of particular value:

(a) Practically every section of SOE before its dissolution produced a narrative of its work. These vary enormously in quality and in the number of references they give, but they are all in a sense primary sources, as they were generally written by junior officers who had been actively engaged in the section's work: most of them were also checked by senior officials.

(b) A War Diary for the London HQ of SOE was kept in considerable detail by a separate section set up in 1941. This section did not always receive all the necessary material, nor did it have much grasp of policy: but the Diary is nevertheless invaluable for reference, especially as there goes with it a card-index of names.

(c) When SOE was being wound-up a 'Technical Handbook' was compiled from contributions by branches, in order to leave behind a comprehensive picture of the methods used. This deals with methods, not with events, and it has not been much used here as a source except to explain points of detail: but it is important to note that it exists and covers a great deal which is not included in this History.

(d) There are certain series of branch files which are of particular importance on the level of policy. These are the papers of the Minister's chief assistant, mainly in the AD/S.1 series: the papers of the successive holders of the post of CD: the papers of the Regional Directors: and those of the Section (COS/Plans) responsible for liaison with the COS Committee. So far as possible all these have been kept together in the archives.

Apart from the archives of SOE the author has used no official source except the files of Cabinet and COS papers in the Cabinet Office. The papers of other departments are referred to only when originals or copies appear in the SOE archives. The narrative is therefore written primarily from the point of view of SOE: it makes no claim to speak with authority as regards any other department.

Printed sources are already accumulating in embarrassing profusion. The author has covered fairly thoroughly such reminiscences as have appeared in English: but there is a vast literature in every European language, and it has only been possible to use rather random samples of this. These are referred to in footnotes where relevant.

The author is particularly obliged to Lord Selborne for granting the use of his own set of demi-official correspondence affecting SOE; and to all those members of the SOE staff who have helped him so much by comment or reminiscence. It has been a pleasure and an honour to work with them.

W.J.M.M.
September 1948

PART I

ORIGINS

CHAPTER I

First Steps

The year 1938 opened in an atmosphere which stimulated discussion of revolution and subversive warfare. The Spanish Civil War was at its height, and General Queipo de Llano's reference to the 'Fifth Column' in Madrid had already passed into common usage. The German 'tourist' was a familiar figure in the Balkans and had made his first practical contribution to war in Spain. Austria, Czechoslovakia and Danzig were being harassed by internal disorder stimulated from outside; the 'Cagoulards' were a staple topic of politics in France, Russia had turned the light of publicity on Trotskyist subversion and German intrigue. The Middle East was exposed to a well-contrived propaganda campaign, Italian as well as German; outside complicity in the Arab disorders in Palestine was a matter of fact, though its extent was a matter of speculation.

The general outline of the plan of warfare envisaged by the new Germany and the new Italy was therefore plain to any shrewd observer. Rearmament had already been accepted as a necessity by all but a small minority in Britain, and with it went the scrutiny of existing plans and the completion of a skeleton organisation for expansion in war. It was natural that many minds should turn to the necessity for meeting a subversive enemy by offensive as well as by defensive action, and there was considerable British experience on which to draw. Much of this was defensive – the experience of guerilla warfare in South Africa, in Ireland, in Palestine, on the North-West Frontier of India, sabotage as practised by the IRA in the 'troubles' of 1919/20, and by Von Papen's organisation in the USA before 1917. But the British had also a subversive tradition of their own; this was dramatised in the popular mind by 'Lawrence of Arabia', and by the 'Northcliffe propaganda' on which the Germans cast much of the responsibility for their earlier defeat, but it goes back much further into the history of the 'small wars' which made the British Empire.

It was also natural that these ideas which were in the air did not engage much of the time of the higher levels of government, and that such planning and organisation as there was lacked coherence and clear purpose. A policy of active subversion does not go well with

Parliamentary government, nor with organs of administration shaped by the traditions of Parliamentary government. In 1938 the importance of subversion was obvious; the dangers of incompetent subversion were no less obvious, and over-burdened Ministers and staffs were not anxious to meet them halfway. In the event, three separate organisations emerged, which at the outbreak of war had hardly gone beyond the stage of research and experiment: their objectives were obscure and overlapping, their relations to older departments ill-defined and often bad-tempered.

1. D Section

The first of these in order of time was Section IX (later D Section) of the Secret Intelligence Service. Some time in April 1938 Admiral Sir Hugh Sinclair, KCB, (who was head of SIS until his death in the autumn of 1939)* secured the seconding from the War Office of Major Lawrence Grand, RE,** for a limited period, in order to study and report on the possibilities of a British organisation for offensive action on the lines already made familiar by Germany and Italy. No record has been found of authorisation from a higher level, but it is scarcely likely that this initiative was taken without the concurrence of the Foreign Secretary;† the step was quite non-comittal, and circumstances were pressing – Austria had been occupied by the Germans a few weeks before. Major Grand was a regular officer in the RE, then engaged on work on 'motorisation' in the War Office; he was without experience in secret service work, but was a man of energy and ideas, to whose personal force tribute is paid by all who worked with him.

Major Grand's first task was to write his own directive. His first report[1] was dated 31st May 1938, and consisted mainly of a list of possible sabotage objectives in Germany such as electricity supply, telephones, food supplies, warships, aeroplanes, agriculture: a very heterogeneous list, with which 'moral sabotage' was oddly coupled as 'Item 12'. Methods of working into Germany were conceived to be:

(i) The use of organisations already existing in Germany, e.g. the Communists.

---

[1] SOE Archives File 1/470/2 (first document).
* [1873–1939; in *DNB*, *Missing Persons*.]
** [1898–1975, major general 1949; to be in new *DNB*.]
† [E. F. L. Wood, 1881–1959, Viceroy of India (as Lord Irwin) 1926–31, KG 1931, Foreign Secretary (as Lord Halifax) 1938–40, Ambassador in Washington 1941–6, Earl of Halifax 1944, OM 1946; in *DNB*.]

   (ii) Lone workers to carry out isolated and specially dangerous acts of sabotage.

   (iii) 'Moral sabotage', i.e. 'whisperings', etc., possibly organised by the Jews.

It was also made clear that representatives would be required in neutral countries on the German frontiers, both for action against goods in these countries *en route* for Germany, and to act as bases and supply depots for workers within the country. It was not suggested that action should be taken on any of these items in time of peace; the immediate programme should be:

   (i) Research into sabotage devices and production of stocks.

   (ii) Investigation of targets.

   (iii) Organisation of depots and establishment of contacts in neutral countries.

The cost of this programme was put at £20,000.

This document was circulated within SIS – apparently not outside it – and was received 'with a combination of alarm and fascination'.[1] The upshot of the comments made was that extreme caution would be necessary to avoid diplomatic incidents in time of peace, and that the planning of operations should be concentrated in the first instance on the transport of iron ore from Sweden and of oil from Roumania. Approval for action on these lines was given by Admiral Sinclair, and Major Grand's posting was confirmed for another two months, with a possible extension to the end of 1938.

Section IX was thus constituted originally within the SIS, with terms of reference which were narrow, in that they precluded any aggressive action in time of peace, but also wide, in that they left a free choice as to the investigation of means, and included such embracing terms as 'moral sabotage'. The political significance of the means which came to hand, and the natural progression from 'sabotage' through 'moral sabotage' to propaganda and politics, were to make much trouble for Section IX and for the organisation which followed it.[2]

2. Electra House

The other two components of the future SOE were MI(R) (War Office) and 'Electra House'. The latter is the less important to us, as its later fortunes linked with PWE, not with SOE, and it may be dealt with briefly first.[3]

---

1 SOE War Diary.

2 Apparently CSS explicitly extended Colonel Grand's task to propaganda in September 1938: see Note on p. 34.

3 Mr David Garnett's 'History of PWE'. [1892–1981, novelist; in *DNB*. His history of PWE awaits clearance.]

The importance of propaganda was just as obvious in the years immediately before the war as was that of an active 'Fifth Column', and there was no lack of competitors for the right to organise it. The Foreign Office, the embryo Ministry of Information, the BBC, the Admiralty, the War Office (PR and MI7) and the Air Ministry, as well as D Section, all had a finger in the pie; and the confusion was never finally resolved. The history of Electra House seems to begin with a request from Admiral Sinclair to Sir Campbell Stuart* during the Munich crisis in September 1938, to look into the problem of propaganda to enemy countries; Sir Campbell was an obvious choice for the purpose, in view of his close association with the work of Crewe House,** to which extravagant tributes had been paid by the German General Staff after the defeat of 1918. Sir Stephen Tallent's† report[1] to the CID sub-committee on the trial mobilisation of the M of I in September 1938 emphasised that 'the outstanding lesson . . . was the lack of machinery for securing prompt, quick and efficient conveyance of British news and views to potentially enemy peoples'. This led in due course to the appointment of a special sub-committee under Sir Campbell Stuart and to a recommendation (16th January 1939) that an Enemy Publicity Section should be established on a small scale in time of peace. This recommendation was promptly acted on, and Department EH came into being in January 1939 in Electra House, where Sir Campbell Stuart had his office as chairman of the Imperial Communications Advisory Committee.

Its terms of reference do not appear to have been clearly laid down; even apart from developments in D Section, parallel organisations grew up very early in the Ministry of Information and in the BBC. In the former there was a Division for Enemy and Enemy Occupied Countries 'concerned with the collection of news and information from these countries, the distribution of news and information to them, and the conduct of propaganda, and counter-propaganda necessary to meet enemy statements and mis-statements'.[2] Similarly the staff associated with the BBC's German and other foreign language broadcasts construed its duties as requiring much more than the transmission of material provided by other departments.

---

[1] 9th November 1938.
[2] Memo. on organisation of M of I, 21st November 1940.
* [1885–1972, publicist; in *DNB*.]
** [See his *Secrets of Crewe House* (1920: like other books cited below, published in London if no other place is given).]
† [1884–1958, civil servant; in *DNB*.]

The higher organisation of these three bodies is not really intelligible. Electra House was in form a department of the Foreign Office: the extent of its authority over the BBC was obscure, and the latter body complained very early in the war that it was subject to conflicting directives from Electra House, and from the Ministry of Information. A series of fortnightly meetings between Electra House and the Ministry of Information began in December 1939, and in June 1940 an agreement was reached between Sir Campbell Stuart and Mr Duff Cooper,* under which Electra House was to be responsible to the Ministry of Information for policy but was to retain its identity as a department of the Foreign Office, financed from the Secret Service vote. This arrangement broke down almost at once, on the discovery by the Director-General of the Ministry of Information (Sir Walter Monckton)** that Electra House was operating a secret station, 'Das Wahre Deutschland', outside the knowledge and direction of the Ministry of Information.

Department EH's functions were as obscure as its authority: the most that can be said is that it was to be concerned primarily with 'black' propaganda; propaganda that could not be acknowledged as emanating from the British Government, either because of an embarrassing conflict with their official utterances or because it purported to come from some other source. It was responsible for the first British venture (in May 1940) with the device of the 'Freiheitsender' – a short-wave wireless broadcast purporting to be operated by rebels within the country to which it was addressed; and it also experimented, as did D Section, with the production of printed material apparently of German origin and circulated by underhand means within Germany. These techniques proved to be of great importance later, in the occupied countries much more than in Germany itself, and there was a very close connection between their use and the military development of Resistance.[1]

3. MI(R)[2]

The first nucleus of MI(R) is to be found in a section known as General Staff (Research) (GS(R)), whose functions were explained

---

1 See further in the PWE History and WP(R) 105 of 29th March 1940.

2 Apparently most of MI(R)'s papers have been destroyed, lost or merged in the general War Office archives. But after its dissolution a bundle of files on policy was kept together by Colonel Holland's former secretary, Miss Joan Bright,† and went with her to the Cabinet Office. They have now been added to SOE archives.

* [1890–1954, first Viscount Norwich 1952; in *DNB*. See his *Old Men Forget* (1953).]

** [1891–1965, lawyer, knight 1937, Viscount Monckton 1957; in *DNB*.]

† [Miss Bright became Mrs Philip Astley. See her *The Inner Circle* (1971).]

by the S of S for War in the House of Commons on 9th March 1938 in these vague terms:

> When so much instruction is to be gained from present events the absence of any branch exclusively concerned with purely military research is noticeable, and a small section to study the practice and lessons of actual warfare will be established.

Its charter within the War Office was 'Research into problems of tactics and organisation under the direction of DCIGS. Liaison with other branches of the War Office and with Commands in order to collect new ideas on these subjects. Liaison with Technical Research branches'; and its status is illustrated by this quotation from a Minute by DCIGS – 'I have introduced a research section directly under me. This section must be small, almost anonymous, go where they like, talk to whom they like, but be kept from files, correspondence and telephone calls.'[1]

A list of the papers produced by GS(R) is given in a footnote.[2] The variety of topics covered was very wide, and it is not until Report No. 7 that the section began to follow the line which led to practical preparations for irregular warfare. This change of direction reflects the appointment to GS(R) (in December 1938) of Lieutenant Colonel J. F. C. Holland, DFC, RE,* an officer with personal experience of the defensive against irregular warfare in Ireland and India, and a lively appreciation of its technique and possibilities. By this time it was recognised that war was imminent and that investigation must lead very quickly to preparation for action. Contact was established with D Section, and their joint proposals were embodied in a paper by Colonel Grand dated 20th March 1939. The basic ideas of this paper are recognisably those of Colonel Holland; its style and its unquenchable optimism are certainly Colonel Grand's.[3] 'The absorption of Bohemia and Slovakia and the obvious intention of advancing toward and

---

[1] Derived from MI(R) War Diary 'Introduction', (MI(R) File 3).

[2] GS(R) Report No. 1 The Re-organisation of the War Office.

  2 The Employment of Historians by the War Office in a consultative capacity.

  3 Re-organisation of the General Staff.

  4 Army Requirements from the RAF in modern warfare.

  5 Organisation of Armoured and Mobile Units and Formations.

  6 Training of the Army.

  7 Considerations from the Wars in Spain and China with regard to certain aspects of Army Policy.

  8 Investigation of the Possibilities of Guerilla Activities.

[3] SOE Archives File 1/470/1.

* [1897–1956, major general 1943; in *DNB, Missing Persons*.]

absorbing Roumania (and possibly other countries on the North and West) for the first time gives an opening to an alternative method of defence, that is a method alternative to organised armed resistance. This defensive technique, which must now be developed, must be based on the experience which we have had in India, Irak, Ireland and Russia, i.e. the development of a combination of guerilla and IRA tactics.' The scheme dealt with Roumania, Denmark, Holland, Poland, Bohemia, Austria, Germany, Libya and Abyssinia; it suggested the posting of Colonel Holland and some twenty-five other officers, and expenditure of the order of £500,000 – 'should this be approved it will be possible to complete arrangements as regards Roumania in three weeks, and as regards the remainder of the scheme in three or four months, i.e. by July it should be possible to give a date on which there would be simultaneous disturbances throughout German occupied areas'.

A diary of the fortunes of this paper was recorded at the time by Colonel Grand.[1] It was submitted first to the Acting CSS, and by him to the DDMI. On 22nd March Colonel Grand was seen by the CIGS with the DMO and the DDMI, and general approval was given subject to the views of the Foreign Secretary. On 23rd March (Hitler had occupied what was left of Czechoslovakia on 15th March) Lord Halifax discussed the paper with the CIGS, Sir A. Cadogan, the Acting CSS and Colonel Grand. The only points recorded in discussion are the importance of secrecy and the special urgency of the problem of Roumanian oil; in conclusion 'Lord Halifax said that he agreed in principle with the scheme, which he now intended to forget, but that he would raise the matter with the Prime Minister and get him to speak to the Chancellor with a view to obtaining the money'. The CIGS made himself responsible for providing the personnel required, if the Prime Minister's approval were given.*

---

[1] MI(R) File 1.

* [Notes for this paragraph: l. 2 Acting CSS: (Sir) S. G. Menzies, 1890–1968, confirmed as C Dec. 1939, knight 1943, retired 1951; in *DNB*. l. 3 DDMI: Deputy Director Military Intelligence, then W. E. van Cutsem (see page 78 below). l. 3 CIGS: W. E. Ironside, 1888–1959, knight 1919, Chief of the Imperial General Staff Sep. 1939–July 1940, field-marshal 1940, baron 1941; in *DNB*. See *The Ironside Diaries* (1962). l. 4 DMO: Director of Military Operations, R. H. Dewing, 1891–1981. l. 5 Hitler: Adolf Hitler, 1889–1945, dictator of Germany from 1933; see John Lukacs, *The Hitler of History* (New York, 1997). l. 7 Cadogan: A. G. M. Cadogan, 1884–1968, Permanent Under-Secretary (henceforward PUS) Foreign Office 1938–46, knight 1941, OM 1951; in *DNB*; see his *Diaries*, ed. David Dilks (1971). l. 12 Prime Minister: A. Neville Chamberlain, 1869–1940, Prime Minister 1937–40; in *DNB*; see his life by K. Feiling (1946). l. 13 Chancellor: of the Exchequer: Sir John A. Simon, 1873–1954, knight 1910, Lord Chancellor 1940–5; see his *Retrospect* (1952).]

Action followed almost at once. A more specific paper[1] was produced by Colonel Holland on 3rd April, and provisional approval was given by the DCIGS: the CIGS was not able to see Colonel Holland until 13th April, but then approved the paper almost without qualification. The objects of the new Section were defined as:

(a) To study guerilla methods and produce a guerilla 'Field Service Regulations', incorporating detailed tactical and technical instructions, applying to each of several countries.

(b) To evolve destructive devices for delaying and suitable for use by guerillas, and capable of production and distribution on a wide enough scale to be effective.

(c) To evolve procedure and machinery for operating guerilla activities, if it should be decided to do so subsequently.

A limitation was imposed by the CIGS only in (c), which was not to involve participation by Regular Officers 'too openly'.

Colonel Holland's new branch was established first as 'D/M Section' in accommodation adjoining that of D Section.* Its first programme of work[2] is dated 13th April 1939. Although adjacent to Colonel Grand, it was not under his control: funds were provided from Secret Service moneys, but the chain of responsibility appears to have been through the DDMI to the DCIGS. This arrangement lasted only till the outbreak of war, when the Section was transferred to the War Office building and appeared on the official War Office list as MI(R) (sometimes MI1(R)).[3] Its terms of reference were naturally not promulgated, and it was not until 11th February 1940 that the administrative complications arising from this made it necessary for the DMI** to issue a confidential memorandum on the duties of the Section.[4] These were laid down as follows, in terms which cover the work done by MI(R) since its inception:

Duties of MI(R)

The duties of MI(R) are:

(a) General research as required by DMI including examination and preparation of projects involving the employment of special or irregular forces to assist or increase the effect of normally conducted operations, directly or indirectly.

---

[1] MI(R) File 1.
[2] On MI(R) File 1.
[3] Minutes of meeting with DCIGS on 27th June 1939, on MI(R) File 1.
[4] Conduct of Work No. 50, on MI(R) File 1.
* [At Caxton House, 2 Caxton Street, Westminster, next door to St Ermin's Hotel.]
** [F. G. Beaumont-Nesbitt, 1893–1971, Military Attaché Paris 1936–8, Washington 1942, Director of Military Intelligence 1939–40.]

(b) Technical research and production of appliances as required for such projects.

(c) The operation of such projects as may be decided on in discussion between DMI and DMO & P* and when such operation is not the function of any other branch of the War Office or other organisation or headquarters at home or abroad.

(d) The collection of information by special means outside the province of other sections of the MI Directorate.

(e) Interviewing, training and recording of personnel possessing special qualifications likely to be required in conjunction with irregular activities.

Such duties naturally involved serious risk of overlap with the activities of D Section, and relations were by no means happy. No clear 'modus vivendi' was reached before the creation of SOE in the summer of 1940, and the subsequent disappearance of both organisations: but the form of words then suggested indicates the distinction which was more or less observed in practice:

Those activities which can be discussed by British subjects with the authorities of the country concerned and which can be planned and carried out with the knowledge and co-operation of these Authorities, should be the responsibility of the War Office and should be handled in the Field by MI(R) Missions.

Those activities which cannot be discussed officially with the Authorities of the country concerned and which must be carried out by underground methods without the knowledge and even against the will of those Authorities, are the responsibility of D Section and should be handled in the Field by the 'D' organisation.[1]

---

[1] MI(R) No. 309/40 (Report by the DDMI(R), on MI(R) File 6).
* [Dewing had added plans to his remit.]

CHAPTER II

The Work of D Section

It will be convenient first to deal briefly with the organisation of the Section, then to give some account of its operations in various fields. These interlock in a confusing way, and it is not easy to arrange them satisfactorily under headings.

1. Organisation

D Section was in form an integral part of the SIS, sometimes referred to as Section IX. Its head, Colonel Grand ('D'), was responsible to 'C', the head of SIS (Admiral Sinclair, later Brigadier Menzies): the SIS was in turn controlled by the Foreign Office, where the Permanent Secretary himself generally acted in these matters for the Secretary of State. In the first year of the war Lord Hankey,* who was then Minister without Portfolio, appears to have had a special responsibility to the War Cabinet for this field of action, and Colonel Grand frequently dealt with him direct. The chain of command, clear enough on paper, was in practice extremely confusing, and Colonel Grand had in many matters a remarkably free hand.

The organisation in England was at first on a very small scale, and there was no serious expansion of the headquarters staff before the spring of 1939. By December 1939, it included forty-three officers (apart from secretaries, watchmen and so forth);[1] expansion continued during the next six months, and eventually about fifty D Section officers were taken over on the formation of SOE.[2] Many of them were then rapidly disposed of.

Various elaborate organisation charts exist, but it is clear that to the last the Section was run by Colonel Grand on a basis of direct personal dealings with each officer, and that duties were distributed

---

[1] Paper and organisation chart of 13th December 1939 on SOE Archives File 2/340/3.0 (destroyed).

[2] From Aide-Mémoire dated 22nd February 1941 on SOE File 1/470/1.3.

* [M. P. A. Hankey, 1877–1963, secretary to Cabinet 1916–38, knight 1916, baron 1940; in *DNB*. See S. W. Roskill, *Man of Secrets* (3 vols, 1970–74).]

rather at random according to individual ideas and immediate needs. At the very last (11th August 1940) a plan[1] was drawn up for the appointment of a regular Deputy and five Directors (Plans, Operations, Services, Organisation and Special Projects), but the scheme did not come into effect in Colonel Grand's time.

Recruitment also was on a personal basis; this was what happened in most expanding departments in the first year of the war, and it was not altogether inappropriate for a small organisation working in extreme secrecy. The nucleus was provided by a few officers from the SIS, of whom Lieutenant Colonel Chidson* was the most experienced. Colonel Grand's own contacts apparently lay largely in the City, and recruits were drawn mainly from the business world. The list is headed by a few 'big names', such as Lord Bearsted,** Mr Samuel Courtauld† and Mr Chester Beatty,†† who were little more than external advisers; the bulk of the staff were businessmen of lesser note, with a few journalists. On the whole, the London staff and the agents sent out from London were not men with a first-rate knowledge of the countries which concerned them: such experts as there were were mainly recruited locally in the field. The staff as a whole had a great deal of enterprise and ingenuity, as well as a strong personal loyalty to Colonel Grand: a number of them remained with SOE to the end and played distinguished parts. Inevitably they had the defects of a staff collected in such a way. They had little idea of the limitations on individual fancy which are implicit in the work of a government office, or of how to put their own case effectively in higher official quarters. In particular, the Foreign Office and its purposes were mysterious and unattractive to them; this had comparatively little effect in London, but the results were unfortunate for relations with HM Ministers in several countries. Relations with Regular Army officers working for MI(R) were little better.

The organisation was housed at first in the SIS Head Office,‡ and expanded from it in April 1939 into adjacent premises in Caxton House:‡‡ for a short time in the days of D/M Section these were shared with Colonel Holland and MI(R), which returned to the War Office on the outbreak of war. The first premises to be acquired outside London were The Fryth Private Hotel, Welwyn (Station IX), which was taken

---

1   Paper on SOE Archives File 2/340/3.0 (destroyed).
*   [M. R. Chidson, 1893–1957.]
**   [W. H. Samuel, 1882–1948, 2nd Viscount Bearsted 1927, art gallery trustee.]
†   [1876–1947, textile tycoon and art patron; in *DNB*.]
††   [1873–1968, New York-born mining engineer, collector and philanthropist, knight 1954; in *DNB*.]
‡   [Then at 54 Broadway, opposite St James's Park tube.]
‡‡   [Not quite adjacent, but within a furlong.]

over hurriedly for evacuation on the outbreak of war; and Station XII at Aston House, Stevenage, where the early research and supply organisation was housed from October 1939. In addition the Propaganda Section was evacuated to the old Rectory, Hertingfordbury, in September 1939,[1] and Brickendonbury, near Hertford (Station XVII) was taken for use as a demolition school in June 1940, shortly before the formation of SOE.

At this stage D Section mainly relied on the existing organisation of SIS to provide the ordinary administrative services. Finance was controlled by the SIS, although there appears to have been little in the way of detailed supervision; Colonel Grand reported personally to the CSS, and projects were approved or rejected by him without passing through other channels within the organisation.

The importance of Signals had scarcely been realised, and nothing had been done to investigate the problems of wireless communications with agents in the field in war conditions; such signals traffic as there was, was handled through the existing SIS channels, and any small requirements which arose for signals material were met by them. Similarly there had been no investigation of the problem of dispatching material to the field in war conditions, by air or otherwise; the only routes which existed were through commercial channels [PASSAGE DELETED ON GROUNDS OF NATIONAL SECURITY].

The question of training had begun to raise some doubts, and Lieutenant Colonel Chidson had in March 1940 posed the question of how long the system of attaching new entrants individually to more experienced officers for coaching could continue.[2] The project of a school had been approved by June 1940,[3] but nothing was accomplished in Colonel Grand's time.

Research and production had been tackled more energetically under Commander Langley,* who was appointed in December 1938[4] and established Station XII in the autumn of 1939. The investigation of time-fuses for explosives and incendiaries had gone a long way, and in fact later forms of time-fuse did not vary greatly from the types first developed. A good deal of other useful work was done on explosives and incendiaries, and the output of devices from production was considerable, for other users as well as D Section; Colonel Grand

---

[1] After an abortive attempt to join the evacuated 'EH' sections at Woburn. Garnett, p. 14.

[2] Minute of 15th March 1940 on SOE Archives File 2/340/3.0 (destroyed).

[3] Minute by D of 6th June 1940 on SOE Archives File 2/340/3.0 (destroyed).

[4] SOE Early War Diary and Technical Histories, Pt II.

* [RN, retired: distinguish from J. M. Langley, Coldstream Guards and MI9.]

mentions £50,000 a month.[1] Research also diverged into other paths, such as the use of free balloons and the development of 'secure' R/T, which had no future in SOE.

Overseas Organisation

Abroad, D Section had at one time or another in Western Europe officers responsible for work in Sweden, Norway, Holland, and Spain. In France a mission was established on the outbreak of war under Major Humphries,* for liaison with the French 5ème Bureau, and to assist in any projects developing on French territory. Its liaison was mainly on matters of technical development, and it was impossible in the temper of the French Government and people at the time to make any effective approach to the problem of action behind the lines if any French territory were occupied.[2] The mission escaped with difficulty on the fall of Paris, leaving a few explosives with personal contacts of their own; but no organisation of any kind remained in being.

No organisation whatever survived in Western Europe after the fall of France, except a tenuous contact with the ADE in Spain; this was dropped shortly afterwards as a matter of policy.

The situation in the Balkans was better; the organisation was weakened by German diplomatic pressure in Yugoslavia and Roumania, but D Section passed on to SOE considerable assets in all the Balkan countries. The main weakness here was the lack of any effective co-ordination between the Balkan countries, between D Section and other agencies working there, and between the preparations for subversion and those for the conduct of large-scale military operations in the area.[3]

In the winter of 1939–40 there was an awkward three-cornered arrangement: Hanau** in Belgrade, W. S. Bailey† in Istanbul, a certain Mr Goodwill in Greece. The last named was also frequently in Cairo,

---

1   Letter of 5th August 1940 to Mr Gladwyn Jebb on SOE Archives File 2/340/3.0 (destroyed).

2   Some last minute efforts are recorded in SOE Archives File 3/470/7a.

3   D Section had on the outbreak of war sponsored the attachment of Clayton to General Wavell's HQ as GSO1 Publicity (copy of his directive on SOE File 1/470/1) and had provided secret funds for clandestine propaganda among the tribes in Libya and Abyssinia: at an early stage he was absorbed into the military machine and passes out of the picture. [A. P. Wavell, 1883–1950, then C-in-C Middle East, knight 1939, C-in-C India 1941–3, field-marshal, viscount and Viceroy 1943, retired, and earl, 1947; in *DNB*.]

*   [L. A. L. Humphreys, died 1976, after the war, a master at Stonyhurst.]

** [Julius Hanau, real name Hannon, 1885–1943, alias Caesar; see pages 24–5.]

†   [Lieutenant-Colonel S. W. Bailey.]

and had some very vague responsibility for keeping in touch with GHQ Middle East, and co-ordinating D Section's Balkan plans with theirs. By May 1940 it was obvious that communications through the Mediterranean might be closed at any moment, and it was inevitable that in future the Balkan countries should be 'fed' from Cairo, the nearest point at which a dump of stores could safely be established. It was also inevitable that the military authorities there would attempt to exercise some control over an organisation holding a store of destructive weapons held under their supervision and proposing to issue them for action in a theatre of vital strategic concern to the Middle East. At this juncture Major (as he then was) G. F. Taylor,* Colonel Grand's second in command, secured the use of a Sunderland and flew out to the Middle East in haste, while the route was still open, taking with him such stores as he could collect. In Cairo he insisted, rightly or wrongly, that the chain of command lay from London to those active in the field, not passing through GHQ Middle East, except for matters strictly in the sphere of that Command; and to strengthen the case, the main Balkan HQ of D Section was now established[1] at Istanbul, leaving the Cairo Office responsible only for general supervision and supplies and for affairs in Greece.[2] Taylor's personal relations with the soldiers were good, and minor difficulties about stores' allocation and so forth proved manageable; but the organisation then created was the beginning of endless disputes about control. To make matters worse, personal squabbles (which were endemic in the atmosphere of Cairo) broke out between Goodwill, the MI(R) representative, and the DDMI; Goodwill had to be recalled in the autumn of 1940, and he was then replaced by Mr George Pollock,** of whom more hereafter.

2. Scandinavia

It will be remembered that when the creation of D Section was authorised it was asked to concentrate in the first instance on the problems of Swedish iron ore and Roumanian oil, on which great emphasis was laid by the experts in economic warfare. Even after the occupation of

---

[1] For a short time under Lieutenant Colonel Hanau, then under Major Bailey.

[2] Telegrams quoted textually in SOE War Diary, without further reference. See also Taylor's report of 5th June and 27th June in Greek Progress Reports file, and DDMI's letter of 6th June annexed.

* [G. F. Taylor, 1903–79, Australian textile tycoon, one of SOE's strongest formative characters.]

** [(Sir) George Pollock (QC), 1901–91.]

Austria and the drastic exploitation of all native resources by the Hermann Goering Werke, Germany was greatly deficient in iron ore (especially of high grades), and was dependent on the ore of Lorraine, of Spain and of Sweden. The two former would, we hoped, be inaccessible in war. Sweden was therefore the key to the situation.

The Swedish iron-ore mines lie in two main areas, one south of Stockholm with special export facilities through the port of Oxelösund, the other in the far north with exits to Luleå on the Baltic and to Narvik. Annual exports to Germany through these three ports reached 8,000,000 tons or more in a good year;[1] but Luleå was normally closed by ice from December to April, and occasionally Oxelösund was closed – hence the vital importance of the Narvik route. German reactions entirely confirmed the emphasis laid by our experts on the whole complex, and the Swedish Government was equally aware of its importance. Thus D Section's enterprise was in the nature of an attack on an elephant with a pea-shooter; the only favourable factor was that this immense mass of traffic passed through three bottle-necks, any of which might with luck be blocked (at least for a time) by well-directed individual sabotage.

So far as the Narvik exit was concerned, D Section's projects did not go beyond exploration on a map and the collection of information. There was talk of the possibility of sabotaging the power station on which the Narvik–Luleå railway depends: there was also talk of dumping explosives with the aid of a private yacht in some quiet spot near Narvik, in readiness for sabotage, or of sinking two British ships alongside the iron-ore quays.[2] These projects acquired the code-name 'Arctic', but never reached the stage of concrete planning, and the stoppage of the Narvik traffic was very early recognised to be a problem which could not be dealt with on these lines.

Similarly the blocking of Luleå ('Sub-Arctic') hardly attained the status of a plan. There was a suggestion in the air that good effects could be produced by sinking a ship in the fairway, or by clandestine minelaying, and in June 1940 much time was spent on a project for buying and operating under Finnish registry a British-owned ship (the s.s. 'Uleå'). This eventually petered out in the autumn of 1940, after an SOE representative had visited Helsinki, and satisfied himself that the legal complications were insuperable.

Oxelösund on the other hand was pressed to the verge of a serious diplomatic incident, and the history of Operation 'Lumps' is worth

---

[1] Details in Rickman, 'Swedish Iron Ore', Faber, 1939.

[2] A reconnaissance of Narvik was made in a private yacht (by Colonel [Sir] H. H. Hartly, CBE [LMS railway magnate]) in Summer 1938. See Colonel Grand's 'Report and Lessons' d/d November 1946, p. 6; held by SIS.

following in a little detail as an illustration of methods and difficulties. The first step taken by D Section in Swedish business was to engage a certain A. F. Rickman* in July 1938 and to commission him to produce a booklet on the Swedish iron-ore industry. Rickman was the son of the clerk to a well-known barrister; a young man of about thirty with varied experience in Australia and Canada in insurance and in the film industry, whose personal qualities seem to have been admirable, but did not include any knowledge of Sweden, of the steel industry, or of secret work. His book was actually written, and was published by Messrs Faber and Faber in August 1939.[1] It had already served its purpose in enabling Rickman to visit Sweden temporarily and to produce a first secret report on the export of Swedish ore through Oxelösund[2] dated 10th October 1938. The next step was to establish Rickman more permanently in Sweden in some orthodox line of business; this involved much effort, beginning with the formation of a bogus company as a subsidiary to the Aga Company, for which Rickman should act as agent, and ending by his appearance in the summer of 1939 as an agent for the French firm of Odont-Email of Avignon, manufacturers of dental cements. This business cover involved genuine business and occupied much of Rickman's time; but by the autumn of 1939 he was fairly well established with communications to HQ in London by secret messages in his business correspondence and by the use of the diplomatic bag and the SIS transmitter in the Embassy.

The sabotage organisation hardly corresponded to the elaboration of this facade. There were three lines of contact:

(a)   The British colony, exemplified by Mr Ernest Biggs of the Windsor Tea Co., who was brought in primarily to assist in the distribution of propaganda, but collaborated also in the importing of sabotage material under commercial cover.

(b)   Sympathetic Swedes, exemplified by Ture Nermann, a well-known anti-Nazi and publisher of the anti-Nazi paper 'Trots Allt'.

(c)   German refugees, of whom Arno Behrisch was the most prominent and most disastrous.

All three sources of recruitment were watched suspiciously by the Swedish police, which had perhaps certain German contacts and sympathies, but was primarily concerned to avoid incidents likely to compromise Swedish neutrality. Higher authorities in Britain were

---

[1]   'Swedish Iron Ore' by A. F. Rickman. There is some irony in Messrs Faber & Faber's blurb: 'The best technical advice indicated that there was a gap to be filled by this book, and that Mr Rickman was the writer to fill it.'

[2]   SOE Archives, early Scandinavian files, No. 2 on 'Lumps' file – XXX/M/1.

*   [Chidson's brother-in-law.]

anxious that sabotage should not be carried out by British subjects in person, and it was not easy to find reliable Swedes ready to destroy Swedish property; so that the field of choice was further restricted to exiled Germans of various shades.

Active planning for an attack on Oxelösund began in October 1939. Various possibilities[1] such as incitement to strike or the sinking of ships at the quay-side were examined and rejected, and the final conclusion (reached in December) was in favour of an attack on the loading cranes and the conveyor-belt by which they were served. Success in this would certainly have hampered operations at the port, but it is not clear that there would have been a complete stoppage or that much time would have been required to clear the damage. Sabotage material was available in Sweden, Rickman believed that he had some Germans ready to do the job; and the project passed abruptly from the realm of amateurish experiment to that of strategic decision on a very high level. The account which follows is given with some reserve as the documentary evidence is scanty.

The First Lord of the Admiralty (Mr Churchill),* who was especially concerned with the stopping of the Narvik traffic, was consulted on 2nd January 1940, and favoured action. On the next day the Acting Chief of SIS consulted the Foreign Office, and a meeting was held by the Prime Minister at which Mr Churchill, Lord Halifax, Lord Hankey and CSS were present. Action was prohibited, but further investigation was authorised; Sir W. Stephenson** (of SIS) and Captain Fraser† of D Section visited Sweden specially for the purpose. Their reports were favourable, especially in view of unusual weather conditions which had blocked the port with ice and suspended work, so that the area was comparatively deserted; but on 29th January the project was again turned down by the Prime Minister and the Foreign Secretary. Lord Halifax once more discouraged action when approached on 15th February; weather conditions were then again favourable, and there had recently been a round-up of Communists in Sweden, which (it was thought) might give a chance of planting responsibility on them.[2]

---

1 SOE Archives, early Scandinavian files, Minute from D/XE (Captain Dolphin) on 'Lumps' File – XXX/M/1.
2 No. 76 on 'Lumps' file (Note by Colonel Grand).
* [(Sir) W. L. S. Churchill, 1874-1965, SOE's main prop, Prime Minister 1940–45, 1951–5, OM 1946, KG 1953.]
** [(Sir) W. S. Stephenson, 1896–1989, Canadian businessman, headed British Security Co-ordination, New York, 1940–45, knight 1945; in *DNB*. See *British Security Coordination* (1999, though written 1945), his section's in-house history.]
† [Ingram Fraser.]

The next initiative appears to have been taken by Mr Churchill,[1] not by D Section; the First Lord saw Colonel Grand on 5th March and showed some surprise that the plan had not been pressed again by those immediately responsible. The sequence of events was then a further reference to Stockholm (CXG/756 of 6th March); reports from Stockholm on 7th and 8th March (CXG/899 and 905) that conditions were very favourable; informal authorisation of action at once (CXG/762 of 8th March), followed by a formal written authority from Lord Hankey on 9th March, [2] based on a decision of the Prime Minister and Lord Halifax.[3]

The fuse had at last been lit – and nothing happened. The delay had been too much for Rickman's anti-Nazi Germans, and the action party refused to act, ostensibly for political reasons. It is easy but unfair to criticise Rickman for lack of energetic control; it would have baffled any leader to keep such men under discipline in such circumstances. It is less unfair to blame London for its failure to appreciate the conditions in which sabotage operations are planned and executed; but to the end of the war this point was never fully grasped at high levels, and SOE (like D Section) was sometimes too reluctant to make clear how brittle the weapon was which it had created.

The 'Lumps' project was by no means the only D Section activity in Scandinavia. Rickman's organisation was as much concerned with establishing lines of communication to Germany as with sabotage in Sweden; it seems to have been hardly more successful in the former, and the confusion of the two activities was one of the causes of its final disaster. But organisations of German exiles undoubtedly used to pass propaganda material to Germany through Sweden, and there was some attempt to open similar channels through Denmark when Captain Fraser visited Copenhagen in November 1939. Fraser paid a second visit on 2nd April 1940, arriving just in time to be caught by the German invasion; fortunately his passport as a diplomatic courier was respected by the Germans and he was ultimately repatriated with the Legation staff. An office had been opened in Oslo in December 1939 by a Norwegian named Bonnevie,* acting the part of a business agent of Rickman; Bonnevie's object seems to have been simply to open lines for transmission of propaganda to Germany, but there is no record that anything came of it, and the whole thing was swept away by the invasion in April 1940.

---

[1] No. 64 on 'Lumps' file (Note by Colonel Grand). SOE Archives early Scandinavian files.

[2] No. 70A on 'Lumps' file.

[3] The final capitulation of Finland to Russia took place on 12th March.

* [Helmer Bonnevie.]

It is of more interest that the possibilities of small boat operations across the North Sea had been envisaged before the German invasion, which made them a crucial factor in Norwegian resistance. In the summer before the war D Section had exploited the summer holidays of various members of the Royal Cruising Club to carry out an unostentatious reconnaissance of beaches suitable for clandestine landings along almost the entire coast-line from Trondheim to the Finnish frontier;[1] and in the winter of 1939–40 one or two yachtsmen connected with this enterprise had visited Aberdeen and the Shetlands and had begun to explore the possibility of using friendly fishermen to smuggle explosives and other stores to Scandinavia – a necessary alternative route now that commercial channels were blocked. [PASSAGE DELETED ON GROUNDS OF NATIONAL SECURITY.] Lieutenant Commander Holdsworth, RNVR,* visited Norway in November 1939 to explore the other end of this possible route, travelling as a business representative of the firm of Angus Watson, with a keen interest in the canned fish industry. Nothing had developed from this before the German attack, which entirely altered the situation.

There appear to have been no preparations by D Section for such a possibility, and its hasty reaction was to dispatch Holdsworth at once to Stockholm, with inadequate cover as a diplomatic courier and a very wild directive,[2] which instructed him –

   (i) to contact the Norwegian authorities and make arrangements with them to initiate sabotage and the dumping of supplies behind the advancing Germans:
  (ii) to set up a separate and independent organisation of his own to cover occupied Norway:
 (iii) to make arrangements with the local inhabitants to expect a British landing at Trondheim.

Holdsworth reached Stockholm on 13th April, and elaborated an alibi for himself by claiming that he represented a Fund for the Relief of Distress in Norway, sponsored by eminent persons in Britain; an excellent cover, which would give him an easy passage and a warm welcome anywhere in Sweden or in unoccupied Norway, were it not that no such Fund then existed. It was therefore necessary to invent it; it was organised officially on 30th April, under the auspices of the Lord Mayor of London, and it continued to exist blamelessly and efficiently throughout the war.

---

[1] SOE Early War Diary.
[2] SOE Early War Diary.
* [Gerry Holdsworth, 1915–85; see page 235.]

Meantime, on 20th April, Rickman had been arrested. Holdsworth's position: became daily more precarious, and on 4th May he thought it best to leave Sweden in haste via Finland.

The inner history of Rickman's arrest is still far from clear. Its timing and effects were perfect from the German point of view. It practically eliminated the whole D Section organisation in Scandinavia at the moment when it was seriously needed; it left the Swedish public with the impression that the British were sinister and ruthless, while making it clear to the Swedish authorities that they were really incompetent and helpless. All this suggests German planning and instigation, but luck is probably a sufficient explanation. The Swedish Government was very nervous, and its police were efficient. It is fairly clear that Rickman was noticed first as a distributor of Allied propaganda, and that suspicion arose for the obvious reasons, his contacts with Swedes of violent anti-German views and with German exiles who were already under police surveillance and may in one or two cases have played a double game. There is no doubt that the effects of the arrest were exaggerated by the amateurishness of Rickman's arrangements; his stock of explosives – by this time substantial – was still concentrated at Bigg's warehouse, and his papers appear to have been kept in ordinary business-like order at his flat. The Swedish police were presented with the entire story of Oxelösund, and with papers hinting that much more extensive and lethal activities against Swedish neutrality had been planned.

Fortunately there was no direct connection either with the British Legation or with the local SIS organisation. The three British subjects involved (Rickman, Biggs and Gill) did all that was possible at the trial to avoid going beyond admissions to which they were pinned by documentary evidence, and the record is greatly to their credit as individuals, though they were not very competent as secret agents; but the nerves of the Minister* and of SIS's local representative were under severe strain throughout, and their reactions to D Section and its work left a lasting impression in the Foreign Office and in Broadway.

The result of the trial was that Rickman was given a sentence of eight years, of which he served nearly four, and Biggs five years of which he served one; Gill was released on payment of a small fine. Rickman's secretary was given three and a half years, as was the German Social Democrat Arno Behrisch.

---

* [Sir Victor Mallett, 1893–1969, later Ambassador in Madrid and then in Rome. On SOE's affairs in Sweden see (Sir) Peter Tennant, *Touchlines of War* (Hull, 1992).]

3. The Danube

First steps in the Balkans were directed by oil, as those in Scandinavia by iron ore. Till the very last, Germany's oil position continually turned out to be more favourable than was predicted by the experts; but German actions indicated that it was always precarious, and that any serious diminution of supplies from Roumania would have gravely hampered their military operations. A successful military defence of Roumania against German attack was never very probable; but it was reasonable to hope that in the event of war the oil-wells could be effectively destroyed, and that even if Roumania were neutral something could be achieved by sabotage of tank-cars on the railway between Ploesti and Giurgiu and by interference with barge traffic in the Danube. D Section was by no means the only organisation involved in these projects and it is impossible to tell the story without diverging somewhat into the activities of other departments.

The Admiralty were concerned through Captain Despard,* the Naval Attaché at Bucharest, who appears to have thought largely in terms of open naval warfare on the Danube: the Ministry of Economic Warfare took a large part in pre-emptive operations for the control of Danube shipping; MI(R) held a party of RE's in Egypt in readiness to move to Roumania in haste in the event of war, and it was represented in Bucharest; the French, from Gamelin** downwards, were extremely interested, and apparently organised some activities of their own. Meantime His Majesty's Representatives in the Balkan countries were always on tenderhooks lest some of these organisations might provoke an incident diplomatically unfavourable to the Allies. To co-ordinate all this an inter-departmental committee was set up in January 1940 under Rear Admiral Bellairs,† then DNI, as a subcommittee of the Cabinet Committee, with instructions 'to advise on any naval, military or air operations relating to the oil supplies of Roumania or Russia and to transport, which may be referred to them by members of the War Cabinet or by Government Departments'.[1] This committee held numerous meetings and considered various plans, which all petered out even before the military situation changed in the summer of 1940.

---

[1] See POG(D) series of papers.

* [Captain M. C. Despard, DSC, RN (retired), Naval Attaché at Belgrade and Bucharest from 1939 and at Budapest from early 1940.]

** [General M. G. Gamelin, French C-in-C from 1938, dismissed mid-May 1940, survived Buchenwald; see his *Servir* (3 vols, Paris, 1946–7).]

† [Rear-Admiral R. M. Bellairs, 1884–1959, British representative at League of Nations 1932–9, at Admiralty supervising intelligence 1939–45, but not DNI: a post held, 1939–42, by J. H. Godfrey, 1888–1971, in *DNB*; on whom see Patrick Beesly, *Very Special Admiral* (1980).]

Many of these schemes were economic and D Section was involved only because its agents were conveniently placed, and funds could be drawn through it for unacknowledgeable transactions. It was concerned in this way in the purchase of the 'Goeland Fleet' of river craft, which seems to have cropped up first in April 1939 and to have been clinched hurriedly in September 1939 by an arrangement which gave nominal control of the fleet to a Mr Horace Emery, who was then investigating the problem of the Danube on D Section's behalf. Another complicated deal was effected in December 1939 to gain control of the 'Schultz fleet' of six tugs and twenty-six barges, based at Belgrade; and D Section was also involved in a scheme for bribing Danube pilots to refuse employment by the Germans, which was initiated in February 1940 and had some success. All these plots involved the local naval attachés, and led on to the more ambitious project of arming British-controlled Danube shipping for use in the event of war, and of providing a 'stiffening' of British naval personnel introduced as 'tourists' in the first instance. This scheme seems to have been approved[1] with some misgivings by the Bellairs Committee, and the armament required was sent out by D Section on 9th March 1940 in ninety-five cases invoiced as spare parts to the Chrysler agent in Budapest. They were successfully transferred at Sulina on 29th March to one of the Goeland Co.'s barges, controlled by the naval attaché at Bucharest. There D Section's responsibility ended, but unfortunately the story did not. The barge reached Giurgiu on 4th April; the disguised sailors seem to have been indiscreet on shore, and local German 'tourists' successfully directed Roumanian attention to their cargo. Publicity and a minor diplomatic incident followed, well pointed by German propaganda, and a good deal of mud was flung in British official circles; most of this stuck to D Section, which was already *persona non grata* with most British diplomats in the Balkans.

This was unfair. D Section's own business was mainly with various plans for blocking the Danube by direct action; these also ended in failure but not in farce. The three main plans were put forward first after a visit by Mr Horace Emery in the summer of 1939, but their chances of success depended on the personality of Mr Julius Hanau who had become D Section's representative in Yugoslavia in June 1939. Hanau was a South African Jew, who had held a British commission in the war of 1914–18, had finished up in Yugoslavia after fighting on the Salonika front, and had remained in Belgrade, where he had become a successful businessman, in the rather smoky

---

[1] POG(D) series of papers.

atmosphere of business in the Balkans. He possessed a thorough knowledge of Yugoslavia and of the seamy side of Yugoslav affairs; much energy and ingenuity, real hatred for the Germans, and an impish sense of humour which found expression in many harassing attacks on local German prestige: he arranged for instance that a distinguished German orchestra should be howled down in Belgrade, and that suitable publicity should be given to the criminal record of Neubacher, the new German Consul-General. Such incidents drew a good deal of attention to Hanau's activities, and his cover as a secret agent was quite ineffective: but he was in no sense an innocent abroad, as was Rickman.

The three vital points suggested for an attack on Danube transport were:

(a) The Greben Narrows; an area in Yugoslav territory where the river is constricted at a bend in open country by a retaining wall: the destruction of the retaining wall would divert much of the flow of water and would probably make navigation impossible if the water level at the time were low.

(b) The Kazan defile, where the river flows in a gorge, one side of which is Yugoslav, the other Roumanian.

(c) The Iron Gates – the most obvious target and in some respects the most difficult.

The Greben Narrows story is brief. A charge was duly laid against the wall, ready for detonation on proper instructions; unfortunately its custodian was an enthusiastic Yugoslav who could not resist touching it off in November 1939 when a German tug with four oil barges was passing. Two of the barges were sunk, and some inconvenience was caused to navigation: what is more, Hanau succeeded in smothering investigation and in securing the contract for repairs for a nominee of his own, who incorporated a very large destructive charge in the rebuilt wall. But the opportunity to use this never came.

The Kazan defile project was more grandiose, but it had a certain unlikely impudence which gave it more chance of success than ever seemed possible. The river at this point is very deep, but not wide, and it is overhung by high cliffs on the Yugoslav side. The plan was to bury a huge quantity of explosives in these cliffs, so that their detonation would throw a vast mass of rock into the river: it was not certain that it would be blocked, but the speed of the current would be so increased as to make navigation impossible, and clearance would be a very big job. Not unnaturally scepticism was expressed when the project was explained by the CSS to Sir Orme Sargent* and Sir Ronald

---

* [1884–1962, knight 1937, PUS Foreign Office 1946–9; in *DNB*.]

Campbell;[1]* action was prohibited, but not continued investigation and preparation. Accordingly, the same firm of contractors as had repaired the Greben wall was engaged by Hanau to begin quarrying operations above the defile, on the pretext of a search for minerals, and it made considerable progress in removing stone and replacing it with explosive. Unfortunately the preparations were detected by the Germans; perhaps this was inevitable, but there was some suspicion that a British tug had delivered explosives to the site with unnecessary ostentation. This was in December 1939; an official Yugoslav enquiry was inevitable, and (though its report was suitably discreet) nothing more could be done without full Yugoslav complicity. The project became in effect the responsibility of the Yugoslav General Staff, and it was never executed.

The Iron Gates scheme never came so close to maturity as the other two, and to those on the spot it served largely as a cover to distract attention from other projects. Its political background is however of some importance, though little of it can be supplied from D Section's records. The original conception was that some of the Danube barges controlled by the British should be filled with cement and sunk in the narrows; it was also suggested that the line of railway track used for towing at this point should be destroyed and the locomotives flung into the river. It is interesting to find that General Gamelin began to press for action on these lines early in October 1939 and that on 6th October a French memorandum was forwarded to D Section[2] by their opposite numbers, the Cinquième Bureau.[3]

Colonel Grand quite rightly attempted to divert the approach into diplomatic circles; it seems to have been persisted in, and was finally met in early November by a Memorandum[4] forwarded to the French Ambassador** by Sir Alexander Cadogan, in which the Foreign Office case against violent action was very powerfully argued. This ended all idea of action until after the winter; in the spring various troubles overtook British affairs in the Balkans, even before the débâcle in the West. In May 1940 the whole business came up again, with special reference to this Iron Gates project.[5] The case was pressed to the point

---

1   Note by CSS of meeting of 30th September 1939.
2   SOE Archives File 45/470/1.
3   About the same time a M. Wenger was in London and discussed the demolition of the Roumanian oilfields with MI(R) (See MI(R) War Diary 18th October 1939). He had seen Colonel Gubbins in Bucharest in September.
4   Given in full in SOE War Diary.
5   COS (40) 344 of 11.5.40.
*   [1883–1953, Minister in Belgrade 1935–9, knight 1936, Ambassador in Paris Nov. 1939–June 1940, in Lisbon 1940–45; in *DNB*.]
** [Charles Corbin, 1881–1970.]

of a clear decision by Mr Chamberlain, Lord Halifax, Lord Hankey and Sir Alexander Cadogan on 15th May that 'No action must be taken which was likely to precipitate the armed occupation of the river or an early invasion of the Balkan States by Germany': British action should be limited to impressing the need for destruction on the Roumanian and Yugoslav Governments. This did not end the matter, as the COS were pressed by the CIGS to record the opinion that destruction was essential on military grounds and must be prepared at once unless politics made the opposite decision necessary. This point was to be put once more by Lord Hankey to Mr Chamberlain and Lord Halifax: the decision is not on record, but it was presumably again adverse.[1]

D Section also contributed a little to the oil campaign by organising the British colony on the Ploesti area with a view to quiet sabotage of the transport of oil by rail; and a good deal of minor sabotage to German goods and traffic was set on foot in Yugoslavia.

But what is really important in the history of SOE is that D Section, even at this stage, found itself involved in Balkan politics: indeed the men on the spot were convinced that their real work was political, even though London was more interested in the dramatic work of sabotage.

Hanau seems to have been worried as early as December 1939 by the possibility that the lead would be taken (as eventually happened) by the Communists, and he put up a not very happy scheme for intervention in the internal politics of Belgrade University, which was an important centre of intellectual influence. This was very properly turned down, and the next line of approach was a suggestion for action at the elections expected in the spring of 1940 – it was suggested that a relatively small outlay would suffice to bring a majority favourable to the Allies. The elections were postponed and this came to nothing; but Hanau was already working with the leaders (principally Gavrilovic and Mikic) of the Serbian Peasant Party, a small and purely Serbian organisation with some progressive aspirations. At least it stood outside the Government ring, and it was not Communist. Their organisation appears to have been used for minor sabotage of German interests before there was any question of paying them or instigating a coup d'état; large ideas were not broached until the spring of 1940, when a subsidy of £5,000 a month was proposed by Hanau. This figure was ultimately beaten down to £1,000 a month, and this was

---

[1] Following papers and conclusions refer: COS(40)344 of 11.5.40; COS(40)129 Mtg of 13.5.40, Item 3; DCOS(40)73 of 16.5.40; COS(40)372 of 21.5.40; COS(40)145 Mtg, Item 2, and DCOS(40)79 of 25.5.40. See also letter from Lord Hankey to Mr Dalton summarising the story – 14th January 1941 (on SOE Archives File HD/44b – early AD/S.1 files).

accepted in the summer of 1940, after complex discussions with HM Minister* and the Foreign Office.

This gave the British some basis for action in Serbia. In Croatia the political atmosphere was unfavourable, but there were somewhat similar developments in Slovenia, where D Section's representative was Mr A. C. Lawrenson, [PASSAGE DELETED ON GROUNDS OF NATIONAL SECURITY] on excellent terms with local Slovene leaders. The most promising field was in those groups which were both nationalist and progressive, or at least anti-conservative. There were various Slovene organisations which felt strongly enough about the position of Slovenes in Austria and Italy to undertake minor sabotage of railway vehicles en route for Germany, even against the policy of their own government. Quite considerable quantities of explosives and equipment were also passed to the Slovenes beyond the frontiers, and some successful attacks were made on railway lines in the Slovene areas of Carinthia, even before Yugoslavia entered the war in the spring of 1941. A good deal of propaganda material was also circulated, both in German and in Serbo-Croat. When the German invasion came two W/T sets were left behind, along with a small quantity of sabotage equipment; but this attempt to keep open a line to occupied Yugoslavia was not successful. It is possible that one of SOE's earliest casualties was incurred here in July 1940, when Frodsham, Lawrenson's deputy, was found dead in circumstances suggesting murder faked as suicide.

In Bulgaria D Section from April 1940 onwards opened similar contacts with a variety of political parties, which might be called Left Centre, although their moderation in theory did not exclude tendencies to violence in action. The three main elements here were the Veltcheffists – the Army faction then in eclipse; the Protogueroffists, descended from one of the bands involved in the Macedonian imbroglio; and the Bulgarian Peasant Party, under the leadership of George Dimitrov (not to be confused with the more famous Bulgarian Communist**). All these contacts proved useful in minor ways; they were kept open all through the war, and the parties concerned played some part in the Bulgarian government of the armistice, till they were displaced by the Communists. The Foreign Office seems to have approved the establishment of these contacts and their use for propaganda and sabotage, but no more. Unfortunately, in August 1940, Mr Julian Amery† (who was not himself employed by D Section) appeared

---

* [(Sir) R. I. Campbell, 1890–1983, Minister in Belgrade 1939–41, knight 1941, in Washington 1941–5, Ambassador in Cairo 1946–50.]
** [G. M. Dimitroff, 1883–1949, acquitted of firing Reichstag 1933, secretary, Comintern 1935–43, Prime Minister of Bulgaria from 1945.]
† [H. J. Amery, 1918–96, son of L. S., Conservative MP 1960–92, baron 1992.]

in Sofia, apparently encouraged by D's Balkan representatives, and began to preach revolution to D's Bulgarian friends. The Minister, Mr (now Sir George) Rendel,* had not been consulted, and there was not a shadow of Foreign Office authority.[1] This was another black mark for D.

Hanau's activities had inevitably made him conspicuous and the Germans were beginning to press for his removal even before the end of 1939. This was a considerable tribute to his success in causing them annoyance, in spite of their vastly superior resources; but it put the British Minister in a difficult position, as it was not to our advantage at that stage to force the Yugoslav Government to choose once and for all between Britain and Germany. Its unpopularity was so great that a firm British stand might have brought it down; but we could do nothing effective to support a pro-British government in its place. In April Colonel Grand was invited by Lord Hankey to address a meeting of all the British Ministers in the Balkan countries, who were then in London for consultation,[2] and to explain his plans and problems. His exposition seems to have been received with sympathy. But almost at once there followed the sequence of German victories in the West, and their pressure on the Balkan Governments was intensified. Nothing was to be gained by frontal opposition until the situation had improved, and British policy was very cautious until in the autumn the Italians compromised Axis prestige by their defeats in Greece and in Libya.

Hanau was finally withdrawn from Yugoslavia in June, his assistants, Bailey and Head, were expelled in July, and D Section's representative in Skoplje was expelled in August. Similar troubles followed in Roumania. Young and other representatives were expelled in July; and when Marshal Antonescu** came into power in September and the Roumanian frontiers were brusquely redrawn by Hitler, the heads of the British organisation in the oilfields were arrested and mishandled by the police and were only rescued after the lavish payment of blackmail; de Chastelain, who then represented D Section, was also withdrawn. These losses did not leave the same complete vacuum as

---

1 Belgrade telegram to Foreign Office No. 573 of 16.8.40.
2 Ciano records that the 'records' of this Conference were purloined by the Italians from the British Embassy in Rome and that he passed a copy to the German Ambassador: it does not appear whether Colonel Grand's contribution was included. (Ciano Diary, under 8th May 1940.) [G. Ciano, 1903–44, son-in-law to Benito Mussolini, 1883–1945, who was Italian dictator 1922–43; Foreign Minister 1936–43. See M. Muggeridge (ed.), *Ciano's Diplomatic Papers* (1948).]
* [(Sir) G. W. Rendel, 1889–1979, later with Yugoslav Government in London; see his *The Sword and the Olive* (1957).]
** [Ion Antonescu, 1882–1946, Roumanian dictator 1940–44.]

D Section's disasters in Scandinavia; a new and very competent representative, Mr T. S. Masterson, was sent to Belgrade in November 1940, and D Section's interests in Bucharest were taken over by the MI(R) representative there. The position was very weak, but there was a slender thread of continuity in the Balkans which did not exist in Western Europe.

This continuity is clearest in Albania, Greece and Turkey, where D Section's small beginnings were not swept away in the 'Great Slump' of 1940, and were carried over intact into the SOE organisation. None of these carried out any effective operations in D Section's time, and it will be convenient to postpone discussion of them for the present.

Note: Colonel Grand records ('Report and Lessons' dated November 1946, p. 14, held by SIS) that in July 1938 CSS was 'directed by the Cabinet' to 'blow up the Skoda Works at Pilsen'. Colonel Grand was in Czechoslovakia with this in mind in the summer and again in October 1938: the directive bore no relation to practical possibilities, but apparently some discussion on technique took place with the Czechs.

4. Other Political Activities

On Colonel Grand's interpretation of his charter his third main objective was to take advantage of any elements of German discontent for work into Germany itself either for sabotage or for political subversion. The most obvious approach to this was through Germans in exile, and much time and trouble was spent from 1938 onwards in contacting and testing various refugee organisations. Of the official groups the most important were the German Social Democratic Party, the 'Neubeginnen' Group, the 'Reichsbanner' (the 'fighting' organ of the Social Democrats) and the Internationaler Sozialistische Kampfbund (ISK). The first three were worthless, except for the distribution of the milder forms of propaganda; the fourth was more international, more radical and more inclined to action, and it supplied one or two contacts who were of practical value on a small scale.

But the only German organisation which showed much spontaneous life and activity seems to have been the private affair of Karl Otten and Karl Groehl, two eccentric old gentlemen who kept alive a little of the nineteenth-century spirit of conspiratorial terrorism. Their organisation, known variously as LEX and PROBST, made no large claims, but it did seem when tested by performance, that it could achieve what it undertook, an unusual characteristic in German émigré politics.

Contact with 'the two Karls' was apparently opened in December 1938; Groehl was domiciled in Paris, and after the outbreak of war contact was maintained through D Section's Paris office, which was then opened under Major L. Humphries. Groehl was taken into custody by the French in September 1939, and some difficulty arose in securing his freedom at the cost of sharing with the French the direction and possible profits of the organisation.

The main dividends were in the distribution of propaganda and the collection of information. Demolition schemes were continually pressed, and were not rejected; but very few of them looked like bearing fruit. One scheme suggested the demolition of installations at the Tullinger Hügel, which was believed to be an important control centre for the southern part of the Siegfried line. Explosives for the purpose were actually transferred at Basle to one of LEX's agents, and an explosion took place within the expected area on the expected date in February 1940. The explosion was certainly not at the Tullinger Hügel, but LEX's agent claimed that he had seized a convenient opportunity of using the explosives on a munition dump of importance. Another project for an attack on the Rheinfelden aluminium plant reached the stage of transfer of explosives to LEX, but went no further.

The only other fruitful contact with existing organisations of the Left was that with the International Federation of Transport Workers, which was in effect a section of the International Federation of Trade Unions, the TU body affiliated to the Second (or Socialist) International. [PASSAGE DELETED ON GROUNDS OF NATIONAL SECURITY] early in 1939 D Section began to be aware of the possibilities of the organisation. Fimmen* himself had been thinking in terms of obstructing German iron-ore traffic by industrial action, and the agents of his Federation had gone to Narvik, Luleå and Oxelösund in January 1939 with this in mind. D Section were thinking on parallel lines, and it was not difficult to reach a rather vague understanding when Lieutenant Colonel Chidson visited Fimmen at Antwerp in May 1939. The affiliated Unions were sounded by Fimmen at the meeting of the IFTU General Council at Geneva in June 1939, and the results were very disappointing; the prospects in Sweden were dismissed as hopeless, those in Norway rather better, but not likely to go beyond an unofficial strike – which would cost £720 a day.

In spite of this disappointment the contact with the transport workers remained alive all through the war; there was some true community of feeling among European railwaymen not entirely dead even in Germany, and outside Germany the 'Ca'canny' attitude of 'cheminots' everywhere was a considerable factor in limiting German industrial exploitation on some occasions, as at the time of 'Overlord',

---

* [Eddo Fimmen, international socialist, *floruit* 1928–39, died 1942.]

transport workers made a contribution of substantial strategic importance.

[PASSAGE DELETED ON GROUNDS OF NATIONAL SECURITY.]

There are two other political connections opened by D Section which are worth mentioning here, as they have their place in history.

One of these was with the Jewish community throughout the world, who had ample reason to be active enemies of Germany. [PASSAGE DELETED ON GROUNDS OF NATIONAL SECURITY.] In the West the only concrete project of importance was the support given in April 1940 to the formation of a Jewish Boycott Committee, in order to run a blackmail of Jewish firms trading with the enemy and to threaten them with the hostility of the Jewish community. This seems to have had some repercussions in the Antwerp diamond trade in the early days of May 1940; and the contacts made were of value to Lieutenant Colonel Chidson when he visited Amsterdam on 13th May 1940, while the Germans were at the gates, and induced the diamond dealers to confide to him a very valuable treasure of stones for removal to England.[1] But the idea of using the Jews in Europe was swept away by the Western campaign, and an attempt to transplant the idea to America bore very little fruit. Contacts with the Jewish Agency in Palestine were opened also by D Section; this was a dangerous enterprise as things stood in the Levant and it had later repercussions. These are mainly important for Jewish propaganda regarding their assistance to the British cause: the Jewish secret armies would probably have arisen in much the same form if D Section had not intervened.

Political contacts with the Spanish Opposition also proved somewhat embarrassing, but in the spring of 1940 it seemed certain that Spain would enter the war with Italy, as soon as there was any substantial German success, and it would have been foolish to do nothing. Overt action against General Franco's* régime was out of the question until he chose to enter the war, but D Section was permitted to open relations with the Opposition parties, excluding the Communists (then tainted by the Russo-German pact), and to encourage the formation of a united front. There was at least one small flirtation with the Monarchists, but the main line of activity was support of the Aleanza Democratica Espanola which was formed in the latter part of 1939, with headquarters at Foix in France. The men associated with it were

---

[1] This admirable exploit was the only demonstrable net profit which D Section ever realised. [See David Walker, *Adventure in Diamonds* (1955).]

* [F. Franco y Bahamonde, 1892–1975, Spanish general, led revolt against republic in civil war 1936–9, thereafter Spanish dictator.]

Spaniards of good standing, politically of the second rank and comparatively untainted by earlier Republican wrangles. They ranged from
members of the Spanish regular Army and Navy to representatives of
the two Trade Union Federations, the UGT and CNT, and they put
forward a programme of 'Spain for the Spaniards', to the exclusion
of foreign influence, whether Axis, Allied or Russian. The programme
was one which any honest Spaniard could heartily endorse, and the
movement had a real life which kept it in existence even after indirect British support had been withdrawn.[1]

The Aleanza managed to initiate a conspiratorial organisation
within Spain which seems to have maintained it fairly well for some
time. This organisation was used once or twice in 1939–40 for the
distribution of leaflets, produced with British complicity; no diplomatic complications arose and the leaflets were at least read and
circulated in fair numbers, though naturally they had no dramatic
effect.

Franco did not, as was expected, follow Mussolini into the war,
and during the winter of 1940–41 it was touch and go whether the
next German move would be a push through Spain to Gibraltar. Sir
Samuel Hoare* reached Madrid as Ambassador in June 1940 and
advised a policy of extreme caution – a humiliating policy, justified
only by its success. One of its first fruits was the abandonment of
British support for the ADE, and this was for the present the end of
D Section work in Spain.

5. Propaganda

So far the political activities described have had some possible relevance to active sabotage or subversion, though the only immediate
dividends were in propaganda. Colonel Grand's interpretation of his
directive went a good deal beyond this, and he involved his Section
in much propaganda work which has little relevance to the later work
of SOE. In logic there may be no dividing line between subversion
and propaganda, but the organisers of the British machinery had
decreed otherwise, and Colonel Grand was pretty bold in his encroachment on the field of other departments even if we judge him by the
easy standards of 1939 and 1940. His main excuse is the contrast
between his own energy and the confusion and ineffectiveness of the

---

[1] Report and further details on SOE Archives File (AD/S.1) Sc. 55/1.

* [1880–1959, baronet 1915, Foreign Secretary 1935, Home Secretary 1937–9,
Ambassador in Madrid Sep. 1940–Dec. 1944, Viscount Templewood 1944; in
DNB. See his *Ambassador on Special Mission* (1946) and *Nine Troubled Years*
(1954).]

competing organisations, the British Council and Electra House, to which was added on the outbreak of war the Ministry of Information.[1] [TWO AND A HALF PAGES DELETED ON GROUNDS OF NATIONAL SECURITY.]

Colonel Grand also got it into his head that short factual films on aspects of British life could be cheaply produced and readily distributed in neutral countries – a very superficial notion of the complexities of the film trade. This project advanced so far as the formation of a private company – 'Fact Films Ltd' – in July 1939, but seems to have died unhonoured on the outbreak of war.[2]

In tackling the German problem D Section's business in the narrow sense was only to carry material manufactured elsewhere, and SOE in the end kept fairly strictly within these bounds. But no one seems to have thought, until November 1939,[3] of laying down any clear line between the functions of D and those of EH, and Colonel Grand was not the man to be stopped by scruples about organisation. D Section's ingenuity was freely applied both in finding new methods of access to the German eye and ear, and in preparing its own rendering of the British case.

Reference has already been made to the use of D's agents in neutral countries as channels for passing printed matter into Germany and circulating it there, by post or otherwise; it is quite impossible to estimate the results, but this responsibility certainly took much of their time and a good deal of material was disposed of in one way or another. Three other promising lines were also taken up; 'Whispering', exploitation of the British censorship, and radio broadcasts.

The principle of the 'whisper' is very closely set out in a paper written by Colonel Grand in November 1938,[4] which envisages an elaborate 'chain' organisation for the introduction of rumours into Germany and adjacent countries. D Section agents were apparently expected to do anything they could on these lines on their own initiative; but the scheme never became a system in D Section's time, and its effective exploitation lay with PWE.

The censorship project was one which could operate wherever mail destined for Germany or occupied territory from neutral countries passed through a British censorship station. In its simplest form it involved the enclosure of D's normal propaganda matter in envelopes

---

[1] Mr Garnett's 'History of PWE' (p. 6) records that Colonel Grand claimed to have had instructions from CSS on 26th September 1938 'to form immediately a section for the dissemination through all channels outside this country of material to enemy and neutral countries'. There is no trace of this in SOE papers.

[2] SOE Archives File 2/340/4 (destroyed).

[3] Indirect reference on SOE Archives File 2/340/0 (destroyed).

[4] SOE Archives File 1/470/1.

addressed to recipients in Germany and made up to appear as if posted by some person in a neutral country; [PASSAGE DELETED ON GROUNDS OF NATIONAL SECURITY.]

Broadcasting openly from England was of course a matter solely for the BBC; the 'Freedom Station' idea in its early stages was a preserve of Electra House, on which D did not encroach. There was left the possibility of using foreign stations to broadcast matter planted on them by the British. In its simplest form this could be done by 'buying time' on the air from commercial stations, and the three stations first considered were Luxembourg, Strasbourg and Liechtenstein, which were conveniently placed and probably already had some audience in Germany; some progress was made with a more elaborate scheme for the establishment through intermediaries of an additional 'commercial' station in Liechtenstein on D's behalf.[1]

Colonel Grand was in contact with the Director-General of the BBC as early as July 1938,[2] and some progress had already been made when he consulted Sir Stephen Tallents in October 1938.[3] One problem was to find some nominee to make the necessary commercial contacts on D's behalf. There was first an abortive project for the use of a bogus agency to advertise the delights of travel in England.[4] Then Miss Hilda Matheson, formerly Director of Talks at the BBC, was brought in, and in March 1939 she was in contact with the Directeur des Émissions of Radio Strasbourg on behalf of 'some people in this country who are interested in promoting "goodwill" broadcasts from foreign stations, especially Strasbourg, with a view to developing closer intercourse between the Nations of Europe'.[5] At the same time these 'interested persons' were being hastily assembled, as justification for the claim that a 'Joint Broadcasting Committee' existed; and the Committee possessed premises and a list of distinguished members by the beginning of April 1939.

Unfortunately it became clear at a very early stage that the political censorship imposed by commercial stations in their own interests would make it impossible to broadcast any material with sufficient 'bite' to be of value in approaching a German audience. From this point the Joint Broadcasting Committee continued to develop under

---

[1] D Section does not appear to have been involved in the affairs of the commercial station Radio Normandie at Fécamp, which caused a good deal of friction between the Allies in the winter of 1939–40.

[2] Adverse comments on its methods in SOE Archives File 1/430/3 under date 12th November 1939.

[3] SOE Archives File 1/430/3, first item.

[4] SOE Archives File 2/430/3 Item 6 (The Hendon Travel Agency) (destroyed).

[5] SOE Archives File 1/430/3.

its own momentum on the line laid down in its public prospectus:[1] that of preparing 'cultural propaganda' in foreign languages and distributing it free to neutral broadcasting stations, with no political implication except that publicity would be given to England and its ways. On these lines it seems to have been efficient and successful, though open to the usual attack on all such enterprises, that it cost a great deal and there was no means of assessing what it achieved.[2] Most of the expense was borne by the Ministry of Information and the contribution from Secret Funds was limited to £350 a month, in respect of special work done for D Section; the most important part of this was the production of miniature gramophone records of violent anti-Nazi propaganda, intended for distribution with other material through D's own channels. Full control passed to the Ministry of Information in February 1941, and with it the obligation to meet any requirements SOE might have for the production of recorded material for its own purposes.[3]

The Joint Broadcasting Committee produced a certain amount of original material in German, which was apparently never used. There was also a small organisation, sponsored by two ladies, Mrs Holmes* and Miss Stamper (now Mrs Lefeuvre), for the production of printed material in German. They seem to have done the work themselves, with casual contributions from various sources and with the assistance of various refugees to translate, compile lists of recipients and to address envelopes. Even the printing arrangements were made by them direct with a private printer. Few specimens of their work survive, but it was certainly amateurish judged by later standards, both in content and in the technical steps taken to disguise its origin. Most of the material distributed by D seems to have come from this source, though a certain amount was provided by political organisations in exile.

6. Conclusion

The impression left by a study of D Section's operations is one of great energy and ingenuity spread thinly over an immense field. This is one reasonable way of approaching an unexplored problem, in which no one can say what is practicable and what is not, except by the expensive process of trial and error. But fortunately D was overtaken by war before the process of experiment had gone very far, and in war the survival of government departments depends more than at other times on their capacity to produce visible results. This D Section

---

[1] SOE Archives File 2/430/3, Item 18 (destroyed).

[2] Various reports of material produced and used in SOE Archives File 1/430/3.

[3] SOE Archives File 1/430/3.

* [Clara Marguerite Lockington Holmes, *née* Bates.]

could not do, nor could any other department in the first phase of the war; and it was not the only organisation to produce, for its own encouragement and that of others, optimistic reports tainted with the style of the false prospectus. Its demonstrable achievements were sadly few; there was Colonel Chidson's haul of diamonds at Amsterdam and a minor raid on Norway, which will be referred to later:[1] some railway sabotage in the Balkans, some propaganda distributed in Germany, certain contacts with political groups of the Left Centre in various parts of Europe. There had been one or two notorious failures, and German countermeasures had led to some annoying diplomatic incidents, not very serious in themselves, but effectively exploited by an active enemy. Relations with other government departments were distant and on the whole unfriendly; D Section and all its works were a nuisance to the Foreign Office, the Secret Intelligence Service, and the War Office alike.

There were therefore many people who were anxious to make a case against D Section, for not achieving what no one could have achieved in the conditions of the time; and these accusations were freely spiced with suggestions of nepotism and extravagance. There is plenty of evidence to justify this line of argument, yet it is not altogether fair; on the whole there are few departments which did much better in 1939–40. What SOE regretted later was not that D accomplished so little but that it left so little organisation behind it. Being wise after the event, one can see that the right policy was to go quietly and build for the future: months and perhaps years could thus have been saved. But this was no one's wisdom at the time.

---

[1] Below p. 195 ff.

CHAPTER III

The Work of MI(R)

The activities of MI(R) were very wide but they are much easier to classify and summarise than those of D Section. MI(R) had from the start a reasonably clear programme and charter, and it was to some extent controlled in the execution of it; not so much by the supervision of the DMI (this was probably not much more detailed than CSS's supervision of D Section), as by the necessities of existence within a highly-organised department such as the War Office. MI(R) had various projects which led beyond the original scope of the branch; but most of them were picked up and regularised as soon as they became 'going concerns', either by absorption in an older branch or by the creation of a new one. Though it was largely financed from Secret Funds, MI(R)'s establishments were controlled in the normal way, and there was never an unregulated expansion such as blurred the outlines of D Section. The difference from D Section was also one of temperament and personnel; MI(R), though adventurous enough in some of its projects, had always a keen sense of realities and of the advantage of presenting a case in a hard and realistic light. Its personnel were limited in number, but well selected, and the original selection was in almost every case justified by their later records.

It will be simplest to follow the classification given in the DMI's memorandum of February 1940, which has been quoted above.[1]

1. General Research

It will be remembered that when D/M was set up in April 1939 one of its first tasks was to be the production of Field Service Regulations for guerilla warfare.[2] These had already been begun by Major Gubbins[3] who had been brought into GS(R) by Colonel Holland to assist in the

---

[1] Above pp. 10–11.
[2] Above p. 10.
[3] Later Major General Sir Colin McV. Gubbins, KCMG, DSO, MC. [1896–1976, knight 1946; in *DNB*. See Peter Wilkinson and Joan Bright Astley, *Gubbins and SOE* (1993).]

preparation of his guerilla warfare papers, and they were completed early in May 1939. In their final form they consisted of three slender pamphlets printed on rice paper and bound in brown cardboard covers without indication of their contents. The original intention was to have them translated into various languages, but it is not at all clear what use was eventually made of them. They were entitled 'The Art of Guerilla Warfare' (twenty-two pages), 'Partisan Leader's Handbook' (forty pages), 'How to use High Explosives' (sixteen pages plus diagrams).[1]

The last two need little comment: the Handbook was designed as a handy collection of practical tips for the aspiring guerilla leader on the lower levels; the notes on explosives were equally technical and practical. 'The Art of Guerilla Warfare' is more ambitious, and invites comment in the light of later experience. It is unfortunately not easy to summarise; there are some twenty pages of it, which contain a compressed bible of general principles without much superfluous verbiage and without any illustration of specific cases. It is plain however that the doctrine is largely drawn from British experience in the offensive under Lawrence,* on the defensive in Ireland, Palestine, the North-West Frontier and Russia, in fact from the German experience of Wassmuss** and Von Lettau-Worbeck.†

It is an ambitious doctrine; it is conceived that it is possible by guerilla warfare 'so to weaken the enemy's main armies that the conduct of a campaign becomes impossible'. There are three main types of guerilla warfare:

(a) The activities of individuals, or of small groups working by stealth on acts of sabotage.

(b) The action of larger groups working as a band under a nominated leader, and employing military tactics, weapons, etc., to assist in the achievement of their object, which is usually of a destructive nature.

(c) The operations of large guerilla forces, whose strength necessitates a certain degree of military organisation in order to secure their cohesion and to make and carry out effectively a plan of campaign.

---

[1] Copies on MI(R) File 1: the third was written by Major M. R. Jefferis. [Knight 1945; on whom see R. Stuart Macrae, *Winston Churchill's Toyshop* (Kineton, 1971).]

* [T. E. Lawrence, 1888–1935, 'of Arabia'; in *DNB*. See his *Seven Pillars of Wisdom* (1935) on theory of irregular warfare.]

** [W. Wassmuss, *floruit* 1914–16, German agent in Persia.]

† [P. von Lettow-Vorbeck, 1870–1964, undefeated German commander in East Africa, 1914–18.]

The development of the guerilla moves from stage (a) to stage (c), but to be most effective it should include all three together. The 'Nine Points of the Guerilla's Creed' are also worth quoting:

(a) Surprise first and foremost, by finding out the enemy's plans and concealing your own intentions and movements.
(b) Never undertake an operation unless certain of success owing to careful planning and good information. Break off the action when it becomes too risky to continue.
(c) Ensure that a secure line of retreat is always available.
(d) Choose areas and localities for action where your mobility will be superior to that of the enemy, owing to better knowledge of the country, lighter equipment, etc.
(e) Confine all movements as much as possible to the hours of darkness.
(f) Never engage in a pitched battle unless in overwhelming strength and thus sure of success.
(g) Avoid being pinned down in a battle by the enemy's superior forces or armament; break off the action before such a situation can develop.
(h) Retain the initiative at all costs by redoubling activities when the enemy commences counter-measures.
(i) When the time for action comes, act with the greatest boldness and audacity. The partisan's motto is 'Valiant yet vigilant'.

As regards organisation the main stress is in the personality of the leader: granted good local leaders, the rest of the organisation can be and must be very flexible. *Some* higher organisation is essential and the attachment of some regular officers will be valuable and even necessary: but they must not presume on their professional knowledge, which will often be irrelevant or dangerous.

The prime guerilla weapon is the 'tommy-gun' – a very early appreciation of this on the British side. The bayonet is merely a nuisance: a dagger is better, and bombs of any type which can be secured are also important.

Finally, there is throughout emphasis on *morale*: on the strength which guerillas can draw from a friendly population, and on the way in which, in an indifferent population, the spirit of revolt can be awakened by resolute partisan warfare.

This is all sound: indeed there is little in the pamphlet which was disproved by later experience. But there are a few notable omissions. There is for instance no reference to air supply as a means by which a friendly Power can sustain and guide a partisan movement; and it was in the end air supply which made possible the growth of Resistance in Europe. Again, there is no indication of the effects on a partisan movement of reprisals against the civilian population on whose support they ultimately depend.[1] The British, though ruthless enough at times, have always been reluctant to adopt the hostage system on a large scale, or to attempt to control the guilty by executing the innocent, enslaving their families, and looting their goods. The Black and Tans tried reprisals – very mild reprisals by German standards – in the Irish war of 1919–21, and the Irish were shaken by the experiment; but it was disclaimed by His Majesty's Government and had a good deal to do with the final abandonment by public opinion in Britain of the idea of holding Ireland by force. The Germans had no such scruples, and their planned policy of large-scale execution and destruction had serious effects in distorting and confusing the Resistance movements in areas otherwise very suitable for guerilla warfare. Finally, Major Gubbins had then perhaps little inkling of the political confusion which always accompanies guerilla warfare. He sees clearly T. E. Lawrence's dilemma – a mission attached to guerillas must 'be prepared, at the risk of future regrets and disillusion, to identify themselves in every way with the peoples they are to serve' – but he could hardly be expected to foresee the internal struggle for power 'after the war' which racked almost every Resistance in Europe, and was sedulously fomented by the enemy, as one of his best means of self-defence. In practice, the guerilla leader, and the officer attached to him, had to be as much politician as soldier, and it was rarely possible to undertake serious operations without considering political consequences.

From May 1939 until May 1940 MI(R)'s staff were busy with problems and projects involving immediate action, and there is not much development of doctrine until the revolution in policy which followed the fall of France, and which is discussed below.[2] But it is worth mentioning[3] the final version of GS(R) Report No. 8 on 'The Possibilities of Guerilla Activities' dated 1st June 1939, which is annotated to the effect that an abridged copy had been passed to the CIGS and to General Gamelin; MI(R) Report No. 1 on 'The Progress of Para-Military Preparation',[4] dated 10th July 1939, of which a copy was passed to the French General Staff; and MI(R) Report No. 2, dated 8th August, which surveys the ground so far covered and includes an elaborate report by Captain Peter Fleming* on the possi-

---

[1] General Gubbins's recollection is that this was deliberately omitted, as a point best passed by in silence.

[2] Below p. 59.

[3] MI(R) File 3.

[4] Copy, in French, is on SOE Archives File 1/470/1.

* [R. P. Fleming, 1907–71, traveller and author; in *DNB*. See his life by Duff Hart-Davis (1974).]

bilities of action against the Japanese in China. The pessimism of its conclusion is interesting, as compared with the buoyancy of Colonel Grand's forecast in March:[1] 'Apart from the Polish arrangements, nothing that is likely to have an immediate effect has been achieved yet. Nor is substantial progress likely to be made without something more assured in the way of financial arrangements. . . . It is impossible to avoid the feeling that, on the present scale, the work is little more than busy-bodying.'

During this period 'research' was mainly a matter of dealing with special problems as they arose: a report on security organisation in the Middle East was made and approved in September 1939 and was followed up by a visit by Colonel Elphinston of MI(R); in October 1939 the branch put up a proposal[2] for the formation of an organisation to assist escaping prisoners of war. This led in December 1939 to the formation of a new branch, MI9, under an MI(R) officer, Major Crockatt,* which came to play a very large and novel part in the lives of prisoners of war. It was not until France collapsed that there was for the first time a real urge in high quarters to secure good estimates of the possible range and effectiveness of subversive activities. MI(R) had a large hand in drafting JPC and JIC** papers in which these considerations were important and which eventually became the basis of higher policy. Under its own name, it contributed an Aide-Mémoire on 'The Co-ordination of Subversive Activities in the Conquered Territories',[3] and papers on 'The Possibilities of Revolt in Certain Specified Countries by March 1941'.[4] Research projects, like others, profited from the greatly increased emphasis on subversion in the summer of 1940, and approval was given shortly before the dissolution of MI(R) for the establishment of a series of Bureaux, covering various countries and regions, and intended to act as planning and research staffs on which the encouragement of revolt could be based. These never came into being, but one important piece of research was done at this stage. This was an elaborate report[5] by Major Kenyon, circulated on 19th September 1940, on 'Quasi-Military Organisations and Activities': a most able and comprehensive analysis of the Nazi

---

1   Above p. 8.
2   MI(R) War Diary, MI(R) File 2.
3   Report No. 6a, d/d 6th July 1940, on MI(R) File 4.
4   Report No. 7a, d/d 25th July 1940, on MI(R) File 4.
5   No. 4 d/d 19th September 1940, on MI(R) File 5.
*   [N. R. Crockatt, 1895–1956, Royal Scots, later brigadier and DDMI. See M. R. D. Foot and J. M. Langley, *MI9* (2nd ed., Boston, 1980).]
** [JIC=Joint Intelligence Committee, chaired by V. F. W. Cavendish-Bentinck, 1897–1990, Ambassador to Poland 1945–7, last Duke of Portland 1979; in *DNB*. See Patrick Howarth, *Intelligence Chief Extraordinary* (1986).]

technique of subversion, which draws excellent conclusions on measures of defence and on the adaptation of the technique to our own purposes.

2. Technical Research

As soon as D/M Section was authorised in April 1939, Major M. R. Jefferis, RE,[1] was brought in to work on any technical developments which would be useful in guerilla warfare.[2] His section MI(R)c was originally concerned with such things as boring devices to produce camouflets for road demolition; time-delay fuses; fuses sensitive to the vibration of vehicles; booby-trap switches; 'limpet' magnetic bombs for the sabotage of ships or barges. Devices on all these lines were later produced and used in large quantities, and MI(R) certainly contributed much to their development. There was apparently no MI(R) research establishment in the ordinary sense until June 1940, when premises were taken at 35 Portland Place; at this stage the civilian staff numbered twenty. Earlier, most of the development was done by small firms working on MI(R) projects, and development work passed easily into small production contracts for urgent requirements. There was thus an obvious risk of conflict with the orthodox channels of research and supply, and minor discord arose in this way. There was also an obvious overlap with the D technical section under Commander Langley, and there were no arrangements except by personal co-operation for the adoption of particular devices as standard, or for their production and allocation in bulk. This trouble was in due course overcome by the absorption of both sections into SOE.

MI(R)'s technical reputation however rests on various projects which soon passed beyond the scope of guerilla warfare. The 'Royal Marine' operation, which played a minor but complex part in relations with the French in early 1940, grew out of Major Jefferis's invention of a floating mine which could be used to attack bridges and barges on the Rhine. The section also developed the 'sticky bomb', which was for a time in great favour as a simple anti-tank weapon for use by the Home Guard or other lightly armed troops. The 'Blacker Bombard',[3] which had a similar vogue, was originated by Lieutenant Colonel L. V. S. Blacker* in the early summer of 1940 while he was on the staff of MI(R).

---

[1] Later Sir M. R. Jefferis, KBE, MC.
[2] Information mainly from note in MI(R) File 3.
[3] Papers in MI(R) File 8.
* [1887–1964, soldier, inventor and explorer; in *DNB*.]

Another project[1] of some interest was the development of the helicopter as an Army weapon, for use by modern 'light cavalry' on raids or reconnaissance into occupied territory. Colonel Holland pushed discussions of it to a high level in the autumn of 1940, and the ideas worked out then had their part in later tactical developments of airborne operations and 'air observation posts'. But that summer the pressure in the aircraft industry was too great for anything serious to be done.

3. Special Projects and Intelligence

These two points in MI(R)'s charter are best taken together. In practice any special project involved a mission, and a mission on odd jobs in odd places collected much news that would not otherwise have reached the War Office. The division between 'operations' and 'intelligence' is always a little arbitrary: in irregular operations it is almost meaningless. One of the difficulties found later in the division between SOE and SIS was that SOE's activities involved the collection of much odd information which was in its own way as important as their offensive projects. So here it is not possible to classify MI(R) missions formally: their only common feature was that they arose out of particular crises and particular projects which did not fall neatly within the sphere of any existing War Office branch.

The projects which mature first are naturally those which affected Poland and Czechoslovakia – the country immediately threatened, and the one in which it was hoped that conditions for resistance already existed. Authority to contact military attachés and to take unofficial soundings as to the possibilities of guerilla warfare appears to have been given early in May 1939. In that month Major Gubbins visited Poland and the Baltic States, made contact with the British military attachés,* and tentatively approached the Polish General Staff. The results were relatively encouraging. The Polish tradition had much in it which fitted well with MI(R)'s ideas, and even at that stage (in spite of their great self-confidence) the Poles were prepared to think in terms of guerilla warfare and underground resistance. There was limited disclosure of Polish plans, and interest was shown in British devices and the possibilities of British assistance. Tentative arrangements were made for assistance with supplies and for the reception of an MI(R) section as part of the British Mission in the event of war.

---

[1] Papers in MI(R) File 8.

* [In Poland, Major E. R. Sword; in Estonia, Latvia and Lithuania, Major C. S. Vale, MC.]

This MI(R) Mission (No. 4 Military Mission)[1] was formed in haste when war became imminent, and left by air for Poland on 25th August. It reached Poland after some vicissitudes on 3rd September, but in the prevailing confusion there was little to be done. One of its officers, Captain Davies,* was flown back to England on 6th September, to report on behalf of General Carton de Wiart** to the Chiefs of Staff, and was seen by the Chiefs of Staff on arrival; his report was discussed at their meeting on 9th September.[2] The Mission itself was evacuated with some difficulty to Roumania on 18th September, where a number of its officers were left to assist the MI(R) representatives there, to keep touch with the Polish organisations and to make any possible use of routes from Roumania to Poland. In October Colonel Gubbins saw General Sikorski[†] and General Ingr (the Czech Chief of Staff) in Paris, and an MI(R) Mission was established there in November to keep contact with the Poles on all matters affecting resistance in Poland. It was charged at the same time with similar duties vis-à-vis the Czechoslovak government in exile.

The question of Roumanian oil was next in order of priority, and Major Gubbins's second trip was to the Balkans, in July 1939; he explained the role of MI(R) to the military attachés in all the Balkan countries except Bulgaria, which he did not visit, but he had no contacts with the local General Staffs. The chance of effective action by the Roumanians appeared in sight, and it was essential to prepare for British assistance, and possibly for independent action. A preliminary appreciation had been made in London, and some local reconnaissance was carried out during July and August.[3] On 24th August Commander R. D. Watson, RN, was flown out in haste as local representative of MI(R); and simultaneously Major G. A. D. Young proceeded to Egypt with a small party to arrange for a Field Company RE to be available to proceed to Roumania at once in case of need. Commander Watson's party was reinforced after the fall of Poland by

---

1   Colonel Gubbins was head of the MI(R) Mission, which included a section responsible for work into Czechoslovakia; he was also GSO1 to General Carton de Wiart as chief British military representative.

2   COS (39) 8th Meeting. Item 2 and Annex. (The diary and report of the Mission has not come to hand.)

3   Commander Watson's Report on MI(R) File 5.

*   [F. T. ('Tommy') Davies, 1906–c. 1982, Grenadier Guards, another of SOE's leading figures.]

**   [Sir A. Carton de Wiart, 1880–1963, born in Brussels, VC on Somme 1916, knight 1941, led missions to Poland, 1939, and China, 1944–6; in *DNB*.]

†   [W. Sikorski, 1881–1943, Polish Prime Minister 1922–3, army general, Prime Minister in exile from 1940 till killed in air crash at Gibraltar. See J. Garlinski, *Poland, SOE and the Allies* (1969).]

officers from Major Gubbins's mission, and was concerned in the Roumanian end of the confused story of the attack on Roumanian oil: Major Young's Field Company had an equally complex history, and in the end was never used, though on one occasion it got as far as Turkey. There was talk of its transport by air, which involved the possibility of landing in neutral territory in Turkey or Greece, and led to complex negotiations with these two; there was also talk of its transport by warship, or by a merchant ship which would cruise in the Black Sea till required. All this occupied the time of many high-placed persons and committees, and was of potential importance – the destruction of the oilfields would have been a decisive act of war; but it would be aimless to trace the details now.[1]

Another early project, which broke down on Foreign Office objections, was for the despatch of Captain Peter Fleming and Captain Michael Lindsay* to China to assist in organising guerilla activities against the Japanese. Foreign Office objections also limited action in the Middle East before the Italian declaration of war, but MI(R) was in the field early with plans for raising the tribes in the Western Desert and in Abyssinia. Colonel Elphinston visited the Middle East more than once in the latter part of 1939, and eventually (in April 1940) Lieutenant Colonel Adrian Simpson went out to form an 'MI(R) Section' in HQ Middle East (later known as G(R)). This was an integral part of General Wavell's HQ, and MI(R) as such had no responsibility for the preparation of the Abyssinian rising. But it acted as the expert 'rear link' in London, and most action at the London end depended on its briefing and its persuasion. It was also responsible for such preliminary investigation as was done (it amounted to little) with a view to raising trouble in the Caucasus if relations with Russia deteriorated further; and it fathered various other missions sent to overseas theatres to harass the Italians, to resist German penetration, or to advise on technique. These included:

Captain Rodd to Lagos, June 1940
A reconnaissance in the Azores, July 1940
No. 19 Mission to the Belgian Congo, July 1940[2]
No. 101 Mission to Abyssinia[3]
No. 102 Mission to Libya (for Sienussi tribes)

---

[1] The story can be traced very fully in COS, DCOS, POG, POG(D) and ISPB series of papers. DCOS (39)51, Annex II, is the best single review.
[2] Some details in Note 'Aims of Missions and Personnel', on MI(R) File 3.
[3] Note on MI(R) File 3 (this was the Sandford Mission). [D. A. Sandford, 1882–1973, long resident in Abyssinia, plucked to this task from the chancellorship of Guildford Cathedral.]
* [1904–94, son of A. D. Lindsay, Master of Balliol, 2nd baron 1952.]

No. 103 Mission, to 'inspect' British Communities in South
America[1]

No. 104 Mission to Australia, October 1940[1]

No. 105 Mission to the Canaries[1]

No. 106 Mission to Aden[2]

No. 107 Mission to Kenya[3]

There were also projects for establishing officers in Portugal and
Spain. The former was vetoed completely by the Foreign Office; a
certain Captain Peter Kemp* (a veteran of the Spanish Civil War) was
actually dispatched as Press Attaché to Madrid in June 1940, but was
turned back by the Ambassador.

In other Balkan countries, as in Roumania, MI(R) operated under
great difficulties and all its labour produced little fruit. Albania at this
stage was the only 'occupied' country, and it would be ripe for guerilla
activity should Italy declare war; but it would have been unwise to
take undue risks there while Italy's action was in the balance. In addition D Section was already involved in Albanian affairs and there was
a good deal of jealousy and confusion between local representatives.
Elsewhere in the Balkans the Foreign Office representatives were
already perturbed by the activities of D Section, and were distinctly
hostile to the idea of another secret organisation with a penchant for
the clandestine transport of explosives. Besides it was never easy to
discuss with a Balkan General Staff the action which ought to be
taken after German occupation; in Balkan eyes this was an admission
of Britain's inadequacy as an ally, and a recommendation to accept
German influence without too much fuss.

In Hungary the main problem was of assistance to the Poles in
communications across the frontier, and an Assistant Military Attaché
(soon on the worst of terms with the local D representatives) was
appointed in April 1940.

Apart from visits by Major Gubbins and Captain Davies, the first
action in Yugoslavia was the 'unofficial' mission under General Sir
John Shea, GCB, KCMG, DSO,** who went out on the indirect invitation of the Yugoslavs in November 1939, to make contacts with the
Yugoslav General Staff and to try to make some estimate of the country's military potentialities. A project for the establishment of a permanent mission under cover as AMA† was turned down on the suggestion
of the British Minister in June 1940: but representatives were sent

---

1 Some details in Note 'Aims of Missions and Personel', on MI(R) File 3.

2 See Mr Gordon Waterfield's book 'Morning will Come'.

3 Some details in Note 'Aims of Missions and Personnel', on MI(R) File 3.

* [1916–93; see his *Thorns of Memory* (1991).]

** [1869–1966, GOC Eastern Command, India, 1928–32.]

† [AMA=Assistant Military Attaché.]

under similar cover to Athens in June 1940 (Major Barbrook, for work into Albania), to Sofia in August 1940 (Captain K. J. Elliott);* Mr Pendlebury** (the well-known archaeologist) went to Crete as Vice-Consul at Candia; and other men with local knowledge were held available to reinforce them if necessary. A number of these men distinguished themselves later, but the missions achieved nothing of note, either before or after the dissolution of MI(R).

MI(R)'s Scandinavian missions had a much more lively history. As we have seen, D Section had very early become involved in schemes for the denial of Swedish iron ore to Germany. In its purely military aspect the Russo-Finnish war, which broke out on 30th November 1939, was very relevant to the same problem: a complete Russian occupation of Finland would have left the Gellivare mines and the port of Luleå open to attack by Russia over the long open frontier between Sweden and Finland. Narvik and Northern Norway would have been equally difficult to defend, and the potential threat from an ally (even a doubtful ally) of Germany required investigation and planning. MI(R) was not the only department concerned in the Finnish question – it had no responsibility for instance for the raising and training of the British 'volunteers' – but it was involved in much of the negotiation, and various officers visited Finland on its behalf in December 1939 and January 1940.[1] The first plans for a Scandinavian operation grew out of the Finnish problem; the 'Avonmouth' and 'Stratford' expeditions were intended to occupy Narvik, Trondheim, Bergen and Stavanger, to secure lines of communication to Finland, and if possible to advance to the Gellivare iron-ore region. MI(R) was involved in the preliminary secret reconnaissance of an area where open action by British officers was impossible. Parties visited Norway and Sweden in February and March 1940, but most of their members were withdrawn when the prospect of action receded[2] – Finland capitulated on relatively moderate terms on 12th March 1940. MI(R) was also involved in the preparation of security and cover plans for the operation, and was partly responsible for the formation of a proper inter-departmental organisation for the purpose; the Inter-Service Security Board,[3] which came into existence on 20th February 1940,

---

[1] See reports by 2nd Lieutenant Scott-Harston, Captain Croft, Lieutenant Munthe and 2nd Lieutenant Whittington-More, on MI(R) File 5. These parties left for Scandinavia on 19th and 21st December 1939, returned 23rd and 27th January 1940.

[2] Details of their departure and return in MI(R) War Diary: no reports available.

[3] JIC(40)8(S) of 18th February. See also JIC(40)11(S) of 5th March 1940.

* [See *I Spy* (1999) by his son, Geoffrey Elliott.]

** [J. D. S. Pendlebury, 1904–41, curator at Knossos 1930–34.]

with Major Coombe* of MI(R) as its Secretary, and played a very important part in all deception planning later. MI10, the War Office branch concerned,** was formed under Major Coombe in September 1940.

The Scandinavian plans revived abruptly at the end of March, when the Cabinet finally accepted the plan for a minefield in Norwegian waters, to be backed if necessary by reconstituted 'Avonmouth' and 'Stratford' expeditions, and MI(R) was again called on for reconnaissance. On 2nd April arrangements were made for officers to be established as 'Assistant Consuls' in Narvik (Captain Torrance), Trondheim (Major Palmer), Bergen (Captain Croft),† and Stavanger (Captain Munthe).†† Unfortunately they were barely in position when the German attack began on the night of 7th/8th April; Major Palmer was captured, the other three escaped with much danger and difficulty.[1]

The hasty extemporisations to meet the German invasion included four[2] MI(R) parties, one of them abortive. This was the 'Knife' expedition which was to have landed by submarine in the Sogne Fjord area to harass German communications; it set sail on 23rd April, but the submarine 'Truant' which carried it was damaged by enemy action and had to put back to Rosyth. The first party to leave was that flown out to Namsos under Captain Peter Fleming on 13th April; this consisted only of Captain Fleming and two Signals Sergeants, with a W/T set, and their role – a little vague – was apparently to report direct by wireless to the force which followed on 16th/17th April, and to do anything that could be done to facilitate their landing. In fact they failed to make radio contact with the British naval force, and they achieved little, although they remained in Namsos till the evacuation.[3] Major Jefferis, of the MI(R) technical section, was somewhat similarly associated with the British forces which landed at Andalsnes, though his main concern was with demolitions rather than reconnaissance. The expedition landed early on 19th April, and Major Jefferis (with one sergeant) was flown out the same day with 1000 lbs of explosives and various small demolition stores, including pressure switches. He at once went forward with 148

---

1 Reports by Major Torrance and Captain Croft on MI(R) File 5.
2 The Independent Companies are dealt with separately below.
3 On MI(R) File 5.
* [Major E. E. Coombe; see references in Astley, *Inner Circle*.]
** [By 1942 MI10 had become the branch dealing with enemy equipment (personal knowledge).]
† [Andrew Croft, 1905–98; see his *A Talent for Adventure* (Hanley Swan, 1996).]
†† [Malcolm Munthe, son of Axel (1857–1949), Swedish author.]

Brigade which reached Lillehammer. As appears from his report[1] he was just beginning work in his proper role of instructing the Norwegians in demolitions and of carrying out demolitions himself, when the position crumbled; for the rest he was involved in infantry fighting and extracting parties of British stragglers, and was finally evacuated by air on 28th April.

The third party was more formally designed, as No. 13 Military Mission, which left via Stockholm on 16th April with instructions 'to act as DMI's representative at Norwegian HQ, and to proceed there as quickly as possible, reporting direct to the Norwegian C-in-C on arrival: to encourage every aspect of guerilla warfare, if necessary by personal appearance with the Norwegian forces: to carry out liaison duties between all British and Norwegian forces'. Other MI(R) officers were to be brought into contact with No. 13 Mission if possible, and to come under its orders with a view to assisting the Norwegians in guerilla warfare. The Mission consisted of Major A. W. Brown, MC, RTR, Captain R. B. Readhead, 12th Lancers, and Sergeant Dahl, RAPC (Interpreter): when it set out, the plan for a direct attack on Trondheim was still being considered, and discussions were to be opened with the Norwegian authorities on that basis. Major Brown and Sergeant Dahl reached General Ruge's HQ at Oyer in the Gudbrandsdal on 19th April, and in the confusion of the time they were mainly ongaged on keeping such contact as they could with General Ruge.[2] Captain Readhead was delayed by transport difficulties, but eventually got through on 22nd April, in time to take part in the only serious attempt made to cut in on German communication. This involved the use of two parties of Norwegian ski-troops to operate against the Gudbrandsdal road from the hills to the east and west. Unfortunately the troops were inexperienced, Norwegian leadership was poor, and equipment was almost lacking. The western party, to which Major Brown was attached, was forced to break off after two days, and Major Brown was back with Norwegian HQ on 26th April, being withdrawn finally through Molde. The eastern party, with Captain Readhead, similarly disintegrated in a few days, but Captain Readhead with some Norwegians remained and gathered round them various parties of British stragglers; at one time there were sixty-three British together, many of them unarmed and practically all without skis or snow-shoes, except what could be improvised. This party moved north parallel to the German advance, and by extraordinary efforts held together, and even inflicted damage on the enemy, until 2nd May, when they heard of the evacuation of Andalsnes and Molde.

---

[1] On MI(R) File 5.
[2] See Report by Major Brown, on MI(R) File 5.

Their only chance was then to split into small parties and make for the Swedish frontier, which Captain Readhead reached in ten days with three other British, after a journey of some 200 kms over very difficult country.[1]

There was little for MI(R) to do in the Battle of France; the French were naturally not disposed to accept British assistance for demolitions or guerilla warfare in France, and when the crash came it was too sudden for much last minute organisation. A little was done by D Section to leave stocks and personal contacts, nothing by MI(R).[2] The latter did however make some plans (which were never executed) for demolitions in Holland and Belgium; and from 13th to 15th May Captain Davies paid a hasty trip to Amsterdam to destroy or remove securities held in the National Bank there. In this he was successful.[3]

It should also be mentioned, for the record, that MI(R) was probably the first to send a party across the Channel into occupied France. Unfortunately the party's report has not come to light, but some details are given in the MI(R) War Diary. It consisted of three officers and set out on 2nd June for the Boulogne-Etaples area, which the Germans had overrun about 25th May: its mission was to rally and withdraw any British stragglers it could contact, in fact to 'try it on' and see what possibilities there were. Only one straggler was found, but all returned safely on 10th June, after a week abroad and thirteen hours at sea in a rowing boat.

The end of the campaign in France overlapped with the first preparations for a 'resistance' movement in England – the organisation known as 'Auxiliary Units', which will presumably be covered by a separate narrative.* The idea seems to have arisen independently in D Section and MI(R). There is a D Section paper[4] headed 'Pessimism' dated 22nd May 1940, which puts the proposal in a nutshell; on 25th May Captain Fleming (back from Namsos) was 'attached to Home Forces for the purpose of training LDVs** etc. in fighting behind the German lines in case of invasion of this country'.[5] The Inter-Service Project Board[6] set to work to sort out this competition; the project

---

1 Captain Readhead's Report, on MI(R) File 5.
2 See D Section papers on SOE Archives File 3/470/7a. MI(R) provided one officer who carried out a very successful demolition of oil storage at Gonfreville near Le Havre on 7th June. See report by 2nd Lieutenant Mayler, on MI(R) File 5.
3 MI(R) War Diary, MI(R) File 2.
4 SOE Archives File 1/470/7.1.
5 MI(R) War Diary, MI(R) File 2.
6 See below pp. 57–9.
* [This, if written, has never gone public.]
** [The Local Defence Volunteers, renamed the Home Guard, provided cover for the Auxiliary Units.]

was discussed at the Board's meetings of 27th May,[1] with the conclusion that 'a memorandum should be submitted by the Board, setting out their view that activities in England should be controlled on a military basis and that –

(a) The Regular Defences require supplementing with guerilla type troops who will allow themselves to be overrun and who will thereafter be responsible for hitting the enemy in the comparatively soft spots behind zones of concentrated attack.

(b) The SIS (i.e. D Section) should be prepared similarly to organise and execute action of a technical sabotage kind requiring special equipment.

(c) The whole population whether in formed or loose formations, or whether as individuals, must be instructed in the sort of contribution they can make to assist the services, and must be encouraged to make their contribution should the need arise, with the same ruthlessness we may expect from the enemy, whether he is provoked or not.'

The first of these conclusions led directly to the formation of 'Auxiliary Units' under Colonel Gubbins, and his G2 was Major P. A. Wilkinson,* who had been with him in Poland; the date is given in the MI(R) War Diary as 17th June. The third was met by the famous 'Official Instructions to Civilians' which were issued by the Ministry of Information on 18th June and were given immense publicity at the time; an excellent document, in the drafting of which Major Kenyon of MI(R) was much concerned. The second conclusion, which affected D Section, proved less happy, as military control lay with the War Office and GHQ Home Forces, and it was not easy to fit in a body ultimately responsible to the Foreign Office. D Section with its usual energy speedily created a network of local representatives, operating in the deepest secrecy: this had to be dissolved, and there were many complications, humorous and otherwise.[2]

4. Recruitment

There are two main lines to be followed on this side of MI(R)'s activities; the card-indexing and training of men with special qualifications to form the 'officer corps' of guerilla activities, and the development of field training for a British rank and file. In the early stages the possibility of actual British guerillas was rather in

---

[1] Copy in SOE Archives File 1/470/7.3.

[2] Papers on SOE Archives File 1/470/7.1.

* [(Sir) Peter Wilkinson, born 1914, soldier and diplomat, knight 1970. See his *Foreign Fields* (1997).]

the background; but it was obvious that Britain had an immense potential asset in its resources of men who possessed special knowledge of odd corners of the globe. The business of collecting names had begun before the outbreak of war,[1] on the basis of personal knowledge or indirect recommendation; the idea of training was put forward first mainly as an excuse for getting promising men together, and looking them over unostentatiously, without giving too much indication of what was in mind. Two small courses of about thirty men each were run in London in May and June 1939, more or less out of MI(R)'s own resources; this had to be dropped when war broke out, but the project was revived again in the autumn. Arrangements were made for OCTU courses for selected men, and Lieutenant Colonel Gubbins and others visited Cambridge in November 1939[2] with a view to establishing a so-called 'Politico-Military' course there. The University authorities collaborated warmly and the first course opened for about forty officers on 15th January 1940; it ended on 9th March, when the VCIGS* was present in person. The project was then regularised by transferring it to the Directorate of Military Training (MT7). On this side of MI(R)'s activities the main asset which passed to SOE was a card-index of about 1,000 potential recruits for unlikely projects.

The idea of British guerilla companies matured later, largely in response to the Norwegian campaign. A proposal for training Czech guerillas was made and rejected in September 1939. In October 1939 there was talk of incorporating a training wing in the Lovat Scouts,[3] but nothing came of it at the time, and the scheme was still in the air in the spring of 1940. But in April the Lovat Scouts were dispatched to the Faroes, the idea of using them was hastily replaced by a new scheme for Independent Companies. This was formally submitted to the CIGS on 13th April and was approved in principle at once. Details were agreed at a meeting with DDSD** on the 15th, and ten Companies had been formed by the 25th, under the command of Lieutenant Colonel Gubbins, as he now was. There could be no question of special training in these circumstances; the Companies began to move to Norway on 1st May, and were at once heavily engaged in the Mosjoen area. Their later history belongs to the narrative of that

---

1   See note on 'Personnel Section of MI(R)' Appendix H, in MI(R) File 3.
2   MI(R) War Diary, MI(R) File 2.
3   MI(R) War Diary, MI(R) File 2.
*   [(Sir) P. Neame, VC 1914, briefly DCIGS 1940, captured in Cyrenaica 1941, escaped 1943, knight 1946.]
** [A. E. Nye, 1895–1967, Deputy Director of Staff Duties 1940, VCIGS 1941–6, High Commissioner in India 1948–52, in Canada 1952–6; in *DNB*.]

campaign and to the story of the Commandos and of Combined Operations. They speedily became 'regular' shock troops, rather than the 'irregulars' envisaged by their founders; and their main legacy to SOE was the training school and training area near Loch Ailort on the west coast of Scotland. DMT's approval for a centre for guerilla warfare training for up to 500 men was given on 9th May, and the Centre opened on 3rd June: instruction was first provided by the MI(R) officers who had been trained for the abortive 'Knife' expedition to Norway. This remained one of the centres of Commando training: SOE in due course took over a house not far off, near Arisaig, originally requisitioned as an auxiliary school by MI(R), and from this developed the para-military side of its training organisation.

5. Conclusion

MI(R) was certainly extremely successful as a research department, in the widest sense. There is always argument about the exact origin of any scheme which proves successful, but it is safe to say that MI(R) was one of the really live spots in British military organisation, and that it launched or helped to launch a number of projects which had an important future. There were for instance aid to escaping prisoners (MI9), strategic deception (the ISSB and MI10), the Independent Companies, from which came the Commandos, the guerilla training centre at Loch Ailort, the Politico-Military courses at Cambridge. These were all projects which have left a deep mark on our ideas of training and organisation for war, which are not likely to be forgotten. It should be noticed that MI(R) was successful as a research department largely because it was also allowed to assume some executive responsibility. Its job (as construed by Colonel Holland) was not only to think up new schemes, but to drive them through the clogging medium of War Office discussion till they worked and stood on their own legs.

It is not so easy to sum up its value in the narrower field of subversive warfare. It was unquestionably superior to D Section in all matters of technique: its schemes have a harder and more practical air than those of Colonel Grand, it had no conspicuous and damning failures, and there was never any suspicion that its position was being misused. Its men were more carefully picked, and they were better schooled in the discipline of organisation, possibly because there was a nucleus of regular soldiers; in spite of this, it was not inferior to D Section in enterprise and vigour and esprit de corps, though these were D Section's strong points. It had perhaps less sense of the endless political ramifications of subversive warfare, but it was certainly not blind to them, and it suffered much frustration in the attempt to impress them on more orthodox sections of the War Office.

Yet it is impossible to claim that it achieved much subversion, or that it left much organisation on which SOE could build. There were its contacts with the Poles and Czechs, which were never broken, and in the Middle East its missions had a considerable future, largely outside the scope of SOE. But in the West its organisation was swept away as completely as that of D Section, and its Balkan contacts were also very flimsy. It must be admitted that both organisations were insufficiently pessimistic about Allied prospects, and did little to prepare for the situation which actually arose in the summer of 1940. But that, of course, was a matter above their heads.

CHAPTER IV

Reorganisation

There is plenty of evidence that the problem of co-ordinating clandestine activities was present to various minds at a comparatively early stage. But the essence of the problem was not to see that co-ordination was needed but to decide who should co-ordinate and how far his powers should reach. The first considered paper on this subject is one prepared by D in June 1939.[1] Along with various proposals for expansion, this suggests (p. 8):

Co-ordinating machinery
(27) Various ministries and organisations are each primarily concerned with certain aspects. It is recommended that they now need special sections.
(28) These special sections should within the sphere of their ministries be co-ordinated by CSS, using D Section for the purpose.

The special sections envisaged are to be at the War Office and Admiralty; there is no mention of Electra House – it is quietly assumed that D Section can be responsible for all clandestine propaganda – nor of the Air Ministry, which ultimately proved to be of vital importance as a 'common carrier'. The Ministry of Economic Warfare and the Ministry of Information are also omitted, but this is less surprising, as they had no official existence until the outbreak of war. The proposal then is that each Ministry should retain control of the activities developed by it, but that D Section should be the senior and co-ordinating organisation; its responsibility would be to the Foreign Secretary through the CSS.

The only project in this paper which came to anything was the development of D/M Section into MI(R) at the War Office, and no formal co-ordinating machinery existed in the early months of the war. MI(R) was controlled by the CIGS through the DMI, D Section

---

[1] Recommendations with regard to the control of 'extra-departmental' and 'paramilitary' activities, dated 5th June 1939 – on SOE Archives File 1/470/1.

by the Foreign Office through the CSS. Electra House also owed allegiance to the Foreign Office independently. The Ministry of Information also had some ill-defined responsibilities for propaganda to the enemy, and it was harassed chiefly by difficulties with the British Press and existed only on a precarious tenure. The BBC was to some extent under the control of the Ministry of Information, in virtue of powers inherited from the Post Office, but the extent of these powers in war time was obscure. The Ministry of Economic Warfare, which had some responsibility to the Foreign Office, had inherited the work of Major Morton's* Industrial Intelligence Centre, on which much of the planning for sabotage was based. So far as clandestine operations were concerned, Lord Hankey, then Chancellor of the Duchy, acted as arbiter and chaperone on behalf of the War Cabinet; his experience and prestige gave him great influence, but he possessed no department and departmental control of any kind.

The first practical step toward co-ordination was the constitution (under the aegis of Lord Hankey's War Cabinet Committee on German oil) of an Inter-Departmental Committee on River Transport, to sort out various competing projects for action on the Danube.[1] This first met on 8th January 1940 and continued to sit at intervals until June, under the chairmanship first of Vice-Admiral Sir C. E. Kennedy-Purvis** (then President of the Royal Naval College, Greenwich) and later of Rear-Admiral Bellairs, the DNI. It cannot be said that it achieved much, as the projects considered were without exception abortive, but at least it brought together some of the parties to the existing confusion.

The next initiative seems to have come from the DMI (Major-General Beaumont-Nesbitt), doubtless inspired by MI(R). The text of his proposals has been lost, but there is a record of his discussion with Colonel Grand on 29th February 1940.[2] The DMI had suggested an Inter-Service Board, on the lines of the Joint Security Board and including representation of the French. To this Colonel Grand had two objections; first, that the Foreign Office and the Ministry of Economic Warfare had important responsibilities, but were not to be represented, second, that it would be impossible to adjust British inter-departmental conflicts and disputes on a board including a French representative. He admitted the need for co-ordination – indeed he complained sharply

---

[1] Its activities are recorded in the POG(D) series of papers in the Cabinet Archives.
[2] On file 1/470/7.2 – SOE Archives.
* [(Sir) D. J. F. Morton, 1891–1971, ran industrial intelligence centre in 1930s, Churchill's private secretary in charge of secret affairs 1940–45, knight 1945. See R. W. Thompson, *Churchill and Morton* (1970), a disgruntled book.]
** [Knight 1939, Deputy First Sea Lord 1942–5, died 1946.]

of War Office encroachment on his own field – but what he suggested to the CSS was 'a joint Inter-Services D Project Board, parallel with and similar in constitution to the Inter-Services Security Board'; it 'should not be inter-Allied, anyway at this stage', and should include an MEW representative; the Foreign Office should not normally be represented, but should retain liberty to traverse the Board's recommendations on a higher level if necessary.

This idea seems to have been combined with the War Office proposal in a scheme which the JIC put forward to the COS on 21st March,[1] and which was taken by them on 1st April.[2] The paper is a little deprecatory in tone – 'such' (irregular) 'activities when taken by themselves may not be of great importance, but if properly co-ordinated and directed, they should make an appreciable contribution to the main strategy of the war': and its conclusion was only that there should be a consultative Inter-Service Projects Board which 'will not normally be responsible for putting into effect any project which is approved'. The proposal was pressed by the Foreign Office representative and DMI and was not resisted by CSS, although he stressed the somewhat increased risks of leakage: the First Sea Lord was more sceptical, but in the end the scheme was accepted in outline, subject to his promise that 'it was made quite clear that the Board should not impose delay on action being taken and did not interfere with Departmental action'.

The paper was then referred back to the JIC for re-drafting with these points in mind, and a revised version was produced on 26th April[3] which contained little change of substance, although rather more emphasis is laid on the secondary and consultative character of the Board. This re-draft was apparently accepted informally by the Chiefs of Staff on 1st May.[4] The essential points in this paper are:

(1) 'The Board will consist of representatives of the Service and Intelligence Departments on the level of Commander; The Ministry of Economic Warfare and Electra House should be asked to detail officers to attend when their Departments are affected. The War Office will provide a permanent secretary, accommodation, and clerical staff.'

(2) 'The Board will be primarily an advisory and consultative body and will not have executive functions.'

(3) 'The Board is set up to provide machinery for the co-ordination

---

[1] COS(40)271 (JIC(40)15).

[2] COS(40) 62nd Mtg, Item 2.

[3] COS(40)305(JIC) (JIC(40)36).

[4] MI(R) War Diary, 1st May 1940: no record in COS Minutes.

of projects for attacking the enemy by sabotage or other "irregular" operations, with the object of ensuring:

(a) that there is no overlapping or misdirected effort in connection with such projects;

(b) that full use is made of "irregular" activities in order to assist the objects of "regular" operations and economic warfare;

(c) that no project of value, which cannot be put into force immediately, is allowed to lapse;

(d) that the inter-departmental consultation necessary when any project affects more than one department, is facilitated.'

(4) 'Contact with the Foreign Office will be maintained through the Foreign Office representative on the JIC.'

(5) 'It will be for the JIC to consider when and how the French should be consulted.'

This was a cautious and comprehensive scheme, which brought in all likely interests – the importance of the Ministry of Information and the BBC hardly became clear till later. Its obvious weakness was that departmental responsibilities remained unchanged and that the Board had no executive authority; but this was mitigated by the fact that the War Office provided the Chairman (Colonel Holland), and a full-time Secretary (Major Kenyon), and that the Charter was so drafted that additional full-time staff could if necessary be put up by the War Office to act on the Board's business. In fact, the Board was a first step on a line of advance which might lead to centralisation under the War Office; a tentative beginning, but as much as was practicable at the time.

The Board met frequently during the next month; eight meetings were held between 3rd and 20th May, there was a special meeting[1] on Danube projects on 24th May, at which Lord Hankey was present, and there were meetings on 27th May, 10th June and 5th July. There is no record of further meetings, and the Board vanishes when SOE is set up. It had certainly achieved something, in that it ensured for the first time that projects were put down on a common list and seen by all departments interested. There is however little to be found in its minutes which ever came to anything, except the organisation of the Auxiliary Units in England, and the preparations for intervention in Abyssinia; but this is hardly surprising in the circumstances.

By this time, German successes in the West had transformed the attitude in high quarters to the potentialities of subversion. By the end of June Holland, Belgium, Denmark and Norway were fully occupied; France had signed an armistice surrendering half its territory to

---

[1] See DCOS(40)79 of 25th May 1940.

occupation; Italy was at war, the Mediterranean was closed to all normal traffic, and the fate of North Africa was in the balance. Even at the end of May it was already evident that the West was lost and that in Eastern Europe Britain could impose no military check on further German expansion. What this meant may be indicated by quoting two passages from the paper which the Chiefs of Staff submitted to the War Cabinet on 25th May[1] –

Ability to defeat Germany

14. Germany might still be defeated by economic pressure, by a combination of air attack on economic objectives in Germany and on German morale, and the creation of widespread revolt in her conquered territories.

Subversive Activities (in Annexe)

59. The only method of bringing about the downfall of Germany is by stimulating the seeds of revolt within the conquered territories. The occupied territories are likely to prove a fruitful ground for these operations, particularly when economic conditions begin to deteriorate.

   In the circumstances envisaged, we regard this form of activity as of the highest importance. A special organisation will be required and plans to put these operations into effect should be prepared, and all necessary preparations and training should be proceeded with as a matter of urgency.

In other words, a British victory was possible on the basis of naval blockade, air bombardment and subversion. The first two would undermine the German position, but British manpower, heavily committed to the Navy and the RAF, could not provide an army large enough to deliver the *coup de grâce* single-handed; only the occupied countries could so disperse and demoralise the German army that it could be destroyed by a relatively small British striking force. This was the dominating strategic concept in the early summer of 1940,[2] and it at

---

[1] COS(40)390 also WP(40)168 of 25th May 1940. The earliest reactions are summarised in a paper put up to the Joint Intelligence Sub-Committee by the DMI on 15th July 1940 proposing a great expansion of MI(R)'s activity – 'Subversive Activities in Enemy and Conquered Territory', JIC(40)180 of 18th July 1940. [See P. M. H. Bell, *British Policy in a Certain Eventuality* (Farnborough, 1974).]

[2] It remained dominant *on paper* until both the USSR and the USA were at war in 1941; but *in practice* (though nothing could be said) ultimate American intervention was accepted as pretty certain once Roosevelt had won the election in November 1940, and the breach between Germany and Russia became visible in the spring of 1941. This is important for the later history of SOE: its status soon receded from what had been expected in the enthusiasm for its creation. [F. D. Roosevelt, 1882–1945, President of USA from 1933.]

once raised the problem of subversion to a level not inferior to any other strategic task. It was this factor, rather than the known short-comings of D Section and Electra House, which made thorough re-organisation inevitable.

Reorganisation was therefore being discussed in many quarters from the early days of June 1940, and it is unlikely that the documents available give a complete story. But the views of many of the parties are on record, and the choice open to them was fairly limited. No one pretended any longer that the drive and initiative needed could be provided by a committee; it was common ground accepted that respon-sibility must be centralised and laid on one man. But the type of man required and the nature of his responsibility were not so clear; the problems may be tabulated somewhat as follows:

(a) Should he be a politician, a service officer, or a civilian official?
(b) The appointment of a politician would in effect imply respon-sibility direct to the War Cabinet, perhaps primarily through one of its members. If a non-political head were appointed, he must necessarily fall within the field of some existing depart-ment, and there could be only two serious claimants, the War Office and the Foreign Office, the latter acting possibly through the CSS.
(c) It was pretty well agreed that unity of purpose must be imposed on all the subversive organisations, ranging from the clandes-tine propaganda of Electra House to the open guerilla warfare planned by MI(R). It was not clear whether Electra House, D Section and MI(R) could retain separate identities under a 'Grand Co-ordinator' or whether they should be amalgamated to form a new department; nor was it easy to provide for the 'frontiers' of the new organisation, on the one hand with diplo-macy and open propaganda, and on the other hand with ortho-dox warfare as handled by the Service Departments through the existing organisation.

The first stages of the discussion can be traced in the papers of MI(R). On 3rd June 1940 the DMI saw the VCIGS[1] with a paper by Colonel Holland on the scope of MI(R) and its possible extension,[2] and these proposals were embodied in a formal minute dated 5th June,[3] which puts vigorously the case for a very great expansion of all irregular

---

[1] MI(R) War Diary under date 3.6.40 (MI(R) File 2).
[2] In MI(R) File 6 – on Branch folder, paper headed 'Duties of MI(R)' (ref. MIR/M/I/1 d/d 2.6.40).
[3] In MI(R) File 6 – on Branch folder.

activities. Its conclusion is: 'I recommend therefore the early creation of a separate directorate of the War Office to plan and carry out all operations and activities of an irregular nature. . . . The Director should work under the general direction of the VCIGS. It will be necessary for the directorate to co-ordinate and exercise a measure of control – the extent to be a matter for discussion with the parties concerned – over SIS and the Campbell Stuart organisation,[1] and it should be directly responsible for all shadow missions, School of Irregular Warfare and the special Cambridge course.' It is clear from Colonel Holland's paper that there was hesitation within the War Office about accepting responsibility for anything more than the coastal raiding parties which were the first task of Combined Operations; VCIGS's views are not on record, but it seems clear that though he accepted the idea of co-ordination by a soldier in the War Office he did not press it heartily.[2] However, Colonel Holland saw Mr Eden* (then Secretary of State for War) on 6th June[3] and the DMO on 8th June,[4] and a letter embodying the scheme for a War Office Directorate of irregular operations was sent by Mr Eden to the Prime Minister.[5]

The first inter-departmental discussion recorded was a meeting[6] between Lord Hankey, Colonel Menzies, Colonel Grand and Colonel Holland on 13th June 1940 'to discuss certain questions arising out of a possible collapse of France'. The crucial point is in para. 4:

No adequate machinery for such co-ordination at present existed. It was suggested that this machinery might consist of:
(a) A representative of three Service Departments, who should be a Director in the War Office, employed whole-time on this work and with naval and air force officers attached to him.
(b) A representative of the Secret Service.
(c) A representative of the organisation for propaganda in enemy countries.
All the above should have direct access to a Minister who would also be employed whole-time in this work.

---

[1] i.e. Electra House.
[2] Brief for DMI by MI(R) d/d 6.6.40, MI(R) File 4.
[3] MI(R) War Diary, MI(R) File 2.
[4] MI(R) War Diary, MI(R) File 2.
[5] MI(R) War Diary, MI(R) File 2. The letter is not available, but was sent on or shortly before 12.6.40.
[6] MI(R) File 6 'Re-organisation'.
* [(Sir) Anthony Eden, 1897–1977, Foreign Secretary 1935–8, 1940–45, 1951–5, War Secretary 1940, KG 1954, Prime Minister 1955–7, Earl of Avon 1961; in *DNB*. See his *The Reckoning* (1965).]

It was agreed that a draft scheme on the above lines should be drawn up, after which Lord Hankey might take informal soundings of individual Chiefs of Staff before putting up the proposal more formally.

This is clearly based on the War Office line of thought, but there are two important new suggestions:
- (a) That a full-time Minister should be appointed: a new and very important idea, probably suggested to Lord Hankey by the analogy of Lord Swinton's* position in relation to the Home Defence (Security) Executive.[1]
- (b) That the 'governing body' should continue to be a board, containing naval and air representatives, as well as spokesmen of SIS and Electra House.

Apparently no objection was raised by the CSS to the proposal that D Section should be transferred to the War Office outside his control and that of the Foreign Office.

The 'draft scheme' referred to (if it ever existed) has not been found, nor is there any record of Lord Hankey's discussions with the Chiefs of Staff. Possibly the matter was confused by the creation on 15th June under the Admiralty of the Directorate of Combined Operations, under Lieutenant General Bourne, RM,** which cut sharply across the line of development proposed by the War Office. The next stage is to be found in a minute[2] from Sir Alexander Cadogan to Lord Halifax dated 28th June, in view of a meeting to be held under the latter's chairmanship on 29th June (postponed in the event to 1st July). The last paragraphs of this are worth quoting in full; as will be seen, they largely endorse the War Office proposals, and do not insist at all strongly on the Foreign Office's interest in the political implications of subversion:

> Para. 9. They should be concentrated under one control. They should probably be divorced from SIS, which is more concerned with intelligence, and has enough to do in that sphere, and placed under military authority as an operation of war.

1   WP(40)172 of 27.5.1940 and WP(40)271 of 19.7.40, paras 1–3.
2   On SOE Archives File 2/340/3.0 – with pencil comments by Mr Dalton (destroyed).
*   [P. Cunliffe-Lister, 1884–1972, knight 1920 (as Lloyd-Graeme), Viscount Swinton 1935, Air Minister 1935–8, headed Security Executive 1940–42, Earl 1955; in *DNB*. See his *I Remember* (1948) and *Sixty Years of Power* (1966).]
** [(Sir) A. G. B. Bourne, 1882–1967, Adjutant-General Royal Marines 1939–41 and briefly director of combined operations 1940.]

10. If this is accepted, it might seem wise to amalgamate the 'D' organisation with MI(R), the whole thus coming under control of the DMI. If possible, the staff should be housed in the War Office.

11. If that were accepted, the DMI would take over the whole 'D' organisation, and be responsible for (1) sabotage, (2) subversive activities, and (3) to some extent propaganda in all countries.

12. The DMI, who would be the chief executive, would thus be responsible, in regard to his various activities, to War Office, Foreign Office and Ministry of Information.

(1) On sabotage in enemy and enemy-controlled countries, he would be assisted and advised by MEW and would be responsible to the War Office.

(2) On sabotage in neutral countries, the same would apply, but he would have to obtain the consent of the Foreign Office.

(3) On subversive activities, he would be responsible to the War Office, but should seek advice of the Foreign Office.

(4) On propaganda, he should seek direction from the Ministry of Information, who have a sufficient liaison with the Foreign Office and with Sir Campbell Stuart.

13. The DMI would arrange for proper liaison with DNI and DAI and CSS.

14. An officer from the Foreign Office could be provided, if desired, to form a permanent liaison with the new organisation.

15. The funds required would have to come from the SIS vote and could be paid through the Director of the SIS, who might be able, from his experience, to give advice as to their application.

The meeting to discuss this paper was attended by Lord Halifax (in the Chair), Lord Lloyd* (then Secretary of State for the Colonies, and Chairman of the British Council), Lord Hankey, Mr Dalton,[1]**

---

1 Mr Dalton seems to have been drawn into the matter a few days earlier; see his letter of 27th June to Mr Attlee, forwarding a note on the work of MEW (SOE Archives File 1/470/7). [C. R. Attlee, 1883–1967, led parlimentary Labour Party 1935–51, Lord Privy Seal 1940–42, deputy Prime Minister 1942–5, Prime Minister 1945–51, earl 1955; in *DNB*. See his *As It Happened* (1954).]

* [G. A. Lloyd, 1879–1941, baron 1924, High Commissioner in Egypt 1925–9, had worked with Lawrence; in *DNB*. See his *The British Case* (1940).]

** [E. H. J. N. Dalton, 1887–1962, anti-Nazi labour leader, MP 1924–31 and 1935–59, Minister of Economic Warfare 1940–42, Board of Trade 1942–5, Exchequer 1945–7, baron 1960; in *DNB*. See his *Second World War Diary*, ed. Ben Pimlott (1986).]

Sir Alexander Cadogan, the DMI, Colonel Menzies, Mr Desmond Morton (representing the Prime Minister) and Mr Gladwyn Jebb* (then Sir Alexander Cadogan's private secretary). There was no representative either of the Ministry of Information or of Electra House, which were then engaged in private warfare of their own as to their respective powers. The Minutes, which are on record,[1] are of great interest since the proceedings virtually decided the future form of SOE, even though no firm conclusions were recorded. The main points put in opposition to the joint Foreign Office-War Office view were as follows:

(a) Mr Dalton 'held that there was a clear distinction between "war from without" and "war from within", and that the latter was more likely to be better conducted by civilians than by soldiers'.
(b) Lord Hankey was inclined to defend the existing machinery and to attribute the failure of major sabotage schemes to 'the reluctance of the Foreign Office to authorise them, or at any rate to authorise them until too late'.
(c) 'There was a general feeling, voiced by Lord Lloyd, that what was required was a Controller armed with almost dictatorial powers.'
(d) Mr Morton appealed to the analogy of Lord Swinton's position in relation to the Home Defence (Security) Executive. 'Lord Swinton, he explained, presided over a committee on which all the various bodies dealing with this question were represented. If he differed with the view of any particular department, he was at liberty to take the matter up direct with the Prime Minister.'

The current opinion thus set sharply against the limited action proposed in Sir Alexander Cadogan's paper, and it does not seem that either the Foreign Office, the War Office or the SIS were anxious to insist on adding this unlimited commitment to their existing responsibilities. There was general agreement that there should be a Co-ordinator, who, 'provided he was the right man, would be able to look at the problem as a whole, and, subject only to the approval of the Prime Minister, would be able to override if necessary any departmental objections. Whether any reform of the existing machinery was required could safely be left to him to decide, after he had had some experience of its working. He should in any case devote his whole

---

[1] Garnett's 'History of PWE', p. 30.
[2] On MIR File 6 'Re-organisation'.
* [H. M. G. Jebb, 1900–96, diplomat, Dalton's private secretary 1929–31, ran SOE 1940–42, knight 1949, Ambassador to Paris 1954–60, Lord Gladwyn 1960.]

time to the work.' This clearly implies (though it is not stated) that the Co-ordinator should be a Minister, not an official.

The meeting then broke up, on the understanding that names would be suggested and a report should be made to the Prime Minister by Lord Halifax, after a further meeting.

Almost at the same time a paper[1] on the reorganisation of irregular activities was put forward to the Chiefs of Staff by Lieutenant General Bourne, RM, then DCO; this pointed in the same direction, though it laid more stress on the position of the War Office. Its origin is explained in para. 1:

> Since taking up my appointment as DCO I have daily been impressed with:
> (i) The need for co-operation between, and single control of, all the activities which reach overseas, of which my department is one.
> (ii) The political implications which continually arise in these activities, and which need to be rapidly resolved.

The essence of its conclusions[2] is that MI(R), MO9 (the 'raiding' section of the War Office), D Section and Electra House should be amalgamated to form a new Directorate in the War Office (Colonel Holland's proposal of the 5th June); that a Minister should be appointed to control this Directorate, SIS, MI5 and DCO; that the administration of these departments should remain as at present, though their policy would be a matter for the new Minister. It will be seen that this was the most ambitious project for centralisation yet put forward.

The War Office in its brief on this paper (dated 5th July)[3] warmly supported the appointment of a Minister, but it did not accept the proposal for a separate War Office Directorate, which had come first from Colonel Holland early in June – 'the duties of such a Director could well be done by DMO and P, and DMI. I suggest that D Section and "CS" (i.e. Electra House) should be placed under the control of DMI.' It is clear once again that prevailing opinion in the War Office scarcely appreciated what was involved in the development of irregular activities on a large scale and was not desperately anxious to take control. Colonel Holland's attitude was much more energetic. This is to be seen in his Aide-Mémoire[4] of 6th July and the Strategical

---

[1] COS(40)523(0). Copy on MI(R) File 6, under date 30.6.40.
[2] Given very clearly in the chart at Appendix II of the paper.
[3] Copy on MI(R) File 6.
[4] Copy on MI(R) File 6 (also 6a on MI(R) File 4).

Appreciation attached to it, which are designed to show the vast importance of irregular warfare in the situation of 1940 and to establish that its ultimate objective is strictly military and can be reached only by proper attention to technique and to the canons of strategy. 'All subversive activities must eventually aim at open rebellion, either as a forerunner to, or an auxiliary of, direct military action.' 'What has to be welded into one whole campaign to the one end of promoting open rebellion is subversive propaganda, minor sabotage (which, after all, is only incidental), and irregular warfare.' This is a clear-cut view which contains much truth, and its operation can be traced throughout the history of SOE: it is sharply opposed to the view put forward with equal conviction by Mr Dalton, that subversive activities are 'too serious a matter to be left to soldiers' and that it is by no means self-evident that the final stage must always be open rebellion; political subversion and economic sabotage may also play a great part without leading to open warfare.

DCO's paper came before the VCOS* on 5th July;[1] discussion on the lines of the War Office brief is recorded, but a decision was postponed until DCO and the Directors of Intelligence could be present. The paper was taken again by the VCOS in their presence on 8th July[2] when there was full discussion. The points which are of most interest in the light of later history are the following:

(a) There was a tendency to plan and carry out certain types of 'irregular' operations without the knowledge of the Chiefs of Staff. There was, in consequence, a danger that such activities might not contribute towards the effective strategical conduct of operations, and might even prove detrimental.

(b) There was a risk, under the present organisation, that activities that were strategically desirable might be initiated before, or without, their political repercussions had been properly assessed.

(c) It was emphasised that as the Chiefs of Staff were responsible to the Government for strategical advice, they must be kept informed of all activities that might affect the conduct of operations.

The conclusion reached was that DCO's diagnosis was sound but that his reorganisation scheme was open to some objections; the Secretary was instructed to draft and circulate a report in the light

---

[1] COS(40)210th Mtg, Item 2.

[2] COS(40)212th Mtg, Item 1.

* [Vice Chiefs of Staff.]

of the discussion. But the problem had already been taken up on the political level; the report was never prepared and no later Chiefs of Staff discussion is recorded until after the creation of SOE.

These political discussions were decisive, but they cannot be traced in detail from the papers available, nor is it possible to assess precisely the weight carried by political opinion outside Ministerial circles. The existence of the problem was by this time obvious to the intelligent public, and outside interest and pressure is shown by a paper[1] on 'Guerilla Warfare' which was produced on 2nd July by a Committee of MPs consisting of Vernon Bartlett, Commander Fletcher, Mr L. H. Gluckstein and Commander King-Hall,* and was widely circulated, as well as by an Evening Standard 'leader' of 8th July[2] which calls pointedly for the establishment of a Ministry of Political Warfare parallel to the Ministry of Economic Warfare. There were also many 'bright ideas' on these lines submitted about this time by members of the public of varying degrees of eminence and intelligence.[3]

So far as the evidence goes, the sequence of events was as follows:

3rd July Mr Dalton discusses with Mr Attlee by telephone: suggests Brigadier Spears as Chief Executive, with himself as Minister responsible and Mr Attlee as War Cabinet member in general charge.[4] Probably writes to Lord Halifax on similar lines.[5]

4th July Letter from Mr Dalton to Mr Attlee making the case for Brigadier Spears'** appointment.

---

1 Copies on MI(R) File 4.
2 Copies on MI(R) File 4.
3 Copies on MI(R) File 4.
4 Letter of 4th July from MEW to the Lord Privy Seal, on SOE Archives File 2/340/3.0 (destroyed).
5 Letter of 5th July from Lord Halifax to MEW, on SOE Archives File 2/340/3.0 (destroyed).
* [C. V. O. Bartlett, 1894–1983, journalist and broadcaster, independent MP 1938–50; in *DNB*. R. T. H. Fletcher, 1885–1961, Labour MP 1935–41, commander RN 1939, Lord Winster 1941; in *DNB*. (Sir) I. H. Gluckstein, 1897–1979, Conservative MP 1931–45, territorial colonel. W. S. R. King-Hall, 1893–1966, sailor and educator, independent MP 1939–45, baron 1966; in *DNB*.]
** [Sir E. L. Spears, 1886–1974, Paris-born (as Spiers), soldier and businessman, ensured Anglo-French army liaison 1914–17, Conservative MP 1922–4 and 1931–45. Rescued de Gaulle 16 June 1940, quarrelled with him in Syria 1942. See Max Egremont, *Under Two Flags* (1997).]

5th July Letter from Lord Halifax to Mr Dalton accepting the latter's argument for civilian control, expressing some doubts as to whether a member of the War Cabinet need be involved, and undertaking to see the Prime Minister.[1]

7th July Mr Dalton discusses with Mr Attlee.[2]

8th July Letters from Mr Dalton to Lord Halifax and Mr Attlee stressing need for first-class executive officer, and urging the latter to see the Prime Minister that day.[3]

At this point it seems that Mr Neville Chamberlain, then Lord President, was asked by the Prime Minister to look into the position and report. There is no record of his action, but his report was in draft and had been discussed with Mr Dalton before 16th July.[4] It envisaged an organisation 'to co-ordinate all action by way of subversion and sabotage, against the enemy overseas'. Mr Dalton is appointed as Chairman, to be assisted by Sir Robert Vansittart,* and is to refer to the Lord President for assistance and arbitration when required. The various departments concerned 'will, for the time being, continue to be administered by the Ministers at present responsible for them'. Provision is made for delimiting subversive and regular operations and for co-ordination with the Foreign Office and the Chiefs of Staff.

On 16th July the Prime Minister wrote formally to Mr Dalton acquainting him of these proposals and asking him to accept the task.[5] On 19th July, Mr Chamberlain's paper, the formal charter of SOE, was circulated as WP(40)271, and on 22nd July it was formally approved by the War Cabinet, with one minor amendment. The effective decision had already been taken by the Prime Minister in consultation with the Ministers concerned, and the Minutes add only the Cabinet's opinion that 'it would be very undesirable that any

---

[1] Letter of 5th July from Lord Halifax to MEW on SOE Archives File 2/340/3.0 (destroyed).

[2] On SOE Archives File 2/340/3.0 (destroyed).

[3] On SOE Archives File 2/340/3.0 (destroyed).

[4] Prime Minister to Mr Dalton, 16.7.40, on SOE Archives File 2/340/3.0 (destroyed). This must have been the last, or almost the last important political action of Mr Chamberlain's career. His first operation was on 24th July, and he was never effectively at work again.

[5] Prime Minister to Mr Dalton, 16.7.40, on SOE Archives File 2/340/3.0 (destroyed).

* [R. G. Vansittart, 1881–1957, diplomat, knight 1929, PUS Foreign Office, 1930–38, baron 1941; in *DNB*. See his *The Mist Procession* (1958) and Ian Colvin, *Vansittart in Office* (1963).]

(Parliamentary) Questions in regard to the SOE should appear on the Order Paper'.

This solution was clearly to some extent a compromise in between political interests. A concentration of power such as DCO had suggested would have been politically impracticable, even in the summer of 1940, and it was appropriate that a Labour Minister should be appointed to SOE to balance the appointment of Lord Swinton to the Home Defence (Security) Executive, and the control of SIS by the Foreign Office under Mr Eden. This Labour responsibility was balanced in its turn by making the Minister responsible through Mr Chamberlain rather than through Mr Attlee, as at first suggested. After Mr Chamberlain's retirement nothing more is heard of the Lord President in connection with SOE. It also seemed appropriate that a Labour representative should be in charge of subversion, which was expected to rely mainly on the forces of the Left in Europe. There was some case on practical grounds for the association of SOE with MEW, as subversion activities required close collaboration with economic warfare both in intelligence and in planning, but politics enter into this also, as the responsibilities of the MEW were in themselves hardly adequate to a Minister of Mr Dalton's status holding Cabinet rank.

But as a matter of organisation the charter was an almost complete victory for Mr Dalton's point of view, and it was secured without serious opposition from any quarter. In form he was a mere chairman and the existing departmental administration remained in existence. But he was a chairman authorised to recruit his own staff,[1] and the old administration was reprieved only 'for the time being' (para. 4(e)).

The time proved to be very short. Control of D Section and of Electra House was formally transferred to Mr Dalton by Lord Halifax on 16th August.[2] The Foreign Office acted apparently without further consultation with the CSS, who wrote on 4th September[3] that he had only that day become aware of the transfer of control, and predicted sadly the difficulties which would follow when two sets of secret agents worked independently into the same territory.

Mr Dalton also at once raised the question of absorbing the subversive side of MI(R) into the new organisation; he writes[4] on 19th August: 'what I personally would like is for MI(R) in so far as it is responsible for military operations to be somehow absorbed in the Operations side of the War Office, and for its other functions to devolve

---

[1] WP(40)271, para. 4(d).

[2] Two letters Halifax to Dalton 16.8.40, on SOE Archives File 1/460/1.

[3] 'C' to Mr Gladwyn Jebb, ref: C/4824 of 4.9.40, on SOE Archives File 1/460/1.

[4] Para. 3 of Annex I to Paper on Subversion circulated by Foreign Office in October 1940: copy on SOE Archives File 1/470/1.

on the reformed D organisation. If certain of the particularly gifted junior officers of MI(R) could gravitate towards the latter, nobody would be more pleased than I.' Like the CSS, MI(R) had not foreseen that action would entail the disappearance of the old organisation, and it had continued actively to develop its own plans during July and August. But Mr Dalton's ideas were accepted with little hesitation by the higher authorities of the War Office. Brigadier Wyndham was appointed over Colonel Holland's head as DDMI(R) to report on the future of the department, and on 25th August he recommended its dissolution and a partition of its empire. His proposals were largely endorsed by VCIGS on 3rd October,[1] and the formal dissolution of MI(R) followed later that month.[2]

---

[1] Papers on MI(R)309/40 – now in MI(R) File 6.
[2] MI(R) War Diary, MI(R) File 2.

PART II

THE MAKING OF A WEAPON

CHAPTER V

The Beginnings of the Organisation

When Mr Dalton took over in July 1940, he was given wide powers and almost unlimited objectives, and the existing organisation contained little on which to build. The steps to be taken were:
  (i) To recruit directing staff, and through them to frame an organisation.
  (ii) To define the task more closely and to secure higher approval for the line to be followed.
  (iii) To delimit the frontiers between SOE and other departments.

1. Staff and Internal Organisation

Mr Dalton's charter had attached Sir Robert Vansittart to him as assistant and had empowered him to recruit such additional staff as they might find necessary.[1] Sir Robert continued until his retirement in June 1942 to fill the post of Chief Diplomatic Adviser to the Secretary of State for Foreign Affairs, and his attachment to SOE was neither executive nor full time; he seems at first to have been consulted regularly on matters of high policy, but his influence grew less and disappeared as the organisation found its feet. The first full-time officer recruited[2] was Mr Gladwyn Jebb, who was then Private Secretary to Sir Alexander Cadogan, and was thus familiar with the genesis of SOE; he took up his duties almost at once, bringing with him as assistant Mr Philip Broad,* also a Foreign Office Official. Mr Jebb's post was that of Chief Executive Officer; apparently there was not at the time any Office Instruction or other official paper setting out his duties, but it is clear from correspondence that he was in effect to act as Permanent Under Secretary. The ordinary business of the office would be conducted by him on behalf of the Minister, and papers for the Minister's attention would normally pass through him

---

[1] WP(40)271 paras 4(c) and (d).
[2] See correspondence between Mr Dalton and Sir Alexander Cadogan, dated 17th, 18th and 19th July 1940, on SOE Archives File 2/340/3.0 (destroyed).
* [1903–66, Consul-General in Istanbul 1955–60.]

to the Minister with no intermediary except the Minister's Private Secretary. Mr Jebb was accommodated with the Minister in the Ministry of Economic Warfare's offices in Berkeley Square House, under cover of Foreign Policy Adviser to the Ministry of Economic Warfare and with the rank of Assistant Under Secretary in the Foreign Office; Mr Hugh Gaitskell was the Private Secretary nominated as the sole channel for SOE business.

The first obvious need was to obtain reports on the works of the three existing departments, MI(R), D[1] and Electra House, and to take decisions about their future. As we have already seen,[2] the conclusion was reached early in August that D Section and Electra House should be taken over by SOE *in toto*; while MI(R) should be absorbed in part by SOE, in part by other branches of the War Office. After collecting opinions[3] Mr Dalton decided that the existing heads of D and Electra House could not continue to hold their posts. Sir Campbell Stuart (who was then in Canada) was courteously dismissed,[4] and was replaced as chief of propaganda by Mr R. A. Leeper,[5]* then head of the Political Intelligence Department of the Foreign Office, which continued to exist as cover for the subversive propaganda organisation; Mr Valentine Williams,** Sir Campbell Stuart's second in command, remained in charge of Electra House's 'Country House' at Woburn.† It proved more difficult to find a suitable replacement for Colonel Grand, and it was not until late in August that the post was accepted by Sir Frank Nelson,†† a man of business and formerly a

---

1 See final form of D's Report on 'Great Britain's only Successful Experimental in Total Warfare', dated 27th August, in SOE Archives File HD/P. 370, with extremely adverse comments by CSS; also lists of D Section officers employed, with functions and symbols, sent by D to Jebb 14th August 1940, on SOE Archives File F/138 (AD/S.1).

2 Page 70.

3 See files HD/P. 370 (Colonel Grand) and HD/S/72 (Sir Campbell Stuart) (AD/S.1).

4 Letter of 16th August 1940 on SOE Archives File HD/S/72 (AD/S.1). (See also File F/138 (AD/S. 1) notes from CD/XX/252 of 16.11.40 – para. B.)

5 Suggested in letter from SO to Mr Duff Cooper, 26th July 1940, on SOE Archives File HD/S/72.

* [(Sir) R. W. A. Leeper, 1888–1968, Sydney-born diplomat, Ambassador to Greece 1943–6, Argentina 1946–8, knight 1945, director of de Beers 1950–65. See his *When Greek Meets Greek* (1950).]

** [1883–1946, journalist, MC on Somme.]

† [Stuart had requisitioned the bulk of the palace of the Dukes of Bedford, some 40 miles NW of London.]

†† [1883–1966, India merchant, knight 1924, Conservative MP 1924–31, Consul at Basle 1939, CD of SOE 1942.]

Conservative MP, [PASSAGE DELETED ON GROUNDS OF NATIONAL SECURITY]. There was an awkward interregnum during August, and at first it was intended that Colonel Grand should continue as Sir Frank Nelson's second in command (as D under Nelson as CD);[1] this soon proved unworkable and Colonel Grand left the organisation about the end of September.[2]

These personal changes were in themselves difficult and important decisions, but they did not affect the main problem, the forging of the three conceptions of propaganda, sabotage and open revolt into a single 'fourth arm' of war. To anticipate, it may be said here that this problem was never solved, in spite of the breadth of Mr Dalton's own conceptions and the very wide charter given to him by the Cabinet. Electra House and D Section were re-christened SO1 and SO2, but they remained separate organisations which grew apart rather than together. The decisions which made this inevitable were taken in the summer of 1940, although their consequences did not emerge for some time.

One factor was the acceptance of the Minister of Information's claim that he should retain control of overt as distinct from covert propaganda.[3] Another was the breakdown of the plan for regional 'Bureaux', which appears first in Mr Gaitskell's paper of 31st July.[4] As there outlined, the project was that the centre of the organisation should be a series of 'Bureaux' (the name perhaps derived from a similar project conceived by MI(R));[5] small but highly qualified bodies, on a 'country' basis, each to be divided internally into three 'Sectors' – the Propaganda Sector, the Organisation and Personnel Sector, and the 'Activities' Sector. The Bureaux should be concerned with intelligence, in the sense of gathering all relevant information from other departments and putting it in shape for the purposes of SOE; and with planning, which should include the drafting of propaganda directives and the preparation of plans for destructive operations. The Bureaux might even, at some stage, become responsible for directing some operations; but they were not to be executive bodies. Indeed, they would be flanked by three other main departments, the Directorate of Propaganda, the Directorate of 'Activities', and the Directorate of Technical Matters and Supply; and projects would pass for approval from the Bureaux through the relevant Directorate to the

---

[1] See interview between CD and D of 26th August 1940, and D's letter of 29th August, in SOE Archives File 2/340/3.0.

[2] Letter from Grand to SO dated 29th September 1940, on SOE Archives File HD/P/370.

[3] Dealt with more fully below, p. 96.

[4] On SOE Archives File 1/470/1 Vol. I.

[5] Above pp. 46–7.

Chief Executive Officer and the Minister. The Bureaux might draw staff from the corresponding sections of D and of Electra House; but they would in themselves be weak bodies, with no head comparable to Mr Leeper and Sir Frank Nelson, and with no corporate existence as a driving force in the organisation. This plan may have been to some extent forced on the Minister by the inescapable fact that Electra House and D already existed as living and working departments; but it was doomed from the outset by the failure to give the Bureaux (known for a period as SO3) an effective weight equal to that of SO1 and SO2. Mr Broad was at one time head of this 'Planning and Intelligence' Department in Lansdowne House, with Brigadier van Cutsem as Director of Intelligence;[1] appointments clearly not of the same status as those of Mr Jebb, Mr Leeper and Sir Frank Nelson. SO3 as such had already disintegrated by the end of September 1940, and what was left then ranked as the Intelligence and Planning Department of SO2; this in its turn was abolished in January 1941 and its stronger personalities were absorbed elsewhere in the organisation.[2]

The problem of centralisation was made worse by the ambiguity of Mr Jebb's position as Chief Executive Officer; according to the original plan he was to be responsible for the working of the department as a whole, and when the Bureaux broke down he was left as the only possible central point. His role as 'Permanent Secretary' is indicated quite clearly in the letters regarding his original appointment, in Mr Dalton's paper of 19th August on 'the Fourth Arm', and in the description of the organisation prepared by Mr Jebb early in October.[3] Unfortunately it was in practice ambiguous, largely as a result of the problem of relative standing as between himself and Mr Leeper (who was much his senior), aggravated by the vested interests of the two existing departments. Mr Jebb's original position was virtually abandoned in Mr Dalton's letter[4] of 17th August to Mr Valentine Williams, offering him the post of head of the country establishment of SO1 – 'Mr Leeper . . . will act under the general direction of myself as responsible Minister and of Sir Robert Vansittart. He will rank on an equality with Mr Jebb who will be my Chief Executive Adviser' (sic) 'under Sir Robert Vansittart for a wide range

---

[1] CEO's paper of early October 1940, on SOE Archives File 1/470/1. (See also AD/S.1 File F/138 – notes from CD/XX/252 of 16th November 1940, para. F.)

[2] Letter from Mr Jebb to Mr Cadett (PID/1576 of 14th January 1941) refers, on SOE Archives File 2/340/3.1. [Thomas Cadett, former and future *Times* man in Paris, joined SOE's F or independent French Section.]

[3] Printed copy on SOE Archives File 1/470/1.

[4] On SOE Archives File 2/340/3.0. Mr Leeper had said the same thing to Mr Valentine Williams on 13th August (Garnett, 'History of PWE', p. 31).

of activities, extending beyond propaganda, with which I have now been charged by the Prime Minister and the Cabinet.' This is clinched by an amendment[1] circulated by Mr Jebb on 17th October to his paper on 'Subversion', obviously in response to an objection. The operative sentences are: 'Mr Leeper, of course, is in no way directed by me, who am responsible for the "operations" side. In practice, all major questions are discussed at a periodic meeting of the Minister, Sir Robert Vansittart, Mr Leeper and myself. CD also attends this meeting, when necessary. At the same time all papers for submission to the Minister come through me, and I, therefore, act as a central, co-ordinating link.'

The plan at this stage is somewhat as follows:

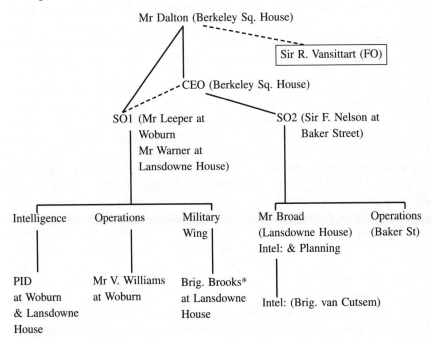

The link interposing Mr Jebb between SO1 and the Minister has become very tenuous, and soon vanishes, leaving Mr Jebb as Chief Executive Officer of SO2 alone; the Bureaux have disintegrated into their elements, and are nominally attached to SO2, which in practice can find no use for them. Geography played almost as much a part in this confusion as did personalities; whatever the personalities, it is

---

[1] On SOE Archives File 1/470/1.

* [Dallas Brooks.]

hardly conceivable that a unified force could have been built with the Minister in Berkeley Square, one of his Directors in Baker Street, and the other in Bedfordshire; the latter represented in London only by a 'holding party', itself geographically separated from the rest of the Ministry.

The internal organisation of SO2, with which we are mainly concerned here,[1] was equally fluid and it would be a waste of time to follow it through each stage of its development. Many of the 'old hands' remained throughout, but their roles changed continually, and in addition innumerable new solutions were tried as new problems arose.

At first the main framework was inherited from D Section. Its 'country sections' were retained, and Colonel G. F. Taylor, who had been Grand's second in command, also remained as AD, chief assistant to CD. The first important additions were:

(a) The introduction of Squadron Leader (later Group Captain) Venner,* a very experienced professional accountant, as Director of Finance, a position which he continued to hold to the end, with the warm approval both of SOE and of the Treasury.[2]

(b) Colonel Davies (a Courtauld's Director), who had been one of the most successful 'amateur' members of MI(R), was at first the only representative of the MI(R) tradition: he came in as 'Personal Assistant'[3] to Sir Frank Nelson, and was required in the first instance to advise him on organisation at home. His interests were thus turned mainly to the 'general services' side of the organisation, to which he continued to devote himself: he ultimately became a Director of Research and Supply in the autumn of 1941, and continued to hold that post to the end.

(c) One result of Colonel Davies's period as PA was a very far-sighted report on training;[4] this laid down a programme for the provision of schools, which never required fundamental alteration. The Training Section, set up as a result of this report,

---

[1] As will be seen later, SO1 became PWE and SO2 took over the name SOE: hence some confusion in terminology in the narrative.

[2] See CD's letter to Jebb, No. 92 undated, on SOE Archives File (AD/S.1) F/138, paras 12 and 13.

[3] This is made completely clear in CD's 'Office Instruction on Higher Organisation', of 22nd March 1941, copy on SOE Archives File 2/340/3.1.

[4] Dated 12th October 1940, copy on SOE Archives File 1/270/02. See also Chapter 1 page 2 of Training History, and below p. 729.

* [J. F. Venner, 1902–55, an accountant of genius.]

was in the first instance in the charge of Lieutenant Colonel G. S. Wilson,* an old Indian policeman, now a leading figure in the Boy Scouts Organisation, who was later head of the Scandinavian Section.

(d) Colonel Gubbins (now a Brigadier) was released on 18th November 1940[1] from the organisation of Auxiliary Units for guerilla warfare in England, and came back into the organisation. He had been in MI(R) from the first, and was excellently qualified to maintain its tradition within SOE. He retained the old symbol 'M' from the days of D/M, and he was charged both with the supervision of training and with the actual conduct of operations planned and prepared by the Country Sections; a somewhat clumsy arrangement which in practice meant that M became a 'Director-General' of Country Sections so far as their operations were based in the United Kingdom, with no clearly defined control over the political bearings of their work. To confuse matters further, he retained sole responsibility for Poland and Czechoslovakia, which were both old MI(R) commitments.[2]

(e) In October 1940 (after an unsuccessful attempt[3] to secure offices in St James's Street) the organisation moved to 64 Baker Street and assumed the cover name of 'Inter-Services Research Bureau.'[4] Other offices in the same area were gradually added as the HQ expanded.

These were the main points on which some stability in organisation had been reached by the spring of 1941; in other respects it was still very fluid:

(a) The provision of a personal or 'high-level' planning staff to assist the head of an organisation is not a matter which can be settled by any simple formula, since so much depends on his personality; and there would be little point in working through the various solutions adopted by SOE. At this stage the position was particularly unsatisfactory, since the Intelligence and Planning Section, under Colonel Anstruther,** had hardly yet recovered from the confusion created by the original Bureaux.

---

1 London War Diary Vol. I, pp. 31 and 54.
2 Chart of M Section as at February 1941 on SOE Archives File 2/340/3.1.
3 5th Meeting of SO Board, 3rd October 1940; copy on SOE Archives File (AD/S.1) '103.a'.
4 7th Meeting of SO Board, 10th October 1940; copy on SOE Archives File (AD/S.1) '103.a'.
* [1880–1960.]
** [P. N. Anstruther, 1891–1960.]

Its theoretical role is set out in para. 8 of the 'Aide-Mémoire on SO2', submitted to the Joint Planning Committee on 26th March 1941. The first step in examining a project is that its appropriateness for SO2 should be considered by CD and his Council; the second stage is a decision on its feasibility in consultation with the Country Sections concerned. Only then does it pass to the Intelligence and Planning Section for the preparation of an appreciation, for which Brigadier Gubbins's Training and Operations Section is jointly responsible. This does not give 'Planning' a position of much serious importance, and a more rational solution was reached in July 1941[1] when Intelligence was separated from Planning, and Air Commodore Boyle* (till then Director of Intelligence at the Air Ministry) took responsibility for the former, along with other duties. Planning thereafter passed through various vicissitudes; first as a 'Chief of Staff's' office attached personally to CD, later as virtually the liaison section with the COS and the JPS. It was only in this last phase that some stability was reached.

(b) There was no Director of Personnel until the appointment of Air Commodore Boyle, who added this responsibility to that of the Intelligence Section.

(c) An 'Admin' section under Major G. Courtauld existed from an early date. But this was concerned mainly with minor routine matters, and on larger issues each Directorate, Station or Section had to look after itself; if no one inside the organisation could help, the Section itself went outside it. On the whole this method at first made for speed and good service, as an officer from SOE could generally claim high priority for the relatively small facilities he required. But in the long run it created confusion intolerable in a large organisation, and the appointment of a Director of Organisation was very much overdue when the post was finally filled in November 1943 by Mr M. P. Murray,** then an Assistant Secretary in the Air Ministry.

(d) It is also worth noting that, with the exception of a few Regular Army Officers, the whole staff from top to bottom was amateur, and the organisation lacked entirely the minor 'bureaucracies' of a government department, which were provided as a matter of course for other new Ministries – for

---

[1] CD/OR/317/AD of 2nd July 1941, Pt 1 para. 2; copy on SOE Archives File (AD/S.1) File 138.
* [A. R. Boyle, 1887–1949, said never to have made a personal enemy.]
** [M. P. Murray, 1905–79, rose to be deputy secretary Ministry of Power 1961–5.]

such in effect SOE was. There was no Central Registry, with the usual accessories of archives and library; no central filing system; no central branches for routine personnel matters, or for the allocation of rooms. This is something of a grievance to the historian, as papers were kept separately for each section; it is impossible to find any complete series of routine records, for organisation and duties, postings, movements, and so forth, and there is not even a continuous record of policy decisions. There was some real justification for this on grounds of security, but the minor forms of 'red tape' were badly missed when the organisation grew to its full size. In the early stages they were hardly necessary, and they could not be introduced later without a dislocation which would have been intolerable.

A chart of the organisation of SO2 as it began to emerge from this first stage is given in Appendix B, which refers to March or April 1941. There is not much to be said for it as a theoretical distribution of the functions of a great department; but practice was a little better than theory. The 'old hands' of the organisation formed a fairly small and compact group, which was given formal existence as an executive council, whose title varied at different stages.

At the outset the old Inter-Services Projects Board was in effect continued as the D Board (or SO Board),[1] including representatives of the Director of Combined Operations, SO1 and SIS, as well as the three Services liaison officers and the leading members of SO2. Its first meeting[2] was held on 30th August 1940, and some records are extant up to its twenty-fifth meeting on 27th February 1941.[3] It is not clear that it was then formally abolished, but it had undoubtedly become too large and vague a body for anything more than 'inter-departmental co-ordination', *alias* pious platitude.

The effective organ was now the Committee of heads of branches, constituted as the 'SO2 Executive Committee' on 5th December 1940.[4] This was known as the 'Board of Directors' from November 1941, and simply as 'the SOE Council' after February 1942: and it continued to meet with varying membership once or twice a week

---

[1] For this title see Minutes of 7th Meeting of the Board, para. 1, dated 10th October 1940, on SOE Archives File 1/360/3.

[2] See letter from CEO, to Colonel Grand, ref: 0/1106/26 of 26th August 1940, on SOE Archives File 1/360/3.

[3] SOE Archives File (AD/S.1) '103/a'.

[4] See CD/XX/42/PA of 30th November 1940, on SOE Archives File 2/340/3.1 convening first meeting and giving list of those summoned: see also CD's Minute of 1st December 1940 on SOE Archives File (AD/S.1) HD/138.

throughout SOE's history. It was in a real sense the Directorate of SOE – a corporate body of experienced persons – although formal responsibility rested solely on CD. 'Council' was not the 'governing body' of SOE; the chain of command and responsibility led from the Minister through CD to the Directors and their subordinates. But all major matters of organisation and policy (not necessarily of operations) were laid before it, and through it was expressed the 'corporate opinion' of the department.

2. The Definition of Policy

In a sense the settlement of policy was at this stage a matter of secondary importance, as no instrument yet existed with which to execute it. But the early discussions of the role of SOE still possess more than academic interest.

The first step is to be found in Mr Dalton's paper of 19th August[1] entitled 'The Fourth Arm', which was discussed by the Vice-Chiefs of Staff on 21st August.[2] The bulk of this paper is concerned with questions of organisation and liaison which are dealt with elsewhere, but its opening paragraphs contain some general principles of great importance. Their drift is best seen by putting together a few sentences from the paper itself. 'The Germans have shown that success in war can, to a large extent, be achieved by 'Subversion', by which I mean not only propaganda, but subversive activities in the widest sense . . . . Subversion, I suggest, is an essential element in any large-scale offensive action: *per contra*, it is of little or no value when the main strategy is defensive . . . . Indeed, I imagine that such considerations are now very nearly axiomatic.'

'It has, I think, already been laid down by the Chiefs of Staff that, if we are to win the war, we must, at some stage, pass to the offensive on the Continent of Europe. The preparation for such an offensive is naturally the business of the Fighting Services, but it is probable, to say the least, that their plans will be very materially assisted if Subversion is planned on the broadest scale *now*.'

'During the last fortnight I . . . have reached certain general conclusions. One is that the selection of the right men is even more important than the creation of the right machine. Another is that I shall be able to achieve little or nothing unless I have the confidence and the co-operation of the Fighting Services . . . . A third conclusion is that it will be essential for my activities to be within the framework of some strategical plan. I have no views on strategy as such and I shall

---

[1] Annex I to the Print circulated in October 1940, on SOE Archives File 1/470/1.
[2] COS(40)276th Mtg, Item 2, of 21st August 1940.

certainly not attempt to formulate any. But clearly I must be told what *not* to do as well as, within broad limits, what I am to do . . . . My last conclusion (which is really elementary) is that no one of the Fighting Services is in a better position than another to run "Subversion". It seems to follow from this that Subversion should be clearly recognised by all three Fighting Services as another and independent service.'

The Vice-Chiefs of Staff recorded that they 'found themselves in general agreement with the organisation as set out in Mr Dalton's paper', and discussed in detail only the question of Service Liaison Officers on the 'D Board'. Their attention was clearly not directed to the far-reaching implications of Mr Dalton's axioms, and in particular not to his claim that Subversion was in effect a 'Fourth Service'. Mr Dalton himself had not pressed this very far: he had not claimed for his organisation a share in strategic decisions – it would have been laughable to make such a claim for an organisation which did not yet exist even on paper – and he had left much of the propaganda field in the hands of the Ministry of Information. But the logic is difficult to evade. It can fairly be held that Subversion in the widest sense is one of the major arms of modern war and that it cannot be handled as a side-line by one of the Fighting Services. The implication of this must be that the Head of Subversion is entitled to a status equal to that of the other Chiefs of Staff, and that his subordinates must be consulted on each level in the preparation of the strategic plan.

This logic did not work out so clearly in practice. For one thing SOE never attained an inclusive control of Subversion. Later, when it had grown to maturity as an organisation, its claim to rank as a Fourth Service was taken up more earnestly; but propaganda was by that time entirely outside its scope, and the Foreign Office had reasserted control over the political aspects of its work. SOE was charged only with the organisation of sabotage and the preparation of guerilla warfare – a very large and important task, but not in itself comparable with that of any of the three Fighting Services and certainly not sufficient to sustain an equality of status with them. The second difficulty is more theoretical, but not without practical implications. The position of the Chiefs of Staff as a technical advisory committee rests on the assumption that the Fighting Services are concerned with the means and not with the end; that a clear distinction can be drawn between the objects of strategy and its technique – the first is for the political Cabinet, the second for the Chiefs of Staff. This distinction is not easy to sustain even for the Fighting Services in modern war, but it is a lifeline to which they must cling; if it gives way, the soldier is merged in the politician, and the tradition of the 'profession of arms' is broken. It would be almost impossible to make such a distinction for a Subversive Service in the full sense, charged with policy and execution, both for propaganda and for the resistance which breeds in ground made fertile by propaganda. Policy in these respects is concerned with war aims, not with war strategy; at every step it raises the question of what situation is to be aimed at 'after the war'. Shall we strengthen the Left, or the Right, or the Centre? Is it our policy to reduce an enemy country to ideological and political chaos on which nothing can be re-built? Unless we are to accept the political nihilism which was Hitler's policy for every country except his own (and which eventually involved his own), these questions are for the highest political authority to decide; they go far beyond even the scope of the Foreign Office as it is usually conceived, and 'technical advice' from a reorganised Chiefs of Staff would advance matters very little.

These questions are indicated here because they raise the most complex of all the issues illustrated in the story of SOE. For the moment we are concerned with the practical problems of the autumn of 1940, debated to the accompaniment of the Battle for Britain and the first of the 'winter blitzes' of 1940–41.

Some indications of policy can be gathered from reports[1] by Mr Dalton to Mr Attlee (on 16th August) and to the Prime Minister (on 2nd September), but these papers are mainly concerned with organisation, and some time was required in which to frame a policy formally for submission to the Chiefs of Staff. In this formative stage the main contributions are:

(a) A paper submitted to D by A/D (Major Taylor) on 'The Functions of D Section', dated 23rd August.[2]

(b) A paper by Brigadier van Cutsem (Director of Intelligence in the 'Bureaux') on 'Subversive Action against Germany and Italy', dated 14th September.[3]

(c) Sir Frank Nelson's first Report on the existing organisation of D Section, dated 23rd September 1940.[4]

(d) Mr Jebb's paper on 'Subversion: A Description of the Special Operations Machine and some Suggestions as to Future Policy', dated 5th October.[5]

---

[1] On SOE Archives File 2/340/3.0 (destroyed).
[2] Original on SOE Archives File 1/470/1.
[3] Annex III to Mr Jebb's Print of October 1940, copy on SOE Archives File 1/470/1.
[4] Original on SOE Archives File (AD/S.1) HD/138.
[5] Print on SOE Archives File 1/470/1.

All these papers must be read in relation to the comprehensive COS paper[1] on Future Strategy dated 4th September, and approved by the War Cabinet on 30th September. This included as an Annex a paper on the possibilities of revolt in occupied Europe based primarily on material supplied by MIR,[2] and it devoted some paragraphs to the discussion of 'Subversive Activities'. The passage is difficult to summarise and is worth quoting in full to illustrate the higher attitude to subversion now that the first shock of French collapse was past.

Extract from COS(40)683 of 4th September, paras 195–9
195. The review of the state of readiness and ability of the enemy peoples and subject populations to rise in revolt, contained in paragraphs 51 to 57, has indicated that with the exception of Poland and Czechoslovakia none of these countries is likely, from its own resources, to initiate risings on an effective scale. Nevertheless, the stimulation of the subversive tendencies already latent in most countries is likely to prove a valuable contributory factor towards the defeat of Germany. By such means the enemy will be compelled to increase his armies of occupation and to make inroads into the resources required for offensive operations elsewhere. A general uprising, coinciding with major operations by our forces, may finally assist to bring about his defeat.
196. Subversive operations must be regarded as a strictly supplementary course of action, and must conform with regular operations undertaken as a part of our strategic plans.
197. The objectives of subversive operations will be as follows:
(a) Sabotage of key plants, commodities and communications, to supplement the effects of the blockade and air attack.
(b) The containing and extending of as many of the enemy's forces as possible, thus forcing him to expend his military resources.
(c) The preparation of the requisite conditions for a general rising of subject populations to synchronize with the final military pressure we exert on Germany and Italy or to coincide with land operations in any particular theatre.
198. Successful results will require careful planning and detailed organisation. If successful revolts are to be organised in German-occupied territories the following conditions must be fulfilled:

---

[1] COS(40)683 of 4th September, also WP(40)362 of 4th September, approved by the War Cabinet on 30th September. WM(40)262nd Mtg.

[2] JIC 198, 199, 200 of 25th July; copies on SOE Archives File 1/470/1. [The MIR paper is in David Stafford, *Britain and European Resistance 1940–1945* (1980), as appended Document 1.]

(a) Adequate preparations to provide the necessary material and physical assistance and support for the revolts. The provision of this support must be clear beyond all doubt.

(b) A carefully prepared scheme of propaganda.

(c) A clear policy as to the economic and political future of Europe.

199. It will be important to ensure that subversive movements should not be allowed to break out spontaneously in areas that individually become ripe for revolt. No appreciable results can be expected in the early future and we should organise these activities on a large scale so that they are timed to mature in relation to regular operations undertaken as a part of our general policy. In the interim we should endeavour to obtain the assistance of individuals and small factions to carry out sabotage and to co-operate with our harassing action on the enemy coasts.

There is a considerable difference of emphasis between this passage and the earlier references to subversion in the days of June[1], when it ranked with sea power and air power as an essential to the defeat of Germany – the only means by which the necessary manpower could be found in the final crisis.* There is now a much more cautious estimate of the difficulties and possibilities of revolt; and its importance has been reduced to that of 'a valuable contributory factor' which 'may finally assist to bring about the enemy's defeat'. The solution contemplated was now American participation in the war, and not a European rising: American opinion had moved a long way since June – the Destroyer/Bases deal was announced on 3rd September 1940, and the USA were now scraping the bottom of the barrel to find arms for Britain. It was therefore not as pessimistic as it might seem to include Para. 207 – 'We believe that the active belligerence of the United States has become essential for a successful prosecution and conclusion of the war. Without this it is difficult to see how or when we can pass from a grim defence to a resolute offence.'

In some ways the most important of the other papers is CD's review[2] of the resources he had inherited, which strongly reinforced this more modest view of the possibilities of subversion. The results of the paper can be tabulated very simply:

---

[1] Quoted above p. 60.

[2] See also a similar review by Major Taylor on 11th November 1940, on SOE Archives File 1/470/1.

* [See David Stafford, 'The Detonator Concept', in *Journal of Contemporary History*, x. 185 (April 1975).]

Country	Agents in the Country	Notes
USA	3	[PASSAGE DELETED ON GROUNDS OF NATIONAL SECURITY.]
S. America	Nil	
Eire	Nil	
Norway	Nil	(6 or 8 Norwegians training)
Sweden	Nil	(2 D agents in gaol)
Finland	Nil	(except a man trying to buy the s.s. 'Uleå', see above p. 17)
Holland	Nil	
Belgium	Nil	
France	Nil	(some chance of reviving contact with 5ème Bureau in Lisbon)
Switzerland	Nil	
Portugal	Nil	
Spain	Nil	
French Africa	Nil	
Italy	Nil	(except for Slovene Irredentists in Istria)
Poland	Nil	(this was MI(R)'s concern, as was Czechoslovakia)
Hungary	3	[PASSAGE DELETED ON GROUNDS OF NATIONAL SECURITY.]
Yugoslavia	9 British 3 Serbs	'Definitely the best of our organisations'
Roumania	7 British	
Bulgaria	Nil	(banned by HM Minister)*
Greece	7	
Turkey	6	HQ of Balkan Organisation
Middle East	Vague	Control vested in C-in-C ME
Russia and Far East	Nil	

---

* [(Sir) G. W. Rendel, 1889–1979, knight 1943, Minister in Sofia 1938–41, with Yugoslav Government in London 1941–3, at UNRRA 1944–7; see his *The Sword and the Olive* (1957).]

These figures speak for themselves.

Brigadier van Cutsem's contribution was a very sound technical analysis of what ought to be sabotaged, doubtless written in ignorance of the facts set out above; it was to take two years of hard work to bring its proposals within the range of practical politics. Major Taylor's paper on the other hand is directed to the immediate problem of organisation, and his specific proposals were rather important in the first phase of SO2's development. They include much detail which need not be covered here, but the following points of policy are significant:

(a) There should be a basic distinction between a 'Special Projects Force' and a 'Field Force'. The former would consist of a relatively small force of selected 'toughs' of all nationalities, who would be trained and held in readiness for 'butcher-and-bolt raids of a type more irregular than those of Combined Operations. They should be under a first-class British leader.' This force would be the only weapon available for the execution of sabotage until the Field Force had been patiently built up, and it was therefore essential at present; but even later it would have a valuable part to play.

(b) The Field Force on the other hand would consist essentially of local and permanent organisations in the occupied countries. 'It cannot be too strongly emphasised that under present conditions we are, for subversive work, almost entirely dependent upon the support of such local underground organisations . . . . Our object must therefore be to lay down as our Field Force a network of agents who will get in touch with all the organisations (mostly underground) which are prepared to work against the common enemy . . . . The ultimate object of the whole of this work must be to raise Europe against German domination at the moment when the hold of the German army upon the Continent can be seen to be weakening.'

(c) 'It is my view that these Field organisations in the Balkans area' (as yet unoccupied) 'will become less and less concerned with direct sabotage projects, and more and more concerned with the development of their contacts with anti-German organisations in the various countries . . . and the fostering and directing of their activities.'

These three points are all illustrated with some accuracy by what followed.

Mr Jebb's paper was for the most part a condensation of the earlier papers in a form suitable for outside circulation, but it is worth noting that it does not in any way disguise the nakedness of the land: 'For the moment, and probably for some time to come, we are simply not in a position to effect any major sabotage operation in Western

Europe[1] . . . or do anything at all in these areas beyond sending in an occasional man for the principal purpose of collecting our own type of intelligence.' Its main new contribution is on the political side. Here Mr Jebb's ultimate aim was a Europe which would, under the guidance of Britain and the USA, gradually grow more conscious of its own unity of history and of interest. But, in the short run 'what really counts at this time, when the spirit of Europe, its mind and intelligence, have been very nearly broken, is simply Power; Power and the ability to provide people with bread . . . . There is surely no objection to our employing any particular slogan at any time and in any place which may seem desirable. We may even find it necessary in certain countries, to encourage the Right and the Left simultaneously.' This line of action was never then or afterwards formally endorsed on a higher level, but it was followed in action with reasonable consistency, partly for the sake of immediate practical objectives, partly because it made it possible to evade problems which seemed insoluble. Whether it was the best policy, morally or practically, is a controversy not likely to be set at rest for a long time to come.

The issues involved on the Propaganda side were being handled separately through SO1, and discussions in which the Minister took part led through the Joint Planners to the Chiefs of Staff, and finally to the approval by the War Cabinet of a paper on Propaganda Policy put forward jointly by the Ministry of Information, the Ministry of Economic Warfare and the Chiefs of Staff.[2] There is little in this to affect SO2 directly, but the SO2 papers already mentioned led up to the preparation of a similar directive for violent subversion. The Joint Planners were at work on this early in November in consultation with Mr Broad and Brigadier van Cutsem, and while it was in preparation[3] Sir Frank Nelson attended a meeting of the Chiefs of Staff on 12th November[4] and gave a general review of the situation of his organisation. The Chiefs of Staff paper on 'Subversive Activities in Relation to Strategy', which arose out of this meeting, constituted SO2's formal directive for the first phase of its activity. The Chiefs of Staff express rather unwonted enthusiasm for subversion – 'We are very conscious of the important and even decisive part which subversive activities may play in our strategy . . . . We feel that if we are to exploit the use of subversive activities to the full, these activities must be planned on a very big and comprehensive scale. Our aim, in fact, should be

---

[1] Underlined in the original.

[2] The refs. are COS(40)858(JP) of 23rd October, COS(40)375th Mtg, Item 1, of 5th November, WP(40)444 of 15th November, and WM(40)292nd Mtg of 20th November.

[3] As JP(40)631(S).

[4] COS(40)386th, Item 2, of 12th November.

to get subversive activities laid on and ready for execution in all areas where there is any chance that they may be needed, so that, wherever the fortune of war may require action, the ground will be prepared in advance.' The detailed programme put forward corresponds to this introduction; the long list can be roughly summarised as follows:

Priority 1 Italian morale.

Railway traffic between Italy and Switzerland.[1]

Communications and supplies of enemy forces in France, Belgium and Holland.

Communications from Roumania to Germany and Italy.

Enemy communications in the Middle East, and oil.

Preparations to destroy communications in Yugoslavia and Bulgaria.
Ditto. in Spain and Portugal.

Preparations for co-operation with our own forces in the Atlantic Islands, Tangier, the Balearics, Spanish Morocco and S. Spain.

Enemy shipping in neutral ports.

Priority 2 Preparations for co-operation with our own forces in Tunisia, Sicily, Sardinia and S. Italy.

Priority 3 Similar preparation in S. Norway, Brittany, Cherbourg and the Bordeaux area.
Ditto. in Holland and Belgium.

It is difficult to decide whether SO2 were wrong to accept such a directive. It bore no relation to their existing resources, the poverty of which had been freely confessed, and it tended to lead to excessive claims later in an attempt to measure up to the task. But the strategic sequence of the programme was sound enough – as witnessed by later events – and no organisation could refuse to assume power and responsibility offered to it for a task in which it believed profoundly.

This first phase of policy formation may be suitably concluded by quotation from a letter[2] which the Prime Minister addressed to Mr Dalton on 20th January 1941, in reply to a report by the Minister. 'Pray press on with any useful scheme to cause trouble to the enemy in his own country or occupied territories. Should you meet opposition from any of your colleagues in regard to any special scheme

---

[1] A paper on this subject was put up to the COS (i.e. COS(40)9(0) of 28th September), and considered at COS(40)345th Mtg, Item 1, of 11th October. SOE Archives File (AD/S.1) SC/48.2 also refers.

[2] DO(41)3rd Mtg of 13th January. No record of this point in Minutes.

about which you hold strong views, I shall always be glad to give the matter my personal consideration if you will bring it to my notice .... Local action ... and the organisation in occupied territories of passive resistance to the enemy may embarrass enemy plans out of all proportion to the energy expended or the risk of loss incurred .... As a result of the Defence Meeting[1] on Monday last you are now empowered to proceed urgently with action to prevent Roumanian oil reaching Germany. If you wish for authority to pursue other major plans elsewhere I shall be glad to consider them.'

With such encouragement, SO2 had some excuse for a lively sense of its own importance and of the obstructive lethargy of older departments.

3. Inter-Departmental Relations

These debates on policy raised another problem, that of SOE's appropriate sphere of action, in relation to those of other departments, and of the mechanics of co-operation between departments.

As regards the Chiefs of Staff and the Service Departments, the matter was handled, at least in London, as one of mutual assistance rather than of rivalry. The principles of a solution were fairly simple and were established early: there was a good deal of controversy about the details of their operation, but the system itself was never seriously disturbed.

These main principles were –

(a) 'Advisers', or liaison officers, should be appointed by the Service Departments to live and work within SOE.

(b) These representatives should be full members of the 'Inner Council' of SOE, should have free access to all the facts, and should be entitled to state their views at an early stage in the formulation of plans.

(c) The converse of these arrangements was that CD himself, or officers on his behalf, should have direct access to the Joint Planning Committee or to the Joint Intelligence Committee on any matters that concerned the department, and should be fully aware of the general strategic 'picture' and of any particular operations under consideration. If necessary, CD should be invited by the Chiefs of Staff to be present when matters affecting SOE were discussed. SOE sometimes went so far as to demand equal participation in all the work of the Chiefs of Staff and their Sub-Committees; but this was never within the sphere of practical politics, and the looser system proved perfectly adequate so long as personal relations were good.

---

[1] DO(41)3rd Mtg of 13th January. No record of this point in Minutes.

There was however one special case which might have raised 'boundary disputes' with the Services, that of Director of Combined Operations, Admiral of the Fleet Sir Roger Keyes,* with whom Mr Dalton opened discussions on 20th July 1940.[1] The territory of Director of Combined Operations was ill-defined and potentially unlimited, and there might have been difficulties if the Director had been another man. But subversive warfare was the last thing to which Sir Roger was likely to turn his hand, and in any case his mind was running on projects quite beyond the scale of SOE's ideas.[2] A rather vague but amicable 'agreement' was concluded in December 1940.[3] The clearest point which emerges is that DCO's raids will normally be made by parties of fifty or more British troops, to be withdrawn after the operation, whereas SO2's operations will be primarily carried out by not more than thirty men, usually foreigners and capable of 'fading into the landscape': apart from this, the 'agreement' deals only with informal co-operation on training, intelligence, equipment and so forth. At this stage Commander Fletcher, MP, sat as the Director of Combined Operations' representative on the 'SO Board': but the Board disappeared in February 1941, and for the time being no formal liaison was left.[4]

The Foreign Office was to raise very serious difficulties later, but at first it showed little uneasiness about the position. It had itself concurred readily in the creation of SOE; Mr Dalton, himself a former Under-Secretary of State for Foreign Affairs, was advised by a former Permanent Under-Secretary, Sir Robert Vansittart, who still worked within the Foreign Office: his principal aides, both in SO1 and SO2, were active members of the Foreign Service. This seemed to give the essentials of control, and there was no attempt at first to create more formal machinery.

The SIS had equally been acquiescent in the creation of SOE; but CSS's agreement had been given only under the mistaken impression that he would retain full administrative control of D Section,[5] and he

---

[1] Letters of 20th, 22nd and 23rd July 1940, on SOE Archives File 2/340/3.0 (destroyed).

[2] Para. 5 of Mr Dalton's paper of 19th August 1940.

[3] PA/XX/95 of 14th December: copy on SOE Archives File (AD/S.1) SC/75. See also record of meeting between Colonel Davies and Captain Knox, RN, on 16th December (same file).

[4] See further below p. 361.

[5] See memorandum written by Commander Arnold-Forster after D Board meeting of 30th August 1940, and CSS's letter of 4th September 1940, both on SOE Archives File 1/460/1.

* [R. J. B Keyes, 1872–1945, naval hero, fought in Dardanelles 1915, knight 1918 on raiding Zeebrugge, Admiral of the Fleet, Conservative MP 1934–43, baron 1943; in *DNB*.]

saw serious difficulties when it became clear that the divorce was to be complete. Sir Frank Nelson was however familiar with the SIS side of this issue, and a first agreement[1] was reached without much trouble on 15th September 1940. It presupposes that 'D is intimately associated with C both on historical and on practical grounds, and if he is to function efficiently, it must be with the friendly co-operation of C': and it provides rules to cover Projects, Transport, Communications, Spheres of Interest and Recruitment of Agents. On the first two, the rules only provide for reference to 'higher authority' in the event of disputed priorities – and in fact there was no common higher authority below the Chiefs of Staff and the Defence Committee of the War Cabinet. On the other three points D (i.e. SO2) is strictly limited: W/T traffic will be handled through C, who will have liberty to reject it: any intelligence collected by D must be passed to C before circulation even within D: D may take the initiative in recruiting agents, but may not proceed further without C's consent. These limitations were very reasonable from the point of view of CSS, as the advocate of a single centralised Secret Service, in the interests of good administration, good security, and good intelligence; but experience very soon showed that they were incompatible with the licence to grow which had already been given to SOE by the War Cabinet. The dispute came to a head early in 1942, and was then in part adjusted: but incompatibility of temperament remained to the end.

SO2 began early to fight for freedom from control by SIS; conversely it was the proponent of centralisation as against SO1, which soon became anxious to have its own representatives in countries overseas, and to put agents in the field itself in order to spread propaganda and to report on its effects. The original understanding was that all 'operations' beyond the shores of England were a matter for SO2.[2] SO1, in its later guise as PWE, fought hard on this issue and secured the right to establish its own missions in friendly territory overseas,[3] but it was never allowed to establish a third Secret Service (a fourth if we include MI9),* although many agents trained jointly by SOE and the Political Warfare Executive were sent into the field under SOE's auspices to perform tasks designated by the PWE.

This frontier dispute was interlocked with that between SO1 and the

---

[1] Printed as Annex II to Mr Jebb's Subversion Paper of 5th October 1940, on SOE Archives File 1/470/1; see also File 1/470/14.

[2] Minute from CEO to Mr Leeper, ref. 0/26 of 21st December 1940; copy on SOE Archives File 1/270/3.

[3] Below p. 378 ff.

* [In fact there were nine British wartime secret services: the Auxiliary Units, the security, intelligence and decipher services, the Radio Security Service, the escape service, SOE, PWE, and the deception service.]

Ministry of Information; an organisation much buffeted in the first year of the war, which was now (under Mr Duff Cooper) fighting hard to gain some efficacy and prestige. The controversy concerned control of subversive propaganda, not of operations, and it is therefore not directly relevant to the narrower field to which SOE was eventually reduced. But some account of it is essential to explain the early collapse of the original conception of a union of propaganda and subversive operations as a single weapon of war, and it will be convenient to introduce this here although it leads us some distance forward into 1941.

The first step was taken in a memorandum[1] circulated by Mr Duff Cooper on 18th July 1940 to the Prime Minister, the Lord President, the Foreign Secretary and Mr Dalton. In this paper the Minister attacks the old organisation both on administrative grounds, and because it rested on an illogical distinction between propaganda to enemy and occupied countries (Electra House) and propaganda to unoccupied countries (Ministry of Information). As a remedy he proposed –

(a) to make a distinction between European and non-European, and not between occupied and unoccupied; the whole propaganda side of Electra House should be 'fused with the Foreign Policy Department' of the Ministry of Information, which would be headed by a senior diplomat.

(b) that all open propaganda 'that is to say, propaganda by leaflet and by broadcasting should remain' (sic) 'under the Ministry of Information'.

What this amounts to is that the Ministry of Information is to be given sole charge (under the Foreign Office) of all propaganda policy and that the new SOE will be its agent in the limited role of distributor through 'black' channels. The idea of a 'Ministry of Subversion' would go by the board; the decision taken in WP (40)271 is challenged even before it has been formally placed on record. The ruling given in that paper, that SOE should 'co-ordinate all action, by way of subversion or sabotage, against the enemy overseas' is at first sight flat and unqualified: but 'subversion' is not defined, and a loophole can be found in a later paragraph of the paper where the reference is to 'secret subversive propaganda', a hint perhaps that 'non-secret subversive propaganda' would be outside Mr Dalton's control.

The first stage of the argument was decided by a meeting between Mr Dalton and Mr Duff Cooper on 1st August, and by an agreement which arose from it.[2] Mr Dalton's initial position was in essence the

---

[1] On SOE Archives File (AD/S.1) 'CD/I.10/2a'.

[2] See Mr Dalton's Aide-Mémoire of 1st August, his letter of 2nd August with Memorandum of Agreement, the revised version in Mr Duff Cooper's letter of 3rd August; Mr Dalton's letter of 3rd August and Mr Duff Cooper's of 6th and 15th August: all in SOE Archives File (AD/S.1) CD/I.10/2a.

converse of Mr Duff Cooper's, though perhaps a shade less posses-
sive. SOE would assume sole responsibility for all propaganda to
enemy and enemy-occupied territories, including the whole of France,
and her possessions in Africa; but the Ministry of Information would
deal with the rest of the world. The solution reached in August 1940
was an unhappy compromise, doubtless accepted (as Mr Dalton said
later) because the immediate problems of SOE were a sufficient burden
for any man. The vital point is in para. 1 of the Agreement: 'From a
practical point of view the best dividing line would be between those
activities which might be discussed in Parliament and those which
might not. Mr Duff Cooper would control the former, Mr Dalton the
latter. Thus public broadcasts which anyone might listen to must fall
on one side of the line, while leaflets and the Country House, regarding both of which it has been laid down that Parliament would be
refused information, must fall on the other.' As a corollary (para. 3):
'Mr Duff Cooper would be free to establish in his Ministry Sections
or Departments dealing with all foreign countries and Mr Dalton likewise would be free to undertake with the knowledge and approval of
Mr Duff Cooper appropriate activities, not only in enemy and enemy-
occupied countries but in neutral territories.'

It would surely be hard to invent, 'from a practical point of view',
any less workable arrangement than this division of propaganda policy
between two parallel organisations, one 'overt' and the other 'covert',
both covering the entire field. It was certain that there would be further
controversy very soon.

The first re-statement of SOE's claim is to be found in Memoranda
of 11th and 18th October,[1] on the second of which the Minister has
minuted 'hold in suspense, till D gets under way'. Soundings 'on the
official level' were quite ineffectual, and the issue was forced to the
notice of Ministers by a Cabinet decision of 18th November to set up
a Committee under the Chancellor of the Exchequer (Sir Kingsley
Wood)* to examine 'what changes, if any, were necessary in the constitution and management of the BBC, in order to insure its effective
control by HMG.'[2] This was important because in practice open BBC
broadcasts were the only means of propaganda to the enemy and to
occupied territory at the Ministry of Information's disposal; and the
controversy therefore turned fundamentally on control of the policy

---

[1] One by Mr Gaitskell, the other unsigned (? by Mr Leeper), both on SOE Archives
File (AD/S.1) CD/I.10/2a. [H. T. N. Gaitskell, 1906–63, then Dalton's assistant,
Labour MP from 1945, Exchequer 1950–51, Party leader from 1955.]

[2] WM(40)290 Item 4 of 18th November.

* Kingsley Wood, 1881–1943, solicitor, knight 1918, Conservative MP since 1918,
Air Minister 1938–40, Exchequer since May 1940; in *DNB*.]

of these broadcasts, although it strayed into many side-issues. The immediate result of the battle of memoranda which followed was the appointment (by the Prime Minister) of Sir John Anderson (then Lord President of the Council)* to arbitrate on the frontier dispute[1] since the Cabinet Committee concerned held that this vital point was outside its terms of reference.

The opposing points of view may be indicated briefly. Mr Dalton was strong[2] – indeed impregnable – in theory: 'all subversive activity should be under unified control', he had been entrusted with such control, and 'subversion . . . clearly should include all propaganda having a subversive object'. But practical considerations made it hard for him to suggest that all propaganda should be transferred from the Ministry of Information to SOE, and short of this it was not easy to find a logical halting-place. One of the gravest problems in constitutional theory is to distinguish between subversion (which must be judged criminal) and fair political persuasion, which is the essence of free government; and even arbitration by Sir John Anderson was not likely to produce a definition which would end that controversy. Mr Dalton's practical proposal was that he should be responsible for all enemy and enemy-occupied territory, to which he added any other country in which HMG desired to create subversion – the Foreign Secretary to pronounce in each case whether HMG's policy was or was not 'subversive'.

Mr Duff Cooper also opened his argument with a large generalisation: 'all propaganda should, if possible, be directed by one Department in order that control may be centralised and a consistent policy pursued'[3] – a proposition which Mr Dalton could neither refute nor follow to its logical conclusion. From this premise it was easy for him to make hay of distinctions between 'subversive' and 'non-subversive' propaganda, or between occupied and unoccupied territory. But his paper ends with a more practical and more conclusive argument – 'All foreign propaganda should be controlled by one Department, that Department may be the Ministry of Information, or the Ministry of Economic Warfare, but if it be transferred to the latter, the activities of the Ministry of Information would be so reduced as hardly to justify its continuance as a separate Department of State.'

---

[1] Mr Dalton's note of 18th December, on SOE Archives File (AD/S.1) CD/I.10/2a.

[2] Paper of 15th December, on SOE Archives File (AD/S.1) CD/I.10/2a.

[3] Paper of 13th December, on SOE Archives File (AD/S.1) CD/I.10/2a.

* [J. Anderson, 1882–1958, administrator, knight 1919, PUS Home Office 1922–32, Governor of Bengal 1932–8, independent MP 1938–50, ran home front for coalition 1940–45, Exchequer 1943–5, adviser on atomic energy 1945–8, Viscount Waverley 1952; in *DNB*; and see his life by J. W. Wheeler-Bennett (1962).]

It is clear from Sir John Anderson's letter[1] of 23rd December that his terms of reference were based on this premise – 'I should find it difficult to reconcile with the continued existence of a Ministry of Information the removal of "open" broadcasts of any character from the sphere of their responsibility'; the result of his enquiry was therefore prejudged within narrow limits, and it served little purpose except to keep the *status quo* in being for a time. There were some sporadic and ineffective discussions between officials, but no progress was made until in March 1941 disputes arose within the Foreign (Allied) Resistance Committee[2] regarding the control of policy for propaganda to France. There were renewed Cabinet discussions, and the Lord President was again called upon to arbitrate.[3] He met Mr Duff Cooper and Mr Dalton on 16th May, and embodied his conclusions in a memorandum[4] dated 19th May; but Mr Duff Cooper then fell sick and it was some time before his comments were available. The interval was enlivened by discussion of a minor 'gaffe' by the Prime Minister on 15th May, when he admitted in reply to a Supplementary Question[5] in the House of Commons that there were some propaganda questions on which the Ministry of Economic Warfare might answer in the House – in spite of the clear Cabinet ruling that SOE should not be the subject of Parliamentary discussion.

The 'Anderson Award', which was finally submitted to the Prime Minister on 4th June,[6] was in the end merely an endorsement of the old distinction between 'overt' and 'covert' propaganda; the only change was that the Foreign Office secured a rather distant responsibility for the formulation of propaganda policy. The Lord President did indeed suggest that there should be various co-ordinating committees, ranging from a Standing Ministerial Committee to working committees for countries and groups of countries; but no-one believed much in the value of 'co-ordination', and there was no visible effect except the appointment of Mr Bruce Lockhart as the Foreign Office's 'Co-ordinator of Propaganda'. The Award was overtaken almost at once by another 'Ministry of Information crisis', brought on by the imminence of a debate in the Commons.[7] Lord

---

[1] On SOE Archives File (AD/S.1) CD/I.10/2a.

[2] The 'Morton Committee'.

[3] See Garnett's PWE History, Vol. II, p. 67.

[4] SOE Archives File (AD/S.1) CD/I.10/2a.

[5] Hansard, 15th May 1941.

[6] Minute by Sir John Anderson on SOE File (AD/S.1) CD/I.10/2a.

[7] Mr Duff Cooper minuted the Prime Minister on 6th June about all the troubles of his Dept, copy on SOE Archives File (AD/S.1) CD/I.10/2a.

Beaverbrook* this time made a personal investigation on behalf of the Prime Minister, which gave rise to much Cabinet discussion:[1] but he decided at once that the Anderson Award should stand,[2] and the rest of the controversy did not involve SOE.

But the respite was very brief, two meetings of Mr Bruce Lockhart's Standing Committee are recorded,[3] and then the whole issue was reopened by Mr Brendan Bracken;** Mr Bracken had been appointed to the Ministry of Information (on 20th July) in consequence of the Commons debate of 3rd July[4] in which no-one had a good word to say for our propaganda services. He opened the campaign by circulating on 31st July the draft of a Cabinet Paper proposing the creation of a Department of Political Warfare, 'to be regarded as a secret body, furnished with officers and a secretariat independent of any Ministry', with 'the right to create and lay down policy for every Government organ concerned with political warfare' – i.e. for the BBC European Services and for SO1 as well as for some parts of the Ministry of Information. This new Department should be supervised by the existing Ministerial Committee (the Foreign Secretary, Ministry of Information and Ministry of Economic Warfare), and should be directed by an Executive Committee under the Chairmanship of Mr Bruce Lockhart (BBC) and consisting of Brigadier Brooks (M of I), Mr Kirkpatrick† (BBC), Mr Leeper (SO1) and Major Desmond Morton. This is curiously reminiscent of the old Inter-Services Projects Board – a committee with licence to become a Department by recruiting its own staff – but at least it gave some hope of progress, in that the Ministry of Information made it clear that it was at last prepared to surrender part of its responsibilities to an autonomous department provided that other Ministries did likewise. Matters were driven forward with great rapidity by Mr Bracken, seconded by Mr Bruce Lockhart's Committee and by judicious

---

1 WP(41)137 of 21st June, WP(41)139 of 24th June, WP(41)142 of 26th June, WP(41)147 of 28th June, WM(41)64th Mtg, Item 7, of 30th June, and WP(41)149 of 2nd July refer.
2 Minutes from Lord Beaverbrook to Prime Minister d/d 11th June, on SOE Archives File CD/I.10/2a.
3 See letter from Mr Eden to Mr Dalton d/d 4th July 1941, and Minutes of Meetings on 20th July and 1st August: all on SOE Archives File (AD/S.1) CD/P.5/23.
4 Hansard, 3rd July 1941, Cols 1529 ff.
* [W.M. Aitken, 1879–1964, Canadian newspaper magnate, knight 1911, MP 1910–17, Lord Beaverbrook 1917, Minister of Aircraft Production 1940–41, in War Cabinet 1940–42; in *DNB*. See his life by A.J.P. Taylor (1972).]
** [B.R. Bracken, 1901–58, Conservative MP 1929-51, Churchill's private secretary 1940–41, Minister of Information 1941–5, Viscount 1952; in *DNB*.]
† [(Sir) I.A. Kirkpatrick, 1897–1964, diplomat, European adviser to BBC 1941–4, knight 1948, PUS Foreign Office 1953–6; in *DNB*. See his *The Inner Circle* (1959).]

pressure in the Commons.[1] On 8th August the Foreign Secretary, the Minister of Information and the Minister of Economic Warfare met and reached cautious agreement on principles;[2] an Official Committee was set up under Mr Bruce Lockhart to consider ways and means; by 19th August[3] this Committee had produced a specific plan for amalgamation. The Ministerial Committee met and blessed this on 21st August, in face of some protest from Mr Dalton,[4] and the official Committee – now the Executive Committee – was authorised to begin work at once. A Minute dated 27th August and initialled by Mr Bracken and Mr Dalton authorised it to prepare arrangements 'for the complete fusion of the personnel of the Ministry of Information, the BBC and SO1 now engaged in propaganda in war zones'.[5]

The Committee's proposals were ready on 1st September, and were endorsed at once,[6] subject only to the proviso by Mr Dalton that 'all activities of the Political Warfare Executive outside Great Britain will be conducted through the medium of the Special Operations Executive'.[7]

SO1 was therefore at an end, and we are concerned now only with SO2, which inherited the title 'SOE'. It was a sad breach of principle that the great idea of Subversion should have fallen to pieces, leaving two independent departments united only by that most tenuous of bonds, a Ministerial Committee. But the separation was a relief from sore frustration, and it is worth repeating the 'unanimous opinion' of the Executive Committee 'based on intimate knowledge of all the facts,

(1) that for twelve months the energy of our whole propaganda

---

[1] cf. Commander King-Hall's demand for a Political Warfare Department: Hansard, 5th August (a question which received a negative reply) and 6th August, Col. 1991 (in a general war debate). Doubtless the question was also ventilated in the Press, but I have not pursued this.

[2] Letter from Eden to Dalton d/d 8th August on SOE Archives File (AD/S.1) CD/P.5/23 and attached memorandum. This latter document, which was initialled by the Prime Minister on 19th August on his return from 'Arcadia', was regarded by PWE as its foundation charter.

[3] On SOE Archives File (AD/S.1) CD/P.5/23.

[4] Letter, Dalton to Eden d/d 20th August, on SOE Archives File (AD/S.1) CD/P.5/23.

[5] On same file as Ref. 3.

[6] The formation of the Political Warfare Executive (PWE) was announced by the Prime Minister on 11th September in answer to a question by Commander King-Hall.

[7] Mr Jebb's Minute of 5th September on SOE Archives File (AD/S.1) CD/P.5/23. This Minute also makes the point that the old SOE no longer exists, and that the title should now pass to SO2.

effort which should have been directed against the enemy has been largely dissipated in inter-departmental intrigues and strife:
(2) that in view of the fact that today propaganda is assuming new and vital importance which has been recognised by the Defence Committee it is imperative this deplorable state of affairs should be ended immediately.'

CHAPTER VI

Operations in Yugoslavia

In the preceding chapter we have sketched briefly the very loose initial organisation of SO2, the development by which it became SOE, and the tasks imposed on it at the outset. In order to follow these central issues further, we must turn next to operations in the field. The general principles enunciated in London were not exactly false, but they were lifeless until they had been tested on flesh and blood: the real organisation grew from below and not from above.

There was no country with which SOE dealt that did not contribute something individual to the character of the organisation as a whole: but time and space are limited, and it is proposed to deal in some detail here only with France, Norway, Greece and Yugoslavia, countries which present a wide variety of conditions and of ultimate political consequences. Other countries must perforce be dealt with briefly and in relation to these four.

It will be convenient to begin with Eastern Europe, as SOE was at work there before the German invasion came: it had some contribution to make from the first, so that it was involved in major issues in the Balkans while in Western Europe it was still struggling to establish single agents.

As we have seen, D Section's Balkan organisation had been seriously affected by German political pressure in the summer of 1940, but an organisation of a kind still existed when SOE took over. There were two headquarters, one in Istanbul for the Balkan countries except Greece (under Major S. W. Bailey), the other in Cairo, for Greece and the area of Middle East Command (under Lieutenant Colonel Pollock). In Cairo there were also G(R) (the MI(R) branch of GHQ) under Lieutenant Colonel Adrian Simpson; an offshoot of Electra House, under Lieutenant Colonel Thornhill, which became SO1; and an Arab section of GHQ known as GS1(K), under Colonel Clayton.* This organisation was useless as an HQ, as the division of functions between

---

* [A. F. H. S. Simpson, 1880–1960, in Russia 1914–15, telegraph manager 1922–7, Press Attaché Beirut 1944–6. C. J. M. Thornhill, 1883–1952, Military Attaché Petrograd 1916–8, fought in north Russia 1918–19. I. N. Clayton, 1886–1955, Arabist, knight 1949.]

the various organisations was unintelligible even to those directly concerned, and their control over their local representatives was very tenuous. What effective action there was came only from the local organisations; it will be best therefore *first* to follow their work up to the summer of 1942 which marks a break of fundamental importance. A general Allied offensive was then contemplated seriously for the first time; *then* to explain the tangled history of the Cairo HQ over the same period.

1. The Origins of the Coup d'État

When SOE was set up, the existing organisation in Yugoslavia had been seriously reduced by the expulsions described earlier;[1] D Section had now no senior representative in the country, and its Belgrade office was being run by the Assistant Naval Attaché, Lieutenant Commander Glen, RNVR (a young explorer of note),* and by Mr J. S. Bennett,** supervised by the Naval Attaché and the Passport Control Officer. Lawrenceson's connections in Slovenia were maintained, and Major D. R. Oakley Hill, formerly of the Albanian gendarmerie, was sent out in December 1940 with a view to work into Albania. There was heavy pressure on HM Minister from the Yugoslav authorities (including the Prince Regent himself)† to close down subversive activities entirely, for fear that they might provoke a German invasion; and during August and September 1940 there were a series of telegrams from Mr Campbell in which he pointed out to the Foreign Office the dangers involved.[2] It was common ground in London that it was not in British interests that Germany should be needlessly provoked in the Balkans; the SOE counter-argument was generally to the effect that the Germans were very unlikely to be 'provoked' until they decided that the time was ripe – and then they would need no provocation. This defence was effective in preventing a complete 'shut-down', and SO2 activities continued in Yugoslavia, though on a much reduced scale. There was no further conspicuous activity on the Danube; sabotage continued, but was generally of a minor and less traceable kind. A subsidy to the Serbian Peasant Party

---

[1]   Above p. 29.

[2]   A number of these are on SOE Archives File (AD/S.1) HD/34, but the series is
     not complete.

*   [(Sir) A. R. ('Sandy') Glen, born 1912, explorer and travel expert, knight 1967.]

**   [1911–70, directed British information services Istanbul 1943–5, Consul at
     Houston 1952–4, at Khorramshahr 1955–60, High Commissioner in Barbados
     from 1966.]

†   [Prince Paul, Regent for his nephew Peter II (1923–70) after Peter's father
     Alexander was assassinated in Marseilles in 1934.]

was however formally sanctioned in September, and payments of £4,000 a month were started through the agency of a bogus company floated for the purpose with Mr Chester Beatty's assistance.[1] The notion of a coup d'état had been in the air since July 1940,[2] but this was obviously out of the question then: the subsidy was intended to keep things sweet, not to promote immediate action. Gavrilovič, the leader of the party, was now in Moscow, and the main contact was with his deputy Tupanjanin. Contacts were also established with other nationally minded bodies, such as the Narodna Odbrana and Ilija Trifunovic's 'veterans' organisation'.

This pause was ended by Mussolini's Greek adventure, launched on 28th October 1940. When the Italian advance was checked, German intervention became increasingly probable. At the same time the risk that it would be precipitated by ill-timed action grew less, and it became more urgent to do everything possible to impede it, especially when the decision had been taken to put British forces into Greece.[3] SOE had now found a now senior representative for Yugoslavia, Mr T. S. Masterson,* a businessman with oil interests in Roumania and an intimate knowledge of the Balkans, who reached Belgrade early in December.[4] The Wavell offensive was launched that month in North Africa, German intervention became more certain as the Italian position deteriorated, and by the end of December it was pretty clear that the Balkans must be treated as a theatre of war, without further respect for diplomatic *convenances*. SO2's part was to do what could be done now to make trouble for the Germans, and to arrange for some organisation to remain in being after the occupation, which was militarily inevitable – indeed German penetration had already gone very far in Hungary, Roumania and Bulgaria.

The new policy is very plainly set out in a telegram sent to Colonel Bailey by Colonel Taylor about the middle of January 1941:[5]

2. We must be in position provoke widest possible upheaval Roumania at some suitable date prior to first April and probably about 15th March with primary object of causing damage

---

[1] SOE Archives File (AD/S.1) HD/F.34.4.
[2] Mr Campbell's telegram No. 482 of 25th July on SOE Archives File HD/34.
[3] First landing 12.4.41.
[4] SOE Archives File (AD/S.1) HD/F/34.
[5] Copy on SOE Archives File (AD/S.1) HD/SC.44/12. No date or reference, but probably CXG.700-7 of 10th January. cf. Mr Jebb's Minute of 14th January to Mr Dalton, which is on similar lines.
* [T. S. Masterson, 1881–1944, Balkan expert; see references in B. Sweet-Escott, *Baker Street Irregular* (1965).]

to oilfields, refineries and all oil communications. Secondary object of causing prolonged transport hold-up which would hinder supplies from Roumania reaching Germany and impede possible German advance through Roumania. Whole of above plan may be altered by Germans taking initiative with early invasion Balkans in which case we must simply do everything we can to cause them trouble.

3. In Yugoslavia we must concentrate firstly on inducing Yugoslav General Staff to complete Kazan scheme[1] with the idea that we should be able by bribery or other means to have charges fixed at appropriate moment regardless of attitude of Yugoslav Government. Secondly on preparations for destruction of communications in front of German advance and maintenance of guerilla warfare behind them.

4. In Bulgaria concentrate on same objectives as secondly in Yugoslavia . . . .

6. You must understand our function Balkans under new policy more military than political and therefore upheaval Roumania and destruction of communications in front of German advance should have priority . . . . General political conversations on lines hitherto approved by us should only be continued in so far as they are necessary for carrying out of specific schemes indicated above . . . .

8. Whilst you must issue necessary detailed instructions to all stations under your control for carrying out of above policy, you should reveal the contents of this telegram to nobody repeat nobody and destroy all copies as soon as memorized.

One of the weaknesses of a subversive organisation in such a crisis is that reinforcements cannot be rushed to the threatened point; the work must be done with the organisation already there, since a new one cannot be built quickly. The D organisation had never been really strong, and it had been weakened by German action and by the period of extreme caution between June and December. So that the full task was quite beyond its powers: a little was done, and it is remarkable how much it was.

HQ in London could assist only by seeing that money was available, and by sending out a senior officer with adequate status and powers to pull the Missions together and to focus their small resources on the key points of policy as they were seen in London. Major Taylor was chosen for this purpose, and went out with the local rank of full Colonel and Counsellor in the Foreign Office; his visit was announced to His

---

[1] See above p. 25.

Majesty's Representatives in the various capitals on 11th January,[1] but he does not seem to have reached Cairo till the end of that month. He spent a few days in Cairo, Ankara and Istanbul, went on to Belgrade via Sofia, then back to Greece, where he spent some time in consultation with the British Military HQ there. He was back in Yugoslavia in time for the coup d'état, which took place on 27th March.[2]

By that time SO2 had shot its bolt both in Bulgaria and in Roumania. In the former country[3] there was a chance of some ruthless and disinterested support, drawn from George Dimitrov's* wing of the Peasant Party, from the Protogerovist Macedonians, and from the Military League. But it was not till August 1940 that HM Minister approved nogotiations, and matters developed slowly even then. The necessary subsidies (which were small) were available, and a certain amount of propaganda was printed and distributed; but there were great difficulties in importing demolition stores and in training agents in their use. When Colonel Bailey received his new directive early in January 1941, only Dimitrov's party was prepared to contemplate violent action, the organisation had not progressed far when it was broken by precautionary arrests in the third week of February. The only result reported was one train wreck – carried out by one man with one crowbar – which destroyed forty trucks of oil.[4]

Dimitrov himself was smuggled out to Turkey [PASSAGE DELETED ON GROUNDS OF NATIONAL SECURITY], then he travelled to Belgrade, where the Yugoslavs were helpful.[5]

The Regent's 'appeasing' government fell on 17th March and a small 'irregular expedition' was then organised to infiltrate across the Bulgarian frontier. But its departure coincided with the German attack on 6th April and no more was heard of it. Further arrests had taken place in Bulgaria after the German occupation, and most of the remaining British stores and contacts were rounded up. SO2 therefore had practically nothing in hand except Dimitrov and a few other Bulgarians in exile. But the old political organisations still existed, and there was always a slender chance that contact might be resumed.

---

[1] Foreign Office Tel. No. 80 to Ankara of 11th January: repeated to other Missions.

[2] Major Taylor's reports d/d 10th February (Istanbul), 26th February (Athens), 11th March (Athens) are on SOE Archives File (AD/S.1) HD/SC/44.12. Copies of a general report d/d 24th June by Taylor and Masterson are on File HD/34.

[3] See 'Bulgarian History' by Mr Norman Davis – SOE Archives.

[4] SOE London War Diary, February 1941, p. 209.

[5] See CXG.861 of 12th March from Belgrade; copy on SOE Archives File (AD/S.1) HD/34. [Details of escape in Rendel, *Sword and Olive*, p. 174, and in Elliott, *I Spy*, pp. 52-4.]

* [This was not the same Dimitroff as the secretary of the Comintern (see p. 28).]

In Roumania[1] Axis counter-action began earlier and was more effective. W.R. Young and some twenty other oil engineers had been expelled early in July 1940; the Antonescu dictatorship was inaugurated on 6th September, and there followed attacks by Iron Guard thugs on Treacy and other members of the organisation, who were rescued and evacuated with some difficulty by a judicious combination of bribery and diplomatic pressure. The Antonescu régime involved the acceptance of the Vienna Diktat of 27th August 1940, in which Roumania lost a large part of Transylvania, and it was therefore not based on much popular support; but the Germans were present in force in the lost area of Transylvania and had infiltrated military 'instructors' in large numbers into what was left of Roumania, so that there was little in the situation to encourage Roumanians in the idea of active resistance. Nevertheless, SO2 was able to make contact with M. Maniu,* the veteran leader of the National Peasant Party, himself a Transylvanian, who was one of the few Roumanian politicians with a reputation for personal honesty; Maniu declared himself ready to work with the British, to accept subsidies as a 'loan', and to make preparations for sabotage.

In that field there was one purely British project, that for the blowing up of the Yalomitsa bridge, on the railway from Ploesti to Guirgiu, which might have exercised a certain effect on oil traffic; this might have been possible for a party from outside, without Roumanian aid. From October to December arguments pro and con were bandied between Bucharest, Istanbul and London; HM Minister in Bucharest** believed that action would mean the immediate expulsion of the Legation, and was therefore on the whole not worthwhile. The argument continued until the Danube froze up for the winter, and it was then clear that nothing need be decided for months.[2]

Maniu's own plans for sabotage in the oilfields were carefully made conditional on the bombing of the Ploesti region by the RAF; serious bombing would have provided perfect cover for sabotage, even a token raid would have given some moral support. At this time there was a clamour in many quarters for an air attack on the oilfields, and

---

[1] See narrative by Lieutenant Colonel de Chastelaine – SOE Archives.
[2] Very full papers on SOE Archives File (AD/S.1) HD/SC/44/1. [A few details in M. Minshall, *Guilt-Edged* (1975).]
*   [I. Maniu, died in prison 1947.]
** [Sir R.H. Hoare, 1882–1954, Minister in Teheran 1931–5, Bucharest 1935–41, banker; in *DNB*.]

the discussion went much beyond the sphere of SOE.[1] There were strong arguments against action. It was technically a very difficult air operation from any of the bases available, and RAF resources were already committed up to the hilt in other spheres of at least equal importance. In addition, Greek airfields would be necessary and their use raised serious questions of the Greek attitude in face of German pressure: the neutrality of either Turkish, or Bulgarian, or Yugoslav air would have to be violated en route; and Roumania itself was still technically neutral, though virtually under German occupation. In the end, the decision was that action should be taken, but it would be proved quite impossible to do anything. There was indeed an American attempt from the Middle East in 1942, but this was a lamentable failure, and serious raids began only in 1944, when circumstances were very different. It is not at all clear that Maniu would have lent much support in 1941 even if bombing had taken place; it was certain that without it he would do nothing.

The British Legation, including the last SO2 representatives, was withdrawn[2] on 10th February (a month earlier than had originally been planned). A wireless set was left under the charge of Maniu, and contact was made with this on 8th April. It proved useful as a source of information, but SO2 failed to persuade Maniu to leave the country and head a Roumanian movement in exile; more than once he accepted and then thought better of it at the last moment. This first period was ended by a series of arrests in August 1941; Maniu remained at liberty but the wireless set was lost, and contacts had to be laboriously renewed by other means.

Action proceeded much more briskly in Yugoslavia. The significance of the coup d'état of 27th March 1941 has been overlaid by later events, and it has been half forgotten that it was an action which demanded skill and courage from the Yugoslav plotters as well as desperate patriotism, and that at the time it gave immense encouragement to Britain and her one fighting ally, Greece. The scheme was executed primarily by Serbian nationalists, in some ways narrow and short-sighted, and their main support came from the younger men in the officer corps; the impending attack on Russia was perhaps already suspected, but the Communist Party was still pinned to its earlier line and took no part in events. Yet if it had not been for 27th March there would have been no national resistance on which Tito might build,

---

[1] The following refer among others: WM(40)297th Mtg, Min. 1 Confidential Annex: WP(40)1 of 4th January: COS(41)3(0) of 8th January: DO(41)3rd Mtg of 4th and 13th January: COS(41)40(0) and COS(41)62nd Mtg, Item 7, of 20th February: COS(41)67th Mtg, Item 6, of 24th February and CIGS's telegram from Greece attached. SOE Archives File (AD/S.1) HD/44.6 refers.

[2] COS(41)75 of 6th February refers.

and it will be interesting to see how the mythology of Yugoslav history will be adapted to explain this.

One cannot assess precisely the share of credit to be given to SOE;* on the one hand, the impetus came primarily from the national spirit of the Yugoslavs themselves, on the other hand there were contributory agencies besides SOE – other unofficial contacts (for instance through the Air Attaché), and the impression of the American attitude left by Colonel Donovan during his visit to the Balkans in the winter of 1940–41. But the SO2 representatives in Belgrade held most of the strings in their hands, and it is worth giving a short account of events from the point of view of Taylor and Masterson.[1]

The régime in power was virtually that of the Prince Regent himself, governing through a few minor politicians of Serbian origin, but without popular support except from Dr Maček's Croat Peasant Party, which had made a deal with the régime in August 1939 for local reasons of its own. The old and somewhat discredited Serb political parties – Nationalists, Liberals and Democrats – were in rather ineffective opposition; the nationalist associations – Narodna Odbrana, Cetniks and so forth – were hardly political bodies, but they were a much more real power than the political opposition, as their sentiment was very close to the traditions of the Serbian army. The Serb Peasant Party, in which SO2 had invested the larger part of its stake, was in an ambiguous position. It was temperamentally in opposition to the Regent, but also to the old Serb parties, which were now themselves in opposition; and as a step in its own development it had accepted a share in the Government – its leader, Milan Gavrilovič, was Minister in Moscow, and it was represented in the Cabinet by Dr Cuvrilovič. But this was essentially a Trojan horse accepted by the Regent as the price of retaining a small element of Serb support; the main force of the party, under Tupanjanin, its deputy leader, was under no official restraints, and was in opposition to much of the Regent's policy,[2] in particular to his tendency to compromise with the Germans, which became progressively clearer during the winter of 1940–41.

There are hints that the Regent was interested in securing his own position at the expense of the young King; but they need not be too literally believed – there were plenty of reasons why a ruler of Yugoslavia should feel it to be in his people's interest to compromise rather than to fight. German infiltration had gone very far in Roumania and Bulgaria, and the military position was now indefensible, except with British aid on a scale known to be impossible; memories of the

---

[1] See their report of 24th June, on SOE Archives File (AD/S.1) HD/34.

[2] See SOE Archives File (AD/S.1) HD/34.

* [See David Stafford, 'SOE and the Belgrade coup d'état of 27 March 1941', in *Slavic Review*, Sep. 1977.]

heroic resistance to the Austrians in 1914 and the final disastrous retreat did not encourage cooler heads to sacrifice everything for national honour a second time. There was not on the face of it any reason to suppose that the Germans would treat Yugoslavia as it had treated Poland – unless it resisted like Poland.

A train of thought of this kind would lead naturally to a gradual weakening in face of German pressure until the point of possible resistance was passed. It may be that the Germans were too closely bound by the timetable they had set themselves for the summer of 1941, and pushed matters a little too fast. It became clear by the middle of March that they would no longer tolerate the Regent's old policy of neutrality; Yugoslavia's accession to the Tripartite Pact would be demanded and would probably be conceded. In other words Germany was now determined on a Balkan campaign which required free use of the Morava Valley with security for the good behaviour of the Yugoslavs. The Regent visited Germany secretly on 3rd March; there is little doubt that from that time his course was set, and that his further dealings with the British and with the Opposition were directed only to secure the quiet adoption of the Tripartite Pact.

The Pact was to come before the Yugoslav Cabinet on the morning of 20th March, and a meeting at the British Legation on 19th March decided that all possible action must be taken to bring down the Government, either before or after the Pact was signed. There is no SOE record of authority given from London for this policy.

The advantage of the position of the Serb Peasant Party was now plain. Its own Minister, Dr Cuvrilovič, was prepared to resign, and with him would go Budysavlević, the leader of the Independent Democrats, another small party subsidised by SO2; pressure was brought to bear on a third Minister, an independent named Constantinović, who was with some difficulty kept in line. The resignations of these three were submitted immediately after the Cabinet meeting which had approved the Pact against their dissentient votes. The Prime Minister (Cvetkovič) and the Foreign Secretary (Concar Markovič) set off to Vienna, where the Pact was signed on 25th March 1941: but there was now in Yugoslavia a small nucleus of effective opposition, working feverishly to undo the *fait accompli*. The higher officers of the Army were pessimistic and cautious, and the initiative came from the younger officers, in particular Knesević, then Minister of the Court, and General Bora Mirkovič, the Deputy Chief of Air Staff. SO2 knew of the conspiracy in advance, but they were not concerned in its details, and it surprised them when it exploded in the small hours of 27th March, twenty-four hours before the due date. The effective forces were supplied only by the Air Force, a Tank brigade, and a battalion of Royal Guards commanded by Knesević's younger brother; but there was no serious resistance, and General

Simovič, Chief of the Air Staff, (who had been no more than a figure-head) was installed as Prime Minister by 4 a.m.

There was a meeting of the Defence Committee[1] in London that night, and General Ismay* wrote to Mr Dalton on the Prime Minister's instructions 'that it was a source of great satisfaction to the Committee that the careful and patient work of your people had reaped such a rich reward', and asked the Minister 'to convey to all concerned, both in London and "on the spot", their cordial congratulations'.

The situation was certainly satisfactory, but all was not yet clear. The Simovič government was formed not of the real leaders of the movement, but of the old Serb political parties which had been in opposition to the personalities of the régime rather than to its policy; when suddenly they found themselves in power, after a coup d'état which they had not made, their first instinct was to reopen negotiations with the Germans. The insult to German vanity had been far too direct to leave room for further discussion, and the only effect of this interlude was to delay Yugoslav proparations for war. Simovič was not himself a very serious leader, and he might not have done much better even if he had been free from the politicians; but these last few days of hesitation contributed to the completeness of the Yugoslav débâcle.

2. Collapse and Resumption of Contact

The German attack began early on 6th April, and was instantly success-ful in dislocating organised resistance. SO2 had expected early Yugoslav defeat, and was making plans for post-occupational sabo-tage and guerilla warfare. In particular it had been ceaselessly press-ing the Yugoslav General Staff to make effective preparations to block the Danube at once in the event of war. The evidence of what actu-ally happened is very scanty, but clearly something was done – not enough to hold up traffic for long, but sufficient to impose a few weeks delay. Other demolition projects were even less successful, and nothing is established beyond doubt except for the destruction of one important bridge near Maribor by a Slovene associate of Lawrenceson. Similarly nothing effective could be done with the few wireless sets and small quantity of stores available. Two sets were left in Slovenia and disappeared without trace; another two sets in Serbia also disap-peared. To make matters worse, almost the entire SO2 staff was captured; Taylor and Masterson were given the benefit of their diplo-

---

[1] Personal letter from Ismay to Dalton, d/d 28.3.41, on file HD/34 'Activities in Yugoslavia' – SOE Archives.

* [H. L. Ismay, 1887–1965, knight 1940, deputy secretary (military) to War Cabinet 1940–5, baron 1947, KG 1957. See his *Memoirs* (1960) and his life by Sir R. Wingate (1970).]

matic cover and were repatriated a few weeks later with the Minister and his staff, but Lawrenceson [PASSAGE DELETED ON GROUNDS OF NATIONAL SECURITY] was held in internment for the rest of the war.

There was thus for the moment a complete blank in Yugoslavia, as in the rest of the Balkans (except for Greece); but the Germans at first made no serious attempt to clear the hills and it is probable that resistance never really ceased, although it was some time before news reached the outer world. SOE's effort had to be made from Middle East, and details are not always easy to follow, as many Cairo papers were destroyed in the summer of 1942, but the general outline is fairly clear. In May SOE in London was already urging Middle East to formulate plans for re-establishing communications and encouraging guerilla warfare.[1] Early in June, Bailey was in charge of Yugoslav affairs at the Middle East end, and he had established relations with the Yugoslav government in exile, with a view to building up a joint organisation based on Istanbul.[2] Circumstantial reports of resistance began to arrive during July and were piling up during August.[3] It is clear that these reports did not take long to reach the highest quarters: on 25th August the Prime Minister wrote to Mr Dalton:[4]

> I understand from General Simović that there is widespread guerilla activity in Yugoslavia. It needs cohesion, support and direction from outside.
>
> Please report briefly what contacts you have with these bands and what you can now do to help them.

Mr Dalton in fact had nothing but rumour to report,[5] but preparations for action were well advanced. Some early attempts had been made to infiltrate agents overland, but the crucial step was the despatch of Captain Hudson* by submarine from Malta on 7th September. This project was known to the Russians, and SOE were informed of a parallel plan for infiltration from Russia.[6]

---

[1] Telegram to Jerusalem d/d 19th May 1941; copy on SOE Archives File (AD/S.1) SC/34/1.

[2] CXG.230 of 3rd June from Jerusalem; copy on SOE Archives File (AD/S.1) '34 – Activities in Yugoslavia'.

[3] e.g. Letter from Djon Djonović (an old Peasant Party friend of SOE) to Colonel Masterson d/d 17th July: and a summary by Mr Broad of reports received up to 20th August. Both in SOE Archives File (AD/S.1) HD/SC/34/9.

[4] Original letter on SOE Archives File (AD/S.1) HD/34/9.

[5] Copy of his reply d/d 30th August 1941, on SOE Archives File (AD/S.1) HD/34/9.

[6] Minute from Colonel [J. S. A.] Pearson to Mr Jebb d/d 22nd September 1941, on SOE Archives File (AD/S.1) SC/34/9.

* [D. T. Hudson, mining engineer, 1911–95. See pages 117–19.]

The situation into which Hudson was intruded was one of a complexity quite unsuspected by the outer world.[1] It was some time before it became reasonably clear to Hudson himself, and it is doubtful if it was ever fully understood in all its implications by any organ of the British Government. The development of British policy would only be fully intelligible against a background of the information which flowed into London from all its sources, of which SOE was only one, and it is important to realise how limited and tainted these sources were at the periods when crucial decisions of policy had to be taken.

Some brief description of the situation is essential here as a prologue to events, but it should be clear that it was not and could not have been available to any of the actors at the time.

The Yugoslav State before the war had been held together by a precarious coalition of moderate Serb opinion with Dr Maček's Croat Peasant Party and with the Slovene Clericals: and where this broke down on irreconcilable local differences the only alternative was a Royal dictatorship, founded largely on the Serbian elements in the Army, but stopping short of the extreme demands of Serbian nationalism. Both these solutions were swept away by events in the spring of 1941. The Regent was under suspicion of treachery to the nation, the King was a boy and in exile, accompanied by a government of 'runaways': the politicians of the old parties were insignificant in conditions of war and occupation. The leadership was thus thrown to two elements which had hitherto remained in the background.

On the one side, was the tradition of militant Serbian nationalism, founded on the very proud Serbian record of resistance to the Turks, and thinking politically only in terms of Greater Serbia. The only real fighting in April 1941 had been carried out by Serbian units on Serbian soil; the Army was scattered rather than destroyed, and while some of its units dispersed to their villages others remained in being in the hills with some discipline and some equipment. The main instinct of its leaders was for the preservation of Serbia, and this was strengthened in the summer of 1941 by an outbreak of terror against the Serb population in all districts where it had been a minority. For this the main responsibility rests with the Croat extremists under Pavelič doubtless tacitly supported by the Italians and possibly by the Moslem

---

[1] There is a very valuable first-hand account in Christie Lawrence 'Irregular Adventure' (February 1947 – published since the above was written). Lawrence was a Commando officer captured in Crete in May 1941: he escaped while in transit to Germany and was with the guerillas during the rising of September 1941, and the subsequent breach between Mihailovitch and the Partisans. He is particularly illuminating on the relations between Neditch, Kosta Pechanats, Mihailovitch and the local 'chieftains' loosely allied to one or other of them.

population in Bosnia. The old Serbia had lost one million out of 4,500,000 inhabitants in the war of 1914–15, and it was natural that its leaders should be concerned above all to avoid the recurrence of the same catastrophe. There was agreement on this over a wide band of opinion, which stretched from the 'Quisling'* Government of Nedić** in Belgrade to Mihailović† in the hills, with differences on personalities and tactics rather than on principle. The object was to preserve Serbian life and interests now, and to emerge from the war in a position which would make possible a more effective Serb control of Yugoslavia within its old borders.

Even the Nedić Government, on the extreme 'Right' (if it may be so called) of this movement, cannot be dismissed as pure 'Quisling';[1] for the present, at least, Croatia was an Italian puppet, and it was natural to get closer to the Germans as the only available counterweight. With the Nedić Government went the 'Cetniks', in the sense in which that word would most naturally bear in Yugoslavia. They had behind them the long tradition of guerilla resistance to the Turk, but the most recent association of the word was with Kosta Pečanač, who had been dropped behind the enemy lines in Macedonia in 1916 and had stimulated a useless revolt, suppressed by large-scale massacres. Pečanač had survived and had been something of a national here to his Cetniks, who became virtually a veterans' association of those who had fought for Serbia in 1914–18. He now put such weight as he had on Nedić's side, and his Cetniks were a natural source of recruitment for Nedić's forces.

Mihailovitch differed profoundly from Nedić only in that he was from first to last convinced that the Germans would lose the war; it would therefore be fatal to Serbia that she should be nothing more than a minor jackal of the Nazis – some continuity of resistance was essential to her national future. Mihailovitch was himself therefore a convinced 'resister': very little solid evidence has ever been produced of his personal collaboration either with Nedić or with German or Italian authorities. But this was qualified in two ways. *First*, his primary object was the preservation of Serbia, and he would have no truck with action which might please the Allies and even serve their

---

[1] Even to the Right of Nedić there was the small faction of Fascists adhering to Ljotič.

* [Vidkun Quisling, 1887–1945, assisted Germans' attempts to Nazify Norway and became a byword for collaboration with them, tried and executed at end of war.]

** [General Milan Nedić.]

† [Colonel D. Mihailovič (later spelt Mihailovitch by Mackenzie), 1893–1946, raised revolt against Germans, lost civil war against Partisans, captured March, executed after show trial July 1946. See David Martin, *Patriot or Traitor* (Stanford, Calif., 1979).]

strategy, but would entail such Serbian losses as had been incurred by Pečanac in the autumn of 1917. *Second*, he deliberately encouraged his well-wishers to remain for the most part on the right side of the law, and if possible to hold positions where they would be allowed possession of arms, access to supplies, and some strategic advantages for the future. It was never a secret that Mihailovitch had 'his men' in Nedič's forces,[1] and that his subordinate leaders made local deals with the Italians: indeed, the British Government in qualified terms approved these tactics.[2] Unless Britain had been in a position to supply arms and food on a vastly greater scale it is hard to see what other policy was possible for those who considered the problem primarily in terms of Serbian interests.

The other new factor in the situation was the Communist Party, which had been formally suppressed in 1921. The suppression was only moderately effective in practice, and Marxist doctrine was a common enough line of thought for the poor but energetic University student in the years between the wars. What is more, the Communist Party gained in prestige by its air of mystery, and by the fact that it had no share in responsibility for any of the manifold errors and vested interests of the old Yugoslavia. It had no popular basis, but it did possess a party organisation experienced in underground methods, and a considerable fund of non-party sympathy among the young, energetic, and frustrated.

The Communists had no share in the coup d'état of March 1941; the popular response to it was so great that there could be no question of their opposing it at the time, though their attitude today appears to be that it was a wicked attempt by the Allies and by native reactionaries to exploit Yugoslav patriotism for their own purposes. Communist policy was only released from this ambiguity by the German attack on Russia in June, 1941; evidence for what happened in these early days is very scanty,[3] but it seems that from the first they adopted the policy which followed throughout – one of resistance *à l'outrance*, regardless of consequences. This had a working basis (as Mihailovitch's policy had not) in a determined party

---

[1] The first report appears to be a claim by Mihailovitch himself, transmitted by Hudson on 19th November 1941.

[2] Aide-Mémoire d/d 21st July 1942, left with M. Jan Maisky by Mr Eden on 27th July 1942. Copy with documents in support of White Paper, Part II, Section B. [I. Maisky, 1884–1975, Soviet Ambassador in London 1932–43, deputy Foreign Minister 1943–6.]

[3] The first 'Partisan' rising is said to have been in Montenegro on St Peter's Day (13th July) 1941. Ciano's diary under 14th and 15th July 1941 confirms the importance of this rising, which was related to an attempt to put an Italian puppet on the throne of an 'independent' Montenegro.

organisation free from local and social ties, and carrying with it a fringe of young and able intellectuals almost equally free from commitments; and to some extent it grew by the momentum of its own policy. Each village which was sacked, each batch of hostages who were shot, swelled the numbers of the embittered men who became the Partisan Army, moving homeless about the country and stirring fresh trouble and fresh resistance wherever they came.

The original incompatibility between Communism and the 'Serb Idea' was intense; the Communist strain among the Partisans grew less conspicuous as the Partisan movement grew broader, but the incompatibility of policy did not decrease. The Communists stood for a type of action which to Mihailovitch seemed reckless and destructive; in addition, their main strength lay at first in Croatia, and to Mihailovitch they appeared as a new manifestation of Croat nationalism – perhaps allied with Pavelić and his Ustashi, certainly indistinguishable from them in their consequences.

Captain Hudson, who had been selected by SOE to investigate the first rumours of these two rival guerilla factions, was a young mining engineer, then aged thirty, who had already worked for five years in Yugoslavia. He knew the language and the people well, and was a man of courage and good sense, though with no political and little military experience. His equipment included a substantial sum in sovereigns[1] and a moderate amount of arms and other stores: he was also provided with two wireless sets, one of which was a battery set too weak for regular contact with his base, the other a more efficient set but dependent on electric mains – a poor prospect in the interior of Yugoslavia.

The party included also two Yugoslav officers, Major Ostojić and Major Lalatović, nominated by the government in exile, and a Yugoslav wireless operator. It should be remembered that it was in form a mission sent by the Yugoslav government in exile to establish contact with any resistance there might be in its own country; Captain Hudson's role was of crucial importance, but he was not formally in command. When the mission set out, nothing was known of Mihailovitch or of civil war in Yugoslavia: whatever directive may have been given to its own officers by the Yugoslav Government, Captain Hudson's instructions were certainly in general terms, to contact, investigate and report on all groups offering resistance to the enemy, regardless of race, creed or political persuasions.[2]

---

[1] No record of the exact amount has come to light.

[2] No copy of this directive can now be found, but the above is confirmed by all who were concerned with it, and is entirely compatible with the circumstances of the time.

The party was put ashore from HM submarine 'Triumph' on the coast of Montenegro on 16th September 1941, and made contact first with a group calling itself 'The Montenegrin Freedom Forces', which included several Communist leaders later prominent in the Partisan movement. This group received them well, and passed on Hudson with one of the Yugoslav officers to the headquarters of their movement, which had then been driven into western Serbia by enemy pressure further north and west. There Hudson met Tito,* and was well received and favourably impressed; but on all practical details, such as arrangements for British aid and for wireless communications, Tito was extremely cautious. Indeed it was clear that he rated the possibilities of active British assistance pretty low at this time, and was not prepared for its sake to incur the political liability of 'strings' attaching him to the British Government and to the Yugoslav government in exile.

Meantime, communication had been established between Malta** and a transmitter in Serbia, which claimed to be speaking for the Royal Yugoslav Army in the field, headed by Colonel Dragolub Mihailovitch; this claim was confirmed by the arrival in London by an emissary who stated that he came from Mihailovitch himself. Accordingly, instructions were sent to Hudson to make contact with and investigate this movement, and he moved on 25th October from Tito's Headquarters to those of Mihailovitch, who was established not far off – in fact this Serbian territory was Mihailovitch's ground, recently invaded by the Partisans, and their relations were already on the verge of open war. Hudson was politely but not cordially received; it was made clear to him that further contact with the Partisans was incompatible with relations with Mihailovitch, who claimed from the outset that he was the senior representative on Yugoslav soil of the Royal government in exile, and was thus the only legitimate authority in the whole of Yugoslavia. Hudson's only channel of communication with his base was now the set already used by Mihailovitch, and under the latter's control; so that his messages were short and fragmentary, and were often garbled in transmission.

Meanwhile matters had made substantial progress in London, before any communication had been received either from Hudson or from Mihailovitch. On 3rd October General Simović saw Mr Eden and

---

* [Josip Broz, 1892–1980, codenamed Tito (= Do this), secretary, Yugoslav Communist Party from 1937, led Partisan revolt against both Germans and Yugoslavs who disagreed with him, Marshal 1943, thereafter dictator of Yugoslavia. See W. Roberts, *Tito, Mihailović and the Allies* (2nd ed, Durham, N.C., 1987).]

** [But see Bill Deakin, 'The Emergence of Colonel Mihailović by Radio', in K. G. Robertson (ed.), *War, Resistance and Intelligence* (1999).]

appealed for assistance 'to arrest the extermination of the Yugoslav people' – not for Mihailovitch, whose role was as yet unknown: on 13th October King Peter himself saw the Prime Minister, and the same night the question of military aid was referred to the Chiefs of Staff for their advice. It is in this interval between 3rd and 13th October that the name of Mihailovitch is first seriously mentioned, as a result of the coincidence of the opening of Mihailovitch's own wireless communications and of the arrival in London of the emissary sent out through Istanbul. In a Minute to the Prime Minister, dated 14th October, Mr Dalton is already referring to 'the rebels under Colonel Mihailovitch'.[1] It is at this point that Mihailovitch is seized on both by the Yugoslav Government and by SOE as a symbolic leader of resistance, and Hudson is moved on SOE's instructions from Tito's Headquarters to those of the man who proved to be Tito's worst enemy. At this stage, before the lines of cleavage had set, there was perhaps a chance of 'reserve', of a careful choice of policies: but SOE's business was to back resistance, and no one could question that there was real resistance, in desperate need of aid – it would have been unthinkable to pause and scrutinise the credentials and policy of its leader. No evidence was available or could be available about such details: and resistance might be wiped out before it could be collected. The crucial decision was therefore taken at once, and taken blindly.

On 15th October the Chiefs of Staff telegraphed to the Cs-in-C, Middle East, to ask them to give such help as they could 'without prejudice to other operations'. This proviso deserves emphasis. The Germans in Russia had encircled Leningrad, had cut through to the sea of Azov and seized most of the Ukraine, and were engaged on vast operations directed straight at Moscow: North Africa was the only theatre in which a diversion could be made, and an operation to relieve Tobruk and exploit success was in a late stage of preparation. It was launched on 18th November, with equipment which was barely adequate, and it forced the relief of Tobruk on 9th December – 'a damned nice thing, Creevey, the nearest run thing you ever saw in your life', as the Duke [of Wellington] said after Waterloo. It is not surprising that the Chiefs of Staff were lukewarm about Mihailovitch – 'From our point of view revolt is premature, but patriots have thrown their caps over the fence and must be supported by all possible means.'[2]

---

[1] Copy on SOE Archives File HD/34/9. Cf. the paper prepared by Mr Jebb on 14th October 1941 for the COS; copy on SOE Archives File (AD/S.1) SC/34/9.

[2] 95880 Cipher (MO5) 15/10: discussed by the COS on 14th and 15th October (COS(41)353rd Mtg, Min. 2, and COS(41)354th Mtg, Min. 4). Copy of cipher on SOE Archives File (AD/S.1) SC/34/9.

On 22nd October the Soviet Ambassador, M. Maisky, had approached the Foreign Secretary with the suggestion that the Yugoslav revolt should be encouraged in every possible way, and that the British and Russian Governments should work closely together for that purpose.[1] Mr Eden saw M. Maisky again on 29th October,[2] and gave him a certain amount of information about the situation as known to the British: it appears that SOE's representatives had already had some discussions with the NKVD both in Moscow and in Constantinople about the Yugoslav situation, and the information given to M. Maisky was rationed a little for fear of 'crossing wires' with this other and more delicate channel.[3] It is at least plain that the Russians were then pressing the British to give all possible aid to a diversion in Yugoslavia, irrespective of its political colour; and that the British warmly agreed in principle and were fairly frank about their own line of action.

The problem was briefly referred to at a War Cabinet meeting on 30th October, when Mr Eden mentioned that it might be necessary to bring the problem before the Defence Committee.[4] On the same day General Simovič forwarded to the Foreign Secretary a telegram from Colonel Mihailovitch – 'In God's name send us help while the weather is still fine. In a few days we can build up a large and powerful army. We need:- Revolvers, machine-guns, Bren guns, hand grenades, mortars, ammunition, surgical and medical supplies, and money. We are ready for your arrival. Ostojitch and companions' (i.e. Hudson) 'are here.' This appeal was the basis of discussion at a Staff Conference held on 4th November at which the Prime Minister presided and Mr Eden and Mr Dalton were present, as well as the Chiefs of Staff. The meeting had before it a paper by Mr Eden,[5] as well as one by the Chiefs of Staff, submitting a draft telegram on policy to the Cs-in-C, Middle East.[6] As was to be expected, the Chiefs of Staff did not favour

---

[1] Dispatch by Mr Eden to Sir Stafford Cripps at Kuibyshev, d/d 22nd October 1941. [R. S. Cripps, 1889–1952, labour lawyer, knight 1930, MP 1931–50, Ambassador to Russia 1940–42, Minister of Aircraft Production 1942–5, Exchequer 1947–50; in *DNB*. See his life by Colin Cooke (1957). As the Germans approached Moscow late in 1941, the diplomatic corps (and others) were moved 400 miles east to Kuibyshev.]

[2] Dispatch by Mr Eden to Sir Stafford Cripps at Kuibyshev, d/d 29th October, 1941.

[3] See letter from Mr Jebb to Sir Orme Sargent, d/d 27th October 1941, on SOE Archives File (AD/S.1) SC/34/9.

[4] WM(41)107th Mtg, Min.3, of 30th October. There had been previous references on 23rd October, WM(41)105th Mtg, Min. 1, and at the Defence Committee on 17th October (DO(41)65th Mtg).

[5] DO(41)24 of 31st October 1941.

[6] DO(41)26 of 3rd November 1941: the draft was discussed by the COS on 31st October, COS(41)374th Mtg, Item 10.

any large diversion from operations then in progress – 'Rebels are located in difficult hill country, whence they may well be able to keep movement in being for a long time, but probably only as a nuisance to the Axis and not much more. For revolt to develop into a nation-wide rebellion the movement would have to spread to the towns where in absence of British forces it would certainly be quelled by the Germans with extreme ruthlessness. This must be avoided. Our policy should therefore be to provide rebels with supplies necessary to maintain movement in the hills.' Mr Eden's paper was more encouraging to the rebels in its tone, but did not make a serious issue of aid to Yugoslavia in any form which might imperil British operations. In these circumstances the issue was prejudged; the conclusion of the meeting was merely 'to invite the Admiralty in consultation with the War Office and SOE, to examine, as a matter of urgency, the possibility of sending arms and supplies to the Yugoslav rebels by sea from Malta and Middle East'.[1] The results of this reconsideration were embodied in a telegram to the Cs-in-C, Middle East, dated 7th November,[2] which was on the lines of the earlier draft, but added in plain terms 'at present we are not in a position to give the Yugoslavs substantial military aid'.

This meant in effect priority of the second grade; assistance was not refused, but it was clogged by shortages of all kinds: aircraft, submarines, parachutes, weapons, wireless sets, men were needed still more urgently for the battles of Tobruk and Malta, and the files are full of disheartened and recriminatory telegrams about requirements and the failure to meet them. For instance, SOE Cairo's telegram of 29th November 1941:[3]

2. It is obvious that Balkans revolt is not looked upon as a serious proposition.
3. In spite of the fact that Serbian guerillas are retaining approximately six German divisons apart from many Italian divisions Serbia Bosnia and Montenegro practically no effort is being made on our side to support these forces in the hills.
4. In spite of directives given from highest quarters from COS in London . . . so far it has not been possible to render more than a paltry help of 400 kilos of material.
5. From directives received from London and here we promised Hudson that during this moon help would be forthcoming and this was held out by Hudson as an offer to Mihailovitch and

---

[1] COS (41)35th (0) Mtg of 4th November.
[2] COS(41)379th Mtg, Min. 2, of 7th November, and telegram COS197 of 7th November to Cs-in-C ME.
[3] On SOE Archives File (AD/S.1) SC/34/9.

partisans to reconcile (see his telegram No. 5 of 21st November).
6. The moon is already up and we race from pillar to post looking for planes.
7. If facts mentioned in para. 3 are accepted then Balkans essentially Yugoslavia must be considered as a permanent front and not repeat not one which can be treated as side show and help given only if and when time and material permit.
8. If help is not forthcoming immediately repeat immediately there is grave risk of disintegrating this front and wiping out most enemy troops now immobilised in Balkans.
9. A continuation of this attitude will have disastrous effects on neighbouring Balkan countries and especially in Greece where revolt can be looked for in due course . . . .

This is annotated by Mr Dalton in Ministerial red ink 'Pretty desperate and I don't wonder!'

There is no doubt that Cairo's attitude was shared by SOE London: to take two instances among many:

Brigadier Gubbins to Sir Frank Nelson on 29th November:[1] 'Quite obviously the Yugoslav rebellion is of major importance and we, the British, shall be culpable of the grossest ineptitude and negligence if it is not supported to the utmost . . . . At this moment, in my opinion, supplies dropped in Yugoslavia are worth any number of bombs dropped in Germany. We have in the former country a third land front against the Germans which, if supported, may hold for months and can be a constant running sore.'

Lord Glenconner* to Mr Jebb on 4th December:[2] 'It is now quite evident that the Cs-in-C and the Chiefs of Staff are opposed to diverting any of our forces to assist the insurgents, and we have, therefore, as usual, fallen between two stools, and are endeavouring to work a compromise between two opposite and conflicting policies. I say that we have fallen between two stools because I am confident that, if the Germans were in our place they would either decide to back the revolt or leave it alone . . . .'

This aspect of the matter was much more fundamental at this stage than the question of whether to back Mihailovitch or Tito. Unless substantial aid could be given, SOE's efforts would only result in

---

[1] Original (which was shown to the Foreign Office) on SOE Archives File (AD/S.1) SC/34/9.

[2] Original (which was shown to the Foreign Office) on SOE Archives File (AD/S.1) SC/34/9.

* [C. G. Tennant, 1899–1983, 2nd Lord Glenconner 1920, on SOE's Balkan desk 1940–41, head of SOE Cairo 1942–3.]

useless massacre; nor could it hope to mobilise all resistance under one leader unless that leader was established as a single channel through whom arms, money and stores would flow copiously to those who accepted his leadership. Pearl Harbour followed three days after Lord Glenconner's Minute, and it became clearer than ever that substantial aid could not be given:[1] but by that time the word of the British Government was committed to the support of revolt in Yugoslavia, and in particular of revolt under the leadership of Mihailovitch.

The possibility that the revolt might be transformed into a civil war did not emerge until shortly after the important Staff Conference of 4th November. The first clear indication was a signal from Hudson which reached London via Malta and Cairo on 9th November:[2] 'Impossible to establish communications with Partisans. Mihailovitch insists that communicating your message will end relations between us. Fighting between Cetniks and Partisans broke out yesterday and continues in Pozegar, Ćaćak, and Uziće. Mihailovitch hopes to liquidate differences shortly . . . . Urge appropriate broadcasts from Moscow and London.' This was amply confirmed by a message from Mihailovitch himself received on 13th November: 'The Communists have attacked us and forced us to fight at the same time against Germans, Communists, Ustashis and other factions. In spite of this the whole nation is for the King . . . .' It is worth quoting also from Hudson's first impressions of the political situation, received on 13th November and the following day: 'Communists at head of Partisans are genuine anti-Axis. Montenegro is Partisan-organised and Mihailovitch has only just started there. Mihailovitch uncompromising towards Partisans and leading Cetniks state openly rather Nedič than Communists. Partisans would compromise but Mihailovitch believes he holds all the trumps. Mihailovitch and his officers completely loyal to crown. Both parties have withdrawn large forces from German front. Many who join Partisans because they started first will go over to Cetniks if latter backed by British. Civil war will be a long affair and nothing substantial against Germans for months.' And on 14th November: 'Suggest you tell Mihailovitch full British help not forthcoming unless attempt made to incorporate all anti-Fascist elements under his command. This attempt to be made by my personally discussing terms of such incorporation with Partisans at

---

[1] Cf. letter from General Ismay to Mr Jebb, d/d 13.12.41. On SOE Archives File (AD/S.1) SC/34/9.

[2] Copy in series of 'Bullseye' (i.e. code name for Hudson's telegrams) messages in SOE Archives File 18/400/78. Messages to Hudson were dispatched via Cairo, and it seems that all copies there were destroyed in the 'evacuation' in June 1942: the series of outgoing messages is therefore very incomplete.

Uziće and reporting same to you . . . . Such attempt to be preceded by strong appeal for unity by Moscow broadcast to Partisans.'

Both the British and the Yugoslav Governments reacted promptly on the lines suggested by Colonel Hudson. General Simovič at once asked M. Maisky in London and his own Ambassador in Kuibyshev to persuade the Russian Government to use its influence for unity behind Mihailovitch. On 13th November he wrote to Mr Eden to ask for his intervention with the Russians through Sir Stafford Cripps; and on 15th November he broadcast an appeal for unity himself. The King was to make a similar broadcast on 1st December, the Yugoslav National Day. The Foreign Office took parallel action with M. Maisky and in Kuibyshev.[1] Neither M. Maisky nor M. Vishinsky* (whom Sir Stafford Cripps saw on 18th November)[2] contributed anything but platitudes on the virtue of unity, and the important messages were those sent from the Yugoslav Government to Mihailovitch, and from SOE to Hudson. The essential parts of the former, which was sent on 19th November, read as follows: 'HM King Peter, the Government and myself are absolutely in agreement. We are maintaining the Yugoslav policy. We are using every means in our power to extend you material aid . . . .

'We have taken measures for the Partisans to discontinue unnecessary action, and to place themselves under your command as in my speech of 15th November. Endeavour to smooth out differences and refrain from any kind of vindictive action.' The rest of the telegram was concerned with the promotion of Colonel Mihailovitch to the rank of General – a step of pretty considerable importance in Yugoslav military politics, which serve to soften still further the rather mild injunctions to compromise. The British message transmitted to Hudson on 16th November was scarcely stronger:[3] 'HMG now considers fight should be Yugoslavs for Yugoslavia and not revolt led by Communists for Russia, if it is to prosper. HMG therefore asking Soviet Government urge Communist elements to rally to Mihailovitch, collaborating with him against Germans putting themselves unreservedly at disposal of Mihailovitch as national leader. Simovič will also instruct Mihailovitch to refrain from retaliatory action.' Good

---

[1] See letters from Sir Alexander Cadogan to M. Simovič dated 16th and 18th November, and Foreign Office telegrams to Kuibyshev No. 155 of 16th November and R.10199 of 29th November; copy on SOE Archives File (AD/S.1) SC/34/9.

[2] Foreign Office telegram dated 20th November in White Paper dossier. SOE also attempted to use what influence it had through its liaison with the NKVD, without recorded effect: see telegram from Lord Glenconner to SOE's Moscow Mission dated 22nd November 1941. Copy on SOE Archives File (AD/S.1) SC/34/9.

[3] Copy on SOE Archives File (AD/S.1) SC/34/9.

* [A. J. Vishinsky, 1883–1954, Soviet chief prosecutor from 1936.]

intentions could hardly have been expressed less tactfully, or with less relevance to the realities of the situation.

The conference between Mihailovitch and Tito to which these moves led up took place on 20th November, and was a total failure. Hudson's report was plain enough: 'Attended Cetnik-Partisan conference. Conveyed your attitude. Partisans insist on keeping identify under joint GS with Cetniks. They consider Simovič slack. Partisans' leading part in revolt shows Yugoslav Government's ignorance of situation. Partisans consider people lost all confidence in former Yugoslav officers who were responsible for collapse. They suspect Mihailovitch helping Nedič and other pro-Axis elements fighting Communists. Partisans will continue fight Mihailovitch unless combine on their terms. Mihailovitch has now agreed to recognise Partisans. I told him of both sides turning against the Germans. Believes immediate British aid at his disposal and we could help him establish himself as unconditional C-in-C.' To which Hudson added in a separate signal: 'My attitude to Mihailovitch has been that he has all qualifications except strength. At present Partisans stronger and he must first liquidate them with British arms before turning seriously to Germans. He told me today lack of ammunition will force him to retire from Ravnogora if Partisans continue fight.' This is harshly expressed, but it conveys an obvious truth: further negotiation was useless until Mihailovitch had received sufficient British support to become an effective rallying point.

Mihailovitch's own report is less plain. 'I have done everything and succeeded in breaking off the fratricidal strife provoked by the other side. In the fighting up to now against one and the other I have exhausted almost all my ammunition. I am making the greatest efforts to unite all the nation's forces and to complete reorganisation for decisive struggle against the Germans. It is most urgently necessary to receive arms, munitions, money, clothes, boots and then the rest.' This meant the same as Hudson; but by some odd piece of wishful thinking the British, as well as the Yugoslav Government, accepted it as a report of provisional unity and sent congratulations both to Hudson and to Mihailovitch.[1] They were thus committed to the policy of building up Mihailovitch as a national leader by giving him a monopoly of British supplies; and they were in no position to provide sufficient supplies for the purpose. The seal was set on this policy by the fall of the Simovič Government on 9th January 1942, and its replacement by a new government under M. Jovanovic, who attempted to strengthen a weak position by the formal inclusion of General Mihailovitch as Minister of War.

---

[1] Bullseye Tel. of 22nd November 1941; copy on SOE Archives File (AD/S.1) SC/34/9.

After the abortive Uziće conference darkness falls on the scene. A German offensive sweeps over the area in which Tweedledum and Tweedledee had been at their battle, and the contestants react in accordance with their respective tactics. The Partisans gather their nucleus of professional resisters and breakthrough encirclement into new territory in south-east Bosnia: Mihailovitch's men dissolve into their elements and go under cover as innocent villagers, or even as members of Nedič's security forces. Hudson is cut off from Mihailovitch while on a journey to what had been Tito's HQ, where he recovered one of his useless wireless sets; he is prevented from resuming contact until June 1942 – at first by the fortunes of war, later by Mihailovitch's resentment of his attempts to promote a compromise with the Partisans. Mihailovitch himself is off the air for most of December, and when he begins to transmit again in January 1942 it is some time before any satisfactory proof is given that the transmissions are genuine and not under German control. But even when accepted they are for practical purposes worthless; a mixture of tirades against the Communists, demands for aid, intelligence of rather a poor grade, and endless details about the promotions and decoration of individual soldiers. This last category was much the largest and was a source of much annoyance and delay to the SOE signals organisation.

During this period London and Cairo were helpless but not inactive. SOE made repeated attempts to open new channels of communication, but was quite unsuccessful until the end of August 1942. Two parties (known as 'Hydra' and 'Henna') left Malta by submarine on 22nd November 1941, but were recalled before they could land as there was a sudden need for the concentration of all available submarines in the central Mediterranean. The crisis of the second Libyan offensive had just been reached. Another two parties ('Desirable' and 'Disclaim') were formed in Middle East, with a view to parachute landing from an aircraft based on Malta: this too was abandoned early in January, as a result of heavy enemy attacks on the Malta airfields. Finally, 'Hydra' and 'Henna' were landed by submarine on 25th and 27th January. 'Henna' consisted of two Yugoslavs and simply disappeared without trace. 'Hydra' was led by Major Terence Atherton, a British officer who knew the country well, and it included one Yugoslav and one British NCO: no W/T traffic was ever received from it, though there were early rumours of Major Atherton's death. From the evidence available later it appears that he and his British NCO were murdered for their money and stores while trying to make their way across country unescorted.* A further party

---

* [More on Atherton's murder in F. W. D. Deakin, *The Embattled Mountain* (1971), pp. 174–7.]

('Disclaim'), consisting of Major K. J. Elliott, one British NCO and two Yugoslavs, were dropped into Bosnia on the night of 5th February and were captured almost at once by Croat troops.* 'Desirable', which was to have been led by Major G. H. Head, was standing by at the same period but was held up by all sorts of adverse factors, and was eventually abandoned.

All parties dispatched so far had been sent in 'blind'; a dangerous gamble, which appeared to have failed totally, as even Captain Hudson had for the time being disappeared. This experience, as well as short-age of aircraft, shortage of supplies, shortage of suitable personnel, held matters up for a time. There were some who felt that with more skill and energy more could have been done,[1] and this was one of various factors which led at this time to dissatisfaction with SOE's Cairo organisation – that organisation was bad but the difficulties were real nevertheless. Attempts to send in stores were almost equally unsuccessful, and the supplies received by Mihailovitch up to August 1942 were ridiculously trivial in relation to his needs.[2]

The next agent sent in exemplified more than one of the problems involved. He was a Yugoslav national named Branislav Radojevic, who had been recruited by SOE's New York office, on the strength of the fact that he was a trained ship's wireless operator who had been dismissed for anti-Nazi propaganda: he appears to have been drunken, talkative and reckless, and also near-Communist in his political views – but hardly a fair specimen of the Communist type as it appeared in Yugoslavia. The original plan had been to drop him blind in some area where he could contact Tito's partisans, a task for which he had some qualifications; but no fewer than nine attempts at the operation were made without success between April and August 1942. Eventually, it was decided in haste to drop him to Mihailovitch's HQ, which was the only place where some reception could be arranged: he arrived there successfully on the night of 29th August 1942, under the pseudonym of 'Captain Charles Robertson'. This was the first reinforcement Hudson had received since his arrival in September 1941, and it was followed up shortly after by the arrival of a British signals party consisting of Captain P. H. A. Lofts and two NCO's.

Thus for the first time Hudson was provided with an adequate chan-nel with which to report: at the same time he had attached to him a reckless Yugoslav whose outlook was entirely antipathetic to Mihailovitch and who was in a position to report direct to Cairo on his own wireless set. 'Robertson' was known outside to be biassed

---

[1] Cf. Major Head's report of 1st May 1942 on SOE Archives File 18nc/470/1.

[2] See list attached to letter of 5th June 1942 to Mr P. J. Dixon, Foreign Office, on SOE Archives File 18/360/30: even this list seems to be inflated.

* [Details in Elliott, *I Spy*.]

against Mihailovitch; and his tirades may have had a negative effect, in that their irresponsibility cast some doubts on what Hudson himself had to say to Mihailovitch's discredit in his cautious estimate of the situation.[1] There was still room for sharp controversy within SOE as to the realities of the situation.

All through this period the success of SOE's efforts depended primarily on the transport at its disposal, and this meant submarines and long-range bombers; the idea of using caiques, as in the Aegean, fell through, in face of the distances involved. The submarine problem was comparatively simple; on the First Sea Lord's showing[2] only two submarines were left in the Mediterranean suitable for transport, and these were required for the supply of Malta; all other suitable submarines had been withdrawn to meet the Japanese threat in the Indian Ocean. The Chiefs of Staff had no hesitation in saying that Malta and the Indian Ocean should have priority over General Mihailovitch. The aircraft situation was more confused, and the essentials became lost in a maze of technicalities about the ability and usefulness of Liberators, Halifaxes, Wellingtons, Whitleys, even obsolete Wellesleys and captured Heinkels. SOE's extreme claim was for the exclusive use of a squadron of long-range transport aircraft based in the Middle East; the Yugoslav Government went further and proposed to man such a squadron (and a submarine) with their own men.[3] Neither of these suggestions bore any relation whatever to the availability of aircraft; and when the fog had cleared a little, it became plain that the only aircraft which could reach Yugoslavia while Malta was out of use were Liberators, which had to be specially converted for the purpose. Only two converted Liberators were available; additional aircraft were coming forward very slowly, especially when the USA began their own full mobilisation after Pearl Harbour; Liberators were the key to the Battle of the Atlantic as well as to the Battle of Yugoslavia. Here again there could be no real hesitation about priorities.[4]

The same ground was gone over three times during this period: in December 1941 on the initiative of Mr Dalton;[5] in February 1942 on the initiative of Mr Eden;[6] and in April as a result of a direct approach

---

[1] See summary dated 23rd February 1943 of his PLOZ series, on SOE Archives File 18/360/30.

[2] COS(42)117th Mtg, Min. 5, of 13th April.

[3] To confuse matters further they put in an independent application for Lease/Lend aircraft from the USA, which had to be headed off. See Foreign Office Tel. USLON No. 100 of 9th November 1941, in SOE Archives File (AD/S.1) SC/34/9.

[4] COS(42)117th Mtg, Min. 5, of 13th April.

[5] DO(41)36 of 14th December and DO(41)72nd Mtg, Min. 3, of 15th December.

[6] COS(42)139 of 26th February, COS(42)67th Mtg, Min. 8, DO(42)7th Mtg, Min. 2, of 2nd March.

by the Yugoslav Government to the Prime Minister, as well as of a memorandum by Sir Frank Nelson.[1] The results in each case were similar. The Yugoslav case was supported by the Foreign Office, and less forcibly by the War Office – whose Order of Battle showed that there were in Yugoslavia in March 1942 seventeen Italian, five German and four Bulgarian divisions: the Admiralty and the Air Ministry could not be moved from the position that aid was possible only at the expense of interests which all agreed to be more vital. It was in fact the most disheartening, if not the blackest, period of the war; vast American production was in sight, yet policy in every field was dominated by aching shortages.

The most curious attempt to break the deadlock was an approach to the Soviet Ambassador in March 1942: M. Maisky saw Mr Eden on 27th March and received from him an Aide-Mémoire setting out that His Majesty's Government had lost touch with General Mihailovitch and that 'it occurs to Mr Eden that the Soviet Government may have means of communicating with General Mihailovitch. If so, would they be prepared to assist His Majesty's Government in making with the General such arrangements as are necessary to enable supplies to reach him from British sources, or could they let His Majesty's Government know where they believe him to be, so that they can drop wireless sets?'[2] M. Maisky's reply, given a fortnight later, was (not unnaturally) that 'he had received a message from his Government to say that, unfortunately, they had no communication with Yugoslavia at all'.[3] Mr Eden thanked the Ambassador, and went on to say 'that, in the interval since I had put my question to him, we had, I am glad to say, been able to re-establish communication to some extent with General Mihailovitch. The Ambassador then said that he would be grateful if we could keep him informed of any news of importance which we received from that quarter. I undertook to do so.' SOE had now satisfied themselves that the Mihailovitch messages were really from him and not from the Germans; and Mr Eden returned to the charge with M. Maisky on 27th April.[4] He explained that Mihailovitch complained 'that he is being constantly disturbed in his work by the "Communists" who, he has proof, are being helped by the occupying powers, who are anxious that both sides should be kept busy this

---

[1] COS(42)80(0) of 30th March, and COS(42)102nd Mtg, Min. 8, of 6th April: COS(42)215 of 10th April and COS(42)117th Mtg, Min. 5, of 13th April.

[2] Dispatch to HM Ambassador at Kuibyshev No. 81 of 27th March 1942 (Ref. R.2079/178/G). (Copy in White Paper Dossier.)

[3] Ditto No. 112 of 15th April 1942 (Ref. R.2515/178/G). (Copy in White Paper Dossier.)

[4] Letter to M. Maisky (Ref. R.2515/178/G) of 27th April 1942. (Copy in White Paper Dossier.)

spring fighting each other'; 'I realise that in the circumstances it is difficult for the Soviet Government to maintain any control over those "Communists": it seems to me, however, that a word of authority broadcast from Moscow would probably carry influence with them.'

There is nothing to show what the Soviet Government made of this sort of stuff; it is unlikely that they even suspected that it was put forward in all truth and innocence as between Allies. It may well be that there was a real change in Soviet policy at about this time. When Moscow was under immediate threat in the late autumn of 1941, the Russians themselves had taken the initiative in pressing the British to assist the Yugoslav insurgents, irrespective of their political colour;[1] but in April 1942 things looked better and a more considered policy was possible. Already M. Bogomolov, the Soviet Ambassador to the Yugoslav government in exile, was expressing doubt to his British colleagues about Mihailovitch's *bona fides* and was asserting that the Soviet Government did not intend to get mixed up in Yugoslav quarrels.[2]

Events were developing fast within Yugoslavia. The Partisans had been attacked again in Bosnia in January 1942 and were driven south into Montenegro (the 'second offensive'); there was more fighting there from March to May (the 'third offensive') and they were again forced to shift their ground. It is probable that each of their moves involved 'incidents' with Mihailovitch's troops or with the fringe of 'Cetniks' who could plausibly be described as Mihailovitch's troops. Certainly Mihailovitch kept up a ceaseless barrage of complaint against the Communists; and evidence from independent sources began to accumulate which showed pretty conclusively that the Partisans were engaged in heavy fighting with Axis troops and that Mihailovitch was not. It is also probable that at this stage Moscow established direct contact with Tito by wireless; a member of the Soviet Embassy staff (one Lebedev) may have been with him from the beginning. Early in the summer a 'Free Yugoslav' wireless station began to broadcast from the neighbourhood of Moscow; it issued 'Partisan communiqués' which showed very recent knowledge of the situation, and it heartily adopted the Partisan line of violent attack on Mihailovitch as a traitor and assassin. It is quite impossible to say whether the Partisans dragged Moscow into supporting civil war, or whether the influence was the other way. There is no doubt that by June 1942 at latest the Russian Government was fully committed to exclusive support of Tito.

---

[1] Above p. 120.

[2] Letter from Sir George Rendel to Mr Howard, Southern Department, d/d 28th April 1942.

Matters came to an open diplomatic break in July. Early in July Mr Eden directed Sir A. Clark Kerr* in Moscow to approach the Soviet Government once more with a view to a combined effort to stop the civil war.[1] Later on the same day Mr Eden saw M. Maisky, who gave a blank refusal based on his Government's knowledge that Mihailovitch was in touch with the Quisling Government of General Nedič. The instructions to Sir A. Clark Kerr were cancelled, but Mr Eden tried again on 27th July, when M. Maisky was presented with an Aide-Mémoire[2] setting out that Mihailovitch had always admitted, and had claimed it as a source of strength, that many of Nedič's officers were loyal to him; such tactics were not to be regarded as evidence of bad faith. The Soviet answer to this was the submission of a memorandum which they had presented to the Yugoslav Ambassador in Moscow, bluntly accusing Mihailovitch of treason.[3] Replies to this were sent by Mr Eden on 20th August,[4] and by the Yugoslav Government on 2nd September; and there the correspondence ceased.

This open break marked the beginning of a new phase. It was pretty clear that the Partisans existed and were fighting. It was also clear that the Russians would not intervene to stop the civil war; if it was to be stopped, the British must intervene themselves. This indicated that some method must he found of making independent contact with the Partisans. In addition, the military situation had changed. In October 1941 the Yugoslav revolt was 'premature', more trouble than it was worth; now the North African landing was in prospect it was worth supporting any diversion which could distract German attention and pin down their troops. Just at this time the Greek guerilla movement was beginning, and a good deal was being done to assist it and to incite it to attacks on German communications. So long as North Africa was in Vichy hands and the 8th Army stood behind Alamein, Yugoslavia was too far away to receive assistance on a similar scale; but Yugoslav resistance was strategically even more important than that of Greece. It became therefore a strategic question of some importance to decide whether the Partisans or Mihailovitch were the better military investment.

The internal memoranda which passed within SOE (both in London and in Cairo) on the subject were endless, and were based on so little fresh evidence that it is hardly necessary to summarise them. The best

---

[1] Telegram R.4400/G of 13th July, in White Paper Dossier.

[2] Aide-Mémoire of 21st July 1942.

[3] Letter of 5th August 1942, in White Paper Dossier.

[4] Letter No. 5254/178/G of 20th August 1942, in White Paper Dossier.

* [A. J. K. Clark Kerr, 1882–1951, knight 1935, Ambassador to Iraq 1935–8, China 1938–42, USSR 1942–5, Lord Inverchapel 1946; in *DNB*.]

of them is perhaps a paper produced by Mr Hugh Seton-Watson* in Cairo on 9th November 1942.[1] It is a cool and realistic explanation of Yugoslav internal politics between the wars, and the way in which they were likely to work out under the occupation; and it is odd and interesting, in view of Mr Seton Watson's record, that Brigadier Keble,** SOE's Chief of Staff in Cairo, should have noted on it – 'the attached is an excellent appreciation, written, I should say, by a Communist and one who is definitely anti-Mihailovitch'.

In fact, although there was a certain ideological flavour about the debates, SOE was not internally divided on ideological lines, and its action was settled within narrow limits by the facts of the situation. It was not possible to make any immediate contribution to Allied strategy except by using Mihailovitch, since we had no communications with the Partisans. It could hardly seriously be proposed (after nine failures with 'Captain Robertson') that a new mission should be dropped blind in Partisan territory – no one knew what was Partisan territory – until the existing connection with Mihailovitch had been fully tested. Furthermore, it was clearly necessary to relieve Hudson, who had been in the field in severe conditions for a year, and to send in a new senior officer, if possible one with greater political experience, as soon as possible. The field of choice was not large, and in the end the man selected was Colonel W. S. Bailey, another mining engineer, then thirty-seven years old, who had been a right-hand man of Colonel Hanau in the old D Section days in Belgrade, had played a prominent part in the SOE organisation in Middle East, and had been withdrawn to other duties (under a slight cloud) in the reorganisation of August 1941.[2] His mission was decided in September 1942, but for various reasons he did not reach Yugoslavia until Christmas Day 1942; for the present the whole complex responsibility rested on the shoulders of Captain Hudson.

---

1 Copy on SOE Archives File 18/360/30 (Colonel Bailey's papers).
2 Below p. 180.
* [G. H. N. Seton-Watson, 1916–84, son of R. W., recruited in Belgrade, at SOE Cairo 1941–4, professor of Russian history, university of London 1951–83, author; in *DNB*.]
** [C. M. Keble, died 1945. See page 189.]

CHAPTER VII

Operations in Greece[1]

In the early stages of the war the position of Greece differed from that of the other Balkan countries in that no German communications of vital importance ran through it; nor was German property there of sufficient value to make a case for violent action in a friendly neutral country. In addition, Greece was not under immediate strategic pressure from Germany; the enemy on her borders was the Italian Army in Albania (occupied at Easter 1939), and the Metaxas* Government never showed any weakness for the Italians, though by temperament and tradition it had little antipathy to Germans or to Nazism.

To begin with, therefore, the roles of D Section and MI(R) were comparatively passive. In Greece itself it was enough to frame long-term plans for action in the event of occupation, and to purvey anti-Italian propaganda to a very willing market: the only activity which might cause trouble was the use of Greece as a transit point for activities into the other Balkan countries (in particular Albania), and into the Dodecanese.

A D Section representative, one Shotton, of the Ingersoll Rand Company, was appointed in September 1939, but he was employed only part-time and does not seem to have been very effective. Mr Goodwill visited Greece in April and May 1940, and made much more elaborate arrangements, some of which stood the test of time. There is a record[2] of his discussions on 15th April with HM Minister (Sir Michael Palairet),** who 'absolutely declined to have his diplomatic

---

[1] The events in the field for this period of Greek affairs are covered by a narrative by Mr Ian Pirie, which contains an excellent collection of material, though its conclusions should be accepted only *cum grano*. [See also Phyllis Auty and Richard Clogg (eds), *British Policy Towards Wartime Resistance in Yugoslavia and Greece* (1975), C. M. Woodhouse, *The Struggle for Greece 1941–1949* (1976), and Mark Mazower, *Inside Hitler's Greece* (1994).]

[2] On SOE Archives File 19/340/1.

* [I. Metaxas, 1871–1941, general, dictator of Greece from 4 August 1936.]

** [C. M. Palairet, 1882–1956, Minister in Vienna 1937–8, knight 1938, Minister in Athens 1939, retreated with King of Greece 1941, Ambassador to Greek government in exile 1942–3; in *DNB*.]

mission involved in our work in any way which might conceivably compromise it with the Greek Government'. This meant that the organisation must be built up under business cover, and a number of leading members of the British community were enlisted under the cover name of 'Apostles'.[1] The 'No. 1', known as 'Mark', was chief engineer of the Athens and Piraeus Tramways Trust, a British Company, and the inner circle included the Lloyd's agent and two engineers connected with the Lake Copais reclamation scheme. A full-time officer was to be sent out from London under the cover of ARP officer for the British community, to act as No. 2; Mr Ian Pirie arrived in this role on 31st May, having been specially flown out to the Middle East. The organisation added to itself British residents in Salonika, (Major Menzies, the British War Graves Commissioner), in Patras, and in Jannina (near the Albanian border). About the same time Major Barbrook joined the Legation as representative of MI(R), and Mr Pendlebury,* a famous expert in Aegean archaeology, returned to Crete on their behalf.

The D organisation received with Pirie a directive[2] from Major Taylor – a comprehensive essay which must have been somewhat alarming to an organisation newly recruited from the business world. Summarised briefly it covers:

(a) *Communications and Supplies* 'This is a matter of using Greece as a channel of communication for the supplying of materials to other countries in south-east Europe, and particularly Yugoslavia.'

(b) *Sabotage work in Greece* 'Our object here is to put ourselves in a position where useful sabotage could be carried out in Greece itself *after* she has been involved in the War – which in practice means after an Italian invasion. I cannot emphasise too strongly that, as things are at present, we are not allowed to commit any acts of sabotage in Greece which would be against the interests of the Greek Government' – including their interest in maintaining their neutrality.

(c) *Albania* 'There is, of course, no need to emphasise how delicate this job is and how cautiously we must proceed.'

(d) *Other anti-Italian Activities*
  (i) Corfu
  (ii) Dodecanese.

---

[1] See Goodwill's Report of 16th May, and further report 'received 19/5/40', on SOE Archives File 19/340/1.

[2] Dated 25th May and quoted in full in Pirie's narrative, p. 5.

* [See page 144.]

(e) *Underground Propaganda* 'I do not know how far such work would be:

(a) practicable in Greece, or

(b) desirable from the point of view of our wish not to antagonise the Greek Government. We can come to a decision when I arrive'

(on the tour which Major Taylor carried out shortly afterwards).

This first organisation seems to have been somewhat shaken by two or three unlucky incidents in its early stages. An attempt to smuggle explosives into Albania was 'blown', luckily without involving any British subject, and a firm directive was received from C-in-C Middle East, on 6th July, telling D to avoid all trouble on the Albanian border.[1] A Greek MI(R) agent who was put into Crete to contact anti-Metaxas politicians was caught at once, and could only be extricated with difficulty.[2] A cargo of scrap-iron, doctored with explosive, which had been loaded with Jewish assistance at Haifa, failed to secure delivery to the German consignees for whom it was intended, and finished up in the Piraeus, where it proved a particularly exasperating white elephant.[3] None of these incidents were the fault of the 'Apostles', but they cut rather near the quick for respectable businessmen, and it seems to have been agreed informally at the D Section Conference at Istanbul on 26th/27th August[4] that Pirie should quietly take over the duties of No. 1 in Athens.

Italian intentions became fairly plain from 15th August 1940, when the Greek cruiser 'Hellé' was torpedoed without provocation and without warning while at anchor off Tenos, and para-military preparations became progressively easier, although the Italian attack was not launched until 28th October. At the same time SO2 became for the first time involved in Greek politics, on lines which were very significant later. Pirie himself attributes this turn in part to his growing knowledge[5] of the complexities of the situation through intimacy with Mr Graham Sebastian,* the British Consul-General, and the honorary Vice-Consul, Mr Thomas Bowman; in part to a visit from Colonel S. W. Bailey in the latter part of October 1940,[6] which impressed him

---

[1] Greek History (Pirie), pp. 16–17.

[2] Greek History (Pirie), pp. 17–18.

[3] Greek History (Pirie), pp. 18–19.

[4] Minutes on SOE Archives File 19/340/1, and Greek History (Pirie), p. 21.

[5] Greek History (Pirie), pp. 21, 28.

[6] See Colonel Bailey's personal report to Major Taylor, dated 18th November 1940, on SOE Archives File 19/330/22.

* [E. G. Sebastian, 1892–1978, Consul-General Athens 1940–41, Gothenburg 1942–4, Antwerp 1944–50, Milan 1950–52.]

with the political work being done in other Balkan countries.[1] It was specially laid down by Bailey that 'any political activity, as opposed to soundings, must be frankly discussed with HM Minister', and financial support for such work would only be forthcoming from London if the Minister agreed:[2] no evidence has come to hand of any authority going beyond this. Nothing more than 'sounding' was contemplated and little money was spent; but even these first steps coloured later events.

The reasons which made these approaches very desirable from the local SO2 point of view are hard to set out without a comprehensive essay on Greek politics; and Greek politics are almost inexplicable except in terms of personalities. Thucydides' chapter in Book III of his History, on the civil strife in Corfu in the fifth century BC, is still as good an introduction as any. Class division counts for something, and so do local differences. Almost everyone is interested in politics, yet there had hitherto been little true political organisation either locally or on a class basis; régimes and Ministries rose and fell through the dealings of a relatively small number of army officers, civil servants, and professional politicians, all intimately acquainted with one another's family history and political record. The only constant division was between the 'Ins' and the 'Outs'; this line of cleavage varied very rapidly, but each past division had left deep traces in Greek memories. There was (first) the division between pro-German monarchists and pro-British monarchists – King Constantine and King Alexander;* then when the German issue was no longer present, there was a new division between the monarchy and the republic, which was set up in 1922, on the ruins of the Greek adventure in Asia Minor, and maintained itself stormily until 1935: a final cleavage was added by the King's support of the Metaxas régime of 4th August 1936, which rested on '4,000 men with 4,000 tommy-guns' and proscribed a very wide range of opposition leaders, in the Army, judiciary and Civil Service, as well as in political circles. To complete the confusion, the Metaxas proscriptions were justified to the public as the suppression of an impending Communist revolution, although the Communist Party had been practically negligible as a factor in Greek politics. There was plenty of hatred of the rich, and Communist methods made some appeal to the conspiratorial genius of the Greeks; but Communist doctrines were almost

---

[1] Greek History (Pirie), p. 44.
[2] Greek History (Pirie), p. 46.
* [1893–1920, King of the Hellenes during first abdication of his father, Constantine. Constantine, 1868–1923, married 1889 a sister of Kaiser Wilhelm II, King 1913–17, resumed throne on his son's death, re-abdicated 1922.]

meaningless to the Cretans, the islanders and the more comfortable peasants, while the mountain villages and the town workers were as yet scarcely within the ambit of political calculation. It remains to be seen whether the conditions of the Resistance have permanently changed their political status.

The personalities through which this confusion was expressed are innumerable, and their personal relations are always obscure and frequently important. It may be useful to insert here a brief key to those of general importance in this phase.

Metaxas himself was essentially King Constantine's man: a staff officer trained in the best German school, successful professionally in the Balkan wars, and marked politically by his very well-reasoned opposition to intervention on the Allied side in the 1914 war, and to Venizelos's vision of a new Byzantine empire of the Aegean directed by the Greeks.

Panagiotis Kanellopoulos was a Professor of Political Economy at Athens: more significantly he was the nephew of King Constantine's Prime Minister, Goumaris, who had been executed after the fiasco of the Turkish War in 1922. He was founder and leader of the small and recent 'Party of National Union', which opposed Metaxas, but stood for national unity (with a touch of Liberalism) behind the King.

General Gonatas and General Plastiras had as Colonels gained some glory in the campaign against the Turks in Asia Minor, essentially a 'Venizelial' war. In September 1922 they made the coup d'état which expelled King Constantine for the second time, and after it they were responsible for the execution of certain of his Ministers, a serious breach with the traditions of Greek politics, which were (by Balkan standards) very merciful to fallen enemies. The military régime which followed had been primarily that of Plastiras, who in December 1923 expelled also Constantine's successor King George II, after an abortive attempt by Metaxas to make a coup d'état in the King's interest. Gonatas was now living quietly in Athens, at peace with the restored régime of George II. Plastiras was of tougher metal: he had been implicated in the futile Venizelist 'putsches' of March 1933 and March 1935, and was now in exile in France.

Colonel Bakirdzis, the 'Red Colonel', belonged to a rather younger generation, and had also been associated with these Venizelist 'coups'.

General Pangalos is chiefly known as the 'dictator' who had seized power at the expense of the Republic in June 1925, and had himself been ignominiously expelled by *General Kondylis* in August 1926. Pangalos' political position is obscured: he had overthrown a Venizelist government, but his enemy Kondylis (who does not appear in this story) had been largely responsible for the restoration of George II in November 1935. Pangalos was thus deemed to be of the Right, but not wholly committed to the Metaxas régime.

The mantle of *Venizelos** had been parted between many heirs, whose claims could with difficulty be reconciled. Of these we need mention here only *Sophocles Venizelos*, now in exile, a son who inherited little but his father's name: *Sophoulis*, a very old and very energetic islander from Samos, who had been a leader in politics since that island was part of the Turkish Empire: *Kaphandaris*, who had made a creditable showing as leader of the Venizelist party before the somewhat irresponsible resurrection of the great man himself in 1928.

To this perhaps should be added some mention of the 'Popular Party', associated with the name of *Tsaldaris* the elder, who had led it as a constitutional Conservative party, hostile to Venizelos and favourable to the monarchy but not to military intrigue or non-Parliamentary rule: it had naturally abetted and welcomed the restoration of George II in 1935, but it was not as a party associated with the semi-Fascist claptrap of Metaxas' dictatorship. The nephew of the older Tsaldaris appears as its leader, and eventually as the King's Prime Minister from the elections of April 1946 to January 1947.

This very incomplete outline may suggest why it was essential to look beyond the Metaxas régime when seeking a basis for action in the event of German attack and for the occupation which would inevitably follow it. The Metaxas régime had responded fairly well to the Italian attack; Greek opinion was almost solidly resolved on resistance and proud of its success, and Metaxas went some distance in conciliating the 'Outs'. A large number of politicians were released from internment in the islands, and a number of proscribed officers returned to their posts, though only in the lower commissioned ranks. But if one looked further ahead, prospects were bad. The Metaxas clique was well penetrated by German sympathisers, and it was doubtful if it would stand up at all in face of a German attack. If Metaxas did not fight, a coup d'état might be necessary to displace it, and its success would have been as popular as that of the similar coup in Yugoslavia. But even if Metaxas fought, his Government would be useless as a government in exile: German propaganda could make havoc of its record, and there were plenty of Greek politicians who would come in readily enough on a German programme of 'Down with Metaxas'. On a less political level, there was little or nothing to be hoped for in the way of determined underground work either from the Metaxas party or from the normal run of politicians; day-to-day sabotage could only be carried out by unknown 'men of the people', with the tacit support of ordinary Greeks, not of the politicians of Athens.

---

* [E. K. Venizelos, 1864–1936, Cretan, repeatedly Prime Minister of Greece, a strong liberal.]

This train of thought led to contacts in various quarters,[1] which seem roughly to have been as follows:

(a) The first of them was between the 'Apostles' representative in Salonika and the Zannas family; three sons of a father who had been prominent in Macedonian affairs since before 1914. The oldest of these, George, was head of the Greek Red Cross; the second, Alexander, was a politician and controlled what was left of the Venizelist party machine in Macedonia and Thrace. This provided a ready-made organisation which was useful later.[2]

(b) Contacts were also made with politicians of various shades of anti-Metaxas feeling who had returned to Athens from exile in October; General Pangalos and Professor Panagiotis Kanellopoulos are perhaps the best known. It was suggested that contact should be made with General Plastiras in Nice and with Sophocles Venizelos in New York; both suggestions were turned down by London Headquarters.[3]

(c) Pirie's assistant, Pawson, was in touch from January 1941 through a violently anti-Metaxas lady, Miss Elli Papadimitriou, with the well-known 'Red Colonel', Colonel Bakirdzis (Prometheus I), who had been 'purged' after the abortive revolt of 1935;[4] his views were radical Republican rather than 'Red', but he was more a man of action than SO2's other contacts in the political world, and he was therefore from SO2's point of view a rational choice as head of their main post-occupational

---

[1] Very neatly set out in this chart by Pawson, drawn up in August 1941: on SOE Archives File 19/340/2:

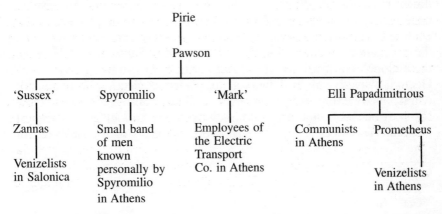

[2] Greek History (Pirie), p. 22.
[3] Telegram of 9th November 1940, quoted in Greek History (Pirie), p. 47.
[4] Greek History (Pirie), p. 97.

organisation. To him and his friends was entrusted the only wireless set available, which was handed over at the very last moment on 24th April;[1] and they also had access to a stock of some $1\frac{1}{2}$ tons of sabotage stores, made up in suitable containers with money and instructions, and distributed and hidden before the British evacuation. This was the 'Prometheus' organisation of which more will be heard in the sequel. Its most active individual member was Prometheus II, Lieutenant Commander Koutsoyannopoulos, RHN, also a victim of the 1935 purge.

(d) Pirie mentions[2] that 'we also left in Athens supplies and a small amount of cash with certain Communists (probably), also recruited for us by Elli Papadimitriou, and with certain men recruited for us by Milto Spyromilio'. This is the only evidence of any Communist connection at this stage, and nothing more was heard of this line of contact.

(e) 'Mark', the chief engineer of the Tramways Company, arranged for some twenty tough working-men among his employees to be given training at the small sabotage school set up by SO2 on Suda Island off Crete. These men were an isolated and non-political group, and were not likely to be a nucleus of expansion. The one trainee of this school who appears prominently in the story was a certain Gherassimos (or 'Odysseus'), a smuggler and small-boat sailor of much resource and doubtful reputation, who was employed by SO2 before the fall of Crete to establish a series of ports-of-call for caique traffic across the Aegean; these proved invaluable later.

These political activities consumed comparatively little of the Mission's time during the winter of the Italian campaign. It was laid down[3] by Brigadier Whiteley, who visited Athens on General Wavell's behalf early in November 1940, that MI(R) (still controlled by HQ, Middle East) should operate in Crete, D Section (now under SO2) on the mainland; a gloss was added which gave D Section the islands of the archipelago, including its school on the island in Suda Bay. When General Wavell was in Athens a little later, D Section were forbidden[4] to move explosives in the area south and west of the Vardar even for post-occupational use, and they were put under the orders of General Heywood* of the British Military Mission for sabotage or

---

[1] Greek History (Pirie), p. 112: and SOE Archives File 19/340/2 – paper entitled 'Proposed SO2 Activities in Crete and Occupied Greece', dated 19th May 1941.

[2] Greek History (Pirie), p. 97.

[3] Greek History (Pirie), p. 38.

[4] Greek History (Pirie), p. 94.

* [T.G.G. Heywood, 1886–1943, in Russia 1939, in Holland 1940, in Greece 1940–41, retired in India.]

demolition to be conducted in Greece during an enemy advance; they retained, however, full discretion to lay plans for sabotage after an enemy occupation, without consultation with the Greek Government or General Staff. The position became plainer[1] early in 1941, when British troops began to land and the policy of holding the Olympus line was agreed. Anything north of that line became the responsibility of the Greeks themselves and of the British Military Mission assisted by D Section; south of the line demolition before evacuation was a British military responsibility, to be executed in part through MI(R), if so determined by the C-in-C.

When the German advance began, Menzies and Alexander Zannas, in company with Major West's party of sappers, did a very thorough job of demolition in the Salonica area, including the harbour and harbour defences.[2] There was more difficulty in Athens, where the city power station and the oil stocks in the Piraeus were left undamaged. The controversy over responsibility for this did not really concern either D Section or MI(R), though the Minister felt called upon to defend them; the position was apparently that the Greeks, from the King downwards, were prepared to resist by force if necessary, and that General Heywood was not prepared to use force to overcome resistance.[3]

The demolition of the Corinth Canal had also some 'high-level' history, which need not be pursued in detail. The idea had been proposed and vetoed after considerable dispute while Greece was still at peace,[4] and discussion of how a block-ship could be obtained was proceeding slowly when Italy attacked Greece. Greek co-operation in demolition was very doubtful, and when the time came a rather ramshackle arrangement was improvised by which Lieutenant Commander Cumberlege took D Section's auxiliary schooner 'Dolphin' through the canal on 26th April and unostentatiously sank a dinghy laden with $2\frac{1}{2}$ tons of explosive. The explosive was well primed with delayed action fuses set to go off about six days later; it is not clear what happened, but apparently something went wrong, as the demolition was at best only partially effective.[5]

[1] Greek History (Pirie), p. 99.

[2] Menzies' Report dated 30th April 1941, in Greek History (Pirie), p. 101.

[3] See Pirie's Report of 5th May, in Greek History (Pirie), p. 104: Cairo telegram of 29th May (Pirie), p. 109: and Pirie's own account at p. 110. See also London HQ papers, including Mr Dalton's Minute to the Prime Minister of 10th June, on SOE Archives File (AD/S.1) HD/61.

[4] Greek History (Pirie), p. 35.

[5] Pirie's report of 5th May 1940, in Greek History (Pirie), p. 106; and Memo. of 8th September 1942 on File HD/F.61 Pt II.

Action into the Dodecanese and Albania was not very successful and left few traces. Various contacts were made with exiled Dodecanesians but (to quote Pirie) 'our researches soon unearthed no fewer than twenty-four secret societies in Athens for the recovery of the Twelve Islands'[1] – none of them very serious bodies. Some caiques were also bought with the idea of 'trading voyages' to explore the lie of the land, but this project was cut short by the Italian attack and there was no organisation in existence which could be of any value in war.

Albanian affairs were equally complex and slightly less negative; some propaganda was distributed, some arms were smuggled, and small raids were made on the Italians by Albanians from the hills – there was a report, for instance, passed on by Mr Dalton to the Prime Minister, that the Italian Governor's Palace at Tirana had been looted by Albanians in January 1941.[2] But no British agents were sent in, and there was no question of any general Albanian revolt, such as was planned by the British 'co-ordinating committee' at Istanbul, under Colonel Stirling,* formerly of the Albanian gendarmerie.[3] The opportunity might have come when Yugoslavia entered the war and the Italian forces were momentarily in a position of extreme difficulty. Major Oakley Hill then set off with a band of Albanians from the Yugoslav side, but circumstances turned against the Allies almost at once; the party was dispersed and Major Oakley Hill was captured.

D Section's share in the organisation of British propaganda in Greece was substantial and enterprising, on the usual lines of clandestine leaflets, unauthorised bill-posting, whispering campaigns. Relations with the Director of Publicity (Mr Gerard Young) and the Press Attaché (Mr David Wallace) were excellent, with the Services less good, and it was not till January 1941[4] that a Propaganda Committee was created to bring all British interests together. Propaganda is writ in water, even when it is good propaganda, and it would be useless now to try to estimate the value of what was done. The most novel enterprise,[5] and one which bore some fruits, was that of 'pan-Balkan' broadcasts from Greece, a project which was warmly taken up by the Greek Government once they were at

---

[1] Greek History (Pirie), p. 23.
[2] See the Prime Minister's letter of 20th January 1941, on SOE Archives File 1/470/1.
[3] Greek History (Pirie), p. 41.
[4] Greek History (Pirie), p. 69. SOE Archives File 19/270/01 refers to this Committee, with comments and copies of some of the Minutes.
[5] See Searight's Report of 4th November 1940, in Greek History (Pirie), p. 59.
* [W. F. Stirling, 1880–1958, fought in South Africa, in Gallipoli and with Lawrence, adviser to Albanian Government 1932–3, in Syria 1942–9, narrowly surviving attack in 1949, died in Tangier; in *DNB*. See his *Safety Last* (1953).]

war with Italy. Colonel Bailey saw in this the germ of the future 'Jerusalem station', for which he had been collecting potential broadcasters in various Balkan countries: 'I intend', he wrote on 8th November 1940,[1] 'the service to serve principally as a training ground for the pan-Balkan station which I propose setting up . . . should it be necessary to institute this after the occupation of the Balkans.' This was officially a Greek service, but British influence on it was very strong through various channels, and 'come-backs' from the Balkans were favourable.[2] Once British troops were established in Greece, Pirie began to press matters further, with the object of opening Britain's own broadcasting station in Greece – 'The Voice of Britain speaking from Greece'.[3] Matters were hastened by the Yugoslav coup d'état of 27th March 1941, and the Yugoslavs then also interested themselves in the idea of 'time on the air' under their own control. The station actually went into operation on 7th April,[4] using a spare transmitter borrowed from 'Cables and Wireless'; but the main Balkan speakers were marked men who had to be evacuated as soon as German occupation became probable, and the 'Voice of Britain' was soon silenced. But, as had been planned, some of the speakers turned up again in the various 'Freedom Stations' established in Palestine.

This brings us to the military débâcle in Greece, and the political thread must be resumed.

It should be made clear that the account given here is based solely on papers in the SOE archives from London and Cairo, which include only a small part of the Foreign Office material, and practically nothing on the work of SIS and MI9. The story is told from SOE's point of view, although not biassed in its favour: a complete narrative of British policy would require much further research.

General Metaxas had died suddenly on 29th January 1941,[5] but the problem of reconstructing his government had been shirked, and the Premiership had been taken over by M. Koryzis with no serious change of personnel or policy. M. Koryzis committed suicide on 18th April 1941 as the German breakthrough became complete: Greece was left without a government, and it was essential that one should be formed

---

1 Greek History (Pirie), p. 61.
2 Bailey's letter of 27th November: Greek History (Pirie), p. 62.
3 Empax No. 69 of 12th March, and Pirie's telegram of 15th March refer. Greek History (Pirie), p. 83, and SOE Archives File 19/270/01 – letter from Pirie to Taylor dated 30th March 1941.
4 Greek History (Pirie), p. 88.
5 See account of the circumstances in Greek History (Pirie), p. 53, and his report of 7th February 1941, on SOE Archives File 19/100/43 'Greece Political'.

at short notice to maintain the continuity of the Greek state, which it was hoped could be maintained on Greek soil in Crete. It was impossible to go very far to the Left, as the C-in-C insisted[1] on security grounds on the temporary retention of Maniadakis, Metaxas's Minister of the Interior and the 'Himmler' of the régime, who was personally distasteful to those whom he had 'purged' – including almost all the Moderate politicians in Greece. After hasty and intricate negotiations, the post was accepted by M. Tsouderos, a Venizelist banker of Cretan origin, who had been one of the victims of the Metaxas purge.[2] But few other politicians of the same colour could be found to join; Maniadakis and his friends were removed when the Government reached Crete, but in spite of this M. Tsouderos came to be regarded pretty early as a renegade in the Royalist camp rather than a representative of the Venizelists.

The SO2 party was successfully evacuated to Crete by caique on 29th April, with one disaster: the loss of the caique 'Irene' with the codes and signal plan for the wireless set which had been left with Koutsoyannopoulos (Prometheus II), the only prearranged link available.[3] In Crete an SO2 Headquarters was established at Canea and a fresh start was made. The programme is described in a telegram[4] from Cairo to London dated 22nd May, which embodied the result of discussion with General Wavell. There was no opportunity to execute this programme, and the only point of interest is that it clearly laid down that the Greek Government should not be taken into consultation regarding the use of the organisation left by SO2 on the mainland.

The party reached Egypt safely on the fall of Crete, with the exception of Pendlebury, who had been seriously wounded and was shot in his bed by the Germans as soon as he was identified. Another serious mishap was that contact was lost with 'Odysseus', on whom Pirie had been relying to act as courier to the organisation in Athens, and it was some months before he reappeared. After this evacuation the only British officer who deliberately remained in Greece was Captain O'Brien McNabb,[5] an MI(R) representative evacuated from Bucharest, who had volunteered to remain in the Peloponnese to assist in the evacuation of British stragglers and to organise guerilla activities if possible. He did good work and remained at large for many months,

---

[1] Greek History (Pirie), p. 55.

[2] See Pirie's version of the circumstances, Greek History (Pirie), p. 55 ff.

[3] Pirie's report on the evacuation sent to London HQ on 9th May 1941 is on SOE Archives File 19/340/2. Papers on this file give clear picture of the reorganisation of SO2 (Greece) after the German drive.

[4] Greek History (Pirie), p. 120.

[5] Greek History (Pirie), pp. 111, 122.

but wireless contact was never established; eventually he was betrayed and captured about May 1942.[1]

Even after the occupation of Crete, Greece was in many ways easier territory for SO2 than the other Balkan countries. Caique traffic in the Aegean could not be stopped or fully controlled by the enemy without destroying the livelihood of the population, and a fairly continuous stream of Greek refugees, generally with some political affiliations, reached Turkey and other countries in the Levant without the aid of any British organisation. Caique traffic in the reverse direction was also a relatively easy matter compared with work in Yugoslavia, Bulgaria and Roumania. In addition, there were large and wealthy Greek communities in Egypt and other countries of the Levant. An atmosphere of active politics therefore followed the Greek government into exile, and they only evaded it temporarily by moving first to South Africa, then to London in September 1941. It is understood that the Egyptians were not then willing to have an exiled government established in their territory; but Palestine was available, and it is not clear why the Greek Government should have moved to London except to strengthen their own position by closer contact with the British authorities and by relief from active Greek political pressure in the Levant.

Little emerged during the first months in Cairo, except for the establishment, with the co-operation of the Greek Government, of a training school at Haifa for Greeks who would work back into Greece. This was under the charge of Major Barbrook, MI(R)'s former representative in Athens; and the King's brother, Prince Peter, was nominated as chief liaison officer.[2] An effective British organisation only began to emerge when SOE's affairs were taken over by Mr Terence Maxwell in August 1941. His first organisation will be referred to in detail later; in essence it amalgamated D Section (now the Directorate of Policy and Agents), MI(R) (now the Directorate of Special Operations), and SO1 and GS1(K) (now the Directorate of Subversive Propaganda), without seriously modifying their roles.[3] Colonel Masterson, formerly of Belgrade, became Director of Policy and Agents, with Pirie and Pawson in charge of his Greek Section. At the same time their old friends Sebastian and Bowman, Consul-General and honorary Vice-Consul in Athens, became 'Advisers on Greek affairs to the British Embassy in Cairo',[4] later transferred to the

---

[1] Greek History (Pirie), p. 319. See also Athens telegram CX.22640/41 of 30th April and a narrative by M. Asimakopoulos dated 10th December, both on SOE Archives File (AD/S.1) HD/61.

[2] Greek History (Pirie), p. 125.

[3] See Greek History (Pirie), p. 130: and below pp. 182–3.

[4] Notes on conversations between Bowman and Tsouderos are reported to London under date 6th June 1941; copy on SOE Archives File 19/340/2.

Minister of State's office: they worked very closely with a certain Milto Spyromilio, an old SOE contact, who had been left in Cairo by M. Tsouderos as his personal representative for all subversive matters.[1] The senior Greek Minister in the Middle East at this stage was Admiral Sakellariou, Vice-President of the Council and Minister of Marine, who was politically marked as a man who had not been purged by Metaxas.

Behind everything that follows is a bitter controversy as to whether SOE's representatives in Cairo took upon themselves more than was implied in their general directive, which authorised them to take all action possible to damage the Italians and Germans in Greece by stimulating resistance: in particular whether they were led to pursue a foreign policy of their own which conflicted with that of His Majesty's Government. The Foreign Office policy was one of firm support to King George* provided he stood by Great Britain; it went back at least to Mr Eden's visit to Athens in the first days of March 1941, and the later documents are summarised in a Foreign Office print of 26th February 1942.[2] The following indicates the position in October 1941: 'It was laid down by the Secretary of State (after discussion between King George and Mr Churchill) that our policy is to support the King of Greece and the present Greek Government. In fact, we are pledged to see them through to the end. It was recognised that if the King and the present Government were to be received back into Greece, we must work for a Greece united in support of their King and Government, and we are entitled therefore to expect that the Greek Government should not antagonise their nationals . . . . To ensure this the King and Government must themselves do all they could to dissipate the mistrust which undoubtedly existed as to their political intentions.'

Within the limits of this policy, it was clearly legitimate – indeed essential – that SOE, which was in a position to be well-informed, should submit its views regarding the concessions required to 'dissipate mistrust'. Such 'mistrust' was plainly a dangerous obstruction to SOE's work in Greece, and it would probably also be legitimate that SOE should use such influence as it possessed to bring about the concessions necessary to remove it. But these concessions, it turned out, would not be made willingly by the Tsouderos Government, and SOE was therefore early marked down as a centre of influence hostile

---

[1] Greek History (Pirie), p. 127. List of SOE personnel working in Greek Section Cairo as at 18th September 1941 on SOE Archives File 19/340/2.

[2] R.1362/112/19 of 26th February 1942 'The Greek Constitutional Question, April 1941–February 1942'; copy on SOE Archives File (AD/S.1) HD/F.61 Vol. 2.

* [George II, 1890–1947, King of the Hellenes 1922–4 and 1935–47.]

to that régime. This led on to accusations that SOE had gone a step beyond the limits of its duty; that it was not only reporting the existence of mistrust, but was deliberately exaggerating it and was even fomenting it for political purposes of its own – in fact that SOE was pursuing a foreign policy contrary to that of His Majesty's Government.

These charges of deliberate malice certainly go much too far. On the other hand, it is important to realise that SOE was placed in a position of serious embarrassment between two masters – the Foreign Office, whose primary aim was to maintain the monarchy in Greece, both as a matter of pledged loyalty to an excellent ally, and as a matter of long-term policy; and the soldiers, whose only concern was to hit the enemy as hard as possible wherever he might be found. By temperament, the leaders of SOE leant towards the latter view. Three quotations will suffice to illustrate this. On the Foreign Office side: 'It is the sincere belief of His Majesty's Government that the best interests of the Greek people will be served by the return of the King, since they believe that a liberal constitutional monarchy is likely to be the régime best suited to Greece . . . . A democratic régime from which the moral and symbolic force of monarchy is lacking would be likely in the future, as in the past, to perpetuate in Greece those internal political dissensions to which the Greek people throughout their history have been prone.'[1] On the SOE side: 'SOE is interested only in promoting unity inside Greece for the purpose of resisting the occupying forces and in organising eventual revolt, and we are not interested in post-war Greece.'[2] Or this – 'There is thus a very clear conflict between the policy for SOE as determined by the interests of the C-in-C and that imposed upon us by the Foreign Office under pressure from the Greek Government. On any intelligible theory of SOE's functions and certainly on the theory which is both explicitly and implicitly contained in our treaty with the Foreign Office, the interests of the military authorities, so far as SOE's work is concerned, should certainly prevail in enemy-occupied countries, and to put it bluntly, I do not think we are entitled to take a directive from the Foreign Office which is flagrantly at variance with the requirements of the C-in-C, without at least referring the matter to the Chiefs of Staff.'[3]

---

[1] Foreign Office to Washington No. 3337 of 24th May 1942, à propos of the possible attitude of M. Sophocles Venizelos; copy on SOE Archives File 19/100/61.

[2] Letter from Lieutenant Colonel Boxshall to Colonel Masterson, on 15th January 1942. On SOE Archives File 19/100/61 (or 'Greece' 5B, Pt I).

[3] Extract from report by Colonel G. Taylor to Mr Hanbury-Williams, ref: AD/105 of 21st September 1942.

It can now also be seen that the anti-monarchist elements in Greece were able to use assistance given by SOE to strengthen their own political position. This assistance was given them in good faith in order to attack the enemy, and was honestly paid for by them in the form of damage to the Germans which could not otherwise have been achieved: nevertheless its political consequences reached far beyond its military purpose.

All this put SOE in a bitterly invidious position; SOE was primarily responsible for what was certainly a bad business, yet the fault lay outside its control in the absence of a complete marriage between British foreign policy and British military policy. The best proof of this is that the difficulty was not eased in the slightest by M. Tsouderos's success in his campaign for the removal of those members of SOE whom he considered to be his enemies.

After this prologue, it will be convenient next to set out in bare essentials the mechanism of the lines opened into Greece in the winter of 1941–2, and to recur later to their political bearings.

The earliest two-way contacts were through open missions from Greece on the subject of Greek relief. There was an alarming lack of food, as the occupation had interrupted normal sources of supply, and the question of passing supplies through the blockade was one of great urgency. The pressure of starvation in itself was likely to drive the population to the Left, and food was thus of great political importance. The first of these missions was of an anti-Metaxas Royalist character, under M. Mavromichalis and General Reppas: it arrived in Istanbul at the end of September 1941, and had full discussions on the situation with Sebastian and Bowman and with Pirie, but nothing conclusive emerged and it took no message back.[1] This was succeeded by a Republican mission under Bakalbasis, who was able to some extent to speak for SOE's earlier contacts, such as Bakirdzis and Alexander Zannas. He was interviewed by Pawson on 16th November 1941; and Pawson's view, as then recorded 'from information received from different people of all political opinions', was 'that the King and his Government have only a very small following and they are hated and looked upon as traitors by the vast majority of the people'.[2]

There followed a number of more deliberately planned contacts:
  (a) One Lekkas *alias* Kip, a henchman of Tsouderos's representative Spyromilio, was put into Greece by submarine on 24th October 1941, with a verbal message from Tsouderos to Kanellopoulos.[3] He attempted to return in December, but did

---

[1] Greek History (Pirie), p. 194.
[2] Greek History (Pirie), p. 200.
[3] Greek History (Pirie), p. 132 (Operation 'Fleshpots').

not in fact reach Smyrna till 4th April 1942, when Kanellopoulos came with him.

(b) The same submarine also carried a Greek officer named Abatzis, alias Alexander, sent on behalf of the Greek Government to report on the supposed 'Kyrou' right-wing resistance movement: when he returned in November 1941 he reported unfavourably both on this and on another organisation of the Right, called the 'Under Thirty Association'.[1]

(c) SOE's old friend 'Odysseus' had found his way out to Smyrna on 14th September 1941 after Homeric adventures on the way.[2] He was sent back by SOE early in November, without the knowledge of the Greek Government, with instructions to contact the organisations left by SOE and to supply Prometheus II with codes and a signal-plan to replace those lost in the evacuation.[3]

(d) This mission was successful, and Prometheus II's set (Station 333) came on the air on 20th November 1941. Full two-way communication began on 23rd November and continued till Prometheus II and his operator were caught red-handed on 2nd February 1943.[4] Attempts to pass other wireless sets to more Conservative groups failed. It is of crucial importance that this was the only SOE wireless channel to Greece until June 1942; and the sets then added were from the outset in the hands of EAM.[5]

On 28th November this channel was used to pass a message to Kanellopoulos urging him to come out, in addition to that carried by Kip: this was duly delivered by Odysseus and the tone of the interview is plain from his report.[6] 'When I approached him and communicated your message, he started making theory about future Pan-Europe – United Europe – and he quoted to me extracts from the chapter of Marx on economic disequilibrium, and it seemed as if he was conversant with the secrets of economic equilibrium of Europe . . . . After several reserves, I was obliged to admit that he was right in everything he said so as to save myself from the affluence of his

---

[1] Greek History (Pirie), pp. 179, 181.

[2] See his report of 7th October, Greek History (Pirie), p. 140.

[3] See his directive in full, Greek History (Pirie), p. 168.

[4] Greek History (Pirie), p. 171. After this the Germans operated the set until 27th March – copies of these signals can be seen in SOE Archives File 19/490/11 Pt 2.

[5] NIKO on the air 17th June 1942 (Odysseus): COSTA on the air 9th July (Eumaeus *alias* Tsimas of EAM): Greek History (Pirie), p. 274.

[6] Greek History (Pirie), p. 135.

rhetoric in the matters of economic science of Mr Kanellopoulos . . . . And as I was in a hurry to leave in order to look after another matter regarding the organisation of a system of daily information on the movement of shipping in the port of Piraeus, I bade him good-bye.' This gem of malice illustrates what was involved in the use of Station 333 as a political channel.[1]

(e) Also in November 1941, a young Athenian called Ladas was infiltrated on behalf of the Greek Government, and saw Kanellopoulos and General Gonatas. Unfortunately he was captured on his way back in December.[2]

(f) On 10th December 1941, Station 333 telegraphed:[3] 'No serious work can be done without enough money. We need to organise services both for intelligence and for sabotage. We are the only people able to fix the needed money in each case. The sum of 10,000,000 drachmas must be in our hands to be in a position to work seriously.' This was backed by hard facts. Excellent shipping reports were being regularly transmitted from the Piraeus, with the assistance of the harbour pilots:[4] one German ammunition ship had been sunk:[5] and there had been various other minor acts of sabotage. SOE had plenty of evidence that value could be obtained for money, and they replied agreeing. 'Odysseus' reached Istanbul from Greece early in January 1942 and returned to Greece in March, taking with him money, messages for '333', as well as a wireless set intended for General Gonatas. The General's response will be seen later.[6]

(g) About 20th November Alexander Zannas's brother, Sotiri Zannas, reached Smyrna with a very important letter from General Gonatas;[7] and a little later a courier came through from Zannas's organisation. The latter had extremely favourable reports of sabotage carried out,[8] including the destruction of a 5,000-ton ship, a Greek destroyer, and thirteen bridges, and an explosion at Tatoi aerodrome which killed seventy-nine Germans. The Zannas organisation seemed to have justified itself, as had that of 'Prometheus', and it was a matter of mili-

---

[1] Compare Odysseus's interview with Gonatas – Greek History (Pirie), p. 274.
[2] Greek History (Pirie), p. 133.
[3] Greek History (Pirie), p. 171.
[4] Greek History (Pirie), p. 172.
[5] Greek History (Pirie), p. 146.
[6] Greek History (Pirie), pp. 268, 273; and below p. 153.
[7] Greek History (Pirie), p. 214 (see below pp. 153–4).
[8] Greek History (Pirie), p. 186.

tary necessity to feed it with money and materials, although it was Republican in politics. Unfortunately Zannas's courier could not safely be sent back, and this accident led to a disaster for which SOE as an organisation was responsible though it was much disputed where the responsibility lay within it.

(h) Zannas's courier had come out in company with an MI9 officer named Atkinson, and Atkinson was about to return by submarine to Greece on behalf of MI9. SOE took advantage of this operation[1] (Operation 'Isinglass') –

(i) To send in the same submarine a Greek wireless operator, with a set, codes, and a signal plan for Kanellopoulos; this was well-known to the Greek authorities, though they were not given access to the SOE code.

(ii) To add to Atkinson's mission (without MI9's knowledge) two others: one to Kanellopoulos, assisting him with money and urging him to complete his organisation and then leave Greece to join the Greek Government; the other to Zannas, sending money and urging him to co-operate with Kanellopoulos. It is not clear that the Greek Government saw Atkinson's political directive,[2] but it was prepared mainly by Sebastian and Bowman, the responsible officials of the Foreign Office and it was exactly in line with the programme concerted with the Greek Government. Kanellopoulos represented the point furtherest to the Right at which there was any chance of forming a serious centre of resistance in Greece: if other organisations could be linked to that centre and would accept Kanellopoulos as their head, there would be a fair chance that resistance inside Greece would be prepared to look for leadership, at least for the present, to a government of which Kanellopoulos was a member.[3]

The intentions of 'Isinglass' were therefore good; but it was a bad breach of technical doctrine to heap so many responsibilities on a single agent. Further, it was an inexcusable dereliction that a complete list of SOE's contacts in Greece should have been prepared for Atkinson's use; that he should have been permitted to take it on board the submarine; and that he carried it with him when he went ashore. Payment was exacted in full. Atkinson was captured

---

[1] SOE Archives File 19nc/370/1.

[2] Greek History (Pirie), p. 190.

[3] See 'Notes on Tsouderos's conversations with Bowman', on SOE Archives File 19/340/2.

on landing at Antiparos, the wireless operator 'Diamond' disappeared, and HM submarine 'Triumph' was lost in returning from the operation. The first news came in a telegram from Station 333 dated 3rd February 1942.[1] The Italians made less than they might have of their windfall, but the effects were bad enough. The Kanellopoulos organisation and our contacts with it were completely broken at a critical stage in their development: the Zannas organisation was almost as badly compromised. Kanellopoulos left Greece, but when he reached Turkey on 2nd April 1942[2] it was as a fugitive and not as the leader of an effectively unified resistance. There was never another chance of resistance under a Royalist leader.

(i) The next major operation was equally fruitful in a different sense, though scarcely better organised. Station 333 had signalled as early as 29th December 1941 to ask for arms to be landed near Kymi in Euboea.[3] It had asked for machine-guns, grenades, revolvers, and ammunition, which were not at first sight the best weapons for a sabotage campaign; but it clearly meant business of some sort, and there was no choice but to support it. The original idea of a submarine operation was dropped after the 'Isinglass' disaster, and an air operation was arranged in its place. With curious absent-mindedness the same location was chosen for air dropping as for submarine landing, in spite of entirely different operational requirements; and when three Liberators and a Wellington eventually did the job on 2nd/3rd March 1942 a great deal of their cargo fell into Italian hands; but some of it reached the agents of Station 333,[4] and it put ideas into their heads. To quote the personal report of Prometheus II a year later: 'Although this dropping proved unsuccessful as such, it was instrumental in proving how it is very well possible to supply groups on the ground from the air, provided the signals on the ground are well recognised by

---

[1] Greek History (Pirie), p. 250. Copy of Station 333 signal – No. 42 of 3rd February – on SOE Archives File 19/490/11 Pt II.

[2] Greek History (Pirie), p. 250. Copy of telegram Cairo to London B/798 of 8th April 1942, reporting his arrival at Smyrna on SOE Archives File 19/100/72 – 'Greece – 5/a Kanellopoulos'. Also on same file statement by M. Kanellopoulos on his arrival in Turkey, concerning conditions in Greece – in which he states he did not sign the protocol against the King of Greece (below p. 156).

[3] Greek History (Pirie), p. 175: Station 333 signal Nos 14–15, on SOE Archives File 19/490/11 Pt II.

[4] Greek History (Pirie), p. 177: Station 333 signal No. 67 of 3rd March 1942, copy on SOE Archives File 19/490/11 Pt II.

experienced pilots who should effect dropping from the lowest possible altitude, with a perfect system of parachutes and packing. It was then that the formation of Andartes' (Guerilla) 'bands came first to the surface and could be considered as realisable'.[1]

(j) Finally there were two formal political messages of importance. The first of these was a formal message[2] from Tsouderos to Kanellopoulos dated 21st January, asking the latter to leave Greece and take office in the Government[3] on very favourable terms. SOE Cairo were in doubts as to the wisdom of transmitting the message as it stood, and some time was spent in discussion, which was not settled before the 'Isinglass' disaster. Thereafter Kanellopoulos was a fugitive; it was decided to attempt to transmit the message, but it did not reach him till he was on Turkish soil.[4] The second was the reply to General Gonatas's message brought out by Sotiris Zannas in November;[5] this was in the form of a Foreign Office telegram[6] forwarding a message from M. Tsouderos and attaching the comments of His Majesty's Government, which were irreproachably loyal to M. Tsouderos's regime and correspondingly disheartening to the Opposition in Greece. SOE Middle East, as well as Mr Sebastian, were in some doubt as to the wisdom of this message, but it was eventually forwarded with the co-operation of a Finnish courier and reached General Gonatas's 'cut-out' on 30th March 1942[7] – some five months after his original letter had left Greece.

This is not an exhaustive list of contacts with Greece and sources of information in the winter of 1941–2, but it includes the main links and illustrates the type of channel which was open. The picture presented at the time was shifting and fragmentary, and the conclusions then available were the guess-work of experts, not demonstrable by solid evidence. But now that one can look back on the period as a whole the picture is fairly clear.

In the first place, SOE's original contacts with the Left Centre and Moderate Left (if these terms can be used of Greek politics) had been fruitful: it was beyond doubt that they had aided the Allies to the utmost of their power. Unfortunately it was clear from the 'Gonatas

---

[1] Quoted in Greek History (Pirie), p. 178.

[2] Text in Greek History (Pirie), p. 226.

[3] Tel. London to Cairo No. 4820 of 21st January 1942, copy on SOE Archives File 19/100/61.

[4] Greek History (Pirie), p. 229.

[5] See p. 150, and below p. 154.

[6] Dated 2nd February 1942: text in Greek History (Pirie), p. 229.

[7] Greek History (Pirie), p. 268.

letter', written as early as October 1941, that they were resolutely against the King. 'All political parties now in Greece are united in their desire for the establishment of a republic, and except for a few persons attached to the monarchy by personal ties, and certain officers, there is no one who supports the King.'[1]

Second, this had been confirmed by contacts established on behalf of the Greek Government itself with certain so-called Royalist resistance movements. These organisations had been tested and found wanting by the Government's own agent.[2]

Third, Professor Kanellopoulos had begun to form a group based primarily on his own students of the University of Athens, on the slogan of 'Support the Government for the war: a free choice after the war'.[3] He was not personally associated with the Metaxas régime, and he had contacts both to the Right and to the Left: he appeared therefore to offer the best centre for a 'National Front' on lines palatable to the King and the government in exile.

Fourth, this concentration rather to the Right of Centre was being dogged by a rival combination well to the Left of Centre. This begins to emerge in the late autumn of 1941,[4] and the best early description is in a report[5] written by 'Odysseus' in January 1942 on his work during the two months preceding: 'I managed to persuade the Communists of both sections' (his story includes a theory that there was an 'old' and a 'new' wing of the Communist Party) 'to unite themselves with the Popular Front, because, by working separately, I told them, they cannot succeed in enforcing a Soviet Government on the country, even if the country would have at the end to remain without any troops of occupation for fifteen days and the Government without a head . . . . I told them that they could only establish Soviets in Greece if the Russian troops would advance in the Balkans reaching Greece, in which case it would be natural that all action' (e.g. by the Communists to seize power) 'would be unnecessary on the appearance of regular Soviet troops in Greece. I thus arrived to the conclusion which they accepted, that they are obliged to take an active part in the liberation struggle, collaborating with all Greeks of the Left and others, with no reservation, and to let things take their way naturally, because, I told them, if they were not to work for the liberation

---

[1] Cairo Tel. to Foreign Office No. 90 of 7th January 1942, para. 3, quoting Gonatas letter. Quoted in Foreign Office Print R.1362/112/19 of 26th February 1942.

[2] Above p. 149.

[3] Greek History (Pirie), p. 202 – Asimakopoulos's report in SOE Cairo telegram of 4th December 1941.

[4] EAM officially regards its own foundation date as September 1941. This is likely to be too early.

[5] SOE Archives File 19/370/3.

struggle, they would lose all prestige and esteem in the eyes of the whole nation.' The whole document is most acute and farsighted, too acute to be quite convincing, and the exact origins of the Popular Front, the Ellenike Apeleutherotike Metopon, EAM, are not likely to be cleared up from evidence in British hands. But this grouping well to the Left of Centre existed before the end of 1941, and it was linked on the one hand with the Communists, on the other with the energetic group of Republican officers who controlled Station 333. It was a native phenomenon, not conceived or instigated by SOE; but undoubtedly their agent 'Odysseus' was deeply involved, and their wireless station, and the supplies and money which it could charm out of the air, made a focal point on which the organisation could form.

Fifth, in the early months of 1942 this new grouping took the offensive and displaced both the Kanellopoulos organisation and the Kanellopoulos slogan from the centre of the stage. This was in accordance with all the laws one can trace in the development of resistance movements, and was expedited by sheer starvation in the streets of Athens; but SOE by ill-luck and ill-judgment contributed to the breakdown of Kanellopoulos – by ill-luck in its failure to deliver to him a wireless set of his own, by ill-judgment in the 'Isinglass' disaster, which 'blew' both Kanellopoulos and the Zannas organisation, the least 'Left' of the active movements. The decisive turn is marked by the telegram[1] from Station 333 on 14th February 1942, ten days after it had reported on 'Isinglass'. 'The leaders are united and categorically against the King. The Greek people are very Anglophil and decidedly for the struggle. They are astonished however and angry at the British Government's attitude in favour of the Greek King. A very strong Democratic' (i.e. Republican) 'organisation exists, capable of valuable services to the British Government.' A few days later the Station reported[2] that a formal declaration had been signed to this effect, with the following adherents:

Sophoulis	Peter Rallis
Kaphandaris	Stephanopoulos
Mylonas	Kirkos
Papandreou	Theotokis
Sophianopoulos	General Gonatas
The Labour Socialists	Maximos
The Communists of	
the Popular Front.	

---

[1] Greek History (Pirie), p. 233. Copy of telegram No. B.181 d/d 28th February 1942 on SOE Archives File (AD/S.1) HD/61 – Greece Vol.1.

[2] See SOE Archives File 'Greece, Reports – Smyrna Office, Pt II'.

'The only ones who did not sign were Tsaldaris'[1] (the Royalist Prime Minister of 1946), 'Mavromichalis,[2] George Petzamoglou. This declaration contains proof of King's treason against the country and against England.'[3]

It is now clear that the Foreign Office reactions to these developments were panting behind events; hardly surprising in view of the scantiness of the evidence and the vigorous efforts of the Tsouderos Government to resist pressure and confuse counsel. In October 1941 that Government had begun badly by proscribing six prominent (and very provocative) Venizelists in Egypt, and by securing British aid in expelling them from the country: it did not help matters that one of them (Miss Elli Papadimitriou) was an old friend of SOE whom they continued to use, and that another (Doganis) continued to be employed by the SOE radio unit in Jerusalem. But thereafter M. Tsouderos had made certain constitutional concessions, drop by drop,[4] and he had consented to a widening of the Government to include M. Kanellopoulos. The terms he offered appeared generous toward M. Kanellopoulos, in that he was offered the reversion of the post of Prime Minister on the return to Greece: but they hedged on the issue of the régime – 'we propose after the war to restore a free constitutional régime in harmony with post-war political and social conditions. This régime must receive the people's sanction.'[5] This is soothing but evasive; and was disastrously glossed by M. Tsouderos's message to General Gonatas contained in the Foreign Office telegram of 2nd February[6] – 'after the war a free and democratic constitution under the King, will be established in Greece, of a kind which shall correspond to the new political and social conditions resulting from the war – which constitution must, in any event, be subject to popular approval'. In other words the monarchy will be restored without a plebiscite: there will be a plebiscite only on the new constitution granted by the King.

SOE in Cairo (loyally supported by the London Office) was baffled by this attitude and pressed hard – perhaps too hard – for some improvement.[7] But it was apparently more bad luck (and bad

---

[1] Station 333 Signal No. 59-60 of 25th February 1942; copy on SOE Archives File 19/490/11 Pt II.

[2] See above p. 148.

[3] B.181 of 28th February from Cairo; copy on SOE Archives File (AD/S.1) HD/61.

[4] Details in Foreign Office Print R.1362/112/19 of 26th February 1942; copy on SOE Archives File (AD/S.1) HD/61.

[5] Full text in Greek History (Pirie), p. 226 – date 21st January 1942.

[6] Greek History (Pirie), p. 229.

[7] E.g. Cairo telegram No. B.805 of 2nd February 1942, copy on SOE Archives File (AD/S.1) HD/61 – 'Our policy cannot be to back the Tsouderos Government, but rather to back all elements in Greece resisting the Axis forces.'

organisation) that at this juncture (on 6th and 7th February) the SOE 'Free Greek' station in Palestine celebrated by a disastrous gaffe one of M. Tsouderos's concessions, the dismissal of Metaxas's Minister of Labour, M. Dimitratos, who had hitherto remained in office. 'So the Fascist Dimitratos has gone at last! But who appointed Dimitratos? Metaxas, Who appointed Metaxas? The King. Who is therefore the arch-Fascist?'[1] This was indefensible, and fatally weakened SOE's position. It was now pressing the Foreign Office for permission to give unofficial assurances to leaders in Greece that His Majesty's Government would not impose the Greek King on his people at the end of the war without some prior expression of popular opinion.[2]

A letter dated 21st March from Lord Glenconner, then Director in charge of Middle Eastern affairs at London Headquarters,[3] drew only an acid reply from a junior official[4] – 'it seems to us that the only sound basis on which we can found our relations with Greece is the closest possible adherence to the official policy, and I hope this will be impressed on all SOE agents in the Middle East dealing with Greece.' The incident came at a difficult time in SOE's relations with the Foreign Office,[5] and there could be no question of taking the matter further. On 19th April Lord Selborne, who had succeeded Mr Dalton on 22nd February, minuted on a paper by Lord Glenconner, 'I certainly do not approve of pursuing a policy at variance with that of the Foreign Secretary. SOE policy in Greece, as elsewhere, must be in conformity with that of His Majesty's Government. Please impress this on all concerned. We cannot all be Foreign Secretaries.'[6]

M. Tsouderos signed a 'Lend/Lease' agreement with Great Britain on 9th March, and the King returned to the Middle East with his Government on 14th March 1942. M. Kanellopoulos reached Turkey from Greece on 4th April and negotiations began at once for his inclusion in the Government. SOE's part in these negotiations was rigidly

---

[1] Text as paraphrased in Greek History (Pirie), p. 242. Broadcast 6th and 7th February 1942. See also Sir Charles Hambro's interview with King George on 17th February 1942. Copy on SOE Archives File 19/100/58.

[2] See Lord Glenconner's Memo. of 2nd April, on SOE Archives File (AD/S.1) HD/61, and Greek History (Pirie), p. 245.

[3] Copy on SOE Archives File (AD/S.1) HD/61. See also Mr Jebb's letter F.3370/61 of 5th March to Sir Orme Sargent, and reply – R.1520/40/G – of 16th March, on same file.

[4] On SOE Archives File (AD/S.1) HD/61.

[5] Below p. 343 ff.

[6] On SOE Archives File (AD/S.1) HD/61.

controlled, on Lord Selborne's personal direction. Mr Sebastian, who had been in general agreement with their views on Greek politics, was 'recalled for consultation' in March, and was replaced by Mr Edward Warner.[1] Apparently Spyromilio, once M. Tsouderos's ally and link with Sebastian, disappeared from office at the same time.[2] M. Tsouderos explicitly expressed his distrust of Lord Glenconner, head of SOE's Greek Section in London,[3] and this distrust was echoed by the Minister of State's office in Cairo – 'I fear however that (SOE) are fundamentally hostile to King and present Government and tend to regard our efforts to promote reconciliation between the King and Opposition elements in Greece as a waste of time and even as a hindrance to their subversive plan in Greece.'[4] Finally, SOE's London HQ gave explicit instructions that SOE Cairo were not to associate themselves with the discussions:[5]

4. We know you will take every precaution to ensure that SOE personnel do not prompt or advise Kanellopoulos or take any part in these negotiations in any way.

5. Moreover, the Minister is most emphatic that we should not allow ourselves to be drawn into a matter of foreign policy such as this which is essentially the province of the Foreign Office.

6. In the circumstances, it is also his wish that you should confine yourself to reporting the political situation in Greece as known to you and not to advocate policy or that the official policy should be changed. If however a change is desirable, the Minister will be prepared to consider taking the matter up with the Foreign Secretary.

7. We here therefore will not make any representations to the Foreign Office except in the manner indicated in para. 6 above, nor should you continue to urge your views on Monckton or the Minister of State except in the manner set out in the first sentence of para. 6 above.

On Kanellopoulos's arrival in Middle East, he had been met by Pirie and Spyromilio, and had expressed views entirely in accord with

---

1 Mr Bowman apparently remained till September 1942.

2 Minute dated 11th September from Colonel Pearson to Mr Sporborg; copy on SOE Archives File (AD/S.1) HD/F.61/Pt II.

3 Telegram No. 244 of 24th April 1942 to Cairo; copy on SOE Archives File (AD/S.1) HD/61.

4 Minister of State's Office to Foreign Office No. 506 of 27th April; copy on SOE Archives File (AD/S.1) HD/61. See also Mr Dixon's suggestions to Lord Glenconner on this, SOE Archives File 'Greece – Political Pt II', 19/600/16.

5 Telegram No. 256 of 28th April 1942 to Cairo on SOE Archives File 19/100/72.

those held by SOE[1] and with his own earlier slogan.[2] On 26th April they submitted a memorandum[3] to Sir Walter Monckton, the acting Minister of State, in which they emphasised that the addition of M. Kanellopoulos to the Government would be of no value unless it carried with it a declaration that the King's position would be submitted to popular vote at the end of the war. At this point their interventions were cut short by the explicit instructions from London quoted above, and they had no share in the compromise reached. M. Kanellopoulos now took office as Vice-President, and was made responsible for resistance in Greece, but he was given no firm assurance regarding a plebiscite and there was no thorough purge of the old Metaxist elements in the Government.

M. Kanellopoulos took office on 3rd May: on 8th May Station 333 replied[4] to a request to assist one of his emissaries:

> It must be understood that the Greek people, military leaders and organisation believe that Kanellopoulos and all people round the traitor King are themselves traitors. We do not accept in any circumstances your proposal because it will destroy all built-up work . . . (signed) Prometheus II.

Matters in Greece had now progressed another stage beyond the solution which might once have been acceptable, and a new phase began in Greece one step ahead of the new phase in Cairo.

The first scene of the new act in Greece was the organisation by EAM (the 'Greek Liberation Front', as the Popular Front had now become) of a General Strike in Athens in mid-April 1942.[5] This had a solid unpolitical background in the starvation of the people;* and the basic demand was for food – one cooked meal a day for the families of the essential workers in Athens, tramwaymen, railwaymen, Post Office employees, bank clerks, civil servants. On 'Odysseus's' showing, 'the Communists, as more experienced, played a great part in this': but the essential point is that the strike was successful. The ordinary Greek people had stood up to the invader and had won. 'This strike had given birth to a revolutionary disposition, and acted as a tonic to the morale of the people.'[6]

---

1 Pirie's report and Cairo telegram of 19th April, in Greek History (Pirie), p. 215. [PASSAGE DELETED ON GROUNDS OF NATIONAL SECURITY.]
2 See above p. 154.
3 Text in Greek History (Pirie), p. 254.
4 Station 333 signal No. 24 of 8th May 1942; copy on SOE Archives File 19/490/11 Pt 2.
5 See 'Odysseus's' account of 19th May 1942, in Greek History (Pirie), p. 275. Copy of original report on SOE Archives File 19/370/3 – 'Greece 1/A, Odysseus'.
6 *Ibid.*
* [See Mazower, *Inside Hitler's Greece*, p. 23 ff.]

The second step was the beginning of a guerilla movement in the hills, as distinct from underground organisations in the towns. Banditry was endemic in Greece even in peace, and it was fed by economic distress: so that it is not easy to say when men outside the law ceased to be bandits and became fighters for their country – 'Klephts', as the word was used in the wars of liberation against the Turks. The same report of 'Odysseus' contains an account of these scattered beginnings: parties of ten or fifteen men raiding Italian ports, occupying villages for a few days, living out of reach in the mountains between spells of activity. On 'Odysseus's' own showing, Communists were early in the field in attempting to make these gangs into an army, but the argument was one which would appeal to any Greek of spirit. 'I am of the opinion that all our attention should be concentrated on this. It will strengthen highly the morale of the people who are fed up with words only and want to see action. Naturally, this may cause reprisals on the part of the occupation forces, but what does it matter? There are some 5,000 people who daily die of hunger in Greece: if there were some 50 persons to be shot daily, the total would become only 5,050 . . . . It is a shame for us, when the Serbs are working so well in the mountains in their guerilla war, to remain hidden in our holes like foxes.'[1]

'Odysseus' was by this time pretty close to the Communist Party, and to the left wing of the EAM. But the same conception was beginning to take hold of the Venizelist officers, who also had access to Station 333, and a military grouping of Republican Colonels to the right of EAM was reported by Prometheus II as early as 27th March.[2] Some of these man were resolute and active enough, others seem to have been bar-room strategists of a poor type: but none of them were by class, origin, or early training so well adapted to the life of the mountains as the leading spirits of EAM. Two separate guerilla organisations eventually emerged from them, known as EDES[3] and EKKA, identified eventually with the names of Colonel Zervas[4] and Colonel Psaros. Their early history and political affiliations are obscure, but it is pretty clear that both arose out of the group of which Colonel Bakirdzis was the leading figure in Greece,[5] and which looked to

---

[1] 'Odysseus's' Report, Greek History (Pirie), p. 278; copy on SOE Archives File 19/370/3.

[2] Telegram quoted in Greek History (Pirie), p. 264. Copies of Station 333 signals can be found on SOE Archives File 19/490/11.

[3] First mention traced is in 'Odysseus's' report of 19th May 1942 – see ref. 1.

[4] Minister of Public Order in M. Maximos's Government, from 23rd February 1947.

[5] See (e.g.) Station 333's telegram of 2nd May in Greek History (Pirie), p. 279: also report of Colonel Bakirdzis's own views in Greek History (Pirie), p. 287.

General Plastiras abroad.[1] The first to take the field was Zervas; but talk of his guerillas began in April and it was not until August that he could be extricated from Athens. The impression left by the documents is that the Colonel was an ingenious rogue, of great personal charm and some force of character. [PASSAGE DELETED ON GROUNDS OF NATIONAL SECURITY.][2]

This guerilla movement was none of SOE's making. On Pirie's showing, the Cairo office had begun with a totally different conception, that of the underground organisation of sabotage, coupled with quiet preparations for a general revolt timed to coincide with some crisis of the war. Once the Andartes movement was launched, there was no choice but to support it. Supply dropping to the mountains began in June, with reasonable success; two new wireless sets were in operation about the same time;[3] and further developments in supply to the guerillas were now mainly a matter of the development of technique and the availability of aircraft. The policy was initiated without much thought: it was only when it was in full operation that controversy began as to the military role of a guerilla movement in Greece and its value in face of the political consequences involved.

The third new development was a great intensification of the sabotage campaign in the Piraeus, coinciding with the crisis of the 'Battle of Knightsbridge' in Libya and specifically called for by the British as a matter of vital importance during Rommel's pursuit to Alamein.[4] Between 26th May and 6th July the score reported (and fairly well authenticated) was:

26 May	2 'limpets' on Italian ship. Fuses failed.
27 May	Limpets on German ship. Fuses failed.
11 June	German ship 'Plouton' sabotaged and put in dry dock.
	Mail-ship 'Ardena' sabotaged (damage to electrical equipment).
12 June	Italian ship with MT for Rommel sunk by limpets in Saronic Gulf.
6 July	One tanker damaged by limpet and docked for six weeks.
	A second tanker damaged and put under repair.[4]

This run of successes was broken by arrests in the middle of July, and four of the organisation were shot in October: but the effort was good, and served to confirm SOE's belief in the soundness of their own judgement.

---

[1] Prometheus II's report of March 1943 – Greek History (Pirie), p. 285.
[2] [NOTE DELETED ON GROUNDS OF NATIONAL SECURITY.]
[3] Above p. 149.
[4] SOE Archives File 19/490/11 Pt 2 – Sabotage Report.

Finally, on 15th September, the situation began to be affected by the imminence of 'Torch' and the battle of Alamein: Cairo telegraphed to Pawson in Istanbul: 'Axis supply position in Libya is at present so acute that any action undertaken against their lines of communication *now* will have a result very disproportionately greater than action taken even in a few weeks' time. C-in-C personally asks that SOE collaborators in Greece should undertake the most vigorous possible immediate action. Their success or failure will largely determine the support we and they may expect from other services in realisation of our long-term aims.'[1] The results were (first) the spread and intensification of the Piraeus dock strike which began about this date,[2] (second) the well planned and executed attack on the Papadia railway bridge, cutting rail communications to the north. This was politically a turning point, in that for the first time the guerillas called for the assistance of Allied parachutists – a course which they had so far been careful to avoid. Station 333 replied on 21st September to SOE's suggestion of this target: 'For successful sabotage of the railway bridges the following must be carried out exactly. We shall wait at Giona from the night of 28th September to 3rd October. You must drop about ten parachutists of which two are experts' (i.e. in demolition or sabotage). 'Parachutists should carry between them 1,000 sovereigns for the job and more explosives. At the same time you must drop at Milsaesa for Zervas explosives and weapons, and one officer with two W/T sets to act as liaison officer between the Andartes and yourselves. Zervas has his own operators.'[3] This was Operation 'Harling',[4] which dropped on the night of 30th September: its results will be related later.

Politically confusion continued. On the one hand SOE Cairo had been permitted to resume contact with Kanellopoulos, and were framing with him a programme which was virtually that which they had advocated throughout. 'Kanellopoulos confirms that two possible alternative régimes are likely to be established in Greece after the war: either –

(i) a Liberal Republic

    (a) Looking to Britain and USA for guidance and alliance.

    (b) recognising foreign and private investments.

    (c) willing to participate in an independent Balkan Federation.

---

[1] Quoted in Greek History (Pirie), p. 323. Copy on SOE Archives File 19/410 Telegrams from Cairo to Smyrna – No. 1346 of 15th September 1942.

[2] Greek History (Pirie), p. 325.

[3] Text in Greek History (Pirie), p. 326, and SOE Archives File 19/490/11 Pt 2 – Station 333 Signal No. 87 of 21st September 1942.

[4] SOE Archives File 19/490/11 – Operation 'Harling' directive.

or (ii) a Republic of the Extreme Left,

    (a) Looking to Russia for guidance and alliance.

    (b) not recognising foreign and private investments.

    (c) probably preferring to form part of a greater USSR.

Our task there is to attempt to induce the supporters of the latter to transfer their allegiance to the former, while remembering always that the latter are at present the best organised and most active anti-Fascists and we must on no account therefore lose their support . . . .[1]

The practical steps contemplated were to build on what was left of Kanellopoulos's own 'Action Committee' in Athens embracing roughly the following (reading politically from Right to Left):

        Kanellopoulos's own party.
        Gonatas (mild Republican).
        Plastiras (moderate Venizelist).
        Bakirdzis (extreme Venizelist).

This scheme had been badly shaken by the aftermath of 'Isinglass'; but it was rational to build on it and to attempt to tie into it Zervas (who appeared to be an offshoot of Plastiras), Psaros (who had connections both with Kanellopoulos and with Bakirdzis) and EAM. The natural tactics were to build up the Committee by making it the channel of money and supplies to all Resistance movements, including EAM; and for this £150,000 a month was requested from the British Treasury.[2]

The Foreign Office on the other hand remained obstinately suspicious of SOE's tactics: 'unless these large sums are spent with the full co-operation of the Greek Government the result may be to strengthen opposition elements in Greece and render more difficult the return of the Greek Government and the King . . . . You will no doubt bear in mind importance of avoiding giving M. Tsouderos any impression that M. Kanellopoulos is going behind his back.'[3] The Minister of State (Mr Casey had taken over from Mr Lyttelton on 28th March 1942) replied on 10th June:[4] 'when I saw the King of the Hellenes and the President of the Council' (M. Tsouderos) 'before their departure' (they were expected in New York on 8th June and

---

[1] Telegram of 10th May – text in Greek History (Pirie), p. 288.

[2] Telegrams Nos 1505-7 of 20th July 1942, Foreign Office to Minister of State, give Foreign Office's views on financing of Greek operations. Para. 3 of 1506 stresses that Kanellopoulos should accept full responsibility for the financing of organisations which were admittedly in opposition to the Greek King. Copy on SOE Archives File 19/100/97.

[3] Foreign Office telegram to Cairo No. 1136 of 29th May 1942; copy on SOE Archives File 19/600/17 'Greece/General G.1 (AD.3)'.

[4] Cairo Telegram No. B/2058 of 10th June; copy on SOE Archives File 19/100/97. Quoted in Greek History (Pirie), p. 292.

arrived in London on 19th July 1942) 'I asked both of them whether I could take it that Kanellopoulos fully represented the views of the Greek Government. Both assured me that he did, and I could accept his recommendations as having full authority. I am therefore personally satisfied that in subsidising *inter alia* the EAM we shall not be running counter to the wishes of the King and Greek Government.'

In spite of these assurances the provision of £150,000 a month was not finally approved until 24th July,[1] and expenditure from it was placed under the supervision of an 'Anglo-Greek Committee' in Cairo,[2] under the chairmanship of Mr Maxwell, Controller of SOE in Middle East, and consisting of M. Kanellopoulos and a representative of the Minister of State, with Pirie as Secretary. The first meeting was held and the first allocation of funds was made on 30th July:[3] but unfortunately the Greek Government itself was now going two ways. In the Middle East Kanellopoulos's views were not far from those of SOE: he recalled the six Republicans banished in October 1941, including SOE's friend Elli Papadimitriou, he abolished Prince Peter's post as Greek liaison officer, and his control of the school at Haifa, he substituted as a recruiting agency the 'Hellenic Information Service' under a Republican, Commander Zangas. At the same time an effort was made to straighten out the troubled affairs of the Greek forces in the Middle East. In London M. Tsouderos's war with SOE continued. On 5th August he presented a powerful Aide-Mémoire[4] to the Foreign Office on the crookedness of the 'British Intelligence Service', concluding with a strong statement of the national character of his own Government and the inevitable trend of Greece towards unity behind it, if it were not hampered by SOE.[5] On 21st August he saw Lord Selborne, and after anxious thought the Minister agreed to the request that Pirie should be recalled. 'The King of Greece and his

---

[1] Greek History (Pirie), p. 294. See also note of meeting with Sir Orme Sargent on 2nd July, on SOE Archives File 19/100/58.

[2] On 3rd October 1942 Sir Orme Sargent wrote to CD regarding support for Left organisations in Greece and asking that Glenconner should be instructed that *all* contacts with Greece must come before the Anglo-Greek Committee. Ref: R/6171/40/G; copy on SOE Archives File 19/100/58. SOE Archives File 19/100/42 refers to setting up of Anglo-Greek Committee.

[3] Telegram from SOE Cairo dated 31st July in Greek History (Pirie), p. 294, and the Foreign Office instructions in full in Nos 1505-6 of 9th July to Minister of State; copy on SOE Achives File 19/100/97.

[4] Text of Aide-Mémoire on SOE Archives File 19/100/46.

[5] Forwarded by Mr Eden to Lord Selborne on 15th August (copy in Lord Selborne's correspondence). See extracts in Greek History (Pirie), p. 315. See also full comments by Colonel Taylor dated 19th August in SOE Archives File (AD/S.1) HD/F.61 Vol. 2.

Government are *our Allies* and it is *intolerable* that any British organisation should assist in endangering his throne by the use of British
influence and British gold. Any of our Agents who can be held guilty
of such conduct must be dispensed with . . . . I am not saying that
Tsouderos's complaint against Pirie is justified, but if any of our Allies
conveys to me that one of our principal agents with whom they have
to contact is *persona non grata*, the matter at any rate calls for serious consideration. This is particularly so in the case of an Ally who
has been so magnificently loyal to us as the Greek Government.'[1] In
the event Pirie was retained in Cairo until December 1942 to assist
with technical preparations for 'Harling' and operations related to it,
but he was no longer in a position of political importance.

On 21st August, Mr Maxwell had been replaced by Lord Glenconner
as Controller of SOE in Middle East, and a thorough internal reorganisation took place. One of Lord Glenconner's earliest acts was
to inform his directors that 'any employee of SOE Middle East will
be dismissed if he is found guilty of expressing sentiments in public
which are hostile to the King and his Government'.[2]

The practical accompaniment of this political campaign was a
determined attempt to establish contacts outside the old orbit of
Station 333: four of these are worth mentioning. The first two were
conducted through the agency of SOE and there was much delay in
dispatching them, which was naturally reckoned to be deliberate by
SOE's opponents: but in the light of endless experience in all theatres
of war it is fair to accept Pirie's clear statement that the delays were
inevitable.[3]

(a) An experienced agent known as 'Sphinx' was sent in on 14th
July, after delays in part due to Prometheus II's refusal to
assist any agent of Kanellopoulos.[4] He acted as
Kanellopoulos's representative in discussion with many
important politicians: [PASSAGE DELETED ON GROUNDS
OF NATIONAL SECURITY.] However he was back in

---

[1] Lord Selborne's letter to Lord Glenconner of 10th September; copy on SOE
Archives File (AD/S.1) HD/F. 61 Vol. 2. See also Lord Selborne's telegram of
22nd August, and Lord Glenconner's reply of 27th August (Cairo Alpha 537–8
of 27th August 1942 – précis in London HQ War Diary, Mid-East & Balkans,
Vol. 1, p. 73). There was a further meeting between Lord Selborne and M.
Tsouderos of 15th September – see File HD/F.61 Vol. 2, and Lord Selborne saw
King George on 16th September (letter to Mr Eden of 16th September on SOE
Archives File 19/100/99.1).

[2] Copy on SOE Archives File 19nc/460/5.

[3] Greek History (Pirie), p. 276.

[4] Above p. 159.

Smyrna in person on 30th July and reported at once.[1] His contacts were very wide and the report is a long one, but its gist can be given in a few sentences. 'They all agree not to oppose Kanellopoulos but are all convinced that he will turn out Royalist and they do not believe in him. They consider the King of the Hellenes and the Tsouderos Government as a present necessity . . . . Everybody said however that neither the King nor the Tsouderos Government will be permitted to return to Greece until the question of the future form of Government is settled.'

(b) The second expedition was Operation 'Thurgoland', carried out on the night of 27th/28th July 1942, an elaborate affair led by a Greek officer, Major John Tsigantes, who had recently escaped from Greece. One objective was to attack the Corinth Canal; another was to make contact with Tselos and Kanellopoulos's own party, on Kanellopoulos's behalf. Tsigantes took with him 12,000 sovereigns, three wireless sets and a somewhat obscure directive.[2] He was a man of extreme bravery, but apparently both indiscreet and quarrelsome. He was captured and shot by the Italians in January 1943, and the story of his adventures will probably always remain obscure. One clear practical result was a telegram from him on 16th September – 'Following for Kanellopoulos personal. Necessary that Smyrna' (i.e. SOE) 'break off independent contacts and sending of money' (i.e. to Prometheus II and 'Odysseus' for EAM). Another was a quarrel with Kanellopoulos's trusted lieutenant Tselos, who came out to give his personal version of events on 25th September.

(c) It is worth mentioning briefly as a third contact the arrival in Cairo in August of two agents of what was known as the Lavdas organisation, claiming to be a body of generals of Royalist views. These representatives were sponsored by Prince Peter: but the conclusion reached by the Defence Security Officer in Cairo was that they were certainly valueless and possibly enemy agents.[3] This impression was confirmed by Sphinx's report.[4]

---

[1] Text in Greek History (Pirie), p. 303. (Interrogation Reports ISLD and SOE on SOE Archives File 'Greece – Smyrna Reports, Pt 2 – also Foreign Office report on 'Political Feeling in Greece' of 28th August 1942, copy on SOE Archives File 19/100/82, was based on 'Sphinx's' report.)

[2] Greek History (Pirie), p. 297, and London HQ War Diary, Mid-East & Balkans, Vol. 1, p. 147. Directive on SOE Archives File 19/490/11.

[3] Report in Greek History (Pirie), p. 300.

[4] Greek History (Pirie), p. 304.

(d) A further check was provided by an American Greek [PASSAGE DELETED ON GROUNDS OF NATIONAL SECURITY] but his report was not available till 12th September. It contained a sharp and not altogether ill-founded attack on the reputations of 'Odysseus' and Zervas, as well as on McNabb and Atkinson, and poured much cold water both on the sabotage campaign and on the guerillas. But [NAME DELETED] contacts were somewhat shy of taking an initiative themselves: their solution was that they 'would like to have a suitable British officer sent in with instructions, a man under whom they could combine for sabotage work. They want to bring all sabotage elements (including EAM) together under military control.'

In spite of the implied attack on SOE this chimed well enough with policy as it was developing in Cairo. Operation 'Harling' began to frame itself a few days after this report was submitted, though the British officers went in in the first instance to EAM in the hills, not to the Liberals in Athens. And Tselos, Kanellopoulos's own man, who arrived about the same time, and remained there as his deputy, reported that there already existed a Military Centre of Co-ordination in Greece. This was reported at the third meeting of the Anglo-Greek Committee on 5th October:[1] 'The Army itself had set up an organisation, which relieved us of the necessity of setting up a Centre of Co-ordination of our own. This Military Centre, consisting mainly of Colonels, all regular officers fully proven in Albania, would take charge of the continuation of the war in Greece – it was "the Greek State in Greece".'

This was the 'Six Colonels' organisation, which held the field as the 'non-political' centre of Greek resistance when British officers began to join the guerillas. Unfortunately 'non-political' is not a term applicable to any part of Greek politics: and the Colonels, perhaps innocent themselves, were labelled by their origin as men who had held high military rank under Metaxas. Station 333 with its usual flair for the effective argument stressed, not this point, but their uselessness as irregular leaders. 'Please impress on Cairo that the formation of Greek Guerillas is due on the one hand to the misery of the mountain people and on the other to their desire to perpetrate sabotage. Their success depends on your help and our capability. Unfortunately many officers will not take the risks which guerilla work entails. We have applied to many of Colonel's rank but all have refused. It is ridiculous, as they think to try and conduct guerilla warfare from

---

[1] Quoted in Greek History (Pirie), p. 329. See also Kanellopoulos's report to Tsouderos in SOE Cairo telegram No. 1678 of 6th October on SOE Archives File (AD/S.1) HD/F.61, Pt 2.

salons . . . . If all their people had their headquarters in the mounains instead of in salons these questions would be solved.'[1]

There we may leave Greece for the present. Contact has been solidly established, and some dividends have been earned: the Allied High Command is asking anxiously for money. There is good reason to hope that their requests can be met somehow: but not through the political channels prescribed by the British and Greek Governments.

---

[1] Telegram quoted in Greek History (Pirie), p. 333; copy on SOE Archives File 19/490/11, Pt 2 – Station 333 signal No. 03 of 14th October 1942.

CHAPTER VIII

SOE Organisation in the Middle East, up to the Autumn of 1942

1. Miscellaneous Activities

These two cases, Yugoslavia and Greece, furnish the best examples of the political and practical difficulties of work from the Middle East. The responsibilities of SOE Middle East of course extended much further. Events in Albania, Bulgaria and Roumania have already been mentioned, and a good deal of effort was put into the problem of re-establishing communications with these countries, and even with Hungary, after the breakdown in 1941.

Penetration of Crete had began earlier than that of Greece itself, largely because of the urgent MI9 problem posed by the numbers of British stragglers still at large, and the first SOE officer reached the island in October 1941.[1] Luckily the Cretans posed fewer political problems than did the mainland of Greece, and the story was relatively straight-forward. Continuous violent activity was impossible in face of the number of German and Italian troops in the island (in 1943 there was one enemy soldier to every five Cretans): but the organisation lived and kept up its morale, and British Officers came and went with relative freedom.

SOE in Turkey raised awkward political questions, as there were considerable German interests there, in chrome and other commodities, which could have been attacked by sabotage at the expense of some danger to our relations with Turkey. This was another case where there was a clash between the instincts of SOE and the cautious policy of the Foreign Office; luckily events did not develop in such a way

---

[1] Dolbey's Greek History, Appendix III A, p. 12. Operation 'Stiletto' – infiltration of Smith-Hughes, SOE Archives File 69/400/1 refers.

as to force a major crisis.[1] The main practical contribution in Turkey in this stage was the development of a 'caique' base at Smyrna, under the aegis of SIS and with tacit Turkish connivance.[2]

The guerilla expeditions which contributed to the downfall of the Italian Empire in Ethiopia had been in part initiated by MI(R); when it disappeared, they were conducted by GHQ acting through G(R), a limb of MI(R) which survived the death of its parent. The question of the amalgamation of G(R) and D Section did not arise until the former had completed its work in the East African war and was looking around for fresh worlds to conquer.

One curious incident was that of the 'Yak Mission',[3] a party largely formed on MI(R) lines, which left England in great haste in April 1941 to assist in raising irregular forces from the anti-Fascist Italians among General Wavell's prisons:[4] it was headed by Captain Peter Fleming and included five officers, among them Captain W. Stirling, who had been chief instructor at Loch Ailort School.[5] The anti-Fascist saboteurs were soon found to be a myth; the Mission charged itself with some miscellaneous duties in Greece, and withdrew on the Legation yacht at a later stage of proceedings. In the Middle East it disintegrated – part of the staff was absorbed by the SOE training school in Palestine: Captain Fleming returned to England: Captain Stirling, after taking no small part[6] in the campaign which led to the reorganisation of SOE Middle East in August, found more congenial employment in the development of the Long Range Desert Group.*

---

[1] SOE Archives File (AD/S.1) '83.Turkey' largely covers Turkish activities. The following correspondence between Lord Selborne and Mr Eden cover the relations between SOE and FO in regard to Turkey.

    F/3493/83.3 of 31.3.42 to Mr Eden
    R/2174/386/G of 6.4.42 to SO – in reply
    F/3529/83.3 of 10.4.42 to Mr Eden.

Copies with SO's papers – under corres. with Foreign Secy.

[2] See reports by Captain Harris and Captain Skelly – SOE Archives File Turkey/490/11, Pt 1.

[3] Cipher 93391 dated 18th November 1940 from War Office to C-in-C Middle East, advises of this Mission – 'Dalton informs us at the instance of the Prime Minister SO2 are to recruit and train Italians and other foreign subjects . . . please give them all possible assistance.' Copy on SOE Archives File 60/470/1.

[4] See 'Charter' in SOE Archives File (AD/S.1) SC/68.2 – Yak Mission.

[5] Above p. 54.

[6] See his contributions to the 'Anti-SO2 dossier', SOE Archives File (AD/S.1) HD/F.68.3(a), Items 7, 12, 14 and 18.

* [See W. B. Kennedy Shaw, *The Long Range Desert Group* (1945) and David Lloyd Owen, *The Desert my Dwelling Place* (1957).]

SO2's Jewish 'Friends'[1] were engaged both in the Iraq fighting and in that in Syria, and certainly supplied a large number of active agents. Their exploits however are vaguely and tendentiously reported, and it is not easy to see how far they were interested in SO2's objectives rather than their own. The sabotage of sixteen Northrop aircraft of the Iraqi Air Force in April 1941 is pretty well authenticated;[2] there is much more doubt as to achievements in the Syria campaign – probably there was a little fire behind the rich smoke of claims.[3]

Some beginnings were made in the opening of contacts in the Caucasus, with Armenians and others, both when Russia was hostile and when it was an ally in some danger of collapse. But there was no activity in the field here, and the organisation of exiles involved were without exception unimpressive. In addition, the mere hint of preparation for such activities was enough to make the Foreign Office seriously uneasy.[4]

The remaining activities of SOE Middle East were mainly related to propaganda, and involved difficult relations with other organisations dabbling in the same field. Bailey's scheme[5] for a series of 'Freedom Stations' in Palestine was realised in the late summer of 1941, and clandestine broadcasts were initiated from the so-called 'Jerusalem Station' to Yugoslavia, Greece, Roumania and Bulgaria, purporting to come from resistance movements within these countries. The policy of such broadcasts was admittedly a matter for SO1 (or PWE) and the latter's directives were ostensibly accepted on matters of propaganda: but direct control was resisted, first on the ground that SO1 was not under its charter entitled to run establishments overseas, later because the day-to-day running of such stations involved the safety of our missions in these countries and could only be effectively controlled by the organisation concerned with operations.

[PARAGRAPH DELETED ON GROUNDS OF NATIONAL SECURITY.]

---

[1] SOE Archives File (AD/S.1) 'Zionists' refers.

[2] Arab World History, p. 3.

[3] See reports in 'Anti-SO2 dossier' – ref. 6, p. 170 above.

[4] On 21st March 1942 Lord Selborne wrote to Mr Eden (F/3441/68.4(O/14) – 'In regard to Kurds, Armenians and Georgians, etc. I am informed that the only steps that Maxwell has taken has been to recruit several individuals from these nationalities and have them by him in Palestine, so that in the event of the Foreign Office deciding that broadcasts to those nationalities would be advisable, (e.g. if Turkey was overrun by Germany) the personnel would be to hand in order to carry out the task. No such broadcasts will be made, or any further steps taken without your advice. I hope you will be content to let the matters rest there.'

[5] Above p. 143.

2. 'The First Organisation and its Breakdown', August 1940–August 1941

All these problems produced work and friction, and required policy decisions. Let us now follow the organisation which attempted to co-ordinate them, in its development up to the autumn of 1942.

We have seen above[2] that relations between D's representative (Mr Goodwill), Colonel Adrian Simpson (MI(R)), and the DDMI (Brigadier Shearer) had become impossible in the summer of 1940. It appears that there was then some idea that D Section in Middle East should be absorbed into G(R).[3] Mr Dalton saw General Wavell in London on 12th August, and they agreed that Mr George Pollock, then on his way out (with the rank of Lieutenant Colonel), should be permitted to take over; and that a general settlement should await a visit from Major Taylor or some other more senior official.[4] When Major Taylor eventually visited Cairo early in 1941, his attention was directed to much more pressing matters in the Balkans; there were difficulties and bad luck in finding an alternative 'inspector' and matters developed without serious supervision until a crisis was reached in the summer of 1941.

One difficulty was certainly the vagueness of Colonel Pollock's directive: in fact no directive is on record, but its general tenor is plain from a letter from Mr Dalton to General Wavell dated 5th January 1941, after a visit by Pollock to London, bringing with him a memorandum[5] approved by General Wavell.

1. Henceforth the distinction between SO1 (in Cairo Colonel Thornhill) and SO2 will only apply in this country and will consequently disappear in your area. There will henceforth be only one SO organisation in the Middle East, under the general control of Pollock who, while responsible to me, will operate under your direction.
2. The functions of the SO Department will cover:
   (a) Subversive Propaganda
   (b) Political Subversion
   (c) Raiding and Sabotage.

---

[1] [NOTE DELETED ON GROUNDS OF NATIONAL SECURITY.]
[2] Above p. 34.
[3] Minute by Colonel Taylor dated 7th August 1940, on SOE Archives File (AD/S.1) HD/68.
[4] Minute by Dalton dated 12th August 1940 on SOE Archives File (AD/S.1) HD/68.
[5] Not found. But cf. ME(M)(40)28 of 5th December, which contains the views of the Cs-in-C, Middle East, about open propaganda and the weakness of the existing arrangements, and S.50/23 of 6th January 1941 which discussed it. See also Mr Garnett's account in his 'History of PWE', p. 59.

Full details will be explained by Pollock personally and many problems, including that of personnel, will have to be worked out on the spot. I authorise Pollock to do this on my behalf.

I should like you to know that I have excellent reports of Thornhill's work and I hope that he will play an even more important part under the new arrangements.[1]

Colonel Thornhill protested violently against this subordination: the Minister instructed Colonel Pollock to seek a compromise. But the telegram giving these instructions was not shown to Thornhill by Pollock and this served only to exacerbate relations.

This left much to Pollock's initiative, and was hardly workable without support in high quarters in Middle East. The Cs-in-C were conscious of the dangers of enemy subversion, especially in the Arab World, and of the possibility of developments such as took place a little later in Syria and Iraq: and their first interest was in an improvement of British propaganda within their area, without much regard to the relatively minor question of the roles of SO1 and SO2, or to the distant prospect of subversion in the Balkans.[2] So far as they were concerned, the most urgent matter was that a single authoritative representative should be appointed to co-ordinate all propaganda, both open and secret; the para-military operations of SO2 would in that event virtually pass under the control of the General Staff.[3]

On the other hand it was politically impossible in the light of controversies then in progress in London that a representative of the Ministry of Information should be empowered to co-ordinate part of Mr Dalton's organisation.[4] It was also unpalatable that the notion of a unified subversive organisation should break down in the Middle East, at a time when it was already under a severe strain in London; and it was particularly distasteful that 'the military' should reassert in Middle East the control of subversion which had been wrested from them at home.[5]

---

[1] Copy on SOE Archives File (AD/S.1) HD/68. See also General Wavell's reply of 3rd February 1941.

[2] The following refer: ME(M)(40)28 of 5th December, ME(M)(41)1 of 2nd January: S.50/23 of 6th January, and S.50/23 of 17th January: these and further papers on SOE Archives File (AD/S.1) HD/SC/68.4.

[3] See General Wavell's cipher 1/70116 of 4th June, on SOE Archives File (AD/S.1) HD/SC/68.4.

[4] See exchange of letters between Mr Dalton and Mr Duff Cooper in March 1941 – on SOE Archives File (ADS.1) HD/SC/68.4.

[5] See in particular Mr Dalton's cipher 71810 (MO1) of 11th June; copy on SOE Archives File (AD/S.1) HD/SC/68.4.

'The Military' were however limited in their grasp by the boundaries of the Middle East Command, whereas the work of SOE, whether in operations or propaganda, flowed across geographical boundaries, and even when it was based within a military command it affected much more than the work of that Command. The local Commanders-in-Chief could therefore make good a claim that they should control SOE's work in so far as it concerned their own operations: but it was not plausible to extend this to the complete absorption of everything controlled by SOE Headquarters in Cairo. This dualism runs through the whole history of SOE's relations to the military organisation in Cairo, though the picture changes somewhat with each change in Command areas.

The Commanders-in-Chief made no progress in their wider proposal for a 'M of I Co-ordinator' for all propaganda based on Middle East; and they appear next to have taken the initiative in a proposal for co-ordination of such activities as were quite clearly within their own boundaries. The C-in-C and AOC-in-C* telegraphed on 15th May:[1]

Setting up of Bureau in Jerusalem being proceeded with on the following lines:

Title: Jerusalem Bureau.

Objects: Under the direction of Cs-in-C ME:

(i) To formulate policy for and to co-ordinate and direct activities designed to ensure satisfactory attitude of native population in area East of Mediterranean and Red Seas, South of Turkey and West of Iran:

(ii) To organise any assistance they can give in furtherance of strategical plans:

(iii) To counter enemy subversive movements.[2]

Mr Dalton was clearly right in feeling that this arrangement cut across the charter of SOE; but recent events had shown the direct military dangers of enemy subversion in this area to be so great that

---

[1] Cipher 9343 15/5 to War Office; copy on SOE Archives File (AD/S. 1) HD/68.

[2] Telegram 1/67064 of 23rd May 1941 from C-in-C ME to War Office states – 'Charter of Bureau expressly lays down that Bureau will direct activities of local SO representative in whispering and other forms of propaganda. SOE ME is under direction and control of C-in-C and will be used to the full in any implementation of plan AQ or other activities which may be subsequently formulated by JEB. Operational activities in these connections of SOE will be directed through General Staff as is case in all other spheres of action of SOE propaganda and political activities will be directed through JEB as laid down in charter.' SOE Archives File 52/470/1.

* [A. W. Tedder, 1890–1967, knight 1942, baron 1946, deputy commander for 'Overlord' 1944–5, was just taking over from A. M. Longmore, 1885–1970, knight 1935, C-in-C Middle East 1940–41, Inspector of RAF 1941–2; both in *DNB*.]

it would have been unfair and impolitic to resist the judgement of the Commanders-in-Chief as to what was required. The Jerusalem Bureau was therefore accepted, subject to minor reservations.[1]

This still left untouched the problem of 'higher co-ordination'; the line of approach agreed in London is clear from discussions at the Middle East (Ministerial) Committee:[2] for instance, on 16th June 'it was emphasised that the officer appointed would in fact direct both propaganda and subversion in the area and would require to be of equivalent status with our Ambassador in Cairo and the three Commanders-in-Chief'. This line of thought led in due course to the appointment on 1st July 1941 of Mr Oliver Lyttelton,* as Minister of State in Middle East, with Cabinet rank: the scope of his authority went far beyond the limits of SOE, but its particular problem was provided for in his Directive:[3]

> Para. 3 The principal task of the Minister of State will be to ensure a successful conduct of the operations in the Middle East by –
> (a) relieving the Commanders-in-Chief as far as possible of those extraneous responsibilities which they have hitherto been burdened; and
> (b) giving Commanders-in-Chief that political guidance which has not hitherto been available locally;
> (c) settling promptly matters within the policy of His Majesty's Government but involving several local authorities.
> Para. 4 Examples of (a) above are:
> . . . .
> (iv) Propaganda and subversive warfare.

A civilian authority was thus provided who was not a representative of any of the Ministries in London, but could act with great force as an arbiter between their warring agents in Middle East.

The internal position of SOE gave rise to as much anxiety as its 'foreign affairs'. D Section had made an unfortunate name for itself with most other British agencies in the Balkans; but during the winter and spring of 1940–41, SO2 in the Balkans had been fighting a real war and had emerged not without credit. Money was of course spent freely, and without much accounting: but visible results followed, and there was a decrease in allegations of pure inefficiency and extrava-

---

[1] Mr Jebb to Brigadier Mallaby, 10th June 1941, on SOE Archives File HD/68: also signal of same date to General Wavell from Dalton – copy on SOE Archives File 60/470/1. [A. W .S. Mallaby, 1899–1945, Indian Army, deputy DMO 1941–2.]

[2] ME(M)(41)1st Mtg, para. 5, of 30th May: and 2nd Mtg, para. 2, of 16th June.

[3] WP(41)148 of 28th June 1941.

* [O. Lyttelton, 1893–1972, son of Alfred, businessman and politician, conservative MP 1940–54, Minister of State, Middle East 1942–3, Minister of Production 1943–5, Viscount Chandos 1954, KG 1970; in *DNB*. See his *Memoirs* (1962).]

gance in the Balkan areas, though SO2's policy there was frequently under fire. There was however confusion as to responsibilities: it was not clear how far (if at all) Bailey's Balkan HQ in Istanbul (later in Jerusalem) was controlled by Pollock and through him by the Commanders-in-Chief, nor was it clear who was responsible for Greek affairs after the capture of Major Taylor in Yugoslavia.[1]

There were in addition grave doubts about the efficiency and even the honesty of the management of SO2 affairs within the Middle East area. Uneasiness seems to have grown in the London Headquarters independently of outside reports from Middle East. Pollock's recall had been suggested by the beginning of April 1941,[2] but General Wavell had then spoken well of him and had discouraged the idea. By the beginning of May, London was clear that matters could not continue as they were.[3] Apparently this view was now confirmed by General Wavell.[4] The problem was to find at short notice a man with the experience and standing to command confidence and make sweeping changes. One or two early efforts were unsuccessful, and the choice fell on Brigadier Taverner, a regular soldier with a record of ten years service in India and a knowledge of East Africa. His directive[5] gave him very wide powers over the internal affairs of SO2; it also directed him to consider and report on its relations with the Commander-in-Chief and his Staff, the Jerusalem Bureau, G(R), His Majesty's representatives in the various countries of the Middle East, and with SO1. Evidence of extreme strain between SO1 and SO2 in Cairo was already reaching London, and the last point was of special importance. It should be noted that at this stage the Minister was entirely satisfied with SO1's work within its own sphere and telegraphed to Colonel Thornhill in this sense on 18th June suggesting his up-grading to Brigadier, to match Brigadier Taverner.[6] This of course implied that it was then in mind that the two branches should henceforward be co-equal and independent of one another. The shadowy primacy enjoyed by Colonel Pollock would disappear.

Unluckily Brigadier Taverner was on board the flying-boat 'Golden Fleece' which was shot down in the Bay of Biscay; he was rescued and taken prisoner, but the search for a solution had to begin again.

---

[1] Above p. 112. Correspondence on this subject on SOE Archives Files 60/470/1 and 60nc/470/11.1.

[2] Mr Dalton to General Wavell 60156 (DMI) of 5th April (not found): referred to in General Wavell's reply 1/56802 of 14th April on SOE Archives File HD/SC/68.4.

[3] E.g. CD's Minute of 3rd May on SOE's Archives File HD/68: 'there was no less than 21 telegrams outstanding to the ME to which we are still awaiting replies'.

[4] Mr Dalton's memo. to CIGS of 27th May, on SOE Archives File (AD/S.1) HD/68.

[5] Dated 17th June; copy on SOE Archives File (AD/S.1) HD/SC/68.4.

[6] Telegram of 15th June, on SOE Archives File (AD/S.1) HD/SC/68.4.

The interim answer is to be found in the telegram of 26th June, addressed both to Pollock and to Bailey.[1]

The effect of this telegram was to abandon decisively the attempt to centralise SO2 work under the Cairo Office: the telegram is from SO2 and contains no mention of SO1, but its drift was hardly likely to strengthen Pollock's authority over the other branch. Its contents were briefly:

(a) Balkan Section for Hungary, Yugoslavia, Bulgaria, Roumania to be independent (under Bailey) reporting direct to London.

(b) Iran to be an independent section, reporting direct to London.

(c) Malta and Tunisia to continue as independent sections, reporting direct to London.

(d) Turkey to be made into an independent section as soon as possible.

(e) Pollock to control a curtailed ME section (Egypt, Palestine, Syria, Transjordan, Iraq, Saudi Arabia, Cyprus), with a limited role: no more para-military activities, no underground politics, no schemes for pre-occupational demolition, no propaganda except within political directives of Jerusalem Bureau: in fact nothing except preparations for sabotage in the event of German occupation; and a little Arab propaganda.

(f) Greece to pass to Balkan Section if possible which should be responsible only for political contacts in collaboration with Mr Sebastian of the Cairo Embassy: all para-military plans for Greece to be the concern of G(R) within GHQ.

The process by which this solution was reached is not clear, but it was scarcely plausible except as a desperate remedy. It would stop what was believed to be the damaging influence of the Cairo office, and of the Cairo atmosphere, and it might be hoped that it would stop wrangles with 'the military'. But it reduced the status of SOE as a unified organisation in the Middle East almost to vanishing point, and it foreboded the administrative nightmare of five independent sections sharing the same base areas and similar strategic problems, with no common centre except London. It was in any case overtaken at once by the initiative of the Minister of State immediately after his arrival in Cairo.[2] General Wavell was succeeded by General Auchinleck at about the same time.

---

[1] No. 4065 to Cairo on SOE Archives File (AD/S.1) HD/SC/68.4.

[2] See Cairo telegram No. 2178 of 10th July, Foreign Office to Cairo No. 2443 'Twist' of 12th July, Cairo No. 225 of 16th July, Foreign Office to Cairo No. 2526 of 18th July – all on SOE Archives File (AD/S.1) HD/SC/68. Also the Minister of State's telegram to the Prime Minister No. 2340 No cop of 27th July on the general propaganda organisation (same file).

On 10th July Mr Lyttelton telegraphed Mr Dalton: 'Preliminary enquiries which I have made into the activities of SO2 organisation in Middle East point to alarming state of affairs. Information in the possession of HQ Middle East reveals inefficiency, extravagance and even corruption. It is essential that a senior and responsible officer, proferably head of SO2 organisation itself, should come to Cairo at once to investigate.' After an exchange of telegrams it was agreed to send Sir Frank Nelson by air to look into the affairs of SO2.[1]

His terms of reference were unfortunately confused by the fact that the search for a replacement for Brigadier Taverner had now been successful. The choice fell on Mr Terence Maxwell,* a director of Glyn Mills, and son-in-law of Mr Neville Chamberlain, whose energy and business capacity were highly spoken of: it was unfortunate but almost unavoidable that the man chosen should be without experience of SOE work. He was not, like Brigadier Taverner, to be concerned only with SO2, but was to be Mr Dalton's 'representative in Middle East, in charge of all SOE activities, both SO1 and SO2'.[2] 'You will review the existing organisation of SO1 and SO2 throughout these areas and are empowered to make such changes as you think necessary to promote efficiency and eliminate causes of personal discord. If you decide to liquidate any prominent personalities, you should submit recommendations to me before action. I undertake that you shall have a quick reply.'

Mr Maxwell's directive was thus very wide, and its tenor had been endorsed by the head of SO1:[3] that of Sir Frank Nelson was apparently narrow, and had certainly been regarded as a matter purely for SO2.[4] But in fact when the party reached Cairo on 5th August, matters affecting both branches were handled by Sir Frank Nelson, and the vital telegrams were sent in his name, although with the express concurrence of Mr Maxwell and of higher authorities.

It is unnecessary to follow in detail the discussions in Cairo with the

---

[1] The Prime Minister minuted Mr Dalton on 23rd July, deprecating the idea of a formal Court of Inquiry: M.701/1 on SOE Archives File (AD/S.1) HD/SC/68/3.

[2] Draft Directive with Mr Dalton's amendments – on file HD/SC/68/3: annotated to be telegraphed out 4th August – telegram not found.

[3] See Mr Leeper's telegram to Colonel Thornhill, dated 26th July – SOE Archives File HD/SC/68/3.

[4] A paragraph which in effect gave him full powers until Mr Maxwell wished to take over was deleted by Mr Dalton from the latter's directive.

* [A. T. Maxwell, 1905–91, married daughter of Sir Austen Chamberlain, businessman, in Middle East 1941–2, at Allied Force HQ 1943–4, returned to City after war.]

Minister of State, Lieutenant General Sir Arthur Smith (the CGS),* Mr Rucker (of the Minister of State's office)** and others involved.[1] The case against SO2 was documented in a collection of papers known colloquially as the 'Anti-SO2 Dossier',[2] which was apparently put together under the authority of Sir Arthur Smith. It includes derogatory comments on SO2's operations, security and expenditure gathered from a variety of sources, as well as some fairly convincing attacks on the reliability of SO2's claims of sabotage in Syria: but there is no first-hand documentary evidence except a few telegrams abstracted from SO2's files, which prove only its incapacity to execute some of London's more optimistic directives. None of this would have held water in a Court of Law or a Court of Enquiry: but when supported by the unanimous voice of Cairo gossip it was at least proof of such general mistrust that the present SO2 organisation could not be maintained.

There were no similar charges against SO1; but common talk, and the compilation of the dossier in which SO1 took some part, proved the existence since the beginning of 1941 of what Sir Frank Nelson calls 'blood-thirsty internecine warfare . . . between two parts of the same entity'.[3] Sir Frank Nelson made no claim to have investigated the internal affairs of SO1 or to have found them wanting: though it should be added that 'he formed the poorest opinion' of Colonel Thornhill's judgement.[4]

The result of these rapid investigations is embodied in a telegram of 11th August[5] addressed to Colonel Taylor for the Minister, which had the approval in detail[6] of the Minister of State, the Ambassador and the CGS, as well as of Mr Maxwell: the Minister of State confirmed his approval separately[7] – 'I am entirely satisfied with his recommendations . . . . He has carried out a difficult and unpleasant task with the utmost tact and firmness.' CD's conclusions are best given in his own words:

---

1 See Sir Frank Nelson's Report on SOE Archives File (AD/S.1) SC/68/3.
2 SOE Archives File HD/F.68/3a.
3 Sir Frank Nelson's Report – 1. above.
4 Nos 4 and 5 of 11th August, on SOE Archives File (AD/S.1) HD/SC/68/3: see also file 60nc/330/11.
5 Nos 4 and 5 of 11th August, on SOE Archives File (AD/S.1) HD/SC/68/3: see also file 60nc/330/11.
6 Last paragraph of 1. and Sir Frank Nelson's Report, p. 5.
7 Cairo telegram No. 2498 of 11th August, on SOE Archives File (AD/S.1) HD/SC/68/3.
* [A. F. Smith, 1890–1977, Coldstream Guards, Chief of Staff Middle East 1940–42, knight 1942, C-in-C Eastern Command, India 1947.]
** [(Sir) A. N. Rucker, 1895–1991, knight 1942, deputy secretary Ministry of Health 1943–8.]

b. Senior personnel of SO2 have lost confidence of all British authorities. As a result work of SO2 is stultified. Inquiry was therefore urgently necessary and drastic action must be taken at once . . . .

g. The position has been greatly exaggerated by intrigues on all sides, facilitated by parallel communications, by clashing of personalities, by slinging of mud and by orgy of gossip.*

h. Behind this I believe the truth to be:

i. Results are inadequate.

ii. There has been extravagance, and probably some improper expenditure.

iii. Control has been lax and ineffective.

iv. In any case and above all, situation is now out of hand because confidence has been largely impaired.

On these premises the inevitable conclusion was the immediate recall, before Mr Maxwell took over, of the senior officers in both branches: Colonel Thornhill and Colonel Wetherell of SO1, Colonel Pollock and Colonel Bailey of SO2. To this was joined the recall of a third SO1 officer, Lieutenant Colonel Johnstone, who had been sent out to assist in special propaganda in Greece, but had arrived too late and appears to have been retained by Colonel Thornhill to assist him in developing Balkan propaganda, in spite of clear directions that he was to return to London.[1]

Unfortunately Mr Dalton was on leave when this recommendation arrived, and the papers had to be sent to him outside London: so that opportunities for discussion were limited. Mr Leeper as head of SO1 submitted a reply suggesting that action on Thornhill's case should be delayed until his defence had been received and reported to London.[2] Mr Dalton clearly felt that this was impracticable in face of the united representations of all high authorities in Cairo, and he drafted his own telegrams to Sir Frank Nelson and to the Minister of State, accepting their recommendations *in toto*.[3] However it might be softened or disguised as 'recall', this was in effect the dismissal of SO1 officers whose work for SO1 had not been called in question:

---

[1] See Mr Dalton's cipher 99101 of 28th January to General Wavell, the latter's reply 1/39261 cipher of 3rd February, and Colonel Johnstone's original terms of reference of 31st March, on SOE Archives File (AD/S.1) HD/SC/68/4, and a summary of telegrams about his recall in 'Anti-SO1 Dossier' – File HD/SC/68/4a.

[2] Draft dated 31st August, on SOE Archives File HD/SC/68/3, and Mr Dalton's letter to Mr Leeper – on same file.

[3] Nos 12, 13 and 14 of 14th August, to Cairo – on SOE Archives File (AD/S.1) HD/SC/68/3.

* [See Lady Ranfurly, *To War with Whitaker* (1994) and Sweet-Escott, *Baker Street Irregular*, esp. pp. 73–4.]

and it was natural that they should be defended, and their fate resented, by their superior officers in SO1.[1] The situation was not eased by the crisis in London which was at this time leading up to the formation of PWE, and there were one or two accidental aggravating circumstances. For one thing Colonel Bailey was permitted to remain in Middle East for a few weeks until he could be relieved by Colonel T. S. Masterson (who had been very successful in Belgrade),[2] and Lieutenant Colonel Johnstone (whose fate was really a separate issue) had been added to the two SO1 'deportees': so that there were three immediate victims from SO1 and one only from SO2, which had been the first cause of scandal. Further, Mr Dalton had asked that all four victims should leave Cairo as soon as possible (so as to clear the air), but had not asked for air passages for them to England, in view of the many urgent claims on the inadequate air transport facilities available. This was natural enough, but its effect was that Colonel Thornhill did not reach London to state his case until 1st October,[3] and the matter was then very cold.

It is worth mentioning these trivial points only because of the resentment left in the 'corporate mind' of SO1, and transmitted by it to PWE. There was undoubtedly a feeling, which bore no relation to the facts, that SO2 had on this occasion recklessly and unscrupulously defeated SO1 on an important personal issue. It is equally curious, and much more important, that the SOE organisation had for the first time been formally unified in Middle East, just as it was splitting into two separate departments in London. It was inevitable that war should break out again later on this front; but the situation was accepted for the moment by PWE. It may be that this was due, at least in part, to the acceptance at last of the request of the Commanders-in-Chief for a co-ordinator of propaganda, and the appointment of Sir Walter Monckton (hitherto Director-General at the Ministry of Information) to fill this post under the Minister of State.[4]

The last important point decided during CD's visit was the constitution of a sub-committee of the Middle East War Council to co-ordinate the activities of the various secret organisations in the Middle

---

[1] On 17th August Mr Leeper declined to take further responsibility for the affairs of SO1 in Middle East (letter on SOE Archives File (AD/S.1) HD/SC68/3); presumably matters were set right by the creation of PWE on 19th August – p. 101 above.

[2] Above p. 105.

[3] Note of interview by Mr Dalton, on SOE Archives File (AD/S.1) HD/SC/68/4(a).

[4] See ME(M)41 3rd Mtg, Item 5, of 11th July, and Minister of State to Prime Minister No. 2340 Nocop of 27th July 1941 – copy on SOE Archives File (AD/S.1) HD/SC/68/3, and the Minister of State's letter of 2nd October to Mr Dalton on file HD/SC/68/4.

East.[1] This would meet under the Chairmanship of the Minister of State, and would include the Commanders-in-Chief, or their representatives, as well as those of SOE, SIS, G(R), MI9 and the 'Strategic Deception' organisation: in practice an impossibly multifarious body, which perished early. In November it was replaced by a more restricted 'SOE Sub-Committee', consisting only of the Minister of State, the representatives of the Commanders-in-Chief, and Mr Maxwell.[2] It was agreed at the same time 'that the amalgamation of SOE and G(R) was desirable in principle but that definite action to that effect should be deferred for the time being'.

3. Mr Maxwell's Régime, August 1941–August 1942

The progress of Mr Maxwell's reorganisation[3] is not easy to trace closely, as many of the Cairo files were destroyed in the 'great panic' of June 1942, and it is obvious from the London papers that Baker Street was somewhat in the dark as to details. But the main lines were simple enough.

> On paper unison was complete: the new organisation had four
>   main divisions[4] –
> Directorate of Special Operations (Colonel Airey)*
> Directorate of Policy and Agents (Colonel Masterson)
> Directorate of Special Propaganda (Mr Euan Butler)
> Directorate of Finance and Administration (Mr G. P. S.
>   Macpherson).**

To these may be added a few subsidiary branches – security, secretariat and an independent Italian Section. In practice matters were much as before, except for the addition of Mr Maxwell, as a co-ordinator unsupported by a strong personal staff or by the corporate feeling of his organisation.

DSO (Directorate of Special Operations) was in fact G(R), still passing under that cover-name, and manned by soldiers on military principles, including 'approved war establishments' and the rapid and random posting of officers in and out of the organisation. G(R) had in this conversion lost certain para-military activities directly ancil-

---

1   Minutes of Meeting of 13th August, Minister of State in the Chair, on SOE Archives File (AD/S.1) HD/SC/68/3.
2   Alpha telegram 119 of 21st November, on SOE Archives File (AD/S.1) HD/68.
3   There is a brief and unilluminating report by Mr Maxwell on his Mission as a whole; copy on SOE Archives File (AD/S.1) 68, Vol. 2.
4   See note dated 3rd October 1941, on SOE Archives 'Middle East Establishment File' (AD.3).
*   [(Sir) T. S. Airey, 1900–83, commanded in Trieste 1947–51, knight 1951.]
** [1903–81, accountant.]

lary to the war in the Western Desert: and a considerable line of progeny descended from what was left with GHQ – the Long Range Desert Group, the SAS and the Raiding Forces in the Aegean and Adriatic. This closer association with the military coincided with the first full consideration by the Staffs of the military implications of subversive activities based in Cairo: the results were embodied in a full and careful paper[1] by the JPS, Middle East, which contained little new matter, but put an official seal on plans and conceptions already in existence.

DPA (Directorate of Policy and Agents) was D Section, manned by civilians in or out of uniform, still responsible for political work, and for the control and dispatch of agents connected with it and with clandestine sabotage. This line between operations by agents (DPA) and operations by irregular British forces (DSO) could have no reality in the field, and appears to have broken down at once in practice. On 21st November[2] Mr Maxwell informed London of a further reorganisation by which DSO became responsible for all operations, and DPA (retaining these initials) was transformed into the Directorate of Political Advice, in two sections, for the Arab World and for the Balkans. Concurrently with this change it was agreed that G(R) officers should now be put freely at the disposal of the organisation as a whole, and should be held by DSO on an SOE establishment for personnel on loan from the Services: i.e. that there should at least be a formal merging of G(R) and SOE. London was in some doubt lest in practice it should be G(R) which had swallowed SOE and these doubts were reinforced by the resignation of Colonel Masterson, an old SOE hand, on the ground that the new organisation gave no scope for the true technique of subversion – 'preparations for eventual uprising of people of Near East, especially in Balkans, can better be achieved by more flexible methods of a conspiratorial nature than within the more rigid framework of a military organisation such as has now been decided upon'.[3] He was persuaded to withdraw his resignation; but this was merely temporary and he returned to London on 21st April 1942, leaving SOE Middle East with no experienced senior officer in the tradition of D Section.

---

[1] ME JPS Paper No. 73, dated 5th December 1941, circulated in London as JP(41)1074 of 26th December; copy on SOE Archives File (AD/S.1) HD/68. See also preliminary paper by DSO dated 18th November 1941, SG(R)/43 on SOE Archives File 32nc/470/1.

[2] Alpha telegrams Nos 115-19 of 21st November 1941, on SOE Archives File (AD/S.1) HD/68.

[3] Alpha telegram No. 126 of 30th November, on SOE Archives File (AD/S.1) HD/F.34.1.

DSP (Directorate of Special Propaganda) like DSO retained an old cover-name, that of GS1(K), but it represented a more real consolidation, as it brought together under one head practically all the 'odd jobs' of secret propaganda based in Middle East:[1] broadcasting to the Balkans and to the enemy from Jerusalem Station, [PASSAGE DELETED ON GROUNDS OF NATIONAL SECURITY] 'whispering' campaigns in Middle East: the preparation of propaganda leaflets: and the organisation of Army propaganda companies. This was locally a gain, but it confused the issue of higher control still further. PWE was responsible for the direction of propaganda to the enemy and to enemy-occupied countries in Europe, and was itself conducting secret broadcasts to the Balkans from stations in England: SOE was prepared to accept its Directives for the Jerusalem Station and other Balkan propaganda, but held that it must have discretion to neglect them where the needs of operations in the field required it. Within the Middle Eastern area PWE had no responsibilities; open propaganda was the duty of the Ministry of Information, 'subversion' of a multiplicity of authorities of whom SOE was one. SOE could in part obtain directives from the Arab Bureau in Jerusalem, in part it took its own line with such local guidance as it could find. Internecine warfare in this jungle paused for a little after the constitution of PWE in August 1941, but it broke out again on the report of a Committee under Sir Walter Monckton in December 1941,[2] and raged fairly continuously until SOE's interest in it was practically eliminated in March 1943.

All these factors, in the over-charged atmosphere of Cairo, made Mr Maxwell's position uneasy from the outset. To sum up the difficulties, most of which have been indicated elsewhere:

(a) There soon grew up a feeling in London that Mr Maxwell's personal qualities were inadequate for so great a task – he was felt to be too 'academic' and 'organisational'.[3] This distrust deepened as time went on.

(b) London believed that 'the military' had almost swallowed up the operational side of the organisation, and that they were not conducting it very efficiently. Junior officers came and went too frequently, and they hardly regarded a job in DSO as a serious step in their military career. One or two opera-

---

[1] See summary prepared for Lord Selborne, dated 30th March 1942, on SOE Archives File (AD/S.1) HD/SC/68/4.

[2] See Cairo telegram No. 3806 of 3rd December 1941 – on SOE Archives File (AD/S.1) HD/SC/68/4: and below p. 375.

[3] See CD's record of discussion with Minister of State in London on 2nd October 1941, on SOE Archives File (AD/S.1) HD/68.

tional mistakes can certainly be traced to this department.[1]

(c) The whole position of DSP was under heavy attack, and it gave one or two good openings to criticism by the Foreign Office: for instance, the celebrated attack on the King of Greece,[2] and some (fairly inoffensive) preliminary steps to arrange for the subversion of Kurds, Armenians and Georgians.[3]

(d) The Balkan political situation was harassingly difficult for all concerned, and SOE attracted many of the kicks that were freely distributed by the Foreign Office. SOE's part in Yugoslav and Greek politics has been considered in some detail above: there is no end to argument as to the degree of SOE's responsibility, but it is at least clear that there was no effective political head of SOE in Cairo.

This dissatisfaction can be found fairly early on the 'working level' in London: the most important personality here was Lord Glenconner, who became head of the Balkans and Middle East Section in October 1941, and was promoted to Director and member of the SOE Council in April 1942. But it was not until the spring of 1942 that the time was ripe for a new departure. By that date Mr Dalton had been succeeded by Lord Selborne, and Sir Frank Nelson by Sir Charles Hambro, while Mr Sporborg a little later became Principal Private Secretary to the Minister, with a role similar to that hitherto held by Mr Jebb. Mr Lyttelton had ceased to be Minister of State on 18th February; his successor, Mr Casey,* was not appointed until 15th March, and could not then take over at once, so that there was an interregnum during which Sir Walter Monckton acted in his place. Lord Selborne saw Mr Casey before he left London, but little could be done with SOE's problems while this major reshuffle was in progress.

The first general statement of London's criticisms is to be found in a Minute[4] put forward by Lord Glenconner on 3rd April: one paragraph of this is worth quoting: 'Directing SOE activities, whether they be in occupied countries or making preparations against invasion, is

---

[1] For instance Operation 'Isinglass' to Greece (above p. 151), the first supply-dropping operation to Greece (above p. 152), Hudson's wireless equipment (above p. 117): the failure to reinforce Hudson in the winter of 1941–2 was also held against them, less fairly.

[2] Above p. 157.

[3] See Mr Eden's letter of 12th February 1942, on SOE Archives File (AD/S.1) HD/SC/68/4, and correspondence between Mr Jebb and Sir Orme Sargent arising out of it and above, p. 171.

[4] On Middle East Establishment File (SOE Archives).

* [R. G. Casey, 1890–1976, Australian Minister to USA 1940–42, Minister of State, Middle East 1942–3, Governor of Bengal 1944–6, Governor-General of Australia 1965–9, KG 1969.]

not an affair which can be conducted either on big business and' (sic) 'still less on military lines. The success of SOE operations depends on their secrecy, the most laborious and closest attention to detail, and on the most intimate knowledge of the countries concerned. If this is not present, the patient work of months can be thrown away by one mistake or ill-judged action. Moreover, each country constitutes a different problem requiring its own treatment and solution. We should look therefore to what I may call the "handcraft principle" as opposed to that of mass production, and to throwing responsibility as much as possible on to the officer responsible for each country section.'

This is an excellent statement of the 'professional outlook' of SOE, as it had already developed; and there was a clear contrast between this and the form and spirit of the Cairo organisation. There were minor contributory causes of disagreement: requests for staff from Cairo which seemed to show little sense of realities, and recriminations[1] about Cairo's failure to keep London fully briefed so that it might exercise due control and fight Cairo's case in Whitehall. But the breaking point came on proposals for reorganisation. Full proposals were telegraphed[2] by London on 26th May, indicating with some tact that it would be in the best interests of SOE that the Cairo organisation should conform to the London model; the specialists of the 'Country Sections' should carry the primary responsibility for matters of detail, and the para-military work, which represented the G(R) tradition, should be segregated or expelled entirely. Maxwell's reply was a flat *non possumus* – 'a major operation such as CD suggested was not required, and was in fact undesirable'; this was qualified only by the suggestion that a personal visit from a high official from London might give a chance of satisfactory discussion. It is essential to remember that the organisation in the Middle East now consisted of some 1,100 people, widely dispersed geographically, of whom perhaps a dozen had some connection with the early days of the organisation in the Balkans and Middle East, and only four or five had any knowledge of the London Office.[3] SOE Middle

---

[1] Cairo Alpha telegram 374–6 of 26th May – quoted in SOE London HQ War Diary, Mid-East and Balkans Section, p. 3835.

[2] Alpha 286–7 to Cairo of 27th May: final draft in SOE Archives 'Middle East Establishment File' (AD.3). See also SOE London HQ War Diary – May 1942, p. 3831.

[3] Figures in draft letter to Foreign Office, dated 6th June 1942, in SOE Archives 'Middle East Establishment File' (AD.3):

Paid by SOE	399 (of whom 220 were engaged in propaganda).
Paid by Army	209
Army personnel attached	444
	1,052

East lived its own life, and had not much conception of its place in a wider organisation.

Greater events intervened at this point. Rommel launched his offensive on 27th May, Tobruk fell on 20th June, and Alamein was reached by 1st July; there followed the 'Cairo panic', in which most of SOE's staff were evacuated to Palestine, and many of their papers were burnt. For the moment nothing was done but to dispatch a team of 'junior' experts, which had been under preparation for some months: but by 24th June the recall of Mr Maxwell and his replacement by an officer from London was under discussion. The person proposed was Lord Glenconner himself; by 10th July this had become a firm decision,[1] although the decisive telegram[2] was not dispatched until 29th July, when the situation on the Alamein front was fairly stable. It expressed very full appreciation of the value of Mr Maxwell's work, but indicated that a new phase had begun and that it would be in the interests both of Mr Maxwell and of the organisation to make a change.

4. The Appointment of Lord Glenconner, August 1942

Mr Maxwell accepted his own displacement with a good grace, but on the principles involved he appealed at once to Mr Casey, the Minister of State. Here he found strong support, and a difficult exchange of telegrams followed between Lord Selborne and Mr Casey, complicated by the fact that Lord Glenconner had taken advantage of one of the rare opportunities of air passage to leave for Cairo before final agreement had been reached. The incident indicates one of the reasons why Cairo and London had grown so far apart: it was impossible to arrange a regular interchange of higher officials, as passages by air were almost unobtainable (especially after the heavy attacks on Malta and the loss of Cyrenaica) and the length of the sea voyage was prohibitive.

The Minister of State's views, formed in discussion with the Commanders-in-Chief, are expressed in his telegram[3] of 6th August. 'The fact is that SOE can only work effectively if it is in closest possible touch with the three Services. SOE plans must be intimately related to military operations and SOE are dependent on the Services for air and sea transport. Success depends therefore on complete confidence between the Controller of SOE and the Commanders-in-Chief

---

[1] Cf. Lord Glenconner's Minute of 10th July, on SOE Archives 'Middle East Establishment File' (AD.3).

[2] Alpha telegram 356 of 29th July: text on SOE London HQ War Diary – July 1942, p. 4; copy on SOE Archives File (AD/S.1) F/68/13.

[3] No. 1244 of 6th August; copy on SOE Archives File (AD/S.1) F/68/13 – and file 60/470.3 refers.

and their staffs. Maxwell during his tenure of office has been at pains to win this confidence and is to be congratulated on results he has achieved. Co-ordinating machinery, the details of which are known to you, has been built and is working well. But the Commanders-in-Chief and I believe more is needed and that best results can only be secured by appointing as head of SOE a service staff officer of adequate seniority. It is in our view immaterial from which service he is chosen, but we think that he should be, or have been, a regular officer and have passed the Staff College.' The officer suggested was Colonel Jennings, who had succeeded Colonel Airey as DSO in April 1942.

SOE Headquarters would have admitted the premise, that the confidence of the Services was essential: it denied absolutely the conclusion that this could or should be given only to a regular soldier. In this it could count on support from the Foreign Office, who well understood the political consequences of the view that nothing counted but 'killing Huns'. SOE in London had been brought to accept Foreign Office guidance with a reasonably good grace, and Glenconner himself had won the confidence of the Foreign Office: if SOE Cairo became a wholly military organisation the whole battle would be fought again. This point was stressed in the further exchange of telegrams,[1] in which Lord Selborne insisted that the Cairo proposal was impossible and stood firm on the appointment of Lord Glenconner: the only concession offered was that a regular soldier might be appointed as his 'No. 2'.

All this meant, however, that when Lord Glenconner reached Cairo on 13th August, he was on very difficult ground. It was an indispensable condition of SOE work in Middle East that the confidence of the Services should be retained, but this beginning had been inauspicious. His task as seen in London could be summarised in four points:

(i) To reassert the general control of the London Office over policy, subject to the immediate control of the Commanders-in-Chief over operations.

(ii) To keep matters on the right lines politically.

(iii) To expel the G(R) influence – the tendency to become paramilitary rather than subversive.

---

[1] No. 1790 to Cairo of 8th August: Cairo No. 1278 of 10th August: No. 1822 to Cairo of 12th August (drafts of London telegrams on SOE Archives File (AD/S. 1) F/68/13). See also Lord Selborne's letter to Mr Casey of 8th August – draft on same file; and Lord Glenconner's directive dated 20th August (original on SOE Archives File 60nc/460/4). Mr Eden was away and his personal agreement was not received till 18th August – telegram No. 1882 to Cairo of 18th August – copy on file F/68/13 mentioned above.

    (iv) To reorganise internally on his own 'handcraft principle', so that operations should be conducted by expert and semi-autonomous sections, not on military lines.

At first sight none of this was practicable politics in Cairo, but it did prove possible to save something from the wreck. In the first place, Mr Eden's personal intervention induced the Cairo authorities to accept the appointment without further debate and to arrange a meeting for 21st August between Lord Glenconner and the Commanders-in-Chief. At this meeting a memorandum[1] was presented setting out Lord Glenconner's conception of his task; and this too was accepted in general both by the Minister of State[2] and by the Commanders-in-Chief. What they had accepted was an able but general statement on Subversion and its technique; what they obtained in exchange was a form of organisation which secured the essence of control for the military authorities in Middle East, while Lord Glenconner was left free of detailed work to do what could be done on the political level.

The main changes effected[3] were that the Controller of the Mission was provided with a Chief of Staff; the Directorate of Political Advice disappeared, the Directorate of Special Propaganda remained – and its relations with PWE are a separate story. The post of Chief of Staff was held by Lieutenant Colonel C. M. Keble (later upgraded to Brigadier), a regular soldier of strong personality and narrow views: in effect, all operations into the field now came under his control, through two Directors of Special Operations; Group Captain Domville for the Arab World, and Colonel G. R. Tamplin for the Balkans. Within these Directorates there existed on paper country sections on the London model: in practice experts were rare and the working posts were filled by soldiers, some professional, some amateur – some competent, others the reverse. This organisation was driven hard by Brigadier Keble, and in time acquired an efficiency of its own; but on the lower levels it was not acutely sensitive to political impressions, and it tended to judge success by military criteria – the number of Allied 'bodies' bearing arms in the field, the numbers of 'Huns' and 'Eyties' slain. Lord Glenconner's personal influence undoubtedly improved the handling of political matters on the higher levels, and the tone of relations with the Foreign Office

---

[1] Copy No. 14 on SOE Archives File 60/470/1.3.

[2] See his Arfar telegram No. 8 of 31st August – copy on SOE Archives File 60nc/460/1, and Lord Selborne's reply No. 2035 of 2nd September, on SOE Archives File (AD/S.1) F/68/13.

[3] See Operational Standing Orders for SOE, ME, dated 25th September 1942, on SOE Archives File 60nc/460/4.

on Balkan questions never again sank to the earlier level: in addition, the principle had been preserved that SOE Middle East was a Mission responsible primarily to Headquarters in London, not an agency of the Middle East Command. Beyond this little had been gained. SOE Cairo continued to be a body which had little in common with SOE London.

CHAPTER IX

Western Europe – Norway*

Introductory

We have now traced the development of the Balkan resistance and of the SOE organisation in Middle East up to the late summer of 1942: a period which marks a turning-point both in the internal development of resistance and in the role which the Allies expected of it. Hitherto it had been a matter of making contacts, building movements, incidentally doing minor damage to the enemy while strategically the Allies fought a rearguard action: now substantial guerilla forces were openly in the field, both in Yugoslavia and in Greece, and the problem was to supply and control their operations so as to make a useful contribution to an Allied offensive.

The same period can be taken as a turning-point in Western Europe. It was here another eighteen months before military operations had to be brought directly into relation with the work of the Resistance: but the launching of 'Torch' was, nevertheless, a crisis in French history, and the story of the Resistance in the West is primarily the story of France. 'Torch' merged the Occupied and Unoccupied Zones, it re-established a Free French Government in territory which ranked as the soil of France, above all it profoundly altered the 'morale' of the situation.

Belgium and Holland, though they have interesting histories, must be treated briefly, and their military and political weight was relatively small. The Scandinavian countries are rather differently placed: they were never called upon to play a part in the main Allied offensive, although their underground movements made remarkable contributions of their own. But what is of great general interest is that both

---

* [Besides Cruickshank's official history, see also Knut Haukelid, *Skis against the Atom* (1954), B. Nokelby and O. Riste, *Norway 1940–1945: The Resistance Movement* (4th ed., Oslo, 1984) and Patrick Salmon (ed.), *Britain and Norway in the Second World War* (1995). There is also a large literature in Norwegian, beginning with Jens Chr. Hauge, *Frigoringen* (Oslo, 1970) on the circumstances of the Germans' first arrival.]

Norway and Denmark present cases where internal political division were of comparatively little importance in face of the enemy. A narrative which dealt in detail only with France and with the Balkans would present on the whole a depressing picture of the Resistance and of the ultimate results of SOE's work in the political field: it would leave the impression that an underground movement can only grow at the cost of political turmoil and ceaseless jealousy – great sacrifices are made and great deeds done, but the question is left as to whether they were worth the price. Might it not have been better for Europe if we had left it alone?

The stories of Norway and Denmark are valuable as an antidote to this view. They had grave political probelms of their own, and there were crises in their collaboration with SOE: there were also a few bad technical mistakes in the practical developments of their movements. But in neither country were internal feuds of much importance; nor could any political party be seriously accused of using British aid for its own purposes at the expense of the national cause.

Norway is the most favourable case of all, and therefore the most suitable for discussion in detail: it is also of value in illustrating conditions which differed greatly both from the wild partisan warfare of the Balkans and from underground work in a heavily garrisoned and thickly populated country such as France: Denmark will be dealt with briefly.

Norway[1]

1. The Background

A few general remarks are necessary to introduce the Norwegian story.

Politically the main points are these:

(a) In spite of the great role played by the Norsemen in the early Middle Ages, Norway has long stood outside the main current of European history. It was annexed to the Danish Crown for some 400 years up to 1814; and was thereafter subject to Sweden (with independent institutions of its own) until 1905. The memory of this long period rankles a little, and has left its mark on the present feelings of Norway toward the other Scandinavian countries: but there was little of conquest, subjection, spoliation about Danish or Swedish rule. Till the German invasion of 8th April 1940, Norway had not shared the common European experience of foreign conquest: nor had it played any aggressive part in European politics. It had a proud past as a great

---

[1] An excellent history of the Norwegian Section of SOE was prepared by Colonel Wilson. There is also a useful account by Miss Janet Gow of the SOE Mission in Stockholm.

nation, but a very distant one. When invasion came, the national spirit was shocked and outraged: there was no question of submission, but little idea of how to resist. All good 'Jøssings' were anxious to get at the Germans, but they were ignorant and often very innocent about how to do it and what the cost would be.

(b) The national tradition is strong, and there is plenty of life in organisations on a national scale such as the political parties, the Church, the Trade Unions, the Universities. But the most typical feature of Norwegian institutions is the combination of high national standards in social services with an administration fully decentralised to elected local authorities. There are over 700 elected local authorities for a population of some 3,000,000: so that the average constituency is very small, and the local representative is close to those he represents. Yet most of the administrative services are provided by these small units, and local taxation is much heavier than that levied by the national government. In addition, the countryside still stands its ground against the towns: Oslo, Stavanger, Bergen, Trondheim have grown in population and importance, and show the usual social stratification of Western Europe. But they are in no sense dominant, and the typical Norwegian of this story is the peasant farmer and fisherman, holding his small freehold on the old 'odel' tenure, which virtually entails it in the family from generation to generation: often he will take his surname from his farm.

(c) Political parties were pretty evenly balanced between moderate Right and moderate Left, with a slow but steady trend toward the Left.[1] Party views were strongly held and strongly expressed, but domination by one party was unthinkable, and even democratic rule by a strong Parliament majority of one party (as in Great Britain) was rare. Compromise was essential for government and was usually attained. King Haakon's* own role was not attended by much publicity or ceremony, but since his arrival from Denmark in 1905, his identification with Norwegian unity and Norwegian national interests had been absolute, and he had added to his prestige by his own experiences in the German invasion. He and his Government remained in

---

[1] The Labour Party formed a government in 1935 which was still in power in 1940: at the 1936 elections the four main parties polled as follows:

Labour	618,616
Conservative	329,560
Liberal	239,191
Farmers' Party	168,038

Quisling's Nasjonal Samling polled only 26,577 votes.

* [Haakon VII, 1872-1957, King of Norway since 1905.]

the country to the very last, and when they left it was with the good-will of all political parties. The 'Quislings' were an insignificant and odious fraction of the population.

(d) The Norwegian, in spite of geography, is not a creature isolated from the world. The country has always lived by shipping, fisheries and foreign trade, and there are comparatively few Norwegians who have not been abroad and absorbed at least a working knowledge of some foreign language, generally English. Indeed at any given time a pretty high proportion of the population will be overseas, in merchant ships, on the whaling grounds, or in other fisheries. The Norwegian Government in England was at the head of a substantial Norwegian community, with valuable revenue-producing assets; it was less conspicuously a government in exile than any of the other London governments.

The geography of the country presents some paradoxes which will become clearer in the sequel. The mountains at first sight present ideal territory for resistance; the Hardanger Vidda and the Jotunheimen among others, present vast tracts of tangled mountains which could never be swept clear without fantastic expenditure of manpower. Yet they are traversed by many foot-tracks and tolerably equipped with ski-huts and saeters, so that a small tough party can move fairly freely on foot or on ski, summer or winter. There are plenty of instances of individuals who lived safely in the mountains for long periods under German occupation, but the difficulties of building up any large-scale guerilla bands were in reality prohibitive. The mountains were almost foodless and supplies must come either from the valleys or from abroad. The valleys were thinly populated and easily watched, and, however loyal the population, a new face or a strange course of action would be very soon marked. Supply to the mountains from abroad meant air supply, which also had exceptional difficulties. Weather was at all times uncertain. From May to September there was practically no darkness and air operations were impracticable. The terrain was dangerous for parachutists, and it made landing operations nearly impossible except in frozen lakes. To these difficulties of supply it must be added that the problem of internal communications was worse for guerillas than for the enemy. Even if wireless sets had been avail-able, they would have been a serious danger to security: the post and telephone conversations were easily checked, and it was scarcely possible to concert action except by messengers, running the gaunt-let of road controls, or moving slowly over the hills out of reach of the enemy.

The sea-coast was at first much more favourable than the moun-tains. It was some time before the Germans thought it worth while to introduce a really close system of coast-watching: anything less was useless during the winter months, and at first Norwegians came and went pretty freely across the North Sea in small boats. There was a steady trickle of active men coming out as refugees to England: and it was not till the winter of 1942–3 that it became really dangerous to return by fishing-vessel and land in remote corners of the coast. But even in these early days activity by sea was almost impossible in the summer months.

Finally, there was the Swedish frontier, which runs for a thousand miles through wild country, and could never be effectively patrolled. Escape by this route, given reasonable luck, was easy: but the Swedes were morbidly anxious to give no pretext for a complaint that their territory was being used as a military base. The SOE Mission at Stockholm played an important part in Scandinavian operations, but it was never so central a point as seemed possible on paper. It was handicapped not only by Swedish caution, but by the difficulty of passing between Sweden and Britain. The Stockholm air service was grossly overburdened, and its development was a problem which was pressed to Cabinet level more than once. SOE had probably the largest requirement for the transmission of goods to Sweden and the evacuation of passengers to England: but the MEW, PWE and SIS had all vital interests in the service, and strongly supported SOE in pressing for its expansion.[1] But the shortage of aircraft, and particularly of transport aircraft, was felt just as acutely in every other aspect of the war, and it was not till the summer of 1942 that it became possible to operate an air line to Stockholm with reasonable regularity. Even then its capacity was behind requirements, and the demands for its expansion continued till the last stages of the war in Europe.

2. The First Attempts

The story opens with an expedition[2] conceived by D Section as early as 11th May 1940, while fighting was still in progress at Narvik and the Norwegian Government was still on Norwegian soil at Tromso. The plan contemplated landing a small party of Norwegian-speaking civilians in the Sogne Fjord area, to gather information and to do such damage as they could to communications. Naturally no resources

---

[1] The efforts made by SOE to keep this link alive can be traced in SOE Archives File 20/470 – Vols I and II. The question often reached Cabinet level: the following papers among others refer: WM(40)285th of 8th November; Dalton's personal letter to the Prime Minister of 19th November 1940; WM(40)296th of 26th November 1940; WM(41)29th of 17th March 1941.

[2] This narrative is drawn largely from the early SOE London HQ War Diary: see also SOE Archives File XXX/b/6 (63/1940 and early files) which contains a full report by the leader of the demolition party.

existed for such an expedition, except D Section's stocks of demolition stores. Norwegians had to be found and trained, and sea transport had to be arranged and equipped. In the event, action followed the idea with astonishing speed: approval was given by the CSS for the expedition (at a cost of up to £1,000) on 14th May, and it set sail from Aberdeen on 25th May.

The party consisted of twelve Norwegians, and one Norwegian-speaking Swede: they were recruited mainly through the Norwegian Chamber of Commerce in London and the Norwegian Seamen's Association. As was to be expected, they were all untrained and proved to be a very mixed bag. The leader of the expedition, Field, was enterprising but unstable, and the effective leadership devolved upon the Swede Kronberg, ably assisted by Rubin Langmoe, who was one of SOE's best men (under the name of Rubin Larsen) throughout the Norwegian story, and survived to return home with the Independent Company in 1945. The pilot was a pastor named Olaf Leirvaag, who was later Chief Chaplain to the Norwegian forces: his brother, Oscar, who went with him, was also a reliable man.

A 60-ft Esbjerg fishing vessel, the 'Lady', was bought at Buckie and was moved to Aberdeen, where it was overhauled and fitted out with the energetic co-operation of the local authorities between 21st and 25th May. The equipment included 700 lbs of plastic explosive, 600 time-fuses, 2 machine-guns and 5 sub-machine guns, as well as other weapons and a rather limited supply of ammunition. No portable wireless set was taken. The expedition's directive included a large number of industrial and communications targets, between the Sogne Fjord and the Hardanger Fjord, in the area behind Bergen: it was also instructed to gather any useful information it could, and to dump unused arms and ammunition in safe places for future use.

The 'Lady' left Aberdeen on 25th May, reached Lerwick in the Shetlands on the 27th and left for Norway at 9 p.m. on the 29th, the day after the Allied capture of Narvik. It made its landfall about 10 p.m. on 30th May, and anchored early the next morning in a small fjord some way south of the Sogne Fjord. There was no sign of Germans, but three of four Norwegians 'on the run' found the party and were apparently admitted to join it without ceremony. The party then divided. Kronberg and Langmoe set out with four men and a large stock of demolition stores to reconnoitre the Voss area: Field with one man and a new recruit went off to Bergen. The latters' adventures there are mysterious: Field claimed to have passed himself off as a Nazi to the local German authorities, and he certainly brought back a formal German licence for the 'Lady', under the name of the 'Hospiz'; he also claimed to have contacted a large number of patriots in Bergen, and to have been responsible for the burning down of two match factories in Larvik. All that can be established is that he was an unreliable witness, and that a request was later received from Norway that he should not return there as he had been dangerously indiscreet. He was back on board the 'Lady' by 9th June, and it was then agreed that some of the party (who were clearly nervous) should return to Scotland at once: they secured another boat and were back in the Shetlands on 11th June, with various reports and a request that a wireless set be sent out to those who remained.

Meantime Kronberg and Langmoe had made a much more serious experiment in guerilla warfare, although their four men proved a liability and had to be sent back to the 'Lady' where they joined the first evacuation party. It was probably as well that they were cleared out of the way at once. The two who were left covered some 200 km, largely on foot, in the days from 3rd June to 10th July. Their route took them up the road from Dale on the Bergen railway to Voss, across to the Hardanger Fjord at Aalvik, where there is an important aluminium works served by the power station at Bjölvefossen: thence by the shores of the Sogne Fjord, across to the head of the fjord on which Bergen stands and so back to their starting point. The journey was partly on main roads, partly on mountain tracks: Germans were fairly numerous, but quite unsuspecting, although the whole area contained many industrial plants and communications targets of importance, some of which were guarded. There was no difficulty in finding friendly and discreet inhabitants to give minor assistance; and there was sleeping accommodation in farm houses or mountain huts.

Kronberg and Langmoe kept a rendezvous in the mountains with Field on 14th June; then set out again at 1 a.m. on 15th June to take action on the basis of their reconnaissance. They arrived at Aalvik that night, after a march of some 30 kms; next morning very early they climbed high up the mountain side and attached charges with long-delay fuses to the water intake of the power station. A little later in the day, but still early, they set charges to demolish four telephone pylons, some high tension cable masts, and two weak spots in the main road by the side of the Hardanger Fjord. They had planned to complete the job by a demolition on the Bergen-Oslo railway, but their journey was held up a little by bad luck with a motor-boat and they were not in time to lay further charges before the delayed explosions of their first day's work raised the hunt. They were back on board the 'Lady' on 17th June, sailed that night, and were in Lerwick within twenty-four hours.

This was the first Allied raid into occupied Europe: its practical results were real but very small – an important power station out of action for two or three weeks, a little minor damage, and a good deal of fairly reliable information. But it was most valuable as an indication of what good Norwegians could do in their own country. It was clear that the North Sea was not a serious obstacle to small boats well handled, and that the Germans would find it hard to cover the country in any way which would check the movement of active men.

3. Internal Organisation

It seems that D Section succeeded in sending to Norway the wireless set which this party had called for, but it failed to come on the air as expected on 30th June, and no more was heard of it. For some time there was no other attempt to follow up the initial success – Norway could not be expected to bulk very large in the British scheme of operations in the summer of 1940 – but there was a great traffic of exiles across the North Sea to Scotland.

SO2 obtained the services of some of the best of these men, and began to train them in its first school (Station XVII at Brickendonbury, Herts.) in the latter part of September 1940. About the same time the Norwegian Government appointed as its liaison officer with SO2 Captain Martin Linge, an actor by profession but also an experienced officer of very high personal qualities, who had been wounded in the fighting in Norway: typically, he drew his name from the family farm at Linge in Norddal, where he was a neighbour of Lieutenant Chaworth-Musters, then in charge of SO2's Norwegian section. With Captain Linge's appointment recruitment was put on a more regular basis with the Norwegian authorities: further men were added and in June 1941 a separate Norwegian 'holding-school' was opened at Fawley Court, Henley-on-Thames (STS 41). Practical courses were given in the Commando schools in the Arisaig area and in the parachute school at Ringway: but the Thames Valley was poor country in which to hold Norwegians in training for guerilla work in the mountains, and [a] really suitable arrangement was not found until the School (now known as STS 26) was moved to the Aviemore area in November 1941. There three lodges were requisitioned in the area between the Spey and the Cairngorms: away from any centre of population and facing a wild mountain country, which is more similar to Norway, winter and summer, than any other tract of Britain. STS 26 remained here and prospered to the end of the war.

At first the men had been civilians, under the general direction of Captain Linge. It was not until they had taken a successful part in the first Lofoten raid that they were incorporated into the Royal Norwegian Army, as the Norwegian Independent Company, or Linge Company[1] as it was generally called. At the same time a regular programme for the enrolment of 20–25 men a month was agreed with the Norwegian

---

[1] Appendix 'B' of Colonel Wilson's Norwegian History gives an account of the Linge Company.

authorities, and was maintained from March 1941 until May 1943, when it was decided that the strength of about 250 at that date was sufficient for the work in sight. It was kept at about this figure by necessary replacements until the winter of 1944–5, when an additional fifty men were added to strengthen it for the final operations in Norway.

Another essential preliminary step was to establish transport facilities on a sound footing. Dropping operations to the interior of Norway were never popular with the RAF – weather conditions over the mountains were unpredictable and always dangerous for low flying at night – and in any case aircraft were hard to come by in the summer of 1940. Sea transport was therefore essential; small boats were escaping from Norway in large numbers and they could go back. In December 1941 an SIS officer visited the Shetlands on behalf of that organisation and of SOE, chartered four Norwegian fishing vessels, and obtained volunteer crews from among Norwegian fishermen in the Shetlands.[1] A house at Flemington was taken as Headquarters, and as a billet for agents, while the crews lived on board their boats at Lerwick or Cat Firth. The first operation took place on 22nd December 1940. After the experience of the first season, in which eight or nine trips were made without loss, the period of short summer nights was used to reorganise and prepare. Twelve boats were obtained, and crews for six; the men were put into Norwegian naval uniform, although they retained their civilian status and took part in operations only as volunteers. It was necessary to find a more remote anchorage and some spare accommodation for the crews, and at the beginning of August a move was made to Lunna Voe, some thirty miles north of Lerwick. Operating conditions were harder in the winter of 1941–2: forty-three operations were sailed, thirty of them successfully, but three boats and two crews (fourteen men) were lost by enemy action (out of ten boats available at the start of the season); and a storm in November did great damage and overstrained the maintenance organisation so badly that there was a serious break in operations in midwinter, with the inevitable effects in the field. Summer 1942 was therefore again a period of active reorganisation, and at the same time the Norwegian authorities began to show anxiety about the conditions under which the men were working. The main base was now moved to Scalloway, where there was a village and tolerable repair facilities, and in addition a subsidiary base was opened at Burghead on the Moray Firth. The British staff was strengthened: and a Norwegian

---

[1] Appendix 'A' of Colonel Wilson's Norwegian History gives an account of the Shetland Base. [And see David Howarth's classic adventure story, *The Shetland Bus* (1951).]

officer was attached to look after the interests of the men, who were now to be known as the Norwegian Naval Independent Unit. The men themselves insisted on remaining civilians and volunteers, paid on special rates under British command, and it was not till 1944 that they were fully absorbed into the Royal Norwegian Navy.

In spite of this careful preparation the season of 1942–3 was a very difficult one. The German defences and control systems had been greatly improved in face of various forms of British pressure – Commando raids, air attacks, and MTB operations, as well as the activities of SOE – and it became clear that the 6 or 7 knot fishing-boats had seen their day as a means of war transport. The morale and efficiency of the crews remained good, and forty trips were made, twenty-three of them successfully: but six boats and thirty men were lost out of a strength at the beginning of the season of about twelve boats and seventy men. This ended the first phase of the Norwegian Naval Independent Unit: it was clear that men could no longer be called on to operate at such a casualty rate, and that fishing-boats had ceased to be a possible means of supply. The search for alternative vessels was eventually successful, as will be related later.

The third important preliminary was the re-establishment of the Stockholm Mission, which had been effectively destroyed by D Section's disaster there in April 1940. One of MI(R)'s representatives, Captain Malcolm Munthe at Stavanger, had remained in Norway and had eventually made contact with Norwegian forces and escaped to Sweden after two months' travel on foot. There he was established in July 1940 as Assistant Military Attaché, charged with opening 'lines' into Norway for the encouragement of resistance and the intelligence channels of SIS. This arrangement was put on a more formal basis in October, when Mr Charles Hambro, then head of SO2's Scandinavian Section, visited Sweden for the purpose. The arrangement then reached was that Mr Peter Tennant (the Press Attaché) should be responsible for SOE's work in Sweden and into Germany, Captain Munthe for Norway, and an additional officer (Mr Turnbull) for Denmark. These arrangements stood through the war with minor personal modifications, the most important of which was the withdrawal of Captain Munthe in July 1941, in face of heavy diplomatic pressure by the Swedes.

The most striking of SOE's efforts in Sweden at this stage was Operation 'Rubble', by which five Norwegian ships of some 25–30,000 tons in all, were manned, equipped and taken out of Gothenburg under the noses of the German Navy. All five escaped safely to England in January 1941, with cargoes valued at over £1,000,000. The responsibility for this coup was shared with Mr George Binney of the Iron and Steel Control, and was the first of a series of naval adventures of the same kind. Much of the story has already been made public, and it would take us too far afield to include it here.[1]

Connections with Norway were less dramatic, but of great importance from the first, as they afforded quicker contact than any other means with the growth of more or less centralised resistance movements in Norway. The Swedish frontier presented no serious difficulty to active Norwegians, but refugees in Sweden at this stage found the Swedish authorities hostile and their own Legation passive: so that they were almost compelled to turn to the British Mission for guidance and assistance.[2] A few violent coups were organised from Stockholm with the assistance of such refugees. The Bergen-Oslo railway was sabotaged in November 1940 with SOE equipment, and its agents were useful in guiding the RAF to the same target by flares in December 1940. There was even a plan to assassinate Himmler on his arrival in Oslo in March 1941, which broke down through a change in his programme. Activities of this kind were particularly distasteful to the Swedes, and violent action was dropped almost entirely after some unfortunate incidents in the summer of 1941 – in June the Swedes arrested and sentenced two of SOE's agents, and in July a train en route to the Germans in Norway blew up prematurely in Swedish territory. But the Swedes did retain some fellow-feeling for Norway – or perhaps their caution prompted them to a little reinsurance, even at the height of German power – and they were not prepared to destroy the SOE organisation entirely, provided it limited itself to political contacts and messages. Some of these were valuable; and contact was kept open with organisations in Oslo, Bergen, Trondheim and the Stavanger area. It is impossible to trace from SOE's papers the process by which a central leadership of the Home Front developed; indeed there is probably no record except in the memories of the participants, and few of them could have any picture of the situation as a whole. It is at least pretty clear that the idea of a central organisation had emerged early in 1941. As early as June of that year[3] SOE's Scandinavian Section committed itself to the view that –

---

[1] See narratives of Operations 'Rubble' (January 1941), 'Performance' (April 1942), Bridford (1943–4), 'Moonshine' (1945), in SOE Archives Files 20/230 series). Mr George Binney and Mr Charles Hambro were both knighted for their parts in 'Rubble'. [And see R. Barker, *The Blockade Busters* (1976).]

[2] For the first stages of this development see report by the British Military Attaché Stockholm, dated 21st June 1940, on SOE Archives File 6/490/2. There is also interesting material on the early days in Max Manus, 'Det Vil Helst Gå God' (Oslo, 1945): Manus was arrested on 16th January 1941, and escaped from hospital with outside aid on 13th March.

[3] Colonel Wilson's Norwegian History, p. 23, quoting from report to King Haakon – SOE Archives File 6/490 N.36/2, Vol. 1, folio 7a.

There is a Military Organisation in Norway consisting of some 20,000 persons, apart from various small organisations which have been built up more as a local force than anything else. The main Norwegian organisation is divided into three main groups, firstly Political, secondly Secret Army, and thirdly a Sabotage Group. The Sabotage Group really forms part of the Secret Army Group, and both these groups take no active interest in politics.

The Military Organisation is divided into a staff with its various committees and sub-sections. There is an active group in all the principal towns, and separate groups for Organisation, Air, Red Cross Supplies, Maps, Transport, Propaganda, Messenger Service, Finance, Intelligence, Communication between Norway and England.

This is no more than a pretty picture, and it is important mainly as an indication of what SOE in its early days was prepared to believe about the organisation of resistance movements. On the other hand, there certainly was a tendency toward centralisation and over-organisation in the early months of 1941,[1] which led in due course to breaches of security and to a wave of arrests in the late summer and autumn of 1941. So far as can be judged, the trend was then reversed: the Central Leadership continued to exist, but the important work was done locally, and it was not till Allied invasion became a real possibility that the Military Organisation as a unity again became important.

4. Operations 1940–41

All these preparatory steps – Linge Company, Shetland Base and Stockholm Mission – were satisfactorily begun in the winter of 1940–41: but only the Stockholm Mission was sufficiently developed to be the basis of any plan for that winter – operations from the United Kingdom, which later became much more important than those from Sweden, were tentative and unco-ordinated.

SOE's first operation took place in November 1940, and was an attempt to land two men, Konrad Lindberg and Frithof Pedersen, in south-west Norway, for the purpose of establishing wireless communication. The men got ashore safely from a fishing-boat, but no more

---

[1] See e.g. the report of Captain J. Schive dated 12th November 1941 – SOE Archives File 6/100 'File 99 Anglo-Norwegian Collaboration'. Captain Schive had apparently found himself leader of the central organisation, almost by accident, in the spring of 1941. See also report from the Central Organisation to the King dated (?) June 1941, and the reply drafted by SOE on 17th July – both on SOE Archives File 6/490 'N.36/2 Military Organisation in Norway'.

was heard of them: it appeared later that their wireless set had failed, and that they were arrested by the Germans shortly after landing. They were shot for espionage on 11th August 1941, the first casualties in the campaign to reopen Norwegian resistance.

The next attempt was successful: a young Norwegian named Starheim (later Captain Odd K. Starheim, DSO, but always affectionately remembered by his code-name 'Cheese') was landed from a submarine in January 1941 in the Egersund area of south-west Norway, from which he had escaped in a small boat in August 1940. He landed in bitter weather, soaking wet, and suffering from a sharp attack of fever, and his hardships at first were extreme; but he kept alive in the open country and brought his wireless set on to the air on 25th February 1941[1] – the first message which SOE received on the air from occupied Europe. After this difficult beginning he did splendid work: over 100 messages came from his set (including one which reported the 'Bismarck' as she passed Flekkefjord on her last voyage to destruction on 27th May), and he was safely brought off in June 1941, leaving behind him the nucleus of an organisation in the Agder area of the south-west.

Finally, in April, a party was landed in Trondelag to attack the railway between Trondheim and the Swedish frontier at Storlien. They consisted of Norwegian refugees who had been recruited and trained in Sweden in December, had slipped across the Norwegian border in February and took ship from Norway to the Shetlands. The attack on the railway was successful, but unfortunately the party were arrested on their escape to Sweden and were sentenced to terms of imprisonment for the illegal possession of arms – a sharp lesson on the limits of Swedish toleration.

Apart from these operations, a few trips were sailed from the Shetlands to lay mines, to dump stores on uninhabited outer islands, to carry out tasks for SIS. But the only other development of significance in this first winter was the beginning of Combined Operations on the Norwegian coast, with the assistance of Norwegian guides and interpreters drawn from the Linge Company. Thirty officers and men took part in the first Lofoten raid ('Claymore') in March 1941,* and a party also went with a small raid on a herring-oil factory at Oxfjord, north of Tromso, in April. Both operations were militarily successful, and gave great encouragement to British opinion. They were also valuable to SOE: they showed that Norwegian morale was high and they raised it higher by demonstrating Allied strength, German weakness

---

[1] SOE Archives File 6/3701.1 contains copies of the 'Cheese' messages.

* [The strategic importance of this raid lay in the help it gave in solving German naval 'Enigma' keys; of this SOE knew nothing.]

The Secret History of SOE 1940–1945

and the possible fate of Quislings. At this stage there was little on the reverse side of the picture – the damage done by the Allies to Norwegian livelihood was small, and German reprisals were not severe.

5. Summer 1941

As usual, sea and air operations to Norway were impracticable from April to September: Starheim's wireless set was the only one operating in Norway and it went off the air when he returned to England in June: the Swedish attitude severely limited action from Stockholm. The summer of 1941 was therefore for SOE one of inactivity in the field, and of reorganisation and planning at home. Nevertheless matters did not stand still in Norway or elsewhere, and much happened which affected the resistance campaign of 1941–2.

The most important single factor was the German attack on Russia. Morally, this sharpened the atmosphere in Norway as much as it did elsewhere, for it renewed the feeling that Norway was still an active theatre of war. Rumours of an imminent British landing were current as early as September 1941, possibly spread by the Germans for their own purposes. Anticipation grew livelier as German difficulties in Russia increased and clamour arose for a 'Second Front': it was very natural to deduce that, with their limited resources, the Western Allies would find Norway the best field for an operation to make a lodgement on the Continent and draw German forces from the Russian front.

It seems probable that German forces in Norway were seriously reduced in numbers during the summer: there is no doubt that good troops were replaced by poor ones, that German nerves grew worse and with them German behaviour to the Norwegian population. There was a corresponding change in the attitude and methods of the German Government. Quisling's original Government of 9th April 1940 had been thrown aside by the Germans after five days of futility; Terboven* was appointed Reichskommissar and a Norwegian 'administrative council for the occupied districts' was formed on the initiative of the Supreme Court. During the rest of the summer the Germans made determined efforts to find a basis for a broader Norwegian Government by negotiating indirectly for King Haakon's abdication. This line proved fruitless, and on 25th September 1940 Terboven, on his own authority and without a shadow of legality, deposed the King, dismissed the King's Government and dissolved the Storting. At the same time new Quisling Ministers were set up, responsible only to

* [J. Terboven, 1898–1945, Nazi, committed suicide.]

the Reichskommissar, and on 10th October nominees of Quisling were intruded into positions of authority on the elected local councils. In December the Supreme Court resigned in protest against a parallel attack on the integrity of the judicial system, and the whole constitutional framework of Norway was dissolved, leaving nothing but naked force in the hands of the Germans and their puppets. The civilian side of the Norwegian national organisation at home grew out of the storm of protests which rose from every organised group of society in face of these usurpations.[1]

In spite of this wide discontent German repressive measures did not become severe until the Russian campaign was under way: but a new tone was clear by about September 1941. In that month Trade Union opposition broke out in strikes in the Oslo area, possibly provoked by the Germans:[2] these do not seem to have represented any very new or serious threat to German authority, but for the first time repression was comparable in severity to that in other occupied countries: there were many arrests, and two Trade Union leaders, Hansteen and Vikstrøm, were shot. Two SOE agents, Lindberg and Pedersen,[3] had been shot as spies in August, after some months' imprisonment: in September there was also an attempt to break up the central Norwegian leadership (Milorg) by further arrests.[4]

Up to the end of the winter season of 1940–41 the emphasis in London had been on stimulating the Norwegian spirit of resistance by a persistent offensive, in readiness for comparatively early action:[5]

---

[1] Up to date (January 1947) the best accounts of the development of Norwegian feeling in the summer of 1940 are to be found in:

F. Schjelderup (one of the Supreme Court Judges), 'Fra Norges Kamp for Retten: 1940: Høyesterett'.

Bishop Berggrav, 'Da Kampen Kom: noen blad fra Startaret'.

There is also an important report by a Committee of the Storting (which I have not seen): 'Instilling fra Undersøkelser kommisjon 1945', Oslo (Ascheborg) 1946. This deals with Norway's preparedness for war and the events of 1940. [See also Magne Skodvin, 'Norwegian Non-violent Resistance during the German Occupation', in Adam Roberts (ed.), *Civilian Resistance as a National Defence* (1967).]

[2] See Dispatch by Mr Collier (British Minister to Norway) dated 12th September 1941, on SOE Archives File 6/100/5. [(Sir) L. Collier, 1890–1976, Ambassador to Norway 1942–50.]

[3] See above p. 203.

[4] See above p. 202.

[5] See following papers –

	SOE Archives File
6.8.40 Rebellion in Norway	6/110 Norway/Policy
11.12.40 Norwegian Policy	6/110 Norway/Policy
16.12.40 Subversive Operations in Scandinavia – Note for Minister	63/110/1
26.1.41 Letter to Major D. Morton	6/110 Norway/Policy

during the summer the emphasis changed with the atmosphere. The essential thing now was to hold back Norwegian enthusiasm from action which might be suicidal and would certainly break their confidence in Allied support:[1] at the same time to build up a decentralised organisation which would be more secure in face of German counter-action than the first amateurish Norwegian efforts at conspiracy. The effective use of Stockholm as a centre was barred by recent experience of the Swedish attitude:[2] it was therefore necessary to create district organisations in direct touch with the United Kingdom. Improved facilities for sea operations from the Shetlands, and some air assistance, might make this feasible: in any case there was no alternative.

There were two other factors affecting policy on the British side. First, the Combined Operations organisation was growing in strength and confidence, and the Norwegian coast was an area in which the Germans might be attacked without serious risk of an unlimited commitment; it might even be possible to effect a permanent lodgement in some defensible area. Second, the Ministry of Economic Warfare was increasingly interested in the economic assistance which Germany drew from Norway, and it pressed during the summer of 1941 for an ambitious programme of sabotage attacks on industrial objectives.[3] This line of thought, which proved important later, was very fully worked out in the latter part of 1941: numerous objectives were investigated and plans laid. But the main scheme ('Clairvoyant') suffered all sorts of set-backs during the 1941–2 season, mainly from lack of air transport, and not a single party was dispatched under it.[4]

6. Operations 1941–2

From SOE's point of view, therefore, the programme for 1941–2 was (a) to build up a series of district organisations in communication with the United Kingdom; (b) independently of these, to execute *coup de main* sabotage operations on important industrial targets; (c) to assist CCO in his operations and advise him on their effects in relation to Norwegian resistance.

---

[1] Cf. paper on Scandinavian Policy for Joint Planning Staff dated 16th April 1941 – File 63/110 Scandinavian Policy.

[2] Imprisonment of the 'Barbara' party in April (above p. 203), imprisonment of two members of Major Munthe's organisation in June, premature explosion of a German train in Sweden (July), expulsion of Major Munthe (p. 200).

[3] SOE Norwegian History, p. 37.

[4] The first steps to attack the heavy water plant at Vemork and the pyrites mine at Orkla were taken this season 1941–2, but the main operations came later (below pp. 653 and 655).

The progress made with the first of these tasks can best be shown by an annotated list of the main Missions put into the field during the season (reference to a map here is essential):[1]

Nordland. A party of four ('Archer')[2] was put into the Mosjøen area by fishing-boat on 16th December 1941: this was the furthest north which the Shetland fleet had yet come, some 600 miles from its base. The original idea was that it should form part of a Combined Operations plan to out the northern railway and isolate German forces to the north ('Ascot'): this fell through, but 'Archer' remained as the nucleus of a resistance organisation in the area. It was reinforced by further parties of five men in March and six men in April 1942, and it received twenty-four tons of provisions and warlike stores, of which at least seven tons were moved inland. In spite of all sorts of difficulties, physical and personal, it was still in the field at the end of the season (under a Swedish officer Lieutenant Sjøberg), in wireless communication with base and well supported by the local population in the whole area round the Nordland railway between Majavatn and Mosjøen.

Trondheim ('Lark')[3] Two men had been landed in February 1942, two more in April: wireless communication was established on 27th May.

Aalesund ('Antrum')[4] Two visits were paid by K. J. Aarsaether, from September to November 1941 and from December 1941 to January 1942; useful contacts were made and a fishing-boat was brought back to Shetland, but an attempt to get a man through to Trondheim failed. Aarsaether's brother, Knut, went out with a wireless set in January 1942, and established his station successfully with a local operator. It remained in operation for a long time, although there were a number of arrests in the spring of 1942, and Knut Aarsaether himself had to escape to England in March.

Sogn ('Mallard')[5] Two men with a wireless set were put ashore at Bulandet in April, and contact was established on 29th April 1942: their job was to make contacts over a large area, including Bergen – obviously too much for so small a party. They were detected and arrested on 30th May, and were later shot.

Voss ('Raven')[6] Four men were dropped by air on 18th April, and made wireless contact: there was intensive German counter-activity

---

[1] A statistical summary of the season's work is at Appendix C.
[2] For full report on Mission see SOE Archives File 6/370/20.1. This is a very impressive story.
[3] SOE Archives Files 6/370/18.1 to 18.5 refer.
[4] SOE Archives Files 6/370/13 refer.
[5] SOE Archives Files 6/370/21 refer.
[6] SOE Archives Files 6/370/11 refer.

in the area, which kept them in the mountains all the summer, but they remained at large.

Haugesund ('Arquebus')[1] Two men were landed in October 1941, but their wireless set failed, and the chief of the party was lost at sea in attempting to return to England. The wireless operator remained, but it was impossible to get a new set to him until October 1942. Thereafter he remained in Haugesund and in continuous touch with the United Kingdom until VE-day.*

Stavanger ('Penguin')[2] Here there was the first serious disaster. An organiser with a wireless set had been put ashore at Nesvik on 17th April for the Stavanger area, along with a wireless operator who was to be guided overland to Vestfold, the area just west of the Oslo Fjord. Unfortunately the same landing place had been used very openly by an SIS vessel only a few days before, without consultation with SOE, and the local population were well aware that a Gestapo search was likely to follow. In spite of this the two men remained together in the same area, were betrayed, and were trapped by the Gestapo in the loft of a farmhouse. They fought it out: three Gestapo officials were killed and one of the SOE men – the other was severely wounded but survived to be executed later. German reactions, for the first time in Norway, were such as might have been expected of them elsewhere in Europe. At Televaag eighteen Norwegians (unconnected with the affair) were arrested and shot out of hand; some seventy buildings were burnt down. The Norwegian Government stood up well to the shock of these reprisals, and boldly accepted them as casualties of war: but the affair increased Gestapo rigour and Norwegian caution up the whole west coast.

Vest-Agder ('Cheese')[3] Odd Starheim, who had been a pioneer in this area early in 1941, was dropped with a wireless operator on 2nd January 1942 – the first air operation to Norway. In February he had a very fortunate escape in a Gestapo round-up in Oslo: and he found thereafter that even his own area was too hot for him and that the only safe course was to return to England. The weather was exceptionally wintery and nothing could be arranged from the Shetlands: but with his wireless operator and four other friends he successfully boarded and took over the coastal steamer 'Galtesund', a 600 ton vessel on its usual run from Oslo to Bergen. The crew and passengers were coerced or persuaded, and the ship was brought safely into

---

[1] SOE Archives Files 6/370/9 Vols 1–6 refer.

[2] SOE Archives Files 6/370/22 and 6/370/25 refer.

[3] SOE Archives Files 6/370/1 – Vols 1 & 2 refer to 'Cheese' missions.

* [This was unknown at Combined Operations HQ when an attack was mounted on Haugesund in 1943; on which see Foot and Langley, *MI9*, pp. 148–9.]

Aberdeen on 17th March, through appalling weather. A locally-trained operator remained in charge of the 'Cheese' wireless set, which was still on the air, and the area was reinforced by another party ('Swan'), which landed in August from a submarine – the only communication available in the summer months. In addition, two men had been dropped in Telemark in April ('Cockerel') and had moved into 'Cheese's' area in Vest-Agder to act as instructors for local recruits.

Telemark ('Grouse') In March a certain Einar Skinnarland had been dropped in the mountains of Telemark to prepare for action against the heavy water plant at Rjukan. His adventures were important and will be related later.[1]

Vestfold ('Anchor')[2] An organiser was landed on the west coast on 23rd February, and succeeded in making his way across country to Drammen: but he was wounded and captured there, and his wireless operator (who landed in April) was one of those lost in the disaster at Televaag.

Ostfold ('Crow')[3] An organiser had been landed in February and had succeeded in reaching his area, which included Oslo and the Oslofjord: but his wireless operator did not arrive and come on the air till May. The organiser then returned to England, and shortly after the operator was captured by the Germans, who continued to work his set. This trick was detected almost at once.

Opland ('Anvil')[4] A wireless operator had reached the Lillehammer area from the west coast in March, and came on the air on 27th April: his organiser did not arrive till June, and was at first under suspicion by the local military organisation as an agent provocateur – a sign of the growing 'canniness' of Norwegian resistance at this stage.

Each of these expeditions has a saga of its own, often told by the participators in narratives which have the authentic ring of saga-style. Their stories are likely to be preserved and honoured in Norway for generations; but their historical value is mainly in the detailed picture they give of the development of a united movement among a highly individual people, and it would be impossible to summarise any of them adequately here.

It will be seen that SOE's plans had provided for a network of decentralised organisations to cover every important province of Norway, as far north as Nordland. In addition considerable quantities of military stores had been dumped in the outer islands. The men sent had in theory been of three types: Organisers, to give guidance to

---

[1] Below pp. 653 and 674.
[2] SOE Archives File 6/370/25 refers.
[3] SOE Archives File 6/370/12 Vol. 2 refers.
[4] SOE Archives File 6/370/24 Vols 1 & 2 refer.

existing local movements or to build them up if they did not exist; Instructors, to give training in the use of arms and demolition materials; Wireless Operators, to put each organisation directly in touch with England – there was to be no internal wireless communication. In practice the three types necessarily overlapped. They were all Norwegians, young men of similar type, many of them of magnificent courage and ingenuity: all were members of the Linge Company, and thus part of the Norwegian forces, but their training had been conducted entirely by SOE, and they operated at first on a purely British plan under British operational control. Their casualties had been heavy, but the position reached in the summer of 1942 was not altogether discouraging, in view of the novelty of the problem and the scanty means available to solve it. Twelve areas are included in the list given above, covering most of Southern Norway, and in the late summer SOE agents were still active with varying success in eight of them: six wireless sets were on the air, out of fifteen which had been sent in, and London was thus in touch with Nordland, Trondelag, Aalesund, the 'Raven' party in the hills behind Bergen, the Cristiansund (S) area and the Lillehammer area. This meant that London had some first-hand knowledge of the organisation and requirements of those areas, and there was at least a possibility of co-ordinating Norwegian action against the Germans in a crisis. On the other hand, the means of supply available were very limited, and Gestapo pressure was increasing and becoming more efficient, through the usual techniques of informers, searches and reprisals: so that SOE's action might govern the fate of large sections of Norwegian people. In fact, SOE had in a sense assumed responsibility for the leadership of the Norwegian people, in so far as they could be guided by SOE's men in the field; and this was not a responsibility that it was anxious to bear alone. It had from the first placed much reliance on the sense and good faith of the Norwegian Government, and it was anxious to share responsibility with them: the problem was to find a machinery which would combine the political responsibility of the Norwegians to their people with SOE's responsibility to the British Government for operations conducted from British soil and intimately related to British military plans.

The urgency of finding a solution was increased by two other factors – the development of the political situation in Norway, and CCO's* operations in the winter of 1941–2.

---

* [Keyes had been succeeded as Chief of Combined Operations by Lord Louis Mountbatten, 1900–79, cousin of King George VI, knight 1922, CCO 1941–3, Supreme Commander South-East Asia 1943–6, KG 1946, last Viceroy of India 1947, earl 1947, First Sea Lord 1955–9, Chief of Defence Staff 1959–65, OM 1965, murdered on holiday off Ireland; in *DNB*. See his life by Philip Ziegler (1985).]

As we have seen, repression had grown more intense in the autumn of 1941, and this in itself made the Norwegian Government in London more keenly aware than ever of their responsibility for the direction (and if necessary the restraint) of resistance at home. For some reason – possibly Hitler's personal intervention – the Germans added to their own difficulties by saddling themselves with another attempt to set up Quisling as the constitutional government in Norway. By 31st January 1942 these plans had developed so far that the Quisling 'Ministers' were permitted to demand publicly the appointment of a National Government by Quisling, the leader of the only legal party, the Nasjonal Samling. The Storting and the old parties had been dissolved, the Supreme Court had resigned and been replaced by German nominees, the local authorities had been brought under control: so that there was a political vacuum which was ostensibly filled by the appointment of Quisling as Minister-President on 1st February, and by a series of decrees by his 'Government' reorganising Norway on a 'corporate' model. The reaction to this silly provocation must have startled the Germans: it certainly complicated their task enormously. Twelve thousand out of fourteen thousand schoolteachers refused to join the new Nazi teachers' organisation: practically the entire national Church followed suit, and used its position of authority to organise public protest: there were wholesale resignations of lawyers, doctors, and other indispensable civil servants. There was in fact a demonstration of quiet, resolute and almost unanimous national feeling; apparently it was spontaneous in its origin, but out of it grew a real 'Civil Organisation' of the 'Home Front', with much deeper roots than the existing Military Organisation.[1] There were wholesale arrests, and leaders who could be identified were removed to concentration camps: but the protest was so widespread and so orderly that it made it very difficult for the Germans to apply the ordinary means of repression. It is probable, too, that the local Nazi authorities were for the time being pretty busy saying 'I told you so' to higher authority in Berlin.

CCO's operations in 1941–2 coincided fortuitously with the early stages of this explosion of feeling, and had unexpected political repercussions.

The first of them ('Kitbag I') was directed against Florø, but failed to keep its schedule and returned ineffectively,[2] with two accidental

---

[1] Cf. report by J. E. Skappel dated 21st July 1942, on SOE Archives File 6/490 'Military Organisation', (N.36/2 Vol.2).

[2] Report by 2nd Lieutenant Isene dated 13th January 1942, on SOE Archives File 6/480 'Archery'.

casualties to Captain Linge's men on board.[1] The second Lofoten raid ('Anklet'), which sailed on 22nd December, did some damage to the Germans and brought out six 'quislings' and 266 refugees: but the Lofoten population had expected the expedition to stay, and had put themselves unreservedly at its disposal. Bitter disappointment ensued at its withdrawal, and there were severe German reprisals. 'Archery'[2] which was directed against Vaagsø and Maaloy, on the 'inner lead' for shipping on the Norwegian coast, was moderately successful as a military operation: but it also led to disappointment and to reprisals, and it was a particularly severe blow to SOE that Captain Linge was killed by a German sniper during the Vaagsø attack on 27th December.

The Norwegian Government protested very sharply against these operations – indeed it was almost the only occasion when there was a note of exasperation in their relations with the British. Their complaint was directed not so much to the nature of the operations (although their wisdom was somewhat doubtful), as to the manner in which they had been planned. No Norwegian authority had been consulted at any stage, although in the calculation of profit and loss on the operations political repercussions in Norway were bound to be of paramount importance: did the damage done to the Germans outweigh the destruction of Norwegian livelihood, the danger of wide-spread reprisals, the blow to Norwegian morale through hope deferred? The Norwegians were ready enough to recognise the problems of security involved and to make suggestions for meeting them: but their whole position as a government was involved in the claim to be consulted on political issues profoundly affecting their country. The 'Home Front' was absolutely loyal to the King, as the symbol of national unity, but its confidence in the London Government was not without limits, and there were murmurs even in 1941 that direction of Norwegian resistance should be in the hands of those who had lived under the occupation, and knew what its conditions were.[3] With

---

[1] Mid-December. This operation was sailed again on 6th January 1942. It had some success but no landing was made.

[2] Full operational report, with names of Norwegian personnel, and report on Captain Linge's death, in SOE Archives File 6/480 'Archery'. See also Supplement to The London Gazette d/d 2.8.48, which gives report of this operation.

[3] E.g. Report from Milorg to King Haakon, dated 10th June 1941 – on SOE Archives File 6/490 – No. 36/2 Vol. 1 – 'The *idea* behind our organisation is to make available a military machine to support an internal government, secret or official sanctioned by the King, and acting under direct responsibility to the King. This *internal* government shall decide if and when the military machine will function. It is of vital importance to us that this fundamental idea should be approved.' This was rejected in the King's reply, and the rejection was accepted, subject to recognition by the King of the legality of Milorg's authority within Norway (on same file).

this went the natural suspicion that the London Government might use its legal status and its central position to secure its own political future when Norway was freed. Both these reactions were normal pieces of resistance psychology, well understood and carefully fostered by the German propaganda machine. Fortunately their incidence was less violent in Norway than in any other country; but this was in part because the London Government was exceptionally sensitive to them.

The latter was disposed of finally by the proclamations of Christmas 1942 and 9th April 1943, which made it clear that on its return to Norway the London Government would place its resignation in the King's hands, and that a new government would be formed to conduct elections as early as possible. The demand for a share in leadership was met, as well as might be, by bringing Home Front leaders (such as Captain Rognes and Professor Tronstad) to London for consultation and to take part in the direction of operations: and the Government was considerably strengthened by the appointment in November 1941 of M. Oscar Torp as Minister of Defence, and the creation in January 1942 of the post of Commander-in-Chief of all the armed forces, filled by a relatively junior officer, General Hansteen. SOE worked henceforth largely with these two men, and had the greatest respect for them.

The position was thus somewhat eased. But it was still essential that the Government should press the British hard for more effective consultation, and its claim was not one which could be pushed aside. Apart altogether from the services of Norway in merchant shipping and in other ways, British expeditions depended largely on the co-operation of Norwegian guides and interpreters, mainly from the Linge Company: the Company operated very loyally under British orders, but it consisted of Norwegian patriots, not of hired agents, and there was no doubt that its services would cease if the Norwegian Government withdrew their approval.

There were three related problems to be solved:
(1) Norwegian participation in Allied plans for large-scale military action against Norway.
(2) The use of the Linge Company in support of regular operations.
(3) Collaboration between SOE and the Norwegian Government in the development and control of resistance.

The first two of these might have proved insoluble in practice if CCO's operations had developed to the point of a full-scale Allied assault in Norway: in such a case military security must have paramount weight, and would make it almost impossible to disclose plans in advance to an authority which had no serious military contribution to make. Fortunately (from this point of view) the question did not arise, and the compromises reached were not brought to the test.

First, the Chiefs-of-Staff agreed in principle on 13th January 1942 that M. Torp himself should be kept informed of impending operations on the Norwegian coast, subject to a prior decision by the Chiefs-of-Staff in each case.[1] In addition they considered on 24th January a letter from Defence Minister Torp to General Ismay asking for the institution of a Joint Anglo-Norwegian Planning Committee to co-operate in planning the future reconquest of Norway. The letter had been drafted in close consultation with Sir Charles Hambro, and asked only for what was reasonably practicable: the Chiefs of Staff welcomed the approach and agreed to consultations with the Joint Planners – a tenuous agreement which involved no specific commitment as to premature disclosures.[2] *Second*, Sir Charles Hambro assured M. Torp that the Linge Company would not be used for any SOE purpose without prior consultation. But if it were called upon to assist a regular operation, the secret would not be SOE's, and it would not be within SOE's discretion to arrange consultation: Sir Charles could undertake only that SOE would use its best offices with other departments concerned.[3]

SOE's own collaboration with the Norwegian authorities had been friendly but informal up to the autumn of 1941: there are plenty of records of discussions and of exchange of information, on all levels, but British and Norwegian operations in the field proceeded separately – in theory the Norwegian Home Front organisations were to grow parallel to SOE's organisation and independently of it. It became pretty clear early that this conception was in practice difficult and even dangerous: in spite of its size on the map, Norway is a small country in population and in channels of communication, and independent organisations were bound to cut across one another's work.[4] SOE was thus itself inclined to press for more formal consultation and full exchange of information, and was well aware that this could only be achieved if the British as well as the Norwegians contributed freely to the common pool.

---

[1] COS(42)13th Mtg, Item 6, of 13th January.

[2] COS(42)27th Mtg, Item 11, of 24th January. See also General Ismay's letter to M. Torp dated 31st January 1942 – both on SOE Archives File 6/100 'Anglo-Norwegian Collaboration'.

[3] See Sir Charles Hambro's letter to M. Torp of 14th January 1942, on SOE Archives File 6/100/2: also his letters to CCO of 5th and 28th February, and CCO's reply of 5th March – all on SOE Archives File 6/100 'Anglo-Norwegian Collaboration'.

[4] One instance of this was the break-up in September 1941 of the SIS 'Skylark' organisation in Trondheim, which SIS were inclined to attribute to 'crossing of wires' with the Norwegian Military Organisation, and thus indirectly with SOE. See Folio 49A, and others, on SOE Archives File 6/490/– No. 36/2 Vol. 1.

The initiative therefore came from SOE, before matters came to a head on the Norwegian side, in December 1941, and was contained in a long paper on 'Anglo-Norwegian Collaboration regarding the Military Organisation in Norway', which was completed on 24th November 1941.[1] The main thesis of this paper is that 'The British cannot get on without the work of the Norwegians in Norway, and the Norwegians in this country cannot help their compatriots at home without the direction, equipment, transport and facilities of communications which only the British can supply': and the solution follows plainly from these unchallengeable premises. 'Control can best be exercised by means of an Anglo-Norwegian Joint Committee in London to consist entirely of people actively engaged in the work. To maintain the necessary links between the Committee and the Norwegian and British Governments will be the duty of the senior members of the Committee of each nationality, since it is not practicable or desirable, owing to the very secret nature of the work to have Ministers, Chiefs of Staff or Commanding Generals as members . . . . It is desirable that there should exist power for the Committee to co-opt additional members from time to time as they may be needed, and this is particularly important so as to enable representatives of the Military Organisation in Norway to attend meetings of the Committee in the event of their coming to this country for consultation.[2] It will be the duty of the Committee to keep in close contact with the directing council of the Military Organisation in Norway, but it must be remembered that this council cannot of necessity be in very close touch with all the District Organisations . . . . It would therefore appear desirable that the new Committee in London should be in direct touch with each District Organisation in Norway as far as this is possible.' It will be noticed that this solution avoids the thorny problem of 'channels of command'; the Committee is a consultative body, not an executive one, and orders will continue to flow through the existing channels, British or Norwegian. But these orders will be framed in consultation, and can if necessary by-pass the Oslo Headquarters of the Military Organisation: it was permissible to hope that (if all went well) the Committee would in effect become the headquarters of the Norwegian Resistance, and that unified action would follow the plans agreed at its meetings.

This paper was discussed by Sir Charles Hambro and Mr Sporborg with M. Torp on 27th November, shortly after his appointment as

---

[1] Copy at Folio 2A – SOE Archives File 6/100 'Anglo-Norwegian Collaboration'.

[2] An indirect reference to Captain Rognes, who had recently reached London, and became one of the first members of the Committee.

Minister of Defence:[1] the matter had been discussed with the Chiefs of Staff by Sir Charles Hambro that morning.[2] M. Torp received the proposals with rather inconclusive goodwill; and expressed much more serious anxiety as to the lack of prior consultation on regular operations. He understood however that the Chiefs of Staff might have grounds for thinking that Norwegian headquarters were not altogether secure. CCO's Lofoten and Maaløy operations were then in preparation, and no doubt the Norwegians had wind of them: the question of their scope and their effects was much more pressing than that of collaboration with SOE. The decision on this latter point was not taken until 14th January 1942, when Sir Charles Hambro was again received by M. Torp: the conclusions reached are embodied in a letter written the same day:[3] 'You approved in principle our suggestion . . . for a joint Anglo-Norwegian Committee . . . to take charge of secret work in Norway, such a Committee, on the Norwegian side, to report direct to you . . . . It was agreed that the Committee should not have any written terms of reference at first, but that we should learn by experience and only reduce terms of reference to writing when we have found out in practice the scope which the Committee can usefully cover' – a British method of procedure which would probably have proved unworkable with any other Ally: in this case it proved the happiest of solutions for the problems of sovereignty and command. So far as can be traced no terms of reference were ever written.

The Committee met for the first time on 16th February 1942, and sat regularly, at first once a fortnight, later once a month, until 26th April 1945.[4] Its meeting-place was the Norwegian Section's flat at Chiltern Court, where a junior Norwegian Officer was permanently stationed for liaison. Unfortunately, it was not practicable for Norwegian officers to work in SOE's own offices: partly on security grounds, partly because of the repercussions of other less-favoured Allies. The membership of the Committee varied with the transfers and promotions of its members, but its main pillars were, on the British side, Colonel J. S. Wilson, who became head of SOE's Norwegian Section in January 1942: on the Norwegian, Professor Tronstad, of the Technical College at Trondheim, and Lieutenant Colonel Öen. Once the Americans were fully involved in Europe, there were added to it successively Major Frederic Cromwell, US Army, and

---

[1] See note by Mr Sporborg at Folio 4A on SOE Archives File 6/100 'Anglo-Norwegian Collaboration'.

[2] COS (41) of 26th November, Item [?].

[3] Folio 13A of SOE Archives File 6/100 'Anglo-Norwegian Collaboration'.

[4] Its Minutes are to be found on SOE Archives File 6/360 'Anglo-Norwegian Collaboration – Minutes of Meetings'.

Commander G. Unger Vetlesen, USNR, both of OSS,* who proved thoroughly effective collaborators.

The spirit of the Committee on the British side is neatly summed up in a scribbled exchange of notes after the first meeting[1] – 'I feel that from Trondheim South we must pool our resources which will mean that we should lay our cards on the table. (So-&-so) may not like it, but we cannot remain as two ostriches presenting a stern view to each other!' 'I absolutely agree. We must give a thorough trial to the method of *complete* collaboration – we are absolutely committed to the attempt and, in spite of obvious difficulties (I fully appreciate (so-and-so)'s point of view) I believe we can make it work.' Defence Minister Torp was equally definite when he wrote on 27th April 1942 to Sir Charles Hambro on the latter's promotion to succeed Sir Charles Nelson as CD.[2]** 'You will recall that I was a little doubtful of the advisability of setting up a Joint Anglo-Norwegian Committee for handling such delicate questions as those mentioned in your memorandum of 24th November last. However, I have been kept regularly informed of the work of the Committee by my secretary, Mr Bøye, and I am now convinced that our Committee is the right instrument for dealing with these questions. It is both with regret and with satisfaction I note that the general lines of co-operation are now laid down so firmly that it may no longer be necessary for you to devote your time to the day to day work.'

---

[1] Attached to Minutes of 2nd Meeting – ref. 4., p. 216 above.
[2] Folio 39A of SOE Archives File 6/100 'Anglo-Norwegian Collaboration'.
* [Donovan's Office of Strategic Services, 1942–5, which did the work both of SOE and of SIS for the USA. See George C. Chalou (ed.), *The Secrets War* (Washington DC, 1992).]
** [Sir Frank Nelson, mistakenly called Charles by Mackenzie.]

CHAPTER X

Denmark*

Development in Denmark was very different in character from that in Norway, though it can be dealt with here only as an appendix to the latter.[1]

In the first place, Denmark was the only country in Western Europe which succumbed to Germany without a struggle; at first it was handled very gently by the Germans, in the hope that passivity might in due course lead to co-operation, and that Denmark might serve as a model for other small countries of the West in their relations with the New Order. The Danish King remained in Copenhagen; the Government, the Rigsdag and the political parties, as well as the staffs of the Danish armed forces and police, were left intact until a crisis (in line with SOE's policy and at least in part of SOE's making) arose in August 1943. The Danes were not pro-German, by temperament or by history; if their Government had called for war in 1940 they would have fought hard. But they were peace-loving and a little passive, and the work of creating a resistance had to begin from nothing. A political centre as well as an active organisation had to be created.

In the second place, the physical conditions of the country are a contrast to those of Norway. It is thickly populated, flat and largely agricultural; at first sight very unpromising terrain for underground war. In practice, the difficulties were not so bad as might have been anticipated; they were much less for instance than in Holland or in the more remote countries of Eastern Europe. Sea transport from the United Kingdom was difficult, as it led through the well-guarded waters close to German bases: a little was done by transferring stores to Danish fishing-boats at sea, but this was never of major importance. But Denmark lay very open by sea toward Sweden; the crossing was short and difficult to guard, and there was always a pretty

---

[1] There is a competent narrative of SOE Danish Section by Major Alasdair Garrett, from which this account is largely derived.

* [Besides Cruickshank's official history, see Jorgen Haestrup, *Secret Alliance* (3 vols, Odense, 1976–7) and a mass of literature in Danish.]

regular flow of traffic, even before it was organised through SOE's representative at Gothenburg. Air operations also proved easier than might have been expected: German defences were heavy, but not so heavy as those guarding the short air route to the Ruhr, and the Danish countryside, closely cultivated as it is, contains areas of heath and forest which are not easy to control. The relative density of population in some ways made it easier for the stranger to find cover and friends than in Norway.

In face of obvious difficulties it took some little time for a working plan to emerge. A 'Danish Committee' was formed in the summer of 1940, under the chairmanship of the Head of the Northern Department of the Foreign Office, in order to co-ordinate British action: with its encouragement an Association of Free Danes was formed in London, and in September 1940 a 'Danish Council' was recognised as representing those Danes outside Denmark who desired to assist the Allies. In the first instance, this was mainly a matter of retaining the services of Danish seamen outside the German grasp. The Council was not a very vigorous body, but it went one stage further by opening recruitment for the Allied Forces; volunteers were accepted by the East Kent Regiment (The Buffs) of which King Christian* was Colonel-in-Chief. This gave SOE an opening for its own recruitment, of which it took advantage: but the numbers and quality of the men available were naturally low.

Sir Charles Hambro had had discussions, when he was in Sweden in October 1940, with the Danish author Ebbe Munck,** an enthusiastic opponent of Nazism: but it was not till March 1941 that an SOE representative for Denmark (Mr Ronald Turnbull) reached Stockholm, after a devious journey via South Africa, Turkey and Russia. Another representative (Mr A. E. Christensen) joined him by air at once, and was established as British Vice-Consul at Gothenburg.

The first useful contact was established from Stockholm through Ebbe Munck with an organisation known as 'The Princes', which was at first anonymous to SOE, though known to be connected with the Danish General Staff: as afterwards emerged, its head was Lieutenant Colonel Nordentoft, the Danish DMI, and it possessed the tacit support of the C-in-C, Lieutenant General Gørtz. This was essentially an organisation of a military type familiar in other countries, thinking in terms of the collection of military intelligence and of the maintenance of the cadres of a Secret Army for eventual open use. The intelligence collected and passed through SOE was very valuable: so was the regular military backing given to the Resistance. But here as elsewhere

---

* [Christian X, 1870–1947, King from 1912, Haakon VII's elder brother.]
** [See his *The Spark and the Flame* (1954).]

certain difficulties arose. For one thing, SOE's directive was one for continual harassing sabotage, designed both to hamper the German effort from day-to-day and to raise the temper of the population by ceaseless provocation and counter-provocation. This clashed with the military conception of a conservation of forces for decisive action. Furthermore, 'The Princes' used as 'cover' for their organisation the story that they were preparing counter-action against a possible Communist coup: a good story for the Germans, but unpleasantly like the truth as it emerged in some other countries, and it took some time to convince SOE that the 'Princes' were not likely in the end to provoke civil war from the Right.

Some independent SOE channels were established by sea from Sweden in the summer of 1941, but they were in the first instance used mainly for distributing propaganda material: at this stage a good deal of responsibility rested with PWE for fostering a spirit from which resistance might later develop. It was not until 23rd December 1941 that SOE's first team of organiser and wireless operator was sent in. It was of course impossible to arrange for reception, as wireless communication did not exist; what was worse, the equipment did not function well. The organiser was killed by the failure of his parachute, the wireless set was smashed, and the operator (whose name was Hammer) was left with the whole burden of the Mission. He had few resources and no satisfactory means of communication with England; contact was made with the 'Princes', but there was little else he could do but observe the situation and note further possibilities. The next attempt was made on 16th April 1942, by Captain Rottbøll as organiser, with a fresh wireless operator. All went well, and their first message was received on 17th April.

An attempt was made to follow up this first success promptly, and three 'sabotage instructors' and another wireless operator were put in before the end of August. This group, known as 'Table', was concerned primarily to create a sabotage organisation, and some of Rottbøll's most important contacts were non-political. But there were also the first links with existing political organisations, in particular the 'Dansk Samling' and (to a lesser extent) with the Communist Party.

Progress was also made on the political side, where the first important step was to create some Danish organisation outside Denmark which could speak with authority in favour of active resistance. Invitations were sent in the autumn of 1941 to Hedtoft Hansen, the leader of the Social Democrats, and to Christmas Møller, chairman of the Conservative Party:* the latter was the only member of the

---

* [For Møller see Jeremy Bennett, *British Broadcasting and the Danish Resistance* (Cambridge, 1966).]

Danish Government to take an open anti-German line in 1940, and his resignation had eventually been enforced by the Germans. M. Hansen declined the invitation; M. Møller accepted, after lengthy negotiations, and was eventually smuggled out to Gothenburg with SOE's assistance in April 1942. He proved a controversial but energetic figure: not always 'security-conscious', but invaluable in focusing public interest on Denmark and on its potential value as an ally.

These good beginnings were badly broken by events in the late summer of 1942. Hammer, the first agent, had to be withdrawn through Sweden after the arrival of Rottbøll: one of the latter's wireless operators was surprised while transmitting on 5th September and committed suicide, and Rottbøll himself was killed while resisting arrest on 26th September. This shook the organisation, and two of the sabotage instructors and the other wireless operator were caught while escaping to Sweden in December. Thus all that was left in 1942 was two sabotage instructors, with no wireless communications and a very limited role; and SOE was to all appearance back where it started. It had no one readily available to replace Rottbøll, and the only immediate action possible was to return Hammer to the field. He had reached the United Kingdom on 27th September and was back in Denmark on 15th October. He was so heavily-built a man that it was thought an ordinary drop would be too dangerous, and he was deliberately dropped in the sea, 150 yards off shore: the experiment was successful and he swam ashore safely in Zealand.[1]

SOE thus had very scanty resources in Denmark at the end of this period. The situation was however a good deal better than it would seem on paper. Contacts existed with the Danish General Staff, the 'Dansk Samling', the Communist Party, and there were useful men known to be friendly in the Copenhagen police and elsewhere in government service. In addition there were known individuals, whose energy and patriotism could be relied on later: such men as Flemming Juncker, who did much to organise reception committees and dropping points in Jutland. From London these points of support seemed few and scattered, but they were enough to initiate a rapid development when conditions became more favourable. There was more spontaneous Danish organisation than SOE imagined; the mood of the Danish people was warmly in favour of resistance if it could be shown what to do and given weapons with which to do it.

---

[1] For an account of the development of this technique at the Ringway Parachute School, see Newnham, 'Prelude to Glory', pp. 78 and 153.

CHAPTER XI

France*

SOE's dealings with France are probably the most important, certainly the most complex, part of its story: and it should be said at the outset that a really satisfactory treatment is scarcely possible within the scope of this work.

There are two main reasons for this complexity.

First, France is a Great Power and remained a Great Power even in defeat. This is partly a matter of numbers (the existence of 40,000,000 Frenchmen, and of an overseas Empire of some 65,000,000 souls), partly of material wealth. To a greater extent, it is a matter of civilisation and history: ability and education are widespread, political life is full of energy and ingenuity, the technique which factions use in the struggle for power is immensely sophisticated and intellectual.[1]

Finally it is a matter of military geography: possession of the land of France was the decisive strategic issue of the war – in one of its

---

[1] 'The French nation, tingling as it does to the very finger ends with vivacity, running over with a thousand kinds of talent, and almost unrivalled in the power of giving expression to its thoughts.' Mr Gladstone, in 1858.

NOTE: There are useful continuous narratives for 'F Section' by Colonel Buckmaster [1902–92], and for 'R/F Section' by Major Thackthwaite. In addition, Major Bourne-Patterson has produced notes on 'The British Circuits in France', which have been circulated by the Foreign Office to British Consuls in France.

W. L. Langer 'Our Vichy Gamble' (Knopf, 1947) is a careful account of US policy up to the death of Darlan, based on State Department and OSS papers.

The main sources in France are:

(a) For the history of the FFI: the Service Historique de l'Armée.

(b) For civil affairs: Commission d'Histoire de l'Occupation et de la Libération de la France (Sec., M. Michel), Ministère de l'Éducation Nationale, 12, Rue Guénégaud, Paris, (6e).

(c) The archives of the Conseil National de la Résistance and other political bodies within France are available – it is not clear where. (Dausette: 'Libèration de Paris', Appendix on Sources.)

(d) The archives of General De Gaulle's Government, the BCRA, and his representatives in Occupied France are not available.

* [Besides Foot's official history, there are five volumes by H. Noguères *et al.,* *Histoire de la Résistance en France* (Paris, 1969–81).]

aspects the whole war was the battle of France.

Second. France was the most accessible of the countries occupied by the Germans. Geographically, this is obvious. It has long and open coasts facing the Channel, the Atlantic and the Mediterranean; it has two land frontiers with neutral countries, Switzerland and Spain; it provides a vast area in which air operations, by parachute and even by landing, are possible within easy range of bases in England. What is less obvious, is that the curious quadrilateral of Britain, USA, Vichy and De Gaulle meant that France remained politically accessible through a multiplicity of channels up to November 1942. Britain had no formal diplomatic relations with the Pétain régime, but a Canadian Chargé d'Affaires remained at Vichy, and it was always possible for Vichy diplomats or consuls abroad to open contact with their British colleagues if they wished to do so unofficially: this was the common practice at Madrid in particular.[1] The USA did not break off diplomatic relations until forced to do so by the full German occupation in November 1942: and that very important man, Admiral Leahy,* was at Vichy from January 1941 until April 1942; in addition the USA used its economic strength effectively to force admission to the semi-independent satrapy of North Africa. Thus French political gossip and intrigue worked upon the Allies from many quarters, and SOE was not, as in other countries, the sole (or almost the sole) channel through which relations could be maintained under German occupation.

The narrative which follows cannot therefore pretend to be an adequate account of French political development and relations with the Allies in the years from 1940 to 1945; even the action taken by SOE can be followed in detail only in its first stages.

1. The Battle of France and Vichy

Some relations had been established with the French both by D Section and by MI(R)[2] as far back as June 1939. It was apparently the French who first raised the matter of sabotage in the course of discussions on economic warfare.[3] In July 1939 Lieutenant Colonel Grand was in Paris, where he met Colonel Malraison of the IIème Bureau,[4] and just before the outbreak of war Major L. A. L. Humphreys was established in Paris as D Section's representative, in liaison with its newly

---

[1] Cf. for instance the discussions in the autumn of 1940, published in Cmd 6662.
[2] See above p. 34.
[3] Letter from Major Morton dated 5th June 1939, on SOE Archives File 3/470/7a.
[4] Report dated 17th July 1939, on SOE Archives File 3/470/7a.
* [W. D. Leahy, 1875–1959, Chief of US Navy Operations 1937–9, Roosevelt's Ambassador to Pétain 1941–2, Chairman of US Chiefs of Staff 1942–9.]

created opposite number, the Vème Bureau. Liaison remained friendly if ineffective during the next months: it was mainly concerned with the development of 'devices', and with possible action in Germany, Italy, Roumania and so forth. It was not contemplated that any action would be necessary in France.

That problem became real quite suddenly in mid-May 1940, and on 25th May, Colonel Grand wrote to Humphreys a letter fertile in suggestions – good suggestions, but hardly apt to the French frame of mind. Humphreys discussed this with his contact, Commandant Brochu, and was assured that dumps of materials had been created at Ghent, Antwerp, Brussels, Lille and other places and that at least two men had been left behind at each of these centres: so far as D Section was concerned it could help best by supplying and distributing material.[1] These plans may or may not have had some real existence. Humphreys wrote further to Grand on 7th June;[2] but for the next few days he was away in Switzerland, and he returned on 11th June to find that Paris was being evacuated.[3] His only hope of leaving behind an organisation of his own rested on a casual acquaintance, an energetic Russian taxi-driver who had made some practical suggestions.[4] But the taxi-driver could not be found, and the evacuation of D Section's staff was now itself a very pressing problem. Eventually they left by cruiser from the Gironde on 20th June, after an affectionate and patriotic parting with the Véme Bureau, which expressed its determination to maintain an underground existence in France.

This evacuation made a clean break, and SOE had to begin anew in August 1940 to construct French resistance out of nothing. It is worth recalling the political background briefly. Mr Churchill made his last effort to stiffen the French Government at Tours on 16th June. On that day Reynaud* fell and was succeeded by Pétain: on the 17th De Gaulle** left for London – he made his first broadcast next day. The Armistice was signed on the 22nd: on the 27th De Gaulle formed a Provisional French National Committee in London. This idea of a political committee was dropped at once, and replaced by the concep-

---

1   Report dated 29th May 1940, on SOE Archives File 3/470/7a.
2   Letter on SOE Archives File 3/470/72.
3   See his report on SOE Archives File 3/100/5a.
4   Report of 29th May 1940, SOE Archives File 3/470/7a.
*   [P. Reynaud, 1878–1966, French Prime Minister April–June 1940, prisoner of war 1940–45.]
**   [C. A. J. M. de Gaulle, 1890–1970, captured at Verdun, junior general in French army 1940, escaped to England to found Free French movement, returned to France 1944, retired 1946, again President 1958–69. See his memoirs (3 vols, 1955–60).]

tion of a predominantly military movement:[1] on the 28th His Majesty's Government 'recognised General De Gaulle as Leader of all Free Frenchmen, wherever they may be, who rally to him in support of the Allied cause'.[2] Thus a very junior French general, known only as a good Catholic and a vigorous military theorist, was adopted by Britain as the public symbol of the French nation.

There followed the attacks on the French fleet at Oran, Mers-el-Kebir and Dakar, on 3rd and 5th July; and the severance of relations with Britain by Vichy on 5th July. In August scattered French colonies began to 'rally' to De Gaulle, and most of French Central Africa had been secured by 12th September: but the Dakar expedition, organised belatedly and with much boasting and gossip, failed abjectly on 23rd September. This represented De Gaulle's high-water mark for the moment; and he paused to reorganise. On 27th October a Council for the Defence of the Empire was formed at Brazzaville in the Congo, with a tolerably respectable membership of soldiers, sailors and colonial governors; men of the second rank, and without much political appeal. Wisely, De Gaulle made this the formal centre of his movement: his London followers were a much less reputable band, full of quarrels and intrigue, notoriously indiscreet, and in many cases of extreme right-wing politics: his clientèle in the USA was (if possible) worse.

Vichy meantime had recovered its nerve, and had begun to estimate its political assets and power of manoeuvre. It had two military cards of some value, the French fleet, and the army in North Africa, which was weak enough, but could at least force an enemy to build up and launch a fairly serious operation. These two assets were covered by including Darlan* in the Government as Minister of Marine and by dispatching Weygand as Délégué Général to North Africa: Weygand's scope was effectively limited and checked by the existence of Governors with independent powers within his domain. At the same time German favour was conciliated by Laval's appearance as Deputy Premier and 'Crown Prince'. But probably Vichy's most vital asset was that it was in form the legal government of France. After the abolition of the Third Republic by the National Assembly on 10th July a good lawyer might pick some flaws in Pétain's title but he had a tolerable case, De Gaulle had no case at all. This point of legality undoubtedly carried great weight, even in the abstract, with

---

[1] A 'Comité Militaire' was set up to assist De Gaulle in January 1941.

[2] See CFR(41)207 of 15th December; copy on SOE Archives File (AD/S.1) SC.38/4.

* [J. L. X. F. Darlan, 1881–1942, French admiral, became Pétain's deputy, accidentally overrun in Algiers by 'Torch', shot dead (see p. 559). See his life by Hervé Coutau-Bégarie and Claude Huan (Paris, 1989).]

the ordinary servants of the State, from generals down to postmen: their duty was to serve the State while it stood, and Pétain was the State. This argument of duty was reinforced by more mundane thoughts of pay, promotion, pensions, the welfare of their families; and on the whole the great machine of the French State responded to the directions of Vichy, except in so far as the Germans directly intervened. This control of State power was all the more important in that the ordinary political Frenchman was for the moment badly rattled: the usual clamour of French parties was silent, and the initiative rested with the officials. This was a phase only, and Vichy's position weakened as ordinary political life awoke, even apart from Allied intervention: but for the moment it was strong, within the limits set by the Germans.

This will serve to explain one of the limitations of British policy within which SOE worked from the outset: as early as 29th August 1940 it was laid down by the Minister that 'until instructions to the contrary are received His Majesty's Government view with disfavour any act of aggression by British subjects, or British troops, against persons or objects in unoccupied France'.[1] This came to be known colloquially in SOE as the policy of 'discreet bangs in the Zone Occupée, no bangs without Foreign Office approval in the Zone Non-Occupée': a policy which caused much heart-burning, but was strictly observed until release came in November 1942. The most awkward dispute which it involved arose over the position of Vichy ships not in Vichy ports; these were not strictly covered by the general formula, and were military targets of some importance, both because they might bring colonial products through the blockade and because they were helping, at least indirectly, to maintain Rommel's position in North Africa. The Foreign Office weakened a little under pressure in October 1941, when it permitted attacks without reference to London, provided that the local British Foreign Office representative was consulted in each case.[2] But its grip was tightened again in February 1942; this was at a period when the Foreign Office was in general reasserting control over SOE,[3] but the immediate pretext was the danger of

---

[1] Memo. by 'F.W.' in SOE Archives File 3/470/7a.1. Cf. (for instance) exchange of letters between Mr Jebb and Major Morton, 12th and 15th April 1941, confirming this (on SOE Archives File (AD/S.1) SC.38/2); letter from Mr Hopkinson (Foreign Office) dated 30th April 1941, on SOE Archives File 3/470/2a.

[2] See ruling by CD dated 28th April 1941, SOE Archives File 3/470/2a: Minutes of meeting of 8th October 1941 and letter of 13th October on SOE Archives Files (AD/S.1) SC.38/2 and SC.38/6. For detailed Foreign Office ruling see letter of 3rd December on SC.38/6.

[3] See below p. 344.

disturbing Spanish sensibilities by such pieces of piracy as SOE's 'cutting out' of the Italian liner 'Duchessa d'Aosta' from the harbour of Fernando Po in January 1942.[1] The new rule was that reference should be made to the Foreign Office before any attempt in Spanish or Portuguese colonies which involved anything more violent than bribery:[2] it was scarcely possible for an agent planning sabotage to hold his fire while such discussion proceeded in London (this was a lesson as old as the Rickman case),[3] and the new policy was in effect a ban on 'bangs' in the only areas where Vichy shipping was fairly easy to attack.

Within these limitations SOE's task fell into two parts:

(i) Propaganda from without directed to promote French resistance.

(ii) Action by agents in France, intended to build up the organisation of resistance, and to carry out such sabotage as might be authorised.

The first of these need not detain us long. It was a fruitful subject of controversy, and one in which SOE in its original form was much involved: but it concerned SO1, not SO2, which succeeded to the title of SOE when PWE was formed in September 1941.[4] In so far as it was relevant to SO2's activities, the crux was the problem of the attitude to be taken to Pétain on the one hand and to the French Left on the other. As regards Pétain, SO2 was on the whole more bellicose than the three other partners, SO1, the Ministry of Information and the BBC, or than their agitated foster-mother, the Foreign Office; but it was quite ready to fall in with the general line, that Pétain should be left alone and his subordinates attacked. The question of the working-classes was more difficult. It could be maintained (on the one hand) that an articulate and influential section of French opinion attributed all France's disasters to the Front Populaire,* and that an appeal to the French working-class would frighten off these potential supporters. On the other hand (entirely apart from ideologies) it was plain that the working-class were the people who would have to do the work: for the purposes of sabotage one 'cheminot' was worth ten Inspecteurs des Finances and fifty large 'rentiers'. It was essential that a resistance movement should be based firmly on the workers and the

---

[1] Below p. 327.

[2] Foreign Office telegram of 18th April 1942, on SOE Archives File (AD/S.1) SC.38/6.

[3] See above p. 20.

[4] See above p. 101.

* [The Front Populaire won a general election in 1936 and governed France till 1940.]

peasants: it remained to be seen whether this would involve also an attempt to resuscitate the politicians of the Front Populaire.[1]

The propaganda policy which resulted was necessarily a compromise, and to that extent ineffective; but it was not incompatible with SOE's requirements. Indeed, as will be seen later, there was within SOE itself something of a dualism between the approach to the respectable and the approach to the masses; and it would be absurd to picture SOE as a consistent champion of the Left, and the Foreign Office as sponsor of those official classes whose worth it could most easily appreciate. The matter was far more complex than that.

2. The Problem of Recruitment

The technical means of propaganda existed, in the BBC, and other radio stations, and in the dropping of leaflets by the RAF: those for action by agents did not, and had to be created from nothing. The first difficulties for SO2 were to find the men, and to find means of getting them into France: discussions of policy had a purely theoretical interest for SO2 until some progress had been made with these practical problems.

First, as to men. There were only three methods of recruitment open to SOE, which did not involve going hat in hand to the 'Leader of All Free Frenchmen'. *First*, there were British subjects bilingual in French and English and competent to pass as Frenchmen. These could be found through the 'usual channels', ranging from the personal knowledge of SOE's staff to the indexes kept by the War Office of men suitable for military intelligence work. The whole field was not very large, but it provided a small stream of recruits until late in the war, many of them men of remarkable and heroic quality. To this class should be added a few French-Canadians, but recruitments from this source were not large. *Second*, there were in the early days a number

---

[1] The following papers (among others) are relevant:
   a. Mr Jebb to the Minister summing up the controversy, with a 'Leftish' tendency: 15th November 1940. File SC.38/3.
   b. Meeting on policy under Mr Dalton's chairmanship (Mr Jebb versus Mr Leeper: compromise suggested by Sir Robert Vansittart) 17th November 1940. File SC.38/5.
   c. CFR(40)102 of 26th November (General Appreciation). File 38/9.
   d. Foreign Office paper Z/488/244/17 of 23rd January 1941 (rather to the Right). File SC.38/5.
   e. Meeting of Mr Eden, Mr Duff Cooper, Mr Dalton, on 31st January 1941. File SC.38/5.
   f. Mr Leeper's paper CFR(31)71 of 4th March, and Mr Jebb's comments of 8th March. File SC.38/5.
   (Above files in SOE Archives AD/S.1 series.)

of Frenchmen of the utmost patriotism who could not stomach De Gaulle, or (more particularly) his associates. Some of them already had close English associations of their own, almost all were of upper middle-class or aristocratic origin, but without much previous political connection. Men of this type were admirable material for liaison with non-political resistance, but they were few in number and their potentialities were in some ways limited: they could provide leaders, but not rank and file, and they were not likely to be able to recruit a rank and file of their own. A large-scale movement is hardly possible without politics and all that they involve. *Third*, it early became a rule (though not one accepted quietly by De Gaulle) that any Frenchman recruited by a British agent in France was in a sense British property. If he was brought out of France, De Gaulle had no claim on him as a Free Frenchman, unless the man himself deliberately 'rallied' to De Gaulle. Such men were naturally not encouraged by SOE to transfer their allegiance, and a great many of them did not wish to do so: on the whole, they represented that very useful type of Frenchman, in all walks of life, who hates the Germans and hates his own politicians of all shades only a little less. It was this factor alone which made it possible to build up the 'British Circuits' till their reputation stood high in France, in spite of ideological attacks from many quarters.

These three sources were clearly not enough in themselves. It was in any case high policy (in spite of some reservations and many quarrels) that the leadership of De Gaulle should be sustained and his symbolic importance recognised. For instance the Prime Minister wrote to Mr Dalton and Mr Duff Cooper in February 1941: 'we have never received the slightest good treatment or even courtesy from Vichy, and the Free French Movement remains our dominant policy . . . . I think De Gaulle is the best Frenchman now in the arena, and I want him taken care of as much as possible.'[1] De Gaulle was the undisputed master of those Frenchmen who had chosen to follow him rather than return to France: most of the Frenchmen who escaped from France on their own initiative, in small boats or over the Pyrenees, did so in order to join De Gaulle, since he was the only alternative to Vichy and Vichy policies of which they knew: and it was clearly British policy that spontaneous movements in France should not be discouraged from rallying to De Gaulle, if they wished to do so, although they must not be forced or cajoled. All this gave De Gaulle an importance in SOE's work which could not be evaded, and liaison with him and his officers was vital from the outset.

---

[1] CFR(41)53 of 18th February.

De Gaulle was at first heavily engaged on the affairs of the French Empire, and he was out of England on the Dakar expedition in September and October, so that matters began slowly. Contact was opened between Sir Frank Nelson and Commandant Moret, Admiral Muselier's Chief of Staff, on 8th September, about a wild-cat scheme for landing Admiral Muselier at Beirut:[1] and Major Humphreys (who was in charge of French affairs at this stage) made contact through Moret with the representative of a Colonel Chateauvieux, said to be in charge of De Gaulle's intelligence bureau.[2] From this discussion first emerged the project that De Gaulle should provide men to be trained by SOE and to be put into France under the joint auspices of the two organisations. Sir Frank Nelson's comments on this (which were endorsed by Mr Dalton) are interesting in the light of later developments.[3]

7. The ideal is to allow the Gestapo and the De Gaulle Staff to think that we are co-operating 100% with each other – whereas in truth, whilst I should wish you to have the friendliest day-to-day relationship and liaison with the De Gaulle people, I should wish you at the same time to tell them nothing of our innermost and most confidential plans, and above all, such bases as you may establish in France must be our bases and known only to us . . . .

9. I realise that the demands I make upon you in this respect are extremely difficult, and might even be characterised as impossible – nevertheless it is an ideal which I wish you to follow . . . .

10. I think we might well consider the advisability of making use of Legrain's offer of co-operation on the lines of the creation of a special separate watertight sub-section which would work out a French organisation based on the use of the De Gaullist 2ème and 5ème people. A special officer would have to be in charge of this job, and he would work outside this office and never visit it. The whole of our HQ organisation and its field organisation would be entirely concealed from the French . . . .

This principle of watertight compartments is the crux of SOE's dealings with the French problem until the creation of the combined État Major of the French Forces of the Interior (EMFFI) under General Koenig* on 2nd June 1944.[4]

---

[1] Note by CD dated 9th September, on SOE Archives File 3/100/2(c).
[2] Note by Major Humphreys dated 10th October 1940, on SOE Archives File 3/100/2(c). Cf. also his note of 19th October on File CD/7. (Early CD Files.)
[3] Minutes of 11th October, on SOE Archives File 3/100/2(c).
[4] SHAEF/17245/6/5/Ops(A) of 2nd June 1944.
* [M. P. Koenig, 1889–1970, held off Rommel at Bir Hakeim 1942, commanded (from outside) French forces of interior 1944, Governor of Paris 1944.]

A somewhat similar approach by a certain M. Massip is recorded on the SO1 side by Mr Cadett on 6th November 1940:[1] and Mr Leeper independently took a line not unlike that of Sir Frank Nelson. Control of propaganda and control of agents involved very similar problems, though they were fought out with De Gaulle through different British organisations.

Early in December 1940 SO2's French section was reorganised: Mr H. R. Marriott (who was a Courtauld's representative in Paris up to 1940) took over what became known as F Section, while Major Humphreys was temporarily detached to explore ways and means of communication with France through Iberia. Arrangements were made for training some twenty or thirty volunteers from the Gaullist forces, and the Free French took this occasion to raise again the more general question of joint action; Mr Cadett of F Section was approached by one Schilling, said to be then in charge of De Gaulle's sabotage section, with proposals for co-operation, much like the earlier ones except that they were linked to proposals for sabotage of electric power installations, on which by chance F Section were already working. The only direct response to this was a clear and full restatement by Sir Frank Nelson of his earlier instructions;[2] but SOE now had some of De Gaulle's men in training for its first important French operation, and it was also rumoured that De Gaulle was contemplating special operations of his own. It therefore became important to follow up CD's principle of collaboration through a separate Free French section.

The first step was a Minute from Sir Frank Nelson to Mr Jebb, on 7th January 1941, emphasising primarily the need to extend our control of De Gaulle's activities by offering finance and facilities subject to collaboration in all projects.[3] This was followed by the draft of a memorandum in French, intended to form the basis for an agreement with General De Gaulle – 'En vue d'assurer la collaboration la plus étroite entre les services de la Grande Brétagne et de la France Libre en tout ce qui concerne la campagne d'action subversive dirigée contre l'énnemi commun en territoire français, il est entendu comme suit:

1. Cette campagne sera dirigée d'accord avec le Général de Gaulle par la Section F. du Bureau SO2 . . .' and so forth at length: a programme for direction by the British not at all likely to commend itself to Charles of Arc.

These papers were forwarded by Mr Jebb to Major Morton, as Chairman of the War Cabinet Committee on French Resistance:[4] a

---

[1] Record and relative correspondence in SOE Archives File (AD/S.1) SC.38/4.

[2] Dated 25th December 1940, on SOE Archives File 3/100/2(c).

[3] Copy on SOE Archives File 3/100/2(a).

[4] Letter of 11th January, on SOE Archives File (AD/S.1) SC.38/4.

discussion followed between Major Morton and Sir Frank Nelson, which came rather nearer to the realities of Free French psychology and politics.[1] The next step illuminated the position still more clearly. Eight of the Free French were in training for the important 'coup de main' operation known as 'Savanna';[2] General de Gaulle was approached on 24th January by General Spears, the senior British Liaison Officer, with a formal request that he should authorise their participation in the operation. This was abruptly refused.[3]

The immediate obstacle was overcome, it is not clear how – possibly by the personal intervention of the Prime Minister – and the next step was a somewhat inconclusive conference on 6th February, under the Chairmanship of General Spears, at which De Gaulle's Chief of Staff, General Petit, was present, as well as Mr Jebb and the CSS.[4] The position now was that General Petit asserted De Gaulle's right to conduct independent operations, but admitted that he would depend on His Majesty's Government for their execution; he spoke encouragingly of collaboration, but no more was heard for the moment of the project of a separate Gaullist section of SOE. By this time Colonel de Wavrin,* later so well-known as 'Passy', was established fairly firmly as chief of De Gaulle's 'subversive' organisation (he had appeared on the scene, with ill-defined functions, as early as September 1940), and it was suggested that he would be the proper channel of liaison. De Wavrin was a remarkable character, who was associated from the first with this side of De Gaulle's work and became the subject of bitter controversy in France after De Gaulle's resignation of the Premiership in January 1946. His origins are a little mysterious, but he was clearly a 'man of the Right', and probably concerned in the Cagoulard conspiracy which caused so much alarm in the middle 1930s. Certainly he was an old intriguer, and a very persistent, gallant and successful one, who maintained his position through all the internal wrangles of the Gaullist entourage, and rendered inestimable service to his master in rallying the independent resistance movements.

---

1 Letter by Major Morton to Mr Jebb dated 14th January, and note by CD dated 15th January, both on SOE Archives File (AD/S.1) SC.38/4.
2 Below, p. 244.
3 Aide-Mémoire for discussion with De Gaulle d/d 20th January, and Aide-Mémoire for the Minister d/d 28th January, on SOE Archives File 3/100/2(c).
4 Record by Mr Jebb on SOE Archives File 3/100/2(c).
* [A. de Wavrin, 1911–98, remote cousin of the De Wavrin who belonged to the *deux cent familles*, French military engineer, survived Norwegian campaign, appointed head of De Gaulle's secret services 1940, survived two missions into France, framed, arrested, released 1946, went into business. Misstated by Mackenzie to be far to the right in politics. See his life by G. Perrier (Paris, 1999).]

Whatever his ultimate political objects, there was no doubt at all about his courage and skill.

A new paper[1] on the 'Basis for Collaboration' was prepared after this meeting, on much more promising lines. 'A bureau will be established in which will be housed personnel delegated by both organisations . . . . Projects of common interest will be planned and agreed upon and joint recommendations will be made to General De Gaulle and the Chief of SO2 for approval. Brig. Gubbins will, in conjunction with General Petit, decide upon the final operational order and be responsible for making the final arrangements.' This document was handed to General Petit on 25th February, and no more was heard of it. Collaboration seems to have gone on smoothly enough; the atmosphere improved and there was some informal negotiation. There was however one scare at the end of May, when the Swinton Committee on Home Security recorded a decision that henceforward no government department should be permitted to engage or use French 'volunteers' except with the express permission of General De Gaulle.[2] This would of course have put SOE's work in France entirely under De Gaulle's control, and SIS was no less alarmed; the two secret services intervened in unison, and the decision was interpreted or revised so as to refer only to Frenchmen who had deliberately chosen to enter the service of De Gaulle.[3]

Finally, a formal dinner-party was convened by Sir Frank Nelson on 12th June to put the finishing touches to an agreement already informally worked out between Mr Sporborg and De Wavrin:[4]

1. In principle the plan for any operation should originate from Col. de Wavrin and should be worked out only in very broad outline in collaboration with Capt. Piquet-Wicks (of SOE).
2. The plan in this original form should first be shown to Mr Sporborg, and if approved by him it will be passed on to Col. Barry,* who is in charge of the SO2 Operations Section.
3. Provided that Mr Sporborg approves the plan and that Col. Barry agrees that it is feasible, Col. de Wavrin should then submit it to General Petit personally and secretly so as to obtain his approval in principle.
4. If the plan is of sufficient magnitude and importance to require the approval of the COS, or the War Cabinet, Mr Sporborg will

---

[1] Copy on SOE Archives File 3/100/2(c) (date of paper 20th February 1941).

[2] Home Defence (Security) Executive, (Paper HD(S)E.81 para. 5) of 26th May 1941, and meeting of 28th May 1941, Min. 5. SOE Archives File 3/100/7(c).

[3] Minute from ACSS to CD d/d 13th June 1941, on SOE Archives File 3/100/7(c).

[4] Copy on SOE Archives File (AD/S.1) SC.38/4.

* [R. H. Barry, 1908–98, Gubbins's Chief of Staff 1943–6, Military Attaché Stockholm 1947, on North Atlantic Council 1959–62, joint master Hampshire Hunt.]

be responsible for obtaining this approval directly he hears that General Petit is in agreement.

5. The necessary consents in principle having thus been obtained, the following action would be taken . . .

and so on at length and in detail.

This was far from the original dream that a new sub-section of SO2 should control the political operations of De Gaulle: but it was at least the working model of an organisation related to the practical needs of the two parties and evading all issues of principle. There is no written record of its acceptance by the French: De Gaulle himself was abroad, much engaged with operations in Syria (which began on 8th June), and it may have been unwise to set pen to paper in his absence. But matters went on in practice much as laid down in the 'agreement', except when disturbed by local storms of temper, and the system was very little modified in principle until the final merger under EMFFI in June 1944.

As part of this system a new French section was formed in May 1941, under the title of DR/F Section (later known as R/F Section), and was housed separately for a short time at No. 72 Berkeley Court, then at No. 1 Dorset Square, so that Free French visitors need not be admitted to Baker Street. Its heads successively were: Captain Piquet-Wicks to August 1942, Lieutenant Colonel J. R. H. Hutchinson* to December 1943, Lieutenant Colonel L. H. Dismore to November 1944 (latterly within EMFFI).

3. The Problem of Communications

So much for the problems involved in recruitment. Those of communication were equally important in shaping the organisation, and equally complex. Only three elements are open, sea, air and land, but each of them admits of infinite variations and perplexities. It must always be remembered that the least part of the problem is to get a man in: it is only if he (or others) can be got out again that communication becomes a system, and not a series of gambles.

The most convenient form of sea transport is a submarine, which can be used with relative safety to land men or stores at night on a deserted beach. But a prearranged meeting with a shore party is essential in order to get anyone out, and it is also useful for a landing; yet the keeping of a fixed rendezvous is a matter of extreme danger which may hazard many lives and a valuable vessel of war on a compara-

---

* [(Sir) J. R. H. Hutchison, 1893–1979, shipowner, mission into France 1944, Conservative MP 1945–59, baronet 1956. See his *That Drug, Danger* (1977).]

tively small venture.[1] It was manifestly unfair to press the Admiralty for the use of submarines except for matters of the highest operational weight: for instance, General Clarke's visit to North Africa on 19th October 1942, or the escape of Giraud from France on 7th November of that year.

Sea transport was thus generally a matter of small vessels or nothing, and the French problem created two miniature navies, one based on Helford in Cornwall, the other on Gibraltar.*

The Helford project was a natural reaction to the situation in the north-west of France. From the fall of France a steady trickle of Frenchmen crossed to the south of England in fishing-vessels of various types: in addition, ordinary fishing operations continued from ports in Brittany and the Bay of Biscay. Surely it would not present serious difficulty to use genuine French fishing-vessels to mix with the fishing fleets or to slip inconspicuously into corners of the Breton coast? The project was floated before the end of 1940,[2] and Lieutenant Commander Holdsworth (an old D Section man) began to collect boats and men early in 1941.

Unfortunately (but naturally) the Germans prohibited all fishing in the Channel except from small open boats, and SOE's sea-going vessels were therefore of no use except to the south of Ushant. For Channel operations it was necessary to depend on speed rather than disguise, and the best vessel which could be obtained was a 41' 6" RAF seaplane tender, which was both too small and too slow. It was remarkable that four successful operations were carried out with this vessel in the early winter of 1941: one of them was a 'Lobster Pot' operation – a simple device by which the British party could 'plant' letters or stores in a moored 'pot', to be collected at leisure by those on shore. But in January 1942 a new directive[3] put operational control of Helford in the hands of NID(C) at the Admiralty, which already ran a larger and slightly more regular flotilla at Dartmouth, and operations with the RAF tender were banned as involving unjustifiable risks. A few operations were carried out later by a gunboat manned by SOE men at Helford, as well as by gunboats of the 15th MGB flotilla: but priority was given to operations for SIS and MI9 (escaped prisoners).

---

[1] See for instance the experience of a submarine which failed to find the 'Josephine B' party, and Brigadier Gubbins's comment – 3rd June 1941, on SOE Archives File (AD/S.1) SC.38/1.

[2] For the earliest stage see Major Humphreys's note of 20th September 1940, on SOE Archives File CD/7.

[3] See below p. 362, where relations with the Admiralty are treated in more detail.

* [On both of these, see Brooks Richards, *Secret Flotillas* (1996).]

The position was even more frustrating as regards operations in the Bay of Biscay. SOE's original 'fishing fleet' was placed under a ban in the winter of 1941–2, on the ground that it consisted of north coast vessels which could not pass muster in the west. Genuine west coast vessels were obtained in the summer of 1942, and all preparations were in hand, when a further ban was imposed: priority was to be given to SIS's well-established 'mail-run' to the west coast, and SOE operations were prohibited on the grounds of possible interference with its security. This decision was a bitter blow to the men at Helford, but other means of communication were now fairly well established, and London HQ acquiesced in the decision without fighting to the last ditch. A good many of the Helford men were transferred to the Mediterranean in the winter of 1942–3, and the base (which was formally controlled by the Admiralty from 1st June 1943) was thereafter important to SOE mainly as a training centre for small boat work in other theatres.

The Gibraltar flotilla was even odder in its origins, but probably in the end it contributed more. SOE had a representative at Gibraltar early in 1941,[1] and in summer 1941 two very decrepit boats were purchased locally: one of them was used (without success) in attempts to attack Axis shipping in Spanish territorial waters, the other was put at the disposal of the Polish liaison officer in Gibraltar, who used it very successfully for exfiltrating Polish refugees from North Africa. 'The state of its engine may be realised from the fact that it was largely composed of an engine removed from one of the SOE motor-cars.'

This experience led to a reorganisation in 1942, and the creation by the Admiralty of the 'Coast Watching Flotilla', a fleet of tolerably reliable Feluccas: this organisation served all the secret services and was not controlled by SOE, but it was manned in the first place largely by a party of Poles sent out by SOE for other purposes. It was much used (from May 1942 until the events of November 1942) for the transfer of agents to and from the south of France – a long slow sail often in conditions of extreme discomfort, but relatively free from enemy interference.

Even after this reorganisation SOE's navy was perpetuated in the shape of the 'Gibraltar Fishing Fleet', which was created early in 1942 by Captain P. R. Musson, MC.[2] Its primary object was the smuggling of arms into Spain: but this project was soon dropped and replaced by the more orthodox smuggling of tobacco and other comforts, as a method of earning pesetas for His Majesty's Government. The fleet

---

[1] Mr Hugh Quennell.

[2] See account by Captain Musson in Appendix I to the SOE Iberian History.

existed until 1944, and far more than maintained itself by its earn-
ings: its range was too short for operations to enemy-occupied territory and it served the larger purposes of SOE mainly by smuggling
escapees out of Spain to Gibraltar.

The possibilities of sea transport were thus more limited than they
might have seemed on paper. Air transport on the other hand developed beyond any conception which could have been framed before
the war: and in almost every theatre the fate of the Resistance in the
end depended on the numbers of aircraft which could be made available to support it. Much of the later history of SOE depended on a
battle for aircraft allocations against other claimants of high strategical priority. This must be dealt with later,[1] and it is only necessary
here to indicate briefly a few technical factors.

France was close at hand, and any of the aircraft likely to be available had adequate range for dropping operations to any part of the
country. There was not in this case the problem of distance, which
complicated matters in the Balkans, and standard medium bombers
were good enough even if obsolescent for other purposes. Whitleys
were the stand-by in the early days, though Hampdens and
Wellingtons were occasionally used. Bigger bombers came into play
later, and could carry much larger loads: but this was not an unmixed
blessing, as it involved a larger organisation on the ground to find
and conceal before daylight the contents of a Stirling, which might
amount to $3\frac{1}{2}$ tons of stores.[2]

The early days were the days of the 'blind drop': the aircraft, with
no guides but moonlight and dead reckoning, dropped its men a little
vaguely in a neighbourhood which might perhaps be safe and suitable. An error of fifty miles was by no means uncommon, even with
highly trained aircrews, and agents were dropped in forests, in lakes,
on rocks – once on the roof of a police-station, on another occasion
in the midst of a POW camp. A blind drop in 1941 was as big a risk
as has ever been systematically taken in war, yet it was a necessary
first step in practically every theatre.

Once a wireless set had been established in the field 'reception'
could be arranged, and matters were one stage easier. But the difficulties of organisation were still immense. In the first place, once a
place and time had been notified from the field to HQ it still depended
on the weather whether the operation could be carried out, and no
decision could be taken till the last moment. By that time the agent

---

[1] See below p. 363.

[2] Chart of loads carried by various types of aircraft used on SD operations with Air
Ministry letter DO.50/45/A13(USA) of 29th August 1945, on SOE Archives File
2/290/STATS.

in the field would be waiting on or near his ground, and it would be too late to warn him of cancellation through his own wireless set which might be hidden miles away. The answer to this problem was found in the use of the BBC, which could be heard on an ordinary receiver, carried easily or available already in a nearby house. The system of meaningless 'personal messages' was begun in November 1941; many of them were 'dummy messages', mere 'cover' to disguise fluctuations in the traffic, others had been arranged with agents to indicate to them whether or not an operation would be carried out. The normal system was to send a message in the afternoon – either 'cancel' or 'stand-by' – followed by a message in the evening when the final decision was taken. These 'personal messages' could be used for other purposes, but their main value was in 'laying-on' air operations, and their volume to Western Europe was very large at the time when operations were at their height – nearly a hundred a day in the peak period before D-day.

It then remained for the aircraft to find its 'reception committee', and in the early days the flashing of a few torches made the chances very little better than those of a blind drop. Fortunately navigational methods developed very rapidly. 'Gee' (which was introduced in the Special Duty squadrons early in 1943) gave an aircraft a pretty good idea of its position by a technique independent of dead reckoning and of weather. The 'Rebecca-Eureka' system was first used by SOE in February 1943,[1] and provided a method by which an aircraft equipped with 'Eureka' could home on to a 'Rebecca' set worked by an agent on the ground. The set was not unmanageably large, and it had a range of at least fifteen miles in good conditions with the aircraft at 2,000 ft. Finally, in July 1943, the S-phone was introduced: a sort of 'walkie-talkie' which made possible direct communication between the aircraft and the party on the ground.[2] It was not always reliable in field conditions, but when it worked it was very useful both for the exchange of messages and as a precaution against German traps: at least one aircraft is reported to have withdrawn hastily with its passengers on hearing the guttural accents of the Gestapo.

Once the field was equipped with these devices, air supply became less of a lottery, and in the last months the proportion of successful

---

[1] The first record of its potentialities for SOE work is in a Minute dated 8th February 1942 on SOE Archives File 9/170/1 (destroyed). For first use see SOE London HQ War Diary – R/F Section – January/March 1943, p. 193. See also Part 10 of the 'AL Section History'. [Useful diagrams in David Kahn (ed.), Pierre Lorain, *Secret Warfare* (1983), p. 100.]

[2] Range of 10 miles at 2,000 ft, 15 miles at 5,000 ft. See pamphlet on S-phone – SOE Archives. [Useful diagrams in Lorain, *op. cit.*, pp. 96–9.]

operations was relatively high. But these methods were useful only for the outward journey: to return by air presented an even more difficult problem, until the final days of open insurrection when the Resistance could dominate a sufficient area to construct and hold a landing-ground suitable for transport aircraft. Throughout the critical period of SOE's history the normal pattern was that agents and stores were parachuted to the field, agents and written messages came out by sea or by land. There remained however the hazardous resource of 'pick-up' operations by Lysander.[1] The Lysander was ordered in a mistaken hour as a close-support army co-operation aircraft: it was useless for the purpose, but might well have been designed to an SOE specification, if SOE had then existed. It was a sturdy single-engined aeroplane with a cruising speed of 165 mph and a range (out and home) of 900 miles with extra tanks, which enabled it to reach the northern part of the unoccupied Zone of France: with a squeeze it could carry three passengers (besides the pilot): and it could land and take-off on the proverbial pocket-handkerchief. A rough runway of 600 yards was necessary in theory, but in practice much less was adequate. The first SOE operation near Châteauroux, on the night of 4th September 1941, was successful but hair-raising.[2] There was one man to be picked up, and one man to be landed. The former was accidentally detained by a police search and arrived late at the ground, to hear the aircraft circling overhead: a field was hastily chosen at random, and some indication of a flare-path was given with pocket torches. The Lysander pilot got down all right, but in taking off he fouled some unseen telegraph wires and carried a length of wire back to England trailing from the aircraft.

This operation at least showed what could be done, but the RAF could not systematically risk men and aircraft with such complete absence of precaution. It insisted in the first place on a proper notification of proposed landing-grounds, and a careful study of them by the Air Ministry before they were approved. It also required that landing operations should be arranged only with agents who had been given some training by airmen and had at least an elementary understanding of the airman's difficulties and point of view.[3] One of the

---

[1] Section 5 of the SOE 'AL History' deals very fully with these. [H. B. Verity, *We Landed by Moonlight* (1978, often revised); and see his notes in Foot, *SOE in France*, Appendix D.]

[2] Operation Levee/Facade – see below p. 251. SIS had carried out a successful operation as early as October 1940 – 'AL Section History', Part 5, para. 42.

[3] There was serious controversy about the first such operation laid on for R/F Section, in April 1942, when an untrained agent summoned a Lysander on a false plea of urgency. R/F History 1942, para. 14, and below p. 276.

earliest of these specialists was a French civil airline pilot, named Déricourt,* who was trained and sent in for F Section in January 1943 and received fourteen Lysander operations up to February 1944. About that time he came under suspicion of being in touch with the Gestapo, and was withdrawn from operations;[1] but other trained men were then available and no serious gap in operations followed except in a limited area.[2]

The Lysander was the aircraft which made pick-up operations possible, but as conditions improved and experience was gained it was possible also to use Hudsons, twin-engined aircraft with a range of 1,500 miles and capacity which could be adjusted to take up to eight or ten passengers or nearly a ton of stores. Naturally they could land only on tolerably large and level grounds, but twenty-nine Hudson operations were flown to France in the 'clandestine phase', the first of them in February 1943, and they made a big difference to the position. The American Dakota was also brought into use in the summer of 1944, but virtually only for operations to well-secured 'Maquis' areas. The number of pick-up operations carried out from England and from Corsica was as follows:

Year	Operations	Men Carried	
		In	Out
1941	1	1	1
1942	10	15	19
1943	54	103	200
1944	47	140	211[3]

About 900 agents[4] were parachuted to the field in France during the same period, others went in by land or sea: and many of those brought out by air were not agents but Frenchmen who had become promi-

---

[1] SOE Archives File 'AD/E Safe' Gilbert refers. To the time of writing (November 1947) his case is still in dispute and fresh evidence is still coming to light in France: the present impression is that he was guilty and was responsible for the penetration of many Free French 'circuits'.

[2] Major Bourne-Patterson's Report, 'The British Circuits in France', p. 8. See also full list of pick-up operations in Annex to Air Liaison Section History, Pt 5; and the final form of the RAF 'text-book' on 'Night Pick-Up' attached to that History, and notes for pilots by Wing Commander Verity, DSO, DFC, the champion at this form of sport.

[3] From Appendix 'A' to Air Liaison History – chapter on 'Pick-Up Operations'. Only one pilot and two aircraft were lost on these operations.

[4] History of Special Duty Operations in Europe – Appendix H.1 and H.2.

* [1909–62, now proved to have been a double agent, but acquitted of that charge 1947.]

nent within the Resistance. It was thus something of a privilege for a 'London man' to obtain a return passage by air. There was generally something of an emergency character about landing operations, either to bring out quickly some 'VIP' or to withdraw an agent in immediate danger: and they were an essential link in the chain primarily for that reason.

Land communications, by contrast with air transport, were primarily a means of getting men out rather than in. The first stage was spontaneous: a native industry of guides and smugglers already existed on the Swiss and Spanish frontiers (particularly the latter), and it expanded naturally to cope with the increasing market in refugees. But further links were necessary, to bring 'passengers' through occupied territory to the frontier, and to rescue them from internment or mere administrative delay in neutral territory.

Switzerland was relatively unimportant, as it was geographically a 'dead end': SOE had a representative there from February 1941, but his concern was mainly with Germany and Italy. He could pass on messages received across the frontier from France, but for physical communications he was himself dependent on routes through France. Small articles of industrial value passed through from Switzerland in this way, and on one occasion one of SOE's own staff in Switzerland was hastily withdrawn by this route.[1]

The key to the situation was Iberia, and in particular Spain, which was of vital interest to SOE quite apart from any work it might have to do in Spanish affairs.[2] Major J. G. Beevor* was established at Lisbon as Assistant Military Attaché in January 1941:[3] Major Hugh Quennell was sent to Gibraltar early in 1941; at Madrid Mr David Babington-Smith was appointed in February 1941, under the aegis of the Naval Attaché, Captain Hillgarth.** It was of great importance to have someone at Barcelona, the most convenient terminus for a route across the Pyrenees, and Lieutenant H. E. Bell, RNVR, was sent out in January 1941. Unfortunately his arrival had not been previously approved by HM Ambassador in Madrid, Sir Samuel Hoare: it is also probable that he was indiscreet. At any rate, he was sent home almost

---

[1] Miss Hodgson in November 1943. German History, Vol. 1, Part I(f) Switzerland, App. A, p. 3.

[2] See below p. 322.

[3] Major L. H. Mortimore joined him in April 1941, specially to deal with Clandestine Communications.

* [1905–87, entered SOE from Slaughter & May, City solicitors, on leaving Portugal worked under Hambro, then at AFHQ. See his *SOE: Recollections and Reflections 1940–1945* (1981).]

** [A. H. Hillgarth, 1899–1978, at Madrid 1939–43, in Far East 1943–6; in *DNB*.]

at once, and SOE was without a Barcelona representative until Captain Pinsent was finally approved by the Ambassador in February 1943, when it was judged that Franco's position was a little less delicately balanced. Major Muirhead had visited Barcelona in the autumn of 1942 and had been able to arrange some 'underground' lines; thereafter travel through Spain to Portugal or Gibraltar was fairly well organised, though never entirely safe.[1]

The 'Lines' across France were first conceived in February 1941, when Major Humphries visited Lisbon and renewed old contacts with the Vème Bureau. D/F Section, which was responsible for them, did not come into being as a separate section until the spring of 1942. It may seem surprising that there should be yet a third independent section concerned with France, but the arrangement had many merits. In the first place, the section was not concerned only with France; its 'lines' led also to Holland, Belgium and Switzerland, and it was of great importance to these countries. Second, its work was of a kind which could readily be kept separate from that of F Section and R/F Section; indeed it was best that it should be separate. D/F Section will not appear much in the sequel: it had nothing to do with politics and it conducted no operations giving visible military results. The primary duty of its agents was to avoid anything which might draw attention to their existence: and to limit themselves to their defined role of providing 'safe houses' where 'bodies' might stay without suspicion, and of setting the 'bodies' on their way from one house to another with any false papers required. The essence of the matter was in the security precautions involved. Each 'house' must be, so far as possible, detached from its neighbours, so that only the organiser should know the whole chain; 'passengers' would be escorted without their knowledge from one house to another, so that any arrest or suspicious circumstance would be noted and reported back before action against the chain as a whole could be taken by the Gestapo; agents should know as little as possible about the passengers, and the passengers about the agents. Organisation was difficult: the inculcation of doctrine was still more difficult; and it took some time before the system was in working order. No full statistics of its work are available, and the details of it are of purely technical interest. But it is some indication of its importance that in the first six months of 1944 it brought out 131 'bodies' through Spain, and lost only nine: about half of these men were concerned with resistance in France, the rest with other SOE

---

[1] Appendix 'H' of the Iberian History deals with Clandestine Communications through Spain.

activities. During the same period eleven agents entered France over the Pyrenees.[1]

4. Operations

This is a long preface, but indispensable if one is to understand how operations developed. Operations themselves fall naturally into four categories:

(i)   Coup de main parties.
(ii) The activities of F Section agents.
(iii) Activities of De Gaulle agents sponsored by R/F Section.
(iv) The work of D/F Section in building up lines of communication.

Of these (i) is straightforward: (iv) was of great but technical importance, and it is not proposed to describe it here. (ii) and (iii) interlock with one another and with political contacts made through other channels, and the sequence of events is hard to disentangle. It will perhaps be most satisfactory to give first a bare narrative of the action taken up to the summer of 1942; then to return to the political picture which emerged gradually up to that date, and to its effects on SOE's relations with De Gaulle.

(i) Coup de Main Parties

This type of attack was in effect a miniature military operation based on England, carried out by men who wore civilian disguise and were therefore not protected by the laws of war. But for this factor, such operations would have been more appropriate to CCO than to SOE, and they were important only in the first phase of SOE's development. Their importance then was due to two things: first, that SOE was anxious for some visible results which could justify its existence: second, that until an organisation had been built up in the field no sabotage could be carried out except from bases in England. If it is to be economical as an operation of war, sabotage must feed on the soil of the country in which it takes place: the coup de main from outside is unlikely to pay dividends proportionate to the effort expended unless the target is of absolutely first-rate importance – like the heavy-water installations at Vemork.[2]

---

[1] *Note*: A narrative was produced by D/F Section, but cannot at present be found in SOE Archives. There are available only the D/F notes on method contributed to the SOE Handbook, and a statistical report for January–June 1944 (attached to the F Section History).

[2] See below p. 653.

Some mention should be made first of Operation 'Shamrock', though it involved no landing in France. In November 1940 HM submarine (Lieutenant Minshull, RN) entered the Gironde estuary with five agents recruited by SOE. This party seized a tunny-fishing vessel, put some of the crew on board the submarine, and obtained the co-operation of the rest. Thus equipped with a perfect local disguise, they made a valuable reconnaissance of the estuary, already in use as a U-boat base, and sailed the captured tunnyman back to England.[1]

The next four projects were integral parts of a considered policy. They were:

SAVANNA 'A', which was a direct response to German tactics in the night 'blitz'. Coventry and other raids of a similar pattern were led by fire-raising parties from K.Gr.100, a fairly small unit manned by aircrews of very high quality trained in the use of special radio navigational aids. It was reported that they travelled together in buses from their billets to the airfield at Vannes; and it was thought that an attack by a small party on these buses might be very effective.

SAVANNA 'B', was a project suggested by the first stages of the Battle of the Atlantic, and was for an attack on submarine crews (also travelling by bus) at Brest and Lorient, possibly in conjunction with an RAF attack on these ports.

JOSEPHINE 'A' was also related to the Battle of the Atlantic, and was a proposal for an attack on the Focke-Wulf aircraft based on Mérignac airfield near Bordeaux: their shipping reconnaissance continued to be a menace for a long time, and at this stage they were also doing serious damage by bombing attacks in the Western Approaches.

JOSEPHINE 'B' was to be an attack on the big transformer station at Pessac near Bordeaux, which was believed to control electricity supply over a large area both in occupied and in unoccupied France. Unfortunately, there was some dispute later as to the real importance of the target: but before the event it was rated very high by the experts as a target for industrial sabotage.[2]

Savanna 'B' and Josephine 'A' consumed much time and trouble, but eventually fell by the wayside, and they need not detain us here.

Savanna 'A' reached the planning stage at the end of December 1940,[3] and it was then hoped that it would take place in about three

---

[1] SOE London HQ War Diary September–December 1940, p. 25. [See also Minshull's *Guilt-Edged, ad rem.*]

[2] This target was already under discussion in January 1941. SOE Archives Files 3/470/2a and (AD/S.1) SC.38/2.

[3] See Minutes of Meeting dated 30th December 1940, SOE Archives File CD/7.

weeks' time. The party was composed of five 'Free Frenchmen', supplied by De Gaulle's organisation – an attempt at direct recruitment by SOE had proved abortive.[1] Two of them disappeared on the operation and were not heard of again, but it is worth mentioning three – Capitaine Bergé,* OBE (Mil), Adjutant Forman, MC, and Sergeant Letac, MM, who were the first of many, and had distinguished records in the later story.

There were the usual delays over aircraft and weather and De Gaulle's temperament,[2] and the party did not leave until the March moon; they were parachuted successfully into Brittany on the night of 15th March, landing near Vannes during an RAF attack on the airfield there. Unfortunately the scent was cold; the German aircrews now arrived separately by car and there was no single target for a small party to attack: a lesson on the danger of choosing a 'fleeting target' for an operation of this kind, which can seldom be mounted at short notice. But fortunately Capitaine Bergé was a man of initiative, who set to work to make what he could of the situation; his rendezvous with a submarine was not until 30th March, and he dispersed his party to reconnoitre in areas which they knew well. Sergeant Letac visited Brest, Capitaine Bergé and Adjutant Forman travelled to the rendezvous in the south of Brittany via Paris, Nevers, Bayonne and Bordeaux. Their first rendezvous was a failure, but they were met at the second attempt on 4th April by HM submarine 'Tigris'. There were heavy seas and it was only by great gallantry on the part of Captain J. G. Appleyard, DSO, MC (later killed on operations in the Mediterranean), that Bergé and Forman were got on board. Letac had to be left behind.[3]

This was a most useful failure; it was an enormous gain at this stage to know that a party could drop into Occupied France, take trains, stay in hotels, visit their friends, in short behave like normal human beings – and then return safely to England. Sir Frank Nelson's first reaction is worth quoting: 'If Bergé is to be believed, there should be little or no difficulty in putting in our "Organisers" and setting them to work on a long-term basis. We require however (i) wireless facilities (ii) transport by aircraft . . . . The important decision in front of us is – do we send him again to do acts of sabotage, or do we send him in again to "organise" on a long-term basis?'

---

[1] R/F Section History, 1941, para. 3.

[2] Above p. 232.

[3] Detailed and excellent reports by Bergé and Forman are on SOE Archives File (AD/S.1) SC.38/1.

* [Bergé, 1909–97, went on to join SAS, was captured in Crete, and survived to become a French general.]

Josephine 'B', the attack on Pessac, was technically more success-ful. An abortive attempt was made on 10th April (before Savanna 'A' was back in England), with a party of six Poles; it went badly awry, as the stores had to be jettisoned and the aircraft turned back and crashed on landing, injuring the whole party. The operation was then hastily remounted on the basis of the Savanna party, and Adjutant Forman was dropped again with two other Frenchmen on the night of 10th May. Their first attempts were discouraging: they reconnoitred the transformer station on the night of 13th May, and decided that the attack was hopeless because of guards and high-tension fencing; and they failed to make contact with the submarine which attempted to pick them up on 20th May. There was gloom in Baker Street, and the operation was written off as a failure. But curiously enough it was still alive: the party had made contact with Letac, who had been in France since 'Savanna', and they gained from him the energy to try again. The attack was made on the night of 7th June, and was almost completely successful: six out of the eight transformers were blown (the charges apparently slipped off the other two before exploding), and the party got clear away. It was reported later that 250 people were arrested, the Pessac area was fined 1,000,000 francs, and twelve German sentries were shot. Forman, Letac and another man eventu-ally crossed the Spanish frontier, without much difficulty except in Spain, and they were back in England in August.[1] The news had already been received (on 19th June) from one of SOE's first wire-less sets in France, and there was enough independent confirmation for Mr Dalton to report success to the Prime Minister on 25th June.[2] 'We may therefore take it as practically certain that three trained men, dropped from one aeroplane, have succeeded in destroying an impor-tant industrial target. This strongly suggests that many industrial targets, especially if they cover only a very small area, are more effec-tively attacked by SOE methods than by air bombardment . . . . I hope that with the co-operation of the RAF we shall be able to repeat this form of attack during the coming autumn and winter.' This was SOE's first clean-cut and incontrovertible coup, and it was a wonderful tonic to the organisation; it was a pity that the exhilaration was a little marred, in that Mr Dalton gave the Prime Minister one report on the effects of the operation, and Sir Frank Nelson gave a different (and less optimistic) one to the Chiefs of Staff.[3]

---

[1] See their full report dated 5th September 1941, in unnumbered early CD File – marked 'Josephine B', SOE Archives.

[2] Copy on SOE Archives File (AD/S.1) SC.38/1.

[3] See debate about this incident, on SOE Archives File (AD/S.1) SC.38/1.

In fact, Josephine 'B' was not as Mr Dalton anticipated followed by a series of such 'outside jobs'. One of the most important lessons in Forman's report was that 'It is absolutely vital that other operations of this kind should be prepared by members of the organisation on the spot before the actual team is sent over. One cannot always rely on luck.' Once wireless sets were in position, this became practical politics, and sabotage was mainly an incident in the development of bigger organisations and bigger plans. There is only one other 'outside' sabotage operation worth mentioning in some detail.

This was an attack on the Radio-Paris transmitting station at Allouis, near Bourges, by a party of three Frenchmen who had been trained originally for Josephine 'A', the attack on the Focke-Wulfs at Mérignac. They were (perhaps unkindly) described by the D/F Section agent who evacuated them as 'intractable fellows of the pimp type' – 'I had to pay 60,000 francs worth of debts which they had contracted since May': good saboteurs, but a little misplaced in the more political atmosphere of 1942, and the Allouis expedition seems to have been largely an attempt to find a use for them after the collapse of the Mérignac project.[1] Nevertheless, it was a well-executed job, and their MM's were well-earned. They were dropped some 45 km from the target on the night of 5th May 1942; attacked it on 9th May by attaching delayed charges to two of the 500 ft wireless masts; and got clear away without giving the alarm. The station, which was important both for propaganda and for jamming, was out of action for a fortnight. In due course the party reached the Unoccupied Zone, and communicated with London by the slow and uncertain means of a coded letter posted to a cover address. By this time procedure for 'exfiltration' had begun to have something of a routine air: R/F Section minuted D/F Section, D/F Section sent a radio message to one of its agents, and the party came out through Spain on 6th October.[2]

This was in effect the last operation of its type.[3] In February 1942 SOE shared in the provision of men and equipment for the beautifully executed Combined Operation raid which carried off the latest German radar equipment from Bruneval,* and in April 1942 'Passy' and Colonel Sporborg were still talking in terms of 'coup de main'

---

[1] R/F Section History, 1942, paras 15 and 16.

[2] See their report in R/F History, 1942, para. 16.

[3] For completeness one should mention operation 'Garterfish', 31st October 1942, when three men were dropped to attack a transformer station near Saumur. Nothing was heard of this at the time, but one of the men turned up after the Armistice and claimed success. R/F History, 1942, p. 38. For details of operation see SOE Archives File (R/F Section) 'Garterfish'.

* [See George Millar, *The Bruneval Raid* (1992).]

as one of the possible types of operation;[1] but already the resistance had grown beyond this point and the growth of invasion plans for the summer of 1942 gave a different colour to the whole development.

It would be a pity however to omit all mention of the 'Maid Honor' and of No. 62 Commando, which developed from it. In March 1941, Major Gustavus March-Phillips had (under the auspices of SOE) secured command of a 65 ton Brixham trawler, the 'Maid Honor', and had raised a small party of like-minded persons who were based with him at Poole Harbour. He was a devoted small-boat sailor, and the theory was that a sailing-boat with auxiliary engine would be very suitable for small-scale raids on the north coast of France. It is hardly surprising that this did not find favour with higher authority; a tough party was wanted in West Africa, and the 'Maid Honor' made the passage there, literally under sail, with a crew of five in August 1941 – a remarkable exploit in itself, and a comment on the difficulty at that stage of the war of finding more expeditious means of transport.[2] The ship was of no further use thereafter, but the party did a certain amount of reconnaissance of forbidden coasts and was of great value in organising the piratical operation at Fernando Po[3] in January 1942. It then returned to England, where it succeeded in obtaining recognition as No. 62 Commando: a collection of tough men of various nationalities who were based at Blandford, and came under SOE for administration. Operational control rested with CCO, acting in consultation with Brigadier Gubbins and his staff. Their exploits thus lie a little outside the history of SOE, though they caused some stir in their time, when otherwise all was quiet in the West.[4] The most notorious of them was the raid on Sark on 4th October 1942, which led to Hitler's order for the manacling of the Dieppe prisoners of war; but there were others of the same type. Both Major March-Phillips and Captain. Appleyard eventually lost their lives in the course of operations.[5]

(ii) F Section Activities

Attempts to put in agents as 'organisers' had begun as early as September 1940, and F Section was engaged from the first in compil-

---

[1] Letter from Passy to Colonel Sporborg d/d 24th April 1942, quoted in R/F Section History, 1942, para. 15.

[2] See SOE Naval Histories – Section 'Maid Honor'.

[3] Below p. 327.

[4] Cf. the reference in Mr Churchill's speech at Edinburgh on 9th October 1942 to the 'hand of steel out of the sea'.

[5] There is a published account of Captain Appleyard's part in this in 'Geoffry' by J. E. Appleyard, published by the Blandford Press, 1946.

ing lists of suitable contacts in France, as well as in recruiting from the rather narrow field open to it.[1] But the first successful operation was on the night of 5th May 1941, when Commandant Georges Bégué was dropped on the estate of M. Max Hymans, near Châteauroux in the Unoccupied Zone.[2]* Commandant Bégué was a very experienced radio operator, who acted as liaison officer with the British Army in 1939-40; his nom-de-guerre was 'George Noble', and under that name he is famous in F Section history as the slender foundation on which the whole structure of circuits was built up. He had a comparatively short run, as he was trapped by the Vichy police in Marseilles in October 1941, but during that period his work was of the greatest importance. It is pleasant to be able to record that he survived the war.

Bégué landed in the small hours of 6th May, and by 9th May he was in communication with London – the first SOE wireless message from France. So long as Bégué remained free, all F Section's work in France (Occupied and Unoccupied) flowed through this one channel: a dangerous liability, as the existence of the 'radio de Châteauroux' was soon well enough known to the Gestapo and to the Vichy police, and radio detection could not easily be shaken off by moving the set, so long as the same frequencies and signal plan were in use. But at this stage there was no choice. A second radio operator was sent in during the summer for the Occupied Zone, but had a very short run; and all F Section's radio communications were broken from Bégué's arrest in October 1941 until February 1942.

Bégué was followed almost at once by Baron Pierre de Vomecourt ('Lucas'), 'one of the most exceptional men ever to go to the field', as one of the official narratives describes him. He was dropped on 11th May, also to the Châteauroux area, but with instructions to organise work in the Occupied Zone: he had no wireless. His work proved to be as intelligent as Bégué's, and covered a much wider field: with his brothers, Philippe** and Jean,[3] he had social contacts of all levels, both in Occupied and Unoccupied France. He himself built up a very comprehensive organisation in the Occupied Zone, based on Paris,

---

[1] See Colonel Buckmaster's description in the opening pages of the F Section History.
[2] M. Hymans was a former Deputé for Indre and had been a Sous-Sécrétaire in the Blum government of 1936. He came out himself in April 1942, as a representative of the 'Carte' organisation.
[3] Pierre and Philippe survived the war: Jean died in German hands.
* [There is now a memorial to 104 F Section dead at Valençay, near where Bégué dropped, unveiled on the fiftieth anniversary, in the presence of HM the Queen Mother.]
** [See his *Who Lived to See the Day* (1961).]

while Philippe worked on the same lines in Vichy France, Jean in the eastern part of the German zone; all of them had many contacts with spontaneous independent organisations.

Lucas's contacts with London were all through Bégué, and the first F Section supply-dropping operation was organised through this channel in the middle of June 1941: another landmark of some historic importance. With this channel was also linked Lieutenant R. Cottin ('Albert') – also known as Cottin-Burnett – who had been dropped in on 12th May as Lucas's second-in-command in the Occupied Zone.[1] The needs of wireless communication thus enforced over-centralisation, which was in any case always the weakness of young organisations, especially in France; and centralisation was particularly dangerous with an organisation which ramified so widely as that of Lucas and his brothers. Lucas's difficulties increased still further after Bégué's arrest in October 1941: his 'circuits' were in any case in grave danger of Gestapo penetration, but matters were brought to a head by the absolute necessity for recourse to a wireless set – the only source of materials and money. Through a Gestapo woman informer, later notorious as 'Victoire',[2] he contacted a Polish intelligence organisation which was in communication with England; he realised well enough that this organisation was insecure and limited his messages to arrangements for his own temporary evacuation. Eventually he was brought out by sea from Brittany on 25th February 1942, along with Victoire: a curious battle of wits, as the Gestapo connived at his escape in the hope of laying bait for a bigger haul at a more critical time, and the bait was taken knowingly by SOE. 'Victoire' naturally did not return to France.[3]

'Lucas' gave invaluable reports[4] as to conditions in the Occupied Zone, and was able to report a certain amount of minor but specific railway sabotage.[5] His political report was passed to Mr Eden[6] on 9th March, with a request that he might be permitted to see the Prime Minister in order to deliver a message from Michel Clemenceau, the son of the old 'Tiger'.* The Foreign Office took the opportunity to read to SOE a lecture on the limits of its political functions,[7] but the

---

[1] For details see Bourne-Patterson's 'British Circuits in France'.

[2] For a very full report on her case see blue 'Victoire' file (still in use). [See also Mathilde Carre [*dite* Victoire], *I Was the Cat*, tr. M. Savill (1961).]

[3] At the moment (April 1948) she is still awaiting trial in a French gaol. [She was sentenced to death, but secured a reprieve.]

[4] See his political report on SOE Archives File (AD/S.1) F.38/16.

[5] For details see Bourne-Patterson's 'British Circuits in France', p. 2.

[6] Copy of Lord Selborne's letter in SOE Archives File (AD/S.1) F.38/16.

[7] Mr Eden's letter of 18th March 1942, on SOE Archives File (AD/S.1) F.38/16.

* [Georges Clemenceau, 1841–1929, French Prime Minister 1906–9, 1917–20.]

idea of an interview with Mr Churchill (though discouraged) was not rejected: Lord Selborne wrote to the Prime Minister on 23rd March,[1] but Mr Churchill seems at the time to have been overwhelmed by other business.

Lucas saw Mr Eden on 24th March, and shortly afterwards returned to France. He himself chose to return, in spite of full knowledge of Gestapo penetration, in the belief that this was the only means of warning his followers and saving something from the impending wreck. SOE reluctantly concurred.[2]

The decision forced the Gestapo's hand, and was perhaps wisest in the long run; but the immediate consequences were hard. The news of Lucas's arrest reached London on 26th May, and with him were arrested his brother Jean, as well as Lieutenant Cottin and two other F Section agents: Philippe de Vomecourt remained active in the ZNO until November 1942, but the only F Section member of the circuit to escape was Major B. H. Cowburn (another very distinguished name in F Section's annals),* who had already left France through Spain in February 1942. Major Cowburn was an experienced petroleum engineer, long resident in Paris, and had been dropped to the field in September 1941, with the primary object of planning attacks on oil targets:[3] this was the first of four missions which he completed unscathed.

It will be convenient next to refer to several missions of a rather different type: short 'visits of inspection' by British officers who formed part of F Section or could be regarded by it as absolutely reliable and independent witnesses. Three names are important, Major J. Vaillant de Guélis, MBE, Croix de Guerre, MC, Major N. R. Bodington, MBE, MC, and Major Peter Churchill, DSO.**

Major de Guélis was dropped 'blind' (far wide of the mark) early in August 1941; he himself was badly cut and bruised, and his companion, Captain Turck, fell in a quarry, where he was picked up unconscious by the French police next day. De Guélis was brought out on the night of 4th September, by the first SOE Lysander operation, and he submitted a very useful series of reports on his

---

1 Copy on SOE Archives File (AD/S.1) F.38/16.
2 There is an exchange of letters on this very difficult decision, between Mr Eden and Lord Selborne, 27th and 28th March 1942, on SOE Archives File (AD/S.1) F.38/16.
3 Bourne-Patterson's 'British Circuits in France', p. 77.
* [Oil engineer, died 1994. See his *No Cloak, No Dagger* (1962).]
** [P. M. Churchill, 1909–72, three missions into France, the second a wild-goose chase and the third ending in his capture, survived Ravensbrück, married his courier 1947, she divorced him 1955. See his *Of Their Own Choice* (1952), *Duel of Wits* (1953) and *The Spirit in the Cage* (1954). In *DNB*.]

contacts,[1] which were entirely in the Unoccupied Zone. His companion's fate was more ambiguous; the Vichy police by whom he was arrested permitted him to establish contact with the Deuxième Bureau of the French Army, and by its kind offices he was released and established in a villa near Marseilles. He persuaded Major de Guélis (and possibly himself also) that there was an important role for him to play as a secret British liaison with the 'Armée de l'Armistice'. There is not enough evidence to say where the treason lay – it is perfectly possible that the Vichy police double-crossed the Vichy army. The sequel, at all events, was that in October 1941 Turck's villa was raided: a number of agents were found there, and others were swept in later by the same net. In all, Georges Bégué and eight other SOE men were taken, as well as at least four important local recruits. This for the moment almost cleared out the SOE organisation in Vichy territory.

Second, there were two visits by Major Peter Churchill to the Unoccupied Zone in January and in April 1942.[2] Major Churchill came to France again as an organiser in August 1942[3] and remained there (with a short break in March 1943) until his arrest with his courier, Mrs Odette Sansom, GC,* in April 1943. His early reports were less important politically than those of Major de Guélis or of Major Bodington, whose visit took place in August 1942 at a very critical stage of the development of relations between De Gaulle, the British and American Governments, and other currents of French resistance. Major Bodington was an experienced officer with a wide knowledge of France and the French, and he had been associated with the work of F Section from the beginning: his contacts were important and his report carried great weight.[4] Its tenor will be referred to more fully below.[5]

To revert to the construction of F Section's organisation. After Bégué and Pierre de Vomecourt, the next central figure is that of Miss Virginia Hall ('Marie'), an American lady with a wooden leg** (affec-

---

[1] Full set of reports in SOE Archives File CD/7.

[2] Bourne-Patterson's 'British Circuits in France', p. 105; copies of reports on these missions in SOE Archives F Section Files, C-17, Vols 1 & 2.

[3] Bourne-Patterson's 'British Circuits in France', p. 107. SOE Archives F Section File C-17, Vol. 2.

[4] Bourne-Patterson's 'British Circuits in France', p. 108, and Major Bodington's report on SOE Archives File 3/370/54(a).

[5] See below p. 267.

*   [Odette, *née* Brailly in France, died 1996, thrice married; a national heroine on appearance of film *Odette* based on Jerry Tickell's often inaccurate life of her with the same title (1949).]

** [In fact, a brass foot.]

tionately known in F Section as 'Cuthbert') who was sent openly to Lyon in September 1941, under cover as a journalist.[1] She remained there until November 1942, when she came out across the Pyrenees in winter conditions, just before the German occupation: she returned to France by Lysander on 21st March 1944, as an agent of the American OSS, to distinguish herself as a guerilla leader in Nièvre and Haute Loire. Her methods were eccentric and relied too much on the sanctity of American citizenship: Major Cowburn complained that one had only to sit for long enough in the kitchen of 'Marie's' flat to meet all the British organisers in France. But her energy, ingenuity and kindliness were beyond praise, and she saw the F Section organisation through a bad period. It was entirely due to her efforts that wireless communication was reopened in February 1942, after a gap of nearly five months. A wireless operator had been dropped for de Vomecourt, and had gone badly astray: he had lost his set and was trying to get out of the country when 'Marie' contacted him, found him a set left in safe custody by Bégué, and installed him in the Lyon area.

Miss Hall's activities knew no geographical limits, but there were also in this period five more limited developments which deserve description. This does not cover the full list of agents sent in by F Section: some were arrested soon after landing, others were ancillary to the enterprises mentioned.

Lieutenant François Basin ('Olive') was sent in via Gibraltar in September 1941[2] to organise resistance in south-eastern France. His original contact was a certain Dr Lévy ('Philippe') in Antibes, who undoubtedly possessed important political contacts, but proved personally intractable. Like other organisers at this stage, Basin was desperately handicapped by lack of wireless communication, but he maintained some sort of contact with London through Switzerland and through Miss Hall in Lyons, and he was visited by Major Churchill in January 1942. But it was not till the end of April 1942, on Major Churchill's second visit, that he received a wireless operator. Basin himself was arrested on 18th August,[3] and did not leave much organisation behind him: but he had been of importance in early contacts with political movements in the Unoccupied Zone (most readily distinguished by the names of their leaders, most of whom became politically important later). He was in touch before the end of 1941 with

---

[1] Bourne-Patterson's 'British Circuits in France', p. 72, and SOE Archives F Section File 'H.4'.

[2] Bourne-Patterson's 'British Circuits in France', p. 105. See also his report on SOE Archives File 3/370/51(b).

[3] He was released when the Germans marched in, and eventually got back to

the 'Carte' organisation (Girard)[1] and was largely responsible for sending Girard's lieutenant, Major Frager,* out to England in June 1942. He was also known to 'Libération' (Emmanuel d'Astier de la Vigerie),** 'Liberté' (Henri Fresnay), and 'Libération Nationale' (Général de la Laurencie), and was responsible for the evacuation of d'Astier to England in April 1942, an event of some significance in De Gaulle's personal history.[2]

Also in September 1941, Lieutenant Leroy ('Louis') entered the south of France by sea and made his way to the Bordeaux area.[3] Morale in this area was always reported to be poor, and Leroy created no organisation. He left Bordeaux in January 1942, and brought back to London a certain amount of good intelligence as well as some useful contacts for the future. These were taken up by Major de Baissac ('David'),† who was dropped with a radio operator in July 1942:[4] unfortunately the parachute opened badly – the radio operator broke his leg†† and Major de Baissac was injured. He did not reach Bordeaux until September and a new operator (Major Landes)[5] did not reach him until November. About the same time, de Baissac's sister Lise began work in the Poitiers district. The development in these areas must therefore be dealt with later.[6]

At the same time as Leroy, Captain J. G. Duboudin ('Alain') was sent in to develop a local organisation in the Lyon area.[7] This was one occasion in which F Section's judgement of men was badly at fault. Duboudin certainly had personality, but he exercised it chiefly in quarrelling with other agents and in building up a rambling organisation which existed mainly on paper. He quarrelled with Miss Hall, with Major Cowburn, with Philippe de Vomecourt: he baffled an attempt at 'co-ordination' by Major V. H. Hazan, who was sent out

---

1   See below p. 267.
2   See below p. 272.
3   Bourne-Patterson's 'British Circuits in France', p. 36.
4   SOE F Section Files 'B.17'.
5   Famous as 'Aristide': below p. 572.
6   See below p. 571.
7   Bourne-Patterson's 'British Circuits in France', p. 118.
*   [J. H. Frager, murdered in Buchenwald 1944.]
** [There were three d'Astier de la Vigerie brothers: Emmanuel R., 1900–69, propagandist and politician, author of *Seven Times Seven Days* (tr. Humphrey Hare, 1958) and other works; Francois P. R., 1886–1956, Air Force general, Ambassador in Brazil 1945–6; and Henri, 1897–1952, monarchist, who helped prepare Algiers for 'Torch' landings and was suspected of complicity in Darlan's murder.]
†   [The de Baissacs were Mauritian aristocrats.]
†† [This was H. Peulevé, who escaped across the Pyrenees on crutches: see Jacques Poirier, *The Giraffe Has a Long Neck* (1995), pp. 19–39.]

for the purpose in May 1942: and unfortunately in July he persuaded Major Bodington to confirm him in his command. It was not until October 1942 that he was recalled and his organisation handed over to Major Boiteux ('Nicolas'), who had been sent out as second-in-command in June. It was some time before Boiteux could trim away Duboudin's extravagances and reduce the circuit to a smaller and harder organisation.

It will be remembered that Major Cowburn was the sole F Section survivor of Lucas's 'work' in May 1942. He was well-known in Paris, and it was extremely dangerous for him to return there for more than a few days: but the only ready means of renewing contacts was to send him in again with a new officer who could be introduced and then left to rebuild. The risk was accepted, and he was dropped in the Unoccupied Zone in May 1942, with Flying Officer E. M. Wilkinson:[1] unfortunately their wireless operator did not meet them, and they had to make contact with another in the Lyon area. The result of this expedition was that Flying Officer Wilkinson, Captain R. H. Heslop (later Lieutenant Colonel)[2] and the new operator were all arrested at Limoges in August 1942, and held by the Vichy police until November, when they were released.

Major Cowburn was not involved, but his risk had been taken to no purpose; no agent was left in the Paris area except Captain Grover-Williams, a racing motorist who had been sent in May 1942 to build a new circuit from his own friends. He was starting from scratch, and was even without a wireless operator until March 1943. A fresh start was made in October 1942 by dropping Major Suttill ('Prosper') blind near Vendôme with one assistant: his work was important but falls in a later period.

Major Cowburn had also been charged with the separate mission of organising a group in the neighbourhood of the great railway junction at Vierzon, in Cher, to prepare attacks on the railways, on the aircraft factory at Châteauroux and on a transformer station at Éguzon. This had been accomplished satisfactorily by the time he returned to England in October 1942: two aircraft loads of stores had been received and stowed away, and sound men had been recruited. In addition (a rare thing at this stage) a successful attack had been made on high-tension lines and systematic sabotage with abrasives was begun in a piston factory at Châteauroux. No standing contact existed with this group after Major Cowburn's withdrawal, but it was a dependable nucleus for future action.

---

[1] Bourne-Patterson's 'British Circuits in France', pp. 3, 78; and SOE F Section File 'D.9'.

[2] Later famous as 'Xavier': below p. 581. [1907–73; in *DNB*. See his *Xavier* (1970).]

Finally, in July 1942, a young man of twenty, Lieutenant A. Brooks ('Alphonse') was dropped into the Unoccupied Zone with the rather vague mission of contacting Trade Union action groups among the French railwaymen.[1] His only special qualification was a brief lecture on TU organisation, given to him just before he left London: but his personal achievement was remarkable. He was one of the main channels by which an existing organisation, with a powerful corporate entity, could get the supplies and guidance it wanted: what was remarkable was that he gained and kept the confidence of the organisation, gave it what it needed, and turned it in the right direction at the right time. Through him co-ordinated action by railwaymen could be set going in practically all the old Unoccupied Zone except the southwest, and their later contribution was very great indeed.[2] In this period a small beginning was made with the old trick of sabotaging axlebearings with abrasive grease.

The position at August 1942 is statistically summarised by Colonel Buckmaster in his History:[3]

Zone Occupée: Preparations made for receipt of stores.
Six organisers installed.
One courier.
Two wireless operators (only one in contact).
No stores.

Zone non-Occupée: 25 SOE trained organisers.
19 local recruits (at least).
 6 wireless operators (4 in contact).
64 containers delivered.
24 containers scheduled for September moon.
2,000 lbs of stores scheduled for delivery by sea.

To this may be added that F Section sent in about 10,000,000 francs in 1941 and 32,000,000 francs in the whole of 1942: perhaps the equivalent of £150,000.[4]

This is not impressive, and translated into words it was even depressing. The Paris area was at the beginning of a laborious new development from nothing; Bordeaux and Poitiers were planned but untouched, and the only other organisation in the Zone Occupée was a small nucleus at Tours.[5] Miss Hall was a very solid fact at Lyon,

---

[1] Bourne-Patterson's 'British Circuits in France', p. 73, and SOE Archives F Section Files B-20, 4 Vols.
[2] See Bourne-Patterson's 'British Circuits in France', pp. 74–6, for details.
[3] SOE F Section History, p. 4.
[4] Tables prepared for D/Fin 1945 – attached to F Section History.
[5] Bourne-Patterson's 'British Circuits in France', p. 91.

but in bad relations with Duboudin, the area organiser. Basin's political contacts in the south were equally real, though broken by his arrest this month: Bodington's discussions were important. But Cowburn was just beginning near Vierzon, Brooks with the railwaymen: and results were a long way off. There was a certain Lieutenant Pertschuk ('Eugène') with a wireless operator in the Toulouse area, but he was primarily a PWE agent, chosen for his gifts in their field and merely 'carried' by SOE. Once in the field he developed a totally unexpected toughness and leadership, which brought him into F Section's orbit as a leader of sabotage, and entitles him to be regarded as the first of their organisers in this area.[1] But this too was in the future in August 1942.

There could be no question of F Section touching off a revolt in Vichy France, or even conducting major sabotage on a big scale, supposing the Foreign Office should give authority. But there was contact, there was real minor sabotage, and there was a growth of experience and a natural selection of men on whom much could be built.

(iii) The Work of the R/F Section

This account of F Section's beginnings has perhaps been confusing to the reader; the beginnings of the Gaullist organisation are still more difficult to describe, at least from SOE's side. The fundamental difficulty (both for SOE and for its historian) was that SOE had not full control. It handled all De Gaulle's wireless traffic (or so it believed), but it might not know the full directives and the full reports even of the men whom it carried: and it was naturally a cardinal point of De Gaulle's policy that he should put men in by his own means when he could, and evade all supervision by the British – this was difficult for him, but not impossible.

The story therefore is apt to be inconsequent; and where order emerges one cannot be confident that it embraces all the facts.

One rough generalisation may be made at the outset. The division of spheres of recruitment between F Section and De Gaulle was reflected in the type of agent which they secured. F Section was dependent on bilingual British subjects, on Frenchmen with some English background and a special affection for Britain, and on Frenchmen who combined patriotism with distrust for De Gaulle and had the energy and initiative to act independently of his authority. By a process of natural selection (which represented no policy decision) agents of these three types would normally be educated men of a certain social standing, a little detached from ordinary French life and inclined to

---

[1] Bourne-Patterson's 'British Circuits in France', p. 91.

treat all French politicians with scepticism, especially in time of war. It was easy to suspect them of right wing sympathies, and there was perhaps some social bias in that direction: but all (or practically all) were anxious to work outside French politics and to hold the balance until Germany was beaten.

De Gaulle on the other hand had a fairly large pool of plain patriotic Frenchmen, of no great education, and of varying degrees of honesty, but very close to the background of French life. He was less well provided with men of good education, administrative experience, high integrity, and those he had were badly needed to make his organisation outside France reasonably worthy of the name of France. As a result, few of the Gaullists sent in were of the calibre to become leaders of resistance themselves: they were saboteurs, instructors, channels of liaison rather than organisers. If De Gaulle began with the idea of building his own resistance movement, he soon abandoned it and began to draw to him the natural leaders as they emerged within France. What De Gaulle had to offer them (thanks to the British and in particular to SOE) was the tools of their trade – money, arms, explosives, wireless sets, Allied recognition of their movements; and he used this leverage with extreme astuteness to weld together diverse trends, which were led from within France, but to a certain extent took their direction from De Gaulle and through him from the Allied High Command.

The source through which De Gaulle provided men for R/F Section was the Free French training school opened at Inchmery House near Southampton in February 1941. It was not in the first instance under SOE control, though SOE provided facilities and instruction, and as late as December 1941 an SOE inspecting officer reported on its 'lack of discipline and order'. It was not until spring 1942 that De Gaullist agents were passed through the ordinary SOE course of training.[1] This is one point which must be remembered as background to early R/F operations.

The plan of operations as first conceived can be found in a report by Captain Piquet-Wicks in October 1941:[2]

The principles accepted were:
(a) To train FFI agents in organising sabotage and W/T.
(b) To send the agents into the field in teams of two:
    (i) Organiser and sabotage instructor.
    (ii) The W/T operator who, in principle, would be completely under the direction of the organiser.

---

[1] R/F Section History, 1941, p. 17.
[2] Dated 26th October; copy at R/F Section History, 1941, p. 31.

(c) These teams were to be dropped in regions where organisations already existed with the object of:
  (i) effecting liaison between the organisations and this country by means of W/T.
  (ii) instructing the organisations in our sabotage methods.
  (iii) furnishing the organisations with arms and supplies from this country.
  (iv) issuing directives for general sabotage.
  (v) preparing a secret army.
2. It had been verified that France was full of large and small groups of resistance, most of which were impotent as they had no material means of creating large sabotage and no means of liaison with this country and the Free French movement.

   By furnishing them with the required liaison, French territory would be covered by a network of agents all in direct W/T communication with this country.
3. France thus covered and organised, general large scale sabotage could be prepared and the nucleus of a Secret Army formed.

   Meanwhile, isolated teams could be despatched with the object of organising immediate resistance and effective industrial sabotage.

The execution of this scheme fell a long way short of programme, but it is worth following it area by area till it was absorbed in a larger plan.

Savanna 'A' and Josephine 'B', though they preceded the formation of the R/F Section, had both been in a sense 'Gaullist' operations, and had produced valuable information about native resistance. The first R/F operation in the strict sense was the dropping of two men, Labit and Cartigny, near Caen on the night of 5th July 1941.[1] It is worth remembering how late this was: it was more than a year since the fall of France, and Russia was now at war. Their instructions were to gain contact with secret organisations believed to exist in Calvados, to train them and receive stores, and to organise sabotage of aircraft on the Caen/Carpiquet aerodrome. Labit was leader and wireless operator, Cartigny sabotage instructor. Things went badly wrong: they were dropped 45 kms from their nearest contact, they were unable to bury their parachutes, the 'safe houses' given them proved useless. Cartigny is believed to have been caught and shot: Labit escaped (without his wireless set) to the Unoccupied Zone, where he succeeded in reporting home by the hand of Adjutant Forman (of Savanna and Josephine) who came out over the Pyrenees in July 1941.

---

[1] Operation 'Torture' – R/F Section History, 1941, p. 21.

Labit was still game, and accepted instructions to move to the Toulouse area and to get in touch with organisations there.[1] A wireless operator was dropped to him on 10th September: unfortunately the parachutes were found by the police, but the organisers were for the present clear. The set was established in the Municipal Swimming Baths at Toulouse, and on 25th October Labit was able to report that he had been at work for six weeks and thought highly of the possibilities of the local organisation, of which Professor Bertaud* of the University of Toulouse, was said to be the leader. Labit arranged reception on 13th October for the indefatigable Forman,[2] who returned with another wireless operator: and a supply-dropping operation was successful on 6th November.

This was the limit of success for the moment. Both Labit and Forman became known to the police and were on the run: the first wireless operator was arrested: and there were other arrests as a result of attempt to expand at Agen, which also affected the Toulouse organisation. It was not seriously damaged, but development was stopped for the moment and Labit was withdrawn at the beginning of 1942.

This sequence of events had extracted something from initial failure. Very little came of a bold attempt to plant an agent in Vichy itself on 29th August.[3] A young man named Lencement, who was on the staff of the Vichy radio services, obtained three weeks' leave in the first week of August: was in England by 12th August: and was dropped back into France before his leave was up, with instructions to organise sabotage in the radio service. Unfortunately he had at first no communication with London except through the 'Overcloud' organisation in Brittany:[4] a radio operator was dropped for him on 26th November, but was at once in trouble with the police: and in December Lencement himself was arrested for being concerned in a 'reception committee' for another air operation.

There was an equally abortive attempt to establish connections with the Bordeaux area.[5] Lieutenant Donnadieu was dropped on 9th September, with a radio operator, with instructions to contact and train existing organisations, and ultimately to prepare the ground for an attack on the Focke Wulf aircraft at Mérignac.[6] He seemed to be making good progress at first, but wireless contact was lost, and the

---

[1] Operation 'Fabulous' – R/F Section History, 1941, p. 23.
[2] Operation 'Mainmast B' – below p. 274.
[3] Operation 'Trombone' – R/F Section History, 1941, p. 28.
[4] Below p. 261.
[5] Operation 'Barter' – R/F Section History, 1941, p. 18.
[6] This was 'Josephine A': above p. 244.
* [P. Bertaux survived the war to head French security, died 1986.]

next word was that Donnadieu was on the run and far from the Bordeaux area. This put an end to Josephine 'A' – as we have seen the party trained for it were diverted to the operation against Radio Paris.[1]

The next mission gives the first indication of a later, more political approach. It was that of Laverdet, who was dropped with a radio operator not far from Paris on 7th September.[2] He was a Communist or at least had Communist contacts, and his primary mission was to meet the organisation of that party with a view to sabotage in the factories of the 'Banlieu Rouge': it was also important that he should organise the reception of stores from England. In fact, the first organisation which he found was an 'Armée Volontaire', said to be Gaullist in sympathy, 'with 60,000 men in the Occupied Zone', and consisting 'mainly of military administrative personnel and those employed in the public services'. This was as good as the Communists, if true, and the first stage was to exploit it so far as possible. There was difficulty about wireless communication owing to suspected Gestapo activity: in January 1942 Laverdet was reinforced by Sergent-Chef Bourdat and the communications were resumed. But the Armée Volontaire 'blew up' in April 1942; contact with it was severed, and the mission reverted to its original 'Leftist' programme, with Bourdat now in command. It seems already to have been under Gestapo surveillance, and lived very precariously until July 1942 when Bourdat and Laverdet were caught together by the Gestapo: Bourdat was killed, Laverdet escaped to the Unoccupied Zone, bought himself a new identity and remained in Resistance (though out of touch with London) until the Liberation.

Operation 'Overcloud',[3] though a little later in date, belongs also to this phase. It will be remembered that a certain Sergeant Joel Letac had taken part in the abortive attack on K.Gr.100 in March 1941, and had been sent by Commandant Bergé to explore the Brest area, which he knew well. On 13th October he returned to Brittany by sea, with another Breton, De Kergorley, as his wireless operator: their job was of the usual type – to find or form organisations, and to be ready to attack certain objectives at a later date. Wireless contact was made fairly quickly and a written report reached London at the end of 1941:[4] this recorded various contacts – in particular with the former garrison commander of Vannes and with two organisations there, and with

---

[1] Above p. 247.
[2] Operation 'Dastard' – R/F Section History, 1941, p. 17, and 1942, Appendix 'A'.
[3] R/F Section History, 1941, pp. 26, 49: 1942, p. 2, and SOE Archives 'Overcloud' Mission file.
[4] R/F Section History, 1941, p. 49.

a students' organisation and a railwaymen's organisation at Rennes. But it was not optimistic about the chances of finding men tough enough to form sabotage teams – men prepared to risk not only their own lives but those which would be exposed to reprisals. Letac was therefore inclined to deviate into organisation for intelligence and later military action, rather than for immediate attack.

Rather by accident Letac received a second wireless operator on 31st December – a man who was intended for the Ardennes, but never got there.[1] Then on 6th January he and his elder brother (who had been an active resister since 1940) were brought out by sea for consultation.[2] Unfortunately this marked the end of their effective activity: they returned (again by sea) on 2nd February and were arrested shortly afterwards. This cut communications[3] with Brittany and ended a promising venture: but it did not seriously affect the native organisations which Letac had found.

So far we have a mixed record of success and failure. There were some indications of the spirit and organisation of Resistance both in the Occupied and the Unoccupied Zone, but communications were irregular and agents unreliable: there was no indication yet of that united national resurgence which De Gaulle hoped to lead. A new phase begins in October 1941, and is closely associated with the political development of the Free French movement.

De Gaulle had been in the Middle East since July 1941, working hard on French participation in the Syrian campaign. A French division under General Legentilhomme took a distinguished part in the fighting, which was ended by an armistice on 14th July. For the first time De Gaulle had more French weapons than he had men: moreover, the question of administrative control of Syria gave him a *casus belli* against the British on a question of the status of France – a political asset which he used for all it was worth. He returned to England at the end of August, and there is on record an interesting account of a conversation which he held with a French-Canadian on the aircraft from Brazzaville to West Africa:[4] an indiscretion which gave judicious publicity to his political creed. 'Tenez, l'Angleterre, qu'est elle pour moi? Une alliée, une alliée . . . nécessaire. Mais avant tout, je

---

[1] Operation 'Plaice' – R/F Section History, 1941, pp. 27, 30.

[2] Labit (p. 260) and Forman (p. 275) also came out on this operation.

[3] In fact messages continued to come in from De Kergorley's set through most of 1942, but it was under German control. This was detected in May 1942 – see CXG.15 of 21st May 1942 from Overcloud Minor and DR/FFR/368 of 25th May 1942, on SOE Archives R/F Section Overcloud Mission file.

[4] Report by M. René Balbaud dated 29th August 1941; copy on SOE Archives File 3/100/2c.

suis Français, et peu m'importe ce que les Français pensent des Anglais. Ce qu'il faut, c'est les persuader de leur propre valeur . . . la leur!'

His welcome in London was not warm,[1] but at least a temporary understanding was reached with Mr Churchill,[2] and on 24th September 1941 came De Gaulle's Ordonnance No. 16 which constituted the Comité National with De Gaulle as its President. The Ordonnance spoke 'au nom du Peuple et de l'Empire français', and its main doctrine was that 'il importe que les autorités de la France Libre soient mises en mesure d'exercer, en fait et à titre provisoire, les attributions normales des pouvoirs publics'.[3] This was a claim ('*de facto*' and provisional, of course) that Vichy was nothing and that De Gaulle was the French State: full recognition was naturally not to be expected, but the Foreign Office in amplifying earlier declarations gave him perhaps more than he had anticipated – 'HMG in the United Kingdom are prepared to regard the Free French National Committee as representing all Free Frenchmen, *wherever they may be*' (author's italics), 'who rally to the Free French movement in support of the Allied cause.'[4] In other words, De Gaulle's government was recognised as a duly constituted authority for those who accepted it, *inside France* as well as in the outer world. De Gaulle might become the French State, if the Resistance backed him and the Allies won the war.

He naturally accepted this invitation in a spirit larger than was intended.

The first fruits were an interview between General De Gaulle and Mr Dalton on 8th October: it is worth quoting the exordium of the memorandum left with Mr Dalton on this occasion:[5]

The spirit of resistance of the French people has, for the last few weeks, revealed its strength by tangible facts.

On the other hand, it appears certain that Free France is for the French people the symbol of national resistance.

General De Gaulle and the Comité National Français are of the opinion that it is their task to take in hand the effective direction of this resistance in French territory either occupied or controlled by the enemy (i.e. including Vichy territory).

---

[1] CFR (41)54th Mtg, Min.1, of 1st September (The Prime Minister's instructions on dilatory tactics).

[2] CFR (41)55th Mtg, Min. 1, of 15th September.

[3] See Foreign Office Print 16087 (Z8210/8098/17) of 27th September 1941; copy on SOE Archives File (AD/S.1) SC/38/4.

[4] See Foreign Office print 16087 of 27th September 1941; copy on SOE Archives File (AD/S.1) SC.38/4.

[5] Original and translation on SOE Archives File (AD/S.1) SC.38/4.

The purely military side of this action (military intelligence, raids, preparations of a military organisation on the spot) is already now being well provided for by the Special Services of Free France in close collaboration with the British Special Services. But the moment has come to start a political action, which is and must be separate from military action, and must be handled by other men through other means.

General De Gaulle and the Comité National Français wish to initiate political action in France. The co-operation of the Services of the British Ministry of Economic Warfare will be indispensable for this purpose.

In one respect, as Colonel Sporborg noted at the time,[1] this was no more than the reflection of an intrigue by M. Diethelm (Commissioner of the Interior) and M. Dejean (Commissioner for Foreign Affairs) to edge De Wavrin out of his strategic position as sole liaison with the Resistance under the nominal control of General Petit: in another, it was a historic statement of De Gaulle's programme as he now conceived it.

SOE consulted the Foreign Office, and was not quick to reply: so that De Gaulle approached the matter again through a second channel. On 27th October he saw Major Morton and put to him for transmission to the Prime Minister what were essentially the same points, though now with a more Churchillian flavour: 'This (new) organisation would organise the French people for a nation-wide uprising at the appointed time. In the General's opinion this activity should be co-ordinated with future military plans and considered in relation to similar action in other European countries.'[2] This was remitted back to Mr Eden, and drafting proceeded slowly – this was not indeed inappropriate as a means of handling De Gaulle – so that Mr Eden's answer was not dispatched until 22nd November. The phraseology is cumbrous and does not lend itself to quotation: but its effect was –

(i) His Majesty's Government approve a nation-wide resistance movement in France, though they must remain free to co-operate with Frenchmen outside it. They agree that 'in principle' it should be a French organisation and should be led from outside France: i.e. it should be De Gaulle's organisation, subject to detailed agreement with SOE on machinery.

(ii) *But* (a) His Majesty's Government 'cannot associate themselves with' (i.e. they will disapprove but will not stop) 'political

1 Minute of 15th October 1941, on SOE Archives File 3/100/2c.
2 Extract from Major Morton's Minute to the Prime Minister dated 27th October 1941, on SOE Archives File (AD/S.1) SC.38/4.

propaganda designed to secure the post-war establishment in France of any particular form of government or of any particular persons as government.'

(iii) Mr Dalton will do all he can to help in establishing communications. Please deal with the matter through him and do not bother the Prime Minister or the Foreign Secretary again except on major issues.

These terms were accepted by General De Gaulle on 13th December, with greater courtesy and in much better prose:

Il s'agit, en effet, de former, en une organisation massive et fortement articulée, les millions de Français qu'animent la haine de l'oppresseur et la volonté de coopérer à la liberation du pays.

Cet objectif est absolument indépendent de toute préoccupation de régime ou de personnel politique: il est donc dans la ligne de conduite que s'est fixée le Comité National et dont il entend bien ne pas dévier.

In the event, SOE (or possibly Passy)[1] was victorious on the technical point of organisation and avoided the creation of yet another French section: but De Gaulle had obtained all that was necessary for his immediate political purpose.

On 20th October 1941, in the midst of these developments, there arrived in London M. Jean Pierre Moulin (*alias* Robert *alias* Rex *alias* Mercier),* as the accredited representative of resistance in Vichy France: it was not SOE who instigated his journey, nor is it clear who did. But it was singularly opportune. Moulin had been Préfet of the Département of Eure et Loire, a position of some distinction from which he had been dismissed as politically unreliable (in the German sense) in December 1940. He moved to the Unoccupied Zone, and came in contact there with the heads of three 'movements', 'Liberté', 'Libération Nationale' and 'Libération'. These men had met at Marseilles and had sent Moulin as their emissary to De Gaulle. To understand how much and how little this signified it will be necessary to digress somewhat, as it is at this stage that the spontaneous forms of resistance in France became important to the development of the story.

We have seen how local knots of resistance were formed by agents of F and R/F, both in Occupied and Unoccupied France: and how these knots could be linked into an organisation through the personal contacts of a man like Pierre de Vomecourt. The local circuits only

---

[1] His BCRA (Bureau Centrale de Récherches et Action) was organised within De Gaulle's personal staff in January 1942.

* [Jean Moulin, 1899–1943, Prefect dismissed by Vichy 1940, escaped, two missions into France, captured June 1943, died under torture.]

became politically important if linked to a much wider circulation, and such an organisation was not easy to sustain without supplies from outside. As a matter of subversive technique it was best that each locality should be separately in touch with a HQ outside France and isolated from its neighbours; and this was the ideal for which both F Section and R/F Section worked. But such a method could only give slow returns on the small investment possible in the early stages: and it was hardly related to political realities. There were already in existence certain organisations which by their nature linked resistance together on a national scale; and there was also spontaneous attempts from within to create new centralised organisations.

Of the former the most important were:

1. *The 'officiers de réserve'*: men of good education and military background, to whom the military resurgence of France was a matter of personal pride. The IIème Bureau of the Army certainly did not neglect the lesson of the German Army's handling of the Versailles Treaty: and it was prepared to look leniently on movements arising in this milieu. How far it encouraged them, and how far the rest of Vichy connived at such encouragement, are questions which cannot be answered from SOE papers.

Resisters of this type played a prominent and often effective part when the stage of guerilla warfare was reached: but till that time they always disappointed those who relied on them (in particular Giraud) – partly, perhaps, because military training is bad training for underground work, partly because the background of such movements was socially too Conservative to reflect any deep popular feeling.

Three movements of this type (apparently unconnected) are worth mentioning, since they appear in the sequel:

(a) *Libération Nationale*, which is associated with the name of Général de Corel de la Laurencie, KCB, a gallant cavalry officer, in late middle age, who had been Pétain's first representative at the HQ of the German Military Government in Paris; had been recalled and retired early in 1941 for his attitude toward Abetz and Laval: and had later publicly adopted a pro-British attitude.[1]

His patriotism was unquestioned (although he had been since 1934 an advocate of Franco-German rapproachement), and his movement was among those which sent Moulin to De Gaulle. But his 'committee list'[2] was justifiably described by

---

[1] See his own report on his period in Paris, summarised November 1941, on SOE Archives File (AD/S.1) F.38/16: and Foreign Office Research and Press Department report on 2nd January 1942, on SOE Archives File 3/100/15.2a.

[2] See a full report from Switzerland dated 20th November 1941, on SOE Archives (CD) 'De Laurencie' File.

Mr Dalton as 'a collection of aged club bores with extreme Right opinions, commanding no popular support whatever in France, with de Wendel of the Comité des Forges bringing up the rear'.[1]

Furthermore, de la Laurencie was believed to prohibit all association with politicians of the old Front Populaire, which had extended as far to the Right as the Radical Socialist Party; and he was in this period attempting independently to extract assistance from the outer world through Polish and American channels, which put him in touch with SOE The affair was pursued languidly on the British side, and was virtually dropped in March 1942.[2] The General was arrested in May 1942, and his movement was absorbed in others.

With 'Libération Nationale' were associated the clandestine newspapers 'Les Petites Ailes' (or 'Vérités') and 'Travailleurs'.

(b) *The 'Carte' Organisation*, associated with the name of the artist Girard. This was anti-De Gaulle, but moved in the same circles as de la Laurencie, and probably also enjoyed some Vichy tolerance. Girard's speciality was card-indexing: building-up on paper of 'cadres' of those who would be useful when the day came. But in addition he had an admirably persuasive personality and a circle of devoted friends: evidence of Girard's leadership and organisation could be found in many parts of France, and it is impossible now to separate the bluff from reality. News of the existence of 'Carte' began to reach London from Basin[3] toward the end of 1941, and in April 1942 Max Hymans[4] arrived with fuller information. In July Carte's lieutenant Major Frager ('Louba') came out for consultations.[5] Major Bodington who went with him to France in July was greatly impressed by Girard,[6] and when he returned to London persuaded both PWE and F Section to back 'Carte', as being a powerful movement which did not accept De Gaulle. A 'clandestine broadcasting station', 'Radio Patrie', was begun by PWE with the assistance of one of Girard's men; and Major Peter Churchill made his third visit to France in August 1942

---

[1] See Mr Dalton's minute N.S. No. 63 of 10th December 1941, on SOE Archives File 3/100/15a.

[2] See Minute from Brigadier Gubbins dated 3rd March 1942, on SOE Archives File 3/100/15.2(a).

[3] See above p. 254.

[4] Above p. 249.

[5] Above p. 254.

[6] See his report prepared in September 1942, on SOE Archives File 3/370/54(a).

to act as F Section's liaison officer after the arrest of Basin. The ultimate fate of Carte must be told later.[1]

(c) *The Organisation Civile et Militaire (OCM)* was apparently a growth of a similar type in the Occupied Zone. It comes into the story in the Bordeaux area, where it had a rapid rise and a spectacular and most discreditable fall in October 1943.[2]

2. *The Communist Party* in France as elsewhere kept its cadres intact and made no move until the German attack on Russia. It then organised as its effective cover the 'Front National' (FANA),* under the appropriate slogans,[3] and began to take action. It had three great advantages. *First*, it understood underground methods and organisation by cells, and could keep its leadership relatively intact, except where endangered by the necessary risks of war. *Second*, it was prepared to accept casualties in order to damage the enemy: the 'Parti des Fusillés' was its slogan from the first: the more that were shot the stronger the resistance. It was preferable of course that the Fusillés should not be leading members of the Party. *Third*, it had no inhibitions about political and economic change: it could play on all grievances and offer the ordinary man all he wanted – it did not expect patriotism to be enough.

It did not come into relation with De Gaulle until 1942, but from the first it was one of the 'Great Powers' of the Resistance, and other movements were forced to define their political position in relation to it as well as to De Gaulle. Its para-military organisation, (largely non-Communist) was known as the Francs Tireurs et Partisans (FTP).**

3. *The Trade Unions*, still partly associated with the Socialist Party, but gradually penetrated by Communist leadership since the merger of the Conféderation Generale du Travail with the Communist Conféderation Generale du Travail Unitaire in 1936. This process was completed during the Resistance. On the whole, however, Trade Union solidarity was more important than the political colour of particular Unions. It depended on the very nature of industrial life, and could not be broken so long as the men remained at work in their trade – railways, PTT, mines, engineering works and so forth. The problem of harnessing this solidarity to the resistance was not always best

---

[1] Below p. 566 ff.

[2] Below p. 572.

[3] See Colonel R. Brook's paper of 7th September 1943, on SOE Archives File 3/100/15a.

* [Abbreviation for 'fanatiques', used in MI6 to refer to the French Communist Party, mistakenly applied by Mackenzie (and by Foot in his first edition) as if it were used by the French.]

** [See Charles Tillon, their commander, *FTP* (Paris, 1962).]

approached on the political side. [PASSAGE DELETED ON GROUNDS OF NATIONAL SECURITY.] Mr John Price, an authority on the International Labour Movement, was made available for consultation by all Sections from October 1941, and Mr Dalton insisted that he should be consulted.[1] SOE's officers were on the whole not drawn from circles familiar with Trade Union life, and there is no doubt that they required educating in this respect. Particular instances of what was eventually achieved will appear in the sequel: here only three general points need be mentioned.

First, there was the case of M. Jouhaux. M. Jouhaux had been Secretary-General of the CGT since its days of revolutionary syndicalism about 1910, and was a figure of world-wide reputation in Trade Union circles: he was an old established symbol of French Trade Unionism, more Syndicalist than Socialist in its political colour. On the other hand, he was now old and partly crippled with arthritis: and his influence (though he retained his office) was being eaten away by a younger generation of leaders, largely Communists of various shades. [PASSAGE DELETED ON GROUNDS OF NATIONAL SECURITY] there had been a little talk of getting him out. Mr Dalton took up the case that summer, and in September 1941 it was explicitly understood that an attempt would be made by SIS through channels of their own. Nothing happened; the Minister created a not unreasonable storm,[3] and the responsibility for Jouhaux was eventually transferred to SOE in February 1942. But at the end of December Jouhaux had been arrested by Vichy, and SOE was relieved of the necessity of pursuing a project for which it had no great enthusiasm. Major Bodington saw Jouhaux on 17th August 1942, when he had been released 'en résidence surveillée' at Cahors, and there is an interesting record of their interview:[4] but it was not clear that the old man was very anxious to be rescued, and the matter then dropped. It is not likely that his presence in England would have made a serious contribution to the war: and the incident was important mainly for the trouble it caused within SOE and between SOE and SIS. It may fairly be surmised that it was connected with the replacement of Mr Marriott by Colonel Buckmaster as head of F Section in December 1941.

Second, there was the question of subsidising Trade Union funds, which were in some financial difficulty through Vichy's creation of a sort of corporate 'Labour Front'. This was raised at a meeting between

---

[1] See papers about his position on the Jouhaux affair, on SOE Archives File (AD/S.1) F.38/16.
[2] [NOTE DELETED ON GROUNDS OF NATIONAL SECURITY.]
[3] Papers in particular on SOE Archives File CD/F6/33.
[4] Copy on SOE Archives File 3/370/54(a).

M. Henri Hauck, De Gaulle's Director of Labour, and Colonel Keswick,* Colonel Buckmaster and Mr John Price on 2nd February 1942,[1] and was approved later that month.[2] The sum mentioned in the first instance was £3,000. There was some hesitation at the time as to the propriety of financing the French Trade Union movement from British secret funds: but SOE's money found its way in larger quantities into much stranger places, and there is no doubt that this was a sound investment.

Third, the question of evacuating other Trade Unionists arose when the Jouhaux project collapsed; and there is a list of priorities dated 1st April 1942[3] which gives the following names: Lacoste, Bothereau, Philip, Gouin, Moutet. Lacoste refused, and no more is heard of Bothereau till much later: but the others were all important. André Philip, who came out under the auspices of SIS in the summer of 1942, was Finance Minister from January to May 1946 and again in M. Blum's** 'caretaker government' of December 1946. M. Gouin was evacuated about the same time and was President of the Consultative Assembly for a time, then Prime Minister of France from January to May 1946. M. Moutet was Minister of the Colonies from December 1946. This gives a useful indication of the part eventually played by the Socialist side of the Trade Union leadership.

4. *The Catholic Church* is a factor which must be mentioned, though it did not as an organisation intervene directly in resistance. This was partly a matter of doctrine: partly that there was a strong Catholic flavour about Pétain's régime, and resistance to Vichy was associated with such ideas as Republican Spain, the Front Populaire and the 'lois laiques'. But there were always some priests and countless good Catholics for whom resistance came first: details are difficult to trace, but one can see emerging even in 1941 a patriotic and 'social' Catholic movement in the tradition of Comte Albert de Mun and the Democrates Populaires, which in time became the Mouvement Républicain Populaire, led by such men as M. Georges Bidault† and M. François de Menthon. This is not an important factor at our present halting-

---

1 Minutes on SOE Archives File 3/100/15(a).
2 Minute by A/D.1 dated 24th February 1942 (Note: extended later to payments to individual *workers*; SO to Attlee 19th October 1942 on SOE Archives File 3/100/15.1a).
3 Minute by Colonel Sporborg on SOE Archives File CD/F6/33. See also his Minute of 22nd May 1942 on 3/100/2(c).
* [David Keswick, of the Jardine, Matheson family, was then D/R, in charge of France and Low Countries, moved to Algiers late 1942, returned to City 1945.]
** [Léon Blum, 1872–1950, Popular Front leader, survived concentration camps.]
† [G. A. Bidault, 1899–1983, often Foreign and Prime Minister of post-war France.]

place in the autumn of 1941, and at this stage Pétain can count at least tacit support from the Catholic Church, as from the Army and the 'Fonctionnaires'. But the Church is potentially a 'Great Power' in the Resistance, as is the Communist Party; and De Gaulle's plans must take account of both.

So far we have dealt with existing organisations which retained their importance. The old political parties, except in so far as they had some social basis, were dead in public estimation as well as by the Vichy ban: and it remains to describe new movements, made out of the same human material, which arose to fill their place. In almost every case, the centre of such a movement was a clandestine newspaper; its cadres were those who wrote, duplicated and distributed the paper: its supporters were deemed to include all readers of the paper. In the Unoccupied Zone these organisations could only by courtesy be described as 'resistance' movements. They took some risk of a sentence in a Vichy gaol, but it was some time before they even ventured to contemplate the preparation of secret armies for a renewal of the war; still less did they plan for any immediate violent action. But politically they were important as carriers of propaganda, of a type which must in the end breed resistance: and as centres round which different trends could be grouped in some sort of order and on some sort of common programme. In addition, their organisations were of value for the selection and training of men who would later play a more active part.

In the Occupied Zone the Germans appear to have prevented (perhaps unwisely, as a matter of police tactics) any centralisation of this kind until after November 1942; there were minor movements, some of them linked with movements on the other side of the border, but the only centralised force was that of the Communist Party.[1] In the Unoccupied Zone, we have already mentioned General de la Laurencie and 'Libération Nationale'. The three other movements which deserve mention are:

1. *Liberté*, sometimes known by the name of its newspaper as 'Combat'. With this are associated the names of M. Henri Fresnay, later Minister for 'Deportés et Prisonniers de Guerre', of M. Teitgen,

---

[1] The 'official' list given in the EMFFI History (Vol. 2, p. 12) is:
Organisation Civile et Militaire (see above p. 268 and below p. 571)
Ceux de la Libération
Ceux de la Résistance
Front National ⎫
Francs Tireurs et Partisans ⎬ both Communist
Libération (Zone Nord).

Vice-Premier in 1947,[1] and of M. de Menthon, Minister of Justice in Algiers in September 1943, and holder of other offices.[2]

The patriotic sentiments of 'Liberté' were impeccable, but it stood somewhat to the Right; probably to the Right of any part of the old Front Populaire, certainly to the Right of any possibility of association with the Communists. It is misleading to speak of its adherents as if they were a list of persons who could be individually enumerated: but its tone was in general that of the patriotic bourgeois, including Catholics.[3]

It is unfortunately impossible to dissociate Fresnay from his dealings with Darlan's Minister of the Interior, Pucheu, after his arrest early in 1942.[4] Pucheu, who was an enemy of Laval, and perhaps also of the Germans,[5] offered official tolerance on the understanding that 'Liberté' should –

(i) Continue anti-German propaganda.
(ii) Continue propaganda against Trusts.
(iii) Stop propaganda against Pétain and certain ministers.
(iv) Give up its arms.

The hook was baited with the usual Vichy lure: that Pétain was at heart anti-German, and was working by devious means in the national interest of France – the alternative to a Pétain government might be Communism. Fresnay was caught, apparently; then repented and attempted to extricate himself. At least he was released by Pucheu in spite of his confessed offences. The incident was known to other movements and was hard to live down.

2. *Libération*, which is associated with Emmanuel d'Astier de la Vigerie. D'Astier was in the early forties, married to an American: he had begun life as a naval officer, but had early become a freelance journalist. He was well-known in the intellectual circles of the moderate Left, though not then a party politician himself.[6] One of his brothers was Général de l'Air François d'Astier de la Vigerie, who came out

---

[1] R/F Section History, 1941, p. 44.

[2] R/F Section History, 1942, p. 20.

[3] Cf. the report of HM Consul-General at Nice, who was in France until June 1941. Lisbon dispatch No. 198 of 27th June 1941, amplified in SOE Archives File (AD/S.1) F.38/17: and Forman's Report – R/F Section History, 1941, p. 46.

[4] See report by Morandat quoted in R/F Section History, 1941, p. 38, and report by Miss Hall and Captain Basin dated 2nd February 1942, on SOE Archives File (AD/S.1) F.38/23.

[5] He withdrew voluntarily to North Africa in 1943, but was tried and executed.

[6] See note by Colonel Buckmaster d/d 20th May 1942, on SOE Archives File (AD/S.1) F.38/23. After the war he was President of the MURF, a Parliamentary group which generally acted with the Communists.

on 17th November 1942[1] to fight with De Gaulle: another was Henri d'Astier, also a resister, but a man of the Right, who dabbled in Cagoulard and Royalist conspiracy and played some part in the development of resistance in North Africa from early in 1941, under the aegis of the American Consul-General, Mr Murphy.[2]

Emmanuel d'Astier (commonly referred to as 'Bernard')[3] stood, as was to be expected, more to the Left than Fresnay. 'Libération' could appeal in the first instance to the old constituents of the Front Populaire, except for the Communists; but its scope was extended by the 'contamination' of 'Liberté', and it was on the whole the strongest group of this type, and the one most likely to be of value to De Gaulle – if he could get it.

3. *Franc Tireur* was the smallest and least-known of these groups. Its leader apparently was a certain J. F. Levy ('Claudius'),[4] and it seems to have stood well to the Left, short of Communism. It was comparatively unimportant in the sequel.

Having digressed so far, let us return to the arrival of M. Moulin in London in October 1941. The existence of the three movements – 'Libération Nationale' (de la Laurencie), 'Liberté' (Fresnay) and 'Libération' (d'Astier) – had of course been known for some time: but here for the first time was a man high in their councils who could give a detailed account of their resources and plans. Furthermore, he reported[5] that an attempt at unification had been made in July 1941: the leaders met again at Marseilles on 5th September and reached an agreement 'in principle'; 'practical means of collaboration' had still to be settled, but it was likely that the following formula would be accepted:

1. Independence in all questions affecting newspapers.
2. Agreements to be made *re* campaigns, demolitions, etc.
3. One single organisation in spheres of military activity.

It is not clear what in detail were Moulin's instructions from the leaders. Certainly he was not authorised by any of them to accept the political leadership of De Gaulle: on the other hand, military unifi-

---

[1] R/F Section History, 1942, p. 18.

[2] See Renée Pierre-Gosset, 'Algiers 1941–43'.

[3] There had been some SOE contact with him as far back as April 1941, see New York telegram CXG.588 of 15th April 1941, on SOE Archives File 3/100/15.1a.

[4] See a note by Major Morton on an interview with him in November 1943: letter to Lord Selborne of 8th November 1943, on SOE Archives File 3/490/2(c). As 'Claudius Petit' he was later a leader of the Parliamentary group UDSR. Minister of Reconstruction in M. Queville's Government of September 1948.

[5] His report is fully summaried in R/F Section History, 1941, p. 34; copy on SOE Archives File – R/F Mission Files 'REX (Robert)'.

cation had already been agreed 'in principle', and Moulin's primary task was to obtain moral support, arms and money, and to arrange for co-ordination with Allied military action through communication with London. The crucial point is that he came for these to De Gaulle and not to the British Government.

De Gaulle's answer did not force the pace in any way, but it was judicious in securing such key points as could be secured at once. It consisted of:

(i) A short and eloquent letter – 'soyons fiers et confiants!' and so forth – written as an equal to equals, on the theme that 'the task is hard but all Frenchmen will work together to save France'.[1]

(ii) A political directive, which avoids all mention of political leadership: it asks only for an intensification of propaganda, for full and regular reports, and for readiness to transmit and execute 'consignes et mots d'ordre généraux'. It provides 500,000 francs (£2,000 at most) for each organisation at once, and promises regular subventions.[2]

(iii) A military directive – the crux of the matter – which asks in effect that military and political action should be kept strictly separate, that De Gaulle's agents should be accepted for military liaison, and that all military action should be co-ordinated by De Gaulle in London. This was not likely to be acceptable to elements in contact with the Vichy General Staff, which had its own plans for military leadership: but it could not be offensive to anyone else who had thought seriously of the military problems involved in resistance. It was thus an indispensable stepping-stone to the much more difficult problem of political unity.

There were the usual delays, and Moulin did not reach France with these messages until 1st January 1942. He returned there warmly convinced that unity behind De Gaulle was the only ultimate solution to the political problem.

(iv) R/F Operations, Second Phase

Let us now follow the action taken by R/F Section during the remainder of this period, returning later to SOE's political relations with De Gaulle.

Adjutant (now S/Lieutenant) Forman, who had already taken part both in Savanna and Josephine, returned to the field by air on 13th October 1941,[3] to a reception organised by Labit and his group at

---

[1] Dated 5th November 1941, SOE Archives File 3/100/2c.

[2] Also on SOE Archives File 3/100/2c.

[3] Operation 'Mainmast B': R/F Section History, 1941, Appendix B, p. 44

Toulouse:[1] he took with him a wireless operator and 500,000 francs in cash. This was just before Moulin's arrival in London, but Forman had a very wide political charter from De Gaulle, instructing him to contact 'Liberté' and other organisations in the Zone Libre: to promote their unity, and (so far as possible) their allegiance to De Gaulle: then to proceed to Paris and make similar contacts there. In the Zone Libre Forman seems to have travelled a good deal: in particular, he saw M. Teitgen[2] of 'Liberté', who was willing enough to promote a union of the resistance movements in that zone under a committee of their own leaders, without recognition of the primacy of De Gaulle: on his own showing, Forman accepted this policy with misgivings, on the understanding that the combined organisation should accept a liaison officer from the Free French HQ. It is interesting to observe his general attitude, that of the 'good Gaullist' pure and simple. 'In spite of their claim to suppress all party ideas, each of these groups and others like them represented one or another of the pre-war political parties. They aimed at English recognition of them as powerful organisations; funds and materials which they received from England would establish their superiority over the smaller organisations, which they would then be able to absorb, and eventually gain sufficient power to ignore the directives of London which did not fall in with their own wishes.'

Forman apparently became known to the Vichy police, and (most injudiciously) 'escaped' to the Occupied Zone, where he went on confidently with his mission, meeting Yves Letac of the Brittany organisation[3] as well as many others. Towards the end of the year police pressure became too severe: both he and Labit of Toulouse demanded anxiously that they should be evacuated, and they left together by sea on the night of 5th January 1942. Forman's political contacts may have been useful, but his sense of security was very imperfect: *post hoc* is perhaps not *propter hoc*,[4] but certainly many of those he had contacted – M. Teitgen, the Toulouse organisation, the Brittany organisation, Laverdet's Paris organisation[5] – ran into serious difficulties soon after his departure. It will be remembered that Pierre de Vomecourt's F Section organisation was penetrated at about the same period, and it seems most probable that the Gestapo had given all these early organisations (which were recklessly insecure) a good deal of rope, and was gathering its profits in the early months of 1942.

---

[1] Above p. 260.

[2] Later Vice-Premier – January 1947.

[3] Above p. 262.

[4] Cf. on this subject Colonel Sporborg's Minute of 10th April 1942 on SOE Archives File 3/490/3(a).

[5] Above p. 261.

Forman's mission was followed on 6th November 1941 by that of Yves Morandat, a man of a new type:[1] he had been full-time Secretary of the Catholic Trade Union organisation in the Lyon area, and his primary mission was to contact these Trade Unions, and to promote so far as possible a united Trade Union resistance front on a Gaullist basis. Unfortunately he did not receive a wireless operator until June 1942; most of his early reports were made in writing, and SOE did not have access to all of them, so that there is no material for appraising the success of his original Trade Union mission. To judge from his later telegrams, he was politically of considerable importance in promoting unity and Gaullist leadership in the Unoccupied Zone.[2] He eventually returned from France in November 1942.

S/Lieutenant Thomé's mission to St Etienne[3] on 8th December was of relatively local importance, as the intention was primarily to maintain touch with a minor organisation in that area, believed to be Gaullist in sympathy. But he and his wireless operator remained active in the field for some time, and any channel of communication was valuable in these days. Furthermore, a Lysander operation[4] (the first for R/F Section), which Thomé organised on 26th April, was by accident something of a landmark in the development of air operations. The Lysander had been demanded on a false plea of urgency: the landing-ground and flare-path were not set out by Thomé himself, as had been intended: and the passengers sent home were not those for whom the operation had been planned. The aircraft landed and got away successfully, though in exciting circumstances: but the RAF were most reasonably indignant, and refused to consider any further operations unless men whom they had trained were known to be in charge of the field. Hence the genesis of the Bureau d'Opérations Aériennes (BOA) in the north, and of the Services d'Atterrissages et Parachutages (SAP) in the south.[5]

This phase ends with the return of Moulin by parachute on the night of 1st January 1942.[6] With him went Lieutenant Fassin and a wireless operator, to maintain touch between De Gaulle in London and Moulin as the focus of resistance movements in the Vichy zone. This group virtually remained De Gaulle's HQ in France through the

---

[1] Operation 'Outclass': R/F Section History, 1941, p. 37. It is interesting to see that he appears in Mrs D. Pickles, 'France Between the Republics', p. 164, as 'the first man to be parachuted into France': the 'first politician', perhaps!
[2] See e.g. R/F Section History, 1942, pp. 23-4.
[3] R/F Section History, 1941, p. 40, 1942, p. 4 – Operation 'Cod'.
[4] R/F Section History, 1942, p. 4.
[5] Below p. 279.
[6] Operation 'Perch': R/F Section History, 1942, p. 2.

critical period of the year 1942. Moulin was arrested and killed brutally by the Germans in June 1943, after becoming the first chairman of the Conseil National de la Résistance in May: Fassin escaped to England after Moulin's disaster. The material that passed through this channel (also used by Morandat) was primarily political: of considerable importance historically, but too extensive to analyse here.

There followed in the spring of 1942, a gap of three months, during which no R/F operations took place: apparently for reasons outside the control of SOE, though De Gaulle was hardly ready to accept this.[1] In France there was still talk of unifying the resistance, and the two organisations 'of the right', Libération National and Liberté, amalgamated to form Libération Française ('Lifra' or 'Combat') some time early in 1942. But it is hard to see that Moulin had made much real progress as yet.

In April and May 1942 matters moved a step forward. On 1st April a certain Lezinnes was dropped with 3,000,000 francs and instructions to contact 'certain high officials and important political personalities in both zones.[2] The latter end of this mission is obscure and it certainly went somewhat astray. But about the end of March a certain [PASSAGE DELETED ON GROUNDS OF NATIONAL SECURITY] on behalf of the Communist Party, or some fraction of it, and established touch with General de Gaulle.[3] The terms of their accord are not on record: but clearly they were practical and not unfriendly, and there must have been a limited understanding for military support and military co-ordination, with the greatest political reserve on either side. [NAME DELETED] returned to France late in April, and the first-fruits of his visit were the dispatch on 28th May of an instructor (Captain Georges) and a radio operator to establish liaison with the Communist Party resistance organisation 'FANA', in the Occupied Zone.[4] Unfortunately they were arrested soon after landing, and the liaison was not resumed till October 1942, when a wireless instructor and a new wireless operator were sent: a sabotage instructor was added later.[5]

A Trade Union representative is reported to have been in London at the same time as [NAME DELETED][6] and the circle was completed by the unexpected arrival of Emmanuel d'Astier de la Vigerie on 12th

---

[1] See below p. 286.

[2] Operation 'Salmon': R/F Section History, 1942, p. 15. He received a wireless operator ('Eel') at the end of May.

[3] See Colonel Sporborg's Minute of 10th April 1942, on SOE Archives File 3/490/3c.

[4] Operation 'Goldfish': R/F Section History, 1942, p. 37.

[5] 'Carp' Mission: R/F Section History, 1942, p. 38.

[6] Colonel Billotte's letter of 7th April 1942, on SOE Archives File 3/490/3c.

May. He had been sent back unannounced by F Section's agent, Basin, on the submarine which carried Major Peter Churchill to the South of France on 21st April.[1] This was a fair instance of the sort of confusion of channels which could arise, and it is not surprising that d'Astier reacted with horror to the jungle of competing organisations in London:[2] within De Gaulle's Headquarters M. Diethelm and Colonel Passy (under Colonel Billotte) had separate secret departments, and on the British side there were SIS and two separate sections of SOE, to say nothing of the D/F Section with its 'body lines', or of various channels controlled by the Poles. One important proposal made by d'Astier was for the creation of a co-ordinating committee in London,[3] and there is no doubt that he was equally convinced of the need for better co-ordination in France. During his stay in London he had full discussions with SOE, from the Minister downwards: he also had long interviews with De Gaulle and with his staff. At this stage d'Astier made an excellent impression on all who met him: he seems to have been equally impressed by de Gaulle, and although he hardly became de Gaulle's man, as Moulin had done, he warmly accepted him as a symbol of the unity of the resistance. This support was of the greatest importance, as 'Libération' was perhaps the strongest movement in the Vichy area, with some parallel development beyond the dividing line: it had most useful contacts with the CGT: and it was not contaminated (as was 'Combat') with any taint of Vichyism.

Somewhat to SOE's irritation, d'Astier was persuaded by De Gaulle to pay a visit to America and to make an attempt to straighten out the Gaullist organisation there: and it was not until July that he returned to his work in France. But from this period there is visible progress. The BCRA in April was putting forward plans for a new drive to create a centralised organisation on military lines: the idea was adumbrated in De Gaulle's military directive to Moulin, which had reached France in January, but progress so far amounted to very little.[4] The first practical step was the return of Labit[5] (of the Toulouse organisation) on 1st May, with a comprehensive directive on military organisation; he reached the field safely, but lost his life shortly afterwards in a gun battle with German police. On 3rd June an organiser Schmidt[6]

---

[1] Above p. 252.

[2] See report by Colonel D. Keswick dated 14th May 1942, on SOE Archives File (AD/S.1) F.38/23.

[3] See Colonel Sporborg's letter to Major Morton, dated 4th June 1942, on SOE Archives File (AD/S.1) F.38/23.

[4] R/F Section History, 1942, p. 10. See below p. 279.

[5] Operation 'Bass': R/F Section History, 1942, p. 22.

[6] Operation 'Crab': R/F Section History, 1942, pp. 16, 32.

was sent with a wireless operator to establish direct communications with 'Libération' and to develop their para-military organisation. Schmidt was in pretty continuous touch with Moulin and Fassin, and remained important until his return to England in September 1943: the wireless operator was on the air until October 1942, when he was arrested. A sabotage instructor (Michel Gries) went to Clermont Ferrand region on 23rd June[1] on Fassin's request, and an additional wireless operator (Cordier) was dropped for Fassin on 25th July.[2]

This was a little better, and the picture began to take shape. The Resistance movements in the Vichy zone (except for the Communists) came together in July to the extent of forming a 'Conseil Général d'Études':[3] a non-executive body charged with preparing for the 'take-over' by a new government when (and if) Vichy fell – to the British mind a rather aimless and theoretical task at this stage, but none the less important, since it was this formula which created for the first time a central point of unity for the Resistance. About the same time Fassin recruited a regular officer, General Delestraint,* who was designated by De Gaulle as head of the future para-military organisation of the Resistance, and was introduced formally in that capacity in December 1942,[4] under the name of 'General Vidal'. Fassin also organised the Service d'Atterrissages et Parachutages (SAP) for the Vichy zone, and in July this was far enough advanced for him to detach a new agent[5] (Jean Ayral alias Robert Harrow) with his wireless operator to the northern zone to form there a corresponding organisation, the Bureau d'Opérations Aériennes (BOA).

The northern zone was still practically virgin soil: the only R/F Section W/T contact had been through Bourdat and Laverdet, whose organisation was at the best limited, and was practically wiped out in July 1942.[6] The Communist Party had been contacted, but the attempt to establish wireless liaison had failed.[7] Now that there was some progress in the south, Moulin himself moved to Paris in order to attempt a similar co-ordination there. In the south his place was taken by Georges Bidault, the future Prime Minister, who appears first in

---

[1] Operation 'Dory': R/F Section History, 1942, p. 16. He was received by Paul Rivière ('Marquis') who was important later and first appears at this point.

[2] Operation 'Mackerel': R/F Section History, 1942, p. 21.

[3] R/F Section History, 1942, p. 30.

[4] EMFFI History, Vol. 1, p. 20.

[5] Dropped in Operation 'Roach': R/F Section History, 1942, p. 20.

[6] Above p. 261.

[7] Above p. 277.

* [Arrested June 1943, died in enemy hands.]

May as the head of Moulin's information and propaganda service:[1] Bidault had at his disposal the wireless operator Cordier.*

Only four other operations remain to complete this phase. One was the dispatch in September of a Commandant Julitte[2] to assist Fassin: he had no wireless operator until January 1943. The second was the return to France of a certain Collin,[3] who had come out in January 1942 and returned on 29th May to the St Etienne area, primarily to open contacts with Corsica, which he visited in August. Unfortunately the wireless operator who should have accompanied him was killed by his parachute drop, and Corsica remained only a vague possibility for the present. But there was movement there, which proved important later.[4] Finally there was a mission (Nogué) in September directed to penetrate the Gestapo in Paris – an entirely abortive project:[5] and in July a certain Henri Bertrand[6] was sent with a wireless operator and 500,000 fcs to organise resistance in Marseilles. This too was abortive, in circumstances discreditable to Bertrand.

To sum up the mechanics of the situation as they stood in the late summer of 1942. Wireless communications were still on too narrow a basis to be very safe, but they had improved greatly in the last few months. There were at least eight sets in operation, mainly in the Unoccupied Zone. Those serving Lezinnes, Morandat, and Thomé were useful stand-bys but hardly of first-rate importance, and Bertrand's set was wasted. But it was of incalculable value to be in touch with Moulin through Fassin and his operator; with 'Combat' through Georges Bidault and his operator; and with 'Libération' through Schmidt. Things were only beginning in the Occupied Zone, but Jean Ayral's set was available for organising air operations there and it is possible that a set moved in with Moulin in the late summer. The worst set-back was that no effective link had yet been opened with the Communist Party and its affiliates. It was also a disappointment that no set had been established in Corsica.

Apart from wireless sets, the supply position was bad, and the amount of stores dropped was too small to have any practical significance. This was a source of ceaseless worry, both in London and in the field; it is difficult to nourish the offensive spirit for long without

---

[1] SOE London HQ War Diary, May 1942, p. 3798.
[2] Operation 'Chub': R/F Section History, 1942, p. 37.
[3] Operation 'Shrimp': R/F Section History, 1942, pp. 13, 14.
[4] See below p. 543.
[5] Operation 'Hagfish': R/F Section History, 1942, p. 37.
[6] Operation 'Crayfish': R/F Section History, 1942, p. 34.
* [Survived to be Moulin's biographer.]

offensive arms. There was certainly no practical means at this stage of arming these organisations which were independent of Vichy, and violent action on a serious scale could therefore only be carried out with weapons released from Vichy stores. This was important, as it biassed military planners anxious for concrete results toward any scheme which might bring in the Armée de l'Armistice or some elements of it: but it probably did no harm in the long run to the Free French resistance. No organisation existed which could have used a shower of arms in the summer of 1942: if they had been sent before some co-ordination existed, they would have favoured dissension more than unity: the allocation of arms between movements was a fruitful source of jealousy even in the better atmosphere of 1943 and 1944. The only supply which was essential at this stage was money, which was easy to transport and readily available.

R/F's picture was therefore one of a series of popular movements gradually coming together to accept the symbolic status of De Gaulle, and already linked to London by tolerably good communications. The notion of a Gaullist Secret Army was still a vague project, and the movements admittedly had no striking power: no one doubted that they had some adherents who would fight if they could, but estimates of potential forces varied pretty much according to the fancy of the witness. 'The Resistance' might have a political future, but it did not look like a present military asset: and it was certain that it was deeply penetrated by Vichy and Gestapo agents. This was inevitable with large, inexperienced and undisciplined organisations of this political type, and the dangers were increased by the recurring tendency to centralise too much; partly a temperamental failing of individuals, but partly also a necessity in a political situation which made it worth taking risks for the sake of unity and leadership. The prevailing insecurity led to some very serious losses, but in the end the movements as a whole stood up much better than could have been foreseen in 1942.

5. Politics

(i) The Vichy Background

SOE had very little to do with the numerous lines of contact with Vichy which were not properly within its field of action. There was a curious incident in the autumn of 1941, when an American lawyer named Max Schoop attempted to intervene as an unofficial negotiator, and on one occasion actually interviewed Pétain and Weygand: his messages came through SOE's representative at Gibraltar. There was also a contact there in September 1941, with the Royalist pretender, the Comte de Paris, through an injudicious member of

General Gort's* staff.[1] In West Africa there was a vague feeler in February 1942 from Boisson, Vichy's satrap at Dakar.[2] But this sort of thing was not SOE's business, and all these lines were broken off as soon as possible. Nor was SOE concerned in the contacts with Weygand which took place at intervals up to the late summer of 1942. Thus all that is necessary is to give a short chronological summary as background to the Gaullist development.

The first wave of defeatism began to pass in September 1940, when Laval's** position was a little weakened by a reorganisation of the Government and the appointment of Weygand as Délégué Général of the Government in French Africa and Governor General of Algeria. At the same time the policy of conciliation with Germany was pursued up to the Montoire interview between Pétain and Hitler on 24th October, and the strange incident of the return by the Germans of the ashes of Napoleon's son, the Duc de Reichstadt, on 15th December. At this point there was a sudden break, of which the full story is not yet known.[3] On 14th December 1940 Laval was dismissed and arrested, on the ground that he had been planning a coup for his own hand; after an interval Darlan became Vice-Premier, Foreign Minister and 'heir apparent' in his place. This gave Vichy a slightly greater colour of independence; its policy towards Germany was hardly less supple than before, but it now freely took the line (at least in its contacts with Britain and USA) that this pliancy was tactical and did not represent Vichy's real feelings.

This line of development was encouraged by the American policy, adopted in December 1940, of permitting the dispatch of supplies to North Africa on the understanding that American representatives would be admitted in order to ensure that the supplies were not transmitted to the Axis. Mr Robert Murphy arrived as a Consul-General at Algiers in March 1941, and a large staff of Americans was distributed there and elsewhere in North Africa. Mr Murphy's policy in the first instance was to work with Weygand and to strengthen him, in

---

1   The papers on both these affairs are on SOE Archives File SC.38/3: for Schoop see also CD/7.

2   Papers on SOE Archives File (AD/S.1) F.45.

3   It will be remembered that approaches had been made to London in October: see Cmd.6662 of 1945, on dealings with the Vichy Ambassador in Madrid, and with an agent (M. Rougier) in London.

*   [J. S. S. P. Vereker, 1886–1946, VC 1918, 6th Viscount Gort 1902, CIGS 1937–9, knight 1938, C-in-C BEF 1939–40, governed Gibraltar 1941–2, Malta 1942–4, Palestine 1944–6.]

** [P. Laval, 1883–1945, French Prime Minister 1931–2, 1935–6, 1940, 1942–4, favoured co-operation with Germans, tried and executed.]

the hope that the French Army in North Africa would resist further extension of German influence. At the same time Mr Murphy appears also, as a second string, to have kept some contact with the few 'Gaullist' supporters in North Africa. There was no scope in these colonial territories for wide popular movements, and the Gaullists here seem to have been a small knot of conspirators with rather a flavour of the 'Cagoulards' and 'Action Français' – the romantic 'Right'.[1] Henri d'Astier de la Vigerie, brother of the leader of 'Libération', was associated with this from early in 1941.

This situation held during the summer of 1941: Darlan and Weygand* balanced one another, leaning a little towards Germany and the Allies respectively: Laval was kept by the Germans in reserve, as a menace to be applied as necessary: and Laval in turn was threatened with displacement by still more atrocious collaborators such as Doriot and Déat. It was a position relatively favourable to the Allies, and in August there were even suggestions[2] of the possible collapse of Vichy; the police powers of the Government were greatly extended, there was much talk of 'Communist provocateurs', and a great plot was 'discovered' behind the attempt to assassinate Laval at Versailles on 27th August. This was not a process which the Germans could allow to go far, and the screw began to turn in November 1941, as victory in the East receded; on 13th November Weygand was recalled from North Africa, his post as Délégué Général was abolished, and he was replaced as Governor-General of Algeria by the insignificant Yves Chatel. General Juin appears as C-in-C of the Army in North Africa, Vice-Admiral Fénard as Darlan's local representative. The Americans at once ceased supplies to North Africa, and did not resume them until June 1942. Weygand did not break off contact with the Allies, and emissaries from him appear to have been in London in December 1941 and in May 1942.[3] The Armée de l'Armistice had various plans for various hypotheses, such as an Allied landing on the Continent or a German attempt to occupy the whole of France: and they asked for British collaboration. There was a certain symbolic importance, too, in Giraud's** escape from the fortress prison of

---

[1] There is a popular account of these events, which seems very accurate, in Renée Pierre-Gosset: 'Algiers 1941–43'. See also M. Jose Aboulker's Report – with SOE Archives 'AD/E Safe Files'.

[2] See Major Morton's paper CFR(41)158 of 15th August; copy on SOE Archives File (AD/S.1) SC.38/2.

[3] See paper by CIGS dated 12th May 1942; copy on SOE Archives File 3/100/2(c).

* [M. Weygand, 1867–1965, French Chief of Staff 1930–35, briefly C-in-C May–June 1940, allowed to retire.]

** [H. H. Giraud, 1879–1949, French army commander, prisoner 1940, escaped 1942, eclipsed by De Gaulle 1943.]

Koenigstein on 17th April 1942: and it is said that he was interviewed by Darlan shortly after his return to France and promised 'loyalty' on the basis of the General Staff plans.

It is unlikely that much of this was unknown to the Germans, and their counter-action proceeded systematically. Laval was imposed on Pétain as Prime Minister on 14th April 1942, and Darlan was elevated and side-tracked into the position of Head of the Armed Forces, with access to Cabinet meetings, and next in succession to Marshal Pétain. A little later Weygand was arrested and placed 'en résidence surveillée' at Cagnes: and the Germans now had a fairly effective check on the execution of any of the 'Weygand plans'. But at about the same period the German production machine was being geared up for a war longer than had been anticipated, the demand for labour began to weigh on Occupied Europe, and in particular on Laval. The demand developed from financial inducement, through menace, to physical compulsion: it had not progressed far in the summer of 1942, but it was one influence among many in forcing Frenchmen to choose whether they were for Hitler or against him. The Vichy line was to become less and less tenable until it was blown away by the North African landings in November 1942. Already on 1st May and 14th July 1942 public demonstrations against Vichy were staged in many towns of the Unoccupied Zone, with the active support of movements in touch with London.

(ii) De Gaulle and SOE: November 1941 to September 1942

De Gaulle naturally was acutely aware of all these shifts of tendency: watched them anxiously and adjusted his policy to meet them. Some of this can be traced in his dealing with SOE.

As early as 5th November 1941, while Moulin's directive was still under discussion, De Gaulle had begun an offensive on another front. On that day he saw Colonel Sporborg and in the course of discussion on other subjects berated him very soundly for the independent activities of F Section.[1] Again on 20th December he summoned separately Colonel Sporborg and the officer responsible for France within the SIS,* and formally notified them that in view of the many misdeeds of their organisations he had decided to put an end to all collaboration in secret matters, both in the sphere of Intelligence and of Operations.[2] His main grievances were (once more) the independent

---

[1] See Colonel Sporborg's memo. dated 6th November 1941, on SOE Archives File (AD/S.1) SC.38/4.

[2] See Colonel Sporborg's memo. dated 20th December 1941, on SOE Archives File (AD/S.1) SC.38/4 – and draft note by CSS on same file.

* [Lieutenant-Commander K. Cohen, RN.]

activities of British agents; and also delays in handling of his own agents, such as Moulin, which he took to be the result of deliberate obstruction.

These complaints were embodied in an official letter from the General to Mr Eden sent on 22nd December,[1] which repeated his charges with more precision, but made no reference to the menace of suspending all collaboration. As General Gubbins noted at the time, this was not an idle menace – 'we are, in fact, for the moment entirely dependent on him for what we do in France'.[2] It appears from Colonel Sporborg's notes[3] that the more moderate line of De Gaulle's letter represented a real retreat: De Gaulle, it was reported, had been convinced that SOE's difficulties were real and not fictitious, and that it was suffering from a real shortage of resources (particularly of aircraft) in relation to its task: his object now (it was claimed) was not so much to coerce SOE, as to strengthen its hand, by forcing the War Cabinet to consider seriously whether it was worth playing with Resistance at all, if no more help could be given.

There was a general meeting of officials[4] at the Foreign Office under Mr Strang's chairmanship on 31st December to discuss the line to be taken in reply, and Mr Jebb saw M. Diethelm to no great purpose on 8th January.[5] Mr Eden's reply was finally dispatched on 20th January, and was perhaps sharper in tone than is usual in such communications: 'it would not, we fear, be prudent to rely, for the purposes now in question, on the assumption that the National Committee enjoys the adherence open or secret, of a very large majority of French citizens'. This point of view would certainly have been endorsed by most responsible officers within SOE at this stage: to quote Brigadier Gubbins,[6] 'it is clear that we cannot build up a proper secret army in France under the aegis or flag of De Gaulle: *that* we must do through our independent French Section until such time as a combination is practical politics . . . . I can quite see a solution to the problem if and when De Gaulle is replaced by a man who has the general confidence of the French people in France, but with De Gaulle in the saddle it is difficult to know where our support of the F.F. plans in France is leading us.'

---

[1] Copy on SOE Archives File (AD/S.1) SC.38/4.

[2] Minute of 20th December 1941, on SOE Archives File (AD/S.1) SC.38/4.

[3] Minute of 22nd December 1941, on SOE Archives File (AD/S.1) SC.38/4, and of 31st December 1941 on 3/100/2c.

[4] Note by Colonel Sporborg, wrongly dated 1st December 1942, on SOE Archives File 3/100/2c.

[5] Mr Jebb's record on SOE Archives File 3/100/2c.

[6] See his Minute of 22nd January 1942, on SOE Archives File 3/100/2c.

February and March 1942 were quiet months on the De Gaulle front, although atrocious weather had extremely bad effects on air operations, and it seems that no R/F operations took place. De Gaulle was perhaps busy with the affair of St Pierre et Miquelon (which he occupied on 24th December 1941 in defiance of President Roosevelt) and the resulting difficulties with Admiral Muselier, which represented a very serious internal crisis in his movement. But he returned to the charge in April. On 1st April he delivered the famous speech at the Dorchester Hotel, in which he bluntly and publicly claimed full recognition of Fighting France as the 'bloc' of the new French revolution, and mocked at the British and American leaning towards Vichy: on 7th April Colonel Billotte (Passy's immediate superior) lodged a formal protest[1] with Colonel Sporborg regarding the insufficiency of the assistance given to De Gaulle in his dealings with the Resistance: on 14th April De Gaulle himself took advantage of a dinner given to him by Mr Eden, at which the CIGS, General Sir Alan F. Brooke,* was present, to deliver a sharp attack on SOE for the poverty of its support.[2]

A stage in the war had now been reached at which it was possible to think practically of plans for re-entry to the Continent: the 'Round-Up' Planning Committee had been formed by the Chiefs of Staff in April 1942, with a view in the first instance to considering action in the event of a sudden German collapse in 1942. Resistance in France was beginning to be a subject of serious military consideration, and de Gaulle's next step (plainly enough) was to impress his practical importance on the military authorities. On 22nd April Colonel Billotte saw the CIGS on his behalf and outlined, somewhat tendentiously, what De Gaulle hoped he could do to help an invasion: in addition he pressed for any indication that could be given of the time and areas to which organisation should be directed.[3]

Meantime, on 14th April, Laval had become Prime Minister, a fact which was in the end bound to advance De Gaulle's stock. Mr Churchill (who was in close touch with President Roosevelt on this issue) had instructed the Chiefs of Staff to investigate what action could be taken to induce French North Africa to declare for the Allies, and to support it if it did so:[4] the situation he contemplated was one

---

[1] Original on SOE Archives File 3/490/3(c).

[2] See Minute by Colonel Taylor to Brigadier Gubbins dated 15th April 1942, on SOE Archives File 3/100/2c (giving Mr Strang's account of what happened).

[3] Minutes of meeting attached to CIGS's paper of 12th May, on SOE Archives File 3/100/2c.

[4] COS(42)123rd Mtg, Item 1, dated 18th April.

* [A. F. Brooke, 1883–1963, invented creeping barrage 1916, knight 1940, CIGS 1941–6, Field-Marshal 1944, KG, OM and Viscount Alanbrooke 1946.]

to be created by the resignation of Marshal Pétain. An immediate memorandum was prepared by the Chiefs of Staff on 18th April,[1] and the question of further action was referred to Major Morton's Committee on Allied Resistance, whose views were embodied in a paper submitted on 25th April: a similar paper on West Africa was submitted on 28th April.[2] The most essential part of their conclusions was that such a hypothesis was almost inconceivable, a view endorsed by the Foreign Office: the latter were however insistent that the line to be taken must depend on 'highly delicate contacts' then in progress 'on a high level' – in fact with General Weygand.[3] This was enough to hold in suspense most of the Committee's detailed proposals, and no clear directive emerged from the Chiefs of Staff meeting of 27th April, which took the main papers.[4] But the line given to SOE as regards North Africa[5] still relied on Weygand, not on De Gaulle:

Your objects should be:
(a) To prepare the ground for a negotiated agreement with French authorities of sufficient standing to ensure the entry and favourable reception of Allied forces in French North Africa.
(b) To ensure resistance by the French in the event of an Axis attack on French North Africa.
(c) To stiffen French resistance meanwhile to Axis penetration and to counter Axis activities of all kinds.
(d) To guard against premature action by patriots.

The CIGS in his paper[6] of 12th May is equally clear that De Gaulle would be a military liability everywhere except in occupied France, and he was apparently authorised by the Chiefs of Staff on 16th May[7] to open negotiations with Weygand.

These discussions were (it is to be hoped) unknown to De Gaulle: but they would scarcely have made him less inclined to press his case – he was probably not unaware of its weak side. The appearance of Emmanuel d'Astier in London under the aegis of F Section gave a new *casus belli*: and Captain Piquet-Wicks reports two sharp interviews with Passy at the end of April and on 5th May, when the old

---

[1] COS(42)124th Mtg, Item 1, of 18th April, and COS(42)105(0) of 19th April.
[2] CFR(42)11 of 25th April (also circulated as COS(42)112(0) of 26th April) and CFR(42)12 of 28th April.
[3] CFR(42)13 of 29th April.
[4] COS(42)132nd Mtg, Item 4.
[5] COS(42)134(0) of 12th May.
[6] Copy on SOE Archives File 3/100/2c.
[7] This is the impression given in SOE papers: but no record is to be found in the COS series. The first Madagascar landing at Diego Suarez had taken place on 5th May, and had similarly 'by-passed' De Gaulle.

threat of rupture of relations re-emerged.[1] This bore fruit in a letter[2] from De Gaulle himself to Mr Eden on 7th May which (this time) did embody an ultimatum, though a mild one – 'until co-operation of the British and French Special Services can be established on a satisfactory footing, ours will restrict themselves in their relations with yours to matters in hand'. A copy of this was sent with a letter to the CIGS, couched in terms likely to appeal to the soldier's point of view.

The threat remained unexecuted by De Gaulle's staff: Brigadier Gubbins and Colonel Billotte continued to meet, and apparently Billotte again saw the CIGS, this time in company with Gubbins.[3] By this time relations on 'the technical level' were generally good; there was some mutual respect for professional competence, and a pretty accurate knowledge of what cards each held in his hand, so that relations of some sort could be maintained even through political storms. By 22nd May Colonel Sporborg could report that 'Achilles has emerged from his tent, and the Free French are working away with us like beavers': meantime discussions with the Foreign Office on a draft reply went quietly forward[4] and Mr Eden's reply was not dispatched until 9th June.[5] Its most notable point is that it accepts that the CIGS is now an appropriate channel for handling these matters since it takes a letter from him to De Gaulle[6] as the main statement of the British attitude. At almost the same date, the CIGS had written to all heads of Allied governments in London asking them to treat SOE as the responsible British authority for all matters regarding resistance and its parts in British military plans:[7] and Mr Eden pressed this point in his letter to De Gaulle.

The 'détente' on the lower levels progressed, and led on 1st July to a meeting in R/F Section's quarters attended by M. Diethelm, Colonel Billotte and Emmanuel d'Astier, as well as the main SOE officers concerned. All present seem to have agreed on the common-sense proposal that there should be a working committee to exercise effective control of all British and French special operations in France, subject of course to confirmation by higher authority when necessary.

---

1 See his Minutes of 1st and 6th May 1942; on SOE Archives File 3/100/2c.
2 Copy on SOE Archives File (AD/S.1) SC.38/4.
3 See Brigadier Gubbins's Minutes of 14th and 20th May, on SOE Archives File 3/100/2c.
4 See in particular SOE's formal comments on De Gaulle's letter: letter to Mr Strang dated 28th May 1942, on SOE Archives File (AD/S.1) SC.38/4.
5 Copy on SOE Archives File (AD/S.1) SC.38/4.
6 Not in SOE files.
7 Letter of 2nd June 1942; copy on SOE Archives File 1/470/1: COS(42)178th Mtg, Item 7, of 13th June refers. See below p. 359.

On the French side, the idea goes back to Emmanuel d'Astier's proposals in May:[1] the British must inevitably have thought of the Anglo-Norwegian Co-ordinating Committee, just then finding its feet. The membership of the Committee would have been on the French side M. Diethelm, Colonel Billotte, and a representative of Resistance inside France, for the British Colonel Buckmaster, representing F Section, R/F Section and SIS.[2]

As might have been expected, this promising proposal was torpedoed at the outset by General De Gaulle, pending the solution of certain 'grandes questions de principe',[3] and further official letters to the Foreign Office followed. The first of these[4] hammered at the topic of shortage of material aid, and the second[5] at the deplorable British tendency to act in France independently of De Gaulle's direction. The letters bore no ultimatum on the face of them, this time: but they were followed by vast and detailed indictments transmitted to SOE by Billotte and Passy:[6] and they were accompanied by an active hint. De Gaulle was enraged by the delay (due entirely to physical conditions) in carrying out Operation 'Clam', which should have carried dispatches to Moulin and Fassin,[7] and he took reprisals by refusing[8] Free French co-operation in Operation 'Whale'; this was a project for a coup de main against a VLF radio station working to U-boats from the Bordeaux area, which ultimately fell through for other reasons.

Oddly enough, there arrived next day a verbal message from the General's staff that his refusal should be disregarded. To judge from Sir Charles Hambro's comments to Major Morton,[9] SOE were not favourably impressed either by order or counter-order – 'for God's sake send that mad Joan of Arc to inspect his troops in Central Africa'.

There was however an important change under way within the De Gaulle régime: in mid-July M. André Philip arrived from France to take office as Commissaire de l'Intérieur in place of M. Diethelm, and for the first time De Gaulle had in his government a politician claiming some serious consideration in his own right. M. Philip was

---

[1] Above p. 278.

[2] Minutes of Meeting of 1st July, on SOE Archives File 3/100/2c.

[3] Minute from D/R (Colonel D. Keswick) dated 9th July 1942, on SOE Archives File 3/100/2c.

[4] Dated 18th July – Foreign Office paper No. (42)5; copy on SOE Archives File (AD/S.1) SC.38/4.

[5] Dated 5th August 1942, on SOE Archives File (AD/S.1) SC.38/4.

[6] Dated 7th and 12th August 1942; originals on SOE Archives File 3/100/2c.

[7] See SOE R/F Mission File 'Clam'.

[8] See his formal memorandum of 31st July, on SOE Archives File 3/100/2c.

[9] Letter to Major Morton dated 1st August, on SOE Archives File (AD/S.1) SC.38/4.

apparently associated with De Gaulle's letter to the Prime Minister of 21st July,[1] which was sent also to the US military representative in London, Admiral Stark. It presented far-reaching claims for Gaullist participation in operations in the West, 'which, as I see it, should be set in motion during next spring' (1943) 'at latest': these involved immense demands for equipment both for regular forces and for the Resistance. What is more (to quote again), 'it also naturally implies that the French High Command itself should control this material', and the French High Command 'must be equally associated with the organisation of the Allied High Command'. This was referred to the Chiefs of Staff, who gave very little encouragement:[2] so far as the Resistance was concerned, they stood their ground firmly on the necessity for co-ordination with SOE.

On 4th August M. Philip saw Mr Eden[3] and also Major Morton,[4] and painted a lively picture of the disastrous confusion which would arise in the event of invasion if there were no effective co-ordination and no preliminary combined planning with the French. De Gaulle left for the Middle East in mid-August, and the storm-centre moved with him: in September there was an outbreak of violent controversy over Syria, while in London amity was restored and progress was again made toward a working collaboration. Mr Eden had acknowledged General De Gaulle's letters in writing to M. Pleven on 17th August and he wrote to the latter again on 25th August[5] refusing to accept a claim by De Gaulle to jurisdiction over Frenchmen who had joined the British forces. The British Government had issued a communiqué on 13th July on the occasion of a reconstitution of the French National Committee and the change of name from Free France to Fighting France: and De Gaulle built on its wording a claim to direct all French nationals, wherever they might be, who were preparing the liberation of France by a common victory. In one aspect this was a direct attack on F Section: and the Foreign Office replied by making it clear that De Gaulle's authority extended only to volunteers – a large enough jurisdiction, but one which had been conceded long ago.

This was apparently accepted, and the next step was an amicable dinner on the evening of 2nd September at which M. Philip was present with Colonel Billotte and Colonel Passy, and on the other side

---

1 COS(42)212(0) of 25th July – Annex I.
2 COS(42)220th Mtg, Item 5, of 28th July.
3 The paper which he handed to Mr Eden on this occasion is in File F.38/Pt I. On 8th August Mr Eden submitted to the War Cabinet a somewhat 'Gaullist' paper WP(42)349: see below p. 293.
4 Major Morton's report to Brigadier Hollis is in F.38/I.
5 Copy on SOE Archives File 3/100/1(a).

Sir Charles Hambro, Brigadier Gubbins and Colonel Keswick.[1] From this emerged a revival of the co-ordinating committee scheme, this time on two levels, Senior and Junior, concerned respectively with policy and the execution of policy: the latter should be under the chairmanship of the senior air officer of SOE, and should consist of one representative of SOE and one of the Fighting French. As will be seen, this was narrower than the original project – F Section and SIS were not included. The Senior Committee was still-born, but the Junior one began to operate in September 1942, and was confirmed by General De Gaulle on his return.[2] This amounted to little more than a formal recognition of existing practice; but it was at least a first step to the final integration of all command over French Resistance, eventually secured in June 1944.

Conclusion

Here we must pause for the present. In one sense the halting place is a logical one. From late summer 1942 all efforts were concentrated on the North African landing, all action and all political relations with De Gaulle and with other Frenchmen were coloured by its imminence: the success of the landing made a revolutionary change in the whole situation and in the inter-relation of the parties to it, and development henceforward moves rapidly in one direction. In another sense, it is not easy to pause at the outset of this new phase, because there is little solid ground on which to rest. There were several promising lines, but virtually no realisable assets.

F Section's own men in the field were few and their equipment negligible. On the other hand, they were in contact with the 'Carte' organisation, which appeared to be interested more in military action than in politics: it talked in terms of cadres, of training, of military equipment, and there was more than a hint that it was the 'alter ego' of the French Army. Its titular 'second-in-command', Major Frager, had been in England, and Major Bodington was now in France to establish relations with 'Carte' (Girard) himself. A decision on how far it was to be backed as against De Gaulle could be taken only on Bodington's return.[3] Meantime F Section's Directive for the three months to November 1942 was very limited in its scope.[4]

---

[1] There are three records of this: by Sir Charles Hambro and by the French, on SOE Archives File 3/100/2c: a more official SOE record is on (AD/S.1) file SC.38/4.

[2] Note letters from Mr Eden (26th October) and Lord Selborne (27th October) to De Gaulle on his return, 'clearing the record' of his August letters: SOE File 3/100/2c.

[3] See below p. 566.

[4] Dated 26th August 1942; copy on SOE Archives File 3/470/1(a).

De Gaulle had rather more men in the field, and the flow of their messages through the SOE wireless station was much greater than those of F Section. But SOE viewed his activities with doubt and even suspicion.[1] This was in part a matter of exasperation at the 'mad Joan of Arc' and his methods. But it rested also on more solid ground. In the first place, there was good evidence that De Gaulle was personally resented by those Frenchmen who still had arms in their hands, and that his assistance would be an item on the debit side in any operation which involved the French Army and Navy. In the second place, his bent as seen by SOE was political and not military: he was engaged in detaching all groupings of French opinion from Vichy and consolidating them round himself, but not on a basis of an active and persistent offensive against the enemy. He was in contact with groups of all shades, from the Communists on the Left to Colonel de la Rocque's Parti Social Français and the Monarchists on the Right: but all his contacts were men of words and formulae, not of action. They had no arms, and (except for the Communists) they did not show any excessive anxiety to acquire them.

On the other hand, it had to be admitted that De Gaulle had made great strides politically. Free French broadcasting[2] was more effective than was perhaps intended by the British in building him up as the sole symbol of Fighting France and of a national regeneration which most Frenchmen in their hearts passionately desired, however they might differ about its form. At the same time French opinion was awaking from defeatism to a conviction that the Allies were the winning side, and after Laval's return in April Vichy had gone too far to represent any hope for the continuity and future of France in the event of an Allied victory. The only hopes were the Army or De Gaulle, and De Gaulle took the greatest pains to see that politicians of all shades should prefer De Gaulle. It was quite possible that in the event of Vichy bankruptcy the whole game would be thrown into his hands.

All these considerations were argued out within SOE, and SOE's internal debates are reflected on higher levels with (so far as one can trace) little modification from other sources – SIS, PWE and the Americans. The Foreign Office (thought SOE) was becoming 'more

---

[1] See paper of 31st July, 'The Position of General de Gaulle and Fighting France vis-a-vis resistance in France to-day' (copy on SOE Archives File 3/100/2c): draft Aide-Mémoire for the COS prepared by the JPS about 16th August: 'Participation of General De Gaulle in Preparations for Operations in France' (copy in same file): paper by Colonel Keswick dated 1st September 1942 'Relations with Fighting France' (copy in same file).

[2] Apart from facilities given by the BBC, the Free French clandestine station 'Radio Gaulle' was opened by PWE in August 1941. Garnett's 'History of PWE', p. 238.

and more Gaullist as time goes on',[1] and this was reflected in Mr Eden's paper of 8th August[2] on 'Fighting French participation in operations in France'. In particular, Mr Eden suggested that SOE's role as co-ordinator of Resistance should be re-examined, in the light of the memorandum presented by M. Philip on 4th August – a big step towards De Gaulle's position. The War Cabinet verdict[3] on this paper was enigmatic, but not anti-Gaullist; it defined existing policy as –

(a) The continuance of SOE as the 'co-ordinating authority of all secret preparatory action in France' [i.e. stand fast against De Gaulle's claim to operate uncontrolled].

(b) Ensuring closer collaboration between General de Gaulle and the various departments and organisations concerned with secret preparatory action in Occupied and Unoccupied France.

   This should be without prejudice to the maintenance of our present contacts in Occupied and Unoccupied France which need not be disclosed to General De Gaulle's Headquarters. [i.e. be kind to De Gaulle but trust him as little as possible].[4]

(c) The co-ordination by SOE in particular of all operational activities in France to prevent overlapping [a point directed mainly toward PWE and SIS].[5]

Beyond this, the Cabinet directed only that our policy should be further examined by representatives of the Foreign Office and SOE 'in the light of the discussions which had taken place'. The results of this examination are represented by Major Morton's very able paper of 11th September.[6] The last paragraphs of this paper are the distilled and balanced expression of British expert opinion as it stood in September 1942, and will serve fittingly to conclude this section.

General de Gaulle's future in French public life will depend largely on relations between himself and the Generals at the head of the

---

[1] See note by Colonel Sporborg dated 5th August, on SOE File 3/100/2c, reflecting Lord Selborne's view as well as his own. Cf. Mr Eden's amendments to the Anglo-American plan for Psychological Warfare in the French Empire dated 15th October 1942: quoted in Garnett's 'History of PWE', p. 225.

[2] WP(42)349 of 8th August.

[3] WM(42)114th Mtg, Min. 2, dated 20th August.

[4] Cf. Mr Eden's letter to the CIGS dated 27th July on the security of the FFL HQ, a relatively favourable view; copy on SOE Archives File 3/100/1(a).

[5] Cf. the remarks by Major General Kennedy at COS(42)147th Mtg, Item 6; of 11th May, on the importance of centralising under SOE all operational activities in North Africa, and the directive for this theatre given to SOE in COS(42)134(O) of 12th May.

[6] CFR(42)37 of 11th September; copy on SOE Archives File 3/100/1(a).

French Army, who will probably control the military and the immediate political situation when the time for action comes. These
Generals, whoever they may be, will probably be ready to accept
General de Gaulle's co-operation if they think it of value to their
own plans. At present the most they are likely to offer him is a
post as their representative with the Allied Armies. They will not
offer him a High Command of French Forces. Their acceptance of
him at a later date as a political leader in France will depend largely
on the political support he can obtain outside the army, and to no
small extent on the support given to him meanwhile by the British
and American Governments. The belief persists that he is an instrument of British policy.

Meanwhile there is no doubt that, although General De Gaulle
at present carries little weight in France, save as a symbol of resistance, any action by His Majesty's Government interpreted by the
French people as an unjustified betrayal of General De Gaulle,
would seriously alienate French sympathy for this country.

I would emphasize that although these conclusions may be correct
to-day, the shifting sands of French public opinion may invalidate
them a few weeks hence. The situation should be kept under close
review.

CHAPTER XII

The Low Countries*

The cases of Holland and Belgium have a good deal in common; access to both countries was extremely difficult, in spite of their nearness to British shores. The short sea crossing was attractive, but in fact the coasts were from the first too strongly held for it to be of any value: various attempts were made to organise sea operations, but none of them were successful. Air operations were not much easier. Both countries are thickly populated, except for the Ardennes in the south of Belgium, which are inconveniently remote from the main centres of population and industry: so that landing operations were almost impossible and it was difficult even to find suitable dropping zones. What was worse, the direct bomber route to the Ruhr lay across this territory, and the Germans gave it very high priority for all kinds of air defence – guns, search-lights, night-fighters, radar equipment: it was exceptionally unhealthy for a heavily laden aircraft to pause there and circle at a low level to find the faint lights of a reception committee, and the RAF justifiably disliked it.

The military importance of the Low Countries also meant that they were well guarded by the German Security Services, both Sicherheitsdienst (civil) and Abwehr (military). These were on the worst of terms with one another, and they were not otherwise conspicuously inefficient, and their pressure on nascent resistance movements was intense. Their power was increased by mistakes in SOE, due partly to inexperience, partly to the external difficulties: and both in Holland and in Belgium there were setbacks of a disastrous kind, which shook SOE's credit badly and delayed the development of effective resistance. It is not clear that the quality of the SOE Dutch and Belgium sections was lower than that of the other 'Country Sections'; but it was very late in the day before they settled down as working organisations.

Politically, there are again parallels between the two countries: but there were also big differences, and it will be best to treat them separately.

---

* [M. R. D. Foot, *SOE in the Low Countries*, the official history, awaits publication.]

1. Belgium*

Politically the Belgian Government was one of the weakest of the Allied governments in exile. The Cabinet in office in May 1940 had left Belgium soil when it was overrun by the Germans: the King** had stayed, and had surrendered on 28th May with his Army. In France, the Cabinet split: part accepted the view that the more patriotic role was to stay with their own people, the rump reached England in October 1940, under the leadership of M. Pierlot,† and was accepted there as the legitimate government of Belgium. But it was weak in personalities, in manpower, in all other resources (except control of the Belgian Congo);[1] and it lacked confidence in its own position. Out of this situation grew intrigues and suspicions, accusations and counter-accusations, and the files are full of bickerings between SOE and the Belgian Government, which cannot be examined in detail here.[2]

As with most European countries, one basic difficulty was the duality of civil and military authorities within the Government. The '2ème Section' under the Belgian Ministry of Defence in London was staffed by officers of the Belgian Army, and was concerned with matters affecting the renascence of the Belgian Army in Belgium. Over against it was the Sûreté de l'État [PASSAGE DELETED ON GROUNDS OF NATIONAL SECURITY] under a certain M. Lepage,†† who had direct access to M. Pierlot, and was concerned with all secret political matters. [PASSAGE DELETED.] The Sûreté's case against the Army was that the latter was right-wing in its sympathies and above all loyal to the King: it was not interested in sabotage or in any action against the Germans except in order to increase its own strength: and it would use its strength, when the Germans withdrew, to re-establish the King with a 'crypto-Fascist' regime. The Army's case was that

---

[1] The exiled government was in a very sound financial position, and paid all expenses incurred on Belgian Resistance except the pay of agents who belonged to British forces and the 'overhead' costs of SOE for arms, aircraft, training, etc.

[2] SOE Archives File 4/100/2, and D/R Belgian Files contain most of the important papers: there is a useful History of the Belgian Section by Major Amies. In Belgium the collection of material for the history of Resistance is in the hands of a Historical Commission (Sec. Major Lejeune), address Ministère de la Défense Nationale, Office de la Résistance, Historique de la Résistance Belge, 2, Avenue Palmerston, Brussels. [(Sir) Hardy Amies, born 1909, royal dressmaker, knight 1989, head of T section 1943–6. See his *Just So Far* (1954) and *Still Here* (1984).]

* [H. Bernard, *La Résistance 1940–1945* (Brussels, 1968), useful summary by a leading participant.]

** [Leopold III, 1901–83, King of Belgium 1934–51, house arrest 1940–44, prisoner in Germany 1944–5. See Roger Keyes, *Outrageous Fortune* (2 vols, 1984–6).]

† [H. Pierlot, 1883–1963, count 1945.]

†† [Died a baron, *c.* 1990.]

M. Pierlot stood for nobody but himself, and that Lepage was using his position without scruple to hamper and destroy any movement within Belgium which could interfere with the political future of the government in exile. Unfortunately these accusations had some foundation on both sides.

After an early indeterminate phase, SOE's first instinct was to collaborate with Lepage, who had the upper hand within the Belgian Government: as elsewhere, it was difficult to operate without the support of the recognised Government in the recruitment of agents, the assessment of political feeling, the preparation of attacks on industry, and in countless other ways. This policy was associated with Mr Dadson,* who was head of the Belgian Section from December 1940 until about the end of November 1941, when he was replaced by Major C. T. Knight.** It involved the sharing of agents, the planning of missions in common, the pooling of information: SOE kept control of W/T communications, and reserved the right to have its own agents, but it was willing to consider (if need be) control of operations through a joint committee, on the lines which proved successful in Norway.[1]

By the end of 1941 this policy had broken down. Evidence was accumulating that Lepage at least (and probably his masters) were concerned primarily to hamper SOE's policy, both in promoting continuous sabotage and in building up a Secret Army: the former meant (perhaps) provoking reprisals and therefore hostility in Belgium to the exiled government, the latter meant arming the opponents of the government. This total absence of common ground expressed itself in many small ways: difficulty in recruiting agents, secret issue of orders contradicting those of SOE, obstruction of the escape from Belgium of men required by SOE, and so on. The atmosphere within Belgian circles in Britain was full of suspicion, gossip and intrigue; and no frank relations were possible between SOE and their official contacts.

The year 1942 is full of SOE's attempts to escape from this vicious circle. Discussions began in February with a meeting between M. Pierlot and M. Gutt (his Minister of Defence) on one side and Brigadier Gubbins and Major Keswick on the other; a friendly enough meeting, but leading only to an exchange of letters in which M. Pierlot made it absolutely plain that control must rest with M. Lepage. This

---

[1] Difficulties of working with the Belgian Government can be seen from SOE Archives Files (DR/Plans) 'Belgium 3 Vols 1 & 2'.

* [E. Dadson, managed Antwerp gas works 1934–40, head of T section 1940–41, later in PWE, died 1995.]

** [*c.* 1914–96, Coldstream Guards, had worked in military liaison, head of T section 1941–3, later in PWE.]

was accepted but not agreed by SOE, an ambiguity which was a source of trouble later.

By June the matter had reached a 'higher level', Mr Eden saw M. Spaak,* the Belgian Foreign Minister, on 4th June, and did his best to pin him down as regards co-operation with SOE. A few days later M. Pierlot lunched alone with Brigadier Gubbins, and the ground was gone over once again. Brigadier Gubbins's hand was strengthened by the letter on the functions of SOE which General Brooke had sent on behalf of the Chiefs of Staff to all Allied Governments a few days before:[1] but, even so, no agreement of any kind was reached. Lord Selborne was equally unsuccessful at a meeting with M. Spaak early in July.

A little progress was made on 27th July, when Brigadier Gubbins saw M. Spaak while M. Pierlot was absent in the Congo; and Lepage's hand seemed to lie a little lighter. But the agreement was withdrawn as soon as offered. An acid exchange of letters led on 14th August to an essay by M. Spaak in the manner of De Gaulle: 'relations were broken off' on the very 'Gaullish' pretext that SOE had hampered the Belgian Government in its dealings with an emissary of a military organisation, the Légion Belge, who was then in England. SOE laid the matter before Mr Eden and the Chiefs of Staff, and there for the moment it rested.

Relations recovered slowly from this low point. A certain M. Delfosse, a former Minister of Justice, recently arrived from Belgium, was appointed to the Government as Minister of Information and Justice toward the end of September, and was given control both of the Sûreté and of the 2ème Section, apparently with a view to finding a compromise. But he was slow to make advances, and on 29th October 1942 Sir Charles Hambro laid the matter before the Chiefs of Staff, on the basis that SOE were prevented by the action of the Belgian Government from fulfilling their directive, and must make a new departure by independent action in Belgium: he suggested that the Chiefs of Staff should themselves bring pressure to bear on these lines.[2] The Chiefs of Staff evaded direct action, but apparently the hint of it brought a slight concession: Lord Selborne saw M. Delfosse shortly afterwards, and with great reluctance agreed that the Sûreté should continue (under the Minister) to be the responsible Belgian authority, provided that all matters of 'action' were delegated by it to

---

[1] See below p. 359.

[2] COS (42)386(0) of 7th November: taken COS(42)312th Mtg, Item 7, of 9th November.

* [P. H. Spaak, 1899–1972, a founding father of the European Community.]

the 2ème Section, and kept rigidly apart from its other activities.[1] This arrangement rested only on Belgian assurances, and could clearly be no more than a temporary respite.

This political background coloured all activity in the field during the same period. The quality of agents available was low, their training was imperfect and their morale was bad: only a few of those first sent reached a tolerable standard of patriotism and resolution. Nor were they well served by their backers in London, whether British or Belgian.

An outline plan had been produced in May 1941 for the establishment in each of the nine provinces of Belgium of an SOE organiser with his own wireless operator, in order to build up an 'underground' from local recruits; this was in accord with the usual SOE conceptions at this stage, but had very little relation to what happened in practice. The first operation took place on 12th May 1941, and consisted of one team of organiser and W/T operator, and a single agent sent in collaboration with PWE (then SO1) with a political mission to the Liberal and Socialist Parties. This man remained at large for over a year, and eventually returned to England: but the organising team achieved nothing, and at least one of them was arrested early. Rather more progress was made in the third quarter of 1941, when three teams and two independent organisers were put in; the teams do not seem to have been of very high quality, but one of the organisers, the Abbé Jourdain, did good work and eventually returned safely. Wireless communication was opened for the first time, and dividends began to appear in the shape of sabotage reports and news of independent local organisations. As usual, the evidence of sabotage cannot be very strictly assessed; but it is clear that possibilities of action did exist. Two more teams went in towards the end of the year, and the first two supply-dropping operations took place. A Lysander operation was tried in December to bring out two agents, but a German patrol arrived on the ground as the aircraft landed, and the pilot was only able to escape by taking off again instantly in a hail of bullets: an incident which did not encourage the RAF in its dealings with Belgium.[2]

So far, to the end of 1941, developments were relatively favourable: at least no worse than in other theatres. Sixteen agents had gone in, five wireless sets were on the air, and only one arrest had been reported.

---

[1] Reported to the Chiefs of Staff in COS(42)422(0) of 30th November: Taken COS(42)341st Mtg, Item 6, of 6th December.

[2] There were no more Lysander operations to Belgium: one Lysander operation to France was arranged for an agent of the Belgian Section.

There was encouraging news of sabotage and local resistance. At this point German counter-action took effect, and there was a wave of arrests early in 1942; what was worse, two wireless sets were captured and operated by the Germans. The deception was effective for at least six months, with disastrous results in almost the whole fabric of the organisation. The following figures give a clear picture of what happened:

1942	1st Quarter	2nd Quarter	3rd Quarter	4th Quarter
Agents sent (total)	13	9	6	8
Of these, dropped to				
German reception	–	4	5	–
Agents arrested (total)	9	9	13	1
Store-dropping Ops (total)	–	9	7	1
Of these, dropped to				
German reception	–	6	7	1
W/T sets in operation				
during period	9	6	8	8
Of these, operated by				
Germans	2	5	8	7

It will be seen how the arrests early in the year, of which SOE at the time knew nothing, permitted a complete penetration of the organisation, until in the third quarter what the SOE Belgian Section conceived to be its organisation in the field was no more than a mirage created by the Gestapo. At that stage suspicion was aroused in London, and the fourth quarter represents a new departure, in which the joke is to some extent turned against the Germans. The old contacts are avoided, and agents are kept clear of the contaminated organisation; a genuine wireless channel is again established outside the German net.

Penetration of this kind is an ever-present danger in underground operations, and perhaps the worst that can be said of SOE's Belgian Section (and the Dutch Section also) is that in their inexperience they ignored it until taught by disaster. There were many contributory causes. Agents were ill-trained and too readily disposed to take risks and make unnecessary contacts and confidences. The codes used were at this stage relatively simple, and were easily broken and adopted by the Germans. SOE's wireless communications were run by SIS till the early summer of 1942, and it was not possible for SOE themselves to maintain an elaborate check on the form of messages as a clue to the identity of the senders. Belgium was a difficult country for air operations, and there was a temptation to build up too much on a limited number of contacts; yet even a blind drop is safer than one to a 'reception' committee arranged by the Gestapo. It is easy to see – after the event – how the trouble arose and how safeguards could have been taken: it was not so easy to apply them at the time.

In spite of the almost complete 'black-out' in the summer of 1942, there were one or two important developments which give a thread of continuity. The most important of these was the growth of contacts with the 'Secret Army'. The first landmark here was the arrival in England in March 1942 of two officers, Commandant Grisar and Commandant Bernard,* who had been associated with the Secret Army in Belgium: these two were given posts in the 2ème Section of the Ministry of Defence, from which they maintained a somewhat reckless campaign against M. Lepage, in pretty close liaison with SOE. Then, in July 1942, one of SOE's few really good agents, [Comte] P. de Liedekerke, brought back Commandant Glazer, the head of one of the para-military organisations, the 'Légion Belge': de Liedekerke had been sent early in 1942 to contact an organisation known as the 'Chemises Khaki', believed to consist of Royalist officers: he had found that it was politically unreliable, and had turned to other possibilities. Commandant Glazer represented a real patriotic and anti-German movement, though its scope and affiliations were not easy to sort out: but unfortunately he seems himself to have been reckless, obstinate and indiscreet – a dangerous man as an underground leader. Still worse, he appeared in England to represent an SOE and 2ème Section intrigue against the Sûreté: and when he returned to the field in August it was without any proper directive from the recognised Belgian authorities. In his absence from Belgium (it appears) the 'Secret Army' had been reorganised from within so as to leave him on one side: and he did not resume a central position, though he seems to have been leader of a rival faction until his arrest in the summer of 1943. One or two other missions went out in the summer of 1942, under the joint auspices of the 2ème Section and SOE, but they were without exception failures, either through previous Gestapo penetration, or through disasters of their own. There was at the time much suspicion that M. Lepage had in some way counter-worked them: but no confirmation whatever was found for this after the Armistice, and the story can safely be dismissed.

The other point of interest is the part played by PWE missions, which were of particular importance in this phase of bad relations between SOE and the Sûreté. A very narrow line divides a secret mission directed to investigate and support underground propaganda from one sent to further active resistance: but the former could be

---

* [Henri Bernard, later professor at Belgian war college. See his *Guerre totale et guerre révolutionnaire* (6 vols, Brussels, 1960–66), a leading textbook.]

organised through PWE, and PWE's relations with the propaganda section of the Sûreté were relatively good. From the first mission in 1941 PWE in this field had a good deal to do with the development of political contacts, and in 1942 there were some ten missions jointly organised by PWE and the Sûreté on this basis, and sent to the field through SOE's organisation. On the whole, they were kept pretty clear both of the disasters of SOE's own 'circuits' and of the political wrangles which involved the Secret Army; their work provided a very valuable link between this first unhappy stage and the more prosperous and active resistance of 1943 and 1944.

2. Holland[1]*

The Dutch Government, even after the Japanese attack on the East Indies, was much stronger politically than the Belgian. The Queen** and the Royal Family were in England: the Cabinet had travelled with them as a body:[2] and there was no ambiguity about Holland's position in the war – it was clear that there had been no surrender, only a local armistice in face of overwhelming force. Yet in spite of these advantages SOE found difficulties in dealing with the Dutch Government which were curiously similar to those with M. Pierlot and M. Lepage. Dr Gerbrandy, the Prime Minister, took comparatively little part: but there existed a Dutch Secret Service under a civilian, M. Van't Sant, who had great personal influence in Court circles, and who was believed to favour a policy of 'ca'canny' as regards active resistance, though he was keen enough on intelligence and particularly on political intelligence. Over against him stood the Military Intelligence Service (MID) under an officer of the Dutch Marines, Colonel de Bruyne, who was from the first warmly interested in plans for the formation of a Secret Army and eager to co-operate with SOE: but there were the usual doubts as to the role of

---

1   There is a useful history of the Dutch Section by Colonel Dobson and Captain Mills. Some of the political papers are on SOE Archives Files 5/100/2 and 5/470/1, also D/R files on 'Holland'; but these are far from complete. In Holland material for the history of the Resistance is being collected by the Rijksinstituut voor Oorlogs-documentatie (Acting Director Dr L. de Jong), Amsterdam, Herengracht 479: much information is published monthly in the Institute's periodical 'Nederland in Oorlogstijd'.

2   The original Prime Minister (De Geer) lost heart and deserted in the summer of 1940: he was succeeded by the more resolute Gerbrandy.

*   [L. de Jong, Het Koninkrijk der Nederlanden in de tweede Wereldoorlog (14 vols in 29, The Hague, 1969–91), the fullest account of any Nazi-occupied country.]

** [Wilhelmina, 1880–1962, Queen 1890, abdicated 1948, called 'the only man in her cabinet'.]

this Secret Army – was it to attack the Germans at a moment chosen by the Allies, or to emerge only when the Allies had liberated Holland, and then to act in the interests of 'public order' and the suppression of action by the Left?

The intrigues which resulted from this situation led into some curious corners of Dutch politics, but there is no need to follow them in detail. SOE threw such weight as it had on the military side of the battle, quite without success until at last the obvious imminence of invasion forced a change. But though SOE was regarded with little favour by M. Van't Sant, matters were a little better than with Belgium: the Dutch military possessed more resources than the Belgians, they were better able to supply men and advice, and the general tone of proceedings was much less acrimonious.

SOE's original plans, which were discussed with the Dutch and in April 1942 formally embodied in 'Plan for Holland', were on the usual lines.[1] The country was to be divided into districts, each of which would be supplied with at least one organiser, instructor, and wireless operator from England: these agents would work in collaboration with the earliest of the native organisations, the 'Orde Dienst', and would arrange for it to be supplied from England and for its action to be co-ordinated with the Allied plans. Open sabotage was for the present to be discouraged, as likely to expose the population to reprisals: but plans were to be laid for attacks on industrial targets, and the Resistance were to do what damage they could by 'insaississable' methods.

The plan was straightforward enough, its execution was a débâcle which had serious effects both on Dutch resistance and on SOE's standing as a department. As in the Belgian case, the story is best summarised in figures, which necessarily take us somewhat beyond the first phase of SOE's work.

	Agents Dispatched	'Received' by Germans	Survived	Missing or died	Executed
1941					
Sept.	2	–	1	1	–
Oct.	Nil				
Nov.	2	–	1	–	1
Dec.	Nil				
1942					
Jan.	Nil				
Feb.	1	–	1	–	–
Mar.	5	1	–	2	3

[1] See 'Outline of Planning for 1942' – in Dutch Section History under 1942.

	Agents Dispatched	'Received' by Germans	Survived	Missing or died	Executed
Apr.	3	2	–	–	3
May	2	2	–	–	2
June	4	4	–	1	3
July	1	1	–	–	1
Aug.	Nil				
Sept.	4	4	–	1	3
Oct.	11	11	–	4	7
Nov.	2	2	1	–	1
Dec.	Nil				
1943					
Jan.	Nil				
Feb.	8	8	–	2	6
Mar.	3	3	1	–	2
Apr.	2	2	–	1	1
May	3	3	–	–	3
June–Aug.	Nil				
Sept.	1	–	1	–	–
Oct.	2	–	2	–	–
(No further operations till 31st March 1944)					
Totals	56	43	8	12	36[1]

During the same period 544 containers of stores were dropped, all into German hands: they contained *inter alia*:

High Explosive	12,863 lbs
Sten Guns	744
Pistols	2,306
Clams & Limpets (explosive devices)	823

Over 350,000 Dutch florins were issued to agents up to the end of 1943. Eleven RAF aircraft were lost on operations.

This picture is an appalling one. For a period of about fifteen months the Dutch Section had patiently planned the creation of resistance in Holland. It had recruited agents, had trained them elaborately and briefed them for special missions within a general plan: a stream of

---

[1] Most of these men were held until September 1944, then executed together at Mauthausen concentration camp.

wireless traffic had passed between England and Holland: aircraft had been sent on difficult operations, in a heavily defended area, and had delivered men and stores to their destinations in face of heavy casualties. SOE had a full and detailed picture of the organisation thus created, and reported confidently on its potentialities. The reality behind it consisted only of two able German officers of the Abwehr, Oberstleutnant Giskes* and Sonderführer Huntemann; and some forty agents in concentration camps.

There have naturally been elaborate inquests into the consequence of events, and lessons have been learnt, marked and digested.[1] It is not necessary to do more here than indicate briefly what happened.

The first mission was not sent until September 1941, but was relatively successful: nothing very definite was achieved, but the two men kept out of German hands, and one of them got back to England by boat in February 1942 with useful general information. The other seems to have been lost at sea. The next mission, in November, 1941, was the first to carry a wireless set, and it succeeded in establishing satisfactory communication with the United Kingdom and in contacting native resistance. Unfortunately the Germans were already well served by stool-pigeons in the Dutch organisations, and they came to hear of a supply-dropping operation, which had been arranged for 27th February 1942. They secured the stores which were then dropped; this also gave them conclusive proof that some wireless transmitter was in touch with England. The wireless location services went into action at once, and the operator** was caught in The Hague on 7th March. He was speedily persuaded to transmit messages under German control, and the first signal which passed in this way was sent on 18th March 1942. To be fair to the agent, he endeavoured to draw SOE's attention to the trick by omitting the agreed 'secret identity check'; but this was ignored in London, as being merely an instance of the carelessness natural in agents.

Before this turning-point there had been one or two other missions which began work independently of German control. In February 1942, one man was sent to get in touch with the underground press and with the Trade Union movement: contacts were made successfully, but he had no wireless operator and no source of money or

---

[1]   The JIC reported on the affair (so far as then known) in JIC(43)517(0) of 22nd December, and the facts are very carefully recorded in the Dutch Section History and in SOE Archives File 62/470/1.2. There is also an interesting record of the interrogations of Giskes and Huntemann after the Armistice – at present held by Mr N. Mott, MO1(SP).

*   [H. J. Giskes, 1896–c. 1980; see his *London Calling North Pole* (1953).]

** [H. Lauwers, born 1915, wrote appendix to Giskes's book. See also L. Marks, *From Silk to Cyanide* (1999).]

supplies, so that there was not much scope for development. He eventually lost heart and managed to escape via Switzerland, reaching England again in September 1942. Two other missions in March 1942, and one in April, were at first uncontrolled: but their contacts soon led them to 'contaminated' organisations, and by early May all these had been gathered in. All later operations were part of a single chain leading back to the initial error; the first drop to a reception committee controlled by the Germans was made on 27th March 1942, and forty-two other agents went the same way up to May 1943. The system was in theory one of unconnected 'cells': in fact (unknown to London) all these cells derived from a single focal point, which had been occupied by the Germans almost at the outset.

The mystification might have broken down at several points. One agent had an intelligence role, which the Germans felt it was beyond them to counterfeit and he had to be fictitiously 'killed in landing'. There was always the chance that one of the captured men might get away: or that rumours of what was happening would leak out and reach England through the SIS or some other channel. The bluff itself worked perfectly – after all (in the nature of things) the Germans knew far more about Dutch resistance than did SOE, and they were technically more skilled; but they were lucky to be able to maintain it for so long without accidents. Suspicion did not arise until a report was received in June 1943 [PASSAGE DELETED ON GROUNDS OF NATIONAL SECURITY] that eight parachutists had been arrested 'some time ago'. This led to a thorough overhaul by the two British organisations acting together. Wireless contact was maintained through the old channels, but operations were stopped and all messages were thoroughly scrutinised.

In September 1943, began the attempt to build up again. One man was dropped in Paris, in order to make his own way to Holland, and to check a contact given by one of the controlled sets: he visited the man in question, found his surroundings very suspicious, and managed to get back to England himself in November. Two others were to be dropped in October 1943 in Belgium: the aircraft was shot down by a night-fighter but the men escaped and found their way to Brussels. There they made 'resistance' contacts which led only to the German Security Police. One of them was arrested, the other was used as a sop to quiet the suspicions which the Germans could already feel rising in London: he was escorted and assisted, all unwitting, by a German 'stool-pigeon', and eventually got back to England in December.

At this point the gaff was finally blown by the arrival in Switzerland of two of SOE's men* who had escaped in August 1943 from Haaren

---

* [One of these wrote a book: P. Dourlein, *Inside North Pole* (1953).]

concentration camp, where they had been imprisoned since their arrival and very thoroughly interrogated: the interrogation had made it perfectly plain to them that the whole organisation was under German control, and this was the news which reached SOE in unmistakeable form from Switzerland in mid-November 1943.

This total collapse could not be kept dark within the inner circle of government in London, and it had a very bad effect on SOE's reputation at a crucial period of its history.[1] The immediate effect was a ban on all air operations to Holland, which was not raised until the end of March 1944. Wireless traffic was maintained, but in a very non-committal form. The position must thus have become pretty plain to Giskes and Huntemann, and they had definite confirmation from some SIS agents who were caught early in 1944. They 'signed off' in a message dated (appropriately enough) 1st April 1944:

> Messrs Blunt, Bingham and Successors, Ltd London. In the last time you are trying to make business in the Netherlands without our assistance. We think this rather unfair in view of our long and successful co-operation as your sole agents. But never mind, whenever you will come to pay a visit to the Continent you may be assured that you will be received with the same care and result as all those you sent us before. So long.

The best that can be said for this affair is that it did not seriously involve the indigenous resistance movements. The Germans had caught SOE's organisation at so early a stage that there were few threads leading to any real centre of resistance; the Germans could not learn much from SOE that they did not already know. Their chief gain was that until very shortly before D-day they completely thwarted any attempt to build Dutch resistance into the Allied plans and to equip it in readiness for action. The resistance existed and was stubbornly active, though ill-organised and riddled by German agents. The illegal papers, of which the most important were 'Het Parool', 'Je Maintiendrai', and 'Trouw', maintained a continuous existence; and were well written and actively circulated. The 'Orde Dienst', to which reference has been made earlier, also kept its continuity as a loose organisation related to all the old political parties of the Centre. As its name implies, it saw its role primarily that of 'amateur police' to maintain order in the wake of the departing Germans, and it had an anti-Communist flavour about it which lent itself a little to German exploitation: but it represented the real national feeling of the respectable Dutch. Independently, there existed an active organisation

---

[1] See below p. 415.

'Centrum van Sabotage VI' (CX VI),* which was built more on the 'cellular' lines of a revolutionary organisation, and did not disclaim contact with Communism: its purpose was violent and practical action – the elimination of traitors, the provision of forged papers, the destruction of German labour service records, and so forth – and its record for courage and security was good. But at this stage it was lamed by lack of contact with the outer world; and the development of a Secret Army was equally retarded. The central Raad van Verzet (RVV, Council of Resistance), which was to link these rudimentary organisations together, apparently did not emerge until the summer of 1943, after the failure of an ill co-ordinated general strike in May of that year.

Within the limitations imposed by the Dutch terrain, there was plenty of material here for effective action, and it proved possible in 1944 to recover a substantial amount of the lost ground.

---

* [CS6 stood for Corelli Straat 6, the Amsterdam address of one of its leaders, and not (as many subordinates, as well as Mackenzie, supposed) for Centrum van Sabotage 6.]

CHAPTER XIII

Poland and Czechoslovakia

In spite of great contrasts between them in history and temperament, these two countries formed a natural group for the purposes of SOE.[1]

This was in part a historical accident. They were the first non-German countries to be overrun by the Third Reich, and the problem of 'subversion' arose there many months before SOE was thought of. In the early days of the war MI(R) (so far as any allocation of functions existed) was responsible for encouraging guerilla warfare in countries at war with Germany, while D Section dealt principally with action in and through neutral territory. As we have seen,[2] Major Gubbins (as he then was) was attached to the British Military Mission in Poland during the short campaign of 1939, with the task of encouraging irregular warfare. The fighting was over too soon for anything to be achieved, but the 'Gubbins Mission' kept its role and was attached to the Polish government in exile in Paris. As early as October 1939,[3] Major Gubbins was discussing underground warfare there with General Sikorski and his Chief of Staff; and at the same time he opened discussions with the Czech C-in-C, General Ingr. His Mission continued to be responsible for this liaison until he was posted to command the Independent Companies in Norway in April 1940; and his deputy, Major Wilkinson,* took over. MI(R), while it existed, remained the parent department in London, and the liaison mission came with the Polish and Czech Commands when it became necessary for them to leave France in June 1940. It was not until the end of November, when the War Office had finally shaken off the responsibilities for subversion acquired by MI(R), that underground military activities in Poland and Czechoslovakia were transferred formally to SOE. Almost at the same date Brigadier Gubbins was posted to SOE as Director of Training and Operations, and it

---

[1] Useful narratives are available for Poland, 'Polish Minorities', and Czechoslovakia.

[2] Above p. 44.

[3] Memo. dated 31st October 1939: Appendix C to Polish History.

* [(Sir) P. A. Wilkinson, born 1914, fought in Austria 1943, knight 1970; see his *Foreign Fields* (1994).]

was natural (though illogical) that he should resume responsibility for the two countries with whose earlier story he was familiar.

To this it must be added that these two exiled governments – 'résistants de la première heure', in the favourite French phrase – both secured in some respects a privileged status, and enjoyed without question certain rights which were resolutely denied to all other allies, however influential. Both were permitted to maintain their own wireless stations in England, and to receive and dispatch messages uncensored; their signals traffic was quite uncontrolled until the special security precautions taken before the 'Overlord' D-day, and they had discretion to communicate it to SOE or not as they pleased. In addition, they were solely responsible for framing missions and selecting agents, for giving them final instructions on leaving for the field, and for interrogating them on their return. In fact the resistance movements in these cases were organised and directed not by SOE but by the governments in exile: SOE (at least in theory) was merely a supply agency, responsible for the provision of transport, equipment and money, and in part for training. It could influence events only by careful use of its resources; and it was hampered even in this by lack of the latest information from the field, which was judiciously rationed by the Polish and Czech authorities. The two countries are test cases for the experiment of giving virtually a free use of British resources to the exiled government concerned, and the results were not encouraging. But it must be remembered that SOE's archives do not contain material for a real history of resistance in Poland and Czechoslovakia; the disasters stand out plainly, but the train of causes which led up to them is often obscure, and it would be easy to condemn too hastily.[1]

Operational and political conditions also had something in common. Poland was as inaccessible by sea as the 'sea-coast of Bohemia'; access by land was almost equally difficult after the Danube lands had been overrun – one case only is recorded of an agent infiltrated into Czechoslovakia from Istanbul, and his journey from England to Bratislava took eighteen months. Thus everything depended on the air, and air operations were exceptionally difficult. The range was long, even for four-engined aircraft, and it was made longer by the necessity of deviating from a straight course in order to avoid the heavily defended areas of Germany: the flying time required was so long that there was not enough darkness to make the journey in the summer months, until a rather shorter route from the south was opened in 1943.

---

[1] SOE Archives M/Poles/Czechs/1 'Combined Policy' (2 vols) gives details of early relations with the émigré governments.

Politically and strategically the great common factor was that both countries were bound in the end to fall within the Soviet sphere of influence. The pinch was not bitterly felt so long as the Russians were fighting for their lives in front of Moscow and Stalingrad: but from the first it was plain that there could be no support on land from the West – we could give the Secret Armies in Poland and Czechoslovakia no direct help except from the air until the collapse of Germany. A national rising might be of real value to the Western Allies in the invasion of Europe; but it would be a desperate enterprise, which could be tried only once and would finally wreck the Resistance if it failed. Minor sabotage could reasonably be organised from London; but the major enterprise would only make sense as an operation of war if it were related to events in the East, not in the West. The existence of this problem was perfectly plain to both governments, but their reactions to it were very different.

1. Poland*

The root of the trouble for Poland was perhaps that its pre-war governing class (which was strongly represented in exile) had the instincts and traditions of a Great Power – a Great Power of the seventeenth century and earlier, with few resources acquired since that time to justify its claims. What is more, they conceived their country as a great military power, based socially and politically on its army, and they possessed the tradition of a conspiratorial army, part of whose glory was the bloody and unsuccessful revolts of 1830, 1848, 1863 and 1905 – revolts directed primarily against Russia, rather than against the other two partitioning powers, Prussia and Austria. These traditions were embodied in the Polish Army Command in exile, which conceived of its Secret Army in Poland on a grandiose scale, as one of the major military resources at the disposal of the Allies – a far greater potential force (in their eyes) than was available to any other exiled government, far more important too than the Polish Armed Forces outside Poland and already fighting on the Allied side.

The conception was grandiose, but not absurd. The conspiratorial tradition was strong in Poland, and the technique of secret organisation was far more readily grasped there than in Western countries. Polish patriotism in all classes was magnificent, and the nation as a whole could be regarded as enrolled without exception in the fighting forces. The terrain was not unfavourable; in a country with poor communications and wide areas of forest and marsh the nucleus of a guerilla force could maintain itself even in face of the German army

---

* [See J. Garlinski, *Poland, SOE and the Allies* (1969).]

and police. Thus if supplies could be assured (a difficult condition), there was every chance that a real Secret Army could be created: but how could it be used?

The Army's answer would be that Poland, as became a Great Power, should liberate herself; at a moment to be chosen, *before* any Allied Army 'liberated' Poland, the Poles should rise and welcome their Allies, erect and victorious. This was a dangerous picture in itself; and it was further coloured by the feeling that Poland was to meet her Allies as sovereign within the frontiers of 1939 – the Russians no less than the Germans must enter Polish soil on sufferance and not as conquerors. This was a sentiment rather than a policy; it would be hard to find any responsible and intelligent Pole who pursued it logically in all its implications. But few Poles were exempt from the sentiment; and there was no lack of irresponsible Poles to proclaim it and keep it alive. The Russians could not fail to be acutely aware of the atmosphere; and the achievement of collaboration on these terms was possible only by a political miracle.

This strong current of Polish feeling was embodied in exile in the person of General Sosnkowski, Minister without Portfolio and successor designate to the President, under whom the IInd Bureau (later its offshoot the VIth Bureau) was responsible for the organisation of the Home Army (the AK). The counter-current, of prudence, realism, limited objectives, had to some extent gained ground (but always in opposition) in the modern Poland, the Poland of lower middle-class, workers and peasants, and it held real promise for the future. But its political organisation was weak even in Poland, and it was still weaker among the exiles. In the Government it was represented by the Ministry of the Interior, at first under Professor Kot, and from July 1941 (until he became Prime Minister in June 1943) under M. Mikolajczyk; and the thesis of the Ministry was that in Occupied Poland there should be an underground civil government, as well as an underground army – and that the government must control the army.

This direct clash of wills was bridged during his lifetime by General Sikorski – the Polish gentleman who had never accepted Pilsudski and the 'Colonels' régime as a necessary part of Polish tradition. He was a political necessity to the Western Allies, as their sole hope of order and unity within the Polish camp. In addition the authority of his own character and his abilities was very great, and they were backed by the historical claims of Poland, as the country whose sacrifices had been first and greatest in the war with Hitler. He was thus unmistakably the 'doyen' of the exiled governments: less harassing perhaps than General De Gaulle, but infinitely more influential. His status was not so very far below that of the 'Big Three', and in his dealings with SOE he was unmistakably the senior partner.

The outlines of the Secret Army had been conceived even before the fall of Poland, though matters moved too fast in September 1939 for many preparations to be made. Until the spring of 1941 the southern frontier of Poland, which runs through wild country, was relatively accessible by land, and the Hungarians, who held a key position, were not unsympathetic to Polish plans. There is little to show how far progress was made by the Poles during this period: the British share, handled by MI(R), consisted only of the appointment of representatives in Budapest, Bucharest, Belgrade, Szeged and Galatz, to assist in the transport of stores which were supplied (in very limited quantities) from British sources.[1] Apparently also some beginning had been made with the planning of wireless communications, though it is not clear when these were first opened.

When the Polish Government moved to England in June 1940,[2] the question of air operations came to the fore at once: the first mention is made in a memorandum by the Head of No. 4 Military Mission on 7th August,[3] and from that date the subject is never quiet for long during the remainder of the war.[4] The first flight was made on 15th February 1941, after many delays – the first of all SOE's air operations to Europe; and it served to illustrate the extreme difficulties of the undertaking. The operation had been postponed repeatedly on account of weather conditions, and on the night chosen heavy cloud was encountered and for a large part of the course navigation was only possible by dead reckoning. The only aircraft suitable was a venerable Whitley, clumsily converted for parachute operations and equipped with special long-range tanks; its cruising speed was perhaps 120 mph at the best, and it took 11½ hours to do the journey. Three Polish officers were successfully dropped, with some 800 lbs of stores; but they landed thirty miles away from the prearranged point – the men eventually reached safety but all the stores were lost.

It is scarcely surprising that the Air Ministry refused to try again on this basis: no better aircraft could be provided before the long nights of summer excluded operations, and the next six months are a story of intensive 'lobbying' by the Poles in all quarters in order to improve the position for the winter season of 1941/42. Clearly four-engined aircraft were essential, and in 1941 heavy bombers were more esteemed by the Air Ministry than pure gold. The consistent Polish

---

[1] See list of stores in Polish History, p. 14. See also Major Wilkinson's report on the Balkan organisation dated 26th March 1940 (Appendix D to Polish History).

[2] Major Wilkinson of No. 4 Military Mission was with General Sikorski throughout his escape from France: Polish History, p. 13.

[3] Polish History, p. 15.

[4] There is a (very incomplete) list of 'top level' letters exchanged on this subject between 1940 and 1944 at p. 24 of the Polish History, which extends over ten foolscap pages.

demand was for a flight of Halifaxes or Liberators, manned by Polish crews and allocated solely to Polish operations; and it is an index of their political power that they secured as early as this three Halifaxes for which Polish crews were to be trained. SOE for its own purposes (for instance for the air service to Stockholm or for Yugoslavia) could never have obtained so much. The Air Ministry stood firm on the question of a special flight under full Polish control;[1] weather conditions were such that operations to Poland might be possible for only a few nights each winter, and Halifaxes were too valuable to be locked up in 'penny packets' on such terms – the aircraft and their Polish crews must be available when required for 'Special Duty' operations to other parts of Europe. This was a point of operational policy on which there could be no concession.

Thus equipped, the Poles achieved eight successful flights during the winter season of 1941/42, for the loss of one aircraft which forced-landed in Sweden. Forty-five men and about $2\frac{1}{2}$ tons of stores were dropped – a small ration in relation to their needs, but at least a serious beginning. The fate of the men and the growth of their organisation remained a sealed book to SOE, apart from conjectures and hints. The only large project was one for an interruption of German communications in South Poland on the eve of the campaigning season of 1942; this was referred to the Defence Committee and warmly endorsed, but for unknown reasons the project collapsed.[2] Otherwise there is little to report but large Polish projects and occasional reports of sabotage; the claims for 1941 and 1942 included 2,600 locomotives damaged, 75 trains derailed, 8 bridges destroyed, some 700 Germans killed. There was substance behind this – the Poles were certainly fighting – but no evidence for details will ever be available.

Apart from the inexhaustible demand for aircraft, in which the Poles were seconded rather than sponsored by SOE, there were other considerable demands on SOE's resources in support of the Secret Army. Equipment was of course supplied as wanted. Training was from the first in the hands of Polish instructors, but all other facilities were supplied by SOE. At the outset Poles were trained in the first of the SOE para-military schools, at Loch Ailort in Wester Ross; but the policy of establishing separate Polish schools was adopted in January 1944, and the complete scheme as finally established was as follows:

---

1 This point is enunciated as early as Sir Archibald Sinclair's letter to Mr Dalton of 27th January 1941: Polish History, p. 16.

2 DO(42)29 and DO(42)9th Mtg, Min. 1, of 26th March. Some of the papers are on SOE Archives File M/Poles and Czechs/1.

3 The first Polish School was at 'Briggens', Royden, Essex, but was taken over by SOE in March 1942. Audley End was opened in April 1942.

STS 43	Audley End, Saffron Walden	Preparatory and Para-Military
STS 46	Chicheley Hall, Nr Bletchley	Training in underground technique

Polish Wireless School at Polmont.

Stn 18	Frogmore Farm, Herts.	⎧ 'Holding Stations'
Stn 19	Gardners End, Stevenage	⎨ where fully trained agents awaited
Stn 20A	Chalfont St Giles,	⎩ operations
20B	Bucks	

Apart from the Wireless School, all the administrative staff for these Stations was provided by the British – an establishment of about 150 in all.

In addition, there was also maintained a 'Polish Military Wireless Research Unit' at Stanmore, for design and production of radio equipment for secret purposes.[1] This was an active factory employing a staff of about seventy, mainly Poles; and SOE always acknowledged freely that the Poles were from the first ahead of us in the design of miniature sets for clandestine work. We perhaps overtook them towards the end, with superior resources at our disposal; but technical opinion is agreed on the great value of the Polish contribution in this field. They also contributed materially to the early development of SOE's 'forgery' section.[2]

So far we have been considering the work of the Polish Section of SOE, in liaison with the VIth Bureau of the Polish General Staff. There also existed another Section (EU/P – 'European Poles'), which worked in somewhat similar relations to a section of the Polish Ministry of the Interior. This was concerned both with the Ministry of the Interior's work in maintaining a secret civil administration in Poland and with its attempt to keep together and utilise the Polish communities in other countries, both inside and outside the areas of German control. Projects in both these directions can be found as early as 1940, and the EU/P Section came into existence in December of that year: but its main task was set by the special allocation in June 1941 of a credit of £600,000 'for subversive work by Polish organisations in countries other than the USA': SOE were to be responsible for supervising disbursements to the Poles from this fund, in the light of explanation by the Poles of their plans and requirements.[3]

---

[1] See Appendix G to Polish History.

[2] See below p. 334.

[3] See Mr Dalton to General Sikorski 24th June 1941, and General Sikorski to Mr Dalton 5th July: EU/P History, Section I, Appendix 'A'. Reference is there made to a memorandum presented by General Sikorski to Mr Churchill on 20th May, and a letter from Mr Churchill dated 15th June accepting his proposals.

It appears that only £550,000 in all were disbursed from this source up to July 1945, although the original allocation of £600,000 had been intended to cover only the first year.[1] Indeed, SOE were soon complaining of the 'academic' and inactive character of the work being done among Poles outside Poland; and in response to their pressure yet a third Polish authority – the Ministry of National Defence under General Kukiel – was brought into the picture towards the end of 1942.[2] This achievement only made matters worse: to quote Colonel Hazell, for long head of EU/P, 'During a long period, the position was such that this SOE section, was the sole liaison linking these two Polish departments, an impossible but typical Polish situation.'[3]

It was not to be expected that much would be achieved in such an atmosphere. The activities of the Ministry of the Interior in Poland remain a mystery: they may have been a support to morale and a political counterweight to the military clique, but they contributed little or nothing to direct action against the Germans. SOE's opinion of what was achieved in other countries – Belgium, Scandinavia, the Balkans, the Middle East, South America, the Far East – is not much more encouraging; it is pretty clear that SOE was disturbed by the Polish tendency to proliferate a network of comfortably paid offices, the occupants of which waged war with one another rather than with the common enemy. The best that can be said is that these efforts may have had negative value in maintaining Polish national consciousness and in resisting German attempts to secure co-operation.

The position was a little different in France, where a large Polish working population was concentrated in the coal-mining areas round Lille – possibly half a million in all, including demobilised soldiers. This was clearly material from which sabotage 'circuits' might be created in an area of great military and industrial importance, and a good deal of attention was paid to it later. In this period there were only confused beginnings. As early as the end of January 1941 a certain M. Bitner, who became Polish Consul-General in Lille after the German expulsion, was infiltrated by sea to make contact with the local leadership; and on 2nd September an officer (Lieutenant Teodor Dzierzgowski – 'Adjudicate') was dropped (after seven unsuccessful attempts) to investigate the situation on behalf of the Polish General Staff and to stimulate more effective organisation and action. He took with him a million and a half French francs – perhaps £5,000. 'Adjudicate' was brave, quarrelsome, unprincipled; and achieved very

---

[1] See note by Group Captain Venner attached to EU/P History.

[2] See memo. dated 30th December 1942 and related correspondence. EU/P History, Section I, Appendix 'C'.

[3] EU/P History, Section I, p. 4.

little except a 'cause célèbre' – a resounding and confused quarrel both with the Ministry of the Interior and with IInd Bureau of the General Staff. He was eventually withdrawn in haste in April 1942, and the best that can be said for him is that he did not lack energy. A 'circuit' which meant business was created, received stores and carried out a few operations; however insecure and quarrelsome, it did provide a possible nucleus for development.[1]

Naturally, this parallel Polish organisation implied duplication all along the line. It had its own small research station, fathered by SOE, at Mill Hill;[2] it had its own training and holding stations – a main school at Firthampton House, Tewkesbury, opened in February 1942, and three holding stations.[3] These were run, as were the Polish VIth Bureau schools, under SOE administration, but with Polish control of training; they were of course a commitment over and above the credit of £600,000.

As will be seen, there is little here to sum up: one cannot strike a balance-sheet, because SOE knew only the liabilities and had no more than a vague picture of the Polish assets. The liabilities were large – at this stage Poland consumed more time, money and effort than any other country except France, and but for geography General Sikorski would have been a more formidable claimant even than General De Gaulle. The only incontrovertible asset was that Polish resistance was still alive in Poland. No one could say what it was worth in a military sense: but at least it had suffered no major disaster – as yet.

2. Czechoslovakia*

Like the Poles, the Czechs (the Slovaks hardly concern us here) possessed a long tradition of conspiratorial resistance; Czech nationalism played a great part in the break-up of the Austrian Empire, and it had created perhaps the most successful secret movement of the 1914 War. The prestige of Masaryk the elder and of Benes** as resistance leaders stood very high. But the tradition had little else in common with that of the Poles: the Czechs had long forgotten the mediaeval Bohemian Empire, and were consciously a small power –

---

1 The above is drawn principally from EU/P History, Section II, Appendix 'A'.
2 EU/P History, Section V, Part 4.
3 Inchmery House, near Southampton. Warnham Court, near Horsham. Chudleigh, Sussex.
* [See C. Macdonald, *The Killing of SS Oberbgruppenfuehrer Reinhard Heydrich* (1989).]
** [E. Benes, 1884–1948, President of Czechoslovakia 1935–8, 1945–8, and of Government in Exile 1941–5.]

resolute, but canny, and well aware that their first duty to the Czech nation was to exist; they might easily be annihilated, and liberation could not in any event come by purely Czech efforts. From a national point of view the tradition of resistance must be maintained, but it was right that resistance should not be pushed too far. Geography of course seconded this view; Bohemia and Moravia are small and for the most part highly cultivated, and there is no terrain in which a regular guerilla movement can be developed.

The official responsible for the resistance organisation was Colonel Moravec,* head of the Czech Intelligence Service, [PASSAGE DELETED ON GROUNDS OF NATIONAL SECURITY] the important industrial centres of Bohemia and Moravia were relatively safe from bombing; and it was natural to hope that a hostile Czech population could be inspired through SOE to attack German resources at a vital point. But the difficulties were in practice too great – the area was so important to Germany that an open sabotage campaign would have been suppressed by ruthless massacres and deportations, against which there could be no defence. It is reasonable to believe that Colonel Moravec's reserve towards SOE was fully endorsed by President Benes, who was in turn highly sensitive to movements of opinion among the Czechs at home and Czech opinion did not forget Lord Runciman** and Munich.

The Czechs had naturally made preparations for a post-occupational organisation in the period between Munich and the outbreak of war; but this was seriously jeopardised by an injudicious outbreak of resistance in September 1939 (possibly provoked by the Germans), which led to heavy reprisals directed particularly at intellectuals and at the Universities, the seed-bed of Czech nationalism in the nineteenth century. Apparently the existing organisation was seriously prejudiced, and when the Czechs reached England they were keen enough to use SOE to help them in opening new contacts, provided they were not too far committed to SOE's plans. Here they held the key positions in their own hands. They were permitted to use their own codes and to run their own wireless station, free from all censorship until the D-day precautions in 1944. The agents were men whom they selected, and their final briefing was in Czech hands. SOE could therefore only urge and advise; it had no power to supervise the execution even of agreed plans.

The first operation was carried out in April 1941, when a single man was dropped near Prague to open new contacts with the move-

---

* [F. Moravec; see his *Master of Spies* (1975).]
** [W. Runciman, 1899–1949, MP 1899–1937, viscount 1937, mission to beg Czechs to concede to Germans 1938; in *DNB*.]

ments at home. The short nights of summer then interrupted operations, and SOE used the time to urge on preparations for developing sabotage parties on the lines which it sponsored in other countries. A number of good men were put in training, and a fairly elaborate plan was adopted for the winter season 1941–2. Conditions for air operations were almost always difficult over Bohemia, and it required thirteen attempts to achieve five successful operations between December and April. Of these much the most important was the dispatch on 28th December of two Sergeants, Kubis and Gabčik, who had been carefully trained for an attack on Heydrich, Himmler's second-in-command, then 'Protector' of Bohemia and Moravia. The execution was successfully carried out on 27th May 1942.

Operation 'Anthropoid', as this was called, was decided and planned on the authority of President Benes himself, and was undoubtedly the greatest single event of Czech resistance until the final rising in 1945. As a national gesture it was superbly successful; the fact of Czech resistance could not have been more dramatically displayed to the world. But it was very costly: German reprisals were set on foot at once on the most extensive scale, and the organisation which had been growing quietly since the autumn of 1939 was shaken to pieces. The German action had been made ready under Heydrich himself, and might have been touched off at any time, even without this extreme gesture of defiance; but the controversy over the rightness or otherwise of Benes's decision remains a cardinal point of Czech history, closely associated in Czech minds with the problem of relations to the West.

For SOE the disaster was almost complete. Kubis and Gabčik took refuge in St Boromaeus's Church in Prague, where almost all the other agents were already congregated, and eleven of them were arrested there together.[1] Apparently only one man (known as 'Silver A') remained at large, and his wireless set ceased to operate in the latter part of June 1942. He too is famous in Czech history: he was traced by the Germans to the village of Lidice (or Lezaky), and escaped from a German raiding party under cover of resistance by the inhabitants. The fate of Lidice need not be re-told here: it too is a symbol to the world of Czech patriotism, and to the Czechs of the consequences of 'parachutists from England'.

The extent of these disasters was perhaps hardly realised at the time, and summer 1942 was spent, like summer 1941, in urging the Czechs to preparations for a more active policy in the ensuing winter.

---

[1] Two agents, Curda and Gerik, who had been dropped in Czechoslovakia in June 1942, were executed after the Liberation for betraying the party. 'The Times', 30th April 1947.

General Ingr and the General Staff were at least favourable to the laying of plans for the resurrection of the Czech Army, and progress was made towards closer collaboration in this direction, which to some extent forced Colonel Moravec's hand. The first-fruits of this were the creation of an Anglo-Czech Planning Committee, which met for the first time on 23rd September 1942, under the chairmanship of Brigadier Gubbins,[1] and this was to be served by a 'Working Committee' on which Lieutenant Colonel Wilkinson and Colonel Moravec with their staffs could meet and exchange ideas. SOE's control was thus to some slight extent enlarged, but the Czechs still retained the essential points. The wireless station was theirs. The agents (unlike the Poles) passed through the ordinary SOE schools, except for the final 'holding station' for those awaiting operations,[2] but they were selected and finally briefed by Moravec's men, and they acted for their own government and not for SOE. The Czechs were as anxious as SOE to reopen wireless communications with their country, but for the present they had had sufficient experience of German methods of control. If any sabotage was to be done, it must be of the 'insaississable' variety.[3]

---

[1] See SOE Archives File 11/470/1. Lord Selborne gave a lunch-party for President Benes on 24th September: record on AD/S.1 File 59.

[2] At first near Dorking; later at Ardley, near Stevenage.

[3] The Czechs like the Poles possessed a small 'subversive' research station. This was under Dr Malachta in South Kensington, and was concerned mainly with chemical problems – home-made explosives, delay fuses, and so forth.

CHAPTER XIV

Other Activities

So far we have covered developments in the occupied countries of Europe up to the late summer of 1942. The two main enemy countries, Germany and Italy, have been left on one side: they presented such serious difficulties that they could for the present be given only low priority, and at this stage so little was achieved that it will be best to exclude them until later in the story. There were however other developments which had little future, but bulked larged at the time.

One of these was Operation 'Claribel', which was designed to cover all action to be taken by SOE to harass and delay a German invasion of England.[1] It can be judged from the earlier narrative how little could thus have been achieved; but much paper was consumed on the project in the winter of 1940 and in 1941, and it was a factor of some importance in all SOE planning for Western Europe. No part of the scheme was executed, and it is of permanent interest only as SOE's first attempt to harness subversive action to a general military plan.

In the winter of 1940–41 the most obvious alternative to invasion was that Hitler should break out to the south-west: absorb the French in North Africa, crush Spain and Portugal, seal the Mediterranean, and dominate the South Atlantic from the Dakar 'bulge' of West Africa. From there it would be only a step to a series of German and Italian risings in South America, which it would be beyond the power of the USA to control. SOE had an obvious role to play in doing what little was possible to counter this move.[2]

1. Iberia and North Africa[3]

French North Africa and West Africa were understood to be primarily an American concern from the day in March 1941 when Mr Murphy arrived as Consul-General in Algiers; but SOE missions were estab-

---

[1] COS(41)9th Mtg (0) of 31st March – and 'Outline Project'.
[2] Later knowledge of what passed between the Spaniards and the Germans that winter is summarised in two articles in the 'Manchester Guardian', 17th and 18th August 1948.
[3] See Iberian History.

lished at Madrid in February 1941 (under the supervision of the Naval Attaché), at Lisbon in January 1941, at Gibraltar in February 1941, and in Tangier in July 1941. Some reference has already been made to action from these stations which influenced other countries; their local position was much more difficult. It was SOE's duty (as they conceived it) to see that at least *some* Spaniards and Portuguese resisted in the event of an invasion, and they were confident that (given money and energy) this would be easy enough to arrange. The Ambassadors, on the other hand, Sir Samuel Hoare and Sir Ronald Campbell, were clear that such an attempt by SOE would make it certain that neither the Spanish or Portuguese Governments would resist; indeed that they would welcome German invasion if the alternative was to be British intrigues with their domestic Oppositions. Both these contrasting positions were defensible, and they were strongly defended both on the spot and in London, sometimes in good humour, sometimes in bad.

The Spanish story contains many instances of the type of frustration which ensued. SOE in London necessarily set on foot schemes for intervention long before it could be known whether they would be required – it would have been plain negligence to delay. One of these ('Relator') involved the training of a number of English officers ('The Forty Thieves') to operate in Spain as small sabotage and guerilla parties in the event of a German invasion; twenty of these men were trained and ready in Gibraltar by April 1941. Similar steps were taken to recruit and train a body of Spanish Republicans ('Sconce' and 'Sprinkler'), mainly tough characters drawn from the French Foreign Legion; and they too were in readiness in the early part of 1941. But clearly neither of these plans could be put into operation before a German invasion; and it was even difficult to make advance preparations for their reception in Spain. Sir Samuel Hoare (very properly) insisted that he must be fully informed of all SOE's actions and that no contacts should be made with 'Red' groups (however mild) which might be suspected of opposition to the Franco régime. This limited the field to the 'Right' opposition, the nationalist and Monarchist 'Traditionalists' of Navarre; no one could suspect them of Communist leanings, but it was believed that they would resist German invasion on patriotic grounds.

Here again it was virtually impossible to take useful action in advance of the crisis; financial subvention was relatively easy, but until 1942 the Ambassador banned the introduction of W/T sets and dangerous stores into Spain, even to be held unused in readiness. Even when this ban was lifted, it remained difficult for any Englishman to move freely without the knowledge of Franco's police. A beginning was made early in 1942 with wireless training given through a Polish agent; but he proved dangerously insecure and had to be hastily withdrawn. In July 1942 a fresh start was made with a British officer, Major A. C. Holland,[1] who remained in Spain under cover for about eight months, and kept wireless traffic going with Gibraltar for part of the period. But he trained only one Navarrese operator (a priest), and was thoroughly convinced of the ineffectiveness and insecurity of the organisation. It was no surprise when it was betrayed to the police in May 1943: by this time it mattered very little what Franco might think of us, and the Ambassador was perfectly ready to stand up for SOE. Their old representative, Mr Babington-Smith, was voluntarily withdrawn in August of that year, but was replaced by Mr H. F. G. Morris in September.

These frustrations of course are not the full story of SOE's work in Spain. The staple of it was the maintenance of clandestine communications with France, which were worth far more to SOE than any possible intensification of sabotage in Iberia; and there were numerous other minor ways in which the cause could be served [PASSAGE DELETED ON GROUNDS OF NATIONAL SECURITY.]

In Lisbon the situation should perhaps have been easier: Portugal is after all our ancient and faithful ally, and Dr Salazar* is a dictator of a very different stamp from Franco. But he is no more anxious than any other dictator that internal opposition should be fostered by foreign agents, however good their intentions: and in Lisbon the German intelligence services in their various competing forms were scarcely less strong than in Madrid. [PAGE DELETED ON GROUNDS OF NATIONAL SECURITY.]

But this was scarcely a good introduction for SOE's own work, which was to be directed chiefly (so far as Portugal was concerned) to preparing demolitions and post-occupational resistance in the event of a German invasion. This might easily prove less a military asset than a political liability; but the preparations were part of an overall strategic plan and had to be pursued. Contacts at least were more easily made than in Spain: independent organisations were formed in the north, based on Oporto, where SOE had a British representative, and in Lisbon and the south, and there seemed to be a chance of co-operation with some elements of the Legião, the official party of the régime. No attempt was made to introduce arms or explosives – these could be run in by sea at the last moment – but in July 1941 a remarkable figure, Squadron Leader 'Mallory', arrived to give training in W/T. 'Mallory' was an Englishman who had served in the Foreign

---

1 See his report – Appendix 'B' to Iberian History.
* [A. de O. Salazar, 1889–1970, dictator of Portugal 1932–68. For British relations both with him and with Franco, see D. and S. Eccles, *By Safe Hand* (1985).]

Legion, a wireless technician and a hustler, known in the service as the 'human bomb-shell'; incidentally a diarist of merit, who has left a very lively account of his Mission.[1] In about six weeks (while ostensibly 'waiting for an air passage') he managed to establish a wireless set in the Embassy at Lisbon and to train operators for the two SOE 'Circuits' as well as for the Legião.

Unfortunately this good beginning was wrecked in the winter of 1941–2, probably by a deliberate German counter-offensive organised through the Portuguese political police. In January and February 1942 virtually the whole story came out; Dr Salazar's rage was not lessened by the fact that secret staff talks were already in progress between Portugal and the Allies. The Ambassador perhaps took too weak a line; without Foreign Office authority he made full confession, implicating Major Beevor, and for a time there was extreme tension. But in the end Dr Salazar let himself be persuaded that SOE's operations were directed only against Germany and not against the régime, and that they were far less dangerous than the German activities already tolerated by the Portuguese police. The SOE mission was allowed to remain, while Portuguese honour was saved by the 'voluntary' withdrawal of Major Beevor in June 1942. This virtually ended SOE activities in Portugal itself, since the strategic crisis which had inspired them was at an end: but Lisbon continued to be a centre of great importance for contacts involving almost every country in Europe.

From Lisbon Squadron Leader 'Mallory' went on to Tangier, taking with him an operator to be established there. Even after the Spanish seizure of the International Zone in November 1940, Tangier continued to be something of a diplomatic no-man's land, and SOE was able to indulge in more exciting activity there than in Spain and Portugal. Originally the Mission was in part aimed at French North Africa, and it established various lines of contact across the frontier: but here the Americans were far better placed than we, as they possessed a network of consuls with full bag facilities, and the hand was left to them to play once OSS began to operate at the end of 1941.[2] In Tangier and Spanish Morocco there were various Arab leaders anxious to be subsidised and armed with a view (perhaps) to resisting a German invasion; in addition Spanish 'Reds' were more accessible in North Africa than on the mainland and it was possible to form sabotage parties without serious diplomatic danger. The only

---

[1] Appendix 'C' to Iberian History.
[2] Colonel Eddy was appointed by OSS to Tangier in December 1941 (their first post in Europe): they had a representative (Mr Raichle) at Gibraltar early in 1942, and Colonel Solberg was sent to Lisbon in March 1942.

recorded success of these groups was an attack[1] in January 1942 on a secret German radio station in a house in Tangier, which was passing shipping information to U-boats: this was neatly blown up, and no serious consequences ensued. But the Germans were not disposed to let this sort of thing pass unnoticed. In February 1942, the Spaniards arrested SOE's Gibraltar representative and a crew of Poles, while they were cruising innocently in a fishing-boat outside the territorial waters of Spanish Morocco. Their intention had been to land and raid a local rubber store; but this they did not disclose, and HM Consul-General was able to take a high line about Spanish violation of international law, which secured prompt release. [PASSAGE DELETED ON GROUNDS OF NATIONAL SECURITY.]

From Tangier Squadron Leader 'Mallory' passed to Gibraltar; and the wireless station which he established there in the Rock was probably SOE's most important contribution to history in North Africa: it carried all the clandestine signals traffic which preceded 'Torch', as well as all operational messages during the first days of the operation in Algeria – all other communication broke down. His narrative of its construction is a minor classic in the working of 'Système D', in his case a nice blend of French and British techniques of military 'wangling'.[2] Gibraltar's other activities were multifarious but disconnected, and related mainly to communications with other territories.[3]

2. West Africa and Madagascar

After the failure of General De Gaulle's Dakar expedition in September 1940 West Africa hung in suspense. In part it rallied to the Free French, in part it was firmly held by Vichy representatives, men of some determination. Further military operations were out of the question for the present: but the area was strategically vital, and it presented a fair field for subversive experiment, directed either to seduce or to eject the existing French officials. The head of the SOE Mission, Mr Louis Franck, left England for Lagos as early as 6th December 1940, one of the very first of SOE's offshoots overseas. At this time SOE and PWE were still one, so that his task included propaganda as well as sabotage: what is more, he was entrusted with secret intelligence work also, as SIS had hitherto possessed no organisation in West Africa. The Mission was thus an experiment in an 'inclusive' Secret Service organisation, for which there is much to be said, at all

---

[1] Operation 'Falaise': Appendix 'C' to Iberian History.
[2] Appendix 'D' to Iberian History.
[3] See above p. 236.

levels from Headquarters downwards; and it is a pity that it was not tested by more active operations.

At an early stage it was realised that the French colonies were not the only danger in West Africa: there was plenty of scope for enemy activity in the Spanish and Portuguese colonies, and this must be met. Thus in the summer of 1941 the Mission was divided into two: French West Africa (Frawest) under Lieutenant Colonel R. S. L. Wingate,* and Neutral Colonies (Neucols) under Franck.

Frawest was always somewhat thwarted by considerations of higher policy. It laid down an admirable intelligence network, based on the use of native observers: it also conducted an enterprising propaganda campaign, including the use of a makeshift and rather ineffective broadcasting station at Bathurst.[1] It was even permitted to harass Dakar in minor ways, by enticing natives across the frontiers and encouraging forbidden traffics. But 'bangs' were strictly prohibited; as we have seen,[2] the Foreign Office were at one time prepared to concede local discretion for action against Vichy shipping, but the GOC-in-C, West Africa, was most anxious that no pretext whatever should be given for a Vichy attack on his territories. He knew what his military resources were, and he was doubtless right: but Frawest suffered repeatedly from hope deferred, until it was finally abandoned when the devious M. Boisson brought Dakar over to the Allies on 23rd November 1942.[3]

Neucols had less scope for large plans, but much greater local discretion, and it staged two of SOE's most theatrical coups. One of them was the judicious corruption of the Captain of the Vichy ship 'Gazcon', which had been marked down in Lobito Bay (Portuguese West Africa) while running the blockade from Madagascar. An SOE agent was introduced into Lobito Bay in July 1941, under elaborate cover, which included the official blessing of the Portuguese Colonial Minister and of the Governor of the Colony on a project for large-scale production of castor-seed. The rest was relatively straightforward: for a sum of £10,000 the captain raised steam and stealthily put to

---

[1] A full-size broadcasting unit was eventually created by PWE, and was sent out as an independent organisation in December 1942. But it was far too late, and was never brought into use.

[2] Above p. 226.

[3] The main COS references which have a bearing on SOE's part in West Africa are: COS(42)135th Mtg, Item 6, of 30th April (General Gifford present). COS(42)193rd Mtg, Item 10, of 30th June – (COS(42)319 and JP(42)629 refer). COS(42)227th Mtg, Item 7, of 4th August (discussing draft directive to the GOC-in-C, with SOE directive annexed – COS(42)355).

* [(Sir) R. E. L. Wingate, 1889–1978, son of Lawrence's patron, 2nd baronet 1920; see his *Not in the Limelight* (1959).]

sea – to be met outside territorial waters by the seaplane carrier HMS 'Albatross'. His cargo was reckoned to be worth some £300,000: and the ship was a small net gain to Allied tonnage, worth at least another £100,000.

Operation 'Postmaster', the other expedition, was directed against the 7,000 ton Italian liner 'Duchessa d'Aosta' which lay with a German tug and lighter in harbour in the Spanish island of Fernando Po. This involved somewhat lavish expenditure on shore in order to ensure that the ships were deserted by their crews at zero hour and that all harbour lights were extinguished. It also involved a straightforward piece of eighteenth-century piracy, executed by two small vessels, which had come along the coast from Lagos some 400 miles away, with a party of thirty-four Englishmen. Seventeen of these were SOE men, including the party which had sailed out the 'Maid Honor' from England:[1] the rest were respectable Nigerian civil servants who had volunteered for the expedition. There was no hitch. The lights went out as the British vessels appeared: the small enemy parties left on board were easily surprised and locked up: and the expedition withdrew in the darkness with three very valuable prizes. The entire flotilla was then ostentatiously 'captured' on the high seas by HM Corvette 'Violet'. Curiously enough, there were no diplomatic repercussions whatever, although this was January 1942 and relations with Franco were still far from happy.

These two parties realised not much less than £1,000,000 for very small cost, and were manna in the desert to SOE in its early lean years. Madagascar also can be reckoned as one of its successes, although here it required less initiative to earn the dividends. These were due almost entirely to the efforts of M. Percy Mayer, a naturalised Frenchman of British birth, and to the equally brilliant work of his wife. M. Mayer found his way from Madagascar to South Africa early in 1941 in order to put his services at the disposal of the Allies: and returned in March to Tananarive, taking with him a wireless set. This was installed at Tananarive in a false ceiling over the bathroom of the Mayers' house; and an admirable intelligence service was maintained for the next year, largely through the skill of Mme Mayer as W/T operator. One of the reports sent was responsible for the capture of five Vichy blockade-runners by the Navy on 2nd November 1941 – another very valuable dividend.

This however was straight intelligence work. SOE also dabbled in propaganda, by introducing a 'Madagascar Libre' service from the Government radio station on Mauritius, in January 1942.[2] Violent

---

[1] Above p. 248.
[2] Garnett's 'History of PWE', p. 210.

action only became feasible when Operation 'Ironclad' was planned early in 1942 in order to seize Diego Suarez and deny its fortified harbour to the Japanese. SOE had by this time established a small Mission in South Africa: mainly to work into Madagascar, although it was also responsible for Portuguese East Africa.[1] Their trading schooner 'Lindi' managed to land arms and stores for Mayer on 31st March: on 25th April Mayer himself moved to the Diego Suarez area to collect such military intelligence as he could. Here unfortunately confusion followed: 'Lindi' was to have come again and supplied him with a wireless set, but the plan broke down and he was unable to transmit from the battle area. On the night before D-day (4th/5th May 1942) he managed to cut the telephone line from Diego Suarez to the battery which dominated the landing-beaches in Courrier Bay – a very valuable contribution, since when the time came the battery never opened fire. But early on 5th May he was arrested with his intelligence notes in his pocket untransmitted: and it was only the speedy success of the operation which saved his life. This unfortunately 'blew' SOE's one effective agent in Madagascar: elaborate plans were laid for action in support of the later operations to clear the island, but it cannot be said that execution lived up to plans – in fact it was lucky there was no disaster.[2]

3. South America

The USA itself falls outside this story. A Mission was established there under Sir William Stephenson as early as December 1940,[3] but this was a joint enterprise representing SOE, SIS and what was later PWE. Of these three SOE had least scope for direct action in the USA, and there are no SOE operations to record there. The New York Mission was, however, important as a source of supplies, recruits and training facilities, and for the intimacy of the connection which Sir William Stephenson established with both those warring potentates,

---

[1] For its formal directive see COS(42)305(0) (Revise) of 16th October, and COS(42)293rd Mtg, Item 6, of 19th October.

[2] For a frank version of this story see Colonel Taylor's report to General Gubbins on his tour of inspection in 1943 – on private file with Mr Norman Mott, MO1(SP).

[3] First proposed by Colonel Davies, 23rd November 1940 – on SOE Archives File (AD/S.1) SC/76: arrangements concluded with CSS and Sir William Stephenson 24th December 1940 (papers on same file). Lord Bearsted had earlier visited the US on SOE's behalf 13th October, 14th December 1940 (report on same file d/d 28th December), and there was a further visit by Colonel C. G. Vickers early in 1941 (report dated 26th March 1941 on same file).

Mr Edgar G. Hoover* of the FBI, and Colonel 'Wild Bill' Donovan of OSS.

Latin America was also directed by 'British Security Co-ordination' in New York; and before American entry into the war South America belonged to the same strategic picture as Iberia and West Africa.[1] The British commercial community is still strong in most Latin American countries, and it was relatively easy to find good agents with perfect local cover: most of them were given training at the British Security Co-ordination school in Canada, but their most valuable asset was their local knowledge and contacts. When Operations, Intelligence and Propaganda are all controlled together they become inextricably intermingled – as it is proper they should be – and it is not easy to separate out from BSC's narrative what belongs properly to SOE as it existed in other theatres. The main lines to the task were plain enough: to prepare for demolitions and resistance in the event of a German invasion or coup d'état: meantime to identify and harass German agents: to encourage 'spontaneous' movements of support for the Allies: to influence judiciously such politicians as were susceptible to bribery or blackmail. This policy was pursued with effect in almost every part of the Continent. The most valuable results are likely to have been cumulative and are difficult to report and estimate, [PASSAGE DELETED ON GROUNDS OF NATIONAL SECURITY].

This was all hay made by the British before Pearl Harbour: it naturally impressed the Americans, but did not dispose them to leave the field untilled now that the outbreak of war gave them a relatively free hand. In the first months of 1942 the first need was to interest and instruct the Americans in the dangers of Axis influence as we saw them: and the lesson was very readily learnt.[2] Donovan and OSS were excluded by their rivals from the Western Hemisphere, but there were numerous other US organisations to fill the gap, and in 1942 US experts and money were poured into South America. Gradually the South American states were brought into the war and (except in Argentine) potential conspirators were arrested or otherwise rendered

---

[1] See Part VI of the American History, which is very full.

[2] Lord Selborne laid special emphasis on this when he saw General Marshall in London in April 1942 (SOE Archives File (AD/S.1) SC/76): the matter later had considerable history on CCS level – see the series initiated by the British COS in CCS108 of 2nd September 1942. [George C. Marshall, 1880–1959, Chief of US Army Staff 1939–45, Secretary of State 1947–9. See Bruce Lee, *Marching Orders* (NY, 1995).]

* [J. E. Hoover, 1895–1972, director of FBI from 1921, said to know something against every potentate in Washington.]

harmless. By the end of 1942 Latin America was no longer a theatre in which drastic action was required to keep the Axis at bay: but in the bad days of 1941 SOE had, with very limited resources, made some contribution to that end.

4. General

In reading SOE's reports for these first two years 1941 and 1942 one is struck by the high proportion of its successes which came from what have been grouped together as 'Other Activities'. This is not merely a coincidence or an optical illusion. It is quite probable that (so far as these things can be financially estimated) SOE was in these years in a position to 'declare a dividend' on its comparatively small expenditure in unoccupied or neutral territory. It certainly could not do so on the vastly greater proportion of its resources which was devoted to the Resistance in Occupied Europe. Great possibilities existed there for the future, but little concrete damage had been done to the Germans as yet.

This point is worth stressing. It indicates, not a difference in competence between the different branches of SOE, but the vast gap which divides operations in neutral territory from those conducted directly in face of the German army and police. Outside occupied territory it was generally no crime for an agent to be present under suitable cover, so long as he lay low: he might even proceed quietly to create an organisation, and there would be no clash with constituted authority until the organisation began to move from theory to practical execution. Under the Germans it was an operation of the first magnitude even to establish an agent; and every day in which he could be maintained at liberty represented a technical achievement. To put a single agent into France with a chance of survival was as big an operation as the capture of the 'Gazcon'.

SOE (and D Section before it) were doubtless inexperienced and incompetent at first: but it was their misfortune and not their fault that they came to the scene too late to have any chance to learn their business and develop their organisation in the really important countries before the military fronts collapsed. This was the one great advantage which the Communist Party organisations in Europe possessed. Their cadres existed and were well drilled long before German occupation: in policy and execution they were sometimes gravely handicapped by the political liabilities of their past, but at least they were a force in being. This problem of organisation *in time* is one of the gravest which must be faced if the need for an SOE ever arises again.

CHAPTER XV

Internal Organisation
and External Relations

The late summer of 1942 has been chosen as a point at which to break these narratives and consider the general development of SOE because it was a turning-point in the war, and a turning-point also in the character of the organisation. One cannot pin the change of direction to any precise date, nor was it clearly appreciated at the time. But in general terms it can be felt that (in spite of many defeats in Whitehall warfare) SOE rested up to this point on the original conception of a grand strategy of subversion, which would employ all means to break down German morale and to raise their slaves against them in Europe, and which would be as indispensable as any other weapon in enabling the British to defeat a military power which was on paper superior in all the elements of military strength. With the full mobilisation of America and the unexpected military resurgence of Russia, it was no longer necessary to depend strategically on the 'Fourth Arm'. The Allies were entitled to expect victory by superior military strength, and their strategy could again become a matter purely for the three 'old-fashioned' services. Sabotage, guerilla warfare, secret armies could still contribute to the execution of a plan but they were henceforward quite secondary in the making of it. The soldiers had the upper hand of the politicians; and Special Operations tend progressively to share the decline of politics and to become a weapon in the hands of a C-in-C, more complex than Signals or Artillery, but equally controlled by the local requirements of the battle.

It is in this role that SOE (or rather the various SO branches under various Cs-in-C) made its most visible and incontrovertible contribution to the winning of the war: it is also this later period that raises doubts as to whether the military gains were worth the political consequences involved. Ironically (but logically) it was not till the Allies could show the occupied countries that force was on their side that doubters flocked to the Resistance and it became everywhere a mass movement. And at this stage SOE (and the Foreign Office which in theory controlled it in such matters) could not pause to reckon political consequences: the battle was joined, the fate of armies was at stake, and all political forces, from Cagoulard to Communist, must be turned somehow, momentarily, in the same direction, that of military victory.

Thus subversion only began to show serious military results when the balance of military power was already shifting. But this is scarcely sufficient to show that the original, more political, conception had failed. It cannot of course be claimed that anywhere in Europe in the summer of 1942 there existed an organised fighting force taking its directives from Britain. No such force could have been organised in the time and with the means available. But in every country SOE had done *something*: it had shown that Britain's contribution to the Resistance did not consist solely of inspiring words from the BBC or from one of PWE's Freedom Stations. Friends had taken desperate chances to come in person; wireless links had been established; appeals for material help had been answered. All had been done inadequately and sometimes disastrously: but it had been done. It had been proved that Resistance movements could exist, could be fed, could be directed; that the will to resist was there and that the limiting factors were mainly material – more aircraft, better wireless sets, better disguise, more training in the art of conspiracy.

Apart from this moral gain, which can be felt but not measured, there was little to show for the work done. The periodical reports made to the Prime Minister and the Chiefs of Staff are deplorably thin in demonstrable military achievement. There was plenty to say about the movements of opinion in Europe, the plans of the Resistance, and the hypothetical number of its adherents. There were also plenty of reports of sabotage directed against the Germans; but the evidence behind them was always tenuous – it was rarely possible to say who had blown up what, and where he had done it. At best, it can be said that the volume of smoke implied a pretty substantial fire. But it was only outside the area of German control that results could be seen and assessed; there they were handsome, but not miraculous.

1. The Organisation of SOE

In this development SOE had grown piecemeal to a very substantial size.

By July 1942 the total of its staff at home and overseas (apart from agents) is given as 3,226.[1] This can be broken down roughly as follows:

---

[1] Playfair Report, Annex II.

United Kingdom: Headquarters: Officers	247
Junior Staff	444
	691
Research, Supply and Training	1,462
Total	2,153
Middle East (excluding 444 Army personnel attached)	608
North and South America	100
Far East and India	203
Other Missions	162
Total	3,226

These figures doubtless contain errors in detail, but the general pattern is clear enough.

There had been no very drastic changes in the organisation at Headquarters,[1] but every individual branch and section had expanded: the department had outgrown No. 64 Baker Street and occupied a series of buildings in the same area – Michael House, Norgeby House, Berkeley Court and others. It also had various other scattered premises in London, retained as 'flats' where agents could be housed or interviewed without endangering the security of the main organisation. Such for instance were the Norwegian Section flat at Chiltern Court, and that of R/F Section in Dorset Square.

The rest of the organisation in Great Britain had been correspondingly enlarged. The system of training schools had already reached almost its final form, and is dealt with in some detail later.[2] It was only in June 1942 that SOE became independent of SIS in the organisation of its signals systems,[3] and almost the whole of this large development lies outside this period.[4] But the nucleus of the system was already in being at Grendon, near Bicester, where a signals school had been begun as early as October 1941.

Research and production units on a small scale had been inherited both from D Section and from MI(R), and in June 1941 Professor Newitt* of the Imperial College was appointed as Director of Scientific Research. The development and production of explosive devices and weapons suitable for clandestine warfare proceeded mainly at Station IX (The Fryth, Welwyn) and Station XII (Aston House, near Stevenage) respectively:[5] but there was a curious offshoot in naval

---

[1] An Organisation Chart for July 1942 is at Appendix E.
[2] Below p. 729.
[3] See p. 386.
[4] Below p. 736.
[5] Part II of the SOE Technical Histories refer to the work of these Stations.
* [D. M. Newitt, 1894–1980, chemical engineer, in SOE 1941–5, Courtaulds professor at Imperial College 1945–61; in *DNB*.]

development at Staines Reservoir. The miniature submarine had obvious possibilities for operations against shipping in narrow waters; and the Welman and Welfreighter, two types of miniature submarine conceived primarily for special operations at fairly long range in the Far East.

For other types of research SOE was largely dependent on the experts of other Ministries; but the field to be covered was enormous, and it required special knowledge on almost every scientific subject, from poisons and bacteriological warfare to radio devices and the chemistry of forgery. In particular, disguise in all its aspects was almost a science in itself. A 'Camouflage' workshop was opened in South Kensington Museum of Natural History in January 1942, under the charge of an expert in cinema settings, costumes and so forth:[1] and it became a remarkable manufacturory of disguised explosives and arms, 'continental' clothing, cigarettes, toothpaste and an immense variety of the miscellaneous accessories needed to maintain a disguise in Occupied Europe.

The 'Forgery' section,[2] which was a necessary complement to this, was first formed in March 1941 with a Polish staff of three at the original Polish 'school' (STS38) at Briggens. The Poles were technically skilful, but possessed few of the resources required in Intelligence and material, and the unit soon expanded with British staff and equipment, working first for SOE's Polish Section and gradually enlarged to undertake work for other countries. The unit eventually took over all the accommodation at Briggens (as STS14), and at the peak period had a staff of fifty: much work was put out to various firms of private printers. PWE co-operated closely with this Section as regards the production of 'black' propaganda material purporting to be of German origin.[3]

Less specialised supplies presented an easier problem, as SOE could draw on any of the Services for Service stores in ordinary use: a small ordnance depot was opened near Camberley in February 1941, and expanded considerably in course of time. But the main art here was that of maintaining good liaison with 'Q' branches, particularly in the War Office: SOE required only relatively small quantities and could count on pretty high priority so long as personal relations were good. The most specialised task on the supply side was that of packing stores to be parachuted to the field. At first each operation was an event of note, and the work might even be done personally by the

---

[1] An illustrated History of the Camouflage Section is available with the Technical Histories.

[2] See the brief 'history' of Station 14, by Major Ince.

[3] Garnett's 'History of PWE', p. 171. [Also, Ellic Howe, *The Black Game* (1962).]

officers of the Country Section concerned: but by October 1941 it became necessary to open a special packing station at Saffron Walden, and in April 1942 it was moved to Station 61 – Gaynes House, St Neots. There in due course packing became a small industry in itself; for the heavy operations of 1943 and 1944, the contents of containers were standardised in various forms, which could be combined in different patterns to make an aircraft load: it remained necessary of course to make up special packages for special needs.[1]

On the personnel side, recruitment continued to the last to be on a very informal basis, at least for the key personnel who made the character of the organisation. The qualifications either for a section head in London or for an agent in the field were not such as could be prescribed by any central register, and through all this period recruitment was largely a matter of personal introduction and informal scrutiny.

The staff of the Head Office were of very varied types, and it is rash to generalise. But on the whole men were drawn more from the business and legal world, than from other classes, such as journalists and language teachers, who also have some professional knowledge of life in Europe. Most of the staff, in London as well as overseas, were commissioned into the Army: but professional soldiers were very rare until the last phase, except as liaison officers: professional civil servants were almost unknown.

SOE was accused at various times of different forms of political bias, to the Right or to the Left, but this supposed bias is extraordinarily hard to trace in action or in SOE files. The departmental 'esprit de corps' is more noticeable and more intangible than any bias; the interests of SOE and of the Resistance as conceived by them absorbed most of SOE's members heart and soul, and there is a real note of fanaticism in much of their debate, especially in the all-important middle ranks. But no man could come close to the facts of life under German rule without becoming fanatical,* and the energy and labour spent were beyond all praise. SOE was led too far perhaps at times in fighting other departments which it conceived to be deliberately blind to the needs of Europe; SOE was often no less blind to the problems that faced other departments. It was also perhaps led too easily, in its haste and energy, into expenditure of money, materials and manpower, which proved in the end to be wasteful, and it was espe-

---

[1] There is a narrative dealing with the Packing Stations, Part IV of the Technical Histories, and Pt 12 of SOE 'AL History' gives statistics and details of expansion.

* [See for a single example R. Schnabel, *Macht ohne Moral* (Frankfurt-am-Main, 1957).]

cially vulnerable to censure on this ground because the ordinary technique of financial control could not be applied. The financial carelessness and even dishonesty is endemic in the class of men from whom agents – even gallant and successful agents – are drawn, and the final destination of much of the money sent to the field remains uncertain. But no case has ever been alleged of serious peculation by the HQ staff of SOE.

It is worth mentioning one curious exception to the rule of individual recruitment. The FANYs (who have a long history as a corps since the organisation of the Territorials in Lord Haldane's* time) were threatened in the early days of SOE with extinction through the rise of the ATS, in relation to which they seemed a somewhat archaic and undemocratic anomaly. The process by which they were rescued does not belong to this story: but an informal arrangement was reached in the spring of 1941 between FANY Headquarters and SOE by which members of the corps would be attached to SOE for jobs similar to those filled by the ATS – drivers, personal assistants, wireless operators and so forth. In July 1941 this became a regular arrangement accepted by the Ministry of Labour, and as SOE expanded the FANYs expanded with it. This was not of course the only war service on which they were employed, but from small beginnings SOE absorbed much the largest part of the Corps, and thus came virtually to possess a women's auxiliary service of its own. Out of some 2,700 FANYs raised during the war, 2,000 were employed by SOE: largely as wireless operators at Grendon and Poundon, but also in a huge variety of other jobs, even in some cases as agents in the field. Like the other women's services, they became absolutely indispensable; and their discretion was impeccable.[1]

As we have seen, SOE expanded equally overseas, and by the summer of 1942 its organisation was world-wide. Its Middle East Mission presented a whole series of problems in itself, which have in part been dealt with above.[2] In the Far East (which lies outside this story) a beginning had been made later and on a smaller scale with missions sent to Singapore in April 1941[3] and to India in August 1941. By this time these had come together in a Mission at the HQ of the Supreme Commander, South-East Asia, which became (like Middle East) a vast organisation in itself, under the leadership of Mr Colin

---

[1] There is a narrative of the SOE FANY Unit (bound as a section of the Administrative History of SOE).
[2] See p. 169.
[3] There is a London HQ History of the Far East Missions.
* [R. B. Haldane, 1856–1928, viscount 1912, moderniser of the Army; in *DNB*.]

Mackenzie,* who was in charge from 31st August 1941 until the defeat of Japan. This Mission was in touch with Australia (constituted March 1942) for liaison with operations in these Allied theatres.[1]

'British Security Co-ordination' in New York not only handled liaison with the United States of America, but also controlled a network of Missions in the neutral countries of Latin America. Liaison (of a rather formal kind) was established even with the NKVD in Moscow.[2] All neutral capitals in Europe (Stockholm, Berne, Madrid, Lisbon and Ankara) were covered by important Missions, often with 'sub-Missions', such as those at Istanbul, Smyrna and Gothenburg; and on British territory there were representatives at Gibraltar, Malta, Lagos and Durban. In fact there was no relevant part of the globe in which SOE was not represented.[3]

2. The Offensive against SOE and its Results

Yet in spite of this admirably complete organisation it cannot be said that SOE was a department much respected in the early part of 1942. Its shortcomings were obvious enough, and not unusual in a department extemporised to execute a task of an entirely novel kind. But its reputation was out of all proportion to its demerits and took no account of the difficulties which it had to face.

This was partly a result of the workings of the security system. Security was the first lesson hammered into the heads of all SOE's inexperienced staff, and it was a lesson well learnt. From top to bottom, SOE's doings were wrapped in slightly ostentatious mystery. The department itself did business with others only under various aliases – Inter-Services Research Bureau, Room 055A, War Office, later MO1 (SP), War Office, HQ Special Training Schools, the Joint Technical Board, among others – which were introduced at different times and used in dealings with different departments. Precautions were taken to conceal any connection with the Minister of Economic Warfare and with Mr Gladwyn Jebb: similarly the identity of Sir Frank Nelson, Sir Charles Hambro, Brigadier Gubbins and the other leading figures was in theory a military secret of a high category.

All this posed an awkward problem. Security was undoubtedly a first condition of SOE's work: nothing whatever could be achieved

---

[1] SOE Archives File (AD/S.1) '68 – Far East', contains many of the papers regarding the set up of these Missions.

[2] Below pp. 393–9.

[3] 'LS/FE/1803 of 8.5.42' on SOE Archives File (destroyed) 2/340/.1 sets out 'SOE Organisation abroad'.

* [C. H. Mackenzie, 1898–1986, textile tycoon, ran SOE in Far East 1942–5, chaired Scottish Arts Council 1962–70.]

unless the whole organisation was absolutely proof against leakage to the enemy regarding all matters of policy and operations; and with an inexperienced staff it was vital that this principle should be religiously observed at the top of the hierarchy which set the tone to the rest of the organisation. On the other hand it was impossible that a considerable number of eminent men should be withdrawn from their normal occupations without giving rise to gossip: no series of 'cover stories' could be so complete as to provide a convincing picture to their circle of friends of what they were doing in London, when in fact they were doing something entirely different.[1] Similarly in official contacts with other government departments: as SOE's requirements grew, it was impossible that a growing circle of officials should not know, at least in general terms, what SOE was for.

The result of all this was that gossip without knowledge spread fairly widely in influential circles, and that SOE had no means of defence. Its reports on achievement and organisation were documents which could be given only the most limited circulation: and it was not possible for it to justify its *bona fides* even by an appeal to the previous records of its leading men. There is probably no means by which a secret department can shake off this handicap; and it is a real handicap in a system such as our own in which political influence, even in war, depends largely on informed public opinion.

It was worse for SOE in that it had no natural allies among the older departments. The Service departments were to a limited extent its friends, in so far as it could contribute specifically to military operations:[2] but it occupied only a small corner of their thoughts and could not expect much consideration if there were a competition for priorities in a matter of first-rate importance. Such a conflict arose only as regards the allocation of aircraft: but aircraft allocation was a matter of life and death not only to SOE but to all three Services. Even in this first phase, when SOE's needs were relatively small, we have seen the heat generated by the problem of air operations to assist General Sikorski, General De Gaulle and General Mihailovitch.

---

[1] Mr R. R. Stokes, MP [1897–1957], was notably puzzled and alarmed, and conducted a private campaign of his own which culminated in a Parliamentary Question to the Minister of Information on 20th May 1942, regarding the employment of Sir Charles Hambro, Mr Brien Clarke, Mr Sporborg and other SOE officials. Naturally he received no satisfactory reply. (The whole story is set out in Lord Selborne's Minute to the Prime Minister, of 26th May 1942.)

[2] There was a friendly exchange of letters between Mr Dalton and Sir Alan Brooke, when the latter took over from Sir John Dill in January 1942: and CIGS discussed SOE's work personally with Brigadier Gubbins at this time. SOE Archives File (AD/S.1) SC.98, and 1/470/1-Pt II.

The Foreign Office bore more responsibility than any other department for the creation of SOE as a civilian organisation in July 1940. The Prime Minister's intervention through Major Morton[1] tipped the scales, but the decision to remove subversion from the War Office control could not have been taken without the endorsement of Lord Halifax and Sir Alexander Cadogan. Yet the Foreign Office at first took very little heed of its foster-child. It had not stipulated at the outset for any formal control over SOE: Mr Dalton was a 'Minister of Cabinet rank', under the general direction of the War Cabinet, but sharing the responsibility of the Government as a whole: he was in no sense the subordinate of the Foreign Secretary. He does not appear to have asked for any general directive on foreign policy (such as he repeatedly obtained from the Chiefs of Staff on military matters), nor is there any indication that the Foreign Secretary or any other official of the Foreign Office ever attempted to consider or direct the activities of SOE as a whole. But there was ceaseless Foreign Office intervention in inidividual cases; many (but not all) of these have come up in the course of the narrative – Greece, Spain, Portugal, Vichy shipping, the status of De Gaulle, the attitude to be adopted to various Allied governments. There was scarcely a point at which SOE's action did not involve considerations of foreign policy: and each problem was approached by SOE and by the Foreign Office from opposite points of view. The presence of Mr Jebb and Mr Broad in SOE may have eased the situation, but it did little to mend it. From the Foreign Office point of view SOE was an intrusive nuisance with an infinite capacity for diplomatic mischief.

From the Minister of Information nothing could at this time be expected but bitter and deliberate hostility. The battle had been fought in the summer of 1941 for the control of subversive propaganda, and Mr Bracken had secured a firm footing in the tripartite control of PWE, which had once been Mr Dalton's exclusive domain. It was now his business to eject SOE entirely from the nest, and to reign alone, limited only by the joint responsibility of the Foreign Office – which would be far too preoccupied with other matters to exercise it effectively. The issue became in practice largely a personal one; and unfortunately, during the winter of 1941–2 Mr Bracken's great talents as a propagandist were largely directed to discrediting Mr Dalton and all his works, the principal of which was SOE.

SIS must perhaps also be reckoned among the enemies. As has been pointed out,[2] CSS had at the outset drawn attention to the extraordinary difficulties involved in running two separate secret services

---

[1] Above p. 69.
[2] Above p. 70.

in the same territories. The official view of the SIS was that as they were committed to this dangerous experiment SOE must give such assistance as they could; but that SIS's own work must have priority and the two organisations must so far as possible be segregated in order to avoid the contaminating contact of SOE. The danger was a real one: SOE was a raw and untrained organisation, and (even apart from this) it necessarily worked in an atmosphere fatal to the quiet methods of an intelligence service. In the nature of things, an SOE organisation must eventually expose itself by open violence, and even in its beginnings it must indulge in some political activity and move in circles where recklessness of consequences is one of the qualifications for leadership. SIS (rightly) felt that its own work paid dividends which must not be endangered; and in this attitude it could count on some support both from the Chiefs of Staff and from the Foreign Office.

So much for principle: unfortunately there is no doubt that relations between the secret departments were also coloured by more personal feelings – the old contrast between the polished product of tradition and the energetic but injudicious parvenu. This was mainly a matter of small incidents on a lower level in both organisations, and it was only rarely[1] that the trouble involved matters of the slightest historical importance. Formally relations at the top were correct, though distant, in lesser matters the atmosphere was bad; there is plenty of evidence of the suspicion and dislike which existed between various branches of the two organisations, both in London and in Missions overseas.

Too much can be made of all these departmental troubles; at the worst there were always individuals who could co-operate excellently with their 'opposite numbers', in spite of strained relations between departments. But there was certainly in the air early in 1942 a feeling that 'something must be done about SOE'; and the ministerial crisis which arose in February 1942 on quite other grounds was a favourable occasion for a judicious change.

Fortunately for SOE the opposition to it had no alternative programme. No department would lightly put itself forward for the task of taking over and running the organisation: there were various possible candidates – the Foreign Office (direct or through SIS), the War Office, the Ministry of Information – but none of them emerged as claimants for so uneasy a throne. There was some talk of outright abolition: but this would not bear thinking of in cold blood. There were eight exiled governments, every one of them growing daily more clamorous in its demands for effective aid to its countrymen at home,

---

[1] [NOTE DELETED ON GROUNDS OF NATIONAL SECURITY.]

and the cessation of organised assistance would have made life impossible for the Prime Minister as well as for the Foreign Office. The Chiefs of Staff equally were bound to insist on the maintenance of resistance in Europe: any sabotage achieved meantime would be a useful bonus, and it was profoundly important that when the invasion came some native organisations should rise to meet it. In the absence of any effective system of government on the spot, an expedition might easily be strangled by the weight of its commitment for the good order and maintenance of the civil population.

The solution therefore was not drastic. Mr Dalton passed to a higher office, and was succeeded by Lord Selborne, whose personality was in itself an essential part of the solution. He was a Conservative, and as such a sufficient answer to the allegation that SOE was concerned primarily to foment social revolution: yet he was a Conservative who had never been tied closely to the party machine, and no one who knew him could suspect that SOE would now become an organ of reaction. He was an experienced administrator, well-known for his part in the successful campaign to put some energy and humanity into the administration of the Post Office. He was a personal friend of the Minister of Information, and was one of these who had been with Mr Churchill in the wilderness after 1931. He was a grandson of the great Lord Salisbury,* and, though without personal experience at the Foreign Office, he could surely be depended on to understand its point of view and to make it part of his policy to maintain good relations with it.

The only important change in the scope of the department was that the Minister no longer took any part in the direction of PWE. Some changes were later negotiated in its relations to the Foreign Office and to the SIS, which will be referred to more fully below:[1] but they did not involve any drastic change in position. There were also a few internal changes. Mr Jebb had come to the department to give personal assistance to Mr Dalton, and it was natural that he should return to his Foreign Office career as soon as the new Minister had time to establish himself. When he left early in May, the ambiguous post of Chief Executive Officer was abolished, and Mr Sporborg took over in a position more analogous to that of Principal Private Secretary.[2] Sir Frank Nelson had borne the main burden of creating a vast organisation out of nothing, and the permanence of its main framework is the best testimonial to his work. But he was by this time a very sick man, and could not continue. He was replaced in May by Sir Charles Hambro, who had already acted as his Deputy.

---

[1] Below pp. 343 and 383 resp.
[2] SOE Archives File 2/340/3.1, CD/OR/1731 of 8th May 1942, refers.
* [1830–1903, repeatedly Prime Minister and Foreign Secretary.]

Other changes in organisation were mainly minor and consequential. But to meet the charges of maladministration a committee was appointed on 12th May 1942, consisting of an eminent businessman, Mr John Hanbury-Williams,* and an able Treasury official, Mr E. W. Playfair,** to report to the Minister 'on what improvements, alterations or extensions, if any, in the existing SOE machine are necessary or desirable to enable SOE fully to carry out the duties devolving on it under its Charter'.

Their report (dated 18th June) generally endorses what Lord Selborne had already written to the Prime Minister on 10th April,[1] summing up his first impressions of his task – 'much good work has been performed by zealous and patriotic men: if SOE is to function it must receive fair play as well as give it'. The Playfair Report (as it is generally called) acquits the London HQ of SOE of all the charges of nepotism, waste, corruption and incompetence which had been freely circulated, and admits no more than the inevitable incoherence of a newly formed secret organisation. It is less favourable to the Missions overseas, where men had to be chosen hastily, and could not be supervised and quickly replaced (as they could in London) if they proved to be the wrong men for the job. On the larger issues of departmental organisation it analyses the situation excellently, bringing out the impending change in the direction of SOE's work: 'When it first started, it had a programme of its own, correlated with but largely independent of day-to-day strategical developments. In a not very distant future, it may be destined to provide an integral part of the military machine.' Here the main practical problem is that of developing Brigadier Gubbins's Directorate of Operations and Training, so as to become in effect a 'Mission for Western Europe', capable if necessary of detachment from Headquarters so as to work closely with the military command in the event of invasion. The Report considers also the question of appointing a professional soldier as head of SOE; it sums up against it, but recommends that consideration should be given to the appointment of a military Chief of Staff.

As regards details, the main criticism was of the system by which eight separate branches, of approximately equal status, reported direct to CD and D/CD: this organisation (which grew up piece-meal) clearly threw too much weight on the heads of the organisation, and the diffi-

---

[1] Circulated as WP(42)170.

* [(Sir) J. C. Hanbury-Williams, director Bank of England 1936–63, of Courtaulds 1930–62, helped develop cellophane and nylon, courtier, in SOE 1942–5, knight 1950; in *DNB*.]

** [(Sir) E. W. Playfair, born 1909, PUS for War 1956–9 and Defence 1960–61, knight 1957.]

culty had been met in November 1941[1] by creating the post of 'Chief of Staff' (Colonel G. F. Taylor) to perform what were in effect the functions of a central planning and secretariat branch. The Report reaches the conclusion that this had led to duplication and confusion of channels, and it recommends the solution shown in the Chart attached as Appendix E, which gives the position as it was in July 1942. Here the 'Chief of Staff' has disappeared and the hierarchy is made more elaborate. One deputy (this was, from July 1942 to March 1943, Mr Hanbury-Williams himself) is responsible for administrative services, and (through Colonel Taylor) for the affairs of Missions overseas. The other (Brigadier Gubbins) brings together all the Country Sections whose operations are based on England, and with them the services directly ancillary to operations – there were strong grounds for including training among these. This block of directorates would in due course constitute SOE's 'invasion team'.

The other 'Playfair' recommendations affecting HQ turn mainly on details of financial control and on such matters as the pay and promotion of such SOE officials as had been commissioned into the Army. As regards the Missions overseas, their most important suggestion is that a high officer of SOE should be appointed Inspector of Missions and should visit all overseas Missions at least once a year. The Report here puts its finger on an important point. The state of world communications in 1941 and 1942 was such that a continuous interchange of officers between theatres was virtually impossible; once detached on a Mission an officer was out off from home, except for the opaque medium of the cipher telegram, and he would receive visits from high officers of his organisation 'only at moments of crisis when they are bound . . . to appear . . . as something like a witch-hunt'. This would perhaps have cured itself once the Mediterranean was open and aircraft were available in reasonable numbers for communications. The office of 'Controller of Missions' was however set up in July 1942[2] and was held by Colonel G. F. Taylor until its abandonment in April 1943.

3. The Mechanism of Inter-Departmental Relations

(a) The Foreign Office

It is unnecessary to summarise here once again the Foreign Office's grievances against SOE. It should however be made plain that SOE was no less anxious about the damage to British interests which might be done by the Foreign Office. One or two quotations will suffice. 'I

---

[1] 'Re-organisation of London HQ' CD/OR/494/AD of 12th November 1941; copy on SOE Archives File 2/340/3.1.

[2] CD/OR/2473 of 8th July 1942 – SOE Archives File 2/340/3.1.

feel that the Foreign Office still regards us as nasty people who run around with explosives and that they do not really understand what subversive warfare entails.'[1] 'Vacillation, delays, indecision and perhaps even obstruction.'[2] 'My personal view is that the Foreign Office do not wish to be burdened with the responsibility for SOE; but wish to control it by means of a "Treaty" and by means of stead-fast and settled obstruction, until it has been reduced to an innocuous bomb disposal squad.'[3]

Much of this was a matter of overstrained nerves; each department attributed to the other as its settled policy what was merely the result of overwork, bewilderment and bad organisation. But it was not a situation which could be left to settle itself, and the line of approach chosen was the negotiation of a 'Treaty' – a fair specimen of what Sir Frank Nelson in one place calls 'the curious compromises and expedients of British administration'.[4] With all deference to the Foreign Office, it is singular that their approach to the problem of subversion, now that it was forced upon them, was to devise a document laying down at great length what SOE should *not* do.

The negotiations were opened by a letter from Mr Eden on 4th February forwarding a memorandum by Sir Alexander Cadogan,[5] which appeared to imply the reduction of SOE to the status of a subsidiary of the Foreign Office controlled by a high official, on the analogy of SIS. Mr Dalton returned a conciliatory reply on 10th February drawing attention to some of the difficulties which this would involve,[6] and the Ministers met on 12th February. The first draft of an agreement was produced by Mr Jebb on 13th February. Discussion of this did not proceed far before the change of Ministers on 22nd February, which interrupted this piece of business until early April. The 'Treaty' was never formally signed by the two Ministers, nor approved by any higher authority, but both departments accepted as binding the text agreed between Sir Alexander Cadogan and Mr Jebb on 15th May 1942.*

This document is of such importance that it is printed in full as an Appendix,[7] and it need not be summarised here. It was not submitted either to the Prime Minister or to the War Cabinet, or to any other

---

[1] Brigadier Gubbins – M/XX/342 of 18th February 1942.
[2] Sir Frank Nelson – CD/XX/423 of 18th February 1942.
[3] Sir Frank Nelson – CD/OR/550 of 7th April 1942. (Refs 1., 2., 3. SOE Archives File (AD/S.1) F/104/2 refers).
[4] CD/XX/524 of 27th March 1942.
[5] Copy on SOE Archives File (AD/S.1) F/104/2.
[6] Copy on SOE Archives File (AD/S.1) F/104/2.
[7] Appendix D.
* [See Michael Balfour, *Propaganda in War 1939–1945* (1979), p. 88 ff.]

department: yet in effect it is much more than a gloss on the original charter framed by Mr Chamberlain and approved by the War Cabinet in July 1940. In some respects it constitutes a new charter, much more elaborate than the first, but no less anomalous.

First, on the constitutional side. Here two contradictory propositions stand side by side:

(a) As it is put in the Playfair Report:[1] 'SOE is an executive and operational and not a policy-making body.' Its position would be thus analogous to that of a public corporation or of a Commander-in-Chief in the field, not to that of a Department of State. 'While . . . SOE have a right to advance opinions and conduct operations on their own, they execute the policy of His Majesty's Government as laid down in their respective spheres by the Chiefs of Staff, the Foreign Office and other Departments of State.'[2]

(b) Yet it is directed by a Minister of the Crown – a full Minister, not an Under-Secretary – and 'As a Minister of the Crown, the Minister of Economic Warfare has, in his capacity as head of SOE, . . . a general right of appeal against an adverse decision by a Department to any particular proposal of his. On all matters affecting operations the suitable court of appeal would be the Defence Committee.'[3] In other words, SOE is a Ministry and not an 'executive agency': the Minister can challenge the action of any other department by appeal to the Prime Minister, the War Cabinet or the Defence Committee, as appropriate in each case.

Doubt still surrounds the exact constitutional status of that unexpected product of the 'Ministers of the Crown Act, 1937', a Minister of Cabinet rank who is not a member of the Cabinet. But clearly his responsibility (whatever it is) is one which he bears himself. He is perhaps free of responsibility for the general policy of the Government, except for his private responsibility as a member of the Party in power. But as regards the conduct of his department there is no doubt that he is fully responsible, legally to the Crown and politically to Parliament: the responsibility cannot be shaken off or limited by any agreement with another department. It is either nonsensical or irrelevant to add,[4] 'It is understood that the Minister will only exercise his right of appeal in regard to matters which seem to him of the first

---

[1] Para. 4(b).
[2] Foreign Office Treaty, para. 3.
[3] Foreign Office Treaty, para. 6.
[4] Foreign Office Treaty, last sentence of para. 6.

importance from the point of view of the conduct of special operations': this is not a matter on which the Minister can be bound without ceasing to be a Minister.

These constitutional points are of some substantial importance; the British constitution may be only a matter of 'working arrangements' – but this is certainly not an arrangement which will work. The more precise instructions as to SOE's work are equally elusive. For one thing, it is clear that the Foreign Office were hankering after a convenient distinction between 'sabotage' and 'subversion': war which is a matter for the Chiefs of Staff, and politics which is a matter for the Foreign Office.[1] This is strangely archaic in itself, and the earlier narrative will have shown that it was meaningless in relation to the operations of SOE. With rare exceptions (Norway and Denmark are the strongest cases), every saboteur and guerilla was a politician: not every politician was a saboteur, but every politician's career depended on harnessing the potential saboteurs to his own purposes. Nothing could be done by SOE which did not have political implications: SOE saw this and believed that the Foreign Office could not be blind to it except of set purpose – they *must* be attempting to control and strangle the whole work of SOE, under the plea of specious distinctions. In fact, the Foreign Office seem to have believed in all seriousness that a valid distinction existed.

This is borne out by the care which was taken to divide the whole world into five zones, to each of which different considerations should apply.

(a) Enemy and occupied territories. Here military directives are paramount: only the 'political line' is to be taken from the Foreign Office.

(b) Vichy territories – the 'Foreign Office have a special interest in those areas', and nothing is to be done without *general* Foreign Office authority.

(c) Neutral territories. 'Here the interests of foreign policy are predominant' (whatever that may mean), and there is no action without *specific* Foreign Office authority.

(d) In unoccupied Allied countries: SOE's interests are small, but can be freely pursued, on agreement *by SOE* with the Allied government concerned.

---

[1] e.g. Mr Jebb's F/3299/104 of 17th February 1942 to CD – 'We (Sir Alexander Cadogan and Mr Jebb) had a long argument on this point and I more or less got him to say that in practice the two' (sabotage and subversion) 'could not be sharply distinguished: but he nevertheless was very keen on some specific reference to sabotage being put among the "purposes of SOE".'

(e) Finally, Latin American states (whether belligerent or neutral) are to be as much a Foreign Office preserve as neutral countries.

It cannot be said that any of these provisos are at all clear, except (c) and (e), which relate to areas of little importance in the general picture of foreign policy. The vital countries of occupied Europe – France, Poland, Yugoslavia, Greece – remain in a position as ambiguous as before: and the position as regards enemy countries is almost equally vague, except that all peace feelers must at once be referred to the Foreign Office.

It is impossible to believe that the 'Treaty' did anything to improve the conduct of business, and major rows were not much less common than before. But on the whole minor friction decreased. This was partly due to increased experience on both sides, partly also to the growing paramountcy of the military, in particular of the Americans; but it was also important that Lord Selborne made it a cardinal point of his policy that SOE should go along with the Foreign Office in all cases where co-operation was possible. We have already seen his attitude in regard to Greece,[1] and there will be other examples later.

There was also some talk at this stage of improvement in formal arrangements for liaison, in particular of the appointment of a Foreign Office liaison officer to SOE – after Mr Jebb had left there was no professional diplomat in SOE's staff. No action was taken on this until August 1943 when Mr Houstoun Boswall, CMG, MC,* was given an office in Baker Street for liaison duties. The only step forward at the moment was the constitution of a Foreign Office-SOE liaison committee,[2] which met once a fortnight from 19th May 1942: the representatives at first were Sir Orme Sargent, Sir Maurice Peterson, Sir David Scott and Mr William Strang on one side,** Sir Charles Hambro, Mr J. Hanbury-Williams, Colonel George Taylor, and Lieutenant Colonel Sporborg on the other. This too must have helped to ease matters on minor issues, though major disturbances were beyond its scope.

---

1   Above p. 157.
2   SOE Archives File (AD/S.1) F/104/5 gives early correspondence and Minutes of first meetings.
*   [(Sir) W. E. Houstoun-Boswall, 1892–1960, Minister at Beirut 1947–51, knight 1949.]
** [Sir M. D. Peterson, 1889–1952, knight 1938, worked under Lloyd in Cairo, Ambassador to Baghdad 1938–9, to Madrid 1939–40, to Ankara 1944–6 and to Moscow 1946–52; in *DNB*; see his *Both sides of the Curtain* (1950). Sir D. J. M. D. Scott, 1887–1986, Assistant Under-Secretary in Foreign Office, knight 1941. (Sir) W. Strang, 1893–1978, knight 1943, PUS Foreign Office 1949–53, baron 1954; in *DNB*; see his *Home and Abroad* (1956).]

(b) The Chiefs of Staff

Relations with the Foreign Office were thus essentially negative: SOE asked for no general directives and was given none.[1] A much more positive attitude was adopted throughout by the Chiefs of Staff and the Joint Planners, and there is a long series of papers which constitute SOE's strategic directives. There was no formal liaison[2] until Lieutenant Colonel D. R. Guinness was appointed as SOE liaison officer with the Chiefs of Staff Secretariat in January 1942: and even then he was accommodated in Baker Street, not in the Cabinet Offices.[3] But personal relations were excellent between SOE's officers on the one side and the Chiefs of Staff Secretariat and JPS on the other. Things went a little less smoothly on the higher levels: Mr Jebb, Sir Frank Nelson or Brigadier Gubbins would nominally be summoned to a Chiefs of Staff meeting where SOE was directly concerned, but there were some mishaps, and in any case SOE was not summoned if its interest (though real) was only indirect. There was complaint that chances were thus missed, because SOE was not consulted in the formative stage of discussion: and at intervals SOE reasserted the view[4] that it was the Fourth Arm of modern war, and could not be effectively used unless it were given full membership of the COS, the JPS and the JIC.[5] But debate on this controversy was never pushed very far, and the system worked happily enough without a solution of the point of principle.

We have already dealt with the general directives which prescribed SOE's task in the autumn of 1940.[6] These documents were all couched

---

[1] The only *positive* proposal by the Foreign Office which I have found is a suggestion for the recruitment of suitable British to act as a 'fifth column' in neutral countries, which was brought up to the JIC in March 1941 (JIC(41)127). This contrasts oddly with the Foreign Office's usual attitude and its origin is obscure. The approach was rather crossly received by SOE, which felt it had the job in hand already, and the discussion petered out (some papers on SOE Archives File 1/470/1).

[2] Fortnightly progress reports were made by SOE to the COS from 11th January 1942 to 1st March 1942: thereafter monthly. These are not very intelligible taken by themselves, and were rarely discussed by the COS.

[3] Minute from CD to CEO dated 22nd January 1942, on SOE Archives File (AD/S.1) SC/98. This was the upshot of discussion at a COS meeting in December 1941 – mentioned in memo. CD to CEO of 22nd December 1941, on SOE Archives File (AD/S.1) SC/98. Lieutenant Colonel Guiness was succeeded by Lieutenant Colonel Rowlandson in December 1942.

[4] For the formal authority for it, see above p. 84.

[5] In this period see for instance Brigadier Gubbins to the JPS 22nd April 1942, on SOE Archives File 1/470/1 Pt II.

[6] Above p. 91.

in very broad terms, and gave almost unlimited scope. In due course a point was reached at which SOE could be given limited and attainable objectives within a detailed operational plan: but only the first steps in this development had been taken by the summer of 1942.

Many of the more detailed references in Chiefs of Staff discussion have already been mentioned, and it is not necessary to revert to them: they became progressively more numerous as the war goes on, until finally there is scarcely a COS meeting which does not contain some reference to SOE. Perhaps five 'sequences' of general discussion can be traced separately in this period, though the division is in some ways arbitrary.

First, there was the COS meeting of 31st March 1941,[1] which had before it papers on 'The Organisation and Method of Working of SO2',[2] on SO2 projects, and on SO2's outline plan for 'Claribel' (action in the event of German invasion). SOE's generalities were still very general, and skated over a great many uncertainties with an air of confidence. There is nothing on strategic policy which represents any new departure, and the Chiefs of Staff do not appear to have discussed the policy paper at length, although it was 'noted with approval'. The main points recorded in the Minutes are in relation to 'Claribel'. 'Claribel' was to be kept in being, although no 'target date' for completion should be given. But it was not to be given absolute priority: some of the personnel earmarked for 'Claribel' could be employed on other secondary tasks, others could treat 'Claribel' for the present as secondary. This to some extent cleared the decks of a cumbrous and unpromising operation, though it remained formally in existence for some time longer.

From this develops almost at once a second step, in which SOE is working pretty closely in combination with the F.Ops Section of the JPS (under Mr Oliver Stanley)* on the preparation of a detailed study of the future course of the war. Part of the development of their ideas can be traced from SOE papers. On 2nd April Colonel Anstruther (who was then SOE's 'Planning Officer') had a long discussion with F.Ops, on which he reports[3] that they were looking ultimately to the creation of a British striking force of six armoured and four infantry divisions; so small a force could only be effective in conjunction with 'a universal uprising of oppressed peoples'. 'The harassing and mopping up of the German armed forces will have to be done by

---

[1] COS(41)9th Mtg, (0) Item 1, of 31st March.

[2] Dated 26th March 1941, copy headed 'SO2' on SOE Archives File 1/470/1.

[3] Copy on SOE Archives File 1/470/1.

* [O. F. G. Stanley, 1896–1950, son of 17th Earl of Derby, Conservative MP from 1924, War Secretary 1940, Colonial Secretary 1942–5; in *DNB*.]

irregular bands of nationals of the countries. This means that SOE will have to organise and equip guerillas on a vast scale.' Here the Sten gun, the characteristic weapon of the Resistance, appears in SOE's papers for the first time, and a requirement for a million of them is suggested.[1] But what the F.Ops want is a more detailed estimate of SOE's requirements for all-out guerilla war.

There were two SOE answers to this request. One was a general paper on 'The Prospects of Subversion',[2] which rehearses yet again the case for subversion – 'Subversion is a weapon which we can use offensively and continuously wherever the enemy's interests can be reached. Intangible and elusive, it is a form of attack which exerts a constant pressure and constitutes a continuous strain on his resources and his will.' It is all very ably done – is indeed right and convincing – but it does not advance matters much. Its conclusion is to ask the Chiefs of Staff to endorse the policy suggested, and 'to make available to SOE the men and materials' (particularly aircraft) 'necessary for carrying it out'. But it does not indicate how many men and how many aircraft – what is the Allied commitment involved? It admits (as it must) that subversion 'ultimately depends for its success on the armed forces': but it does not attempt to show how much the armed forces will have to be weakened in order to strengthen the guerillas. As General Ismay wrote to Mr Jebb in acknowledging receipt of the paper, 'Much as we may deplore it, the COS are at present faced with the problem of having to feed many hungry mouths with bread, on which the butter has to be spread very sparingly . . . . To sum up, I feel sure that the COS would agree, in principle, with your paper, but I am positive that they would not be prepared to give you the carte blanche for which you ask.'[3]

This problem of specific material requirements was tackled for the first time by Brigadier Gubbins in a paper dated 21st May 1941, with explosive effect.[4] Here the plan emerges more clearly, in three phases:

(1) The organisation and equipment of a sabotage system in the occupied territories.

(2) The organisation and equipment of underground armies in occupied territories.

(3) The ultimate revolt, which can only be effective if given some regular stiffening: for this purpose the Allied contingents in

---

[1] At least 650,000 were in the end used by SOE (App. B, to Section A of 'Supplies History'). [See Kahn & Lorain, *Secret Warfare*, pp. 118–21, for diagrams.]

[2] Copy on SOE Archives File 1/470/1.

[3] Letter of 24th April 1941 – quoted in 'History of Special Duty Operations in Europe', p. 14.

[4] Copy on SOE Archives File 1/470/1.

Britain must be retrained as airborne shock troops, who must be flown in as soon as the guerillas can receive mass drops of parachutists and capture an airfield.

This is unmistakably the correct solution, and it was in effect that ultimately adopted – and where it was not adopted risings failed catastrophically. But its implications were alarming, when worked out for three typical countries, Poland, Czechoslovakia and France. A few figures will illustrate this.

A. *Sabotage Groups of 7 men*

	Poland (1,000 Groups)	Czech (700 Groups)	France (350 Groups)	*Total*
Sub-machine guns	7,000	4,900	2,450	14,350
Wireless sets	1,318	962	458	2,758
Plastic Explosives (lbs)	54,000	58,800	28,400	171,200 lbs (77 tons)
Parachute containers	5,000	3,500	1,575	10,075
Aircraft Sorties	1,250	875	394	2,519

B. *Secret Armies*

	Poland (84 Bns)	Czech (100 Bns)	France (70 Bns)	*Total*
Light machine-guns	5,124	6,100	4,270	15,500
Sub-machine guns	13,112	16,800	11,760	42,000
Pistols	43,680	52,000	36,400	132,000
Wireless Sets	1,260	1,500	980	3,770
Containers	10,500	12,500	7,875	30,875
Aircraft Sorties	2,625	3,125	1,968	7,718

These are merely extracts: the original paper gives the scale of equipment in detail. In some senses the figures are no more than a 'pipe-dream': Brigadier Gubbins did not forget that there were all sorts of incalculable factors – it would be a remarkable piece of organisation (for instance) if the equipment reached the Resistance with less than 25–30 per cent wastage from enemy action: abortive aircraft sorties must be allowed for: and so forth. But most of these imponderables tended to increase rather than reduce his figures: and no one could say that his scale of equipment was too high for guerillas whose target was to be the German army, even in its decline, or that rebellions would have been worth staging with smaller forces. Yet this very limited force would require some 8,000 aircraft sorties: what that meant in aircraft would depend on how many months were allowed – if the job were to be done by the spring of 1942 it would require

444 aircraft, practically all of which must be heavy bombers and would not be available for any other operations at moon periods. This would be reduced if a longer period were allowed: to allow till spring 1943 would almost halve the aircraft commitment. Finally there remained the shock and support troops on whose arrival the fate of the risings would depend: as always, the aircraft requirement for airborne troops depends on how many must be taken in one lift, and what wastage is expected on each lift. The figure for 620 aircraft for this purpose is the only figure in the paper which might with good fortune prove to be a maximum.

Even in the autumn of 1941 SOE had eight Whitleys and five Halifaxes available in No. 138 Squadron: in the Mediterranean it had two antique Wellesleys. When Brigadier Gubbins's paper was written the operational strength of Bomber Command included only ninety heavy bombers.[1] The Blitz was not yet over, the invasion of Europe was still a distant dream, and the minds of strategists and plain men were full of the possibilities of the Bomber. The Air Staff were working on a new programme which contemplated a force of 4,000 heavy bombers by the spring of 1943:[2] a project which was only within the bounds of possibility granted absolute concentration both of British and American resources on this one target. There could not be a less favourable time at which to talk of the diversion of aircraft from the attack on Germany: and when it was put in this way the problem of subversion at once began to come into sharper perspective.

Brigadier Gubbins's paper was forwarded to the F.Ops on 24th May 1941: on 27th May they discussed it with Lieutenant Colonel R. H. Barry, on 29th May with Mr Sporborg. Their comments are recorded in Minutes by Brigadier Gubbins[3] and Mr Sporborg, and traverse the whole basis of SOE's programme. There are two lines of argument –

(a) First, that of broad strategic theory. It is admitted by Mr Sporborg 'that our secret army however good and however well equipped could never retake Norway itself. It could play an extremely useful role resulting in considerable economy of force, but it could never play a principal role.'

From this admission the reasoning runs as follows:

If a Secret Army can only act as an auxiliary and not as a principal, it cannot be used except in the event of the British landing a force in its territory.

---

[1] Out of a total operational strength of 842. Figures supplied by Air Ministry (Central Statistical Branch).
[2] JP(41)374(0), 4th Draft, para. 197.
[3] Both dated 30th May 1941, in SOE Archives File 1/470/1. See also Sir Charles Hambro's Minute of 1st June.

There can be no British landing in face of overwhelming German land forces until we have overwhelming air superiority.

When we have air superiority and are fully armed, we will probably find that our air superiority can be decisive without any military operations at all.

On the foregoing assumptions, the Secret Army would never be used, except perhaps to stage a final massacre of Huns about a week before the Armistice.

This is logical enough but too absolute to be convincing. So long as we stood alone, it was true that an army of ten divisions could not defeat one of 250 divisions unless a miracle was achieved by the air superiority which was undoubtedly possible with the resources of America at our backs: and it was defeatism to doubt the miracle. Such a force as 4,000 heavy bombers would introduce a new scale of destruction into war, and all things were possible for it. But there was scarcely enough analysis of what the miracle would look like when it came to pass: it must clearly in the end be a psychological rather than a physical miracle – no physical destruction from the air would be enough to redress the balance – and the right make-up of the bomber loads might well turn out to be as much a question of politics and psychology as of high explosives.

(b) Thus far SOE had a reasonable though unpopular case: but it was on weaker ground if strategy were looked at more concretely. The sabotage plan would require 15 per cent of the existing bomber force, the Secret Armies would require 40 per cent: a large part of this would be directed to creating risings in Poland and Czechoslovakia, because they gave the best geographical and political scope for secret armies: but when the time came these risings could not be given the air support (and the supplies and reinforcements from the air) which would be necessary to give them a fair chance. As an operation of war, then, Secret Armies in the East must be abandoned, and effort must be concentrated on France, Belgium, Holland and Norway, where something real might be achieved with a very much smaller expenditure of aircraft. This appears conclusive on its own ground: but unfortunately it reckoned without the Poles and Polish politics – it is hard enough to leave an army to perish unsupported, impossible to leave a nation.

F.Ops great paper[1] was by this time already in draft and allocated a large role both to sabotage and Secret Armies. The former figured prominently in the programme for economic war (paras 156–60): the

---

[1] JP(41)374(0) of 2nd June 1941.

plan for the coup de grâce was based entirely on the latter (paras 255–80). So important a place did SOE fill in the picture that at one point (paras 159–60) the F.Ops by implication endorsed SOE's claim to be a Fourth Arm, entitled to equal representation on every level: but the two points set out above, which answered Brigadier Gubbins's paper, were not included, and it was left to future discussion (para. 273) to work out the detailed implications of the final rising.

All this labour (unfortunately) was overtaken by events. It was already clear to a small circle that the attack on Russia was impending, and it came on 22nd June. The F.Ops had allowed for this contingency: but only as a contingency, and their paper as a whole could not be based on it. It therefore became obsolete at once, and perished in draft.[1] On 3rd July Mr Jebb saw Mr Oliver Stanley and the F.Ops, who were then about to set to work anew. Their labours ultimately bore fruit in COS(41)155(0) of 31st July, which got a little further, but seems also to have perished before reaching the Defence Committee. In this the references to Subversion (paras 33–5) were greatly watered down; it was plainly hinted that its priority for aircraft must be relatively low, and no more was expected from it than that 'these methods will make a substantial contribution to the offensive'. In fact, now that Russian manpower was in the field the manpower of Occupied Europe became a rather secondary matter. Furthermore, the political situation had become confused and unpredictable.

For the purposes of this revised paper F.Ops had called in haste for a moderate and practical plan by SOE for operations in the immediate future. This took shape as the 'Outline Plan of SO2 Operations from 1st September 1941 to 1st October 1942', dated 15th July, which deserves separate treatment. The paper was forwarded by Mr Dalton to the Prime Minister on 16th July and referred by him to the Chiefs of Staff:[2] SOE's operational programme was thus submitted for decision independently of the proposed 'bible' of British strategy, and before any 'bible' had been adopted.

The paper is a formidable document, which occupies sixteen foolscap pages with its annexes (many of them in statistical form): so that it cannot be summarised very fully here. For the first time one has a statement of policy that looks like a General Staff study and not like an academic essay on the theory of modern war. Discussion

---

[1] Cf. the Prime Minister's remark at the Defence Committee Meeting of 25th June (DO(41)44th) which had before it JP(41)444: 'he was not convinced of the value of such papers for distribution to Dominion Governments or Cs-in-C. Much of the contents became rapidly out of date and statements were falsified before they were read.' See also Mr Jebb's Minute of 3rd July 1941 on SOE Archives File 1/470/1.

[2] Circulated by them as COS(41)147(0) of 21st July.

of the general role of Subversion is concluded in a single paragraph, and the paper proceeds to give 'the minimum programme which will make a really effective contribution without excessive demands on the RAF' (para. 4). The assumption is made that the earliest date for action is the autumn of 1942, and confirmation of this is requested.

The plan itself clearly shows the effects of comment on Brigadier Gubbins's trial balloon of 21st May. The scale of operations is greatly reduced, and the Secret Armies of Poland and Czechoslovakia have been abandoned. The programme is now (for a date postponed by six months) reduced to:

	Saboteurs	*Secret Armies*	Aircraft Sorties *1 Sept. 41 to 1 Oct. 42*
Norway	500	19,000	315
Denmark	500	–	36
Holland	1,000	5,000	265
Belgium	700	6,000	300
France	3,000	24,000	1,200
Poland	2,000	–	130
Czechoslovakia	1,200	–	88

This has come down from 10,237 aircraft sorties to 2,334; these cover more territory, but much of it within a more economical range of operation. Only sixty sorties are asked for to the Balkans.[1] SOE wisely refrain (para. 13) from estimating how many aircraft would be needed to do the job – there are too many imponderables such as weather conditions, navigational equipment, casualty rate, range and speed of aeroplanes available. But as an illustration one may say that the programme involved an average, summer and winter, of about 180 successful sorties a month: on the average, an aircraft would do well to find its target and deliver four times a month. Thus the scale indicated is an establishment of forty to fifty medium bombers: say three squadrons. This was more than the Air Ministry was likely to accept: but it was not an unreasonable allocation to demand out of a bomber force which had now reached squadrons.

The paper was also reasonable in stressing that the Chiefs of Staff need not accept the programme as a whole: Secret Armies could be eliminated, or some countries might be cut out. But there must be a plan: 'without a regular plan on a considerable scale, thought out and

---

[1] In the event there seem to have been 280 successful aircraft sorties from the UK during the period contemplated: there are no proper figures for the Balkans, but there cannot have been more than twenty successful sorties there, at the most.

approved well in advance, there is grave risk that, if at some future date (which may well coincide with a most critical phase of the war) SO2 are ordered to press the button which would cause a European explosion, the result would be either a succession of feeble reports, or a flicker and a splutter'. The immediate conclusion is that there must be a very early decision, which would constitute authority for detailed collaboration with the Air Ministry, the War Office, SIS (for wireless communications), and Allied Governments.

The Joint Planners commented fully on this paper on 9th August.[1] It was inevitable that a good deal of water should be added to SOE's wine. Sabotage is to be adjusted to the bomber plan (para. 3): 'it would be unsound to sacrifice the effectiveness of our bombing effort to subversive activities' (para. 12): the requirements of SIS must not be interfered with (para. 12): the demands for equipment must be postponed to the equipment of British forces (para. 15). But the Joint Planners did recommend the increase of No. 1419 Flight to a full squadron: a great increase in wireless facilities: an allocation of 25 per cent of what was required for Secret Armies in France, Holland and Belgium by the spring of 1942. They did give a specific order of priority – Northern France, Belgium, Holland, Norway, in that order – and some other explicit suggestions. The greatest set-back perhaps was that they refused to accept SOE's document as a true 'Outline Plan': it must be treated as 'more in the nature of a target to be aimed at' (para. 17) – a 'Cock-shy' which was probably too ambitious, but could hardly even be criticised until more experience had been gained. The framing of a real 'plan' was adjourned to the spring of 1942.

SOE decided not to fight on any of these issues[2] – after all the JPS were on very strong ground – and there was no serious controversy before the Chiefs of Staff, who discussed the paper with the Joint Intelligence Committee on 14th August,[3] and with Mr Jebb and Brigadier Gubbins on 15th August.[4] On policy, it was minuted only that 'subversive activities should be given every encouragement',[5] but certain practical points were covered which implied authority to go ahead with the plan:[6]

---

1 JP(41)649 of 9th August.
2 Mr Jebb to General Ismay 12th August 1941, on SOE Archives File 1/470/1.
3 COS(41)287th Mtg, Item 10, 14th August.
4 COS(41)288th Mtg, Item 14.
5 See also Brigadier Gubbins's Minute giving a fuller account, dated 17th August 1941; copy on SOE Archives File 1/470/1.
6 On 18th August Mr Jebb asked General Ismay to write Mr Dalton more specifically on this point: I have not found any such letter from General Ismay.

(a) Sabotage should be generally directed in accordance with the bombing policy aim.
(b) The Air Ministry would provide a squadron as soon as possible.
(c) The provision of sorties for SO2 should not be allowed to interfere with the requirements of SIS.
(d) The War Office would report on the availability of arms and equipment, and Secret Armies would then be discussed again.
(e) The Admiralty would try to provide a suitable ship at Gibraltar for infiltration into the south of France and North Africa.

On 20th August General Ismay notified the Prime Minister of the Chiefs of Staff conclusions, and there matters rested for the present.[1] No. 138 Squadron was formed in the autumn of 1941 out of No. 1419 Flight, and a second squadron (No. 161) began to form in February 1942. The CIGS reported that the equipment required for Secret Armies could in the main be made available if adequate notice was given.[2] On 24th October CD formally called on all heads of Country Sections to prepare detailed plans in consultation with Brigadier Gubbins's department, and to keep careful records of achievement during the winter's campaign.

One summary[3] gives the following figures which serve to indicate what became of this first concrete plan:

1st September 1941–15th January 1942

Country	Successful Sorties	Unsuccessful Sorties (no details)	Agents Dropped	Containers and Packages
Norway	1		2	2
Denmark	1		2	1
Holland	2		4	–
Belgium	4		8	7
France	13		27	14
Poland	3		15	6
Czechoslovakia	2		8	6
Totals	26	27	66	36

[1] Copies on SOE Archives Files 1/470/1 and SC.98 (AD/S.1)
[2] COS(41)536 dated 31st August 1941, approved by COS(41)309th Mtg, Item 4: also COS(41)219(0) of 28th September, and COS(41)339th Mtg, Item 1, of 1st October.
[3] Progress Report from 'AD' to 'CEO', dated 18th January 1942, on SOE Archives File (AD/S.1) SC.98.

We have already seen what this meant in preparation and perplexity in each of these countries: the effort it represented was very much larger than would appear, either from the figures or from the visible development of resistance. But it was far from satisfying the Allies, and their discontent became a general offensive in the spring of 1942 under the leadership of General Sikorski. The issue was also forced by General Marshall who was in London in April, pressing for a resolute attempt to plan the invasion of Europe in 1942. These two threads, relations with the Allies and plans for invasion, run closely parallel, but it may be clearest to follow each in isolation.

General Sikorski had intervened at what was obviously a decisive crisis of strategy with a paper strongly supporting the creation of a Second Front in Europe.[1] One passage in this was aimed directly at SOE. The resistance of the occupied countries 'will carry far greater significance than is generally supposed, provided that *the effort of the united nations will be directed on uniform lines, prepared methodically and co-ordinated with the whole war plan'*. '*A common Staff should be established for all the countries in Europe under German occupation.* This Staff should consist of General Staff officers of those occupied countries which may be seriously considered in connection with the future armed risings.' This 'common Allied staff' would in effect take over the directing role of SOE, which would be reduced (if it continued to exist) to the status of a supply and transport agency.

Here at last was a claimant for the inheritance of SOE: but not one likely to appeal to the military instincts of the Chiefs of Staff. The Joint Planners were briefed on their answer[2] largely by SOE,[3] and they took a firm line. They adhered to the view that 'An airborne invasion of Poland and Czechoslovakia is impossible. The transport of arms for the "secret armies" of those countries is not at present possible. Even if possible, it would not be justifiable at the expense of the bomber offensive, except on a small scale for diversionary activities by special groups.' They also accepted SOE's arguments against a 'Common Allied Staff':

(a) It would be dominated by the Poles.
(b) It would be incapable of reaching agreement.
(c) It would be hopelessly insecure.
(d) If it did reach agreement, it would be able to bring undue pressure to bear on the Chiefs of Staff.

---

[1] COS(42)101(0) of 15th April, COS(42)122nd Mtg, Item 5, of 17th April, and related papers.
[2] JP(42)465 of 1st May 1942.
[3] JP(42)423(S) of 19th April, and Brigadier Gubbins's Minute to the JPS dated 22nd April 1942 – on SOE Archives File 1/470/1 Pt 2.

SOE had reverted in its brief to the 'Fourth Arm' theory and had suggested that all Allied Governments should be formally notified of its status. The JPS (once more) evade this awkward issue, but agree that it should be impressed on General Sikorski that 'SOE acts as the co-ordinating authority charged with dealing with the General Staffs of the occupied territories'. The COS accepted this,[1] along with the JPS's other recommendations, and the CIGS wrote to General Sikorski accordingly. It then became clear that it was essential that other Allied Governments should be similarly directed into one channel, that of SOE, and on 1st June the Chiefs of Staff agreed upon a letter to all the exiled Governments, to be dispatched over the signature of Sir Alan Brooke as Chairman of the Chiefs of Staff Committee:[2] copies were sent to the Joint Staff Mission in Washington and to all Cs-in-C abroad.[3]

This letter[4] (though in some cases the Allied Governments took care to forget its terms) was an important landmark for SOE: like the 'Foreign Office Treaty' it was in effect a new charter under the guise of an interpretation. Unlike the 'Treaty', it extended only to the occupied countries, but within that area it had far more reality and weight. It was clear that Resistance might have some day some military value: it was still clearer that it possessed already immense power to waste the time of the Chiefs of Staff and possibly some power to endanger important strategic decisions. From the Chiefs of Staff point of view there *must* be some 'buffer state', to soothe the Allies, to disentangle their demands and so far as possible to align them with the main plans: SOE was there in readiness for this role, and the role would inevitably give it great power, 'as the agent to whom the General Staffs should refer on all matters in connection with sabotage and the organisation of resistance and secret armies'.

The Foreign Office had been consulted and appear to have concurred.[5]

There had been some general discussion during April of SOE's part in the attack on oil targets.[6] But this was not a field in which SOE

---

[1] COS(42)137th Mtg, Minute 11, of 2nd May, and COS(42)141st Mtg, Minute 5, of 6th May. See also COS(42)142(0) of 19th May and COS(42)159th Mtg, Minute 15, of 23rd May.

[2] COS(42)274 (Revise) of 21st May, and COS(42)166th Mtg, Minute 11, of 1st June.

[3] COS(42)178th Mtg, Minute 7, of 13th June, and COS(ME)No. 271 of 13th June.

[4] Reproduced as Appendix F.

[5] Letter from Colonel G. R. Price (COS Secretariat) to Mr W. Strang, dated 3rd June 1942; copy on SOE Archives File 1/470/1 Pt 2. [C. R. Price, 1905–87, military assistant secretary to War Cabinet 1940–46, DMI 1956–9.]

[6] COS(42)102(0), COS(42)113(0), COS(42)138th Mtg, Item 7, and related papers refer.

could contribute much as yet: and the main point of strategical interest is the drafting of a directive 'in order that action by SOE should conform to the general plan for an offensive proposed by General Marshall'.[1] Home Forces were consulted, as they were then (with CCO) primarily responsible for invasion planning, and they testified that their liaison with SOE was already close: what they wanted was what SOE would find very difficult to give, 'rather more exact appreciations' of what could be expected from the general population. Home Forces also undertook to keep SOE closely informed of 'the areas in which the action of patriot forces and sabotage can be most effective'.[2]

The document which resulted[3] was severely practical, indeed Puritanical: its formal military phrasing contrasts oddly with the human struggle and confusion which was SOE's standing army in the field. But it was full of meaning. It informed SOE specifically of forthcoming operations, enumerated the authorities responsible, and enjoined continuous collaboration: SOE had been accepted as a military authority with a clear place in the hierarchy. What is more, 'SOE should endeavour to build up and equip para-military organisations in the area of the projected operations'. There is all the difference in the world between the languid concurrence in a trial of Secret Armies, given in August 1941: and the precise directive to create them for one or more specific operations. This is not a plan: but it is in effect an instruction to go ahead and damn the political consequences. It is not known if the Foreign Office were consulted or concurred.

(c) The Service Departments

So much for higher strategy. The guidance given had not been very continuous nor always very clear: but liaison had been reasonably well maintained. On the whole, the same may be said as regards the individual Service departments and organisations at home: as we have seen, the position in Middle East was more awkward.[4]

Since July 1940, the War Office had never shown any anxiety to control or absorb SOE: SOE on the other hand had to some extent assimilated itself to the War Office. It had an office at the Horse Guards: its normal cover for doing business was that of MO1(SP), a

---

[1] Secretary of JPS to Brigadier McNabb, GHQ Home Forces, dated 21st April 1942. SOE Archives File (AD/S.1) 'SC/76 USA' has a section on 'SO and General Marshall'.

[2] BGS (Plans) to Secretary of JPS, April 1942, on SOE Archives File 1/470/1 Pt 2.

[3] Reproduced an Appendix G. JP(42)479 of 6th May, and COS(42)133(0) of 12th May, approved by COS(42)147th Mtg, Item 5, of 11th May. Modified in detail by COS(42)231st Mtg, Minute 2, of 5th August.

[4] Above p. 169.

War Office branch: it did not contain many regular soldiers, but most of its staff were in military uniform, and some of them had military experience. There was thus no great problem of 'War Office liaison', as a matter of external relations, and no centralised machinery for it was required.[1] It was a matter of effective collaboration through a large number of separate channels: personnel, ordnance, other stores, accommodation and so forth. Each of these presented a whole series of problems,[2] but they were too technical to be worth treating here.

Until the creation of 'Cossac'* in March 1943, the main executive authorities concerned were GHQ Home Forces, CCO and the Airborne Division. Home Forces were already beginning to consider the invasion problem, and were in touch with SOE: the Airborne Division could usefully draw on SOE's experience and on the development work in progress at Station IX. But neither of these was engaged in operations, and there was no need as yet for any formal definition of relations.

The position was rather different as regards CCO.[3] Formal liaison had ceased with the disappearance of the 'SO Board' in February 1941: there is a record of a detailed exchange of projects in March 1941,[4] but little more emerges on the policy level until the appointment of Lord Louis Mountbatten as 'Adviser on Combined Operations' in October 1941.[5] From this time dates the real development of Combined Operations as a development organisation, whose operations all played some part in the growth of a new technique. Lord Louis Mountbatten could always be reckoned as one of SOE's 'friends', both in London[6] and later in South-East Asia: and he did not hesitate to make full use of SOE's resources. The first liaison officer with Combined Operations Headquarters (Major D. A. Wyatt, RE)

---

[1] There was a junior officer in the Liaison Section until summer 1945. (The AG Section is still in existence in the SOE Liquidation Section – August 1947.)

[2] See SOE Technical Histories – Part III Supplies for ordnance.

[3] There is a brief but useful narrative of this by Miss Winifred Close.

[4] SO2 list dated 27th March 1941: DCO list about same date. Both on SOE Archives File (AD/S. 1) SC/75. (In addition SOE supplied an Italian – who was captured and executed – for the first regular parachute operation in Southern Italy in February 1941.)

[5] Directive in COS (41)629 of 17th October.

[6] See for instance record of talk between Lord Louis Mountbatten and Mr Dalton, 9th January 1942, on SOE Archives File (AD/S. 1) SC/75.

* [Chief of Staff to the Supreme Allied Commander, not yet appointed, for the invason of North-West Europe (later codenamed Operation 'Overlord': i.e. (Sir) F. E. Morgan, 1894–1967, fought in France 1914–18 and 1940, drafted invasion plan, deputy Chief of Staff to supreme commander 1943–5. See his *Overture to Overlord* (1950). In *DNB*.]

was appointed in December 1941, and it is pretty clear that he was useful to ACO in putting at his disposal what had so far been achieved by the SOE Technical Directorate.

SOE also took a very practical part in the active operations of the next few months. It supplied men and information for the Norwegian raids, probably somewhat to its own disadvantage. It contributed equipment and training both for the Bruneval raid of 27th/28th February 1942, and the St Nazaire raid of 27th/28th March: in addition a Sudeten German was picked by SOE for each of these operations, and two French officers accompanied the St Nazaire raid.[1] Major Wyatt, the SOE liaison officer, was killed in the Dieppe operation (19th August 1942), and his post was left vacant for some months: by this time relations had become so close that direct contact was made between all the branches concerned on both sides,[2] and the need for formal machinery was less pressing. The CO liaison branch however remained in existence on a small scale as a central point of reference up to the end of the war.

SOE had a tiny but far-flung Empire at sea, with bases in the Shetlands, at Burghead, Leigh-on-Sea, Helford and Gibraltar, as well as in the Levant and the Red Sea: so that there was a substantial administrative problem involved, as well as a danger of operational conflicts. But fortunately SOE's various 'private navies' were never on a scale to disturb the Admiralty's feelings, either on a point of principle or through a serious clash of priorities. Relations with regular naval operations presented no serious difficulties: but there was always an uneasy feeling in SOE's mind that SIS as the older organisation on the whole got more consideration from the Navy than it deserved.[3] There was in addition the question of what assistance SOE could give the Admiralty in its strategic tasks: the attack on enemy shipping, the anti-submarine campaign, even the destruction of enemy capital ships. SOE could never do so much for the Navy as it could for the Army; but it had something to offer which could not be neglected.[4]

SOE had practically no naval officers on its ordinary establishment: and the machinery for handling relations with the Admiralty was as a result always largely centralised in a special naval branch, which

---

[1] See detailed list of SOE's contributions to Combined Operations dated 16th April 1942, on SOE Archives File (AD/S.1) SC/75.

[2] See Appendix 'A' to SOE 'COHQ Liaison History'.

[3] Cf. for instance the question of Brittany and the west coast of France: above p. 236.

[4] See the brief but comprehensive list in Appendix A to SOE 'Naval Section History'.

assumed various forms. At the outset Commander R. D. Watson, RN,*
(who had been MI(R)'s representative in Roumania until September
1939) formed part of a special liaison section with Army and Air
representatives. In May 1941 he fell ill and was replaced by Rear
Admiral L. S. Holbrook,** who remained liaison officer until April
1942. A more direct solution was then adopted. The Naval Liaison
Section became the Navy Section of SOE, under Captain H. A.
Simpson, RN; it took over from Brigadier Gubbins's Directorate the
responsibility for all sea operations based on the United Kingdom,
and was also in charge of SOE's naval administration – personnel,
stores, technical liaison and so forth – except for the special problem
of Norwegian personnel. This Section was in form part of the
Directorate of Naval Intelligence, under the cover name of NID(Q):
parallel to it was NID(C), in similar relations to SIS.

Finally, in April 1943 the Section was up-graded to the status of a
Directorate, under Rear Admiral A. H. Taylor,† who became Naval
Director with a seat on the SOE Council. Shortly afterwards NID(Q)
and NID(C) were amalgamated under the Operations Division of the
Admiralty as DDOD(I), which asserted Admiralty 'responsibility for
clandestine operations by sea in all theatres': the Norwegians at
Lerwick and the 'Levant Fishing Patrol' were governed by separate
local arrangements, but on the whole the Admiralty had reasserted its
position. The 'private navy' had disappeared, and the Admiralty had
accepted responsibility for a number of highly irregular commitments
which it would certainly not have welcomed in 1940. Needless to say,
they were efficiently discharged.

The RAF presented much the most difficult problem of co-operation. On the one hand, there was comparatively little that SOE could
do to help the RAF in its battle with the German Air Force. Various
sabotage devices were invented such as bombs fused barometrically,
which could be secreted in an aircraft so as to explode when it reached
a given height: and there were projects for bigger things such as the
attack on the crews of KG.100 at Vannes, or on the Focke-Wulfs at
Mérignac.[1] But airfields in Western Europe were well guarded and
did not make easy targets: there were one or two minor successes,
but nothing very striking[2] – and certainly nothing such as the Long
Range Desert Groups were able to achieve in North Africa. SOE

---

[1]   Above p. 244.
[2]   Except perhaps the attack on the Iraqi Air Force by Jews in April 1941, which
      apparently destroyed sixteen aircraft.
*   [(Sir) R. D. Watson, 1904–88, knight 1959, Fourth Sea Lord 1955–8.]
** [1882–1974.]
†   [1886–1972.]

could of course (once its organisation was established) attack small industrial targets which were beyond reach of bombing: and it later proved pretty conclusively that more locomotives could be immo-bilised by the 'cheminots' than by the RAF, with less loss of Allied life. But in 1942 this was largely speculative and in the future; and it was not at all easy to demonstrate to an unsympathetic Air Marshal that a ton of agents and equipment would achieve more than a ton of bombs.

On the other hand, SOE very soon found that its own operations were impossible without the RAF, and that its requirements for air support were practically without limit. Everywhere (except perhaps in Norway) the tempo was set by the number of aircraft which could be made available: SOE was in fact controlled by the Air Ministry, and the Air Ministry had troubles enough on its hands without extend-ing air operations to a new field. Furthermore, the operations involved were of a very awkward kind. An airman could see there were few people in SOE who had any conception of the technical difficulties involved, and that it would be a miracle if SOE's agents in the field were not a great deal worse than their masters. Even a dropping oper-ation was like trying to get home in the dark to an aerodrome controlled by irresponsible amateurs: and it was many times worse for landing operations. The aircrews concerned took fantastic risks with great coolness and skill: but it pressed awkwardly on their superiors that they should have to send men on such errands without some guaran-tee that reasonably 'airmanlike' precautions had been taken.

It is unnecessary to rehearse the various controversies about aircraft allocation and control which have already appeared almost every-where even before the end of 1941. The amount of air support avail-able can be summarised fairly briefly. No. 419 Flight was formed at North Weald in August 1940 with an establishment of two Lysanders. In October it moved to Stradishall and in February 1941 to Newmarket – it was then renamed No. 1419 Flight. By this time its establishment had been increased[1] to three Whitleys, one Lysander and one Maryland: this to suffice for the needs both of SIS and SOE.

---

[1] Cf. JIC(41)63 of 8th February 1941, COS(41)55th Mtg, Item 1, of 14th February, Mr Jebb to General Ismay of 22nd February, to DCAS (Air Marshal Harris) of 6th March, and DCAS's reply of 10th March; Mr Dalton to the Prime Minister of 6th March. CSS to Mr Jebb dated 10th March and the latter's reply. Letters on SOE Archives Files (AD/S.1) '133' and F.112/3. [(Sir) A. T. Harris, 1892–1984, deputy CAS 1940–41, knight 1942, C-in-C Bomber Command 1942–5, Marshal of the RAF 1945, baronet 1953; in *DNB*. See his *Bomber Offensive* (1947) and Sir Charles Webster and N. Frankland, *The Strategic Air Offensive against Germany 1939–1945* (4 vols, 1961).]

In August 1941 came the first serious calculation of the air implications of SOE,[1] and the undertaking given by CAS to the Chiefs of
Staff. The establishment of Whitleys in No. 1419 Flight was increased
to six; and shortly afterwards it became No. 138 Squadron, with eight
Whitleys, two Halifaxes, and one Lysander. The Halifaxes were a
special concession to the needs of Poland, and the squadron had on
its establishment one Polish and one Czech crew.

The demand for expansion continued throughout that winter and
there was another substantial improvement early in 1942. No. 161
Squadron was formed in January, under Wing Commander Fielden,*
out of the King's Flight, with an establishment of four Whitleys, six
Lysanders, two Wellingtons, and one Hudson; and in February the
two squadrons were grouped together as No. 107 Wing and moved
to Tempsford, near St Neots, Huntingdonshire,[2] which is the airfield
mainly associated with air support to the Resistance in its critical time.
The picture by this time was:[3]

No. 138 Squadron	4 Halifaxes
	12 Whitleys
No. 161 Squadron	6 Lysanders
	4 Whitleys
	2 Wellingtons
	1 Hudson

The main burden of SOE work fell on No. 138 Squadron: all landing operations were carried out by No. 161 Squadron's Lysanders,
while its Whitleys were intended primarily for SIS. The other three
aircraft were on special duties of a different kind.

No. 138 Squadron was now gradually re-equipping with Halifaxes,
which meant a considerable improvement in range and load: but this
process was not complete until the autumn of 1942.

This represented a small but effectively organised force based on
the United Kingdom: development was slower in the Middle East.
The first period of heavy pressure was in the autumn of 1941, when
Mihailovitch came to the fore: there was much discussion and little
progress, as there was almost a total lack of aircraft with sufficient

---

[1] Above p. 355.
[2] There is a short history of the RAF Station at Tempsford – SOE Archives 1/420/18.
From April 1942 to May 1945, deliveries to the field were: 29,000 Containers,
over 1,100 Agents, nearly 10,000 packages – Tempsford History, p. 2.
[3] Minute from Colonel Barry to CD dated 1st February 1942, on SOE Archives
File (AD/S.1) '133'.
* [(Sir) E. H. Fielden, 1903–76, commanded Royal Flight 1936–62, knight 1952.]

range based on North Africa. A special flight was promised[1] and did not materialise: two Whitleys were given and proved too slow to reach Mihailovitch during the hours of darkness: two Wellesleys were given and proved useless: four Whitleys were flown out from England and three of them were destroyed on the ground at Malta. Liberators were the only real hope: and there were only three Liberators with the necessary modifications in Middle East. No more could be provided except at the expense of Coastal Command. It was not until October 1941[2] that a real 'Special Duty' flight was organised in Egypt, and it was then equipped with only two Whitleys from 138 Squadron. We have seen what this meant to Mihailovitch and to Captain Hudson.[3]

In spite of these prevailing shortages, a good deal of progress was made in these two years in creating an efficient organisation in the United Kingdom on the 'working levels'. The full procedure for a single operation in its final form[4] involved twenty-three stages and seven different authorities: so that there are technical complexities which cannot be unravelled here. The original picture was that (under Brigadier Gubbins as Director of Operations) Lieutenant Colonel Barry was responsible for 'laying on' all air operations. To him came all Country Sections with demands for operations: he in turn went to the Air Ministry through the Air Liaison Section, which was also AI10 in the Air Ministry Directorate of Intelligence. Through one of his branches (AI2(c)) the Director of Intelligence checked the projected operation against all known information of the terrain and the enemy's dispositions, and decided whether it was possible: through another (its title varied at different times) he exercised detailed operational control of the SD Squadrons. These Squadrons came for administration at first under No. 11 Group, Fighter Command: later under No. 3 Group, Bomber Command, but it was not until August 1943 that operational control was devolved by the Air Ministry to Bomber Command.[5]

This organisation grew in complexity both on the side of SOE and on that of the Air Ministry. Ultimately there was a 'Conference Room' in Norgeby House where a detailed War Room of operations was maintained: there were a Pin-Pointing Section, a Q Section, and a Radio Section within SOE's air operations organisation: in the country

---

1   COS(41)339th Mtg, Item 2, of 1st October.
2   From 'Summary of Position regarding, provision of Aircraft for SOE Cairo and Malta' dated 1st November 1941; copy on SOE Archives File (AD/S.1) F/68.14.
3   Above p. 127.
4   As set out in Squadron Leader Braithwaite's excellent paper on 'Air Operations – SOE', dated 13th November 1945; copy with SOE Histories.
5   COS(43)491(0) of 25th August, Annex. I.

there was a vast packing station at Gaynes Hall, St Neots,[1] where there was also a 'hotel' for agents awaiting transport: there was a parachute section under RAF charge at Henlow:[2] there were special courses for agents in the organisation of air landing operations and in the use of Rebecca/Eureka. The main lines of the organisation however remained quite constant: all demands for operations were centralised in one section of SOE, and the final discretion as to the conduct of operations rested with the RAF and not with SOE. These are fixed points on which any future organisation would necessarily be based.

Relations on a higher level were not so happy. SOE felt that this was in part due to the RAF's lack of knowledge of the purposes of SOE and of confidence in its internal organisation: and it was anxious to draw the RAF into a fuller share of responsibility. On the RAF side the difficulty was to find the men: an office job could not be expected to be popular with regular officers in such a period of RAF expansion. The first experiment[3] was the appointment of Group Captain Grierson to Brigadier Gubbins's staff in April 1942, to take a full part in the organisation as Director of the Operations Section, with other responsibilities besides those for air operations. Day-to-day efficiency continued to improve under this régime: but it proved to be no answer to the problem of improved mutual comprehension.[4] SOE and its ways were still a somewhat tedious mystery to most responsible officers of the RAF, and in particular to the AOC-in-C Bomber Command.

(d) Propaganda

We have already traced the story of SOE's relations with the Ministry of Information up to September 1941, when the original

---

[1] Packing became so vast that in October 1943 an outside firm of packers (Messrs Carpet Trades Ltd Kidderminster) were employed to pack 'standard loads', so that a reserve supply was built up for the 1944 deliveries, for example in 1941 95 containers were packed – in 1944 56,464. [Details of standard loads in Foot, *SOE in France*, pp. 475–7.]

[2] See SOE 'Air Liaison History' – SD Parachute Section, by Flight Lieutenant Bunn.

[3] Originally proposed by Sir Frank Nelson: letter to ACAS(1) dated 30th January 1942, to Air Vice-Marshal Medhurst on SOE Archives File (AD/S.1) '133'. Cf. also Minute from Brigadier Gubbins to CD dated 24th February 1942 recording a meeting with DCAS on the whole problem. [(Sir) C.E.H. Medhurst, 1896–1954, assistant CAS (intelligence) 1941, (policy) 1942, air C-in-C Middle East 1945–8.]

[4] There was a proposal in May 1942 that Air Commodore L.G.S. Payne, then a Director in SIS, should act as 'high-level' liaison officer. This was turned down by SOE. Papers on SOE Archives File (AD/S.1) '133'.

conception of unified subversion broke down. The narrative of operations has illustrated at almost every turn what this meant. De Gaulle's position rested in part on agents maintained in the field by SOE and on SOE's money, arms and wireless transmitters: but in the first stages it probably meant more to his success to have at his disposal open broadcasting facilities on the BBC and it was equally important to him to have access to a secret station sponsored by PWE. The attitude towards him adopted in the BBC's own transmissions and other direct British propaganda was also important, though not always in the sense which its authors intended. The same situation reproduced itself everywhere in Europe; in relations between Mihailovitch and the Partisans, between King George of Greece and EAM, between the Right and the Left in the smaller countries of the West. In order to grow and fight the Resistance needed a voice as well as weapons, and these two necessities of life could not be handled in isolation.[1]

Unfortunately they were so handled, and it is not possible in this narrative to present a complete story of subversive policy or even of the relations between the 'subversive' departments. We must be content to trace briefly SOE's own position up to the late summer of 1942.

In its own person the Ministry of Information continued to overlap with SOE only in regard to the United States of America, Russia, the Far East, the Arab World, South America and the unoccupied countries of Europe. Each of these presented serious problems, but the urgency of the need was much less great than in the territory of the Political Warfare Executive, where every move was a matter of immediate life and death for someone. The Far East is of course a vast subject in itself: but the other territories mentioned did not afford very serious room for friction, and the problem of co-operation proved perfectly tractable except at periods when the Ministers were in personal disagreement. The Arab World was part of the general confusion of responsibilities in the Middle East, but it was not an area in which SOE was operating very actively:[2] in the other areas all that was needed was a working liaison between the heads of Sections concerned, and the provision of liaison officers for any minor matters which did not fit the existing arrangement. This position was reached

---

[1] As Lord Selborne wrote to Sir Orme Sargent in another context on 16th April 1943: 'If my officers say one thing to the Greeks and Yugoslavs and the BBC say something quite contrary, they will be liable to have their throats cut, and that is a responsibility that rests on your shoulders as well as on mine.'

[2] [NOTE DELETED ON GROUNDS OF NATIONAL SECURITY.]

fairly satisfactorily by the summer of 1942, when a memorandum[1] was drawn up setting out the general principles to be followed and the detailed arrangements for each area. The essence of this was that SOE would not indulge in 'subversive' activities in the Ministry of Information area unless asked to do so by the Foreign Office or by the local Commander-in-Chief: and that if these activities involved propaganda of any kind the Ministry of Information should be generally informed of their scope. SOE would not disseminate open propaganda at all except at the specific request of the Ministry of Information: but it would be the normal channel of 'unacknowledgeable' propaganda, unless the Ministry of Information wished in some area to break into this field themselves. Finally, SOE representatives would not involve the local Ministry of Information officials in any activities which could not be reported to the Ministry and duly authorised by them.[2]

This agreement might not have stood the test if SOE had ever become involved in 'unacknowledgeable' propaganda on a serious scale in the areas concerned:[3] but the scheme proposed is a relatively intelligible one. The Foreign Office and the 'military' in concert call for a campaign to further some specific end: 'open' propaganda is handled by the Ministry of Information, 'secret' by SOE. This was one possible theory of the 'decentralisation' of subversion: and its practicability was certainly not disproved by this experiment.

Unfortunately the Minister of Information was also the principal begetter of the Political Warfare Executive, which was based on the opposite principle of the unity of propaganda in war zones. There were in a sense three levels: the Foreign Office in concert with the Chiefs of Staff responsible for the general lines of policy; the Political

---

[1] Forwarded to Lord Selborne by Mr Bracken on 2nd June 1942: Lord Selborne's reply dated 9th June is on SOE Archives File (AD/S.1) 152 'Liaison with M of I'. The memo. was returned with slight amendments by Mr Sporborg to Mr Grubb on 10th June, confirmed in Mr Grubb's letter of 2nd July and Mr Sporborg's of 28th July: all on same file '152'. [(Sir) K. G. Grubb, 1900–80, controller in Ministry of Information 1941–6, knight 1953; in *DNB*.]

Earlier papers which refer are draft 'Notes on Co-operation between M of I and SOE' prepared by Mr Jebb on 9th October 1941 and put aside by Mr Dalton with the note 'These points can be usefully raised if we ever succeed in getting a *sensible* discussion with M of I on "ministerial level" – or with "Ministerial approval on official plane"': (SOE Archives File (AD/S.1) 131 Vol. I – PWE) and draft 'Treaty' with M of I submitted by Mr Jebb to Lord Selborne on 31st March 1942 (on same file). See also note for CD by Mr Sheridan on liaison arrangements as they existed at 19th June 1942 (on same file).

[2] The last section of this 'Charter' is printed as Appendix H (para. 9(a)–(f)).

[3] [NOTE DELETED ON GROUNDS OF NATIONAL SECURITY.]

Warfare Executive responsible for working out policy in more detail so far as it affected the German 'Empire'; Special Operations Executive responsible for the execution of PWE's directives anywhere outside the United Kingdom. Each of these levels had its own Minister, with independent access to the 'highest quarters'.

This was clearly an unstable arrangement: yet SOE's part in the scheme was vital so far as it affected the dispatch of agents into territory held by the enemy. There were already too many British 'travel bureaux' concerned in that field, and any conflict between their arrangements was a source of great and immediate danger. PWE thus accepted fairly readily SOE's operational control of its agents in the field: we have seen that men of this type were going into Belgium and France by the summer of 1942.[1] When it came to work in the field, they were in every respect as other agents, except that their directives gave primary emphasis to special tasks, in particular to assessment of public opinion and support of the underground Press. These men were 'graduates' of SOE's ordinary schools, but had generally also been given special training in what was usually called the 'Hackett School' after Major Hackett its first commandant. This was established first at Beaulieu under the Political Warfare Executive, then in October 1941 a new school incorporating the old staff (who were known as STP) was opened at Pertenhall, twenty-five miles from the country headquarters of PWE. In May 1942 the school moved for a second time to premises within six miles of the PWE country headquarters. In the spring of 1943 it was brought into line with other SOE establishments, and transferred to Wall Hall, Aldenham, as STS 39, under the control of SOE. It continued to operate until May 1944, and handled some 200 pupils in all. The Political Warfare Executive continued to be intimately concerned with the training given.

But the case was not so strong for what may be called 'base areas' overseas, of which the most important were Gibraltar, West Africa, Middle East, and the USA.[2] No logic could exclude from these areas the principle of unity of propaganda which had been adopted in Great Britain: if the Political Warfare Executive was to be a true 'specialist' service, only very strong practical objections could prevent it from sending its own specialists to discharge its functions overseas. Unfortunately there already existed in each of these areas missions based on the alternative principle of the 'unity of subversion': and their interests had been reserved when Mr Dalton gave his agreement

---

[1] Above pp. 293 and 302.
[2] There was also a minor difficulty about the dispatch of Miss Wiskemann by PWE to Switzerland in September 1941. SOE Archives File (AD/S.1) F.48/3(c): also Garnett's PWE History, Vol. II, pp. 125–9.

to the formation of the Political Warfare Executive. In Britain PWE had come into being in order to unite discordant organisations: in the overseas theatres it could only begin to operate by breaking up what was already united and in working order.

West Africa and the United States of America both gave rise to serious disputes, and there were grave doubts as to the wisdom of the decisions taken. In the USA Mr David Bowes-Lyon* arrived in July 1942 to take over a substantial part of Sir William Stephenson's organisation:[1] the PWE Mission in West Africa was much delayed, and did not begin work until December 1942, when it was much too late to be of any practical value in attacking Vichy territory.[2] The Gibraltar case was also difficult, since PWE at once proposed to establish their own team of propagandists in the congested confines of the Rock,[3] and to set up a broadcasting station. This was settled in June 1942, by the constitution of a joint PWE/SOE Mission: but PWE's broadcasting arrangements fell through, and their part of the team was withdrawn in September 1942.

The problem of the Middle East remained to trouble the waters for many months to come. In September 1941 Mr Dalton had only recently succeeded in imposing a unified solution on the original chaos of SOE Middle East,[4] and it would be administrative madness to disturb the new organisation so soon. In addition, the Balkans were already envisaged as an area of open guerilla warfare,[5] and there was every reason to maintain unity of control over agents in the field and the 'secret' broadcasting stations which purported to be working with them. Many of the broadcasters were natives of the occupied states who had been brought out earlier in 1941 by SOE's field representatives, as they withdrew in front of the Germans: and these SOE representatives were many of them still present and active in the Cairo organisation.

For these reasons there was not at first a frontal attack on SOE's position in the Middle East: the question was of fundamental importance, but not yet quite ripe for practical solution, and the disputes

---

[1] Garnett, 'History of PWE', p. 120. As regards PWE's Mission to Switzerland (Miss E. Wiskemann), see Garnett, p. 125. [E. Wiskemann, 1901–71, author, in PWE 1941–5, suicide; see her *The Europe I Saw* (1968); in *DNB*.]

[2] Garnett, 'History of PWE', p. 130 sqq.

[3] Correspondence regarding this on SOE Archives File (AD/S.1) F/71.8a, 'PWE Gibraltar', and Garnett, 'History of PWE', p. 127 sqq.

[4] Mr Maxwell had been sent out in August 1941, above p. 178: see also Mr Dalton's letter of 22nd September 1941 to Mr Eden, on SOE, Archives File (AD/S.1) 131 – Vol. 1.

[5] The first news of Mihailovitch almost coincided with these events.

* [(Sir) D. Bowes-Lyon, 1902–61, brother-in-law to King George VI, banker, in PWE 1941–5.]

by which the Ministerial Committee was wrecked seem to have turned rather on general propaganda policy, for which Mr Dalton still bore a share of responsibility, although the propagandists of the old SO1 had virtually passed out of his control.

We need not here consider the line suggested in his formal paper of 6th December 1941 'suggested particularly by the recent Conference of the ILO in the United States, at which the Lord Privy Seal' (Mr Attlee) 'represented His Majesty's Government, and by the evidence, which steadily increases, that it is the working class, and especially the industrial working class, which are our best allies in the occupied territories, and our best prospective allies in the enemy countries themselves.'[1] It is however important that on 9th December Mr Dalton handed to Mr Attlee a memorandum[2] in which he sharply retorted on Mr Bracken's view 'that SOE should not have anything to do with any kind of propaganda whatever': in his own view Mr Dalton had not abandoned SOE's special interest in subversive propaganda, but had put it into a common stock to which the Minister of Information had merely contributed one vital element, his control of the BBC.

On 30th December, while Mr Attlee was acting as Prime Minister in the absence of Mr Churchill in Washington, Mr Dalton took matters a stage further by forwarding to him a 'Proposal for a Ministry of Economic and Political Warfare'[3] – 'Let there be a clear-cut line between the responsibilities of the Minister of Information and myself. Let him have charge of all publicity and propaganda for the Home Front: for the British Empire, both Dominions and Colonies and India; for the Americas, both USA and Latin America: for the USSR and such other neutrals as may still be left. This, together with the Censorship, should surely be a full-time job. Let me, on the other hand, have charge of all propaganda directed towards enemy and enemy-occupied territories (the present Middle-East set-up can, I suggest, be left as it is, under Lyttleton and Monckton). I should then become in effect Minister for Political as well as for Economic Warfare, and my Department might be renamed accordingly. I should then be able to simplify and improve many of the present arrangements. On the one hand Political Warfare could be closely welded in with SOE, and on the other the Intelligence could be closely co-ordinated.' This is sound sense, and Mr Dalton could quote Mr Duff Cooper as a reluctant convert to the logic of the position:[4] but Mr

---

[1] Copy on SOE Archives File (AD/S.1) '131 PWE' Vol. 1.
[2] Copy on SOE Archives File (AD/S.1) '131 PWE' Vol. 1.
[3] Copy on SOE Archives File (AD/S.1) '131 PWE' Vol. 1.
[4] Letters to Mr Attlee and Mr Eden dated 7th January 1942, enclosing copies of Mr Duff Cooper's letter of 6th June 1941. SOE Archives File 131 Vol. 1. (AD/S.1).

Bracken was of sterner metal than Mr Cooper and it was clear that only a political tug-of-war could decide whether Mr Bracken or Mr Dalton should be ejected from the Ministerial Committee controlling the Political Warfare Executive.[1]

This found its issue on 22nd February in the promotion of Mr Dalton to the Presidency of the Board of Trade and the appointment of Lord Selborne as Minister of Economic Warfare without a share in responsibility for the Political Warfare Executive. The change was publicly announced in a Parliamentary answer on 18th March: 'The Secretary of State for Foreign Affairs will continue to be responsible for policy, but the Minister of Information will be solely responsible for administration of the Political Warfare Executive. All forms of propaganda will thus be brought under the administrative control of a single Minister.' This text had been submitted to the Prime Minister for approval by Mr Eden on 13th March, after agreement with Lord Selborne, who had insisted only that close liaison must be maintained with SOE: 'I do not think it is possible for SOE to function at all if it is dissociated from all work connected with secret subversive propaganda. If you will visualise the position of any agent we send to enemy occupied territory, it will be clear that he can only function by gathering a band of like-minded inhabitants around him, and his procedure in so doing could not be described otherwise than "secret subversive propaganda".'[2] This one vital reservation was again hammered home in letters from Mr Jebb to Mr Bruce-Lockhart on 23rd March, and from the Minister to Mr Bracken on 25th March.[3]

There is no doubt that the tension was almost at once relaxed by this change. Personal relations between the three Ministers concerned were now excellent, and their staffs on working levels were in the main perfectly ready to collaborate. Formal liaison arrangements had been suggested when the Political Warfare Executive was formed: Mr David Bowes-Lyon was appointed principal PWE Liaison Officer, with free access to Baker Street,[4] and liaison meetings took place on 7th and 28th October with Sir Charles Hambro in the chair.[5] By

---

[1] The SOE papers throw very little light on the details of this. On 3rd February Mr Jebb briefed the Minister on the impending attack (copy on SOE Archives File (AD/S.1) 131): and on 4th February Mr Eden wrote to Mr Dalton and negotiations for the Foreign Office Treaty were opened.

[2] Letter of 9th March; copy on SOE Archives File (AD/S.1) 131 – Vol. 1.

[3] Both related to the PWE 'Re-organisation Memo' of 20th March: all on SOE Archives File (AD/S.1) 131 – Vol. 1.

[4] Mr Jebb's Minute to Mr Dalton of 15th September, on SOE Archives File (AD/S.1) 131 – Vol. 1.

[5] Minutes on SOE Archives File (AD/S.1) 131 – Vol. 1.

February 1942 these occasional meetings had given birth to a 'Planning Committee' 'to examine and report to what extent operational propaganda, with particular reference to instruction in sabotage, can be made use of in open broadcasting',[1] this Committee apparently did not meet until 24th April, when Mr David Garnett presided over representatives of the three Service departments as well as of MEW and SOE.[2] The Committee was reorganised in June on a higher level with Mr Ivone Kirkpatrick (the Foreign Office representative at the BBC) in the chair and without the Service departments: and it was responsible for the launching of a general 'operational propaganda' campaign which was approved by the Chiefs of Staff 'provided that it does not endanger either the formation of Secret Armies and the general uprising of patriots, or sabotage connected with actual operations'.[3] The story of this first 'phased' campaign, which was directed primarily against transport, belongs to the history of PWE; the verdict recorded in SOE's papers is that in its first phases it was astonishingly effective, but that it proved politically impracticable to follow the 'hard' line of specific incitement to sabotage, which the later stages of the plan required – the risks of violent repression by mass reprisals could not be taken.[4] However this may be, such collaboration brought the two departments into contact in quite a new way, and by March 1943 Sir Charles Hambro was able to write most warmly to Lord Glenconner in the Middle East about the excellent practical working of the agreed division of responsibility.[5] Indeed during the winter of 1942–3 matters had gone so far that the two departments were now tending to pull together against the restraining hand of the Foreign Office.

In this atmosphere formal liaison had a chance to work, and it expressed itself on three levels.[6]

---

[1] Minutes of Mr Bruce-Lockhart's meeting of 16th February, on SOE Archives File (AD/S.1) 'PWE Vol. 1'. This problem had already arisen over 'Colonel Britten's' V-campaign in 1941: Garnett, 'History of PWE', p. 87 sqq.

[2] Minutes on SOE Archives File 1/270/3. See also Committee's first paper PW(Op.)(42)1 of 20th April, on same file.

[3] PW(Op.)(42)3 quoted in Sir Charles Hambro's letter to Mr Bruce-Lockhart of 12th June 1942, on SOE Archives File 1/270/3. The COS reference cannot be traced: presumably approval was given informally.

[4] Mr Sporborg and Mr Robin Brook were SOE's representatives. See Mr Brook's reports to CD of 7th September and 16th October (among others) on SOE Archives File 1/270/3. [(Sir) R. E. Brook, 1908–98, assistant to Dalton 1940–42, D/R in SOE 1942–4, head of special force headquarters at SHAEF 1944–5, flourished in City, knight 1974.]

[5] Various letters and telegrams in SOE Archives File (AD/S.1) 68/4.

[6] This is in part set out in Sir Charles Hambro's letter to Mr Bruce-Lockhart of 12th June 1942, on SOE Archives File 1/270/3.

(a) A PWE/SOE Policy Committee, which began in February 1942 and met in general fortnightly on the 'highest official level'.[1]

(b) Direct liaison between heads of Regions and Country Sections, and frequent meetings, either regular or *ad hoc*.

(c) A 'low-level' liaison officer, for minor practical matters, in the branch 'D/Q', which was responsible also for liaison with the Ministry of Information in its other aspect.

Disagreements were still inevitable in so complex a field, but they no longer tended to become deadlocks.

The practical problem was thus largely in process of solution in London: it remained to find some formal expression of it, and to apply the solution to the much more intractable question of the Middle East.[2] These two things were intimately connected. We have seen[3] the establishment of Mr Maxwell as SOE's Controller in Cairo, in circumstances which caused great bitterness in the Political Warfare Executive: the creation of his Directorate of Special Propaganda under Mr Euan Butler; the formation of the Jerusalem Bureau, [PASSAGE DELETED ON GROUNDS OF NATIONAL SECURITY] and the final agreement to their demand for a 'high-level co-ordinator' of propaganda from Cairo. Sir Walter Monckton arrived in Middle East in this capacity in the autumn of 1941. A somewhat acrimonious dispute was already in progress in London between the Foreign Office, the Political Warfare Executive and SOE as to responsibility for the backwardness of propaganda plans to support the offensive of November 1941 in North Africa;[4] and this was not at first eased by the Minister of State's telegram[5] of 3rd December, reporting the recommendations of a Committee which had met under Sir Walter Monckton to 'survey all machinery for publicity radiating from Cairo'. This did not in fact involve any change in SOE's position: but no copy was sent to Mr Dalton and his first instinct was to protest sharply.[6] Mr Maxwell however made it clear that he had concurred in Sir Walter Monckton's recommendations throughout and indicated that there was no cause for alarm.[7]

---

[1] Minutes in SOE Archives File 1/270/3.1.

[2] For the PWE side of this story see Garnett's 'History of PWE', p. 136.

[3] Above p. 178.

[4] Mr Dalton to Mr Eden, two letters dated 18th November 1941: replies from Mr Eden 19th, 20th and 27th November 1941; copies on SOE Archives File (AD/S.1) 68/4 Pt I.

[5] No. 3806 of 3rd December 1941 – on SOE Archives File (AD/S.1) 68/4 Pt I.

[6] No. 138 of 6th December 1941 to Mr Maxwell – SOE Archives File, (AD/S.1) 68/4 Pt I.

[7] No. 133 Alpha of 7th December to Colonel Taylor – SOE Archives File (AD/S.1) 68/4 Pt I.

Meantime in London 'plans for political warfare' were being produced by PWE, in more or less close touch with SOE, but not without recriminations as to the scope of PWE's authority: and the next stage is marked by Mr Maxwell's visit to London in January 1942. A meeting at which he was present was held at the Foreign Office on 23rd January, and a formula was reached between PWE and SOE: the essential parts of this read as follows:[1]

PWE will lay down policy from time to time, which they will communicate to Sir Walter Monckton, who will issue directives for both overt and covert political warfare to the propaganda organisation in the Middle East working under his guidance. SOE propaganda from the Middle East will, therefore, conform to the directives received by them from Sir Walter Monckton. Any deviation from the settled policy which SOE may desire to introduce for operational reasons must be referred to Sir Walter Monckton for the Minister of State, who will refer to PWE London if in doubt . . . .

Finally, co-ordination will be completed by the representation of Mr Dalton on the PWE Council of Ministers, and by the close liaison already established between SOE and PWE Regional Heads in London. The Controller of SOE, Middle East, and the Director of Special Propaganda sit on the Monckton Committee, which ensures co-ordination in Cairo.

The last paragraph is sufficient to explain the fate of this promising approach: the Minutes were never accepted by the Foreign Office, and in effect the Foreign Office reply is given in Mr Eden's letter[2] of 12th February to Mr Dalton – 'I am bound to say that I was perturbed to find that SOE in the Middle East are handling propaganda at all. It is surely the case that for SOE to carry on any propaganda, either overt or subversive, is contrary to the division of functions laid down, whereby PWE were entrusted with propaganda in enemy and enemy-occupied countries, and the Minister of Information with propaganda in neutral countries.' (A little disingenuous, this, in face of Mr Dalton's repeated statements since August 1941 that SOE must act as the Political Warfare Executive's agent overseas.) The letter proceeds to attack SOE for preparing without authority to broadcast to Kurds, Armenians and Georgians:[3] and concludes by an attack on Sir Walter Monckton's position as co-ordinator, as an attempt to extend the

---

1 Copy of revised Minutes dated 1st February 1942, SOE Archives File (AD/S.1) 68/4 Pt I.

2 Original on SOE Archives File (AD/S.1) 68/4 Pt I.

3 A controversy of very minor importance, explored further in Mr Jebb's F/3243/68/4 of 16th March to Sir Orme Sargent, and related papers, in part in SOE Archives File (AD/S.1) 68/4. Above pp. 171 and 185.

Minister of State's influence beyond that laid down in his Directive. The implication in fact is that there is a tendency for PWE, SOE and the Minister of State's office in combination to oust the Foreign Office from control of British policy towards the Balkan States.

Lord Selborne found this letter on his table when he took over on 22nd February, charged in particular with the task of seeing that SOE whole-heartedly backed the foreign policy of His Majesty's Government; and negotiations were thus to begin again in rather a new light. Meantime, on 6th and 7th February, SOE's 'Free Voice of Greece' station in Palestine had made its resounding attack on King George of Greece, which greatly discomfited the Foreign Office,[1] and greatly weakened SOE's position. Against this must be set the strong views of most of SOE's directing staff and in particular of those on the spot in the Middle East: 'SOE covert broadcast now forms integral part of military plan for this Command and any impediment to its progress would, I feel sure, be strongly deprecated by Cs-in-C.'[2] Lord Selborne's reply to Mr Eden's letter[3] was couched in mild terms; but the DSP, Colonel Euan Butler, was summoned home from Cairo to back SOE's case, and Mr Jebb on 20th March put SOE's arguments with considerable force to Sir Orme Sargent.[4] The Foreign Office on its side were pressing SOE to abandon any projects for subversive activities in Turkey,[5] and was equally anxious about Gibraltar [PASSAGE DELETED ON GROUNDS OF NATIONAL SECURITY] and about SOE's plans for Portuguese East Africa.

Opinion within SOE was absolutely agreed on the 'unity of subversion': 'black' propaganda was an essential part of subversive operations. But there was some divergence as to the line to be pressed against other departments. Mr Jebb's view, expressed in various papers,[7] was that an agreement could and should be negotiated with the Political Warfare Executive to give a formal blessing for the existing compromise and to establish a basis of real co-operation between the departments. Colonel Taylor could see no logical halting-place short of assumption by SOE of responsibility for all 'black' propa-

---

[1] See above p. 157.

[2] Mr Maxwell's telegram Alpha 202 to CD dated 5th March; copy on SOE Archives File (AD/S.1) 68/4 Pt I.

[3] Dated 21st March 1942 – in Lord Selborne's papers.

[4] Copy on SOE Archives File (AD/S. 1) 68/4 Pt I.

[5] Lord Selborne to Mr Eden on 31st March, and further correspondence in Lord Selborne's papers.

[6] [NOTE DELETED.]

[7] Minute to Lord Selborne dated 1st March, with draft 'Treaty' with PWE: Minute to CD dated 12th April, copy to Lord Selborne on 13th April: Minute to Lord Selborne dated 18th April – all on SOE Archives File (AD/S.1) 131 Pt I.

ganda from the United Kingdom as well as from the Middle East: the Ministry of Information could deal with 'overt' propaganda everywhere, SOE with 'covert' – in fact, Mr Dalton's solution of December 1941.[1] The matter was for the present settled by personal discussion between Lord Selborne and Mr Bracken, in which the latter very frankly accepted the position in Middle East as it stood.[2]

There matters rested, as it seems, until the Foreign Office took the initiative in proposing a more radical solution. A proposal[3] was submitted by Sir Orme Sargent on 5th June for the full transfer of responsibility for covert propaganda in the Middle East from SOE to the Political Warfare Executive: this set out very convincingly the case for regarding the Middle East as a 'base area', parallel to the United Kingdom, in which the Political Warfare Executive should be entitled to set up its own specialist organisation. The paper was discussed with Sir Charles Hambro and it was also forwarded by Mr Eden himself, with his full endorsement, on 22nd June.[4] Lord Selborne's reply was not dispatched until 24th July,[5] but it represented the result of very full and careful discussion within SOE. The case for unity was well and fully argued: but unfortunately it proved too much – it proved that most of PWE's activities in the United Kingdom should properly be united with those of SOE – and the difficulty could hardly be concealed by claiming that SOE's stations in Palestine dealt with real resistance movements, while those of PWE in England dealt with fictitious ones. Lord Selborne's policy was however to co-operate with the Foreign Office on all reasonable occasions – 'I am extremely anxious that SOE in all its activities should possess your confidence and deserve it' – and the argument led up to compromise proposals. The essence of these was that the existing SOE stations should be maintained in Middle East: but that a Director of Propaganda and Information should be appointed to ensure full conformity by SOE to the policy of the Foreign Office and PWE and that if the Director thought fit PWE should be entitled to set up its own stations in the Middle East. Mr Casey, the Minister of State, almost simultaneously submitted proposals[6] of a very similar nature, in which he recognised

---

[1] Minute of 1st April, on SOE Archives File (AD/S.1) 131 Pt I. Cf. above p. 372.

[2] Lunch discussion on 8th April, and letter from Lord Selborne to Mr Bracken dated 21st April – draft on SOE Archives File (AD/S.1) 131.

[3] Copy on SOE Archives File (AD/S.1) 68/4 Pt II.

[4] Original in Lord Selborne's papers.

[5] Copy in Lord Selborne's papers, and on SOE Archives File 1/270/01: it refers to a letter of Mr Eden dated 27th June – this is almost certainly a mistake for 22nd June.

[6] No. 1134 of 24th July 1942; copy on SOE Archives File (AD/S.1) 68/4 Pt II.

the disadvantages of breaking up the existing SOE organisation but asked as matter of urgency for a successor to Sir Walter Monckton, for a senior PWE representative, and for a Press Adviser. This telegram was not available to SOE until Mr Eden wrote to Lord Selborne on 12th August[1] rejecting SOE's proposals for a compromise, and pressing for the continuation of the negotiations already in progress between SOE and PWE. Lord Selborne's advisers were now unanimously in favour of renewing the battle in concert with Mr Casey: the Minister took his own line – the only line which gave promise of peace – and insisted on the immediate conclusion of the proposed agreement with PWE.[2]

From this point matters went ahead quickly in London: 'Heads of an Agreement' were already in existence, and a draft was cleared between Mr Leeper and Sir Charles Hambro in letters exchanged on 20th and 21st August.[3] The Foreign Office still saw a loophole, which Sir Orme Sargent formally closed in his letter of 22nd August – a belated intervention accepted reluctantly by SOE.[4] The Agreement itself is printed as an Appendix, with the Foreign Office amendments. As will be seen, it explicitly concedes the handing over to the Political Warfare Executive of SOE's broadcasting Stations [PASSAGE DELETED ON GROUNDS OF NATIONAL SECURITY] in Middle East, and it accepts PWE's rights to similar facilities elsewhere. The Political Warfare Executive on its side is to provide SOE with 'special clandestine broadcasting facilities for operational purposes', and arrangements are foreshadowed for keeping these in line with propaganda policy: and in addition 'PWE will not put, or permit their overseas missions to put, agents into the field' for any PWE purpose – SOE will act as the sole 'travel agency' for PWE in Occupied Europe.

Here at last was a working arrangement for mutual co-operation between two specialist services, each of which recognised the other's right to exist. It was no answer to the fundamental problem of subversion, it was indeed a very timid compromise compared with the dramatic design of 1940: but PWE and SOE were henceforward in reality much closer to one another than ever SO1 and SO2 had been, and the major issue did not arise again.

It must however be mentioned, by way of appendix, that the Agreement in its plain terms was not brought into force in the Middle East until March 1943. This represented a rearguard action conducted

---

[1] Original in Lord Selborne's papers.
[2] D/CD(A)'s Minute of 14th August, and Lord Selborne's reply, on SOE Archives File (AD/S.1) 68/4 Pt II.
[3] Copies on SOE Archives File (AD/S.1) 68/4 Pt II.
[4] The final text of the Agreement is dated 3rd September 1942 – see Appendix J.

with skill and energy by Lord Glenconner in Cairo; but it raised no new issue of principle and need not be followed in detail here.[1] First, there was delay in getting Mr Vellacott,* PWE's representative, to Cairo. Then argument broke out in Cairo on the meaning of 'broadcasts for operational purposes': did it mean propaganda campaigns of a general kind or messages related to particular operations? When this was resolved, agreement was reached on 7th December between Lord Glenconner and Mr Vellacott for a transfer of the broadcasting facilities to PWE, reserving SOE's right to maintain its own teams to broadcast to Yugoslavia, Roumania, Bulgaria and Greece, with the possibility of extension. No sooner was this agreement reached and reported to London than it was in effect repudiated by Sir Orme Sargent, who insisted that the covert Yugoslav station 'Karageorge' should be closed down. This was a 'Mihailovitch' station, and it is clear that SOE did not in fact supervise the Yugoslav broadcasting team as closely as was necessary. To make matters worse, the instructions sent by the Foreign Office through PWE were simply ignored in the Middle East.[2]

It is not therefore surprising that on 10th February 1943 Mr Eden wrote somewhat brusquely to Lord Selborne, repudiating absolutely SOE's claim that operational propaganda could include 'continuous propaganda in support of any body or movement in an enemy or enemy-occupied country merely because SOE were in contact with such a body or movement': he would accept no solution but the complete control of all propaganda from Middle East by the Foreign Office through PWE. This was not altogether sensible: it was useless for the Foreign Office to grasp control of words, while accepting the right of the military to direct SOE as regards arms, money and operations. But SOE were in no position to negotiate further, and after an exchange of letters between Ministers it was left to the officials to negotiate a new and less ambiguous agreement, this time in London. It is clear from Sir Charles Hambro's messages to Lord Glenconner early in March that SOE London were now satisfied with their working arrangements with PWE in England, and were not prepared to fight further to maintain the Directorate of Special Propaganda in Cairo. The matter was however abruptly clinched by Sir Orme Sargent

---

1 The main London papers are on SOE Archives File (AD/S.1) 68/4 Pts II and III: Lord Glenconner's Cairo papers are on two Middle East Propaganda Files – dated December 1940 to March 1943.
2 On the incitement of Lord Glenconner who was then in London – see his telegram 657 of 26th December 1942; copy on SOE Archives File (AD/S.1) 68/4 Pt II. The SOE papers imply that PWE were in sympathy with this defiance.
* [P. C. Vellacott, 1891–1954, headmaster of Harrow 1934–9, thereafter Master of Peterhouse, directed political warfare Middle East 1942–4.]

who took the matter to the Prime Minister on 16th March, on receipt of a telegram from Lord Moyne.[1] Some of Sir Orme's statements might be tendencious or even false, but there could be no further dispute on the main point at issue. The agreement was concluded on 20th March 1943, and made it plain beyond all doubt that the Jerusalem Station and all responsibility for broadcasting must be handed over, as well as all responsibility for the composition of leaflets. SOE retained only some technical personnel at the Station, and their own printing press. The Prime Minister himself as Foreign Secretary asked Lord Moyne to ensure that the agreement was promptly and completely carried out.* This marked the last stage of SOE's career as a Ministry of Political and Subversive Propaganda.

(e) The Secret Services

By a series of historical accidents the three main Services supported from secret funds were during the war under independent Ministers. The SIS was the responsibility of the Foreign Secretary; the Security Service (or MI5) was from the summer of 1940 run by the Home Defence (Security) Executive, under the chairmanship first of Lord Swinton and later of Mr Duff Cooper; SOE belonged to the Minister of Economic Warfare. This was scarcely defensible on administrative grounds: it clearly involved a duplication of common services, a danger of confusion in the handling of agents in the field, and undue delay in the pooling of essential common information. Administrative logic at first sight seems to point to the unity of the Secret Service. Political logic in a democracy points the other way: the withdrawal of funds from the scrutiny of Parliament is in itself a danger to the public control of government. The disposal of secret funds is traditionally a source of political power: and it is clearly safest for the public that it should not be grasped by a single hand. It is therefore fortunate that the administrative arguments do not all tend in the same direction. The three Secret Services were similar in method but not in purpose; each was drawn toward different groups of open departments and used somewhat similar methods to promote different ends.

MI5 was concerned primarily with internal problems: the other two were largely external. The collection of intelligence put the SIS primarily at the disposal of the Intelligence divisions of the Service departments and to a lesser extent of the Foreign Office. The promotion of

---

1 Mr Churchill was acting as Foreign Secretary with Sir Orme Sargent as his senior official.

* [W. E. Guinness, 1880–1944, Conservative MP 1907–31, Lord Moyne 1932, Colonial Secretary 1941–2, Minister of State in Cairo 1944, assassinated by Jewish terrorist gang which included a future Prime Minister of Israel; in *DNB*.]

Subversion drew SOE first towards Political Warfare in a broad sense, then towards the offensive operational side of the Services. From this divergence of purpose there developed considerable divergence of method, and the creation of a single Secret Service was never a project of practical importance during the war.

As regards MI5, there was very little conflict of interest: indeed there was a strong community, as SOE were profoundly interested in maintaining the security of their own organisation.[1] The problem therefore was in practice only one of securing efficient liaison between MI5 and SOE, as between MI5 and other departments. At first SOE's security section was controlled by Lieutenant Colonel Calthrop, who acted also as liaison officer with SIS, and a Scotland Yard officer was attached to his section in January 1941 for liaison with the police. But the problem of security soon outgrew this organisation and in July 1941 the Section was reconstituted on a larger establishment, under Major General G. Lakin* [PASSAGE DELETED ON GROUNDS OF NATIONAL SECURITY]. At about the same time a meeting was held between the heads of the two organisations to discuss all points of friction outstanding:[2] but the practice of high-level meetings did not develop further. The principle adopted was that all matters of Security, as regards agents and as regards SOE's own organisation, should be canalised through the Security Section, which worked on a footing of mutual confidence with MI5. This confidence was well established in General Lakin's time and was maintained after his retirement to a less onerous post in September 1942, when he was replaced by Commander Senter. The only formal machinery was the system of joint 'Panels' envisaged in July 1942:[3] there were to be four of these –

(a) To discuss problems of mutual interest arising out of SOE training.
(b) To consider the security of SOE operations.
(c) To consider the security of SOE signals and communications.
(d) To arrange the exchange of information between MI5 and SOE Country Sections.

Panel (b) was found to be unnecessary in practice, as MI5 shortly afterwards attached an officer to the Special Security Section of SOE, which had been set up in January 1943 to interrogate all returning

---

[1] This account is drawn largely from the SOE History of the Security Section, and comments thereon by Commander Senter, RNVR, head of the Section from September 1942. [(Sir) J. W. Senter, 1905–66, QC 1953, knight 1958.]

[2] Meeting of 18th July 1941: Minutes on SOE Archives File (AD/S.1) SC/94.

[3] Details in Security History of SOE p. 4.

* [J. H. F. Lakin, 1978–1943, Indian Army, major-general 1933.]

agents with a view to checking the security of their organisations and to conduct any special investigations regarding enemy penetration in the field. Panel (d) also turned out to be an arrangement more formal than was required: but Panels (a) and (c) continued to be very useful channels of collaboration.

Relations with SIS presented much more serious difficulties. D Section had been formed within SIS and had been removed from its control without its prior agreement and in face of a strong protest made by CSS as soon as the decision came to his knowledge.[1] There was undoubtedly serious danger that confusion would arise from the existence of separate organisations working into enemy territory, and there were the best reasons for insisting on very close liaison. Arrangements for this were throughout satisfactory enough in form. Sir Frank Nelson [PASSAGE DELETED ON GROUNDS OF NATIONAL SECURITY] appears to have visited the CSS with Mr Jebb at frequent intervals and to have informed him of SOE's plans and progress. Lieutenant Colonel Calthrop, who was well-known and liked in both organisations, acted as a junior liaison officer, and from May 1941 (after the disappearance of the 'D Board') the ACSS,* [PASSAGE DELETED] was given a room in Baker Street and assumed personal responsibility for maintaining good relations;[2] he also occasionally attended meetings of the SOE Council.[3] Direct relations were assumed to exist between Heads of Sections in SOE and their opposite numbers in SIS: in one case, that of France and Belgium, a joint Committee[4] was created in December 1941 in order to pool information and resources as far as possible.

In spite of all this machinery relations during 1941 and the early part of 1942 were a continual story of friction and recrimination. No intelligible issue of principle was involved, and each particular incident is an individual problem of great intricacy: no useful purpose would be served now by attempting to scrutinise any of them in detail. The matter can be summed up as one of faults on both sides and psychological incompatibility. From SIS's point of view SOE was an upstart organisation staffed by amateurs not one of whom understood the elements of secret work. It was invading SIS's territory with much

---

[1] Above p. 71.
[2] CD's circular Minute of 4th May 1941; copy on SOE Archives File (AD/S.1) '134 – Liaison with C'.
[3] Minute by Mr Jebb to the Minister (March 1942, undated) on SOE Archives File (AD/S.1) F/134/1.
[4] This was the Westmacott Committee: Sir Charles Hambro's letter to the ACSS on 1st December 1941, on SOE Archives File (AD/S.1) '134'.
* [Identified in *DNB, Missing Persons*, as (Sir) Claude Dansey, 1876–1946, knight 1943.]

sound and fury, and (as we have seen) it could not in its first two years expect to achieve anything proportionate to the disturbance which it caused: SIS's intelligence, (it would be claimed) scanty though it might be, represented a concrete gain for the Allied war effort, and there was no reason why it should be endangered by bungling amateurs. For SOE the same set of facts assumed quite a different aspect. They were admittedly amateurs, but they had been entrusted by the War Cabinet with a task of an entirely novel kind, which was of the greatest importance to the whole Allied strategy. SIS's assistance could be of the utmost value, but it must be given as between equals and not as a matter of patronage. SOE complained that while they were called upon to reveal all their projects to SIS they got very little by doing so except discouragement: and there was no reciprocal attempt by SIS to put its cards on the table and invite the co-operation of SOE. In all practical fields – wireless communications, sea transport, the recruitment of personnel – SIS claimed absolute priority for intelligence: and its secretiveness could be as dangerous to SOE's agents as SOE's inexperience was to SIS.

Like so much in the development of SOE, this issue came to a head in the early part of 1942. Even apart from the general tension of the period, the time was then ripe for a new settlement. SOE had gained much hard experience which fully justified it in claiming technical independence from SIS: it was probably already the larger organisation – apparently by the spring of 1942 it was sending three or four agents to the field for every one sent by SIS: and it was looking to a future in which it would be required to expand further and faster in order to support the Allied invasion of Europe.

Relations were at this stage formally governed by the agreement of 15th September 1940,[1] under which the CSS retained a measure of control over communications and the recruitment of agents, as well as the right to know SOE's projects and to appeal against them if they conflicted with the requirements of intelligence. The only important modifications up to the end of 1941 were that SOE obtained the right to handle its own 'main line' signals traffic to its Missions overseas, and also to organise clandestine wireless communications to agents, except from the United Kingdom: the building up of an SOE 'War Station' was begun in Egypt in December 1941[2] for communications to the Balkans.

By the end of 1941 there was some agreement that the old arrangements were in many respects obsolete: but the only question of imme-

---

1 Referred to above p. 95.
2 SOE Signals History – Section on Middle East. SOE Archives File (AD/S.1) SC/68/5 refers to early wireless arrangements in Middle East.

diate practical importance was that of the organisation of clandestine wireless communications from England. Hitherto SOE's traffic to its agents had been handled by SIS, in SIS's ciphers. There was a certain moral grievance in that SIS thus had knowledge of all SOE's traffic, whereas SOE had no corresponding access to SIS's signals: but the practical issue was that the scale of SOE's traffic was already large, and that SOE was necessarily laying plans for the very much greater expansion which would be needed if resistance in the West, in Poland and in Czechoslovakia, passed into open guerilla warfare. This involved a signals organisation on a completely different scale from anything which SIS would ever contemplate for its own purposes, and the difference of scale was certain in due course to bring a difference in kind; SOE's communications would ultimately more closely resemble those of a military organisation than those of a Secret Service.[1]

There was some preliminary argument as to whether the old document of September 1940 was an agreement between departments which they could revise at their pleasure, or an edict which must stand until modified from above. SOE was clearly in the right here, in maintaining that the relation between the departments had never been laid down by higher authority;[2] and negotiations appear to have been opened just before Christmas 1941 by the presentation of a new draft by SOE.[3] This was discussed between CD and CSS on 2nd January 1942,[4] and elicited a counter-draft prepared by SIS.[5] This really only contains two points of substance which are not in the original agreement: *first* a proposal for a joint fortnightly meeting of senior officers to discuss SOE's projects, *second*, a consolidation of all secret communications from England under the existing SIS controller. Both points were profoundly unwelcome to SOE, but the comments of SOE's officers concentrate less on them than on the 'undertone of condescending patronage bordering on the impertinent',[6] which can certainly be felt in various minor turns of style. The decision taken was to let matters rest until a report was made on SOE's signals

---

[1] Cf. CSS's 'dismayed' Minute to CD of 5th February 1942, inspired by a preview of SOE's plans – on SOE Archives File (AD/S.1) F.134/1.

[2] The only basis for the opposite view was that the agreement and SOE's charter from the Cabinet had both been printed as Annexes to Mr Dalton's paper of October 1940.

[3] Referred to in CD's Minute to AD of 3rd January 1942 on File 1/470/14. (AD also wrote a brief for SO on communications, after his interview with CSS) – on SOE Archives File 1/170/1.

[4] SOE Archives File 1/470/14.

[5] Copy on SOE Archives File (AD/S.1) F/134/1.

[6] Note by CD to CEO dated 18th January 1942, on SOE Archives File (AD/S.1) F/134/1.

problem by a technical officer shortly to be appointed: then to take matters before some higher court – possibly Sir Alexander Cadogan.[1]

At this point Lord Selborne took over, and he was from the first aware of the importance of the problem. Fortunately much of the sting went out of it when on 26th March the CSS formally agreed to SOE's claim for its own communications system in the West: in doing so he stipulated that SOE should not 'pirate' frequencies, but should operate 'an overt system under the constitutional control of the W/T Board', which was responsible for the allocation of frequencies between competing claimants.[2] The concession was unexpected, but eminently reasonable. SOE's requirements were now such as to reduce the old clandestine system to nonsense, and there was little practical advantage in maintaining unified control of signals when it did not exist in other fields.

This was one controversial issue out of the way. The other major point was SIS's proposal for a joint board to control the operations of SOE, and of this no more was heard. In its place emerged a new suggestion, for periodical meetings of the heads of the two organisations presided over by a Conciliator: their object would not be to concert plans, but to smooth out such wrangles as might arise between subordinate sections of the two Services. This was put forward to Mr Eden by the Minister in a letter of 31st March, which refers to an earlier conversation with the Foreign Secretary and Sir Alexander Cadogan: as the Minister said, 'the friction develops from a series of small incidents . . . . These occur *de die in diem,* therefore the only way to deal with them is a regular weekly meeting such as I have suggested.'[3] Lord Selborne recurred to this proposal in the Report which he submitted to the Prime Minister on 10th April, and again in a letter to him of 20th April,[4] and the upshot was the appointment as Conciliator of Sir Findlater Stewart.* The terms of reference were agreed with Mr Eden early in May and the 'Liaison Committee' was constituted 'to review such points of mutual interest to C and SOE as may be brought before it by C or CD, and to determine their

---

1 Mr Jebb's minute of 20th January, and Mr Dalton's note of 24th January, on SOE Archives File (AD/S.1) F/134/1.
2 Meeting of 20th March 1942: CD's letter of 21st March, CSS's letter of 26th March, and CD's of 27th March, which together constitute a formal agreement; copies on SOE Archives File (AD/S.1) F/134/1.
3 Copy on SOE Archives File (AD/S.1) F/134/1. With the letter were enclosed a memo. by Mr Jebb, and a note by Sir Frank Nelson on individual instances of friction.
4 Copy on SOE Archives File 1/470/14. This letter is also the origin of the administrative enquiry by Mr Hanbury Williams and Mr Playfair.
* [Sir S. F. Stewart, 1879–1960, PUS India Office 1930–42, knight 1932; in *DNB*.]

solution. In the event of the Committee not being unanimous on any matter it shall be open either to C or CD to raise the question with their respective Ministers.'[1]

This was never a very promising experiment in the field of government, and it perished without even a trial.[2] Apparently CSS protested at once against Mr Eden's decision and the debate began again. This time the matter was taken through Sir Desmond Morton to the Chiefs of Staff, whom he met in May in order to discuss SOE/SIS relations.[3] Apparently no final conclusion was recorded by the Chiefs of Staff: but the upshot was that the machinery was improved in two very practical respects. First, SIS was instructed to maintain close liaison with the JPC regarding operational requirements, on the same basis as SOE: second, a fortnightly meeting was arranged between SOE and the Foreign Office, and the CSS was invited to attend. These steps provided for proper co-operation on the level of policy, both civil and military. Clearly friction on the lower levels could not be eliminated until such co-operation existed: once it did, minor disputes would fall into their proper place, to be judged in relation to a wider agreement. It cannot be said that this agreement was ever completely achieved or that SOE and SIS ever worked as a whole in perfect harmony: but major disturbances did not recur, and in many sections very close and helpful relations developed undisturbed.

Like so much else in the story, this reflects not only improvements in organisation but the general turn in the course of the war from the autumn of 1942: when all was moving prosperously towards a clearly seen objective, there was far less excuse for backbiting and inter-departmental feud than in the early days of ill-organised rear-guard action. This in part explains why the idea of the unity of the Secret Service never came seriously under discussion. It was brought up by Mr Maxwell in January 1942 as a possible solution of certain difficulties in the Middle East: Mr Jebb's reaction was the very practical one – 'There would be much to be said for such an arrangement in a sensible world, but it would mean removing any control of the SIS from the Foreign Office, and it would therefore, I should have thought, be impossible to propose it at the present time.'[4] Sir Frank Nelson in his paper on relations with SIS seems to have recurred to the idea of

---

[1] Signed by Mr Eden and Lord Selborne on 4th May 1942: sent to Sir Findlater Stewart by Lord Selborne on same day. (Copies in Lord Selborne's papers.)

[2] Sir Findlater Stewart to Lord Selborne 4th June 1942: Lord Selborne to Sir Findlater Stewart 9th June. Copies in Lord Selborne's papers.

[3] CD to Major Morton 31st May 1942; copy in SOE Archives File (AD/S.1) F/134.

[4] Memorandum of 6th January 1942 and Mr Jebb's note to the Minister of 2nd February 1942, on SOE Archives File (AD/S.1) F/134/1.

unity – a larger unity embracing MI5 – as the administrative ideal: but the idea went no further in the negotiations of 1942.[1] It only appears once more in the course of the war in an ably argued paper by Mr Duff-Cooper dated 23rd March 1943,[2] where the administrative argument is stated in relation to the problem of maintaining an efficient nucleus of the three Secret Services in time of peace. The Prime Minister would have none of it: 'Every Department which has waxed during the war is now considering how it can quarter its officials on the public indefinitely when peace returns. The less we encourage these illusions, the better.' He would consider nothing but the creation of a regular monthly meeting between the heads of the three Services and Major Morton.[3] This Committee met once and (as Mr Churchill doubtless had foreseen) forthwith recommended its own dissolution, as no business could be found which was not already handled through other channels. The three Secret Services continued, not without success, in their several independent courses.

4. Co-operation with the USA and the USSR

It remains to give some account of the organisation for collaboration with the two major Allies, both of whom were, in very different ways, inclined to take energetic action on lines parallel to those of SOE. An attempt to describe their organisation (or lack of organisation) and objectives would lead very far afield, and could not be satisfactorily documented from SOE's papers: so that this account must be limited fairly strictly to SOE's side of the story.

(a) USA

Reference has already been made[4] to Sir William Stephenson's Mission, which opened a channel of communication with Mr G. Edgar Hoover's FBI toward the end of 1940. Colonel Donovan comes into the picture as a roving Presidential agent at about the same time. He paid a visit of investigation and encouragement to the Balkan countries early in 1941: in February he saw Sir Frank Nelson in London[5] and was given a 'conducted tour' of selected SOE stations. The

---

[1] Page 7 of Mr Jebb's Minute of March 1942 (undated) to Lord Selborne; copy on SOE Archives File (AD/S.1) F/134/1.

[2] Copy on SOE Archives File (AD/S.1) F/138/15.

[3] Prime Minister's Minute M.231/3 of 4th April 1943; copy on SOE Archives File (AD/S.1) F/138/15.

[4] Above p. 328.

[5] No record of meeting, but it was authorised by the Minister on 12th February. (Papers on SOE Archives File SC/76 (AD/S.1).)

Minister himself had seen Mr Hopkins* in London in January but had limited his discussions to the official business of the Ministry of Economic Warfare.[1] His first official approach to the US Government on SOE affairs appears to have been a discussion on 9th May with Mr Averell Harriman,** then in London as a special representative for matters relating to Lease/Lend – the Defence Aid Act was passed in March 1941.[2] This was on delicate ground as regards revelation of Sir William Stephenson's status and activities in the USA: but it led to a fairly frank discussion of the nature of SOE's work and the ways in which the USA could assist it. Mr Harriman undertook to approach the President through Mr Hopkins as to the possibility of a meeting of representatives to discuss collaboration in detail.

The next stage was the emergence of Colonel Donovan as Co-ordinator of Strategic Information: a post created on 18th June 1941, with a vast and indefinite charter, reporting direct to the President.[3] From this grew in June 1942 the Office of Strategic Services, which had a complex and troubled history, full of quarrels with competing departments – the FBI, the Office of War Information, the Co-ordinator of Latin-American Affairs, and the two fighting services. If these could be traced in detail they would afford interesting parallels to the development of SOE, and would probably also show in a relatively favourable light the various make-shift arrangements by which SOE was fitted into the general British system of war government. The ultimate upshot (after various permutations) was that OSS became an 'all-embracing' agency for 'black' work, whether Secret Intelligence, Special Operations or unacknowledgeable propaganda: it embraced the work of SIS and SOE and in part that of PWE. But it had only a limited jurisdiction as regards propaganda, even of a subversive kind, and its sphere was geographically limited. It was excluded by its charter from the Western hemisphere, and by the hostility of the local commanders from the Pacific Theatre. It was thus very far from having a free hand to run subversive warfare as a whole, and in its dealings with SOE it had always to be 'looking over its shoulder' at possible repercussions on its position in Washington.

---

1 Record of luncheon discussion in SOE Archives File (AD/S.1) SC/76 – (date 22nd January).

2 Record of dinner meeting on SOE Archives File (AD/S.1) SC/76.

3 Account of the circumstances by Mr David Eccles, dated 24th June, on SOE Archives File (AD/S.1) SC/76. [D. McA. Eccles, 1904–98, diplomat and politician, Conservative MP 1943–62, Board of Trade 1957–9, viscount 1964.]

* [Harry L. Hopkins, 1890–1946, Roosevelt's closest confidant. See R. Sherwood (ed.) *The White House Papers of Harry L. Hopkins* (2 vols, 1948–9).]

** [W. A. Harriman, 1891–1986, American diplomat, envoy to England 1941, Ambassador in Moscow 1943–6.]

Official contact between the organisations began with a visit by Colonel Davies to the USA in September 1941, for discussions with Colonel Donovan, in which Sir William Stephenson took part. The essential points were, on the one hand, British aid to the USA, by a sharing of experience and in particular by opening a school in Canada where organisers and agents could be trained on US as well as on British account: on the other hand US aid to Britain, in men, in materials and in the provision of channels and contacts in those countries to which the Americans had access more freely than the British. There seems to be no record of an agreement on paper at this stage – a rather delicate stage in the development of the US attitude towards the war – but friendly relations were established and there was henceforward a reasonably free exchange of information and facilities. As can be imagined, most of the assets were at first on the British side: Colonel Donovan came into the field at an even later date than SOE, and his initial problems of organisation were enormous – in most occupied countries OSS was to the last dependent on channels opened up in the first instance by SOE. It was only in French North Africa and the territories related to it that there existed some American organisation – that of Mr Murphy – on which to build, and it was in this region that OSS's first active local officers were established after America's entry into the war.[1] Colonel Donovan himself was in London in November 1941, and was given a very full picture of SOE's methods. He left a representative in London and an OSS representative (Mr Mauran) was also established in Cairo early in 1942.

The first need for formal agreement arose out of this OSS Mission to Middle East, which had big ideas, and was not at all inclined to submit to British control. From February 1942 onwards Mr Mauran was demanding the development of an independent American field organisation: and the British were pointing out the intolerable political consequences of such a step.[2] A temporary solution was embodied in a letter from Colonel Donovan to the newly appointed Minister of State, Mr Casey, dated 5th April:[3] British and US Secret Intelligence organisations would operate independently, their Special Operations would be closely linked and would be directed by the country which had military command in the theatre. The British would thus have the controlling interest in the Middle East and Balkans, and there would be some chance of pursuing a coherent policy.

---

[1] Captain Eddy at Tangier, Colonel Solberg at Lisbon, Mr Raichle at Gibraltar – all in December 1941 or early 1942.

[2] Cf. papers of the SOE Sub-Committee of the MEDC, in February 1942 and exchange of telegrams with SOE London. SOE Archives File 60/470/12.

[3] Copy on SOE Archives File 60/470/12.

As was so apt to happen in dealing with the USA, this high level agreement had very little effect on what American officials did in practice: and by May 1942 it was obvious that the danger of unco-ordinated action was still there[1] – there were suggestions for instance of the direct allocation of aircraft by the Americans to the Yugoslavs in order to assist Mihailovitch, and of similar direct aid to the Poles, which would have been administratively quite unworkable. In addition, provisional arrangements had been made for joint operations in North Africa and Iberia,[2] and these would require higher confirmation. It was thus appropriate that the whole field should be covered by discussions between Sir Charles Hambro, Colonel Donovan, and their staffs, which took place in London, in June 1942. The agreement which issued from these discussions was finally confirmed in September, under the authority of the Chiefs of Staff and the US Joint Chiefs of Staff.[3] The documents involved are very detailed and bore too little relation to later practice to be worth quoting in full. But the principles involved were simple enough in themselves, and proved to be fairly stable (though very complicated) in application:

(a) Close collaboration between the two Head Offices, through liaison officers in London and Washington.

(b) The division of the world into British and American areas, in which ultimate control would rest with the British and American authorities respectively.

(c) In the Balkans and Middle East a rather loose arrangement by which the head of the OSS Mission would accept 'direction and instructions' from the SOE Controller, but would have the right of direct appeal to Washington in the event of disagreement.

(d) In the rest of Europe a distinction between

(i) 'Invasion Countries' (at this stage Norway, Belgium, Holland and France) in which there should be only one integrated Field Force controlled jointly by SOE and the London Office of OSS

---

[1] See long Minute by Lord Glenconner dated 28th May, on SOE Archives File 60/470/12.

[2] Copy of agreement dated 5th May 1942 in SOE Archives File 1/470/12 (subject to confirmation by Colonel Donovan and the British COS).

[3] Copy of exchange of letters and summary of agreement on SOE Archives File (AD/S.1) F.76/9. Full note of discussions – SOE Archives File 1/470/12. COS approval given by letter from Brigadier Hollis to CD dated 3rd September on SOE Archives File 1/470/12: the Joint Planners had earlier pressed for a closer integration than was provided for in the agreement – JP(42)632 and 707.

* [(Sir) L. C. Hollis, 1897–1963, in War Cabinet Office 1939–45, major-general 1943, knight 1946; see his *War at the Top* (1959); in *DNB*.]

and
(ii) 'Non-Invasion Countries', in which there was no objection to an independent OSS Field Force, provided that it was controlled by OSS London in close liaison with SOE.

In general this worked well in Western Europe and North Africa, poorly in the Balkans, very unevenly in India, China and the Far East. In Western Europe OSS's ambitions were relatively limited.[1] In France and the Low Countries it was anxious only to contribute 'teams' to assist in the final rising, and it did not interfere seriously with the preliminary 'build-up' of resistance: when D-day approached integration under the control of SHAEF became complete. In Norway OSS wished to be more fully associated with the work from the start: but luckily a joint Anglo-Norwegian control already existed and OSS fitted very well into the existing framework, with joint responsibility for all operations, and a particular responsibility for the area north of Namsos. In the other countries – Germany, Poland and Czechoslovakia in particular – the activities of both organisations were so tenuous that there was no serious chance of friction.

In the Balkans there were continual difficulties, beginning with a proposal in August 1942 for an OSS mission on a grand scale under a certain Colonel Hoskins, whose powers appeared to be likely to approximate to those of a Minister of State. This was repressed with some difficulty, but left a legacy of friction. A joint controlling committee with Lord Glenconner as chairman and arbiter was set up in February 1943: in June the Commanders-in-Chief expressed uneasiness about the weakness of SOE's control and proposed a new arrangement for a committee under the CGS, reporting to the Commanders-in-Chief.[2] This was in the eyes of SOE a serious breach in the position of the organisation as one exercising world-wide control of subversion from Headquarters in London. Lord Selborne protested to Mr Casey[3] and was mollified by an assurance that real control would still rest with SOE: but the decision was in effect a stage in the development (to be referred to later) by which Special Operations in the Balkans became more and more a matter of military policy for which SOE London bore comparatively little responsibility. This did not in itself reduce friction: it was for obvious reasons the policy both of the Foreign Office and of the Commanders-in-Chief that American

---

[1] The original agreement was amplified and made more precise on these points in a document signed in January 1943; copy on SOE Archives File 1/470/12.

[2] Telegram giving the Cs-in-C's conclusions No. 1527 of 24th June 1943; copy on SOE Archives File (AD/S.1) F.76/9: cf. CCS conclusions of 3rd July reported in JSM1027 on same file.

[3] Letter of 29th June 1943 on SOE Archives File (AD/S.1) F.76/9.

attempts to develop independent field organisations in the Balkans should be tactfully resisted, and the burden of resistance fell on SOE. It was only in 1944 that the American and British organisations working into the Balkans grew into the habit of easy collaboration which generally prevailed in Western Europe.

So bare an account as this does less than justice to the lively nature of the collaboration. There was political friction fairly frequently, personal incompatibility less frequently: but there was real freedom in the exchange of operational information, of however secret a character, and there were many fields in which OSS and SOE worked as one single organisation. From 1942 onwards each occupied a very large part in the other's thoughts and plans. OSS could hardly move without British organisation and British knowledge, cramping though it sometimes found them: SOE drew largely on American stores, above all on American aircraft, and American brains and energy contributed much to the liveliness of an organisation which might easily have become narrow and over-tired as the war went on. One can believe little of what is published or hinted in America about the American creation of resistance in Europe: but there was nevertheless an American contribution of the very highest importance.

(b) Russia[1]

The Russian story is very different, and illustrates once again the type of difficulty which hampered our dealings with the USSR in all fields. With the Americans there was quarrelsome but intimate and lively co-operation. With the Russians every attempt was made to initiate co-operation on formal terms, but formality never developed into practical cohesion in pursuit of a common object. In this the fault was by no means entirely on the Russian side.

The idea of active co-operation with the Russians in subversion seems to have originated[2] with Sir Stafford Cripps, who went to Moscow as Ambassador in June 1940: and the first thought was of indirect contact, possibly through the Czechs, who were always careful to maintain intimate relations with Moscow. This was not pursued, but direct contact was opened towards the end of July by the dispatch of Lieutenant Colonel Guinness to Moscow for discussions with the NKVD.* This organisation, it should be explained, was the only one

---

[1] There is a useful History of the Russian Section by Major McLaughlin.

[2] Mr Dalton's Minute No. 30 of 25th June 1941; copy on SOE Archives File (AD/S.1) F.85/5.

* [Narodny Kommissariat Vnutrennich Dyel, the Soviet secret police, then under L. P. Beria, 1899–1953, executed on death of his master Stalin (J. V. Djugashvili, 1879–1953).]

among the Allies (or among the enemy for that matter) which approached the theoretical conception of an all-embracing service dealing with all subversion and also with all 'black' activities of whatever kind. It embraced within itself all the activities dispersed among various secret or semi-secret organisations in Great Britain – MI5, the 'Special Branch', SOE, SIS, PWE: it also had pretty large general responsibility for propaganda, internal and external: and (like Himmler's* organisation) it tended in some senses to become a State within a State. In relation to this body SOE was a junior organisation dealing with one which had great power and endless ramifications outside SOE's sphere: the direct contacts which SOE possessed were only with one corner of NKVD – the internal reactions of that organisation as a whole remained mysterious to the end.

Colonel Guinness naturally was not sent without the concurrence of the Foreign Office and the Embassy. Unfortunately his Report has not been found, so that there is no material available on the course of the negotiations, which resulted in a full draft agreement early in September. This was brought to England by Colonel Guinness early in September, and was sent to Sir Orme Sargent at the Foreign Office for his information.[1] Colonel Guiness then returned to Moscow, where the Agreement was signed on 30th September by him and by General Nikolaev for NKVD.[2]

The agreement itself provides fully and explicitly for co-operation between the Allies in subversive action in all countries, outside the USSR on the one hand and the British Commonwealth on the other; and it is accompanied by a survey of objectives indicating the type of target to be attacked by sabotage in the main areas concerned. 'Co-operation' (in subversive activities) 'is not only desirable and practicable but essential for our common aims in defeating the enemy.' 'Co-operation in all other countries . . . will be decided by the Heads of the British and Soviet organisations and will be based on a common policy. Such a common policy includes:

(a) The co-ordination of sabotage activities and the allocation of targets.
(b) The co-ordination of propaganda intended to incite the local population to insurrection, active sabotage and other subversive activities.

---

[1] Letter of Mr Jebb of 17th September on SOE Archives File F.85/5. This is worth noting, as the Report and Agreement were returned to SOE on 8th October (Sir Orme Sargent's letter of that date), and in later discussions the Foreign Office denied having seen and approved the document (Sir Alexander Cadogan's letter of 10th February 1942).

[2] Text at Appendix I of SOE Russian Section History.

* [H. Himmler, 1900–45, headed Nazi SS from 1929, suicide on arrest.]

(c) The timing of any particular operation, especially where it affects the political or operational plans of the other party.'

Liaison missions would be exchanged between SOE and NKVD: each country would 'give all possible assistance in introducing each other's agents into occupied territory': each 'would consider the possibility of permitting the establishment in their own territories of the other party's W/T terminals'.

In fact, the agreement was more precise and far-reaching than that arrived at with OSS almost a year later, and much of it was formally fulfilled. Missions were exchanged, under Colonel Hill* in Moscow and Colonel Chichaev in London, and they were in fairly frequent contact with the organisations to which they were accredited. It is not known what was the real status of the supposed 'high contacts' on the Russian side: on the British side two different individuals were successively 'passed off' as CD, the head of the organisation. Information on technical devices was exchanged: but only on those already commonplace and in regular use. Plans were begun for liaison with NKVD in other theatres – the Middle East, Persia, the Far East and China in particular – but nothing ever came of them. It was however an item to the Soviet credit that they put at the disposal of the Government of India a certain Bhagat Ram, an agent working for the Germans on Russian orders in Afghanistan: he proved to be of considerable value, and the Russians had a reasonable complaint that they got no adequate *quid pro quo* from the British as regards intelligence in Central Asia.

SOE's counter-claim would have been that there was a more than adequate *quid pro quo* in the 'Pickaxe' parties which they transported for the Russians to Western Europe. No similar facilities were ever given by the Russians in the East, although they permitted the dropping of one British agent in Estonia[1] and seem to have done a certain amount to trace and to extricate British parties in the territories which they overran. But the Russians would certainly not have admitted that the British handling of the 'Pickaxe' parties was such as to call for gratitude.

To strike a balance on this matter (which was of some substantial importance in Anglo-Soviet relations) one would need to know (as we do not) how seriously the Russians regarded 'Pickaxe': was it a

---

[1] His Mission was an abject failure: Operation 'Blunderhead' – see Section V of SOE History of Polish Minorities Section. [The agent, Ronald Seth – later author of works on espionage technique – had trouble explaining why, when overrun in 1945, he was dressed as a captain in the Wehrmacht.]

* [Hill, as the Russians must have known, had been the case officer for the notorious Sidney Reilly, on whom see Gordon Brook-Shepherd, *Iron Maze* (1998).]

real part of their plans or merely an attempt to test British good faith?
It would also be necessary to penetrate the fog of wrangling which
surrounded almost every one of the parties. The statistics of the story
can be put fairly shortly:

1942

For France	One agent by sea	Two months' delay in UK
For France	Three agents by air	One month's delay in UK
For Belgium	One killed in a crash; one delivered to Holland after twelve months' delay.	
For Holland	Two: one dropped with wrong luggage by SOE's error, of which the NKVD became aware. One month's delay.	
For Austria	Four who 'mutinied' and attempted to escape from NKVD with SOE's connivance. Two dispatched in an aircraft which failed to return. Two months' delay.	

1943

For Germany	Two dropped	Five months' delay
For Germany	One dropped	Four months' delay
For Austria	Two dropped	Five months' delay
For France	One dropped	One month's delay
	Three dropped	Two–four months' delay.
For North Italy	One landed after much delay and recrimination.	

1944

For Austria	One dropped	Little delay
For Germany	One dropped	Four months' delay
	Two dropped	Two months' delay
For France	Three dropped after a good deal of recrimination.	

The total was thirty-four 'Pickaxe' agents of whom twenty-five went
to the field, three were killed in aircraft lost and six were abortive. From
SOE's side this was technically not too bad. The housing and care of
the agents was very troublesome: their false papers and cover stories
were often poorly organised by the NKVD and had to be provided
afresh by SOE: the delays were in no way beyond comparison with

those which SOE's own agents endured through lack of transport facilities. But NKVD could hardly be expected to admit its own technical deficiencies or to sympathise with SOE's transport problems: if it wanted evidence of double-crossing or at least 'administrative delays', it could find it fairly easily in the record.

It would certainly have been encouraged to do so if it had known the political history of the matter on the British side. The Foreign Office (though it is pretty certain that it had the papers at the time) was clearly unconscious of the implications of the 'Moscow Agreement' until it was faced early in 1942 with the first specific Russian request for the delivery of an agent to France.[1] It was then (not unnaturally) startled by the implications of delivering Russian agents to the territories of countries whose 'Free' governments were in most cases rabidly anti-Communist: and the debate which ensued occupied most of 1942. SOE (supported on the whole by HM Ambassador in Moscow) represented that the Russians would inevitably regard the matter as a test case, just because it was politically so delicate, and that no growth of easy co-operation could be expected unless we met reasonable Russian requirements promptly and efficiently. The Foreign Office maintained its reluctance to permit the dropping of agents whose true tasks were unknown to us without the consent of the Governments concerned: it also showed some disposition to bargain (e.g. for an improvement of the Russian attitude to Mihailovitch) about the fulfilment of an obligation which we had plainly accepted in the 'Moscow Agreement.'

The final upshot was a letter from Sir Charles Hambro to Sir Alexander Cadogan in December 1942,[2] confirming agreement reached verbally:

(a) Agents to be introduced freely into all countries fighting with the Axis.

(b) Agents not to be introduced into occupied Allied countries without consulting the Government concerned.

(c) Agents not normally to be introduced into occupied France without consulting the Free French: but exceptions to be possible.

(d) Agents not normally to be introduced into neutral countries.

This was confirmed and made slightly more stringent in Sir Alexander's acknowledgement.[3]

---

[1] Mr Loxley to Colonel Taylor on 5th January 1942; copy on SOE Archives File (AD/S.1) F.85/5.

[2] Letter of 2nd December; copy in SOE Archives File (C.D.) 'Russia/3'.

[3] Letter of 11th December; copy in SOE Archives File (C.D.) 'Russia/3'.

This was of course a one-sided abrogation of the Agreement. But there is no reason to believe it was known to the Russians, and it had already become pretty clear that there was not to be a gradual growth of friendly collaboration. This was a phenomenon to be observed in other departments of Anglo-Russian relations in the same period, and it must not be referred only to the local difficulties in SOE's sphere. From this time onward are to be found regular representations from Brigadier Hill about the futility of his work in Moscow, and the SOE Mission was retained there mainly because it was convenient in minor ways to the Ambassador and the Military Mission. Brigadier Hill was for instance given excellent conducted tours in the Leningrad area and in White Russia in 1944, when other British officers were much less freely received: and he had some opportunities for meeting unofficial Russians, as no guard was placed outside his flat. He was thus able to produce some interesting general appreciations of the Russian attitude: but relations on the NKVD front were a matter of dinner-parties and deadlocks.

A few of these troubles are worth referring to as specimens. In Yugoslavia there was first the complaint that the British had refused on grounds of impracticability to send a Russian party to Tito in 1943, and had then sent a party themselves without prior consultation in April 1943. Then in 1944 a Russian officer was put in to maintain liaison with Brigadier Maclean's Mission and had to be withdrawn after a brief stay on grounds of incompatibility of temperament. In Greece a Russian party succeeded in getting itself dropped to ELAS in July 1944 by a curious and rather childish stratagem, and there was trouble about British Liaison Officers' relations with escaped Russian prisoners. In Roumania it was a serious grievance that Colonel de Chastelain was dropped in uniform in December 1943 without prior Russian knowledge: was he intended to intrigue against Russia with reactionary Roumanians? In the West the worst dispute[1] was over British attempts to find some means of exploiting the large number of Russians fighting in German uniform: a military factor of very serious importance. They had been pressed into German service by the most brutal methods; and were held to it by the conviction that they could expect nothing from the Allies but execution as traitors. This was a grave matter of high policy which had many aspects: SOE's share in it was to segregate and train some Russian prisoners with a view to their use as agents. This was done after no more than a general intimation of the plan to NKVD, and when the action taken was admitted there followed a great storm and an absolute refusal to co-operate. The whole scheme had therefore to be dropped.

---

[1] See SOE File (CD) 'Russia/4' for the full story.

By this time the Russians on their side had abandoned the 'Pickaxe' programme entirely, and in 1944 and 1945 there was little ground of co-operation left. The idea was broached once or twice of negotiating a new agreement for collaboration against a Nazi revival: but it was not pursued very seriously on either side, and the SOE Mission was finally withdrawn from Moscow in September 1945. It had been a failure, but not for reasons within SOE's control.

PART III

THE OFFENSIVE

CHAPTER XVI

Introductory

We have now reached a point at which SOE can be regarded (at last) as an established Department of State. It was in many ways oddly adjusted to the rest of the machine, it possessed a very well-developed set of departmental idiosyncrasies and inter-departmental quarrels, and it was not very highly rated by the comparatively small outside circle to which its work was known. But it could now stand on its own feet as one of the strongest of the lesser Ministries, at least the equal in influence and in the abilities and energy of its staff to such bodies as the Ministry of Economic Warfare, the Ministry of Information and the Political Warfare Executive; and it had developed by bitter experience a pretty clear idea of what its purpose was and within what limitations it must be pursued. Above all it had a sense of mission, the intensity of which varied from one 'Country Section' to another, but effectively pervaded and united the organisation.

There remain in the next period some disasters, some constitutional crises, some allegations of inefficiency and corruption; but we are henceforth concerned less with warfare in Whitehall and more with the pattern of the ultimate European rising, and its relation to regular military operations.

Here too there is a change of atmosphere and of tempo, varying a little in different countries, which affects the character of the narrative. Hitherto the Resistance has been to a great extent a matter of the individual and his problems; irrevocable steps were taken as a result of the idiosyncrasies or accidents of individuals – the contacts made by Pirie in Greece, the ill-luck which dogged Hudson in Yugoslavia, the influence of single Frenchmen, such as Moulin or Emmanuel d'Astier or 'Carte'. The narrative has thus far been one of detail – perhaps too much detail. In the summer and autumn of 1942 the atmosphere begins to change. It is partly that SOE is now fully organised: it can train its agents better, it can dispatch and handle more of them more efficiently, and it is less dependent on pure luck. Each agent has his own story which can be followed in detail from the records; but there is also an intelligible story of movements largely independent of individual fortunes, for there is in most countries an organisation sponsored by SOE which continues to play its part in spite of individual disasters. It is even more important that in most countries the Resistance is now visibly the winning side; the immediate dangers are no less, but common sense now tells on the same side as political idealism in rallying the boldest and most far-sighted elements in the population to the Allied side. This broadening of the Resistance was undoubtedly aided by the German policy of conscripting labour almost at random for deportation to Germany, which drove many active 'unpolitical' men into the 'Maquis' in its various forms, and greatly increased the numbers of those living underground and outside the law. If they could be given arms and training there was here in most countries the nucleus of a guerilla force permanently mobilised and backed by the warm sympathy of the population. This part must be concerned more with the general pattern of this mass movement than with the multitude of incidents in which each part of it was involved.

The general plan is *first* to follow the development of events in Yugoslavia, Greece and (more briefly) Albania – countries which the Germans evacuated without Allied invasion. *Second* to deal shortly with SOE's limited activities in Roumania, Bulgaria and Hungary – countries which were liberated by the Russians. *Third*, Poland and Czechoslovakia, where SOE exercised little control, but the political aspects of Resistance were of the highest importance, both at the time and later. *Fourth*, to follow the pattern of Special Operations in support of Allied operations into the Mediterranean from the West in 1942 and 1943 – North Africa, Sicily, Sardinia, Corsica, Italy. *Fifth*, the whole problem of France, in relation to the great invasion operations of 1944, 'Overlord' and 'Anvil', to which Belgium and Holland form an appendix. *Sixth*, Norway and Denmark, where the technique of industrial sabotage was pushed perhaps to its highest point, but the occasion for the final rising never came, and the most important work of the Resistance was its peaceful assumption of control. *Finally*, the attempt to organise or counterfeit Resistance in Germany and Austria, an enterprise begun too late to be a serious test of what might in other circumstances have been achieved.

It will be seen that there is a broad division between the first three of these chapters, which are dominated by the problem of relations with Russia and the movements sponsored by Russia: and the last three, in which the overriding influence is that of Allied military operations from the West.

The narrative must throughout postulate a general knowledge of the progress of the campaigns and the changing patterns of the Allied command organisation, which cannot be set out here. But it may be useful (at the risk of some duplication later) to cover two general topics briefly at the outset: *first* the development of the 'command organisation' of SOE in the field, *second* the general directives given to it on policy, with which is interlocked the problem of aircraft allocation.

1. SOE Field Organisation

The Mediterranean

At the outset SOE's only important headquarters outside Great Britain (so far as concerns the 'German war') were SOE, Middle East, in Cairo, known for cover purposes as MO4.* As guerilla activities developed during 1943 in Greece and Yugoslavia, this assumed more and more a para-military character, and in consequence it acquired in November 1943 the additional 'cover-name' of Force 133. Its position was complicated by the advance from Egypt to the west and then into Italy, which meant that the base for Force 133's air operations to Yugoslavia moved forward first into Cyrenaica, then to Tunis and finally to Brindisi. Its control thus became increasingly remote, and in October 1943 an 'Advanced HQ of MO4' was formed in Bari,[1] primarily to supervise sea communications with Yugoslavia.

Meanwhile at the western end of the Mediterranean a special Mission ('Massingham' or ISSU6) had been formed to work with General Eisenhower's** invasion force, and after the success of 'Torch' it became responsible for special operations in support of further advances, as well as for working with SOE London to assist resistance in France. It was subject to control by General Eisenhower only as regards activities related to his own operations. A smaller Mission ('Brandon') was attached to the First Army for the Tunis campaign. In October 1943 'Massingham' in Algiers sent forward an offshoot into Italy (No. 1 Special Force or 'Maryland') to deal with operations in Italy, and beyond it to Austria ('Clowder') and to Poland ('Torment').

The Americans of OSS were only partly integrated in these arrangements. In the East they were formally independent, but in general accepted the guidance of Force 133. In the West a joint operational HQ, known as SPOC, was finally set up in Algiers in May 1944. In Italy there was no proper formal arrangement for common action,

---

[1] London HQ War Diary, ME & Balkans Section, p. 1123.
* [This had been the name of the body that had supported Lawrence and the Arab Revolt in 1916–18.]
** [D. D. Eisenhower, 1890–1969, US general commanding 'Torch' and 'Overlord' in turn; President 1953–61. See his *Crusade in Europe* (1948) and Stephen E. Ambrose, *Eisenhower* (vol. 1, NY, 1983).]

though informal arrangements were fairly satisfactory.

This confused situation late in 1943 was the reflection of an equal confusion of organisation on the highest level, which led to the decision of the Sextant Conference at Cairo in December 1943 to create a unified Mediterranean Theatre under a single commander – General Maitland Wilson* – with HQ at Algiers and Advanced HQ at Caserta. The Middle East Command came under his control for all operations against the Germans, though not for its vast administrative responsibilities.

One of the first tasks of SACMED was to achieve some rational organisation for Special Operations based on his command, and the plain solution was to bring all existing forces together under a single HQ adjacent to his own working HQ in Italy. It was agreed with SOE in London in January 1944 that a HQ Special Operations Mediterranean (SOM) should be set up in Italy under Major-General Stawell,** who had succeeded Lord Glenconner in Cairo after a period of crisis in September and October 1943. This was delayed by the resistance of the C-in-C Middle East, who wished to retain control of the only active operations still within his sphere, those into Greece, Bulgaria and Roumania. It was in the end, in March 1944, agreed that HQ Force 133 should remain in Cairo under the operational control of the C-in-C Middle East, but administratively within SOM: Advanced Force 133 (now known as Force 266) was detached from it, and its responsibility was limited to Greece, Bulgaria and Roumania.

SOM thus came into being in March 1944 as a military headquarters directly responsible to SACMED: it included OSS as well as SOE, and was therefore no longer a subordinate formation of SOE HQ in London. But its military position remained obscure. On the one hand, there was a staff branch (G3 Special Operations Section) in AFHQ, under an American Brigadier-General, who was interposed between SOM and the SAC as co-ordinator of SOM's requirements with those of other 'special' formations – secret intelligence, psychological warfare, strategic deception and so forth. On the other hand, SOM had only a limited control over its own lower formations, which looked for operational directives to various other commanders and were on the administrative side very well accustomed to look after themselves. Arrangements altered repeatedly in detail during 1944, but the following 'composite picture' gives a working idea of SOM's sub-units.

---

* [H. Maitland Wilson, 1881–1964, commanded British troops in Egypt 1939–40, Greece 1941, Syria 1942–3, C-in-C Middle East 1943, Mediterranean 1944, in Washington 1945–7, knight 1940, field-marshal 1944, baron 1946. See his *Eight Years Overseas* (1949); in *DNB*.]

** [W. A. M. Stawell, 1895–1987, a DDMI 1940–42, major-general 1943.]

Sub-Unit	Responsible for	Controlled by
Force 133	Greece Roumania Bulgaria	C-in-C, Middle East
Force 399 (formerly 266)	Yugoslavia Albania Hungary	HQ Balkan Air Force
No. 1 SF ('Maryland')	Italy	15th Army Group
ME 43 ('Clowder')	Austria	SHAEF (later AFHQ)
Force 399 ('Torment')	Czechoslovakia Poland	SOE London
ISSU6 ('Massingham')	South France	SHAEF (partly through the 'Anvil' force)

These names and command relations are in the highest degree confusing, and the best that can be said is that in practice the formal diagram was of much less importance than the relations of each sub-unit to the Commander directly concerned with operations: and these were in this phase almost uniformly excellent. HQ SOM remained a good idea in theory which came too late in a period of rapid movement to have much chance of finding its feet.[1]

In the West the picture is much simpler. From a very early stage the 'Country Sections' within what was later the SHAEF area were brought together in groups under two Regional Directors, for France and the Low Countries, and for Scandinavia respectively. In the reorganisation of summer 1942 both these Directors came under Brigadier Gubbins, as DCD(O), and there thus existed in effect a 'Mission' in London responsible for the Western countries, which was readily detachable for work with the Supreme Commander when he was appointed. The next stage, reached in November 1943, was the creation of a unified organisation (SOE/SO HQ)[2] with the OSS for all these countries – a fairly simple step forward from the existing collaboration. On 1st May

---

[1] The first section of the elaborate history prepared by G3 (SO) at AFHQ gives a great deal of detail about this organisation. There is also available in SOE records 'A Short History of SOM HQ' by Lieutenant Colonel J. G. Beevor.

[2] Under Brigadier Mockler-Ferryman, CBE, MC, and Colonel J. S. Haskell (US).

1944 this joint body, under the command of Brigadier Mockler-Ferryman,* who had been 'Director' for Western Europe within SOE since June 1943, became Special Force Headquarters, fully under the control of SHAEF, without changing its location in Baker Street (Norgeby House) or its personnel. This was now in form an Anglo-American military command reporting direct to General Eisenhower, through a special staff branch (in G3) known as 'Musgrave', under Lieutenant Colonel H.N. Saunders: in practice it still worked so closely with SOE and so much on the old lines that there was no serious break within the organisation. SFHQ threw off detachments to subordinate Commands and Armies, and the logic of its position was confused by the removal of its French Section on 6th June 1944 to form part of the État Major, Forces Françaises de l'Intérieur (EMFFI) under General Koenig, who was independently responsible to General Eisenhower and was in practice controlled by General de Gaulle. But this did not (as in the Mediterranean) mean that the real control of operations rested with the sub-units. All operations almost without exception were to the end carried out from Britain, all signals flowed through SOE's stations at Grendon and Poundon, and an effective central control remained in being.

We must revert later to the general problems of control of Resistance in the field, when we have seen how the Resistance developed in action: but this brief summary may serve as a glossary to some of the terms which will be met with in the narratives.

Policy Directives and the Allocation of Aircraft

In retrospect it seems often that the higher policy of SOE grew out of events rather than anticipated them: but this was not for lack of resolute attempts to look ahead and plan ahead.

Up to the end of 1942 SOE was still working under the 'Invasion Directive' of May 1942:[1] this did not deal with individual countries in much detail, and it was in any event rendered obsolete by the success of 'Torch'. It was therefore essential to replace it early in 1943 by a document more in line with the existing situation. In six months the fortunes of the Allies had been transformed, and with them the prospects of SOE. Work began at the end of January 1943, a necessary sequel to the decisions of the Casablanca Conference,[2] and it led finally to the 'Directive for 1943', issued by the Chiefs of Staff on

---

[1] COS(42)133(0) of 12th May 1942: reproduced as Appendix G.
[2] 14th–24th January 1943.
* [E. E. Mockler-Ferryman, 1896–1978, chief of intelligence for 'Torch', AD/E in SOE 1943–5 in charge of North-West Europe; in *DNB*.]

20th March.[1] This is a document of a very different type from that
of May 1942: it extends to seven foolscap pages, it deals separately
with every country of importance, and it bears evident marks of careful consultation and compromise with every departmental interest
concerned. As a result, each paragraph is so shaded that general principles do not stand out clearly, and no short summary is possible. The
general drift of the paper is that SOE's work must be carefully geared
to strategy and to foreign policy, that SOE must co-operate closely
with all the other authorities concerned, and that (for the present and
on the whole) sabotage has priority over the building of secret armies.
The most tangible part of the Directive is the strategic order of priority (para. 36):

1. The Italian Islands, Corsica and Crete.
2. The Balkans.
3. France.
4. Poland and Czechoslovakia.
5. Norway and the Low Countries.
6. Far East.

The relevance of this to the general situation is obvious: but SOE's
resources were hardly flexible enough as yet for any real strategic
concentration to be possible.

The Directive indicated that it was to be 'followed up' in two directions (paras 37, 38): *first*, SOE were to submit as soon as possible an
Appreciation based on the Directive, from which could be deduced
the additional resources required to execute it: *second*, SOE were to
report to the Chiefs of Staff, through the Joint Planning Staff on 1st
November 1943, on their success in executing the Directive, so that
it might then be revised or replaced as required.

The second of these lines can be followed readily. SOE's report
was duly laid before the Chiefs of Staff under cover of a brief note
by the Joint Planners:[2] the report covers twenty-five foolscap pages
of print, dealing with the areas of the Directive one by one, and no
great issue of policy emerges. Indeed it was now doubtful in theory
how far the Chiefs of Staff were entitled to give Directives on policy,
as operational control of SOE was now passing to the theatre commanders in each area – COSSAC in Western Europe, AFHQ and the
Cs-in-C Middle East in the Mediterranean, SEAC in the Far East –

---

[1]   The main papers are JP(43)72 of 24th February: JP(43)105(S) of 10th and 16th
      March: COS(43)142(0) of 20th March. [This last paper is document 7 in Stafford,
      Britain and European Resistance, pp. 248–57.]
[2]   JP(43)397 of 18th November 1943.

all under the general direction of the Combined Chiefs of Staff in Washington. Only in Central Europe (Poland and Czechoslovakia) did SOE now look directly to the Chiefs of Staff for guidance, and a separate directive for this area had recently been issued.[1] The Chiefs of Staff therefore confined themselves to giving a new order of priority in place of that contained in the March Directive:[2]

1. The Balkans.
2. Enemy-Occupied Italy.
3. France.
4. The Aegean Islands and Crete.
5. Poland, Hungary and Czechoslovakia.
6. Norway and the Low Countries.
7. Far East.

The question of a general directive only came before the Chiefs of Staff once more, a year later, in November 1944, and they then merely reissued with slight modifications those parts of the March Directive of 1943 which dealt with SOE's relations with other government departments: there is no indication of strategic policy except for Central Europe, which was not within the sphere of any Supreme Commander.[3]

Thus the last formal guidance given by the Chiefs of Staff was in March 1943: but this did not mean that SOE thereafter ceased to be regulated in its policy by the Chiefs of Staff, or even that the Chiefs of Staff were less occupied than before with SOE business. Whatever the formal authority of the Combined Chiefs of Staff and the Supreme Commanders, the power of decision rested with the Chiefs of Staff so long as SOE's plans competed for British resources with other British services: and even when the flow of American production ended this competition, there were lesser points of conflict continually in need of decision – both in 1943 and 1944 Special Operations fill a very substantial part of the Subject Index of COS papers. The main field of competition is heavy bombers, and until this conflict ends early in 1944, the Chiefs of Staff (and on occasion the Defence Committee) continue indirectly to bear the entire responsibility for finding SOE's place in Allied strategy as a whole. We must thus to complete the story of SOE's general directives pursue briefly the complicated history of aircraft allocation during 1943.

The formal starting-point is the Appreciation prepared by SOE

---

1 JP(43)356 of 16th October 1943: taken at COS(43)255th Mtg, Minute 13.
2 COS(43)289th (0) Mtg, Item 10, of 26th November 1943.
3 JP(44)261 of 6th November 1944 and COS(44)957(0) of 9th November 1944: amended as regards Czechoslovakia by COS(45)54(0) of 18th January 1945.

under para. 37 of the March Directive and submitted on 24th April
1943[1] with the clear conclusion (para. 53): 'Finally, it must be put on
record that, owing to the inadequacy of air transport, resistance in the
occupied territories cannot be further increased. It is even open to
doubt whether it will be possible with existing resources to maintain
resistance at its present pitch throughout the coming autumn and
winter.'

There followed the second Washington Conference (Trident) from
11th–27th May, which held up action on SOE's paper until the major
decisions on strategy had been taken, and it was not until 10th June
that the Joint Planners put forward their views on SOE's requirements
to the Chiefs of Staff.[2] They had also before them a paper[3] by the
Committee on the Equipment of Patriot Forces (a committee concerned
primarily with the equipment of Allied forces in liberated areas *after*
liberation), which had estimated at 300,000 the total of Resistance
groups which should and could be equipped. Authority had already
been given by the Chiefs of Staff for the production and allocation
of the necessary weapons.[4] The Joint Planners now considered SOE's
areas of activities one by one and reached the fairly obvious conclusion that the areas which promised most were Corsica, the Balkans,
France and Poland: what was more important, they supported SOE's
immediate claim for the allocation of additional aircraft on the basis
suggested by SOE.

	Present	*Addition*	*Future*
United Kingdom	16	10	26
North Africa	–	4	4
Middle East	14	4	18
Totals	30	18	48

These additional aircraft could only be heavy bombers, and could only
be obtained at the expense of Bomber Command's offensive, now at
a critical stage: Hamburg had been destroyed, the Battle of the Ruhr
was at its height, and the US 8th Air Force was incurring heavy losses
in its very effective daylight raids. These air operations were very
costly, both in aircraft and in aircrews, and they had the highest strategical priority. The airmen, at least, still hoped that they might win
the war without a land battle. It was therefore a considerable step for
the Joint Planning Staff to back SOE's initial request for another

---

[1] COS(43)212(0) of 24th April.
[2] JP(43)170(Final) of 10th June (on instructions given at COS(43)96th Mtg).
[3] COS(43)267(0) of 22nd May.
[4] COS(43)111th (0) Mtg, Item 7, of 25th May.

squadron of heavy bombers: and it says still more for the potential importance of SOE's work that the Planners did not reject out of hand the estimate of some ninety more aircraft which was put forward by SOE as the implication of its full programme.

The Chiefs of Staff took this paper on 17th June[1] and in general endorsed it. The Air Ministry had already accepted the request for eighteen aircraft; they were asked to consider and report within ten days what could be done to meet the larger requirement, which envisaged a force of ninety-three aircraft at home and forty-eight in the Mediterranean.

So far this appears to be a model of cool and business-like method: but parallel with it ran a somewhat melodramatic crisis in the affairs of SOE in Yugoslavia: this was the time of decision between Tito and Mihailovitch, and on the extent of British support to Tito.[2] On 23rd June was held a Staff Conference[3] at which the Prime Minister directed that deliveries to the Balkans should be stepped up to a rate of 500 tons a month from 30th September 1943.

A direct and precise instruction from the Prime Minister was thus superimposed on the rather vague target of the Equipment for Patriot Forces Committee: SOE's priority was greatly enhanced, and it could only be achieved at the expense of Bomber Command – a weapon not less close to Mr Churchill's heart.

In the following weeks the promised increases were made in SOE's aircraft establishment, and air operations from North Africa were begun; while in London the staffs calculated in detail what was implied in this new step forward. The final picture, agreed between SOE and the Air Staff, was this:

	Present	Additions Required	Total
United Kingdom and North Africa for Western Europe	33	31	64
Middle East for Balkans	14		
(i) Original EPF Programme		24	
(ii) Additional for Prime Minister's Programme		15	53
	47	70	117

---

[1] COS (43)128th (0) Mtg, Item 4, of 17th June.

[2] Below p. 422.

[3] COS(43)135th (0) Mtg, Item 2, of 23rd June. On the same date a paper by VCNS on SOE's Sea Transport requirements was circulated (COS(43)338(0)) – this raised no issues of major importance.

Bomber Command at this stage had forty operational heavy bomber squadrons: SOE had three and it required about four and a half more – a diversion of seven and a half squadrons in all. This was a claim considerable in itself and felt more keenly because Bomber Command also faced serious claims for the diversion of heavy bombers to anti-submarine operations and to airborne forces. The question of aircraft for SOE was now a large one in itself: it was still larger in relation to the main strategic issue – was the bomber force to be the main pillar of British offensive strategy, as had been envisaged when British plans were re-made after Dunkirk, or was it to be dissipated squadron by squadron on attractive and indecisive projects? The question was one which merited the earnest attention of the high authority.

The Chief of the Air Staff* on 25th July laid before the Chiefs of Staff what was in effect a compromise.[1] SOE operations in the Balkans should be pressed home, since 'they exploit our present successes and should give us good and immediate results': in Western Europe the resistance was less highly developed and the fruits of it could not be gathered until 1944, unless the bomber offensive broke down German resistance earlier. He therefore proposed an allocation of fifty-eight heavy bombers in all up to the end of 1944 – an increased establishment of eleven only instead of seventy asked for, but so distributed that thirty-six should be available in the Mediterranean, twenty-two only in the United Kingdom. The only additional hope held out was that Bomber Command might on occasion be able to divert the effort of other squadrons to SOE without prejudice to the main offensive. The Chiefs of Staff adopted Sir Charles Portal's arguments;[2] but the issue had already been laid by Lord Selborne before the Prime Minister,[3] and by him before the Defence Committee: in Mr Churchill's words: 'A political and not only a military appraisal of the profit and loss must be sought.'[4]

At the Defence Committee meeting on 2nd August[5] the Prime Minister pursued this train of thought further: he 'emphasised the immense value to the war effort of stimulating resistance amongst the people of Europe. He recognised that acts of rebellion against the Germans frequently resulted in bloody reprisals, but the "blood of the Martyrs was the seed of the church", and the result of these incidents had been to make the Germans hated as no other race had ever been

---

[1] COS(43)404(0) of 25th July 1943.
[2] COS(43)173rd (0) Mtg, Item 11, of 27th July.
[3] Letter of 21st July 1943 – History of SD Operations, p. 41.
[4] DO(43)17 of 30th July.
[5] DO(43)7th Mtg, Minute 1, of 2nd August.
* [C. F. A. Portal, 1893–1973, held this post 1940–45, knight 1940, KG, OM, Marshal of the RAF and viscount 1946. See Denis Richards, *Portal of Hungerford* (1978).]

hated . . . . Nothing must be done which would result in the falling off of this most valuable means of harassing the enemy.' Mr Eden scarcely went so far – for the Foreign Office SOE meant more work than profit in Greece and Yugoslavia – but at least he lent support to an expansion of operations in the Balkans. Yet somehow these weighty considerations of high politics made little difference to the facts of aircraft supply. The Chief of the Air Staff's offer stood – thirty-six aircraft in the Mediterranean, twenty-two at home – and was qualified only by an ambiguous hint of further resources potentially available –

   (ii) that Bomber Command should undertake the responsibility for carrying out such additional work for SOE as SOE required to be undertaken, subject to the directive on priorities as decided by the Chiefs of Staff.

   (iii) It is open to the Minister of Economic Warfare to appeal to the Defence Committee, if at any time he considers that SOE requirements are not being given a sufficiently high priority.

This debate had raised SOE to a higher status in world affairs than it had hitherto attained, and the seal was set on this new dignity by the attention paid to Resistance at the 'Quadrant' Conference, which ensued at once – Mr Churchill was in Canada and the USA from 10th August until the middle of September. For the first time air supply and guerilla resistance found a place in the conclusions of a conference on this, the highest, level.[1] This change in status was the occasion of renewed discussion of the proper place of SOE in the British war organisation and of the adequacy of existing means of co-ordination. There was some reference to this at the Defence Committee meeting of 2nd August; SOE for its part claimed (with more plausibility than hitherto) that it should rank as a Fourth Service represented equally with the others on the Chiefs of Staff Committee: for the Chiefs of Staff (and in particular for the Chief of Air Staff) the question was rather one of asserting more effective control over SOE now that it had established a claim to a very substantial share of military resources. The solution of this problem was much less than SOE had claimed, as much as it could reasonably hope.

   (a) Operational and administrative control of the Special Duties Wing at Tempsford was transferred from the Air Ministry to Bomber Command. In return, Bomber Command was to provide a 'supplementary effort' on supply operations to France by ordinary bomber squadrons.[2]

---

[1] A fairly full account is in 'History of SD Operations', pp. 51–9.
[2] COS(43)491(0) of 25th August and Annex.

(b) Since 14th May 1942 an experienced Air Staff officer, Group Captain C. McK. Grierson, had been a full member of SOE's staff, first as head of the Operations Section and later as Director of Plans. He was not however a member of the SOE Directing Council, and it was now agreed to appoint to it Air Commodore H. N. Thornton,* with full responsibility as a member of SOE.[1] An Admiralty representative, Rear Admiral A. H. Taylor, CB, OBE, was added at the same time.

(c) As a result of the Defence Committee meeting of 2nd August the Chiefs of Staff appointed[2] a special sub-committee under Brigadier Hollis to inquire into the improvement of liaison with SOE. This Committee reported somewhat inconclusively early in October:[3] equal status for SOE as a Fourth Service was ruled out from the start, and the firm recommendations of the Committee were merely that SOE should in future circulate a weekly report to the Chiefs of Staff, and that members of its planning staff should be very closely associated with the Joint Planners, although there was not to be any SOE representative on that body.

It cannot be said that these arrangements had any happy result. One of the Prime Minister's last acts before leaving for Quebec had been to adjudicate in SOE's aircraft requirements: when he returned he found waiting for him the whole question of SOE's organisation in Middle East, which he settled at a meeting of Ministers on 30th September.[4] No sooner had he left for Teheran at the end of November than matters broke out again, and the last and greatest of the crises over SOE's aircraft allocations raged almost without intermission until his return in January 1944. There is no doubt that in this crucial phase of its development SOE and the Resistance movements which it led were sustained very largely by the personal influence of Mr Churchill.

The immediate occasion of the new breach was the final and conclusive proof of German control of the SOE wireless station in Holland.[5] This had been suspected for months: there had been an investigation by the JIC (moved thereto by SIS) in July 1943 of allegations about

---

[1] He was succeeded in February 1944 by Air Vice Marshal A. P. Ritchie, CBE, AFC.

[2] COS(43)180th (0) Mtg, Item 5, of 4th August 1943.

[3] COS (43)505(0) of 4th September, and COS (43)240th Mtg of 7th October.

[4] Minutes circulated by Cabinet Secretariat; copy on SOE Archives File (AD/S.1) '97 Defence Committee'. See further below p. 511.

[5] Above pp. 303–7.

* [1896–1971, Air Attaché Stockholm 1940–41, Washington 1941–3.]

penetration in France,[1] and SOE was now fully on its guard about Holland, though it had not given up hope of saving something from the wreck. On 30th November the AOC-in-C, Bomber Command, (now fighting the desperate and inconclusive battle of Berlin) abruptly countermanded all SOE air operations in Western Europe, without prior consultation with SOE – an act justified only by the relatively high rate of aircraft losses in Holland, and by his comprehensive ignorance of the effects of this action on the Resistance in other areas. The paper war which followed was fought with quite exceptional bitterness, and is perhaps not worth now recording in detail.[2] The ban on operations was lifted at once for all countries except Holland, Denmark and Poland, which presented real cause for anxiety, and the two latter were cleared rapidly by the JIC. That Committee however proceeded (on the instructions of Mr Attlee's Staff Conference of 1st December) to a full investigation of the work of SOE, conducted in no very friendly spirit, and leading to an attack on the existence of SOE as a separate organisation which went far beyond the terms of reference of the JIC and the evidence before it. It was in fact (as SOE described it) an 'SIS and Foreign Office-minded' report, and indicated the existence of a hopeless deadlock between extreme views – the SOE theory that it should be a Fourth Service with equal representation on the Chiefs of Staff Committee, and the Foreign Office theory that it had no right to separate existence and should be abolished in short order. The month of January 1944 was no time at which to debate fundamental (and rather academic) issues of this kind: the Defence Committee met on 14th January under the shadow of a telegram from the Prime Minister to Lord Selborne – 'We will certainly go into this on my return'[3] – and its conclusions were essentially

---

1   COS(43)173rd (0) Mtg, Item 11, of 27th July, JIC(43)325(0), and COS(43)178th (0) Mtg, Item 12, of 2nd August.

2   It can be traced very clearly in the 'History of Special Duty Operations' pp. 69–97. The main papers are a Minute from General Ismay to the Deputy Prime Minister on behalf of the VCOS (1st December), Minutes of a Staff Conference held by Mr Attlee at 5.45 p.m. on 1st December: letter of 2nd December from Lord Selborne to Mr Attlee, Staff Conference held by Mr Attlee on 6th December; JIC(43)517 of 22nd December on German penetration of SOE: COS(43)781(0) of 22nd December on SOE's aircraft requirements: DO(44)2 of 11th January (rejoinder by Lord Selborne): DO(44)2nd Mtg of 14th January: COS(44)15th (0) Mtg, Item 14, of 19th January.

3   Letter from Mr Peck of the Prime Minister's Office to Lord Selborne's PS. This was elicited by a telegram from Lord Selborne to 'Colonel Warden' dated 7th January (SOE Archives File 62/370/1.2). See also Lord Selborne's letter to the Prime Minister of 12th January 1944 (in Lord Selborne's papers). [(Sir) J. H. Peck, 1913–95, private secretary to Prime Minister 1940–45, knight 1971, Ambassador in Dublin 1970–73. See his Dublin from Downing Street (1978).]

inconclusive and to that extent a victory for SOE. Aircraft sorties to Holland were to be resumed, the Chiefs of Staff were encouraged to give high priority to SOE operations, and a general blessing was given to the development by which the control of Special Operations was progressively passing from Baker Street to the Headquarters of the Commanders-in-Chief concerned. Practical consequences followed in two directions only:

(a) As a result of a meeting between Lord Selborne and the Secretary of State for Air on 2nd December, arrangements for co-operation between SOE and the RAF were thoroughly over-hauled. Discussions continued during December and January, in which the C-in-C, Bomber Command, fought a losing battle for complete operational control: and they ended in February 1944 with the transfer of the Special Duties Wing in England from Bomber Command to No. 38 Group, the RAF Transport Group in the Allied Expeditionary Air Force. At the same time responsibility for SOE business in the Air Ministry was consolidated in the hands of a new Director (D of I(R)), and RAF representation at all levels within SOE was greatly strengthened.[1] This development was now formally blessed by the Defence Committee.[2]

(b) The problem of adequate air transport at last came within sight of solution.

On 18th December SOE had put up to the Chiefs of Staff a recalculation of its aircraft requirements in the now familiar form,[3] which was held in suspense while dispute proceeded on a higher level. The paper was finally taken by the Chiefs of Staff on 19th January,[4] when the Chief of Air Staff reverted once more to the difficulties of Bomber Command which was 'between 70 and 80 Halifaxes short of their expansion programme target'. From British sources he could promise only four more Halifaxes at home (up to an establishment of twenty), and in the Mediterranean the execution of past promises which would bring the British aircraft strength up to forty-six. The RAF could help further only by a supplementary effort with Stirlings, now retired as obsolete from Bomber Command and transferred to air supply operations under No. 38 (Air Transport) Group. No priorities however high could push the RAF contribution beyond this, and the Chief of the Air Staff saw no further hope

---

[1] For the resulting directives to the Air Adviser to SOE and the Air Transport Organisation of the SOE London Group see Apps. B and C to the 'History of Special Duty Operations'.

[2] DC(44)2nd Mtg, Conc. 1, of 14th January.

[3] SOE(43)PLANS/350, circulated as COS(43)781(0) of 22nd December.

[4] COS(44)15th (0) Mtg, Item 14, of 19th January.

except in American aid: two Liberator squadrons (twenty-four aircraft) were already in training in England and should be ready shortly, and he proposed to ask for one more USAAF squadron for the Mediterranean. This was accepted by the Chiefs of Staff, and it represented the utmost limit of RAF assistance – Nos 138 and 161 Squadrons at Tempsford, Nos 148 and 624 in the Mediterranean, *plus* substantial assistance from No. 38 Group which would increase as the resources of that Group increased.

On paper this seemed very little, in practice it proved to be enough. This was in part due to the general increase in the margin of Allied air superiority, in part to specific American allocations of aircraft: but in essence it was due to a recognition, spreading downwards from the highest levels, that assistance to the Resistance movements was a matter of cardinal importance, both politically and in strategic relation to operations planned for the immediate future. Support to the Balkan partisans occupied a good deal of the time of the Sextant Conference at Cairo in December[1] and was placed on the agenda for Teheran; the Polish question was already advancing to a position of primary importance;[2] and the French Maquis in many areas was in open revolt[3] and in grave danger of disaster. Above all, General Eisenhower was now in London, and air support for the Resistance in the West took a high place in the anxious phase of 'softening up' the German defences against invasion. A few figures, not perhaps reliable in detail, will show clearly what happened – the third quarter of 1943 is included because operations at the end of the year suffered badly from weather.

There are no figures to show how this enormously increased effort was distributed between the specially allocated squadrons on the one hand, and the supplementary effort provided by transports and bombers on the other. But it is clear that it was the extent of this extra contribution which solved the problem, and in particular the contribution made by the transport services of the two air forces, which did not otherwise operate at full pressure except for the few great airborne operations – Normandy, Arnhem and the Rhine crossing. Once a really substantial force of transports was available the allocation problem fell to a lower level and could for the most part be dealt with by a Supreme Commander and his Air C-in-C as a matter of operational decision from day to day. Airpower had recovered its proper flexibility, and we hear no more of the problem of long-term allocation of aircraft carried to the Chiefs of Staff and the Defence Committee:

---

1   History of Special Duty Operations, p. 76 ff.
2   History of Special Duty Operations, p. 97 ff.
3   History of Special Duty Operations, p. 94 (the Prime Minister's meeting with M. D'Astier de la Vigerie on 27th January).

Successful Sorties from the United Kingdom

	France		Belgium		Holland	Norway	Denmark	
	RAF	USAAF	RAF	USAAF	RAF	RAF	RAF	USAAF
1943								
3rd quarter	327	–	10	–	1	3	8	
4th quarter	101	–	6	–	1	12	5	
1944								
1st quarter	557	52	13	5	–	13	3	
2nd quarter	748	521	24	40	2	23	7	
3rd quarter	1,644	1,336	119	22	37	2	12	9
4th quarter	46	–	19	–	152	50	71	–
1945								
1st quarter	–	–	–	–	25	326	54	36
2nd quarter	–	–	–	–	76	170	114	89

Tonnage dropped by aircraft from the Mediterranean (no figures available for distribution between RAF and USAAF, or for sorties)

	France	Italy	Yugoslavia	Greece	Albania	Poland
1943						
3rd quarter	1	4	144	395	57	–
4th quarter	6	1	125	234	76	–
1944						
1st quarter	172	92	251	290	121	3
2nd quarter	794	398	2,602	201	81	153
3rd quarter	1,100	650	3,014	219	259	163
4th quarter	–	780	2,398	428	463	24
1945						
1st quarter	–	1,669	3,347	–	34	–
2nd quarter	–	875	1,158	–	5	–

'aircraft for SOE' still occur frequently in their Minutes, but the issues are now those of sudden crises where there is political pressure to divert aircraft swiftly from other tasks to assist a Resistance movement which had little strategic value in proportion to the cost of support – the Vercors rising in France, the battle of Warsaw in Poland. These crises will be seen most clearly in perspective as they arise in the narrative of the countries concerned.

CHAPTER XVII

Yugoslavia[1]

Introductory

We left the Yugoslav situation at the point in the late summer of 1942 when it was decided to send in Colonel Bailey to replace Captain Hudson. A year earlier the British reaction to Mihailovitch's revolt had been that it was premature, an adventure without military significance which could only be supported at the expense of British needs in Libya and the Mediterranean. The position was now reversed: it was the British who were anxious that Mihailovitch should attack and were suspicious that (as the Russians insisted) he had perhaps no real intention of doing so. Parallel with this argument, and confused with it, goes the older debate as to the military value of Tito's Partisans: a relatively simple problem in itself but complicated by the political necessity of making an absolute choice. Almost everything conceivable was done to bring Tito and Mihailovitch to co-operate, or to maintain them independently and in parallel without co-operation: and the event proved, as conclusively as anything can be proved in history, that they were oil and vinegar, incapable of coalition. The story falls into four main stages –

(a) Bailey's Mission and the attempt through other British Liaison Officers to draw Mihailovitch into an active policy: December 1942–Spring 1943.

(b) First period of decision on policy, Spring to August 1943: Brigadier Maclean* with Tito, Brigadier Armstrong** with Mihailovitch.

(c) The parallel missions, the Teheran conference, and the decision

---

[1] The main continuous sources here are: Draft 'White Paper' prepared by Colonel Bailey in collaboration with FORD in 1946, and annexed documents. Colonel Bailey's report on his Mission written in April 1944. A continuous history by Lieutenant Colonel W. D. Wilson: clear and useful though second-hand.

* [(Sir) Fitzroy H. Maclean, 1911–97, diplomat, Conservative MP 1939–74, in SAS 1942–3, in Yugoslavia 1943–5, baronet 1957. See his *Eastern Approaches* (1949) and *Disputed Barricade* (1957).]

** [C. D. Armstrong, 1897–1985. See pages 431–2.]

to abandon Mihailovitch – August 1943 to January 1944.
(d) Full support for Tito: January 1944 to the race for Trieste in May 1945.

Colonel Bailey's Mission

Hudson had at last in August 1942 received the dubious reinforcement of 'Captain Robertson' and a little later the more substantial aid of Captain Lofts and his Signals Unit. During September 1942 the aircraft situation was (for these early days) relatively good, but it was used only to send in (mainly during September) about a dozen SOE-trained Yugoslavs, whose mission was to give instruction and encouragement in sabotage methods to Mihailovitch's subordinate commanders. With them went a very limited quantity of stores. There is no doubt now that this policy (although it worked well in some other countries) was here misconceived, both politically and as an inducement to military action. These Yugoslavs were briefed privately by the Yugoslav Government, on lines which quite probably ran counter to British policy: certainly they could not provide political reports which would be of value to the British. On the military side it is doubtful whether it was technical knowledge which Mihailovitch wanted: explosives, fuses and ammunition were much more seriously required than men, but the main deficiency was the will to fight.

As communications improved, the nature of the problem became increasingly obvious from Hudson's reports, and the weeks of preparation for Alamein and 'Torch' were the occasion of the first 'test case'. This was posed by a message sent by General Alexander* on 21st September, calling explicitly for an all-out attack on Axis communications and hinting very plainly that great operations were impending in North Africa. This was backed by a telegram from M. Jovanovic, the Yugoslav Prime Minister, on 23rd September – a message which he reiterated in most emphatic form on 6th November, when the Alamein breakthrough was complete and 'Torch' was already at sea. To all these approaches General Mihailovitch's reply was that he had ordered 'stronger action', that sabotage was in progress, that no more could be done without more arms.[1]

This was irrefutable so far as it went; there was some sabotage in Mihailovitch's areas, British support was certainly inadequate. But the real sense of Mihailovitch's policy remained elusive; it was clear

---

[1] Papers with the 'Bailey Documents' (with the FORD).

* [H. R. L. G. Alexander, 1891–1969, knight 1942, C-in-C Middle East 1942–3, 18th Army Group 1943–5, field-marshal 1944, KG 1946, Governor-General of Canada 1946–52, earl 1952, Minister of Defence 1952–4, OM 1959; in *DNB*. See his memoirs (1962).]

only that his assurances could not be taken quite at their face value, and that it might be necessary to look elsewhere for active support. How did Tito stand at this stage?

In the first place, this was a crucial period in the development of the Partisan movement. After the 'Third Offensive' against them in Montenegro in the spring of 1942, the main Partisan forces had concentrated in Bosnia and Hercegovinia and remained almost undisturbed there for a considerable period. Moscow was now fully committed to them, and their story was being given world-wide publicity through 'Leftist' channels. Internally the movement began to evolve some kind of rough military organisation in Divisions and Brigades: what was more important, it began to make high political claims. The decisive formality was the meeting at Bihac, on the borders of Bosnia and Croatia, of the 'Anti-Fascist Council of National Liberation', on 26th November 1942: a body of delegates, of ambiguous origin, who in effect claimed to be the supreme constitutional authority of the new Yugoslavia. In the light of later events, this is the first working model of the form of government which was by 1947 dominant in the 'Soviet Zone' of Eastern Europe.* Its nature was from the first known intimately to Mihailovitch, though he saw it through a haze of local prejudice: it was quite obscure to the British. But the British knew at least that a rival movement of importance was now on foot.

Thus (*in the second place*) from the late summer of 1942 Hudson was pressed to supply any information he could as to the real nature of the Partisan movement and of Mihailovitch's attitude to it;[1] 'Robertson' was asked to answer the same questions. Hudson's replies[2] were unfortunately too well-balanced to be conclusive: he knew the limitations of his own range of observation and he knew how much there was to be said for Mihailovitch from Mihailovitch's point of view. But they made it pretty plain that Mihailovitch was principally concerned to fight a political battle for the future control of Yugoslavia: assistance to the Allies was only an object to him in so far as it conduced to the restoration of a particular form of government after the war; and that government would be founded on the domination of Yugoslavia by a narrow Serbian tradition, not exactly 'Undemocratic' in so far as it affected Serbs, but certainly in the literal sense 'reactionary'.

In the third place, all independent evidence which could be collected, from intercepts and other 'Most Secret Sources' indicated that the Partisans were a thorn in the flesh to the Axis and that Mihailovitch was not. Some minor sabotage might be attributed to Mihailovitch's

---

1 See (e.g.) 'questionnaire' in telegram of 1st September in 'Bailey's Documents', App. F (with FORD).

2 There is a good summary of them in 'Bailey's Documents', App. G2 (with FORD).

* [See Hugh Seton-Watson, *The East European Revolution* (1950).]

forces, but it was perfectly clear that they were not engaged in open guerilla warfare and that no serious attempt was being made by the Axis to eliminate them. For what it was worth, this tended to confirm the Moscow thesis that Mihailovitch was at least as ready to make a deal with the Axis as with the Allies.

The dispute was therefore fully engaged before Bailey went in. On the whole, the Foreign Office and SOE were still playing the line to which they had been committed by events in the autumn of 1941, of creating unity behind Mihailovitch as the representative of the only legitimate Yugoslav Government; but there was already a lurking feeling (expressed mainly by some dissidents within SOE) that this was a policy with no future. Doubts were increased by the fatuity of the exiled Yugoslavs, particularly over the control of their regular troops in the Middle East; there was an open mutiny in November 1942, which does not seem to have been due to any malicious agitation from outside.[1] Bailey's mission was therefore not a military one, to arrange for British support to Mihailovitch subject only to military considerations. On the contrary, it was essentially political; Bailey's role was on the one hand to inform His Majesty's Government of the situation, on the other to press British policy on Mihailovitch with all the force at his command.[2] He was in fact an Ambassador acting under technical difficulties which are not frequently met with by the Foreign Service; but he also experienced the common difficulty of British diplomats, that the policy he was to follow was indicated only in platitudes which had little relevance to the situation as he found it.

He did not drop until Christmas Day 1942, partly as a result of illness, partly through operational delays: the waste of time was not fatal in itself, but it shortened the period in which his assessment of the situation could shape itself and impress itself on opinion at home before the crisis which arose in the spring of 1943. The Prime Minister, when in Cairo in January 1943 had seen Brigadier Keble and had expressed the liveliest interest in the Yugoslav situation:[3] but at this stage the mind of SOE in Cairo was still running mainly on the aircraft shortage – as Keble reported a month earlier: 'it is quite useless repeat useless sending any strong or other message from His Majesty's Government to Mihailovitch with a view to spurring him to further

---

[1] Note also the incident of the Yugoslav Government's request to be allowed to use its own cyphers in communications with Mihailovitch. This was agreed by the Foreign Office in October 1942, then refused under pressure from SOE, the Minister of State, the Cs-in-C, Middle East, and the Chiefs of Staff. (Papers mainly in SOE Archives File (AD/S.1) F.34.)

[2] See (e.g.) his own 'Notes' on his Mission dated 12th November 1942, on SOE (CD) file 'Yugoslavia – Political'.

[3] See SOE telegram 'Alpha 824' of 29th January; copy on SOE Archives File (AD/S.1) F.34.

activities when we lack almost entirely means of supporting him'.[1]

The *first* influence in breaking into this prevailing view was the very carefully weighed and delivered survey and recommendations which came in from Bailey and Hudson, acting in close consultation, in the latter part of January. The gist of this is contained in Bailey's long telegram of 21st January,[2] backed by a still longer report from Hudson which was greatly delayed in transmission.[3] There was no discrepancy in their views as to the nature of Mihailovitch's movement, and they held out no prospect that there could be any reconciliation between Mihailovitch and Tito, even temporarily. Bailey's recommendation was that a boundary should be drawn between them, which should if possible permit Mihailovitch to expand into Bosnia and Hercegovinia while the Partisans moved further north; and that if this were accepted equal support should be given to both parties.

Second, in accordance with the general line of policy then prevailing in Middle East, an increasing number of British parties were being trained and dispatched to Mihailovitch's areas in order to organise and press forward attacks on particular military objectives; the Belgrade-Nish–Salonika railway, the Danube, the copper mines at Bor, the chrome mines at Allatini, among others. The first of these Missions (Major Greenlees) joined Colonel Bailey in February, and other parties continued to arrive until May.[4] Few of these men knew much of the

---

[1] Tel. COS 3407 of 28th December 1942; copy on SOE Archives File (AD/S.1) F.34. Cf. also a memo. by Lord Glenconner left with Sir Orme Sargent in January 1943, and Sir Chas. Hambro's comment (on same file).

[2] Copy in 'Bailey Documents', App. G2.

[3] Full transcript sent to the Foreign Office on 9th February 1943; copy on SOE Archives file (AD/S.1) F.34.

[4] The main parties were:

February	'Cavern'	Major Greenlees	near Kragojeva
18 April	'Enamel'	Major Greenwood	Homolje (near Danube and Bor mines)
19 May	'Excerpt'	Major Rootham	Homolje (near Danube and Bor mines)
19 May	'Rupees'	Captain Hargreaves	Homolje (near Danube and Bor mines)
20 April	'Rhodium'	Captain Wade and Captain More	Kopaonek
23 May	'Rhodium'	Major Selby	Kopaonek
19 April	'Neronian'	Major Sehmer	Pristina area (Nish railway)
20 May	'Neronian'	Captain Hawkesworth	Pristina area (Nish railway)
15 April		Major Morgan	Pristina area (Allatini chrome mines)

Major Rootham has written a good book on his experiences – 'Misfire', published by Chatto & Windus. Full list of Missions with Chetniks and Partisans as at 17th September 1943 appears in SOE HQ War Diary, Middle East and Balkans Section, p. 1022.

Balkans, but they were desperately anxious for action against the enemy, and thus provided a fair test for the dispositions of Mihailovitch's subordinate commanders. Formally, these Missions were subordinate to Colonel Bailey, but for good practical reasons their wireless communications all led direct to Cairo, and they were thus felt to be an independent and unbiassed source of information; indeed Bailey complained that his task was made unbearably difficult by his ignorance of where they were and what they were doing and saying. Without exception their reports were unfavourable to Mihailovitch's men as a fighting force: Mihailovitch's politics appeared more nakedly among his subordinate commanders, and it frayed the nerves of active British officers that they should be frustrated and cheated at every turn in the attempt to carry out the specific tasks set them by the British Command. A number were lost, mainly in purposeless skirmishes with Bulgarian troops, but no major operation of any kind was carried out. This experience undoubtedly carried great weight with Brigadier Keble and the military side of SOE's organisation in Cairo; and through them with the military staffs in Middle East.

Third, internal politics developed one stage further in the early months of 1943. In January the Germans launched the 'Fourth Offensive', against the Partisan 'Republic' at Bihac and drove the Partisan main body south towards Mihailovitch's territory: a strategy which was doubtless deliberately chosen in order to force Mihailovitch to make a choice. There is no doubt that his decision was to keep the Partisans out of Serb territory at all costs. In this he succeeded only in part, in spite of serious fighting in tacit alliance with the Axis: Serbia itself was not invaded, but the Partisans broke through Mihailovitch's lines and found temporary refuge in Montenegro, which had been one of their first homes. In the midst of this crisis Mihailovitch chose an opportunity (at a wedding party) to make in Bailey's presence a violent attack on the Western Allies, and on all their works;[1] he indicated, as clearly as need be, that if the British would not give him arms the Italians would, and that he had found the latter to be the better allies. This outburst of 28th February 1943 had some justification: the British had only sent in three tons of stores since Bailey's arrival, a trifling amount compared with what could be extracted from the Italians by intrigue, bribery and blackmail. In addition, the BBC had (since about October 1942) been indulging in a rather ill-coordinated campaign of advertisement for Tito, which infuriated Mihailovitch without coercing him. When he made the speech, Mihailovitch calculated perhaps that the Partisans would shortly be eliminated by the Axis and that a little later the Axis would be

---

[1] On 28th February, see Bailey's telegram of 1st March; copy in 'Bailey's Documents', App. G2.

eliminated in its turn, leaving him as the arbiter of the situation: certainly he did not rate Bailey highly, either as a political mentor or as a source of money and supplies. But this was the turning-point in his relations with the British: after this incident he broke contact with Bailey for some six weeks, while the battle with the Partisans was in progress on the Neretva front, and in the interval there was a decisive turn in British policy.

2. The First Period of Decision

From the receipt of Bailey's recommendations late in January there were almost continuous discussions between SOE and the Foreign Office on policy,[1] and doubtless argument in Cairo was no less keen. Cairo's official line at this stage[2] was still that of a mixture of pressure and support directed to Mihailovitch alone. In London the question was posed[3] as one of choosing between –
  (a) Unconditional support to Tito.
  (b) Unconditional support to Mihailovitch.
  (c) Drift.
  (d) Equal support to both parties.
The balance was now swinging towards course (d), but the decision was hedged a little for the present.[4] Officers should be sent in to Tito; but Tito should not be 'supported' until their reports had been received, and until one more attempt (which was quite ineffective) had been made in Moscow. Meantime Mihailovitch should continue to receive support.

Three events followed before the decisive turn. *First*, early in April the Yugoslav Prime Minister was induced by the personal intervention of Mr Churchill to protest to Mihailovitch about his outburst of 28th February.[5] Mihailovitch's answer[6] was a well-drafted statement of his whole case, insisting on his grievances but recurring to his absolute loyalty to the Allies. *Second*, on 21st April two parties of Croats of Canadian and American nationality were dropped blind to establish contact with the Partisans in Croatia and Bosnia. They succeeded in reaching local Partisan HQ, and reported very

---

1 Many papers on SOE Archives File F.34 and elsewhere.
2 As expressed e.g. by Lord Glenconner in his telegram No. 959–61 of 6th March; copy on SOE Archives File F.34.
3 Sir Orme Sargent's paper of 18th February, on SOE Archives File F.34.
4 Sir Orme Sargent to CD on 23rd February, and CD to Sir Orme Sargent: both on SOE Archives File F.34.
5 Copy of telegram in SOE London HQ War Diary, Mid-East and Balkans Section, p. 576 (and Mihailovitch's reply, p. 581).
6 Dated 16th April; copy in 'Bailey Documents', App. C.

favourably: admittedly they were men of 'Leftist' views, but their stories were connected and credible. On 7th May Cairo sent a message saluting the Partisan effort and offering the assistance of small highly trained British parties: this offer was accepted 'in principle' on 17th May. *Third* on 7th May, after most careful consultations, Mr Eden invited the Yugoslav Prime Minister to dispatch to Mihailovitch a directive which in effect threatened to withdraw support unless satisfactory assurances were given on all the old points of controversy: strategic direction by the C-in-C Middle East, no contact with the Axis, no aggressive action against the Partisans. This message was apparently dispatched to Mihailovitch from London shortly after 12th May; his reply was not received until 1st June.[1]

Meantime the affair had been 'brusqué' by Middle East, in rather mysterious circumstances. *First*, on 18th May a British party had been dropped to one of the earlier Missions in Croatia, under Major W. M. Jones, DSM and bar, a Canadian of much gallantry and little judgement: a later witness reports that the natives thought him 'mad but holy'.[2] His primary task was to attack the Fiume railway, but he very soon found much else to do. Much more important, Cairo accepted an invitation to send a liaison officer to Tito's GHQ, and without consulting London dispatched on 25th May, Major F. W. Deakin,* a young history tutor at Wadham, who had worked with Mr Churchill on his book on 'Marlborough'. He arrived in the midst of the 'Fifth Offensive', the greatest effort yet made against the Partisans: he and Tito were both wounded slightly by the same bomb, and he took part at once in one of the most sensational of the Partisan marches.[3]

Second, on 26th May SOE Cairo dispatched through Bailey what was in effect an ultimatum requiring Mihailovitch to withdraw east of the River Ibar and to leave to the Partisans all territory not strictly Serbian. This telegram was prefaced by a highly controversial reading of the tactical situation within Yugoslavia. Bailey (rightly or

---

[1] Mihailovitch's reply is in 'Villa Resta' telegrams Nos 1597–8 (Summary in London HQ War Diary, Mid-East and Balkans Section, p. 603). (Final version of message sent to Mihailovitch is in same section of War Diary, p. 583.)

[2] See also his report to Mr Mackenzie King, dated 5th May 1944, in SOE Archives File (AD/S.1) F.34. [W. L. M. King, 1874–1950, Liberal Prime Minister of Canada 1921–6, 1926–30, 1935–48.]

[3] Full account in SOE London HQ War Diary, Middle East and Balkans Section, p. 625 (his directive appears on p. 623).

* [F. W. D. Deakin, born 1913, survived Missions to Tito, founder warden, St Antony's College, Oxford, knight 1975. See his *The Embattled Mountain* (1971) for an unusually vivid picture of how muddled irregular warfare is on the ground.]

wrongly) decided that if a tough policy was to be pursued it must be tough, and presented to Mihailovitch the entire text of the telegram: thus facing him with incontrovertible evidence of the authority under which Bailey spoke and the contemptuous view which Middle East held of Mihailovitch's value as an ally.

These actions together effectively committed the British to a policy of supporting both parties, with some bias towards Tito. As regards the 'Ibar telegram', at least, SOE Cairo were explicitly covered by the authority of the Middle East Defence Committee; and the new line was not one which SOE Cairo in its corporate capacity had advocated. The origin of the break (which was scarcely an accident) must therefore lie outside SOE in the realm of General Staff policy, which looked for immediate action and military success. It must be remembered that the Eighth Army had vanished from the ken of Cairo (it broke through the Mareth line into Tunisia on 21st March), the invasion of Sicily (which took place on 10th July) was now impending, and Middle East could contribute to the battle only by action in the Balkans. The influence of the military view within SOE Cairo grows visibly stronger from this point, until a crisis is reached in September 1943.

Intense debate ensued in London on the highest levels,[1] and occupied much of June, but the issue was so far prejudged that it is hardly necessary to set out these discussions in detail. The most important point is that Mr Churchill's interest was for the first time continuously engaged by the problem of resistance in Yugoslavia, as well as by the parallel problem of Greece, and from this point events are affected by his highly personal policy of support for Tito in Yugoslavia, hostility to ELAS in Greece: an apparent inconsistency, for which there is much to be said that need not occupy us here. Apart from this personal factor, there were only three decisions of substance:

(a) That 'subject to operational requirements elsewhere' the Air Ministry and SOE should together work out a plan to increase the delivery of supplies to Yugoslavia and/or Greece up to ultimately 500 tons a month.[2] Twenty-five tons had been dropped to Yugoslavia in May, by far the best month hitherto: so that this meant a huge change in the scale of operations, a change that would in itself almost take them outside the scope of SOE as it had existed hitherto.

---

[1] The very numerous COS references are to be found in the COS subject-index for 1943: the crucial meetings were the Prime Minister's Staff Conference on 23rd June (COS(43)135th (O) Mtg) and a meeting held by Mr Eden at the Foreign Office on 24th June (Record by CD in SOE Archives File (CD) 'Yugoslavia 5').

[2] COS(43)135th (O) Mtg, Item 2, of 23rd June. See also Brigadier Hollis's letter on SOE Archives File (CD) 'Yugoslavia 5', as regards the 'qualifying clause'.

(b) That Mr Fitzroy Maclean, Conservative MP for Lancaster, and a former member of the Foreign Office, should go to Tito's HQ as the personal representative of the Prime Minister: he was formally a member of SOE, but on matters of major importance his allegiance lay elsewhere.[1] He reached Yugoslavia on 18th September, with a staff of four officers and a strong signals unit.

(c) That a regular officer should be sent to Mihailovitch's HQ, and that Bailey should henceforth rank only as that officer's political adviser. Some protest was made by SOE on Bailey's behalf, but the action was a sensible one in itself: a professional soldier might well be the best man to impress upon Mihailovitch the reasons why his policy must inevitably alienate the Allies from him. But such a choice at this stage emphasised the different lights in which His Majesty's Government now viewed Tito and Mihailovitch: the one a key post for a rising politician, the other a matter of routine for a man of limited professional competence. Brigadier Armstrong, RE, DSO, MC, who was chosen (and proved an excellent choice) reached Yugoslavia on 24th September, with a considerable staff, including two representatives of OSS.[2]

3. The Parallel Missions and the Abandonment of Mihailovitch

These three decisions emphasise that we have reached a point at which SOE has played its part and must shortly withdraw from the stage. Yugoslavia is no longer a matter of 'clandestine warfare' or 'unacknowledgeable means'. It is in part diplomacy, in part irregular war: both conducted in rather odd circumstances, but on orthodox enough lines. Individuals trained by SOE and carried on its books continue to play an important part; but SOE as a body is progressively less concerned either with the formulation of policy or with its execution. The story cannot however be abandoned at this point.

One result of the policy debate in London was that Middle East's 'Ibar ultimatum' was cancelled, and, as a substitute for it, an attempt was made to pin Mihailovitch more closely to the terms of the

---

[1] See his directive as re-drafted on 11th August; copy on SOE Archives File (CD) 'Yugoslavia 5'.

[2] Copy of his directive in SOE HQ War Diary, Middle East and Balkans Section, p. 823.

Directive which had been sent to him in April. A telegram in this sense was dispatched from London on 17th July,[1] and a fairly explicit acceptance was at last received on 21st August.[2] This made little difference in the ordinary routine procrastination, and on 24th August Bailey (in a mood of exasperation) pursued the 'tough' line one step further by presenting a written ultimatum in the name of GHQ Middle East, which informed Mihailovitch that no further support would be given until there was an improvement in his attitude. This was unauthorised and was disclaimed by Middle East, so that no practical effects followed; indeed, the effect may have been merely to weaken further Mihailovitch's belief in the authority with which Bailey spoke.

Then followed the Italian surrender, on 7th September, and a period of confusion in Yugoslavia, as elsewhere, in which Mihailovitch's objectives for once coincided with those of the Allies. There was a brief period of activity while he gathered in such spoils as he could on the borders of his territory. In the midst of this Brigadier Armstrong arrived, and at first matters looked much brighter. But (as was inevitable) the Partisans were expanding also into the vacuum left by the Italians, and there was soon a prospect of renewed civil war; on Brigadier Armstrong's orders Mihailovitch in the end resentfully withdrew his forces from some of the territory he had gained, but the brief 'honeymoon' was over. During October and November Armstrong and Bailey, in complete accord, were again pressing against Mihailovitch's obstinate procrastination. There was a formal interview on 20th October, which seemed to produce some temporary effect, and formal letters were sent on 15th November and in the following week. At the end of this series of experiments Armstrong and Bailey on the 18th November reported to Cairo[3] that further pressure was in their judgement hopeless: the alternatives were a complete abandonment of Mihailovitch's territory or an attempt to displace Mihailovitch from his position of authority. It would not (they thought) have been sufficient that the Yugoslav Government should depose him from his office as Minister of War, his personal standing in Serbia was too high for action from outside to be effective. But many of his troops were keen to fight the Axis, and there was none of his subordinates who could replace him; there was therefore a chance that if he were somehow 'removed' a resistance movement would remain alive in the Serb lands and would fall naturally under Tito's leadership.

As Mihailovitch's stock thus depreciated, Tito's rose. It was at

---

[1] Copy in 'Bailey Documents', App. C.
[2] See SOE HQ War Diary, Middle East and Balkans Section, pp. 802/804.
[3] Copies of telegrams in SOE Archives File (CD) 'Yugoslavia 5'.

the period that the Partisan movement was seen in the most roseate light by the outside world. This was in part a matter of propaganda: it was impossible to resist the concert of advertisement by Russia and the BBC, with Mr Churchill at intervals personally intervening. In part it corresponded to important military events. The Partisans survived the Fifth Offensive in May 1943, and when Italy fell in September the 'underbelly' of the Balkans was for a moment exposed along the Adriate coast; for a brief period the Partisans were masters of most of the coast and of the islands, and it was of vast potential importance that these gains should be held. By ill luck or ill judgement a great proportion of the Allied effort was sucked into the campaigns of Salerno, the Liri Valley and Anzio, and too little was left to hold off the German counter-attack in Yugoslavia, which was remarkably prompt and efficient. By the end of the year the 'Sixth Offensive' had cleared all key points on the coast and all the islands except Lagosta and Vis. The German grip on the strategic position was restored and they could no longer be dislodged by guerilla forces: but for a moment the Partisans had held a position of the highest military value, and though they were beaten back here and suffered severe losses, in the central hill country of Yugoslavia the Germans could henceforth intervene only sporadically and for limited objectives.

The essence of the Partisan movement is hard to grasp even now. On the one hand it was beyond all doubt a great moment in Yugoslav history: virtually by its own unaided efforts a people was breaking out from the shadows and re-establishing itself as a nation in Europe. Every young Yugoslav was by instinct behind Tito and for the new birth of his country, a country now for the first time something greater than the local loyalties of Croat or Slovene, Macedonian or Serb. 'Bliss was it in that dawn to be alive' can be applied here without irony, even in the light of later events and of the intense national suffering of the time. The British Liaison Officers[1] were without exception impressed, and rightly impressed, with the vigour and idealism and enthusiasm of the movement. But it must be added that Tito and his staff were very clever men; and that the British Liaison Officers were largely innocents abroad, who knew nothing of guerilla warfare and very little of Yugoslav language or history or politics. Their reports were at this stage almost without exception more lyrical and less realistic than those of the old warriors Hudson and Bailey; and in part for that very reason they were more

---

[1] Basil Davidson has written a full account of his life with the Partisans in 'Partisan Picture' – published by Bedford Books Ltd. [B. R. Davidson, born 1914; see also his *Special Operations Europe* (1980).]

influential at home.[1] Hence arose most naturally the widespread conviction that the Partisans were 'not really Communist', and that Tito could in due course be tamed to co-operate in a new 'national' government of Yugoslavia, recognising the legitimacy of King Peter. All Yugoslav history and the whole political character of the movement made this impossible; no middle course was open. But at all times the British are reluctant to believe in the necessity of an absolute choice of alternatives, and the evidence here was not of a kind to convince any but experts – and there were few of these.

The main events of the summer and autumn on the British side were these:

(1) First, in mid-June, while debate still proceeded in London, Cairo arranged the first supply-dropping operation to Deakin; no other answer could be given (little though London then liked it) to his suggestion of specific operations against railways in Tito's area.

(2) Then in July and August, once policy had been agreed, new Missions began to flow in to the subordinate Partisan HQs, some of them manned by British officers, others by Canadian Yugoslavs. The first American liaison officer (Lieutenant Benson) reached Partisan HQ on 21st August. By December there was an extensive network of Missions, each with its wireless set, throughout Tito's area of penetration; there were eleven of them, excluding Maclean's Mission and the Missions to Mihailovitch, on the 'situation map' in December, and they extended from Italian Slovenia to rather indefinite 'partisan' areas on the borders of Bulgaria and in Southern Macedonia. Supplies were not sent in any reasonable proportion to the number of Allied Missions, and it is a little doubtful whether the Missions served any purpose except to give adventurous occupation to a number of very tough young men. Their reports were useful, though limited in value by their ignorance of the general political problem, and they saw a good deal of active guerilla war. But they were observers, not leaders: very few actions were fought which would not have been fought without them, and half a ton of ammunition and explosives would in most areas have been more effective than half a ton of British Liaison Officers.

---

[1] There is a sad note by Bailey in the spring of 1944 recounting how much the Prime Minister and Mrs Churchill seemed to be moved by Randolph Churchill's snapshots of the Partisans, and regretting that it had never occurred to him that evidence of that sort might have helped the unlucky Mihailovitch. [Churchill had married 1908 Clementine Ogilvy Hozier, 1885–1977, who sustained him thereafter, and was made Baroness Spencer-Churchill on his death 1965. Their only son Randolph, 1911–68, MP 1940–45, went into Yugoslavia with Maclean.]

(3) On 18th September Brigadier Maclean and his staff arrived at Tito's HQ; they were warmly received and no difficulty was made about the condition that Tito should refrain from civil war. The moment was one of great strategic possibilities, and Brigadier Maclean very properly constituted himself the spokesman of Tito's unlimited needs; first for military aid in holding the great gains made on the Dalmatian coast, then for help in succouring the vast numbers of refugees who left their homes in terror of the German 'Sixth Offensive'. SOE, Cairo, in October pushed forward an Advanced HQ of 'Force 133' to Bari with a view to exploiting sea communications to Dalmatia. Unfortunately little came of this in the short period during which the door remained open, and there was no serious improvement in supplies until the aircraft position improved towards the end of the year.

(4) With his military advance Tito also made politically a bound forward, symbolically expressed in the second conference of the Anti-Fascist Council which met at Jajce on 26th November. This now assumed without qualification sovereign rights as the ruling body of Yugoslavia: it denounced King Peter and the government in exile, it proclaimed the new federal Yugoslavia, it sent telegrams of greeting to Churchill and Roosevelt, it raised Tito to the dignity of Marshal. Rightly or wrongly – probably there was little choice, so well had the moment been chosen – Maclean became the spokesman of these larger claims as well as of the urgent practical needs of the battle. He supported an appeal from Tito (on 25th October) to be permitted to send a mission to Middle East; he insisted that liaison officers should not be sent to Tito's subordinate formations without Tito's consent – a crucial point in strengthening Tito's position; and his reports, both by signal and when he came out temporarily in November, were well-balanced and well-argued and uniformly emphasised the strength and cohesion of Tito's movement and its decisive importance for the future of Yugoslavia.

The stage was now set for another period of decision, initiated by the Teheran Conference. The first item in the Conference's military conclusions, initialled on 1st December, reads:[1] 'The Conference agreed that the Partisans in Yugoslavia should be supported by supplies and equipment to the greatest possible extent, and also by commando operations.' Mr Eden had already agreed that a mission from Tito should be received in the Middle East on a purely military basis, and after serious technical difficulties Colonel Velebit was flown out on

---

[1] Cmd 7092.

his first mission by an Allied aircraft which landed on an improvised landing-ground at Livno – the first operation of this kind in Yugoslavia – and reached Alexandria on 4th December. There he was excellently received, and met separately in conference the C-in-C Levant, the C-in-C Middle East, and the AOC-in-C Middle East. The main topic of the conferences was the possibility of an operation to secure a permanent bridgehead in Dalmatia, which proved abortive, but the whole tone of the discussions was that of rational military consultation between experts of equal status – Colonel Velebit played politics supremely well by excluding them entirely.[1] This private recognition of the Yugoslav Army of National Liberation as an allied force in the field was blessed ceremonially by a public allusion by Mr Eden in a speech made shortly afterwards.

It remained only to dispose of the problem of Mihailovitch. The Partisans had contributed effectively to this by the careful compilation of dossiers on Cetnik collaboration which were made available to Maclean: the evidence (though carefully selected) was not faked and did not seriously conflict with the picture of the situation given by Hudson and Bailey from the first. Documentary evidence has however an odour of sanctity which does not attach to the reports of unknown agents, and it helped His Majesty's Government in making the difficult final decision. By the beginning of December SOE Cairo were officially convinced that no more could be made of Mihailovitch, and this decision was confirmed by higher authority, subject to one last chance of penitence. This was given in a signal dispatched on 8th December, under the authority of the C-in-C Middle East; it instructed Mihailovitch to attack two specified railway targets by 29th December or to forfeit all claim to Allied support. This was presented by a junior British Liaison Officer (Mihailovitch was now so exasperated that he was not prepared even to meet Brigadier Armstrong), and was answered on the usual lines of acquiescence followed by procrastination. Mihailovitch at this stage began at last to hint at the possibility of compromise with the Partisans. It is not known how matters went at this eleventh hour within Mihailovitch's close political circle; whether he himself procrastinated, or whether he pressed for action and was baffled by his subordinates. The bridges were not attacked: Brigadier Armstrong was not given facilities when he demanded permission to carry out the attack himself.

Already in December SOE were making preparations for the difficult task of withdrawing the British Missions from Mihailovitch's territory, and on 15th December all who wished to do so were given permission to make their own way to the Partisans. Mihailovitch had

---

[1] Minutes of two of these conferences on SOE Archives File 18nc/470/1.

behaved hitherto with extraordinary loyalty to his guests, who were never in danger of betrayal to the Axis, however unpopular they might be with the Cetniks: but British intentions were now fairly plain, and there must be a limit even to the Balkan code of hospitality. Two Missions and Captain Hudson took advantage of this, and three officers and four other ranks were eventually evacuated: Captain Hudson was thus withdrawn after some two and a half years in Yugoslavia. He had done as much as any man could do, and it was no credit to the organisation that he was not brought out at all costs for consultation earlier.

The final decision was not taken until 17th February – an agonising period of meaningless delay for the missions in the field. The decision was communicated to the world in the course of Mr Churchill's speech in the Commons on 22nd February, in which he stated very fully and frankly the case as it then presented itself to His Majesty's Government and wholeheartedly adopted Tito as the hero of Yugoslav nationalism.

Colonel Bailey accompanied by two of Mihailovitch's men was withdrawn separately by sea, after a very difficult cross-country journey, and he was not in London until 3rd March, after the decision had been taken:[1] it will be noticed that he was the first man of substance, British or Yugoslav, to come out with first-hand knowledge of Mihailovitch's story. The other Missions had first to be concentrated at Mihailovitch's HQs, a matter of the greatest difficulty in a bad period of the mountain winter: there were serious difficulties from illness and injuries, but only two officers were lost in this phase by enemy action. The concentration was not complete until 20th May, and there then followed the desperate excitement of evacuation by air from an improvised landing-ground close to the enemy and covered only by the uncertain loyalty of Mihailovitch and his men. So far, the situation though tense had not been one of open hostility. Mihailovitch himself had kept away from his own Headquarters and had avoided all contact with the Missions since the decision to withdraw, and his subordinates had been passively unco-operative. But there had been no treachery and no attempt at enemy interference. This held to the end, although there was a last minute threat to detain Brigadier Armstrong as a hostage: Dakotas landed safely on three nights from 28th to 30th May, and 110 persons in all were withdrawn. These included fifty-four members of the Missions (and escaped British prisoners who were with them) and forty-two Allied airmen who had crashed in Mihailovitch's territory, as well as twelve Poles.

The Americans, after agreement on withdrawal, backed out on the

---

[1] His report and recommendations dated 14th March are on SOE Archives File (AD/S.1) F.34.

express instructions of President Roosevelt[1] and left an 'Intelligence Mission', which was deemed not to imply moral support to Mihailovitch. There were still dividends to be gathered, in the shape of intelligence and of aid to crashed airmen and escaped prisoners, and the President had a good case: but it was useless to pretend that his decision had no political implications. The British break was now complete, apart from a few accidental contacts which formed no part of a political plan.[2]

4. Full Support for Tito

The commitment to the 'new Yugoslavia' was now final and it remained only to find a formula by which it could be legitimated without disloyalty to our ally King Peter. There had been acrimonious mutual defiance between Tito and the Puric Government in December, and the process of reconciliation was a complicated one which was not formally complete until June. King Peter then accepted as his Prime Minister Dr Subasic, who had been Governor of Croatia in the short period in 1939 when the Regent was seeking to conciliate Croat local feeling: Tito recognised this régime as the legitimate government of Yugoslavia. SOE was consulted throughout these delicate negotiations,[3] and the solution was on the whole the best that they could envisage. But their responsibility was limited. Maclean's position was itself ambiguous; his discussions with SOE in London in April were friendly – more friendly than their previous relations – and there was some talk of bringing him more effectively within the SOE organisation. But there was little regret in London when on 23rd June the matter was cleared up by a unilateral decision of the SACMED, and 'Macmiss' became an organ of that Command. There was similar ambiguity regarding SOE's responsibility for Velebit when he was in London on his second Mission in May; there was some complaint which reached the Cabinet[4] from left-wing circles to the effect that he had not been given proper facilities, and SOE earned an unmerited reproof.

The same loosening of responsibility was in progress in Italy in other ways. The whole trend of events was now towards a control of

---

1 Dated 4th April 1944; copy on SOE Archives File (CD) '02 OSS'.
2 These are set out in an annex to Bailey's 'White Paper': the most awkward was an exchange of wireless messages between Mihailovitch and some Poles who had access to an SOE wireless station in Italy.
3 Hudson, Bailey and Maclean had long private discussions with the Prime Minister in April: Bailey's notes on SOE Archives File (CD) 'Yugoslavia 5'.
4 WM(44)67th Mtg, Item 2, and letter from Lord Selborne to the Prime Minister, on SOE Archives File (CD) 'Yugoslavia 1'.

operations from that theatre. In January 1944 the RAF supply-dropping squadrons concerned completed the move forward from North Africa to the Brindisi area, where their range and carrying capacity were immensely improved. At about the same time British troops began to land on the Adriatic islands in order to hold the few vital bases which still remained to the Partisans. No. 2 Commando and a US Operational Group reached Vis towards the end of January, and they were considerably reinforced in February and March. All these troops at this stage came under 'Advanced Force 133', still responsible in theory through SOE Cairo to the C-in-C Middle East. There was some technical need for this chain of command, because all wireless communications from Yugoslavia still passed through SOE's 'War Station' in Egypt, and it was very easy to open new links from Italy to the field. But it was unfortunate that there should be delay and argument regarding the principle of transferring control from Middle East to AFHQ and about the constitution of HQ Special Operations Mediterranean. Neither step was complete until April 1944, and in the meantime there was no effective control either by SOE or by any other authority. In truth, the time for SOE control was past, and the problem was now to find a system of military control over the very considerable regular forces now committed to the support of irregular operations. This complication was eventually resolved by the creation of the Balkan Air Force on 15th June,[1] under the command of Air Vice-Marshal Elliott,* who had a tenuous but effective primacy in committee with the military commander of 'Land Forces Adriatic' (LFA), and the Flag Officer, Taranto (FOTALI), with whom rested operational control of the extensive minor naval operations involved.

The SOE organisation in Italy now remained responsible only for the organisation of the supplies to be carried in to Tito, by sea and air; a very large task in 1944 and 1945, best illustrated by a few figures:

	By sea	By air	Personnel evacuated by air
1943			
Last quarter	1,857	113.5	–
1944			
First quarter	6,398	321	–
Second quarter	5,679	3,023.4	3,390

---

[1] See COS(44)552(0) of 21st June.

* [(Sir) W. Elliott, 1896–1971, director of plans, Air Ministry 1942–4, commanded Balkan Air Force 1944–5, Fighter Command 1947–9, knight 1946.]

Third quarter	7,072	3,380.3	8,915
Fourth quarter	15,005	2,405.7	1,124
1945			
First quarter	15,748	3,263.8	(no records)
April/May	7,699	1,187.4	(no records)
Totals	59,458	13,695.1	13,429

This covered all needs, relief stores for a destitute civil population, as well as all the requirements of an army of at least half-a-million men, which was trying to transform itself from a medley of guerilla bands into the armed forces of a state. The tonnage sent represented an immense effort of organisation, but it was little enough in relation to the nature of the case. Operationally much the most significant part of it was that carried by air to numerous rough landing-grounds in the interior: it was not till the very end that it was possible for the Partisans to move stores from the sea-coast to the areas where they were needed in the battle. It was in fact the largest experiment made during the German war in the maintenance of an army by air (there were larger enterprises of the same kind in the East), and it belongs properly to the development of that branch of tactics rather than to the story of SOE.

The last series of operations which have the characteristic flavour of SOE work were those for the development of the Partisan movement in Mihailovitch's own territory in Serbia. This was of great military importance to the Allies, as it was strategically a crucial area, and at this time, early in 1944, was not heavily held by German troops. The political difficulties are obvious: on Tito's side it was vital that he should before the final collapse establish the reality of his régime in this last recalcitrant area: for the British, it was an awkward manoeuvrs to push the development of the Partisans within Mihailovitch's own pale while Mihailovitch still held the British Missions and other Allied subjects as hostages.[1]

At the end of 1943 SOE knew only of scattered Partisan bands in the area between the Morava Valley and the Bulgarian frontier, and the only British officer in the region was Major Mostyn-Davies, who had arrived in November after a hard march from Albania, with the intention of contacting Bulgarian resistance under the auspices of the Partisans. In the confusion which would follow the break with Mihailovitch, it would be important to maintain some British contact here, and on the 28th November 1943 Major Dugmore was dropped

---

[1] For the high policy involved see Mr Eden's paper COS(44)412(0) of 11th May, JP(44)133 of 24th May, and COS(44)174th (0) Mtg, Item 13, of 27th May.

to Major Mostyn-Davies's party: it had been intended that he should join Brigadier Armstrong, and the plan was changed at the last moment, without prior reference to Tito. For the next four months he was alone in the area, and it was not till March that Tito was satisfied with the British break with Mihailovitch and authorised the sending of other Missions. Five of these (including an SIS and an OSS Mission) arrived during April, and the stage was set for a great expansion based on the rather feeble and scattered bands with whom Major Dugmore was in contact. During this period various Partisan commanders were attempting to break into the area on foot from territory which they already held; but none of these infiltrations was successful on any large scale and till July the movement in Serbia was built up largely by British staff-work and supplies. Five more Missions and reasonably plentiful munitions came in, and the tiny minority of Partisans grew rapidly into a substantial guerilla force, well-organised and aggressive. For the Serb peasantry, all motives now told the same way: eagerness to be on the winning side, frustration with long inactivity under the Cetnik régime, political confidence inspired by the presence of British officers and stores. At least one of Mihailovitch's commanders, Djuric, deserted with his men; and doubtless many who had been Cetniks were swiftly transformed into Partisans. For the first time there were fairly continuous guerilla attacks on the crucial traffic lines through the Morava Valley, not of course decisive but effective within their limits: German troops had to be brought up in May and there were various counter-offensives, in the end abortive.

This seems to have been one of the least frustrating periods of SOE work in Yugoslavia; but the spell was broken by the arrival on 10th July 1944 of a complete new Partisan HQ, flown in from Bari by the British and accompanied by a Russian Mission. Henceforward, this area (like the rest) was tightly controlled from Partisan GHQ, and the British Liaison Officers sank to the status of junior representatives of a friendly but alien power, whose task was to produce supplies, not to advise on policy.

The honeymoon was already over elsewhere in Yugoslavia. From the end of the Sixth Offensive early in 1944 there was a fairly stable balance of power between Axis and Partisans. The Germans held all key towns and could not be dislodged by guerillas; and they could always secure freedom of movement for strong bodies of troops along the main lines of communication. But in the hinterland the Partisans were now an effective state, becoming rapidly more highly organised and disciplined. There was never again any serious threat from the Germans to the organisation as a whole; there were various local offensives but the one dangerous period was at the end of May 1944, when the Germans nearly brought off a very well-planned coup directed at Tito himself. By good fortune he and the Missions with him were just outside the area of the German airborne landings, and they were safely withdrawn to Italy for the time being. Apart from this, the Partisans were regularly on the offensive, within the well-defined limits of their equipment and tactics. The most important single series of operations was 'Bearskin', a concerted attempt to wreck communications in Slovenia, timed to coincide as closely as might be with 'Overlord' and with the corresponding offensive in Italy. All reports from British Liaison Officers indicated very active and well-concerted operations, with some striking passages such as the destruction of the Stampetov viaduct by four Partisan batallions on 12th June.

Against successes of this kind must be set growingly unfavourable reports from British Liaison Officers in many areas. Something must be allowed for an increase both in the weariness of British officers and in the sharpness of their observation in surroundings which had at first been strange. But a general picture emerges of a more official atmosphere, a more terroristic and centralised régime, and a growing scorn for the Western Allies. A large Russian Mission had been with Tito since December 1943, a Russian transport squadron was based on Bari from the spring of 1944,[1] and the shadow of the Russian Army was over the Balkans from the time when they reached the Carpathians and the Pruth about the end of March 1944. But there is no need to seek for an explanation of the change in Russian intrigue: it was not a situation in which there was room for gratitude. If the new Yugoslavia was to stand morally on its own feet, the essential myth was one of liberation by its own efforts; this might be mortifying to BLOs, but it was not too far from the truth. Allied help was substantial in 1944, but that was very late in the day. In their days of need, before June 1943, the Yugoslav Army of National Liberation had received nothing; it was a grievance that Mihailovitch, their arch-enemy, had received anything – but even he had till then received no more than perhaps 50–60 tons of stores. The Partisans had risen with arms taken from the enemy, not by the grace of the capitalist world. This was in essence a home truth, rather than a myth: but the instinct of the Partisans was now to emphasise it ceaselessly, to the point of rudeness, and to let it be seen on all occasions that they were masters in their own home.

There remained only one more major concerted operation. This was the attack on communications throughout Yugoslavia, known as 'Ratweek', which opened on 1st September, to coincide with an attempt to rush the Gothic line and break through into North Italy.

---

[1]   London HQ War Diary, Mid-East and Balkans Section, p. 1327 (Maclean's report of 11th May 1944), and Russian Section, p. 102.

More fortuitously, it also coincided well with the collapse of Roumania – the Russian armies under Malinovsky* entered Bucharest on 31st August, on 5th September Tolbukin entered Bulgaria, on the 8th Bulgaria was at war with Germany. 'Ratweek' was an unqualified success as a guerilla operation: rail and road communications were broken in hundreds of places throughout the country, and all enemy movement was greatly restricted.

But this was still guerilla war; communications could be broken but not blocked. Its limitations were shown up badly in the next month, when circumstances were very favourable to the destruction of an entire German Corps of some thirty to forty thousand men, the 21st Mountain Corps in Montenegro. The Russians and Bulgarians had broken into the Morava Valley early in October, the Russians and Partisans together had beaten the Germans outside Belgrade and entered the Yugoslav capital – the Partisans leading – on the 18th. This cut the obvious German line of escape into the Hungarian plain; at the same time, the Partisans helped by British air and sea support and some British artillery were taking Dubrovnik and other towns on the coast, cutting this alternative route. The Germans in Montenegro could now escape only through the mountains, where the Partisans were at their strongest. But the Russian drive had swung away to the north, to more important objectives in the Hungarian plain and there was no aid from the Russian army; British artillery support was offered, was sent in without Yugoslav consent, and was then so misdirected by the Yugoslavs that it took no effective part in the battle. The German corps began its retreat from Montenegro and Northern Albania late in November; by 18th January 1945 it had reached temporary safety in the area of Sarajevo, with a vast loss of stores but otherwise virtually intact.

The last phase now opened in an atmosphere of the greatest cordiality, with the reception of Field Marshal Alexander by Marshal Tito in his own capital at Belgrade on 21st February 1945. Here there was a series of meetings in which politics played little part, and there was no precise agreement on the bitterly vexed question of Trieste and its hinterland. The main discussions were on timing and supplies for the final offensive, in which the Soviet Marshal Tolbukin was also concerned. In Yugoslavia this began on 20th March with a vigorous push forward in Croatia. The Allies attacked in Italy on 8th April, and crossed the Po on 25th April. Meanwhile the Partisan advance had continued on the other side of the Adriatic, and the final rush for Trieste began in the last days of April. On 30th April a Partisan division was on the outskirts of the city and reported that resistance had

---

* [R. Y. Malinovsky, 1898–1967, liberated Dnieper basin 1944, Soviet Minister of Defence from 1957.]

ceased. On 1st May they met the 2nd New Zealand Division at Monfalcone: the New Zealanders pushed straight through them into Trieste and found a German garrison still holding out, whose surrender they accepted next day.*

An offensive begun in concert had finished in competition. This section may suitably conclude (as does one of SOE's files)[1] with Mr Churchill's telegram of 6th May to Field Marshal Alexander: 'In order to avoid leading Tito or the Yugoslav commanders into any temptation, it would be wise to have a solid mass of troops in this area and with a great superiority of modern weapons and frequent demonstrations of the Air Force.'

5. Conclusion

What in summary is to be made of this mass of experience? There are three problems worth considering separately:

   (i) First, what did Resistance in Yugoslavia contribute to the defeat of Germany?

   (ii) Second, what did SOE contribute to the making of Yugoslav resistance?

   (iii) What was the cost?

As regards the first question, Mihailovitch's part was certainly small; some minor sabotage, a few skirmishes with Axis troops, the evacuation of a substantial number of Allied escapers. Damage to the Axis was never the dominant motive in his mind, and he was at best a 'non-belligerent' ally rather than a neutral.

Defeat of Germany was not the sole end of the Partisans either, but it was an essential part of their programme that they should be active combatants in the war against Fascism, and their claims are such that they must be taken seriously. There are three main heads:

   (a) *Axis forces contained*: First, the number of Axis divisions pinned down in Yugoslavia so that they could not intervene on other fronts. If one looks at the situation maps, one finds for instance in August 1943, 17 Italian, 7 German, 5 Bulgarian and 3 Croat 'Ustachi' divisions in Yugoslavia. In December 1943, if we include Slovenia, there are 18 German divisions, 6 Bulgarian and 4 Croat divisions. Clearly the German divisions are the key point here; the others were not likely to be of use on any other front. Even so the figures remain impressive: but one must qualify further. In the first place, these German divisions were not incurring wastage at rates comparable to those of other fronts: doubtless some men got killed

---

[1] SOE Archives File (CD) 'Yugoslavia 5'.

* [See Sir G. Cox, *The Race for Trieste* (1992).]

in unpleasant circumstances and the whole atmosphere was bad for discipline and for morale, but there were no serious losses of men until the final collapse. In the second place, if one looks more closely, for instance, at the eighteen 'German' divisions in December 1943, one finds among them the SS Nederland Division, the SS Prinz Eugen Division, the 1st Cossack Division, two German-Croat divisions: the German element is eked out very carefully with 'subject races', and even among the supposedly 'pure German' divisions there are a number of low category formations. There is no means by which these factors can be weighed precisely: one must take refuge in the obvious – the Resistance did indeed hold back a substantial Axis force from other fronts, but not so many as it would have us think.*

(b) *Damage done:* Second, the destruction to Axis resources by guerilla war. Industrial sabotage was here of no significance: the only important industrial targets were the mines in Mihailovitch's area, which remained intact to the end. There was no Axis port of importance on the Adriatic coast, and if any sabotage of shipping took place there it was a minor matter. Strategically therefore the issue turns on the destruction of railways and highways, which are targets notoriously difficult to put out of action for any length of time. Here an immense amount of action took place, but the problem is primarily one of timing: continuous attack is of some value in destroying rolling stock, tying up repair gangs, slowing down all movement, but its value is enhanced many times if a whole series of bridges can be blown together in widely separate areas, at the same moment, and that a moment at which the enemy is particularly anxious to move troops. There were only two big operations of this kind, 'Bearskin' in June and 'Ratweek' in September 1944, and they were both very successful: how far successful could only be ascertained from German papers. Certainly there is a credit balance here, though smaller than would be thought from the endless list of bridges, viaducts, cuttings and so forth destroyed.

(c) *'Mopping-up':* In other theatres one of the greatest contributions made by the Resistance was in making straight the way for invading troops, and in cleaning up and organising behind them. In Yugoslavia the only invasion was the Russian and Bulgarian breakthrough into the Morava Valley: it seems pretty clear that the Partisans in that case were valuable. In the rest

---

* [Some enemy troops were also drawn to the Balkans by deception: see Michael Howard, *Strategic Deception* (1990), pp. 135–7.]

of the country the case did not arise: but it was still an asset
that in the last weeks of the war there were forces at hand to
harass and round up the retreating Germans. It was even an
asset of importance (politics apart) that there existed a strong
government 'underground' which emerged at once, without
confusion or civil war, as the new Yugoslav State: if there had
not been such a government the problem of inventing one
would have been nearly insoluble – as it proved in Greece –
and would have eaten up Allied resources, British and Russian,
long after the Armistice.

Second, what was SOE's contribution? One dominant motive which
runs through SOE's records is the bitterness of regret that more could
not have been done in the early years, from October 1941 to May 1943.
From the Minister downwards, there is a feeling that Mihailovitch did
not have a fair deal. If only we had been able to give him adequate
supplies while his movement was young, if only we had opened such
channels of communication then as would have made it inescapably
clear what the Allies asked of him, he would at least have had a chance
to rise above his origins and to lose his Serbian nationalism in the wider
vision of a new Yugoslavia, which could have rallied Slovenes and
Croats, Moslems and Montenegrins behind him and not behind Tito.
As events developed, his moves were predetermined: in the interests of
Serbia as he saw them, he had no choice but to play his ambiguous
part to the end. A judgement on such an issue must be highly personal:
but to the author at least it appears that no other course was open to
the British at the time when they decided finally to back Tito alone.
Mihailovitch was a leader, a man of courage and ability, a man of patriotic feeling: but he and those on whom he rested lived in an older world
whose passing they could not realise. Effective aid to Mihailovitch as
late as 1943 and 1944 would have led only to more intense and savage
civil war, involving the Great Powers in a dispute to which there could
be no rational issue.

If this is a true judgement, Mr Churchill's policy of backing Tito
was the right policy, in spite of the false optimism which surrounded
it at the time. SOE Cairo pressed for it, but only after a late conversion, SOE London disliked it but had no workable alternative: so that
SOE's voice was too uncertain to be decisive in the choice of policy.
Once the decision was taken, SOE played an essential part in carrying it out. Perhaps the most important thing here was the smoothness
of the technique which had been developed after painful trial and error
for pushing in liaison officers to strange places, establishing communication, and following it with supplies. The technique may to some
extent have become an object in itself: but it is impressive to see the
speed with which 'Tito's country' is opened up and made accessible
in the summer and autumn of 1943. In a period of six months there

is development from the stage of desperate adventure to one in which the problem is to control the number of 'tourists' anxious for relief from tedium of regimental life.

On this technique was based the supply organisation which began to operate on a really large scale in the spring of 1944. Until that time British supplies were no more than gestures of encouragement; they were not operations of war. It is thus perfectly fair to claim, as Yugoslavia does, that the Partisan movement in its origins owes nothing to the West: but we must claim on our side that it was only our action in 1944 which equipped it to the point at which it could not be threatened by civil war within and could assert itself as a power the instant that the German hold weakened.

This last stage was entirely beyond the scope of SOE, but it was only the earlier work of SOE which made it possible.

Third, what was the cost? To the Yugoslavs, it was (on their own figures) 1,800,000 lives out of a population of 16,000,000, and almost universal destruction of facilities of human life wherever the Partisans and their hunters had passed. Communications have been fairly swiftly restored, and there were never many industrial installations to destroy: but the loss of the miserable houses and steadings of the peasant villages is an immense disaster in a primitive economy. Certainly these losses are out of all proportion to the damage inflicted on the enemy, and illustrate how much reason there was in the policy of Mihailovitch and even of Nedič: they are a heavy burden of responsibility to bear. The British surely need bear little of it. Their material aid was negligible till late in 1943, when the whole pattern of guerilla raids and reprisals and civil war was already well established. At first, in the autumn of 1941, they deprecated resistance: later they did what they could, by advice and propaganda, to foster it. But these counsels had little effect in themselves, and even if they had been withheld Russian precept and example would have carried great weight.

For the British and Americans, the cost in material and human lives was fantastically small, and (if we regard this solely as an operation of war) the balance is heavily on the credit side. In all some 215 SOE personnel were sent to Yugoslavia, of whom about twenty-five[1] were lost: a low ratio compared with the losses in Bomber Command or the Merchant Navy, or an Armoured Division engaged in heavy fighting. The tonnage of stores was at the beginning negligible, in the later stages still negligible in relation to the resources which the Allies then possessed. The same may be said of the numbers of aircraft involved and the losses which they incurred.

It can be argued that the Western Allies by their aid to Tito created for themselves a political problem which they could not solve. As has

---

[1] [Footnote not supplied by Mackenzie.]

been suggested above, an opinion on this issue must be highly personal: but there is at least good ground for believing that the political problem was none of our making, and that in the end good rather than harm was done by the presence with the Partisans of many British officers, who were warmly in sympathy with the aims and temperament of the new Yugoslavia. If greater international events permit it to develop, there exists already a ground for sentimental rapprochement. The story of the Partisan movement will for generations be the central 'myth' of Yugoslav national politics: and it is one in which the British played a part which no propaganda can permanently distort or obliterate.

CHAPTER XVIII

Greece[1]

Introductory

The centre of the Greek story has hitherto been outside Greece, and it has been concerned primarily with the confused attempts, through various imperfect agencies, to discern and evaluate what was happening behind the curtain of Axis occupation. From October 1942 the story has two points of focus, one at the HQ of the British Mission in the mountains, the other in the outer world. Communications between them gradually improve, but there is never true mutual comprehension, and events in the two spheres are continually a little out of step. It is thus not possible to present a single continuous story; each strand has to be taken separately, and it must be left largely to the reader to set them side by side and match one set of dates against the other. In spite of the high value set by the outer world on its own decisions, the initiative really rested throughout with the mountains, and it will be best to present their history first in each phase, until the two sides are drawn together and confronted at last by the German withdrawal from Greece. The order of the narrative will therefore be:

(1) The British Mission in Greece from October 1942 until August 1943, when Brigadier Myers reaches Cairo with six Greek leaders.
(2) The outer world in the same period.
(3) The British (now Allied) Mission until the Lebanon Conference in May 1944.

---

[1] There is a very able official narrative by Colonel Woodhouse of the work of the British Military Mission, and a shorter account by Brigadier Myers of his period – 'Inside Greece' (imperfect copy of the latter in SOE Archives File (AD/S.1) F.61): there is also a survey of all SOE's work in Greece and the Aegean, written for the C-in-C Middle East, by Lieutenant Colonel Dolbey and including valuable detailed appendices. To these must be added Colonel Woodhouse's book 'Apple of Discord' and Colonel Hammond's 'I Fell among Greeks'. [See also E. C. W. Myers, *Greek Entanglement* (1955) and L. Baerentzen (ed.), *British Reports on Greece 1943–1944* (Copenhagen, 1982).]

(4)   The outer world in the same period.
(5)   The German withdrawal.
To this must be added two important appendices:
(6)   The clandestine organisation in Athens and the Piraeus.
(7)   Special Operations in Crete and the Aegean.

1. The British Mission October 1942–August 1943

The British Military Mission to Greece became in the end a large organisation, and contained many remarkable men: but its creation was entirely the work of Lieutenant Colonel E. C. Myers* and Captain C. M. Woodhouse** (as they were then), a fortuitous combination which made one of the strongest teams which SOE ever sent out. The former was a regular Sapper officer, then aged thirty-six, entirely without knowledge of Greece or of subversive politics, picked at short notice because an engineer was needed for a big demolition: the latter was a young classical scholar of academic distinction (then only twenty-five), who had already worked in occupied Crete and had a good knowledge of modern Greek and of the Greek political background. 'Colonel Eddie' and 'Colonel Chris', as they became, are figures of some importance in modern Greek history.

Their original mission was a plain military one[1] – to destroy one or more of three viaducts on the only railway connecting Southern Greece with Central Europe, and so to hinder the dispatch of reinforcements to Rommel through the Piraeus or the movement out of Greece of German troops for use elsewhere: Colonel Myers was thereafter to be withdrawn, leaving Major Woodhouse with a small party to maintain liaison with Zervas. We have already seen[2] the invitation extended by Prometheus II in control of Station 333 in Athens: his plan was the excellent one of sending one party to Zervas, another to an agent of his own who would put it in contact with ELAS guerillas. Zervas was some sixty very difficult miles from the scene of the intended operation: but none the less this double contact would be a useful reinsurance. It was sound politically: Prometheus II (to quote Colonel Woodhouse)[3] 'disliked and distrusted EAM–ELAS and Zervas about equally', and he was thus politically

---

[1]   The best published narrative of the Gorgopotamas operation is Denys Hamson's 'We Fell among Greeks'.
[2]   Above p. 162.
[3]   History of British Military Mission, p. 3.
*   [E. C. W. Myers, 1906–92, regular engineer, married Sweet-Escott's sister 1943.]
**   [C. M. Woodhouse, born 1917, classical scholar, in Tehran 1951, Conservative MP 1959–66, 1970–74, 5th Lord Terrington 1998.]

not committed too far, nor had he committed the British. The party of twelve was not complete until 28th September, the morning of the day intended for the operation: that night they took off (in three Liberators) but returned unsuccessful, as they could find no signal fires in the target areas. They took off again on 30th September: this time the signals (or the aircraft's navigation) were again wrong, but two out of the three parties jumped at random. Major Woodhouse was lucky: he did not find Zervas, because Prometheus's signal had been corrupted in transmission and the area to which he was sent was thirty miles from that in which Zervas was waiting; but he found another reception committee, which was awaiting a supply-dropping operation to Major Tsigantes.[1] Colonel Myers had less good fortune: Prometheus's man had been arrested by the Italians, and he met first with a band of villagers who looted the expedition's stores, second with a self-styled guerilla leader, with three or four cut-throat followers, who recovered the expedition's stores but soon made it clear that their main object was to monopolise the source of supply. It was a week before the two British parties met, on the slopes of Mt Giona, high above the railway which was to be their target.

Stores were dropped to them on 9th October, messages were dispatched to Prometheus and Tsigantes, various hangers-on (some useless, some invaluable) joined the party; there was trouble in evading an Italian man-hunt and the party and its stores withdrew to a very secure cave high up on the northern spur of Giona. The next stage was to dispatch Major Woodhouse sixty miles across country to meet Zervas: the journey took nine days and Woodhouse found Zervas sporadically engaged in fighting with the Italians. But he readily detached himself with half his troops – 100 men in all – and returned with Woodhouse.

Meantime the third British party had dropped at random dangerously near an Italian garrison, and had at once made contact with an authentic ELAS guerilla, who appears in this story as Ares Veloukhiotis: his real name was Athanasios Klaros, a Communist in theory but essentially a professional condottiere or gang leader, who had plied his trade for years on the seamier side of European politics: like many of the best Communist fighters, he had been with the Republicans in the Spanish War. Ares in the end was killed obscurely in a minor skirmish in the spring of 1945: Zervas at the time of writing is Minister of Public Security in the Maximos 'Right Centre' coalition.[2] They differed in temperament, but both belonged to the ancient

---

[1] Above p. 166.
[2] He was turned out of office under US pressure when M. Sophoulis took over, in September 1947.

profession of those who live by their wits; the social difference between them was that Ares had fallen from grace originally through a conviction for a homosexual offence, Zervas was a professional soldier who had in 1928 been expelled from the Greek Army on political grounds.

After manoeuvring a little in hope of other advantages, Ares too decided to co-operate, and on 14th November he with a hundred and fifty men met Woodhouse and Zervas with one hundred at the small village of Viniani in West Roumeli: a force ill-fed, ill-clad and ill-shod (a quarter of them were barefoot) but all armed somehow and ready to fight. Sixty of Ares's and sixty of Zervas's men were left to distract Italian attention to the Viniani area: the rest by forced marches reached Mt Giona and the vicinity of the British cave on 17th November.

Colonel Myers meantime had reconnoitred the railway, had chosen the Gorgopotamas bridge as his objective, and had framed a plan of attack.

There was still some delay, while Ares's final decision hung in doubt. The peculiar nature of the ELAS system of command was already important: Ares was the commander or 'Capetanios' of the band, but with him was associated a Political Adviser and a Military Adviser (the latter in this, as in most cases, insignificant). The Political Adviser had first to be convinced: and behind him lay the invisible and unintelligible system of the EAM higher command. It took some days for this machine to reach the fairly obvious political conclusion that it would be disastrous to leave all the credit of success to Zervas, and still more disastrous to cause a failure which could be laid to the discredit of EAM: or perhaps in the end Ares took action on his own responsibility. Zervas was put in command of the joint guerilla forces for the operation (an occasion of note in Greek history), and the attack was made on the night of 25th November 1942.

The Greeks fought well, in their disorderly fashion: Captain Barnes, RE, performed miracles in making up demolition charges under fire for attack on a structure which was totally different from what he had been led to expect: and by 2 a.m. on 26th November all was over. The bridge was down and remained closed to traffic for thirty-nine days, and the Italian garrison of about eighty was wiped out.

Cairo was overjoyed at the news, as it had good right to be: up to this time it had never organised a coup so neat, so well-timed, and so incontrovertible, and the political aspect of the affair was just as satisfactory. It seemed to indicate that a real striking force of guerillas existed in the Greek mountains, ready to co-operate under the guidance of British officers and awaiting only supplies to maintain a continuous offensive. Myers and Woodhouse were in no position yet to explain the underlying complexities, which they scarcely knew themselves: and Cairo proceeded to take advantage of the position with great energy. It is clear[1] that the Anglo-Greek Committee in Cairo were consulted and that M. Kanellopoulos and the Minister of State were thus aware of the position: but there is no indication that the new departure in policy was debated as a political issue. It was later made to appear in some quarters as a sinister reflection of SOE's attitude to the Greek King that it took such prompt action to assist ELAS: this was indeed the consequence of its action, but it was not one which anyone could have envisaged at the time. Cairo's military picture was one of ragged non-political fighters of the hills, calling for arms with which to attack the invader: there was much truth in it, and there was no one to point out the elements of falsehood. The related political picture of the six Colonels in Athens, who would form the directing centre on behalf of Kanellopoulos and the exiled government, was wholly false: but that was scarcely SOE's fault.

The decision was that Colonel Myers should remain in Greece, with the rank of Brigadier, as commander of all British troops in Greece: Major Woodhouse (now Lieutenant Colonel) was to go to Athens to keep contact with the legendary 'Six Colonels', and strong British Missions should be sent to every mountain area where there were rumours of guerilla activity. By the late spring of 1943 there were ten of these Missions, one in Mt Olympus, one in Macedonia, one in East Roumeli, one on Parnassus, one in West Roumeli, two in the Peloponnese, two in Epirus, one in West Thessaly. Communications between Brigadier Myers and local Missions were for a long time possible only through Cairo: and at first his own wireless station was immobile, so that he could not go on tour without losing touch with his base. Thus it was not until about mid-summer 1943 that Brigadier Myers and his HQ were able to hold most of the threads in their hands and to give a reasonably accurate picture of the situation as a whole. This is an important point as regards relations with EAM, which was highly centralised from the first.

For the British Mission the period immediately succeeding the Gorgopotamas operation was one of some confusion. They parted on good terms with Ares, giving him 250 gold sovereigns, and a letter to the EAM Central Committee, a mysterious entity which they were anxious to reconnoitre as cautiously as they could. They then moved west through the mountains, Myers to keep a rendezvous with a submarine on the coast of Epirus, Woodhouse to take up his post with Zervas. They parted on 12th December: on 17th December an officer,

---

1 See Lord Glenconner's memo. of 10th December 1942, on SOE Archives File F.61/II. This bases the new organisation on the 'Six Colonels': a revision to meet their 'explosion' is outlined in Lord Glenconner's telegram No. 273 of 16th February, on same file.

Lieutenant Jordan, arrived with the new instructions from Cairo, and a runner had to be sent to recall Myers. The latter did not get back until 8th January 1943, after twenty-seven wasted days in which he was out of all contact both with Cairo and with Woodhouse.

Meantime, EAM were as anxious to reconnoitre Woodhouse as he was to know more of them; and he received three visits from different ELAS detachments, while he was out of contact both with Cairo and with Myers. The last of these visits was paid on 31st December by Ares himself with several hundred men; this expedition at first threatened open war and the violent elimination of Zervas. Woodhouse brought matters to a conference,[1] the first of many endless mountain debates on unity, academic on the surface, intellectually and oratorically keen, and covering deadly intentions. This brought a good deal of character and psychology into the open; but unity was no closer, and little had been done to elucidate the problem of EAM. Ares left on 1st January taking with him 250 more British sovereigns: beyond this Woodhouse would not go without authority, except to promise one aircraft sortie of supplies. Unluckily this failed through bad weather and served only to give EAM a reason, or at least a useful pretext, for doubting the British word.

The British party, reunited on 8th January 1943, was based for the next few months at Botsi, just west of the River Akheloos. There Myers remained to work out a detailed plan in touch with Cairo.

Meantime Woodhouse carried out his Mission to Athens. This took place in the last week of January and was important mainly in a negative sense. Of the two old British contacts, Tsigantes had been surprised and killed by the Italians a few days earlier: Prometheus II was caught on 2nd February and Woodhouse only escaped being involved through the efficiency of EAM.[2] Zervas's representative, Petmezas (alias Nikitas), was away in the mountains. Woodhouse met Colonel Spiliotopoulos (later Military Governor of Athens in December 1944) and one other of the Six Colonels: but they were extremely timid and evasive, and clearly had no intention whatever of becoming involved in rough work in the mountains. It may be added, parenthetically, that they were simultaneously 'blown' in Cairo,[3] by the interception of a report to Kanellopoulos's coadjutor, Tselos, which made it clear that the whole extent of their plan was to seize power in Athens on the withdrawal of Germany, and then with a revived Greek Army to stake out post-war claims in Albania, Yugoslavia and Bulgaria.

---

[1] The 'Rovelista Conference'.

[2] Prometheus I (Colonel Bakirdzis) left Greece at this stage and returned in a very different role in August.

[3] Cairo's telegram No. 273 to London dated 16th February; copy on SOE's Archives File (AD/S.1) F.61/II.

Woodhouse also had two meetings with what purported to be the central committee of EAM: on the first occasion with the important Communist Tzimas,[1] the non-Communist Tsirimokos,[2] and three unknown representatives of unknown parties affiliated to the National Liberation Front: on the second occasion with Tzimas, Tsirimokos and the Secretary of the Greek Communist Party, George Siantos.[3] No promises were made on either side, and the only point of permanent importance was a suggestion, made by Woodhouse and welcomed by EAM, that they should send a representative to Cairo for discussions. It was clear that Communist experience lay behind the conspiratorial efficiency of the arrangements: it was not clear how far the Front was merely a 'front' for the Communists. Woodhouse records that Myers was not convinced of this until April 1943, he himself not until August.

Woodhouse's only other significant contact was with Yanni Peltekis (a stockbroker by profession), later famous as 'Apollo', who rescued Prometheus II from gaol, took over what was left of his organisation, and became one of the most successful sabotage leaders in Europe.[4] He was back in the mountains (escorted out of Athens by a Communist, 'Thomas') early in February, and found that matters there were moving fast politically, though action against the enemy was at a standstill and the main body of the Mission was chafing in inactivity.

EAM on its side was now putting forth its maximum effort to create and control armed resistance. Woodhouse bears witness to the awakening of spirit and the immense growth of organisation in the early months of 1943. EAM sent its organisers round the villages, and in this phase at least it was widely accepted at its face value as the symbol of resistance and of national spirit: in a few months a sort of working government of unoccupied Greece emerged from the previous morass of famine, despondency and brigandage. It was not an amiable government, and it soon provoked a reaction; this reaction could have been foreseen, but in Woodhouse's judgement EAM had guessed wrong not about Greek politics but about the course of the war. The siege of Leningrad was raised on 18th January 1943, Rommel* was driven into Tunisia on the 29th, Von Paulus** surrendered at Stalingrad on the 30th: there was good reason to believe that

---

[1] *Alias* Evmaios, *alias* Vasilis Samariniotis.
[2] Later an EAM member of the Papandreou Government.
[3] Died of heart failure, 20th May 1947.
[4] Below p. 479.
* [E. J. E. Rommel, 1891–1944, commanded Hitler's bodyguard 1938–9, German forces in Africa 1941–3, suicide under threat of arrest.]
** [F. von Paulus, 1890–1957, invested Stalingrad 1942, surrendered there 1943, released 1953.]

the German position was near collapse, at least in the Mediterranean, and that it was a matter of urgency for EAM must at all costs become the *de facto* government of Greece quickly before the *de jure* government returned.

Zervas on his side was restrained from any such activities by Brigadier Myers; they were plainly political, not guerilla, warfare, and it could be no part of any military plan to encourage them. In this EDES was perhaps handicapped by the British; its pompous initials never had a chance to develop into anything more than an alias for Zervas. But Zervas himself was temperamentally disinclined for such work, and his principal political coadjutor in the mountains, Professor Komninos Pyromaglou, seems to have been equally indisposed to patient organisation. As for the supposed EDES committee in Athens, it played no part whatever except to give EAM good ground for suggesting that Zervas's movement was secretly in touch with the occupying powers. On this side the most important reaction to Allied successes was the drift to the mountains of a motley collection of soldiers and politicians, who began to think that their interest lay there. Of these the most important were the Venizelist Colonel Sarafis, prominently associated with the abortive coup of 1935: and another Venizelist, Colonel Psaros, a more soldierly and independent figure, backed by the politician Kartalis.[1]

Out of these elements Colonel Myers had to make a plan and to reach agreement on it with Cairo. His own conception was one of a division of mountain Greece into guerilla areas, each to be controlled by the captain of a band accompanied by a British Liaison Officer. Through his BLO each captain would be operationally controlled by GHQ in Cairo: and the whole network would be loosely co-ordinated by Myers's own control of the BLOs. Cairo was anxious for a more centralised scheme, in which control would be exercised from a centre in Greece where Myers should have great authority. EAM for very different reasons was also an exponent of centralisation: and this coincidence of view did not at this stage predispose Cairo to discard their own solution. There were only two wireless sets working to Cairo from the mountains: that of Myers, which did not present a wholly unfavourable picture of EAM, and that of Major Sheppard, widely separated from him in Mt Olympus, which painted a very favourable picture indeed. Sheppard knew little Greek and had lost his two Greek-speaking officers in their parachute drop: he was well handled by the local political commissar, Karayiorgis, and for some months gave Cairo EAM's picture of themselves – a national uprising, which the British must support so that the democratic parties in the movement might be strengthened to control the Communist minority.

---

[1] Minister of the Press in the Papandreou Government of 1944.

From this debate there evolved first the project of the 'National Bands', which corresponded closely with Myers's ideas. As a basis there would be Zervas in Western Greece, Psaros on Parnassus and Giona, Sarafis in Western Thessaly, possibly a shadowy organisation known as PAO in Macedonia: other leaders (such as Bakirdzis, the original Prometheus, now in Cairo) could be introduced from outside or might arise locally. It would be open to EAM to take the lead in areas where it was competent to do so, on a basis of mutual toleration with other bands. This might have worked if it had come earlier, but it must be remembered that the non-EAM leaders were all strong Republicans, and it was only EAM's policy which in the end threw them into the arms of the government in exile. M. Tsouderos and his government would have fought hard to prevent the British supporting them at an earlier stage, when the support might have been effective.

By the spring of 1943 EAM was confident and aggressive, and would tolerate no rivals. Its instant reaction was to attack and destroy such new captains as took the field before they could gather strength. Sarafis was attacked and captured early in March; they harassed and drove off a minor soldier, Vlakhos, in Western Thessaly, and turned out his BLO: they burst into the southern part of Zervas's territory and effectively loosened his control there: they put down all attempts at independent bands in Macedonia. Zervas and Psaros were relatively strong, and were not attacked as yet: but they were subjected to an intense war of threats. EAM's forces undoubtedly acted with great brutality in the areas which they invaded, and the whole operation, though it strengthened them militarily, was the first serious breach in their moral position. The horror stories were of course denied: but they were increasingly believed.

As the position developed it became steadily clearer that no solution would work which did not take primary account of EAM: either their assistance against the Germans must be bought at their own price, or it must be made the first British object to defeat them, as it was EAM's first object to eliminate political rivals. The latter course was ruled out on all grounds, political and military: Cairo was not even ready to stop supplies to EAM. It remained therefore to make a deal, and it became more urgent for the British to make a deal as the time of the next forward step in the Mediterranean approached. The SOE plan of action in Greece in support of the Sicily invasion was known as 'Animals': a simultaneous attack on communications designed in part to assist the cover plan of an impending attack on the west coast of Greece, in part to prevent the withdrawal of German troops for use elsewhere. It was eventually timed to begin in the third week of June 1943.

It is unnecessary to follow in detail the negotiations which preceded this. *First*, in the latter part of March, Myers (lately recovered from pneumonia) set out on a tour of his diocese with a draft agreement for presentation to any responsible EAM authority whom he could find. This led to little progress in dealing with the Greeks, except that it may have hampered some local EAM hostilities, and it had the disadvantage of withdrawing Myers from contact with Cairo at a time of crisis in the Greek Government there. But it greatly consolidated the British Military Mission and increased their knowledge of the general situation: in particular Myers for the first time met Sheppard, who had hitherto been an unwitting mouthpiece of EAM. This process of British consolidation was helped by improvement in communications; and also by a tour of inspection made by Lieutenant Colonel Stevens, head of SOE Greek Section in Cairo, who entered Greece in the middle of April and saw much which was valuable, although unfortunately he was not back in Cairo until August.[1]

Second, there was the first general conference, that at Liaskovo in the first week of June 1943. Its background was a vicious EAM offensive against Psaros in Parnassus in May and again during the conference: but at least the parties had for the first time been brought to a meeting. The EAM delegation was in theory the 'High Command' of their military organisation, ELAS, in the usual tripartite form: Tzimas as Political Commissar, Ares as Capetanios, and (of all men) Sarafis, the Venizelist Colonel whom they had crushed in March, as their professional military adviser with the bogus status of C-in-C – a mere bait to attract other trained soldiers. The immediate result was deadlock between Myers's version of the agreement and the version brought by Tzimas from Athens. The debate continued with acrimony and eloquence for two full days, then broke up on 7th June.

'Animals' was now a matter of extreme urgency – its opening was set for 21st June. Cairo gave authority to Myers to accept Tzimas's terms, in the last resort: and Myers set out on tour, with his newly equipped mobile wireless station, to check plans finally with his BLOs and also (if possible) to secure the co-operation of the ELAS high command on their own terms. The BLOs had in many areas excellent relations with local EAM bands, and all was ready for action – if ELAS gave the word. This led to the *third* stage: a meeting with main ELAS personalities at Avdhela, near the junction of Macedonia, Epirus and Thessaly. The 'National Bands' project in its original sense was dead: ELAS had had its own way except in the very limited areas of Zervas and Psaros. But it was necessary to sign something, as a preliminary to 'Animals', and the EAM

---

[1] A summary of Lieutenant Colonel Stevens's report can be seen in SOE HQ War Diary, Mid-East and Balkans Section, pp. 862–70.

version was accepted on 14th June.[1] This provided for a joint HQ
to control all guerilla activity, under the direction of the C-in-C
Middle East: Zervas and Psaros would be represented at this HQ,
and fair words were included about tolerance for all patriotic bands.
The orders of C-in-C Middle East would be transmitted through
Brigadier Myers: but in effect it would rest with EAM to say whether
they should be obeyed.

After these ironical preliminaries it is pleasant to be able to record
that 'Animals' was a brilliant success. It opened auspiciously with an
astonishing attack on the Asopus railway bridge on 21st June: the
guerillas had declined this as beyond their strength and it was carried
out by a party of five British and one Arab (an escaped prisoner)
under the command of Major Gordon-Creed. They climbed down a
gorge so precipitous that it had been left unguarded: they lived at the
bottom of it for several days within 400 yds of German posts: and
they eventually carried out the attack by stealth in the full glare of
German searchlights. The bridge collapsed again while being rebuilt
and was out of action for nearly three months. Elsewhere the guerillas played their parts excellently, steered tactfully by British Liaison
Officers: within the next three weeks there were forty-four major cuts
in the few road and rail communications, as well as countless minor
operations. In addition there was a five-day strike of transport workers in the Piraeus. It is understood that the operation was entirely
successful also in its major role as part of the deception plan for
'Husky', which landed in Sicily on 10th July.

The stage was thus admirably set for the first meeting of Joint HQ,
which was to be based at Pertouli in the mountains overlooking the
Thessalian plain from the west. There assembled there on 18th July
all the BLOs available in Northern Greece, and also the representatives of EAM, Zervas and Psaros: a halcyon moment of goodwill in
a troubled story. There for the moment was the united government of
'mountain Greece', which was (to quote Woodhouse) now 'overlaid
like tracing paper on a map' over enemy-occupied Greece. The inhabitants of each could move freely in their respective areas, their paths
often crossing but never running for long together: they were at war,
but hostilities were far from continuous, though very bitter when they
broke out.

In this government, which was far more than a military HQ – indeed
it had very few military functions – the British Mission played an important part, Zervas and Psaros, or their representatives, a trivial one. It
was in fact EAM's government of Greece: and the respectability they
had gained was further sanctified by the arrival late in July of Major

---

[1] Official British summary at Appendix B of Woodhouse's History of British
Military Mission.

David Wallace,[1] to act as representative of the Foreign Office, reporting to HM Ambassador with the *de jure* Government in Cairo. A point seemed to have been reached at which EAM need take only one step further to crown its work by assimilating that Government to itself.

Their opportunity was apparently at hand when (in response to an invitation first made during Woodhouse's visit to Athens in January) a delegation was taken out by Dakota on 9th August from an airfield built under British Military Mission directions. The delegation consisted of (for EAM) the Communist Tzimas, and with him Roussos, Despotopoulos and Tsirimokos, whose position was less clear: for Zervas, Komninos; and for Psaros, Kartalis. This was a party of great dignity and weight in their own world; with them went Brigadier Myers and Major Wallace.

To understand why their contact with the other, outer world proved a fiasco we must re-trace our steps and follow briefly the troubles of the British and Greek Governments since September 1942.

2. The Outside World September 1942–August 1943

An earlier period of disturbance had ended in the late summer of 1942 with the appointment of M. Kanellopoulos, (who marked perhaps the extreme Left of the old-fashioned Royalist movement), as Vice-President of the Council with special responsibility for resistance in Greece. M. Tsouderos's government remained in London: M. Kanellopoulos was in Cairo with full powers locally as a member of the Anglo-Greek Committee, on which SOE and the Minister of State's office were the other parties. Kanellopoulos's solution was to be given a fair trial, although (as we saw earlier) the conception on which it was based had already been exploded by developments within Greece for which SOE bore some responsibility.

The experiment did not last long, but its breakdown was not due to the really fundamental problems which first arose in the winter of 1942. Kanellopoulos was in London early in November 1942, and all then seems to have been well as regards his relations with the King and the King's Government.[2] But on 13th November His Majesty's Government made a declaration of its intention to restore the independence of Albania[3] – a declaration very welcome to SOE and accepted by the

---

[1] Exchange of letters between Sir O. Sargent and CD on his terms of reference, 2nd and 3rd June 1943, copies on SOE Archives File (CD) 'Greece 3 – Political', and Foreign Office Telegram No. 72 of 9th June to Cairo.

[2] Note of conversation between Kanellopoulos and Lieutenant Colonel Pearson on 4th November 1942, on SOE Archives File (AD/S.1) F.61/II.

[3] SOE London HQ War Diary, pp. 328 and 466 of Mid-East and Balkans Section refer.

Greek and Yugoslav governments in exile – which produced a storm in Greek nationalist circles, and particularly in the armed forces in the Middle East. Kanellopoulos made himself the mouthpiece of this very unrealistic reaction, and by the middle of December[1] there were threats of resignation and demands for the reconstruction of the government. Kanellopoulos arrived in London again on 30th December with something in the nature of an ultimatum.[2] In the cooler atmosphere of London it was possible to smooth matters over for the time being, but the position was now clearly unstable, and a new and more serious crisis broke out early in March, when there was a serious mutiny among the Greek troops in Palestine. The origins of this lie outside SOE's story, but apparently the trouble was Venizelist Republican rather than Communist in its origin: it is pretty clear that SOE's old ally Miss Elli Papadimitriou had a finger in the pie.[3] The immediate result was the resignation of Kanellopoulos and the destruction of the carefully constructed mechanism of the Anglo-Greek Committee.

This time a more determined effort was made to reassert the prestige of the Greek Government. The War Cabinet discussed the matter on 8th March 1943,[4] in the absence of Mr Churchill, and Mr Eden then indicated a policy of full support for the Greek King and his Government, even at the expense of some loss of active effort against the occupying powers: he also suggested that the King should be advised to move to Cairo as soon as possible. This was followed by a sharp cross-fire between British departments. On 13th March Sir Charles Hambro wrote to General Ismay to draw the attention of the Chiefs of Staff to the military considerations neglected by the Cabinet:[5] on the 14th Sir Orme Sargent attacked[6] Sir Charles over the instructions given to Brigadier Myers to rally the guerillas under the banner of the C-in-C Middle East, rather than under that of the Greek Government. On the 17th the Chiefs of Staff considered a Foreign Office memorandum on policy and submitted comments in which they expressed 'their earnest hope that political considerations will not be allowed to hamper or reduce the good work which is being done by

---

1   See telegram from Colonel Taylor (then in Cairo) dated 19th December; copy on SOE Archives File F.61/II.
2   See note of interviews between Sir Chas. Hambro, M. Tsouderos, M. Varvaressos and M. Kanellopoulos on 31st December 1942 – on SOE Archives File (AD/S.1) F.61/II.
3   Note of interview with her in October 1942 by Pirie, dated 9th March 1943, on SOE Archives File (AD/S.1) F.61/III.
4   WM(43)38th Mtg of 8th March.
5   Copy on SOE Archives File (AD/S.1) F.61/III.
6   Copy on SOE Archives File (AD/S.1) F.61/III. Sir Charles replied effectively on 16th March.

the guerilla bands'.[1] To confuse matters further, Zervas, the old Venizelist, entered the lists at this point with two telegrams,[2] one to the King, one to the British Government in which he asked for understanding of the position of the fighting men and offered unity 'with all true patriots, both Royalists and Democrats. We wished to work the same with the Communists, that is EAM. Though Greece is enslaved Communism now seeks to impose itself by force and has already declared revolution.' He would accept the King, if this was the will of the people: he would even accept it if it were merely the will of England, based on good reasons of England's own.

There is no indication that the outer world, Greek or British, grasped at the time the significance of this reaction to the first wave of EAM aggrandisement in the mountains. The issue for the politicians outside was still 'King or no King': not 'for or against EAM', as it was for those in the mountains. The formal statement of British policy which followed turns entirely on the former of these issues: a long, well-drafted, and carefully hedged document, with little relevance to the mountain world.[3] Its key passage as regards SOE (para. 7) reads as follows: 'In view of the operational importance attached to subversive activities in Greece, there can be no question of SOE refusing to have dealings with a given group merely on the grounds that the political sentiments of the group are opposed to the King and Government, but subject to special operational necessity SOE should always veer in the direction of groups willing to support the King and Government, and furthermore impress on such groups as may be anti-monarchical the fact that the King and Government enjoy the fullest support of His Majesty's Government. In general nothing should be neglected which might help to promote unity among the resistance groups in Greece and between the latter and the King and Government.' It will be seen that the point of view of the Chiefs of Staff has here in practice prevailed; and that (in many words) the C-in-C Middle East, and SOE on his behalf, are given very wide discretion as to the form of organisation they are to encourage. Myers had now full authority to proceed on the lines of the

---

1   COS(43)47th (0) Mtg, Item 2, of 17th March and Annex II. The following also refer: COS(43)135(0), MEDC telegram CC.201, COS(43)50th (0) Mtg, Item 6, and COS(ME) 364.

2   Woodhouse claims to have suggested these messages: Myers says that they were sent by Zervas spontaneously: presumably the former is right. Text in Woodhouse's History of British Mission, Appendix D. See also his 'Apple of Discord', p. 74.

3   No. 871 of 18th March 1943 to the Minister of State as amended by No. 913 of 20th March (copies of both on SOE Archives File (AD/S.1) F.61/III). It proceeded from the Prime Minister, as he was then in charge of the Foreign Office, but there is no indication of Mr Churchill's own hand in its wording.

'National Bands Agreement' which Sir Orme Sargent had attacked so sharply on 14th March.

On the constitutional issue, the directive discouraged the idea that there should be a constitutional plebiscite shortly after the return of the King and his Government to Greece. Curiously enough, the King himself had already gone beyond this in his reply to Zervas:[1] 'after his return to Greece, His Majesty will base himself on the will of the people and will follow the opinion which they will freely express on all questions affecting them'. In the next phase, this is the main issue for the politicians: there will be a plebiscite as regards the monarchy: is it to be held before or after the King's return to Greece? It will be understood that in Greek as in other Balkan elections the verdict is expected to be in favour of the government holding the elections: the question posed is therefore not one of academic principle, it is the vital one 'Is the King to "make" the elections?'

Subject to these underlying ambiguities, the political situation had for the moment been brought under control. The King and M. Tsouderos reached Cairo in the third week of March, accompanied by Mr Leeper as British Ambassador: and a new government was formed under M. Tsouderos with an admixture of Republicans, of whom the most important were M. Roussos (no connection of the EAM Roussos), M. Emmanuel Sophoulis (nephew of the old Liberal leader), and M. Karapanyotis, one of the six expelled from Egypt in the summer of 1941.[2] From SOE's point of view the most important change was that Mr Leeper now in effect took over the functions of the Anglo-Greek Committee in controlling all political aspects of SOE's work in Greece.[3] This solution was imposed by the Foreign Office without prior consultation, a discourtesy hotly resented by Sir Charles Hambro: Lord Selborne very wisely declined battle and the instructions went into force after a merely formal protest to the Prime Minister.[4] Their principal demerit was that they provided no continuous machinery for co-ordinating military and political policy, and trouble was thus stored up for the future. But at first liaison between Mr Leeper and Lord Glenconner, as well as between their subordinates, appears to have been close and friendly.

The next crisis was plainly not of SOE's making, though SOE proved

---

[1] Cairo's telegram No. 226 of 24th March to Colonel Myers; copy on SOE Archives File (AD/S.1) F.61/III.
[2] Above p. 156.
[3] Foreign Office dispatches to Mr Leeper, No. 46 of 22nd March and No. 48 of 23rd March; copies on SOE Archives File (AD/S.1) F.61/II.
[4] Lord Selborne's Minute of 25th March on SOE Archives File (AD/S.1) F.61/II: letters to the Prime Minister 26th March and 8th April, letter from the Prime Minister on 8th April, in Lord Selborne's papers.

to be a useful scapegoat for all parties involved, and its position was in consequence seriously affected both inside Greece and in the Middle East. During May and June the ideas of Mr Leeper and Lord Glenconner developed on parallel lines on the two main points at issue:[1] *first*, the steps to be taken to conciliate the old Republican politicians inside and outside Greece, *second*, the line to be followed by Brigadier Myers in his discussions with EAM, which eventually opened at Liaskovo in the first week in June. In London the Foreign Office and Lord Selborne also kept closely in step with one another, though not quite in step with Cairo; both were on the whole more anxious than Cairo that nothing should be done which might suggest a weakening of British support for the King.[2] There was concurrence in the dispatch to Myers of a telegram authorising the creation of the Joint HQ;[3] there was also agreement on the text of a new statement on the constitutional issue which was eventually broadcast by the King on 4th July.[4] In this the King for the first time went so far as to promise explicitly that elections to a constituent assembly would be held within six months *after* his return and that he would abide by its decision as to the future of the monarchy.

The reactions to this carefully agreed policy were in the highest degree disconcerting. On 8th July a new mutiny broke out in the Greek forces and had to be suppressed by British troops: the issue of what action was to be taken against the convicted mutineers was in itself sufficient to divide the Greek Government from top to bottom.[5] EAM for its part at once repudiated the King's offer.[6] It was even more disturbing to the Greek Government that (as soon became clear) it was repudiated just as forcibly by the café politicians of Athens. On 16th July Mr Leeper still followed Royalist reports from Greece and considered it possible that a new centre of resistance might emerge on the basis of the King's speech;[7] he and M. Tsouderos both at that moment seem to have contemplated a disclaimer of SOE's work for the Joint

---

[1] Cf. (for instance) Lord Glenconner's telegram No. 1009 of 26th May to CD, Mr Leeper's telegram No. 107 of 27th May and his dispatch of 24th May: all on SOE Archives File (CD) 'Greece 3 – Political'.

[2] Many papers on this period on SOE Archives Files (AD/S.1) F.61/III and (CD) 'Greece 3 – Political'.

[3] Foreign Office draft telegram cleared between Sir Orme Sargent and Sir Chas. Hambro, 11th–12th June 1943, SOE Archives File (AD/S.1) F.61/III.

[4] Final text in SOE Archives File (AD/S.1) F.61/IV. The USA was also consulted and agreed in cautious terms – Washington No. 3073 of 6th July to Foreign Office; copy on SOE Archives File (CD) 'Greece 3 – Political'.

[5] Mr Leeper's telegram No. 188 of 4th August; copy on SOE Archives File (AD/S.1) F.61/IV.

[6] Myers's telegram 'Mobility 160' of 4th July; copy on SOE Archives File (AD/S.1) F.61/IV.

[7] Dispatch No. 16 of 16th July; copy on SOE Archives File (AD/S.1) F.61/IV.

HQ, and the discovery of some new solution on the lines of the old 'Six Colonels'.[1] But early in August there arrived from Athens a certain M. Exindaris, fully briefed by Lambrakis, Gonatas, Sophoulis, Kaphandaris and others far to the Right of EAM. His escape had been aided by SOE's agent 'Apollo', who himself left Athens on 10th August, bringing with him a full dossier of correspondence from these politicians.[2] Their attitude was uniformly hostile: the King must not return until *after* a plebiscite, to be conducted by a coalition government under a Regency. It may be noted that (unlike Zervas) none of these politicians had yet grasped the fundamental change in the position brought about by the rise of EAM.

Mr Leeper saw M. Exindaris for the first time on 7th August;[3] it was clear that the latter would find considerable support within M. Tsouderos's Government, already *en plein crise* over the matter of the mutineers. There were thus already two concurrent crises in full swing when Brigadier Myers appeared almost unheralded with his strong party of mountain politicians on the morning of 10th August. It was true that such a mission to Cairo had been offered and welcomed ever since February, and that the date of its arrival was known shortly before:[4] nevertheless it came as a very severe shock. Hitherto there had been much careful debate but no one had quite appreciated the real and formidable existence of the Joint HQ and the 'free state' of mountain Greece.

Mr Leeper's first reaction was favourable: 'I cannot help feeling that the appearance on the scene here of men who have been actively resisting the enemy at home cannot but have a refreshing and stimulating effect on the Greek Government and might in fact modify their present standpoint and that of the King also.' The position had indeed suddenly become fluid, and any of the three serious parties, the British, the King and EAM, might be able to extract great advantage from it by rapid manoeuvre. The intricate movements of the next few days can be followed in some detail from SOE papers:[5] but the British hand was played by Mr Leeper and not by Lord Glenconner, and there

---

1   The last words of the above Dispatch: on 17th July Tsouderos wrote attacking SOE's policy and its effects. See SOE's reply dated 29th July; copy on SOE Archives File (CD) 'Greece 3 – Political'.

2   It is not obvious when these reached Cairo; copies dated 18th September on SOE Archives File (AD/S.1) F.61/IV.

3   His No. 195 of 7th August; copy on SOE Archives File F.61/IV.

4   See note on the sequence of events sent by Lord Selborne to Sir Orme Sargent on 3rd September; copy on SOE Archives File (CD) 'Greece 3 – Political'. The exact date depended on the speed with which a decent landing-ground could be prepared in Thessaly: that end of the story is excellently told in Denys Hamson's book. [*We Fell among Greeks* (1946).]

5   Woodhouse's account in 'Apple of Discord', p. 151 ff, is by no means complete, though good so far as it goes.

is no indication that the latter intervened directly in politics, though he was at first fully consulted. By 15th August the position had again hardened. Mr Churchill and Mr Eden were both in Quebec; the instructions from London were those purely of the Foreign Office, and they followed unhesitatingly the established line of British policy: 'the King himself must decide on his course of action, but it is still our policy to give him all the support we can and full use should be made of our influence if the King requires it'.[1] This reached Cairo early on the 18th, and later that day the King dispatched a message to the Prime Minister and President in which he asked for advice but clearly indicated his own preference for a line of scepticism and resistance in face of EAM.[2]

This decided the issue in a sense which was perhaps best in the end for the Greek dynasty, though it led immediately to a series of embarrassments both for the King and for the British.[3] The British attitude in Cairo changed instantly without further guidance from Quebec.[4] Mr Leeper virtually broke off relations with Lord Glenconner:[5] he attempted to hustle the entire guerilla party into an instant return to Greece; and he proceeded to attack SOE bitterly as having wantonly caused the whole imbroglio. Lord Glenconner naturally represented strongly that irreparable harm would be done if the Greek representatives were packed off in such circumstances: harm not only to the military work of the Joint HQ but also to the King's own cause, for among the representatives were those of Zervas and Psaros, the only defence which remained against a complete EAM domination of the mountains. The Minister of State and the C-in-C[6] backed Mr Leeper, and 'the six' were only rescued because SOE's conducting officer permitted them to interview M. Tsouderos before they left. M. Tsouderos intervened in their favour (an act later reck-

---

[1] No. 131 dispatched 11.40 p.m. on 17th August.

[2] Quoted in telegram 'Concrete No. 374' of 19th August to Quebec; copy on SOE Archives File (CD) 'Greece 3 – Political'.

[3] On 19th August Lord Selborne wrote to Sir Orme Sargent, who was then virtually in charge of the Foreign Office, and (as the only Minister concerned who was in London) whole-heartedly backed the Foreign Office's inclination to take a firm line: this was before he knew of the King's decision. Copy on SOE Archives File (AD/S.1) F.61(c).

[4] The Prime Minister's Welfare 349 of 25th August and Welfare 490 of 31st August – both on SOE Archives File (AD/S.1) F.61(c).

[5] Alpha 035/38 from Cairo of 25th August – on SOE Archives File (AD/S.1) F.61(c). There had been no discrepancy in view up to 18th August: Lord Glenconner's Alpha 029 of 18th August on SOE Archives File (CD) 'Greece 3 – Political'.

[6] The latter had a painful interview with 'the six'; record on SOE Archives File (AD/S.1) F.61/IV.

oned by the Foreign Office to the discredit of SOE) and they were permitted to remain for the time being. In the end they did not leave until 16th September and SOE doubtless did what it could to salve their wounded vanity. But the political and moral gap between Cairo and the mountains had reopened and now seemed irreparable.

3. The British Mission September 1943–May 1944

Even while the Mission was in Cairo the situation had developed rapidly. The Italian Armistice was signed on 3rd September, on 9th September the Allies landed at Salerno, on 16th the British moved into Cos and Leros and for a moment seemed likely to clear the Aegean.[1] As early as the beginning of August (Mussolini fell on 25th July) some feelers had been put out to the British Mission by Italian officers in Thessaly. Nothing came of these at the time, but the negotiations prepared the ground for prompt action when the news of the Armistice broke. Isolated Italian garrisons were in some cases swiftly disarmed by the Germans, in others by EAM: but in Thessaly BLOs were the first on the spot and opened negotiations with General Infante, in command of the Pinerolo Division at Larissa, and with Colonel Berti in command at Trikkala. Under General Infante's leadership the Division was brought over to the British side almost intact, with some of its artillery, and the first agreement for Italian co-belligerency in any theatre was signed between him and Colonel Woodhouse on 12th September.[2] In this Woodhouse undertook to support the Italians financially at the same rate as the guerillas: an agreement first repudiated, then endorsed by Cairo.

The Germans cleared the plain of Thessaly without much difficulty: but the Italians fought stubbornly and successfully against German attempts to push westwards into the hills, a success resented for their own good reasons by EAM, who at once took steps to disperse the Italians in small units, so as to weaken their cohesion and fighting strength. Woodhouse negotiated hard for a reversal of this policy, and secured EAM's agreement to a concentration of the Pinerolo Division in a single sector. This agreement was achieved on the morning of 14th October, the day after the Italians declared war on Germany: the same evening EAM simultaneously surrounded and disarmed all the isolated Italian units and put many of their officers under arrest, on the ground that they were planning a 'Fascist plot' in concert with Zervas.

---

[1] Appendix V(F) to Colonel Dolbey's Greek History gives details of SOE work in the Aegean Islands.

[2] Photostat of the agreement and photographs of the conference on SOE Archives File F.61/IV.

This ended Italian co-belligerency in Greece: henceforward the disarmed Italians were merely a problem in poor relief, which caused Woodhouse infinite anxiety. He seems to have been remarkably successful in preserving a fairly high proportion from starvation on the mountains or in EAM concentration camps: though EAM (as always) succeeded in diverting to other purposes some of the money provided for relief.

Simultaneously with the Italian surrender and the German counter-stroke, the C-in-C Middle East called for an all-out effort from the Greeks to assist the British in their difficulties in Cos and Leros. The crux of this came on 29th September, when the C-in-C called for an attack on all German aerodromes in Greece in order to reduce the weight of air attack in the Aegean. The orders were accepted by ELAS at Joint HQ, but the offensive proved almost a complete fiasco. In only one instance, that of Larissa, did a party succeed in entering an airfield and attaching charges to eight aircraft: none of the charges exploded. This was a party led by British and consisting largely of Italians: where plans were dependent on the Greeks they failed completely. This was in part due to the unsuitability of the guerilla organisation for a co-ordinated series of 'set piece' operations of this kind; but this was a weakness which they could overcome when they were so resolved, and the trouble lay fundamentally in the political situation.

When the Cairo party returned to Greece on 17th September it came without Myers and Wallace: the former had been held back because he was suspected of too great favour to EAM.[1] Woodhouse had therefore to face single-handed and inadequately briefed the most difficult situation which had yet developed. He was now assisted by a junior American officer of OSS, Captain Ehrgott, whose judgement appears to have been amiable but erratic: it was not till December that a more senior American, Major Wines, came in as second-in-command of what was now the Allied Military Mission. General Bakirdzis ('Prometheus') also accompanied the party.[2]

First, there were a series of rows on minor points within the Joint HQ: not in themselves raising new issues, but symptomatic of the end of the period of day-to-day co-operation which had begun with 'Animals' in June. Wounded vanity played its part: but the failure of the Cairo Mission had in any event thrown EAM back on a policy of

---

[1] According to Woodhouse ('Apple of Discord', p. 157) King George threatened to abdicate if Myers returned to Greece.

[2] He was later EAM Commander in Salonika, and in that capacity was a factor making for conciliation both during the German withdrawal and in the Civil War of December 1944. He was interned by the Greek Government and committed suicide in 1947.

violent aggression, since peaceful penetration had failed. They judged that the end of the occupation of Greece was near and that there was just time left in which to seize sole power in the mountains and to prepare to rush the towns. Their plans for this were as meticulous as those for the attack on airfields had been shoddy. Psaros had been neutralised by an agreement made under duress, which isolated him for the moment from Zervas. On the night of 9th October the scattered adherents of Zervas in Macedonia, Thessaly, Roumeli and the Peloponnese were quickly rounded up and disarmed. Simultaneously an offensive began against Zervas's main stronghold in the southwest, where Zervas was sufficiently alert to clear up minor ELAS bands before the offensive developed. On 13th October a New Zealander, Lieutenant Hubbard, was shot down by ELAS men while they were clearing a Zervas village: it was never certain whether or not they knew at the time who he was.[1] On 14th October the Italians, as we have seen, were efficiently eliminated as a military factor. Only Zervas now remained, holding a constricted mountain area, with perhaps 5,000 men in arms against ELAS's 25,000.

The Germans were not passive spectators of these operations. They had already begun to draw off troops from the Peloponnese, and thus confirmed in EAM's mind the notion that complete evacuation of Greece was not far distant. These troops were at hand when the civil war broke out, and in October they made various drives through the northern mountains. There was very little armed resistance, but they burned, destroyed and massacred with great efficiency and impartiality. The HQ of EAM, Zervas and the Allied Mission were all scattered and 'on the run': the Joint HQ at Pertouli ceased to exist.

The German tactics were not only those of violence. Now that they were in sole control, they began to develop a much more purposeful use of 'Quisling' Greeks, modelled closely on the use made of Nedič and the most extreme flank of the Cetniks in Serbia. They encouraged the formation and arming of 'Security Battalions' in the villages.[2] To the villagers themselves their role appeared to be one of protection against EAM blackmail and the German reprisals that followed the payment of blackmail: for the Germans the main advantage was that they progressively transformed the war against the invader into a civil war, which the invader could permit to develop at his ease.

The other arm of this policy was to put it about through all the channels of 'black' propaganda, that the British favoured the Security

---

[1] A useful summary of the later history of this incident dated 5th March 1944 is on SOE Archives File (CD) 'Greece 1 – Operational': see also Lord Selborne's Minute of 6th December to the Prime Minister (in Lord Selborne's papers).

[2] According to Woodhouse, 'Apple of Discord', General Gonatas and General Pangalos were both to some extent implicated.

Battalions as the answer to 'Communism' and that a realignment of forces was not far off in which the British and Germans together would confront the Russians and their allies EAM. EAM itself could be made to assist Dr Goebbels* in this line, since this was exactly the line they used themselves to cast suspicion on the King, the British and their ally Zervas. By ill-luck some circumstantial confirmation was provided. A 'brave but simple man' (as Lord Selborne described him later), Captain Stott, DSO, one of the heroes of the Asopos bridge operation, was infiltrated into Athens for other purposes about this period, and was deluded into accepting contacts with the Gestapo, who talked of negotiating German 'surrender'. This was a plain case of the use of surrender talk in order to gain material for the German propaganda plan, and it was one of 'Apollo's' great services to the Allies that he heard at an early stage of what was happening and reported it to Cairo. Captain Stott was instantly and peremptorily recalled, but some harm had already been done. Confusion in Greece was further confounded, and the incident has in a distorted way become part of the German version of the history of the war: it was used for instance in Jodl's defence at Nuremburg.[1]

The Germans in fact had evolved a technically sound answer to the Russian doctrine of continuous partisan warfare nourishing itself on the enemy's attempts at repression. The new technique was as effective on the political level as in the villages. On the one hand, Zervas could with reason complain that EAM were playing the German game, not only because they fed the Security Battalions and played Dr Goebbels's propaganda line, but also because they actually attacked him while he was attempting to resist the Germans. EAM on its side could circumstantially demonstrate that Zervas through the EDES Committee or Committees in Athens was in touch with persons who were certainly in touch with the Germans. These cross-currents were inevitable: it was largely a matter of personal accident in which camp any individual Greek appeared at each stage

---

[1]   Cooper, 'The Nuremburg Trials' (Penguin), p. 238. It seems also to have come up in the trial of Neubacher by the Yugoslavs in November 1947. Contemporary summaries of the Stott affair are on SOE Archives Files (CD) 'Greece 3 – Political' and (AD/S.1) F.61: his own later report is referred to but has not been found. There were other local negotiations later, in the Peloponnese, in the Yannina area and in Athens, and there was an attempt through deserters to negotiate a mutiny in a German penal regiment: but all these contacts were carefully controlled and restricted and caused no political disturbance. (For feelers by Von Lang and Neubacher in Athens in September 1944 see File 9/100/12 Pt III: for the negotiations regarding No. 999 Regiment in April 1944 see File 9/100/12 Pt II.)

*   [J. Goebbels, 1897–1945, Nazi propaganda chief since 1930, suicide. See 3 vols of his *Diaries*, 1939–41, ed. and tr. F. Taylor (1982), 1945, ed. H. R. Trevor-Roper, tr. R. H. Barry (1978), and Selections, ed. Louis P. Lochner (1948).]

– ideals and ideologies counted for very little in so confused a struggle for existence. EAM had some success in labelling Zervas as the 'Greek Mihailovitch' – Zervas had unwisely conducted a long-range flirtation with Mihailovitch early in 1943, while the latter was still 'respectable'. But Zervas, whatever his intrigues, was always clearly distinguishable from Mihailovitch in one vital respect: he was always willing to accept orders from the British for the effective conduct of the war, and to carry them out to the best of his ability without cavilling or obstruction. He was a very weak ally, but wholly loyal to the alliance.

The last months of 1943 were a period of great bitterness for the Allied Military Mission. Almost every liaison officer was on bad terms with the local ELAS command and was continually on the run in order to avoid German activity or the movements of the civil war: the danger of being caught by the Germans was probably less than that of random murder by one of the contending Greek parties. Activity against the enemy was at a standstill. Zervas, who was eager enough to attack the Germans, continued to receive arms from the British, but was none the less getting the worse of the civil war, and might soon be unimportant as a military factor. Arms to EAM were stopped, and it was bombarded with stern warnings from Cairo against its policy: but it seemed to get stronger as its relations with the British grew worse. Indeed it had probably looted more arms from the Italians than it ever received from the British. BLO's became bitter and disillusioned; there was argument between them as to policy, and irritation with the interventions of the outer world. They functioned, if at all, as a relief organisation and not as a military force. The lowest point was reached early in December, when Woodhouse despaired of Zervas and recommended on military grounds that he should be abandoned and our sole reliance placed on EAM.[1]

This, fortunately, was disregarded, as matters then began to mend a little. Zervas held his ground on his own mountains, and even regained some territory: regular meetings were resumed between Woodhouse and the ELAS HQ; and by the third week in December 1943, negotiations were in progress for the termination of the civil war. EAM's terms indicated that it was prepared to revert to its earlier line. Its ill-tempered coup had proved a failure, and had merely led to a break-up of the 'mountain state' of the summer of 1943: it was now again ready to seek official recognition and to participate in the Cairo Government, on terms which would give it a chance to extend its influence. The crucial stage was reached early in January, when Cairo proposed a 'military plan' (which was more political than military in its intention) for co-ordinated operations to harass a German

---

[1] Woodhouse's History of Greek Military Mission, p. 146.

withdrawal – Operation 'Noah's Ark'. D-day was set for April, though
the British knew well enough that the operation was not likely to be
required so early: Greece was to be divided into guerilla areas, two
of which would be reserved for Zervas and Psaros respectively: British
and American units were to be infiltrated to stiffen the guerillas: and
the Allied Military Mission's chain of command was to be made at
once more flexible and more effective. The political implication latent
in the military phraseology was that EAM would again be given a
chance to become 'respectable', if the civil war were stopped and the
'frontiers' of Zervas and Psaros recognised.

It will be clear that this was a delicate device not likely to lead to
precise lines of agreement: but the first stage was achieved when on
18th January[1] Sarafis accepted the plan in outline on behalf of ELAS
and signed operational orders to his local commanders: but Zervas's
area was not covered and the civil war continued. There followed on
28th January a conference (at Neokhori) of all the BLOs who could
be assembled, to discuss their parts in 'Noah's Ark': and while it was
in progress Ares launched a final attack on his old ally and enemy
Zervas. This gained much ground, but was held finally on the River
Arakhthos. EAM were now ready to negotiate.

They opened negotiations with proposals for a 'united' guerilla
army, for a joint political committee in the mountains, and for a public
denunciation of collaborators, so framed as to cause the maximum
embarrassment to Zervas. The usual endless and ingenious debates
followed, in a series of the usual squalid and half-wrecked mountain
villages: a period broken by two incidents, Mr Churchill's sharp attack
on EAM in his speech of 22nd February and the first really notable
operation since 'Animals' – a German troop-train was thrown bodily
off the lines into the Vale of Tempe, without casualty to British or
guerillas, and at least 500 Germans were destroyed.[2] The negotiations
ended at last on 29th February 1944, after four weeks of anxiety, in
the 'Plaka Agreement',[3] which put a stop to civil war and provided
a bare basis for mutual toleration and military action without clear
commitments on the political issues.

EAM naturally did not rest at this point. The Plaka Agreement
was from their point of view a failure, as it gave them only a military status: and late in March they tried a new line, the creation of
the 'Political Committee of National Liberation' (PEEA), a body
with tasks ostensibly administrative which could easily assume the
guise of a parallel government. It was strongly staffed with non-
Communists: General Bakirdzis, the old 'Prometheus', who was

---

[1] Woodhouse's History of the Allied Military Mission, p. 157.
[2] Full report by Captain Lake on SOE Archives File (AD/S.1) F.61/V.
[3] Woodhouse's History of Allied Military Mission, Appendix E.

seduced from his first allegiance to Psaros of EKKA: Professor
Svolos, Professor of Constitutional Law at Athens, who had suffered
under Metaxas for his Socialist views: General Mandakas, who had
been a successful guerilla leader in Crete: Askoutsis, a former Liberal
Governor-General of Crete: and other able and respectable persons
qualified to revive the rather faded legend that EAM represented the
best and most liberal spirit of Greek national unity. This went well,
except that Zervas and Psaros still held aloof: and (very injudiciously) EAM let loose at them the other barrel of its policy. On
16th April 1944, Ares attacked Psaros: his bands were destroyed or
forcibly converted, and he himself was murdered. EKKA vanished
completely from the scene, and it seemed likely that a fresh attack
on Zervas would follow. Cairo's reaction was to order the instant
withdrawal of the Allied Military Mission: but Greek politics in the
Middle East were now turning another way, and the order was countermanded. M. Tsouderos had fallen at last, and M. Papandreou*
had been brought out from Athens to take his place, with a new
programme and a broadened government. Delegates from the mountains were invited to meet him in the Lebanon, under Mr Leeper's
eye; and eventually arrived there in mid-May. Meantime, there had
been in the mountains one more conference, the Koutsaina
Conference, designed to clear up certain questions left unsettled at
Plaka, in particular that of Zervas's 'frontiers'. It broke up on 8th
May with no results: the only fresh twist was a violent and unsuccessful effort by EAM to discredit Woodhouse with the Allied High
Command.

4. The Outside World September 1943–August 1944

In October 1943 SOE in London had lost its old rather ill-defined
responsibility for the policy of SOE Middle East, now Force 133, and
control had passed to a new Special Operations Sub-Committee of
the Middle East Defence Committee, in which the C-in-C's representative and Mr Leeper had the deciding voice. Lord Glenconner and
Brigadier Keble, both men with very positive views on policy, had
gone, and Force 133 was now commanded by Brigadier Stawell, an
innocuous professional soldier uncontaminated by previous experience in SOE. In Middle East, as eventually in other theatres, a final
stage had been reached in which SOE as a Ministry was no longer
responsible for policy, except as a supply agency and an adviser
frequently disregarded. It is therefore not necessary to the history of
SOE to follow in much detail the later developments of Anglo-Greek

---

* [G. Papandreou, 1888–1968, Prime Minister of Greece 1944–5, 1963, 1964–5.
See page 476.]

diplomatic relations. A brief sketch will be sufficient as a background to the final execution of 'Noah's Ark', the plan to harass German withdrawal from Greece.

The first phase occupied the autumn of 1943. A reconsideration of policy was in any case inevitable after the August fiasco, and the need for it was emphasised by the outbreak of the first civil war in Greece and by a new crisis raised early in October by those members of the Tsouderos Government who demanded a plebiscite on the monarchy before the King's return. M. Tsouderos's own attitude was weakened considerably by a report in the same sense from a reliable agent of his own who returned from Athens early in October.[1] At first Mr Leeper and the Foreign Office were for a downright policy of attacking and weakening EAM by every means in our power.[2] This was resisted by Lord Glenconner and Brigadier Myers, who were then both in London, as likely to sacrifice all chance of military advantage and to defeat its own ends by strengthening EAM politically – it would be broadened rather than isolated by an unbending policy. Mr Eden was in the Levant during the Greek crisis there in October (on his way to Moscow), and from his telegrams there emerges the possibility of a Regency under the Archbishop Damaskinos, as a preliminary stage before the return of the King.[3] This is pushed one stage further by SOE's comments in London, of which the most interesting is a paper[4] by Lieutenant Colonel Stanley Casson, a distinguished archaeologist with long experience of Greece, who had just been brought into SOE as an unbiased adviser. This paper for the first time suggested Regency *plus* plebiscite, in the form in which they were ultimately carried through in 1945 and 1946: it was forwarded by Lord Selborne to the Prime Minister on 4th November with a Minute which regretfully endorsed its conclusions and warned the Prime Minister of the dangers of opposition to EAM à l'outrance.[5] Brigadier Myers's advice told in the same direction.[6] The paper submitted to the War Cabinet by Mr Eden on 16th November adopted the policy of Regency and plebiscite,[7] though still requiring extreme toughness with EAM. The Cabinet,

---

1 Copy on SOE Archives File (CD) 'Greece 3 – Political'.
2 Draft Foreign Office paper of 20th September; copy on SOE Archives File (AD/S.1) F.61/V.
3 Nos. 1935, 1942, 1943 of 16th October – same file as 2. above.
4 Dated 26th October – same file as 2. above.
5 Prime Minister's Minute to Lord Selborne 3rd November and Lord Selborne's reply of 4th November – same file as 2. above.
6 Appreciation dated 2nd November on SOE Archives File (AD/S.1) F.61/V: Woodhouse's telegraphic report of 19th October is also important.
7 WP(43)318 and WM(43)155th Mtg, Minute 2.

in some indecision, adjourned matters for advice by the Chiefs of Staff, who replied on the basis of a plan worked out between the Cs-in-C Middle East and Mr Leeper.[1] This solution accepted the fact that EAM's present military value was not high, and proposed to bargain with the King on the basis that no more British support should be given to EAM provided that he accepted the policy of Regency and plebiscite. As a further stage, if this went well, Zervas's forces should be incorporated into the Royal Hellenic Army and subordinate EAM leaders should be induced to follow him. But the lives of the British Liaison Officers, who were virtually hostages in the hands of EAM, should not be endangered by a clean break and an attempt to withdraw them. These proposals were adopted by the War Cabinet on 22nd November.[2] Their first stage (no Royal return until after a plebiscite) represented the triumph of a view long held on the lower levels of SOE and among their 'old Republican' allies: the latter stages were speedily rendered obsolete by the progress of the civil war.

The next phase was an attempt to substitute an agreed truce with EAM for the piecemeal liquidation of its forces which had been hoped for. The military side of this campaign was the 'Noah's Ark' plan, which Woodhouse began to sell to EAM early in January 1944. M. Tsouderos's part was to broadcast an appeal for peace on 31st December, and on 15th January to offer discussions on participation by EAM in the Government, provided that a military agreement was first reached.[3] Colonel Woodhouse for a time acted formally as representative of the Greek Government as well as of the British. In February the C-in-C Middle East forced a formal reconsideration of Cabinet policy by reverting to the view that EAM's assistance was of serious military value and suggesting that as a gesture of reconciliation Brigadier Myers should return to Greece.[4] The way was now cleared for the Plaka Agreement of 29th February, which entailed in turn the opening of political negotiations between the Greek Government and EAM. M. Tsouderos wobbled a little, and was ready to evade the issue, but he was pinned to it both by British guidance

---

[1]   COS(43)283rd (0) Mtg, Minute 4, and 284th (0) Mtg, Minute 5: CC/346 of 19th November from Cs-in-C Middle East gives the appreciation on which this was based: this in turn rested on an investigation of the evidence by an independent sub-committee of the SOC, dated 17th October. See also Mr Leeper's telegrams circulated as WP(43)526.

[2]   WM(43)160th Mtg, Item 2.

[3]   Telegram to the field; copy on SOE Archives File (CD) 'Greece 3 – Political' Pt II.

[4]   General Wilson's 47851 of 5th February to COS, COS letter to Foreign Office – COS155/4 of 7th February.

and by the pressure of events.[1] The formation of EAM's strong provisional committee (PEEA) in the mountains was backed by a revolt within M. Tsouderos's Government and by a fresh mutiny in Middle East; and M. Tsouderos's long troubled reign ended at last on 3rd April 1944.

After an interlude of Sophocles Venizelos, Tsouderos was replaced on 26th April by M. Papandreou, who had much to recommend him as a compromise candidate. He had lived in Athens under the Occupation and had come out secretly: he was thus free from the disrepute of the government in exile, and could speak with some authority for the politicians of Athens, though not for 'mountain Greece'. He was a Republican and vaguely 'of the Left': but as leader of a 'splinter party', the Social Democratic Party, he was not committed wholly to the vested interests of Republican politics. Certain places in his Government were reserved for leaders from within Greece, and the Lebanon Conference with the EAM leaders opened on 16th May under auspices much more favourable than those of August 1943. The situation was also handled much better, both by Mr Leeper and M. Papandreou, and the first phase closed at the end of May with an appearance of agreement; an agreement which proved to have the immense tactical advantage of separating EAM's delegates in the Lebanon from the party leadership in the mountains. For the latter finally repudiated their delegates early in July, and there followed another period of crisis initiated by a letter from the King of Greece to Mr Churchill on 7th July, in which he asked once more for the 'clean break' with EAM.[2]

The British debate on policy was resumed, but this time it did not reach an issue: on 9th September the high command of EAM reversed its decision and agreed to appoint six Ministers to M. Papandreou's Government. What this meant was that EAM had abandoned the idea of seizing power as the Germans moved out, and of presenting the British with a situation in which they must either accept EAM or use force against a 'democratic' ally, at a time when all resources were needed against the Germans. It is not easy to follow the reasons for this decision, which apparently meant abandoning EAM's best chance; but it is practically certain that Russian influence played a part. At the Moscow Conference in October 1943 Molotov* had expressed complete lack of interest in Greek affairs, and there was no evidence

---

1   Mr Leeper's telegram No. 140 of 4th March, and Lieutenant Colonel Keswick's comments: Lord Selborne to Mr Eden 14th March, and Mr Eden's reply 23rd March; copies on SOE Archives File (CD) 'Greece 3 – Political' Pt II.

2   Mr Leeper's telegram No. 493 of 7th July; copy on SOE Archives File (AD/S.1) F.61/VI.

*   [V. M. Molotov, 1890-1986, Soviet Foreign Minister 1939–49.]

at any earlier stage of EAM's career of Russian guidance or Russian support. On 26th July 1944 a Russian mission had landed in Greece in a Russian aircraft from Italy, which had deceived the British as to its destination. But in spite of this trickery, what followed was a softening, not a hardening, of the EAM attitude towards the British, and it is natural to see here the effects of the first clear guidance as to Russian policy. For the Russians it was plain common sense to avoid all trouble in Greece at this juncture. Their offensive against Roumania was to open on 20th August, and the lines on which it must be developed were quite plain. It was impossible that Russian troops should be diverted to Greece: it was essential that fresh German divisions from Greece should not appear intact on the flanks of the Russian spearheads.

5. The German Withdrawal

All was thus ready for the long-delayed execution of 'Noah's Ark'. There had been changes in the Allied Military Mission meanwhile. The Peloponnese had for some time been a separate command under Colonel Stevens: a heartbreaking task, as ELAS had here succeeded in liquidating all 'patriotic' rivals and was concerned solely to fight a continuous civil war with the Greek Security Battalions. In June Colonel Woodhouse was withdrawn at last, after carrying a great weight of responsibility, in most arduous conditions, for twenty months.[1] He did not return until mid-September, and meantime Colonel Hammond* was in charge, assisted for part of the time by Major Wallace who returned as Foreign Office representative in July.[2] During August Brigadier Barker-Benfield,** now in command of Force 133, made a tour of inspection through Greece, in which he spoke kindly to the EAM leaders and was on the whole favourably impressed with their military value.

Late in August Roumania collapsed, and it became plain that the Germans intended to withdraw; their retreat was heralded by new raids and atrocities designed to ease their escape and to discourage their own men from taking refuge among the Greeks. The problem was to lay a military plan which would enable the Greek Government to return to Athens with the smallest possible expenditure of military force, and which would also inflict the greatest possible damage on

---

[1] There are interesting reports made by him while he was out; copies on SOE Archives File (CD) 'Greece 3 – Political' Pt. II.

[2] He was killed very unluckily by a stray German bullet in September.

* [N. G .L. Hammond, born 1907, classical archaeologist.]

** [K. V. Barker-Benfield, 1892–1969, military attaché, Vienna, Budapest and Berne 1935–8.]

the retreating Germans. The former was a matter for General Scobie*
and Force 140, which consisted of little more than 10,000 men of all
arms: the latter was for the Allied Military Mission and the guerillas
aided by two or three hundred special service troops and the Allied
Air Forces.

The most important preparatory step was the conference at Caserta
early in September, attended by Sarafis and Zervas, for ELAS and
EDES, at which a rough division of responsibilities was agreed: still
more important, it was accepted that Athens was 'out of bounds' for
guerillas and that the Greek command there should be in the hands
of General Spiliotopoulos, one of the 'Six Colonels' of earlier note.
Lieutenant Colonel Sheppard, a very experienced British Liaison
Officer, went into Athens early in September to handle British interests.[1] The agreement to send no guerillas into Athens was honoured
by EAM mainly in the breach; but at least it excluded one town of
the utmost importance from the race for control between Zervas and
EAM. In the same month M. Kanellopoulos[2] entered the Peloponnese
on behalf of the Papandreou Government, and there struck up a very
temporary and uneasy alliance with Ares Veloukhiotis.

'Noah's Ark', after some earlier skirmishing, began officially on
10th September, ten days before the British landings in the
Peloponnese, and it continued until 1st November, when the last
German detachments crossed the Greek frontier, leaving only isolated
garrisons in the islands. It was a serious of individual episodes out of
which it is impossible to make a narrative; but on the whole it was a
success. Naturally the guerillas held back a large proportion of their
men and arms for their own purposes, EAM more than Zervas: but
both parties fought well, at least in areas where they were backed and
stimulated by good liaison officers and Special Service troops. The
main battles were fought on the only two escape roads, in the east
and west of the mainland, and there were here a series of minor 'battles
of Thermopylae' in reverse, in which the Germans were held in defiles
until forced to deploy and mount regular attacks. There were also
ambushes and a number of very successful attacks on loaded trains,
as well as continuous sabotage of the permanent way. Woodhouse (a
most cautious witness) estimates German losses by action on the
ground as 100 locomotives, 500 motor vehicles and 5,000 men killed.
To this must be added the damage done by the air forces to traffic
jammed on the roads by guerilla action: these air forces were able to

---

1   Directive in SOE Archives File (CD) 'Greece 3 – Political' Pt II. He was later
     killed by a landmine while in the service of UNRRA in Greece.
2   He was later Minister of the Interior in the Maximos Government of 1947.
*   [(Sir) R. MacK Scobie, 1893–1969, GOC Malta 1942, GOC Greece 1944–6,
     knight 1946.]

leap-frog very swiftly forward to advance landing-grounds in guerilla territory. Finally, there are the uncertain factors of time lost, morale weakened, and equipment destroyed or abandoned because it could not be moved in time. These are all substantial, though the last must be discounted a little by the deliberate German decision to leave what arms they could into the hands of EAM as the seed of future trouble. But, using all possible caution, one must conclude that 'Noah's Ark' paid a dividend much higher than the whole British expenditure on special operations in Greece, and that it did not in itself cost much in Greek lives. Furthermore, it was accomplished in the way least favourable to an armed bid for power by EAM. Their rising in December 1944, which lies outside this story, was a last throw made at a time when all the odds were against success.

6. The 'Apollo' Organisation

One very important strand has hitherto been kept apart from this narrative. Athens and the Piraeus together form an industrial town and seaport of very considerable importance – much more important than any other in the occupied territory of the Balkans – and SOE's plans had at the outset been laid not for guerilla warfare but for secret sabotage of objectives of this kind. The 'Prometheus' organisation had first been conceived in this sense, although it later proved also to be an important link in the development of open resistance in the mountains, and it had achieved considerable successes against shipping at an important time in the summer of 1942:[1] it had also proved a reliable source of shipping intelligence. Early in 1943 Prometheus II (Koutsoyannopoulos) was caught and his organisation was broken up: a certain John Peltekis, a stockbroker, came out to Smyrna to report, and was there taken into the service of SOE by Major Pawson. He returned to Athens, rescued Prometheus II from gaol by an ingenious ruse with a forged release order, and proceeded to rebuild the organisation. Peltekis became 'Apollo' and the organisation 'Yvonne'. It continued to prosper, and during the rest of 1943 it was able to report a continuous series of successes against shipping, as well as some minor industrial sabotage. It is useless to present a total for ships of all sizes sunk, damaged and delayed, as the figure would be statistically meaningless. But some details can be given from a fairly well-authenticated summary which runs from June 1943 to September 1944.[2] Some fifty ships, ranging from two Italian destroyers down to harbour tugs and caiques, were attacked, most of them with at least partial success. Only one of the larger vessels sank at sea, but half-a-dozen others were damaged in

---

[1] Above p. 161.
[2] Exhibit 2 of the 'Apollo' Court of Enquiry; copy in SOE Archives.

harbour and were in dock for long periods. Most of the smaller vessels were total losses. In addition, there were six good pieces of railway sabotage and two successful attacks on munition dumps. Finally a serious strike and popular demonstration was staged in June 1943, after the Germans had shot eighteen hostages as a reprisal for the sinking of a 7,000-ton ship in the Piraeus. In addition, the Yvonne 'escape route' was used successfully by at least a hundred persons.

Peltekis was in the Middle East for a short time in July 1943, and he came out again in May 1944 after his organisation had been badly broken by arrests in March. He was back in Athens in June for a short visit to reorganise, which he did with good effect. Shipping sabotage continued, and in the last days of the occupation the organisation performed a great service by attacking and putting out of action a floating-crane and several vessels which the Germans had intended to use as blockships. This much accelerated the opening of Athens as a port.

So far this is a 'success story', achieved at the cost of 2,500 sovereigns a month, a small supply of 'limpets' and other explosive devices, and very few Greek lives. Peltekis was (and is) a man of the highest ability, a Greek patriot with an almost equal scorn of all Greek politicians. But no Greek is non-political, and Peltekis did not refrain from expressing views on politics. His views were highly intelligent, and approached more nearly to impartiality than those of any other Greek: but they were sharply expressed and were keenly felt by a number of influential Greeks. In July 1943 Peltekis was the bearer of bad tidings to M. Tsouderos in the shape of a budget of letters from the Republican politicians,[1] and there is little doubt that he confirmed their views in personal discussion with M. Tsouderos. During that winter rumours began to circulate, and were apparently accepted by Mr Leeper's staff, that Peltekis was in some ill-defined way fraudulent: a 'double-agent' employed by the Germans, a Russian agent, a supporter of EAM. In May 1944 he met M. Papandreou, whom he already knew slightly, and they parted on bad terms. M. Papandreou's Chef de Cabinet, M. Vassiliades, was from this time a central source of rumour intended to discredit Peltekis.

This chain of causes led to a most unpleasant incident in August 1944. M. Vassiliades reported to M. Papandreou a story current in Smyrna that Peltekis was receiving money from SOE for the support of an EAM organisation: Mr Leeper was then in England, and the report was transmitted by his deputy to the Foreign Office in a form which magnified an unsupported rumour into an accusation of deliberate evasion by SOE of Foreign Office guidance.[2] The Foreign Office

---

[1]   Above p. 465.
[2]   Telegram No. 604 of 15th August 1944; copy on SOE Archives File (CD) Greece 4.

replied insisting on the letter of SOE's charter and rebuking the C-in-C Middle East for his lack of control:[1] the Prime Minister (then in Italy) intervened with an even sterner rebuke: 'There should be a Court of Enquiry held to ascertain the official guilty of this neglect or perversion of his duties. Someone must have been responsible. That person should be ascertained and immediately dismissed from any share in our affairs. Nobody ever gets punished for doing these kind of things.'[2]

The necessary consequence was that the dispatch of funds to 'Apollo' was stopped and that a military Court of Enquiry was convened by the C-in-C Middle East. The Court examined most painstakingly a cloud of witnesses, British and Greek, including 'Apollo' himself, but much crucial evidence was missing: in particular Mr Leeper evaded all attempts to examine him or his staff, and the Greek politicians from whom the reports came could not be called. On the evidence before it the Court entirely exonerated Force 133 and Apollo, and very sharply censured the Foreign Office officials responsible. Seventy-one of Apollo's men were in gaol and fifty-nine of them were executed by the Germans just before they withdrew: he believed that if the monthly subsidy had continued they could have bought their freedom. He is a good judge of such matters, and it is to be feared that he was right.[3]

7. Crete and the Islands

The Aegean was from the beginning a highway rather than a no-man's land, and Allied caique traffic was surprisingly little hampered by enemy action. The first caique operation from Smyrna sailed for the Piraeus in September 1941, and the route became so well established that in July 1943 SOE obtained facilities for a caique base of its own at Egrilar, on the Chesme peninsula, fifty miles west of Smyrna. In August 1943 a corresponding base was established on the coast of Thessaly, north of Skopelos, through which the British Mission and the guerillas received a considerable proportion of their supplies.

But the islands themselves were not promising ground for SOE, except as ports of call. There were few objectives calling for sabotage: the Axis garrisons were too large and the areas too restricted

---

[1] Telegram No. 393 of 19th August 1944; copy on SOE Archives File (CD) Greece 4.

[2] Chain No. 174 of 23rd August; copy on SOE Archives File (CD) Greece 4.

[3] The Report of the Court of Enquiry is available, with a full dossier of evidence, in SOE Archives: see also SOE Archives File (CD) Greece 4. Lord Selborne continued up to the end of the Coalition Government to press the Foreign Office unsuccessfully for some amends or apology.

for guerilla warfare: and, for the same reasons, EAM was not able to make much headway by its usual tactics of provocation and counter-provocation, so that political dispute was relatively muted. Three phases can perhaps be distinguished, in a tangle of small incidents.

First, up to the Italian surrender, the main interest was in in Crete, which was at that stage a point of great strategic importance. SOE officers had been infiltrated and had operated there in plain clothes as early as October 1941; they were at first serviceable mainly in helping the escape of British troops who had been harboured by the Cretans. During 1942 they were in contact with guerilla bands, which were necessarily small and scattered and were not encouraged by the British to take any violent action. Towards the end of that year it was decided to build upon this basis a 'Secret Army' which could be mobilised in the event of a British invasion. This was never required, but the foundations seem to have been well laid.

In 1943 some progress had also been made in Samos, Chios and Mytiline, as well as in Rhodes, Scarpanto and Symi in the Dodecanese. These Missions were still feeling their way when the news of the Italian surrender broke in September 1943.

This was followed at once by intense activity. Lieutenant Colonel Dolbey, of SOE's Cairo HQ, parachuted into Rhodes and opened negotiations, in the end fruitless through no fault of his, with the commander of the Italian garrison. General Carta, the Italian commander in Crete, made contact with an existing SOE Mission and offered co-operation, but his troops were too weak to fight without British military support; he himself was evacuated, but the Germans suffered only very minor losses in small local disturbances. An SOE Mission also dropped into Corfu and for a short space held the island in co-operation with the Italians: but the latter showed very little resolution in resisting the German counter-attack.

The one area in which the British felt strong enough to act was that of Cos, Leros and the Adriatic coast, and here SOE went ahead of the British regular forces. It held Cos with local forces until the RAF arrived: it seized Samos and accepted the surrender of an Italian division there: and it also briefly controlled Chios and Mytiline.

In this phase SOE was able to perform in an unusually precise and military manner just what was required of it, and it bears no blame for the subsequent débâcle, which unfortunately wrecked much of the preparatory work.

A new phase began in 1944, when the policy of GHQ, Middle East, was to harass and subvert without taking the risk of frontal attack. Regular forces were organised for hit-and-run raids, and there was a well-planned campaign against enemy-controlled shipping by the small naval and air forces available. Force 133 provided an indispensable background for this plan. For the first time small Missions in disguise were spread widely among the islands, and were in position as sources of intelligence and as local guides and friends for raiding forces by land and sea. They played an independent part mainly in the 'caique enticement scheme', designed to reduce enemy resources by bribing and blackmailing Greek skippers to desert, and their final 'bag' amounted to about 100 caiques of various sizes.

There was also in Crete Major Leigh-Fermor's* admirably executed coup which removed from the island Major-General Kreipe, the commander of the German 22nd Division.[1] The utmost care was taken to avoid involving the Cretans in reprisals, and these were in this instance successful. But unfortunately in July and August 1944 the Cretan Andartes broke out into open attacks, not instigated by SOE. The Germans lost about 120 killed and a dozen motor vehicles, but reacted instantly by burning thirty villages and executing over 1,000 innocent Cretans. The game was not worth pursuing on these terms; and the final objective, in Crete as in the other islands, was to harass steadily and to make preparations for a quiet transfer of control when the Germans surrendered or withdrew. This fortunately was achieved almost entirely without political complications: EAM existed, especially in Crete and Samos, but it had no wide popular backing and in the end authority was transferred without difficulty to the Greek Government.

The story of the Islands is on a small scale a very favourable instance of the correct and careful use of SOE methods in their developed form, and has left behind it little bitterness and historical controversy.

8. Conclusion

The public verdict on this story, which is in its broad outlines public property, is that the British Government created EAM and made a rod for its own back by doing so. The movement achieved little against the Germans and it led to a disastrous civil war which has created new divisions in Greek political life, as irreconcilable as the old ones. In addition, some 800,000 lives were lost out of a population of some 6,000,000: at least some of these might have been saved if the mountain war had never begun. Those who know a little more of the story emphasise this verdict by pointing to the success of Prometheus II and Apollo and lamenting that SOE was ever diverted by the schemes of military men from its proper clandestine role.

Colonel Woodhouse has already answered this line of argument

---

[1] Report of the capture of General Kreipe is given in SOE HQ War Diary, Mid-East and Balkans Section, p. 1365. [See also W. S. Moss, *Ill Met by Moonlight* (1950), an eye-witness account.]

* [P. M. Leigh-Fermor, born 1915, author.]

publicly, with convincing effect.[1] EAM was conceived without British instigation, and it began its campaign in the hills in 1942 with Communist leaders and under the inspiration of the Russian partisan technique. The raw material was already there. The mountains were full of men outside the law: this nucleus could be bound together and expanded by determined and aggressive leadership which only the Greek Communist Party could give. Once they were in the field the British supplied them: from October 1942 to October 1943 they were given arms, thereafter only gold and supplies. It was certainly of considerable importance that after the brilliant success at Gorgopotamas in November 1942 SOE in Cairo pushed ahead with large plans for guerilla war. British supplies undoubtedly nourished EAM through a difficult period: but in the end, when they made their bid for power, they had secured from German and Italian sources far more arms than the British ever gave them, and it is practically certain that they could have survived and obtained these arms even without British aid. EAM could hardly have been stopped except by a concerted and deliberate British attempt to crush it, even at the expense of the German war: and such an attempt could have succeeded only in the early stages of EAM's growth, perhaps not later than the spring of 1943.

To this it must be added that the one guerilla movement in Europe which was clearly sponsored, fed and controlled throughout solely by the British was that of Napoleon Zervas: whatever may be said to Zervas's discredit, there is no doubt that he proved a political card of great value against EAM. EAM were not left with a monopoly of the heroic myth of resistance: Zervas could neither be wholly destroyed nor wholly discredited. Greek governments since the Liberation have extended dangerously far into the collaborationist world: but they have never been simply the collaborationists in face of those who fought for Greece; the Communists did not secure a monopoly of resistance.

In the narrow military sense the guerillas at least repaid the small effort which they cost: but the margin is narrower than in Yugoslavia. It can be made to seem that a number of Axis divisions were held in Greece by partisan warfare, but this is an illusion: it was inevitable in any case that the exposed peninsula should be fairly strongly held. On the credit side there is only the damage done: this was considerable, and included serious interference with chrome and nickel production, but it was on the whole ill-coordinated, except for the short golden days of 'Harling', 'Animals' and 'Noah's Ark'. The Greek guerillas did not lack fighting spirit or ability, but they were a smaller and less effective military force than were Tito's Partisans in their best days.

---

[1] Letter to 'The Times', 14th January 1947.

There were also wider and less tangible military advantages. SOE was not itself an intelligence organisation, but the presence of some eighty British officers in Greece, with innumerable Greek contacts, was inevitably a rich source of information. When Sicily was invaded, and in a lesser degree on other occasions, SOE was able to play a useful part in strategic deception. It helped to rescue many British and Allied nationals: it was a relief organisation of some importance: it was at hand to negotiate with the Italians when they surrendered, and it was a useful channel of propaganda to German troops. Finally, it was able to do a little to impede the German policy of 'scorching the earth' as they withdrew. All these things were necessary and useful; we should have been so much the poorer if there had been no BLOs ready to turn their hand to a great variety of tasks.

British policy is therefore defensible and was probably inevitable in its main outlines. But its development in detail is a history of confusion and back-biting, and the British were perhaps lucky that the political consequences were not more serious. EAM at times looked capable of greater mischief than it ever achieved; in October 1944 General Scobie's forces could not have faced the EAM attack which they held off with difficulty in December, and it would have been politically impossible to eject EAM if it had once been installed in Athens. This must be set in part to the credit of the Russians. But the Greek Communist Party had in any event a stiffer task than that of Yugoslavia, and it was less well equipped to handle it. For one thing it had nothing serious to offer. Unlike Yugoslavia, Greece can never be rich except through commerce, and there are few Greeks however radical who can face with equanimity the idea of being locked up in their mountains to build the Communist State. For another, a 'Five Year Plan' and 'Soviet Federalism' make sense in Yugoslavia but not in Greece. The Greek Communists had been 'underground' only since 1935, and they were not (in spite of Metaxas's efforts) the only symbol of opposition to the régime: plenty of other equally ingenious politicians had also suffered mildly for their faith, and were now occupying their active minds with the problem of the succession to Metaxas. EAM thus, as it rose, bred opposition which was not reactionary opposition; it realised that this was the real enemy but it was never quite strong enough to beat it down. All it achieved was to create a new line of cleavage in Greek politics, now (1947) reinforced by the Slav alignment of EAM; this new cleavage may destroy Greece, but it is at least more mature and rational than the old personal rancours bequeathed by Constantine and Venizelos.

Prompt awareness of these new alignments was essential to a sound British policy towards Greece during the war: but at each stage awareness lagged fatally behind reality, and the British Government was never quite quick enough to control rather than follow the eel-like wrigglings of the politicians in exile. The problem of liaison with occupied Greece is an interesting one, as the experiment was here made in relatively favourable conditions. Britain was excellently represented in Greece, and from about January 1943 communication with Myers and Woodhouse was relatively free. But the difficulties were most formidable. As Woodhouse says in one of his reports, within Greece 'no one is ever free from the struggle for existence: everything else is secondary to it. This is why no one outside Greece can speak for the Greeks in Greece. Five minutes after leaving Greece, anyone is out of touch with the reality in Greece and disqualified from speaking for the Greeks . . . . I doubt whether any of the Greeks now discussing their country's future in the Middle East can even state the problems they are trying to solve.'[1] Voices penetrate thinly through this barrier, and at each stage there is delay. Myers and Woodhouse delay a little before committing officially to paper their first impression of each intangible change in the situation: they know that the cypher and signal staff is overburdened, and that there is no use wasting men's time with anything but 'firm' news. The lower levels in Cairo delay a little and bungle a little before forming a coherent picture of what is new, and attempting to impress it upon Directors and Brigadiers and Ambassadors. There is again delay here in transmitting firm and agreed recommendations to the high and icy levels on which policy is finally decided; and at each stage British decision is fogged by the conflicting advice of able but interested Greek exiles. High policy is set on the 'Six Colonels' while EAM and Zervas are becoming realities in the mountains: it is set on a brisk military development of the united guerillas while Myers and Woodhouse are gradually elucidating the political basis of EAM. In the autumn of 1943 it is set on expanding Zervas into the Greek Army *in partibus infidelium* while Woodhouse is beginning to despair of the possibility of keeping Zervas in the field at all. The time-lag between fact and the reaction to it was never less than two or three months and it was often longer.

There are not many devices which were left untried to overcome this. The agents employed were men of mutually complementary gifts, whose agreement ought to have carried great weight in circles which would normally disagree. A great technical effort was made to give them the communications they required. Woodhouse was certainly kept in Greece too long without a break, but Myers at least came out as soon as was reasonable: it took a man some months to grasp the realities of the new world in the mountains and a really quick relief of agents would have been worse than useless. Cairo was active in

---

[1] Report of 26th May 1944, p. 11; copy on SOE Archives File (CD) Greece 3 – Pt II.

sending men from the offices to see what was happening in the field – Colonel Stevens and Colonel Budge in 1943, Brigadier Barker-Benfield in 1944. Full facilities were given to the Foreign Office to be independently represented, though it did not use them to the full. Even the exiled Greeks had pretty free access through agents of their own to political circles within Greece.

There is in fact little more that can be suggested on the technical level. It is only possible to draw attention to the problem and to the immense gifts of adaptability and imagination which must be found in high quarters if British policy is to maintain initiative and cohesion in such circumstances.

CHAPTER XIX

Albania[1]

Albania belongs to the same pattern as Yugoslavia and Greece: it was a 'guerilla country', in which the chief political problem was set by the emergence of a 'Popular Front' cast in the mould of Tito's Partisans and the EAM. The complexities of Albanian politics even exceed those of Yugoslavia and Greece, although they are on a more primitive level: national unity is split by three religions, Catholic, Orthodox and Moslem, and by innumerable tribal allegiances. The educated class is so small that these divisions and cross-divisions are very superficially coloured by Western ideas, and the situation is ultimately explicable only in terms of very primitive and very complex feuds and loyalties. SOE was early interested in Albania, as it had been occupied by the Italians in April 1939, two years before the fall of Yugoslavia and Greece: but its later fate was never of much significance, either in politics or in strategy, and a very brief account must suffice.

The Italian annexation of Albania had been recognised by the Chamberlain Government, and there was thus no legitimate government in exile. King Zog* was however at large and maintained certain connections with Albania, so that his claims played a part in the pattern not altogether dissimilar to those of Peter of Yugoslavia and George of Greece. The situation can be set out (somewhat diagrammatically) as follows:

(1)   The 'Quisling' Governments, at first nominated by Italy, after September 1943 by Germany.

(2)   The Zogist or 'Legality' movement, headed by a certain Abbas Kupi.

(3)   The 'Ball Kombetar', in effect the 'right wing' of pre-war opposition to Zog.

(4)   The FNC (National Liberation Front) to which was related the

---

[1]   There is a very full narrative of the Allied Military Mission April 1943–January 1945 by Lord Harcourt. [1908–79, 2nd viscount 1922, banker]. See also Anthony Quayle's novel 'Eight Hours from England' (by one of the British Liaison Officers), and Julian Amery's 'Sons of the Eagle', which deals thoroughly with the politics of Northern (Gheg) Albania.

*   [Ahmed Zogu, 1895–1961, King of Albania 1928, exiled 1939.]

Albanian National Liberation Army (LNC, or using the English translation ANLA): this was in effect the left-wing of opposition to Zog, organised and controlled by the Communist Party.

This development was not clear in all its aspects until late in 1943, and it must always be remembered that behind it lay feudal, tribal and religious rivalries: the intervention of the Great Powers, Western, Axis, and Russian, and their barrage of propaganda gave it an air of simplicity which was quite superficial.

The first SOE attempt at penetration, made from Yugoslavia in April 1941, was assisted by a very mixed party of anti-Zog Albanians: the attempt broke down and Major Oakley-Hill, who led it, was captured, but many of his Albanian supporters remained at large. SOE made no further attempts until April 1943, but the endemic brigandage had in 1942 grown to the status of a guerilla movement. The 'National Liberation Front' programme was proclaimed at the Peza Conference in September 1942, on lines exactly parallel to those set out a little earlier in Yugoslavia and Greece: liaison at long range was established both with Tito and with EAM. The reactions were in outline of a very normal pattern: the FNC grew by a policy of active resistance, and at the same time it created by its own activities an anti-Communist wing of the resistance, the Ball Kombetar, which was at first equally anti-Axis, or at least anti-Italian. Like EAM, the FNC used such of the old leaders as it could: Abbas Kupi, a Zogist, was one of its first military commanders.

The first SOE Mission, under Lieutenant Colonel N. L. D. Maclean,* was dropped to EAM reception in Northern Greece in April 1943, and worked its way up into Albania with the assistance of EAM. Maclean very shortly found himself involved in the usual type of Balkan negotiation, and was present at the conference of Labinot in July which held out some temporary prospects of unity. (At that moment, it will be remembered, there was a similar temporary appearance of unity in Greece, and relations between Tito and the British were at their best.) In July and August 1943 four other SOE Missions were infiltrated, and Albania began to be (by SOE's standards) relatively open territory. One of the main objectives given these missions was the Albanian oil-field, almost the only important economic target in the country, and an elaborate plan was made for an attack by BLOs and guerillas. But the latter would not move without air support – not readily available on the eve of Salerno – so that the whole scheme fell through.

In September there broke the great alarm of the Italian surrender. The Germans were alert and had already begun to move troops to

---

* [1918–86, Conservative MP 1954–64; distinguish from Sir Fitzroy Maclean.]

strategic positions (hitherto Albania had been held almost entirely by Italians): but on the other side British Liaison Officers, Italians, and guerillas were all equally taken by surprise. One BLO, Major Seymour, penetrated to Italian HQ in Tirana: but while he negotiated resistance in one room, the Italians were negotiating surrender with the Germans in another, and the situation elsewhere was similar. There was a little sporadic resistance, and several thousand Italians took to the hills: but the rest were quietly rounded up and disarmed, and a comparatively small part of their weapons reached guerilla hands.

The Albanian political situation was by this time occupying at least a fraction of the time of higher authority, and it was decided in September 1943 to send in a more senior officer fully briefed for an effort to unite all good Albanians against the Axis. Brigadier E. F. Davies, MC,* was chosen for this task, and before he left was interviewed both by the Minister of State, Mr Casey, and by the C-in-C, General Wilson: his detailed directive laid it down (*inter alia*) that 'The policy of His Majesty's Government . . . in Albania is to support all anti-Axis elements, wherever they may be . . . provided always that they continue to combat the Axis actively and wholeheartedly.'[1] This was an intermediate stage between policy in Yugoslavia (where Mihailovitch was shortly to be abandoned) and policy in Greece (where the Foreign Office was now primarily concerned to reduce the power of EAM): but when Brigadier Davies reached Albania, it very shortly proved that he had little choice but to throw in his lot with FNL. German political warfare was proving extremely efficient: the Germans played on Albanian nationalist aspirations for expansion at the expense of Yugoslavia and Greece, which had necessarily been passed over in silence by the Allies; and they held open ample opportunities for Albanians to get money and arms in the German service. The Communists ably abetted them by making their first target those Albanian resisters who remained outside the FNC,[2] and by proclaiming their affiliation with movements in Yugoslavia and Greece, traditional enemies of Albania. Sporadic civil war broke out in November and December 1943, and inevitably drove Ball Kombetar into the arms of the Germans. At the same time the Germans were very active in offensive drives through the mountains, which FNC was quite unable to resist even with limited British help, and the winter proved a very hard one both for FNC and for the British. From the middle of December Brigadier Davies was 'on the run' and out of wireless contact, and he was eventually wounded and captured in the high

---

[1] London HQ War Diary, Mid-East and Balkans Section, p. 1095.
[2] A very interesting Communist Party directive of 3rd November 1943 is at Appendix A to the Albanian History.
* [Nicknamed Trotsky; see his *Illyrian Venture* (1952).]

mountains on 8th January 1944. His second-in-hand, Colonel Arthur Nicholls, got away, but was so badly frost-bitten that he died shortly afterwards.[1]

Ball Kombetar was now hopelessly compromised, by co-operation with the Germans, but one last effort was made to find a centre of resistance independent of FNC. Colonel N. D. L. Maclean had come out after his replacement by Brigadier Davies,[2] and it appeared from reports from the field that Abbas Kupi was proclaiming the existence of a new anti-Axis movement acknowledging the leadership of Zog. It was proposed that Colonel Maclean should return to Albania and see what could be made of this. Much discussion arose, involving the Foreign Secretary and the Chiefs of Staff: the Mission was in the end carried out, with a directive so carefully hedged as to avoid all danger-ous commitments, and it proved conclusively that Kupi had been driven by FNL too close to the verge of collaboration to be of any value.[3]

In 1944, therefore, action against the Germans was possible only through FNC, who recovered and expanded quickly after the set-backs of the winter. They were supported effectively. Supplies came in well by air and sea.[4] Land Forces Adriatic conducted active commando operations on the coast: and the Balkan Air Force was able to give some useful close support. In addition some forty men of the Long Range Desert Group were dropped to the Peza area in September 1944 and gave invaluable assistance in the last stages of the battle. The evidence suggests that the Albanians fought well in the final German withdrawal, which was complete by November 1944: attacks were pressed well home, particularly when air support was available, and some 6,000–7,000 German troops were killed, and 500 captured, with a considerable loss of stores. The 21st Mountain Corps had already been severely handled in Albania before it ran the gauntlet of the Partisans in Yugoslavia.[5]

These final operations had been discussed amicably in a series of meetings between Lieutenant Colonel Lord Harcourt and FNC repre-

---

1 He was posthumously awarded the George Cross. [He had gone to Albania from a post at Court in St James's.]

2 See his report dated 14th December 1943, summarised in the SOE HQ War Diary, Mid-East and Balkans Section, p. 1291.

3 Mr Julian Amery went with this Mission and has told Abbas Kupi's story fully in his 'Sons of the Eagle'.

4 Full figures in Albanian History, App. P. They include (e.g.) about 7,000 rifles, 2,000 MGs, 5,000 Stens. The money sent in amounted to 75,000 sovereigns, 6,000 gold 'Napoleons' and 36,000 paper 'Napoleons'. FNC received about 33,000 gold sovereigns, other Albanians (except by theft) only about 7,000. (Albanian History, p. 162.)

5 Above p. 443.

sentatives at Bari late in July 1944,[1] and there was no serious friction in the field. The British had not seriously interfered with FNC's political plans, and FNC was not ashamed to accept military advice and guidance where they met its own interests. The BLOs, and their American colleagues, played an active part in the fighting, and they carried out a number of small but brilliant operations of their own, often virtually without support. In February 1944, Squadron Leader Hands, with two British sergeants, very effectively sabotaged the chrome mines at Kan; and in June Major Smiley and a small party of Abbas Kupi's guerillas laid explosives on an important bridge at Gjolos while German traffic was passing overhead, and thus put the main Durazzo-Tirana-Scutari road out of action for a considerable period. These are merely two notable episodes among many: the most unusual of them perhaps was the successful evacuation in mid-winter 1943–4 of a party of fifteen American nurses whose aircraft had crashed in the heart of Albania.*

This was clearly a case in which a small but useful military dividend had been earned by limited investment in the guerilla movement: and the political consequences, though unwelcome, were of no great significance on the international level.

---

[1]   Minutes dated 23rd August as App. K to Albanian History.
*   [See Foot and Langley, *MI9*, pp. 187–9.]

CHAPTER XX

The South-Eastern Satellites

General

In spite of local divergencies Bulgaria, Roumania and Hungary for SOE purposes formed a group as clearly marked as that of Yugoslavia, Greece and Albania. All three countries, though perhaps anti-German at heart, had entered the war on the German side in the hope of satisfying ancient national ambitions, and so long as that hope was alive there was a fair degree of national unity on the Axis side. But when the tide turned the main national problem was to change sides in such a way as not to lose all, and more than all, that they had gained from Germany.

In each of these countries the army and the police systems held together very well, and had long experience in dealing with internal trouble-makers: in addition the terrain was relatively unsuitable for partisan warfare. Access was impossible by sea, by air it was not easy, even after the invasion of Italy. Thus SOE's work was technically difficult, and in addition these countries were strategically more relevant to the Russian front than to the Allied offensives in the Mediterranean. Their priority was thus relatively low, and low priority was quite inadequate to solve the technical problem: so that SOE's dealings with them are largely a story of individual gallantry and frustration.

1. Bulgaria[1]

Bulgaria was in some ways the most promising of the three. SOE had been able to do little there before the collapse in 1941,[2] but it had useful contacts with the main opposition parties: the Peasant Party and George Dimitrov, to whom fell the inheritance of the great peasant leader Stamboliski, murdered in 1923: the Military League, inspired

---

[1] Good short narratives by Mr Norman Davies and Major Ian Macpherson are available with the SOE Histories.
[2] Above p. 107.

by Colonel Damian Velchev, who had created the short-lived 'progressive' government of Kimon Georgiev in 1934: and the Protogerovist Macedonians, perhaps the less disreputable wing of the Macedonian Revolutionary Organisation. Furthermore, Slav sentiment had been too strong in Bulgaria to permit a declaration of war on Russia, the creator of their country, and a Russian Minister remained in Sofia throughout the war. SOE's activities followed naturally from these two lines of approach.

The first line was to develop contacts with the opposition parties and to use the Jerusalem station for 'black' propaganda in their names. The main asset here was the assistance of George Dimitrov, who had escaped from Yugoslavia after the abortive attempt to infiltrate Bulgaria from that quarter in April 1941. Ceaseless efforts were made from Istanbul to reopen some line of communication with his friends, and there were times at which messages were successfully exchanged through slow and complicated channels. But no wireless station was ever established in Bulgaria, no arms or supplies were infiltrated, and so little came of this that it would be useless to follow the course of events in detail. The opposition was well watched; and perhaps saw little advantage in taking risks.

There were moments when the other line of approach looked much more promising. In August 1942 the Russian 'black' station broadcasting to Bulgaria launched a campaign on behalf of the Patriotic Front (OF), which purported to be a coalition of all democratic parties against Fascism, and this slogan was spontaneously re-echoed by SOE's Jerusalem station. This was clearly part of the general Russian 'political warfare' plan for the Balkans, slightly adapted to the special conditions of Bulgaria, and there was a stronger case in Bulgaria than in any other area for accepting the Russian lead without question. There was in addition some independent evidence of the affiliation of the non-Communist opposition to such a 'Front', and even of partisan warfare on a very small scale.

SOE's first active step was to brief Bailey in December 1942 to ask Mihailovitch for facilities to establish contact with the OF: but for obvious reasons Mihailovitch and his political advisers took all possible steps to obstruct such a development. This was particularly unfortunate, as Mihailovitch's territory was of crucial importance. The Bulgarian frontiers had been advanced on the west to include most of Macedonia, and even part of Serbia itself, and there was here a frontier of mixed population in difficult country, through which infiltration should be possible. As Mihailovitch was obstructive, the only course was to enlist the assistance of Tito's Partisans, who had strong reasons of their own for wishing to establish contact. In September 1943 Major Mostyn-Davies and a small party were dropped in Albania, and made an arduous march across country to East Serbia, under

Partisan escort. The intention was to establish there a base area to which supplies could be dropped if it proved that the Bulgarian partisans possessed sufficient reality to be worthy of support. In December Mostyn-Davies succeeded in meeting a Bulgarian leader, 'Ivan': conditions in the area were extremely difficult (it will be remembered that this was the time of the final British break with Mihailovitch), but it was decided that the importance of Bulgaria justified a desperate attempt to build something on this basis. Some supplies were dropped successfully, and in January 1944 Major Frank Thompson joined Mostyn-Davies with a small British party. The plan was that he should build up the base area, while Mostyn-Davies did his best to push forward into Bulgaria.

Major Thompson[1] has become a figure of some significance in Bulgarian history. He was the son of Edward Thompson, an author of distinction, and was himself a poet of great promise: he was also a convinced and idealistic Communist, like many of his contemporaries who had grown up in the period of the Spanish Civil War and Munich. His first work for SOE had been as a BLO in Greece, but he had found it impossible to keep in line with British policy towards EAM and had asked for employment elsewhere. His Bulgarian expedition unfortunately was doomed almost from the outset by the conditions of the time in Serbia: it had no firm base except in Partisan support and at this time desperate efforts were being made by all parties, Germans, Bulgarians and Cetniks, to crush the Partisan movement in Serbia before it got beyond control.[2] It was not till the late spring of 1944 that Force 133 and Tito in alliance were able to get the upper hand, and meantime the small British party was ceaselessly harassed. Finally, on 22nd March, Mostyn-Davies and some others were captured and shot by the Bulgarian police: Thompson narrowly escaped.

In spite of these great difficulties he kept contact with his base and managed to equip some 500 Bulgarian partisans. This party in May 1944 recklessly launched itself on an expedition into Bulgaria: and Thompson felt that it was his duty to go with them, though the chance of survival was clearly negligible. They were ambushed and captured, and Thompson was eventually shot in Sofia, after a mock trial in which he greatly impressed all by his nobility of bearing. He alone, of all the SOE officers who died in Eastern Europe, is thought of kindly by the country in which he fell: his memory is publicly cele-

---

[1] See in particular the memorial volume 'There is a spirit in Europe', with a note by Thompson's father, the late Edward Thompson. [E. J. Thompson, 1886–1946, missionary and poet; in *DNB* with brief mention of his elder son, W. F., 1920–44; his younger son was E. P. Thompson (1924–93), the radical historian.]

[2] See above p. 427.

brated, a village has been named after him, his family have been cere-
moniously received as official guests of the State. This is of course
not done without ulterior motive: but it is none the less important that
a generation of young Bulgarians will associate the name of England
with the martyr of Bulgarian liberation, Frank Thompson.

Bulgarian affairs were not too easy for SOE to handle at this stage,
as the Bulgarian section of Force 133 remained in Cairo under the
C-in-C Middle East, while the sections responsible for Yugoslavia and
Greece, the only lines of access to Bulgaria, moved forward into Italy
and came more directly under the control of AFHQ and later of the
Balkan Air Force. Expenditure up to £50,000 on the Patriotic Front
was sanctioned by the Treasury in February 1944, and it was acknowledged on all hands that it was of extreme importance to force Bulgaria
out of the war.

The only other line of entry, if the Serbian frontier proved impossible, was from the strip of Greek territory on the Thracian sea-
board which had been annexed to Bulgaria. Here there was some
Greek resistance under a loose and ineffective confederation of semi-
brigands known as the 'Capetanos', who maintained a precarious
existence harassed both by the Bulgarians and by EAM. In April
1944 Major Harrington was established here, under difficulties
almost as great as those of Mostyn-Davies in Serbia, but it was not
until July that he made any useful contact with the OF guerillas. He
had been joined in July by Major Ian Macpherson, and by Captain
Riddle in August. Early in August Harrington and Macpherson
entered Bulgaria, intending to make for the Provdiv and Sofia areas
respectively and there to receive supplies. The OF partisans proved
to be poorly armed, but much better in spirit than had been expected;
the two British officers were confident that with a very small supply
of arms they could give a decisive shock to the wavering spirit of
the Bulgarian army. In Yugoslavia, too, things were looking better:
after a good deal of delay Major Strachey was established in
Macedonia on 21st August and made contact almost at once with
OF representatives from Sofia.

But all this came too late. The Russians attacked in Roumania on
20th August, and it was announced on the 24th that Mushanov, the
rather ambiguous representative of the ambiguous Bulgarian government of Muraviev, had arrived in Cairo to ask for an armistice. Supplies
to the SOE Missions with the OF were stopped while these negotiations with the 'legitimate' government were in progress: but the
Russians had no such delicate scruples. On 5th September they
declared war on Bulgaria; within forty-eight hours a coup d'état had
been made by the OF and the Military League, and on 8th September
the Bulgarians were at war with Germany. Harrington and Macpherson
quietly made their way to Sofia, and declared themselves to the

Russians, who (with the utmost courtesy) expelled them from the country on 24th September.

SOE could extract little comfort from this conclusion, except that George Dimitrov was received in Sofia with enthusiasm: four of his Peasant Party followers joined the new Government, and Colonel Velchev was its Minister of War. But (as it proved) even their tentative relations with the West were sufficient to exclude them from any real share of power, and their organisations were branded as traitorous and dissolved in the summer of 1947. Such of their leaders as could be caught were executed by the Communists.

2. Roumania[1]

From August 1941, when SOE's original wireless station was captured,[2] until September 1943 radio communication with Roumania was cut, and the primary object was to restore it. SOE's Roumanian section in Istanbul were able through a wide range of agents to maintain indirect contact with the Maniu and Bratianu groups, and the Roumanian talent for intrigue exercised itself in devising similar contacts in the neutral capitals, Lisbon,[3] Berne and Stockholm. But these channels were ambiguous and slow; of some value for intelligence, but practically useless for the encouragement of resistance or for effective negotiation. In December 1941 a fairly precise offer of collaboration was received from Maniu, and in March 1942 two radio sets were actually infiltrated by a shady Turk, who possessed diplomatic cover as honorary Consul for Finland. One of these reached Maniu, but for unknown reasons it was never used: possibly Maniu was alarmed because the Turk was subsequently, on other grounds, arrested in Budapest. It was clear that the politicians of the old opposition were concerting action and biding their time, and that the Antonescu régime was not prepared to take decisive steps against them; but the prospects of organised political action against the Axis remained at this stage of the war extremely remote, and the chances of sporadic resistance and guerilla war were even worse. An attempt was begun in June 1942 through SOE's 'black' Roumanian station in Jerusalem to sponsor an active movement, led by a legendary hero 'Vlaicu', and two agents were actually infiltrated to distribute 'Vlaicu'

---

[1] With SOE Histories Narrative by Lieutenant Colonel de Chastelain with useful annexes by Lieutenant Colonel Boxshall. [E. G. Boxshall, 1899–1984, born in Bucharest, on SOE's Roumanian desk in London, Foreign Office SOE adviser 1959–82. See also I. Porter, *Operation Autonomous* (1989); Porter (born 1913) was on de Chastelain's Mission, described on page 498 below.]

[2] Above p. 109.

[3] Note Ciano's reference to a leakage about this in his Diary, 29th January 1943.

propaganda: but this was an activity which could never have more than a minor 'nuisance value'.

This was discouraging. Nevertheless, Roumania was important and by the spring of 1943 there were British Missions working with fair success in Yugoslavia, Greece and Albania. It was therefore natural to consider whether the deadlock could be broken by the dispatch of a mission to establish proper communications and to apply some continuous impulse to the Roumanian politicians. Several mixed British and Roumanian teams were put in training, and steps were taken to recruit further Roumanian volunteers in Canada. Maniu was approached as to the possibility of receiving a British Liaison Officer, but his reply was delayed and was evasive when it came, and it was decided to go ahead without his approval. Captain David Russell, MC, and a Roumanian wireless operator named Turcanu, were dropped into Mihailovitch's territory in June 1943, with the object of infiltrating into Roumania across the Danube. Mihailovitch was co-operative – the Roumanian brand of opposition politics was less unsympathetic to him than the Bulgarian Patriotic Front – and the two men crossed the Danube with a Serb guide on 22nd August. They were successful in contacting the local representatives of the National Peasant Party, in establishing a good hiding-place, and in opening wireless communication. But this good start was followed by a disaster never completely explained. One day early in September Turcanu returned to the hiding-place in the woods to find Captain Russell lying dead and the hut stripped of everything worth stealing: the Serb guide had disappeared. This was probably a plain case of murder and robbery: at least it was not followed by any enemy action, and Turcanu's wireless set remained in use.

During this period a rather curious one-way channel of communication had also been opened to Maniu by means of coded messages in the BBC German broadcasts: the code had been sent in to Maniu by hand, and the BBC German service was used because it was actually better received in Roumania than the Roumanian service, which was heavily jammed.

Through these channels arrangements were made to receive another party, consisting of Colonel de Chastelain, Major Porter and a Roumanian officer, and after a series of failures they finally dropped into Roumania on 22nd December 1943. But they landed 14 kms from the dropping area and were captured next day by Antonescu's police. The sequence of events which followed was much the most important part of SOE's interventions in Roumania, and it is unfortunate that it cannot be made fully intelligible without a detailed study of the intricacies of Roumanian politics and personalities, and of the discussions which took place between and within the Foreign Offices of the great Allies. What follows is no more than a rough outline.[1]

As early as May 1943 Maniu had put forward a plan for a coup d'état against Antonescu; this was known then as 'Colonel Black's Scheme', and depended on the co-operation of certain friends well-placed in high official positions. Later in 1943, when Colonel de Chastelain's Mission was being prepared, Maniu had indicated by radio that Antonescu was now ready to 'stand down' in favour of the plotters: so that Antonescu himself was in some sense implicated in the plot. This knowledge, and the civility with which they were treated, encouraged his British prisoners to treat with Antonescu as equals and to transmit to him verbally and in writing messages encouraging him to dispatch envoys asking for an armistice. This was apparently well enough received; the prisoners were well treated and were given facilities to send out a coded message explaining their position. The Russian winter offensive of 1943–4 was now in full swing, and had made plain to all what should already have been sufficiently obvious, that the Roumanian annexations in South Russia were absolutely valueless. The disputed territories of Bessarabia and Bukovina, annexed by the Russians in 1940, might also have to be abandoned, but there was still a chance that co-belligerency might regain the part of Transylvania lost to Hungary by the Vienna Diktat in 1940. Antonescu therefore sent out an envoy, Prince Stirbey,[2] who reached Cairo on 15th March: somewhat injudiciously, the British permitted Stirbey's arrival to be published in the Press, and (whether as a result or not) Antonescu was summoned to the presence of the Führer, to be personally chastised and 'stiffened'.[3] A message from the C-in-C Middle East, urging him to refuse and to resist, was not delivered until 25th March on his return from Hitler's HQ.

Meanwhile, early in March 1944, the last phase of the Russian winter offensive had opened, and at the end of the month it swept through Bessarabia and its spearheads were in Moldavia with nothing but their own exhaustion to stop them from walking forward to Ploesti.

Conditions were thus exactly right for a Roumanian coup d'état and declaration of co-belligerency: the Roumanians had something of value to offer to the Allies, and the Germans were in no position to stage a counter-stroke. It was perhaps unfortunate that there were two separate *foci* of negotiation. In Cairo Stirbey negotiated with the Ambassadors

---

[1] There is a very detailed chronology of events from 1st March to 30th April 1944 annexed to the SOE 'Roumanian History' (Colonel de Chastelain's narrative).

[2] He was brother-in-law of Lieutenant Colonel Boxshall, the head of SOE's Roumanian Section in London.

[3] The other German move to consolidate the south-east in this crisis was the occupation of Hungary: see below p. 504.

of the three Powers; and the three Powers cumbrously agreed on Armistice terms, which were not handed to Stirbey until 13th April. In Bucharest De Chastelain, though formally a prisoner, had become in effect an Allied envoy, negotiating both with Antonescu and with his ally or adversary Maniu. Antonescu had asked De Chastelain to use his radio set to dispatch Antonescu's reply to General Maitland Wilson's message: De Chastelain rejected the first draft, which dwelt uselessly on the need for guarantees against Russia, and received a new draft for transmission on 29th March. It was then found that the essential crystals had been stolen from the wireless set, and De Chastelain's only recourse was to reveal that Maniu possessed an SOE wireless set, that brought in by the ambiguous Turk in 1942 but never used. He was permitted to see Maniu, and on 2nd April he urged on him privately the importance of making his coup at this unique moment: Maniu agreed and undertook to rise 'next week'. There was again a technical delay and Antonescu's message was not finally transmitted until 13th April: on the same day SOE sent the Armistice terms to De Chastelain for delivery to Antonescu and Maniu. Through the same channel Allied air support was promised for the Roumanian change of sides.

From this point, which should have been the point of decision, the tide recedes and dies away in useless bargaining. The Russians had halted: the Germans were counter-attacking a little in Eastern Galicia and were doubtless pulling every lever they could reach in Roumanian politics: the Allies on 4th April had bombed Bucharest with heavy loss of civilian life – a method of hastening the Roumanian decision which SOE was convinced would defeat itself. In Antonescu's circles the overwhelming fear of Russian occupation and vengeance reasserted itself: Maniu made no open move. Early in May De Chastelain was prevented from sending further messages and on 23rd May the prisoners were put under close arrest. At the same time the Russians began to take a high line about the British treachery in secretly sending an envoy to Roumania to treat with Antonescu, without prior consultation among the Allies. Maniu was still in wireless touch, but this Russian protest effectively scotched plans for putting in further SOE/OSS parties: the Russians, it must be admitted, had reasonable enough ground for suspicion in Antonescu's ambiguous attitude and the little they knew of De Chastelain's dealing with him.

This was an important opportunity missed; and the weakness of the SOE position inside Roumania certainly contributed to the failure. The Roumanians would never have been anything but evasive: but a strong British party (or parties) at liberty and working closely with Maniu might well have forced their hands by a blend of threats and cajolery and promises of Allied aid.

The final coup was staged without any such close co-ordination. On 5th August Antonescu, still undecided, paid his last visit to Hitler, and failed to make good his vague intention of withdrawing from the Axis. In the same period Maniu's coup was being brought up to scratch once more, and it appeared at last to be firmly appointed for 26th August. But the Russian offensive in Moldavia on 20th August produced an instant débâcle: on its first two days the Russians broke through completely, and there was no longer a Roumanian front. On the night of the 22nd Mihai Antonescu approached De Chastelain with the offer to revolt independently against his brother, Marshal Antonescu: on the 23rd King Michael* arrested the Marshal and set in motion the whole machinery of the Maniu plot, which its original sponsor had never ventured to use. The coup worked perfectly: the Government was taken over without the slightest friction, and De Chastelain in effect became once more the envoy of His Majesty's Government. The SOE wireless set held by Maniu had broken down again: so on 24th August De Chastelain was flown out to General Wilson's HQ in a Roumanian aircraft, leaving Major Porter to maintain liaison in Bucharest. A simple signals plan was brought into operation using Roumanian sets, and next day, Turcanu, the original operator of Captain Russell's party, was released from gaol and restored one of the SOE sets to working order. Through these channels it was possible to arrange the well-timed Allied air support which enabled the new Roumanian Government to hold Bucharest against German counter-attack.

From this point the story is one of military action and of diplomatic negotiation through ordinary channels. It had been a disappointing one for SOE. 'Colonel Black's Scheme' in the end worked perfectly, but it was too late to be more than the recognition of a *fait accompli*, of little use either to the Allies or to Roumania. It might well have come sooner, if luck had favoured SOE a little. The death of Captain Russell and the capture of De Chastelain were both disasters outside its control. They showed how high the chance of failure was: SOE might perhaps have re-insured by doubling and re-doubling the number of attempts, but there is a limit to the number of 'forlorn hopes' for which a commander can call, and it would have been a hard decision to put more brave men in peril for so uncertain a gain.

3. Hungary[1]

The political situation was less favourable in Hungary than in any other country in Eastern Europe. The Horthy** régime had been the stable centre of Magyar national feeling ever since the fall of Bela

---

[1] SOE 'Hungarian History' by Major G. I. Klauber.

* [Born 1921, King of Roumania 1927–30 and from 1940, abdicated under Communist pressure 1947.]

** [M. Horthy, 1868–1957, Austro-Hungarian admiral, Regent of Hungary 1920–44.]

Kun's* Communist régime in 1919. Parties of the Left Centre, both Socialist and Peasant, were permitted to exist and even to conduct a little harmless propaganda, but they were far too effectively controlled to constitute a dangerous opposition. The Communists were held within very narrow limits, and the régime was much more in danger from the Right, where there were a number of demagogic groups largely financed by Germany and spouting various adaptations of Nazism, anti-Semitic, anti-bourgeois and intensely nationalist. In 1939 Germany had permitted the Magyars to gain at the expense of Czechoslovakia, and in 1941 at the expense of Roumania and Yugoslavia. This was far from satisfying the Magyar passion for the historic frontiers of the Kingdom of St Stephen; intelligent Hungarians knew that they were being played with by the Germans, and they hated them. But they could expect nothing from the Allies: plainly an Allied victory would cost Hungary all it had gained from Czechoslovakia and Yugoslavia, and it would perhaps also mean the full restoration of Roumania – only on this last point was there any room for diplomatic manoeuvre.

SOE had thus never a chance of organising an opposition in Hungary: on the political side it could only work through individual believers in the Allied cause, and hope for contacts within the circle of the Horthy régime. [PASSAGE DELETED ON GROUNDS OF NATIONAL SECURITY.] D Section's activities (which were strongly discouraged by HM Minister in Budapest)** had wide ramifications and bore very little fruit. A good deal of clandestine propaganda was produced and circulated: use was made of the sentimental link between Hungary and Poland to encourage work into Poland:[2] and a small group was established which was willing to accept explosives and consider direct action. This group remained in existence after the break with Hungary; but was finally liquidated in April 1942, when one of its members was executed and others imprisoned for planning an attack on an armaments factory at Györ.

Mr Davidson was withdrawn just before the German attack on Yugoslavia: he was captured with Sir Ronald Campbell's party from the Belgrade Legation, but secured his release under diplomatic cover. He had succeeded in evacuating a small party of Hungarians to play their part in Bailey's general plan of clandestine broadcasts[3] to the

---

1 [Footnote deleted.]
2 MI(R) were involved in this as well as D Section.
3 Above p. 142.
* [Born 1886, founded Hungarian Communist Party 1918, seized power March, fled August 1919, victim of Soviet purge *c.* 1939.]
** [(Sir) O. St C. O'Malley, 1887–1974, Minister in Budapest 1939–41, Ambassador to Poland 1942–5, to Portugal 1945–7, knight 1943.]

Balkans: Hungarian transmissions were begun from SOE's Jerusalem station, but otherwise there was no effective contact with Hungary, and the work was to begin again.

The weakness of SOE's position in what followed was that at each stage the initiative lay with the Hungarian Government, or with a section of it, and SOE never possessed any independent leverage by which to force action upon it. The old Prime Minister, Teleki,* had committed suicide in April 1943, in despair at the unlimited success of Germany: his successor, Kallay, was less distasteful to the Germans, but he was also anxious to reinsure against Balkan rivals, and still more against the Russians, by keeping a link open with the Western Allies. SOE's Hungarian Section was at first based on Istanbul, and from quite an early stage was obtaining useful economic intelligence from within the Hungarian Legation in Ankara and the Consulate in Istanbul. By June 1942[1] there were feelers from official circles, intensified during the winter of that year. A distinguished scientist, Professor Szentgyörgy,[2] appeared in Istanbul, with a scheme for an anti-German coalition government in which he should be Prime Minister: and there were other SOE contacts in Madrid. One of these led to the first attempt to introduce an agent: a Hungarian, Lieutenant Klement, was dropped in Poland in March 1943 and a wireless set was taken in to Budapest for him by a Croatian diplomat. Klement reached Budapest successfully, but so long after the appointed date that the Croat had destroyed the wireless set: Klement remained at large, and occasional messages came from him through Poland, but he was of no practical value as a contact.

These tentative approaches were brought together into a single channel in August 1943, a critical point of the war; a minor Hungarian official, Veres Laszlo,** then appeared in Istanbul and offered unconditional surrender on behalf of a powerful group within the Government, consisting of the Prime Minister (Kallay), the Minister of the Interior, and the Chief of the General Staff. Once the authority of this approach had been established, this negotiation was a matter of diplomatic history, with which SOE was not very intimately

---

1   SOE HQ War Diary, Mid-East and Balkans Section, Vol. I, p. 105. Matters were further confused by the activities of the Archduke Otto and of Tibor Eckhardt and the 'Free Hungarians' in the USA. (The Italians had at least an inkling of what was going on: Ciano's Diary 29th January 1943.)

2   Nobel Prize Winner in Biochemistry, discoverer of Vitamin C, Hon. D.Sc. of Oxford July 1947. [1893–1986, emigrated to USA 1947.]

*   [Count P. Teleki, 1879–1941, Prime Minister of Hungary 1920–21, 1939–41, killed himself when German troops crossed Hungary to attack Yugoslavia – Mackenzie misdates his death by a slip in next line.]

**   [For Laszlo Veress, 1908–80, see his widow L-L. Veress, *Clear the Line* (Chapel Hill, NC, 1995), ed. by his daughter Dalma Takacs.]

concerned. In spite of the apparent boldness of the Hungarian initiative, the Hungarians contemplated no action until they had some guarantee that the Anglo-Americans in Italy would reach Hungary before the Russians (as then seemed possible), and would protect the existing régime against 'Communism'. The British on their side would give no guarantees, and demanded action against the Germans as evidence of Hungarian good faith. This is perhaps the essence of a complicated story; negotiations dragged on for a long time, and it fell to SOE to attempt to extract some advantage from them by putting Hungarian goodwill to the test. The first step was the establishment of a wireless set in the Hungarian Foreign Office to maintain contact: the second was to press the Hungarians to accept an SOE Mission – a military, not a political mission – which would advise and stimulate the Hungarians regarding active resistance to the Germans. The Hungarians accepted this, after some hesitation, and the Mission was organised in the late autumn of 1943. But the Foreign Office was justifiably anxious as to the effects on Moscow of the dispatch of a British Mission (however non-political) to an Axis government of a violently anti-Russian colour, and they withheld their consent throughout the winter. Agreement was finally given in the middle of March 1944: almost at the same moment the Russians broke the German front in the south and swept up to the Carpathians and the Pruth. The German reaction was to brush aside the temporising Government of Hungary, whose moves they knew well enough, and to take direct control of the country. SOE London telegraphed firmly to Cairo that it was still our policy to infiltrate agents to Kallay and his group: but in fact SOE were back again at what one document calls the 'traditional scratch position'.

The only surviving contact was that provided by a Mission under Mr Davidson (now Major Davidson) with Tito's Partisans in Slavonia, near the new Hungarian frontier with Yugoslavia. This had been dropped in Central Bosnia in August 1943, and had worked its way northward with instructions to encourage sabotage in Hungary and Hungarian-occupied territory and to do what it could to build a resistance movement out of the Hungarian Left. The Partisans co-operated to the best of their ability: but the physical difficulties were extreme, and it is doubtful whether there was any effective Hungarian Left on which to build. Major Davidson did spend some time in Hungarian-occupied territory, and his Hungarian wireless operator, Markos, was actually infiltrated into Hungary and overrun by the advancing Russians late in 1944. But the Mission through no fault of its own was quite ineffective for its main purpose.[1]

---

[1] Mr Basil Davidson has published a book on his work with the Partisans: 'Partisan Picture', Bedford Books, 1947.

The remainder of the story consists of a series of desperate attempts to find and support the resistance which ought in theory to have been created by the German coup d'état: there were plenty of named contacts within Hungary, given by Veres Laszlo, but no wireless communication on which to build, and these operations were a series of blind adventures, which involved a number of very brave British officers, as well as all the limited force of trained Hungarians at SOE's disposal. The record of gallantry should be set out briefly, though it had no historical consequences.

1. In April 1944 a Hungarian, Lieutenant Agoston, was dropped blind with a wireless set near Szeged: he never came on the air, and it was found later that he had been captured almost at once.

2. In May part of the Mission which had been designed for work with the Kallay Government was dropped in Northern Yugoslavia (further west than Major Davidson's party): it succeeded in putting a Hungarian-Canadian, Lieutenant Bodo, across the frontier in June, but he was captured almost at once. His captors made an attempt to maintain bogus contact in his name, which was at first successful.

3. In June another attempt of the same kind was made near Varazdin, where Hungary, Austria and Yugoslavia meet: this party had no success and was ultimately withdrawn.

4. Early in July a party under Lieutenant Colonel Boughey was dropped blind in wild country near Lake Balaton, where there was thought to be a nucleus of resistance: they landed far from their dropping-point and were captured next day. Luckily they managed to secure acceptance of their cover-story that they were escaped prisoners of war, and two of them survived: the other two were killed in an RAF raid.

5. An attempt was made to take advantage of the supposed establishment of Lieutenant Bodo in safety in the Pecs area, and a party of one British officer and two Canadian-Hungarians was dropped blind there on 13th September. As usual, they were dropped wide of the target, and all were rounded up within five days: like Colonel Boughey's party, they stuck to their story that they were escaped prisoners in spite of ill-treatment, and were held in Budapest in an internment camp. All three escaped, and were at large in Budapest when the Russians cleared it in February 1945.

6. Finally a last attempt was made from another quarter. Part of the Slovak Army had revolted on 29th August 1944 and held a considerable mountain area round Banska Bystrica.[1] Major

---

[1]   See below p. 528.

Sehmer, who had already served with SOE in Yugoslavia, was dropped here on 18th September with three others, and established wireless contact from the Slovak HQ. It was made plain that his task was to work into Hungary, not to assist the Slovaks, who had contacts through other channels, and he made determined efforts to get across the frontier, which led to the infiltration of one Hungarian into Budapest. But the collapse of the rising in October left Sehmer's party in an impossible position; they joined forces with an OSS officer and some escaped American airmen and kept going until December. Sehmer and his operator, Sergeant Davies, were ultimately caught, on 27th December 1944, and were apparently shot out of hand: the two Hungarian members of the party were not with them, and in the end escaped. By this time the Russians had swept through Eastern Hungary and up to the gates of Budapest, creating a new Hungarian government as they came: there was no further need for British action.

This record of failure has been set down here simply as negative evidence: there was no apparent lack of gallantry and skill, there was obstinate and even unreasonable persistence by the SOE command, but nothing came of it. It is worth setting this against the numerous cases where important results followed from enterprises which seemed even more hopeless: Hudson in Yugoslavia, 'George Noble' in France, Odd Starheim in Norway. Pure luck is a factor which one is apt to forget in an academic analysis of this kind.

CHAPTER XXI

The Cairo Organisation

Some indication was given at the outset of this volume of the lines on which the SOE organisation developed in the Mediterranean from September 1942 onwards.[1] This requires to be supplemented by an account of the last crisis in the history of the Cairo HQ, which was also a crisis in the history of SOE as a whole, and which is intelligible only in the light of what had happened in Yugoslavia and Greece.

It will be remembered[2] that in September 1942, after an earlier crisis, SOE Cairo had been reorganised under Lord Glenconner, with Brigadier Keble, the nominee of the C-in-C Middle East, as his Chief of Staff. The burden of the work in five of the six countries covered in the preceding chapters was borne by the Director of Special Operations (Balkans) (DSO(B)) Colonel Tamplin: control of the sixth country, Hungary, alternated between London and Cairo, but even when control lay theoretically in London most of the work had to be done from bases in the Middle East. DSO(B) also had to handle, as agent for London, a good deal of work for Poland and Czechoslovakia and a little for other countries. London, on its side, had to work closely with Cairo even for the countries fully under Cairo's control, as there were many important contacts, open and secret, carried on through London and through the SOE Missions in the USA and in the neutral capitals. The other side of SOE's Cairo work was that of DSO (Arab World) (Group Captain Domville); no attempt is made to deal with this further here, partly because it was of little relevance to the German war after 1942, partly because the threads of its activities lead on into the post-war history of the Middle East.

Full control of military operations in the countries within their sphere (Yugoslavia, Greece and Albania) lay with the Cs-in-C Middle East: political control was primarily exercised by the Foreign Office through SOE in London, under the 'Foreign Office Treaty' of May 1942.[3] The Minister of State had however certain rather ill-defined powers of local co-ordination: and there were special arrangements

---

[1] Above p. 169.
[2] Above p. 187.
[3] Above p. 344.

for Greece, at first through M. Kanellopoulos's Anglo-Greek Committee, then after the fall of Kanellopoulos through Mr Leeper as Ambassador to the Greek government in exile. These arrangements were vigorously attacked by the Middle East Defence Committee at the end of August 1943, and radical alterations were proposed which would in effect have abolished SOE, Middle East.[1]

The origins of this attack, which are only in part stated in the MEDC paper, were both political and military. On the political side, Lord Glenconner proved to be by far the best chief whom SOE Cairo ever had. As a man of sense, he was bound to have views of his own regarding the general lines of British policy in the Balkans, and it was his duty to state his case, which was at times unwelcome both to the Foreign Office and to his own HQ in London. But his points were always put with moderation as well as with force, and there is no evidence that he did not loyally follow the line of policy laid down even when he disagreed with it.[2] Indeed, he had been on good terms both with the Minister of State's office and with Mr Leeper until the incident of the six EAM representatives in August 1943. There was then an abrupt change, and the blame for the August crisis in Greek affairs was thrown violently onto the shoulders of SOE in general and Lord Glenconner in particular, who were openly accused of a deliberate attempt to sabotage the British policy of support for King George of Greece – an accusation which M. Tsouderos had been spreading for a long time past. When the accusation was challenged it was somewhat sulkily withdrawn,[3] but there was substituted for it the allegation that Lord Glenconner had failed effectively to control his subordinates.

There was more truth in this, but the exact measure of truth is only comprehensible in terms of the military side of the organisation. It had been the understanding in September 1942 that Lord Glenconner should leave control of operational matters to Brigadier Keble and the soldiers, subject to a reorganisation which would assimilate the Cairo organisation to that of SOE in London. On the face of it Brigadier Keble's reorganisation was enormously successful. To take one instance: in September 1942 the only SOE officer in the Balkans was Captain Hudson, who was just beginning, after intense difficulties, to

---

1 CC/285 of 31st August 1943 from the MEDC, and their paper of 2nd September, circulated in London as COS(43)519(0) of 7th September 1943.

2 The only exception was in regard to control of the SOE broadcasting station in Palestine (above p. 380): but here the responsibility is shared with SOE London, and even with PWE, and it concerned not policy but the instrument for its execution.

3 E.g. in Sir A. Cadogan's letter of 20th October 1943, to Lord Selborne; copy on SOE Archives File 60/470/1.1.

receive some not very satisfactory reinforcements: on 12th September 1943 the Minister of State reported to the Prime Minister:[1] 'In August SOE dropped 243 tons arms ammunition etc., into Greece and Yugoslavia, as well as 79 individuals, 37 tons of PWE leaflets and 26 wireless sets. September target was double above tonnage but will not be reached owing to necessity of diverting aircraft to widespread leaflet dropping on Italian collapse and for droppings into Dodecanese.' In the space of a year the three occupied countries had become the stamping-ground of numerous parties of British officers: there was a network of wireless communications: a respectable quantity of arms and very substantial sums of money[2] had been sent in.

But there were many serious blots on this achievement. *First*, there was the personality of Brigadier Keble, who established something of a reign of terror within the organisation and commanded very little confidence outside it, even in military circles. *Second*, there were the curious notions which arose in the military mind as to the nature of Balkan resistance. Even the MEDC paper (para. 1) lends itself to these delusions by describing the guerillas as 'numerically equivalent to three Army Corps': and SOE was not above endorsing the claim that this force was at the time of the Italian surrender holding in check fifty-six Axis divisions. GHQ was apt to think (now that the Eighth Army had vanished from its ken) that the Balkans were a theatre of war where the C-in-C through various agreements commanded large and well-organised Allied forces and where the military duty of 'killing Germans' should be the ruling consideration for all concerned. This view was not shared by all Brigadier Keble's staff: but it was unfortunately one which the organisation as an organisation had a vested interest in encouraging.

This leads to the *third* point, the effects on internal efficiency of over-rapid expansion. It was only very hard driving which made the expansion possible at all, and credit must be given for this where it is due: but the cost in inefficiency was very high, and by September 1943 the effects were becoming visible. Probably the most noticeable of these, to those outside the office, was the inadequacy of the signal facilities, more especially the cypher staffs, in face of the immense stream of new traffic. Decyphering was days, even weeks, in arrears, and it was easy for important operational or political messages to be delayed until they were worthless. One of the Foreign Office's most serious grievances was that a whole series of telegrams from Major Wallace, the Political Adviser with Brigadier Myers in Greece, had been held back and did not reach Mr Leeper until Wallace himself

---

[1] MOS 84 of 12th September; copy on SOE Archives File 60/470/1.1.
[2] Exact figures not available: roughly the equivalent of £300,000 to Yugoslavia and £1,000,000 to Greece in the year 1943.

had arrived in Cairo and described them. There was a Court of Enquiry into this, which exonerated SOE from charges of malice, but it severely censured the efficiency of its office organisation.[1] SOE in London was as badly irritated as anyone else by blunders of this kind.

The grievances of the officers in the field did not make themselves felt so readily, but they were equally serious. It was a cardinal doctrine of SOE's work that nothing can be too good for an agent in enemy territory: he cannot be efficient unless he has absolute confidence in the organisation behind him, and his requests (even absurd requests) must be promptly and sympathetically met at all costs. This was not the experience of many of the Missions in the Balkans.[2] Signals were left unanswered or were answered late and at cross purposes: orders were often incomprehensible or absurd: stores were promised and were never sent: large quantities of useless articles were included in the cargoes of aircraft which had been eagerly awaited in conditions of extreme discomfort and anxiety. It is easy to see how impossible it was for the staff in Cairo to do better: it consisted largely of regimental officers without SOE experience or knowledge of the Balkans: it was intolerably overworked: the dispatch airfield was a vast distance from HQ even when it was still at Derna in Libya. It would be unfair to blame individuals: but it is not unfair to question the policy. Was it wise to pour Missions into the Balkans when they could not be given the support necessary to their efficiency?

This leads us *finally* to the question of political control. Very few of the British officers concerned had any real knowledge of the countries to which they were sent. They were young men endowed (almost without exception) with remarkable qualities of energy and initiative, and quite a number of them were intellectually outstanding and possessed an excellent political flair. But few of them went in with more than a smattering of the language of the country concerned: they were inadequately trained on the political side: and they were briefed to act as military liaison officers and instructors to organised Allied formations – and to avoid politics like the plague. This instruction, though pleasing both to the GHQ Cairo and to the Foreign Office, was fantastically unreal. Each of these Missions was dropped in

---

1 Copy of the Evidence and Findings on SOE Archives File (AD/S.1) File 97.
2 One story will serve to illustrate all this. The first British Mission was dropped in Greece at the end of September 1942, and (not through negligence) received no mail from home until February 1943. It then had various complaints about silly censorship and so on, which it sent to Cairo signed by the Christian names of the officers concerned; it had been agreed to use these as their code names to cover their true identities. Cairo's reply was 'Owing to reorganisation, previous records mislaid. Who are Tom and Martin and Denys? Please give proper names.' Hamson 'We Fell Among Greeks', p. 149.

isolation to act alone within a large area: the guerilla chiefs with whom they dealt were far below the level of sophistication at which the politician is a character clearly distinguishable from the soldier: and whether they liked it or not, the young British officers were forced to act as the sole plenipotentiaries of His Majesty's Government for all purposes, political, military, propagandist, civil relief, intelligence and everything else. No one could tell them what to do: the wireless links with Cairo or with the HQs of Myers and Armstrong and Maclean were broken reeds in a real emergency. A line had to be taken, and once taken it was accepted by the guerillas as the official line of the great and cunning British Empire.[1] There were no means by which the working of the British machinery of government could be made intelligible to a Greek or Yugoslav mountaineer.

It was only in this sense that Lord Glenconner had not effective control of his subordinates: he did not control the expansion of the Missions, because that was a matter of military policy, and he did not control their political activities because it was impossible for anyone to do so. Reliance on the political judgement of British subalterns was extraordinarily well justified in most cases: but of course there were slips, and the Foreign Office was not always as well served as it would have been by experienced professional diplomats – if some 200 professional diplomats could have been found to share the life of Balkan guerillas. The only alternative was a policy of fewer Missions, each of them more carefully picked and trained, and more fully supported: it may seem curious that this alternative was not carefully canvassed at the time, but it is easily explicable. On the one hand, directives from the highest quarters called for all possible support to the guerillas. On the other, the conditions of life in the Balkans were not really understood in the outer world until the British Missions had been sent in and widely scattered. The picture given by the first centralised Missions was incomplete, and was in any case so strange that it was not really believed until it was illuminated from all sorts of angles by a large number of independent and credible observers. The policy of multiplying Missions thus had some political justification in the end: there were also some military advantages both in the exploits of the BLOs and in those of guerillas who would not have moved without them. But it was a pity that the implications of the policy were not better understood by any of those concerned.

Out of this situation grew the alliance between the Foreign Office and GHQ Middle East, the results of which were embodied in the MEDC paper. The paper reported (first) that, (as was within their powers), the MEDC had decided that Special Operations within their sphere should in future be 'co-ordinated' by a new Special Operations

---

[1]   All this is extremely well brought out in Rootham's book 'Miss Fire'.

Committee (SOC) on which should be represented the three Cs-in-C, the Ambassadors to Greece and Yugoslavia, SOE and PWE. But this was considered insufficient: they demanded also that SOE Cairo should in effect be abolished, except for its work in the Arab World, and that Special Operations in the Balkans should be controlled by a Director in the General Staff, supervised by the SO Committee. This was to satisfy two criteria: *first*, that Balkan operations 'had now assumed the character and magnitude of a military campaign' (para. 13), and should be directly under military control; *second*, that the Foreign Office should have effective political control. The new Directorate of Special Operations would deal direct with SOE London only 'on matters of finance and certain matters of administration'.

This posed a problem of absolutely first-rate importance for SOE: in the course of debate on the line to be taken the Minister parted company with Sir Charles Hambro, who was replaced as CD early in September 1943 by Brigadier (now Major General) Gubbins, who had been one of the pillars of the organisation since the primitive days of MI(R). It is a point of some general importance that in this final stage of the war it was thought right that the executive head of the organisation should be a soldier and not a civilian.

There were two lines to be taken in opposition to the MEDC proposals. *First*, there was the sound debating point that they were really impracticable: the Balkan Directorate of SOE in Cairo was organised as part of a world-wide network, the duties of which went far beyond the limits of the MEDC's sphere, and it could not be amputated without gravely hampering the whole work of SOE, not only in the rest of the Mediterranean but in other countries of Europe and even beyond. This could be established and documented in detail without difficulty. *Second*, and much more important, was the issue of the whole future of SOE in this last phase of the war. General Eisenhower had accepted SOE in the Western Mediterranean as being in fact but not in theory a 'Fourth Service': he gave it strategic and tactical tasks, but its internal organisation was a matter between it and SOE HQ in London, provided that it served efficiently the needs of the Supreme Allied Commander. Any local political guidance required came from the SAC's local political advisers, in this case Mr Murphy and Mr Macmillan:* but a political line could also be given from London direct through the Foreign Office and SOE. This system was perfectly satisfactory where personal relations were good, and where the SAC was carrying the burden of

---

* [Harold Macmillan, 1894–1986, Conservative MP 1924–9, 1931–45, 1945–64, Minister of State, Algiers and Caserta 1943–5, Housing Minister 1951–4, Exchequer 1955–7, Prime Minister 1957–64, OM 1976, Earl of Stockton 1984; in *DNB*. See his *War Diaries* (1984) and his life by Alastair Horne (2 vols, 1988–9).]

offensive operations on such a scale that he had no wish to add to his detailed responsibilities. It was continued (*mutatis mutandis*) by General Eisenhower for 'Overlord'; it was warmly endorsed at this time by Lord Mountbatten,[1] now about to take over the SEAC, and it was used by him there with brilliant success. But neither of the essential conditions was met in Middle East, where tempers were on edge and GHQ had virtually no offensive operations to conduct except those of the guerillas in the Balkans: and if the MEDC were to succeed in absorbing SOE Cairo it was practically certain that the Cs-in-C in other theatres would follow suit. The result of such an amputation of all its limbs would be not only to destroy SOE's conception of a world-wide interlocking machinery of subversion but also to reduce the functions of SOE HQ to those of a Directorate of Training, Finance and Technical Research.

The question was thus, after much debate within SOE, posed by Lord Selborne as one of principle. All concessions would be made to the MEDC's reasonable requirements for military and political control: but the principle of amputation could not be conceded. If the MEDC's principle were accepted, there would be no future for SOE as an independent organisation: it should be reduced to the status of a Directorate in the Foreign Office or the War Office – and it was made pretty clear that most of the existing staff would wish to resign with the Minister.

It is not necessary to deal in detail with the battles in the campaign which followed. The main stages were *first* an inconclusive meeting of the Defence Committee on 14th September, presided over by Mr Attlee in the absence of the Prime Minister in Canada. The Committee had before it on one side the MEDC paper, warmly (and somewhat offensively) supported by Mr Eden: on the other, a paper by Lord Selborne, posing the issue of principle but offering the essentials of control, which were accepted as sufficient by the Chiefs of Staff. *Second*, an attempt was made by Mr Oliver Lyttleton, then Minister of Production, to find a compromise, by accepting the MEDC principle and linking to it such practical concessions as were absolutely vital to SOE's work in other theatres. *Finally*, on 30th September the Prime Minister presided over a special meeting of Ministers, at which he decided the issue unequivocally in Lord Selborne's favour.[2]

---

[1] See his note of 24th September 1943 on SOE Archives File 60/470/1.1.

[2] All the essential papers are on SOE Archives File (AD/S.1) File 97, and Archives File 60/470/1.1. The main references are COS(43)210th (0), Item 7, of 8th September, COS(43)215th (0), Item 11, of 14th September, DO(43)8th Mtg of 14th September, which had before it COS(43)519 (0), 522 (0) and 531 (0): Minutes of Meeting of Ministers on 30th September 1943, which had before it these papers and also DO(43)21 by Mr Lyttleton and DO(43)22 by Lord Selborne. See also Lord Selborne's letter of 22nd September to the Prime Minister, copy on SOE Archives File 60/470/1.1.

The solution can be stated briefly as follows, including some loose ends which were tied up at a meeting between Lord Selborne and Sir Alexander Cadogan on 7th October and were embodied in the Minutes of the Prime Minister's meeting:

(i) The SOE organisation to preserve its integrity.

(ii) The main policy of SOE to be settled in London between SOE and the Foreign Office, subject to arbitration by the Prime Minister and the Cabinet.

(iii) 'The execution of SOE policy in Greece, Yugoslavia and Albania will be under the sole control and direction of the Cs-in-C Middle East, because they are operational theatres: and this principle will apply to any new operational theatres.' The Cs-in-C would receive political guidance from the Foreign Office through a Committee consisting of the Ambassadors to Egypt, Yugoslavia and Greece.

(iv) SOE London will continue to make all important appointments to SOE Cairo, but the C-in-C may 'call for the dismissal of any personnel whom he may consider unsatisfactory'.

(v) The Foreign Office to appoint an officer to act as Political Adviser within SOE Cairo.

(vi) The Chiefs of Staff to keep in close touch with SOE operations on all levels and to express their views to the Minister of Defence as necessary.

These proposals were accepted by the MEDC,[1] with the minor modification that the Committee of Ambassadors should be omitted, and the role of 'final local arbiter' should be taken over by the MEDC, acting nominally through the newly created Special Operations Committee. This meant in practice that the Minister of State as chairman of the MEDC was brought back into the picture and Lord Killearn,* the Ambassador to Egypt, was excluded: but the Foreign Office did not object.

The immediate practical effects were the removal of Lord Glenconner, Brigadier Keble and Colonel Tamplin (DSO(B)) as *personae non gratae*: Colonel Tamplin died of heart failure almost at the moment of his removal. Brigadier Keble's post of Chief of Staff was abolished, and Major-General Stawell became head of the organisation, with Brigadier Barker-Benfield in charge of Balkan operations. Major-General Gubbins visited Middle East in October to consider the organisation as a whole, and sundry minor changes were then also made. The most important of these was the appointment as Political

---

[1] CC/326 of 15th October 1943; copy on SOE Archives File 60/470/1.1.

* [M. W. Lampson, 1880–1964, diplomat, knight 1927, Ambassador in Cairo 1936–46; Lord Killearn 1943; in *DNB*. See Trefor Evans (ed.), *The Killearn Diaries 1934–1946* (1972).]

Adviser of Mr C. E. Steel,* who was also to act as Foreign Office specialist on Albania.

The atmosphere in Cairo was henceforth much pleasanter, though there was still at times trouble such as that over Peltekis ('Apollo') in the summer of 1944:[1] and there was a gain in efficiency which might have come in any case once the hectic period of expansion was past. But the whole problem of SOE's organisation in Cairo was pushed into the background very shortly by the creation of the SACMED and the transfer of the centre of activity to Italy. The real importance of this episode was not in relation to subversive work in the Balkans. The decisions of the Prime Minister on 30th September were a vital amplification of SOE's charter, and they decided the course of its development for the remainder of the war.

---

[1] Above p. 480.
* [(Sir) C. E. Steel, 1903–73, knight 1951, Ambassador in Bonn 1957–63.]

CHAPTER XXII

Poland and Czechoslovakia

1. Poland

Resistance in Poland had been a big issue from the first. From June 1940 to June 1941 Poland was the only serious ally whom we had: its forces in the West and its resistance at home were factors of importance, its leader, General Sikorski, stood very close to Mr Churchill, and his staffs were ceaselessly at work pleading and driving forward the Polish case. Poland's strategic value diminished with the entry of Russia and America into the war, but its political importance did not: if anything it grew, as Poland became the test case for the future relations of East and West in Europe, and the Warsaw rising of August 1944 appears now (in a perspective which is still very short) to have been a turning-point of history.

Most of this lies quite outside the scope of a history of SOE. Poland always occupied a large proportion of SOE's time and trouble: but in spite of SOE's efforts Britain could contribute comparatively little to Polish resistance, and as it could not contribute it could not effectively control. SOE's papers are full of interesting material on Polish affairs, but the role of the organisation was mainly that of intermediary and interpreter between the Allied and the Polish Commands, and it does not bear any large share of responsibility for the turn which affairs took in Poland.

It has already been explained that Polish Resistance plans were dominated from the outset by the conception of a National Rising in which Poland would free herself by her own efforts. The continuous war of sabotage and subversion was important enough but secondary to this 'Big Scheme'. The essence of the tragedy which followed is that the turn of the war in favour of the Allies was to bring this dream within sight of realisation, yet the tide of victory meant also the advance of Russian power, as implacably hostile to Polish nationalism as had been the German invader.

The year from October 1942 to October 1943 is one in which the Poles continuously press the Western Allies to supply the resources needed for their 'Big Scheme': while the Allies elude them and Polish relations with Russia deteriorate. The scheme reached the Joint Planners with SOE's comments in October 1942,[1] and (though it was not rejected) it was made plain that there was no hope that the resources required could be made available in the foreseeable future – the Poles imagined for instance that the Polish air force would be flown in to operate from Polish airfields, and that 400 transport aircraft would be provided to move in troops and supplies. In March 1943 SOE's general directive from the Chiefs of Staff[2] laid it down that priority should be given to supplies for immediate sabotage, and implied that the equipment of the Secret Army was a matter of political rather than of military importance. From June to September 1943 the Poles pressed their case before the Combined Chiefs of Staff in Washington,[3] with frequent recourse to the President and the Prime Minister. On 24th September the Combined Chiefs of Staff finally recorded their rejection of the Polish requirements, but undertook to provide (eventually) for Polish *and other* resistance movements one squadron of heavy bombers in Italy and two in England – provided that this did not prejudice the bomber offensive.

This was merely 'jam tomorrow', and not much jam at that; and it came at a time when air operations with existing resources were going badly. Since the autumn of 1941 two or more Polish aircrews had been operating with Halifax aircraft in No. 138 Squadron, for the general purposes of the squadron as well as to Poland. In January 1943 President Roosevelt was induced to request the diversion of six Liberators for Polish needs out of US allocation to Britain, and the establishment of Polish crews was then raised to six, though in the end only three Liberators appeared and the other three crews had to be content with Halifaxes. Even these small resources meant a very great expansion during the winter of 1942–3. Up to April 1942 there had been only nine successful sorties to Poland in all, landing forty-eight men and a negligible quantity of stores. There was a gap during the short nights of summer: then operations began again in September, and from September 1942 to April 1943 there were sixty-two sorties, forty-one of them successful. These involved 119 men and some 23 tons of stores – not much, but something, and only two aircraft were lost. Operations broke off in the short nights of summer 1943, and when they began again in September it was soon found that German defences had been greatly strengthened to meet the intensification of the bomber offensive which had intervened. In September twenty-two sorties were flown, and six aircraft were lost: this included one night when four aircraft were lost out of eleven sent. This could not go on,

---

[1] Appendix A to SOE's History of the Polish Section.
[2] COS(43)142(0) of 20th March 1943.
[3] See the CCS/267 series of papers.

and the RAF insisted that a new and more circuitous route must be followed to evade the defenders: this meant that a very large part of Poland would be out of range. In October there were only nine sorties to this reduced area, of which seven were successful for the loss of one aircraft: and in November there were none. It had been decided, after fresh protests and debates[1] that a decent scale of operations could now be maintained only from the south, from North Africa or Italy, and there was a complete gap while the movement of the base was being carried out.

What was the nature of the movement which these imperfect communications were designed to serve? There was at this stage little good evidence by which to judge it. There were some wireless sets on the air (twelve in January 1944, the first date for which a figure is available): but no Pole could escape from Poland to make a personal report except through fantastic delays and dangers. The first high-grade report available was that of General Tabor, the DMO of the Secret Army, who was brought out by Dakota in April 1944: and there was no direct British evidence until the 'Freston' Mission was sent in December of that year. The picture given by these reports is probably fairly accurate even for this earlier stage.

The central organisation for resistance was the Home Army, the AK, which had been formed late in 1942 or early in 1943 out of the resistance groups of four political parties ranging from moderate Right to moderate Left. It had civil and military sides, acknowledging the authority of the London government and the C-in-C of the Polish Forces, and it was organised primarily as a secret administration of Poland, designed to ensure the continuity of the Polish nation and state. For the most part it was a clandestine organisation of men and women normally engaged on other tasks: but its military chain of command was so organised that quite large forces could be mobilised at short notice. Estimates of numbers vary from 100,000 to 500,000; there were a good many light weapons available, stolen from the enemy or hidden by the Polish Army in 1939, but not enough to arm more than a small proportion of the troops. The policy of the AK was not at first one of open partisan warfare, though there were at each level within it 'semi-professional' sabotage and execution squads, which could be (and were) used for special tasks against the enemy. But the policy of the AK was undoubtedly limited by the necessity, in the interests of the nation, of avoiding an increase in reprisals and repression to the point of annihilation.

The AK occupied a central position. To its Right was the NSZ,

---

1   SOE to the COS 17th October 1943 – App. J to SOE Polish History: COS(43)255th Mtg of 20th October (and JP(43)356(0) of 6th October). Lord Selborne to the Prime Minister, 31st October. New CCS discussion on 5th November.

which had grown from the semi-Fascist wing of the National Democratic Party – the Radical National Camp. This was only in part collaborationist, but its existence was undoubtedly a convenience to the Germans, as its line of propaganda was at least as much anti-Russian as anti-German. To the Left was the People's Army (AL), launched by the Polish Communist Party sometime in 1943, mainly as a political instrument to coerce the 'London Government' and to prepare the way for a peaceful Russian occupation. The AL stood theoretically for the familiar Russian policy of open resistance *à l'outrance* regardless of consequences: but it was created at a later date than the corresponding Partisan movements of the Balkans, and in quite different political conditions, so that its doctrine does not seem to have been executed very literally in practice. It did not acknowledge the legitimacy of the AK's chain of command, but it was a great deal weaker morally and numerically, and it never ventured to treat it as Mihailovitch or Zervas were treated.

Civil war broke out only between the AL and the NSZ, representing small extreme fractions of the Left and Right of the Polish nation. The Russians naturally supplied and inspired the AL, but they do not seem to have put much faith in its military value: in 1944, at least, 'partisan warfare' on German communications was waged by substantial parties of Russians dropped for the purpose and operating independently of all Polish organisations.

There seems thus to have been a fairly stable organisation of the main body of national opinion: subject of course to political dispute and very severely repressed by the Germans, but never broken either by internal or external troubles. And at least while General Sikorski was alive, it fully acknowledged the legitimate authority of the London Government: his unhappy death in July 1943 did not at once break up the organisation but it made it more vulnerable. There had already been a break with the Russians over the affair of the Katyn massacres in April 1943: but if Sikorski had lived the Russians would have found it hard to build anything on the narrow basis of the AL and the Lublin Government.

Until April 1944 the links between this Polish situation and London remained tenuous and ineffective. The Polish flight (now No. 1586 Flight)[1] began to operate from North Africa in December 1943, and moved forward almost at once to Brindisi, where it formed No. 334 Wing together with No. 148 Squadron RAF. Here there grew up a considerable Polish base organised as part of SOE's Force 139 (*alias* 'Torment'): as well as an operations section, there were a training school, a packing unit for airborne supplies, and a signal station in touch both with Poland and with London – all these manned by Poles under general

---

[1]   Also responsible for Czechoslovakia: it later became No. 301 Squadron.

British supervision. Operational results were at first most discouraging: weather conditions proved to be no better than in the north (this was the winter of cold and mud before Cassino and in the Liri Valley), and from January to March 1944 there were only two successful operations out of twenty-three attempted. But a real change began in April: this was due largely to weather conditions, but partly also to more generous allocation of aircraft – a change of policy which falls into line with the increased support given to the Resistance everywhere in Europe in anticipation of its value on the D-day of the Western invasion.[1] The increase in strength was gradual, but by July 1944 No. 1586 Flight had reached an establishment of eleven Halifaxes and three Liberators, and the Poles had a rather indefinite right to further assistance from the rest of No. 334 Wing. There was an unhappy gap in June 1944 but the figures for April, May and July speak for themselves.

1944	Total Sorties	Success-ful	Aircraft lost	Men dropped	Stores dropped
April	135	65	3	60	76½ tons
May	120	76	2	44	96 tons
June	–	–	–	–	–
July	63	33	3	10	46¾ tons

The percentage of successes was still low, and the stores dropped still bore very little relation to the inexhaustible Polish needs and demands: but air supply was at last working on a serious scale.[2]

In addition, there were three air-landing operations[3] by Dakotas of No. 267 Squadron: a small total of very great practical importance. The plan in each case was that there should be a local mobilisation of a battalion or brigade of the Secret Army to defend an improvised landing-ground: the transport aircraft would land, collect its passengers and instantly depart: the Secret Army would melt away before dawn. The first operation was approved in February 1944, but could not be carried out until 15/16 April, when it brought out General Tabor (the Director of Military Operations of the AK), the chief of their air reception organisation, and two politicians of some note.[4] The second

---

1   For Poland the main references appear to be SOE(43) Plans/410 of 18th December 1943: DO(44)4th Mtg, Item 2, of 3rd February. COS(44)43rd Mtg, Item 7, of 10th February.
2   Cf. the grateful message from the Polish GOC in Warsaw, dated 5th June 1944, quoted as App. K to SOE Polish History.
3   The 'Wildhorn' operations.
4   M. Berezowski and M. Stanislawski, later Minister of the Interior and Secretary at the Ministry of the Interior in the 'de-recognised' London Government.

(on 29/30 May) was designed to fetch M. Retinger, General Sikorski's right-hand man, who had dropped into Poland some months before (at the age of sixty-two) to carry out a mission on behalf of M. Mikolajczyk. M. Retinger was on this occasion unable to reach the landing-ground in time, though other passengers of importance were taken. The last operation was the most serious of all: for the Poles it was a matter of regaining personal contact with the Secret Army as the day of decision approached, for the British it was perhaps more important to secure the intelligence material regarding the 'V.2'[1] which had been collected by the Polish 2nd Bureau of the AK from the testing grounds in Poland. The landing took place on 25/26 July and was dangerously near failure: the ground had been soaked with rain during the day and it took 2½ hours of effort (with German units within two or three miles) before the aircraft shook itself free of the mud. But the V.2 plans were secured: and so were the persons of M. Retinger and M. Arciszewski, who was later to replace M. Mikolajczyk as Prime Minister.

This last episode leads straight to the Warsaw rising of 1st August, but there are certain other preliminary matters of importance. *First,* the Russians had already during the winter offensive of 1943–4 entered the Poland of 1939 – territory claimed by Russia on many grounds but dear to Polish hearts – especially those of the Polish 'Right'. Apparently one division of the AK was mobilised in Volhynia in February 1944, two others in the Palatinates of Novogrodek and Vilna in March.[2] These divisions certainly fought the Germans: and the story which passed into currency among the Poles was that the Russians stood by and let the Germans escape, then disarmed and interned the Polish forces. The evidence for this is second or third hand, but Polish belief in the story is certain and important. *Second,* General Tabor (who had been brought out in April) saw both the British Chiefs of Staff and the Combined Chiefs of Staff,[3] and all possible efforts were made by the Poles to secure further promises of Allied assistance for a general rising. These efforts were not successful: no promises were given, indeed the difficulties were made very plain, and the Allies still called only for sabotage and diversionary action by the Poles.[4] But (and this is the *third* point of importance) no attempt was made to control or to prohibit a general rising: this was explicitly left to the Poles to

---

[1] The first rocket landed in London on 8th September 1944.
[2] 'Six Years of Struggle for Independence': an official account of the 'London Poles' published in 1947 (Montgomeryshire Printing Co., Newton). See 'The Times', 22nd May 1947.
[3] On 12th June.
[4] COS(44)165th Mtg of 20th May.

decide, and in particular to the Polish GOC on the spot. A British censorship of Polish wireless traffic was introduced for the first time as part of the security precautions for 'Overlord': but it was relaxed after D-day, and it was not used at any time to control Polish policy. The British had at least washed their hands publicly and unmistakeably, and they can (if it is a comfort to them) disclaim responsibility for the events which followed one another swiftly and in confusion in the latter part of July.

On 16th July a great Russian offensive opened towards Lvov: on 18th July the British broke out beyond Caen and were checked with difficulty: on 20th July Hitler narrowly escaped assassination in East Prussia.* Then on the 23rd the Russians announced the capture of Lublin, which meant in effect the disappearance of the German front covering central Poland: the same day they broadcast the proclamation of the Polish Committee of National Liberation, formed out of the 'Moscow Poles' and backed by the People's Army and by the rather dubious Polish divisions formed in Russia under General Berling and General Rola-Zymierski. This Committee was recognised at once by Russia as the legitimate authority in the liberated territory of Poland: and it called on all good Poles to rise and attack the beaten Germans. The 'Lublin Committee' was promptly denounced by M. Mikolajczyk's Government in London: but the Russian troops were already sweeping ahead beyond Lublin and their 'government' could not be ignored. M. Retinger arrived in Italy from Poland by Operation 'Wildhorn III' on 26th July: on 27th July it was announced that M. Mikolajczyk would go at once to Moscow to negotiate with the Russians for the formation of a combined government recognised both by Eastern and by Western Allies. On the same day the Americans broke through at St Lô and the end of the German defence in Normandy was in sight.

These dates are necessary to put the Warsaw rising in intelligible perspective, as an operation of war and of politics. There were hints of the coming decision in Italy on 27th July:[1] on 29th July General Tabor saw General Gubbins, informed him that the London Government had given full discretion to the authorities in Poland, and asked for aid:[2] on 1st August at 5 p.m. both the AK and the People's Army rose in Warsaw.[3] It is to be assumed that the final decision lay with General

---

[1] SOE 'Polish History' Appendix R, p. 1.
[2] SOE 'Polish History', p. 49.
[3] The AL is accused not of hanging back (as one might expect from the later Russian attitude) but of rising before H-hour, out of bad discipline or anxiety to make the commitment irrevocable.
* [See Peter Hoffman, tr. R. H. Barry, *The History of the German Resistance 1933–1945* (1977), pp. 397–523.]

Bor-komorowski* in Warsaw, and that he was moved to it by the appearance of small Russian forces some ten miles from Warsaw on 31st July. On the military maps available after the event[1] it can be seen that these troops were not a spearhead but the extreme left flank of a wide turning movement, dangerously exposed to counter-attack, and that there was no strategic justification for an immediate Russian attack on Warsaw. But even if General Bor knew this (and probably he could not), the decision was still a rational one. On the military side the situation had gone a little beyond text-book strategy: the Germans were visibly beaten and in disorder, and there was good reason to exploit that disorder in all quarters before the moment passed. Politically, it was the last chance of the old Poland to rise and stand on its own feet: if it remained passive the initiative must pass irretrievably to the Russian puppet government at Lublin. The decision to rise had tragic consequences, but it was not irresponsibly taken.

Once the Poles had risen aid could not be refused – at least by the Western Allies. It was of course more logical that aid should come from the East: Russian aircraft could operate at short range and it was surely a clear strategic gain to the Russians to keep the rising alive. Much debate arose out of this, and it is worth quoting M. Vyshinsky's decisive letter of 15th August to the American Ambassador:

> In connection with your letter of August 14th addressed to the People's Commissar for Foreign Affairs, V. M. Molotov, stating that a unit of American Air Forces has received an urgent directive to clear with Air Forces of the Red Army the question of the possibility of carrying out a shuttle flight from England so that the bombers and fighters should proceed across to bases in the Soviet Union and also a proposal regarding the necessity of concerting with Soviet Air Forces of a similar attempt to drop arms in Warsaw if such an operation should be undertaken on that day from the Soviet side, I am instructed by People's Commissar to state that the Soviet Government cannot go along with this. The outbreak in Warsaw into which Warsaw population has been drawn is purely the work of adventurers and the Soviet Government cannot lend its hand to it. Marshal I. V. Stalin on the 5th August informed Mr W. Churchill that it could not be supposed that a few Polish detachments, the so called National Army, could take Warsaw when it does not possess artillery, aviation or tanks at a time when the Germans had assigned for defence of Warsaw four tank divisions.

---

[1] See Allen & Muratoff, 'The Russian Campaigns of 1944–45' (Penguin) – Map 13.

* [T. Komorowski, 1895-1966, codenamed 'Bor', survived his rising, prisoner of war, overrun 1945, settled in England.]

The Russians were a little better than their word: they allowed an American operation to take place on 18th September, and at that late stage of the rising they also sent some liaison officers and supplies of their own. But it was in their ultimate interest (as they believed) that the rising should fail bloodily, and they took little pains to hide that opinion.

The onus therefore fell on the Western Allies, and from 1st August to the final surrender on 2nd October there was unending passionate discussion up to the highest levels, in which SOE was continually involved. There is little point in following the process of decision in detail: how much and how little was done can be set out fairly briefly.

At the outset no technical preparations had been made for air supply: it was a new and puzzling problem to drop with reasonable accuracy to points in a half-ruined city which was also a battle area. It seemed possible that a daylight operation by American Liberators would be the only feasible method. Force 139 knew of the rising on 2nd August and an operation to Warsaw by No. 334 Wing was arranged for the night of 3/4th August, and then abandoned because of bad weather. On the 4th Air Marshal Slessor* countermanded all air operations to Warsaw, whether by night or by day; it looked like madness to undertake an operation of this character at some 700 miles range while the Russians lay a few miles off Warsaw. Operations were flown elsewhere in Poland that night by No. 1586 (Polish) Flight, and the results made good Air Marshal Slessor's point: out of fifteen aircraft sent four were lost and two crashed on their return. But Polish resistance in Warsaw had already been split into pieces, and no further Russian advance was reported: it was morally impossible to sustain the ban. On the nights of 8th, 9th and 12th August eighteen sorties were flown by No. 334 Wing (six of them by British crews), and ten aircraft managed to drop their loads on the city without loss.

This relative success weakened RAF resistance to moral pressure, and it was agreed to strengthen No. 334 Wing with the equivalent of two squadrons of night-flying Liberators.[1] The squadrons made their first effort on 13th and 14th August: there were fifty-four sorties to Warsaw, twenty-three successes, eleven aircraft lost, and as many more unserviceable through damage done by light flak as they went in low over the house-tops. A very warm telegram of thanks was received from Warsaw on the 16th:[2] but clearly this could not be continued. At this rate there would soon be no long-range aircraft or trained crews available for night operations from Italy.

---

[1] Nos 31 and 34 Sqdns SAAF and No. 178 Sqdn RAF.

[2] SOE Polish History, p. 52.

* [Sir J. C. Slessor, 1897–1979, knight 1943, RAF C-in-C Mediterranean 1944–5, Marshal of the RAF 1950; in *DNB*. See his *The Central Blue* (1956).]

On the 15th therefore Air Marshal Slessor again stopped operations to Warsaw, but he permitted dropping to the woods of Kampinos outside the city, where the Poles could receive stores and get them into Warsaw. This was tried on the 15th and 16th: twenty-seven sorties, fourteen successes, and (on the second occasion) six aircraft lost out of eighteen dispatched. This rate of loss was still far higher than could be borne continuously: there were other resistance movements dependent on the same resources. The additional British aid was therefore withdrawn, and all that could be conceded was that the Poles of No. 1586 Flight might fly to Kampinos woods or elsewhere in Poland if necessary. They persisted in this during the period of bright moonlight from 17th to 27th August. During that period there were twenty-one successes out of forty-six sorties, and on the last two nights half the aircraft engaged were lost and others returned damaged. No. 1586 Flight was reduced to two or three serviceable aircraft out of its establishment of fourteen, and it was only kept going by 'loans' from No. 148 Squadron which could never be repaid.

The situation in Warsaw grew daily more desperate, and Polish appeals to British honour were heartrending. The nights were now moonless, and one more effort was made with additional RAF forces on the 10/11th September: out of twenty sorties only five were successful and five aircraft were lost – a final proof that aid from Italy was not an operation of war. The Russians at last began to send some small assistance on 13th September, and there was a great effort from England on 18th September, when 110 US Fortresses flew over Warsaw to Russian airfields: they dropped their stores from 15,000 ft, but even from this height 30% of them reached the right hands and only two aircraft were lost. Such an operation unfortunately needed much preparation and was only possible in almost perfect weather: so that the opportunity did not recur before the surrender on 2nd October.

Apart from this one large-scale operation, the statistics of the siege are painfully simple:

Sorties to Warsaw or Kampinos woods	161
Successful	79
Aircraft lost	27

In addition there were thirty-one sorties to relieving troops of the Secret Army elsewhere in Central Poland: eight were successful for the loss of four aircraft. These figures are sufficient in themselves to show that aid could not have been pressed harder without destroying the force available: but it is easy to understand Polish bitterness and distress.

The end of the Warsaw rising in effect meant the end of the Polish resistance movement. In London it tore the exiled government to pieces: first by the dismissal of General Sosnkowski in September as a result of his bitter attacks on Allied failure to aid Warsaw, then in November through the replacement of M. Mikolajczyk by the irreconcilable anti-Russian, M. Arciszewski. The Lublin Government were virtually left in possession of the field, and it was they who were established on the ruins of Warsaw when the Russians at last entered on 11th January 1945. The AK had, since the failure at Warsaw, remained passive, and its standing orders were to disband quietly and conceal its weapons on the approach of Russian troops: it was the AL who met the Russians in January and February 1945 as the representatives of Polish resistance.

SOE was naturally to some extent concerned in the efforts made on the highest level to patch up this irremediable situation: but these efforts lie outside the history of Resistance, and there was only one other SOE action of importance in occupied Poland – the dispatch of the 'Freston' Mission in December 1944. The idea of a British Mission in Poland had never been rejected by the Poles: but until communications improved in the spring of 1944 the difficulties were more than men could reasonably be asked to face. Even then they were very great: but the project was taken up seriously early that summer and it was delayed not because of its dangers but because of the known jealousy of the Russians, which had caused grave difficulties elsewhere.[1] Foreign Office scruples were not overcome until October 1944; four Missions were then prepared, but the first of them, 'Freston', was not able to reach the field until 26/27th December, and the others were never launched.

The leader of 'Freston'[2] was Captain (now Colonel) D. T. Hudson, who played an equally honourable part in Yugoslavia; and he was accompanied by three other British and by one Polish interpreter. The party (after three failures) was dropped to an AK 'reception' committee in wooded country not far from Czestochowa, in the south-west of Poland, and it was at large in that area until 15th January, when it was overrun by the advancing Russians. Conditions were perhaps easier than they had been in the days of German strength: the Mission was able to move fairly freely, to meet the working members of the local AK administration, and to hold one formal conference with the GOC of the Home Army. Time was too short to accomplish much, but the situation as portrayed in Colonel Hudson's report contains much food for thought. It is clear that it would have been possible for British Missions to work in Poland earlier: they would not themselves have been able to exercise much influence over Polish politics,

---

1   Especially over the dropping of De Chastelain into Roumania in December 1943.
2   See the Official Report – SOE Archives File No. 8/400/1.

but their reports might have had fundamental effects in London and Washington. There would of necessity have been a clearer view of the Polish situation: and it is possible that a clear view might have forced the Western Allies to adopt one Polish policy or another, while there was yet time. As matters developed, the crisis of Warsaw (which was the final crisis) came and was over before it was even realised that a policy was necessary.[1]

There is little more to be added in the way of summary and conclusion. It may be said cynically that SOE's only essential role in Polish affairs had been to act as buffer and shock-absorber between Polish importunity and the harassed Allied High Command. But SOE had also done what it could for the maintenance of Polish resistance and national spirit in Poland, and it had done much, although it was too little to have a serious effect on the course of political history. On the military side it is especially difficult to make an assessment, since there were no British witnesses and the Poles cared little for detailed records. The 'Secret Army' (it is fairly clear) was primarily concerned (and rightly concerned) to remain an 'army in being' and to prepare for the final rising and resurrection of Poland: it did not follow a policy of reckless and continuous offensive, which might perhaps have suited the Allies better, but would have been finally disastrous to Poland. Its service to the Allies consisted in part of endless small-scale local actions: in part in the spirit of passive resistance and undetectable sabotage which it kept alive: most of all perhaps in that Poland remained under German occupation a country at war, in which the commitment for the maintenance of internal security always pressed heavily on the Germans and drew away an important part of their resources, both physical and moral. These were substantial gains and they cost us little, though they cost the Poles much.

2. Czechoslovakia

It has been explained earlier that after the execution of Heydrich in May 1942 the Czechs in London were cautious, and their organisation at home was badly broken: it required steady pressure to induce them to formulate any aggressive plans at all, and the technical difficulties were very great. It was thus nearly two years before a serious new start was made.

During the winter of 1942–3 only one party[2] was landed, in spite of seven attempts: apparently one member of it was in wireless touch

---

[1] At that juncture apparently the only British reporter was an escaped RAF prisoner (Flight Sergeant Ward), whose messages the Poles sent over their own wireless, as those of a valuable independent witness.

[2] 'Antimony', 25th October 1942.

with London until May 1943, when contact was again lost.[1] But the Czechs still controlled their own communications, and an agreement for full disclosure to the British was not made until January 1943.[2]

Nothing could be done during the long summer nights of 1943, but in the autumn the responsibility for Czech communications (as for those with Poland) was transferred to the Mediterranean: in theory operations by No. 1586 Flight began from North Africa in December 1943 and from Italy in January 1944. But the Czechs, like the Poles, suffered from the hopeless weather conditions of that winter, and it was not until April 1944 that there was a real success. In that month four parties, consisting of thirteen Czechs in all, were safely landed in Czechoslovakia and wireless touch was resumed. From this point there were two lines of development, the first leading to the Slovak rising of August 1944, the second to the rising in Prague in the early days of May 1945.

A beginning was made in Slovakia by the dropping of a Czech party of three on 9th June 1944, and there was thus opened a channel of communication between London and the anti-German elements in the confused politics of the Slovak puppet state. Plans were laid early in July for open resistance by the Slovak forces in the event of a German attempt at a complete occupation of the country: President Benes accepted full responsibility for the decision,[3] and it seems that adequate steps were taken to secure Russian approval in advance. The expected German move came on 27th August, as the Russians thrust forward into the Carpathians from the north and through Roumania to the south-east: on the 29th four very weak 'divisions' of the Slovak Army revolted and joined hands with so-called 'partisans' to control a considerable area (including two airfields) in the mountainous centre of the country. The Western Allies already had on their hands the bad business of the Warsaw rising, and they wished for no more commitments within the Russian zone of operations. Fortunately in this case the Russians did their best. As early as 6th September they flew in thirty transport aircraft with stocks of arms, as well as 700 men of the Czech parachute brigade: and they also sent twenty-four Czech fighter aircraft, with rather inadequate supplies. Nevertheless, Russian aid was not nearly sufficient in the absence of a further advance by the Russian armies, and the rising was gradually compressed and overwhelmed by a concentration of German forces. On the Western side

---

[1] SOE Czech History, p. 14 and note of interview with Colonel Moravec 11th January 1943, on SOE Archives File (AD/S.1) 'File 59'.

[2] Note by V/CD, dated 19th June 1943, on SOE Archives File (AD/S.1) File F.128.

[3] See dispatch No. 124 from the British Ambassador to the Czechoslovak Government, dated 30th August 1944, which gives Dr Ripka's account of the origins of the revolt. (SOE Archives File (CD) Czechoslovakia 2.)

it was made plain throughout that no formal support could be given. Two US Fortresses flew in on 17th September, and six more on 7th October: they carried such supplies as they could, but their primary mission was to bring out escaped US airmen who were with the rising. On the second occasion there went with them Lieutenant Colonel Threlfall, the head of SOE's 'Torment' Mission in Italy, and he had a brief interview with the Slovak commander, General Golian: but on Lieutenant Colonel Threlfall's side the main point made was that the Slovaks must look to the East for help – and the Slovaks were not too well pleased with what they had received from that quarter.[1]

Major Sehmer's 'Windproof' party[2] was already with the Slovaks attempting to make its way into Hungary, and it was forced by circumstances to act as a liaison mission with the Slovaks until their collapse in November. A more regular liaison mission was planned, but could not be sent before the end. Beyond this SOE was not permitted to go.

British policy as regards support for resistance in the heart of Czechoslovakia was similarly affected both by experience of the disasters of the open risings elsewhere – Warsaw, Domodossola, the Vercors – and by diplomatic nervousness regarding the effects of interference in a Russian zone. SOE's policy for Czechoslovakia was still that enunciated in the COS Directive of March 1943,[3] to give priority to sabotage, but not to exclude the preparation of a Secret Army in so far as it was consistent with the immediate task. A Secret Army in Bohemia and Moravia had not been in the realm of possibility until communications began to improve in the summer of 1944. The excitement of the Warsaw rising interrupted the programme badly, but nevertheless things looked so promising in September that the Czech C-in-C, General Ingr, approached first Major General Gubbins,[4] then the CIGS, with requests for increased aircraft support for his army at home. The question was discussed on 7th October by the Chiefs of Staff,[5] who seem to have been shaken somewhat both by the request and by SOE's support of it: they were inclined to blame SOE (unfairly) for the emergence of another major military nuisance. The final upshot of the discussions which ensued was an instruction given by the COS on 21st December that supplies to Czechoslovakia from the West should be limited to about twenty successful aircraft sorties a month.[6]

---

[1] SOE Czech History, Appendix C.
[2] Above p. 505.
[3] COS(43)142(0) of 20th March, para. 29.
[4] Letter of 11th September on SOE Archives File (CD) Czechoslovakia 2.
[5] See Note from Mr Brook to Colonel Price of 6th October: COS(44)331st (0) Mtg, Item 12: and General Gubbins's note to Major General Hollis of 13th October.
[6] COSMED203 of 21st December 1944: see also COS(44)957(0).

This would be enough only for liaison missions and specialised supplies; anything else must come from the Russians. What the Russians did is unknown: certainly not much was achieved from the West except to keep open a slender channel of communication. During the whole final period from April 1944 to May 1945 SOE sent in only thirty-five men (including seven to Slovakia) and 42 tons of stores. Conditions remained difficult almost to the end: out of 101 aircraft sorties in the first months of 1945 only twenty-three were successful, and only two parties of agents reached Czechoslovakia. Both of these parties were of some importance: the first ('Manganese') split into two parts, one going to Prague whence it maintained a link with London throughout the final rising, the other organising reception of air supplies in Eastern Bohemia: the second was a single man ('Bauxite') who provided a wireless channel for the Czechoslovak National Council in Moravia.

Through these agencies some 28 tons of stores were put in during April 1945 – a vast increase on any previous figure – and plans were laid for four parties (including British Liaison Officers) to go in for the final rising. But when Prague rose at last, on 5th May, air communication with the West had been blotted out once again by bad weather. No operations had been possible since 25th April and the shut-down continued until the final arrival of the Russians on 9th May. During that period the Czechs fought unsupported (except for the dubious aid of the Cossack 'Quisling', General Vlassov),[1] they received no supplies from the West, and General Patton's army remained stationary at the boundary of its operational zone. SOE received continuous bitter appeals for aid over its radio links, but it could do nothing. Liberation came as a gift from Russia, and it was very small comfort that Colonel Perkins, head of SOE's Polish and Czech Section, was the first British officer to enter Prague after the Liberation: such was the fear of complications that he slipped in disguised as a Czech and withdrew again almost at once.

SOE had done its best: but the whole story, from Munich in 1938 to the Prague rising of 1945, will serve mainly to teach future generations of Czechs that in a crisis little is to be expected from the West.

---

[1] See an interesting narrative in the 'Manchester Guardian' of 2nd May 1947. [A. Vlassov, 1900–46, Soviet army commander, captured July 1942, changed sides, recaptured 1945, hanged 1946.]

CHAPTER XXIII

The Western Mediterranean and Italy

Our next task is to follow the part played by SOE in the series of campaigns which led Allied Armies from the West through North Africa, Sicily and Italy to the Alps. SOE's contribution here was relatively less important than in Western Europe or the Balkans, but the experience gained was of great value and the operations conducted were by no means insignificant.

1. French North Africa

The project of detaching French North Africa from the Axis was not a new one in 1942, but the initial organisation of a Fifth Column there had hitherto been left entirely to the Americans: the work was begun by Mr Murphy when he became Consul-General at Algiers in March 1941, and OSS became formally responsible after its creation in June 1942.[1] The original American wireless network linked the Consulates at Tunis, Algiers, Oran and Casablanca to that in the International Zone at Tangier, where Colonel Eddy was posted as senior American representative at the beginning of 1942. We have already mentioned the SOE station established by Squadron Leader 'Mallory' at Gibraltar in December 1941:[2] this served in the first instance as a link to Tangier, but steps were also taken to ensure that direct contact could be made with the other American stations in North Africa.

Concrete discussion between SOE and OSS on the requirements of Operation 'Torch' began early in August 1942, and led to an agreed division of responsibility. OSS could contribute the existing American contacts, which consisted in part of high officers in the French North African command, in part of a small French 'action group' composed of curiously diverse elements, to which a flavour of ultra-nationalist reaction was given by Henri d'Astier de la

---

[1]   See SOE Archives File (AD/S.1) SC/76 – USA.
[2]   Above p. 323.

Vigerie, the Royalist brother of De Gaulle's supporter Emmanuel d'Astier.

But the Americans were badly off for experienced men, for specialised equipment of all kinds, and for base facilities, so that SOE's co-operation in these respects was indispensable. The organisation agreed was set out on three distinct levels:

(a) There was to be an SOE/OSS Mission at Gibraltar, commanded by Colonel Eddy, with Mr Brien Clarke of SOE as second-in-command: this unit would be under the orders of General Eisenhower for the purposes of the operation.

(b) Small SOE technical elements with signals equipment were allocated to each of the three Task Forces, at Oran, Algiers and Casablanca. All of these proved useful in minor ways, and that at Casablanca was invaluable, as the naval signals equipment on shore was out of action for several days and all Admiral Hall's messages were put through the SOE station. But the only really important mission on this level was that to be attached to the Eastern Task Force (British 1st Army and US 2nd Corps) in its dash for Tunisia: this was known as 'Brandon'.[1]

(c) Finally, General Eisenhower gave his consent to the establishment in North Africa, as soon as possible after the Liberation, of what was to be in effect an outpost of SOE HQ, working from another angle into territories such as France, Corsica and Italy which SOE was already attempting to open up from England. This was known as ISSU6,[2] or 'Massingham'.

'Massingham' was important later, but it had a unity of its own only as a HQ providing common facilities for operating sections whose policy was laid down elsewhere. The work of these sections can only be dealt with in the general narrative for the countries concerned, in particular France and Italy. But it must be remembered that 'Massingham' base provided the facilities in training, signals, stores, conduct of air operations, and so forth, which made that work possible. A general history of 'Massingham' could deal only with the administrative morass in which all Allied services in North Africa were floundering, and it would not be very instructive in this context. It is necessary here only to make it plain that, from a tiny beginning under Lieutenant Colonel J. W. Munn and Lieutenant Colonel David Keswick on 17th November 1942, it grew to be a big affair, employing at its peak nearly 800 British staff

---

1 There is a short account of the 'Brandon Mission' with the SOE Section Histories. [Plenty of detail in Richards, *Secret Flotillas*.]

2 Inter-Services Signals Unit 6.

(including a considerable FANY unit) and working with at least equal numbers of Americans and French.[1]

The Gibraltar HQ and the fate of 'Brandon' must be dealt with a little more fully.

(a) SOE's Part in 'Torch'

The success of 'Torch' was conclusive proof (if proof is needed) of the military value of good 'underground' preparation. Strategically the operation might have been impossible without the well-planned and executed appearance of Giraud: it would certainly have been impossible without the support of Mast, Béthouard and other highly-placed officers in North Africa. Tactically, the small and ill-armed French 'action group' in Algiers was remarkably successful in holding key-points for a vital period of a few hours at the right time, though the Americans were perhaps a little too cautious in taking advantage of their work.

But all these preparations were American, and it is unnecessary to repeat here the well-known story of General Mark Clark's* visit, the fluctuations of Giraud and the final coup. SOE's part was purely ancillary, but in one respect vital.[2] *In the first place*, it had already supplied a good deal of equipment to be infiltrated by the Americans through Tangier, and at the last moment an attempt was made to run in a larger consignment by sea to a beach near Algiers. A determined effort was made by the small vessel 'Minna', which lay off the Algerian coast from 3rd till 5th November: but something went wrong with the rendezvous and the 'action group' had to make its coup without some vital stores. *In the second place*, the entire burden of secret communications with North Africa was borne by Squadron Leader 'Mallory's' station at Gibraltar from General Eisenhower's arrival on 5th November until two or three weeks after D-day. The American signallers failed at first to solve the technical problem of establishing wireless communications from the Rock to North Africa, and important messages were still carried by the SOE station long after the Allies were established in Algiers.[3]

---

1   There is an SOE history of 'Massingham', with useful Appendices by Captain Jacqueline Porter, FANY; this deals mainly with operations, but also covers the chief points of administration.

2   There is a good short account by Mr Brien Clarke, at Appendix F to the 'Iberian History'.

3   A set of the most important messages is at Appendix E to the 'Iberian History': this may be of some historical value, as the US representatives in North Africa destroyed all their papers on D-day, and it is doubtful if General Eisenhower's HQ ever had a complete set.

*   [M. W. Clark, 1898–1985, American general, visited Algeria by submarine before 'Torch' landings 1942, commanded Fifth US Army in Italy 1943–5.]

(b) 'Brandon'

'Brandon' on the other hand was almost entirely SOE's affair; it was on the whole a failure, but a very instructive failure. It consisted in the first instance only of two British officers, Lieutenant Colonel Anstruther and Major Watt Torrance, with a W/T operator, who landed at Algiers very early in the operation, on 8th November 1942. With them was an OSS representative for Algiers; other OSS men were supposed to take over further east, but they do not appear in the sequel. The party's brief was far from clear, and they were given no official channel for drawing stores from the British 1st Army, although they were under General Anderson's orders as Commander of the Task Force. There were no existing SOE contacts in Tunisia, and apparently none were handed over by the Americans: so that 'Fifth Column' work in the normal sense was impossible without further preparation. It was contemplated apparently that 'Brandon' should raise and train as swiftly as possible a guerilla force from any active pro-Allied elements they could find in North Africa, and that they should use it for raiding and sabotage behind the enemy front; this was likely to produce something more like the Long Range Desert Group than a 'Fifth Column', except that its men would have an intimate knowledge of the country and might on occasion operate in civilian clothes.

From this vague conception three lines of action developed:

(i) *Training*: Lieutenant Colonel Anstruther at once got in touch with the French youth organisation, the 'Chantiers de la Jeunesse', which had played a part in the Algiers rising, Vichy creation though it was. He was well received, and training arrangements were hastily made at a temporary HQ near Algiers. A small force was quickly raised here, half-trained but bold and energetic. During November the Mission moved forward to a more permanent and secluded base at Guelma, where training was continued on a better footing: then in December the French withdrew the Chantiers de la Jeunesse party from British control, on reasonable enough political grounds, and offered in its place an arrangement in regard to the new 'Corps Franc d'Afrique'. This was to be a force of foreign volunteers, particularly Republican Spaniards, many of whom had been imprisoned by the Vichy authorities in North Africa: it would be under French military control, but 'Brandon' would help to train it and could draw on it for its own purposes. It was from this source that most of 'Brandon's' men were provided: some 300 at its peak period, good material, but less than half-trained and in bad physical condition from recent hardships.

(ii) *'Special Detachments'*: 'Brandon's' first reinforcement was the vessel 'Minna', which arrived at Bone on 17th November under an

SOE officer, Lieutenant Brooks Richards, RNVR,* with some stores and some partly-trained volunteers from Gibraltar. Brooks Richards worked along the coast with the 'Minna' and on 2nd December took possession of the lighthouse at Cap Serrat in the mountainous no-man's land on the extreme left flank of the Allied advance. Here his party successfully maintained itself, six hours from the nearest Allied troops, until the final Allied breakthrough, and contrived to annoy the enemy in a number of minor ways. This useful cover on an open flank suggested the idea of another 'Brandon' post, under Major Torrance at Sedjenane, in the same wild country on the Allied left.

One unforeseen problem of the unforeseen front in Tunisia was the Arab population, which passed freely through the very loose front lines and was on the whole inclined to aid the Axis rather than the allies of their masters the French. Arab espionage and theft became a serious nuisance which the Field Security Police could not control, and 'Brandon' (who had a fair number of men with local knowledge) were called in to assist. They did so not unsuccessfully, and after this experience they were reinforced and expanded for this purpose by 5th Corps, which now controlled them under 1st Army. Four 'Special Detachments' were formed early in January 1943 (in addition to that at Cap Serrat), as No. 1 Group under Major Torrance. In addition No. 2 Group was formed early in February and attached to 2 (US) Corps.

But clearly this police work was not proper work for SOE, and it appears that First Army were somewhat baffled by 'Brandon', a band of unclassified thugs with no obvious function and no normal channels of supply. Complaints reached SOE in London both through the War Office and through Colonel Eddy of OSS in Algiers; and, when Brigadier Gubbins was in North Africa at the end of January 1943, one of his main tasks was on the one hand to explain 'Brandon' to the military, on the other to put the administration of 'Brandon' on more orthodox lines. The results of his discussions were embodied in a directive, circulated by First Army to 2 Corps, 5 Corps and 19 Corps on 12th February 1943:[1] this explained briefly what the Special Detachments were, and laid it down that their functions should be:

(a) To enlist active Arab support.
(b) To prevent enemy use of the Arabs.
(c) To provide guides and interpreters for operational purposes.
(d) To distribute propaganda leaflets behind the enemy lines.
(e) To carry out sabotage of communications in the enemy's rear.

---

[1] 50/G.Ops of 12th February 1943, reproduced as Appendix C to SOE 'Brandon' History.
* [(Sir) F. Brooks Richards, born 1918, knight 1976, Ambassador in Athens 1974-8.]

(f)   In the event of major operations, to undertake guerilla operations of longer duration behind the enemy's lines.

The administrative paragraph is short and precise and may be quoted
in full, as it was the parent of many similar arrangements in the field,
in Italy, France, Norway and elsewhere:

Special Detachments in First Army area consist of a Headquarters
and two Groups. SDHQ works operationally and administratively
under Army HQ. One group is attached to 2 Corps and the other
to 5 Corps. Each Group is under both operational and administrative command of the corps to which it is attached and all requirements will be met through the normal channels.

From this point 'Brandon' was 'married in' successfully to the military hierarchy, and performed its minor role with efficiency, though
not with great distinction. The possibilities of deep penetration were
practically at an end when Rommel arrived in Tunisia and the front
'thickened up' early in 1943: so that a sensational guerilla offensive
was quite out of the question. There were some successful raids into
the enemy front lines, propaganda was distributed, intelligence was
collected and help was given in the hard task of controlling the Arab
population; at least enough to show that irregulars had some value
even on a rather static front.

(iii) *Long-range operations*: 'Brandon' HQ was also responsible
for the deep penetration of Tunisia, either to contact resistance or
to attack particular objectives. This part of the story is short and
unhappy. Two raids were attempted on railway bridges on the east
coast of Tunisia: one party of twelve landed from a submarine on
the night of 28/29th January, but was captured without achieving
anything: another party of eight landed by parachute on 25/26th
March – it also was captured, but it first destroyed its objective and
succeeded in delaying railway traffic for twenty-four hours at an
important time. The first attempt to organise internal resistance was
the landing of two Frenchmen near Bizerta on 4/5th March: their
wireless set was stolen by Arabs, so that they never made contact
with base, and they were eventually captured when trying to get
back through the German lines. They had been able to do a little
small-scale organisation in the Bizerta area. The second attempt
was a more serious disaster. Squadron Leader 'Mallory', a very
energetic character whom we have met before,[1] was sent into Tunisia
by sea on 29th January with two French agents to organise resistance in Tunis. The party was captured almost at once: the enemy
took possession of their codes, wireless set and signal plan, and
opened communications with the Massingham W/T station. The
Germans omitted the secret security check, which was unknown to

---

[1]   Above p. 323, etc.

them, and Massingham disregarded the omission. It was thus readily beguiled into landing ten more agents by sea on 6th April, to be gathered in at once by the Germans: and two other parties would have followed but for the end of enemy resistance. It was an unhappy episode, and the best that can be recorded is that 'Mallory' and eight others were eventually found alive in German concentration camps.

What was to be learnt from 'Brandon's' experience, which was (with the minor exception of Madagascar) SOE's first attempt to contribute directly to an Allied offensive? The lessons were clear and simple, and were not forgotten:

(i) *First*, what SOE can contribute depends on preparation long beforehand. Fifth-column methods were invaluable in Algeria and Morocco, where they had been well-prepared: they might have been even more important in Tunisia, if they had been prepared in time. But it was useless to imagine that they could be extemporised.

(ii) *Second*, Special Operations Detachments in the field must be geared into the normal military chain of command and supply, so that they are for administrative purposes orthodox units, however unorthodox their functions.

(iii) *Third*, the military authorities must be given a reasonably clear picture of what 'Special Operations' can do and cannot do. Hitherto SOE had wrapped itself in absolute darkness: it was now plain that it would not be properly used unless all responsible authorities knew at least in outline what its functions were. This did not mean that its methods should be explained in detail, except to those directly concerned.

(iv) *Fourth*, there are a surprising number of things to which 'irregulars' can turn their hands and can do more easily and economically than regulars. There is no reason why this adaptability should not be fully used, provided that it does not divert effort from the bigger conception of building up the 'Fifth Column' to play its part in the strategy of a major offensive.

2. Italy[1]

Little has been said of Italy hitherto, because SOE had achieved little. SOE was backward in its attempts to penetrate the main enemies, Germany and Italy, chiefly for two reasons:

---

[1] See (SOE) general narratives by Lieutenant Colonel Roseberry and Lieutenant Colonel Hewitt, the brief account and large dossier of documents in the AFHQ (G3) History of Special Operations: 'Corsica' narrative, bound with SOE 'Massingham' History.

(a) The policy of 'unconditional surrender'[1] (which was probably the only formula which could have kept the USA and the USSR in coalition for so long) meant that no serious attempt could be made to corrupt or seduce any part of the governing oligarchy either in Germany or in Italy. As has become clear since the Armistice, there were plenty of high Nazi and Fascist officials anxious for reinsurance; and we need have felt no moral scruples about dealing with them and double-crossing them, as they had so often done to others. But the political danger of opening a rift between the three Allies was too great, and SOE ventured rarely and nervously on this ground, although it was the line of approach most likely to confuse and break up the Axis régimes from within. Instead, almost everything had to be built on the very slender foundation of authentic anti-Nazis and anti-Fascists, an ill-organised and almost powerless minority.

(b) In the second place, although Colonel Grand and D Section had originally thought of Germany and Italy as their main targets, the position had been transformed by the German victories of 1940 and 1941. There was now a vast area of occupied territory which provided much more favourable ground for subversive action: and SOE was undoubtedly wise to concentrate its small resources where they could give the quickest results. But there arose in consequence the apparent paradox, that the British subversive organisation was very late in making a serious attempt to subvert the main enemy.

(a) The First Phase

There had been a good deal of talk of attacking Italian morale during the period of disasters which befell Italy in the winter of 1940–41. SOE accepted a directive from the Chiefs of Staff [2] which put the railways linking North Italy to Germany high on the priority list: and a little was done from Switzerland to encourage 'insaisissable' sabotage of Italian rolling-stock in transit. There was also an idea that something could be done with the Italian prisoners taken in the Wavell offensive, and the original purpose of Major Peter Fleming's Yak Mission[3] was to recruit and train patriotic prisoners as saboteurs. This was a failure, but a less abject failure than the attempt to recruit 'democratic' Italians in the USA and to ship them to India for work among

---

[1] The formula was not announced until the Casablanca Conference in January 1943, but the policy had its effect much earlier.

[2] Above p. 92.

[3] Above p. 170.

the prisoners there: these 'democrats' proved to be a very awkward band of spongers, who were only got rid of after months of humiliating wrangle between British departments.[1] The only positive contribution which SOE made in this period was to send a trained Italian as guide and interpreter with the first British regular parachute operation, that to South Italy in February 1941:[2] the man did well, but was captured and shot by the Fascists.

This frustration was to some extent due to confusion of responsibility. Operations were conducted partly from Switzerland, by SOE's representative there, Mr John McCaffery, partly from Malta and Egypt, partly from various neutral capitals. Such general direction as there was came from a section in the Cairo HQ: and the Cairo HQ was crippled by the deadlock between Colonel Pollock's SO2 organisation, and the SO1 organisation under Colonel Thornhill, which was actively and independently engaged in clandestine propaganda to the Italians in Libya and in the prison camps. CD reported in gloomy terms on the Italian position to Mr Dalton in October 1941,[3] and carried out a reorganisation by which an Italian Section (J Section) was set up in the London HQ under Lieutenant Colonel C. L. Roseberry: policy was to be directed from London, and the Missions in Switzerland, Malta and Cairo were each to play subordinate parts in its execution.

(b) J Section in Control

The next phase extends from the creation of J Section until the Allied invasion of Italy in September 1943. On the political and propaganda side matters now improved, although penetration by agents was still totally unsuccessful. The propaganda attack on Italian morale by broadcasts, leaflets, 'whispers', and other means seems to have had considerable success – backed as it was by convincing military and political arguments. SOE was able to help here in minor ways, by smuggling material into Italy by various channels. In addition it was the channel for two important political contacts.

One of these was with Emilio Lussu,[4] a Sardinian anti-Fascist associated with 'Guistizia e Libertà', the most active of the anti-Fascist groups in exile, from which later grew the small but important 'Partito

---

[1] There is a full account of this comedy in Mr David Garnett's 'History of PWE'.

[2] Operation 'Colossus' – COS(41)52nd and 56th Mtgs refer. For a personal recollection of the Italian (Picclei), see Newnham 'Prelude to Glory', p. 24.

[3] Minute of 15th October, quoted in Roseberry's narrative p. 1. At this stage Mr Bracken was attacking Mr Dalton violently for the ineffectiveness of his political warfare preparations to support the Auchinleck offensive in Libya.

[4] SOE Archives file (AD/S.1) SC/77/5 refers. [See his *Enter Mussolini* (1927).]

d'Azione'. Lussu came out of Vichy France with his wife on his own initiative in November 1941, and approached the British with a proposal that he should be infiltrated into Sardinia, where he expected to be able to rally a strong movement against Mussolini. This was a serious project, put forward by an able and resolute man of considerable political standing, and J Section was heartily in favour of it. But Lussu (to his credit) would not accept the role of a British agent conspiring to defeat his own country except in return for a clear understanding that Italy's pre-war frontiers in Europe would be respected. This was naturally impossible, and he returned to France in July 1942 without commitments of any kind to SOE. When Mussolini fell, he found his own way into Italy and played an important part in organising resistance in Rome.

The second was a much larger project, put forward first in Switzerland by an Italian industrialist named Rusea, who was in contact with Marshal Badoglio* and other anti-Fascist and anti-German Italians of high standing. The matter was broached late in 1942, and early in 1943 it had reached a point at which it was possible to lay authentic proposals from Badoglio before the War Cabinet.[1] His offer to make a coup d'état was firm, but not unconditional: no date was set for the seizure of power but it was suggested that an Italian army should be raised at once outside Italy from prisoners in Allied hands. Elaborate arrangements had already been made to fly Badoglio's envoy, General Pesenti, from Italy to Cyrenaica.

After reference to the Chiefs of Staff,[2] the proposal was turned down by the Cabinet in January 1943, while Mr Churchill was away:[3] it was revived in March 1943 and the Cabinet then decided that General Pesenti should be encouraged to come to Cyrenaica.[4] But it was stipulated by the Cabinet that no undertakings of any kind should be given to General Badoglio before negotiations were opened: and this was sufficient to break off discussions. Badoglio after the Armistice made much of the opportunity which the Allies had missed on this occasion: a rising in Italy timed to follow swiftly on the fall of Tunis would have made an immense difference to the whole aspect of the war, and the risk of German intervention in force was much less than

---

[1] These were embodied in WP(43)27 of 14th January, which is not in the Cabinet archives: possibly all copies were destroyed.

[2] Copy of CD's Minute to General Ismay dated 7th January 1943, on SOE Archives File (AD/S.1) File 77 Activities in Italy.

[3] There is no record of this in the Cabinet archives.

[4] WM(43)42nd Mtg of 18th March 1943 (Confidential Annex on Secretary's Standard File): communicated by Sir Orme Sargent to Sir Chas. Hambro in letter of 20th March 1943 on SOE Archives File (AD/S.1) File 77 Activities in Italy.

* [P. Badoglio, 1871–1956, Italian Chief of Staff 1940, head of government 1943–4.]

at the time of Salerno. But the political risks of negotiation were obvious: so also were the technical difficulties of mustering sufficient forces for a landing and providing them with air cover while Sicily was still in enemy hands. The balance of arguments lay very even, and the decision taken was certainly one of critical importance.

This important contact had come through SOE's Mission in Switzerland; and that Mission was also endeavouring to reach the remains of the left-wing movements, Liberal and Socialist, in North Italy. Such movements did exist, and they were mildly active in sabotage and propaganda, but SOE was badly tricked in its attempts to support them. It was deceived through two separate channels; both by the Military Intelligence Service (SIM), who ran for it a 'resistance' organisation under the auspices of a certain Dr Klein (alias Almerigotti), and by the Fascist police (the OVRA)* which had a variety of bogus 'resistance circuits', known as 'Wolves', 'Tigers', 'Cubs', and so forth. This meant that the British diverted some useful material into Fascist hands and swallowed a good deal of fraudulent information, but luckily no harm was done to the real resistance: even a W/T operator who was infiltrated from Switzerland to Dr Klein was carefully preserved by SIM as a hostage, and was eventually rescued after the Armistice. Outside these police networks there was one other contact, with a certain Cavadini, who appears to have been genuine, and a British wireless operator, Lieutenant Mallaby, was dropped to him in August 1943: but the quiet country area in which he landed was that night filled with a swarm of refugees from an RAF attack on Milan, and Mallaby was arrested almost at once. Nevertheless he proved useful later.[1]

When the Allies invaded North Africa a small Italian section went with 'Massingham' to do what they could from the south. One area now easily accessible was Sardinia, which had hitherto been closed territory, and a Mission of two men (one an Italian-speaking Hungarian, the other a Sardinian) was landed by submarine on 11th January 1943. They had ill-luck and were captured almost at once: the usual trick was played with their wireless set and signal plan, but fortunately this time it was speedily detected. 'Massingham' kept up the interchange, and even fed the enemy gently with supplies, as evidence of their good faith: the deceivers did not suspect deception, and the channel played an extremely valuable part in the cover-plan for 'Husky' (the invasion of Sicily), which the Italians believed almost to the last was to be aimed at Sardinia. This was the only contribution made by the resistance in Sardinia: when the surrender came, an OSS officer, Lieutenant Colonel Serge Obolensky, dropped into

---

[1] Below p. 543.

* [Organizzazione di Vigilanza e Repressione dell'Antifascismo.]

Sardinia at once, with a mixed Anglo-American party, and he was followed in a few days by a larger party under Brigadier-General 'Teddy' Roosevelt.* But they could do no more than maintain liaison with the local Italian general, who had no intention whatever of fighting the retreating Germans.[1]

'Massingham' was responsible also for collecting such suitable Italians as it could find in North Africa, for training them, and for forming an SOE party to assist in the invasion of Sicily. New adherents in North Africa were not numerous: but in America and elsewhere Italians of a better type were ready to co-operate with the Allies, now that the interests of Italy lay clearly on the Allied side. The first hints of the newly formed Partito d'Azione began to reach Switzerland in June 1943, and it included already many distinguished names: and SOE was able to supply 'Massingham' with such men as Tarchiani (later a member of the Naples Government and Ambassador in Washington), Cianca (a member of the first Bonomi Government), Weiczen (a member of the Central Council of Resistance in North Italy) and Max Salvadori, Lussu's brother-in-law and a very good friend of the British.**

All this promised much better than 'Brandon', even though contacts within Italy were still slender; but 1st Army's view of 'Brandon' was on the whole unfavourable, while 8th Army had brought with it echoes of the turbulence which always surrounded SOE in Cairo. There was therefore some 'sales resistance' in Algiers to the proposal that an SOE Mission should land with 'Husky', and it required a personal visit by Lieutenant Colonel Roseberry to overcome it. The result was the 'Brow' Mission, under Major Malcolm Munthe,[2] whose father was Dr Axel Munthe, the author of 'The Story of San Michele'. Five parties went in with the invading troops, including a number of admirable Italians; there was no organised resistance in Sicily for them to raise, but there was great spontaneous goodwill, and the 'Brow' Mission fulfilled the same sort of miscellaneous role as 'Brandon', but under much more favourable auspices.

This raised SOE's stock somewhat with the soldiers: but its fortune in Italy was made, a little luckily, by the part which it played in the Armistice negotiations. Mussolini fell on 25th July, and the envoys of the Badoglio Government reached Lisbon on 20th August, in

---

1   See Lieutenant Colonel Obolensky's Report attached to Section VI of the AFHQ History.

2   He had served earlier with MI(R) in Norway and for SOE in Sweden: above pp. 49, 200.

*   [1887–1944, brigadier-general, died in Normandy; cousin of the President.]

** [See *Max Salvadori, l'uomo, il cittadino* (Fermo, 1996), proceedings of a conference in his memory.]

circumstances of considerable danger to themselves. One of the most pressing problems was how to maintain contact after their return to Italy, which could not be long delayed, and Lieutenant Colonel Roseberry was flown out to Lisbon at once, taking with him a wireless set and a signal plan. These were handed to the Italian delegates, who were hastily instructed in their use; and, to make doubly sure, they were told of the existence of the W/T operator, Mallaby, then in gaol in Milan, who was thus available in Italy to provide expert assistance. Mallaby was quietly brought to Rome by Badoglio, and it was he who used this set of Roseberry's ('Monkey' was its code name) to carry all messages between Badoglio and Eisenhower in the breathless days which preceded the Salerno landing – arranging the movements of negotiators and technical experts, the infiltration of General Taylor into Rome, the exchange of vital information of all kinds. This improvisation of a wireless link was an impressive conjuring trick rather than a planned success; but it was of great immediate value, and it also gave SOE a much higher prestige in Italian affairs than it had ever enjoyed in North Africa.*

We have already seen how difficult the Italian surrender was to handle in the Balkan and Eastern Mediterranean theatre. Security forbade SOE to give any prior indication or guidance to British Liaison Officers or to plan contacts with the Italians before the surrender was announced and our forces landed at Salerno (8/9th September 1943): Badoglio, presumably on the same grounds, had also left Italian forces without a plan or even a general lead. As it turned out, security was already hopelessly compromised, and Allied secrecy meant only that the Germans made preparations while SOE could not: in fact both the Allies and Italians might well have lessened their risks by a bolder policy.

That was however an issue above SOE's head, and it had in this phase at least one success to show, that of its part in the reoccupation of Corsica. This is worth some discussion as it was the first case in which the rising of an Allied 'fifth column' was smoothly and accurately combined with an offensive operation. Corsica had not been occupied by the Italians until Vichy France was overrun in November 1942, and the earliest SOE feelers had been made through one of the Gaullist agents in 'Vichy-land'.[1] With the occupation of North Africa the attempt began again from the south: Corsica (after all) was the home of the original 'Maquis', and it was not likely to accept Italian occupation quietly. The first party infiltrated (early in December 1942) was a Franco-American one, whose fate is not clear from SOE records:

---

[1] Above p. 280.

* [See C. M. Woods, 'A Tale of Two Armistices', in K. G. Robertson (ed.), *War, Resistance and Intelligence* (1999), p. 1 ff.]

on 31st December a 'Gaullist' party was dispatched by the French submarine 'Casabianca' under the auspices of 'Massingham'.[1] Its leader, Captain Scameroni, was a Corsican of great courage and energy and no great discretion, and under his guidance resistance grew rapidly, sporadically and dangerously. Wireless touch was lost on 15th March 1943, and it was found later that the party had been betrayed and the leader had killed himself in prison.[2]

This meant a fresh start, and the man now chosen was Captain Colonna d'Istria, a Corsican of old family who was working in the 'gendarmerie' at Algiers and was put forward on behalf of General Giraud. He was a man of first-rate ability, who needed comparatively little training, and he was put ashore in Corsica on the night of 6th April, with two Corsican assistants and a young English wireless operator. Colonna succeeded very rapidly in pulling together the divergent trends of the Resistance – Gaullist, Giraudist, Communist and pure brigand – into the semblance of a military organisation: at the end of May[3] he was able to report that 'All patriots, approximately 9,000, are under single command and organised in "cadres" in towns and villages with the view to enrolling 95% majority of the population, which is in sympathy, but so far left out for security's sake. Chain of command is established and based on administrative division of terrain and allotment of tasks – targets have been catalogued and studied.'

The next problem was one of arms, and it proved relatively simple, by the standards of SOE. The range for aircraft was fairly short from North Africa and the French submarine 'Casabianca' was available for landing operations: the total reported infiltrated before D-day was 8,000 Stens, 1,000 rifles, 150 German M.G. 34's, 98 Brens, 12 2" Mortars, with a moderate allotment of ammunition and explosives – an impressive total, when added to the arms already kept in hiding by the Corsicans, but of course adequate only for guerilla war.

Colonna came out for a visit during July, and was back in position early in August with some idea of what was to be expected. Even before the Armistice he had been in touch with Colonel Gagnoni, the Italian commander in Bastia, who was anxious to fight; and when the 8th of September came Colonna went straight to the Italian C-in-C, General Magli. Magli could not be persuaded to take the initiative, and the only Italians who fought were those under Gagnoni: but at least the Italians were neutralised and Colonna's forces were in control of a large part of the island, in which all enemy demolitions were

---

1   Operation 'Sea-Urchin' – RF Section History, 1943, pp. 2/3.
2   Details in SOE 'R/F History', 1943, p. 1.
3   Appendix A to SOE Massingham History, p. 3.

prevented. The Germans at once decided to abandon Sardinia and to evacuate their troops through Corsica; so that for them the only important thing was to keep clear the eastern coast road to Bastia. There was no obstacle in their way except Gagnoni's Italians at Bastia, backed by the Corsicans, and these were pushed aside (after some sharp fighting) by 13th September. On the same day French destroyers arrived at Ajaccio, where Colonna's men were fully in control: they brought a French Bataillon de Choc and a small SOE Mission, and other French troops arrived shortly after, accompanied by Major de Guelis, an old SOE hand.[1]

Up to this point the Corsicans had done exactly what was asked of them, and it is unlucky that there was some friction in the last days. Colonna fell sick and Commandant Clipet, who represented Giraud's 2ème Bureau, became responsible for the guerillas: partly of necessity, partly from lack of comprehension, an attempt was made to treat them as regular troops and to use them in a formal way in the French attempt to break through the German rearguards from 20th September onwards. For such a purpose they were neither equipped nor trained nor temperamentally fitted; very few of them were of any real use away from their own homes, and the Germans finally left Bastia almost undisturbed on 4th October. From SOE's point of view (and a great share of the credit goes to Colonna) it had been a well-executed little affair, and an instructive demonstration of what guerillas could and could not do.[2]

(c) The Resistance in Italy, September 1943–May 1945

Major Munthe's 'Brow' Mission, now re-named 'Vigilant', played a useful part at the Salerno landing: and thence continued its irregular skirmishing of the west coast of Italy. It rescued Benedetto Croce* from under the noses of the Germans at Capri in September 1943;[3] it took part in the Anzio landing in January 1944; and similar parties from Corsica were active in raids on the small islands of the Tyrrhenian Sea and prepared the way for the French occupation of Elba in June 1944. But these invaluable 'odd jobs' henceforward fell into the background.

There was a legitimate Italian government at Brindisi, in close military collaboration with the Allies: Italy from Naples to the Alps was

---

[1]   Above p. 251.

[2]   There is a detailed report on the Corsican Campaign available with the SOE 'CD Reports' files.

[3]   SOE Archives File 21/480/18 gives Major Munthe's account of the escape.

*   [1866–1952, Italian philosopher. On this operation, see A. Gallegos, *And Who Are You?* (1992), pp. 57–68.]

now an occupied and not an enemy country: the vast majority of Italians looked to the King's* Government as the symbol of Italian patriotism, and Mussolini's Republic had no more national authority than Laval or Doriot.** The question of Italian resistance was thus transformed instantly: what had been barren soil for SOE became at once capable of immense growth and fertility.

It is a pity that time and space make it impossible to do justice here to the political importance of Italian resistance. It flowered very quickly in what had seemed to be a barren land, and was in the end one of the greatest Resistance movements in the West, second only to that of France. It was a movement primarily of the North (and to a lesser extent of Central Italy), excluding most of the more primitive Italy which has always created a dualism in Italian politics: and it was thus a movement of a Western character, a product of the cities rather than of the mountains, combining various sophisticated political trends and weaving them together, as best it could, into an instrument of action against the Germans. It says much for the capacity of the Italian people that after twenty years of Fascism political life sprang into existence at once; confused, varied, and passionate, yet capable of successful co-operation with the constitutional framework of the National Liberation Movement.

The focus of SOE's Italian operations was now with the Italian Government and the Allied armies in Italy, and the old arrangements for control by J Section in London with a sub-section in Algiers immediately became obsolete. Unfortunately it was some time before a workable alternative was found: in the interim period there were three claimants. *First*, there was the small SOE Mission which had given technical assistance at the Armistice negotiations and which landed at Brindisi with the first Allied arrivals, in order to maintain liaison with the Badoglio Government. This party became a very useful part of the Allied Control Commission; and it was reinforced by Lieutenant Colonel Roseberry himself, who still held a post on the establishment of London HQ, with power to act for it on the spot. *Second*, there was No. 1 Special Force, or 'Maryland', which arrived from North Africa in October 1943, and eventually established its HQ at Monopoli near Bari. This was commanded by Lieutenant Commander Holdsworth, RNVR, who had been mixed up in most of SOE's para-naval activities from the days of Colonel Grand's 'cruising club' in the summer of 1939:[1] it was conceived only as an operational 'out-station', not a directing HQ, and was designed primarily to take prompt

---

[1]   Above p. 21.

*   [Victor Emmanuel III, 1869–1947, King of Italy 1900–46. See F. W. Deakin, *The Brutal Friendship* (1966) on fall of Mussolini.]

** [J. Doriot, 1898–1945, lapsed Communist, ardent supporter of Pétain.]

advantage of a new jumping-off ground, which would be useful for many destinations besides Italy.[1] In theory it was merely parallel to the small para-naval unit 'Balaclava',* which was pushed forward at the same time to the northern tip of Corsica to work into South France and North Italy: in practice it proved to be 'the man on the spot' for practically all Italian operations, and the ends of many strings dropped naturally into its hands. *Third*, 'Massingham', now under Lieutenant Colonel Dodds-Parker,** was still at Algiers: 'Maryland' was its child, and 'Massingham' was in form responsible for the policy which 'Maryland' was to carry out. The strength of 'Massingham's' position lay in that it was at hand in Algiers, close to the Allied Supreme Commander and his political advisers, and it was the official recipient of his directives.[2] In this respect it was not only in control of 'Maryland', it was also virtually independent of SOE HQ in London except for administrative matters. The first ruling by AFHQ was that co-ordination by HQ 15th Army Group in Italy should cover special operations only up to a line running just north of Rome:[3] SOE work beyond that line would be controlled through 'Massingham' by AFHQ in Algiers. The line was afterwards moved forward to La Spezia–Rimini, but it remained a nonsensical division: Italian resistance could not be fed and controlled in two sections from two separate centres, one in Italy, the other in Algiers.

The result of this confusion was that relations between Lieutenant Colonel Roseberry in Italy and Lieutenant Colonel Dodds-Parker in Algiers became increasingly distant and acrimonious, since they disagreed not only on responsibilities but on policy; the former stood for long-term political preparation, the latter for quick military gains. This rather unedifying dispute was primarily the result of the confusion of command relations on a much higher level, and it could not be resolved until the SACMED was appointed and had moved his advanced HQ to Caserta at the end of 1943. The centre of the Mediterranean theatre was now in Italy and so also was the centre of Mediterranean special operations; after March 1944 these were controlled in theory through G3 (Special Operations) at AFHQ and

---

1 Operations across the Adriatic were taken out of its hands when 'Advanced Force 133' arrived from Cairo in November 1943. (See SOE HQ War Diary, Middle East and Balkans Section, p. 1309.)

2 See e.g. that of 18th August 1943: App. A to AFHQ History, Section IV.

3 AFHQ directive of 30th September 1943: Annex B to AFHQ History, Section IV.

* [Croft ran 'Balaclava' (see page 49.)]

** [(Sir) A. D. Dodds-Parker, born 1909, long stop in Khartoum for Abyssinian expedition, headed 'Massingham', moved forward to Caserta, Conservative MP 1949–59, 1964–74, knight 1972.]

at 15th Army Group, and through HQ SOM under Major General Stawell. 'Massingham' in Algiers was now concerned only with the penetration of France from the south in close concert with the London organisation in the north, and it was important to the Mediterranean theatre only in relation to the 'Dragoon' landings in the south of France. Lieutenant Colonel Roseberry was at this stage withdrawn to London, where he became 'regional head' for Switzerland and Italy: some useful co-ordination could be done there, but the centre of policy lay in Italy. There the control of G3(SO) and HQ SOM over 'Maryland' was in practice very slight: 'Maryland' was now virtually responsible for all British special operations in Italy under the supervision of HQ 15th Army Group and Mr Harold Macmillan, the British political representative. The Americans were not integrated in 'Maryland', and OSS policy was in practice regulated independently through an American chain of command: fortunately collaboration on the lower levels was close and friendly, and there does not seem to have been much trouble over collaboration in detail, though there was some confusion of purpose and much confusion of organisation.

It will be simplest to complete here the story of 'Maryland's' development in this final phase. At first its main HQ was near Bari, while its dispatch airfield was near Brindisi: a Tactical HQ went with 5th Army through Rome and up to Florence, and was responsible for all the work of close collaboration with the Partisans in the field. The connection with the 8th Army on the Adriatic coast was less close, but a liaison mission was established at their HQ in December 1944.[1] In February 1945 both HQ SOM and 'Maryland' moved to Siena, and their internal organisation was there linked and simplified: at the same time the main dispatch centre was moved forward from the Brindisi airfield to that at Malignano on the west coast. Rosignano near Siena was also sometimes used.

The structure of this chain of command remains almost unintelligible on paper: but in practice it provided in the end the two things necessary – a single controlling centre for resistance, in close touch with the military and political high command: and tactical detachments operating with the advancing troops down to Army level and below.

There are perhaps four phases distinguishable in the twenty months from September 1943 to the beginning of May 1945:

(i)   *First*, the confused alternations of hope and despair from the Salerno landing in September 1943 until the Allied breakthrough to Rome in the latter part of May 1944.

(ii) *Second*, the summer of 1944, a period of all-out offensive

---

1   SOE Archives File 21/480/12 gives details of 8th Army Liaison: Captain E. P. Macdermott was the first Liaison Officer.

action by the Italian partisans, accompanied on the one hand by political consolidation, on the other by an Allied attempt to secure better military control.

(iii) *Third*, the winter of 1944–5, which was marked by effective German counter-action and a decline in guerilla activity, and also by Allied nervousness about the political fruits of the Resistance: a period of damping down.

(iv) *Fourth*, the German peace-feelers and the final liberation, March–May 1945.

(i) The First Phase, September 1943–May 1944

In spite of 'Massingham's' claims to primacy, the burden of the new phase fell in the first instance on Lieutenant Colonel Roseberry's Mission in Brindisi and on 'Maryland'. The former were in confidential relations with the Badoglio Government, and were also authorised by AFHQ to work closely with the Italian Ministries and in particular with the surviving parts of the Military Intelligence Service (SIM), an old enemy which was now a valuable source of information. 'Maryland' had to handle the practical aspects of co-operation – the supply of Italian agents, trained, untrained, and half-trained, the utilisation of small Italian naval vessels for coastal activity, and of Italian aircraft for air supply.

Naturally order did not emerge at once: but great progress was made. By the end of October 1943 six Italian Missions had gone to the field with wireless sets, among them the 'Rudder' Mission to Rome, which kept open a link of great importance through the days of Anzio in January 1944 up to the liberation of Rome on 4th June: and during the next six months eighteen other Italian Missions (forty-one 'bodies' in all) went to the field. The supply position was not very brilliant,[1] but at least some 200–300 tons were got in by air during the winter and an equal amount by sea: in addition, the Italians had been able to divert a good deal of equipment of their own from German control.

Politically, old landmarks began to re-emerge. The 'Six Parties'[2] became recognisable as formed bodies, with leaders and principles and clandestine newspapers; and (in spite of divisions and cross-divisions as regards the monarchy, religion, property and almost everything else) there arose in most towns a Committee of National Liberation (CLN) representing all the parties, backed by a Corps of Volunteers of Freedom (CVL) which included all active fighting elements irrespective of party affiliation. The general pattern of activity was that in the mountains there would be bands of deserters,

[1] See SOE Monthly Review of Activities and App. E to SOE Italian History.
[2] Liberal, Democrat, Action Party, Christian Democrat, Socialist, Communist.

fugitives from Fascist conscription, 'broken men' of all kinds, quietly but warmly supported by the peasantry; poorly armed, but on the whole good fighting material. Among them were a surprising number of escaped Allied prisoners of a variety of colours, creeds and nations. Each major town would have a circle of active politicians, who combined mutual suspicion with mutual support, and exercised a rather shadowy collective influence over the partisans in the mountains; the latter were dependent on the towns for many things – money, forged papers, information of enemy movements, technical supplies of many kinds, sometimes even for food.[1]

Fortunately it was only the Communist Party which attempted to tie these bands to itself so as to form a private army; this policy, cut according to their standard pattern, had enough success to alarm the Western Allies, especially after the civil war of December 1944 in Greece, but it never attained the military monopoly achieved by the Communist Party in Yugoslavia, Albania and Greece. It is doubtful whether it was even as strong as the Communist 'FANA' and 'FTP' in France.

Other political parties were too weak and inexperienced to compete on this ground. There were however a certain number of individuals who became in effect independent leaders of their own organisations, with no more than a nominal attachment to the hierarchy of the CNL and CVL. Those of Dr Balduzzi and Lieutenant Sogno are worth mentioning.

Balduzzi was a distinguished brain specialist in Genoa who made contact with 'Maryland' by courier shortly after the Armistice and received three of the first Italian Missions sent into the field. With their help he opened wireless contact and made arrangements to receive stores by sea from Corsica ('Balaclava') and by air. For six months his 'Otto' organisation grew rapidly and was a valuable channel of intelligence and of assistance to escaping prisoners. But it was 'blown' during March 1944 and collapsed completely.

Lieutenant Sogno also began independent organisation in the winter of 1943–4, under the name of 'Franchi': this was based on Milan and had a certain 'liberal' or anti-Communist political flavour, though it professed to operate on a non-political basis and accepted the direction of the CLNAI in Milan. Sogno was a man of great courage and enterprise, and his organisation was of service in many ways, though its security was bad and it was from the spring of 1944 frequently shaken by arrests. Nevertheless fragments of the organisation remained vigorous: Sogno himself was instrumental in bringing a delegation

---

1   This is the background of the Italian film 'Open City', which deals with the atmosphere of Rome during that winter, brilliantly and (so far as one can judge) most faithfully.

south from Milan in November 1944 to confer with the Allied Command and the Italian Government. His career ended in a gallant but unsuccessful attempt in January 1945 to rescue Ferruccio Parri, in which Sogno was himself captured.[1]

In this first phase there was not so much an organisation, as a mass of raw, energetic, untrained recruits, anxious to hurt the enemy, but ignorant of conspiratorial method and apt to attack without co-ordination in circumstances where (through the hostage system or otherwise) they suffered much more damage than they inflicted. To the Allies the small Italian successes and the irritation and delay they caused were almost pure gain. But they were a large net loss to the Italians, except in so far as they created a cooler and a more experienced hatred for the Germans. The winter of Cassino and Anzio was the blackest time of all for Italy.

(ii) The Summer of 1944

As we shall see later, the planning of 'Overlord' in the West included the first thoroughly prepared scheme for the utilisation of a resistance movement in support of an Allied offensive. There was no native material for so elaborate an organisation in Italy, nor was the SO organisation at AFHQ strong enough to plan it. Nevertheless something was done to canalise the spontaneous outburst of Italian energy and optimism which followed the breakthrough to Rome and the simultaneous great offensives in East and West: and it became important to do more, as Allied troops were drained away from Italy for the 'Anvil' landings in the south of France and General Alexander was left to conduct a policy of continuous offensive with ground forces numerically inferior to those which opposed him.

Thus in the summer of 1944 the Italian Partisans become for the first time potential allies of importance; the Allied policy is to supply and encourage them, without too much thought for the political morrow, and reasonably good priority is given to their needs. Supply arrangements improve in quantity, quality, promptness; British officers begin to arrive as representatives of the Allied High Command and to give ocular evidence of the doctrine proclaimed publicly by AFHQ in July 1944, that the Partisans belong to the regular forces of the Allied Italian State and are entitled to the full protection of the laws of war.

Between June and September 1944 seventeen British Missions (thirty-seven British 'bodies', seventeen Italian) arrived in the field; they were not the only cause, but an important one, of the increase of Partisan military efficiency. They were now better trained, better armed and better led, and their attacks were on the whole relevant to

---

[1] Both Balduzzi and Sogno survived the war.

the main military operations in hand. There is ample evidence[1] of the burden which these activities imposed on Marshal Kesselring's* command, and so long as he was holding on desperately in face of a series of major offensives he had no troops to spare in order to bring the situation under control. It was not until October 1944 that the Germans were at leisure to turn and hit back systematically.

There was similar consolidation in the towns. The CLNAI (Committee of National Liberation of Northern Italy) is said to have been formed as early as October 1943 to federate the CLNs of the towns of the Po Valley, but it only emerged as a serious force in the spring of 1944. It had by that time an elaborate paper organisation of Regions and Zones, which had even a certain limited control in practice, where local circumstances permitted: and its central committee in Milan was of sufficient authority to treat as an equal with the Italian Government in liberated territory. Similarly there existed in theory, and to a limited extent in practice, a chain of military command (parallel to the CLNAI) and controlling the Corps of Volunteers of Liberty; the 'Volunteers' were in part fully mobilised as 'partisans' in the hills, in part awaited the call in their ordinary jobs in the towns. Contacts with this organisation were opened through Switzerland in the winter of 1943–4: in June 1944 an Allied subsidy of 100,000,000 lire a month was begun: and in August General Cadorna (son of a victorious general of 1918) was parachuted into North Italy, accompanied by a British Liaison Officer, Major Oliver Churchill, to act as Military Commander under the direction of AFHQ. Under him were two joint Chiefs of Staff: Longo, a Communist, and Ferruccio Parri of the Action Party, Prime Minister from June to November 1945.

There is no simple means of striking a military balance-sheet for Italian resistance in this period. There is plenty of evidence to prove the damage done by small attacks on German troops and stores and the anxiety which they caused the Germans, and there are plenty of dramatic stories: that for instance of the telephone line which kept communications open across the Ponte Vecchia over the Arno at Florence to Partisan HQ behind the enemy lines, while the Germans faced the 5th Army over the river. The best-known story perhaps is one of disaster, the ill-timed rising in the Val d'Ossola, which held the upper part of the Simplon line for thirty-two days in September and October 1944, until overrun by strong German forces. It was unfortunately a case in which the typical vices of Italian politics had

---

1   See the photostats of German documents obtained after the Armistice and attached as Annexes to the AFHQ History, Section IV.

*   [A. Kesselring, 1885–1960, Chief of Staff of Luftwaffe 1936–8, Field-Marshal 1940, German C-in-C in Southern Europe 1941–4, in NW Europe March–May 1945. Sentenced to death 1947, reprieved, released 1952.]

the upper hand over individual courage and energy.[1] There was thus a great volume of guerilla activity, but once the Germans were back on the short line north of Pisa to Ravenna their communications were not highly vulnerable at crucial points to attacks of this kind. The Po Valley was bad territory for Partisans, the mountains of the Swiss frontier had little military significance, and the vital roads and railways to Austria and Yugoslavia were restricted objectives and not difficult to protect. The situation was thus very different to that in France, where the area of operations was much wider; the military value of guerillas was necessarily limited.

On the other hand their political significance was considerable. The real reconstruction of the Italian State dates (oddly enough) from the return to Italy of Togliatti, the very able Communist leader, at the end of March 1944. He at once proclaimed an abrupt turn of Communist policy, which permitted the Party to accept office in a royal government under the leadership of the 'reactionary' Badoglio: this recantation forced the hand of the other parties, and the first 'six-party' government was formed by Badoglio on 21st April. When Rome was reoccupied Badoglio gave place to Bonomi:* but the principle of 'national coalition' was maintained, and the transfer of the Government to Rome made it once more in point of prestige a true government of Italy. To complete its status it required the allegiance of those Italians who were still under enemy occupation; and the politics of the summer turned largely on its relations with the CLNAI, and in turn on the extent of the control which the CLNAI could exercise as an organ of government in the North. These problems were on the whole solved by the autumn of 1944, and in their solution the activities of the Partisans were of primary importance as a symbol of political unity and the national will to resist.

(iii) The Winter of 1944–5

The end of this phase can be marked formally by the visit of a Mission from the CLNAI to Rome in December 1944, escorted by 'La Franchi' (Lieutenant Sogno). The Party consisted of Dr Alfredo Pizzoni (known as 'Pietro Longhi'), an 'Independent' who was President of the CLNAI; Parri of the Action Party, joint Chief of Staff to General Cadorna; and the Communist Mare. Long discussions with the Bonomi Government and AFHQ led to a series of carefully-drafted agreements, in which the Bonomi Government formally 'delegated the CLNAI to represent it in the struggle' in occupied Italy; the CLNAI accepted the Bonomi

---

[1] See Report made in 1945 by Lieutenant George Paterson, an escaped British prisoner who was sent in as Liaison Officer by SOE from Switzerland, and was captured. SOE Archives File 21NE/400/71.

* [I. Bonomi, 1873–1951, anti-Fascist, Italian Prime Minister 1944–5.]

Government as the legitimate authority in such territory as the Allies returned to it, and agreed to accept the military directives of Field Marshal Alexander: the Allies on their side undertook to make available 260,000,000 lire a month.[1] This was on paper satisfactory, but the state of Italian politics was already deteriorating once more as the date of final liberation approached. Bonomi's first government had fallen at the end of November, and there was an interregnum of hard bargaining before a new government was formed, without the Socialists and the Action Party, after a squabble with the Allies about the proposed appointment of Count Sforza as Foreign Minister.

The Allies on their side were becoming nervous about the condition of Italian politics, and in particular about the danger of Communist influence growing beyond bounds and reproducing the situations of Greece and Yugoslavia. The Communists had been the chief architects of the Six-Party coalition – a cause for suspicion in itself – and there was enough in the reports of Liaison Officers in the field to suggest that the Communist 'Garibaldi Brigades' had much more in mind than resistance to the Germans. The situation was particularly disturbing in north-eastern Italy. The Slovene population there gave allegiance to Tito and was organised by his men on the usual lines: in spite of racial antagonisms, this 'open door' into Eastern Europe seems to have enabled the Communists to organise exceptionally strong 'Garibaldi Brigades' of Italians, who were as likely to co-operate with the Slovenes after German withdrawal as with the more conservative Italian elements with which they were formally united in the CVL. The north-east was clearly the danger-point, and the situation there was well documented by reports from successive British Liaison Officers, Major Vincent and Major R. T. S. Macpherson.[2] But there was also cause for anxiety elsewhere, particularly as regards Communist influence over the industrial workers in the large towns.

There was thus a deliberate change of Allied policy as the continuance of the war through the winter became certain. The idea of relatively large Partisan forces was abandoned: the Italian role would no longer be to eke out the slender Allied strength by a sustained guerilla offensive, but to continue minor sabotage, to take steps to prevent 'scorching' of Italian resources by the Germans, and to be ready to maintain order when the collapse came.[3] This meant that military

---

1 Appendices K, L and M to AFHQ History of Special Operations.
2 Roneoed copies circulated by No.1 Special Force – REF MN/859 of 29th November 1944, and J/Circ/83 of 30th December 1944; copy with SOE Archives 'CD' files.
3 This is embodied in Field Marshal Alexander's directive of 4th February 1945 (App. O to Section IV of AFHQ History of Special Operations), but was certainly in force earlier.

supplies to North Italy would be substantially reduced and aircraft diverted to other purposes: that Liaison Officers would be asked particularly to watch the political situation and keep some control of the destination of supplies: and that the main plan would not be one for armed rising but for 'counter-scorch' and a peaceful take-over in what were commonly known as 'Rankin' conditions – those of a German collapse or voluntary withdrawal. There was thus no important expansion during the winter except for the detachment of sub-missions by 'Maryland' to Nice and Grenoble in December 1944, with a HQ later at Avignon. These were designed to organise and encourage Italian resisters driven over the mountains by enemy activity, and to work back into Italy from this new angle, both over the mountains and along the coast. They had some success, accompanied by a good deal of diplomatic difficulty; the French unfortunately lacked enthusiasm for the re-birth of Italy and were on the whole obstructive.[1]

This change of policy was depressing for 'Maryland', as well as for Liaison Officers in the field and for the Italians themselves. As Allied pressure relaxed on the main front, German attention had been turned to the areas dominated by the Partisans, and these had in many cases been temporarily cleared at the cost of comparatively small casualties to the Germans. Winter aided the process of dissolution, and the active strength of the CVL dwindled rapidly, though their battle casualties were not high. At the same time there was vigorous police activity in the towns: as we have seen, Parri and Sogno were captured early in 1945 and there were other losses. Italian Resistance was thus in any event hard-pressed, and the decrease in Allied support was keenly felt. Nevertheless, the political basis of the new policy was probably sound: and it did not so weaken the Italians as to cripple their action when spring came and the Allied offensive was renewed.

(iv) The Last Phase

The end at last came quickly: Field Marshal Alexander's final offensive was launched on 12th April, the Argenta Gap was forced on 17th April, the Po was crossed on the 25th and the German surrender was signed on the 29th. But there had been signs and portents since the beginning of 1945. German local commanders tended to make local 'arrangements' for mutual toleration with the Partisans: copious hints of approaches on a higher level began to reach SOE and OSS through well-to-do Italians who kept a foot in both camps: and in February there were well-authenticated proposals from the German High Command in Italy. The handling of these was entrusted to Mr Allan

---

[1] For further details see Chapter XX of SOE Italian History and Annex P to AFHQ History of Special Operations.

Dulles,* the OSS representative in Switzerland, and they led on 8th March to the arrival in Berne of Waffen SS General Karl Wolff,** the chief SS officer in North Italy, accompanied by a representative of the High Command.[1] The complex negotiations which followed need not be described here: they led first to the release by the Germans of Ferruccio Parri, as a guarantee of their good faith; then to a meeting between Major General Lemnitzer[†] (US), Major General Airey[††] (British) and General Wolff in Switzerland on 21st March, and on 13th April to the dispatch of an Allied wireless operator (a Czech named Hradecky) to German HQ in Milan to make possible continuous direct communication. At each stage there were complex reservations and references back on each side, and no formal agreement of any kind had been reached when the Allied offensive was launched on 12th April. But the German High Command had by this time moved far from the Wagnerian vision of North Italy in flames and a last stand in the German Alps: resistance was now relevant only to the timing of surrender and the preservation of 'military honour' – the necessary qualification for a military career in the 'next Reich'. The channels already opened led directly to the dispatch of German representatives who reached Switzerland on 27th April, *en route* for Caserta where they signed unconditional capitulation on 29th April: the surrender was publicly announced on 2nd May, when the Allies were already well on their way towards the Austrian frontier.

Inconclusive though they were, these negotiations greatly simplified the task of the Resistance in North Italy.[2] A period of maximum effort was timed to coincide with the Allied offensive, and it opened splendidly with general strikes in Turin and Milan on 19th April. When the breakthrough came two days later, all was in readiness to harass the German retreat, to block their plans for destruction, and to aid the Allied pursuit towards the Swiss frontier and the Brenner. Fortunately the German High Command was now itself in sympathy with those purposes, and the Italians had to reckon only with German

---

1 There is a detailed account by Mr Dulles at Annex Q to AFHQ History of Special Operations.

2 There is a detailed narrative of this phase by Lieutenant Colonel Hewitt: 'Report on No. 1 Special Force Activities during April 1945' dated 3rd June 1945. Ref. MI/P/19/354.

* [A. W. Dulles, 1893–1969, younger brother of J. F., Roosevelt's man in Switzerland 1942–5, head of CIA 1953–61. See his life by James Srodes (1999).]

** [1906–84, pre-war Chief of Staff to Himmler, SS commander in Northern Italy 1943–5.]

† [L. L. Lemnitzer, 1899–1988, deputy Chief of Staff, Fifteenth Army Group.]

†† [(Sir) T. S. Airey, 1900–83, in SOE Cairo, knight 1951, commanded in Hong Kong 1952–4.]

commanders on a lower level who misunderstood the situation or deliberately chose a Götterdämmerung of their own. In all this the Italians were brilliantly successful. Destruction was almost completely stopped: numerous small German units were harassed into surrender: and a number of towns of great importance – Turin, Milan, Venice, Bergamo among others – were firmly in Italian hands before the Allies arrived. 'Maryland's' part was to send forward detachments of experienced officers with the leading troops of the Fifth and Eighth Armies. These proved extremely valuable in making contact with British Liaison Officers and in establishing a working understanding between the Allied regular forces on the one side and the confused enthusiastic outburst of Italian feeling on the other.[1]

The enemy was already beaten and the direct military importance of SOE's work here lay mainly in the hours, perhaps days, which it allowed the Allies to gain by following up their breakthrough *à l'outrance*, in absolute confidence that they were advancing through a friendly population which possessed at least the rudiments of political and military organisation. In the light of later events, the speed thus gained perhaps proved most vital in the New Zealand Division's rush for Trieste: but at the time it was at least equally important to cut the German Army into pockets beyond hope of recovery.

Politically the Resistance counted for much more. It was a political gain to the Allies that in every town and village Committees of National Liberation emerged at once as a provisional organ of government, with the co-operation of all political parties, the allegiance of a vast majority of the population, and the habit of command. The passage from the régime of the CNLs to that of the normal authorities of the State prevented difficulties later, both for Allied Military Government and for the Italian Government in Rome: but at the time they played a part in the maintenance of the framework of public order which could have been achieved in no other way. And for this it was important that they had behind them the 'myth' of the Partisan movement. The Allies (it would be admitted) had won the battle: but it was the Italians themselves who had risen and taken back their towns from the invader. For a brief space there was Italian victory and Italian harmony: the mood was soon dulled by the harshness of the post-war world, but it was a moment of importance in Italian history, in which the Allied special forces played an honourable part.

---

[1] There were in North Italy on 1st April fifty-nine British officers and sixty-six other ranks, as well as ninety-two Italians recruited and trained by 'Maryland'.

CHAPTER XXIV

France

The earlier chapter on France has perhaps done enough to illustrate the complexity of French affairs, even when Resistance was in its infancy. In the great period of French Resistance this complexity increases, the available evidence is enormous and on all points of detail conflicting. A great historian in future may be able to do it justice, and he is more likely to be British than French: conflicting 'myths' of the French Resistance are already woven into the substance of French thought and politics. All that can be done here is to impose a somewhat arbitrary order on the mass of material, and to concentrate mainly on the part played by the Resistance in the military plans of the Allies.

The plan of this chapter is briefly as follows. *First*, as a convenience for reference, to sketch briefly the political history of the French outside France and the changing pattern of British and French organisations designed to assist Resistance. *Second*, to trace the growth of effective organised forces within France, organised on the one hand by F Section, on the other by the French themselves in collaboration with R/F Section. *Third*, to assess the value of the offensive action by these forces in the period before D-day, 6th June 1944. *Fourth*, to trace the evolution and effects of the plans made to assist the invasion. Each section interlocks with and overlaps the others.

1. Politics and Organisation Outside France

During the preparations for 'Torch' the British were, rather faintly, 'Gaullist': the Americans strongly hostile to De Gaulle and inclined

---

Note: The main continuous sources not used earlier are:

The History of SFHQ, prepared by SOE. A 'tripartite' history of EMFFI (very unsatisfactory).

A History of the 'Jedburgh', prepared by J/Cdr K. Keble (very useful).

There are also references of some importance of General Eisenhower and General Maitland-Wilson. General Montgomery's Dispatch has only one minor reference (London Gazette of 4th September 1946, p. 4433).

to some sort of 'Weygandist' solution – a fairly intelligible programme for North Africa, but (as it soon proved) quite irrelevant to the problem of France itself. General Giraud, extracted from France in some haste and embarrassment on 5th November, was the *deus ex machina* expected to produce a conclusion acceptable to both parties. De Gaulle (whatever he may have suspected) was shut out from all formal knowledge of the plan until Mr Churchill and Mr Eden saw him on 8th November, the day of the operation itself. He then reacted well: he expressed great willingness to co-operate with Giraud, and delivered a most helpful broadcast. This happy start was wrecked by the extemporised flirtation with Darlan.[1] Darlan, armed with the authority of Marshal Pétain, undoubtedly made a most important contribution to the military success of the operation: indeed he represented the only means by which the Allies might win the race for Tunisia. But politically he was a blind alley, or worse: and it was an undisguised blessing when he was assassinated on Christmas Eve, whatever the origins of the assassin.

The way was now open for Giraud. Darlan had constituted an 'Imperial Council' of high officers and officials: the Council, on the strength of a 'secret ordinance' signed by Darlan before his death, elected Giraud as High Commissioner for Military and Civil Affairs in all the North African territories. The appointment rested really on the authority of General Eisenhower, but there still clung to it a faint flavour of legitimacy derived from the Maréchal at Vichy: perhaps still an asset in French colonial circles, but a political millstone for the future.

There were now two French governments in exile, both concerned to secure their position in France. De Gaulle in London continued to operate through 'Passy' and the BCRA, in collaboration with the R/F Section of SOE. A more military air was however given to the old arrangements by the institution in May 1943 of the État Major F. under Général de l'Air Cochet, charged with the planning of Resistance activity to assist an Allied invasion.[2] Cochet was a good professional soldier, who had been intended earlier[3] to act as Chef d'État Major of the Gaullist Secret Army in France, and was brought out to England in the spring of 1943. His immediate superior was for the present De Gaulle himself: later Général de l'Air François d'Astier de la Vigerie, brother of the head of 'Libération', who had come out in November 1942, and was for a time commander of

---

1 Text of the Agreement with him in Foreign Office Print No. Z/10522/8325/17 of 23rd December 1942; copy on SOE Archives File 3/100/1(a).
2 COS(43)261(0) of 19th May; copy on SOE Archives File 3/470/1a.
3 Note of meeting with 'Passy', 10th September 1942, on SOE Archives File 3/100/2(c).

French Forces in the United Kingdom and Délégué to the Allied High Command:[1] 'Passy' and the BCRA were nominally his subordinates.

Giraud in North Africa set to work, much less efficiently, to build what he could out of the Armée de l'Armistice, now demobilised: the Deuxième and Cinquième Bureaux of his Staff, which were responsible, were directed by Colonel Rivet, under the supervision of General Ronin, his Chief of Staff. In North Africa SOE collaborated with him first through Colonel Keswick, who arrived on 17th November with the 'Massingham' Mission from Gibraltar and remained until April 1943,[2] then through Colonel Dodds-Parker who took over 'Massingham': Lieutenant Colonel Anstey was from September 1943 his chief assistant and was largely concerned with French affairs. In London a certain Captain Lejeune arrived in February 1943 as Giraud's representative for this work, and a separate 'Giraudist' sub-section was set up within F Section.

At Casablanca, in January 1943, Giraud and De Gaulle were induced to shake hands, but this small concession was achieved only by the combined authority of the President and the Prime Minister, and negotiations then stood still for months, while the parties sparred for position. Giraud weakened himself by demonstrating publicly his dependence on Vichyist administrators, such as Bergeret, Boisson and Peyrouton:* De Gaulle through 'Passy' worked indefatigably to unify the Resistance behind himself. In March Giraud made a sharp turn away from the Old Vichy associations: a meeting planned for April was postponed at the direct request of General Eisenhower until the final crisis in Tunisia was past. Finally, through the mediation of General Catroux,** the two Generals met in North Africa on 31st May, accompanied on the one side by General Georges and M. Jean

---

1   He made an important 'reconnaissance' for De Gaulle in North Africa in December 1942. For his later position as 'Délégué Militaire' of the 'Comité d'Action' in France, see M. Viénot to Sir A. Cadogan 18th December 1943, on SOE Archives File 3/100/1a.

2   He returned for a visit in July 1943, while acting as Director of both SOE's French Sections. See his Directive dated 19th July 1943 on SOE Archives File F.38/II.

*   [J. M. J. Bergeret, 1895–1956, Vichy's Air Minister 1940–2, supported Darlan in Algiers, resigned March 1943, in prison till 1945. P. Boisson, 1894–1948, Governor of Dakar 1940–43, in prison 1943–5. M. Peyrouton, 1887–1983, colonial administrator, ran repressive police for Pétain 1940–41, Ambassador in Buenos Aires 1942–3; briefly Governor of Algeria 1943 till purged by Gaullists; see his *Du service public à la prison commune* (Paris, 1950).]

** [G. A. J. Catroux, 1877–1969, Gaullist commander in Syria 1941, governed Algeria 1944, French Ambassador in Moscow 1945–8.]

Monnet,* on the other by M. André Philip and M. Massigli. From this meeting emerged the CFLN – Comité Française de Libération Nationale – which was to meet under the joint chairmanship of General Giraud and General De Gaulle and to consist of seven members, with the possibility of adding others. The other five members were General Catroux, General Georges, M. Massigli, Jean Monnet and André Philip: a balance of Gaullists and Giraudists which was not likely to endure. Almost at once there was a flurry about the possible enlargement of the Committee, which led Mr Churchill to threaten extreme action against De Gaulle by cutting off supplies to the Gaullist Resistance: but this blew over for the time being. Varying degrees of recognition were extended by the United Kingdom, the USA and the USSR.[1]

General Giraud was now C-in-C of all French forces, and in effect Minister of War: M. Philip was Commissaire de l'Intérieur. Hence there was an immediate clash of responsibilities for the Resistance in France, solved temporarily by the institution of a committee consisting of Giraud, De Gaulle and Philip. This committee was charged with making recommendations for the recognition of the 'Special Services'; as was to be expected, it deadlocked at once, and their competing activities continued as before. The only immediate change was that the centre of 'Passy's' activity shifted to Algiers, to which he transferred himself in June, in spite of an American attempt to stop him.[2] Politics required that 'Passy' should be in North Africa, but England was still the main channel of communications with France, and the French organisation there was of immense importance. The London Branch of the BCRA now became the Bureau de Renseignements et Action à Londres – BRAL – under 'Passy's' nominee, Commandant Manuel. Manuel was nominally under the command of General Cochet, but that good soldier was intensely dissatisfied with his own limited power of control over an organisation which worked largely for political purposes under the independent direction of Algiers.[3]

It was soon clear that the balance of votes in the CFLN counted

---

1 See Foreign Office Print Z/6774/6504/69 of 22nd September 1943; copy on SOE Archives File 3/100/1a.

2 Minute by Colonel Sporborg to CD dated 15th June 1943; copy on SOE Archives File F.38/II.

3 In mid-July an attempt was made to unseat him (Note by Colonel Buckmaster dated 31st July 1943 – copy on SOE Archives File 3/100/2(c)). His strong letter of protest to De Gaulle dated 13th July is on SOE Archives File 3/100/6c.

* [A. J. Georges, 1875–1951, commanded armies in north-east France 1940, refused to take political stance. M. Jean Monnet, 1888–1979, a founding father of the European Community.]

for little in practice. De Gaulle's political position was impregnably based on the fact that the Conseil Nationale de la Résistance in France,* which was formally constituted on 5th May 1943, was for him and against Giraud. They made it perfectly clear that a government standing politically to the Right of De Gaulle could only be imposed on France by force of arms; this was undoubtedly true, and it needed little Gaullist prompting to have it effectively said. His political line was a judicious mixture: on the one hand, strong Nationalism in face of 'Anglo-Saxon' encroachment, and a strong defence of the needs and powers of the Resistance: on the other, an insistence on the democratic will of the French people, a gentle move to the Left in social policy, and a bid for Russian support against the 'Anglo-Americans'. Against this combination American hostility was powerless: it was indeed an asset, as it strengthened De Gaulle's position in France, both with Nationalists and with 'anti-capitalists': and as his position in France became stronger it became less and less possible for the Americans to challenge the authority of the only man who could summon French assistance to save American lives on D-day.

The crisis came during November 1943. For months past De Gaulle had been at work on the project of an Assemblée Consultative, half of whose members should be 'Resisters' brought specially from France. Early in November Emmanuel D'Astier (SOE's old friend 'Bernard' of 'Libération') succeeded André Philip as Commissaire de l'Intérieur: and there was a blast of publicity about his Resistance record and the neglect of Resistance by the Allies – implying also the negligence of Giraud. In this political atmosphere an old professional soldier could not hope to retain influence except by military force. On 9th November Giraud resigned his position as a member of the CFLN: for the moment he remained C-in-C of the Armed Forces, but on 4th April 1944 he abandoned this also, and retired fairly cheerfully into private life. Politics were not his métier.[1]

De Gaulle as sole chairman of the CFLN was now in effect both President and Prime Minister of the only government which could claim to represent the French nation. The next step was the proclamation of the CFLN as the Gouvernement Provisoire de la République Française, on the invitation of the Assemblée Consultative: this did not come until 15th May, and Allied recognition was slow to follow. But the rest was certain, given Allied military success.

The Committee on 'Special Services' had at the end of August

---

[1] For General Wilson's view of Giraud's position at this stage see his Report pp. 15–16.

* [See R. Hostache, *Le Conseil National de la Résistance* (Paris, 1958).]

come to an agreement on unification,[1] but it was not till early in November that General Cochet was summoned from England to take charge of the single organisation to be formed in North Africa, under the direction of the Committee.[2] This compromise broke down at once, on Giraud's fall from power. Cochet was replaced by M. Soustelle,* a clever young anthropologist with political ambitions,[3] and the dominating influence in the amalgamation was that of the BCRA. The cover-name of the new Directorate of Special Services was 'Direction Générale d'Etudes et Récherches' (a graceful tribute perhaps to the 'Inter-Services Research Bureau'!): and it was responsible to a committee consisting of De Gaulle, D'Astier and Le Trocquer – the last a Socialist resister who was designated later as Commissaire-Général in France for the period of the Liberation. Thus, very late in the day, there was at last an intelligible pattern in French organisation; Consultative Assembly, CFLN, 'Steering' Committee, DGER. But there remained the confusing factor of division of responsibility between Algiers and London. There General Koenig, the 'hero of Bir-Hakim', in April 1944 succeeded Emmanuel's brother, François D'Astier, as commander of French forces in Great Britain: and in May he was given command of the newly invented FFI – Forces Françaises de l'Intérieur. It was his business to co-ordinate the action of Resistance with that of SHAEF; and he had a relatively straightforward task now that the outlines of a political solution were clear.

The development of SOE's own French organisation is much simpler. In April 1943 there was constituted a 'Western European Region', embracing all countries likely to be affected by invasion from the West. This was designed specifically for collaboration in the invasion plans of 'Cossac', and was throughout commanded by a regular soldier, Brigadier Mockler-Ferryman, CBE, MC. Within this there was a French Directorate (from November 1942 under Colonel R. E. Brook), which controlled the operations of the three French Sections, F, R/F, and D/F, as well as those dealing with Holland and Belgium. The policy of 'Massingham' as regards operations into France was also directed from London through Colonel Brook's Directorate, though there was much which had to be settled locally.

Integration with the Americans was also relatively straightforward.

---

1 Resident Minister in Algiers No. 2443 of 21st November to Foreign Office; copy on SOE Archives File 3/100/2(c).
2 Note by Major Desmond Morton of interview with him on 3rd November 1943; copy on SOE Archives File 3/100/2(c).
3 Prominent in 1947 as an organiser in De Gaulle's political party, the Ralliement du Peuple Français. Vol. I of his Memoirs has been published, but only goes up to the autumn of 1942.
* [J-E. Soustelle, 1912–90.]

There was close contact and exchange of officers with the OSS organisation in London from the summer of 1942 onwards; and when SHAEF was formed in January 1944 the branches of SOE and OSS concerned with the SHAEF area came together as an integrated organisation (SOE/SO) under the operational control of SHAEF through G-3 Division of the Staff (Major-General Bull, USA). More for euphony than anything, this was rechristened Special Forces Headquarters (SFHQ) in April. There was a similar Anglo-American integration in North Africa in May 1944, when the 'Special Projects Operational Centre' (SPOC) was formed at Algiers under Lieutenant Colonel Anstey of 'Massingham' and Colonel Davies of OSS.[1]

For security reasons there could be no question of integration with the French until 'Overlord' was launched: but on 20th June there was one final transformation. In North Africa the French moved into SPOC, and Général de l'Air Cochet returned to favour as Délégué Militaire Opération Sud (DMOS) working independently of SPOC but in close collaboration with it – closer than his collaboration with the Soustelle organisation! For the purposes of the 'Dragoon' landings, operational control was assumed by General Devers.* In London there were good political reasons against bringing the French into SFHQ, in what would seem a very subordinate role: the Anglo-American Sections concerned with France were therefore abruptly removed from SFHQ to form part of the État Major des Forces Françaises de l'Intérieur (EMFFI) under the command of General Koenig. There was little physical movement, so that the change was not so disastrous as it sounds – EMFFI remained close to SFHQ in Bryanston Square. But it was far too late to make any serious attempt at tripartite integration, the perfect theoretical solution: EMFFI's short life, till its dissolution in September 1944, was passed in considerable confusion, and the best that can be said for it is that the main lines of action had been cleared before it came into existence.

2. The 'British' Organisations in France

F Section was in theory above French politics, and it is remarkable how large the field was in which this unlikely theory could be applied. But there were several points of serious strain, and it may be convenient to take these first: they are effectively a small part of the whole, but unfortunately the enemies of F Section (who were many) found their motives and their best material here, so that these political controversies have in France attracted a publicity out of all proportion to their importance.

---

[1] See Section V of the SOE 'Massingham' History.
* [J. Devers, 1887–1979, commanded 'Dragoon' landings and fought on into Germany.]

The prime source of the trouble was the cleavage between Giraud and De Gaulle, behind which lay a less profound divergence between British and American policy. The British (or most of the British) were sceptical of the possibility of rallying the French nation behind Giraud; but it was not their policy to refuse assistance to any organisation which was prepared to fight, simply because it accepted Giraud or repudiated De Gaulle. Such a refusal would have been a direct repudiation of the compromise agreed with the USA, it would indeed have been an intervention in French politics in aid of De Gaulle, and neither the Prime Minister, nor the Foreign Office nor SOE ever loved De Gaulle enough to yield consciously to that temptation. But if 'non-Gaullist' movements were to be given a fair chance, the business could not be handled by the 'Gaullist' Section, R/F. Short of the monstrosity of inventing yet another French Section, it could only be taken on by F; and to that extent F Section was turned aside from its primary role – a mistake, as events showed, but not one that could well have been avoided in the autumn of 1942.

'Giraudist organisation' in the strict sense amounted to very little. There was a possible basis for it in the 'Armée de l'Armistice' and in the work which had been done by the Deuxième Bureau under the Vichy régime to prepare clandestinely for the military resurgence of France. On 11th November 1942, when the Germans invaded the Free Zone, a fragment of the 'Weygand plan' was put into effect by General de Lattre de Tassigny, apparently on his own responsibility:[1] but apart from this local resistance the army submitted to demobilisation without a struggle and in so doing dissipated the last remnants of its prestige. It had lost its claim to leadership: as General de Lattre put it a year later, it was necessary that 'the new army of France' should 'reflect the same tendencies and views as those of the resistance leaders'.[2] There remained two assets only. *First*, there were trained officers and NCOs now demobilised. There were few, very few, convinced Vichyists among them: but there were many too conservative or too cautious to venture on resistance under the leadership of De Gaulle, an insubordinate officer, and of a collection of unknown and probably untrustworthy politicians of the Left: if they were to play a part at all, it would be to resist 'Communism' – a broad term – after the Liberation. Equally dangerous were those resolute and patriotic officers, who could conceive of Resistance and

---

[1] He was brought out in the autumn of 1943 after a long period of captivity.

[2] There is on SOE Archives File 3/100/1(a) an interesting record of his views as given to the US Ambassador in London on 10th November 1943. [See Verity, *We Landed by Moonlight*, pp. 129–31, for details. J-M. G. de Lattre de Tassigny, 1889–1952, fought hard in 1940, arrested 1942 for opposing German invasion of Vichy France, escaped, commanded First French Army 1944–5.]

guerilla warfare only in terms of military hierarchy and field service regulations. Setting aside these two classes there were still left a large number of officers and NCOs whose contribution in skill and energy was inestimable: but it was generally best given in subordinate positions within other organisations. The *second* asset was that the Army had not disappeared quite without preparation: there were secret stocks of weapons and military stores at the disposal of the Deuxième Bureau. It is impossible to say what they amounted to, but there are instances where they proved of great value to groups insufficiently supplied from elsewhere.

Out of these elements Giraud certainly constructed the theory of an 'Armée Sécrète',[1] a source of some confusion with the 'Armée Sécrète' of the Gaullist Resistance movements: but it is not easy to discover what became of it in action. There were certainly some 'Giraudist' wireless sets on the air, and SOE helped to put in a few 'Giraudist' agents. The ORA claimed that in the summer of 1944 it contributed some 600 officers and 30–40,000 men to the strength of the FFI, in which it was then incorporated; its head in France at that time was General Revers who had been Secretary General of the Ministry of War at Vichy, and had presided over the Vichy court-martial which condemned De Gaulle. It is probable that politically the ORA had no positive programme after the fall of Giraud in November 1943 and could offer no alternative leader in place of De Gaulle: the maintenance of order was the sum of its military creed, and De Gaulle now represented order against Communist anarchy, in spite of his own past lack of respect for the military hierarchy. There is no doubt that in the final battles some members of the ORA did excellent service; others proved to be an unmitigated nuisance, either because they were incapable of grasping the nature of guerilla tactics or because the Communist bogey worked them into a state of mind in which they were more afraid of the FFI than of the enemy.

'Carte' was a much more serious affair.[2] We have already seen the first stages of contact, through Basin, Max Hymans and Major Frager. The decisive stage for the British was that of discussion on the report of Major Bodington, who saw 'Carte' himself in August 1942 and returned to England in September. The considered verdict, reached in consultation with SIS, was that 'Carte' was either a 'cover' for the secret organisation of the Armée de l'Armistice or a 'private venture' closely related to it. On this basis SOE put before the Chiefs of Staff a proposal to send a liaison officer to 'Carte', to make experimental deliveries of

---

1   More officially known as ORA: Organisation de Résistance dans l'Armée.
2   For the first contacts with it see above pp. 267 and 291. A selection of the most important papers are to be found on SOE Archives Files 3/370/54(a) and 3/490/2(b).

arms, and to put at its disposal a secret broadcasting station in England.[1] The decision was an anxious one: it was not only a political challenge to De Gaulle, it also raised problems of military security in view of the imminence of 'Torch'. The Chiefs of Staff's answer was to accept SOE's recommendations and to let matters proceed as normally as possible, so as to give no hint of an impending operation.

One result of this was the opening by PWE of the station 'Radio Patrie',[2] the source of violent altercation with De Gaulle, until it was finally merged in May 1943 with the Gaullist station, as 'Honneur et Patrie de la Résistance Française'. The main broadcaster was M. Gillois (Diamant-Berger), formerly of Radio-Cité, who had come out with Major Bodington. Another result was the appointment of a liaison officer, Major Peter Churchill, who had already arrived in France on his third visit at the end of August. Unfortunately the best contact with 'Carte', Lieutenant Basin, was arrested about a fortnight before Churchill's arrival, and Churchill's job of liaison proved much harder than had been anticipated.

In the confusion which followed 'Torch', 'Carte's' organisation – if it ever existed in its full glory – was virtually dissolved. The problem was now not one of paper schemes framed with the connivance of important elements in the Government itself, but of hard and dangerous work under a German régime. Fragments of the organisation undoubtedly survived, but from top to bottom it was torn by disputes, and by a process of natural selection it lost a very large number of purely theoretical resisters. The details of the story are now beyond research, but there are ample records of the violence of the quarrel which divided the 'fighting men', Churchill and Frager, from the scheme-maker, Girard. The quarrel had begun by the beginning of December, and furious telegrams continued until in January 1943 Girard was threatening Frager with proceedings for treason and Churchill was pleading for the hasty removal of Girard to England. There were the 'usual delays', and the two parties could not be withdrawn to the cooler atmosphere of London until March: but once F Section had seen and talked to Girard they agreed with Churchill that he was virtually mad. To complete his tragedy, his wife and children were arrested while he was in England: he demanded to be sent back to France and SOE refused to let him go – it would have been suicide for him and death to many of his followers.[3]

---

[1] The relevant papers are COS(42)314(0) and 315(0), taken at COS(42)29th Mtg, Minute 7, of 16th October 1942.

[2] Garnett's 'History of PWE', p. 240 ff, gives details of the life of 'Radio Patrie'.

[3] He nearly succeeded in transferring his allegiance to the Americans, in circumstances which do not reflect well on them. See CD's letter to Sir Alexander Cadogan, dated 25th May 1943; copy on SOE Archives File 3/370/54(a) – 'Carte'.

The dream which had been broken was SOE's as well as Girard's, and SOE, perhaps unwisely, allowed itself to be convinced by Frager that much could be saved from the wreck. The new plan was that the 'Carte' Empire should be divided into three parts, isolated from one another: Frager himself in the north, Churchill in the centre and south-west, and a new organiser, Captain F. Cammaerts,* in the south-east. These were still wide and straggling kingdoms, but the plan now looked much more practicable and serious, and there was plenty of confirmation later that local fragments existed and were prepared to fight. Frager was, it seems, in his way a first-rate man, of a much harder and tougher type than Girard: but unfortunately he too had a fundamental and disastrous flaw. He accepted at its face value the story of a certain Colonel Verbeck (known as 'Heinrich') of the German Intelligence Service, that he was an Alsatian and an anti-Nazi, anxious to reinsure himself with the Allies. This story was doubt-less 'proved' by much help in minor matters, but it was broken to pieces by two facts. It was Colonel 'Heinrich'** who arrested Major Churchill and Mrs Sansom[1] two days after Churchill's fourth return to France in April 1943: and in the end, in August 1944, he arrested Frager himself, and Frager was executed in Buchenwald a month later.

The infection of Colonel 'Heinrich' spread through all that Frager touched, and it is not possible now to say what was healthy and what was unsound. Undoubtedly much of the work he inspired was absolutely outside German control: but he was a dangerous man to work with. His own organisation was now limited to the north, and it reported considerable activity in widely-separated areas – the Dordogne, Jura, Lorraine, Mantes, Normandy, the Yonne. It received a British Liaison Officer and a wireless operator in May 1943, and there were nineteen successful supply operations to it that summer. In October 1943 Frager came out to England, and while he was away the Liaison Officer, Captain Jones, was betrayed and arrested, as was the wireless operator. In February 1944 Frager returned, with instruc-tions to reduce his field still further to the Yonne and Côte d'Or only, and there are well authenticated reports of the work carried out there between D-day and the final arrest of Frager early in August.

Frager was also intricately entangled through Colonel 'Heinrich' with the affairs of F/O Déricourt, who entered France as a Lysander expert in January 1943[2] and was responsible during the next year for

---

[1]   Mrs Odette Sansom, GC, now Mrs Churchill.
[2]   Above p. 240.
*   [Son of the Belgian poet; survived to become an English professor of education.]
** [He was not a colonel at all, but Sergeant Hugo Bleicher of the Abwehr: see E. Borchers, tr. I. Colvin, *Colonel Henri's Story* (1954). Bleicher retired after the war to keep a tobacconist's shop in Bavaria.]

fifteen landing operations, all of them apparently successful. But Colonel 'Heinrich' suggested to Frager that Déricourt was in German service, and there was some slight confirmation from less tainted sources. After Frager's denunciation Déricourt was recalled to England in February 1944; at the time SOE's verdict was 'Not Proven', but at present (1948) Déricourt is still held under suspicion in France.

The affair of Roger Bardet and Jean Kieffer rests on much more than suspicion: there is no doubt these two trusted lieutenants of Frager acted also for the Germans. Roger Bardet, hero of two sensational 'escapes' from the Gestapo, was Frager's second-in-command, and was undoubtedly responsible for the arrest of the British Liaison Officer, Captain Jones, and his wireless operator while Frager was in England in November 1943: he may also have been responsible for the break-up in April 1943 of Lieutenant Pertschuk's Toulouse organisation,[1] which had some affiliations with 'Carte'. Kieffer was Frager's organiser in Normandy; he was overrun there by the Allies after D-day, and supplied glowing accounts of his own successes – which were probably largely mythical.

The third legatee of 'Carte' (besides Churchill and Frager), Captain Cammaerts, was severely tested at the outset. Many of his 'reception committee' were arrested shortly after he arrived: and one of them sent to him Colonel 'Heinrich' with a letter of recommendation and confidence. To make matters worse, Bardet (who was in charge in Frager's absence) warmly espoused the idea of negotiations with the good Colonel. Cammaerts most wisely distrusted the smell of the whole affair; he cut all contacts with Bardet – and four weeks later he heard from Churchill's radio operator of the arrest of Churchill and Mrs Sansom. From this point there was a clean break with 'Carte', and Cammaerts began again from scratch as an independent organiser in the south-east. With one break (November 1943 to February 1944) he remained there until the area was liberated by Operation 'Dragoon' in August 1944, and he was largely responsible for its excellent organisation and co-operation with the invading army. At the last moment he and several of his staff were arrested, and were only rescued by the superb self-possession and bluff of his assistant, Christine Granville.[2]*

Another small legacy of 'Carte' appeared in the Annemasse area, close to the Swiss frontier. Here there was an anti-Frager group of

---

[1] Above p. 257.

[2] He finished as Lieutenant Colonel Cammaerts, DSO, Légion d'Honneur, Croix de Guerre.

* [Cover name of the Polish countess Krystyna Gisycka, *née* Skarbecka, 1915–52, who ran escapers out of Poland into Hungary 1939–41, escaped to Cairo, was taken on as an SOE agent, rescued Cammaerts, and was murdered in a Kensington hotel. See Madeleine Masson, *Christine* (1975). To be in new *DNB*.]

'Cartists', which appears sometimes as 'Radio Patrie', so-called after the 'Carte' radio station in England. During 1943 their leader at Annemasse, a certain Mesnard, made contact with SOE through Switzerland: but the proposal was not taken up until March 1944. There then arrived a first-rate organiser, Captain de St Genies, with Flight Officer Yvonne Baseden, as wireless operator: in the next few months he carried out some really fine sabotage, in particular on the Rhône–Rhine Canal. Unluckily at the end of June, just after receiving very large supplies by a daylight Fortress operation, de St Genies was killed in a gun-fight with the Gestapo near Dôle and the organisation was broken up. This was one 'Carte' disaster not due to any original sin in that organisation.

Another interrelated series of events was begun by the Mission of Major J. A. F. Antelme,[1] a British subject born in Mauritius, who had been a successful businessman in Madagascar. He left England on 18th November 1942 on what was primarily a mission of political reconnaissance. He had excellent contacts in French official and financial circles, and had no difficulty in reaching, directly or indirectly, a number of important politicians, for instance Reynaud, Herriot,[*] Jeanneney, and Paul Clémenceau. His political report was made when he came out for a brief interval at the end of March 1943, and the essence of it can be given briefly in his own words: 'Implicit trust and hopes in General De Gaulle and General Giraud, the former having a far wider popularity, but I wish to make it clear that the "Comité National" of "Fighting France" neither enjoys the prestige nor the authority attaching to General De Gaulle's person and is not in the least readily accepted in France.' To this may be added that he found no one who could suggest a possible alternative leader: and that there was some feeling that in North Africa General Giraud had let himself be entangled by Vichyists – though (belatedly) he began to turn away from them in the middle of March. In addition to this political report (which was undoubtedly correct for the vast mass of French opinion), he brought back much useful intelligence, and two interesting projects, which had been worked out with the assistance of important officials: one for the provision of French currency for an invading army, the other for accumulating food stocks for the Allies. These plans went no further in their original form, and they were drawn up without much knowledge of military needs and technicalities: but they contained excellent material.

In June 1943, Antelme was involved in the break-up of Major

---

1   His reports are on SOE Archives Files (F Section) B.51 and A.21.
*   [E. Herriot, 1872–1957, French Prime Minister 1924–5 and 1932, President of Chamber of Deputies 1940 and of National Assembly 1947–52.]

Suttill's organisation,[1] with which he was in touch, and he had to be recalled: on his last Mission in February 1944 he was arrested shortly after landing, and died whilst a prisoner of war at Ravitsch. But from his original work there came a considerable progeny.

In the Le Mans area he originated a circuit directed by Emile Garry, with the Princess Inayat Khan* as his radio operator: this survived the break-up of Major Suttill's organisation, but Garry was caught and killed in October 1943, and this area remained unorganised until April 1944 when it was taken in hand by Major C. S. Hudson (later DSO).

In the Troyes area Antelme prepared the ground for Major Cowburn, who arrived in April 1943 on his third Mission to France, and once more did an extremely effective job. His 'tour of duty' ended in September 1943, and he handed over to Major Dupont a sound non-political 'réseau' which remained very active to the end.

For our present purposes it is more important to follow what emerged from Antelme's contact with the Organisation Civile et Militaire (OCM): he describes this very succinctly and accurately in his report of March 1943 as 'a Secret Organisation which mostly comprises legal people and which is mainly concerned with the main-tenance of order when the invasion takes place, and a better orienta-tion of the French population towards social, religious and political matters. They are rather in favour of General Giraud, but are not hostile to De Gaulle himself but on no account do they accept his Comité Nationale. They have got branches in every town in France.' OCM was at this time being drawn into the circle of Gaullist resis-tance,[2] and it was eventually represented on the Conseil National de la Résistance. But it stood well to the Right within that body, and in its present state of indecision it could scarcely be handled by R/F Section. Fragments of OCM appear in many areas, but it is impor-tant here chiefly for its part in the Grandclément affair in Bordeaux. There Major Claude de Baissac had begun work in September 1942, and his sister, Lise de Baissac, had been responsible for receiving Antelme in the Poitiers area. About February 1943 Antelme put de Baissac in touch with Grandclément, who claimed to have at Bordeaux 3,000 men organised by OCM. This association appeared to bear very rapid fruit. By the middle of 1943 the 'Scientist' circuit claimed to be able to mobilise 17,000 men, and it received 121 air supply oper-ations between November 1942 and August 1943 – including *inter*

---

[1] Below p. 574.
[2] See 'Seahorse Mission', below p. 588.
* [Noor Inayat Khan, GC, 1914–44, half-Indian, half-American, born in the Kremlin, RAF wireless operator, sent to France June 1943, arrested three months later, murdered in Dachau.]

alia 7,500 Stens, 300 Brens and 1,500 rifles. This was a big affair –
too big in any case to survive intact until a D-day so far distant as
June 1944. The disaster came in September 1943 when Grandclément
was arrested in Paris and was effectively 'turned' by the Gestapo: on
grounds of conscience, so he claimed, because the real enemy was
Communism and it could be fought effectively only with German aid.
Whether sincere or not, this theory was disastrously convenient to the
whole German scheme of political warfare: and its immediate consequence was the betrayal by Grandclément of the whole circuit and
the loss of its rich store of arms.[1]

Fortunately de Baissac was in London at the time, and his second-
in-command Major Roger Landes ('Aristide') avoided arrest and
informed SOE at once of what had happened. After taking the first
steps to salvage something from the wreck he withdrew through Spain
in November 1943. In March 1944 he was back in Bordeaux, and by
D-day he had constructed a good working organisation in a difficult
region. It was 'Aristide' in collaboration with 'Triangle', the Free
French Délégué Militaire of the Region, who took possession of
Bordeaux for the Allies on 28th August. This ended unfortunately
three weeks later in a majestic row with General De Gaulle, who
contumaciously dismissed both 'Aristide' and his collaborator
'Triangle' from their posts. 'Aristide's' operations may have been in
some ways a little flamboyant, but his real offence was that he, an F
Section agent, had assumed in France an authority not delegated to
him by De Gaulle.

This complex sequence of events left in the end two sound organisations for use in the final battle, those of Lieutenant Colonel
Cammaerts in the south-east and Major Landes round Bordeaux.
Unfortunately it also left three notable 'affaires' to occupy the French
popular press after the Liberation – those of Bardet and Kieffer,
Déricourt and Grandclément: it also furnished a line of gossip to the
effect that the British preferred anti-democratic organisations and
cared less for the future of France than for stopping Communism. It
is satisfactory to record that this is balanced by official allegations
that F Section was dangerously inclined to favour the Communists.
Fighting French complaints about F Section never ceased, and never
remained long on the same ground, but the clearest instance of this
particular line was M. Massigli's approach to the Resident Minister
in Algiers on 2nd November 1943. To quote the Minister's telegram[2]
reporting M. Massigli's words: 'We (the British) did not realise that
in most cases active and energetic leaders of local opinion, as we

---

[1]   Grandclément himself was kidnapped, interrogated, and executed by 'Aristide'
in June 1944. SOE History of R/F Section, 1943, p. 22.

[2]   No. 2217 of 3rd November 1943; copy on SOE Archives File 3/100/2(c)).

thought them to be, were in fact Communist agents who had been planted there. His fear was that all villages and towns would be seized by Communist self-elected bodies immediately on liberation. We should not pursue this separatist method but work with the Committee (of National Liberation) . . . . The only hope of preventing a complete seizure of power by the Communists would be for the Allied armies to work in the closest harmony with the Committee with a view to imposing immediately on liberated territories prefects of the Committee's choice. If that were not done, the Communists would hold the field.'[1] This provoked an inquiry by the Prime Minister, a firm reply by Lord Selborne,[2] and an equally firm telegram from the Foreign Office to Algiers.[3]

It is much more difficult to find plausible evidence for this mare's nest on the Left than for the corresponding structure on the Right. Of course F Section organisers were in touch locally with the Communist organisation, the FTP, and they used it and equipped it where it seemed loyal and serviceable: indeed the division between 'Communist' forces and others was much less clear in the field than it looked from Algiers. Research shows only one case where anything that could be twisted into the semblance of a Communist 'réseau' was sponsored by F Section. This is the intolerably confused affair of the Groupes Vény.[4] These seem to have begun with a Gaullist intelligence réseau, the 'service Froment', which had developed by the end of 1942 into a para-military organisation (sometimes called 'France au Combat') linked to the Socialist Party and led by Colonel 'Vény' (Général de Brigade Jean Vincent). After various approaches and withdrawals, Vény split the organisation in July 1944 and linked the section which followed him to the Communist FTP. The main centre of his activity was the southern part of the Massif Central, and an F Section agent, Major Hiller (later DSO), was sent to 'Vény' in one of his phases of independence in January 1944. Hiller did a remarkable job in extracting military action out of political chaos, and his groups did some good work after D-day in the Départements of Lot, Lot-et-Garonne and Tarn. In addition he was responsible in March 1944 for introducing to the Vény organisation in the Limoges area Major Percy Mayer, who had already earned an OBE by brilliant work for SOE

---

[1] A similar line was taken by M. Viénot with Sir Orme Sargent in London on 8th November (Minute on SOE Archives File 3/100/2(c)).

[2] Lord Selborne to the Prime Minister, 9th November 1943; copy on SOE Archives File F.38/II.

[3] No. 2638 of 14th November 1943; copy on SOE Archives File 3/100/2(c).

[4] Explained at some length by Major Bourne-Patterson, in 'British Circuits in France', pp. 97–100.

in Madagascar.[1] Here Mayer certainly found that Vény's contacts were closely affiliated to the Communist Party,[2] and one of his main jobs was to secure some working co-operation between the Communist FTP and the other Resistance organisations and to persuade both parties to act on SHAEF Directives. In this he seems to have had great success: at least his aid was welcomed by De Gaulle's Délégué Militaire Régional, and in the fighting after D-day the DMR put Mayer in command of all French forces, including the FTP, in northern Creuse.

There was another offshoot of the Groupes Vény in the Marseilles–Nice area, where Major Boiteux, MC, MBE, was sent in March 1944, after an earlier mission at Lyon.[3] He also had an exceptionally difficult time in sorting the real from the imaginary Resistance, and in getting serious unpolitical support: but after D-day the Socialist Party organisation looked to him to give it some ground for claiming a part in resistance, and Boiteux's groups did good work in clearing Marseilles and in Maquis warfare in the surrounding area.

In spite of their collaboration with 'Communists', it looks as if the work of Major Hiller, Major Mayer and Major Boiteux was one of F Section's best achievements in persuading the French to subordinate politics to the needs of war.

Little more need be said about the politics of F Section. By the time D-day came F Section had sent some 390 agents to the field, and it had forty-five wireless sets on the air. Of these only a small part belonged to the 'political' organisations described above. It is impossible to describe fully here how the rest of this complicated structure was built up. All that can be done is to refer briefly to one or two local 'empires' which were broken before the day came, and to indicate the most important of the 'circuits' which were then fit to fight.

The largest of these early 'empires' was that of Major Suttill, who had been dropped blind near Vendôme on 1st October 1942, and rapidly created an organisation based on Paris but extending over some twelve Departments round the capital. In principle these areas were covered by separate 'réseaux' connected only in the person of Major Suttill and his immediate staff: but they ramified through other earlier F Section connections, such as those of 'Carte' (though Suttill greatly distrusted Frager's methods) and of Antelme. The stage was thus set for rapid expansion and catastrophe. Up to June 1943 the whole Suttill circuit had received 254 containers of stores, and in ten days in June

---

[1] Above pp. 327–8.
[2] Details in Bourne-Patterson's 'History of the British Circuits in France', pp. 85–8.
[3] Above p. 255.

it beat all records by receiving 190 more containers. By this time it was the Gestapo's main target in the Paris area: about 24th June, Suttill was caught, and with him disappeared his courier, Mlle Borrel, and his wireless operator, Major Norman ('Archambaud'). None of them returned, and the circumstances of the disaster were never cleared up: but in dealing with such an organisation the Gestapo must have had scraps of information from many sources, and there is no strong reason to suspect treachery. 'Archambaud's' wireless set continued to operate, but SOE were warned quickly through Antelme.[1]

Operations began in the north-east with the dropping of two agents, Major Bieler and Captain Trotobas, in November 1942. Bieler was expected to build on some contacts of 'Carte', and he worked from Paris until March 1943, when he went to the St Quentin area: Trotobas was at Lille from the first. One indication of their success is the record of sabotage in the area during 1943 – the biggest affair was the destruction of twenty-two transformers which halted production at the Fives-Lille engineering works in June 1943: another indication is the intense loyalty to the memory of Trotobas – 'Captain Michel' – which SOE found in Lille after the Liberation. According to Suttill's report in May 1943: 'Captain Michel is known to move in a very tough circuit of "*maquereaux*" and race-horse gangs: apparently he fits into this world, and is doing very good work.' Certainly in 1944 SOE found Trotobas's 'crowd' in excellent order and discipline as the 'Organisation Franco-Anglaise du Capitaine Michel', wearing 'War Office' flashes on their battle-dress and boasting of the British alliance and their contempt for French politics. But Trotobas had been killed in a gun-battle in November 1943, and Bieler was caught and executed in January 1944. Their organisations survived, but this corner of France was an extremely difficult area for the RAF to reach and it was not possible to restore communications and stores until April 1944. This was eventually done through Commandant Dumont-Guillement who had come to France in February 1944 with a list of targets, of which the most important (and unlikely) were to kidnap a leading German V.1 expert and to stage a mass rescue of the prisoners in Fresnes gaol. In the end his greatest service was to keep the movement in good heart in the north-east, mainly by running stores to it in lorries from the Paris area: but his groups were also in action in Paris and were involved in heavy fighting in the region of Meaux.

In the Rouen area also a fine organisation had been largely broken up before D-day. This was the work of Major Philippe Liewer and Lieutenant Chartrand (a Canadian), who arrived in May 1943 and had a small tough sabotage organisation going by that autumn. It was

---

[1] Major Bodington made his second visit to France in July 1943, in order to assess what could be rescued from the ruins.

distinguished for instance for the sinking of a 900-ton minesweeper in Rouen harbour and for some good industrial sabotage. But there were a series of arrests while Liewer was in London in February 1944, including that of his second-in-command, the brother of the novelist André Malraux:* ninety-eight members of the organisation were rounded up and removed to Germany. Liewer returned for a short time in April, but found that enemy pressure was too great for a new beginning.

The Lille and Rouen disasters can be regarded as cases of 'normal casualties'; their organisation in itself was good and could have been restored without too much difficulty if air-supply had been easier. Major Suttill's tragedy was of a different type and will serve to mark the end of a phase in F Section's development. Up to the autumn of 1942 its organisers had been doing an uphill job rather against the mood of France. After 'Torch' the mood changed, but the spirit of resistance still lacked technical skill. F Section knew in principle that large organisations were dangerous, but the movement grew too fast for it. Organisers were few, and there were vast numbers to be organised. There was thus a great upswing from November 1942 until the summer of 1943, and an invasion then would have found a loose and ill-armed but energetic organisation on quite a large scale. That summer there was an inevitable reaction: F Section suffered the disasters to 'Carte', Grandclément and Suttill, and the Gaullist organisations were also hard pressed.[1] During the winter and spring of 1943–4 it was a matter of sealing-off the sound parts of the old sprawling organisations and doubling and redoubling the number of organisers and wireless sets, so as to create a very wide network of 'Circuits' of moderate size each directly and independently controlled from London.

F Section's organisation at D-day was thus governed by one great principle, that there should be no centralisation within France: but it had no other logic than that of local needs and local history. An attempt has been made to show the pattern roughly on a map:[2] but even this rough sketch is to some extent misleading. There were no defined boundaries, no pattern of organisation appropriate to a 'circuit', no disciplined relationships of command or subordination with other Resistance organisations. The 'circuits' were in effect the zones of influence of resolute and able men, well supplied with money and arms. As one witness says of the south-west: 'At the time of the Liberation, the whole of the area was in the hands of a series of feudal

---

[1] Below p. 590.
[2] Appendix K.
* [A. G. Malraux, 1901–76, Minister of Culture 1960–69. He lost two brothers in F Section circuits, and worked briefly in one himself in summer 1944.]

lords whose power and influence were strongly similar to that of their 15th century Gascon counterparts. Among these barons, "Hilaire" (F Section's Captain (later Lieutenant Colonel) G. R. Starr)* was, without any question, the most influential.'[1]

With these reservations we may roughly divide France into three areas, and see what each contained:

(a) The Zone of Invasion from England, stretching across the north of France from Brittany to the Belgian frontier.

(b) The Zone of Invasion from the south, penetrating up the Rhône Valley and eventually swinging eastward into Alsace.

(c) The rest of France: a great area of the centre and south-west where the British and American armies never came in force, and the French fought their own battle: first harassing German divisions moving to attack the Normandy bridgehead, then clearing up isolated pockets of the enemy, and finally besieging the Germans in the Biscay ports.

(a) The Northern Invasion Zone

(i) F Section had no early contacts in Brittany. But at Nantes an eminent racing-motorist, Captain Robert Benoist, began to build up an organisation in October 1943, and by D-day he had his plans laid for attacks on the HT pylons there: he also had Maquis groups available in other areas (Rambouillet and Compiègne). Unluckily he was caught in July 1944 and did not survive.**

(ii) In the Le Mans area, due south of the Normandy front, there was Major C. S. Hudson (later DSO), who had been in France before but did not begin work here until April 1944. At D-day he was in control of three large 'Maquis' in the Sarthe; but these were broken up by German offensives and he reformed his forces in sabotage groups which did very effective work on railways, roads and telephones.

(iii) To the east, in Loire et Cher (the Blois area) there was a circuit north of the Loire run by an officer of OSS, Lieutenant Henquet: there was also Baron Philippe de Vomecourt, brother of SOE's very old friend 'Lucas', who was to be responsible for the southern area. He had been arrested in November 1942, but broke loose in a mass escape from prison in January 1944, along with Major C. S. Hudson. Philippe (like 'Lucas') was a man of infinite energy and resource, and his empire tended to grow on very

---

[1] Quoted in Bourne-Patterson's 'British Circuits in France', p. 92.

* [G. R. Starr, 1904–80, mining engineer and saboteur; in *DNB*.]

** [He was among a score of F Section agents who were murdered in Buchenwald in September 1944.]

old-fashioned lines. F Section was hard put to it to keep him in his designated area, but what he did there was excellent. It was also largely due to him that organisers were at the last moment established on his eastern flank: Lieutenant Dedieu in the Chartres-Dreux area, and Captain G. A. Wilkinson near Orléans. They had a short period of work, but an active one.

(iv) In Normandy there had been for a long time an organisation of doubtful efficacy under Frager's lieutenant, Jean Kieffer.[1] Effective organisation by F Section did not begin until Lieutenant J. Dandicolle arrived in January 1944, followed by Major Claude de Baissac in February and by de Baissac's sister Lise in April. This was exceptionally dangerous work, as de Baissac was already pretty well known to the Germans:[2] open guerilla warfare in such an area was out of the question, but there were plenty of men and arms for small ambushes and attacks on communications. In the end the zone was split into two: de Baissac in Mayenne, Orne, and Eure et Loire, Dandicolle in the actual invasion area, Calvados and Manche. Curiously enough, the aristocratic de Baissac was on excellent terms with the FTP, (in particular with an important group under Yves Tangui at Rennes), whereas he became involved in a row of the usual pattern with high Gaullist authorities.

(v) F Section never had a plan for resistance in Paris itself and it made little or no attempt at sabotage in the city. But its many organisers from the first worked in and through Paris to areas outside it. 'Lucas' had worked there, so had Antelme, Suttill, and the racing-motorists Grover-Williams and Benoist: in the summer of 1944 Frager was still in and out of Paris, and Dumont-Guillement was there. His main job, as it turned out, was to keep the Lille area going, but he also claimed the support of 6,500 men in Paris (1,500 of them armed) and he had good contacts with the gendarmerie. Outside Paris to the east there was Captain P. Mulsant in Seine-et-Marne, unfortunately caught in the middle of July, as a result of some rather injudicious SAS activities in the Forêt de Fontainebleau: Captain Dupont as successor to Major Cowburn's circuit in the Troyes area: and Major Bodington (on his third mission) in the Haute Marne, where he distinguished himself by arranging an RAF attack on the HQ of the harassed Field-Marshal Von Kluge* at Verzy.

---

[1] Above p. 569.
[2] Above p. 571.
* [G. H. von Kluge, 1882–1944, nicknamed 'Kluge Hans' after a circus horse, German army commander 1940–41, army group commander from December 1941, C-in-C western front July–August 1944, suicide.]

(vi) To the north-east of Paris the situation was difficult, and we have already seen the problem set by the fate of Major Bieler and Captain Trotobas. But it will be convenient here to refer to the Polish circuits in the area, though they were not of F Section's making.

These had originated with the Missions of M. Bitner and 'Adjudicate' in 1941,[1] and there is no doubt that in 1942 the Poles in the north-east of France were well-organised as a national group, the 'Monica' organisation. They were however discouraged by General Sikorski from active sabotage, for fear of reprisals, and they were also the occasion of one of the many disputes between the civil and military sides of the Polish Government. In January 1943 the relevant section of SOE was working on a plan to extract some value from the organisation when the time came to invade France: and by April provisional agreement had been reached with the Polish Government.[2] This provided for the creation of a para-military organisation capable of harassing and delaying the Germans after D-day, and for the training of Polish 'Jedburghs' to be sent in when the time came to give leadership and communications. Some of these men were already in training, and over 100 in all went through STS 63 at Inchmery and later at Warnham. A Polish officer, Major Zdrojewski, went to France in June 1943 as senior military representative of General Kukiel, and in September 1943 the organisation was visited by Major F. Chalmers Wright of SOE's EU/P Section, who came out through Spain in April 1944. In all twenty-eight agents were sent to 'Monica', of whom seven lost their lives.

As an organisation this was excellent, but unfortunately the question of command continued to give trouble. The 'Bardsea Agreement', drafted early in 1943, was not finally signed until 27th February 1944; and even then difficulties remained. The Polish Government (reasonably from its own standpoint) were not anxious to transfer fully to a foreign commander responsibility for committing their countrymen to a desperate battle, and the original agreement laid it down that the organisation should not be called out until 'it can reasonably be expected that an Allied advance will overrun the particular district concerned within a period of two or three days': and further, that 'no action will be taken until the appreciation of the position has been placed before General Sikorski or a single officer delegated by him'. These were, from the point of view of SHAEF, very serious limitations, and SHAEF's request for wider discretion was placed before

---

[1] Above p. 316. See further SOE History of the E/UP Section, and SOE Archives File (AD/E) 'Bardsea'.

[2] SOE History of EU/P Section, Section II Appendix B.

M. Mikolojczyk by Lord Selborne on 22nd May 1944.[1] Hard negotiation followed, but in the end the Poles co-operated well: the final
letter[2] on 10th June from the Deputy Prime Minister, M. Kwapinski,
gave SHAEF full discretion, subject only to close co-operation with
General Koenig and the FFI and to the avoidance of unnecessary
reprisals and bloodshed.

All was now ready, and the warning signals were sent on 20th
August: but bad weather held up the operation and the final date
chosen, 2nd September, was too late: the Americans were already on
the verge of the operational area. The only action completed was the
dropping of Major Chalmers Wright in the Belgian Ardennes at the
end of August: unfortunately he injured his back in landing and did
not reach Lille until 13th September, when he linked up with Major
Hazell and SPU22, then in process of formation[3] for work into
Germany.

This was an unlucky end to good work. The Poles in 'Monica' had
done much quiet service, especially in minor sabotage and in collecting information on the V.1 and V.2, but their big chance did not come,
through no fault of their own. As regards the 'Bardsea' parachute
parties – trained men of first-rate quality* – the first Polish reaction
was to demand that they be sent to help Warsaw which was at that
moment in desperate need:[4] but this was clearly impossible, and there
was little chance left of using them. A few were used by SPU22:
others were held in readiness for Operation 'Dunstable', an abortive
plan to assist and to use the Polish workers in Germany:[5] a few others
went in to central Germany with the SAARF at the end of April 1945.[6]
But for the most part they contributed nothing to the final effort. This
was waste, but waste of a kind inevitable in war. Expensive plans had
been laid to meet a contingency which did not arise: but the contingency was a probable one, and might have been of very serious importance, and the plans were well laid.

---

[1] Copy on SOE Archives File (AD/E) 'Bardsea'.
[2] Actually drafted by the SOE Polish Minorities Section; copy on SOE Archives
File (AD/E) 'Bardsea'. Lord Selborne's reply, conveying SHAEF agreement, is
dated 26th June.
[3] Below p. 710. It had also been planned that a few British and US teams should
go with the main 'Bardsea' operation.
[4] Letter from M. Mikolajczyk to Lord Selborne, dated 5th September 1944, copy
on SOE Archives File (AD/E) 'Bardsea'.
[5] The 'Dunstable' Agreement is at Appendix D, Section I of the SOE History of
EU/P Section.
[6] Below p. 712.
* [Gubbins once described them privately as the finest body of troops he had ever
encountered.]

(b) The Southern Invasion Zone

These circuits in the north were working largely in thickly populated country, either urban or agricultural; internal communication was easy and the Germans were very thick on the ground. Their activities were therefore mainly a matter of harassing small-scale sabotage, with much useful intelligence as a by-product, and the work was less openly dramatic than that in the rest of France, where the regular armies were less intensely engaged.

(i) Taking the 'Dragoon' area from the south, we have already seen the work done by Major Boiteux[1] in the Marseilles–Nice area, and by Lieutenant Colonel Cammaerts[2] in the area stretching back from the lower Rhône to the Alps. It must also be remembered that Major Brooks[3] was at work continuously from July 1942 with the railwaymen in a zone stretching across the south and centre.

(ii) Lyon itself had been very active in the days of Miss Virginia Hall, and Major Boiteux on his first Mission began to extract some order out of confused enthusiasm there after he had got rid of Duboudin ('Alain') in October 1942. He was severely harassed by the Germans and was without wireless communications from November 1942 to May 1943: shortly afterwards he was so hard-pressed that he had to be evacuated with some of his best lieutenants. He could not himself safely return to this area, but his wireless operator was still there, and his organisation left a considerable progeny. In October 1943 Flight Lieutenant Brown-Bartrolli arrived to maintain liaison with the large Maquis near Cluny, which dominated Sâone-et-Loire after D-day: early in August it beat off an attack by 3,000 Germans, and as the Allied forces broke through early in September the French themselves cleared a large area round Mâcon. With it were associated (to the north) Captain Régnier's organisation round Châlons-sur-Sâone, and to the south Captain Marchand at St Étienne. Still further south near Le Puy there was 'Gaspard', an independent French organiser at the head of some 15,000 rather ill-armed men who received an F Section Mission in April 1944.

(iii) To the east there was 'Xavier', Lieutenant Colonel R. Heslop, whose organisation in Ain, Isère and Savoie deserves a history of its own.[4]

---

1 Above p. 574.
2 Above p. 569.
3 Above p. 256.
4 There is an impressive glimpse of him, as well as of Miss Rochester, his courier, in George Millar's book 'Horned Pigeon'.

He had originally been intended by F Section to work with a Giraudist group of the 'Organisation de Résistance dans l'Armée' (ORA), which was reported to exist in Haute Savoie. Eventually, after political complications, his Mission became a joint one with the Fighting French, and he was landed in France by Hudson aircraft in September 1943 with 'Cantinier', Lieutenant Pierre Rosenthal. They were back in London to report for a short time in October: their joint plan now was to make as much as possible of the large but ill-armed and ill-trained Maquis in the Alpine valleys. Heslop was instructed by F Section also to create and maintain as an insurance small independent 'British' groups. Both branches of the plan worked well: the Maquis was kept relatively small (perhaps 5,500 men in Ain, Jura and Haute Savoie), but well-trained and relatively well-armed, with plenty of potential reserves. It stood up well in heavy fighting at the Plateau des Glières in Jura in March 1944, and round Bellegarde in June: and finally at the end of August and beginning of September it cleared the mountain territory as far as Bourg. There ensued the usual coldness with the Gaullist authorities: but Heslop's services were in the end decently recognised by the Légion d'Honneur and Croix de Guerre.

(iv) To the west of Dijon, in Yonne and Côte d'Or, was Major Frager on his last Mission: his methods seem to have been dangerous to the end, for an agent (Lieutenant A. Woerther) who was sent to him in July to take up work in the Nancy area found that his contacts were mainly contacts with the Gestapo. Lieutenant Woerther eventually shook himself free, but he had not advanced very far in organising Meurthe-et-Moselle when General Patton's* tanks arrived early in September. Another separate Mission (Captain Pearson and Lieutenant Breen) attempted the same area in August, through another line of contact: it was luckier but little more successful.

To the east of Dijon there is a long interlocking story of effective work. The 'Radio Patrie' organisation under de St Genies at Annemasse[1] is outside this: and the main development begins with the arrival of Captain B. D. Rafferty in September 1942. His own concern was with the Clermont-Ferrand area, but he also found contacts round Dijon and Montbéliard. These were followed up by Captain Harry Ree,** who arrived in April 1943, and eventually took over Montbéliard himself. There he played a most important part in the attacks on the Peugeot

---

[1] Above p. 569.

* [G. S. Patton, 1885–1945, American cavalry commander, fought in Sicily, Normandy and into Germany, killed in road accident.]

** [H. A. Ree, died 1991, professor of education at York.]

works at Sochaux: important particularly as it set going the policy of 'blackmail' operations, by which the threat of RAF bombing was used to induce 'inside' sabotage.[1] In November 1943, by sheer ill-luck, he ran into trouble with the Feldgendarmerie and had to escape to Switzerland after a fantastic Hollywood fist-fight with an isolated German. From Switzerland he was able to keep some contact with his organisation, and in May 1944 he was replaced by an American officer, 1st Lieutenant E. F. Floege: Floege had some first-rate quarrels with the local FFI, but his groups were well in the fighting at the end.

In the Dijon area Captain Ree established Captain J. A. R. Starr ('Bob') and his wireless operator in June 1943: Starr was arrested in July,[2] and his successor Lieutenant Jean Simon carried on under serious difficulties until February 1944, when he was shot down in a café in Montbéliard. The new man found for the job was Comte Maze-Sencier de Brouville, whose character is sharply sketched (under his *nom-de-guerre* of 'Albert') in George Millar's two books.[3] Matters were not then very far advanced, but before D-day he had ready an organisation adequate to cut all railway lines leading through Dôle and to obstruct canal traffic seriously. Arms were in very poor supply until August, as all this area was difficult for aircraft to reach during the short bright nights of June and July: so that there was not much open guerilla warfare.

From this circuit was thrown off to the east that of Captain George Millar in the Besançon area: his work was important, and so is his book 'Maquis', which is at present the only good account in English of the Resistance work and atmosphere.

(c) The Rest of France

We have already seen briefly what happened in Bordeaux, where Major Landes ('Aristide') survived to receive personal chastisement from General De Gaulle: we have also seen Major Percy Mayer's work with the ambiguous 'Groupes Vény' round Limoges, and that of Major Hiller in Lot, Lot et Garonne and Tarn. The rest of SOE's work in this zone came from three main sources – Squadron Leader Southgate, Lieutenant Colonel G. R. Starr, and Major H. Peulevé.

Southgate arrived at Clermont-Ferrand with a courier, Jacqueline Néarne, in January 1943, with instructions to pick up the contacts left by Major Cowburn. He also inherited the beginning made by Captain Rafferty, who was arrested in the spring of 1943. The field originally allotted him was thus impossibly wide – very much in F Section's

---

[1] Below p. 600.

[2] At the moment (April 1948) J. A. R. Starr is under arrest in France on suspicion of betraying more than was necessary to the Germans.

[3] 'Horned Pigeon' and 'Maquis'.

'early bad manner' – stretching right across the centre of France from Châteauroux to Pau and Tarbes in the foothills of the Pyrenees. Fortunately he had excellent lieutenants, some of them sent to him, others recruited locally, and he was able to decentralise considerably. His 'empire' was distinguished long before D-day both for effective sabotage and as a 'reception area' for F Section organisers proceeding to other parts of France.

Southgate was in London for a brief spell from October 1943 to January 1944: after his return he retained his wide responsibilities, but when he was caught through a momentary lapse of caution in May 1944[1] F Section took the opportunity to impose a more formal decentralisation.

The outlying Tarbes–Pau area was split off under a local recruit, Captain Rechenman. In the main central kingdom a new officer, Major P. Liewer ('Staunton'), (who had already done good work at Rouen),[2] arrived to take over the southern part of Haute-Vienne with the Dordogne. The northern part of Haute-Vienne fell to Southgate's radio officer, Captain Maingard (DSO, Croix de Guerre avec Palmes), whose influence extended into Charente, Deux-Sèvres and Vienne. Indre and northern Vienne were run by Southgate's courier, F/O Pearl Witherington, who had the distinction of receiving the Croix de Guerre and of refusing the MBE (Civil) on the ground that she had been engaged in purely military work.* These three circuits were all engaged in heavy fighting in the last phase, and Captain Liewer had the pleasure of negotiating the surrender of Limoges with the German General Gleiniger. With few exceptions their relations with the local FFI organisations were singularly pleasant.

Lieutenant Colonel G. R. Starr on the other hand is for ever memorable for his altercation with General De Gaulle on 18th September 1944. There is a record of their remarks, which is at least persuasive. Starr's final answer to De Gaulle's rebukes for interference in French affairs was 'Mon Général, je vous connais comme chef du Comité Français de la Libération Nationale, et même comme Président du Gouvernement Provisoire de la République, mais pas comme un officier supérieur, et je vous emmerde.' De Gaulle in fury ordered him to quit France instantly, with all his staff, French or British: and then at the end shook him by the hand – 'Il y a une chose de vrai dans ce qu'ils m'ont dit de vous . . . que vous êtes sans peur et que vous savez dire "merde".' Starr got his Croix de Guerre avec Palmes as well as the DSO and MC.

---

1   He survived Buchenwald and received a well-earned DSO and Légion d'Honneur.
2   Above p. 575.
*   [She later accepted a military MBE.]

Starr had arrived originally in November 1942 to share in the wide empire of Philippe de Vomecourt, inherited by him from his brother 'Lucas'.[1] Philippe was arrested shortly after Starr's arrival (fortunately before contact had been made): and on Pertschuk's betrayal by Roger Bardet in April 1943, Starr fell heir also to his large circuit in the Toulouse area. These troubles meant that Starr had no wireless set until August 1943 and his earliest reports were made by couriers through Spain and Switzerland: the first direct contact was one of the very early uses of the S-Phone (on 22nd July 1943) for conversation between an aircraft and the ground. He was now established as a gentleman farmer of respectable antecedents, Deputy Mayor of Castelnau-sous-l'Auvignon in the north of Gers: and once supplies were assured he built up a very powerful organisation round this base. His home ground was in Gers and part of Landes, and his chief lieutenant Philippe de Gunzbourg (an old ally of Pertschuk) ruled to the north in southern Dordogne and the north part of Garonne. There was heavy fighting here after D-day against German reinforcements moving to the bridgehead: and on 21st August when the break came Starr and de Gunzbourg marched with the FFI into Toulouse and hunted the Germans toward Carcassonne. Eventually their troops were included in those blockading the Germans in the Royan pocket. Starr was not an easy man, and he left enemies: but this was one of the most dynamic of all the F Section Circuits.

Finally there was the circuit founded by Major H. Peulevé, who arrived on September 1943 to take up contacts in the Corrèze given by the Grandclément (OCM) organisation in Bordeaux. By good luck Peulevé just avoided destruction in the Grandclément disaster: but he had to begin work independently. His chief contact at the outset was André Malraux,[2] the novelist, whose political position is obscure: from a position close to the Communists he has now shifted to the side of De Gaulle, and is one of the important figures in the Ralliement du Peuple Français. At this stage he worked, it seems, mainly with the FTP, and Peulevé's supplies went in part (by no means exclusively) to the Communists: a fair instance of how an F Section Mission designed to work with OCM on the Right could adapt itself equally to the needs of the FTP on the Left. Peulevé himself was arrested in March 1944,[3] but his work was carried on by his lieutenant, Jacques Poirier,* who provided a line of communication for a miscellany of groups in Dordogne, Corrèze and Lot. One of these, though Poirier did not reveal it at the time, was an intelligence réseau directed by

---

[1] Above p. 251.
[2] His brother had already been associated with F Section in Rouen: above p. 576.
[3] He survived Buchenwald and received the DSO.
* [See his *The Giraffe Has a Long Neck* (1996).]

his father, Commandant Robert Poirier. There was heavy fighting here after D-day, and these groups claim to have imposed seven days' delay on the movement to the bridgehead of 2 SS Panzer Division.

3. The Fighting French Organisations in France

F Section's method, as we have seen, was essentially individual. Men like Southgate, Cammaerts, Heslop, Starr, de Baissac constituted together a formidable team, and they were handled as a team. But the captain of the team was in London, and it is not unjust that they should be inscribed in French history as the 'Réseaux Buckmaster': Colonel Buckmaster was an 'anxious mother' to each and everyone of his 'boys'. The 'native' organisations on the other hand strove towards political unity and administrative centralisation within France. R/F Section, as was its duty, contested this fiercely on grounds of security and of military command: they were right, but so were the French. It was only by centralising Resistance within France that the will of France at home could be given political expression and political weight in face of the intrigues – often quite patriotic intrigues – of exiles, and the military power of the Allies. Unless there was a government of the Resistance within France, the government of France after liberation must come from without, and could derive its political authority only from the armed force of Britain and the USA. It was part of De Gaulle's strength that he saw this clearly from the outset and that he made no attempt to force order on the Resistance from without until the Resistance had itself given De Gaulle the victory in his contest with Giraud. Thenceforward he put his full strength behind the construction of an underground administration of the Republic, and at the end the framework of government was in readiness in France. It was unstable and inefficient, and not always popular, but it was the Resistance government, and it worked.

This section of the history is therefore mainly the story of the central organisation in France under German occupation. It is necessarily incomplete, in part because the crucial documents (if they exist) are in French hands, in part because much of this political complexity is foreign to the main work of SOE, though it consumed endless time. From the military point of view the essential part of the machine was not the Conseil National de la Résistance and its Regions, but the local groups of fighting men: these groups could remain effective so long as they had a link with London or North Africa to produce for them money, arms and instructions. This spontaneous decentralisation was extensive: by June 1944 R/F Section had perhaps seventy wireless sets working to London and North Africa,[1] and the forty-five or

---

[1] It is impossible to give an exact figure as SOE's control was not comprehensive.

so sets run by F Section were also available (if security allowed) for the reinforcement of any local group in trouble.

The point reached in July 1942 in the Vichy Zone was that 'Combat', 'Libération' and 'Franc-Tireur' (Fresnay, D'Astier and 'Claudius') had come together to form a Conseil Général d'Études (CGE) without executive powers:[1] and there were in France Moulin ('Rex') and General Delestraint ('Vidal') as civil and military advisers on behalf of De Gaulle, whom the Resistance movements accepted as a symbol of resurgence rather than as a leader. After a good deal of debate and difficulty Fresnay and D'Astier were brought out in September 1942 (D'Astier for the second time): the result of their discussion with De Gaulle, the Foreign Office and SOE was a considerable step forward. There would be, in addition to the CGE, a Co-ordinating Committee of the three movements, under the Presidency of Moulin as representative of De Gaulle's National Committee: and he would be assisted by General Delestraint, who would form a single Armée Secrète out of the para-military organisations of the three movements. For this purpose France (Occupied and Non-Occupied) was divided into Regions, which came to be of considerable importance later.[2]

It was impossible to return D'Astier and Fresnay to France before 'Torch' began, and the project of reorganisation had to be communicated to Moulin by telegram on 10th November 1942.[3]

In imposing the plan Moulin was greatly assisted both by the total German occupation of France on 11th November and by the spontaneous reactions of Frenchmen to the Darlan affair: out of the confusion of these days he produced (by means unknown) the very important message of 17th November,[4] endorsed by the three Movements, by the CGT and the Catholic Trade Unions, and by all non-Vichy political parties except the Communists – Socialists, Radicals, Démocrates Populaires (the later MRP), and Fédération Républicaine. This opened with polite words, but continued with a sting:

> . . . We salute gratefully General Giraud and all Frenchmen who have rallied spontaneously to General De Gaulle, the unchallenged leader of Resistance who now (more than ever before) has the whole country behind him.

> We can in no circumstances admit that those guilty of military and civil treason should secure pardon for their crimes by turning their coats now.

> We demand that at the earliest possible moment liberated North Africa should be placed under the control of General De Gaulle.

---

[1] Above p. 279.
[2] A map showing this is given at Appendix L.
[3] SOE History of R/F Section, 1942, p. 29.
[4] Text in SOE Archives File 3/100/2(c).

This said a great deal, though perhaps a little less than is at first sight suggested by the fervour of its language. It does *not* (in fact) hail De Gaulle's Committee as the legitimate Government of France: its object is to force De Gaulle – personally and without his Committee – upon the Allies, as the nominee of an assembly speaking for almost all shades of patriotic opinion within France. With this card in his hand De Gaulle could bid pretty confidently against Giraud and even against Roosevelt; and his confidence was all the greater in that SOE had now organised secure communications with Moulin. His only weakness was that it was still possible to be honestly sceptical about the *'bona fides'* of Moulin's 'constituency': it was hard to believe that his 'Committee' had much behind it except the rather academic organisations of the old Vichy zone.

The next stage therefore was to transform the Committee of Co-ordination in the Vichy Zone into a committee for all France; in England this phase was seen largely through the eyes of the 'Seahorse' Mission. This consisted of the indomitable 'Passy' ('Arquebuse') and of Squadron Leader Yeo-Thomas (later GC) ('Seahorse'), second-in-command of R/F Section and the first Englishman to go into the field on its behalf.* With them went Captain Brossolette ('Brumaire'), also a hero of some note.** They reached France in mid-February 1943 and returned on 15th April. While they were there, Moulin and Delestraint were in England.[1]

Already in January the three 'Southern movements' had moved one step further: the old names remain, but their movements have a special position henceforward as the 'Mouvements Unifiés de la Résistance' (MUR).[2] This Co-ordinating Committee assumed executive powers under the Presidency of Moulin; Fresnay (who had once been an Army officer) became director of military activities, D'Astier (who stood more to the Left) was director of propaganda and 'politics'. In each region the 'cells' of the movements were to remain distinct, but there was to be local unity of command under a regional chief.[3] The next step, as Yeo-Thomas and 'Passy' saw it,[4] was to filter out from the confusion of lesser movements those which could make some solid

---

[1] Major Antelme (above p. 570) was on a political mission for F Section in rather different circles at the same time: his report on all important issues confirmed that of Yeo-Thomas.

[2] At the beginning of 1944 MUR incorporated three very minor northern groups and became the Mouvement de Libération Nationale (MLN): this new set of initials causes a good deal of confusion, but makes little difference in practice.

[3] SOE History of R/F Section, 1943, p.11.

[4] 'Seahorse' Report; copy at Appendix A to SOE R/F History, 1943.

* [See Mark Seaman, *Bravest of the Brave* (1998), a biography of Yeo-Thomas.]

** [See the life of him by his widow (Paris, 1985).]

contribution either to political unity or to military striking power. Five
such movements were discovered:

(a) *OCM* We have already seen the 'Conservative' tone of this
     organisation, and its ultimate responsibility for the
     Grandclément disaster at Bordeaux.[1]

(b) & (c) *Ceux de la Libération (Vengeance)* CDLL or CDLV and
     Ceux de la Résistance (CDLR) remain a little vague: they
     appear to have been 'patriotic Conservative', but less clearly
     political than OCM. In post-war French politics their leaders
     appear in the 'old-fashioned' Conservative Party, the Parti
     Républicain de la Liberté (PRL). The former had connexions
     with 'Transport Routier', the national road transport
     organisation.

(d) *'Libération Nord'* was an offshoot of the original 'Libération'
     in the Vichy Zone, as yet not highly developed. It claimed that
     there were affiliated to it the Comité d'Action Socialiste, the
     CGT and the Catholic Trade Unions.

(e) *'Front National'* (FANA) was the 'popular front' sponsored by
     the Communists after Russia entered the war. Its ostensible
     leadership included an array of national figures extending as
     far to the Right as M. Louis Marin and M. François Mauriac;*
     and its para-military side, the FTP, was largely non-
     Communist, except for a limited number of key-men. The
     'party line' was at this stage visible only in an insistence on
     the Russian policy of continuous offensive at all costs – the
     solid basis of the Communist 'myth' of the Parti des Fusillés
     – and in a strong disinclination for a merger of FANA troops
     with those of the Gaullist Armée Secrète. None the less FANA
     gave full political support to De Gaulle.[2]

Moulin was back in France at the end of March 1943, and he collaborated with 'Seahorse' in working out a compromise between a rather
rigid London plan and the material as it existed in France. Their joint
project was accepted at a meeting with the Movements on 14th April
just before 'Seahorse' left for London: the new Conseil National de
la Résistance (CNR) was formally constituted on 5th May and met
for the first time on 27th May, under Moulin's presidency. It included
one representative each from the three 'Southern' Movements and the

---

[1] Above p. 571.

[2] According to Dansette, 'La Libération de Paris', p. 29, these 'Northern' move-
     ments formed a Comité de Co-ordination in the spring of 1943, which generated
     a Commission d'Action Militaire (COMIDAC): there are a few traces of this in
     SOE's papers, but it does not seem to have been of much importance. It is to be
     distinguished from COMAC – below p. 597.

* [1885–1970, leading Roman Catholic novelist.]

five 'Northern' Movements: one each from the CGT and the Catholic Trade Unions: and one each from six political parties – Communists, Socialists, Radicals, Démocrates Populaires, Alliance Démocratique (M. Reynaud's party) and Union Démocratique Républicain (M. Louis Marin's party). A membership of seventeen was of course too large for useful action under the eyes of the Gestapo, and the effective work of the CNR was done by its Bureau. At the time of liberation this consisted of:

M. Bidault	(MRP)
Avinin	(Franc-Tireur)
Bloc-Maseant	(OCM)
Saillant	(CGT)
Guisburger	(FANA)

The balance was thus roughly one 'bourgeois' nationalist, one progressive Catholic, one Socialist, one 'fellow-traveller', one Communist, a fair microcosm of the politics of the Resistance.

The creation of the CNR was both an end and a beginning. There now existed a symbol of French unity within France, and in the June negotiations with Giraud at Algiers De Gaulle had this unity on his side: his victory over Giraud was thus in the end certain, for Giraud could command no section of French opinion except that of the ORA, which was politically nil. But as the old struggle ended another began, this time between the Resistance and 'le premier résistant de la France'; the former seeking to assert the premacy of the CNR, the latter seeking to develop from the CFNL the French State of the future. In the next phase the CNR and De Gaulle both set themselves, in a curious mixture of rivalry and collaboration, to build an effective administration, which could exist under German repression and could step forward when that repression was withdrawn to exercise instantly the full authority of the French State.

At this moment the Germans struck. On 21st June 1943, Moulin, Delestraint* and fourteen others were taken at Calliure near Lyon: and with them went some 7 million francs, the HQ files of the Secret Army, and many other important papers. None of the victims survived, and the circumstances surrounding the tragedy provide one of the great 'affaires' of the Resistance. There was at one time a tendency to throw the blame on SOE through the instrumentability of Déricourt:[1] but at present (spring 1948) the confessed traitor is Colonel René Hardy,** a man whose record was otherwise excellent and who had

---

[1]　Above p. 568. An investigation of SOE's security in France was made at this time by the JIC with very inconclusive results (JIC(43)325(0) of 1.8.43).

*　[A slip: Delestraint had been arrested a few days earlier, in Paris.]

**　[Hardy ran 'Sabotage Fer', a large French railway sabotage organisation; his case is still the subject of dispute.]

been one of the heroes of the anti-Communist wing of the Resistance. He had already been triumphantly acquitted once, and was rearrested in the spring of 1947 as a result of a piece of new evidence – a sleeping car ticket – which proved that he had been in the hands of the Gestapo for a brief period just before the disaster. The case is now fabulously complex: all that need be said of it is that it is inconceivable that the Gestapo had not many separate sources of evidence for each aspect of Moulin's work. The whole organisation – though vital to the future of France – was technically damnable: it could only be a matter of time until the Gestapo put out their hand and took it, and any one individual out of thousands might have provided the final occasion for action. The moment which they chose was fortunately a bad one: it was too late to affect the political situation and too early to destroy the military organisation, for none existed except on paper.

Here it may be convenient to turn back and trace the rather separate history of the 'Relève' and the 'Maquis'. The story begins in the early summer of 1942 with the negotiation by the German Labour Minister Sauckel* of an agreement with Laval by which 50,000 French prisoners in Germany would be exchanged for 150,000 'voluntary' skilled workers. This bait proved unattractive, and by September 1942 the Germans had begun to put the screw on Laval. Compulsory labour service was introduced by Vichy that month, and SOE's political intelligence summary already reports in October 1942 that 'the situation in France has been dominated during the last month' by the question of the Relève.[1] The Germans secured their first 150,000 men one month behind time; by 31st March 1943 they had squeezed out 250,000 more: and when this was achieved the demand went up to another 400,000.[2]

Resistance to these exactions was entirely spontaneous. Young men liable to compulsory service 'lost' themselves at new addresses: or obtained false papers from friendly officials, or fled to the country and slept out in camps protected by sentries and by local vigilance. This whole swarm of 'refractaires' constituted the 'Maquis' in the broad sense, a great reservoir of active men living outside the law. In a narrower sense a camp of 'deserters' in difficult country constituted 'a Maquis' – which might be anything from a semi-criminal slum to a first-rate body of disciplined men.[3]

---

[1] Copy on SOE Archives File 3/100/5(a).
[2] See Report on the Relève by Lieutenant Colonel Hutchinson; copy on SOE Archives File F.38/Pt II.
[3] Some confusion is caused by the use of the term 'Corps Francs' in some contexts. This generally means such bodies of men as were permanently mobilised for armed action even during the clandestine phase: and a 'Corps Franc' will generally (but not always) correspond to a 'Maquis'.
* [Hanged 1946 for his work as a slavemaster.]

As early as February 1943 Bidault's wireless set was reporting French anxiety about the fate of these men:[1] and in March De Gaulle attacked Mr Churchill personally on the subject. The Chiefs of Staff, to whom this letter was referred, considered it in close consultation with SOE,[2] and devised a draft reply for the Prime Minister in which he promised SOE's assistance but urged De Gaulle to limit the numbers in the open 'Maquis' and to discourage any provocation of the Germans. It would be most unwise to jeopardise the whole organisation in France and to waste resources in fighting without strategic value. Another urgent appeal (on behalf of the Savoy Maquis in particular) was made by General Cochet in June, and Brigadier Gubbins did his best with the Air Ministry – unfortunately Savoy was beyond the range of Halifaxes of No. 138 Sqdn during the short summer nights, and the situation was pretty hopeless.[3]

In France, meantime, the lawyer Michel Brault ('Jérome') had in June 1943 been put at the head of a specialised organisation designed to aid the 'Maquis'. The Resistance Movements had not created the 'Maquis', and at this stage it was for them a problem of 'relief work' rather than of military organisation. 'Jérome' was responsible for 'relief', while in practice responsibility for military training and armament lay where it fell, in spite of various paper schemes: a 'Maquis' might be taken in hand by an F Section officer, or by one of the CNR hierarchy, or by the Communists – or it might be left in dirt and idleness. But by June 1944 there were few 'Maquis' which had not some arms, some military discipline and some chain of command.

The Savoy 'Maquis' had always been one of the largest and most advanced, and in January 1944 R/F Section took part in a Mission specially designed to help it. This consisted of a French officer, Lieutenant Colonel Fourcaud,* an American Marine, Captain Ortiz, and Captain Thackthwaite of R/F Section, with a French wireless operator.[4] When they were in the 'Maquis' they worked in uniform, and they were thus the first open Allied Military Mission in France since 1940. In theory they were a liaison Mission attached to the French command, with powers to investigate but not to act; in practice their role (and those of other similar R/F Missions) was not so very different from that of the F Section organisers like Lieutenant

---

1   SOE History of R/F Section, 1943, p. 29.
2   COS(43)45th(0) Mtg, Item 1, of 15th March, and COS(43)48th(0) Mtg, Item 6, of 18th March: relevant SOE papers are on File F.38/Pt I.
3   Papers on SOE Archives File F.38/Pt I.
4   There is much first-hand information about this in the SOE R/F History, which was compiled by Thackthwaite. Operational instructions to Mission appear in the SOE War Diary, R/F Section 1944.
*   [P. Fourcaud died aged nearly 100 in 1998.]

Colonel Heslop.[1] Some temporary order had to be found in the confusion of personalities and politics, and an Allied Mission (whether F or R/F) possessed a special authority derived from its impartiality in French politics, as well as from the weight of Allied resources which it could command, or was thought to command.

Thackthwaite was recalled to London on 3rd May 1944 to take over the position of second-in-command of R/F Section on the arrest of Yeo-Thomas (on his third Mission), and Ortiz also returned a little later. To ease the strain on Fourcaud, now left alone, a fresh Allied Mission (including two British officers, Major Longe* and Captain Houseman) was dropped on 25th June into the middle of the open revolt on the Vercors plateau, where the tricolore was flying over the villages. They fought there until resistance collapsed in the middle of July, and then withdrew to Switzerland.[2]

Two other similar R/F Section Missions may be mentioned here. The advance party of 'Citronelle' was dropped to the French Ardennes in April 1944 and was reinforced in June: it saw hard fighting there in very difficult conditions up to the Liberation at the end of August. The other ('Benjoin')[3] was sent in May 1944 to help the large Maquis in the Massif Central (Cantal and Corrèze). There was considerable confusion here between the 'official' French organisation and that of 'Gaspard'[4] (who possessed an F Section liaison officer): but order of a sort emerged, and the battles in June and July were on the whole better directed than those of the Plateau des Glières and the Vercors.

To return now to the central organisation of the Resistance. Politics naturally did not cease with the constitution of the CNR. To the Right, outside the Council, was the Giraudist ORA under General Revers, president of the court-martial which had condemned De Gaulle in 1940: patriotic, but concerned mainly with the prestige of the Army and the future careers of Army officers, and not immune from the German 'anti-Communist' trick which had caught Grandclément. Within the Council Fresnay, it seems, leant a little in this direction and had some hopes of special American favour. On the Left were the Communists, strongly Gaullist, but equally determined to maintain their own fighting policy and their own plans outside the control of the military hierarchy. There was thus ample scope for manoeuvre,

---

[1] In Savoy they worked pretty closely with Lieutenant Colonel Heslop and Captain Rosenthal (above pp. 581–2).

[2] There was an allegation that they had given up too easily, which was rebutted by a formal Court of Enquiry; copy of Enquiry with SOE Archives Files, CD Reports.

[3] The chief British representative was Major Cardozo.

[4] Above p. 581.

* [D. E. Longe, 1914–90, Norfolk notable, became chairman of Norwich Union insurers.]

and yet fundamentally the position was more stable than it looked. It was soon pretty obvious to the Right that their only hope (take it or leave it) was De Gaulle. On the Left it is plain now (and it was plain to discerning observers even then) that there could be no question of a Communist coup d'état unless by some miracle the Russian armies brought liberation from the East. The Communists could not make a revolution against the American and British Armies; they kept their powder dry for all eventualities, but their first concern for the moment was to establish themselves as a 'national' party, the true Resisters, the 'Parti des Fusillés'. To achieve this they must make themselves chief spokesmen and agents of French hatred of Germany: and (in spite of all later exaggeration) there is no doubt that in most areas the FTP under Communist leadership fought the Germans, and fought well.

R/F Section's battle was largely against 'politics', in every shape and form: in spite of its faith in the future of De Gaulle its policy was dominated (as French policy could not be) by Allied military needs – French unity of purpose was for the British primarily a means to save British lives on D-day. For the same reason R/F fought hard on the issue of centralisation, and it never ceased to ply the French with the lesson of the Calluire disaster. After the loss of Moulin his office was divided: M. Bidault became President of the CNR, M. Bollaert[1] Délégué Général of the CFLN. In this latter post he was succeeded (after his arrest in January 1944) by M. Parodi.[2] But on other fronts centralisation proceeded in the teeth of British warnings.[3]

The trouble which arose over the decentralisation of Brault's Maquis organisation may have been due to genuine misunderstanding: at least the 'Union' Mission in January 1944 found that an agreement on organisation reached in London had not been observed.[4] But the clash regarding military decentralisation in October 1943 was open and unpleasant. Two important officers, Colonel Maréchal (alias Morinaud) and Colonel Mangin, son of General Mangin,* were then going to the field on behalf of the CFLN, and it was agreed that they should *not* be given general responsibility for the Zones of France,

---

1   A former préfet of the Rhône Department and an ally of M. Herriot, at Lyon.
2   M. Parodi was an eminent civil servant, 'Maître des Requêtes' at the Conseil d'État.
3   At Appendix M is an official French chart released after the Armistice by the DGER: this is helpful, though in parts tendentious.
4   SOE History of R/F Section, 1944, p. 8. There was similar trouble about the excessive centralisation of air operations within France by the amalgamation of the BOA and SAP, see R/F Section History, 1943, p. 24.
*   [C. M. E. Mangin, 1866–1927, took part in Fashoda expedition 1896–8, army commander on Western Front 1918.]

North and South. At this time the French sent their messages in French code from SOE's signal station: a copy of the code was kept by SOE on trust that it should not be used except in emergency. R/F Section noticed that the coded message was longer than the text agreed, and they had it broken by SOE's cypher section – who found that it contained a few vital words constituting a Délégué Militaire Zone Nord and a Délégué Militaire Zone Sud. The message was withdrawn, and the row followed, with innuendoes of trickery on both sides.[1] A fortunate by-product was that the French were persuaded at last of the insecurity of their codes, and went over to the British 'One Time Pad' system.[*] But in practice it was quite impossible for R/F Section to prevent French centralisation if the French were set on it. Maréchal and Mangin took up their appointments as Zonal Delegates: Maréchal was arrested almost at once and Mangin found himself responsible for both Zones, virtually in the position of Délégué Militaire National. Finally, in April 1944, Delestraint's old post was formally reconstituted and was filled by an able young Inspecteur des Finances, M. Delmas ('Chaban').[2] The theory of centralisation had won.

There was similar trouble over the 'Zonal Secretariats', which were constituted in Paris to assist M. Bollaert in the late summer of 1943: M. Serreulles ('Sophie') for the North, and M. Bingen ('Cadillac') for the South, who ranked eventually as Délégués Généraux Adjoints.[3] At the end of August 1943 Squadron Leader Yeo-Thomas went to the field with Brossolette on his second Mission, the 'Marie-Claire' Mission, and their accounts shattered all illusions about the efficiency of the Secretariats.[4] There were many grounds of criticism: political intrigue and the diversion of funds to further personal ambitions: total neglect of security: administrative inefficiency which left the Regions without funds and equipment readily available at the 'Head Office'. Yeo-Thomas backed this report in person on his return to London in November, and in the end Serreulles was recalled in January 1944.

---

[1] There was another unpleasant incident in November 1943, when there came into SOE's hands a letter from D'Astier to the acting head of 'Libération' discouraging all co-operation with the 'Anglo-Saxons', who are accused of attempting to seize command for themselves; copy on SOE Archives File F.38/Pt II.

[2] Chaban-Delmas was at first appointed provisionally pending the arrival of Colonel Billotte (above p. 278 etc.). but Billotte arrived only at the head of one of the Brigades of the Leclerc Division, and Delmas thus held the post to the end. [J-P-M. Delmas, born 1915, added Chaban- to his surname after war, Prime Minister of France 1969–72.]

[3] SOE History of R/F Section, 1943, p. 49.

[4] The 'Marie-Claire' report is on SOE Archives File (AD/S.1) F.38/Pt II.

[*] [See Marks, *Between Silk and Cyanide*, *passim*, on his reinvention of one-time pad (which the Foreign Office had been using all through the war), and on the insecurity of French codes.]

M. D'Astier fought hard in his interests, but SOE flatly refused to let him return to Paris.[1] Its case was strengthened by a fresh series of disasters in January and February 1944, in which Bollaert was caught and Brossolette and many others were killed. In April Yeo-Thomas on his third Mission fell into German hands: Fassin (a very old hand),[2] Bingen and Colonel Langlois (the head of OCM) lost their lives. On each occasion the Gestapo made considerable hauls of documents and money, and the circle of arrests widened.

Fortunately by this time the Délégués Militaires Régionaux were finding their feet, and the parallel civil organisation of Commissaires de la République – in effect regional préfets – had been set going by M. Bollaert. These men varied much in personal and political quality, but at least they represented legitimate French authority at a level not too far above the confusion of the battle. Still more important, the supply situation improved greatly in the early months of 1944: now that each local authority had direct contact with London or Algiers its hold on its locality was greatly strengthened and its allegiance naturally flowed towards the CFNL rather than towards the CNR and the Movements, which could give orders only through slow and dangerous underground channels. Thus by the time D-day came in June a fairly sound system of decentralisation existed in practice, and the effective strength of resistance had not been much weakened by Gestapo successes against the titular leaders.

But in principle centralisation was maintained. Politically it was of the greatest importance that in March 1944 the Bureau of the CNR formulated the Charte de la Résistance, a programme of moderate socialism and social reform put forward as the first sketch of the Fourth Republic.[3] On the military side it was possible in January 1944 to draw the necessary deductions from the elimination of Giraud and the inclusion of two Communist Ministers in the Government. The Forces Françaises de l'Intérieur were then called into being to incorporate all existing military formations: the Giraudist ORA, the Gaullist Armée Secrète, and the Communist FTP did not lose their identity and local organisation, but all alike accepted in theory the operational direction of the Allied High Command. For the moment F Section's circuits remained outside the hierarchy, and were subject to obscure menaces as 'Traitors to France', but this last gap was closed when EMFFI was set up on 17th June.

---

[1] SOE Archives Files 3/370/46(c) and (AD/S.1) F.38/Pt III. He was eventually replaced by M. Roland Pré.

[2] Above p. 276.

[3] Apparently this was never submitted to a full meeting of the CNR. At least two right-wing members of the CNR, M. Laniel and M. Muther, later dissociated themselves from it (Dansette, 'Libération de Paris', p. 24).

This did not in practice mean that there was even now a single intelligible chain of military command. De Gaulle and the CNR were both, as against the British, exponents of centralisation; and centralisation had won at least on paper. But there were still two independent hierarchies. On the civil side the CNR and a chain of Regional, Departmental and local Liberation Committees were balanced by the Délégué-Général, M. Parodi, the Secrétaires-Générals designated to take provisional charge of the various Ministries, the two Delegates for the Northern and Southern Zones and the Regional Commissionaires de la République. On the military side there was the Gaullist hierarchy of Délégué Militaire National, Délégués Militaires for the two Zones, and DMRs. There was also in parallel the État-National of the FFI, created by the CNR early in 1944 against the protests of the BCRA, and below it États-Majors for Regions and Departments. Early in May the CNR challenged De Gaulle by creating its own Comité d'Action Militaire (COMAC),[1] composed of three civilian members, who claimed to exercise control of the FFI through the États-Majors on various levels. If COMAC had been able to operate effectively, the authority of General Koenig as Commander of EMFFI would have been reduced to a shadow; and wrangling continued over this piece of organisation throughout the second battle of France.[2]

But De Gaulle, through the work of SOE, held the whip hand. It was London alone who possessed wireless communications with every part of France, and London alone had power to decide what arms and reinforcements should be directed to one area or another. De Gaulle was weak only in that he was not himself present on the spot, and when the time came he set to work to remedy this with immense energy and ruthlessness. Until D-day he had fought off the conclusion of a Civil Affairs agreement with the Allies, and at the earliest moment (on 14th June) he descended on Normandy and imposed on the protesting Allies a hierarchy of French local officials. In Paris a rising broke out almost spontaneously on 18th and 19th August, and by a mixture of luck and judgement De Gaulle's nominees installed themselves at once in the Ministries and in the Prefectures of Police and of the Seine Department. On the 22nd a burst of pressure broke down General Eisenhower's opposition to a direct march on Paris, and the Leclerc Armoured Division was unleashed. On 25th August (before the firing had quite ceased) De Gaulle himself appeared as

---

[1] These were 'the three V's', 'Villon', 'Valrimont' and 'Vaillant' (actually Ginsburger, Kriegel and de Vogüé). General Revers of ORA was associated with them in form as 'technical adviser'.

[2] The CNR 'found a formula' on 17th August, when it was too late to be of any practical importance.

the symbol of the French State in liberated Paris: and in the days of wild excitement which followed he swept through France using the whole force of his immense prestige to confirm his chosen delegates in authority. The République Française was back. F Section packed its bags and slipped out as gracefully as it could; the native Resistance Movements were left searching for a political future in a disappointing post-war world.

4. The Sabotage Campaign

Nothing is so tedious and so unilluminating as a bare list of acts of sabotage. Yet each incident in detail is dramatic: sabotage is probably the least boring form of war, and it suited the French temperament very well. Unfortunately there is no means of reducing the mass of incidents to a statistical summary. The evidence for their authenticity is of all shades of merit: the best saboteurs do not keep very perfect records; and such statistics as there are cannot be added together to produce a grand total which means anything.

On the whole Allied policy from 'Torch' until 'Overlord' was to damp down spontaneous minor sabotage. Action of some sort was essential to keep the troops in good heart, but it must be action under a coherent plan against objectives of serious military importance: the Communist policy of ceaseless offensive involved useless danger to valuable lives, and to still more valuable organisations.

Some of the more important attacks have already been mentioned: for instance Trotobas's attack on the Fives-Lille works, the sinking of a minesweeper at Rouen, Heslop's coup at the Annecy ball-bearing plant. These were the work of F Section; if a star turn is to be chosen on the R/F side it must be the 'Armada' team.[1] This was built round the fireman Basset and the garage mechanic Jarrot – famous as 'Marie' and 'Goujon'. After working their own way into resistance they came out to England over the Pyrenees at the end of 1942, and their first Mission (in August 1943) was directed against the power supplies of the Creusot works. After a great success here they went to the field again in October 1943 with two Missions, to attack the electricity supplies of Paris and the canal system – in particular the links which enabled the Germans to move small submarines and Flak ships between the North Sea and the Mediterranean. With their satellites – among whom should be named 'Pakebo' (Lieutenant Pellay), a distinguished canal-wrecker, and 'Khodja', who specialised in the execution of Gestapo agents – they had a long run of well-authenticated success. Finally in July 1944 'Marie' and 'Goujon' arrived a third time to organise the scattered 'Maquis' round Lyon and Châlons-

---

[1] SOE History of R/F Section, 1943, p. 39.

sur-Sâone, and at the end 'Marie' marched on Lyon at the head of some 15,000 men.[1]

'Armada' is perhaps the best that France has to offer to set along-side the work of 'Noric' in Oslo and of 'Apollo' in the Piraeus: there were few gangs as good, but there were many who achieved at least one first-rate coup without disaster. In addition, there was much 'small beer': some of it reported *en bloc* by SOE agents, some the unrecorded work of 'private enterprise' or the FTP. The best evidence of its cumu-lative effect is the lamentations recorded in German official papers, in the loud public denunciation blending 'saboteurs' and 'terrorists' with 'Communists' and 'Jews', and in the ferocity and scale of repres-sion. Germany doubtless made some profit on the occupation of France, but after November 1942 it was meagre and hard-earned.

Two problems of general strategic importance arose out of the work of sabotage: those of RAF attacks on locomotives, and of 'blackmail' attacks on factories.

During 1942 and 1943 the RAF had as part of a general campaign against the Axis transport system carried out persistent low-level fighter attacks on locomotives on the French railways. It was never thought likely that this would destroy many locomotives: but in theory the serviceable stock could be greatly reduced by increasing the burden of repairs and by attacking the repair sheds. The results are succinctly described by a report from a French railway engineer who reached England in December 1943:[2]

Aircraft attacks on Locomotives
Since the beginning of 1943 650 locomotives have been hit (an average of 70 a month) out of 10,200 in service.

The damage is generally very slight and the average period of repair is a fortnight. There are therefore on an average 35 loco-motives under repair, about 0.34% of the total.

In order to achieve this derisory result 78 railwaymen have been killed and 378 wounded since the beginning of 1943.

Sabotage of Locomotives
40 locomotives on an average were sabotaged each month, but the repairs required were much more serious. The average time required has not yet been established. But if we take it as six months, this means 240 locomotives under repair, 2.40% of the total, eight times as many as those damaged by aircraft.

---

[1]   His diary of this campaign is in SOE R/F Section History, 1944, Appendix B.
[2]   Dated 14th December 1943; copy on SOE Archives File (AD/S.1) F.38/Pt II.

Fortunately the policy had been reversed before this was written. The question had been raised by SOE without success in February and again in August 1943: by October the volume of protests became so great that the matter was pressed once more, with Lord Selborne's personal support. Fortunately the MEW (Lord Selborne's *alter ego*) took the same view on economic grounds, and Fighter Command gave way. Every effort was made to bring the situation home to the railwaymen and to step up sabotage, and the results were certainly good, as demonstrated by the large number of German railwaymen moved into France early in 1944.[1] The statistics are swallowed up in the crescendo of attacks on transport which preceded and followed D-day, and there is no means of making neat comparisons. But there can be little doubt which policy was correct.[2]

The 'blackmail' issue arose in rather similar circumstances. High-level bombing attacks on factories (generally by the USAAF) were often effective – far more effective than the low-level attacks on locomotives: but they were not popular in France. The wholesale destruction of French economic potential was disliked – especially by its owners: and it often happened that a small bombing error caused large civilian casualties. In the end some 55,000 French civilians were killed by Allied bombing. A fair share of these were lost in the bombing of Atlantic ports at the behest of the Admiralty, and many others in the mass attacks on railway targets which preceded D-day; but the attacks on industry contributed largely to the losses.[3] The test case was that of the Peugeot works at Sochaux near Montbéliard. Here there was an ineffective and costly RAF attack in the summer of 1943: Captain Harry Ree arrived just at this time and was fortunate enough to get in touch with a Peugeot director whom he found to be enthusiastically interested in sabotaging his own factories. London was with difficulty persuaded to call off further RAF attacks meantime: and on 5th November there was a very well-executed 'outside' attack on the transformers and compressors at Sochaux. SOE followed this up at once with the Air Ministry,[4] and they were helped by Heslop's brilliant attack on the Annecy ball-bearing works on 13th November –

---

[1] An interesting map of their distribution is on SOE Archives File (D/R) D.1(0) under date 20th April 1944.

[2] SOE's paper on the subject was put up to the Bombing Targets Committee on 5th November 1943, Lord Selborne wrote to the Prime Minister on 15th November, and the matter was decided by the COS on 24th November (COS(43)287th (0) Mtg, Item 7). An incomplete set of the papers is on SOE Archives File F.38/Pt II.

[3] For consultation with SOE regarding these railway attacks see Archives File (D/R) P.1(b).

[4] From this point the story is pretty clear from SOE Archives File (D/R) France 7(c).

which also followed an ineffective air attack. What they secured (at a meeting on 20th December) was in effect the first close co-ordination of attacks by bombing and attacks by sabotage. Of the list of priority targets in France some were allocated exclusively to the RAF and USAAF, and others exclusively to SOE: for a third category SOE was given a limited period in which to secure the co-operation of the management (or the workmen) under threat of bombing. Thus emerged the list of 'blackmail' targets, which was watched over by a sub-committee of SOE, OSS, the Air Ministry and the USAAF. Some reinforcements came later: the scheme was extended to Belgium: and the CGT was brought into it, in return for an undertaking that after the war the British would use their best efforts to replace any machinery destroyed.[1]

Earlier in the war SOE's organisation was perhaps inadequate to 'sell' the scheme and to test it in practice: but unfortunately 1944 was rather late for an experiment which must be cut short at D-day. The RAF obliged in March by a very successful attack on 'Michelin' at Clermont-Ferrand, which followed swiftly upon a refusal to pay 'blackmail' to SOE.[2] SOE on their side continued to harass Peugeot at Sochaux, which remained exempt from bombing: at Annecy continued sabotage alternated with RAF attacks: at Toulouse Lieutenant Colonel Starr arranged a thorough-going attack on the explosives factory: at Figeac the Ratier airscrew works were successfully sabotaged. On the other hand there were some 'blackmail' targets where SOE proved to be unable to place agents in the short time available. The experiment remained a little inconclusive: but it is at least a first-rate precedent for future collaboration between airmen and saboteurs. Even this short trial was enough to show that the effectiveness of both arms is increased if they can learn one another's powers and limitations, and can choose the method to fit the circumstances: and the circumstances include important moral and political factors.

5. Preparations for 'Overlord'

(a) Resources and the Problem

What has preceded can give only a dim picture of the mixture of energy and patriotism, muddle, political ambition and even treachery, which made up the atmosphere of the Resistance. The picture was even less clear in the summer of 1944. The one certain fact was that

---

[1] Correspondence between Lord Selborne, Mr Oliver Lyttelton, Mr Dalton and General Koenig on SOE Archives File (D/R) France 7(c).

[2] Unfortunately at Berliet they hit the factory at the moment when SOE's man was negotiating with the management.

on D-day SOE's main wireless station was in touch with 137 active stations behind the 'Atlantic Wall' in France. There was no means of measuring the military qualities of the men whom these wireless sets represented: even their numbers and armament were obscure.

In May 1944 SOE's best estimate was that there were 100,000 men with arms who would take action on orders from London. Almost at the same date 'Jérome', head of the Maquis organisation, gave the number of 'well-armed' men as 35,000–40,000, of whom only 10,000 would have munitions for more than one day's fighting; behind this, in loosely organised bodies, were 350,000 unarmed men of the Armée Secrète (with perhaps another 350,000 in close personal touch with them), 500,000 railwaymen and 300,000 Trade Unionists. Thus in the widest sense, including all who might co-operate in passive resistance or in a general strike, the Resistance numbered perhaps 3,000,000 men, a very large proportion of the working population of France.[1]

This illustrates the problem of numbers. As regards arms there are fairly satisfactory figures for those delivered by SOE up to 11th May 1944: the main heads of these are:

	F Section	R/F Section	Total	Known losses	Net Total
Stens	30,936	45,354	76,290	2,159	74,131
Pistols	10,385	17,576	27,961	914	27,047
Rifles	6,694	10,251	16,945	450	16,495
Brens	1,609	1,832	3,441	146	3,295
L.M.Gs	2	402	404	–	404
Bazookas	272	300	572	–	572
Piats	119	185	304	–	304
Mortars	17	143	160	–	160
M.M.Gs	–	54	54	–	54
A.T. Rifles	32	18	50	–	50

From this must be deducted the unknown losses, which were very much larger than those known: on the other side of the balance sheet are fairly large quantities of grenades and demolition equipment sent by SOE, as well as an unknown quantity of arms derived from other sources, in particular from stores hidden by the Armée de l'Armistice.

Armament was thus almost as uncertain as numbers: but on any basis it was clear that the FFI, in spite of SOE's efforts, were pitifully equipped for modern war. Their fighting value depended entirely on their skill, discipline and enthusiasm, and here again the Allied High Command was in the dark, except for the personal assessments of SOE and of SOE men who had been in France. It was not possible

---

[1] Both estimates are on SOE Archives File (D/R) D.1(a).

to give the staff planners any neat picture of the available striking-power, translated into the formal military language of Divisions, Battalions and Platoons. On the other hand the strategic location of the FFI was potentially of immense importance, and their value was likely to be enhanced by the loyalty of Frenchmen of all classes, and in particular of Frenchmen in public services on which the enemy was greatly dependent. It was an extremely hard technical problem to make a military plan out of such material: it had never been done before, and there are no final lessons to be learnt from the single experiment of 'Overlord'. But many points of great interest emerge.

(b) Liaison

As early as May 1942 there had been discussions between Brigadier Gubbins, Home Forces and CCO regarding SOE's role in the reoccupation of Western Europe, but the first serious experiment was made during the 'Spartan' exercise in March 1943. In this a few platoons were widely distributed to represent 'the resistance' and eleven SOE teams (leader, second and wireless operator) were dropped to them to provide leadership and communications. These were known as 'Jedburghs'. This very small expenditure of effort was justified by substantial successes in local actions and in the collection of tactical intelligence; what is more, it gave the Army some confidence in SOE in general and in the 'Jedburgh' scheme in particular.

As laid down in SOE's report on the exercise, the requirements for successful co-operation were as follows:

(a) W/T Communication with England.
(b) Adequate arms and equipment.
(c) Clear and definite orders or instructions.
(d) Adequate leadership.
(e) Preparation for replenishment of supplies generally.[1]

At that stage of Resistance development it was thought unlikely that these requirements could be met by SOE's clandestine agents, who were still few in numbers, and in any case might not be the right men to fight an open battle. The original plan was that 'Jedburghs', in uniform, should be dropped on D-day or shortly before it, to give a quick and sudden impetus to local organisations in the areas immediately behind the bridgehead. By the spring of 1944 the Resistance had greatly extended and so had SOE's organisation and wireless network: so that the role of 'Jedburghs' required some adaptation. They now became 'strategic reserves' for the Resistance all over France: a comparatively small number would go at once to the battle area, and the rest would be held ready to reinforce any other district

---

[1] Appendix Ic of SOE 'Jedburgh' History.

which needed them. In this new role the 'Jedburghs' might have to remain with Resistance for weeks or months before being overrun, and they might, on occasion, have to operate in civilian clothes. They thus became 'agents' rather than 'special troops', and occupied a position intermediate between SOE's long-term workers and the 'striking parties' provided by the SAS.

Ultimately the standard team was made up of three men: one 'SHAEF' officer, either British or American, one officer from the country concerned, and a wireless operator. The programme was to provide seventy-five teams for France, six for Belgium and six for Holland, with some ten–twelve teams in reserve to cover casualties and failures in training: the British contribution was to be sixty officers and forty wireless operators. The men were most carefully selected, with a view to political adaptability and tact as well as military leadership; in January 1944 they began training together, and early in February they moved to the special 'Jedburgh School' (ME65) at Milton Hall, Peterborough.[1] There they worked up to advanced training on 'schemes' under field conditions, and so far as possible they were encouraged to choose their own team-mates, as temperament and friendship moved them.

In the event the pace of advance through Belgium was so fast that no Jedburghs were used there; seven teams were sent to Holland, but things moved slowly there and they had to act virtually as long-term secret agents.[2] In France operations went closely according to plan. In all ninety-three teams[3] were used, sixty-eight sent from England, twenty-five from North Africa, and they were spread pretty evenly over all the areas of France where open resistance was in progress.[4] Each party normally took with it arms for 100 men. The casualties were twenty-one killed, prisoner or missing, and twenty-one wounded.

The general lines on which they were used are fairly plain, amid a mass of adventurous detail. First, on D-day and in the following week nine Missions were distributed over the main resistance areas: the rest were held back meantime until the development of operations became clearer – only four more Missions went during the rest of June. Then in mid-July there were ten Missions, all but one of them to Brittany. This is a good instance of the flexibility of the 'Jedburgh' idea: at this moment Brittany was the key point – Resistance had developed well there, the Allies were badly represented (there had been no F Section circuits), and co-ordination was badly needed at

---

1   For details of 'Jedburgh' training, see SOE Training Section History, p. 59.
2   SOE 'Jedburgh History', Pt VIII.
3   One of them ('Isaac') included the previous head of R/F Section, Lieutenant Colonel J. R. H. Hutchinson.
4   SOE 'Jedburgh History' – Map at App. X(b).

the moment when the Allies began (with the attack beyond Caen on 15th July) the series of punches designed to extricate them from the bridgehead.[1] The main stream of Missions did not go until August, when there came the breakthrough in the north and (on 15th August) the 'Dragoon' landing in the south. In the north events moved so fast that this last wave of Jedburghs was in the main overrun before they could do much: but the Resistance played a great part in easing the invasion from the south and in harassing the escaping Germans, and the Jedburghs there and in the centre were pretty busy. When all was over, several of the Missions were retained in France at French request, to help in converting the FFI into a reborn army.

The Jedburgh experiment showed up some sore points. The ordinary arrangements for 'briefing' were hardly adequate to cope with operations on this scale, and 'Jedburghs' did not always have a very full and clear picture of what they would find in their area and what they ought to do with it. On some occasions SOE's 'old hands' in the field complained that they would have preferred more stores rather than more inexperienced 'bodies' to nurse. On others, the 'Jedburghs' themselves felt that EMFFI had sent in more Missions than it could supply with the aircraft available, and that it did harm rather than good to provide an extra channel of communication which produced more orders but no arms with which to execute them.

There was some confusion too as regards the relation of the 'Jedburghs' to the SAS and the American OGs which came into the planning rather later.[2] The latter were in theory 'striking forces' on their own, with specific and limited objectives: whereas the 'Jedburghs' were intended to provide communications and leadership for the French. But (as might have been foreseen) the ordinary 'Maquisard' knew nothing of such distinctions, and the two organisations had to operate under very similar conditions. The admirable thugs of the SAS were not selected or trained for such a role, and some of their rank and file seem to have been a little heavy-handed in their dealings with the natives. In addition, the chain of command was baffling: if a 'Jedburgh' and an SAS team were side by side the chain of command for one led back through EMFFI, for the other through HQ Airborne Troops, who were in turn under 21st Army Group.[3] This was mitigated by the presence of an SAS liaison section

---

[1] An amphibious and airborne operation against Brittany was planned for this phase, but was not required: Eisenhower's Report, p. 47.

[2] There is a note of what seems to be the first 'co-ordination' meeting on 1st March 1944 – see SOE Archives File (D/R) 'Overlord'.

[3] SHAEF/17240/8/Ops(A) of 24th May 1944 is directive on joint operations by Resistance Forces and SAS troops. HQ Airborne Troops later came under First Allied Airborne Army.

at SFHQ, but EMFFI was not given operational control of SAS parties in the field until 5th August.[1]

These troubles are worth mentioning because they were easily avoidable: they do not much affect the main issue. The 'Jedburgh' scheme was conceived as a device of leverage; a small expenditure of Allied force might greatly increase the total force at our disposal. How much Resistance was mobilised by the 'Jedburghs' which would otherwise have remained ineffective? There is no means of measuring this: but practically every 'Jedburgh' which was in the field for any length of time found much to do on the lines intended for it – reconciling factions, suggesting targets, bringing supplies, instilling good guerilla doctrine. They were certainly a reinforcement to Resistance out of proportion to their numbers.[2]

The 'Jedburgh' problem, like that of SOE's long-term agents, was from the military aspect mainly one of liaison with the lowest formations in the scale of command: there was also a problem at the upper end of the scale. Relations between SOE, Home Forces, and 'Cossac' were always close and friendly, and when SHAEF appeared in January 1944 there was no serious trouble in securing integration with the Americans: SOE/SO, later SFHQ, soon became a sound working organisation.[3] We have already seen[4] that the question of liaison with the Chiefs of Staff had been scrutinised pretty carefully by the 'Hollis Committee' in August 1943;[5] this repulsed SOE's claim for parity with the other Services but its practical results were satisfactory. Liaison at the top was mainly the responsibility of Colonel R. H. Barry, OBE, a young professional soldier who had been CD's Chief Staff Officer since July 1943 and was in continuous and friendly contact with the Joint Planners. This arrangement was informal but efficient, and SOE had no further reason to complain that it was left in ignorance of plans in the formative stage.

Liaison with the French Command was for various reasons much more difficult. On security grounds the French were excluded from all knowledge of the 'Overlord' plan, and the action of the FFI could therefore not be related to it in advance except in very broad terms.

---

1   SHAEF/17240/25/Ops(C) of 5th August 1944.
2   There is a set of reports on most of the 'Jedburgh Missions' in SOE Archives.
3   The first draft of a Directive by Cossac (27th September 1943), and the first draft of the SHAEF Directive (10th January 1944) are on SOE Archives File (D/R) D.1(a). The final SHAEF Directive SHAEF/17240/Ops is dated 23rd March 1944 (amended 10th May 1944). Copy on War Office File 'France SOE-OSS', now with SOE Archives.
4   Above p. 415.
5   COS(43)505(0) of 4th September.

The French themselves were in some confusion. Their main channel of communication with France led from London; theoretically it was controlled by General Cochet, General D'Astier and General Koenig in succession, in fact it was disputed with them by their nominal subordinates of the BRAL. In addition there was much signals traffic to France from North Africa, and in North Africa were generally present the main political wirepullers – De Gaulle, Emmanuel D'Astier, André Philip, Soustelle, 'Passy', and the rest. The final conflation of the French Section of SFHQ with General Koenig's staff to form EMFFI did not come until 6th June:[1] it was logical and politically necessary, but it came so late and at such a vital stage in the operation that on the whole it probably reduced the efficiency of the support given to those in the field.

Finally, there was the question of liaison with the 'Political Warfare' organisations which had given so much trouble in the early history of SOE. The organ finally responsible on this side was the Anglo-American Psychological Warfare Division of SHAEF, under Brigadier General Robert McClure, reporting to the Supreme Commander through G6 of SHAEF. Goodwill now reigned between SOE and PWD, and SOE was consulted in Psychological Warfare plans in so far as they affected it.[2] But their lines of action led in different directions – PWD's towards the problems of 'presentation' of the offensive as a whole and of attack on German morale, SOE's towards the organisation of the whole technical and tactical maze of small-scale operations; the time was past for any renewal of the original 'grand design' of a unified weapon of subversive warfare.

The problem of liaison with Allied armies on a lower level of command had virtually been solved by the Mediterranean experiments from 'Brandon'[3] onwards. The lessons there learnt were that Commanders in the field must have at their immediate disposal advisers on the possibilities and organisation of Resistance: that these advisers must have adequate signals facilities and transport under their own control: and that they must be part of the organisation of the Command, and not 'foreign bodies' externally attached to it. The resulting picture was fairly simple:

HQ 21 Army Group: No. 3   Special Force Detachment
2nd British Army: No. 1   Special Force Detachment

---

[1] SHAEF/17245/6/5/Ops(A) of 6th June 1944; copy on SOE Archives Files (AD/E) 'Command and Control of French Resistance', 'French Integration' and 'Koenig Chain of Command' on which are the most important of the relevant papers.

[2] E.g. Annexe II of the Draft PWE/OWI Outline Plan of October 1943; copy on SOE Archives File (D/R) Command and Control of French Resistance.

[3] Above p. 534.

First Canadian Army:	No. 2	Special Force Detachment
First US Army Group:	No. 12	Special Force Detachment
First US Army:	No. 10	Special Force Detachment
Third US Army:	No. 11	Special Force Detachment

In addition to these No. 4 Special Force Detachment was formed and trained in Algiers, to operate with Forces taking part in the invasion of Southern France. The leading echelons of these Detachments went ashore on D plus 3 day, and they had their independent signals channel to SOE's main station through which they could pass messages fairly speedily to any of the stations behind the enemy lines, as well as to HQ EMFFI. In periods of rapid movement they were able to throw off Detachments down to Corps level. The picture was finally completed, when SHAEF moved forward into France on 1st September 1944 and EMFFI was dissolved, by the attachment of Colonel R. E. Brook to SHAEF as liaison officer on behalf of SOE and SIS.[1]

This part of the scheme worked perfectly, and a difficult problem was smoothly overcome. There is no record of trouble between subordinate Allied commanders and Resistance groups, and agents were recovered without difficulty as their areas were overrun.

(c) Planning

Within SOE itself there was no great emphasis on formal plans for the details of action in the field. At Headquarters the greatest problems were those of liaison, air supply, signals communications, security and effective 'cover', which could be and must be handled in England and North Africa on strict and efficient military lines. But in the field it was essential to have flexibility of operation within very broad outline plans. For security reasons it was quite impossible to give agents in the field an exact plan for action relevant to a landing in Normandy and nowhere else. The possible 'D-day targets' – in particular communications – were examined in great detail; each organiser had a list of possible objectives and he was so far as possible given the equipment with which to attack them. But beyond that SOE could not go: the direction of the Allied attack could not be revealed, and the circumstances of each organiser at a given date could not be foreseen. The best method was to call each organiser into action separately as the need for him arose: in fact to make SFHQ the battle HQ of the Resistance.

On the French side planning was much more grandiose and elegant. In most cases (though not in all) these plans were formulated in

---

[1] There had since March been a 'SF Detachment' at HQ SHAEF under Brigadier 'Eddie' Myers (of Greek fame), but it was not of much importance until this final stage.

consultation with SOE: but they were formulated without full knowledge of Allied intentions, and they were in any case too perfect for the real Resistance world. Their importance was therefore not so great as the labour expended on them deserved.

First there was the series of 'Colour' plans. These were produced in consultation between the French and R/F Section in the early summer of 1943. The theory was that comprehensive lists of 'D-day Targets' should be prepared under different categories: that stores for each category should be sent to the field in containers labelled with the colour of the plan: and that these stores should be put aside for 'the day'. Each plan would be put into effect by special BBC messages, in different forms for different regions. The complete set was:

Plan Vert:	attacks on railways.
Plan Tortue:	attacks on reinforcements moving by road.
Plan Violet:	dislocation of telecommunications.
Plan Jaune:	attacks on munition dumps.
Plan Rouge:	attacks on oil fuel.
Plan Noir:	attacks on enemy HQs.

In addition there was Plan Grenouille, for the sabotage of railway turn-tables, which was to be put into effect before D-day as part of the preparatory attack on communications. All these plans were set going; some of them unfortunately were sent to the field complete and may have fallen into enemy hands. But by January 1944 SOE was reporting that 'the only plan on which definite progress seems to have been made is Plan Vert for dealing with the railways. We have no progress reports for any of the other plans (Rouge, Noir, Jaune, etc.) and I feel that, in the time now available, it will probably not be possible completely to organise separate teams for each of these objectives.'[1] This was agreed with the French on 2nd February 1944, and those which survived were Plan Vert, Plan Tortue and Plan Grenouille.[2] All these were in the end put into action, raggedly but with good effect.[3]

There is more mystery about what sometimes appears as the 'Plan Vidal'. The French (or some of the French) held that certain areas of France could and should be liberated by the French themselves as soon as possible after D-day: that they could be held by the FFI against any counter-attacks which were probable; that they would serve as

---

[1]   Draft letter to General D'Astier dated 24th January 1944; copy on SOE Archives File (D/R) D.1(a).

[2]   Note by DR/P dated 3rd February 1944; copy on SOE Archives File (D/R) D.1(a)

[3]   There is a fine account in George Millar's 'Maquis' of an application of Plan Grenouille at Besançon.

'ports of entry' through which supplies (and possibly airborne troops) could be received in substantial quantities; and that from them raiding parties could dominate sections of the German lines of communication. This was damned firmly by SOE/SO in February 1944.[1] To their mind it was inspired partly by French political ambitions (not discreditable in themselves), partly by a false doctrine, accepted too readily by professional soldiers, that in prepared positions guerillas could hold a line against well-equipped regular troops; it was likely to lead to a demand for a diversion of Allied resources, hard to resist yet strategically useless. But it does not seem to have been killed. Major Thackthwaite found it in general circulation in Savoy when he arrived there on Mission 'Union' in February 1944;[2] and it reappears (excellently presented) in a paper on 'The Military Role of the French Resistance', prepared by the BRAL in March 1944.[3] In the end it was put into effect in the Vercors Plateau, and (with rather less rigidity) in the Massif Central: and the result justified SOE's caution.

Two other plans are interesting because they came from inside France. One of them was a railway plan prepared by someone in authority in the Société Nationale des Chemins de Fer, which reached London early in May 1944.[4] This contained an excellent and detailed allocation of targets between bombers, fighters, sabotage parties, and 'inside' work by the railway staffs, which was pretty close to SOE's own ideas. It is historically interesting that the SNCF believed strongly in the bombing of marshalling yards, the 'Tedder' or 'Zuckermann'* policy which cost many French lives and much searching of Allied consciences.[5] 'Les responsables estiment que les bombardements joueront un rôle décisif. Ils permettront à la SNCF de créer un embouteillage inextricable sur les tronçons intacts.' For this reason (among others) the SNCF were against a general strike: local strikes might be useful, but on the whole the railwaymen could do more harm by sticking to their jobs and tending the 'embouteillage inextricable'.

The PTT also contributed. There was said to be available an organised group of 'some 700 men working in connection with the long distance underground cable system', and the possibility of using them

---

1   See draft reply for General Eisenhower to a letter from General D'Astier dated 24th February 1944; copy on SOE Archives File (D/R) D.1(a).

2   SOE History of R/F Section, 1944, p. 8.

3   Dated 6th March 1944, filed separately with SOE Archives D/R files. An ambitious version of this plan was presented to General Wilson by General De Gaulle in the course of planning for 'Dragoon'. See General Wilson's Report, p. 26.

4   Text and summary dated 6th May 1944; copy on SOE Archives File (D/R) P.1(b).

5   See Eisenhower Report, p. 21, for a brief discussion.

*   [S. Zuckermann, born Cape Town 1904, anatomist, scientific adviser to COHQ and RAF 1939–46, to Defence Department 1960–66, OM 1968, baron 1971.]

was discussed pretty thoroughly in April 1944.[1] The conclusion was that attacks on the telephone system were best made by outside saboteurs secretly instructed by inside experts. The 700 experts themselves should at all costs keep out of German hands so that they would be on the spot to restore the system promptly for Allied use. The cables might be attacked, but the repeater stations and other irreplaceable equipment should be left alone,[2] and if possible safeguarded from German attacks.

'Plan Violet' in the end thus merges into the 'Counter-Scorch' plans.[3] In France these never assumed the same importance as they did in Norway in the winter of 1944–5. The enemy were too strong, and the needs of 'Overlord' were too great. But the question of saving the ports was considered in great detail: unfortunately without much success except in the south. This was of great importance strategically: the French laid great economic weight on saving the basis of the hydro-electric system, and General Koenig wrote personally about it to Lord Selborne on 25th April.[4] Fortunately, in the mountain areas where the dams are, the Germans collapsed quickly, and they had no time to make a serious attempt at wrecking.

(d) Air Supply

We have already seen[5] that the last three months of 1943 were a bad period in SOE's relations with the RAF. There was a bitter quarrel with Air Chief Marshal Harris, and in addition a period of bad weather cut down operations far below programme. Not unreasonably, Emmanuel D'Astier raised the question publicly at one of his press conferences, and in a broadcast delivered shortly after he took office as Commissaire de l'Intérieur (in November 1943); and he kept at it when he saw Lord Selborne in London on 13th December.[6] Meantime Mr Churchill was convalescing at Marrakesh, while SOE in London was embroiled in a wrangle with Bomber Command. On 12th January he saw General De Gaulle at Marrakesh, and it is a fair conjecture that one of the General's main themes was the need for more aircraft.[7] At least this was one of the first problems Mr Churchill tackled after

---

[1] See SOE Archives File (D/R) D.1(p) Plan Violet.
[2] On this point the FFI in the Paris Region was issuing precisely opposite orders! Dansette, 'Libération de Paris', p. 464.
[3] SOE Archives File (D/R) D.1(d) Counter-Scorch.
[4] Copy on SOE Archives File (D/R) D.1(d) Counter-Scorch.
[5] Above p. 416.
[6] Lord Selborne's memo. of interview; copy on SOE Archives File F.38/II.
[7] On 4th January M. D'Astier had staged another vigorous Press Conference on the subject. See Mr Rooker to Foreign Office No. 4 of 9th January 1944; copy on SOE Archives File 3/100/2(c).

his return to London on 18th January. On 27th January there was a meeting[1] under his chairmanship at which were present Sir Archibald Sinclair, Sir Charles Portal, Lord Selborne, General Ismay and M. D'Astier. These great men were hustled by the Prime Minister in his inimitable way: 'He wished and believed it possible to bring about a situation in the whole area between the Rhône and the Italian frontier comparable to the situation in Yugoslavia. Brave and desperate men could cause the most acute embarrassment to the enemy and it was right that we should do all in our power to foster and stimulate so valuable an aid to Allied strategy. He enquired what additional aircraft could be provided so as to arm and supply the Patriot forces in question.' This was perhaps a dangerous incitement to the 'Plan Vidal', but it was incomparably effective. The immediate consequence was a directive to Bomber Command that (subject to the needs of SIS) the order of priority after the air offensive against Germany should be:

(a) The Maquis
(b) Other SOE operations
(c) 'Crossbow' operations
(d) Sea-mining.

The second result was a really substantial acceleration of the aircraft programme.[2] The additional forces were, in detail:

1 USAAF squadron of 12 Liberators (long promised and delayed)
60 sorties by Transport Aircraft of No. 38 Group (RAF)
Two RAF squadrons, each of 16 Stirlings.
120 additional sorties from the Mediterranean.

This should mean 186 successful sorties to the Maquis during February, and enough arms for 16,000 men, in addition to SOE's normal programme.

This was vigorously followed up in all quarters during the spring. A special committee was formed in London, and Lord Selborne reported monthly to the Prime Minister, who appended cheering comments – 'Good. Press on' and such like. The French continued to grumble in Algiers, and to lobby the Americans and the CCS in Washington. March produced twelve more USAAF Liberators, thirty-three more Stirlings and thirty more sorties by No. 38 Group, and the score of successful sorties mounted steadily –

---

[1] Recorded in War Cabinet paper (unnumbered); copy on SOE Archives File F.38/III.

[2] Details in COS(44)125(0) of 3rd February.

	RAF	*USAAF*	*A/C Lost*	*Total*
1943 Oct.–Dec.	101	Nil	6	101
1944 Jan.–March	557	52	15	609
April–June	748	521	26	1,269
July–Sept.	1,644	1,336	28	2,980

In addition there are the figures for North Africa:

1943 Oct.–Dec.	4
1944 Jan.–March	91
April–June	396
July–Sept.	593[1]

This great effort was small in proportion to the need, but it came at the right time. Earlier, it might have inflated Resistance dangerously before the Allied armies were ready to assist it. Now there was a steady crescendo up to D-day and beyond, and the French met the invasion with strong faith in Allied support.

(e) Security and Deception

In the months before D-day all SOE's planning was dominated by the need to conceal the date and place of the main operation. This was an overriding principle: it could only be satisfied by sacrificing some of the possibilities of Resistance, but this sacrifice made security a relatively simple problem. The Fighting French knew nothing of the 'Overlord' plan, and there should therefore be no danger of leakage through the capture of their agents, unless they had knowledge from other means. Similarly F Section agents were told nothing which would be dangerous.

The time of the landing was further masked by giving Resistance a 'target date' well in advance of the true date of the operation – in the first instance 1st April 1944. A timed programme could never be exactly realised in the Resistance, and an effort directed to an early date did not involve much risk of a premature explosion: at the worst it meant a little more nervous strain for agents and friends. The place of the operation could only be concealed by ensuring that all plans known within France would cover a landing anywhere on the Channel coast. Plans for cutting railways and other communications must be designed to encircle not a particular beach-head but the whole northern area: and until 6th June agents (and the volume of signals traffic

---

[1] All these statistics are drawn from the Appendices to the Narrative of Special S/D Operations in Europe: there seem to be no detailed figures of air operations in the archives, but there is an excellent set of statistics of arms sent to France by F, R/F and Massingham from 1941 onwards. SOE Archives – with Appendices to F Section History.

to agents) must be distributed as evenly as possible over that area. This meant a considerable waste of effort; but the needs of security were adequately met.[1]

New problems were set by the Cabinet's decision early in April to suspend diplomatic privilege, to censor all messages out of the United Kingdom, and to exercise a strict control of travellers.[2] SOE's own men and messages presented no special problem, but there was a danger that if reprisals were taken by neutral countries SOE would be cut off from its representatives with diplomatic missions abroad. This eventuality (which did not arise) might have been met by providing clandestine wireless stations for them, and plans were laid with this in view. Agents, British and foreign, were still sent to the field, provided that the operational need for their Mission was established; but all documents to be carried by foreign agents were to be deposited three clear days in advance, and any cyphers in use were to be held by SOE. This ban could be enforced pretty effectively by a strict search at the airfield, but there was of course no effective check on verbal messages, and communications between exiled governments and their own countries were certainly not brought fully under British supervision. The Polish and Czech wireless stations presented an awkward special case; in the end (under the seal of absolute secrecy) Mr Churchill released the Poles (and the Poles only) from the obligation to deposit their cyphers with the British, subject to the submission of '*en clair*' versions of all messages, verified by the Polish word of honour.[3] In France this affected the important Polish organisation in the Lille area;[4] but there is no reason to believe that the Poles cheated or that any other Ally came to hear of their special privilege.

Deception posed awkward problems of its own. SOE possessed

---

1 One of the main 'panics' before D-day arose from the shooting down in Northern France of Air Commodore Ivelaw Chapman, who had been Director of Policy at the Air Ministry up to January 1944 and knew the plans as they stood at that date. He and a sergeant from his crew came into French hands, and SOE established contact through 'Galilée' (Clouet des Perruches), the chief of the Bureau d'Opérations Aériennes (BOA) in Northern France. Unfortunately Chapman was captured with a number of BOA agents before a Lysander operation could be arranged. While in hiding he heard a Lysander from some other organisation land within a few miles – a comment on the advantages and disadvantages of the isolation of 'réseaux' from one another. (Card from SOE Archives on Air Commodore Chapman and interrogation of 'Galilée' – file 3/370/97(c): personal information.) [(Sir) R. Ivelaw-Chapman, 1899–1978, knight 1951; see Foot and Langley, *MI9*, p. 211, for details of this incident.]

2 The papers are on SOE Archives File 'Overlord Security Measures' – with 'COS/PLANS'.

3 Annex D to JIC(44)169(0) Final of 1st May.

4 Above p. 579.

unique facilities for deception: it could use its own men and through them the civil population as unconscious and convincing agents, and it could produce convincing evidence for the Germans by changes in the volume and direction of its activities, in particular of its signals traffic. In some cases it could even gain direct access to German minds through the wireless sets of agents whom it knew to be in enemy hands. But these opportunities were impaired by the danger of deceiving the Resistance as well as the Germans. This risk attached to all deception plans, and it was the duty of SOE and PWE to explain the limitations which it imposed: it attached particularly to deception by SOE, because such trickery might lead to an irreparable loss of confidence in the good faith of the British and their agents.

SOE therefore took no more than a subsidiary part. For Operation 'Starkey', the 'fake invasion' of September 1943, the plan was that up to D minus 9 SOE should somewhat increase its encouragement to Resistance and should put on the air a considerable volume of bogus traffic in code: on D minus 9 both SOE and PWE should issue a formal announcement that the forthcoming operation was a rehearsal and not the real thing. This seems to have avoided any deception of the Resistance: but apparently the Germans were not deceived either.[1]

For 'Fortitude', the 'Overlord' deception plan, SOE's overriding rules were:[2]

(a) Resistance Groups should not be called upon to take positive action exclusively for the purpose of implementing the deception plan. This is likely to lead to unnecessary reprisals and to have a doubtful effect.

(b) Action in support of the deception plan should not be at the expense of the effort which is directed towards supporting the main 'Overlord' plan.

(c) Action to support the deception plan should not be taken before D-day, as this might have the effect of prejudicing the security of the Resistance Groups concerned.[3]

This meant that until D-day SOE's action was primarily negative: it must avoid prejudicing the deceptive plan, but it could contribute nothing except a very slight bias towards the Pas de Calais area. After D-day the Resistance was largely in the open and the position was easier. The maintenance of the threat was still of enormous importance: SOE

---

1 For SOE plan see SOE Archives File (D/R) 'Fortitude'. [R. F. Hesketh, *Fortitude*, though not published till 1999 was written in 1945, and is decisive.]

2 Papers on SOE Archives File (D/R) 'Fortitude'.

3 Directive for North-West European Region, issued 1st April 1944; copy on SOE Archives File (D/R) 'Fortitude'.

could contribute the use of some enemy-controlled sets;[1] some 'dummy drops' in the areas affected; and a flood of dummy BBC 'déclenchement' messages. These messages were intended in the first instance to go out on 15/16th June: this was cancelled by SHAEF on 13th June, and they were finally dispatched on 1st and 2nd July.[2] It was not until 25th July that the first units of the German 15th Army left the Pas de Calais for Normandy.[3]

There are here negative lessons of some importance. In theory Resistance can be exploited very effectively for deception, in practice it will seldom be possible to accept the political risks involved. The problem posed in practice is that the enemy may draw deductions adverse to the deception plan from the distribution of Resistance activity in particular areas: somehow or other an even flow, or an even crescendo of activity, must be simulated. Deception is thus mainly negative, and merges into Security.

(f) 'Déclenchement'

The final problem was[4] that of an effective starting signal which would neither weaken the French effort by delay nor prejudice the security of the operation. By this time SOE had standardised the method of warning messages on the BBC, followed by action messages, both sets couched in agreed phrases in plain language.* The practice was that Resistance groups should listen for the 'warning' on the 1st and 2nd, 15th and 16th of each month, using either an ordinary civilian set or the special Midget Communications Receiver (MCR) which began to reach the field in large numbers early in 1944. If they then received their 'warning' it meant that they should listen every night until further notice for an 'action' message.

SOE had already had trouble with Mr Bracken and the BBC about the allocation of the extra time required in February and March for the increased traffic involved by increased air operations. Early in April this was resolved by a compromise[5] which gave SOE four minutes each in the 13.30 and 14.30 programmes, six minutes each on the 19.30 and 21.15 programmes – twenty minutes a day. Naturally if this time was not fully required (as rarely happened) it was filled

---

1　There is a nice case on SOE Archives (D/R) 'Fortitude' file of a 'fishing enquiry' from the enemy over such a set.
2　SHAEF order to SFHQ – SHAEF/18202/6/Ops(B) of 22nd June.
3　Eisenhower Report, p. 49.
4　This is very clearly explained in a paper submitted to the BGS Plans 21 Army Group on 11th March 1944: SOE Archives File (D/R) 'BBC Messages'.
5　Copy of letter dated 8th April 1944 from Mr Sporborg, on SOE Archives File (AD/S.1) F.38/III.
*　[Splendid though fictional example in opening minutes of Cocteau's film *Orphée*.]

in with 'dummy' messages to conceal variations in the flow of traffic. The D-day traffic meant a large further increase. At least 315 messages were involved, and the final allocation of time (including ordinary traffic) was forty-seven minutes on each of two days for warning messages, thirty-eight minutes on D minus 1, twenty-two minutes on D-day, followed by a return to normal. There was at this stage no difficulty with the BBC; the problem was that of security. If no warning messages were issued, the Resistance would miss many of the action messages: if there was a great increase in warnings the enemy could deduce the imminence (though not the exact date) of D-day. Some of the conventional messages were probably in enemy hands, but this was not of much importance in itself, as they meant only 'listen to the BBC till further notice'.*

It was decided in the end to accept the risk: warning messages could be broadcast on Y and Y plus 1 days (1st and 2nd June), action messages at H-hour minus $7^1/_2$.[1] This programme was followed, apparently without ill effects. The stream of warnings went out on 1st and 2nd June; the Resistance stood by: the first calls to attack came at 2113 hours on 5th June 1944, and they continued during the 6th. France burst into rebellion: a spontaneous and incoherent rebellion, yet not without leadership and a plan.

6. The Contribution of the Resistance[2]

SOE's role had been to supply this direction from above, but the true impetus came from below, from the hatred and pride of millions of Frenchmen, and its story cannot be told as if it were a military operation. The atmosphere could only be truly built up out of individual narratives. In each group the story is different and in each it is complex: the direction of movement is set by the initiative of individuals and (to a smaller extent) of political groupings. Frustration was always

---

[1] SHAEF order SHAEF/17240/17/Ops of 8th May, on SOE Archives File (D/R) BBC Messages.

[2] Many official attempts have been made to summarise this. The most important are:

SFHQ Report on period 6 June–31 July (7 September 1944).

'SOE Contribution to Overlord': a print circulated to Ministers in App. C to the SOE History of R/F Section: ('Railway Sabotage') (December 1944).

'A Short History of EMFFI': issued by General Koenig in March 1945.

Appreciation by SHAEF: COS(45)146 of 18th July.

Appreciation by SACMED: COS(45)665(0) of 18th November.

* [Jozef Goetz, head of SS wireless counter-measures in Paris 1943–4, claimed privately in 1978 (by which time he was director of education for Westphalia) that by 1 June 1944 he knew of fifteen 'action' messages for Operation 'Neptune', the assault phase of 'Overlord'.]

possible, but in most cases the pent-up national spirit found itself leaders and objectives; the most that SOE could do was to see that there were in France enough arms and enough men trained to preach the right time and the right methods and the right objectives, as they were understood in London. The influence of these men depended on themselves; and those who succeeded had no qualities in common except the quality of leadership. They might be French aristocrats like de Baissac and de Vomecourt and Mazé-Sencier de Brouville: British like Lieutenant Colonel Starr and Captain George Millar: antique colonels of the Armée de l'Armistice or young officers suddenly erected into Délégués Militaires Régionaux; Communist leaders of the FTP; women like Virginia Hall and Pearl Witherington; plain working men like 'Marie' and 'Goujon' and a host of nameless 'cheminots'. All that was best in France was in action and was looking to the future: nothing could have been less like the decadent nation of Nazi myth.

All that can be done here is to summarise somewhat mechanically; first, the temporal sequence of events: second, the various heads of activity.

The course of events can be broken up (not very sharply) into six phases:

(a)   First, the immediate reaction to the action messages on 5th and 6th June. The plan for this phase was that Resistance should concentrate on delaying the German build-up by attacks on communications of all kinds, and it did its part excellently. In the period immediately after D-day there are said to have been 486 rail cuts and 180 derailments, and there were considerable stretches of line in the east and south-east where the cuts were maintained and the Germans had to by-pass the broken line. This pressure was kept up as a supplement to the intensive air attack in the north, and their combined effect was that the Germans were virtually forced to abandon movement by rail except as a specially-planned operation. This drove them on to the roads, and here too the FFI imposed great delay. They could not hold any road against a planned attack, but they laid ceaseless ambushes which forced the Germans to deploy and fight, and they had ample scope for nuisance tactics – puncturing of tyres by spikes and tyre-bursters, concealment of horses and horse-drawn vehicles, falsification of sign-posts. The Germans were moving through an enemy country openly at war.

To this phase belong many of the German atrocities, such as the sacking of Oradour-sur-Glâne:* blind attempts to terrorise an invisible enemy. In this phase also Resistance openly took

---

* [See J. Kruuse, *Madness at Oradour* (1969).]

possession of a number of areas in which for the time being the German writ did not run: notably in the Jura, in Savoy, and in some areas of the Massif Central. This was in the main an outburst of ill-directed local enthusiasm; the French Command doubtless longed to see the tricolore flying over liberated areas of France, but it could not have restrained these outbursts even if it had tried. To the Allies they were unwelcome, and it was not until 4th July that SHAEF issued a directive authorising the development of these areas of overt resistance.[1] Meantime there had in some areas (round the Lake of Geneva for instance) been immediate savage reprisals: others were able to receive fairly large supplies of arms by daylight operations conducted by Fortresses flying in formation.[2] The Resistance in Cantal attracted substantial counter-attacks, without being destroyed: the destruction of the Vercors required a regularly mounted operation by elements of an Armoured Division and an Infantry Division (some 11,000 men) assisted by Stukas and airborne troops. The FFI had only some 3,000 armed men, and the defences broke on 25th July: German losses must have been substantial, but the FFI lost heavily in men and material and there were horrible reprisals in the mountain villages. There was undoubtedly some diversion and dispersal of German forces, but it is doubtful if it was of much strategic importance: the really important loss to the Germans was the loss of time imposed on them by the guerilla war.

(b) The second phase is that of concentration on Brittany; the Allies had not been strongly represented here before D-day, and they were somewhat surprised by the vigour with which Resistance broke out. Two Jedburghs and three SAS teams went in on D-day or soon after, and the SAS organised 'bases' for the reception of further arms: unfortunately the Germans counter-attacked in force in Morbihan on 18th June and over-ran one base with arms for 5,000 men. The SHAEF directive of 4th July envisaged a concentration of effort in Brittany to assist during the 'break-out' phase; we have seen that eight more Jedburghs went in at once, and there was also a substantial reinforcement by French parachute troops. Unfortunately it was held that security precluded a corresponding intensification of air supply operations. Nevertheless, when the Americans swept through on 4th August, they found that their

---

[1] SHAEF/17240/3/Ops(C) of 4th July (EMFFI narrative, p. 12).

[2] 25th June, 14th July and 10th September. Reports of these operations on SOE Archives File (AD/S.1) F.38/III.

way had been made smooth for them:[1] the only disappointment was that Brest was strongly held by the Germans and
nothing could be done to prevent its destruction.

(c) A similar phase followed across the whole of Northern France
when the Falaise gap was closed on 21st August and General
Patton reached the Seine. This time it was a question of harassing an enemy in retreat; destroying his land-lines, sniping his
columns, hindering his demolitions and passing information
of his movements to the Allies. As the Allied spearheads passed
the FFI came into the open: SHAEF rescinded the old order
that they should be disarmed pending reorganisation as regular troops, and they became in effect the civil administration
and the occupying force. The Allies were moving into an organised and friendly country, and the FFI could be depended on
to observe and mop up any pockets of Germans which might
in theory threaten the flanks of the advance.

The greatest single event in this phase was the liberation
of Paris.[2] This was in the military sense a nuisance to the
Allies, as it involved the diversion from the main battle of the
Leclerc Armoured Division and some other troops; but it was
essentially a French operation, well conceived in the interests
of France. SHAEF and EMFFI alike counselled caution, but
the revolutionary spirit of Paris was too strong: the slogan
'Paris will liberate herself' appealed to proud Parisians of all
parties, though the Communists attempted to appropriate it to
themselves. There was a crescendo through a railway strike
on 10th August, police strike on 15th August, seizure of the
Prefecture of Police by the police strikers on 19th August,
general call to insurrection by the CNR and the Liberation
Committee of Paris. On 20th August De Gaulle was in France;
on the 21st General Koenig was appointed Military Governor
of Paris, General Patton reached the Seine above and below
the city, Paris was in open revolt and there followed five days
of confused fighting. Late on the 24th a few of Leclerc's tanks
reached the Hôtel de Ville,* on the 25th the main body of the
division cleared the centre of the city, and early in the afternoon General Von Choltitz surrendered. General De Gaulle
was in Paris within an hour.

---

1 See Eisenhower Report, p. 52.
2 There is an excellent special study of this: Adrien Dansette, 'Histoire de la
Libération de Paris', published by Fayard. [See also H. Michel, *Paris Résistant*
(1982).]
* [J. P. Leclerc de Hautecloque, 1902–47, fought his way from Lake Chad to Paris
1940–44, and then liberated Strasbourg.]

(d) Meantime, the 'Dragoon' landings had taken place on 15th August. Here the Resistance could play a relatively greater part than in the north: the Germans were thin on the ground, the country was more favourable, and the fighting never became stabilised.* In the first stages the FFI cut the Rhône Valley railways and harassed the roads, they destroyed an important RDF station in the Alpes Maritimes, and they sabotaged communications immediately behind the lines. Port de Bouc was seized intact: in Marseille and Sète the 'counter-scorch' plans were largely successful, in Toulon they achieved a little.[1] Strategically it was important that the FFI held the Germans back from escape through the Alpine passes into Italy, and made smooth the way for the small regular force which went straight up the Route Napoléon to Grenoble, which it entered on 23rd August.[2]

(e) As soon as it was clear that there would be no German stand this phase passed into another, that of cutting off the enemy forces fleeing from the south and south-east. This was the time of gallant and crazy incidents – the liberation by the French of Lyon, of Toulouse, of Bordeaux, of countless towns and villages: it was also to the best of French ability the 'killing time'. Of course the FFI could not hold regular troops for long, and such German formations as kept their nerve got back, sadly diminished and stripped of their heavy equipment. The toll of arms and stores was enormous, and the losses in men were heavy, though they cannot be reckoned up. In the south the FFI claimed 42,000 prisoners: on the Loire they certainly delivered into Allied hands an organised body of some 20,000 Germans. Many more surrendered in small packets or were killed in ambush.

(f) The last phase was in part anti-climax. In the east the Allied and French sweep was halted at the 'blue line of the Vosges', and it was necessary to improvise a subversive organisation behind the enemy front in an area technically difficult for such operations. When the French finally broke through to the Rhine in November, the Resistance in Alsace was useful as a source of tactical intelligence, but it could do little more. In the west there followed the long hard winter in which the FFI, ill-fed, ill-trained, and ill-equipped, were virtually the only Allied

---

[1] For the importance of these gains see General Wilson's Report, p. 40. In his narrative 'Dragoon' is shown to have been *primarily* a battle for ports of entry into France.

[2] General Wilson's Report, pp. 34 and 38.

* [Arthur L. Funk, *Hidden Ally* (NY, 1992), an essential text.]

force available to contain the stray German garrisons in Pointe de Grave, Royan, la Rochelle, the islands of Ré and Oléron, and the St Nazaire area. At Lorient and Brest they had some American support, elsewhere there were only a few Jedburghs and other liaison Missions, which did their best to give training and to secure some supplies of arms. For the most part the sieges had to be maintained, as best might be, through the immemorial 'Système D'.

On 23rd September the decision was taken to end the short life of EMFFI and to transfer to the French War Ministry sole responsibility for the reconstruction of the French Army. A 'liquidation section' remained in existence in London until 1st December 1944: but henceforth it was for the French alone to make out of Resistance the framework of a new France.

The most authoritative appreciation of the military value of these operations is that given by SHAEF in a document prepared for the Chiefs of Staff in July 1945: this is supported by a similar report from SACMED in October 1945.[1] The evidence on which these reports are based is a mass of detail, and it will be more instructive to give their conclusions than to reproduce uncertain statistics of railways and landlines cut, and Germans 'contained' or killed. In the view of SHAEF:

Militarily, organised resistance helped the main operations of the Allied Expeditionary Force as follows:

(a) By sapping the enemy's confidence in his own security and flexibility of internal movement.

(b) By diverting enemy troops to internal security duties and keeping troops thus employed dispersed.

(c) By causing delay to the movement of enemy troops:
     1. concentrating against the NORMANDY beachhead:
     2. regrouping after the Allied break-out from the beachhead.

(d) By disrupting enemy telecommunications in FRANCE and BELGIUM.

(e) By enabling allied formations to advance with greater speed through being able to dispense with many normal military precautions, e.g. flank protection and mopping up.

(f) By furnishing military intelligence.

Of these points (a) and (b) need little comment. There is no calculus which will indicate exactly what proportion of German effort was diverted to controlling Resistance in Western Europe: undoubtedly the direct diversion was substantial, the psychological diversion still greater and not less important. The British have been beaten too often by underground warfare – notably in Ireland and in Palestine – to be inclined to minimise its moral effects.

---

1   COS(45)146 of 18th July and COS(45)665(0) of 18th November.

The delay in enemy movement can be documented by the details of some 3,000 rail cuts of varying importance made between 6th and 27th June: by the story of individual attacks on targets which had eluded the attention of aircraft:[1] and by the history of several German divisions.[2] All German reactions to 'Overlord' were clogged and slow, as those of a man in a dream. Near the bridgehead most of the credit goes to the air offensive, but even German divisions moving within the inner circle had much experience of Resistance activity.[3] Further afield the FFI were largely responsible for the delays. Their set piece was a series of actions against the 2 SS Panzer Division which began to move from the Toulouse area on D-day, and was not re-assembled near St Lô until D plus 17: it had to fight most of the way, even before entering the zone of concentrated air attack, and the move probably took between twice and three times as long as would normally be required. 271 Infantry Division from Sète took some seventeen days over a three days' journey: 277 Division from Perpignan and Narbonne was even slower.

The importance of the attack on telecommunications was also illustrated by later interrogation of German commanders: the delays imposed were such that the Germans were driven to increased use of radio, which laid all their traffic open to inspection by Allied intelligence. Tactical intelligence was another valuable by-product. There had originally been a rigid line between the activities of SOE and those of SIS: there was a flavour of conservatism about this, but nevertheless it made sense during the clandestine phase: specialisation is the best self-defence in underground work, and SOE's activities were in their nature 'noisy' and more exposed to continuous enemy intervention than those of SIS. But in June 1944 the Americans found that the existing intelligence system was ineffective in the vital tactical area less than fifty miles behind the enemy lines. A local arrangement was made to send in an SOE officer, and Captain J. B. Hayes ('Helmsman') dropped close to the bridgehead on 10th July, to a reception organised by Major de Baissac.[4] His main task was to recruit local agents who could either find their way through the front lines with tactical intelligence or remain in position until overrun. In all he dispatched thirty-one agents and organised sixteen static observers, and their value was so great that the model was generally adopted: a number of other 'Helmsman' Missions were sent in, and many

---

[1] In particular the crossing of the Eure at Chérisy near Dreux, and various Loire bridges.

[2] See SFHQ narrative of 7th September 1944.

[3] E.g. The Panzer Lehr division from the Le Mans-Chartres area, and 77, 265, 275 Infantry Divisions from Brittany.

[4] Bourne-Paterson's History of the British Circuits in France, p. 12.

organisers were given a 'Helmsman' role in addition to their main tasks.

This was one way in which the organised friendliness of the country could be utilised. It was still more important that French assistance enabled the Allied in their breakthrough to push straight ahead at top speed, brushing the enemy off the roads and discarding all ordinary military precautions. The time subtracted from the speed of German movement was added to that of General Montgomery and General Patton in their thrusts to Antwerp and to Lorraine, and the gross gain was strategically enormous. There was too the additional advantage that the commitment for internal order and security was reduced almost to nothing: a confused but enthusiastic native organisation was standing ready to take over, and all the apparatus of Military Government could be discarded, with the waste of time, temper and manpower which it entails.

Here perhaps comes the line of demarcation between military and political advantages. SOE's enterprise had cost the Allies over the last year of the Occupation the continuous activity of five or six squadrons of aircraft, not all of them modern heavy bombers, and the loss of perhaps 100 aircraft with their crews: they had delivered light arms, explosives and a scanty supply of ammunition for at least 50,000 men: they had sent in something like 500 highly trained men of first-rate fighting quality: and they had spent a very large sum in paper francs. Behind this stood the general organisation of SOE: its signals stations, its training schools, its supply and research services, which were not cheap. All this was a substantial outlay, though it was not large by the standards of the older services. For this investment the Allies had at their disposal the whole diverse and organised effort of the French Resistance. General Eisenhower's comment in his official report[1] is this: 'Our HQ estimated that, at times, the value of the FFI to the campaign amounted in manpower to the equivalent of 15 divisions, and their great assistance in facilitating the rapidity of our advance across France bore this out.' This is phrased with proper caution and indeed it makes little sense to translate the Resistance into an equivalent value of divisions and squadrons, because it did things which no divisions or squadrons could have done: on the other hand it was in some circumstances impotent to perform the work of even a single regular brigade. On any assessment the net military gain to the Allies was very large: by no other means could they have harnessed and directed the great reserves of manpower and human energy which were at their disposal in France.

The military passes imperceptibly into the political: and the resur-

---

[1] Eisenhower Report, p. 11: it is said General Devers verbally rated the contribution of Resistance in the south as the equivalent of four or five divisions.

rection of the French Republic was in itself a political victory of the first order. For this the Western Allies should claim no credit. The whole initiative was French: in part from below, from the impulse of millions of French men and women, whose personal pride required that they should spare no sacrifices called for in the name of France: in part from above, from the political acumen, the energy, the admirable oratory of General de Gaulle. The final political solution was achieved in the teeth of American resistance and with no more than passive sympathy from Great Britain: perhaps otherwise it would have lost some of its finest flavour, as a resolution by Frenchmen, in the face of the whole world, of the psychological problem of France.

It would be a mistake therefore to congratulate SOE upon the miracle of French recovery – for it was a miracle in spite of the anticlimax of the Fourth Republic. SOE in its collective mind was no clearer than any other body of foreigners about what was best for France: F Section warred quietly with R/F Section about policy, and the small weight of SOE in the scales of high politics was never thrown decisively either for De Gaulle or against him. Nevertheless it was SOE alone which made his victory possible. The BBC and PWE had made him a symbol and a name: it was the technical resources and the organisation of SOE which enabled him to link that name concretely with the Resistance within France. Without SOE's training, organisation and technical skill it would hardly have been possible for him even to complete the first stage, which linked De Gaulle in the summer and autumn of 1942 with the Resistance movements of the Vichy Zone. It would certainly have been impossible otherwise to achieve the sustained effort of 1943 and the first months of 1944, which set him at the head of an organisation which (for all its weakness) was still a worthy claimant to the inheritance of the French state. The British can assert only that they held the ring fairly and that they were true to their own doctrine, that French politics must be settled by the French: for that they will deserve French gratitude for ever, provided they do not claim it.

CHAPTER XXV

The Low Countries

1. Belgium

SOE's Belgium affairs never again sank so low as in the autumn of 1942. In England the department was then still at loggerheads with the Belgian Government, in spite of endless effort: in Belgium its organisation had been almost wiped out, and it was known or suspected that all the radio sets 'on the air' were controlled and operated by the Germans.

(a) Reorganisation in London

The improvement in London was first visible in a change of personalities on the lower levels of the Belgian organisation, which doubtless reflected a change of attitude at the top, stimulated by developments in the military situation. Late in 1942 it was agreed that M. Floor, a Belgian industrialist long resident in England and a personal friend of Brigadier Gubbins, should be appointed to act as Liaison Officer between SOE and the Belgian Sûreté, and early in 1943 he was absorbed more fully into that organisation. The plan of the Sûreté, as it affected SOE was now as follows:

M. Delfosse: Minister of Justice
M. Lepage: Head of Sûreté
    1. *'Action' Section*: responsible for liaison with SOE and with all communication to Belgium on SOE business, whether for the Sûreté or the military organisation.
       Lieutenant Floor.
    2. *Industrial Sabotage Section*: (military sabotage was a matter for the Deuxième Direction).
       Captain Guillery.
    3. *Political Warfare Section* (work with PWE)
       Captain Aronstein
       Lieutenant de Liedekerke (an old SOE agent).
    4. *SIS Section*
       Captain Nicodème.

The fourth of these Sections still kept itself strictly to itself, and was undoubtedly influential both with M. Lepage and his superiors and with the British SIS; but in all the other three SOE could count on some understanding and support.

The position in the Deuxième Direction of the Belgian General Staff was also substantially improved. In November 1942 an old regular officer, Colonel Jean Marissal, was appointed to direct it over the heads of those rather irresponsible fanatics, Commandant Bernard and Commandant Grisars, and in March 1943 they were removed altogether. Marissal was something of a military pedant, and he did not move very fast; but he was seriously intent on action, and at the same time made it his first principle to obtain adequate backing from his superiors for each forward step. SOE, one may conjecture, found him at times exasperating, but in the end he did a good job both for the Allies and for his own government. His 2ème Direction was now formally responsible for organising a Secret Army and for sabotage in support of military operations: but its communications with the field had to pass through Lieutenant Floor's Section of the Sûreté. Liaison officers were exchanged between the 2ème Direction and the Sûreté, and their relations grew a little better than they had been in the time of Bernard and Grisars.

In August 1943 there escaped from Belgium a certain M. Ganshof van der Meersch,* who stood very high in the judicial hierarchy[1] and had an excellent Resistance record. He thus already possessed great authority in the world of M. Lepage, and in October 1943 he was given the additional rank of Lieutenant General and was charged with the co-ordination of all clandestine activities in Belgium. This appointment achieved something, but not so much as SOE had hoped: Colonel Jean Marissal stonewalled effectively and was not repressed by his superiors, who were doubtless not anxious to increase M. Ganshof's power without limit. In addition the split in London was now emphasised by a split in Belgium, where the Sûreté sponsored the civilian Front d'Indépendance et Libération as a counter-weight to the Deuxième Direction's Secret Army. There did not ensue any of the disasters which might have been anticipated: nevertheless, the atmosphere remained uneasy.

(b) Organisation in the Field

In describing what took place in Belgium we should have to consider mainly these two broad organisations, FIL and the Secret Army, but

---

[1] He was later appointed to the Presidency of the Cour de Cassation, the highest judicial post in Belgium.

* [General Ganshof van der Meersch, brought out of Belgium down an escape line, reorganised Belgian external resistance.]

much effective work was done outside them, both by agents from London and by 'private enterprise'.

In the summer of 1942 SOE had depended greatly on PWE, and it continued to send out Political Warfare teams to the end; their work naturally inclined more towards direct action and less towards propaganda as liberation approached. In addition, there were one or two successful teams of professional saboteurs, of whom the most famous were Frenay and Woluwe, sponsored by the Sabotage Section of the Sûreté. On their first Mission, which was sent in the spring of 1943, they were 'Mouflon' and 'Jerboa', later (when the Belgian Section of SOE had taken to Shakespeare for its code-names) 'Balthasar' and 'Lavinia'. Their special trade was the demolition of lock-gates: they blocked seven locks between June 1943 and February 1944, imposing long delays on canal traffic, and they also caused a good deal of trouble by sinking barges. But they did not exclude railway and industrial sabotage if the chance came, and SOE records twelve more attacks which they carried out successfully. They came out to England in February 1944, and returned almost at once to resume the canal war in preparation for D-day. In the end they were surprised on 28th April 1944 in an attack on a lock at Menin: Frenay was shot and died later, Woluwe was sent to a civilian concentration camp, and was shot at Sandborstel in April 1945. These two were certainly the greatest Belgian masters of their trade. Another pair who had a long career were Durieux* and Heffinck ('Caracal' and 'Shrew') who went out as PWE agents in the bad days towards the end of 1942, with instructions to impede German conscription of labour by attacking records:[1] they did some good work and in the end got back to England in March 1944.

These isolated exploits were not as isolated as they might seem. They were planned in solitude but their results were public, and they were advertised still more widely by the violent German attempts to repress them by executing innocent hostages. The effect of this was in the main to drive more Belgians into underground opposition, either as members of some organised movement, or as quiet individual saboteurs. The work of these latter can never be recorded, but it was undoubtedly of particular value in Belgium, where the organised groups were poorly supplied from England and were always in danger of being broken up by German penetration. The number of Belgian traitors was not large in proportion to the population, but the Germans spent a great deal of trouble on them, and they were extremely dangerous.

---

[1]   There was a similar campaign in Norway about this time, below p. 666.

*   [See G. Weber, *Capitaine Caracal SSA 2690* (Dinant, 1989), a life of Durieux.]

We have already seen[1] the disturbance which broke out in the summer of 1942 as a result of the appearance in London of Commandant Glazer, whom SOE's agent De Liedekerke brought back to speak for the Secret Army. There was then first elaborated a formal plan for a Secret Army organisation in five zones, with a central HQ. All this collapsed for the moment, but a new start was made on the same basis at the end of 1942. First, there was the Mission of L. A. Livio (a British officer) and J. M. Pans, who went out on behalf of the 2ème Direction, not to contact the Secret Army, but to establish arms dumps to which the Army could later be given access; this they achieved successfully, though on a small scale. Colonel Jean Marissal was now at work on elaborate paper plans for the Secret Army, which were ready in April 1943 and were then endorsed by M. Pierlot and Brigadier Gubbins.[2] It was already intended that the Colonel's younger brother, A. R. E. M. Marissal, should go out to establish formal liaison, but he was too old for a parachute drop and it took some time to make the necessary arrangements for a landing in France. Meantime, several other Missions were sent to open contact and (like 'Livio' and 'Pans') to receive supplies of arms for later use. The younger Marissal did not go until July, and by this time the situation was clearer. Glazer had been arrested, and the Belgians had no longer any cause to fear that his dissident faction was being backed by SOE. Further, on 21st May, SOE was informed that M. Pierlot had appointed Colonel Bastin to command the Secret Army in Belgium: Colonel Gérard was to succeed him in the event of his arrest. These arrangements appear to have been the result of earlier communications of which SOE knew nothing.

Marissal the younger took with him three Special Orders[3] for the Secret Army, which had been worked out with the SOE planners in consultation with Cossac. These covered sabotage of communications on D-day, action in the event of enemy withdrawal, action against enemy armoured reinforcements moving by road. The first and third of these were closely parallel to the French Plan Violet and Plan Tortue. Marissal was back in London in October 1943, with a favourable report. SOE were a little alarmed by the rigidity of the organisation and by the danger that the reserve officers at the head of it would be known to the Germans and would be easily eliminated. But the organisation handled its signals traffic very efficiently, and provided safe and good reception for RAF operations: what is more,

---

[1] Above p. 301.

[2] Belgian History, p. 32; copy on SOE Archives File (Belgian Section) No. 32 'Secret Armies'.

[3] Belgian History, p. 43, SOE Archives Files (Belgian Section) Secret Armies No. 32, and Mission File 'Civet'.

it gave no hint of any political leanings. It thus grew popular in London, and it was relatively well served with agents, wireless sets and supplies during the winter and spring of 1943–4. The first commanding officer, Bastin, had been removed by arrest in December 1943: his successor, Gérard, came out to London (where he made a good impression) in March 1944, and was replaced in Belgium by General Pire.

The Secret Army now claimed to have some 45,000 effectives, of whom perhaps 6,000 had received arms of some sort from SOE and others might have hidden arms in 1940 or stolen them from the Germans. It was organised in five zones, each of which was in wireless touch with London and had with it a London agent. Since the original orders transmitted by Marissal in July 1943, it had received about a dozen others in a form agreed by SOE and based on the Cossac Directive for Belgium issued in November 1943. The detailed plans made in Belgium for the execution of these orders were captured in May 1944, when an agent was caught on his way back across the Pyrenees: fortunately this was too late to affect operations, but it was then known in London only that a detailed scheme of military sabotage existed, and that in addition the Secret Army had organised some seventy 'Refuges' or Bases covering most of Belgium, which could be used as 'points d'appui' for guerilla warfare if the tactical situation made it possible. But the Belgians insisted that there should be no general rising until the Allies were at hand: this was a point on which SOE were extremely ready to give assurances[1] – it was a great relief to find a Secret Army which was *not* over-anxious for regular field warfare.

On the political side, SOE's first contacts (which were doubtless *not* the first contacts made by the Belgian Government) appear to have been made by A. J. Wendelen ('Mandamus'), who went out with a wireless operator in the second quarter of 1942. Unluckily the wireless operator was one of those rounded up by the Germans that summer; but Wendelen escaped and continued to organise sabotage successfully in the Liège area. In addition he was in contact with the Communist Party, which claimed to have carried out industrial sabotage with equipment supplied by him; he was also responsible for initiating an organisation among his friends at Brussels University, which was later famous as 'Groupe G'. Wendelen left Belgium for England in August 1942, but he had difficulties en route which will serve to illustrate one aspect of the Belgian problem: he escaped first to Switzerland and was imprisoned there; was released and escaped to Spain across Occupied France; was imprisoned in Spain also, and did not reach England at last until 28th May 1943.

---

[1]   Copies in SOE Archives File (CD) Belgium General.

Meantime, in February 1943, there had arrived in England a Communist Deputy, Dr Marteaux,[1] whose mission was to advertise the existence of the 'Front de l'Indépendance et Libération' (FIL). This was a 'National Front' typical of Communist tactics at the time. It included genuine patriotic representatives of all the old political parties, except of course those such as the Rexists and the Flemish Nationalists, who were tainted by collaboration; it claimed to be the expression of the will of the Belgian people, more democratically authentic than the government in exile; and it was largely animated by an energetic conspiratorial minority of Communists. It possessed two para-military organisations, not easy to distinguish, the 'Partisans' and the 'Milice Patriotique': intended apparently to be respectively the striking force during the occupation, and the reserves ready for mobilisation at the time of liberation.

This corresponded roughly to the Front National (FANA) in France, but there were not, as in France, strong rival movements outside it. There was Groupe G, which was primarily an action organisation and probably never had more than 2,000 members. There was the 'Mouvement National Belge', which appears to have been mainly interested in the maintenance of public order at the time of liberation; it is said to have been recruited mainly from lawyers and gendarmes, and it certainly did not live up to its grandiloquent title, either in scope or in size. Finally, there was a small group, NOLA, which apparently grew up round certain PWE agents in the coal-mining area of the Borinage, and was ultimately concerned mainly with the important non-political task of preventing the destruction of the mines by the retreating Germans.

It was therefore essential for the Belgian Government, however little it liked it, to work through and with the FIL, and the next stage was the dispatch to Belgium in July and August 1943 of those two experienced agents De Liedekerke and Wendelen ('Claudius' and 'Tybalt'), taking with them two wireless operators. The former had worked in the PWE Section of the Sûreté, and was reckoned to be 'propaganda-minded', as well as a conservative in politics; the latter had an excellent record as a saboteur and had had Communist contacts during his first Mission. In this, as in other respects, they made a good team. The younger Marissal had left almost at the same time to make contact with the Secret Army, and (as the Belgian History puts it)[2] it appeared that 'a great race had begun'.

---

[1] Later a member of M. Pierlot's Cabinet in Belgium, September–November 1944: resigned in the abortive Communist 'Putsch' of November 1944, but returned in the Van Acker Government of February 1945.

[2] SOE Belgian History, p. 36.

De Liedekerke was back on 4th October, Marissal on the 18th, Wendelen not until 6th December. Reports on the FIL were as encouraging as those on the Secret Army: the plan which De Liedekerke and Wendelen recommended was one for the formation of a single organisation to embrace all the civilian resistance movements. This plan gave birth in the winter of 1943–4 to the Comité National de Co-ordination[1] (CNC), whose headquarters were to be divided into four sections, sabotage, propaganda, finance, W/T communications. The third of these embodied the 'Service Solidarité' or 'Socrates' organisation, which was extremely important both in financing resistance by internal loans and in providing for the families of those who suffered for resistance or through deportation to Germany. The last point, the centralisation of W/T communications, was only justifiable because of the extreme shortage of sets and operators.

This was in part due to difficulties natural to the Belgian situation. The last quarter of 1943 was a bad month for air operations everywhere; operations to Belgium were particularly dangerous; France (and above all the 'Maquis') had extremely high priority in the early months of 1944. But within Belgium the FIL and its backer, the Sûreté, worked under special disadvantages. The Sûreté had been later in the field than the 2ème Direction, good material for training was difficult to find, and the time in which to train it was short.[2] The Sûreté drew in men from the Belgian Parachute Company and made vigorous efforts to regain ground; but it was not able to do so until very shortly before liberation. Meantime, the Secret Army was better served by liaison officers and wireless operators; its arrangements for reception were in consequence more efficiently made; and as a further consequence the RAF were much readier to provide operations for it than for 'Claudius'. In the first three months of 1944 there were only eleven supply operations to Belgium in all, among them five to the Secret Army, four to the CNC. In the second quarter there were fifty-five such operations, among them forty-eight to the Secret Army, six to the CNC. From January to September 1944 SOE's deliveries of arms were:

	Secret Army	Civilian Groups
Stens	4,419	375
Brens	278	4
Rifles	547	18
Pistols	1,333	321
Carbines	420	–
Marlines	540	–
Anti-Tank Rifles	24	–

---

[1] Often referred to as 'Claudius', while the Secret Army was 'Osric'.
[2] In addition five precious W/T operators were lost in an aircraft crash in January 1944.

In May 1944 the Secret Army had fourteen wireless sets on the air, the civilian groups two only.

As has been said, there were obvious practical reasons for this allocation: SOE denies that it was moved one way or the other by political considerations, and the Belgian Government (which was now working closely with SOE) had no special reason to favour the Secret Army, which was on the whole Royalist in politics and not very warm towards M. Pierlot. But it was inevitable that there should be political repercussions.

Early in 1944 Captain Guillery, hitherto head of the Sûreté's Industrial Sabotage Section, went to the field as Liaison Officer to the CNC, taking with him 'invasion directives' parallel to those given to the Secret Army. Communications from him were scanty, and it was not at all clear in London that the civilian groups had received these orders; hence in the spring, SOE's old friend, Lieutenant Floor, volunteered for a special mission to inspect the situation, and in addition to take certain financial instructions to the 'Socrates' organisation. He was back in London on 20th May, bringing with him Maître Grégoire, an important member of the FIL: unfortunately Grégoire's views about the political prejudices of London had been reinforced on his arrival in England by a short imprisonment in the 'Royal Patriotic School', and he was not conciliatory as regards the attitude of the FIL either towards the Secret Army or to the government in exile. Lieutenant Floor endorsed Grégoire's statement that there was a serious danger of conflict between the two organisations; and there were hectic efforts at this late hour to improve liaison between them and also to strengthen the position of the FIL. These efforts were not very successful, but at least they showed good intentions.

(c) D-day Action

Finally we come to the action taken by the Belgian Resistance as a whole in the great days of the 'Overlord' campaign. There had been various hitches, and SOE were not very certain how much action would be called forward by the BBC action messages, which began with warning signals on 1st June 1944, as they did for France. In the event all went well.

In the first stage, the campaign was almost entirely one of clandestine operations against communications, in particular railways. As usual, the results are difficult to set out statistically, but it is worth citing some figures for the period from 1st July to the Liberation early in September: action began at once after D-day, but in the early period only the Secret Army was in a position to make useful returns.

	Secret Armies	FIL	Nola	CNC Groupe G	MNB	Partisans	Unspecified Civilians
Cuts in main railways	611	–	–	34	–	22	360
Bridges destroyed	28	1	–	3	1	1	18
Locomotives destroyed	76	–	–	15	–	–	–
Trains derailed	37	1	–	–	–	6	18
Misc. railway sabotage	36	–	30	130	–	–	22

In addition, there was a good deal of canal sabotage, and any number of miscellaneous 'incidents'. Belgium is a small country, and these figures are large enough to indicate that during the vital period the Belgian railway system was not in any ordinary sense in operation. Doubtless, after due preparation, military trains could be pushed through safely on specified lines, but each movement was a military operation, and required preparation and the expenditure of time. All this helped to build up the 'zone of delay' which surrounded the German lines in Normandy.

The second stage, that of open mobilisation, began on 31st August, when the Americans crossed the Upper Meuse and the British entered Amiens and crossed the Somme. On that day seventeen of the Secret Army 'refuges' in Zone V, the Ardennes, were mobilised: Zone V was the best armed of the Zones, and some of its troops were already working with SAS parties.* Zone V was fully mobilised on 1st September, along with Hainault (Zone I): Flanders and Brabant were mobilised next day, when the Allies crossed the frontier, Limburg not until 5th September. The object of these mobilisations was not to begin guerilla warfare, for which the Belgians were scarcely equipped, but to bring formed bodies of Resistance troops into the open to receive the Allies and to see to the maintenance of order and essential services. In this phase the main service of the Resistance was to relieve the Allies of all responsibility for 'mopping-up' and to feed them with tactical intelligence so that they could go straight through to Brussels, Antwerp and the Rhine.

Finally, on 4th September the British reached Antwerp, to find the docks intact. This was the greatest single service of the Belgian

---

* [See J. Temmerman, *Acrobates sans importance* (Liège, 1984).]

Resistance, but it is not quite easy to say from SOE's sources how it was carried out. The preservation of Antwerp took a very high place in the Cossac Directives for action in Belgium, and Colonel Marissal originally claimed the task for the Secret Army. 'Claudius' however was also in the field, and the British Admiralty apparently took to the idea that the dockers themselves were the best men to save the port. General Ganshof gave the task to 'Claudius', and in February 1944 De Liedekerke went out on his third Mission to instruct them. But on arrival he found that an old friend of his was on the local staff of the Secret Army, and on 13th March he reported that they already had the job well in hand. It was therefore in the end left to the Secret Army and they are entitled to claim the credit: but we can be certain that civilian 'private enterprise' also played a very large part.*

(d) The Political Aftermath

On 8th September M. Pierlot was back in Brussels, on 11th September the Americans crossed the German frontier and British patrols entered Holland, on 17th September the Arnhem operation was launched. The front lines had passed swiftly across Belgium and the work of its Resistance was at an end. But its political history was not yet finished. The Secret Army had occasionally given rise to some political anxiety. It had always been a little too inclined to emphasise the maintenance of order, and there was one disturbing incident in the winter of 1943–4 when much needed funds[1] were raised by a loan arranged through M. Plisnier, then Secretary-General of the Finance Ministry in Brussels and therefore tainted with collaboration. This was successfully adjusted between M. Pierlot and General Pire in July 1944,[2] and after liberation the leaders of the Secret Army appear to have been fully occupied with the immense problem of military reorganisation.

The FIL proved much more disturbing. Both SHAEF and the Belgian Government were anxious to disarm the Resistance and to arm the police as quickly as possible, and when the SOE Mission arrived in Brussels on 8th September, one of its first tasks was to arrange for arms to be flown in for the gendarmerie. On 22nd September M. Pierlot resigned his office, in accordance with his undertaking, and he was at once called upon to form a new government. His Cabinet included large representation of the Resistance, including the Communists: but almost immediately the FIL, under Communist inspiration, made new demands, and there was a crescendo of agitation which led to rioting in Brussels on 28th November, and

---

[1]   90,000,000 francs.

[2]   SOE Belgian History, p. 66.

*   [See no. 195 of *Views and Surveys* (Brussels, 1985), report of a 1984 conference at the Imperial War Museum on aspects of Belgian Resistance.]

the attempted 'march on the capital' on 28th November. The situation hitherto had been left to the Belgian Government to handle, but this trouble involved the Allied lines of communication, and it was stopped, gently but firmly, by the use of British troops. The Communists at last gave way, and submitted (after securing some concessions) to the disarmament of the Resistance: they had their 'tit-for-tat' with M. Pierlot and turned him out in February 1945, but the Resistance as a private army had ceased to exist.

Probably this political threat received more attention than it deserved. The situation was entirely different from that in Greece, where the Allies were not anxious to land in force; Allied troops were certain to be present in Belgium in very large numbers, and the Communists would certainly not be permitted to 'transform the imperialist war into civil war' on the Allied lines of communication. It has been suggested, and it may be true, that M. Pierlot forced on the trouble (not deliberately) by over-anxiety about the political dangers of the armed resistance – which was at the best pitiably ill-equipped. Certainly, in the end, political stability was regained without much trouble, except over the personal problem of King Leopold.

(e) Conclusion

On the military side, the operations of SOE showed in the last two years a comfortable profit. The figures for men (and women) employed were:

Agents dispatched		182	
Killed in transit	9		
Injured in transit	3	12	
Arrived in the field		170	(161 Belgian
			9 British)
Killed in action, or executed	36		
Arrested, but survived	23		
Missing	16		

This was a fairly high loss rate, even for SOE's Western operations, but the manpower expended was small even in relation to one single gain such as the preservation of the Antwerp docks, and the expenditure of aircraft and equipment was also negligible. SOE can fairly claim to have shown a handsome profit after a bad start: it is more difficult to decide the case if the losses of the Belgian people are brought into the account. Belgium was notably a country of small individual sabotage, open and secret: it was also a country in which the German policy of deportations and reprisals was ruthlessly pursued. Belgian losses in the war were considerable, and were largely attributable to resolute efforts to obstruct the exploitation of Belgian industry by the Germans. For these efforts SOE was only in part responsible.

2. Holland

The chronological pattern of Resistance in Holland is rather different from that usual in Western Europe. SOE's efforts to establish contact were entirely unsuccessful until the spring of 1944, and there was not the usual steady growth from the days of 'Torch' to those of 'Overlord'. Dutch Resistance was not in a position to contribute much to 'Overlord', and luckily not much was required of it. But the situation continued to improve during the summer, and there was a first great crisis at the time of the Arnhem landing, Operation 'Market'.* The Arnhem landing failed, and Holland was then of necessity abandoned to its most bitter winter of the whole war. Perhaps one-third of the country was free, the rest was almost in the front line; even when the armies paused for breath savage underground war continued in Holland.

We have followed[1] SOE's early plans to the point of their complete collapse in the winter of 1943–4. One result of the disaster was a thorough reorganisation in London. On the British side Commander Johns** was in January 1944 appointed Regional Director for the Low Countries, in February Major Bingham was replaced by Lieutenant Colonel Dobson (previously of the Belgian Section) as officer in charge of the Dutch Section. On the Dutch side there was no change in the arrangements for the secret intelligence branch (BI) which was still the field of M. Van't Sant, acting through Major Somer; but the military side was turned upside down. The organisation previously known as the MID became the BBO: Bureau Bjjzondere Opdrachten – 'Special Tasks'. Colonel De Bruyne was replaced in March 1944 by Major General van Oorschot,[†] and most of the higher staff also disappeared: prominent among the new men with actual experience in Resistance were General van Oorschot's personal assistant, Captain Klijzing, and one of the founders of the sabotage organisation CS VI, Captain de Graaf. General van Oorschot had no authority over the BI, but he was on good personal terms with Major Somer.

In Holland SOE's misfortunes had not left Resistance entirely without communications with London, since SIS was also in the field. But

---

[1]   Above p. 307.

*   ['Market', the airborne element in 'Market Garden', comprised three landings by airborne divisions along the line Eindhoven–Nijmegen–Arnhem: the last of these three failed, as the 'Garden' advance overland did not reach it. D-day for 'Market Garden' was 17 September 1944.]

** [See P. L. Johns, *Within Two Cloaks* (1979), claiming he had been MI6's man in Lisbon before moving into SOE.]

†   [Head of Dutch intelligence autumn 1939, dismissed for complicity in the Venlo incident.]

these communications were extremely bad, and they were not intended (as SOE communications were) to be used to improve the organisation of Resistance as a fighting force. This was one reason for the confused state of Resistance early in 1944; another was the psychology of the Dutch, whose politics are very stable, yet at the same time obstinate and factious: a third reason was the intensity of Gestapo action through informers, who were so active in penetration that no single Resistance organisation could be regarded as fully secure and permanent. The situation may be set out somewhat as follows, though this scarcely does justice to the confusion.

First, there were three main movements with 'para-military' branches:

(a) The Orde Dienst (OD) standing somewhat to the Right. [PASSAGE DELETED ON GROUNDS OF NATIONAL SECURITY.]

(b) The RVV (Resistance Council),* which had emerged late in 1944 to group various movements loosely affiliated to the old political parties of the Centre.

(c) The Knok Ploegen (KP), which had arisen locally to provide assistance for workmen evading German conscription of labour, and had developed into an active working-class sabotage organisation. There was no country in Europe where the Communists were so insignificant as in Holland, but the KP's point of view was closest to that of Communist Resistance, and if a Communist bogey had to be found it could be found most easily in the KP.

To these may be added the small specialist sabotage organisation, CS VI.

Second, there were the non-military organisations, almost too loose to be called organisations.

(a) The Clandestine Press, referred to above.[1]

(b) The National Steun Fonds, the financial organisation of the Resistance.[2]

(c) The Landelijke Organisatie (LO), mainly concerned with the provision of false papers and other assistance to those living underground.

(d) The National Committee (NC), which dealt with welfare work, mainly assistance to the dependants of those killed or deported by the Germans.

(e) The Centrale Inlichtings Dienst (CID), which was designed

---

[1] Above p. 307.

[2] There is an excellent account of this, 'De Bankier van het Verzet', in 'Nederland in Oorlogstijd', for January/February 1948.

* [The Raad van Verzet.]

primarily to watch the working of the German repressive services: it also looked after the construction of a clandestine telephone network, which was of great value to the Resistance in the final stage.

When it came to the resumption of activity by SOE, the obvious lines of approach were to the RVV, KP, CS VI, for the organisation of military action, and (on behalf of PWE) to the Clandestine Press. In mid-February 1944 Lord Selborne and General Gubbins had impressed the importance of a fresh approach on the Dutch War Minister, M. O. A. C. Lidthe de Jeude,[1] and during March permission[2] was given to resume air operations, provided that for the present all agents were dropped blind, so that there should be no risk of 'Gestapo reception'. Priority remained low, compared with that given to France, and conditions were extremely difficult for air operations, so that it is fairly easy to summarise the Missions sent up to the end of August 1944, when the situation was changed by the imminence of the Arnhem operation.

31st March:	*To the Clandestine Press* T. Biallosterski ('Draughts') with a wireless operator 'Bezique' (J. A. Steman): they lost their wireless set in landing, but were eventually provided with another. Biallosterski came out for an interval in July 1944, leaving a local recruit ('Draughts II') in his place. Steman remained to the end and kept his set going in the area of the Hague.
31st March:	One party to contact CS VI, another to contact RVV. All four agents concerned were caught in May 1944, but they succeeded in delivering the directives given them in London.
April:	No operations.
31st May:	Two agents were sent in to organise railway sabotage in preparation for D-day, but the aircraft was shot down over Holland and they were lost with the crew.
June:	No operations.
5th July:	Lieutenant L. Mulholland ('Podex') to make contact with the RVV, Lieutenant A. de Goede ('Rummy') with the KP. They with their wireless operator ('Cribbage') established an extremely important point of contact in Rotterdam; 'Rummy' also worked in Amsterdam.
5th July:	Four others were sent to the RVV in the Veluwe area, but their aircraft was shot down and they were lost.

---

[1] Copy on SOE Archives File 5/100/2.
[2] Correspondence with D of I(R), Air Ministry, concerning resumption of operations on SOE Archives File (AD/E) SOE/Holland.

7th Aug.:   S. Postma ('Sculling') was sent with a wireless operator to make contact with the LO in the Veluwe, and eventually established himself in Utrecht. He and his operator were lost in November and December 1944, but their work was carried on by M. Cieremans ('Cubbing') who provided a very important *point d'appui* up to the Liberation.

9th Aug.:   F. L. J. Hamilton ('Rowing') and his sister ('Tiddleywinks') were sent to take a wireless set for Biallosterski at the Hague and also to help with clandestine propaganda. Miss Hamilton broke a leg on landing, and was in hospital (under cover) almost until the Liberation: her brother did useful work in north Holland, based on Amsterdam. This did not however add to the existing wireless channels.

28th Aug.:   Two agents and a wireless operator were dropped to build up resistance in the Veluwe area – the 'hinterland' of Arnhem: in the confusion caused by the operation they split. One of them went to Rotterdam as an instructor for the RVV; another with the wireless operator ('Charades'), moved to the Overijssel, where they provided essential assistance up to the Liberation for a succession of local Resistance leaders.

28th Aug.:   Three agents intended for Eindhoven were in an aircraft which was shot down; two of them survived, but they were in no position to carry out their Mission.

It will be seen how tenuous were the results. Three aircraft out of nine had been shot down; the remaining expeditions eventually produced four fairly permanent centres of communication, in the Hague, Rotterdam, Utrecht and Overijssel, but so far only three of them were operational. The quantity of stores delivered was negligible – seventy-three Stens and thirty-five rifles, according to one return which gives the *total* up to the end of August 1944. The Resistance possessed a little equipment of its own, and it had now received some Allied directives: but it would have been madness to throw it into the battle of 'Overlord', and in fact it played no organised part. There was of course individual sabotage on a small scale, but there was no question of a concerted attempt to block the Dutch railways: these were in any case of little importance to the German concentration in Normandy.

The situation changed when the British broke through across the Seine in the last days of August: they were in Brussels on 3rd September, in Antwerp on the 4th, patrols entered Dutch territory – after a little slackening of speed – on the 11th. It looked now as if the momentum could be maintained by the Arnhem operation, and all

Holland, or a great part of it, might be liberated at a stroke. Dutch Resistance, ill-equipped as it was, was therefore flung into the balance, and there was a situation of almost open revolt, which called forth extremely violent repression.

On 31st August an order from SHAEF set up the NBS (Nederlandsche Binnenlandsche Strijdkraft – Dutch Forces of the Interior) under the command of Prince Bernhard,* who was in turn directly under the command of General Eisenhower.[1] This appointment was announced on 3rd September, and Prince Bernhard moved his HQ to Brussels on 9th September.[2] There he was assisted by a representative of SOE's Dutch Section,[3] as well as by members of the Dutch civil 'BI'. At the same time in London there was constituted a standing committee of the Dutch BBO and BI, the British SOE and SIS, which met daily. Now that the time of pressure had come there was no longer serious friction between the competing organisations outside Holland.

Unfortunately inside Holland the position was not so easy. The plan was that the NBS should include the para-military wings of OD, RVV and KP, which should retain their political identity, but should be merged for military purposes. The direction in occupied Holland should be in the hands of three representatives, one from each organisation – the Driehoek ('Triangle') or 'Delta Centrum': this was located in Amsterdam. Under its general control Holland should be divided into six Zones, fourteen Regions, and in each there should be a single commander who should if possible be in direct communication with the Allies. This did not go forward smoothly. There were the usual lines of cleavage: on the one hand Resistance as a whole claimed that it be given special rights in the post-war world; on the other hand Resistance fell apart into Right and Left, OD versus KP, with the RVV on the whole inclining towards the latter.[4] These troubles produced sympathetic reactions in the London Government: on 26th January 1945 the Ministry of the Interior resigned over the question of purging collaborationists, and in February Professor Gerbrandy reconstituted his Cabinet. Within Holland the problem was never finally resolved, but it seems to have been tided over by the appoint-

---

[1] SHAEF/17240/28/Ops(C) – GCT 370-19, quoted in SOE Dutch History, August 1944.

[2] Code-name 'Northaw'. The HQ moved to Breda on Dutch territory early in 1945.

[3] SOE helped to fly in arms to Belgium for the equipment of Dutch forces to maintain order in the portion of Holland liberated at this stage.

[4] In the end (January 1945) it appears that of 13 Commanders named, 7 were OD, 4 KP, 2 RVV – SOE Dutch History, under 6th January 1945 (Yellow Annex).

* [Son-in-law of Queen Wilhelmina, husband of her successor (Queen) Juliana, RAF pilot.]

ment of Major General Koot as sole commander of the NBS within
occupied Holland.

Holland now had reasonably high priority, and air operations were
not as dangerous as they had been, since the Allies stood on the land
frontiers of Holland. It will be convenient here to insert the statistics
of deliveries by air until the Liberation.

	Sept.	*Oct.*	*Nov.*	*Dec.*	*Jan.*	*Feb.*	*Mar.*	*April*
Aircraft sorties	86	130	83	22	10	18	40	79
Successful	42	47	40	13	3	4	27	53
Containers for								
SOE	765	996	834	231	53	62	514	1,179
SIS	–	–	1	4	–	10	74	48
SAS	–	–	6	22	–	–	–	–
Packages for								
SOE	71	108	83	25	14	14	92	190
SIS	–	6	4	3	–	–	7	8
SAS	–	4	4	4	–	–	–	–

This shows clearly the burst of activity in September and October;
the reduced activity in the winter months when both the weather and
the Gestapo were at their worst; the relatively low proportion of
successes even at this stage; the final effort in March and April 1945.
Arms dropping was stopped finally on 24th April 1945, in order to
give the enemy no pretext for interfering with the dropping of food
which was then begun.

Even in August SOE had begun to concentrate agents for the area
of possible Allied advance: two parties had already been dispatched
for the Veluwe and one for Eindhoven. When the time came for the
Arnhem operation four 'Jedburghs' (mixed Dutch, British, US) accompanied the Airborne Forces, one with Corps HQ and one with each
of the three divisions engaged: of these only the first, 'Edward', proved
to be of importance in operations. A fifth team, 'Dudley', went into
the Veluwe before the operation: this consisted of Major Brinkgreve
(Dutch), Major Olmsted (US), and Sergeant Austin, the wireless operator (British). Of these only Olmsted survived the war, but Brinkgreve
made a great name for himself in the Overijssel, where his team (with
'Charades')[1] provided the kernel of Resistance up to the Liberation.
Finally on 8th September Biallosterski ('Draughts'), on his second
Mission, went with a wireless operator to Amsterdam to open contact
with the central 'triangle' of the NBS. 'Draughts' himself was mortally
wounded in February 1945, but his work was taken over by a local

---

[1] Above p. 640.

recruit 'Dr X' (Arend), who continued to work with the wireless operator, 'Backgammon'. This was an absolutely vital link in the Dutch chain of command. It should be added that a further party of four was dropped on 15th September; this provided two sabotage instructors for Rotterdam, an additional wireless operator ('Boating') for Amsterdam, and the agent Cieremans ('Cubbing') who ultimately became the chief contact with Utrecht.[1]

On D-day, 17th September, the Dutch Government called for a general strike in the Dutch railways, which was destined to remain unbroken until May 1945. A message from General Eisenhower was also broadcast in which he claimed the status of regular combatants for the NBS and called on the population south of the Lek to stand by to assist the Allies: elsewhere there was to be no general rising for the present. At the same time secret messages through SIS and SOE channels called for railway sabotage[2] and gave more precise instructions for assistance to the airborne troops at Arnhem. It was impossible for these measures, taken at this late hour, to have any serious effect on the movement of German troops by road, but there was for the first time a burst of railway sabotage timed and placed in accordance with an Allied plan; 'Piet van Arnhem' and his men came into the open and gave valuable local assistance; in addition, there were first reports of attempts by Resistance to preserve the port of Rotterdam – the potential blockships 'Borneo', 'Westerdijk', and 'Axenfels' were all sunk at this time.

The failure of Operation 'Market' was plain by 25th September; nevertheless the wave of excitement and sabotage continued into October, and it was not until November that German counter-measures began to have serious effects. German policy had various branches. One tactic was the deportation to Germany of able-bodied men swept up at random in 'razzias' in the streets: very large numbers of men were deported in this way from all the main towns except Amsterdam, where the garrison commander was anxious to 'reinsure'. A good many members of the NBS were thus removed from the scene. Punishments for suspected assistance were brutal and reprisals were taken ruthlessly for any 'incident'; over 400 lives are said to have

---

[1] The Dutch History also refers to an SAS Party ('Regan', later 'Fabian') sent at this time to the Drenthe area: this was reinforced on 9th October by 'Portia II' (later 'Gobbo'). Both parties remained in wireless touch until the spring of 1945, and returned safely. The History expresses some scepticism about their training and security: nevertheless, they survived, and did work of value. ['Fabian' was G. S. Kirschen, later doyen of the Brussels bar; see his *Six amis viendront ce soir* (Brussels, 1983).]

[2] SHAEF Directive SHAEF/17240/28/Ops C of 27th August 1944. SOE Dutch History, September 1944, p. 4.

been exacted for an attack on the Gestapo chief Rauters.* In addition the Germans continued to use cunning as well as force. They were still well served by informers, and they regularly used the old trap of opening local negotiations with individual Resistance leaders on one pretext or another. At the same time the whole population lay under the crushing threat of imminent starvation.

This intense pressure in a confined space was bound to be effective. Arrests were reported from Rotterdam at the end of October. In November SOE's agent Postma ('Sculling') was caught and killed, with twelve local leaders, at Utrecht: Mulholland ('Podex') was accidentally caught up in a razzia in Rotterdam and was deported to Germany. The Rotterdam chief of KP, 'Frank', was killed in December and SOE lost 'Dudley's' wireless operator in Overijssel, the wireless operator in Rotterdam and the wireless operator in Utrecht: communications were kept open with difficulty. The only gain during these three months was the establishment of a good man, P. Tazelaar ('Necking'), with a wireless operator in Friesland; a second operator was got in for Rotterdam and there was a rather unsuccessful political Mission to NBS HQ in Amsterdam, carried out by P. de Beer, who returned to England in January 1945. On the whole, it was necessary for the present to draw back. The population at large was warned to avoid violent action. Air supply operations were suspended for some time at the end of November in order to stop reprisals. SOE's own men were told that their first duty was to maintain themselves in being till the spring and that all contact with Resistance was to be cut except in cases of absolute necessity. The NBS Command was urged to decentralise thoroughly to its Regions: and in each Region to divide the working teams of saboteurs from the military reserves which would take no overt action before mobilisation.

The date at which progress could begin again was set back by the Rundstedt offensive, and the bad times continued until March. In the middle of January there was a serious loss of arms in Rotterdam. In February Biallosterski was badly wounded and captured in Amsterdam, two instructors and a local operator were caught and killed in Rotterdam, in Overijssel the local leader, Evert, was killed, there was a serious wave of arrests in Friesland. The food situation was becoming desperate. On the other side of the account, the SOE wireless contacts were never broken in any area: some of the native Resistance leaders managed to come out (notably 'Rob', the KP leader in Rotterdam, and 'Richard' the RVV member of the Directing Committee), and the political tension was somewhat relaxed: there

---

* [H-A. Rauter, SS chief in Holland, almost killed in early March 1945, exacted over 250 executions in revenge for the attack, was executed himself, after trial, 1949.]

were some excellent reports of rescues and of sabotage – in particular the sinking at Rotterdam of the blockship 'Westerdam' and the giant floating-crane 'Titan'. During January and February 1945 there were only two operations of any importance: an extra wireless operator was sent to the local leader in Overijssel, and 'Rob', the KP leader (M. Van der Stoep), went back to Rotterdam in February, with a special mission from Prince Bernhard to persuade the warring factions to accept the rule of the Commander NBS.[1]

But on 7th March the Americans secured their bridgehead at Remagen, and the main crossing of the Rhine was planned for 23rd March (Operation 'Varsity'). The final stages of preparation for action in Holland are recorded in the Minutes of an SOE Conference on 19th and 20th March.[2] For the zone of the Canadian advance, in Eastern Holland, it was now fairly simple to issue action messages for attacks on railways and roads, for the collection of tactical intelligence, and for the preservation of important installations and technicians. It was more difficult to ensure that this should happen without provoking sabotage and mass reprisals in Western Holland: the Resistance was now relatively well-armed, and the temptation which had to be resisted was very strong, but on the whole discipline held good even at breaking point. The following figures indicate what had been sent by SOE up to 15th March 1945: a good deal of course had been lost.

Explosives	20,905	lbs
Stens	14,344	
Rifles	2,928	
Carbines	765	
Pistols	2,175	
Grenades	20,085	
Brens	362	
Bazookas	286	
Piats	14	

In April the NBS reckoned that they had about 9,350 armed men in the Regions still occupied.

In March there were two Missions designed to reinforce the area of advance, and these were overrun by the Canadians early in the offensive. There was also an additional wireless operator for Rotterdam, and an assistant for Van der Stoep there. There was finally an important Mission carried out by Major J. J. F. Borghouts ('Swish') who had already been distinguished in Resistance as 'Peter Zuid', and was now sent back to Amsterdam to assist the Commander of the NBS, Major General Koot: he played an important part in the negotiations of the last days.

---

1   Code-name 'Scrape'. He was killed in an attack on a Gestapo HQ on 11th April.
2   SOE Dutch History, March 1945 and Appendix.

In the east of Holland, the zone of Canadian advance, matters went straightforwardly, in a fashion now familiar.[1] The Resistance smoothed the way for the advance, and took over responsibility for order without special incident. SOE's men in Overijssel and Friesland were recovered safely, except that the popular 'Dudley', Major Brinkgreve, was killed in action a few days before the final offensive. By the middle of April Holland east of the Ijssel Meer was virtually clear of the enemy, and the Canadian First Corps faced west towards the fortress of Holland. The problem was now to avoid a battle, not to fight one, and it was eventually solved by extremely cautious and complex negotiation, which began in the middle of April and involved Seyss-Inquart, Blaskowitz, the Dutch Government, the Resistance, General Eisenhower, Field-Marshal Montgomery, General Foulkes (of the 1st Canadian Corps), as well as many subsidiary characters.

If it had come to a battle, the most vital task of the Resistance would have been to resist German attempts at 'scorching' the ports or at drowning the soil of Holland in salt; a desperate risk unless the Allies overran German resistance very quickly, but one on which the whole future of Holland depended. Luckily, it did not come to this, and in practice the Resistance's greatest contribution was to ease communications through the lines, in particular by the use of its secret telephone network, which was at the disposal of Prince Bernhard for conversations with the Dutch leaders in Amsterdam. By about 25th April it was pretty clear that the Germans would give way, though it was not until 4th May that Field-Marshal Montgomery received the surrender of the Group of Armies which covered the military command in Holland.

The final problem was that of the maintenance of order while the Allies marched in to disarm the Germans, and this unluckily gave rise to controversy. The NBS at first possessed no arm-bands or other means of identification, and it was felt (rightly or wrongly) both by Prince Bernhard and by General Foulkes that incidents were certain to occur if large numbers of unidentified civilians with arms in their hands were let loose among the hated Germans – who were much more heavily armed than the Dutch. The Resistance was therefore ordered not to carry arms while on duty, until issued with some official means of identification. This was a sensible order; furthermore, it was an order to which the NBS paid little or no attention; nevertheless, it left them with a feeling that their services were perhaps not fully appreciated, and that the great day had been slightly marred.

It is certainly easy to underrate the Dutch Resistance. Its help to the Allies was given mainly in inconspicuous ways, in particular by

---

[1] A joint Jedburgh/SAS team landed in Veluwe on 3rd April and a Jedburgh was sent to Drenthe on the 7th.

supplying intelligence, and it took very little formal or conspicuous part in Allied military campaigns by way of sabotage and guerilla warfare. This was largely a matter of geography. Things were undoubtedly made worse by SOE's early blunders, but these blunders themselves arose in part from geography which made it exceptionally difficult to work into Holland. As it proved, the Dutch for the most part fought their own underground war without much reference to the needs of the Allies, but it must be remembered that it was an extremely fierce and brutal war. The official Dutch casualty figures for losses in the war are 210,000 dead (including about 104,000 Dutch Jews) of whom 23,300 lost their lives as a result of Resistance.[1]

In the last year of the war SOE and its agents worked well, and went some distance towards the creation of a working system of communications and command; but one must still regret that it was not possible sooner to relate Dutch sacrifices to an Allied plan, and either to mitigate them or to draw from them greater military advantage.

---

[1] Dutch Central Bureau of Statistics, quoted in Manchester Guardian of 30th October 1948. The details given are:

Jews deported	104,000
Forced labourers died in Germany	27,000
Resistance: executed in Holland	2,800
died in KZLs in Holland	2,500
died in KZLs in Germany	18,000
Civilians killed by acts of war	20,400
Armed forces and Merchant Navy	7,850
Unclassified	27,450
	210,000

CHAPTER XXVI

Norway

1. The Season of 1942–3

(a) The Plan for the Season

We have seen[1] that at the end of the campaigning season of 1941–2 the Anglo-Norwegian Co-ordinating Committee was firmly in the saddle as the London centre of control for all internal military activity in Norway. It remained to work out together a plan of campaign for the next winter season. The idea of close collaboration had been accepted, but early in the summer of 1942 it was still thought possible that there should be two parallel military organisations in Norway: that of the Home Front, and (isolated from it) a network inspired and maintained by SOE and the Linge Company.[2] By the end of August this conception had been abandoned, and it was clear that from the Trondheim area to the south there could only be one organisation jointly supported by the resources of 'London' and of the Home Front.[3]

One reason for this was the growing realisation that it was not technically possible for two organisations to exist without dangerous overlapping in a country so sparsely populated as Norway.

The decision was made easier by the great development in the Home Front which began in the spring of 1942 and was perceived in London after a short time-lag. The appointment of Quisling as Minister-President on 1st February 1942 had led to a series of insane measures of 'Gleichschaltung', which drove even the most staid members of the community into open opposition. Protests by the Church, the University and the teachers led to persecution and deprivation of offices: and out of these grew a civil organisation the primary purpose of which was to keep in good heart men who had lost everything by refusing to obey the orders of Quisling, and to preserve their families from suffering, or even from starvation. This arose first from

---

1 Above p. 216.
2 See 'Norway – Future Planning', dated 5th June 1942; copy on SOE Archives File (AD/S.1) F/130/17 Vol. 1 Norway–General.
3 Plan of 21st September 1942; copy on SOE Archives File 6/110 'Norway–Policy': copied in part as App. D to SOE Norwegian History.

the natural groupings of professions and trades: the Church, teachers, lawyers, doctors, trade unions. But in the course of 1942 there grew out of these a fairly strong central leadership, with a steering committee in Oslo and a growing comprehension of the technique of clandestine opposition. Naturally this development posed awkward problems for the London Government: there was now in effect a parallel government inside Norway, a possible source of jealousy and of mutual misunderstanding. This danger was never entirely dissipated, and the difficulties were at times picked up and magnified by factions among the Norwegians in exile.[1] But Haakon VII himself held a position above party politics, which was accepted without qualification by all good Norwegians: and on both sides there was much fundamental good sense, even though nerves at times grew ragged. At Christmas 1942 Prime Minister Nygaardsvold for the first time declared formally in public that he would place the resignation of his Government in the King's hands immediately Norway was freed: to still all doubts, this declaration was repeated even more explicitly on the anniversary of the invasion, 9th April 1943. This principle was a firm rock through all later disagreements on lesser matters.

The Central Leadership of the Home Front, thus established in the summer of 1942, effectively ruled Norway beneath the surface of the Terboven and Quisling régimes until the Liberation. It was often shaken by Gestapo action, and it was not free from internal difficulties: but it remained a true 'parallel government' with a real control of every department of national life. Most remarkable of all, perhaps, its Military Organisation (Milorg) remained truly military, and was kept almost entirely free from ideologies and political dissensions: it was with Milorg that SOE were now primarily concerned, and in Norway (as in no other country) it will be possible from this point to pursue SOE's history with little reference to politics.

The first clear report on Milorg, in its new and more efficient form, was received in August 1942 from an officer who had been sent to Oslo for the purpose by General Hansteen.[2] This made it plain not only that Milorg was thoroughly competent to run its own business, but also that it was not prepared to accept the establishment of any rival organisation, at least in the main area from Trondelag to the south. Here was one decisive factor in the preparation of a plan for the new season. Another was the anxiety caused both to the Home Front and to the Norwegian Government by the small 'activist' factions, believed to be under Communist inspiration, which compared

---

[1] For instance the affair of the 'Danielsen petition' in January 1943: and there was later something of a centre of dissidence in Stockholm.

[2] See Colonel Wilson's account of this dated 15th August (ref. SN/1162); copy on SOE Archives File (AD/S.1) F/130/17.

Norway's 'partisans' disparagingly with those of Russia and Yugoslavia and clamoured for action, at all costs. The merits of such a policy were not beyond dispute even in Russia and Yugoslavia: it would have been madness in Norway, where the Germans could have wiped out the entire population in a day or two, almost without inconvenience to themselves. This madness was so plain to all that the policy was not even a sound one for the development of Communism in Norway, and there is no evidence that it ever obtained more encouragement from Russia than could be derived from the casual utterances of Moscow Radio.

The 'activist' tendency never got out of hand, but it remained a minor danger and irritation to the end, and in the autumn of 1942 it led to increased Norwegian emphasis on the necessity for common sense – the proper co-ordination of plans and the avoidance of anything that could cause loss to Norway without compensating military advantage to the Allies. There was a sharp warning of what this meant early in October. Since April 1942 Lieutenant Sjøberg of the 'Archer' party had been working under great difficulties to build up an organisation in the 'waist' of Norway north of Trondelag.[1] On 6th September there was a shooting affray with the Germans at Majavatn in this area, quite a successful little battle in itself: but the Germans responded first by savage reprisals against the tiny village of Majavatn, then in October by the proclamation of a state of emergency in the Trondheim area, and the murder of thirty-four innocent Norwegian hostages. There had intervened a Commando raid at Glomfjord on 20th September, and an SOE coup at Fosdalen on 7th October, which increased German anxiety. Majatavn and the other coups were reasonable operations of war, and the Norwegians firmly accepted the slaughter of hostages as casualties in battle: but such sacrifices could not be accepted except for good reasons, and it must be demonstrated that the reasons were good.

On the British side there were three factors of importance. *First*, there was the Prime Minister's anxiety (related to the imminence of 'Torch' and to the situation on the eastern front) that small-scale raiding should be intensified in the west ('the hand of steel out of the sea')[2] so as to put as much strain as possible on the German garrisons. *Second*, there was the economic warfare plan. Norway's economic resources in total were not great, but there were certain points at which they might be crucial to the Germans: 'heavy water' for the development of atomic piles was by far the most important, but there were others such as molybdenum, pyrites, abrasives, which were believed

---

[1] Above p. 207.

[2] Mr Churchill at Edinburgh, 12th October 1942. The Sark operation which led to the manacling of prisoners had taken place on 4th October, and Hitler's 'manacling' order was announced on 7th October.

to be 'bottle-necks'. *Third*, SOE's activities were to some extent limited by the presence of heavy German warships in Norwegian waters. So long as there was 'a fleet in being' they held substantial British naval forces back from the Far East, and very high priority was given to the securing of intelligence as to their movements.[1] Thus on the whole SIS had priority over SOE on the west coast: SOE was a little cramped even in using the area for transit, and it had to exercise particular care to avoid action which might endanger SIS's sources of information – a curious instance of the indirect effects of sea-power. This limitation continued to have some effect until the sinking of the 'Tirpitz' by the RAF on 12th November 1944.

The result of these considerations was that SOE now had two main lines of action: *first*, the provision of organisers, instructors and wireless operators, to be at the disposal of Milorg for liaison and for the preparation of a secret army against the ultimate day of reckoning: *second*, the dispatch of sabotage parties against particular limited objectives. These latter would be careful to avoid mixing themselves up with the native organisation; they would operate in uniform if they could, and they would seek to leave evidence that their work was an 'outside job'. *Thirdly*, as an addendum to these two points, it was desirable that SOE should do something to open up the difficult territory of Northern Norway, where little had as yet been achieved from Oslo.

(b) Co-operation with Milorg

The first of these tasks was the most intangible and in some ways the most difficult. Here SOE had to face not only the technical problems of subversive warfare, but the psychological problem of proving to Milorg that it had something to learn from the unknown young men of the Linge Company. At first the 'outsiders' were often regarded merely as sources of danger, ignorant of how to live in occupied Norway: at the worst they might be taken for 'agents provocateurs' or allies of the irresponsible 'activists'.

The winter of 1942–3 was technically a difficult one, as the Shetland fishing boats suffered heavily both from storms and from enemy action, and the number of aircraft available was still very small: so that the quantity of men and stores sent in was quite inadequate. But the psychological problem was largely overcome. It is impossible to trace now, step by step, how this was achieved, but there are a few incidents of obvious importance. The first of these was the Mosquito raid in daylight on the Gestapo HQ at Viktoria Terrasse in Oslo. This was timed to coincide with the Quisling celebrations of the anniversary of the effective beginning of his régime in September 1940; it

---

[1] Cf. Para. 6 of COS(43)142(0) of 20th March 1943. (SOE Directive for 1943.)

was the first operation of its kind and the RAF required strong persuasion to attempt it. Fortunately it succeeded to perfection. Viktoria
Terrasse was bombed very accurately for the loss of only one aircraft:
there were few Norwegian casualties, and it was rumoured that a
hundred of the Gestapo had been killed: Quisling was frightened into
the cellars, and resumed his celebrations after an interval, in some
confusion. Most important of all, Norwegian belief in the efficacy of
the link with London was greatly strengthened: London had done
exactly what the Home Front wanted, at the right time, and in the
right way.

This was a good beginning for the season, but much depended on
the work to be done by the rank and file of the Linge Company sent
in to work with Milorg. Two of these parties are worth mentioning.
These were 'Gannet' (O. Doublong and Torbjørn Hoff) who were
dropped in the Gudbrandsdal on 29th November, and 'Chaffinch'
(Stenersen, Olsen and Sandersen) who landed near Drammen on 24th
January 1943. The former were in the mountains till the end of
February 1943, running courses of instruction for Milorg: they held
courses for eleven picked leaders and fifty-nine others, and their pupils
were satisfied that the training given was new and good and that the
'Noric' men were intelligent and absolutely straight. 'Chaffinch' was
equally successful for four months in the Oslo area, and their wireless set was the first direct channel of communication to the Central
Leadership. When they left, Milorg reported of them: 'All three men
have displayed convincing technical knowledge and a striking apti-
tude for imparting instruction. Their conduct and care as regards security have been exemplary.' As Colonel Wilson puts it: 'FO IV' (the
Norwegian Command in London) 'and SOE were over the top of the
hill.'[1] The remaining parties of this type can be given far less space
here than their work deserves: but they contributed much to the
smoothness and discipline with which the Secret Army mobilised in
May 1945.

(c) 'Coup de main' Operations

The responsibility for attacks on specific targets was divided between
Combined Operations and SOE, and it was not easy to say where the
frontier lay. But fortunately the two organisations were in close sympathy, there was healthy rivalry, but no serious confusion. Combined
Operations had two successes – the Glomfjord power station raid on
20th September 1942,[2] and that on the Stord pyrites mine on 25th
January 1943[3] – and one failure, the disastrous glider operation against

---

[1]   SOE Norwegian History, p. 99.
[2]   'Knotgrass-Unicorn'.
[3]   'Cartoon'.

the heavy-water plant at Vemork on 19th November 1942. In all three cases SOE was intimately associated both with the planning and with the execution of the operation. SOE also played a vital part in the Navy's attempt on 31st October at an attack by 'chariots' on the 'Tirpitz' as it lay in the recesses of the Trondheimfjord.[1] The operation was mounted in one of SOE's fishing boats, the 'Arthur', skippered by Quartermaster Leif Larsen (finally DSC, CGM, DSM and bar), who took his vessel in disguise right through the German controls almost to the point at which the 'chariots' were to be cast off for the attack: they were being towed underwater behind the 'Arthur', and by ill fortune they broke loose in heavy seas and were lost. At least SOE had played its part to perfection, and it was warmly thanked by the VCNS.

It is worth recording that all prisoners taken on these operations – which conformed in every way to the rules of war – were shot by the Germans without trial.

SOE's own greatest contribution was the destruction of the entire stock of heavy water at Vemork, the only large source of production in Europe. This magnificent story has now been told in public so fully[2] that no more is required here than a dry recital of dates and facts.

The story begins for SOE in March 1942, when the possibility of atomic warfare was already known to the Allies, and the crucial importance of 'heavy water' was understood. SOE was approached about the possibilities of attack on the production plant at Vemork (where the Germans were understood to be increasing output), and SOE found among those who had come out of Norway with Odd Starheim in the 'Galtesund'[3] one Einar Skinnarland, who came from this valley and was brother of Torstein Skinnarland, the warden of the dam from which Vemork drew its power. Einar ('Grouse' was his later codename) reached England on 17th March: he was given some hasty training and was dropped into the Hardangervidda with a wireless set on 28th March. There he lived and worked until the Liberation: his existence was well enough known to the enemy, but they could never lay hands on him.

---

[1] There is a full account of Operation 'Title' at Appendix I to the SOE Norwegian History.

[2] It was the subject of a British press release after the dropping of the atom bomb on Hiroshima. In Norwegian there are 'Norges Insatts i Atombombkrig' (anonymous but reliable) and an article by Claus Helberg of the 'Swallow' party in the Norske Turistforenings Årbok for 1947. A film reconstructing the story with the original party was under preparation in 1947. The fullest SOE account is at Appendix H to the Norwegian History.

[3] Above p. 209.

In July 1942 the 'heavy water' was given to Combined Operations as an objective, and plans were laid for a British glider attack with Norwegian support. SOE's advance party of four men ('Swallow') were dropped on 18th October, after two failures during September, and they managed after severe hardships to reach Vemork area and open communication on 9th November. A landing place was marked out for the British party, which was to arrive in two gliders, and the operation was attempted in desperate weather on 19th November: one aircraft and two gliders crashed in Southern Norway far from the target, and the survivors were shot by the Germans.

The enemy now knew what the objective was, and the task was so much the harder: nevertheless SOE obtained permission to try again with its own resources, and a party of six men from the Linge Company ('Gunnerside') was put in training for a coup de main. There was one false start during January, then on 16th February they were successfully dropped on the frozen surface of Lake Skrykken, in the heart of the Hardangervidda; on 23rd February they made contact with 'Swallow', which had held out in the depths of the mountains in conditions of bitter cold and semi-starvation. The attack was made on 27th/28th February: it involved a long ski journey, a rock climb of some difficulty (heavily laden with arms and stores) down into the ravine below the factory, and the crossing of a half-frozen torrent. The Germans had justifiably disregarded the possibility of access from this side; the guards at the factory were all indoors in their own hut, and when they heard muffled explosions it did not occur to them at first that saboteurs might be at work within the outer defences. The party thus got clear away with a good start: five of 'Gunnerside' came safely back through Sweden, Einar Skinnarland remained at his wireless post, and the other five dispersed to play other roles in Norway: all of them survived the war. The job had been a supreme test of morale, intelligence and physical skill and stamina, and the whole party deserved the tributes which they received from quarters as diverse as Mr Churchill and General Von Falkenhorst,* the German C-in-C.

The Germans combed Rjukan and the Vemork Valley, closed the Hardangervidda and attempted to sweep it with large forces: but they were apparently satisfied that this was a 'Commando' job, as they took no reprisals against the civil population. It is now clear that German development of the atomic bomb had already at this time been bogged in the quagmire of 'Aryan science', and that 'Gunnerside' was not as it might have been the decisive operation of the war. Nevertheless, it added considerably to the embarrass-

---

* [N. von Falkenhorst, 1885–1968, commanded corps in Poland 1939, commanded German troops in Norway 1940–44, condemned to death 1946, reprieved.]

ments of the German scientists, to whom heavy water was as precious as gold, and it set back their priority still further. Above all, it stands as the perfect instance of the strategic possibilities of sabotage.[1]

It will be well to disregard chronology and complete the story here. London had very full knowledge of the progress of work at Vemork, chiefly through SOE's contacts; SOE was approached in the late summer of 1943 with a view to a second attack, but the guards had now been further strengthened, and SOE could offer nothing but some delay in production by 'insaisissable' sabotage. The job was therefore given to the US Air Force, which made a heavy attack on 16th November 1943: this destroyed 120 lbs of heavy water and retarded production somewhat – unfortunately one bomber group went astray and bombed a fertiliser works in Rjukan, with some loss of Norwegian life. In spite of its imperfect success the raid was apparently enough to make the Germans abandon finally the attempt to keep Vemork in production: this was reported by Einar Skinnarland to London on 31st November, and by February 1944 the Germans were ready to move out the remaining stock of heavy water – some 3,600 gallons. The Norwegians were encouraged to take every possible step to intercept it, even at heavy risk, and a series of plans was laid to catch the consignment at different points on its route. The very first of these was successful: on 20th February Knut Haukelid (of the original 'Gunnerside' party) slipped on board the ferry steamer on Lake Tinnsjø and placed a home-made bomb, which exploded exactly as planned and sank the ferry with its cargo of heavy water in some 200 fathoms of water. This closed a campaign which had been waged continuously for two years since March 1942.

The series of operations against the important pyrites mine at Orkla, south of Trondheim, was of equal technical excellence, though the target was less dramatic. The moving spirit here was the late Lieutenant Peter Deinboll, DSO, MC, son of the engineer in charge at the mine. His first attack ('Redshank') was made in May 1942; with two companions he demolished the converter and transformer station which controlled the power for the railway between the mine and the coast. This cut production by about half for some six months. In February 1943 he tried again.[2] This time the plan was to block loading by sinking a vessel alongside the quay: the German ship 'Nordfahrt' (5,800 tons) was successfully attacked with limpets, but unfortunately she was moved and beached in time and traffic was not

---

[1] The history of German atomic development has now been told fairly fully in Goudsmit, 'Alsos, The Failure of German Science' (1947). This is an account of the findings of the American mission of investigation.

[2] 'Granard'.

seriously interrupted. Deinboll was back again for a third attempt in October 1943,[1] and he chose this time to attack the locomotives on the ore railway, as it was impossible to gain access to the mine itself. There were two attacks, on 30th October and 20th November, and at least five locomotives were put out of action. This was Deinboll's last effort – he was in the end lost unluckily in a missing aircraft in November 1944 – but it was not the end at Orkla. There was another brilliant series of locomotive attacks in May and June 1944 by a party sent in from Sweden: finally in September 1944 the Linge Company's leader in Oslo finished off a locomotive which had been under repair there since Deinboll's last attack. It is hard to say what this cost the enemy in production (for the loss of one man killed and one captured), but it was certainly a high proportion of the output of the mines.

There was another very neat operation at the Fosdalen iron-ore mines in North Trondelag on 7th October 1942, which cut production by a quarter for three months: and there were two disasters – a party sent to the Rødsand iron-ore mine in Møre in November 1942 vanished without trace, and the Norwegian submarine 'Uredd' was lost with all hands in February 1943 while carrying a party to attack the pyrites mines at Sulitjelma. There remains one operation which bore fruit later in more ways than one. Two young Norwegians in training, Max Manus and Gregers Gram,[2] had become the apostles of a gospel of attack on shipping.[3] They knew Oslo well, and (more on their own initiative than on that of SOE) they secured acceptance of a scheme for limpet attacks on shipping in the Oslofjord – a project to all appearance suicidal in narrow waters brightly lit and heavily patrolled. They were dropped near Oslo on 12th March, and managed to recruit a few friends of their own without touching on the main military organisation: by 27th April they had an elaborate scheme ready. Two parties were to attack from the sea in four canoes, and a third party was to work in the Akers shipyard, in such a way that an attack from the sea would be suspected. By sheer nerve the attack was almost perfectly successful: limpets were attached to the 'Ortelsburg' (3,600 tons), the 'Tugela' (5,600 tons), the 'Taiwan' (5,500 tons), one smaller merchant ship, a new mine sweeper, and an oil-lighter. The limpets unfortunately were less efficient than the Norwegians: only eight out of twenty-two exploded, and the total casualties were the 'Ortelsburg' sunk, the 'Tugela' and the oil-lighter

---

[1] 'Feather I'.

[2] Manus was a rolling stone, who had at the outbreak of the war been leading a rather picaresque life in South America, and came back to fight in the Finnish war: Gram was a law student, son of a former Mayor of Oslo.

[3] Their story is told very simply and well in Max Manus's two books, 'Det Vil Helst Gå God' and 'Det Blir Alvor'.

damaged. Norwegian technical inexperience may have been a contributory cause, but the affair led to a very necessary intensification of development work on limpets: it also led SOE to think large thoughts about the possibilities of attack on shipping – if so much could be done with such primitive means.

But the element of luck is beyond insurance in operations on so small a scale. The biggest operation of the season was 'Carhampton', and it could not have been better led and manned: but it was almost completely unsuccessful. The plan was that Odd Starheim (the original 'Cheese', the hero of the 'Galtesund' exploit)[1] should land in his own country near Flekkefjord with a party of thirty men from the Linge Company and ten from the Norwegian Navy, should do such damage as he could to shipping, and should finally join in a Combined Operations attack on the titanium mine at Sogndal near Jøssingfjord. The whaler 'Bodø' was lent for the occasion by the C-in-C, Western Approaches, and landed the party safely on 1st January 1943, after two failures in November: the first disaster was that the 'Bodø' struck a mine off Aberdeen on her return and was lost with all but two of the crew – Lieutenant Commander Marstrander, the first Norwegian member of the Anglo-Norwegian Collaboration Committee, went down with her. 'Carhampton' was well established on shore, and received supplies by air, but it failed in two shipping attacks in Flekkefjord on 11th and 14th January, and had to withdraw to the hills and lie low in bad conditions. The Combined Operations relief expedition was timed for 24th February, and all was in readiness: but it had to be abandoned on account of storms, and Starheim was now left to extricate his thirty-eight men (two had already been withdrawn to Sweden) as best he could. He came remarkably near success. With sixteen of them he seized the coastal steamer 'Tromøysund' and got clear away: but by ill-luck a Focke Wulf found them and the ship was sunk by bombing with all hands. His second-in-command came safely off by fishing boat with eighteen men: four others remained to watch the Knaben molybdenum mines which were to be a target for air attack at the earliest opportunity.[2] 'Carhampton' had been a costly and distressing failure: it had shown that a relatively large force could be kept going in the mountains in winter, but it did not encourage anyone to think that there was much point in attempting such an exercise again.

(d) Northern Norway

The problem of the long 'tail' of Norway north of Trondheim was one which was never satisfactorily solved. The Trondheim region itself was difficult. The Germans were numerically strong there, and they

---

[1] Above p. 208.
[2] They were attacked very successfully by Mosquitoes with Norwegian crews on 3rd March 1943.

thought much of security in view of the district's importance as a naval base and transit area, both for submarines and for surface ships. In particular, they had at their disposal the infamous organisation of Norwegian informers run by Ivar Grande and Henry Rinnan; these scoundrels first came into prominence through a series of betrayals in the winter of 1942–3, which very seriously affected the Home Front in the whole of Trondelag: and they proved to be much the most dangerous of the Norwegian traitors who helped the Gestapo. Grande was successfully 'liquidated' at Aalesund in December 1943,[1] and the value of the gang to the enemy declined as its methods became notorious: but Rinnan and his accomplices remained active to the end, and the Trondelag was never a good area for the Home Front.

Further north conditions were even more difficult. The Norwegian population was scanty, internal communications were limited and offered few alternatives, and the Germans were thick on the ground. Communications with the rest of Norway were very poor, and it was probably easier to get access from Britain or from Sweden than from the south. Not that these were easy alternatives: Swedish co-operation was doled out meanly, and from the west the range of action was so great that sea operations presented serious difficulties and air operations were practically out of the question.

Nevertheless the whole area was of great strategic interest and could not be left untried. The 'waist' of Norway, north of Trondelag, was a bottleneck in all land communications: beyond it lay Narvik and its ore, countless fjords in which German ships could lie concealed, and the base area of General Dietl* and his Alpine troops facing the Russians in North Finland. The first attempt had been 'Archer' and 'Heron' in the winter of 1941–2. This had begun badly: there were dissensions among the original party which arrived on 17th December 1941, and stores and reinforcements were slow to arrive. Sjøberg, the leader, did not reach the Mosjøen area until 15th April 1942: but he then did wonderful work under extreme difficulties in building up a local organisation, assisted by three men of the Linge Company. It was largely by ill-luck that this development was broken by the shooting affray at Majavatn in September: five of the party escaped to Sweden, four to England, and Sjøberg was left to face the winter with a much reduced force. Ill-luck continued to pursue him: it was a winter of storms, and also of increased enemy vigilance – two of SOE's boats were lost in attempting to supply Sjøberg's party – and there was a sickening period of hope deferred. In the end Sjøberg's men could face no more and withdrew to Sweden: he himself remained,

---

1 SOE Norwegian History, p. 212.

* [E. Dietl, 1890–1944, commanded mountain troops in Norway from 1940, killed in air crash.]

and was not evacuated until May 1943, when he was relieved by another party and was flown out by Catalina.

It will be convenient to complete the story of this unlucky area here. Sjøberg returned to the field in January 1944, and there was another period of promising development: he had fourteen men with him on the mainland and in the islands, and there were at one time three wireless stations on the air. But the enemy reacted strongly: Sjøberg was forced to keep on the move, and finally in May 1944, he was killed in a skirmish with a German patrol. All wireless touch was lost and most of his men withdrew to Sweden. This was further proof of the extreme difficulty of the area; London appreciated it well enough, but was reluctant to give up. One more attempt was made in October 1944, interesting because it was led by a British officer, Major J. C. Adamson, and included two other Englishmen – almost the only British sent by SOE into Norway during the occupation. Ill-luck followed these plans to the end: the aircraft missed the reception committee, the drop was visible to the enemy and Major Adamson injured a foot on landing. The rest of the party had no choice but to escape into Sweden at once: Adamson was captured, but he was in uniform and by luck and bluff was able to secure treatment as an ordinary prisoner of war.

We have seen that a plan for a coup de main at Sulitjelma in February 1943 led only to the loss of the Norwegian submarine 'Uredd' with all hands.[1] Two successful landings were made from fishing-vessels in the Lofotens, in December 1942 and January 1943 – almost a Viking voyage from the Shetland base – but the two agents (first-rate men) returned convinced that the area was too cramped and too full of Germans for any useful work to be possible. Finally an attempt was made even further north, beyond Tromsø, in March 1943. A reception party should have gone in from Sweden, but this plan broke down: and the fishing-vessel 'Brattholm' sailed from England unsupported. Her immense voyage was successfully accomplished: but she ran foul of a German patrol boat and the whole party were lost, except for one man who escaped on ski to Sweden – he lost all nine toes from frostbite and survived only by an astonishing display of resolution.

There is little more to tell regarding Northern Norway. The Russians seem to have done little, and that little incompetently. OSS, when it came into the combine for special operations in Norway, had big ideas of using its 'Special Operational Groups' of Norwegian-Americans for guerilla operations in this area: but the problem was too big even for American resources, and in the end only one party was sent to

---

[1] Above p. 656.

North Trondelag, in March 1945. It achieved little but at least involved no new disaster. One cannot see that any real possibility had been left untried: technically the only key to the situation was the free and full use of Swedish territory, and this was denied almost to the end.[1]

(e) Review

The operational season of 1942–3 included many losses that seemed at the time disastrous: but seen as a whole and in perspective, it was a season of great progress. Effective collaboration had been established with the Home Front in Norway, and the Home Front had proved to be politically solid and mature, and technically hardbitten. In London the Anglo-Norwegian Collaboration Committee was working well, and the Americans had fitted comfortably into the existing picture.[2] The triumvirate of Colonel Øen (Norwegian), Colonel Wilson (British) and Commander Vetlesen (American) was firmly united in personal friendship and in agreement on main principles, which held through all the strains of hope and disappointment. In the field there had been successes in the war of sabotage, which had been recognised generously in the highest quarters: there had also been a valuable broadening of the working channels of communication and supply. The number of wireless sets in touch was never stable for long, but in August 1943 there were eleven (as against six in the summer of 1942) and they covered Norway pretty thoroughly, from the Mosjøen area of Nordland to the south.[3]

The black spot was that the days of the Shetland fishing-vessels were clearly numbered: there had been only twenty-three successes in forty sailings, less than in 1941–2, and six boats had been lost with thirty men. The volunteer crews refused to go on at such a casualty rate, and Headquarters were convinced that they were right. This was to some extent balanced by an improvement in the air: nine successful operations had landed twenty-eight men, and there had been four successful supply operations – a great advance on 1941–2, and a further advance could be hoped for. But in Norwegian conditions of weather and terrain air supply could never be the complete answer: there were hardly more than three or four nights a month on the average when conditions made operations possible, and abortive sorties were very numerous.

2. The Season of 1943–4

As usual, the summer was a lull for London, if not for the Home Front, and a lull was essential both for planning and for technical

---

1   See the account of the 'Sepals' bases, below p. 673.
2   Papers on the agreement with OSS are on SOE Archives File 6/470: see also COS papers and Minutes in March 1943, when it was formally approved.
3   SOE Norwegian History, p. 130.

preparation. The new plan was governed in the first instance by the COS directive for 1943,[1] which gave relatively low priority to Norway, but called for continued industrial sabotage and for minor guerilla operations intended to increase the enemy's security commitment. Other factors emerged more clearly during the summer.

It was now perfectly plain that Norway would not be the object of an Allied invasion, as had been almost momentarily expected in the winter of 1941–2: that notion had been put out of count by the success of 'Torch', and it was clear that the problem of Milorg would be different from that originally envisaged – less bold and perhaps more difficult. It was not likely to be called out for a desperate offensive in support of an Allied army, but nevertheless it must remain in being: it would certainly be indispensable in the event of a German surrender, and there were numerous contingencies short of that in which it would be needed. It had therefore to tread a very narrow line. It must organise, train and supply itself: it must provide enough action for its troops to maintain morale: but it must risk nothing which could destroy its own cadres or involve heavy loss of Norwegian life. In February 1943 Quisling had introduced conscription of labour in Norway, to help to meet the insatiable German demand for manpower. Elsewhere this pushed Resistance forward – in France or Italy for instance: but in Norway there was very little chance of an organised Maquis in the hills – conditions were too hard and the population too small. There was thus some danger that labour conscription would work, and there is no doubt that its partial success was having a depressing effect on Norwegian spirits. Here was one target to be attacked: the 'paperasserie' of the call-up was complicated and vulnerable. It suggested also how much there was to be done on the technical side of political warfare; SOE could do much to supply the clandestine press and to send PWE-trained men in to help it in supporting Norwegian morale.

No. 14 Commando in the Shetlands had been disbanded in March 1943, and the policy of major raids was at an end. But there was still industrial sabotage suitable for small parties: there was a chance that action against railways would be needed to check German reinforcements moving to resist an Allied invasion of France; and above all there was shipping, which eventually became the chief target for the season. Various factors conspired towards this: there were MEW reports of the German shipping bottleneck:[2] there was an increase in the number of MTBs available under ACOS in the Shetlands: there were two devices, the 'Welman' one-man submarine and the special

---

1   COS(43)142(0) of 20th March, paras 30–31.
2   Cf. para. 12(a) of COS(43)142(0) (SOE Directive for 1943).

kayak, which SOE's research department was just bringing to fruition: last but not least, there was the dazzling success of Max Manus and Gregers Gram in the Oslofjord in April 1943.

Some of these factors became plainer as the season advanced, but they went with many others of lesser importance to make up the comprehensive joint directive submitted by Colonel Wilson on 23rd June,[1] which stands up well even in the cold light of later experience.

The first problem however was to find some replacement for the Shetland fleet of fishing-boats. The resources of the Royal Navy were turned inside out to no effect: nothing could be spared which was small enough as well as fast and seaworthy – and priority was high, as the Navy itself was dependent on these communications for intelligence of vital importance. It was fortunate that Admiral Stark,* the US naval representative in London, was friendly, and that his influence (combined with that of OSS, ETOUSA, and Norwegian-American opinion) was strong enough to extract three submarine-chasers from the US Navy. It can be said without irony that this was practically all that the USA contributed to subversive war in Norway, but it was an immense contribution. The three boats were delivered on the appointed date, 6th October 1943 – a miracle in itself at that stage of the war: the Norwegian fishermen of the Shetland fleet began to take over on 13th October, and they were almost in sole charge by the 28th: on 17th November the first sea operation of the season was sailed. The ships became the 'Hessa', 'Hitra' and 'Vigra' of the Royal Norwegian Navy: they proved ideal for their purpose – well-armed, fast, seaworthy and quiet – and they ran uninterrupted by the enemy to the end of the war. The figures of their two seasons are worth giving:[2]

Operations	109
Unsuccessful	15
Agents landed	135
Agents picked up	46
Refugees evacuated	243
Stores landed	157 tons

These are large figures for Norway, and may be set against the aircraft figures for the same two seasons, a time when aircraft were relatively plentiful:

---

1   Copy on SOE Archives File 6/470. Briefer indication at p. 123 of SOE Norwegian History.
2   SOE Norwegian History, Appendix L.
*   [H. A. Stark, 1880–1972, US chief of naval operations 1939–41, Roosevelt's naval representative in London 1942–5.]

Sorties successful	696
Agents landed	171
Containers dropped	9,537
Packages dropped	2,717

Twenty-five British and five American aircraft were lost. The two methods were complementary and the air was not able in this case effectively to replace the sea: in particular no tolerable ground for landing operations was ever found in Norway, and (apart for very rare flying-boat operations) the sea remained the only means of bringing men out to the United Kingdom without the tedious delays of passage through Sweden. Much time and many lives were thus saved.

In describing operations, pride of place must necessarily go to the plan for shipping attacks: it was largely unsuccessful, but it was ambitiously conceived and absorbed much capital for a very small dividend. The general conception was that shipping in harbour and in the inner leads should be harassed by raiding parties of various types and driven into more open waters where they could be reached by the MTBs of ACOS. SOE's interest in the raiding took three slightly different forms:

(a) Attacks by men of the Linge Company in special kayaks, developed for them by SOE ('Vestige').

(b) Attacks by 'Welmans', the one-man submarines developed by SOE, which were to be manned partly by the Navy and partly by SOE ('Barbara').

(c) 'Chariot' operations by the Navy, with SOE's co-operation on shore.

All these operations were under the general direction of ACOS.

The 'Vestige' parties fall into two series. Vestige I, II and III were landed by naval MTBs early in September, and had better hunting than any of the later parties. Vestige II at Askevold achieved nothing, but Vestige I limpeted a 2,700-ton ship in Nord Gulenfjord and Vestige III a ship of 6,600 tons in Aalesund harbour: unluckily both ships were beached before they could sink. All three parties were successfully evacuated. After these partial successes, weather proved too much for further landings from MTBs, and it was not till March 1944 that operations were resumed with SOE's sub-chasers and from aircraft. The list is as follows:

5th March	Vestige IV	by sub-chaser for Egersund
16th March	Vestige XII	by sub-chaser for Malm
31st March	Vestige V	by sub-chaser for Sagvaag for Stord
31st March	Vestige XIV	by air for Fredrikstad
12th April	Vestige VIII	by sub-chaser for the Sørdefjord.

Not one of these parties had any chance to make a successful attack, though all were in the end successfully withdrawn.

These were all that went into action out of many 'Vestige' plans: similarly only one 'Welman' operation was actually carried out. Four Welmans, with two British and two Norwegian drivers, were successfully launched from MTBs on 20th November to attack shipping in Bergen Harbour: they had penetrated well into the inner leads when the leading craft fouled an underwater obstruction and had to surface. Its Norwegian driver was captured and was lucky enough to be treated as a British naval POW: the three others escaped (after sinking their 'Welmans') into the protection of the Home Front, and were eventually evacuated by MTB some six weeks later.

It is understood that the various projects for naval 'chariot' operations were equally unsuccessful, and the total score remained that secured by Vestige I and III in September. This was partly due to foul weather: but this is scarcely an unusual phenomenon off Western Norway in the winter, and the plan seems to have been in some other way misconceived. Most careful preparation and great technical resources had produced less valuable results than were secured 'on a shoe-string' by Max Manus and others, both earlier and later. It is probable that the best conditions for this form of coup can be found only by a party which is in a position to wait and watch almost endlessly, until it knows each shift of enemy plans by instinct and can instantly discern the false move which will give the opening. Such a party can be immensely helped by the right kind of special equipment, but its time and knowledge are irreplaceable.

Apart from these shipping operations, outside sabotage was on the wane. There was a good operation on 21st November 1943, which blew the transformers of an important silicon carbide works at Arendal. There were two splended attacks on Orkla, already mentioned.[1] There were also preparations for railway sabotage to assist 'Overlord', which were never called into action.[2] Four parties were specially trained, and were got to the field with great difficulty, two of them in October 1943 and two in March and April 1944, in position to cover the two railways from Trondheim to Oslo and the branch line to Andalsnes. As the Norwegian History records: 'the parties had to be kept on ice – literally so to a certain extent', and when railway attacks were ultimately called for early in 1945 they were executed mainly by Milorg, which was then well placed to do so. But the relation of the plan to general strategy was sound, and it cannot be written off as useless because it was never used.

One reason for this comparative lack of operations was the demands made by the shipping plan: another was the emergence of an effective striking arm of Milorg, reinforced by men of the Linge Company

---

[1]   Above p. 655.
[2]   SOE Norwegian History, Appendix G.

working closely with it. This was not limited to Oslo, but its classic instance is 'Noric (Oslo)', (the Norwegian Independent Company (Oslo)) which had some reason to think itself the best team of saboteurs in Europe. 'Apollo's' gang in the Piraeus were perhaps its closest rivals.

Noric (Oslo) emerged almost unnoticed in the winter of 1943–4: its existence was no part of any London plan, and it was probably not planned by Milorg either, at least in the form which it finally took. Its members were SOE men of the Linge Company, who had gone in primarily for other purposes, and had come together in Oslo. In November 1943 there returned to Oslo Knut Haugland (formerly of the 'Swallow' party at Vemork)[1] and Gunnar Sønsteby* (known usually as 'Erling Fjeld'), who had been in control of courier routes to Sweden on behalf of Milorg. Haugland was intended to act as wireless expert to the central leadership of Milorg, Sønsteby as an expert on courier routes and general 'factotum' in Oslo. Max Manus and Gregers Gram were already there, as they had returned in October: while in England they had been through the Hackett school of Political Warfare,[2] and they were now enthusiasts for propaganda. Their primary mission was to assist Norwegian propaganda, in particular in attacking German morale: but they could not be prevented from laying their own plans for further attacks on shipping – they were not men upon whom the sound theoretical principle of a limited mission could be enforced.

This formed the nucleus, and it is probable that what first brought them together with others into a striking force was the need for some brisk reaction to the Quisling programme of labour mobilisation. This had been attempted first in the spring of 1943, and had been partially blocked by passive resistance and by attacks on the labour exchanges in May of that year. In August 1943, there was an intensification of Quisling's programme of mobilisation and repression: the chief of the civil police in Oslo was executed for obstruction, the police and Quisling's Hird were put under military discipline, and an attempt was made to round up all officers of the Norwegian forces who had been left at liberty in 1940. These measures were met with well-organised counter-action, both by propaganda on the BBC and in the clandestine press, and by another series of concentrated attacks on the machinery of the call-up. This was co-ordinated all over Southern Norway, but Oslo was naturally of crucial importance and the men of the Linge Company were the best that Milorg had available there. Led by Sønsteby, these two parties (with two men who had carried

---

[1]   Above p. 654.
[2]   Above p. 370.
*   [See his *Report From No. 24* (1967).]

out the brilliant attack at Arendal in November)[1] began a series of raids and hold-ups directed at the labour mobilisation mechanism in Oslo: card indexes were stolen and destroyed, offices were bombed, the only card-sorting machine in Oslo was blown up. These attacks were greatly helped both by the passive co-operation of the vast majority of the population and by the active aid of volunteers from Milorg: but the inspiration came from Sønsteby and Noric (Oslo), which could never count on more than eleven Linge Company men in all, of whom two were lost in November 1944. They lived and fought in daily presence of the enemy for over eighteen months – Felmer, the head of the Oslo Gestapo, was to be seen daily going about his business, and his HQ and torture-chambers at Viktoria Terrasse were a familiar landmark: in these conditions the ceaseless freshness, ingenuity, even impudence of their methods is almost more impressive than their physical and moral toughness.

During this winter of 1943–4 their main concerted action was against labour mobilisation, and this could be reckoned by the spring of 1944 to have blocked the German programme effectively: not only by physical destruction of records, but by the continuous inspiration which they gave to the 'little man' to obstruct quietly in his own way.

But Manus and Gram also pursued their private war on shipping. In February 1944 they attacked and sank a newly launched patrol vessel of 500 tons in Oslo harbour. In June they succeeded in slipping down into the space below one of the Oslo quays, where they lived for three days among the rats, awaiting the arrival of the 18,000-ton troopship 'Monte Rosa'. Seven limpets were successfully fixed, almost under the eyes of the German guards: but there was again a technical failure – slight damage may have been done, but it did not delay the ship for long. Meantime they had been working with local help on the development of a home-made portable torpedo: a very well-conceived device for attacks on shipping in narrow waters. With this they paddled out and attacked a German destroyer in the Oslofjord in August, and did quite serious damage. Manus has recorded his indignation that the research resources of London were not turned on to developing this torpedo in proper technical form, and one is bound to feel some sympathy with him: it was a device which could do far more to reduce the strain on the attacker than one-man submarines, submersible canoes, 'Frog-men' suits and other such desperate inventions. The faithful partnership was broken in November 1944: Gram and Tallaksen (also of Noric (Oslo)) were led into a trap baited by the hope of contacting a German who would help them to subvert German troops. Gram was killed on the spot, Tallaksen died in prison: Manus was then in Stockholm, but he returned bent on revenge. His

---

[1]   Above p. 664.

last and best attack was carried out in January 1945, with one locally-enlisted helper: once again he walked through the German sentry-posts in Oslo harbour and attacked with limpets in the full glare of search-lights. His chief victim was the 'Donau', a troopship of 9,000 tons, which sank fully laden in Oslofjord next day: she was beached with only her bows above water, and all the military equipment was lost, probably with considerable casualties to the men and horses on board. There was one limpet to spare, and with it the 'Rolandseck' (1,800 tons) was successfully attacked, though it proved possible to beach her.

We must revert later to other Oslo exploits of 1944–5: in 1943–4 quiet organisation was almost as important as sabotage, but it is not easy to record except in bare figures. There had been eleven wireless stations in August 1943, at the end of May 1944 there were twenty-six:[1] the figure for messages received went up from nine in August 1943 to 249 in May 1944.[2] There were still fluctuations and losses, but the trend was steadily in one direction; what had been an impossible risk was becoming a system.

Another new factor of importance was that the Swedes at last began to pluck up courage a little. In August 1943 they made heavy cuts in German transport of troops and war material across Sweden to Norway: the strict law of neutrality was not yet in force, but at least there had been a gesture of resistance which had produced no answer. Almost at the same time there first arose the project of raising and training a small force of Norwegian police in Sweden. There were plenty of Norwegians there, and the quickest way into Norway was from Sweden: it would be valuable to have a disciplined force which could move fast in the event of German collapse. The project was not without its political difficulties – such as a tendency for Stockholm to emerge as a Norwegian centre competing with London: unrest among the police troops in training: Russian suspicion that they were intended primarily as an insurance against Communism. But the gain from the improvement in the Swedish attitude was immense: and it was also important that the air service from Scotland to Stockholm at last began to improve substantially, and that a new OSS/SOE Mission reached Sweden in October 1943. This 'Westfield' Mission was concerned primarily with Germany, and its sphere in Norway was limited to the north: but the added manpower (especially on the signals side) was a great asset to SOE in Stockholm, which had hitherto been continually cramped by the attentions of the Swedish police.

---

[1] SOE Norwegian History, p. 173. Appendix M gives chart of W/T stations 1941–5.
[2] SOE Norwegian History, Appendix M.

3. The Last Season

The summer of 1944 was not a complete blank for operations, as that energetic Norwegian-American, Colonel Balchen, carried out a few dropping operations in the north in daylight, with the American Liberators which he was operating on the civil air route to Stockholm. But this hardly interrupted the rhythm of summer and winter which was so marked a feature of work into Norway: the new season was again a new problem. 1942–3 had set going a new system of collaboration: 1943–4 had seen it in working order, with steady progress through success and failure: it was clear that 1944–5 would be the final crisis.

Once the Normandy landings had succeeded, it was certain that Germany was beaten: it was also certain that there would be no Allied frontal attack on Norway. A complete German withdrawal from Norway was unlikely, and perhaps impracticable. The main contingencies to be faced were therefore *either* a German surrender including Norway *or* a last German stand in a northern bastion after Germany had fallen. There was some evidence of the existence of this latter plan apart from the emphasis placed on it in German propaganda: it is improbable that it could ever have been executed in the literal sense, as Norway in summer lies open on the Swedish side, and even though (as Colonel Wilson puts it) 'the Swedes were Swedes to the end' they could scarcely have refused to permit Allied action from their territory once the German Reich had fallen. But it was more than probable that desperate elements in the German forces would attempt to stage local 'Götterdämmerungs' for themselves, with results that might impoverish the Norwegian people for a generation. An Allied expedition could not be kept fully mounted in readiness, and Allied troops would therefore not be available except in small numbers for at least a month – perhaps longer. Meantime Milorg would be left to face the Germans: it proved ultimately that there were 365,500 Germans in Norway at the time of surrender, as well as 85,000 Russian prisoners brutalised by starvation, while Milorg's full mobilisable strength was 40,000 men, a quarter of them still unarmed, and the rest with light weapons only. The main problem was therefore one of defence; and Milorg could fairly be called on for offensive action only in so far as it did not grossly prejudice its ultimate role.

Here as elsewhere SOE's organisation was radically modified for the last phase of the war. The Norwegian Section (like the rest of SOE's organisation for Western Europe) came within Special Forces HQ when it was constituted under SHAEF on 1st May 1944. The congestion which this caused in the old offices made it possible for Colonel Wilson to move his section out to new quarters in Oxford Square in July 1944. It had not hitherto been possible for the British,

Americans and Norwegians to work together under one roof without creating awkward precedents for other Allies, and the only common meeting place had been the Section's flats in Chiltern Court, which were fantastically inconvenient. This difficulty now disappeared. The main channel of military liaison was not with SHAEF itself, but with General Sir Andrew Thorne* at Scottish Command, who was responsible under SHAEF for planning Allied action in Norway as commander of Force 134 – 'Allied Land Forces Norway'. Lieutenant Colonel C. S. Hampton, who had been in command of the Norwegian schools in the Cairngorms, was appointed Liaison Officer at Scottish Command, and he was also to command the Special Force detachments which would go in with Force 134.[1]

These were integrated British and American parties, conceived on a model now well-tried in other theatres: there were five main parties (in addition to Lieutenant Colonel Hampton's HQ party for Oslo) intended for Eastern Norway, Trondheim, Bergen, Stavanger and Kristiansand (S), each with a Norwegian liaison officer: three other detachments were added later to work with the Police Battalions moving from Sweden into Oslo, Trondheim and Narvik.

Liaison with the Home Front was also drawn closer. Communication by radio and by courier through Stockholm was now regular and rarely interrupted: in addition it had become relatively easy to make personal contact. Colonel Øen was in Sweden in March 1944 to meet representatives of the Central Leadership: in August Jens Christian Hauge,[2] the young lawyer who had risen to the head of Milorg, was in London for consultations, and he returned again to England in November, with Sønsteby of Noric (Oslo). Finally Colonel Øen was in Stockholm for a long visit in the spring of 1945. This cooperation was clinched by the appointment in July 1944 of Crown Prince Olav** as C-in-C of all Norwegian forces: he had since April 1943 been chief of the Norwegian Military Mission with SHAEF (then Cossac),[3] and his new appointment (apart from its personal merits) had the great political advantage that it set on one side all questions of relative rank and prestige between Norwegian forces inside and outside Norway.

The plan for the last season is not to be found in any single docu-

---

[1] Details of the SF Detachment can be read in Appendix P to SOE Norwegian History.
[2] Later Defence Minister.
[3] COS(43)90th Mtg, Item 7, of 12th April.
* [Sir A. Thorne, 1885–1970, Military Attaché in Berlin 1932–5, C-in-C Scottish Comand 1941–5, knight 1942. See his son Sir Peter's article in *Intelligence and National Security*, vii, pp. 300–16 (July 1992).]
** [Born 1903, succeeded Haakon VII as King of Norway 1957.]

ment: it was worked out with immense elaboration, but its authority came either from its incorporation in the general 'Apostle' plans for the reoccupation of Norway, or from SHAEF directives calling for special action to meet changing situations. Its basic purpose was defensive, but it will be convenient first to deal with its less important offensive side, as the other leads directly on to the final solution of May 1945.

(a) Offensive Action 1944–5

There was only one series of operations from outside in the old style, those inspired by the 'Sleeping Beauty', the submersible motor-canoe which had been developed by SOE to meet a CCO requirement laid down as early as 1942. This was a beautiful piece of equipment, but the 'Salamander' series of operations which used it had no more luck than 'Vestige' and 'Barbara' in 1943–4, and for similar reasons. Two operations only were sailed, both in September 1944, one against Maaløy, the other against the Trondheimfjord, and both went wrong through local accidents which could not have been foreseen in England. Later in the season the water was too cold for further attempts, and the equipment was not used again.

As regards internal operations, the old position was to some extent reversed. London gave the highest priority to maintaining Milorg intact; the leadership at home agreed warmly in principle, but was anxious about the morale of its men, who had waited so long in tedious (and often dangerous) inaction. The Norwegians pressed for active directives, and executed them with alacrity.

The biggest programme from the strategic aspect was the attack on U-boat activities, which were still potentially a serious danger to the Allies. The U-boats themselves were inaccessible, but their supplies, in particular their oil, were vulnerable. The campaign opened in August 1944 with a magnificent attack on the oil storage at Soon on the Oslofjord which disposed of 700 tons of gas oil and 4,000 tons of diesel oil, and it was followed up intensively in the next two months. It is difficult to give a picture by adding totals, and none of the other successes were on the same gigantic scale: but from August to October 1944 there were twenty successful attacks involving millions of litres of oil of different types.[1] The tempo then slackened a little, but from the beginning of November 1944 to the end there were nine more successful attacks, including one by Noric (Oslo) which destroyed 360,000 litres in the Shell Oil storage there. This was one type of steady pressure: there was equal merit in a single-handed attack by a man employed at the Horten Torpedo Store. A fuse was set with twenty-four hours' delay: after twenty-eight hours it acted, and blew

---

1   SOE Norwegian History, Appendix J.

up 184 torpedo war heads and 53 tons of charges as well as stores, barracks and workshops and sundry Germans. This was carried out in January 1945: when hostilities ended the Germans had only five live torpedoes left in south-east Norway.

Another strategic action of importance was the attack on ball-bearings, which had for so long been a favourite 'bottleneck' of the Ministry of Economic Warfare, and a constant target for bombers and for pre-emptive purchase in Sweden. This campaign had passed its prime late in 1944, when a report was received that the Germans were calling for the collection and dispatch to Germany of all stocks of ball-bearings in Norway. Milorg was asked to take action, and in three coups it destroyed all stocks of SKF ball-bearings of which it had knowledge in Norway.

The question of railway transport was also of strategic importance. Milorg was very ready to attack it, but SHAEF was at first disinclined to take any risks for the sake of delaying German withdrawals which might in the end be to the Allied advantage when the time came to reoccupy Norway. Rather reluctantly it gave its consent on 26th October 1944[1] to limited attacks designed primarily to raise Norwegian morale. This meant the resurrection of the plans laid before D-day and abandoned,[2] and the training and dispatch of other special parties – three of these went in the autumn of 1944 and three in March 1945.[3] This time the preparations dovetailed perfectly with strategic needs. The stalemate of the winter changed SHAEF's views about the desirability of German withdrawals from Norway to reinforce the Rhine, and on 5th December a new directive called for 'maximum railway and road sabotage consistent with the maintenance of Norwegian Resistance at sufficient strength for its primary military role'.[4] The campaign began at once and continued to the end: from December to April there were forty-two major attacks thought to be worthy of report, as well as a great deal of lesser sabotage. Mention should be made particularly of the big co-ordinated attack on railways made by well over 1,000 men all over Southern Norway on 14th March; and of the destruction by Noric (Oslo) of the German railway administration's offices in Oslo. SHAEF's estimate was that the Norwegian and Danish sabotage campaigns together reduced the rate of movement from four divisions to less than one division a month,[5] an important result to which Norway contributed its fair share.

---

1   SHAEF/17240/4/Ops(C) – 26.10.42; copy on SOE Archives File – 'AD/E Norway'.
2   Above p. 664.
3   SOE Norwegian History, Appendix G.
4   SOE Norwegian History, p. 208.
5   SOE Norwegian History, Appendix G, p. 4.

On the shipping side the greatest event (apart from Manus's activities)[1] was a coup executed in November 1944 by the shipyard workers in Oslo without reference either to London or to Milorg, in which there were blown up or otherwise damaged six vessels with a total displacement of 35,000 tons.

The best aircraft attack destroyed twenty-eight Messerschmitt fuselages and 150 aero engines in Oslo in August 1944, and there were other attacks on small aircraft repair-shops and stores.

And besides these strategic targets given by the Allied High Command, there was a continual series of attacks on industrial plants, military stores, administrative buildings – targets mainly chosen by Milorg itself – which show that the situation was for the Germans entirely out of hand. The Gestapo could still choose what innocent victims it pleased, and its brutality was unabated, but it was quite powerless to break the Norwegian organisation. At one time for instance it had Jens Christian Hauge and his Chief of Staff under arrest for thirty-six hours and let them go without guessing who they were. It is not known why it did not resort to mass reprisals, which were the only form of counter-action which could have had any effect: but it is possible to guess at the motives which moved German minds at this late stage of the war.

One final set-piece in conclusion. On 2nd May 1945, when the end was in sight, Sønsteby and four men disguised as policemen made their way into the Ministry of Justice and Police: a lorry and six other men drove into the courtyard: quietly and in good order some two tons of documents and a large iron safe were removed from the records of Quisling's Security Police and some half a ton of documents from the Ministry of Justice archives. The party then drove off, laden with evidence for later use.

(b) The Defensive

In the event of desperate German resistance there would be little that Milorg could do, except to protect Norwegian resources so far as possible, and to keep itself in being until the Allied invasion was ready. But there was a good deal which could be prepared in advance even for the worst contingency, and such preparations would be equally valuable if (as was more likely) German violence was only sporadic and unco-ordinated.

The main thing was to develop and sustain Milorg itself by improving communications and supplying arms. The number of radio sets on the air went up to forty-three in January 1945, and to sixty-nine on VE-day – although in March the Gestapo were assuring their superiors that the Home Front was out of touch with London. The air and

---

[1]   Above p. 666.

sea transport situation was satisfactory, and stores went in almost as fast as they could be absorbed: by the end there were light arms available for some 30,000 men.

The ordinary Milorg regional and district organisation remained, and there was only one new development of interest, the plan for 'Milorg bases':[1] mountain areas where fairly large bodies of men could be maintained and supplied, on the analogy of the 'Maquis' areas which had arisen elsewhere. Fugitives from labour mobilisation would probably be available to man them, and their advantages were obvious enough: there was of course the great danger of useless clashes with the Germans, which had led to such painful losses for the guerillas in France and Italy, and there was also the special problem of the Norwegian winter. Out of six bases planned in August 1944 there came into existence 'Elg' some 100 km north-west of Oslo, 'Varg' in the Setersdal mountains of the south-west, and 'Bjørn West' some 120 kms north of Bergen. Special parties were dropped to form them, and men began to gather during the winter: unfortunately Arctic clothing ordered from America did not come through in time. The ultimate strength of the bases seems to have been of the order of 500-600 in 'Elg', 150 each in 'Varg' and 'Bjørn West'. Fortunately none of the possible disasters took place: there were some brushes with German troops but no military pedant emerged to organise a regular defence – the Norwegians dispersed temporarily and little harm was done. When the surrender came, the bases were a useful source of trained and disciplined men, with some stocks of arms beyond their own needs: they might have been much more important in the event of enemy resistance.

Another new move of a somewhat similar character was made possible by increased Swedish co-operation. This was the 'Sepals' plan for the establishment of frontier bases on Swedish territory in the far north, manned partly by the Linge Company and partly by Norwegians recruited in Sweden. Two of these were formed in August 1944, one on the borders of Finnmark, the other on the approaches to Narvik, and a third was added in March 1945 on the borders of Nordland rather further south. Their terms of reference were pretty wide – reconnaissance, raiding, assistance to refugees – and they were active while the war lasted in many minor ways, in spite of the intense difficulties of the climate and the country. But, as matters turned out, their greatest value was when the collapse came; it was most useful then to have on the spot a small force of trained men in wireless contact with HQ.

The most comprehensive new plan of all was for the protection of

---

[1] SOE Norwegian History, Appendix N.

the Norwegian economy against scorching by the Germans.[1] After detailed study the field was in the end divided into six parts:

'Sunshine':   the protection of all objectives in the vital area of water-power and industry in Upper Telemark.
'Polar Bear':   the protection of harbours.
'Foscott':   the protection of the system of electric power.
'Carmarthen':   second priority objectives for protection by Milorg.
'Catterick':   second priority objectives for protection by workers inside the factories.
'Antipodes':   the protection of the vital road and rail communications by which the Norwegian Police Battalions were expected to arrive from Sweden.

Of these 'Carmarthen' and 'Catterick' need not be followed further, as their execution was purely a matter of local initiative. 'Foscott' also was mainly a matter for local forces, but its priority was very high: the essential objectives were carefully analysed and passed down to the localities, plans were called for in some detail, and in many cases Linge Company men were available to train local parties in special methods and to lead them in action. 'Antipodes' was mounted from Sweden at the last minute amid the usual Swedish delays, and the parties meant for it arrived in Norway very late, though in time for the Armistice.

'Sunshine' and 'Polar Bear' deserve a little more description.

The 'Sunshine' party was inspired, thought out and directed by Professor Lief Tronstad* of the Technical College in Trondheim, who had since his arrival in England in 1942 been a very good friend of SOE and an unrivalled source of information on all technical matters, above all on the installations in the Rjukan area which meant so much to the atomic war. He insisted on leading the party himself, and went in by air early in October 1944 with a party of eight, including one British RE officer. They were met by Einar Skinnarland, the doyen of all SOE agents in Telemark, and four other men of the old 'Gunnerside' party also joined them. Their plans went forward very smoothly, and they were confident that with the collaboration of their friends inside they could stop all demolitions, wipe out the local garrisons, and hold the few lines of access for some time against anything but a major counter-attack. It was one of Norway's most serious losses that Professor Tronstad was killed in March 1945: he and one other man had captured and were interrogating the Quisling sheriff of the area, when they were surprised in a lonely hut and shot down by the sheriff's brother. This disaster did not damage the organisation, which went forward as planned: but Tronstad as a technician and as a leader was irreplaceable.

---

[1]   SOE Norwegian History, Appendix O.
*   [Born 1904.]

'Polar Bear' was approved in September 1944, and comprised ten parties, designed to cover all important harbours from Narvik to the Swedish frontier.[1] The plan was that one or two Norwegian naval officers or warrant officers for each port should be given training in German demolition methods, and should be sent in during the winter to organise 'port defence groups' in co-operation with the local leaders of Milorg. Such groups could not be expected to block demolition plans executed at leisure and covered by German regular troops in force: but experience at Antwerp had shown how valuable an 'anti-scorch' plan could be if events went favourably for it, and protection of the ports would be of crucial importance both to Allied military plans and to the future of Norway. Parties were successfully introduced at all the chosen ports except Aalesund and Stavanger; they were not tested in their primary role, but when 'the day' came they were able to emerge at once and take over control of the harbours in good order. Only at Fredrikstad, at the mouth of the Oslo Fjord near the Swedish frontier, was it possible to take overt action before the capitulation: in February 1945 the very enterprising 'Polar Bear' leader there began to move tugs, pilots and potential blockships out of German control into Swedish waters, and before the capitulation he had pretty effectively stopped German navigation of the difficult waters round Fredrikstad.

(c) The Armistice

When the Armistice came on 6th May it was still far from clear what would happen in Norway, and in the confusion of the last few days the Allied High Command had not seen clearly enough to give precise orders to Milorg. It was by the Home Front's own decision that Milorg came into the open on the night of 6th/7th May: an act of great courage which was justified by events. The rank and file moved into position with admirable precision, and in Oslo and each of the important towns there were tense parleys – on one side the local Milorg commander with a tiny bodyguard, in some sort of makeshift uniform, on the other the appropriate high German officer, surrounded by the usual galaxy of staff officers and controlling large heavily-armed forces. The balance of forces was ludicrously disproportionate, but German respect for authority and discipline held good: local agreements were made promptly and were respected, and there was no bloodshed and no destruction.

The Norwegian Police Battalions in Sweden were set in motion on 7th May, accompanied by three of SOE's SF detachments: it was not until 8th May that official Allied representatives arrived, in the person of Brigadier Hilton, as General Thorne's personal representative, with

---

[1] SOE Norwegian History, Appendix O.

Lieutenant Colonel Hampton as his main channel of liaison with the Home Front. At this stage, and for several days more, the clandestine signals network was still of vital importance for all official business. The Airborne Division and the SAS began to arrive on 10th May, and with them the local SF detachments, which were in position by 11th May at Oslo, Trondheim, Bergen, Stavanger and Kristiansand (S): another detachment had already reached Narvik with the Norwegian police troops. Even in the peaceful conditions of surrender, the detachments were kept very busy, as the main channel between the local British commanders and the Home Front in the complicated and nerve-wracking business of disarming vastly superior German forces and shepherding them into concentration areas. When SOE's Norwegian organisation was wound up in June, the detachments were transferred to the establishment of Allied Land Forces, Norway.

4. Conclusion

Norwegian resistance had done substantial damage to the enemy with small resources and at no prohibitive cost in money or in lives: it had risen with perfect timing and discipline to take control of the defeated Germans before local disorders could develop: and, above all, it had given the Norwegians of the Home Front legitimate ground for pride in the part they had borne in the war. But the peculiar nature of its greatness is best indicated in a series of negatives.

It had *not* been rent by divisions between Left and Right, home and exile: its effort to arm itself had *not* degenerated into rival preparations for a political coup: it had *not* refused to accept sensible strategic direction from the Allies: it had *not* been trapped into 'playing soldiers' or challenging the Germans suicidally in the open: its discipline had held and it had *not* been seriously endangered by local factions disregarding the instructions of the Home Front command. Finally, it did *not* when peace came denounce British and American aid to resistance as senseless intrigue and the main cause of all political ills. When Crown Prince Olav reached Oslo on 15th May, Noric (Oslo) were allotted as his personal guard, with Max Manus as bodyguard: the whole Linge Company was in a place of honour the great day of King Haakon's return on 7th June, and Max Manus was again the personal bodyguard: Colonel Wilson and Colonel Vetlesen were honoured guests in the days of celebration which followed.

As the rest of this story has shown, resistance in Norway was remarkable for its boldness and ingenuity, but unique in its combination of solid common sense and political maturity. The Norwegian blend of free initiative and social solidarity rested on old factors with which SOE had nothing to do, and SOE can claim credit only for not mishandling it. But it is to be remembered that where such conditions exist the organisation of a subversive movement does not necessarily lead to an intensification of political rancour. The evil can flower only if the seeds are there: a campaign of subversion may fertilise, but it does not plant them.

CHAPTER XXVII

Denmark

At the beginning of 1943 SOE had only one agent of its own with a W/T set in Denmark, and there was in effect no central resistance organisation. The decisive time began in February 1943. Two successful sorties landed eight men with two wireless sets, and one of the men was Flemming Bruun Muus who was to be SOE's chief organiser in Denmark for the next eighteen months. He was a shrewd energetic businessman who had come from West Africa to volunteer: financially untrustworthy, as it proved, but a fine leader and a man of big ideas. He is entitled to an honourable place in the story, though his career ended in discredit. A little earlier the landowner Flemming Juncker (who had been one of Rottbøll's contacts in Jutland) came out to Stockholm, and returned to Denmark fully briefed on the reception of air operations. He was one of the first to meet Muus after his arrival. Finally SOE succeeded in sending in radio crystals and a signal plan to Duus Hansen (alias 'Napkin'), another of Rottbøll's discoveries, who was a fine radio mechanic and operator: he was able to set up and work his own wireless set, and trained a number of other operators whose work was judged to be excellent by the SOE home station. It was on this triangle of Muus, Juncker and 'Napkin' that SOE's first real progress in Denmark was based.

In March 1943 the Germans still thought highly enough of their 'model territory' to permit the Danes to hold a General Election relatively free from interference. The results were disappointing to the Germans, but not sensational: the old Social Democratic and Conservative parties held their ground, while the two small pro-Nazi parties lost votes to them and to the extreme anti-collaborationist 'Dansk Samling'. In April the sabotage campaign led by Muus's 'Table' organisation began to take effect: six major attacks were reported in April, eleven in May, three in June, eight in July.[1] Most of these were attacks by fire and explosives on shipyards and facto-

---

[1] These figures are taken from one set of SOE Reports, and indicate the trend. Other reports (as is to be expected) give other figures: and it is to be remembered that there were countless instances of *minor* sabotage, which were cumulatively of great political importance.

ries working for the Germans, but they included three or four good attacks on shipping. Their object however was political rather than military, and it was rapidly secured. In the first week of August the Germans demanded that Danish saboteurs should in future be tried by German courts under German law and should serve their sentences in Germany: the Scavenius Government refused and threatened to resign if pressed. Muus now reported to London that a continuation of sabotage would rapidly force the Germans to take over entire control: after discussion in high quarters in London,[1] he was ordered to go ahead.

The programme was faithfully fulfilled: German pressure on Scavenius increased, and late in August he placed his resignation in the hands of the King. The latter refused to accept it, and Denmark was thus left without a government: it was no surprise when on 29th August the Germans seized complete control. All Danish public offices passed into German hands, the Danish Army and Navy were disbanded, and many officers were arrested or fled to Sweden to escape arrest. There was little or no open resistance except by the Navy, which scuttled a number of its ships in harbour and brought one or two minor vessels over to Sweden.

Denmark was now by its own action brought within the ordinary scheme of German occupation, and there could no longer be any doubt as to the proper attitude of patriotic Danes: SOE's task thus became psychologically more straightforward, though it was complicated by the lack of any constitutional leadership of Danish resistance, either inside or outside Denmark. Resistance was still in effect led by SOE, though it encouraged Danish attempts to create a Danish leadership, and left the initiative so far as possible in Danish hands.

The most immediate practical effect was on the 'Princes' organisation of Army officers, with which SOE was in contact in Stockholm. Its main organisers had to flee in August 1943, and one of them was caught: but they left in charge of intelligence Lieutenant Svend Truelsen, a young lawyer and reserve officer, who proved to be a more efficient organiser than his superiors and soon worked up an absolutely first-rate intelligence network. This was not in theory a job for SOE, but the essential contacts had come through SOE and it was agreed that it should not be disturbed: SOE therefore acted as sole agent for SIS in Denmark – an arrangement which created a good deal of minor friction with the older organisation, which appears never to have acquiesced quite wholeheartedly. SOE acted also on behalf of MI9, and on the whole this pooling of resources justified itself: Denmark was far too small for three independent British networks to operate without confusion.

---

[1] This is second-hand information; there seem to be no contemporary papers directly relevant.

Sabotage continued in the autumn, hampered a little by the new German measures. In October the Germans undid most of their own work by attempting to deport all Danish Jews to Germany, not only exasperating the good Danish people but forcing an immense increase in the refugee traffic across the straits into Sweden. SOE's communications were made much easier by this mass movement. In addition, Danes began to accumulate in Sweden in considerable numbers and to create Danish institutions of some efficiency: a Danish refugee office, a press service, a Danish intelligence office, eventually an organisation for supervising the use of illegal routes into and out of Denmark. The Swedish Government co-operated (it will be remembered that in August 1943 it had begun to take a stiffer line with the Germans) or winked at co-operation by junior officials: and it agreed to the formation of Danish Police Battalions, on the same lines as those being prepared by the Norwegians.

But probably the most important event of this autumn was the emergence of the Freedom Council as a directing centre of resistance inside Denmark. It consisted at first of Professor Mogens Fog, an academic Communist, of two other Communists, of two representatives of minor anti-German organisations ('Ringen', and 'Dansk Samling') and of Muus as representative of SOE. It will be seen that the older and larger political parties, Conservative, Liberal and Social Democrat, were not represented, and that the Council had a little the look of a 'Popular Front' on Communist Party lines. It is true that SOE was directly represented, and that Muus had great influence in that he controlled the W/T link to London. In addition, SOE through Stockholm was at this time creating an independent organisation for financing resistance in Denmark:[1] patriotic Danes were induced to advance money to a 'Paymaster in the Field' against a British promise to repay in sterling, and the Paymaster passed funds to the active organisers on specific instructions from London given to him through his own wireless link. Even under this system a good deal of money adhered to various sticky fingers, including those of Muus himself: but it gave far better control than the old method, otherwise inevitable, of sending in agents with large sums in cash.

It was mentioned earlier that SOE had been suspicious from the first of the attitude of the Danish Army, lest its main object be to prepare for civil war against Communism after a German withdrawal. The next stage of SOE's plans, now that sabotage was well under way, was to organise a para-military movement capable of limited but specific action in support of the plans for invasion; doubts of the Army's intentions were still awake, and it seemed wisest to raise the new formations so far as possible outside its control. Muus was in

---

[1] SOE 'Danish History', Appendix VI.

London for a short visit in November 1943, as was Mr Turnbull, SOE's representative in Stockholm, and plans were then laid for the next phase.[1] This involved a temporary slackening in supplies for sabotage in the first part of 1944 in order to increase the delivery of arms: the building up of a military organisation would naturally lead to a growing use of military men, but control was not to pass into the hands of the Danish General Staff in exile. This was a rather precarious line to follow, but on the whole it worked out successfully: there was however friction, particularly in Jutland, between leaders of two different types, the cautious military man and the energetic and unorthodox civilian. Up till D-day in the West supply operations remained on a small scale, judged by military standards. From the beginning of 1943 until June 1944 there were only twenty-nine successful air operations in all, dropping twenty-eight men and 23 tons of stores: it was not until August 1944 that a successful rendezvous was made with a Danish fishing-boat at sea (which took in $6^{1}/_{2}$ tons on a single operation) and the traffic from Sweden, though continuous, was mainly in small items. It was reckoned that only 5,000 men had been armed and organised up to September 1944. Denmark's contribution to 'Overlord' could not therefore be very large, though sabotage was intensified in April and May and the Danish Resistance was used so far as possible to support the general deception plan: this meant inevitably some protests from the leaders in Denmark, who were called upon for action which did not seem to them to make sense, and which in fact did not make sense, as it belonged to a deception plan and not to a real operation.

The SOE Danish Section had from 1st May 1944 been integrated under SHAEF in SFHQ, like the rest of SOE's Western group: even earlier, in February, it had been linked closely with OSS, and an American of Danish birth, Major Winkelhorn, had joined it as Planning Officer. Danish nationals had been excluded from it on security grounds in the period before D-day: but in May and June, two very old and reliable friends, Flemming Juncker and Lieutenant Truelsen, had to quit Denmark in haste, and they joined SOE in London as fully responsible members of the Section.

In Denmark meantime developments proceeded to the accompaniment of continually growing sabotage and repression: the Danish attacks did not at this stage follow any master-plan, and it is difficult to single out special incidents or lines of development. Some figures from SOE's general 'game-book'[2] indicate the progression:

---

[1] These plans were not 'cleared' with the Freedom Council until the spring of 1944, and organisation then began in earnest.

[2] These are of course not *complete* figures.

January 1944	7 incidents
February	7 incidents
March	8 incidents
April	10 incidents
May	10 incidents
June	8 incidents

They included for instance several attacks on the big Burmeister & Wain shipyard in Copenhagen: attacks on radio and machine-tool factories: the sinking of three German naval auxiliaries with limpets: and in this phase there begin to be concerted coups on a fairly large scale by parties of ten, twenty, even fifty armed men.

The Gestapo was now active in Denmark on the usual lines, though in Denmark alone the Germans were checked by some obscure inhibition from using German troops in the policy of random reprisals and execution of hostages which was their first recourse against the Resistance elsewhere. In Denmark the policy of counter-terror was not abandoned, but was left at first mainly in the hands of various gangs of Danish criminals,[1] who were licensed to murder Danish citizens suspected of excessive patriotism (the dramatist Pastor Kai Munck for instance) and to loot and destroy property of value to the Danes. This was intended presumably to confuse Danish public opinion and to spread the belief that all saboteurs were tarred with the same brush – that they were merely criminals making a show of patriotism: but it was transparently ineffective and led only to further exasperation. The next stage was one of reckless German reprisals for an attack by eighty saboteurs on 22nd June on the Dansk Industri Syndikat in Copenhagen which was making guns for the Germans: this led to popular demonstrations, shooting in the streets, and ultimately to a spontaneous general strike in Copenhagen in the first week of July 1944. This was not instigated by the Freedom Council, but they put themselves at its head by demanding the lifting of the curfew and the withdrawal of the Schalburg Corps from the streets: the citizens stood together behind these demands and the Germans in the end gave way.

The Freedom Council was thus put in a position of clear national leadership, and its prestige stood very high. Partly as a direct consequence of this, partly as a result of the imminent collapse of Germany, its political position became more crucial and more controversial. Muus had gradually withdrawn from active work – he married his secretary about this time – and his role as 'SOE's man' was in effect taken over by a politically minded businessman named Dedichen and by a certain Lieutenant Eriksen who had become responsible for intel-

---

[1] These are casually referred to as the 'Schalburg Corps', though this was theoretically distinct: it had been raised originally to fight on the Eastern front, and was now in Denmark as a German auxiliary force under discipline.

ligence after Truelsen's withdrawal and the arrest of his successor. SOE knew neither of these men personally, and was not happy about the position: both men tended to centralise too much in Copenhagen, and also to play anti-Communist 'Army politics', and there seemed in the autumn to be a danger both of a technical and of a political disaster.

At this stage the strategic position in Denmark took a new turn. An Allied landing in Denmark was no longer even a remote possibility, but Denmark now lay not so far behind the German lines, and it also held a strategic position on the reinforcement route by which more German troops could be drawn in from the North. The strengthening of Danish resistance therefore assumed a higher priority, and at the same time the means to supply it were more easily available. In addition, it was important to plan for the 'take-over' in the event of German collapse. On the military side, the important step was the formation of the SHAEF Mission for Denmark early in September 1944, under Major General Dewing, who worked closely with SOE. The supply position was also greatly improved. From October 1944 to the end 239 successful air sorties were flown carrying 582 tons of stores: in addition there were several successful sea operations, and in January 1945 three motor-vessels got through to Sweden from England with a camouflaged load which included about 1,000 carbines and 1,000 Stens, to be smuggled into Zealand. 3,000 Swedish submachine guns were also smuggled across the straits. By the end there were light arms in Denmark for some 25,000 men: and in addition the 'Danish Police' in Sweden were expanded to some 5,000 men, with a fleet of small vessels to move them into Denmark. Plans for 'Danforce', as it was called, were agreed when Major General Dewing was in Sweden in December 1944, and it was also arranged that two British officers should be attached to the force for liaison.

On the communications side there was also great technical improvement. Even at the end there were only twelve wireless stations in operation: but these included an ultra-high-frequency set in Copenhagen which worked to Malmoe in Sweden by automatic transmission at 500 letters a minute, and from Sweden these transmissions were relayed direct to London. There was also available an 'S-Phone' or 'walky-talky' for conversation between Denmark and Sweden across the straits: and one of the telephone cables to Sweden was tapped for use in emergency.

Considerable reorganisation was required internally. One of SOE's objects was to force a decentralisation from Copenhagen to local military areas each of which should be directly in touch with England, and nine Danish military liaison officers were sent in by air for this purpose in October: their object was not achieved without some friction and confusion of channels, but a good deal of flexibility was gained. It was also necessary to find a good replacement for Muus, and a young Dane with a first-rate underground record, Ole Lippmann, was specially trained for this role in England: he was successfully smuggled in from Sweden in January 1945 and did his job well. Finally, at about the same date, it was at last decided that the Danish C-in-C, General Gørtz, should be put in command of the 'secret army', under the orders of SHAEF. This obvious course had been avoided for so long because of its political implications: and the background now was that Danish political common sense had drawn the right lesson from examples elsewhere and had reached a compromise as regards government after liberation. A bargain had been struck between the Freedom Council and the old parties that (pending regular elections) the first Cabinet after liberation should be drawn half from the Council and half from the politicians.

Meantime the situation in Denmark was almost one of continuous warfare. In September the Germans began to remove Danish political prisoners to Germany: the Freedom Council's answer was a forty-eight-hour strike. In reprisal the Germans disbanded the Danish police: about 2,000 were deported to Germany and the rest went underground. Again there was a forty-eight-hour general strike of popular sympathy and solidarity. Gestapo activity and casualties to the Resistance increased: Professor Mogens Fog was arrested in October: late in September Captain Larsen, head of the intelligence network in succession to Truelsen, was caught: Muus at the same time had a narrow escape and had to keep quiet until his final withdrawal in December. The RAF joined the battle with three brilliant attacks on Gestapo HQ, at Aarhus in October, at Copenhagen in March and at Odense in April: in gratitude for the first of these the Jutland Resistance staged a beautiful coup which destroyed twenty German aircraft on the airfield at Aalborg. The whole rhythm of sabotage was stepped up:

October 1944	24 major incidents
November	65 major incidents
December	22 major incidents
January 1945	30 major incidents
February	3 major incidents
March	49 major incidents
April	59 major incidents

These figures are taken a little at random from SOE's 'game-book',[1] but give a pretty good indication of the atmosphere at a time when Denmark was becoming steadily more crowded with Germans fleeing from the Baltic or evacuated from Germany itself. The main concerted campaigns were against registers of population required by the German labour service, and against German rail movements to

---

[1] SOE 'Danish History', Appendix VIII.

the south early in 1945: SHAEF has given a high testimonial to the efficiency of the latter. The rest include attacks on shipping; attacks on factories producing parts for V.2s and other weapons; the removal of tugs and pilots to Swedish waters. The total destruction was formidable, though perhaps not as closely geared to a central plan as in Norway – this was the price to be paid for the late growth of Danish resistance and its relative lack of political co-ordination.

It was in doubt to the last whether it would be necessary for the Allies to fight their way up the Jutland peninsula, and plans were laid for co-ordinating resistance with the invasion and for obstructing German attempts at demolition. Fortunately these were not needed: by 4th May it was clear that all German forces facing the British would surrender unconditionally, and the problem was now that of a smooth transfer of control to Danish and Allied hands. SOE came into this at three points: on 4th May one of the Danish Section officers joined HQ 21st Army Group for liaison with the forces advancing into Jutland, on 5th May 'Danforce' crossed the straits from Sweden accompanied by an SOE liaison officer, Major Ray, who was the first British officer to enter liberated Denmark, on 6th May Major General Dewing was flown in to Kastrup near Copenhagen accompanied by the head of the Danish Section, Commander Hollingworth. As in Norway, the transition was smoothly begun, and it was carried through, in face of immense practical difficulties, with very little shooting and without political complications.

This was one major gain from SOE's work: the Resistance had required delicate handling, but it had in the end been politically successful. Denmark had ended the war with restored pride in its national part, and with complete political unity: SOE's intervention had certainly contributed to both these psychological victories. On the military side, the contribution of Danish resistance had of course not been of major strategic importance, but it had been real and effective: destruction and delay had been caused which was in part unattainable by other means, in part attainable only by a lavish expenditure of bombers and at a high cost in Danish civilian life. The cost in the narrow sense is fairly easily reckoned. Fifty-seven SOE-trained agents (all Danish) were sent in, of whom thirteen were captured and six killed. There were 414 aircraft sorties, of which 285 were successful, for the loss of seventeen aircraft. Some 6,670,000 Danish krones were expended in cash, and repaid later by the Danish Government. Even if one is to add to the reckoning a fair share of the overhead costs of SOE, the margin of gain is very large: and fortunately there are not in this case to be set against it mass reprisals or large-scale destruction of property by the Germans. The idea of the 'clearing murder' – the exaction of five Danish lives for each collaborator killed – was an invention applied particularly in Denmark, but on the whole the

Gestapo avoided mass executions and attempted as best it could to identify and destroy the active Resistance itself. The total loss of Danish life by German action in Denmark is not known, but it was certainly not large by the scale of total war – less perhaps than the number of Danes killed in RAF raids.

CHAPTER XXVIII

Germany and Austria

There are some interesting and perhaps instructive passages in SOE's dealings with the German Reich, but on the whole the story is one of low priorities and hope deferred. It was not SOE's business to make Germany its main objective until August 1944, when it was already 'five minutes to twelve': it was then too late for the experiment to be made seriously, and British subversion played no important part in the internal collapse of the main enemy: the attack on Germany was made mainly in and through the occupied countries. The complexities of German politics under Hitler thus had little effect on the work of SOE, and there is no need to unravel them here.

1. SOE Organisation

SOE's German Section[1] was formed in November 1940, under Mr Brien Clarke, from a small nucleus inherited from Colonel Grand's organisation. It was taken over in the middle of 1941 by Mr R. H. Thornley, who was the man mainly responsible for SOE's German work up to the end of the war. 'X Section' (as it was called) was itself a relatively small body until August 1944, but it served also as the headquarters of a network of representatives working with SOE Missions in the most important neutral countries. In Switzerland it was represented by Miss E. M. Hodgson from September 1941 until December 1943, when she had to be hastily withdrawn through occupied France: a new representative (Squadron Leader Matthey) was sent in with difficulty through France in August 1944.[2] There were similar problems in Sweden: the original X Section representative, Major Threlfall, lasted only from January to August 1942, when trouble arose with the Swedish Security services: he was succeeded first by Miss Forte, then by Major Euan Butler. In Turkey the chief difficulty was to persuade HM

---

[1] There is a very well-documented History of SOE's German activities by many different hands.

[2] See SOE 'German History' Pt I – 2(e) 'Switzerland' for his narrative of adventures en route.

Ambassador* to accept the risks involved, especially as the representative chosen, Mr G. E. R. Gedye** (a very well-known journalist), had already been in trouble with the Turkish authorities, and he was not firmly established in Istanbul until May 1943. Finally, there was from March 1944 a representative (Major Darton) with the SOE HQ (Maryland) in Italy. These representatives (belatedly and with difficulty) covered the main potential lines of access to Germany: elsewhere (in Lisbon for instance) X Section worked through the ordinary SOE Missions. It also did what it could to obtain support from the Sections working with Resistance organisations in occupied territory, but from the records it is clear that they and their agents were generally too hard-pressed by their own business to have time to spare for X Section's problems.

2. The 'German Underground'

This SOE organisation (though ably staffed) was clearly on much too small a scale to make an impression on the enormous technical difficulties of work into Germany. In addition its scope was severely limited by political considerations. What the policy of unconditional surrender meant from SOE's point of view was that no free use could be made of feelers from Germans purporting to be discontented with the régime. There were scores of such 'peace-feelers' of all grades of importance, and progress in subversion could only have been made by following each of them up delicately and ingeniously, with the offer of a little bait to induce *some* Germans from *some* motives to commit themselves to *some* action against their régime. This would have involved grave risks: *first*, the political risk, that any hints thrown out as 'bait' might be employed by the Germans to sow dissension within the rather precarious coalition of Allies, either during the war or after it: *second*, the technical risk, that a high proportion of 'peace-feelers' were put out by Gestapo agents, conscious or unconscious, with a view to entrapping Allied representatives and sympathisers into betraying themselves. It was deliberately decided, on the highest level, that these risks were not worth taking, and X Section itself heartily endorsed and supported this decision.[1] They defended it against all

---

[1] The first formal instructions as to the handling of 'peace-feelers' were issued early in October 1942. SOE Missions and agents were given liberty to contact Germans for subversive purposes, but on any hint of a 'feeler' contact must be broken off and the matter referred to the Foreign Office for decision (SOE Archives File XF/88 Pt I). These remained the guiding principles throughout.

* [Sir H. M. Knatchbull-Hugessen, 1886–1971, knight 1936, Ambassador to China 1936–9, to Turkey 1940–44, to Belgium 1944–7. See his *Diplomat in Peace and War* (1949) and R. Wires, *The Cicero Spy Affair* (Westport, Connecticut, 2000).]

** [G. E. R. Gedye, 1890–1970; see his *Fallen Bastions* (1939).]

comers within SOE, and hammered it home that SOE's reaction to German approaches must always be to mock at them, to break off contact hastily, and to report the substance of the matter to the Foreign Office or its representative. Thus (whether 'unconditional surrender' was right or wrong) it was not a policy forced upon SOE against its better judgement: SOE executed it loyally and with conviction, and (considering how widely SOE extended) it made very few mistakes.[1] Of course the Germans used any channel which came to hand; much happened which did not pass through SOE at all, and some genuine material for anti-British propaganda may emerge from the German archives. But it is pretty safe to say that SOE furnished nothing of importance except the unfortunate negotiations of the excellent Captain Stott in Athens in December 1943, which were broken off instantly as soon as London knew of them.[2]

It is thus scarcely necessary to work through the long list of openings which came to nothing. Before the attempt on Hitler on 20th July 1944, SOE had been made pretty well aware from various sources of the component elements of the plot. But it made no attempt to answer appeals for assistance or concessions, and it remained obstinately sceptical about their sincerity and their freedom from Gestapo penetration. Even after the attack on Hitler, SOE's official view was that there was no real 'resistance' in Germany: at most there were personal jealousies and a divergence of opinion as to the method by which Germany could best attain her ends.

As regards this more or less unified 'opposition movement' SOE's records add little to what has already been published by Mr Allen W. Dulles,[3] the OSS representative in Switzerland, who acted more boldly and perhaps more innocently than SOE. There were other, less concerted, approaches in Greece, in Northern Italy,[4] and in Norway:[5] but these were kept successfully within bounds as local negotiations for local surrender, with (in a few cases) some suggestion of special consideration for helpful individuals. But there are two curious incidents worth mentioning briefly.

One of these[6] was an approach through Stockholm in May 1942 by Helmuth James von Moltke,* great-grandson heir of the Field

---

[1] A good general impression of SOE's policy and the main incidents can be got from SOE Archives File 9/100/12 Vols I–III 'Peacefeelers and Approaches'.

[2] Above p. 470.

[3] 'Germany's Underground', published by The MacMillan Co., New York, 1947.

[4] Above p. 470, 555.

[5] See an interesting paper by Jens Christian Hauge, the head of the Norwegian Milorg, in SOE Archives File 9/100/12 Pt III.

[6] SOE Archives File XF/G/98.

* [1907–45.]

Marshal, Chief of Staff in the war of 1870: von Moltke's mother was a daughter of a Chief Justice of South Africa, and he was himself half English in thought and up-bringing – a sincere Christian gentleman and a dangerously incompetent conspirator. He had maintained some contact with friends in England after the outbreak of war, and wrote to suggest a meeting with one of them in Stockholm in September or October 1942. SOE considered this seriously and proposed to arrange the meeting: but action was stopped on the instructions of the Prime Minister himself. Von Moltke kept the rendezvous in Stockholm in September 1942, but his friend was not there to meet him, and the last contact was a letter which Von Moltke then passed to him through the same channels, gently rebuking the British for their failure to use the 'millions of would-be spies on the Continent'. He was executed in January 1945, although he was under arrest long before the attempt of 20th July 1944 and was not directly implicated in it.[1]

This was the only occasion when SOE reacted to any of the feelers emanating from the 'conservative' opposition, much of which was directly or indirectly linked with Von Moltke.

In December 1942 there was an approach of a very different kind through a certain Dr Söderman, an eminent Swedish criminologist. His story was that he was in contact with leading officials of the German Kriminalpolizei – the old 'legal' police, which was not on the best terms with the Gestapo – and that they were ready to take action at a chosen moment to arrest or execute all leading Nazis (from Hitler downwards) and all the heads of the German security forces.[2] They would require only limited assistance by British airborne forces. The channel through which Dr Söderman wished to pursue this plan (which he took very seriously) was his friend, Sir Norman Kendall,* a distinguished official at Scotland Yard. SOE's immediate reaction was to regard this as a trap and to break off contact: but Dr Söderman was very persistent (and he was also a good friend of SOE in Sweden), and in the end it required the personal intervention of Sir Alexander Cadogan with Sir Norman Kendall to close the episode in March 1943. Dr Söderman recurred once more to his plan, in March 1944, when he made it plain that his contact was with Lieutenant-General Dr Nebe,** head of Kriminalpolizei section of Himmler's Reich

---

[1] A memorial volume of his letters has been published by British friends. 'A German of the Resistance: The Last Letters of Count Helmuth James von Moltke', OUP, 1947.

[2] See papers on CD's personal file, and SOE Archives File XF/G/288 'Operation Shelter'.

* [Sir N. Kendal, knight 1937, assistant commissioner 1928–45.]

** [A. Nebe, 1894–1945?, headed German criminal police 1938–44, bolted, perhaps caught and killed by Gestapo.]

Sicherheits Haupt Amt, and that Count Von Helldorff, chief of the uniformed police in Berlin, was somehow associated with the plot. SOE remained obdurate and would let matters go no further. The aftermath of the '20th July' at least confirmed the claim that the plot existed: Helldorff was arrested and executed, Dr Nebe also was caught after the Gestapo had set a price of 50,000 marks on his head.[1] This is evidence of a real plot, but also of effective Gestapo control: and SOE were doubtless wise to keep out.

3. The Exiles

These contacts with 'Germany's Underground' were both dangerous and unprofitable: contacts with German political groups in exile were merely unprofitable. The ground had already been pretty well explored in Colonel Grand's day, and later experience merely confirmed the findings of D Section.[2] Most of the interlocking and competing groups were interested mainly in their own present survival: they had been in exile too long to have much idea of conditions in Germany and their contacts there were very tenuous. In addition, many of their members were Jews, and therefore of little value for the subversion of an 'Aryan' régime. The total value of their special knowledge was probably considerable: their direct assistance was very slight, and there are only four contacts, out of many, which need be mentioned.

Three of these, 'Lex', the ISK, and the ITF, have already appeared in Part I. The Paris member of 'Lex', Karl Groehl, eventually escaped to London after the fall of France, and resumed contact with his friends in Switzerland. The main 'Lex' representative there was one Karl Gerold, who seems to have been serious enough, though romantic, incalculable and very tedious. Through Miss Hodgson, he was supplied with sabotage equipment and instruction, and a good deal of this material certainly found its way into Germany. There is no corroborated evidence of what happened to it there: but it is certain that some sabotage took place, and the credit for a good deal of it was claimed by 'Lex'. In the end Gerold was betrayed to the Swiss police by his mistress in October 1943, and Miss Hodgson had to withdraw hastily through occupied France. This virtually put an end to the usefulness of Gerold's organisation.

The Internationalier Sozialistische Kampfbund (ISK) also offered useful contacts in Switzerland, mainly through a certain René

---

1 Part of their story is given in Gisevius, 'To the Bitter End' (Cape, 1948), p. 56 and elsewhere. [H. B. Gisevius, 1904–74, German civil servant, agent of A. W. Dulles.]

2 Above p. [18] ff: SOE German History, Pt I (German Exiles), Pt II (c) (Austrian Exiles).

Bertholet ('Charles'), who proved valuable for work into France and Italy as well as into Germany. His activities as regards Germany interlocked to some extent with those of the International Transport-Workers Federation (ITF), which was a valuable line of approach to railway workers throughout Europe, although it did not itself give much leadership after the death of its veteran leader, Edo Fimmen, in December 1942. At least it sponsored railway sabotage, and indicated methods: and the ISK in Switzerland was able to enlist a very resolute Swiss railwayman in the yards at Basel. His gang (and one other party) ran a persistent campaign of sabotage of German rolling-stock from March 1942 onwards, and suffered very little from the Swiss police: this was small-scale work, but of real practical value. The ISK also supplied more than one resolute agent for parachute work: and the wife of one of these agents made three successful trips as a courier to the Reich from Switzerland in 1944.

Some mention should also be made of the Austrian Revolutionary Socialists – a splinter of the Social Democratic Party which favoured the 'Anschluss' with Germany as the only possible basis for Socialism in Austria. They were a small group, largely Jewish, with no possible political future: but they had a good fighting record, and were ready to offer men for serious work. At least four good agents were drawn from this source.

4. SOE's Agents

The land was thus politically naked: there was literally no existing organisation in Germany with which to co-operate, and (till the end) all agents sent in by SOE worked as individuals. Some of their experiences were, however, sufficiently remarkable.

The first attempt (Operation 'Champagne') was made with a young anti-Nazi named Kuehnel, who was captured after the sinking of a German meteorological ship in June 1941. The preparation of his expedition involved the invention and 're-living' of an elaborate cover-story, to explain how he had been set to civilian work in a shipyard at Aberdeen, and had escaped across the North Sea to Norway in a stolen fishing-boat. A suitable boat was found for him and was launched from a British trawler off the coast of Norway in April 1942. Kuehnel was given no wireless set, and could communicate with England only through conventional messages in letters addressed to German prisoners of war here. It is certain that he arrived safely in Norway; and two messages were received, the second in October 1942. In November 1942 there was an obscure report that he had attempted to contact Norwegian Resistance with a view to escaping to Sweden: this might easily be a trap and the Norwegians were warned to keep off. No more was ever heard of

Kuehnel, then or after the war – a first effort 'sunk without trace'.

The second attempt had more remarkable results. The man chosen was a certain Kurt Koenig, a young Social Democrat who had deserted from the German Army and contacted the British in Spain in the summer of 1942: his story was that he had been engaged in sabotage at Bremen, and had escaped when enquiries became dangerous. He was put into training by SOE in November 1942, and was ready for work in February 1943. On the night of 16th February he was dropped to a point just inside the frontier between Germany and Holland, with instructions to contact his old friends in the Bremen and Hamburg areas and to work up a movement for sabotage and subversion: he was not provided with a wireless set. The dropping point was missed, and he landed in the full light of publicity on the roof of a farm-house where a wedding-party was in progress: he escaped for the moment by bluffing the revellers with a story that he was an airman who had 'bailed out' from a burning aircraft, but this was bound to break down as soon as checked, and his position was still extremely dangerous. For the next few days he was on the run in north-west Germany, travelling by train to Hanover, Bremen and elsewhere without serious difficulties. But the strain was too great, and he very soon decided to cut loose and to make for Spain once more. By 1st March he was in San Sebastian and on the 26th he was back in England. This round trip may seem so fantastic as to suggest it was a Gestapo 'plant': but if it was a trick it was one carried out with unnecessary and unbelievable thoroughness – long afterwards three or four police notices giving independent confirmation of the story were found in captured German documents.

Koenig was ready to try again, and his use was approved for a single-handed sabotage mission against German railways. This time (on 15th July 1943) he was dropped successfully on the agreed 'pin-point' in the Rhineland: by 27th July he was back in San Sebastian. He had in the interval travelled over much of Western Germany and had met a few of his friends: and he claimed to have used his small stock of explosives successfully in blowing the railway lines in a tunnel near Oberwesel and in sabotaging a locomotive. There was no independent confirmation of his story, but it stood up well under cross-examination.

Finally on 7th January 1944 Koenig set out for a third time, to drop in the Freiburg area: this time he did not return. It appears that (on his own insistence) he was dropped wide of the pin-point, which could not be found: there was a general alarm in the area and he was caught in Baden the next day. He was executed in February 1945.

These were the only operations into Germany itself before the situation was transformed by the invasion:[1] attempts were also made to penetrate the Sudetenland, with ill-success. Two agents were sent from Sweden in March 1944, but were caught while making the crossing to Denmark. Two others were dropped by parachute in May 1944, and seem to have been at large for some time: in the end one was executed, the other committed suicide to avoid arrest. Various attempts were made to establish contact overland from Turkey, both with Sudetenland and with Austria, and some very tenuous lines of communication did exist: but (except for the dissemination of propaganda material) they led to no practical gain, and on one occasion to a dangerous double-cross by a venal Swiss courier. A great deal of careful work by Mr Gedye in Turkey in the end led nowhere.

There was one other 'open frontier', that of Yugoslavia. It will be remembered that in 1943 SOE began to exploit the state of open war in Yugoslavia in order to work from it into neighbouring countries. Captain Russell found his way into Roumania, Major Frank Thompson into Bulgaria, certain members of Major Davidson's party into Hungary. There remained Austria, and the 'Clowder' Mission destined for Austria was the most elaborate and most desperate of these singularly desperate adventures.*

The project was approved in very general terms in August 1943; the 'usual delays' ensued, and it was not until 3rd December that the advance party was flown in to Brigadier Maclean's Mission with Tito in Bosnia: it was led by Lieutenant Colonel P. A. Wilkinson, and included Major A. C. G. Hesketh-Prichard and CSM G. Hughes. The project was blessed by Tito, and the party set out on 9th December on a 300-mile march to Partisan HQ in Slovenia. About Christmas they reached their destination, some forty-five miles south-east of Ljubljana, and there met the British Liaison Officer, Major Jones, that 'mad but holy' Canadian.[2] As generally happened in the Partisan bureaucracy, Tito's local officials were much more unreceptive and unhelpful than Tito himself: and it took some hard bargaining to establish a working arrangement. From Slovenia the 'Clowder' party went on (in the depth of winter) through the Julian Alps into North Italy and the Slovene districts close to the old Austrian frontier: here they were the first harbingers of British support and were more warmly welcomed. One attempt was made to cross the Austrian border, and another to penetrate southwards to the coast of Istria: both failed, and

---

[1] Among many abortive projects it is worth mentioning a very detailed (but unpromising) study of the assassination of Hitler and other leaders. (See SOE Archives files (German Section) 'Foxley' files 1, 2, 3(a) and (b).) [The Public Record Office published the file on 'Foxley' in 1998.]

[2] Above p. 429.

* [On 'Clowder', see Wilkinson, *Foreign Fields.*]

on 27th February Wilkinson set off on the long journey back to Bosnia, while Hesketh-Prichard remained as 'Advanced HQ Clowder' at the headquarters of the 9th Slovene Corps at Circhno, some twenty-five miles south of the old Austrian frontier in Oberkrajn.

A 'rear Echelon' was now established with No. 1 Special Force in liberated Italy, and in January 1944 air supply began: between January and June 1944 Hesketh-Prichard received thirteen drops, out of seventeen attempts made. Wilkinson came out from Bosnia in the spring and returned to London, where he received approval for the establishment of a chain of British dispatch posts with the Italian and Slovene guerillas along some 120 miles of mountainous territory from the Dolomites to the point where the Drave crosses the frontier. Through these posts it was hoped to infiltrate Austrian agents, and perhaps later British officers. The working-out of the plan falls most readily into two parts, North Italy and Slovenia, which were linked by 'Clowder' HQ in Southern Italy.

The programme was opened in North Italy by the dropping of Squadron Leader Count Czernin with an Italian wireless operator on 14th January 1944: the whole Ampezzo-Belluno area was then in Partisan hands (largely organised in the non-Communist Osoppo Brigade), and it was possible to move fairly freely in spite of occasional enemy sweeps. Squadron Leader Czernin had no difficulty in reconnoitring the Austrian frontier with local guides and in finding routes for courier traffic: but there were as yet no agents ready to enter Austria. Air supply proved particularly difficult, partly from competing priorities, partly from the nature of the country; and it was not until 12th August that Czernin was reinforced by Major G. R. H. Fielding, bringing with him four Austrians. Of these Austrians, only one, Georgeau, could be induced to operate as an agent in civilian clothes, and he made one successful reconnaissance in Austria from 15th to 28th August: he entered Austria for the second time on 9th September, with an Italian guide, and was not heard of again. Another party of four Austrians was sent on 12th October, but by ill-luck they missed the dropping zone and landed among a German patrol – only one escaped to join the British Mission. One more Austrian, a wireless operator intended to work with Georgeau, arrived safely on 17th November, but by that time the Germans were taking active counter-measures as part of their general clean-up of Partisans in North Italy.[1] Life was very disturbed, and it was in any case too late in the season to use the ordinary mountain routes. Determined efforts were made to get this man into Austria, but they failed; there was no point in attempting to sit out the winter, and the whole 'Clowder' Mission in North Italy was withdrawn safely through Yugoslavia in December 1944.

---

[1] Above p. 552.

In Slovenia Hesketh-Prichard was reinforced by two Austrian officers in the spring of 1944, and made a first determined effort to enter Austria at the end of April. He crossed the Karawanken, but found that the Germans had virtually wiped out the Slovene organisation on the north slopes of the mountains towards the Drauthal: he was therefore forced back into Slovenia and moved eastward along the southern slopes of the Karawanken to look for a better line of approach. Meantime (on 14th May) Major C. H. Villiers* dropped to the HQ of the 9th Slovene Corps in the Julian Alps (on the Italian side of the frontier): he soon found that this area was useless for infiltration into Austria and he himself moved east in the wake of Hesketh-Prichard. The latter was now with the East Korosko Odred of the Partisans, reconnoitring ways and means of entering the Drauthal: Villiers set up Advanced HQ 'Clowder' with the West Korosko Odred, while CSM Hughes remained with HQ 9th Corps as a link with its friendly commander. Three Austrians were dropped to him in June, but it proved quite impracticable to infiltrate them and in September they were evacuated with Hughes to Italy.

Meantime Villiers and Hesketh-Prichard were attempting to push the Korosko Partisans into some show of activity: not an easy task. There was some Partisan obstruction and there was some confusion of responsibilities between 'Clowder' and the BLOs of Brigadier Maclean's Mission. But Partisan life here, on the edge of Grossdeutschland, was a different affair from life in the depths of Yugoslavia: the enemy was very active, the population was not 100% reliable, and what the British demanded was action of a very desperate kind. It is a credit to the Partisans as well as to Hesketh-Prichard that he eventually by cajolery and the offer of supplies pushed them into supporting his expedition across the Drave. Some 25 tons of stores arrived to meet Partisan requests between June and September 1944, and their strength in the Korosko was expanded from 200 to 2,000 men. The plan was finally agreed in mid-September, but even then the Partisans would make no diversion in force unless given seventy aircraft loads of stores – a request which was finally turned down in high quarters, since the clash over the post-war Italian frontier was now clearly in view. Hesketh-Prichard, who had pushed the matter for so long, felt that he could not in honour withdraw: and he crossed the Drave on 15th October with a party of some eighty Slovenes. By 20th October they were established in the Saualpen, west of Wolfsberg, and well within Austrian territory. The population (Slovene in part) was friendly but passive: the weather deteriorated rapidly: and it proved impossible to send even one supply aircraft. A reinforcing party of six British officers and two wireless operators

---

* [(Sir) C. H. Villers, 1912–92, knight 1975, chairman British Steel 1976–80.]

was in readiness in Italy, but never started. It is clear from Hesketh-Prichard's messages that his party was increasingly harassed and compressed by the Germans, and that his relations with the Partisans deteriorated. Finally messages ceased on 3rd December 1944. The Partisan story (some forty of them survived in this area until the armistice) is that Hesketh-Prichard was wounded and probably killed by the Germans on that day: one canot exclude the possibility that he was murdered by the Partisans as a danger to their own safety.

This was the end of 'Advanced HQ Clowder'. Major Villiers had been relieved in the Korosko by Major Pickering in September: and the full plan was that once Hesketh-Prichard was established in the Saualpen, Pickering should also cross the Drave to operate further east in Styria. Hesketh-Prichard's failure and enemy reactions on the frontier made this impossible, and Pickering was withdrawn to Southern Italy at the end of December 1944.

So far 'Clowder' had been a brilliant display of gallantry, entirely without practical result: but before writing it off as futile it will be as well to abandon the strict framework of the narrative and to follow what was done in Austria in the last months of the war. The supply of possible agents from among Austrian prisoners of war was now reasonably good, and some thirty of them were put in training in Italy for operations in the spring of 1945. It is worth setting out these operations briefly: apart from some minor infiltrations from Switzerland they constitute the whole of active Austrian resistance so far as sponsored by SOE:

(i)   On 7th February Lieutenant 'O'Hara' was dropped blind with a wireless set near Graz, to contact the local Social Democratic movement: he had already made one attempt single-handed to enter the Tyrol on foot from Bolzano, and when he failed he found his own way back to the Allied front line in Italy. His old contacts in Graz had, he discovered, been seriously affected by Gestapo activity; nevertheless he found some friends and opened wireless communications with his base. Unfortunately he was soon on the run, and it was never possible to send him spare batteries or other stores: first he made contact with a hitherto unknown band of Slovene Partisans in the Kor Alpen, then he attempted to reach Yugoslavia with a small party. About 21st March they were caught while crossing the Drave, and 'O'Hara' was shot.

(ii) On 16th February three Austrians were dropped near Judenburg with instructions to make their way to the Salzburg area. The party was betrayed at once by one of its members, who also attempted (unsuccessfully) to deceive SOE by working his wireless set for the Gestapo.

(iii) On 23rd March a single wireless operator Lieutenant

'Kennedy' was dropped near Krems and succeeded in making his way into Vienna where he had Social Democratic friends. Unfortunately his wireless set was lost in the drop: but he seems to have found in Vienna at least the nucleus of a fighting Resistance, consisting largely of deserters from the German Army; he claims to have been given command of a picked party of 130 men, quite well armed and trained. From the beginning of April until the fall of Vienna on the 13th they were actively engaged in harassing the defenders, and did very useful work: after the Liberation 'Kennedy' found the Russians courteous at first, but he was later arrested and was in a Russian gaol until July.[1]

(iv) On 24th March another single wireless operator was dropped near Murzzuschlag in Styria, where he found friends, and established contact with his base. It appears from his story[2] that there were bands of Austrian deserters in the hills: but he was not in touch with them until after the surrender and he took no open action against the enemy.

(v) On 20th and 24th April three parties, eight men in all, were dropped blind in the area between Graz and Judenburg: their task was to attack railway communications and if possible to secure the aerodrome at Zeltweg which was likely to be of value for the evacuation of Allied prisoners of war. They had bad luck with their wireless and other equipment, but otherwise things went well. The story[3] is one of the confusion of a collapsing régime: bands of Austrian deserters, setting up in business as Partisans, Vlassov Cossacks and Hungarians out of control, village communities organising for their own defence, Wehrmacht officers with no one to give them orders, Gestapo attempting to reinsure their skins with the Western Allies. In the end, SOE's men secured Zeltweg aerodrome and removed the demolition charges, but there was a shift in Allied boundaries and almost at once the area passed under Russian control.

(vi) Finally, there is the star turn of the Austrian Resistance, Albrecht Gaiswinkler. Gaiswinkler had deserted from the Wehrmacht to the Maquis in France in June 1944, taking with him four truck-loads of arms and ammunition, and 500,000 francs: thence he had reached the American lines with seven-

---

1   His account is at Appendix G to the History of the Clowder Mission (SOE German History).

2   His account is at Appendix H to the History of the Clowder Mission (SOE German History).

3   Appendix E and F to History of Clowder Mission (SOE German History).

teen German prisoners in September. On 8th April 1945, he was dropped blind to his own country in the Salzkammergut: the pinpoint was missed and the party lost most of its stores and only escaped by hard rock-climbing in snowbound country. But they came apparently at the right moment. In the Bad Aussee district, well within the Nazi redoubt, Gaiswinkler rapidly raised an active force of 350 men and armed them at German expense. In the last weeks of the Nazi régime he was able to harass the Nazis by a multitude of bluffs: and when the Americans arrived he was in full control of the administration, had his hand on a number of eminent Nazis (including Kaltenbrunner), had effectively stopped all demolitions, and had rescued a number of Nazi treasure hoards, including the 'Mona Lisa' and the Austrian Imperial crown jewels. The Americans at once installed him as Bezirkshauptmann in gratitude for his services.

Other Austrian operations were held up by delay in training wireless operators: nine parties were in readiness when the Armistice came, but they could not be used in time. The work of the last few months was enough to show that in favourable circumstances an Austrian resistance could be created: but it can be argued that there were no favourable circumstances until the end of Hitler's Reich was in sight – the Austrians did not move except to join the winning side. This is doubtless true, but when the time came there was enough kick in the Austrians to suggest that SOE was not mad to expend so much of its resources on 'Clowder'. If contact had been made then, the turn in Austria might have come sooner and might have contributed more. But it was hardly in SOE's power earlier to command success: the physical and political conditions of 'Advanced HQ Clowder' were almost impossible, and the supply of trained and active Austrians was very limited until the stream of prisoners began after 'Overlord'.

5. Foreign Workers in Germany

Apparently the first German plan for the exploitation of Western Europe was that industry should continue to work in the occupied countries for the benefit of the Reich. But it was already clear in 1941 that this policy was politically dangerous and economically inefficient, and the Germans began to move Western workers to Germany to expand production there. This policy was followed from the first in the East, and it was intensified in the West when the winter campaign of 1941–2 in Russia imposed the first serious strain on German manpower. 1942 was in France the year of the 'Relève' and of the birth of the Maquis: in Italy events followed a little behind, but once Mussolini had fallen there were no limits to the conscription and deportation of Italian workers. The exact number of foreign workers – eventually to become 'Displaced Persons' – in Germany will never be known: but it was certainly vast (of the order of 10,000,000) and it represented a huge share in Germany's output of munitions.

This was to all appearances a direct invitation to SOE to penetrate into the heart of German industry – a 'Trojan Horse' introduced by the Germans themselves. This point of view made a great impression on the politicians, the Press and the public, and SOE was not behind public opinion in discovering it: the first directive for the encouragement of sabotage by foreign workers was issued in April 1941, and propaganda directed to maintain their morale and induce passive resistance was always one of the main themes of PWE. Unfortunately there were good reasons why it was impossible for SOE to make much of this promising material. This was not merely a matter of efficient Gestapo control by restriction on the movement of workers and the free use of 'stool pigeons' among them: the technical problem was to find some efficient means of direct contact. We have already seen the extreme difficulty of conducting air operations into Germany itself: and the difficulties would be much greater for operations directed to foreigners whose movement in Germany was restricted by language difficulties. This meant that contact could only be made through SOE organisations in the occupied territories from which the workers were drawn: effective work by SOE's German Section would depend on the other Sections of SOE and the exiled governments with which they dealt. This point was seen quite early, but it was not easy to make much of it. The SOE Sections concerned had sufficient work on their hands in creating their own organisations in the occupied countries, and it was neither reasonable nor practicable for them to divert much effort to the penetration of Germany. In addition, the Allied Governments were by no means enthusiastic about an intensification of sabotage by their countrymen in Germany: their first concern was to keep them out of the hands of the Germans altogether, their second to see that in Germany their conditions of life were not intolerable – and the effect of sabotage would be to restrict their freedom and probably to expose them and their families to mass reprisals.

There is thus little concrete to record about SOE's work in this direction until the last stage, when Allied Governments were again working from their own countries in the West. There was of course passive resistance and 'insaisissable' sabotage by foreign workers: there was also probably much spontaneous organisation among them for resistance and evasion. But this was in no sense directed and controlled by SOE. The most that SOE could do was to instruct its agents in the line to be followed as regards workers in Germany, and to encourage any attempts by the resistance organisations to extend their work over the German frontier. The French in particular had active (but competing) organisations for this purpose. The Trade Unions (CGT) were anxious to keep their movement alive among deported workers; they circulated a good deal of propaganda, and in addition in February 1944 a special team (the 'Mission Varlin') was sent to France to organise the work. There was also the Mouvement des Prisonniers de Guerre et Déportés, under Communist inspiration but primarily concerned with welfare rather than with resistance.

There was thus in effect a deadlock on what appeared to be a vulnerable portion of the enemy's front: and the most important part of the story here is that of the abortive effort to break this down through Operation 'Moon' or 'Braddock'.

This was in essence a scheme to scatter broadcast over Germany vast quantities of cheap sabotage equipment. The mere existence of this would impose a strain on the German security forces: and even a tiny proportion of the whole would be a formidable weapon in the hands of foreign workers and dissident Germans. The genesis of the idea is to be found in two discussions between Lord Cherwell* and Brigadier Gubbins, on 25th September and 22nd November 1941.[1] The Professor was then seriously disturbed about higher strategy: with the equipment then at its disposal the RAF was incapable of hitting any target effectively by night without the aid of a moon, and the prospect of destroying the German army by invasion was so remote as to be out of account. If these two strategic weapons were excluded we should be thrown back on a plan for initiating 'such a campaign of universal sabotage as would eventually reduce German morale to an extent which would lead to their downfall from within'. Lord Cherwell was clear that it was technically possible to produce vast quantities of small incendiary weapons for broadcast distribution. Brigadier Gubbins explained SOE's plans for organised rather than indiscriminate sabotage: and on the whole opposed the scheme, because of its uncertainty, the grave risk of extensive reprisals, and the opposition to it of the Polish and French governments in exile.

There the matter rested until the spring of 1942, when it was taken up by Mr Churchill himself, inspired apparently by Mr John Steinbeck's book 'The Moon is Down'.[2] On 27th July 1942, Lord Selborne submitted to the Prime Minister the first detailed report on the project.[3] It now fell into two parts:

---

[1] Recorded in SOE Archives File 1/470/2.

[2] There seems to be no SOE record of how this happened, or of the original directive by Mr Churchill.

[3] Copy in Lord Selborne's papers, file of correspondence with the Prime Minister.

* [F. A. Lindemann, 1886–1957, born in Baden-Baden, discovered how to cure spin in aircraft 1915, adviser to Churchill 1940–45 and 1951–3, Lord Cherwell 1941, viscount 1956. See Roy Harrod, *The Prof* (1959). In *DNB*.]

Scheme I: for the provision of a small parachute package to fit the standard incendiary containers used in British bombers. It would weigh 4 lbs, and would contain a smooth-bore pistol with ten rounds of ammunition, three pocket incendiaries, a 1 lb grenade, a tyre burster, and some minor accessories. This was designed for dropping in occupied countries, and the German instinct would be to control its use by violent reprisals on a large scale: it should therefore only be used in the crisis of a military campaign.

Scheme II: The Research Section of SOE had developed a tiny incendiary giving a blaze of 2000° centigrade for a period of four minutes, with a cheaply-produced half-hour delay fuze. This could be attached to a card 'no bigger than a bar of chocolate', and could flutter down safely from an aircraft without a parachute: the card would contain instructions for use in many languages, and the whole gadget would be practically indestructible by the weather. One Lancaster could carry 10,000 of these, so that a large raid could without difficulty distribute 5,000,000 in a night. This was for its purpose the perfect weapon: it was easy to produce, easy to handle, easy to conceal – and potentially most destructive. The plan was that this should be used in Germany itself as an addition to the other weapons used by Bomber Command: there would in Germany be willing hands waiting for it, and in Germany a policy of mass reprisals could not be followed without destroying the economy under attack.

This paper was referred by the Chiefs of Staff[1] to the Joint War Production Staff, which reported favourably on the possibility of cheap large-scale production[2] and on 28th September the Chiefs of Staff approved both schemes, subject to further reference to themselves before operations began.[3] Authority was thus given for the production of 30,000 'Attack Packs' and 1,000,000 small incendiaries or 'Braddocks'. The 'Attack Packs' were swallowed up in later and larger plans for supply to the resistance movements: 'Braddock' was designed primarily for Germany, and it remained the most important of SOE's schemes for sabotage in Germany.

The essence of its later history is that, no one wholeheartedly supported it except Lord Selborne himself. The Prime Minister, though he remained vaguely interested, seems to have lost enthusiasm: SOE's German Section was sceptical: the RAF were disinclined to drop anything except bombs, the effect of which they could judge pretty accurately for themselves. Allied Governments were nervous about reprisals: and the workers in Germany had no voice one way or the

---

[1]   COS(42)99th (0) Mtg, Minute 3, of 25th August and COS(42)233(0) of 20th August.

[2]   COS(42)270(0) of 17th September.

[3]   COS(42)274th Mtg of 28th September.

other. There is therefore a long record of official frustration, which it is unnecessary to trace in detail.[1]

The main stages were as follows:

(a) In February 1943 the Chiefs of Staff authorised the increase of the order for 'Braddocks' to 3,000,000.[2]

(b) In April 1943, 700,000 'Braddocks' were ready and production was proceeding at a rate of 300,000 a month. Lord Selborne pressed the Prime Minister for action, and Mr Churchill asked in favourable terms for the advice of the Chiefs of Staff. The latter turned the proposal down: a large operation would be a diversion from the Bomber Offensive and the Battle of the Atlantic, a small one would merely fritter away the secret. Production should not go beyond the existing authorisation for 3,000,000 incendiaries.

(c) Lord Selborne did not accept this without demur: after further pressure he succeeded in securing at the end of May 1943 that production should continue temporarily at the existing rate: i.e. that the existing production organisation should not be broken up until it was clear that the weapon was a failure.[3]

(d) Another push was begun in October 1943, by a Minute to the Prime Minister.[4] This led (through circuitous channels) to another refusal by the Chiefs of Staff towards the end of November, and finally (early in February 1944) to a decision to stop production when 4,000,000 'Braddocks' were complete.[5]

(e) There were now in store $3^3/_4$ million 'Braddocks', D-day was approaching, and with it the end for the time being of all such diversionary operations. The Chiefs of Staff stalled off an approach in February with the suggestion that the right strategic moment for the use of 'Braddock' was after the establishment of 'Overlord': early in May the JIC were pushed to the point of recommending 'that Braddock II should be considered for employment as soon as possible after "Overlord", in

---

[1] The papers are to be found in SOE Archives Files Plans/307/COS 'Braddock', XF/28 Vol. I 'Braddock', and AD/E file 'C. 1' 'Braddock'.

[2] COS(43)33rd Mtg, Minute 3, of 8th February.

[3] COS(43)229(0) of 1st May; COS(43)94th (0) Mtg, Minute 4, of 5th May; COS(43)274(0) of 27th May; COS(43)98th Mtg, Minute 1, of 31st May.

[4] Dated 4th October 1943, in Lord Selborne's papers.

[5] COS(43)252nd (0) Mtg, Item 1, JIC(43)439(0) of 9th November: COS(43)280th Mtg, Annex; COS(43)721(0) of 20th November; COS(43)725(0) of 22nd November (letter of 19th November from Lord Selborne to Mr Attlee); COS(43)287th (0) Mtg, Minute 5, of 24th November; Minute to Prime Minister dated 1st February 1944, initialled by Prime Minister 6th February 1944 (in Lord Selborne's papers).

the light of operational demands'. But at that point (with a sigh of relief almost audible in their Minutes) the Chiefs of Staff reached the conclusion that this matter was now one to be decided by the Combined Chiefs of Staff and General Eisenhower. Lord Selborne had now to begin afresh by converting the Americans.

(f) They at least proved more receptive than the British, and took action as speedily as could be expected in the hustle of that summer. A 'Braddock' operation was actually carried out on 25th September (the day of the Arnhem withdrawal) accompanied by quite a thorough propaganda barrage. But only 250,000 incendiaries were dropped, and they were dropped from Fortresses by daylight, so that the enemy knew roughly where they were, in the area of Frankfurt and Mainz. In spite of these weaknesses the operation was relatively successful, so far as could be judged from the utterances of the enemy: direct evidence of fires could not be expected, but there was ample indirect evidence that the enemy was puzzled and annoyed, and that all Germany was aware of what had been done. Lord Selborne pressed for more action on a larger scale, but unfortunately at this point there was a change in command organisation. The ball was neatly passed back by General Bedell-Smith* to the Strategic Air Forces under the Deputy Chief of the Air Staff and General Spaatz;** thence through the Secretary of State for Air back to SHAEF, which ruled that 'Braddock' should not be reconsidered until 'the situation becomes more fluid'.[1] Lord Selborne tried the Prime Minister once more, again without success,[2] and the hard crust of resistance was only broken by an outflanking move through PWE and the Psychological Warfare Division of SHAEF, which sponsored a scheme for the distribution of 'Braddocks' on a small scale, as part of their plan for an attack on German 'morale' – a bluff rather than a genuine 'Braddock' offensive. SHAEF accepted this on 1st February 1945,[3] and a series of

---

[1] Sir A. Sinclair to Lord Selborne, 7th November 1944: SHAEF letter to DCAS 26th November 1944, copies of both on SOE Archives File XF/28 'Braddock'.

[2] Letter of 28th November to Mr Churchill (copy to Lord Cherwell): COS(44)1063(0) of 30th December: taken COS(45)2nd (0) Mtg.

[3] Signal from Colonel Alms of 4th February, and SHAEF letter of 9th February; copies of both on SOE Archives file XF/28 'Braddock'.

* [W. B. Smith, 1895–1961, Eisenhower's chief of staff 1942–5, Ambassador to Moscow 1946–9, head of CIA 1950–53. See his *Eisenhower's Six Great Decisions* (NY, 1965).]

** [C. A. Spaatz, 1891–1974, observed Battle of Britain 1940, senior American air force commander in Europe 1942–4, in Pacific 1945.]

minor operations began on the night of 20th February with the scattering of 3,500 'Braddocks' in Western Germany by aircraft of the Special Leaflet Squadron.

Some 56,000 'Braddocks' were dropped in this way up to 10th March, when the Prime Minister at last intervened:

Chief of the Air Staff
  Braddock
We have $3^3/_4$ million Braddock incendiaries ready, and the foreign workers in Germany must be very restive by now. Surely the time has come to use this weapon now.
          W.S.C. 10.3.45[1]

It was plainly too late: the COS[2] recommended 'No action' and the Prime Minister submitted. On 7th April General Gubbins formally abandoned the struggle, and SHAEF heartily endorsed his view.[3]

Some three million 'Braddocks' remained, as an awkward problem in the disposal of surplus stock.

It is not easy to estimate how much waste this episode involved, but there was at least the direct labour of 150 women for eighteen months, in addition to the cost of materials and components – none of them in desperately short supply. The story is by no means creditable to British war organisation as a whole: but it is hard to see what more SOE or the Minister could have done. The idea was highly ingenious, the technical development was excellent; it was sponsored by Mr Churchill himself, and SOE acted with full authority at each stage: on every suitable occasion SOE pressed violently for a decision one way or the other – and the decision was never taken. There is no answer to the question whether 'Braddock', as originally planned, was a mare's nest or a war-winner.

6. 'Administrative Sabotage' and 'Black Propaganda'

It will be clear from what has gone before that SOE could not get far in Germany by work on its normal lines of penetration by agents. This was to a small extent compensated by unusual activity in the field which lay on the border between SOE and PWE, that of irritation, humbug and general confusion. No definition of departmental

---

1   Copy on SOE Archives File 0.2(a) 'Braddock'.
2   COS(45)65th, 66th and 71st Mtgs, 12th, 13th and 19th March.
3   General Gubbins's letter to PWE of 7th April, and agreement by Brigadier General McClure, dated 26th April, both on SOE Archives File XF/28 'Braddock'.

functions could have settled who was properly responsible for this: but luckily there was always very close collaboration between Lieutenant Colonel Thornley and Mr Sefton Delmer,* at the head of PWE's section for 'black' activities against Germany, and this was never a field of inter-departmental dispute.

Only a few instances need be selected from this wide range of activities:

(i)   First, there was the attempt to confuse and hamper German administration by the wide distribution of forged ration cards (or even genuine ration cards) of various types, for food, for clothing, for special issues to the 'bombed-out'. This was tried for the first time with 100,000 forged clothing-cards which were dropped by the RAF in July and August 1941. There were sufficient reactions in the German press for the operation to be judged a success, but for various reasons it was not tried again until the spring of 1943:[1] thereafter it was continued with variations until April 1945, when SHAEF closed down operations in view of the imminence of a transfer of administrative responsibility in Germany to the Allies. Operations were never on such a scale as to test fully how German administration and public morals would stand up to an unlimited supply of illicit ration cards: but so far as they went they were successful. It is clear from German documents that the forgeries were very hard to detect except by laboratory methods, and that they could therefore be defeated only by a rapid series of alterations in the form of the genuine documents – at an appreciable expense of German labour and material.

(ii) Subversive propaganda for German troops and U-boat crews was prepared in great quantities by PWE for distribution by SOE, particularly in the occupied countries. The most successful of these efforts was certainly the simple technical guidance on 'malingering', which was issued in many forms, and which elicited a good many counter-blasts from German commanders. This was a weapon with two edges: if German soldiers could secure long leave or exemption from service by malin-

---

[1]   Cf. The Goebbels Diary – a rather doubtful source –

Forged ration cards
16 March 1943
The dropping of forged food-ration cards from English planes is causing a lot of trouble. The use of such cards will be punished severely, in certain cases even by death.

*   [D. S. Delmer, 1904–79, born in Berlin, ran black propganda 1940–45, returned to journalism; in *DNB*.]

gering they were put out of action as certainly as by a bullet: but even the existence of the 'instructions' meant that every German medical officer must think twice or three times during his routine examinations, must waste much time, and might (with luck) even persuade himself that good soldiers were deceiving him with bogus symptons. This scheme culminated eventually in a more elaborate one, which had similar advantages: envelopes were prepared which contained not only incitements to desert but a full set of the necessary papers with which a German soldier could make his way back into Germany – he need only fill in name and details in the right space. This was not done on a large scale: but again there is evidence that the mere knowledge that these forgeries existed (in unknown numbers) was a serious nuisance to the Germans.

(iii) SOE's agents and friends also distributed a good deal of straightforward anti-Nazi propaganda in German, in the usual forms – leaflets, small posters, 'stickers' with anti-Nazi slogans. Much of this was designed so as to appear innocent: a portrait of Hitler with subversive hints on the back, a forged proclamation by General Falkenhorst, the C-in-C in Norway, drawing attention to the frequency of desertions into Sweden, a manifesto purporting to be issued by the SS and denouncing the plots of the Army against Hitler – long before July 1944. Sometimes (as for instance in a clandestine newspaper produced in Stockholm) the material implied that it was issued by German 'underground' movements of various kinds. This was in fact the printed counterpart of the work done by 'Gustav Siegfried Eins' and the other 'black' radio stations of PWE.*

(iv) Finally, there were various hoaxes intended if possible to discredit eminent members of the Nazi hierarchy: or at least to confuse and puzzle. The most famous of these was the 'Himmler stamp', a normal German 6-pfennig stamp with the head of Himmler substituted for that of Hitler. One of these duly arrived in Switzerland, postmarked 'Stuttgart 23rd Sept. 1943', and set going a whole series of interesting speculations in the neutral press on the possibility of a comprehensive plan for Himmler's succession to the role of Führer.[1] The same idea was tried again in April 1945, with a stamp in commemoration of Field Marshal Witzleben,** who had been hung for his part in the July putsch: a mistaken repetition perhaps, but too

---

[1] There is at least one of these philatelic treasures in the SOE Archives – XF/G/82.
* [Again, see Howe, *The Black Game*.]
** [E. von Witzleben, 1881–1944, army commander and field-marshal 1940, retired 1942, was to have headed German Army after 20 July 1944, hanged.]

late to have many repercussions. These two cases were major incidents in a campaign of 'stunts' designed to implicate lesser officials with the Gestapo by planting on them forgeries of various kinds: the tangible results of all this are naturally hard to trace.

Here perhaps (though at the expense of chronological sequence) is the place to explain the greatest hoax of all – at least in intention – 'Operation Periwig'. The real concentration of priorities on the subversion of Germany did not come until August 1944: and it was then clear (at least to some) that it was already too late to create a genuine subversive organisation in Germany. But could not a good deal be achieved, at relatively small cost, by creating an *imaginary* subversive organisation? By the combined organisation and ingenuity of SOE and PWE it should be possible to build up a cloud of evidence of subversion which would at least force the Security Services to divert much of their energy to investigating it. It might even convince them that there was fire behind the smoke, and set the purgative process of July 1944 in motion again: and certainly genuine Allied subversion would operate more easily under this smoke-screen or umbrella.

This was a project of real novelty and great promise, and it is a pity that its possibilities were never seriously tested. The 'Periwig' Planning Section was not set up within SOE until 12th November 1944: it was possible fairly rapidly to produce the outline of an imaginary German resistance movement, in the Army, in the industrial world, in the Church, in the railway system, and to suggest the lines on which evidence of its existence could be built up. But formal approval was not given until 12th January 1945, and even then it was qualified by the condition that no evidence should be manufactured to show that German resistance was backed by the Allies. The reasons for this were partly political, partly the fear that carelessly manufactured evidence might endanger real Allied contacts. The restriction was not removed until 15th February 1945, and in the middle of March SHAEF imposed a new limitation by banning all Allied air supply operations to Germany.

There was thus no serious chance to test the plan, though much of it was set in motion. The kernel of it was a 'picture' of German resistance, which had to be politically sensible and internally consistent, though it was of course subject to continuous modification in detail. Outside Germany SOE had plenty of opportunities to sow rumours which were certain to reach German ears in neutral capitals and in the countries still occupied. Inside Germany what was required was a careful build-up by air operations. This would begin with the dropping of stores and documents to a non-existent reception committee, and the distribution of carrier pigeons. It would culminate in the dropping of German agents who would themselves be convinced of the reality of the imaginary resistance: if they survived they would do real subversive work, if they were caught and examined, they could only add to the deception. The first stages were necessarily hustled: the last was hardly begun. Only four agents in all were dropped, two on 2nd April and two on 18th April, and a fifth was infiltrated from Sweden into Copenhagen: all of them did their best to carry out their imaginary tasks, and all survived and returned to Allied hands. But in April 1945 it was no longer possible to think of 'Periwig' operations in the original sense at all. 'Periwig' (like 'Braddock') is one of the fields of subversion which remains to be explored.

7. The Last Stage

On 2nd August (just as the Americans broke out from the bridgehead) General Gubbins set up a special SOE Committee on Germany with the directive that 'Germany must now be the first priority target for SOE, and all our energies and resources must be concentrated on the penetration of the Reich itself'. SOE's German Section was for the first time to be given a fair chance: it had first claim on SOE's resources, it could operate freely from Allied territory close to Germany, and among the masses of German prisoners potential agents could be found in considerable numbers. Unfortunately it was too late to advance beyond the first stages of organisation.

The scheme of things was somewhat confused by the existence of SHAEF and OSS: but an amicable (if rather vague) arrangement was reached easily enough between them. SOE's German operations would be controlled by the section in London, which was up-graded in October 1944 to the status of Directorate, under Major General G. W. R. Templer, CB, DSO, OBE.* Special Forces HQ, in which OSS had been fully integrated with SOE, ceased to exist, and OSS set out to organise operations of its own on a large scale. Both SOE and OSS were to operate under the general direction of SHAEF, and they did receive various directives from it, generally issued in vague terms after a prolonged period of incubation. In practice co-ordination was largely secured by the presence of Colonel R. E. Brook at SHAEF HQ, as chief British Liaison Officer both for SOE and SIS.

At the same time SOE sent forward various Missions into liberated Europe, partly to 'liquidate' its existing commitments there, partly to act as forward bases for action against Germany. These were:

    (a) ME24 (or SPU24), the SOE Mission which reached Paris in September 1944. This party had its hands full in assisting the

---

* [(Sir Gerald Templer, 1898–1979, knight 1949, KG 1963, CIGS 1955–8; in *DNB*. See his life by John Cloake (1985).]

French to establish the basis of their own SO organisation in France. In spite of harassing disputes between the DGER (under 'Passy' and M. Soustelle) and the Ministry of Prisonniers de Guerre et Déportés (under M. Frenay), a number of training schools were organised for the French in France, and some forty French organisers and wireless operators were put through the SOE schools in England. All this effort produced only two French Missions to Germany: the three men involved survived, but achieved little.

(b) A similar Mission was established in Brussels late in 1944 to work with the Belgian special services: the Belgians set to work energetically and with less misdirected effort than the French, and in the end fourteen agents had been dispatched to Germany in the attempt to reach and organise Belgian workers there. All except three (who were lost in an aircraft crash) survived until the Armistice, but without any striking achievements.

(c) The Dutch problem was more difficult, as the most important parts of the country were still occupied by the Germans and on the edge of starvation. The Dutch could not be very interested in the subsidiary issue of working into Germany while Holland itself was under the threat of imminent destruction. SOE's representative with Dutch HQ at Eindhoven had little success in recruiting suitable workers: and nothing came of attempts to set things moving from inside occupied Holland through SOE's agents there. This remained a dead end.

(d) Finally there was SPU22, which had an adventurous history. It originated in the dispatch to Lille on 3rd September 1944 of Lieutenant Colonel Hazell, of SOE's Polish Section, to investigate and settle the affairs of the 'Monica' Polish organisation in that area.[1] On his advice a small Mission was formed for the 'liquidation' of the 'Monica' organisation and the encouragement of Polish infiltration into Germany. The Mission was established first in the Lille–Roubaix area, then in mid-October it moved forward into the Belgian Ardennes in order to find a suitable base for infiltration through the front lines. Twelve Poles had already been recruited for work into Germany: but there were difficulties (very natural in the political circumstances) with higher Polish authorities. It was not until early in December 1944 that leave for Polish operations was granted, and meantime SPU22 had found valuable occupation in foraging for German identity documents, ration cards, uniforms, and so on, which were desperately needed by SOE

---

[1] Above p. 579.

in London. Lieutenant Colonel Hazell made a valuable haul of these in Aachen shortly after its capture: and it was then decided that this should become one of the official duties of SPU22. At the same time SPU22 found that it was indispensable as a dispatch centre for infiltration of other agents besides Poles: by mid-December it was receiving Germans and Frenchmen also and was becoming dispersed between various houses in the Belgian and French Ardennes.

SPU22 had thus (without a pre-conceived plan) become the advanced HQ for most of SOE's work into Germany overland from the West. Unfortunately its rapid development suffered two serious set-backs. First, at Christmas, it had to withdraw hastily into Northern Belgium in face of the Rundstedt offensive, and it was some time before it could re-establish itself in the Ghent district. Second, it was operating in a US area with the verbal approval of SHAEF but without that of 12th US Army Group and 1st US Army, who were immediately responsible. Lieutenant Colonel Hazell was permitted to remain, although OSS was (for some personal reason) excluded: but he had to draw all his stores from British sources far in the rear, and he was not allowed to infiltrate agents through the most suitable fronts, those of 1st and 9th US Armies: operations had to be limited to the much more constricted areas of 21st (British) Army Group and 3rd US Army.

In these circumstances the effective achievements of this vigorous unit were not very extensive. For 'long-term' work in civilian clothes they managed to infiltrate five Poles and one German: but by the end of March 1945 it was clearly too late to build up any sort of organisation on this basis, and in the last phase the French, Belgian and German agents at SPU22's disposal were used for short-range intelligence and 'commando' work, in collaboration with the SF Detachments in 21 Army Group:[1] some of these operations were (on a small scale) highly successful. In the end SPU22 went forward with 21 Army Group in its advance into Germany, to be absorbed eventually in ME42, SOE's Mission attached to the British occupying forces.

This completes the framework of the organisation in the West: we have already seen the part played by the Missions in neutral countries, particularly Switzerland and Sweden, and the operations directed against Austria from the South. The Directorate in London (at least in principle) co-ordinated all these activities: it was also largely responsible for selecting and training suitable German agents from the endless stream of prisoners: and it was directly responsible for the conduct of air operations into Germany from the West.

---

[1] A special detachment accompanied No. 6 Airborne Division on the Wesel Operation.

Two of these operations are worth mentioning specifically. Early in September an agent called Kappius, provided by the ISK, was dropped 'blind' for organisation work in the Ruhr area. His wife 'Jutta' had worked with SOE in Switzerland, and had already made one trip as a courier to Germany in May 1944: she succeeded in entering Germany again in September 1944 and in January 1945, and in bringing back reports from her husband. Eventually Kappius was overrun by the advancing Americans at Bochum (his home town) in April 1945. His case at least proved that an experienced man could survive and work in Germany for some time: but he found extreme difficulty (in spite of his experience) in starting a working organisation of any kind, and he had no communication with his base except by the cumbrous procedure of a courier to Switzerland.

The other case was that of a very courageous Jew named Becker *alias* 'Captain Baker-Byrne'. He was first used for an attempt to attack a small precision engineering workshop in Berlin, which was believed to be engaged on work for the V.1 or the V.2, and was dropped blind on the night of 26th November 1944: by 3rd December he had reached Switzerland. His Mission had failed, as he had been seen while breaking into the workshop and had to escape hastily: nevertheless, his report contained valuable experience and he was ready to try again, this time as an organiser in the Lübeck area. Unfortunately his dispatch was delayed until almost the last moment: he did not reach the area until 22nd April and he was overrun by British troops before he had any chance to develop an organisation.

The other air operations from England were all carried out by 'Bonzos' – prisoners of war diverted from the stream before their existence as POWs had been officially notified. Fifty-four of these men were put in training, under great pressure of time, and they proved to be good material: but naturally their work had to be limited to relatively simple tasks. In addition, there were always serious limitations imposed by other services on SOE's air operations into Germany: partly by the RAF, on account of the heavy German defences in particular areas, partly by SIS which had priority for its intelligence operations and was anxious to take no risk of compromising its agents. In spite of these difficulties eleven operations, involving nineteen men, were carried out between November 1944 and April 1945: casualties were low, and nine of the Missions were at least in part successful. None of them however established radio contact with their base.

One other piece of organisation is worth mentioning, though it was not specifically the work of SOE. On 17th March the decision was taken by the War Office to form the 'Special Allied Airborne Reconnaissance Force' (SAARF). The object of this organisation was to provide rapid means of establishing communications with Allied prisoners of war and displaced persons in Germany at the moment of final collapse: with the object of keeping them together, protecting them against any lunatic attempts at massacre, and arranging the supply by air of the immediate necessities of life. It was to consist of 120 teams of various nationalities, organised on the 'Jedburgh' plan, two officers and one radio operator in each team. SOE offered to provide twelve teams of trained men: and in addition there fell on it almost the whole burden of extemporising signals arrangements, equipment, and training. In the end the organisation was not required: the Allied advance was so swift that only a few teams were landed, and they were quickly overrun. The episode is chiefly interesting as an instance of the speed with which such an organisation could be extemporised now that SOE existed as a fully equipped and trained branch of the British service: three years earlier (in Middle East for instance) it would have taken a year at least to create what was now extemporised efficiently in a month.[1]

SOE's German experience ended negatively, as it had begun: the whole resources of the organisation could not in the time available improvise an 'underground' in Germany on a scale sufficient to be of much practical value in the last Allied offensive. There were various particular factors in the case, favourable and unfavourable, and one cannot generalise from it too far: but it is the only case in which a really mature and well-equipped attempt was made to build up a resistance at top speed out of nothing. For what it is worth it indicates that the period of nine months from August 1944 to April 1945 was too short. By April 1945 visible progress had been made: a few agents were quite solidly established both in Germany and Austria, and SOE had sufficient experience to send in a number of others for special short Missions with relative safety. But there was still no standing organisation: no wireless sets were on the air, and there were no reception committees; development was still at the stage of the 'blind drop', and there were only the slight beginnings of a native organisation crystallising around SOE's men. These circumstances can never exactly recur: but they give some indication that a year of skilled work, at top pressure and on high priority, is the very shortest period in which anything substantial can be achieved, even by a fully-developed organisation.

---

[1] There is a very full report on SAARF by the CO, Brigadier J. S. Nichols, DSO, MC, bound up with Vol. II of the SOE German History.

CHAPTER XXIX

The Final Form of SOE

So much of the organisation and political history of SOE has already appeared in the context of the events which shaped it that this final chapter must be mainly one of summary and recapitulation. It is however proper in this place to present some comprehensive picture of the organisation as it existed in its prime.

1. Politics

The political history of SOE after the summer of 1942 falls into four phases. In the first phase, which lasts until the spring or early summer of 1943, Lord Selborne's policy of 'appeasement' towards the Foreign Office, PWE, and other hostile departments appears to bear fruit. Areas of conflicting responsibility are defined and delimited, the lower ranks of the organisation become more conscious that they have duties as well as rights in dealing with other departments, and there is some hope that these departments are beginning to respect SOE and to understand what it can and cannot do to help them. Unluckily events in the Middle East renew the atmosphere of acute controversy and lead in September 1943 to what SOE thought of as the 'Middle East Defence Committee crisis',[1] in effect an agreement between the Foreign Office and the military in the Middle East to eliminate SOE as an independent directing body in that area. This is faced by SOE as an issue which affects its future everywhere, not only in the Middle East: and it becomes involved in London with the competing claims of the Bomber Command's 'Battle of Berlin' and with the irrelevant but shocking evidence of SOE's mistakes in Holland. This phase of conflict ended in January 1944. It was closed partly by the resolution of Lord Selborne, partly by the goodwill of Mr Churchill, partly because the imminence of 'Overlord' made the debate seem ridiculous: but it was also important that none of SOE's enemies had any constructive alternative to offer. If SOE did not exist it would have to be invented: it was a going concern, the centre of a web of relationships which could not be handled (for instance) by the Foreign Office or by the War Office without a great change in the

---

[1] Above p. 415.

nature of these departments. It was tacitly admitted that SOE had a job to do: the problem of definition was (very wisely) evaded, but it was now clear that the job was important and that it was not the job of any older department.

In the third phase, roughly from January to September 1944, SOE is reaping the harvest of earlier labours and disappointments: there is little room for inter-departmental disputes while work is so intense and at the same time so exhilaratingly successful. SOE has certainly moved a long way from the original 'grand design' of a unified weapon of political warfare: it is a fighting service, and its relations with the propaganda services are not strikingly more important to it than those of the other organs of the Allied military command. It has not secured the formal adoption of its doctrine of the 'Fourth Arm', but in practice its position and organisation are roughly comparable to those of the Admiralty, War Office and Air Ministry. The 'head office' is responsible for all administrative services – recruitment, training, supply, signals, technical development, the 'doctrine' of the service: its planners work very closely with the COS organisation: but operational control rests with the Supreme Allied Commanders, who work through integrated Special Operations HQs of various types, in which SOE is strongly represented and highly influential.

Pressure relaxes when the summer campaign is over. Scandinavia and some of the Balkan countries remain important, and there is a concentration of resources against Germany: but the greatest of all SOE's efforts had been in France, and all that remains there is the complicated task of 'liquidating' the organisation: tracing the missing, clearing financial claims, piecing together the story of what had really happened and drawing lessons for the future. War in the Far East continued and SOE's work there assumed great importance in 1944 and 1945: but after V-E day in Europe there was no longer a sufficient role for an independent ministry. On 31st May 1945 Lord Selborne retired from office and responsibility for the organisation passed to the Foreign Office: during Mr Churchill's 'caretaker' Government, Lord Lovat,* the Parliamentary Under-Secretary, was specially concerned. Finally, on 31st December 1945, SOE closed down,** leaving only a small nucleus to settle the endless problems of 'liquidation'.

2. Size and Cost of the Organisation

There are certain obvious questions to which the reader will expect to find an answer at this stage. How big a department was SOE? How

---

* [S. C. J. Fraser, 1911–95, 17th Lord Lovat 1933, led commando brigade in Normandy 1944; in *DNB*.]

** [15 January 1946 is the date usually given.]

many did it employ? What did it cost? Unfortunately it is for various reasons impossible to answer as directly as one would wish.

In the first place, it is extremely difficult to say where SOE begins and where it ends. As regards agents in the field, there is a series of delicate gradations. At one extreme are British officers and men, trained, paid and dispatched by SOE. Then there are members of the foreign forces in Great Britain or the Middle East, also sponsored wholly by SOE but dividing their loyalty between it and their own government. There are also agents recruited in the field by these 'men from England'; paid and directed by them but never themselves in direct contact with SOE. Finally, there is the whole mass of resistance workers who took some money, or some arms, or some guidance from SOE, but were not in any sense at all its servants. Even within the circle of British government it is difficult to draw clear lines, because there was in war-time no elaborate system of accounting between departments. SOE was not debited with the cost of the RAF squadrons which served it; nor with the cost of the military and civil stores which it drew through various departmental channels; nor with many of the overhead costs of its training and supply establishments. The proportion of the costs of SOE borne on the open vote of other departments was fairly large, as it was the policy to limit payments from Secret Funds to those which could not with security be made in other ways; and there was a similar tendency to keep down the numbers of those employed directly by SOE. But individual cases were decided on their merits, and no general principle emerges.

In the second place, records of personnel were not kept centrally until a comparatively late stage in the development of the department, partly for reasons of security, partly because selection was highly personal and total figures for establishment and strength were not of much administrative value. This lack of system could not continue when manpower became the main bottle-neck in the war effort, and when many of SOE's formations had to work alongside regular military units: but it was not until September 1943 that a section was set up to keep SOE's manpower figures as a basis for bidding in the regular auction of manpower priorities.

Finally, the one part of SOE's records which has not been available to the historian is that covering its drawings from Secret Funds. These figures would make an interesting series, but there are good constitutional reasons for withholding them; and in any case they are of much less historical importance than seems likely at first sight. They did not cover more than a small part of the total cost of SOE, and their relation to that total cost varied greatly at different stages in the development of the department. Figures for cash expenditure in various countries have been given in the narrative where they are available; these figures are generally those recorded by the Section concerned, but they are not necessarily either accurate or complete.

The upshot of this is that the only sets of figures worth including are those compiled by the Personnel Statistics Section from September 1943. As a starting point it may be recalled[1] that in July 1942 the figures for SOE staff given by the 'Playfair Report' were:

Home:	HQ	691
	Elsewhere	1,462
Middle East	(excluding	
	444 Army personnel)	608
America		100
Far East & India		203
Other Missions		162
	Total	3,226

This included all men and women, civilian as well as service. By June 1943 manpower shortage had become a serious matter and SOE's establishment of *military* personnel was formally limited to a 'ceiling' of 7,000. In August 1943 SOE was anxious that this should be raised to 11,000, and there was much hard bargaining with the DSD at the War Office (Major General Steele).[2]* The highest point reached by SOE on the military side was a British Army establishment of 12,000 in February 1944, subject to a premise that not more than 10,000 personnel should actually be drawn from British Army sources. In October 1944 SOE attempted to secure a little more elbow-room, but this last attack was beaten off fairly easily by DSD, and these maximum figures were not exceeded so far as the British Army was concerned. By the end of 1944 the tide had turned, and throughout 1945 SOE like all other Service organisations was being pressed hard for a swift reduction of staff.[3]

The position as regards Army *establishments* is thus fairly clear: it is much harder to present adequate figures for actual *strength*, and to include 'bodies' drawn from other sources as well as from the Army. The Personnel Statistics section took some time to get into its stride,

---

[1] Above p. 332.

[2] The course of events can be followed fairly clearly in MO1(SP) Folder B.M.546, which also circulated within the War Office.

[3] COS(44)286th Mtg, Minute 12, of 24th August 1944, and ensuing series of COS papers to COS(46)25(0) of 23rd January 1946 (largely on SOE Archives File 1/110/1).

* [(Sir)] J. S. Steele, 1894–1975, director of staff duties 1943–4, knight 1946, C-in-C Austria 1946–7; in *DNB*.]

and its first figures which purport to be complete are for 15th December 1943.[1] They may be summarised as follows:

	Army	Navy	RAF	Civilians	Total
Home	3,833	25	142	1,052	5,052
North Africa	298	51	19	82	450
Italy	143	1	3	17	164
Middle East	2,350	9	93	227	2,679
India	350	7	4	113	474
Other Missions	92	–	–	–	92
Totals	7,066	93	261	1,491	8,911

Within this total the proportion of officers (or civilians of officer status) was high, about 2,000 out of 9,000; and of these 475 were reported to be working at London HQ. There are no figures for the clerical and other junior staff at HQ, much of which was outside 'manpower' categories: but clearly the HQ was much bigger than in July 1942, when 247 'officers' had been served by 444 junior staff.

The figures for 30th April 1944 show a very marked increase, which may in part have been due to improved 'accounting', as the figures are broken down in greater detail in the full table. The main heads are now as follows:

	Army	Navy	RAF	Women's Services	Civilians	Total
Home: HQ	401	12	52	214	816	1,495
Outstations	3,881	2	101	986	429	5,409
N. Africa & Italy	891	53	28	121	–	1,093
Middle East	2,644	9	78	91	166	2,988
India & China	511	11	7	18	139	686
Miscellaneous	73	3	–	–	5	81
Totals	8,401	100	266	1,430	1,555	11,752

Of these 2,222 were officers or of equivalent status.

These complete totals were apparently produced at this stage only as a result of special enquiries, and they do not begin to run as a monthly (eventually a weekly) series until October 1944. The trend during the hectic summer of 1944 can be shown from the series of figures for Army personnel only, which begin at the end of 1943. No-one who has tried to compile such figures will be surprised that this series does not at first sight quite match the totals given by special

---

[1] App. A to paper forwarded on 17th January 1944 – Folio 8A on BM546.

investigations. There is no reason to doubt its accuracy as an indication of the main trend:

	Army Personnel Only			
	15 Dec. 43	*30 Apr. 44*	*31 Jul. 44*	*31 Oct. 44*
Home	3,833	4,202	4,231	4,315
Middle East	2,350	2,663 ⎱	3,709	3,593
N. Africa & Italy	441	801 ⎰		
India	350	428	764	940
Miscellaneous	92	73	92	–
	7,066	8,167	8,796	8,848

From this point the tale is taken up by the series of totals, which purport to be complete except for the exclusion of Indian Army personnel and Indian civilian labour.

		31 Oct. 1944	*31 Dec. 1944*	*31 Mar. 1945*	*30 Jun. 1945*	*30 Sep. 1945*	*30 Nov. 1945*
Home:	'Officer'	1,484	1,410	1,388	1,120	578	379
	Other	6,073	5,492	5,498	4,548	2,342	1,336
Med:	'Officer'	778	686	422	168	23	20
	Other	3,264	3,003	2,287	677	49	46
India:	'Officer'	450	540	676	770	830	563
	Other	843	1,132	1,427	1,878	2,122	1,691
Totals:	'Officer'	2,712	2,636	2,486	2,058	1,431	962
	Other	10,180	9,627	9,212	7,103	4,513	3,073
Grand Total		12,892	12,263	11,698	9,161	5,944	4,035

These figures are quite adequate for our purposes, and may be summed up broadly as follows:

(a) SOE reached its maximum expansion in the late summer and early autumn of 1944, when its total British strength was probably just under 13,000: of these just under 9,000 were drawn from the British Army.

(b) The strength available for 'Force 136' in India continued to increase until after VJ-day: and included much native Indian and other native assistance outside these figures.

(c) The total includes about 450 ATS, 60 WAAF, and 1,500 FANY, as well as nearly 1,200 civilian women: about 3,200 women, of whom about 400 were of 'officer status'.

(d) Apart from the women's services, the proportion of 'officers' was very high. Taking men only, there were about 2,300 officers in a total of under 10,000. Many of these officers were of outstanding quality, either as specialists or as fighting men

– or as both. The 'other ranks' on the other hand were largely of low medical categories engaged in 'housekeeping' duties.

(e) The organisation was now almost entirely military: apart from female secretaries, it included only about 400 civilians in all.

    This is therefore an inconclusive section. The evidence will support only these very general conclusions: and even if there were more evidence, it would not help us to decide whether SOE was 'economically' run and whether it 'paid its way'. Too much of the cost lay outside the direct control of SOE.

3. Internal Organisation at HQ

We have already seen that SOE's internal organisation was always in transition: at any given moment some part of the machine was in process of adaptation to new crises. But some picture of its working can be given by annotating briefly the composition of the SOE Council during the peak period of June 1944.[1]

Chief of the Organisation & Chairman of Council (CD): Major-General C. McV. Gubbins, who was in effect the Commanding Officer, under the general direction of Lord Selborne. 'Council' met weekly, and most issues of policy were discussed by it and recorded in its Minutes: but the organisation was commanded by a man, not by a committee.

Vice Chief (V/CD): Mr H. N. Sporborg (who held the rank of Colonel, but acted normally as a civilian). On the retirement of Mr Gladwyn Jebb in May 1942 there was abolished the old duality between CEO, the Minister's right-hand man or 'Permanent Secretary', and 'CD', the active manager: Mr Sporborg was attached to Lord Selborne rather as Principal Private Secretary (for SOE business) than as 'Permanent Secretary'. When it was decided in September 1943 (after considerable heart-searching) to appoint a soldier to the post of CD, the additional post of V/CD was created and was filled by Mr Sporborg as a civilian. The post of Private Secretary was now taken over by a younger man, Mr Victor M. Cannon-Brookes.

Deputy Chief (D/CD): Mr M. P. Murray, a civil servant of the administrative class who had much experience on the organisation side of the Air Ministry. His appointment in November 1943 represented a rather belated attempt to take advantage of Whitehall experience of large-scale organisation: the more conventional of the war-time Ministries were built from the first on a scaffolding of professional

---

[1] An organisation chart for the spring of 1944 is at Appendix N.

civil servants, who rendered immense service by introducing simple principles of order and inter-departmental co-operation at the outset. Mr Murray assumed general responsibility for problems of internal organisation, served by a Directorate of Organisation and Staff Duties: there was an immense volume of work for this Directorate to do, but it came rather behind events and its job was in the main to clean up rather than to plan ahead.

Assistant Chief (A/CD): Air Commodore A. R. Boyle, who combined the posts of Director of Intelligence, Director of Security and Director of Personnel Services. Intelligence was, it turned out, primarily handled by the Country Sections, and little came of the original plan for a central Directorate of Intelligence, but Security and Personnel were of enormous importance and required the continuous application of persistence, experience and tact.

Chief Staff Officer to CD and liaison with Chiefs of Staff: Colonel R. H. Barry, whose job was virtually that of Director of Plans, as it came to be understood in the Service departments – a post of liaison between strategic policy and the multiple concerns of specialist Directorates.

The remaining posts on this high level fall into three categories:

Regional Directorates

Director of London Group: Brigadier E. E. Mockler-Ferryman, under whom came France, Holland and Belgium (Colonel R. E. Brook), Scandinavia (Colonel J. S. Wilson) and Germany (Colonel R. H. Thornley). Integration with the Americans and French causes some confusion here: from January 1944 there was full integration with OSS (in SFHQ) as regards the whole SHAEF area (which excluded Germany); from June 1944 there was integration with the French in EMFFI for France alone.

Director of Mediterranean Group: Colonel D. J. Keswick, who was the London 'opposite number' of the integrated organisation SOM (Special Operations Mediterranean), which came into being in Italy in April 1944.[1]

Director of Cairo Group (more exactly 'Head of SOM'): Major General W. A. M. Stawell, who was naturally not often present in London.

Director of Far East Group: Colonel G. F. Taylor, a very old SOE hand, who was the London end of all questions relating to the Japanese war.

---

[1]   There is a history of HQ SOM with SOE Archives.

Director of Delhi Group: Mr Colin Mackenzie, SOE's representative at Lord Mountbatten's HQ, who was not frequently in London.

Service Directorates

Director of Finance and Administration: Group Captain J. F. Venner, the pillar of financial orthodoxy and channel of liaison with the Treasury. Under him came a less orthodox financier, Mr Walter Fletcher, who was responsible for all SOE's vast and curious dealings in foreign currencies.

Director of Research, Development and Supply: Colonel F. T. Davies. Here lay the responsibility for research (Professor D. M. Newitt, FRS), and for all SOE's large production activities.

Director of Signals: Colonel F. W. Nicholls,* the enthusiast who had built up the SOE signals system from its beginnings in the spring of 1942.

Advisers

Naval Director: Rear Admiral A. H. Taylor, CB, OBE.

Air Adviser: Air Vice-Marshal A. P. Ritchie, CBE, AFC.

Political Adviser: Mr W. E. Houston-Boswall, CMG, MC: a happy appointment of a regular Foreign Office official, which was unfortunately not made until August 1943.

'Council' was thus a body of sixteen men, two of them normally *in absentia*. It was on the whole a 'functional' body, and most of its members were individually responsible for the conduct of very large operations, administrative or military: there was little provision for 'non-functional' directors and 'long-term thinking', such as is sometimes advocated by professional advisers on administration. There were numerous attempts to produce a long-term planning section, from the ill-starred SO3 in the late summer of 1940 until the appointment of Major Taylor as Chief of Staff to CD, which was abandoned in July 1942:[1] but they all failed. It seemed that in practice such a scheme broke down on a disjunction: *either* the 'long-term' section was so far outside the normal activities of the department that it had no useful experience or material from which to plan: *or* it insisted on consultation to the point of becoming a bottle-neck which slowed up and duplicated the work of other sections.

---

[1] CD/OR/2473 of 8th July 1942, para. 2(a); copy on SOE Archives File 2/340/3.1.
* [1889–1974, expert signaller; in *DNB*.]

In the end the need was met fairly well by that obscure thing, the 'spirit of the department'. Members of Council represented a great variety of experience: out of sixteen there were five regular soldiers (one of them a signaller), two airmen (one 'wingless'), a sailor, a professional civil servant, a Foreign Office man, a solicitor, an accountant, and five businessmen of various types. About half of them had been in the organisation from very early days and had risen with it: Major Gubbins and Mr Taylor had been at work in MI(R) and D Section before SOE was invented, Mr Sporborg, Wing Commander Venner and Major Davies had been in it from the first, and others had come in before the end of 1941. All alike believed passionately in the purpose and possibilities of SOE: the fact that they had heavy administrative duties did not prevent them from speculating and debating on the nature and power of 'subversion'. There was no agreed and analysed 'staff College' doctrine: but there was none the less an immensely strong 'public opinion' within the organisation which expressed itself forcibly on Council level and was felt much lower down. The administration of SOE had many failings which can be defended only by explaining the stress under which the organisation grew: but much had been put right by the summer of 1944, and there was a spirit of excitement and personal concern which atoned for much. The distribution of duties was sometimes obscure or overlapping; but the entire staff was looking for duties, not seeking to evade them. This was not an unmixed blessing, but it meant that things somehow got done, fairly speedily and fairly correctly, though not with perfect economy. Luckily the staff as a whole were relatively young even at the top, at least by Whitehall standards, and many of these physically fit for it had intervals of operational experience: if security prevented them from going to the field, at least they took part in training and in many cases visited Missions and stations overseas. This had two advantages: the organisation was in spirit pretty close to the fighting line, and it suffered less than many departments from sheer physical collapse under the strain of overwork. Few of the 'old SOE hands' were absent from duty through sickness for any long period during the war.[1]

4. Ancillary Services

Enough has already been said of the tangled history of SOE's Missions overseas in the Mediterranean Theatre and in neutral capitals: but it remains to give some account of the great ancillary services in

---

[1] PWE makes an illuminating contrast in this respect: see Sir R. Bruce Lockhart's 'Comes the Reckoning' and a little chart of sickness among directing staff given in Mr Garnett's 'History of PWE'.

England, which lay behind all operational work but have so far been crowded off the stage by the narrative of events for which they were largely responsible. The technical aspects of their work have been fully dealt with in the confidential 'Handbooks' which each Section produced before its dissolution: their administrative problems were extremely complex, but not fundamentally different from those of other war organisations. There were however a number of developments from SOE's work which were new, either in conception or in scale, and it is desirable at least to illustrate these here, though it would not be possible to do them justice except by a more technical account.

The main heads are:
(i)   The design and manufacture of special equipment and its dispatch to the field.
(ii) The training of agents.
(iii) The maintenance of radio communication with agents. It will be simplest to look at these in their developed form, ignoring most of their complex early history.

(i) Research, Production and Supply

First, the *Research Section*, Station IX; some small but valuable assets were inherited from D Section,[1] but the main line of development began early in 1941 at 'The Frythe', Welwyn Garden City, when research was first formally separated from production. Under the Director of Scientific Research, Professor Newitt, there were four main lines of activity – physico-chemical, engineering, operational research and comouflage. The first two of these were built round the problems of fuses and of devices in which to use them. On the physico-chemical side great advances were made in the development of simple foolproof time-fuses and incendiaries, and in the technique of explosive charges to be used for clandestine work: the engineering side arose out of the development of such devices as the magnetic 'limpet' bomb. Chemical research diverged into biochemical fields, such as the investigation of poisons, sleeping doses, suicide pills, and the development of special rations for various operational conditions. Engineering was involved naturally in the design of special fire-arms, silent or easily concealed: less naturally in the production of submersible craft. There was not much logical justification for the development at Welwyn Garden City and Staines Reservoir of such craft as the 'Welman' one-man submarine, its larger brother the 'Welfreighter', and the 'Sleeping Beauty' motor submersible canoe, which should all in theory have been naval responsibilities. But they were well designed and they reached production fairly rapidly; that

---

[1]   See Appendix B to Research and Development Section History.

part of the job was well done, however unorthodox the organisation. But unfortunately it proved in the end that they were not very suitable for SOE's purposes, at least in Europe. In Norway[1] for instance it proved to be safer and more effective for agents to work with simpler weapons; their most important asset was skill, patience and local knowledge, not 'suicide weapons', however ingenious. The trouble was that the research department had pushed on with the development of weapons in advance of any experience from which operational requirements could be framed.

This is the central problem of organisation for all research into weapons, and it was particularly difficult for SOE to solve it. It began its work by the light of nature, entirely without operational experience: and it was hard for it to capitalise experience as it was gained. Saboteurs are not usually good technical observers, nor can they take with them technical advisers, so that Operational Research was not possible for SOE in the same sense as for the other Services. There was a serious danger that the user and the scientist would remain apart, and that research would be wasted on unreal problems. An Operational Research Section was ultimately formed in July 1943, but its work was in practice rather liaison than research: its position was that of the Director of Operational Requirements in the Air Staff, not that of the 'boffin' attached to a night fighter squadron armed with new radar equipment. On the one hand it knew the Country Sections and (when possible) it met their best agents, on the other it knew what technical development had done and could do if asked. Putting these two sides together, it could frame an operational requirement which would be closely related to practical needs: and it would then follow through the development of the new device from this point up to final trials which would precede a decision on production.

This is probably the most that can be done. In the latter days of SOE there was talk of technical missions to the field, and of specialised training for selected agents: but the obvious difficulties were not overcome and it is doubtful if they can be overcome. In the really critical phase of an underground war it is quite impossible to put detached observers in the front line. It requires the highest skill and concentration at that stage for front-line troops even to maintain themselves in being, and they cannot be expected to look after scientists in the field. The most that can be done is to see that the scientists (or selected scientists) live, work, and think with the staff sections which direct the battle.

Second, there was *camouflage*, which had rather a special meaning in this context. Perfection of disguise in every detail was necessary to protect the agent: and in addition rougher but effective

---

[1]   As we have seen above, p. 663 (the failure of 'Vestige').

camouflage was necessary to allow rapid concealment of many ordinary items of stores – containers, ammunition, weapons and so forth. In the early days Country Sections dealt with their own problem individually as best they could, and the first general adviser on camouflage did not arrive until November 1941. This was an energetic film technician, Mr (later Lieutenant Colonel) J. E. Wills, and the inspiration of drawing on the film studios for experts proved to be very sound: a small workshop, with a staff of three, was opened at the Research Station (Station IX) in January 1942, and this small force expanded eventually into an establishment of some 300, including a bewildering range of experts in all sorts of trades.

The final organisation was:

Station XV: the 'Thatched Barn', a road house on the Barnet by-pass, which was the main production centre for the camouflage of stores.

Station XVA: 56, Queen's Gate, SW7, where prototypes were designed for reproduction in quantity. This was also the main centre for 'ageing' clothing to a condition which would match the wearer's story. In addition, it was necessary that the tailoring of clothes should give no hint of British origin: at first sufficient genuine clothing could be secured from refugees or exiles, but in the end production was required on a considerable scale. This was mainly in the hands of outside firms, employing refugee work-people who produced in their own national styles unconscious that there was anything odd about their methods.

Station XVB was buried in the desolate halls of the Natural History Museum in South Kensington, which lay derelict for the duration of the war. Its main purpose was to serve as a centre for the instruction of agents and others in the principles of camouflage: but in course of time its 'Demonstration Room' became a very remarkable museum, displaying SOE 'gadgets' for the benefit of all whom it was desired to impress and to instruct, from HM The King downwards. Some of the 'gadgets' were of intense practical interest: there was for instance a series of agents' wireless sets ranging from the first heavy and clumsy suit-case to the last vest-pocket model; there were standard fuses; there were devices such as the limpet, which saw much hard service. There was also a certain amount of fantasy; explosive rats, designed to cause confusion to any enemy who flung their corpses into a furnace, and Balinese images sculptured out of plastic explosive, in the hope that native agents might be able to sell them (complete with time-fuses) to Japanese departing from the East Indies.

Finally there was *Station XVC*, the photographic and make-up department, accommodated in a small house in Trevor Square.

Closely allied to the problem of camouflage was that of forgery. Convincing documents were as vital as convincing disguise: so vital that there was an independent Documents Section, served by its own production department, Station XIV, at Briggens, near Royden, in Essex. As has already been mentioned,[1] this grew at first out of Polish enterprise.

Production in part developed from Research and Camouflage: SOE made a good deal of its own equipment in its own workshops, and there were occasional outcries about the overlapping of its work with that of the regular production departments. But on the whole SOE produced or purchased directly only small quantities of specialised equipment: its requirements were for the most part met through orthodox channels. Military stores were drawn through the War Office, under the alias of MO1(SP); stores were also drawn, on a much smaller scale, from the Admiralty and the Air Ministry: if special production was necessary, the appropriate supply department was generally willing to give SOE adequate priority for its small needs without serious debate on a high level.[2]

Within the SOE organisation there were certain central points for the handling of stores: the military equipment depot at Knoll School, Camberley: the arms section, which was from the latter part of 1941 at Bride Hall, Welwyn; the Motor Transport Section, with its own repair depot at North Road Garage, Welwyn. These presented no unusual problems: what was new and remarkable was the organisation for making up containers and packages for dispatch to the field.

At first each package was made up individually, generally by the officers of the Section concerned, and the parachutes were packed and attached at the RAF Depot at Henlow, which also packed the parachutes used by the agents themselves. This was a hole-and-corner business, carried out in a mysterious way behind a screen at one end of a large Parachute Repair Shop. By the end of 1941 there had been substantial expansion, and in May 1942 there was set up the 'Special Parachute Equipment Section', with a staff of thirty, largely WAAF: in all from May 1942 to January 1945 it handled 19,863 packages, manufactured 10,900 parachute harnesses, and packed 27,980 parachutes, as well as doing a good deal of repair work. From May to September 1944 the *monthly* rate was 1,692 packages, 775 harnesses, 2,127 parachutes. In addition the unit acted as a research and development centre for the use of parachutes in special operations, and it

---

[1] Above p. 315 – see also History of Station XIV; copy with SOE Archives.

[2] The only serious incident known to the author is the 'parachute crisis' which occurred towards the end of 1943. There was an acute shortage of store-dropping parachutes to meet the needs of Airborne Forces, SAS and other organisations as well as SOE, and this threatened at one time to be as bad a bottle-neck as the allocation of aircraft. A special effort was made, both to increase production and to economise expenditure, and it was in the end successful.

was largely responsible for the development of various 'shock-absorb-ing' containers[1] and of the 'leg-bag' technique for dropping personal stores actually with the agent.

Henlow was concerned with the mechanics of dropping: the contents of the packages were handled mainly by SOE's own pack-ing station, Station 61, which was opened at Audley End, Saffron Walden, in October 1941, and moved in April 1942 to Gaynes' Hall, St Neots. The big expansion began in the summer of 1942, when the idea of the 'standard container' was introduced; various 'contents lists' were standardised,[2] so that an operational section could meet most contingencies from the stock of ready-packed containers which was built up at Station 61. The Packing Station had still to meet special requirements at times, but for the most part it was working on a steady crescendo to build up a reserve stock of containers for D-day. Its record of containers packed was:

1941	95
1942	2,176
1943	13,435
1944	56,464
1945	4,334
Total	76,504 – some 10,000 tons.

The record 'pack' for one day was 1,160 containers on 6th July 1944. At the peak the SOE establishment was about 150, and 96 soldiers and 100 RAF men were specially attached for the final drive: most of these were men of low medical category. The Pioneer Corps was also sometimes called on for further reinforcements.

Even this does not complete the story of packing in Britain. An outside firm, Messrs Carpet Trades Ltd of Kidderminster, were called in to help in November 1943, and packed about 18,500 containers: the Americans at top speed developed their own packing station in 'Area H', which employed over 250 workers.[3] It is to be remembered too that this organisation in Britain served only those countries which could be reached by air from Britain. There was a substantial pack-ing organisation in North Africa to serve the south of France, and Middle East (eventually Italy) had an enormous commitment for main-tenance of guerilla forces in the Balkans.

It was at Station 61, finally, that the different elements came together

---

1 Principally 'Hairlok', 'Koran' fibre, and wire-mesh baskets.
2 Eventually there were fifteen lists for H-type containers, thirty-two for C-type: forty-seven varieties in all.
3 There seem to be no figures for the total number of containers packed by the Americans.

to make an operation. It was the headquarters of the Air Liaison Officers who were in direct touch with the squadrons regarding each night's decision to fly or not to fly: it was the 'hotel' at which agents were kept and comforted through the last ordeal of waiting for weather and perhaps of flying in vain; and the packing station sent with them the stores on which their work depended. The three sections were separately organised, but linked finally under the authority of the head of the 'Personnel Dispatch Section', as the man responsible for the safety and welfare of the agents passing through his station.

(ii) Training[1]

When SOE was set up in the late summer of 1940 it did not inherit much in the way of training establishments from its predecessors. In the spring of 1940 MI(R) had initiated what became an important Commando training centre in the West Highlands, and part of this (round Arisaig) was still under the control of MI(R) when it was merged with SOE. D Section had not become interested in training until very late, and its school of sabotage and clandestine warfare at Station XVII (Brickendonbury, Herts.) was not opened until after the birth of SOE. It was perfectly clear that if SOE was to make any progress with its large plans it must have at its disposal a steady flow of men well selected and trained, and from the first it tackled the training problem with energy. When Major Davies came over from MI(R) in the autumn of 1940 one of his first tasks was to make a plan[2] for training; this plan was adopted at once, and its broad outlines were never altered, though there were important changes in detail.

The plan envisaged four stages:

   (a) *Preliminary Schools*, centres where the capacity and character of students could be assessed without taking them very far into the secrets of the organisation.

   (b) *Para-military Schools*, based on the MI(R) courses at Inverailort: at this stage it might be necessary also to give training in parachuting or in small boat landing. Certain agents, it was thought, would be required only for 'butcher-and-bolt' raids, and their training would finish here: it proved in practice that work of this sort was not SOE's natural business, and in the end almost all agents went on to the next stage.

   (c) *The Finishing Schools*, which would teach the methods of subversive warfare and would hold the agents until required for operations. Each Country Section would have its own School, but the Schools would be grouped round a common centre.

---

[1] There is a very clear summary of developments by Major Forty.

[2] Paper of 12th October 1940, on Archives File 2/160/28.

(d) Finally, each Country Section would also have a flat in London which it would use for the final briefing and dispatch of agents.

What happened to this pattern in practice was briefly as follows:

(a) For *Preliminary Schools* SOE secured in the winter of 1940-41 six large houses in the Home Counties, to which should be added the Free French School, Inchmery House, Beaulieu, Hants.; this last ultimately passed out of SOE's hands and became a depot for the Free French parachute company. These continued to be the main points of entry into the service of SOE until the summer of 1943, but they proved to have some disadvantages in practice. It was not very easy to invent effective courses which gave away no secrets: the students sent to them by Country Sections were not always well selected, yet it was difficult to convince a Country Section of their mistakes at so early a stage of training: Country Sections in a hurry were apt to complain of the delay of three or four weeks which the preliminary course involved, and to try to push their men straight on to a later stage of training. SOE's experience (like that of other services) was that much effort was wasted on students who were eventually rejected at a late stage of training – or (worse still) were passed as fit in the hope of avoiding this waste: and it suffered the additional disadvantage that students rejected late in their training know too much and could not be returned at once to the outer world. Hence the invention of the 'ISRB Workshops, Inverlair, Invernessshire': 'The Cooler', where incompetent or unlucky[1] agents were impounded until their knowledge of secrets was not 'hot' enough to be of any importance. SOE therefore had recourse to the solution favoured by the other Services, and set up in June 1943 a Students Assessment Board (SAB) with a 'country house' (STS 7) at which candidates were submitted to the usual battery of psychological and practical tests. This replaced the Preliminary Schools, and seems to have had some success in reducing wastage at later stages of training: it should however be noted that by this time Country Sections had grown more expert in the initial selection of candidates.

(b) *The Para-military Schools* grew up in a group of ten shooting lodges in the district of Arisaig and Morar, where there was plenty of admirably rough and secluded country. The training here was of the usual 'Commando' type, and requires no description in detail. One of these Schools (STS 23b) was intended for para-naval training, but in the end concentrated

---

[1] This sort of incarceration implied no stigma of treachery, which could be dealt with in other ways.

mainly on training for attacks on shipping, using various specialised devices. Parachute training was primarily the responsibility of the RAF School at Ringway outside Manchester,[1] but SOE's students had to be kept apart except during the actual air training and it was therefore necessary to secure two houses (STS 51 (a) and (b)) in the neighbourhood of the airfield where students could be housed and do their gymnastic ground training.

The Arisaig Group could accommodate up to seventy-five students; the course was at first three weeks, gradually extended to five. STS 51 could take seventy students, and normally gave them at least five days' training: but many went on operations after a much shorter period.

(c) It was intended that *the Finishing Schools* should be grouped in the neighbourhood of Beaulieu, Hants.* Each would be limited to one nationality, but there would be a single staff headquarters for them all, so that instructors could serve more than one school. Eventually eleven houses were acquired, with accommodation for about eighty students for a three weeks' course. The training was organised in five main departments: A – the technique of clandestine existence: B – practical exercises designed to test knowledge of this technique: C – enemy organisation: D – propaganda: E – codes. This original scheme was never abandoned in principle, but there were a number of important modifications in practice.

(i) It was soon seen that it was impossible to use the same establishments both to take agents speedily through courses, and to hold them for indefinite periods and put them in final training for a specific operation; therefore early in 1941 SOE began to acquire houses as 'Holding Schools' (later known as 'Operational Schools') in which students could be segregated according to nationalities. There were in the end seven such schools, which did not prove altogether satisfactory. For one thing it was extremely difficult to plan work effectively under such conditions of suspense; for another the Country Sections often preferred to hold their agents ready for briefing in London rather than in some distant country house. The Training Directorate never felt that it had a complete answer to this problem.

(ii) Certain Country Sections and certain nationalities succeeded in asserting special control over the training of their own

---

[1] Admirably described in Group Captain Newnham's book 'Prelude to Glory'.

* [See C. Cunningham, *Beaulieu* (1998).]

agents. In the case of Denmark this arose naturally from an attempt by the Country Section and the School Commander to find a really effective role for the Danish 'Holding School', STS 45 at Hatherop Castle, Fairford, Gloucestershire. This remained under the Training Directorate, but became in effect Danish headquarters whence students were sent to the other schools and to which they returned for various 'integrating courses'. The Norwegian Holding School (STS 26) at Drumintoul and Glenmore Lodges in the Cairngorms similarly developed into the main HQ of the Linge Company: this was an integral part of the Norwegian Army under its own officers, and in addition Colonel J. S. Wilson, head of the Norwegian Section, took a particular interest in its operational training and had one of his own officers permanently in residence. Eventually, in the summer of 1943, control of STS 26 was transferred to the Norwegian Section.

The Polish and Czech Schools developed in the same direction for different reasons; both these Governments had a privileged position in England and enjoyed considerable 'extra-territorial' rights, and in the end they found it politically expedient to assume full responsibility for their own training. Hence in 1943 the Training Directorate ceased to be responsible for the general Polish School at Audley End (STS 43), for the 'Polish Minorities' School near Horsham (STS 63) and for the Czech School at Chicheley Hall (STS 46): there were of course still certain special courses which had to be provided for Poles and Czechs in other SOE schools.

(iii) There was also a tendency for the centralised plan to break down into 'special subjects'. The main schools of this kind (apart from the Signals Schools, which will be dealt with later)[1] were:

STS 17, the old D Section School at Brickendonbury, which became a centre of training in industrial sabotage, 'counter-scorching', and the manufacture of home-made explosives.

STS 39 or *STP*, more commonly known as 'the Hackett School', which was designed to produce specialists in subversive propaganda and the assessment of public opinion. This mainly served PWE, but it also indicated the general lines of more elementary training in the same field which was given to SOE organisers at the 'Finishing Schools'.

STS 40, the 'Reception Committee' School, which was set up in September 1943 as a result of the introduction into operations of the S-Phone and Rebecca/Eureka, which were often found to fail through

---

[1]　Below p. 739.

mistakes in their use. The School gave a concentrated ten-day course in their use and maintenance, which was particularly important because it gave additional confidence to the RAF in carrying out dropping operations. For air landing operations, which were even more dangerous, the RAF trained SOE's men themselves at Tempsford aerodrome.

STS 3 (later STS 47) specialised in mines and in the use of enemy weapons.

STS 37(a) was a small school which trained a limited number of agents in photography and microphotography.

Each of these specialist schools became also in some sense a research establishment working on the development of operational methods and training technique: STS 17 in particular made remarkable progress not only in methods of attack but in the technique of teaching amateurs quickly how to recognise the key points of complicated industrial installations.

It will be noticed that all these schools, national and specialist, represent another principle conflicting with that of centralisation originally put forward by Major Davies. It is possible to imagine a system in which (after the Students' Assessment Board stage) each Country Section should run its own operational and holding school, as a central point for the general training of all its agents, and should send out its men according to its own plans to obtain special training in a series of specialist schools. These 'technische hochschulen' might be administered by a centralised Training Section, but the nature of their special subjects would mean that each would be much more closely affiliated to the appropriate technical section. Such an organisation has one obvious advantage, for it puts both the operational sections and the research sections directly in touch from the beginning with the pupil, the man who is to be the man of the spot. But there are also serious objections. If it is logically pursued such decentralisation is apt to be administratively expensive; it is not too secure, for it is hard to avoid mixing specialist schools; and if there is no strong centralised training section it becomes much more difficult to bring the experience of different countries to bear on the same problem, so that a doctrine common to the whole organisation can be built up and steadily improved.

The SOE system was built up by *ad hoc* decisions, not without controversy, and it represented a working compromise between centralisation and decentralisation. Some of the Country Sections were little interested in training; others were so interested that they wished to take control themselves. The Training Directorate, on its side, was never altogether happy about its own position. It had begun life as a section under Brigadier Gubbins as Director of Operations and Training, and it was up-graded to the status of Directorate in September

1941. But its Director was never a Member of the SOE Council, to which he was responsible first through Brigadier Gubbins, then through Brigadier Mockler-Ferryman. It thus did not come quite into the front rank of the organisation in London, and it had no status at all overseas. In form it was the training Directorate of the 'HQ for Western Europe' and it had no control over the training arrangements made locally by other HQs of equal rank in North Africa, Italy, Middle East and India. The one exception to this was STS 103 near Toronto, which was planned in the summer of 1941 to assist Colonel Donovan in building up his own organisation in the USA and to give preliminary training to men recruited in the Americas by SOE. STS 103 dealt only with para-military training and propaganda; its first course began in December 1941. In this case the training programme was controlled by the Training Directorate in London, though the School was administered by the New York Mission.*

There was thus no centralised responsibility for the whole of SOE training, and it is not easy to give a comprehensive picture of its methods and output. There are no figures for the number of men trained in the Mediterranean Theatre: the output there was considerable, but (to judge from operational experience) a high proportion of the officers sent to the Balkans were by London standards virtually untrained. In England the organisation provided some 13,500 'courses', covering about 6,800 students, of whom only 480 were British. In this large total there were included various services to other organisations. Some 760 Americans of various origins were trained for OSS, as well as many nationals of other countries recruited by the Americans. Parachute training was arranged for the SIS and some of the SAS: the Jedburghs[1] were trained at ME 65, which was an SOE establishment deliberately kept apart from the other schools so as not to compromise the military status of the Jedburghs: the hasty training of the Allied Airborne Reconnaissance Force[2] in the spring of 1945 was only made possible by setting to work the resources of the SOE training organisation. This large output was naturally expensive to produce: men and women had often to be trained swiftly, always very secretly. In Britain there were something like fifty separate training establishments: each of them was small, and had to handle small courses: often individual pupils had to be trained for special tasks which could not be reduced to a syllabus. The establishment was large relative to the output, probably 1,200–1,400 officers and men at the peak period: yet it could not have been significantly reduced within the terms of the problem set.

---

[1]   Above p. 603.
[2]   Above p. 712.
*   [See David Stafford, *Camp X* (Toronto, 1986).]

Subversive training on this scale was an entirely new thing in England, and it would be easy to find flaws in the organisation while it was learning its job. But in the end it was very expert and very flexible, and it was indispensable to the operational work of SOE. If there is any general lesson to be drawn for the future, it is not that greater weight should be given either to the 'schoolmasters' or to the operational and technical experts, but that the two should be more intimately blended and that the idea of training as a whole should be given the highest possible status within the organisation.

There were two important schemes for 'blending' which were carried out too late and under too great pressure to be effectively tested. One of these was to put the whole HQ Staff of SOE through the training machine, either by making all recruits complete the regular agents' courses or by arranging a special Staff Course on similar lines. Six Staff Courses were run during the summer of 1943, but the project was then swept away by pressure of work and it was not re-started until March 1945. The second scheme was for weekly Training Meetings at which all interested Sections should be represented under the chairmanship of the Director of Training. This was not initiated until July 1944, but it was not pressed very strongly on a high level and it was in any case too late to be of much service.

Both these experiments are obviously of interest for the future, but an improvement in the status of training is also to some extent a matter of organisation at the top. This does not mean that all training activity should be concentrated under a single Director or Dictator of Training, with power to overrule other Directors on matters within his competence. Indeed, it is better to think of a Training Staff than of a Training Directorate. The Training Department will naturally assume direct administrative responsibilities, but their exact scope is not important. What is vital is that the 'chief trainer' should be a man of experience and authority equal to those of any Director within the organisation, and that his field should extend over every activity of the organisation at home and overseas. It is in practice impossible to *impose* training on unwilling clients; it is therefore all the more important to *persuade* on the highest possible level, and to pull together the interests ramifying through the whole organisation which go to make up a proper training plan. Training is a common interest: every part of the organisation has something to gain from it and something to contribute to it. The chief function of the Training Staff is to see that this is never forgotten, and that the right pieces of knowledge are brought quickly to the right places.

(iii) Signals[1]

The easiest way to impress a stranger with the scope and power of SOE in its prime was to shew him the main wireless stations at Grendon and Poundon. To the layman it looked as if there were forests of wireless masts, acres of floor-space, hundreds of girl operators and decoders; a sort of great telephone exchange planted in a corner of agricultural England, an exchange which looked normal enough, but served some very curious subscribers. Wireless and aircraft were the two vital links which bound the Resistance together and tied it to the Allied High Command: their importance is equal, though wireless fortunately never raised the grave issues of priority which made aircraft allocation a matter of high politics. The story of SOE's radio system could be told adequately only by a technician to experts, and the narrative here is no more than a skeleton.

At the outset, even after D Section was divorced from SIS, the signals traffic of SOE was handled entirely by Section VIII of the older organisation. By the end of 1941 it was obvious that this would not do: the problem was of a different kind, and it would shortly be on a different scale. In February 1942 SOE obtained its own Chief Signals Officer, Colonel G. Ozanne, who began to plan ahead: in March 1942 the CSS unexpectedly agreed to SOE's demand for independence:[2] in June 1942 the first station at Grendon in Buckinghamshire began to transmit. In due course the importance of the Signals Section was recognised by raising it to the status of a Directorate, and the Director (Brigadier F. W. Nicholls, OBE) became a member of the SOE Council in September 1943. He was directly responsible for the whole SOE signals organisation in the United Kingdom, for SOE's 'main line' communications throughout the world, for wireless training in England, and for radio research and supply. At each overseas HQ there was a Chief Signals Officer who came within the local chain of command but was also accustomed to work closely with the Signals Directorate in London. The organisation was thus on lines familiar in the older Services, and the only point of special interest is that the Director of Signals ranked high within the organisation: it was fully understood that all operations without exception depended for their success on the efficiency of his Directorate.

(a) The Main Stations
The chain of main stations originally envisaged was as follows:

The UK: three stations at Grendon and Poundon, in Bucks, not far east of Bicester.

---

[1] The Signals History consists of disconnected sections dealing with various topics: much of it is useful.

[2] Above p. 386.

The Mediterranean: main stations at Algiera and Cairo, subsidiary links at Gibraltar and Malta.

Africa: small stations at Freetown and Lagos (for Vichy West Africa) and at Durban (for Madagascar).

Far East: Main stations in India, Ceylon and Australia.

The centre of development in the United Kingdom was Grendon Hall, Grendon Underwood, where the SOE Training Section began in 1941 to give preliminary training for radio operators. The first transmitting station, with twelve channels only, was opened at Grendon in June 1942. In May 1943 a new station was added at Poundon nearby, with forty channels directed to cover Southern Norway, Denmark, Holland and Belgium: Grendon was simultaneously extended to thirty-two channels, directed to France, Spain, North Africa and Northern Norway. Finally, in January 1944, a second station with another thirty-six channels was opened at Poundon; this was erected, equipped and largely staffed by the Americans, and was intended primarily to meet the special requirements of 'Overlord', in particular of the 'Jedburghs', and of the Special Force Detachments which accompanied regular formations in the field. The combined stations, 108 channels in all, were linked to HQ in London by fifteen teleprinter circuits.

To illustrate the work of this group of stations there are annexed as Appendices a graph of the number of groups sent, as well as sketch maps of the stations behind the enemy lines which had to be provided for at the time of 'Overlord'.[1] It will be seen that at the peak period the traffic rose steeply to over 300,000 groups a week, and Resistance stations were numbered by hundreds. Of course not all of these were active: losses were heavy even at this stage. But all had to be provided for in the Signals Plan until they had been formally written off as casualties. The provision made was on a generous scale, but lavishness at this point was a cheap form of insurance. There were virtually no complaints from the field about inefficiency or delay in the signals traffic with England.

The position was not so happy in the Mediterranean where working conditions were bad, operations were highly mobile, and equipment and staff had to be dispatched from England months in advance. The first Balkan Missions were served only by emergency stations hastily provided in office buildings in Cairo, Haifa, Istanbul and Smyrna. In January 1942 a small station was opened at Malta, and it was this station alone which kept in touch with Mihailovitch at a critical stage of his career,[2] when Malta itself was under intense German pressure. An adequate War Station at Cairo was first planned in December 1941, but the plan suffered various set-backs in the summer

---

[1] Appendix O.
[2] Above p. 118.

of 1942: Rommel was for a time at the gates of Egypt, and effort had to be diverted to planning for a signals system which could be used if the Middle Eastern front collapsed. Then in the autumn of 1942 came Allied victories and an immense expansion of the British Liaison Missions in the Balkans. This caught the Cairo War Station unprepared, not entirely as a result of bad signals planning. Traffic went up to something like 100,000 groups a week, while the Station was still finding its feet and half-trained staff were arriving in haste from England. By the spring of 1943 the traffic was at the rate of 150,000 to 200,000 groups a week, and there was a delay at one time of $3^1/_2$ days in handling ordinary traffic: this meant that at least double that time was normally required to dispatch a reply to the stations in the field. There were cases where these delays had serious political consequences, for instance in the handling of David Wallace's political reports from Greece:[1] it was equally unfortunate that the Missions in the Balkans felt themselves to be badly served. The position in Cairo was not under control until the autumn of 1943, and by that time some of the burden was passing to newer stations which had their own troubles.

The Gibraltar station had its great days during 'Torch',[2] but it was never required for work into Spain (one of its main purposes) and by the spring of 1943 most of its responsibilities had passed to the Algiers station. This began in a small way with traffic to Corsica and Sardinia early in 1943; by July it was working under heavy pressure as a result of the Sicilian operation and the Italian surrender, and traffic had mounted to about 160,000 groups a week. There was then a lull, as some of the work passed to new stations in Italy, but there was another peak from May to August 1944, the days of the Special Projects Operations Centre[3] in Algiers, when the station was working with some sixty outstations in the south of France.

The situation in Italy was confusing, because here Algiers and Cairo met. When Italy surrendered one station moved forward from Algiers with the 'Maryland' Mission[4] to Brindisi, and was then established at Monopoli near Bari: its final location was in the Siena area, which was convenient in the winter of 1944–5 both for military HQ and for work into North Italy. From the east in the autumn of 1943 came the forward HQ of Force 133, anxious to improve communications with the Balkans, and it made its own plans for an elaborate station at Torre a Mare, near Bari, which was opened in August 1944. In addition, Force 399, which worked into Central Europe, had its own station at Bari: and (to complete the confusion) the Balkan Air Force also

---

[1] Above p. 509.
[2] Above p. 533.
[3] Above p. 564.
[4] Above p. 549.

had its own signals system for traffic to Yugoslavia and Albania. When SOM was formed in April 1944, the three SOE stations (Monopoli, Bari, and Torre a Mare) all came under its aegis, and it began to be possible to plan more coherently. But it was already too late in the war to think seriously of erecting a new main station in Italy, and the three stations continued to operate independently. Certain HQ facilities were however concentrated under SOM at Siena.

The West African stations and that at Durban were never seriously tested in field operations. Those in South-East Asia were of extreme importance in 1944 and 1945, but their work lies outside the scope of this history. It may be added finally that a station was established at STS 103, SOE's training school at Toronto, which served the purposes of the New York Mission acting both for SOE and SIS.

All these main stations could be put in communication with one another as well as with the field, and SOE thus possessed a world-wide radio network of its own.[1] This was however not the sole channel of SOE traffic; with good code facilities it was perfectly possible to use Cables and Wireless and other normal channels in order to relieve pressure on SOE's staff or to reach Missions in neutral countries not in touch with an SOE main station.

(b) Signals Training
Signals training was begun by the Signals Section early in 1941 in one of the Finishing Schools in the Beaulieu area: in the summer of 1941 the school was moved to Grendon Hall, and finally (at the end of 1942) was taken over completely by the Signals Directorate. Radio operators destined for the field received their wireless training at STS 52 (Thame Park), where they were also taught codes and cyphers: there was an outstation (STS 54B) at Dunbar to provide practice in long-distance traffic in realistic conditions. The complete course was one of six weeks, interrupted in the middle by fourteen days of security training at one of the Beaulieu Finishing Schools. With the co-operation of Scotland Yard and the local police, wireless operators were also given opportunities to practice their work in England in conditions closely simulating those of Resistance. This careful training of diverse men in diverse tongues was a slow and laborious process, and even at the peak period STS 52 was only turning out 16–18 trained men a month.[2] The shortage of operators was often a serious drag on operations in the West, and over the world as a whole the need was only met because each main HQ trained its own radio operators; there

---

[1] A diagram of this is at Appendix P.
[2] In addition something like 135 operators were trained for 'Jedburghs'in the winter of 1943–4.

were W/T schools in Middle East, North Africa and Italy, even in Occupied Greece, as well as in the Eastern theatre.

The Signals Directorate had to train its own staff as well as SOE's agents. In the spring of 1942 there was in England a staff of only about 250: by the spring of 1944 the position was roughly:

HQ	300
Grendon } Poundon I }	600
Poundon II: US	350
British	70
Training Staff	250

a total of 1,220, excluding the Americans. The signals staff throughout the world was probably at its peak nearly 5,000 strong. This total included on the one hand a small proportion of technical experts, on the other a fair number of drivers, clerks and so forth. But the main body were wireless operators and coders, and it was soon found quite impossible to obtain these ready-made through Service channels, or even to recruit civilian labour freely. The main source of recruitment was girls not old enough to be liable to industrial or military conscription, and a really fine body of young women was enlisted through the collaboration of the Ministry of Labour and the FANY organisation. These girls were trained by SOE at STS 54a (Fawley Court, Henley), which could handle courses of 150 girls together, in training as operators and for other duties: in addition some 250 girls in all were trained in London as coders. The girls thus trained were freely used at overseas bases as well as in England, and everywhere they proved to be an unqualified success. They regarded the work as a privilege and a great experience; their morale was excellent, and most of them were quick-witted, adaptable, hard-working, and 'security-conscious' to the point of self-immolation.

So far the signals organisation did not differ radically from that of any other service. The special nature of SOE's work had its effects mainly on the production of equipment for use in the field, and on the various technical devices adopted to ensure security of the operator.

(c) Development and Production
SOE possessed its own radio workshops at Stations 7a, b, c, and d on the outskirts of north-west London[1] for development work, and also for production on a small scale: but production was mainly arranged through the Ministry of Supply, which expended some £2,500,000 on radio equipment built to SOE's specifications.[2] There were perhaps three main technical problems:

---

[1] For location see list in SOE Training History.
[2] Signals History of SOE Chapter VII, and Appendix to that chapter.

(i) Reduction in size and weight without sacrifice of power. In practice all requirements could never be met together in one transmitter/receiver set, but the ratio of weight to performance was steadily reduced. The original suitcase sets weighed some 30 lbs and this was eventually brought down, without loss of performance, to about 14 lbs, within the dimensions of $9^1/_2$" $\times 4^1/_2$" $\times 7^1/_2$". There was also a 'Vest Pocket set' weighing only some 5 lbs and measuring $7^1/_2$" $\times 4^1/_2$" $\times 1^1/_2$": this naturally operated on low power, but it had an adequate range for use in Western Europe in good signalling conditions.

(ii) The provision of power when mains could not be used, either because of security or because of remoteness from civilisation. The maintenance of batteries and the charging of batteries was one of the nightmares of the agent, especially of the liaison officer in wild country; the simple production of electricity by human power seems to be one of the problems which science has not yet tackled seriously. After various rather 'Heath Robinson' experiments, a fairly successful hand generator was eventually produced, but (to judge by the abusive comments of users) it was far from being the perfect solution.

(iii) The third problem was somewhat simpler. For most purposes both a transmitter and receiver were essential, and a set incorporating both was of necessity rather elaborate. But for many purposes a receiver alone would be sufficient, for instance in the final stages of organising a reception committee; and it was a relatively simple problem to produce a receiver which was portable, easily worked and easily concealed. Hence the MCR (Midget Communications Receiver)[1] which began to come into service at the end of 1943 and was distributed in very large quantities: some 26,000 were produced in all.

Two other inventions greatly influenced SOE's operations, the Rebecca/Eureka homing device and the S-phone 'walky-talky': these were however developed originally by other agencies for other purposes.

(d) Signals Security
Security had four main aspects:
(i) First, defence against enemy D/F: German radio security in the West was excellently equipped, and if it had the chance to listen for long to any clandestine transmitter it could find its position quickly within very narrow limits. In SOE's early days the agent was given a signal plan allotting to him a regular

---

[1] Set 9" $\times 2^1/_2$" $\times 3^1/_2$", weight 4 lbs 2 oz: Battery $7^1/_2$" $\times 2^1/_2$" $\times 3^1/_2$", weight 3 lb.

call-sign and regular daily periods during which the home station would listen for his transmissions. This meant that if the Germans heard the agent once they could guess when he would be on the air again and could listen in readiness to 'place' his station. In August 1943 the first flexible signal plans, the 'V Plans', were introduced, and these went through two later and more complicated editions, the 'X Plans' of March 1944 and the 'Z Plans' of August 1944: the last of these did not repeat itself during a period of four months, and it was virtually impossible for the enemy to know transmission times in advance unless he captured a copy of the plan.

Still greater flexibility was gained by two other devices. One was the 'Broadcast Plan', which was not related to the use of the BBC for action messages in plain language. The scheme briefly was that there should be periods of communication in which agents received but did not transmit. One side of the dialogue could thus be conducted in perfect security, and their transmission period (which was the dangerous time) could be kept short. A number of agents would be given the same 'broadcast' time, and in these periods the home station would open transmission with prearranged groups (on a variable plan) to indicate which agents were to stand by for messages during the rest of the transmission period: those indicated would continue to listen until their own message was identified, all others could sign off till the next transmission time.

This was introduced early in 1943, though its general adoption depended on wide distribution of the MCR which did not come until later. The complementary device, the 'Marker Channel system', which gave almost perfect flexibility to the agent in transmission, was only introduced into operations for the SAARF[1] in the spring of 1945. Under this system the base station transmitted call signs continuously on a series of prearranged frequencies: it also maintained listening watch on a second series of prearranged frequencies. The agent would tune to the base-station's call sign, and would then call base (giving his own call-sign) on one of the second series of frequencies, those on which there was permanent listening watch. The base would then listen at once on a third frequency, the agent's own frequency as indicated by the call-sign, and he would begin to transmit his message on that frequency. Thus the base station need keep permanent listening watch only on a limited series of frequencies, yet the agent could

---

[1] Above p. 712.

establish communication at will on his own frequency, selected from so wide a range that the enemy could not watch them all. In addition, the agent's transmission time under this system would be greatly reduced; and various technical devices were invented to reduce it still further. In combination with the 'Broadcast' system of reception this came as near as possible to giving complete security to the agent at his most vulnerable point.

(ii) There was the problem of code.[1] The enemy of course was in no doubt about the existence of Grendon and Poundon and he could listen to them at his leisure; and at first it was relatively easy for him to decode their signals. High-grade cyphers could not be used because agents could not carry code books or any other document which could be identified as a code in the course of a routine search. Hence the codes commonly used were based on some key poem memorised by the agent, and they could be broken by the enemy, if he applied his resources to the problem. At the end of 1942 a special Cipher Security Section was formed at HQ to find the answer to this difficulty, and it developed the WOK (Worked Out Keys) and OTP (One Time Pad) systems in forms which could easily be destroyed and were practically certain to elude a normal routine search. Keys could be reduced by microphotography to a tiny scrap which could easily be destroyed; or they could be printed invisibly on silk handkerchiefs and other articles of clothing. Messages enciphered on these systems could not be read unless the enemy was in possession of the code: and it was the agent's duty (a duty which was apt to be neglected) to cut away and destroy the used section of the 'pad' after each transmission. The new system was still vulnerable to treachery and to human error; but technique could not be carried much further.

(iii) Thirdly, there was the question of identifying the agent transmitting and establishing his *bona fides*. Here there were two independent checks. One was artificial, the introduction of a 'check' by the agent, for example the omission or alteration of a specified letter in a specified word of the message – say the third letter in the fourth word. This could be used even by an agent in the hands of the Gestapo, since he could lie to them with impunity about his check: his base would keep up the traffic with the set even though they knew that it was under enemy control. Second, the signals experts claimed that every individual operator had unmistakeable idiosyncracies – 'fingerprints' or 'hand-writing' – which were visible when his trans-

---

[1] The 'Codes' handbook has interesting specimens of the codes used.

missions were mechanically recorded as a graph, and the 'finger-prints' of all operators were thus taken before they went to the field. It is fair to say that non-experts on occasion expressed scepticism, but there is good evidence of a fair ratio of success. This, in combination with the 'routine check', gave reasonable protection against anything except very thorough treachery.

(iv) Finally, it was necessary to prevent the enemy from deducing anything of importance from the volume and direction of traffic from the home station. The amount of traffic to individual agents would be masked effectively by the variable forms of signal plan, and by the use of efficient codes: but it was necessary also to disguise fluctuations in the total volume of traffic beamed to any one country or area. This could only be done by constructing an 'umbrella' of bogus traffic, so that the total volume of traffic for each area either remained constant or was varied independently of the volume of the real traffic. This was laborious because the false traffic had to consist of intelligible messages properly encoded; the system was perfectly effective, but it consumed a good deal of time and trouble.[1]

This brief layman's account would scarcely satisfy the signallers, and it may not engage the attention of the general reader. But it is not a bad point on which to end this description of the structure of SOE. Nothing can go right with a clandestine organisation unless its signals system is secure, flexible and accurate. SOE as an organisation was slow in starting, but at least some of its early troubles arose from the fact that there was no radio expert to give all his attention in its problems at the beginning. Its communications were not only clandestine, but also military; they involved the co-ordination of the action of considerable forces on a considerable scale. This meant the development of a new technique, quite different from the old 'spy' system. The technique did not exist when the Resistance was in its most difficult and dangerous phase, indeed it was only coming to maturity during the period of intense activity in 1944. But in the end the work was well done, and it is hard to see that it can be carried much further until there is new technical advance in the general field of radio communications.

---

[1] It is rumoured that an 'umbrella' was also used for conventional messages sent on the BBC, but this was certainly not admitted to the BBC who were extremely parsimonious with broadcasting time.

Conclusion

'I always had a horror of revolutionising any country for a political object. I always said, if they rise of themselves, well and good, but do not stir them up; it is a fearful responsibility.'

Stanhope's 'Conversations with the Duke of Wellington'.

It would be useless to attempt to summarise this extraordinary story, since what precedes is itself no more than a summary of activities which touch every part of the political and military history of Europe; and it is dangerous to insert a profit and loss account. It is obvious that in the vulgar sense SOE showed a large military profit. In manpower directly employed it cost less than the equivalent of a division; a rather curious division, in which the officers were the pick of British youth, the rank and file were largely old crocks unfit for active service and girls deemed too young for conscription. Its private air force cannot (on the average) be reckoned at more than four squadrons: its private navy was tiny. The supply services behind these forces were not greater than would have been needed by equivalent regular formations; and SOE's cash expenditure on subsidies to Resistance was probably no greater than its cash gains as a dealer in the European currency black market. The whole of this was by military standards a tiny commitment, and it needs no argument to show that the Resistance contributed to the defeat of Germany far more than the British expended on Resistance. That sum is bound to show a profit, whether we reckon in terms of Germans killed or targets destroyed or administrative effort saved.

But was SOE the lever which moved this immense mass? Or was it merely a small stone thrown into the torrent? It would be impertinent to give a definite answer to such questions. You cannot draw out Leviathan with a fish-hook; you cannot weigh European history in the balance and set up a ratio between the factors out of which it is compounded. SOE was for five years the main instrument of British action in the internal politics of Europe: it was an instrument imperfect in various ways characteristic of the British: but it was an extremely powerful instrument. While SOE was at work no European politician could be under the illusion that the British were uninterested or dead; he might have reason to believe that they were incompetent or sinister, but he was bound to take account of them. The young men whom SOE turned loose on the continent, and the department which backed them, had to be reckoned with seriously by Germany, by Russia, by every political organisation in Europe. They were an important part of history.

Can any lessons be learnt for the future? The academic student should be cautious on this ground. *Venimus ubi tonat fulmen*; these are serious matters, and the only authorities worth listening to are those who carry the weight of responsibility for the life and death and torture of individuals and of nations. But there are some things which can be said about administrative organisation without transferring the discussion to the ground of high politics.

It is to be noted, in the first place, that there have always been in England two currents of opinion about what can now be called 'SOE work'. One of them is represented by the Duke of Wellington's saying quoted at the head of this chapter. The plain Englishman is against it, not so much because it is dirty work, as because he can't see where it leads him: it is a 'fearful responsibility'. In spite of this, England in modern times has always been a centre of subversion – known as such to others, but not to itself. At the periphery our Eastern and African Empires were built up largely by individuals burrowing like termites in the structure of older empires. At the centre England was in the nineteenth century a hotbed of revolutionary conspiracy, which made London seem as horrifying to the Emperors in Europe as Moscow now is to the Americans. In these matters the right hand of His Majesty's Government was careful not to know what the left hand was doing: the disposal of Secret Funds was one of the *arcana imperi*, and in any event most English subversion drew its support from other sources than the Treasury. Hence the strange two-sided picture: England to the outer world was the model of intrigue, subtlety and perfect secrecy, to itself it seemed above all bluff, simple and well-meaning.

There is (in the second place) an impression that in the twentieth century subversion is of much greater importance than it used to be. This is to some extent an optical illusion. From the late seventeenth century there was in Europe in some sense a 'Trade Union of Kings'; dog did not eat dog – beyond a certain point. This understanding was embodied in the practice of diplomacy and in the laws of war: often broken, but on the whole recognisable and on the whole observed. The old structure has now been destroyed in Europe, largely by the action of Germany and of Russia; we lament its destruction and we forget that it never existed except in Europe. The rules were observed by Europeans only in relation to other Europeans; and the great event of European history from the seventeenth to the twentieth centuries was that in these years the Europeans burst their geographical bounds and destroyed every other political structure that existed in the world. In that process the sophisticated abstractions of war and diplomacy had no place; there were no rules to limit the subversion of barbarians.

But (in the third place) though subversion is no new thing, it has certainly as a matter of organisation entered upon a new phase. This is shown not only by the experience of SOE but by that of other nations, some of which were much earlier in the field. 'The Minister' can no longer dissipate the Secret Service moneys through his own shabby agents on the backstairs; the merchant adventurer cannot buy for himself a Grand Vizier or a trading station.* Efficient subversion is now a specialised profession which requires an elaborate organisation for training, communications and supply; it implies the same sort of services at headquarters as Service and Supply Departments provide for the armed forces. In Britain administrative centralisation was enforced by other considerations, which are peculiar to Great Britain but are likely to recur in any future British war. From 1939 to 1945 England was full of governments in exile whose greatest preoccupation was to maintain contact with their own countries; they were all working like beavers to that end, and it was essential that there should be one single department which knew what they were doing, whether to help or to hinder. Their activities were much too multifarious for the Foreign Office to follow, and they were absolutely outside the ken of any of the Service departments. SOE was essential as a 'buffer state'.

These two practical considerations made it impossible in the last resort for SOE's enemies in Whitehall to destroy SOE, and it is quite certain that in some form SOE must be created again in any future war. But the nature of subversion itself makes it extremely difficult to place it conveniently within the administrative hierarchy. There are three sources of difficulty.

In the first place Subversion covers a wide range of activities which are all perfectly distinct from old-fashioned diplomacy and old-fashioned war, as known to international law. At one extreme there is open propaganda, appealing to other peoples over the heads of their rulers, but admitting its origin. Next to this comes 'black' propaganda, which conceals its source. Propaganda of either kind can be conducted from the author's own territory, but its work cannot be completed except by agents on the spot. In the first stage these agents will work under-

---

* [Compare and contrast Elizabeth Sparrow, *Secret Service: British Agents in France 1792–1815* (2000).]

ground; they may have different tasks, intelligence, sabotage, or political leadership, but all alike will employ the techniques of disguise and concealment. Finally, there is open guerilla war, in which the forces nurtured by subversion come into the open as irregular military formations either under the leadership of their own chiefs or of a High Command in the outer world. These types of activity are complementary, indeed essential, to one another, yet in 1938 and 1939 the British Government approached the single subject of Subversion separately from many angles. For 'white' propaganda there was the Ministry of Information, with a shadowy control over the BBC, [WORD DELETED ON GROUNDS OF NATIONAL SECURITY] for 'black' propaganda Electra House, for political agents and saboteurs 'D Section', for intelligence agents SIS, for guerilla warfare MI(R). Each of these five organisations in attempting to do its own job encroached on the field of the other four, and all (except perhaps SIS) were regarded with suspicion and distrust by diplomats and soldiers alike.

Dunkirk and the fall of France shook this kaleidoscope violently: it was suddenly conceived that subversion was of such importance that it must at all costs be unified under one strong hand, and the original charter given to Mr Dalton certainly contemplated the unification of all these services except SIS. This unification, or 'Grand Design', broke down almost at once. There were two fortuitous reasons for this. First, it was administratively quite impossible for Mr Dalton to assume responsibility for clearing up the quagmire of the Ministry of Information as well as those of EH, D and MI(R), which had to be dealt with at once. The Ministry of Information might have been divided and destroyed in the summer of 1940; instead, Mr Dalton agreed with his enemy while he was in the way, and his enemy (rejuvenated by Mr Bracken) survived to break up the original conception of SOE. Second, the surge of interest in the oppressed peoples of Europe and the British Fifth Column soon died down: even by the autumn of 1940 our hopes had been transferred from Europe to America. SOE continued to be important, but it never again had a chance to secure overriding priority.

And overriding priority is certainly necessary to sustain the idea of a unified Ministry of Subversion. Such unification means the concentration of immense power in the hands of one man or of a small group, and it inevitably breeds resistance by rivals. The Nazi Fifth Column, which was so much admired in its day, was run chaotically, by a chaos of conflicting authorities. In Russia there is in theory a high degree of concentration; national policy is primarily a policy of subversion, and the diplomats and soldiers are relegated to a subordinate role below the level on which policy is made; neither soldiers nor diplomats have any place in the Politburo of the Party. But it is still not easy to see where the responsibility lies. There is one concentration of subversive power in the hands of the NKVD (Beria), another in the Secretary of the Russian Party and Secretary of the International Party; in addition the Foreign Minister (Molotov) and the Defence Minister (Bulganin)* both stand high in the Party hierarchy and both are served by secret services of their own. If it is impossible to produce a 'monolithic' system in Moscow, it is certainly impossible to do so in Whitehall, where neither the Foreign Office nor the soldiers have any intention of allowing themselves to be reduced to the level of executive agents of a political party.

This difficulty is all the greater because Britain is a democracy. A Ministry of Subversion is in its very nature exempt from any form of democratic control, and it is not tolerable to us even in war that the vital issue of national policy should be entirely withdrawn from scrutiny by the House of Commons. If they understood the issues, both Parliament and the public would be as hostile to a unified Ministry of Subversion as are the older departments in Whitehall.

The second main difficulty is that the principle of organisation by technique to some extent runs at cross purposes here with that of organisation by purpose. The unity of subversion suggests one kind of organisation, the technique of 'unacknowledgeable means' suggests another. 'Subversion' does not necessarily include all secret service, but secret service has a different unity of its own. On a conservative estimate, there were four British Secret Services in the war of 1939: SIS, SOE, MI9, and MI5. All four had much in common as regards technical development, training, knowledge of the enemy, and at least the first three made much trouble for one another by running independent networks of agents in enemy territory. Both security and economy suggest that some measure of unity at headquarters is essential, even if security requires that agents in the field should be kept distinct.

The third difficulty is that the work of a subversive organisation is not all of one piece. If all goes well with the campaign there will in each field of action be a steady growth, from clandestine work conducted by a few agents in utter secrecy to open resistance closely related to a military plan. The problem begins as a spy's problem and ends as a soldier's problem, and to make matters worse it is not one problem but a series of problems. There is irregular warfare in Yugoslavia while in France the Resistance is still deep underground. When France has reached the stage of irregular warfare, Yugoslavia under Tito has almost attained to the organisation of a state, yet in Holland the work is beginning anew. SOE kept in step with this development by a gradual transition from civil to military in its pattern of organisation, first in the Middle East, then in the West; but the same

---

* [N. A. Bulganin, 1895–1975, Soviet Prime Minister 1955–8.]

department at each stage included men of very diverse habits of mind, and there was always a slight sense of strain between the ghost of D Section and the ghost of MI(R).

For all these reasons it is useless to think that anyone can solve the problem of subversive organisation. There is no correct pattern laid up in Heaven which can be brought down to earth by an administrative genius. The most that can be demonstrated is that some mistakes will be in all circumstances disastrous, and that they must not be allowed to happen again.

In the first place the Foreign Office and the military must, from top to bottom, learn to understand what goes on in this vast field of action which lies between their conventional spheres. SOE has many mistakes to its discredit, but the cause of its worst troubles lay outside its control. The Foreign Office (with certain notable exceptions) regarded SOE as an interloper in diplomacy; it interfered only to prevent SOE from acting. Information from Occupied Europe was extremely scanty and determination of policy was not easy, but the Foreign Office as a whole never grasped how SOE could help it. It did not occur to it that SOE's British agents, great and small, were in a sense diplomats, sent *en mission* in circumstances of extreme danger and responsibility. It took no responsibility for their training and very little for the preparation of their briefs. Surely it would not be impossible for the Foreign Office, even in war, to recruit and train fit young men in the diplomatic service, so that it can use its own men even for desperate ventures?

The military (unlike the diplomats) were perfectly clear that they could find a use for SOE, but that use was merely 'to kill Germans'; it was not understood that sometimes it costs too much to 'kill Germans', when the cost is reckoned in terms of British policy, not simply of British and Allied dead. The Army's experience of 'Civil Affairs', in all its forms, may have been enough to kill this fallacy, but it is one which dies hard in the minds of soldiers.

Second, it is intolerable that the lives of agents and of Allies should be endangered by competition and confusion between British Secret Services. There is every reason for keeping apart in the field intelligence networks, sabotage networks, escape lines, political agents; each has different conditions of work, and they merely endanger one another if they confuse their tasks. It may even be desirable in England that each task should be handled by an independent organisation. But no considerations of security should prevent these organisations from working so closely together that all British agents are in effect handled as a single force.

Third, subversive propaganda cannot in execution be divorced from subversive operations. It may be that each task is so large as to require a separate organisation, but these organisations must work together from top to bottom. If an agent in the field takes a line about British policy, his work will be destroyed if (through sheer muddle) a different line is taken by British propaganda, open or secret. It may sometimes be necessary to repudiate an agent deliberately, even at the peril of his life, but it is monstrous that it should be done by accident. The relations between the Ministry of Information, the Political Warfare Executive, and the Special Operations Executive were generally better at the bottom than at the top; those who knew did their best to work together, but there were times when they were working behind the backs of their superiors. This is one thing that should never happen again.

With these considerations in mind it may be worth hazarding some suggestions for organisation in war. It is clear that the initiative in this whole field must in our system of government come from the Foreign Office, there is no other department competent to take the lead as regards external policy. It is also clear that the Foreign Office as an administrative department cannot single-handedly control the vast ramifications of modern subversive organisation. Therefore let the Foreign Secretary in war become a co-ordinating rather than executive officer; he must stand very close to the Prime Minister, he must be assisted by a small but strong personal staff, and he must have power to co-ordinate and in the last resort decide all issues in the field of external policy. Under him let there be four separate organisations, each headed by a junior Minister and by a high official, to handle orthodox diplomacy, propaganda (white and black together), 'Special Operations' and 'Secret Intelligence'; to these should probably be added (as a fifth) Economic Warfare in the orthodox sense. It will be best to have five separate departments, because the task is so large, and *esprit de corps* and clarity of purpose are stronger in small departments: it will be best to have junior Ministers at the head of each, because these are highly political functions, and a balance between politicians of different shades is in the interests both of efficiency and of public confidence. Nevertheless, each department must be basically a Foreign Office department, even though this involves a change in the character of the Foreign Office; each must secure its fair share of the best brains in the career service. But in addition each must be strongly reinforced by talent from the outer world; and the three 'subversive' departments, the equivalents of PWE, SOE and SIS, will require also strong representation of the fighting services.

This last point is the most difficult of all to secure; in war the best fighting men will struggle to escape from offices in order to command units in the field. It is not wise to compel them to do otherwise, and it is worse than useless to by-pass the difficulty by posting them into subversive departments and out again to their units before they have had time to learn the game. Yet committees on a high level are powerless to co-ordinate military and political demands unless there is already mutual confidence and working agreement on the lower levels. The problem must somehow be solved on these levels. The British Army fortunately has always had its small quota of eccentrics who have loved irregular war, even at the expense of their careers, but the Navy and the RAF have thought little of it; the notion of subversion is at first sight derogatory to the professional dignity of sea power and air power. But this contempt rests on a misunderstanding which it is not impossible to overcome. It is obvious absurdity to suppose that strategy and politics seek different ends by different means; if they are to serve the nation both must seek the same end by all means that come to hand. Subversion is one of the most important of these means. It is not a Fourth Arm or a Fourth Service because its nature is alien to the conception of a profession of arms, but it is indispensable to the professional soldier to understand it and to use it. It is equally indispensable to the professional politician: and national policy can only exist when these two pull the same way.

APPENDICES

Appendix A

Copy

MOST SECRET
WP(40)271
19th July 1940

WAR CABINET
HOME DEFENCE (SECURITY) EXECUTIVE
SPECIAL OPERATIONS EXECUTIVE

Memorandum by the Lord President of the Council

1. The memorandum which I circulated to the Cabinet on 27th May (WP(40)172) gave particulars of the organisation of the Home Defence (Security) Executive, which was set up under the chairmanship of Lord Swinton to co-ordinate action against the Fifth Column.

2. In addition to presiding over the Home Defence (Security) Executive, Lord Swinton has been entrusted with the executive control of MI5 and is thus responsible for counter espionage activities in Great Britain.

3. The Prime Minister has now decided that Lord Swinton shall also exercise operational control over the work of MI6 in respect of all the activities of MI6 in Great Britain and in Eire. MI6 will also continue to place at the disposal of Lord Swinton all information in their possession which may have a bearing on Fifth Column activities in Great Britain or Eire.

4. The Prime Minister has further decided, after consultation with the Ministers concerned, that a new organisation shall be established forthwith to co-ordinate all action, by way of subversion and sabotage, against the enemy overseas. The Prime Minister requested me to set on foot this new organisation in consultation with those concerned. Action is accordingly being taken as follows:

a) An organisation is being established to co-ordinate all action, by way of subversion and sabotage, against the enemy overseas. This organisation will be known as the Special Operations Executive.

b) The Special Operations Executive will be under the chairmanship of Mr Dalton, the Minister of Economic Warfare.

c) Mr Dalton will have the assistance of Sir Robert Vansittart.

d) The Special Operations Executive will be provided with such additional staff as the Chairman and Sir Robert Vansittart may find necessary.

e) The various departments and bodies taking part in underground activities will, for the time being, continue to be administered by the Ministers at present responsible for them.

f) The departments and bodies affected which will now be co-ordinated by Mr Dalton are:

Title	Alternative title	Administrative Authority
Sabotage Service	'D'	FO
MI(R)	–	WO
*Department Electra House	Sir Campbell Stuart's Organisation	Joint FO and Minister of Information

Mr Dalton will also have the co-operation of the Directors of Intelligence of the three Service Departments and of the Secret Intelligence Service (MI6) for the purpose of the work entrusted to him. Mr Dalton will also keep in touch with Lord Hankey.

g) The Planning and direction of raids by formed bodies of British or Allied ships, troops or aircraft will remain the function of the Military authorities, but Mr Dalton will maintain touch with Departments planning such raids in order to afford any possible assistance through the channels he co-ordinates.

h) Any Department obtaining information likely to be of value to Mr Dalton will place their information at his disposal.

i) All operations of sabotage, secret subversive propaganda, the encouragement of civil resistance in occupied areas, the stirring up of insurrection, strikes, etc., in Germany or areas occupied by her will be submitted before being undertaken by any Department, to Mr Dalton for his approval.

j) Mr Dalton will co-ordinate the planning operations of

underground warfare and will direct which organisation is to carry them out. He will be responsible for obtaining the agreement of the Secretary of State for Foreign Affairs or other Minister interested to any operation which is likely to affect their interests.

k) It will be important that the general plan for irregular offensive operations should be in step with the general strategical conduct of the war. With this end in view, Mr Dalton will consult the Chiefs of Staff as necessary, keeping them informed in general terms of his plans, and, in turn, receiving from them the broad strategical picture.

5. Lord Swinton and Mr Dalton will arrange for any consultation that may be mutually helpful or may be necessary to prevent overlapping between the Home Defence (Security) Executive and the Special Operations Executive. Normally, no doubt, consultation between their respective staffs will suffice for this purpose.

6. The Prime Minister has requested that Lord Swinton and Mr Dalton should regard me as the member of the War Cabinet whom they should consult and to whom any inter-Departmental difficulties, should they arise, would be referred.

(Int'd) N.C.

Privy Council Office, SW1.
19th July 1940.

*Note: The organisation of this Department is being reviewed.

Appendix B

Organisation Chart – Spring 1941

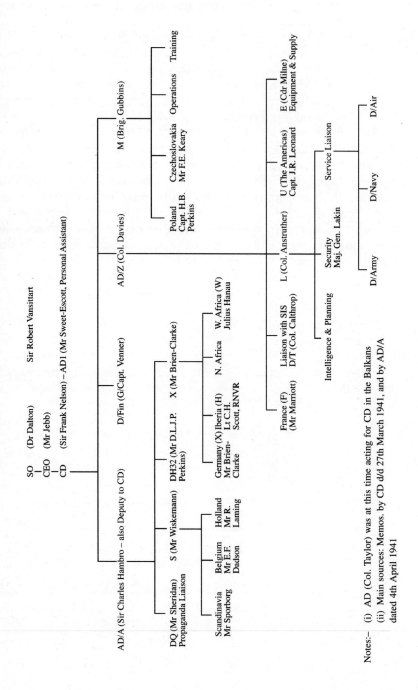

SO   (Dr Dalton)   Sir Robert Vansittart

CEO (Mr Jebb)

CD   (Sir Frank Nelson) – AD1 (Mr Sweet-Escott, Personal Assistant)

AD/A (Sir Charles Hambro – also Deputy to CD)

D/Fin (G/Capt. Venner)

AD/Z (Col. Davies)

M (Brig. Gubbins)

        Operations   Training

Poland
Capt. H.B. Perkins

Czechoslovakia
Mr F.E. Keary

DQ (Mr Sheridan) Propaganda Liaison

S (Mr Wiskemann)

Scandinavia
Mr Sporborg

Belgium
Mr E.F. Dadson

Holland
Mr R. Laming

DH32 (Mr D.L.I.P. Perkins)

X (Mr Brien-Clarke)

Germany (X)
Mr Brien-Clarke

Iberia (H)
Lt C.H. Scott, RNVR

N. Africa

W. Africa (W)
Julius Hanau

France (F)
(Mr Marriott)

Liaison with SIS
D/T (Col. Calthrop)

L (Col. Anstruther)

Intelligence & Planning

U (The Americas)
Capt. J.R. Leonard

E (Cdr Milne)
Equipment & Supply

Security
Maj. Gen. Lakin

Service Liaison

D/Army

D/Navy

D/Air

Notes:— (i) AD (Col. Taylor) was at this time acting for CD in the Balkans

            (ii) Main sources: Memos. by CD d/d 27th March 1941, and by AD/A
                dated 4th April 1941

Appendix C – (a)

Norway – Movement of Personnel and of Arms Dumps for the Period September 1941–September 1942

SOE Agents	Entered Norway	Entered a second time	Returned to UK	Returned a second time	Killed	Captured	In Stockholm	In Norway
Organisers[1]	13	3	2	3	2[2]	2	–	7
W/T Operators	13	–	3	–	1	3	1	5
Assistant Organisers or Instructors	21	–	5	–	–	–	–	16
TOTALS	47	3	10	3	3	5	1	28[3]

[1] Where an Organiser is also a W/T Operator he is shown as the former.

[2] One drowned.

[3] No account taken of probable capture of some of Archer-Heron party except of Archer W/T.

Appendix C – (b)

Norway – Movement of Personnel and of Arms Dumps for the Period September 1941–September 1942

Arms, Explosives	No. of dumps	No. of trips	Approximate Weight tons cwts	Captured No.	Captured Weight tons cwts	Cached No.	Cached Weight tons cwts
Landed by sea	9	18	79 – 4	4	37 – 10	5	41 – 14
Dropped by air	3	3	1 – $1^{3}/_{4}$	1	0 – $2^{3}/_{4}$	2	0 – 19
Landed from submarine	1	1	0 – 2	0	0 – 0	1	0 – 2
TOTALS	13	22	80 – $7^{3}/_{4}$	5	37 – $12^{3}/_{4}$	8	42 – 15

Appendix D

Memorandum

Relations between SOE and the Foreign Office

1. The Special Operations Executive is a secret and independent organisation directed by the Minister of Economic Warfare, for achieving the following purposes:

a) to promote disaffection and, if possible, revolt in all enemy and enemy-occupied countries.

b) to hamper the enemy's war effort by means of sabotage and 'partisan' warfare in those areas.

c) to combat enemy interests and Fifth Column activities by 'unacknowledgeable' means and to create 'post-occupational organisations' in any other part of the world where SOE may be permitted to do so.

2. These purposes shall in all cases be in harmony with the general policy of HM Government and SOE shall be responsible for obtaining the agreement of the Secretary of State for Foreign Affairs to any of their operations which are likely to affect his interests. For their part, neither the Foreign Office nor HM representatives abroad will take action on matters affecting SOE without previous consultation with the latter or their local representatives. The Foreign Office further agree to make available to SOE all information affecting SOE operations or likely to have a bearing upon SOE operations and plans.

3. While it is established that, subject to paragraph 2 above, SOE have a right to advance opinions and conduct operations on their own, they execute the policy of HM Government as laid down in their respective spheres by the Chiefs of Staff, the Foreign Office and other Departments of State. Once this policy is determined, the Foreign Office, so far as they are concerned, will give SOE every facility for carrying it out. At the same time, it is clear that the degree of interest taken by the Foreign Office in the activities of SOE varies in the different areas in which SOE operates, as follows:

i) *Enemy and Enemy-Occupied Territories*
Here SOE work on the directives of the Chiefs of Staff

Organisation (or, alternatively, of the responsible Commanders in Chief) in regard to the tempo of subversive operations, with complete liberty to use their own discretion in regard to the elements with whom they should get in touch. All acts of sabotage and the creation of disaffection against the enemy generally can be undertaken on the initiative of SOE, who will, however, keep the Foreign Office informed of any developments of political significance by means of a periodical report, and by liaison between the Departments concerned. If any organisation controlled by or in touch with SOE is found to be in a position to exercise a political influence in the country concerned, SOE will at once consult with the Foreign Office and the Chiefs of Staff as to the line to be adopted in its dealings with such an organisation, and shall conform to the rulings of the Foreign Office as to the political line to be adopted.

ii) *Unoccupied France and Unoccupied French Overseas Territories*

SOE recognise that the Foreign Office have a special interest in these areas and agree not to conduct operations in them except with the knowledge and (subject to appeal) the consent of the Foreign Office. In these areas the Foreign Office will not normally be informed of the details of subversive operations, but will give (or withold) general consent to their being conducted.

iii) *Neutral Countries*

Here the interests of foreign policy are predominant. Accordingly, the Foreign Secretary assumes full responsibility for deciding whether or not SOE are to conduct activities in neutral countries and SOE will take directives in these areas from him. It follows that save in regard to certain subjects, such as the recruitments of agents or the suborning of ships' masters, where the Foreign Office may give them general authority to proceed, SOE will carry out no operation, and will take no active steps preparatory to operations, except with the knowledge and (subject to appeal to the Foreign Office) the consent of the Head of the local Diplomatic Mission. While it is essential that SOE should select as their Head Representative in any neutral country some competent and trustworthy person, the Foreign Office, for their part, agree that the importance of subversive operations should be impressed on the Heads of the Missions concerned and that, in principle, the necessary preparatory work should be undertaken.

iv) *Alllied Countries (except those in enemy occupation)*

The interests of SOE in these countries lie almost entirely in the recruitment of agents and co-operation with the Governments of the countries concerned in subversive operations. Provided that the Allied authorities concerned are in agreement, the Foreign Office do not wish to be consulted in regard to the recruitment of agents, though they should be kept informed of the main lines of co-operation in subversive matters.

v) *Central and South America*

In all Central and South American States, whether belligerent, non-belligerent, or neutral the interests of foreign policy are also predominant and SOE will only take action in co-operation with an authority duly constituted by the United States Government. Pending the constitution of such authority, no action including preparatory action other than the recruitment of agents shall be undertaken until the approval of the Foreign Office has been obtained and with the knowledge and consent of the heads of the local British Diplomatic Missions.

4. *Peace Moves*

If in the course of their work, SOE should discover groups or parties in any of the above mentioned categories or territories willing and able to embark on anything like peace negotiations, they will at once inform the Foreign Office, who will decide whether, and on what lines, negotiations shall be conducted.

5. *Organised groups of friendly enemy aliens and Exiled Allied Governments*

In addition to the above mentioned areas SOE should have certain relations both with organised groups of friendly enemy aliens and with Exiled Allied Governments.

a) *Organised groups of friendly enemy aliens*

The purpose of SOE in maintaining relations with such organisations outside this country is (i) to obtain recruits, and (ii) to assist SOE Missions abroad to obtain such co-operation as they need from local elements for the conduct of operations in the territories concerned. SOE will keep the Foreign Office fully informed of all dealings which they may have with such organisations and will, in this respect, conduct no policy of their own, but receive directives from the Foreign Office. On the other hand, any communications which such organisations may have with the foreign country concerned should be conducted through SIS or SOE channels since otherwise there would be grave risk of crossing lines and general confusion.

b) *Exiled Allied Governments*

Relations of SOE with Exiled Allied Governments will be restricted to the operational plane. By this is meant, generally speaking, discussions regarding the recruitment and despatch of agents and material, the allocation of priorities (i.e., how best to distribute the available transport facilities and material as between all the Governments concerned) the formation of underground organisations and the exchange of ideas on technical matters. There is nothing to preclude SOE from carrying out the above objects through the agency of Allied nationals who may not be identified with or may even be politically in opposition to the Allied Government in question, provided that SOE ensure that their agents do not encourage any particular political faction or participate in intrigues carried on in opposition to the Government recognised by HM Government.

6. *Right of Appeal*

As a Minister of the Crown, the Minister of Economic Warfare has, in his capacity as head of SOE (and save as qualified in paragraph 3 (iii) above) a general right of appeal against an adverse decision by any Department to any particular proposal of his. On all matters affecting operations the suitable court of appeal would be the Defence Committee. It is understood that the Minister will only exercise his right of appeal in regard to matters which seem to him of the first importance from the point of view of the conduct of special operations.

7. *Propaganda*

The question of the extent to which SOE shall deal with subversive propaganda is excluded from the present paper and forms the subject of separate arrangements between SOE, PWE and the Ministry of Information.

Appendix E

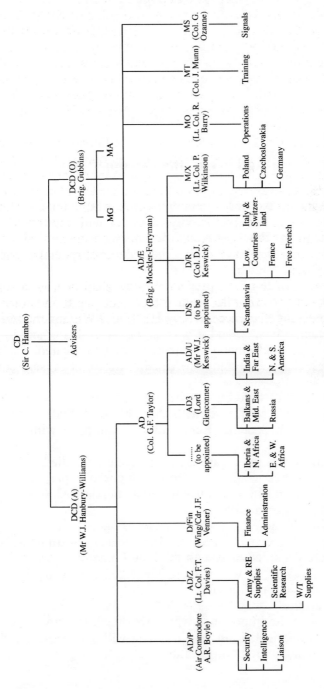

CD
(Sir C. Hambro)

Advisers

DCD (A)
(Mr W.J. Hanbury-Williams)

DCD (O)
(Brig. Gubbins)

MA

MG

AD/P (Air Commodore A.R. Boyle)
- Security
- Intelligence
- Liaison

AD/Z (Lt. Col. F.T. Davies)
- Army & RE Supplies
- Scientific Research
- W/T Supplies

D/Fin (Wing/Cdr J.F. Venner)
- Finance
- Administration

AD (Col. G.F. Taylor)

...... (to be appointed)
- Iberia & N. Africa
- E. & W. Africa

AD3 (Lord Glenconner)
- Balkans & Mid. East
- Russia

AD/U (Mr W.J. Keswick)
- India & Far East
- N. & S. America

AD/E (Brig. Mockler-Ferryman)

D/S (to be appointed)
- Scandinavia

D/R (Col. D.J. Keswick)
- Low Countries
- France
- Free French
- Italy & Switzerland

M/X (Lt. Col. P. Wilkinson)
- Poland
- Czechoslovakia
- Germany

MO (Lt. Col. R. Barry)
- Operations

MT (Col. J. Munn)
- Training

MS (Col. G. Ozanne)
- Signals

N.B. This chart is designed to show only the lines of responsibility of the Directors and does not indicate levels of seniority.

8th July 1942

Appendix F

Memorandum

Subversive Activity in the Occupied Territories

It has been suggested that a common Allied Staff should be formed to deal with all subversive activity in the occupied territories. The special function of this staff would be to co-ordinate and direct such activities in order that they might render the maximum assistance in any future Allied offensive.

2. The importance of the preparation of the peoples of Europe, at present subject to Nazi rule, to take their share in the overthrow of Germany has long been accepted by His Majesty's Government, and by its Military Advisers, and it was largely with this object in mind that the Special Operations Executive (SOE) was created. The functions suggested for this common Allied Staff are at present covered by the SOE.

3. The present method by which SOE works in close collaboration with our planning staff, and with the Chiefs of Staff Committee, enables activities in occupied Europe to be co-ordinated with the whole war plan.

4. We believe that the organisation of a common Allied staff to deal with these activities would serve no useful purpose, particularly as it would not be in a position to relate its recommendations to the requirements of the war as a whole.

5. SOE should therefore continue to act as the co-ordinating authority, dealing with the General Staffs of the Allied governments whose territories are occupied, and with the Free French General Staff, and acting as the agent to whom these General Staffs should refer all matters in connection with sabotage and the organisation of resistance and secret armies.

6. In view of the importance which we attach to subversive activities on the Continent, I am sure that you will give SOE the closest and most whole-hearted co-operation.

Copies of this letter have been sent to the appropriate Belgian, Czechoslovakian, Netherlands, Free French, Greek, Norwegian, Polish and Yugoslav authorities.

(Sgd) A. F. BROOKE.
Chairman, Chiefs of Staff Committee

2nd June 1942

Appendix G

Copy

<u>MOST SECRET</u>
<u>COS(42)133(0)</u>
<u>12th May 1942</u>

WAR CABINET
CHIEFS OF STAFF COMMITTEE

SOE COLLABORATION IN OPERATIONS
ON THE CONTINENT

Note by the Secretary

The attached directive$^{\emptyset}$ to the SOE on their collaboration in Operations on the Continent has been approved* by the Chiefs of Staff.

(Sgd) L. C. HOLLIS

Great George Street, SW1
12th May 1942

$^{\emptyset}$ Annex.
* COS(42)147th Meeting, Minute 5.

ANNEX
Directive to SOE

OPERATIONS ON THE CONTINENT

The War Cabinet has approved* that plans and preparations should proceed without delay for Anglo-US operations in Western Europe in 1942 and 1943, the intention being to develop an offensive in stages as follows:

i)   A series of raiding operations to be carried out during the summer of 1942 on a front extending from the North of Norway to the Bay of Biscay, coupled with

ii) An active air offensive over NW Europe;

iii) A large scale raid to bring about an air battle and/or the capture of a bridgehead in France within the area in which adequate naval and air cover can be given during the summer of 1942 should it be decided to operate on the Continent;

iv) A large scale descent on Western Europe in the Spring of 1943.

2. Responsibility for these tasks has been allocated as follows:

Initiation of offensive preparations	C-in-C, Home Forces and CCO jointly.
Planning and launching raiding operations in 1942	CCO in consultation with C-in-C, Home Forces.
Conduct of Air Offensive	AOC-in-C, Fighter Command in consultation with AOC-in-C, Bomber Command.
Planning of Operations for a large scale raid and/or the capture of bridgehead in 1942. (Sledgehammer)	C-in-C, Home Forces, AOC-in-C, Fighter Command and CCO in consultation.
Large scale descent on Western Europe in 1942	C-in-C, Home Forces in conjunction with AOC-in-C, Fighter Command (and other RAF Commands as necessary) and

CCO, in full consultation with the Naval Staff.

3. SOE is required to conform with the general plan by organising and co-ordinating action by patriots in the occupied countries at all stages. Particular care is to be taken to avoid premature large scale risings of patriots.

4. To this end SOE should work in continuous collaboration with the Planning Staffs of the officers referred to in paragraph 2 above, who will keep SOE fully informed.

5. SOE should endeavour to build up and equip para-military organisations in the area of the projected operations. The action of such organisations will in particular be directed towards the following tasks:

Co-operation during the Initial Assault
   a)   Prevention of the arrival of enemy reinforcements by the interruption of road, rail and air transport.
   b)   The interruption of enemy signal communications in and behind the battle area generally.
   c)   Prevention of demolitions by the enemy.
   d)   Attacks on enemy aircraft and air personnel.
   e)   Disorganisation of enemy movements and rear services by the spreading of rumours.

Tasks after landing
   f)   Provision of guides for British troops. These should know the dispositions of German troops and installations in the immediate neighbourhood.
   g)   Provision of guards for vital points. In the case of personnel that have not been armed and equipped before operations start, this will be completed on the arrival of the Allied expeditionary force.
   h)   Assistance in arranging for the provision of labour for work in docks and on communications and aerodromes.
   i)   Provision of raiding parties capable of penetrating behind the German lines to carry out specific tasks.

6. Copies of this directive have been sent to:

> Commander-in-Chief, Home Forces.
> Air Officers Commanding-in-Chief,
>   Fighter Command and Bomber Command.
> Chief of Combined Operations.

* WM(42)54th Conclusions.

CORRIGENDUM to COS(42)133(0)   *9th August 1942*

At their meeting^ø held on 8th August 1942 the Chiefs of Staff
  '(e) Agreed that paragraph 5 (f) to (i) inclusive of the Directive to
     SOE should be cancelled.'

It is requested that copies of COS(42)133(0) in your possession should
be amended accordingly.

(Sgd) L. C. HOLLIS
ø COS(42)231st Mtg, Min. 2.

Appendix H

(Extract)

Ministry of Information and Special Operations Executive
(Agreement of July 1942)

Para. 9

a) SOE will not engage in subversive activities of any description in areas falling within the jurisdiction of the Ministry of Information unless asked to do so by the Local Commander in Chief or the Foreign Office.

b) SOE will only undertake suberversive propaganda in a neutral country or the Empire at the request of, and on the basis of a plan agreed by the Foreign Office or the appropriate Department. The Ministry of Information will be informed of the existence of such a plan and, very roughly, of its scope.

c) At the same time, if it is the policy of HM Government to indulge in a campaign against any neutral Government or any organised enemy Fifth Column in the Ministry of Information area, SOE will normally be entrusted, as part of a general subversive plan, with operations involving the use, outside this country, of Freedom Stations, rumours, chain letters, bribery and leaflets emanating, or professedly emanating from non-British sources.

d) In any area where the Ministry of Information may have (better) facilities (than SOE) for undertaking all or any of these activities, the Ministry will have the right, if they so desire, of organising them themselves. In any case, the local SOE representative in the Ministry of Information area will always work in close co-operation, so far as use of the above mentioned media is concerned, with the local representative of the Ministry of Information and *vice versa*.

e) Ministry of Information officials in neutral countries should not be approached by SOE representatives in regard to propaganda projects in future unless it is clearly understood that Ministry of Information representatives can and will report fully the nature of these approaches to us.

f) As regards ordinary propaganda, SOE will only act as disseminators of this at the specific request of the Ministry of Information.

Note: Copy of this paper is on SOE Archives File 'CD 110/5 – Liaison with M of I'.

Appendix J

Copy

SOE and PWE

(Agreement of September 1942)

In order to provide the closest measure of co-operation between SOE and PWE in the Middle East, West Africa and any other centres to which it may later be agreed to apply the same principle the two organisations have agreed on the following delimitation of functions.

1. SOE recognise PWE's desire to establish independent missions to conduct all forms of propaganda to the areas assigned to them in their Charter.

2. SOE agree to hand over to PWE in all areas to which this agreement applies, all broadcasting stations which they at present own or control; and not to establish any other stations in their stead.

3. PWE however recognise that SOE, being charged by HMG with all forms of political subversion, have need of special clandestine broadcasting facilities for operational purposes, and undertake therefore to provide these facilities on the following terms:

   a) The broadcasts needed by SOE shall be made, on the stations now transferred to PWE control, by broadcasting teams provided by SOE whose identity SOE are not bound to disclose.

   b) PWE will take the necessary steps to safeguard SOE's security in respect of these broadcasts.

   c) SOE will submit scripts in advance to PWE so that both parties may be satisfied that there is no conflict between the policy laid down by HMG to SOE and PWE respectively.

   d) In receiving these scripts PWE will bear in mind the operational purposes and character of the broadcasting, recognising that the operational policy involved therein is SOE's affair and does not necessarily form part of the propaganda policy which is the business of PWE.

   e) Both parties will do their utmost to make these broadcasting stations pursue a consistent policy in the interests both of SOE and PWE.

f) Any differences on interpretation of policy which may arise will be referred to the Coordinating Committee in London.

3. SOE will transfer to PWE such personnel on the spot as can be released without damage to SOE's operational work or the security of any secret organisation they control and as are willing to be transferred.

4. PWE will not put, or permit their overseas missions to put, agents into the field either for the dissemination of written propaganda or whispers, or to influence the opinions and sentiments of the populations concerned, or to obtain information about the effect of propaganda controlled by PWE in those territories. All such work in the field shall, as heretofore, continue to be done by SOE as agents for PWE.

3rd September 1942

Appendix K

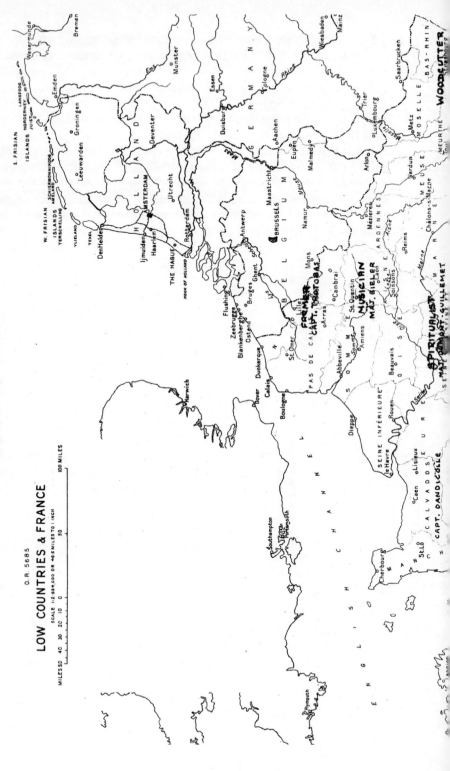

LOW COUNTRIES & FRANCE

O.R. 5685

SCALE 1:2,934,000 OR 46.5 MILES TO 1 INCH

MILES 50 40 30 20 10 0   50   100 MILES

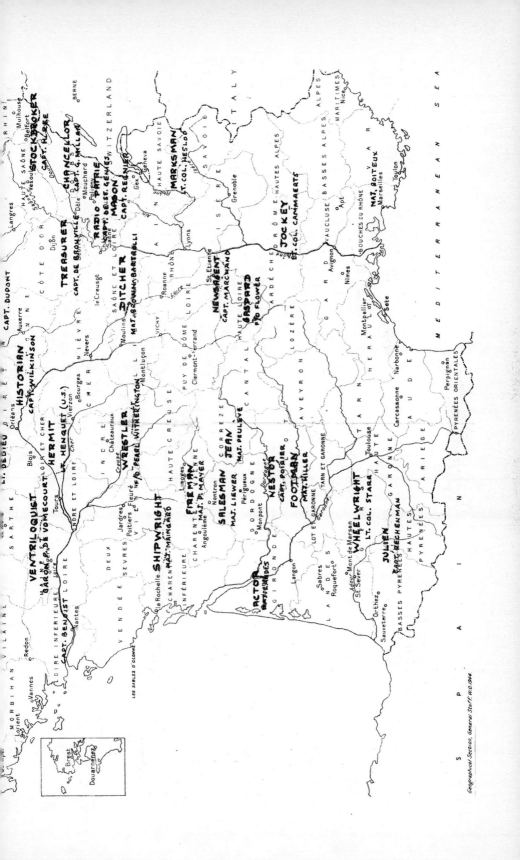

Geographical Section, General Staff. W.O. 1944.

Appendix L

LOW COUNTRIES & FRANCE

U.R. 5005

SCALE 1:2,851,000 OR 46·5 MILES TO 1 INCH

MILES 50 40 30 20 10 0 50 100 MILES

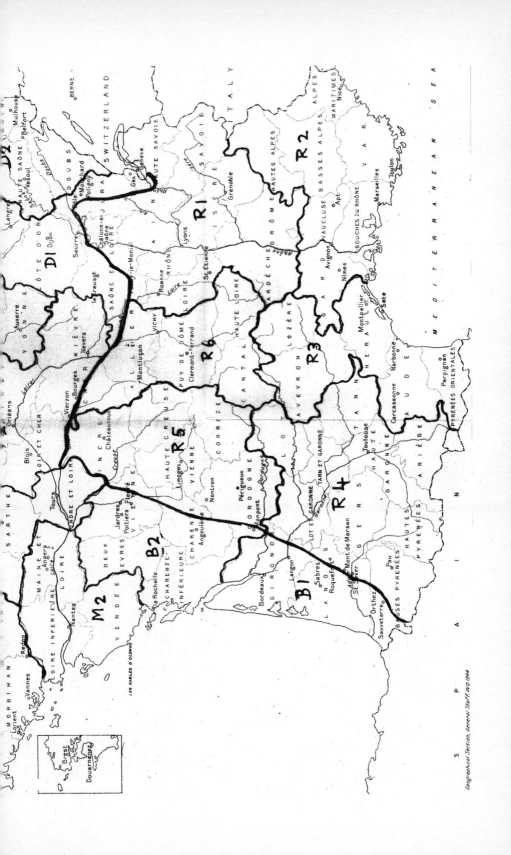

Appendix M

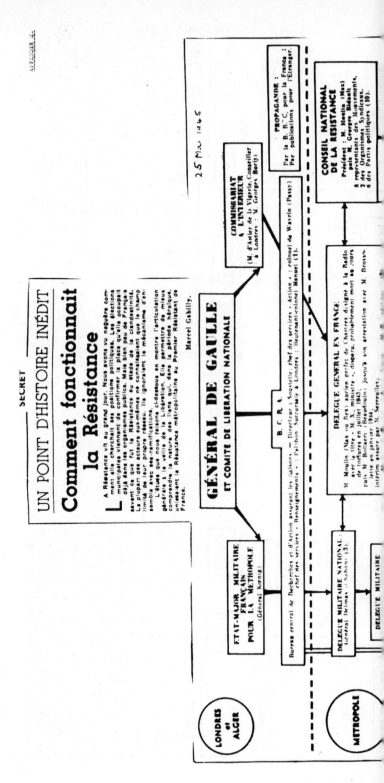

SECRET

UN POINT D'HISTOIRE INÉDIT

Comment fonctionnait la Résistance

La Résistance vit au grand jour. Nous avons vu comment elle cherchait ses positions politiques. Les élections municipales viennent de confirmer la place qu'elle occupait déjà dans les organismes publics. Mais bien peu de Français savent ce que fut la Résistance au stade de la clandestinité. La plupart des acteurs eux-mêmes ne connaissaient que le champ limité de leur propre réseau. Ils ignoraient le mécanisme d'ensemble avec ses ramifications.

L'étude que nous faisons ci-dessous en montre l'articulation générale à la veille de la Libération. Elle permettra de mieux comprendre la nature de la lutte qui, dans la période héroïque, unissait la Résistance métropolitaine au Premier Résistant de France.

Marcel Gabilly.

25 Mai 1945

LONDRES et ALGER

METROPOLE

GÉNÉRAL DE GAULLE
ET COMITÉ DE LIBÉRATION NATIONALE

COMMISSARIAT À L'INTÉRIEUR
(M. d'Astier de la Vigerie, Conseiller à Londres : M. Georges Boris)

PROPAGANDE :
Par la B. B. C. pour la France ; Par publications pour l'Etranger.

CONSEIL NATIONAL DE LA RESISTANCE
Président : M. Moulin (Max) puis M. Georges Bidault, 8 représentants des Mouvements, 2 des Organismes Syndicaux, 6 des Partis politiques (10).

B. C. R. A.

Bureau central de Recherches et d'Action assurant les liaisons. — Directeur : Soustelle; chef des services « Action » : colonel de Wavrin (Passy) chef des services « Renseignements » : Péribon Surrurelé à Londres : lieutenant-colonel Manuel (1).

DELEGUE GENERAL EN FRANCE :
M. Moulin (Max ou Rex) ancien préfet de Chartres désigné à la Radio avec le titre « M. X. ministre », disparu, probablement mort au cours de l'hiver en juillet 1944, puis M. Bollaert (Reaumont) jusqu'à son arrestation avec M. Brossolette en janvier 1944. Intérim assuré par M. Serrurlles.

ETAT-MAJOR MILITAIRE FRANÇAIS POUR LA METROPOLE
(Général Koenig)

DELEGUE MILITAIRE NATIONAL :
(Général Delmas Chaban) (3).

DELEGUE MILITAIRE

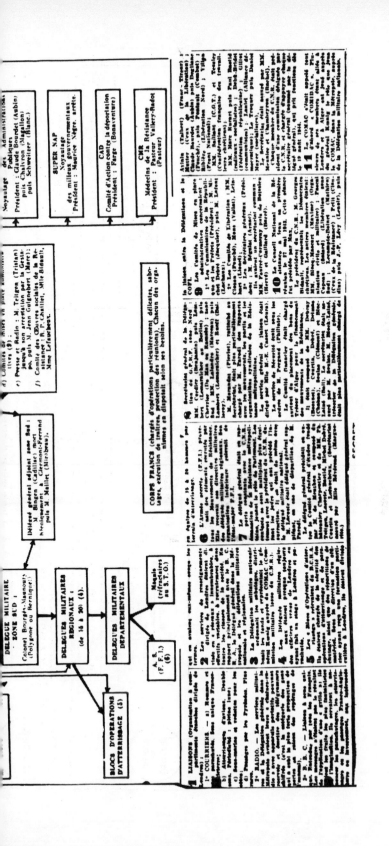

Appendix N

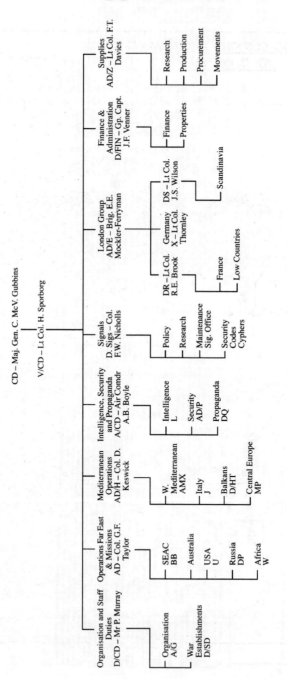

CD – Maj. Gen. C. McV. Gubbins

V/CD – Lt Col. H. Sporborg

Organisation and Staff Duties
D/CD – Mr P. Murray
- Organisation A/G
- War Establishments D/SD

Operations Far East & Missions
AD – Col. G.F. Taylor
- SEAC BB
- Australia
- USA U
- Russia DP
- Africa W

Mediterranean Operations
AD/H – Col. D. Keswick
- W. Mediterranean AMX
- Italy J
- Balkans D/HT
- Central Europe MP

Intelligence, Security and Propaganda
A/CD – Air Comdr A.B. Boyle
- Intelligence L
- Security AD/P
- Propaganda DQ

Signals
D. Sigs – Col. F.W. Nicholls
- Policy
- Research
- Maintenance Sig. Office
- Security Codes Cyphers

London Group
AD/E – Brig. E.E. Mockler-Ferryman
- DR – Lt Col. R.E. Brook
  - France
  - Low Countries
- Germany X – Lt Col. Thornley
- DS – Lt Col. J.S. Wilson
  - Scandinavia

Finance & Administration
D/FIN – Gp. Capt. J.F. Venner
- Finance
- Properties

Supplies
AD/Z – Lt Col. F.T. Davies
- Research
- Production
- Procurement
- Movements

Spring 1944

Appendix O – (i)

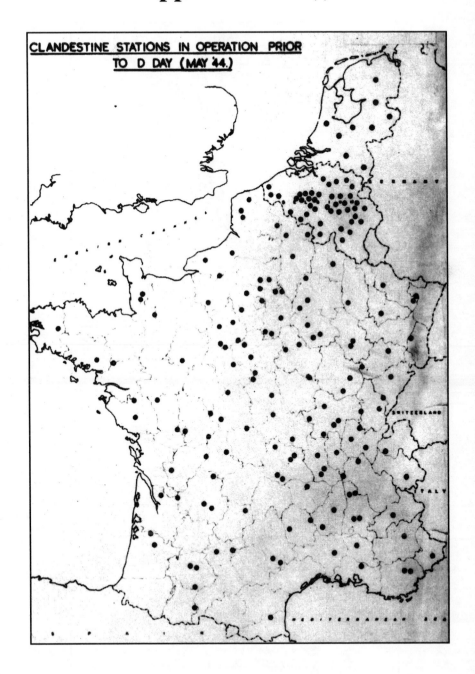

Appendix O – (ii)

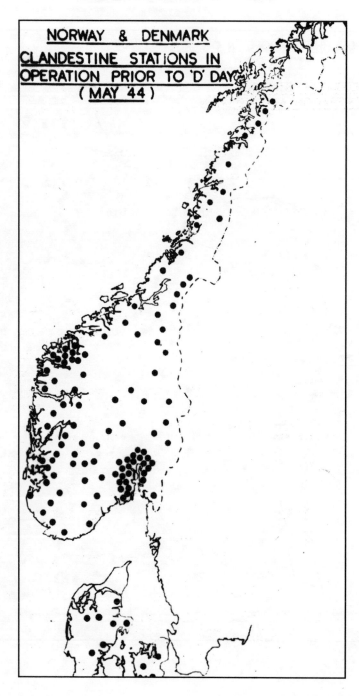

NORWAY & DENMARK
CLANDESTINE STATIONS IN
OPERATION PRIOR TO 'D' DAY
(MAY '44)

Appendix O – (iii)

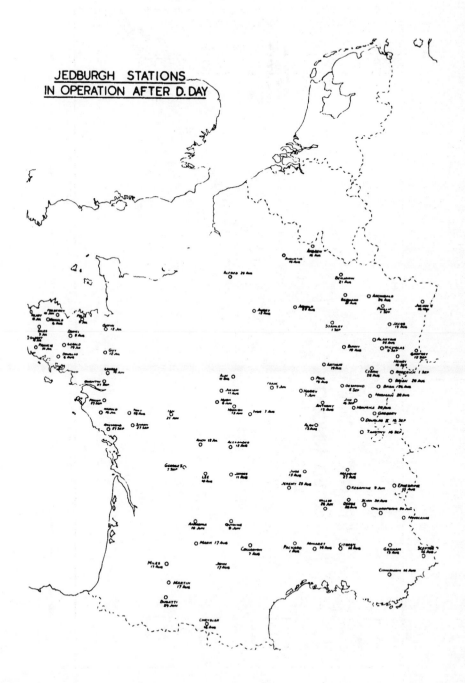

Appendix O – (iv)

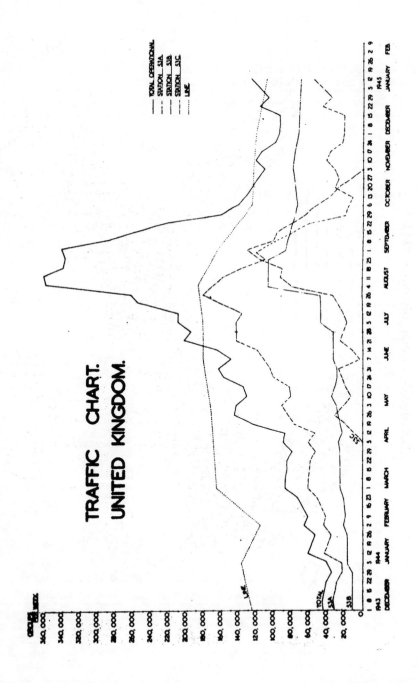

TRAFFIC CHART.
UNITED KINGDOM.

Appendix P

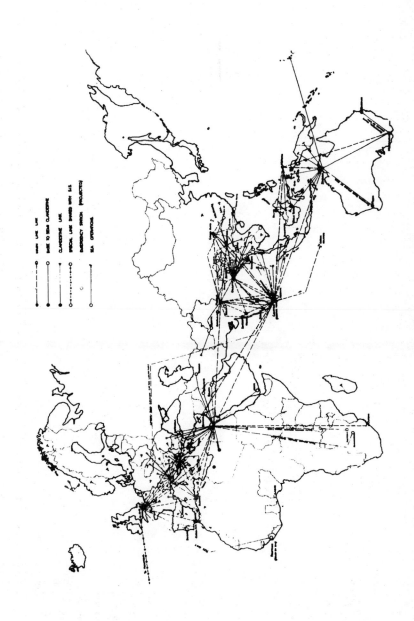

SOE Signals Communications 1942–5

Index

The index covers Foreword, Preface and Appendices. Subheadings are arranged in chronological order of appearance. n following a page number indicates a footnote.